International Edition

# The New Era of Management

## Richard L. Daft

*Vanderbilt University*

**THOMSON**
™
**SOUTH-WESTERN**

Australia · Canada · Mexico · Singapore · Spain · United Kingdom · United States

## THOMSON

### SOUTH-WESTERN

**The New Era of Management, International Edition**

Richard L. Daft

With the Assistance of Patricia G. Lane

**VP/Editorial Director:**
Jack W. Calhoun

**VP/Editor-in-Chief:**
Dave Shaut

**Sr. Publisher:**
Melissa Acuña

**Acquisitions Editor:**
Joe Sabatino

**Developmental Editor:**
Emma F. Guttler

**Marketing Manager:**
Jacquelyn Carrillo

**Promotions Manager:**
Jim Overly

**Production Editor:**
Cliff Kallemeyn

**Technology Project Editor:**
Kristen Meere

**Media Editor:**
Karen Schaffer

**Sr. Manufacturing Coordinator:**
Doug Wilke

**Art Director:**
Bethany Casey

**Production Agency:**
DPS Associates
Cincinnati, OH

**Photo Research:**
Elm Street Publishing Services

**Printer:**
China Translation & Printing Services
Ltd.

*With deep appreciation to Dorothy,*
*the professor, playwright, and partner in my life,*
*and to my parents, who started my life*
*toward outcomes that I could not understand at the time.*

Preface

# Managing in Turbulent Times: Unlocking Creative Solutions

In light of the dramatic and far-reaching events of the early twenty-first century, the central theme being discussed in the field of management is the pervasiveness of turbulent change and its impact on organizations. This edition of *The New Era of Management* was revised to help current and future managers find creative solutions to the problems that plague today's organizations—whether they are everyday challenges or "once-in-a-lifetime" crises. The world in which most students will work as managers is undergoing a tremendous upheaval. The emergence of crisis management, ethical turmoil, e-business, rapidly changing technologies, globalization, outsourcing, global virtual teams, knowledge management, and other changes place demands on managers that go beyond the techniques and ideas traditionally taught in management courses. Managing in today's turbulent times requires the full breadth of management skills and capabilities. This text provides comprehensive coverage of both traditional management skills and the new competencies needed in a turbulent environment characterized by economic turmoil, political confusion, and general uncertainty for the future.

The traditional world of work assumed the purpose of management was to control and limit people, enforce rules and regulations, seek stability and efficiency, design a top-down hierarchy to direct people, and achieve bottom-line results. To unlock creative solutions and achieve high performance, however, managers need different skills to engage workers' hearts and minds as well as take advantage of their physical labor. The new workplace asks that managers focus on leading change, on harnessing people's creativity and enthusiasm, on finding shared visions and values, and on sharing information and power. Teamwork, collaboration, participation, and learning are guiding principles that help managers and employees maneuver the difficult terrain of today's turbulent business environment. Managers focus on developing, not controlling, people to adapt to new technologies and extraordinary environmental shifts, and thus achieve high performance and total corporate effectiveness.

My vision for the international edition of *The New Era of Management* is to explore the newest management ideas for turbulent times in a way that is interesting and valuable to students, while retaining the best of traditional management thinking. To achieve this vision, I have included the most recent management concepts and research as well as showing the contemporary application of management ideas in organizations. The combination of established scholarship, new ideas, and real-life applications gives students a taste of the energy, challenge, and adventure inherent in the dynamic field of management. The South-Western staff and I have worked together to provide a textbook better than any other at capturing the excitement of organizational management.

I revised *The New Era of Management* to provide a book of utmost quality that will create in students both respect for the changing field of management and confidence that they can understand and master it. The textual portion of this book has been enhanced through the engaging, easy-to-understand writing style and the many in-text examples and boxed items that make the concepts come alive for students. The graphic component has been enhanced with several new exhibits and a new set of photo essays that illustrate specific management concepts. The well-chosen photographs provide vivid illustrations and intimate glimpses of management scenes, events, and people. The photos are combined with brief essays that explain how a specific management concept looks and feels. Both the textual and graphic portions of the textbook help students grasp the often abstract and distant world of management.

## Focus on the Future

The international edition of *The New Era of Management* is especially focused on the future of management education by identifying and describing emerging ideas and examples of innovative organizations. Text content has been sharpened and reduced by one chapter, providing greater focus on the key topics that count for management today. Within each chapter, many topics have been added or expanded to address the current issues managers face.

**Chapter 1** introduces the skills and competencies needed to effectively manage organizations in today's turbulent environment, including issues such as managing diversity, coping with globalization and rapid change, and managing crises. Chapter 1 also looks at how societal turbulence and management missteps have contributed to recent ethical and operational problems in today's organizations

**Chapter 2** continues its solid coverage of the historical development of management and organizations and examines new management thinking for turbulent times. The chapter also looks at the shifting world of e-business and effective management of the technology-driven workplace.

**Chapter 3** has been updated to look at current issues related to the environment and corporate culture. A new section illustrates how managers can shape a high-performance culture for innovative response to a rapidly shifting environment

**Chapter 4**'s discussion of the European Union and other global trade alliances has been significantly updated and expanded. In addition, the complex issues surrounding globalization are discussed, including a consideration of the current globalization backlash. Chapter 4 has also been updated with a review of the GLOBE (Global Leadership and Organizational Behavior Effectiveness) Project, which extends Hofstede's assessment of social values to offer a broader understanding for today's managers.

**Chapter 5** addresses the current ethical crisis affecting many managers and organizations and the challenge of restoring public trust and respect in corporate America. Global ethical issues are expanded as well, including a discussion of corruption rankings of various countries compared to the United States. New material in Chapter 5 also examines the sustainability movement and ISO 14001 standards as a response to demands for global environmental responsibility, and the growing interest in social entrepreneurship.

**Chapter 6** includes a new consideration of entrepreneurial activity on a global basis and looks at the reasons entrepreneurship and small business is booming. The chapter continues its focus on practical information regarding small business formation and development, including a look at the characteristics and challenges of high-tech startups.

**Chapter 7** provides an overview of planning and goal setting, including a close look at crisis management planning. The chapter contains a new section on scenario building as a way for managers to prepare for a turbulent and rapidly changing environment. The chapter's final section on planning for high performance has been enhanced by a discussion of event-driven planning for volatile environments.

**Chapter 8** continues its focus on the basics of formulating and implementing strategy. A new section considers the challenges of implementing strategy during turbulent times and looks at how developing a global mindset, paying careful attention to culture, and using new information technology can help managers meet these challenges.

**Chapter 9**'s overview of managerial decision making has an expanded discussion of brainstorming for group decision making, including the current use of electronic brainstorming, or brainwriting.

**Chapter 10** discusses basic principles of organizing and describes both traditional and contemporary organization structures in detail. The chapter includes a new discussion of organic versus mechanistic structures and when each is more effective, and also contains an expanded description of the virtual network organization form.

**Chapter 11** looks at the important role of managing change and innovation in today's turbulent environment. New topics incorporated into this chapter include the trend toward open innovation, the growing use of fast-cycle teams, and the value of taking an ambidextrous approach for facilitating change.

**Chapter 12** includes new material on international human resource management (IHRM), work-life balance issues, downsizing, and the controversy over performance review ranking systems.

**Chapter 13** has been thoroughly revised and updated to reflect the most recent thinking on organizational diversity issues. In addition, the chapter reviews the current debate concerning women opting to leave the corporate workforce (the opt-out trend), and looks at recent research indicating that women may have superior skills for managing in today's environment.

**Chapter 14** provides an overview of financial and quality control, including updated material on Six Sigma and ISO 9000. The chapter also addresses current concerns about corporate governance and finding a proper balance of control that sets and monitors appropriate standards and constraints but does not demean employees or excessively limit their participation in the organization.

**Chapter 15** has been updated to incorporate recent trends in information technology. The section on e-business strategies has been thoroughly revised to look at the two primary reasons organizations use e-business: to expand their markets or to improve productivity and cost-control. The chapter also includes a new discussion of the growing use of business intelligence software for making strategic decisions, and a short section on Web logs (blogs) and wikis, an emerging collaboration tool.

**Chapter 16** has been enhanced by references to new technology used for operations and service management, such as product life-cycle management software, radio frequency identification (RFID) for logistics and supply chain management, and location scouting software for facilities location planning. The chapter also contains a new section on lean manufacturing.

**Chapter 17** contains new or updated coverage of high performance work attitudes, emotional intelligence, the Myers-Briggs Type Indicator, and stress management. Several new exercises have been added throughout the chapter to enhance student understanding of organizational behavior topics and their own personalities and attitudes.

**Chapter 18** includes a new examination of post-heroic leadership for today's turbulent times, focusing on the subtle and often unrewarded acts that good leaders perform every day to keep organizations strong and healthy. This includes updated material on servant leadership, Level 5 leadership, interactive leadership, and e-leadership, along with a new section discussing moral leadership for today's ethically challenged business environment.

**Chapter 19** covers the foundations of motivation and also incorporates some new thinking about motivational tools for today, such as the importance of helping employees achieve work-life balance, incorporating fun and learning into the workplace, giving people a chance to fully participate in the organization, and helping people find meaning in their work. The chapter also includes a new section on goal-setting theory as it relates to motivation.

**Chapter 20** begins with a new discussion of how managers facilitate strategic conversations by using communication to direct everyone's attention to the vision, values, and goals of the organization. The chapter also contains a new section on building personal communication networks to enhance manager power, extend influence, and get things done.

**Chapter 21** includes a new section on how managers achieve the right balance of conflict and cooperation to enhance team performance, improve decision making, and achieve goals. The section on team characteristics has been enhanced by a new discussion of team diversity.

In addition to the topics listed above, each chapter of this text integrates coverage of the Internet and emerging technology into the various topics covered in the chapter. Each chapter contains an *Unlocking Creative Solutions Through Technology* box that features a technologically savvy company or highlights a manager who is using technology to meet the challenges of today's turbulent environment. Each chapter also contains a box entitled *Unlocking Creative Solutions Through People*, in recognition that human capital is essential for solving today's complex organizational problems. These boxes describe various unique, innovative, or interesting approaches to managing people for high performance and creative response.

# Organization

The chapter sequence in *The New Era of Management* is organized around the management functions of planning, organizing, controlling, and leading. These four functions effectively encompass both management research and characteristics of the manager's job.

Part One introduces the world of management, including the nature of management, issues related to today's turbulent environment, the learning organization, historical perspectives on management, and the technology-driven workplace.

Part Two examines the environments of management and organizations. This section includes material on the business environment and corporate culture, the global environment, ethics and social responsibility, the natural environment, and the environment of entrepreneurship and small business management.

Part Three presents three chapters on planning, including organizational goal setting and planning, strategy formulation and implementation, and the decision-making process.

Part Four focuses on organizing processes. These chapters describe dimensions of structural design, the design alternatives managers can use to achieve strategic objectives, structural designs for promoting innovation and change, the design and use of the human resource function, and the ways managing diverse employees are significant to the organizing function.

Part Five describes the controlling function of management, including basic principles of total quality management, the design of control systems, information technology, and techniques for control of operations management.

Part Six is devoted to leadership. This section begins with a chapter on organizational behavior, providing grounding in understanding people in organizations. The foundation paves the way for subsequent discussion of leadership, motivating employees, communication, and team management.

# Innovative Features

A major goal of this book is to offer better ways of using the textbook medium to convey management knowledge to the reader. To this end, the book includes several innovative features that draw students in and help them contemplate, absorb, and comprehend management concepts. South-Western has brought together a team of experts to create and coordinate color photographs, video cases, beautiful artwork, and supplemental materials for the best management textbook and package on the market.

**Chapter Outline and Objectives.** Each chapter begins with a clear statement of its learning objectives and an outline of its contents. These devices provide an overview of what is to come and can also be used by students to guide their study and test their understanding and retention of important points.

**Manager's Challenge.** The text portion of each chapter begins with a real-life problem faced by organization managers. The problem pertains to the topic of the chapter and will heighten students' interest in chapter concepts. At the end of each challenge, students are asked to "**Take A Moment**" to ponder the situation and think about how they would handle it. The Take A Moment questions posed in the Manager's Challenge are resolved in the **Manager's Solution** at the end of the chapter, where chapter concepts guiding the management's actions are highlighted.

**Take A Moment.** The Take A Moment feature is also carried throughout the chapter. This new feature for the seventh edition provides an in-text marginal reference that directs students from the chapter content to the associated end of chapter materials, such as an experiential exercise or an ethical dilemma.

**Concept Connection Photo Essays.** A key feature of the book is the use of photographs accompanied by detailed photo essay captions that enhance learning. Each caption highlights and illustrates one or more specific concepts from the text to reinforce student understanding of the concepts. While the photos are beautiful to look at, they also convey the vividness, immediacy, and concreteness of management events in today's business world.

**Contemporary Examples.** Every chapter of the text contains a large number of written examples of management incidents. They are placed at strategic points in the chapter and are designed to illustrate the application of concepts to specific companies. These in-text examples—indicated by an icon in the margin—include well-known U.S. and international companies such as Verizon Wireless, BMW, eBay, and Nokia, as well as less-well-known companies and not-for-profit organizations such as Remploy Ltd. (United Kingdom), Tom's of Maine (U.S.), Europa Hotel (Northern Ireland), Daily Candy (Internet), the *Milwaukee Journal-Sentinel*, and the U.S. Federal Bureau of Investigation (FBI) . These examples put students in touch with the real world of organizations so that they can appreciate the value of management concepts.

**Unlocking Creative Solutions Boxes.** Two Unlocking Creative Solutions boxes —one focusing on people and one focusing on technology—are presented in each chapter. Describing real companies, these boxes reflect the dual emphasis that today's most successful managers use to unlock innovative solutions and increase organizational performance: the technology side and the human capital side. These boxes provide students with an in-depth analysis of the various issues facing today's organizations and managers.

**Manager's Shoptalk Boxes.** These boxes address topics straight from the field of management that are of special interest to students. They may describe a contemporary topic or problem that is relevant to chapter content or they may contain a diagnostic questionnaire or a special example of how managers handle a problem. These boxes will heighten student interest in the subject matter and provide an auxiliary view of management issues not typically available in textbooks.

**Video Cases.** The six parts of the text conclude with video cases (videos available on the Web site at http://aise.swlearning.com), one per chapter, that illustrate the concepts presented in that part. The videos enhance class discussion because students can see the direct application of the management theories they have learned. Each video case explores the issues covered in the video, allowing students to synthesize the material they've just viewed. The video cases culminate with several questions that can be used to launch classroom discussion or as homework.

**Exhibits.** Many aspects of management are research based, and some concepts tend to be abstract and theoretical. To enhance students' awareness and understanding of these concepts, many exhibits have been included throughout the book. These exhibits consolidate key points, indicate relationships among variables, and visually illustrate concepts. They also make effective use of color to enhance their imagery and appeal.

**Glossaries.** Learning the management vocabulary is essential to understanding contemporary management. This process is facilitated in three ways. First, key concepts are boldfaced and completely defined where they first appear in the text. Second, brief definitions are set out in the margin for easy review and follow-up. Third, a glossary summarizing all key terms and definitions appears at the end of the book for handy reference.

**Chapter Summary and Discussion Questions.** Each chapter closes with a summary of key points that students should retain. The discussion questions are a complementary learning tool that will enable students to check their understanding of key issues, to think beyond basic concepts, and to determine areas that require further study. The summary and discussion questions help students discriminate between main and supporting points and provide mechanisms for self-teaching.

**Management in Practice Exercises.** End-of-chapter exercises called "Management in Practice: Experiential Exercise" and "Management in Practice: Ethical Dilemma" provide self-tests for students and an opportunity to experience management issues in a personal way. These exercises take the form of questionnaires, scenarios, and activities, and many also provide an opportunity for students to work in teams. The exercises are tied into the chapter through the "Take A Moment" feature that refers students to the end-of-chapter exercises at the appropriate point in the chapter content.

**Surf the Net.** Each chapter contains three Internet exercises to involve students in the high-tech world of cyberspace. Students are asked to explore the Web for research into topics related to each chapter. This hands-on experience helps them develop Internet, research, and management skills.

**Case for Critical Analysis.** Also appearing at the end of each chapter is a brief but substantive case that provides an opportunity for student analysis and class discussion. Many of these cases are about companies whose names students will recognize; others are based on real management events but the identities of companies and managers have been disguised. These cases allow students to sharpen their diagnostic skills for management problem solving.

**Continuing Case.** Located at the end of each part, the Continuing Case is a running discussion of management topics as experienced by one company as it is relevant to the material discussed in that part. Focusing on one company, the Ford Motor Company, allows students to follow the managers' and the organizations' problems and solutions in a long-term way.

## Supplementary Materials

**Instructor's Manual.** The Instructor's Manual is available on the Web site (http://aise. swlearning.com). Designed to provide support for instructors new to the course, as well as innovative materials for experienced professors, the Instructor's Manual includes Chapter Outlines, annotated learning objectives, Lecture Notes and sample Lecture Outlines. Additionally, the Instructor's Manual includes answers and teaching notes to end-of-chapter materials, including the video cases and the continuing case.

**Test Bank.** Scrutinized for accuracy, the Test Bank (available on the Web site at http://aise. swlearning.com) includes more than 2,000 true/false, multiple choice, short answer, and essay questions. Page references are indicated for every question, as are designations of whether the question is factual or application so that instructors can provide a balanced set of questions for student exams.

**PowerPoint Lecture Presentation.** Available on the Web site (http://aise.swlearning. com), the PowerPoint Lecture Presentation enables instructors to customize their own multimedia classroom presentation. Containing approximately 350 slides, the package includes figures and tables from the text, as well as outside materials to supplement chapter concepts. Material is organized by chapter, and can be modified or expanded for individual classroom use. PowerPoint slides are also easily printed to create customized Transparency Masters.

**InfoTrac.** Free with the purchase of each textbook, this online database of articles gives students access to full-text articles from hundreds of scholarly and popular periodicals such as *Newsweek*, *Time*, and *USA Today*. Updated daily, this tool allows students to research topics pertinent to classroom discussion and to keep up with current events.

## Acknowledgments

A gratifying experience for me was working with the team of dedicated professionals at South-Western who were committed to the vision of producing the best management text ever. I am grateful to Joe Sabatino, Acquisitions Editor, whose enthusiasm, creative ideas, assistance, and vision kept this book's spirit alive. Jacquelyn Carrillo, Marketing Manager, provided keen market knowledge and innovative ideas for instructional support. Emma Guttler, Developmental Editor, provided superb project coordination and offered excellent ideas and suggestions to help the team meet a demanding and sometimes arduous schedule. Cliff Kallemeyn, Production Editor, cheerfully and expertly guided me through the production process. Bethany Casey and Chris Miller contributed their graphic arts skills to create a visually dynamic design. Michael Guendelsberger, Editorial Assistant, and Anna Hasselo, Marketing Coordinator, skillfully pitched in to help keep the project on track. I also want to thank the team at Elm Street Publishing

Services for their expertise and assistance on several aspects of this project. Crystal Bullen and the team at DPS Associates deserve a special thank you for their layout expertise and commitment to producing an attractive, high-quality textbook.

Here at Vanderbilt I want to extend special appreciation to my assistant, Barbara Haselton. Barbara provided excellent support and assistance on a variety of projects that gave me time to write. I also want to acknowledge an intellectual debt to my colleagues, Bruce Barry, Ray Friedman, Neta Moye, Rich Oliver, David Owens, and Bart Victor. Thanks also to Dean Bill Christie who has supported my writing projects and maintained a positive scholarly atmosphere in the school.

Another group of people who made a major contribution to this textbook are the management experts who provided advice, reviews, answers to questions, and suggestions for changes, insertions, and clarifications. I want to thank each of these colleagues for their valuable feedback and suggestions:

David C. Adams
*Manhattanville College*

Erin M. Alexander
*University of Houston, Clear Lake*

Hal Babson
*Columbus State Community College*

Reuel Barksdale
*Columbus State Community College*

Gloria Bemben
*Finger Lakes Community College*

Art Bethke
*Northeast Louisiana University*

Thomas Butte
*Humboldt State University*

Peter Bycio
*Xavier University, Ohio*

Diane Caggiano
*Fitchburg State College*

Douglas E. Cathon
*St. Augustine's College*

Jim Ciminskie
*Bay de Noc Community College*

Dan Connaughton
*University of Florida*

Bruce Conwers
*Kaskaskia College*

Byron L. David
*The City College of New York*

Richard De Luca
*William Paterson University*

Robert DeDominic
*Montana Tech*

Linn Van Dyne
*Michigan State University*

John C. Edwards
*East Carolina University*

Mary Ann Edwards
*College of Mount St. Joseph*

Janice M. Feldbauer
*Austin Community College*

Daryl Fortin
*Upper Iowa University*

Michael P. Gagnon
*New Hampshire Community
Technical College*

Richard H. Gayor
*Antelope Valley College*

Dan Geeding
*Xavier University, Ohio*

James Genseal
*Joliet Junior College*

Peter Gibson
*Becker College*

Carol R. Graham
*Western Kentucky University*

Gary Greene
*Manatee Community College*

Paul Hayes
*Coastal Carolina Community College*

Dennis Heaton
*Maharishi University of
Management, Iowa*

Jeffrey D. Hines
*Davenport College*

Bob Hoerber
*Westminster College*

James N. Holly
*University of Wisconsin–Green Bay*

Genelle Jacobson
*Ridgewater College*

C. Joy Jones
*Ohio Valley College*

Sheryl Kae
*Lynchburg College*

Jordan J. Kaplan
*Long Island University*

J. Michael Keenan
*Western Michigan University*

Paula C. Kougl
*Western Oregon University*

Cynthia Krom
*Mount St. Mary College*

William B. Lamb
*Millsaps College*

Robert E. Ledman
*Morehouse College*

George Lehma
*Bluffton College*

Janet C. Luke
*Georgia Baptist College of Nursing*

Jenna Lundburg
*Ithaca College*

Walter J. MacMillan
*Oral Roberts University*

Myrna P. Mandell
*California State University, Northridge*

Daniel B. Marin
*Louisiana State University*

James C. McElroy
*Iowa State University*

Dennis W. Meyers
*Texas State Technical College*

Alan N. Miller
*University of Nevada, Las Vegas*

Irene A. Miller
*Southern Illinois University*

Micah Mukabi
*Essex County College*

David W. Murphy
*Madisonville Community College*

James L. Moseley
*Wayne State University*

Nora Nurre
*Upper Iowa University*

Nelson Ocf
*Pacific University*

Tomas J. Ogazon
*St. Thomas University*

Allen Oghenejbo
*Mills College*

Linda Overstreet
*Hillsborough Community College*

Ken Peterson
*Metropolitan State University*

Clifton D. Petty
*Drury College*

James I. Phillips
*Northeastern State University*

Linda Putchinski
*University of Central Florida*

Kenneth Radig
*Medaille College*

Gerald D. Ramsey
*Indiana University Southeast*

Barbara Redmond
*Briar Cliff College*

William Reisel
*St. John's University, New York*

Walter F. Rohrs
*Wagner College*

Marcy Satterwhite
*Lake Land College*

Don Schreiber
*Baylor University*

Kilmon Shin
*Ferris State University*

Daniel G. Spencer
*University of Kansas*

Gary Spokes
*Pace University*

M. Sprencz
*David N. Meyers College*

Shanths Srinivas
*California State Polytechnic University, Pomona*

Jeffrey Stauffer
*Ventura College*

William A. Stower
*Seton Hall University*

Mary Studer
*Southwestern Michigan College*

James Swenson
*Moorhead State University, Minnesota*

Irwin Talbot
*St. Peter's College*

Andrew Timothy
*Lourdes College*

Frank G. Titlow
*St. Petersburg Junior College*

John Todd
*University of Arkansas*

Dennis L. Varin
*Southern Oregon University*

Gina Vega
*Merrimack College*

George S. Vozikis
*University of Tulsa*

Bruce C. Walker
*Northeast Louisiana University*

Mark Weber
*University of Minnesota*

Emilia S. Westney
*Texas Tech University*

Stan Williamson
*Northeast Louisiana University*

Alla L. Wilson
*University of Wisconsin–Green Bay*

Ignatius Yacomb
*Loma Linda University*

Imad Jim Zbib
*Ramapo College of New Jersey*

Vic Zimmerman
*Pima Community College*

I'd like to pay special tribute to my editorial associate, Pat Lane. I can't imagine how I would ever complete such a comprehensive revision on my own. Pat provided truly outstanding help throughout every step of writing the *The New Era of Management,* International Edition. She skillfully drafted materials for a wide range of chapter topics and cases, researched topics when new sources were lacking, and did an absolutely superb job with the copyedited manuscript and page proofs. Her commitment to this text enabled us to achieve our dream for its excellence.

Finally, I want to acknowledge the love and contributions of my wife, Dorothy Marcic. Dorothy has been very supportive during this revision as we share our lives together. I also want to acknowledge my love and support for my five daughters, Danielle, Amy, Roxanne, Solange, and Elizabeth, who make my life special during our precious time together. Thanks also to B. J. and Kaitlyn, and Kaci and Matthew for their warmth and smiles that brighten my life, especially during our days together skiing and on the beach.

Richard L. Daft
Nashville, Tennessee
January 2006

About the Author

Richard L. Daft, Ph.D., is the Brownlee O. Currey, Jr., Professor of Management in the Owen Graduate School of Management at Vanderbilt University. Professor Daft specializes in the study of organization theory and leadership. Dr. Daft is a Fellow of the Academy of Management and has served on the editorial boards of *Academy of Management Journal, Administrative Science Quarterly,* and *Journal of Management Education.* He was the Associate Editor-in-Chief of *Organization Science* and served for three years as associate editor of *Administrative Science Quarterly.*

Professor Daft has authored or co-authored 12 books, including *Organization Theory and Design* (South-Western, 2004), *The Leadership Experience* (South-Western, 2005) and *What to Study: Generating and Developing Research Questions* (Sage, 1982). He recently published *Fusion Leadership: Unlocking the Subtle Forces That Change People and Organizations* (Berrett-Koehler, 2000, with Robert Lengel). He has also authored dozens of scholarly articles, papers, and chapters. His work has been published in *Administrative Science Quarterly, Academy of Management Journal, Academy of Management Review, Strategic Management Journal, Journal of Management, Accounting Organizations and Society, Management Science, MIS Quarterly, California Management Review,* and *Organizational Behavior Teaching Review.* Professor Daft has been awarded several government research grants to pursue studies of organization design, organizational innovation and change, strategy implementation, and organizational information processing.

Dr. Daft also is an active teacher and consultant. He has taught management, leadership, organizational change, organizational theory, and organizational behavior. He has been involved in management development and consulting for many companies and government organizations including the American Banking Association, Bell Canada, the National Transportation Research Board, NL Baroid, Nortel, TVA, Pratt & Whitney, State Farm Insurance, Tenneco, the United States Air Force, the U.S. Army, J. C. Bradford & Co., Central Parking System, Entergy Sales and Service, Bristol-Myers Squibb, First American National Bank, and the Vanderbilt University Medical Center.

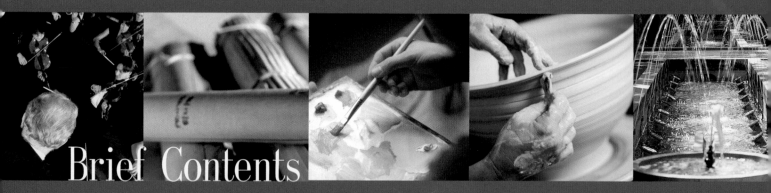

# Brief Contents

# Contents

# Part 4 Organizing, 346

## Part 6        Leading, 618

### Chapter 17     Dynamics of Behavior in Organizations, 620

### Chapter 18     Leadership, 658

International Edition

# The New Era of Management

# Introduction to Management

Artistic movements shake up the world. Art and artists reflect the human condition and use their work to change it for the better. Some art shocks, some comforts, some forces you to rethink how you define art—and how you manage your life.

The creative impulse that fuels innovation also generates turbulence. That upheaval brings in new ideas, new voices. Innovations build on one another, merge, and create new mediums. Turbulence in the arts—including landscaping, painting, architecture, music, and sculpture—brings evolution. Black-and-white photography takes its place in storied art museums. Gospel music begat blues, paving the way for soul, rock and roll, and hip-hop. The world's first skyscraper was built in 1885 with the innovation of a steel, rather than brick, structure.

Today's managers have to be like artists. They work in a global economy where the relationships among nations and corporations, emerging economies, outsourcing partners, and the fast-paced digital revolution create myriad influences, constant shifts and transformations. Flexibility and creativity are vital, but in management, as in art, some principles remain constant. Understanding and communicating information to others, maintaining good relationships with customers and members of the organization, and making clear, rational decisions are key management traits, no matter the time or place.

And despite the changes they face—organizational, cultural, or technological—managers must plan, organize, and lead their staffs, while staying focused to meet goals.

When you look at a painting, view a sculpture, meander through a garden, visit an architectural landmark, or hear an unfamiliar melody, you experience an artist's management of his medium and your environment. Key elements of managing—planning, organization, leadership, and control—are necessary for an artist mastering a medium and creating the work. Artists, composers, and architects harness their creativity to provide their audience a unique experience through their chosen medium. Managers who master the art of management can provide the same impact to their organizations—through people.

Part 1

# Chapter 1

# Managing in Turbulent Times

## LEARNING OBJECTIVES

*After studying this chapter, you should be able to:*

1. Describe the four management functions and the type of management activity associated with each.

2. Explain the difference between efficiency and effectiveness and their importance for organizational performance.

3. Describe management types and the horizontal and vertical differences between them.

4. Describe conceptual, human, and technical skills and their relevance for managers and employees.

5. Define 10 roles that managers perform in organizations.

6. Discuss the management competencies needed to deal with today's turbulent environment, including issues such as diversity, globalization, and rapid change.

7. Explain the leadership skills needed for effective crisis management.

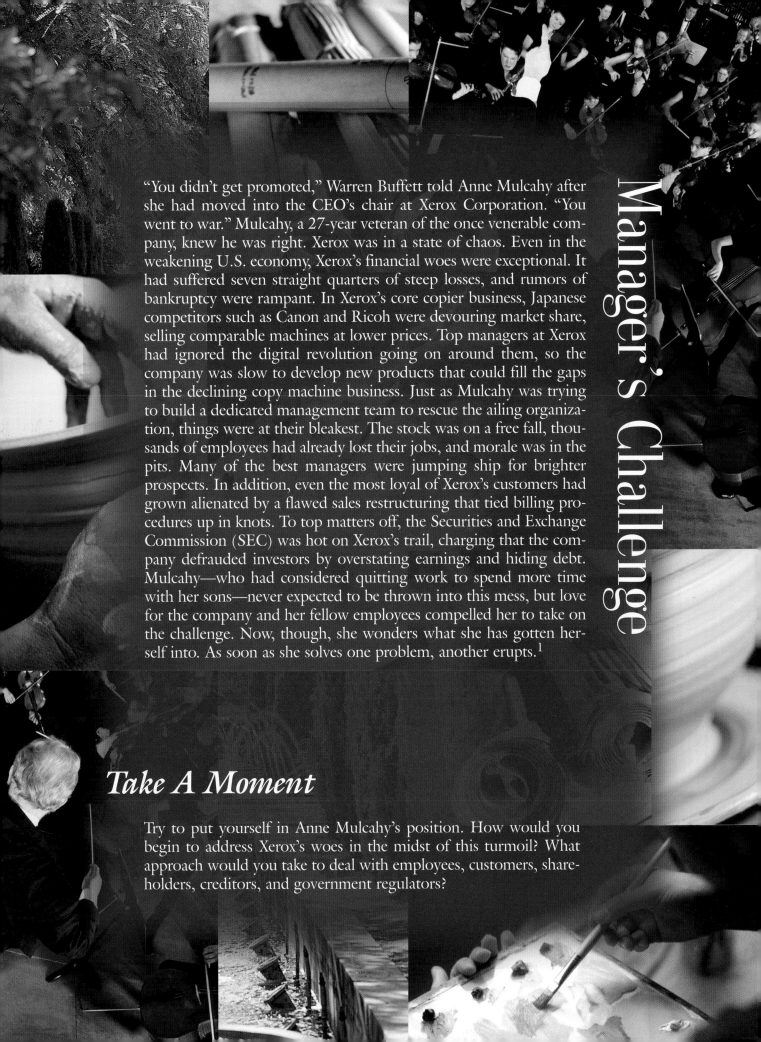

"You didn't get promoted," Warren Buffett told Anne Mulcahy after she had moved into the CEO's chair at Xerox Corporation. "You went to war." Mulcahy, a 27-year veteran of the once venerable company, knew he was right. Xerox was in a state of chaos. Even in the weakening U.S. economy, Xerox's financial woes were exceptional. It had suffered seven straight quarters of steep losses, and rumors of bankruptcy were rampant. In Xerox's core copier business, Japanese competitors such as Canon and Ricoh were devouring market share, selling comparable machines at lower prices. Top managers at Xerox had ignored the digital revolution going on around them, so the company was slow to develop new products that could fill the gaps in the declining copy machine business. Just as Mulcahy was trying to build a dedicated management team to rescue the ailing organization, things were at their bleakest. The stock was on a free fall, thousands of employees had already lost their jobs, and morale was in the pits. Many of the best managers were jumping ship for brighter prospects. In addition, even the most loyal of Xerox's customers had grown alienated by a flawed sales restructuring that tied billing procedures up in knots. To top matters off, the Securities and Exchange Commission (SEC) was hot on Xerox's trail, charging that the company defrauded investors by overstating earnings and hiding debt. Mulcahy—who had considered quitting work to spend more time with her sons—never expected to be thrown into this mess, but love for the company and her fellow employees compelled her to take on the challenge. Now, though, she wonders what she has gotten herself into. As soon as she solves one problem, another erupts.[1]

## Take A Moment

Try to put yourself in Anne Mulcahy's position. How would you begin to address Xerox's woes in the midst of this turmoil? What approach would you take to deal with employees, customers, shareholders, creditors, and government regulators?

Xerox's difficulties might seem exceptional, but Anne Mulcahy is not the only manager who has to deal with uncertainty and crisis on an almost daily basis. Consider the strife and confusion in the music industry, where traditional recording labels and music stores are battling with online services like Kazaa and Grokster that let people download and share music for free. The once-hot Tower Records declared bankruptcy due to the steep decline in music sales through traditional stores. Music industry lawsuits against the file sharing services and threats of legal action against consumers have done little to slow the transition to online music.[2] Managers in all organizations are continually dealing with uncertainty and unexpected events, whether it be something as small as the loss of a key employee or something as large and dramatic as a plant explosion. Moreover, the frequency and intensity of crises have increased over the past couple of decades, with a sharp increase in the rate of intentional acts such as product tampering, workplace violence, or terrorism.[3] Solid management skills and actions are the key to helping any organization weather a crisis and remain healthy, inspired, and productive.

The nature of management is to cope with diverse and far-reaching challenges. Managers have to keep pace with ever-advancing technology, find ways to incorporate the Internet and e-business into their strategies and business models, and strive to remain competitive in the face of increasingly tough global competition, uncertain environments, cutbacks in personnel and resources, and massive worldwide economic, political, and social shifts. The growing diversity of the workforce creates other dynamics: How can managers maintain a strong corporate culture while supporting diversity; balancing work and family concerns; and coping with conflicting demands of all employees for a fair shot at power and responsibility? New ways of working, such as virtual teams and telecommuting, put additional demands on today's managers.

To navigate the turbulence of today's world, managers need to shift their mindsets. The field of management is undergoing a revolution that asks managers to do more with less, to engage whole employees, to see change rather than stability as the nature of things, and to create vision and cultural values that allow people to create a truly collaborative workplace. This new management approach is very different from a traditional mindset that emphasizes tight top-down control, employee separation and specialization, and management by impersonal measurements and analysis. When people are suffering and demoralized, as they were at Xerox when Anne Mulcahy began her job as CEO, an impersonal, highly analytical approach could destroy the company faster than anything else.

Making a difference as a manager today and tomorrow requires integrating solid, tried-and-true management skills with new approaches that emphasize the human touch, enhance flexibility, and involve employees' hearts and minds as well as their bodies. Successful departments and organizations don't just happen—they are managed to be that way. Managers in every organization today face major challenges and have the opportunity to make a difference. For example, Lorraine Monroe made a difference at Harlem's Frederick Douglass Academy when she transformed it from one of the worst to one of the best schools in New York City. Stephen Quesnelle, head of quality programs at Mitel Corp. in Ottawa, Canada, made a difference when he organized "sacred cow hunts" to encourage employees to track down and do away with outdated policies and procedures that were holding the company back. Today, signs of energy, change, and renewal are everywhere at Mitel.[4]

These managers are not unusual. Every day, managers solve difficult problems, turn organizations around, and achieve astonishing performances. To be successful, every organization needs skilled managers.

© ALAN LEVENSON/CORBIS OUTLINE

This textbook introduces and explains the process of management and the changing ways of thinking about and perceiving the world that are becoming increasingly critical for managers of today and tomorrow. By reviewing the actions of some successful and not-so-successful managers, you will learn the fundamentals of management. By the end of this chapter, you will already recognize some of the skills that managers use to keep organizations on track. By the end of this book, you will understand fundamental management skills for planning, organizing, leading, and controlling a department or an entire organization. In the remainder of this chapter, we will define management and look at the ways in which roles and activities are changing for today's managers. The final section of the chapter talks about a new kind of workplace that has evolved as a result of changes in technology, globalization, and other forces, and examines how managers can meet the challenges of this new environment and manage unexpected events.

# The Definition of Management

What do managers such as Anne Mulcahy, Stephen Quesnelle, and Lorraine Monroe have in common? They get things done through their organizations. Managers create the conditions and environment that enable organizations to survive and thrive beyond the tenure of any specific supervisor or manager. Consider Elvis Presley Enterprises, Inc. Elvis died nearly 30 years ago, but managers have created and managed a successful organization with offices in Memphis, Tennessee, and Los Angeles that continues to thrive, employing more than 300 people and bringing in millions of dollars in sales and admission fees to Graceland. The organization's charitable arm supports a transitional housing program in Memphis, provides scholarships in the creative arts, and provides funding for a wide range of programs in the arts, education, and children's services.[5]

A key aspect of managing is recognizing the role and importance of others. Good managers know that the only way they can accomplish anything at all is through the people of the organization. Early twentieth-century management scholar Mary

Parker Follett defined management as "the art of getting things done through people."[6] More recently, noted management theorist Peter Drucker stated that the job of managers is to give direction to their organizations, provide leadership, and decide how to use organizational resources to accomplish goals.[7] Getting things done through people and other resources and providing leadership and direction are what managers do. These activities apply not only to top executives such as Anne Mulcahy, but also to the leader of a security team, a supervisor of an accounting department, or a director of sales and marketing. Moreover, management often is considered universal because it uses organizational resources to accomplish goals and attain high performance in all types of profit and not-for-profit organizations. Thus, our definition of management is as follows:

> *Management is the attainment of organizational goals in an effective and efficient manner through planning, organizing, leading, and controlling organizational resources.*

There are two important ideas in this definition: (1) the four functions of planning, organizing, leading, and controlling and (2) the attainment of organizational goals in an effective and efficient manner. Managers use a multitude of skills to perform these functions. Management's conceptual, human, and technical skills are discussed later in the chapter. Exhibit 1.1 illustrates the process of how managers use resources to attain organizational goals. Although some management theorists identify additional management functions, such as staffing, communicating, or decision making, those additional functions will be discussed as subsets of the four primary functions in Exhibit 1.1. Chapters of this book are devoted to the multiple activities and skills associated with each function, as well as to the environment, global competitiveness, and ethics, which influence how managers perform these functions. The next section begins with a brief overview of the four functions.

**management**
The attainment of organizational goals in an effective and efficient manner through planning, organizing, leading, and controlling organizational resources.

# The Four Management Functions

## Planning

**planning**
The management function concerned with defining goals for future organizational performance and deciding on the tasks and resource use needed to attain them.

Planning defines where the organization wants to be in the future and how to get there. **Planning** means defining goals for future organizational performance and deciding on the tasks and use of resources needed to attain them. At AOL Time Warner, the marketing chiefs of the various divisions—AOL, HBO, Time Inc., Turner Broadcasting, Warner Bros., and a dozen other units—get together every three weeks to talk about future projects and how the divisions can work together to make them more successful. Thanks to careful planning, for example, almost every division was involved in promoting the final film in *The Lord of the Rings* trilogy.[8]

A lack of planning—or poor planning—can hurt an organization's performance. For example, clothing retailer Merry-Go-Round, a once-ubiquitous presence in malls across America, slid into bankruptcy and ultimately disappeared as a result of poor planning. Top managers' lack of vision in perceiving market direction and demographic trends, weak planning efforts regarding acquisitions and growth, and the failure to prepare for management succession helped to kill a 1,500-store, billion dollar nationwide chain.[9]

## Organizing

**organizing**
The management function concerned with assigning tasks, grouping tasks into departments, and allocating resources to departments.

Organizing typically follows planning and reflects how the organization tries to accomplish the plan. **Organizing** involves the assignment of tasks, the grouping of

Exhibit 1.1

**The Process of Management**

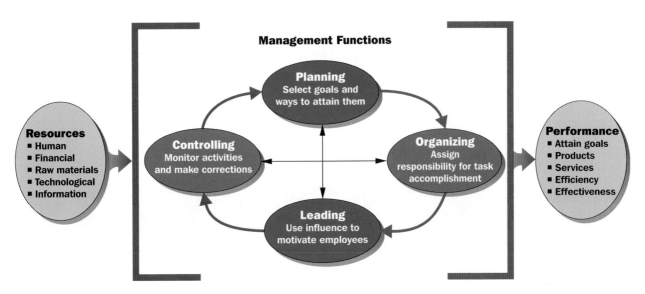

tasks into departments, and the assignment of authority and allocation of resources across the organization. Hewlett-Packard, Sears, Xerox, and Microsoft have all undergone structural reorganizations to accommodate their changing plans. Voyant Technologies, a maker of teleconferencing equipment, revised its structure to meet goals of increased sales and faster product development. By creating a new position specifically to bridge the gap between product managers and engineers, Voyant realized a 25 percent increase in sales, a 20 percent reduction in development costs, and a 40 percent improvement in time to market.[10]

## Leading

Leading is the use of influence to motivate employees to achieve organizational goals. Leading means creating a shared culture and values, communicating goals to employees throughout the organization, and infusing employees with the desire to perform at a high level. Leading involves motivating entire departments and divisions as well as those individuals working immediately with the manager. In an era of uncertainty, international competition, and a growing diversity of the workforce, the ability to shape culture, communicate goals, and motivate employees is critical to business success.

One doesn't have to be a well-known top manager like Bill Gates of Microsoft or Meg Whitman of eBay to be an exceptional leader. Many managers working quietly in both large and small organizations around the world also provide strong leadership within departments, teams, not-for-profit organizations, and small businesses. Valeria Maltoni is a marketing specialist for Destiny WebSolutions, where she leads teams that help clients solve their online business problems. Maltoni's philosophy is that true leaders open themselves up to the ideas and opinions of others.[11] Greg Mortenson runs the Central Asia Institute, a nonprofit organization he founded to promote secular education for girls in northern Pakistan and neighboring Afghanistan. Mortensen's vision, determination, courage, and enthusiasm encouraged others to join him in this new long-term approach to fighting terrorism.[12]

**leading**
The management function that involves the use of influence to motivate employees to achieve the organization's goals.

## CONCEPT CONNECTION

*PaeTec Communications provides voice and data services for mid-sized businesses. The company has increased to more than 1,000 employees while most telecommunications businesses have struggled. This dramatic growth is the result, in part, of a corporate culture that revolves around respect for employees. CEO Arunas Chesonis believes in **leading** PaeTec by putting employees first and then watching those employees voluntarily put customers before themselves. Placing high value on employees is successful for the company: although dealing with 4,000 problem calls a month, the company always answers the phone by the second ring, and the monthly customer retention rate is 99.5% or better since the company was founded in 1998. Every Friday morning, Chesonis demonstrates employee value by communicating with half of his employees.*

## Controlling

**controlling**
The management function concerned with monitoring employees' activities, keeping the organization on track toward its goals, and making corrections as needed.

Controlling is the fourth function in the management process. **Controlling** means monitoring employees' activities, determining whether the organization is on target toward its goals, and making corrections as necessary. Managers must ensure that the organization is moving toward its goals. New trends toward empowerment and trust of employees have led many companies to place less emphasis on top-down control and more emphasis on training employees to monitor and correct themselves.

New information technology is also helping managers provide needed organizational control without strict top-down constraints. Companies such as Cisco Systems and Oracle use the Internet and other information technology to coordinate and monitor virtually every aspect of operations, which enables managers to keep tabs on performance without maintaining daily authoritarian control over employees. Cisco employees have amazing freedom to make decisions and take action, but they also know that top managers keep a close eye on what's going on throughout the company with just a few mouse clicks.[13]

Organization failure can result when managers are not serious about control or lack control information. Particularly in turbulent times, managers need effective control systems to help them make fast, difficult decisions.

## Organizational Performance

The other part of our definition of management is the attainment of organizational goals in an efficient and effective manner. Management is so important because organizations are so important. In an industrialized society where complex technologies dominate, organizations bring together knowledge, people, and raw materials to perform tasks no individual could do alone. Without organizations, how could technology be provided that enables us to share information around the world in an instant, electricity be produced from huge dams and nuclear power plants, and thousands of DVDs be made available for our entertainment? Organizations pervade our society. Most college students will work in an organization—perhaps Sun Microsystems, Toronto General Hospital, Cinergy, or Hollywood Video. College students already are members of several organizations, such as a university, junior college, YMCA, church, fraternity, or sorority. College students also deal with organizations every day: to renew a driver's license, be treated in a hospital emergency room, buy food from a supermarket, eat in a restaurant, or buy new clothes. Managers are responsible for these organizations and for seeing that resources are used wisely to attain organizational goals.

Our formal definition of an **organization** is a social entity that is goal directed and deliberately structured. *Social entity* means being made up of two or more people. *Goal directed* means designed to achieve some outcome, such as make a profit (Old Navy, Verizon), win pay increases for members (AFL-CIO), meet spiritual needs (Methodist church), or provide social satisfaction (college sorority). *Deliberately structured* means that tasks are divided and responsibility for their performance is assigned to organization members. This definition applies to all organizations, including both profit and not-for-profit. Small, offbeat, and not-for-profit organizations are more numerous than large, visible corporations—and just as important to society.

**organization**
A social entity that is goal directed and deliberately structured.

Based on our definition of management, the manager's responsibility is to coordinate resources in an effective and efficient manner to accomplish the organization's goals. Organizational **effectiveness** is the degree to which the organization achieves a *stated goal*, or succeeds in accomplishing what it tries to do. Organizational effectiveness means providing a product or service that customers value. Organizational **efficiency** refers to the amount of resources used to achieve an organizational goal. It is based on how much raw materials, money, and people are necessary for producing a given volume of output. Efficiency can be calculated as the amount of resources used to produce a product or service.

**effectiveness**
The degree to which the organization achieves a stated goal.

**efficiency**
The use of minimal resources—raw materials, money, and people—to produce a desired volume of output.

Efficiency and effectiveness can both be high in the same organization. For example, during the tough economy of the early 2000s, companies like Eaton Corporation, which makes hydraulic and electrical devices, struggled to wring as much production as they could from scaled back factories and a reduced workforce. Managers initiated process improvements, outsourced some work to companies that could do it cheaper, streamlined ordering and shipping procedures, and shifted work to the most efficient assembly lines. At Eaton, these adjustments enabled the company to cut costs and hold the line on prices as well as meet its quality and output goals.[14]

Sometimes, however, managers' efforts to improve efficiency can hurt organizational effectiveness. This is especially true in relation to severe cost cutting. At Delta Airlines, former CEO Robert W. Allen dramatically increased cost efficiency by cutting spending on personnel, food, cleaning, and maintenance. Allen believed the moves were needed to rescue the company from a financial tailspin, but Delta fell to last place among major carriers in on-time performance, the morale of employees sank, and customer complaints about dirty planes and long lines at ticket counters increased by more than 75 percent.[15] Current CEO Leo Mullin came in with a goal to maintain the efficiencies instituted by Allen, but also improve organizational effectiveness.

The ultimate responsibility of managers is to achieve high **performance**, which is the attainment of organizational goals by using resources in an efficient and effective manner.

**performance**
The organization's ability to attain its goals by using resources in an efficient and effective manner.

# Management Skills

A manager's job is complex and multidimensional and, as we shall see throughout this book, requires a range of skills. Although some management theorists propose a long list of skills, the necessary skills for managing a department or an organization can be summarized in three categories: conceptual, human, and technical.[16] As illustrated in Exhibit 1.2, the application of these skills changes as managers move up in the organization. Although the degree of each skill necessary at different levels of an organization may vary, all managers must possess skills in each of these important areas to perform effectively.

## Conceptual Skills

**conceptual skill**
The cognitive ability to see the organization as a whole and the relationships among its parts.

**Conceptual skill** is the cognitive ability to see the organization as a whole and the relationships among its parts. Conceptual skill involves the manager's thinking, information processing, and planning abilities. It involves knowing where one's department fits into the total organization and how the organization fits into the industry, the community, and the broader business and social environment. It means the ability to *think strategically*—to take the broad, long-term view.

Conceptual skills are needed by all managers but are especially important for managers at the top. They must perceive significant elements in a situation and broad, conceptual patterns. For example, Microsoft, the giant software company, reflects the conceptual skills of its founder and chairman, Bill Gates. Overall business goals are clearly stated and effectively communicated throughout the company, contributing to Microsoft's leadership reputation and billion-dollar revenues. As one Microsoft manager pointed out, "Each part of the company has a life of its own now, but Bill is the glue that holds it all together."[17]

As managers move up the hierarchy, they must develop conceptual skills or their promotability will be limited. A senior engineering manager who is mired in technical matters rather than thinking strategically will not perform well at the top of the organization. Many of the responsibilities of top managers, such as decision making, resource allocation, and innovation, require a broad view.

## Human Skills

**human skill**
The ability to work with and through other people and to work effectively as a group member.

**Human skill** is the manager's ability to work with and through other people and to work effectively as a group member. This skill is demonstrated in the way a manager relates to other people, including the ability to motivate, facilitate, coordinate, lead, communicate, and resolve conflicts. A manager with human skills allows subordinates to express themselves without fear of ridicule and encourages participation. A manager with human skills likes other people and is liked by them. Anne Mulcahy, the CEO of Xerox profiled in the chapter opening, has exceptional human skills. Her co-workers describe her as both compassionate and tough, with a willingness to work shoulder to shoulder with subordinates and energize everyone to work toward a common goal.

As globalization, workforce diversity, uncertainty, and societal turbulence increase, human skills become even more crucial. Today's best managers are genuinely concerned with the emotional needs of their employees, not just the physical needs related to their job tasks. Meg Whitman, CEO of eBay, believes her most important contribution to the organization is creating a work ethic and culture that is "fun, open, and trusting." The attention Whitman and other eBay managers give to human skills pays off. Motivated employees have helped the organization expand in the face

Exhibit 1.2

## Relationship of Conceptual, Human, and Technical Skills to Management Level

**Management Level**
Top Managers

Middle Managers

First-Line Managers

Nonmanagers (Individual Contributors)

Conceptual Skills        Human Skills        Technical Skills

---

of stiff competition from larger rivals, and, unlike many Internet companies, eBay has been turning a healthy profit.[18] Human skills are important for managers at all levels, and particularly for those who work with employees directly on a daily basis. Organizations frequently lose good employees because of front-line bosses who fail to show respect and concern for workers.[19]

## Technical Skills

**Technical skill** is the understanding of and proficiency in the performance of specific tasks. Technical skill includes mastery of the methods, techniques, and equipment involved in specific functions such as engineering, manufacturing, or finance. Technical skill also includes specialized knowledge, analytical ability, and the competent use of tools and techniques to solve problems in that specific discipline. Technical skills are particularly important at lower organizational levels. Many managers get promoted to their first management jobs by having excellent technical skills. However, technical skills become less important than human and conceptual skills as managers move up the hierarchy. For example, in his seven years as a manufacturing engineer at Boeing, Bruce Moravec developed superb technical skills in his area of operation. But when he was asked to lead the team designing a new fuselage for the Boeing 757, Moravec found that he needed to rely heavily on human skills in order to gain the respect and confidence of people who worked in areas he knew little about.[20]

**technical skill**
The understanding of and proficiency in the performance of specific tasks.

*Go to the experiential exercise on page 33 that pertains to management skills.*

*Take A Moment*

## When Skills Fail

During turbulent times, managers really have to stay on their toes and use all their skills and competencies to benefit the organization and its stakeholders—employees, customers, investors, the community, and so forth. In recent years, there have been numerous, highly publicized examples of what happens when managers fail to effectively and ethically apply their skills to meet the demands of an uncertain, rapidly changing world. The profusion of company failures is alarming. Companies like Enron, Tyco, and WorldCom were flying high in the 1990s but came crashing down under the weight of financial scandals. Others, such as Rubbermaid, Kmart, and Xerox are struggling because of years of management missteps.

*Steve Jobs is different from many corporate top managers; he is the leader of Apple Computer and Pixar, but he is still deeply involved in using his **technical skills** to run his companies. Jobs takes personal responsibility for what Apple makes and how those products feel to the user. He still directs the design process from start to finish, asking endless questions, pushing the company toward better products. As stated by a fellow technology entrepreneur, Jobs "has the best taste in product design, the best ability as a one-on-one technical manager, and the greatest skill at making the rest of us want to buy stuff we don't strictly need of any American industrialist, ever."*

© ALAN LEVENSON/CORBIS OUTLINE

Although corporate greed and deceit grab the headlines, many more companies falter or fail less spectacularly. Managers fail to listen to customers, misinterpret signals from the marketplace, or can't build a cohesive team and execute a strategic plan. More than 250 public companies declared bankruptcy in one recent year, and the rate seems to be increasing.[21] Although economic factors and other outside forces play a part, the main reason for most failures is poor management. Recent examinations of struggling organizations and executives offer a glimpse into the mistakes managers often make in a turbulent environment.[22] Perhaps the biggest blunder is managers' failure to confront and adapt to the changing world around them. For example, even though Xerox's PARC research center practically invented the personal computer, top managers resisted getting into the computer business until it was too late to even get in the game, much less have a chance at winning. A related problem is top managers who create a climate of fear in the organization, so that people are afraid to tell the truth. Thus, bad news gets hidden and important signals from the marketplace are missed.

Other critical management missteps include poor communication skills and failure to listen; treating people only as instruments to be used; suppressing dissenting viewpoints; and the inability to build a management team characterized by mutual trust and respect.[23] The financial scandals of the early twenty-first century, from Enron to mutual fund mismanagement, clearly shows what can happen, for instance, when top managers pay more attention to money and Wall Street than they do to their employees and customers. As another example, consider what happened at *The New York Times* when it became publicly known that Jayson Blair, a rising young reporter, had fabricated and plagiarized many of his stories. Only then did top executives acknowledge the pervasive unhappiness that existed in the newsroom. Executive Editor Howell Raines, who had created an environment that favored certain editors and reporters, while others were afraid to offer dissenting viewpoints or tell their managers the truth, resigned under pressure following the scandal. The *Times* is still struggling to regain its footing and reclaim its honorable image.[24]

# Management Types

Managers use conceptual, human, and technical skills to perform the four management functions of planning, organizing, leading, and controlling in all organizations—large and small, manufacturing and service, profit and nonprofit, traditional and Internet-based. But not all managers' jobs are the same. Managers are responsible for different departments, work at different levels in the hierarchy, and meet different requirements for achieving high performance. Kevin Kurtz is a middle manager at Lucasfilm, where he works with employees to develop marketing campaigns for some of the entertainment company's hottest films.[25] Domenic Antonellis is CEO of the New England Confectionary Co. (Necco), the company that makes those tiny pastel candy hearts stamped with phrases such as "Be Mine" and "Kiss Me."[26] Both are managers, and both must contribute to planning, organizing, leading, and controlling their organizations—but in different amounts and ways.

## Vertical Differences

An important determinant of the manager's job is hierarchical level. Three levels in the hierarchy are illustrated in Exhibit 1.3. **Top managers** are at the top of the hierarchy and are responsible for the entire organization. They have such titles as president, chairperson, executive director, chief executive officer (CEO), and executive vice-president. Top managers are responsible for setting organizational

**top manager**
A manager who is at the top of the organizational hierarchy and is responsible for the entire organization.

Exhibit **1.3**

**Management Levels in the Organizational Hierarchy**

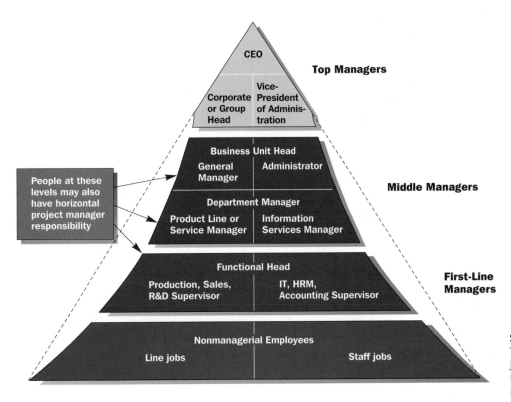

**SOURCE:** Adapted from Thomas V. Bonoma and Joseph C. Lawler, "Chutes and Ladders: Growing the General Manager," *Sloan Management Review* (Spring 1989), 27–37.

goals, defining strategies for achieving them, monitoring and interpreting the external environment, and making decisions that affect the entire organization. They look to the long-term future and concern themselves with general environmental trends and the organization's overall success. Among the most important responsibilities for top managers are communicating a shared vision for the organization, shaping corporate culture, and nurturing an entrepreneurial spirit that can help the company keep pace with rapid change. Today more than ever before, top managers must engage the unique knowledge, skills, and capabilities of each employee.[27]

**middle manager**
A manager who works at the middle levels of the organization and is responsible for major departments.

**Middle managers** work at middle levels of the organization and are responsible for business units and major departments. Examples of middle managers are department head, division head, manager of quality control, and director of the research lab. Middle managers typically have two or more management levels beneath them. They are responsible for implementing the overall strategies and policies defined by top managers. Middle managers generally are concerned with the near future and are expected to establish good relationships with peers around the organization, encourage teamwork, and resolve conflicts.

The middle manager's job has changed dramatically over the past two decades. Many organizations have improved efficiency by laying off middle managers and slashing middle management levels. Traditional pyramidal organization charts were flattened to allow information to flow quickly from top to bottom and decisions to be made with greater speed. The shrinking middle management is illustrated in Exhibit 1.3. In addition, today, line and staff positions are shrinking as well, as companies implement new technologies and procedures that enable them to do more work with fewer employees.

Although middle management levels have been reduced, the middle manager's job in many organizations has become much more important. Recent research shows that middle managers play a critical role in facilitating change and enabling organizations to respond to rapid shifts in the environment.[28] Rather than managing the flow of information up and down the hierarchy, they create horizontal networks that help the company act quickly. People who succeed as middle managers in today's world are those who are constructively critical of the status quo, have a high degree of personal power based on good relationships throughout the organization, are versatile and adaptable, and possess a high degree of emotional intelligence.[29]

**project manager**
A manager responsible for a temporary work project that involves the participation of other people from various functions and levels of the organization.

Middle managers' importance has also escalated because of the growing use of teams and projects. Strong project managers are in hot demand throughout the corporate world. A **project manager** is responsible for a temporary work project that involves the participation of people from various functions and levels of the organization, and perhaps from outside the company as well. Minnie Ingersoll works as a project manager for Google, where she coordinates activities between the advertising, finance, and engineering departments.[30] Today's middle manager might work with a variety of projects and teams at the same time, some of which cross geographical and cultural as well as functional boundaries. Project management makes the middle manager's job much more challenging and exciting.

Another growing trend is using *interim managers*, which means hiring temporary management professionals who work on a specific project or provide expertise in a specific area.[31] This approach enables a company to benefit from specialist skills without making a long-term commitment, and it provides flexibility for managers who like the challenge, variety, and learning that comes from working in a wide range of organizations. While interim managers are used at all levels, they can be particularly valuable for middle management activities.

**First-line managers** are directly responsible for the production of goods and services. They are the first or second level of management and have such titles as supervisor, line manager, section chief, and office manager. They are responsible for groups of nonmanagement employees. Their primary concern is the application of rules and procedures to achieve efficient production, provide technical assistance, and motivate subordinates. The time horizon at this level is short, with the emphasis on accomplishing day-to-day goals. For example, Stephanie Carver, the kitchen manager at a Bennigan's Grill and Tavern restaurant, monitors and supervises kitchen employees to make sure food is prepared in a safe and efficient manner. She is responsible for motivating and guiding young, often inexperienced workers, providing assistance as needed, limiting waste, and ensuring adherence to health and safety rules.

**first-line managers**
A manager who is at the first or second management level and is directly responsible for the production of goods and services.

## Horizontal Differences

The other major difference in management jobs occurs horizontally across the organization. **Functional managers** are responsible for departments that perform a single functional task and have employees with similar training and skills. Functional departments include advertising, sales, finance, human resources, manufacturing, and accounting. Line managers are responsible for the manufacturing and marketing departments that make or sell the product or service. Staff managers are in charge of departments such as finance and human resources that support line departments.

**functional manager**
A manager who is responsible for a department that performs a single functional task and has employees with similar training and skills.

General managers are responsible for several departments that perform different functions. A general manager is responsible for a self-contained division, such as a Dillard's department store, and for all of the functional departments within it. Project managers also have general management responsibility, because they coordinate people across several departments to accomplish a specific project.

**general manager**
A manager who is responsible for several departments that perform different functions.

# What Is It Like to Be a Manager?

So far we have described how managers at various levels perform four basic functions that help ensure that organizational resources are used to attain high levels of performance. These tasks require conceptual, human, and technical skills, which are today being applied in a turbulent environment for many managers. Unless someone has actually performed managerial work, it is hard to understand exactly what managers do on an hour-by-hour, day-to-day basis. The manager's job is so diverse that a number of studies have been undertaken in an attempt to describe exactly what happens. The question of what managers actually do to plan, organize, lead, and control was answered by Henry Mintzberg, who followed managers around and recorded all their activities.[32] He developed a description of managerial work that included three general characteristics and ten roles. These characteristics and roles, discussed in the following sections, have been supported in subsequent research.[33] More recently, research has been conducted on what managers *like* to do. The research found that both male and female managers most enjoy activities such as leading others, networking, and leading innovation. Activities managers like least include controlling subordinates, handling paperwork, and managing time pressures. Interestingly, there was substantial agreement among managers in five different countries on these preferences.[34]

© GAIL ALBERT HALABAN, CORBIS SABA

### CONCEPT CONNECTION

*As a **general manager** of Conoco's Rocky Mountain region, Carin Knickel created a climate of inspiration that cascaded down through the organization. She devised a system whereby her ten subordinate managers coached each other, then coached the people who reported to them, and so on down the line. Results of this team effort included a 12 percent growth in Conoco's share of a large metro retail gasoline market. The success also won Knickel a promotion to vice-president in charge of the company's new carbon-based group, making her Conoco's highest-ranking woman.*

## Manager Activities

One of the most interesting findings about managerial activities is how busy managers are and how hectic the average workday can be. At Google, project manager Minnie Ingersoll never looks at her calendar more than five minutes in advance because her schedule is so frantic and things change so quickly. On a typical day, Ingersoll might have four meetings and a conference call before grabbing a quick lunch and catching up with work on her laptop. Managers at Google use scooters to zip back and forth to meetings in different buildings.[35] Some top managers are even busier. Office Depot CEO Bruce Nelson typically works 14 hour days, visits stores in several different states each week, and is continuously tracking operations at 947 stores in eight time zones.[36]

### Adventures in Multitasking

Managerial activity is characterized by variety, fragmentation, and brevity.[37] The manager's involvements are so widespread and voluminous that there is little time for quiet reflection. The average time spent on any one activity is less than nine minutes. Managers shift gears quickly. Significant crises are interspersed with trivial events in no predictable sequence. One example of just two typical hours for general manager, Janet Howard, follows. Note the frequent interruptions and the brevity and variety of tasks.

| | |
|---|---|
| 7:30 A.M. | Janet arrives at work and begins to plan her day. |
| 7:37 A.M. | A subordinate, Morgan Cook, stops in Janet's office to discuss a dinner party the previous night and to review the cost–benefit analysis for a proposed enterprise resource planning system. |
| 7:45 A.M. | Janet's secretary, Pat, motions for Janet to pick up the telephone. "Janet, they had serious water damage at the downtown office last night. A pipe broke, causing about $50,000 damage. Everything will be back in shape in three days. Thought you should know." |
| 8:00 A.M. | Pat brings in the mail. She also asks instructions for formatting a report Janet gave her yesterday. |
| 8:14 A.M. | Janet gets a phone call from the accounting manager, who is returning a call from the day before. They talk about an accounting problem. |
| 8:25 A.M. | A Mr. Nance is ushered in. Mr. Nance complains that a sales manager mistreats his employees and something must be done. Janet rearranges her schedule to investigate this claim. |
| 9:00 A.M. | Janet returns to the mail. One letter is from an irate customer. Janet types out a helpful, restrained reply. Pat brings in phone messages. |
| 9:15 A.M. | Janet receives an urgent phone call from Larry Baldwin. They discuss lost business, unhappy subordinates, and a potential promotion.[38] |

### Life on Speed Dial

The manager performs a great deal of work at an unrelenting pace.[39] Managers' work is fast paced and requires great energy. The managers observed by Mintzberg processed 36 pieces of mail each day, attended eight meetings, and took a tour through the building or plant. Technology such as e-mail, instant messaging, cell phones, and laptops have intensified the pace. It isn't unusual for a manager to receive hundreds of e-mail messages a day. As soon as a manager's daily calendar is set, unexpected disturbances erupt. New meetings are required. During time away from the office, executives catch up on work-related reading, paperwork, and e-mail.

At O'Hare International Airport, an unofficial count one Friday found operations manager Hugh Murphy interacting with about 45 airport employees. In addition, he listened to complaints from local residents about airport noise, met with disgruntled executives of a French firm who built the airport's new $128 million people-mover system, attempted to soothe a Hispanic city alderman who complained that Mexicana Airlines passengers were being singled out by overzealous tow-truck operators, toured the airport's fire station, and visited the construction site for the new $20 million tower—and that was *before* the events of September 11, 2001, changed airport operations, making them even more complex. Hugh Murphy's unrelenting pace is typical for managers.[40] Management can be rewarding, but it can also be frustrating and stressful, as discussed in the Manager's Shoptalk box on page 21.

## Manager Roles

Mintzberg's observations and subsequent research indicate that diverse manager activities can be organized into 10 roles.[41] A **role** is a set of expectations for a manager's behavior. Exhibit 1.4 provides examples of each of the roles. These roles are divided into three conceptual categories: informational (managing by information); interpersonal (managing through people); and decisional (managing through action). Each role represents activities that managers undertake to ultimately accomplish the functions of planning, organizing, leading, and controlling. Although it is necessary to separate the components of the manager's job to understand the different roles and activities of a manager, it is important to remember that the real job of management cannot be practiced as a set of independent parts; all the roles interact in the real world of management. As Mintzberg says, "The manager who only communicates or only conceives never gets anything done, while the manager who only 'does' ends up doing it all alone."[42]

**role**
A set of expectations for one's behavior.

### Informational Roles

Informational roles describe the activities used to maintain and develop an information network. General managers spend about 75 percent of their time talking to other people. The *monitor* role involves seeking current information from many sources. The manager acquires information from others and scans written materials to stay well informed. The *disseminator* and *spokesperson* roles are just the opposite: The manager transmits current information to others, both inside and outside the organization, who can use it. One colorful example of the spokesperson role is Mick Jagger of the Rolling Stones. The rock band is run like a large, multinational organization with Jagger as the CEO. Jagger has surrounded himself not only with talented artists, but also with sophisticated and experienced business executives. Yet it is Jagger who typically deals with the media and packages the band's image for a worldwide audience.[43]

### Interpersonal Roles

Interpersonal roles pertain to relationships with others and are related to the human skills described earlier. The *figurehead* role involves handling ceremonial and symbolic activities for the department or organization. The manager represents the organization in his or her formal managerial capacity as the head of the unit. The presentation of employee awards by a division manager at Taco Bell is an example

# Exhibit 1.4

## Ten Manager Roles

| Category | Role | Activity |
|---|---|---|
| **Informational** | **Monitor** | Seek and receive information, scan periodicals and reports, maintain personal contacts. |
| | **Disseminator** | Forward information to other organization members; send memos and reports, make phone calls. |
| | **Spokesperson** | Transmit information to outsiders through speeches, reports, memos. |
| **Interpersonal** | **Figurehead** | Perform ceremonial and symbolic duties such as greeting visitors, signing legal documents. |
| | **Leader** | Direct and motivate subordinates; train, counsel, and communicate with subordinates. |
| | **Liaison** | Maintain information links both inside and outside organization; use e-mail, phone calls, meetings. |
| **Decisional** | **Entrepreneur** | Initiate improvement projects; identify new ideas, delegate idea responsibility to others. |
| | **Disturbance handler** | Take corrective action during disputes or crises; resolve conflicts among subordinates; adapt to environmental crises. |
| | **Resource allocator** | Decide who gets resources; schedule, budget, set priorities. |
| | **Negotiator** | Represent department during negotiation of union contracts, sales, purchases, budgets; represent departmental interests. |

**SOURCES:** Adapted from Henry Mintzberg, *The Nature of Managerial Work* (New York: Harper & Row, 1973), 92–93; and Henry Mintzberg, "Managerial Work: Analysis from Observation," *Management Science* 18 (1971), B97–B110.

of the figurehead role. The *leader* role encompasses relationships with subordinates, including motivation, communication, and influence. The *liaison* role pertains to the development of information sources both inside and outside the organization. The former head of Coca-Cola Co., Douglas Daft, placed greater emphasis on the liaison role to address new challenges from the environment. A health scare in Belgium that turned into a public relations nightmare, combined with a failed attempt to take over Cadbury Schwepps without European Union clearance, left Coca-Cola's relationships with European customers, officials, and organizations in tatters. Daft went on a goodwill tour from Brussels to Rome, meeting and talking with governments, investors, and employees to find out what went wrong and how to fix it.[44]

## Decisional Roles

Decisional roles pertain to those events about which the manager must make a choice and take action. These roles often require conceptual as well as human skills. The *entrepreneur* role involves the initiation of change. Managers are constantly thinking about the future and how to get there.[45] Managers become aware of problems and search for improvement projects that will correct them. Oprah Winfrey, head of Harpo Inc., is a master of the entrepreneur role. Although the television talk show *Oprah* is the foundation of Harpo, Winfrey is always looking for new projects. She has branched out into movie production, cable television, the Internet, and even launched a hot new magazine.[46] The *disturbance handler* role involves resolving conflicts among subordinates or between the manager's department and other departments. For example, the division manager for a large furniture manufacturer got involved in a personal dispute between two section heads. One section head was let

# manager's Shoptalk

### Do You Really Want to Be a Manager?

The first training course aspiring managers at FedEx take is called "Is Management for Me?" Becoming a manager is considered by most people to be a positive, forward-looking career move. Indeed, there are lots of appealing aspects to life as a manager. However, there are also many challenges, and not every person will be happy and fulfilled in a management position. Here are some of the issues would-be managers should consider before deciding they want to pursue management careers:

- *The increased workload.* It isn't unusual for managers to work 70–80 hour weeks, and some work even longer hours. A manager's job always starts before a shift and ends hours after the shift is over. Matt Scott, a software engineer promoted to management at Fore Systems, Inc., found himself frustrated by the increased paperwork and crowded meeting schedule.

- *The unrelenting sense of obligation.* A manager's work is never done. Nancy Carreon, an associate partner for an architectural firm, sometimes wakes up in the middle of the night thinking about something she needs to do—so she gets up and does it. George Pollard, a senior human resources official at FedEx, says, "Managers are always on the clock. We're representatives of [the company] even when we're not at work."

- *The headache of responsibility for other people.* A lot of people get into management because they like the idea of having power, but the reality is that many managers feel overwhelmed by the responsibility of supervising and disciplining others. Laura Kelso, who today thrives on the fast pace and responsibility of being a manager, says that the first time she had to fire someone, she agonized for weeks over how to do it. New managers are often astonished at the amount of time it takes to handle "people problems." Kelly Cannell, who quit her job as a manager, puts it this way: "What's the big deal [about managing people]? The big deal is

that people are human. . . . To be a good manager, you have to mentor them, listen to their problems, counsel them, and at the end of the day you still have your own work on your plate. . . . Don't take the responsibility lightly, because no matter what you think, managing people is not easy."

- *Being caught in the middle.* For many people, this is the most difficult aspect of management. Except for those in the top echelons, managers find themselves acting as a backstop, caught between upper management and the workforce. A computer software designer explains why she wanted out of management: "I didn't feel comfortable touting the company line in organizational policies and technical decisions I disagreed with. It was very hard asking folks to do things I wouldn't like to do myself, like put in gobs of overtime or travel at the drop of a hat." Even when managers disagree with the decisions of top executives, they are responsible for implementing them.

For some people, the frustrations of management aren't worth it. For others, management is a fulfilling and satisfying career choice and the emotional rewards can be great. One key to being happy as a manager may be carefully evaluating whether you can answer yes to the question, "Do I really want to be a manager?"

SOURCES: Heath Row, "Is Management for Me? That is the Question," *Fast Company* (February–March 1998): 50–52; Timothy D. Schellhardt, "Want to Be a Manager? Many People Say No, Calling Job Miserable," *The Wall Street Journal* (April 4, 1997): A1, A4; Matt Murray, "A Software Engineer Becomes a Manager, with Many Regrets," *The Wall Street Journal* (May 14, 1997): A1, A14; Hal Lancaster, "Managing Your Career: Nancy Carreon Works Long, Hard Weeks. Does She Need To?" *The Wall Street Journal* (May 13, 1997): B1; and Matt Murray, "Managing Your Career—The Midcareer Crisis: Am I in This Business to Become a Manager?" *The Wall Street Journal* (July 25, 2000): B1.

**CONCEPT CONNECTION**

*In a stunning change of course, Avon Products is targeting 16- to 24-year-olds in a direct attempt to sell to the MTV crowd. Avon shook up its image as a company that sells cosmetics to your mom when it launched "mark" —a trendy cosmetics line for the younger generation. In her* **decisional role as a manager**, *Andrea Jung has to make tough choices about how to position Avon to compete in an over-crowded market. Avon recruits representatives ages 16 and up for its U.S. sales force, who sell to young women at colleges, high schools, shopping malls, and other youth-oriented spots. Response so far has been positive. Even before the introduction of mark, the meetmark.com Web site received 13,000 inquiries about its new line.*

go because he did not fit the team. The *resource allocator* role pertains to decisions about how to allocate people, time, equipment, budget, and other resources to attain desired outcomes. The manager must decide which projects receive budget allocations, which of several customer complaints receive priority, and even how to spend his or her own time. The *negotiator* role involves formal negotiations and bargaining to attain outcomes for the manager's unit of responsibility. For example, the manager meets and formally negotiates with others—a supplier about a late delivery, the controller about the need for additional budget resources, or the union about a worker grievance.

The relative emphasis a manager puts on these ten roles depends on a number of factors, such as the manager's position in the hierarchy, natural skills and abilities, type of organization, or departmental goals to be achieved. For example, Exhibit 1.5 illustrates the varying importance of the leader and liaison roles as reported in a survey of top-, middle-, and lower-level managers. Note that the importance of the leader role typically declines while the importance of the liaison role increases as a manager moves up the organizational hierarchy.

Other factors, such as changing environmental conditions, may also determine which roles are more important for a manager at any given time. A top manager may regularly put more emphasis on the roles of spokesperson, figurehead, and negotiator. However, the emergence of new competitors may require more attention to the monitor role, or a severe decline in employee morale and direction may mean that the CEO has to put more emphasis on the leader role. A marketing manager may focus on interpersonal roles because of the importance of personal contacts in the marketing process, whereas a financial manager may be more likely to emphasize decisional roles such as resource allocator and negotiator. Despite

Exhibit 1.5

## Hierarchical Levels and Importance of Leader and Liaison Roles

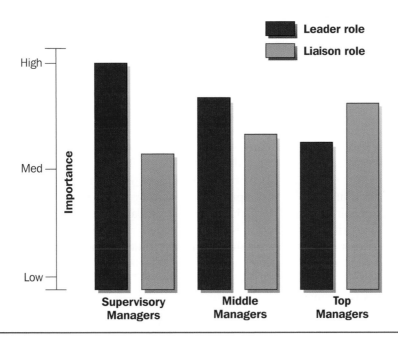

SOURCE: Based on information from A.I. Kraut, P.R. Pedigo, D.D. McKenna, and M.D. Dunnette, "The Role of the Manager: What's Really Important in Different Management Jobs," *Academy of Management Executive* 3 (1989), 286–293.

these differences, all managers carry out informational, interpersonal, and decisional roles to meet the needs of the organization. Managers stay alert to needs both within and outside the organization to determine what roles are most critical at various times.

# Managing in Small Businesses and Nonprofit Organizations

Small businesses are growing in importance. Hundreds of small businesses are opened every month by people who have found themselves squeezed out of the corporation due to downsizing or who voluntarily leave the corporate world to be their own bosses or to seek a slower pace and a healthier balance between work and family life. Many small businesses are opened by women or minorities who find limited opportunities for advancement in large corporations. In addition, the Internet has opened new avenues for small business formation. The huge wave of dot-com start-ups in the late 1990s was driven not just by dreams of wealth, but also by the desire of people to get out of big corporations and start something new and exciting.

Today's environment for small business is highly complicated. Advances in technology, globalization, new government regulations, and increasing customer demands require that even the smallest of businesses have solid management expertise. However, small companies sometimes have difficulty developing the managerial dexterity needed to survive in a turbulent environment. One survey on trends and future developments in small business found that nearly half of respondents saw inadequate management skills as a threat to their companies, as compared to less than 25 percent of larger organizations.[47] Managing in small businesses and entrepreneurial start-ups will be discussed in detail in Chapter 6.

One interesting finding is that managers in small businesses tend to emphasize roles different from those of managers in large corporations. Managers in small companies often see their most important roles as spokespersons, because they must promote the small, growing company to the outside world. The entrepreneur role is also very important in small businesses, because managers have to be creative and help their organizations develop new ideas to remain competitive. Small-business managers tend to rate lower on the leader role and on information-processing roles, compared with their counterparts in large corporations.

Nonprofit organizations also represent a major application of management talent. The American Red Cross, the Girl Scouts, Good Samaritan Ministries, Berea College, Parkland Memorial Hospital, the Boston Public Library, and the Nashville Symphony all require excellent management. The functions of planning, organizing, leading, and controlling apply to nonprofits just as they do to business organizations, and managers in nonprofit organizations use similar skills and perform similar activities. The primary difference is that managers in businesses direct their activities toward earning money for the company, while managers in nonprofits direct their efforts toward generating some kind of social impact. The unique characteristics and needs of nonprofit organizations created by this distinction present unique challenges for managers.[48]

Financial resources for nonprofit organizations typically come from government appropriations, grants, and donations rather than from the sale of products or services to customers. In businesses, managers focus on improving the organization's products and services to increase sales revenues. In nonprofits, however, services are typically provided to nonpaying clients, and a major problem for many organizations is securing a steady stream of funds to continue operating. Nonprofit managers, committed to serving clients with limited resources, must focus on keeping organizational costs as low as possible.[49] Donors generally want their money to go directly to helping clients rather than for overhead costs. If nonprofit managers can't demonstrate a highly efficient use of resources, they might have a hard time securing additional donations or government appropriations.

In addition, since nonprofit organizations do not have a conventional *bottom line*, managers may struggle with the question of what constitutes results and effectiveness. Whereas it is easy to measure dollars and cents, nonprofit managers have to measure intangibles such as "improve public health" or "make a difference in the lives of the disenfranchised." It is more difficult to gauge the performance of employees and managers when the goal is providing a public service rather than increasing sales and profits. Managers in nonprofit organizations must also market their services to attract not only clients but the volunteers and donors on whom they depend. An added complication is that volunteers and donors cannot be supervised and controlled in the same way a business manager deals with employees.

The roles defined by Mintzberg also apply to nonprofit managers, but these may differ somewhat. We might expect managers in nonprofit organizations to place more emphasis on the roles of spokesperson (to "sell" the organization to donors and the public), leader (to build a mission driven community of employees and volunteers), and resource allocator (to distribute government resources or grant funds that are often assigned top-down).

Managers in all organizations—large corporations, small businesses, and nonprofit organizations—carefully integrate and adjust the management functions and roles to meet new challenges within their own circumstances and keep their organizations

# Unlocking Creative Solutions Through Technology

**Click Here for Lower Taxes**

Government agencies are often thought of as plodding, inefficient bureaucracies that waste the public's time as well as money. But new ideas are changing that perception, as some government agencies apply Internet technology to save taxpayers money and make their lives easier.

The U. S. Internal Revenue Service (*http://www.irs.gov*) provides one of the best examples in the government or corporate world of a Web site that is central to the organization's mission. Distributing tax forms has always been an expensive logistical nightmare for the IRS. Hordes of form pullers, envelope stuffers, label-addressers, and so forth are needed to process the millions of mail-in requests for various tax publications and forms. The cost of handling a single request is around three dollars. The IRS recognized the problem and made the distribution of tax forms a major focus when it opened its Web site in the mid-1990s. Today, more than 100 million tax forms are downloaded directly from the site, with each request costing the IRS (and thus the taxpayers) only a fraction of a penny. E-filing of tax returns saves additional time and expense for both taxpayers and the IRS. State governments in the United States are also tapping into the power of the Web by allowing people to renew drivers licenses, file for unemployment benefits, pay quarterly taxes, apply for various permits, find suitable nursing homes, and access a range of other services electronically.

The United States is by no means alone in moving to the Internet. In a study of global e-government success, the consulting and technology services firm Accenture identified Canada as a leader in successfully tailoring government services that meet the needs of citizens as "customers." The Canadian federal government site (*http://canada.gc.ca*) was the sixth most popular Internet site in the country in 2003. In Spain, the government is developing the first Internet ID card. Spanish citizens can insert the card into a reader attached to their home computers and order passports and other government services. Russia launched a $2.4 billion, 8-year-long *e-Russia* project in May of 2003 to stimulate internal cooperation between departments and to make more government information available to the public. And the United Kingdom has a goal of having all public services available online by 2005.

The transition to the Internet is a welcome one for citizens around the world. A market research study of e-government services in 32 countries found that the number of Internet-using adults who have accessed government services online grew to 40 percent in 2003 and continues to increase. The Internet is helping to shatter the image of government workers as paper-shufflers and replace it with one of real people providing real and valuable services to the public.

**SOURCES:** Heather Walmsley, "State of e-Nation: Everyone in UK Will Have Online Access to Government Services by 2005—But Only If We Take Up Those Ideas Successfully Implemented Overseas," *Internet Magazine* (February 2004): 44+; Les Gomes, "Fix It and They Will Come; E-commerce Isn't Dead, Just Broken," *The Wall Street Journal* (February 12, 2001): R4; and "E-Governance A Hit in Metros, Says Survey," Asia Africa Intelligence Wire (December 9, 2003).

healthy. One way in which many organizations are meeting new challenges is through increased use of the Internet. Some government agencies are using the Web to cut bureaucracy, improve efficiency, and save money, as described in this chapter's Unlocking Creative Solutions Through Technology box.

## Management and the New Workplace

Over the past decade or so, the central theme being discussed in the field of management has been the pervasiveness of dramatic change. Rapid environmental shifts are causing fundamental transformations that have a dramatic impact on the manager's job. These transformations are reflected in the transition to a new workplace, as illustrated in Exhibit 1.6. The primary characteristic of the new workplace is that it is centered around bits rather than atoms—information and ideas rather than machines and physical assets. Low-cost computing power means that ideas, documents, movies, music, and all sorts of other data can be zapped around the world at the speed of light. The digitization of business has radically altered the nature of work, employees, and the workplace itself.[50] The *old workplace* is characterized by routine, specialized tasks and standardized control procedures. Employees typically perform their jobs in one specific company facility, such as an automobile factory located in Detroit or an insurance agency located in Des Moines. The organization is coordinated and controlled through the vertical hierarchy, with decision-making authority residing with upper-level managers.

In the *new workplace*, by contrast, work is free flowing and *flexible*. The shift is most obvious in e-commerce and high-tech organizations, which have to respond to changing markets and competition at a second's notice. However, numerous other organizations, such as McKinsey & Company, CNA Life, and Nokia, are also incorporating mechanisms to enhance speed and flexibility. *Empowered employees* are expected to seize opportunities and solve problems as they emerge. Structures are flatter, and decision-making authority is pushed down to lower levels.[51] The workplace is organized around networks rather than rigid hierarchies, and work is often *virtual*, with managers having to supervise and coordinate people who never actually "come to work" in the traditional sense. Thanks to modern information and communications technology, employees can perform their jobs from home or another remote location, at any time of the day or night. Flexible hours, telecommuting, and virtual teams are increasingly popular ways of working that require new skills from managers. Using virtual teams allows organizations to use the best

## Exhibit 1.6

### The Transition to a New Workplace

| | The New Workplace | The Old Workplace |
|---|---|---|
| **Characteristics** | | |
| Resources | Bits—information | Atoms—physical assets |
| Work | Flexible, virtual | Structured, localized |
| Workers | Empowered employees, free agents | Loyal employees |
| **Forces on Organizations** | | |
| Technology | Digital, e-business | Mechanical |
| Markets | Global, including Internet | Local, domestic |
| Workforce | Diverse | Homogenous |
| Values | Change, speed | Stability, efficiency |
| Events | Turbulent, more frequent crises | Calm, predictable |
| **Management Competencies** | | |
| Leadership | Dispersed, empowering | Autocratic |
| Focus | Connection to customers, employees | Profits |
| Doing Work | By teams | By individuals |
| Relationships | Collaboration | Conflict, competition |
| Design | Experimentation, learning organization | Efficient performance |

people for a particular job, no matter where they are located, thus enabling a fast response to competitive pressures. When IBM needs to staff a project, for example, it gives a list of skills needed to the human resources department, which provides a pool of people who are qualified. The team leader then puts together the best combination of people for the project, which often means pulling people from many different locations. IBM estimates that about a third of its employees participate in virtual teams.[52] Teams in today's organizations may also include outside contractors, suppliers, customers, competitors, and *interim managers* who are not affiliated with a specific organization but work on a project-by-project basis. The valued worker is one who learns quickly, shares knowledge, and is comfortable with risk, change, and ambiguity.

## Forces on Organizations

The most striking change now affecting organizations and management is *technology*. Consider that computing power has roughly doubled every 18 months over the past 30 years while the cost has declined by half or more every 18 months.[53] In addition, the Internet, which was little more than a curiosity to many managers a decade ago, has transformed the way business is done. Many organizations use *digital networking* technologies to tie together employees and company partners in far-flung operations. Companies are becoming interconnected, and managers have to learn how to coordinate relationships with other organizations.

The Internet and other new technologies are also tied closely to *globalization*. Global interconnections bring many opportunities to organizations, but they bring many threats, raise new risks, and accelerate complexity and competitiveness as well. Think about the trend toward outsourcing company activities to low-cost providers in other countries. U.S. companies have been sending manufacturing work to other countries for years to cut costs. Now, high-level knowledge work from U.S. organizations is also being outsourced to countries like India, Malaysia, and South Africa. India's Wipro Ltd., for example, writes software, performs consulting work, integrates back-office solutions, performs systems integration, and handles technical support for some of the biggest corporations in the United States—and they do it for 40 percent less than comparable U.S. companies can do the work.[54] *Diversity* of the population and the workforce in the United States is another fact of life for all organizations. The general population of the United States, and thus of the workforce, is growing more ethnically and racially diverse. In addition, generational diversity is a powerful force in today's workplace, with employees of all ages working together on teams and projects in a way rarely seen in the past.

In the face of these transformations, organizations are learning to value *change* and *speed* over stability and efficiency. The fundamental paradigm during much of the twentieth century was a belief that things can be stable. In contrast, the new paradigm recognizes change and chaos as the natural order of things.[55] Events in today's world are *turbulent* and *unpredictable*, with both small and large crises occurring on a more frequent basis.

## New Management Competencies

In the face of these transitions, managers have to rethink their approach to organizing, directing, and motivating employees. Today's best managers give up their command-and-control mindset to embrace ambiguity and create organizations that are fast, flexible, adaptable, and relationship-oriented. The Unlocking Creative Solutions Through People box describes the benefits one company has gained from a new approach to management. In many of today's best companies, *leadership* is dispersed throughout the organization, and managers empower others to gain the benefit of

# Unlocking Creative Solutions Through People

## At Tech Target, Freedom to Leave Makes Employees Stay

Many companies proclaim to be more interested in employees' performance than in their attendance, but few prove it as loudly as Tech Target, an interactive media company based in Needham, Massachusetts. For the 210 people who work there, there are no guidelines dictating work schedules, personal leave, sick days, or vacation time. Amazingly, employees have the freedom to come and go as they please. Sounds like a formula for disaster, right?

Contrary to what many people would think, Tech-Target's open-leave policy makes people more, not less, committed, responsible, and productive. Founder and CEO Greg Strakosch believes the open-leave policy is a competitive weapon, and he attributes increases in revenue largely to effects of the policy. For open-leave to work, managers have to reorient their approach. At Tech Target, supervisors set quarterly goals and timetables, and then employees are given the freedom and independence to achieve them. Managers pay attention to results, not to time, and they learn to trust people to be above-board when it comes to managing their own activities. Tech Target's employees appreciate open-leave for different reasons. For example, those with young children believe the policy eliminates the guilt and worry that accompanies trying to be both a good parent and a good employee, thus enabling them to be better at both.

Far from being lax, Tech Target sets high standards for performance and shows little tolerance for sloppy, lazy, or careless work habits. As Strakosch says, "We don't carry people who underachieve." Tech Target has a stringent hiring process because it wants to hire people with the right attitudes to function in the "loose yet tight" environment. For those who make the grade, it's a great arrangement. Where else could you take the afternoon off for a bike ride?

**SOURCES:** Patrick J. Sauer, "Open-Door Management," *INC.* (June 2003), 44.

their ideas and creativity. Moreover, managers often supervise employees who are scattered in various locations, requiring a new approach to leadership that focuses more on coaching and providing direction and support than on giving orders and ensuring that they are followed.

*Take A Moment*    *Go to the ethical dilemma on page 34 that pertains to managing in the new workplace.*

Success in the new workplace depends on the strength and quality of collaborative *relationships*. Rather than a single-minded focus on profits, today's managers recognize the critical importance of staying *connected to employees and customers*. The Internet has given increased knowledge and power to consumers, so organizations have to remain flexible and adaptable to respond quickly to changing demands or competition. New ways of working emphasize collaboration across functions and hierarchical levels as well as with other companies. *Team-building skills* are crucial. Instead of managing a department of employees, many managers act as team leaders of ever-shifting, temporary projects. At SEI Investments, all work is distributed among 140 teams. Some are permanent, such as those that serve major customers or focus on specific markets, but many are designed to work on short-term projects or problems. Computer linkups, called *pythons*, drop from the ceiling. As people change assignments, they just unplug their pythons, move their desks and chairs to a new location, plug into a new python, and get to work on the next project.[56]

An important management challenge in the new workplace is to build a *learning organization* by creating an organizational climate that values experimentation and risk taking, applies current technology, tolerates mistakes and failure, and rewards nontraditional thinking and the sharing of knowledge. Everyone in the organization participates in identifying and solving problems, enabling the organization to

**CONCEPT CONNECTION**

*One of the hottest television shows of recent years is Donald Trump's* The Apprentice, *where contestants vie for a $250,000-a-year job as president of one of Trump's companies. On one hand, it seems like an exercise in backstabbing. However, on the other hand, it's a search for a leader with* **new management competencies**— *one who knows how to be a team player and build collaborative relationships to help the organization benefit from everyone's creativity and skills. In the photo, Trump chats with hopeful contestants for the hit show.*

continuously experiment, improve, and increase its capability. The role of managers is not to make decisions, but to create learning capability, where everyone is free to experiment and learn what works best.

## Turbulent Times: Managing Crises and Unexpected Events

Many managers may dream of working in an organization and a world where life seems relatively calm, orderly, and predictable, but their reality is one of increasing turbulence and disorder. Today's managers and organizations face various levels of crisis every day—everything from the loss of computer data, to charges of racial discrimination, to a factory fire, to workplace violence. However, these organizational crises have been compounded by crises on a more global level. Consider a few of the major events that have affected U.S. companies within the last few years: the bursting of the dot-com bubble, which led to the failure of thousands of companies and the rapid decline of technology stocks; the massacre at Columbine High School, which prompted schools all over the country to form crisis teams to deal with school violence; the crash of high-flying Enron Corp. due to a complex series of unethical and illegal accounting gimmicks, and the subsequent investigations of numerous other corporations for similar financial shenanigans; terrorist attacks in New York City and Washington, D.C. that destroyed the World Trade Center, seriously damaged the Pentagon, killed thousands of people, and interrupted business around the world; anthrax and ricin scares that altered companies' advertising and marketing plans as they weighed the public's perceptions of the U.S. mail; the uncertainty and confusion associated with reconstruction efforts following the war in Iraq, and continuing terrorist threats against the United States and its allies. These and other events have brought the uncertainty and turbulence of today's world clearly to the forefront of everyone's mind, and crisis management has become a critical skill for every manager.

Dealing with the unexpected has always been part of the manager's job, but our world has become so fast, interconnected, and complex that unexpected events happen more frequently and often with greater and more painful consequences. All of the new management skills and competencies we have discussed are important to managers in such an environment. In addition, crisis management places further demands on today's managers. Some of the most recent thinking on crisis management suggests the importance of five leadership skills.[57]

1. Stay calm.
2. Be visible.
3. Put people before business.
4. Tell the truth.
5. Know when to get back to business.

## Stay Calm

A leader's emotions are contagious, so leaders have to stay calm, focused, and optimistic about the future. Perhaps the most important part of a manager's job in a crisis situation is to absorb people's fears and uncertainties. Leaders have to suppress their own fears, doubts, and pain to encourage others. Although they acknowledge the difficulties, they remain rock-steady and hopeful, which gives comfort, inspiration, and hope to others.

## Be Visible

When people's worlds have become ambiguous and frightening, they need to feel that someone is in control. The Monday following the September 11, 2001, terrorist attacks, the CEO of Young & Rubicam Advertising shook hands with every employee as he or she entered headquarters. Crisis is a time when leadership cannot be delegated. When Russian President Vladimir Putin continued his holiday after the sinking of the submarine Kursk in August 2000, his reputation diminished worldwide.[58]

## Put People Before Business

The companies that weather a crisis best, whether the crisis is large or small, are those in which managers make people and human feelings their top priority. As Ray O'Rourke, managing director for global corporate affairs at Morgan Stanley, put it following September 11, ". . . even though we are a financial services company, we didn't have a financial crisis on our hands; we had a human crisis. After that point, everything was focused on our people."[59]

## Tell the Truth

Managers should get as much information from as many diverse sources as they can, do their best to determine the facts, and then be open and straightforward about what's going on. Following the collapse of Enron Corp. and charges of unethical and possibly illegal activities, top managers at Enron compounded the crisis by destroying documents, refusing to be straightforward with employees and the media, and stonewalling investigators by pleading the Fifth Amendment. Managers at Arthur Andersen, Enron's accounting firm, also reportedly mishandled the crisis by destroying documents and pleading the Fifth.

## Know When to Get Back to Business

Although managers should first deal with the physical and emotional needs of people, they also need to get back to business as soon as possible. The company has to keep going, and there's a natural human tendency to want to rebuild and move forward. The rejuvenation of the business is a sign of hope and an inspiration to employees. Moments of crisis also present excellent opportunities for looking forward and using the emotional energy that has emerged to build a better company.

This is a challenging time to be entering the field of management. Throughout this book, you will learn much more about the new workplace, about the new and dynamic roles managers are playing in the twenty-first century, and about how you can be an effective manager in a complex, ever-changing world.

This chapter introduced a number of important concepts and described the changing nature of management. High performance requires the efficient and effective use of organizational resources through the four management functions of planning, organizing, leading, and controlling. To perform the four functions, managers need three skills—conceptual, human, and technical. Conceptual skills are more important at the top of the hierarchy; human skills are important at all levels; and technical skills are most important for first-line managers.

Two characteristics of managerial work also were explained in the chapter: (1) Managerial activities involve variety, fragmentation, and brevity and (2) Managers perform a great deal of work at an unrelenting pace. Managers are expected to perform activities associated with 10 roles: the informational roles of monitor, disseminator, and spokesperson; the interpersonal roles of figurehead, leader, and liaison; and the decisional roles of entrepreneur, disturbance handler, resource allocator, and negotiator.

These management characteristics apply to small businesses, entrepreneurial start-ups, and nonprofit organizations just as they do in large corporations. In addition, they are being applied in a new workplace and a rapidly changing world. In the new workplace, work is free flowing and flexible to encourage speed and adaptation, and empowered employees are expected to seize opportunities and solve problems. The workplace is organized around networks rather than vertical hierarchies, and work is often virtual. These changing characteristics have resulted from forces such as advances in technology and e-business, globalization, increased diversity, and a growing emphasis on change and speed over stability and efficiency. Managers need new skills and competencies in this new environment. Leadership is dispersed and empowering. Customer relationships are critical, and most work is done by teams that work directly with customers. In the new workplace, managers focus on building relationships, which may include customers, partners, and suppliers. In addition, they strive to build learning capability throughout the organization. An emerging need is for leadership during crises and unexpected events. Managers in crisis situations should stay calm, be visible, put people before business, tell the truth, and know when to get back to business. Human skills become critical during times of turbulence and crisis.

An excellent example of a leader during turbulent times is Anne Mulcahy, CEO of Xerox, described in the chapter opening. Although Xerox's woes are far from over, Mulcahy has gotten the company off the critical list. One characteristic that has gained her the admiration and respect of employees, customers, and shareholders alike is her willingness to tell the truth. "Part of her DNA is to tell you the good, the bad, and the ugly," says one colleague. Mulcahy is also fiercely concerned about people. Even during the darkest days, she refused to consider bankruptcy, preferring instead to focus everyone on rebuilding for the future. Her willingness to work with subordinates on the front lines has expanded her credibility and enabled her to energize people who were previously demoralized and hopeless. Despite the company's financial distress, she rejected a plan to abolish raises, and she implemented symbolic gestures of appreciation, like giving employees their birthdays off. She hid her own fears and insecurities to motivate people with a vision of what Xerox could be if everyone pulled together. Mulcahy definitely believes in being visible. She personally negotiated a settlement with the SEC, believing it sent a signal that the top leader was concerned about ethics and accountability. She met face-to-face with customers to smooth ruffled feathers and with creditors to renegotiate credit agreements and assure them that the company would pay back its enormous debts. When she had to make the tough decision to close the struggling personal computer division and lay off employees, she personally walked the halls to tell people she was sorry and let them vent their anger. "She was leading by example," says one creditor. "Everybody at Xerox knew she was working hard, and that she was

*Manager's Solution*

working hard for them." Employees rallied around her, and there were startling improvements in performance. Costs were reduced significantly, and all the company's divisions returned to profitability. Although it remains to be seen whether Mulcahy can make Xerox once again great, she is masterfully leading it though the greatest crisis in its 100-year history.[60]

## Discussion Questions

1. Assume you are a research engineer at a petrochemical company, collaborating with a marketing manager on a major product modification. You notice that every memo you receive from her has been copied to senior management. At every company function, she spends time talking to the big shots. You are also aware that sometimes when you are slaving away over the project, she is playing golf with senior managers. What is your evaluation of her behavior?

2. What do you think the text means by a management revolution? Do you expect to be a leader or follower in this revolution? Explain.

3. What similarities do you see among the four management functions of planning, organizing, leading, and controlling? Do you think these functions are related—that is, is a manager who performs well in one function likely to perform well in the others?

4. Why did a top manager such as Frank Lorenzo at Continental fail to motivate employees, while a top manager such as Herb Kelleher at Southwest succeed? Which of the four management functions best explains this difference? Discuss.

5. What is the difference between efficiency and effectiveness? Which is more important for performance? Can an organization succeed in both simultaneously?

6. What changes in management functions and skills occur as one is promoted from a non-management to a management position? How can managers acquire the new skills?

7. If managerial work is characterized by variety, fragmentation, and brevity, how do managers perform basic management functions such as planning, which would seem to require reflection and analysis?

8. A college professor told her students, "The purpose of a management course is to teach students about management, not to teach them to be managers." Do you agree or disagree with this statement? Discuss.

9. Describe the characteristics of the new management paradigm. How do these characteristics compare to those of an organization in which you have worked? Would you like to work or manage in a learning organization? Discuss.

10. How could the teaching of management change to prepare future managers to deal with workforce diversity? With empowerment? Do you think diversity and empowerment will have a substantial impact on organizations in the future? Explain.

# Management in Practice: Experiential Exercise

**Management Aptitude Questionnaire**

Rate each of the following questions according to this scale:

5 I always am like this.
4 I often am like this.
3 I sometimes am like this.
2 I rarely am like this.
1 I never am like this.

___ 1. When I have a number of tasks or home-work to do, I set priorities and organize the work around the deadlines. C 4

___ 2. Most people would describe me as a good listener. H 5

___ 3. When I am deciding on a particular course of action for myself (such as hobbies to pursue, languages to study, which job to take, special projects to be involved in), I typically consider the long-term (three years or more) implications of what I would choose to do. C

___ 4. I prefer technical or quantitative courses rather than those involving literature, psychology, or sociology. T

___ 5. When I have a serious disagreement with someone, I hang in there and talk it out until it is completely resolved. H

___ 6. When I have a project or assignment, I really get into the details rather than the "big picture" issues.* C

___ 7. I would rather sit in front of my computer than spend a lot of time with people. T

___ 8. I try to include others in activities or when there are discussions. H

___ 9. When I take a course, I relate what I am learning to other courses I have taken or concepts I have learned elsewhere. C

___ 10. When somebody makes a mistake, I want to correct the person and let her or him know the proper answer or approach.* H

___ 11. I think it is better to be efficient with my time when talking with someone, rather than worry about the other person's needs, so that I can get on with my real work. T

___ 12. I know my long-term vision for career, family, and other activities and have thought it over carefully. C

___ 13. When solving problems, I would much rather analyze some data or statistics than meet with a group of people. T

___ 14. When I am working on a group project and someone doesn't pull a full share of the load, I am more likely to complain to my friends rather than confront the slacker.* H

___ 15. Talking about ideas or concepts can get me really enthused and excited. C

___ 16. The type of management course for which this book is used is really a waste of time. T

___ 17. I think it is better to be polite and not to hurt people's feelings.* H

___ 18. Data or things interest me more than people. T

**Scoring key**

Add the total points for the following sections. Note that starred * items are reverse scored, as such:

1 I always am like this.
2 I often am like this.
3 I sometimes am like this.
4 I rarely am like this.
5 I never am like this.

1, 3, 6, 9, 12, 15   Conceptual skills total score _____
2, 5, 8, 10, 14, 17  **H**uman skills total score _____
4, 7, 11, 13, 16, 18 **T**echnical skills total score _____

The above skills are three abilities needed to be a good manager. Ideally, a manager should be strong (though not necessarily equal) in all three. Anyone noticeably weaker in any of the skills should take courses and read to build up that skill. For further background on the three skills, please refer to the model in pages 8–11.

*reverse scoring item
NOTE: This exercise was contributed by Dorothy Marcic.

# Management in Practice: Ethical Dilemma

### Can Management Afford to Look the Other Way?

Harry Rull had been with Shellington Pharmaceuticals for 30 years. After a tour of duty in the various plants and seven years overseas, Harry was back at headquarters, looking forward to his new role as vice president of U.S. Marketing.

Two weeks into his new job, Harry received some unsettling news about one of the managers under his supervision. Over casual lunch conversation, the director of human resources mentioned that Harry should expect a phone call about Roger Jacobs, Manager of New Product Development. Jacobs had a history of being "pretty horrible" to his subordinates, she said, and one disgruntled employee had asked to speak to someone in senior management. After lunch, Harry did some follow-up work. Jacobs's performance reviews had been stellar, but his personnel file also contained a large number of notes documenting charges of Jacobs's mistreatment of subordinates. The complaints ranged from "inappropriate and derogatory remarks" to subsequently dropped charges of sexual harassment. What was more disturbing was that the amount as well as the severity of complaints had increased with each of Jacobs's ten years with Shellington.

When Harry questioned the company president about the issue, he was told, "Yeah, he's had some problems, but you can't just replace someone with an eye for new products. You're a bottom-line guy; you understand why we let these things slide." Not sure how to handle the situation, Harry met briefly with Jacobs and reminded him to "keep the team's morale up." Just after the meeting, Sally Barton from HR called to let him know the problem she'd mentioned over lunch had been worked out. However, she warned, another employee had now come forward demanding that her complaints be addressed by senior management.

### What Do You Do?

1. Ignore the problem. Jacobs's contributions to new product development are too valuable to risk losing him, and the problems over the past ten years have always worked themselves out anyway. No sense starting something that could make you look bad.

2. Launch a full-scale investigation of employee complaints about Jacobs, and make Jacobs aware that the documented history over the past ten years has put him on thin ice.

3. Meet with Jacobs and the employee to try to resolve the current issue, then start working with Sally Barton and other senior managers to develop stronger policies regarding sexual harassment and treatment of employees, including clear-cut procedures for handling complaints.

Source: Based on Doug Wallace, "A Talent for Mismanagement," *What Would You Do? Business Ethics*, Vol II (November–December 1992), 3–4.

# Surf the Net

1. **Surfing Skills.** To help you get the most out of the "Surf the Net" exercises throughout this text, visit one of the Web sites listed below. If you're new to the Internet, list three things you learned that will help you develop your "surfing" skills. If you're already a proficient surfer, list three items of information you learned that will help you enhance your level of proficiency.
http://www4.district125.k12.il.us/webmeisters/cchausi/tutorial/surfingskills.html
http://www.zdnet.com/zdhelp/howto_help/websearch/search_1.html
http://www.pbs.org/standarddeviantstv/transcript-internet.html

2. **Management Career Opportunities.** The Manager's Shoptalk box in this chapter asked you to consider whether you really want to be a manager. To help you explore a future management career, access one of the online career Web sites, such as Career Mosaic or The Monster Board, accessible at *http://www.monster.com.*

   Click on the "search jobs" feature. You will be asked to enter key search words or select a job title from a list provided. Choose a management career that you are interested in pursuing, such as "sales manager," "financial manager,"

"human resources manager," or any other field that you want to learn about, then click on the search button. The site will return job postings from many different companies. Select at least three, look at the information, and print out the job descriptions. Compile a list of the education and experience requirements as well as any information about the job that appeals to you. Your instructor may ask you to write a memo on what you found and why you think that a management career will or will not be a good choice for you.

3. **Management Skills.** Use a search engine or try one of the Web addresses listed below to locate information about past or present successful managers, such as Sam Walton, Wal-Mart founder and former CEO; the late Dave Thomas, of Wendy's Restaurants; Herb Kelleher, CEO of Southwest Airlines, or Jack Welch, former CEO of General Electric. As you read about these leaders, identify examples of the conceptual, human, and technical skills exhibited in their work.
http://www.en.wikipedia.org/wiki/sam_walton
http://www.wendys.com/dave/flash.html

# Case for Critical Analysis

### Electra-Quik

Barbara Russell, a manufacturing vice president, walked into the monthly companywide meeting with a light step and a hopefulness she hadn't felt in a long time. The company's new, dynamic CEO was going to announce a new era of empowerment at Electra-Quik, an 80-year-old publicly held company that had once been a leading manufacturer and retailer of electrical products and supplies. In recent years, the company experienced a host of problems: market share was declining in the face of increased foreign and domestic competition; new product ideas were few and far between; departments such as manufacturing and sales barely spoke to one another; morale was at an all-time low, and many employees were

actively seeking other jobs. Everyone needed a dose of hope.

Martin Griffin, who had been hired to revive the failing company, briskly opened the meeting with a challenge: "As we face increasing competition, we need new ideas, new energy, new spirit to make this company great. And the source for this change is you—each one of you." He then went on to explain that under the new empowerment campaign, employees would be getting more information about how the company was run and would be able to work with their fellow employees in new and creative ways. Martin proclaimed a new era of trust and cooperation at Electra-Quik. Barbara felt the excitement stirring within her; but as she looked around the room, she saw many of the other employees, including her friend Harry, rolling their eyes. "Just another pile of corporate crap," Harry said later. "One minute they try downsizing, the next reengineering. Then they dabble in restructuring. Now Martin wants to push empowerment. Garbage like empowerment isn't a substitute for hard work and a little faith in the people who have been with this company for years. We made it great once, and we can do it again. Just get out of our way." Harry had been a manufacturing engineer with Electra-Quik for more than 20 years. Barbara knew he was extremely loyal to the company, but he-and a lot of others like him-were going to be an obstacle to the empowerment efforts.

Top management assigned selected managers to several problem-solving teams to come up with ideas for implementing the empowerment campaign. Barbara loved her assignment as team leader of the manufacturing team, working on ideas to improve how retail stores got the merchandise they needed when they needed it. The team thrived, and trust blossomed among the members. They even spent nights and weekends working to complete their report. They were proud of the ideas they had come up with, which they believed were innovative but easily achievable: permit a manager to follow a product from design through sales to customers; allow salespeople to refund up to $500 worth of merchandise on the spot; make information available to salespeople about future products; and swap sales and manufacturing personnel for short periods to let them get to know one another's jobs.

When the team presented its report to department heads, Martin Griffin was enthusiastic. But shortly into the meeting he had to excuse himself because of a late-breaking deal with a major hardware store chain. With Martin absent, the department heads rapidly formed a wall of resistance. The director of human resources complained that the ideas for personnel changes would destroy the carefully crafted job categories that had just been completed. The finance department argued that allowing salespeople to make $500 refunds would create a gold mine for unethical customers and salespeople. The legal department warned that providing information to salespeople about future products would invite industrial spying.

The team members were stunned. As Barbara mulled over the latest turn of events, she considered her options: keep her mouth shut; take a chance and confront Martin about her sincerity in making empowerment work; push slowly for reform and work for gradual support from the other teams; or look for another job and leave a company she really cared about. Barbara realized there would be no easy choices and no easy answers.

## Questions

1.  How might top management have done a better job changing Electra-Quik into a learning organization? What might they do now to get the empowerment process back on track?
2.  Can you think of ways Barbara could have avoided the problems her team faced in the meeting with department heads?
3.  If you were Barbara Russell, what would you do now? Why?

Source: Based on Lawrence R. Rothstein, "The Empowerment Effort That Came Undone," *Harvard Business Review* (January–February 1995), 20–31.

# Endnotes

1. Betsy Morris, "The Accidental CEO," *Fortune* (June 23, 2003), 58–67; Olga Kharif, "Anne Mulcahy Has Xerox by the Horns," *BusinessWeek* Online (May 29, 2003), *http://www.businessweek.com/technology/content/may2003/tc20030529_1642_tc111.htm*, accessed on February 3, 2003; Pamela L. Moore, "She's Here to Fix the Xerox," *BusinessWeek* (August 6, 2001), 47–48; and Cladia H. Deutsch, "At Xerox, the Chief Earns (Grudging) Respect, *The New York Times* (June 2, 2002), section 3, 1, 12.

2. Daniel Roth, "Catch Us If You Can," *Fortune* (February 9, 2003), 64–74; Ian Austen, "Downloading Again," *The New York Times* (May 3, 2004): C12; Christie Eliezer, "Kazaa Case Grinds on in Australia," *Billboard* (April 17, 2004): 60; and Steve Knopper, "Tower in Trouble," *Rolling Stone* (March 18, 2004): 26.

3. Ian Mitroff and Murat C. Alpaslan, "Preparing for Evil," *Harvard Business Review* (April 2003), 109–115.

4. Keith H. Hammonds, "The Monroe Doctrine," *Fast Company* (October 1999): 230–236; and David Beardsley, "This Company Doesn't Brake for (Sacred) Cows," *Fast Company* (August 1998): 66–68.

5. Elvis Presley Enterprises Web Site, "EPE History and Structure," *http://www.elvis.com/corporate/elvis_epe.asp*, accessed on February 6, 2003.

6. James A. F. Stoner and R. Edward Freeman, *Management*, 4th ed. (Englewood Cliffs, N.J.: Prentice Hall, 1989).

7. Peter F. Drucker, *Management Tasks, Responsibilities, Practices* (New York: Harper & Row, 1974).

8. George Anders, "AOL's True Believers," *Fast Company* (July 2002): 96–104.

9. Justin Martin, "The Man Who Boogied Away a Billion," *Fortune* (December 23, 1996): 89–100.

10. Stephanie Clifford, "How to Get the Geeks and the Suits to Play Nice," *Business 2.0* (May 2002): 92–93.

11. Heath Row, "Fearless in Philly" (Company of Friends column), *Fast Company* (June 2001): 36.

12. Kevin Fedarko, "He Fights Terror With Books," *Parade* (April 6, 2003): 4–6; and David Oliver Relin, "With Your Help, He's Fighting On," *Parade* (February 29, 2004): 12–14.

13. Eryn Brown, "Nine Ways to Win on the Web," *Fortune* (May 24, 1999): 112–125.

14. Louis Uchitelle, "Ready for an Upturn. Not Ready to Spend," *The New York Times* (June 23, 2002): Section 3, 1, 13.

15. Martha Brannigan and Eleena De Lisser, "Cost Cutting at Delta Raises the Stock Price But Lowers the Service," *The Wall Street Journal* (June 20, 1996): A1.

16. Robert L. Katz, "Skills of an Effective Administrator," *Harvard Business Review* 52 (September–October 1974): 90–102.

17. Brenton Schlender, "How Bill Gates Keeps the Magic Going," *Fortune* (June 18, 1990): 82–89.

18. Mark Gimein, "CEOs Who Manage Too Much," *Fortune* (September 4, 2000): 235–242.

19. Sue Shellenbarger, "From Our Readers: The Bosses that Drove Me to Quit My Job," *The Wall Street Journal* (February 7, 2000): B1.

20. Eric Matson, "Congratulations, You're Promoted. (Now What?)," *Fast Company* (June–July 1997): 116–130.

21. Ram Charan and Jerry Useem, "Why Companies Fail," *Fortune* (May 27, 2002): 50–62.

22. Based on Sydney Finkelstein, "7 Habits of Spectacularly Unsuccessful Executives," *Fast Company* (July 2003): 84–89; Charan and Useem, "Why Companies Fail"; and John W. Slocum Jr., Cass Ragan, and Albert Casey, "On Death and Dying: The Corporate Leadership Capacity of CEOs," *Organizational Dynamics* 30, no. 3 (Spring 2002): 269–281.

23. Ibid.

24. Matthew Rose and Laurie P. Cohen, "Man in the News: Amid Turmoil, Top Editors Resign at New York Times," *The Wall Street Journal* (June 6, 2003): A1, A6.

25. Heath Row, "Force Play" (Company of Friends column), *Fast Company* (March 2001): 46.

26. Charles Fishman, "Sweet Company," *Fast Company* (February 2001): 136–145.

27. Christopher A. Bartlett and Sumantra Ghoshal, "Changing the Role of Top Management: Beyond Systems to People," *Harvard Business Review* (May–June 1995): 132–142; and Sumantra Ghoshal and Christopher A. Bartlett, "Changing the Role of Top Management: Beyond Structure to Processes," *Harvard Business Review* (January–February 1995): 86–96.

28. Quy Nguyen Huy, "In Praise of Middle Managers," *Harvard Business Review* (September 2003): 72–79.

29. Ibid.; and Jenny C. McCune, "Management's Brave New World," *Management Review* (October 1997): 10–14; "Middle Managers Are Back—But Now They're 'High Impact Players,'" *The Wall Street Journal* (April 14, 1998): B1; and Geoffrey Colvin, "Revenge of the Nerds," *Fortune* (March 2, 1998): 223–224.

30. Dan Tynan, "Jungletalk with . . . Google's Minnie Ingersoll," *MBA Jungle* (October–November 2003): 34–25.

31. Kerr Inkson, Angela Heising, and Denise M. Rousseau, "The Interim Manager: Prototype of the 21st Century Worker," *Human Relations* 54, no. 3 (2001), 259–284.

32. Henry Mintzberg, *The Nature of Managerial Work* (New York: Harper & Row, 1973); and Mintzberg, "Rounding Out the Manager's Job," *Sloan Management Review* (Fall 1994): 11–26.

33. Robert E. Kaplan, "Trade Routes: The Manager's Network of Relationships," *Organizational Dynamics* (Spring 1984): 37–52; Rosemary Stewart, "The Nature of Management: A Problem for Management Education," *Journal of Management Studies* 21 (1984): 323–330; John P. Kotter, "What Effective General Managers Really Do," *Harvard Business Review* (November–December 1982): 156–167; and Morgan W. McCall, Jr., Ann M. Morrison, and Robert L. Hannan, "Studies of Managerial Work: Results and Methods" (Technical Report No. 9, Center for Creative Leadership, Greensboro, N.C., 1978).

34. Alison M. Konrad, Roger Kashlak, Izumi Yoshioka, Robert Waryszak, and Nina Toren, "What Do Managers *Like* to Do? A Five-Country Study," *Group and Organizational Management* 26, no. 4 (December 2001): 401–433.

35. Tynan, "Jungletalk with Google's Minnie Ingersoll."

36. Jennifer Couzin, "Tick, Tick, Tick," *The Industry Standard* (April 16, 2001): 62–67.

37. Henry Mintzberg, "Managerial Work: Analysis from Observation," *Management Science* 18 (1971): B97–B110.

38. Based on Carol Saunders and Jack William Jones, "Temporal Sequences in Information Acquisition for Decision Making: A Focus on Source and Medium," *Academy of Management Review* 15 (1990): 29–46; Kotter, "What Effective General Managers Really Do"; and Mintzberg, "Managerial Work."

39. Mintzberg, "Managerial Work."

40. Anita Lienert, "A Day in the Life: Airport Manager Extraordinaire," *Management Review* (January 1995): 57–61.

41. Lance B. Kurke and Howard E. Aldrich, "Mintzberg Was Right!: A Replication and Extension of The Nature of Managerial Work," *Management Science* 29 (1983): 975–984; Cynthia M. Pavett and Alan W. Lau, "Managerial Work: The Influence of Hierarchical Level and Functional Specialty," *Academy of Management Journal 26* (1983): 170–177; and Colin P. Hales, "What Do Managers Do? A Critical Review of the Evidence," *Journal of Management Studies 23* (1986): 88–115.

42. Mintzberg, "Rounding out the Manager's Job."

43. Andy Serwer, "Inside the Rolling Stones Inc.," *Fortune* (September 30, 2002): 58–72.

44. Betsy McKay, "To Fix Coca-Cola, Daft Sets Out to Get Relationships Right," *The Wall Street Journal* (June 23, 2000): A1, A12.

45. Harry S. Jonas III, Ronald E. Fry, and Suresh Srivastva, "The Office of the CEO: Understanding the Executive Experience," *Academy of Management Executive 4* (August 1990): 36–48.

46. Patricia Sellers, "The Business of Being Oprah," *Fortune* (April 1, 2002): 50–64.

47. Edward O. Welles, "There Are No Simple Businesses Anymore," *The State of Small Business* (1995): 66–79.

48. This section is based largely on Peter F. Drucker, *Managing the Non-Profit Organization: Principles and Practices* (New York: HarperBusiness, 1992); and Thomas Wolf, *Managing a Nonprofit Organization* (New York: Fireside/Simon & Schuster, 1990).

49. Christine W. Letts, William P. Ryan, and Allen Grossman, *High Performance Nonprofit Organizations* (New York: John Wiley & Sons, 1999), 30–35.

50. Harry G. Barkema, Joel A. C. Baum, and Elizabeth A. Mannix, "Management Challenges in a New Time," *Academy of Management Journal 45*, no. 5 (2002): 916–930. The following section is based on Barkema, Baum, and Mannix, "Management Challenges," Michael Harvey and M. Ronald Buckley, "Assessing the 'Conventional Wisdoms' of Management for the 21st Century Organization," *Organizational Dynamics* 30, no. 4 (2002): 368–378; and Toby J. Tetenbaum, "Shifting Paradigms: From Newton to Chaos," *Organizational Dynamics* (Spring 1998): 21–32.

51. Caroline Ellis, "The Flattening Corporation," *MIT Sloan Management Review* (Summer 2003): 5.

52. Carla Joinson, "Managing Virtual Teams," *HR Magazine* ( June 2002): 69–73.

53. Barkema, Baum, and Mannix, "Management Challenges in a New Time."

54. Keith H. Hammonds, "Smart, Determined, Ambitious, Cheap: The New Face of Global Competition," *Fast Company* (February 2003): 91–97.

55. Tetenbaum, "Shifting Paradigms: From Newton to Chaos."

56. Scott Kirsner, "Every Day, It's a New Place," *Fast Company* (April–May 1998): 130–134; Peter Coy, "The Creative Economy," *BusinessWeek* (August 28, 2000): 76–82; and Jeremy Main, "The Shape of the New Corporation," *Working Woman* (October 1998): 60–63.

57. This section is based on Loretta Ucelli, "The CEO's 'How To' Guide to Crisis Communications," *Strategy & Leadership* 30, no. 2 (2002): 21–24; Eric Beaudan, "Leading in Turbulent Times," *Ivey Business Journal* (May–June 2002): 22–26; Christine Pearson, "A Blueprint for Crisis Management," *Ivey Business Journal* (January–February 2002): 68–73; Leslie Wayne and Leslie Kaufman, "Leadership, Put to a New Test," *The New York Times* (September 16, 2001): Section 3, 1, 4; Jerry Useem, "What It Takes," *Fortune* (November 12, 2001): 126–132; and Andy Bowen, "Crisis Procedures that Stand the Test of Time," *Public Relations Tactics* (August 2001): 16.

58. Beaudan, "Leading in Turbulent Times."

59. Paul Argenti, "Crisis Communication: Lessons from 9/11," *Harvard Business Review* (December 2002): 103–109.

60. Morris, "The Accidental CEO."

Chapter 2

# The Evolution of Management Thinking

## LEARNING OBJECTIVES

*After studying this chapter, you should be able to:*

1. Understand how historical forces influence the practice of management.

2. Identify and explain major developments in the history of management thought.

3. Describe the major components of the classical and humanistic management perspectives.

4. Discuss the management science perspective and its current use in organizations.

5. Explain the major concepts of systems theory, the contingency view, and total quality management.

6. Describe the learning organization and the changes in structure, empowerment, and information sharing managers make to support it.

7. Discuss the technology-driven workplace and the role of enterprise resource planning and knowledge management systems.

Cementos Mexicanos (Cemex), based in Monterrey, Mexico, has been making and delivering concrete for nearly a century. The company specializes in delivering concrete in developing areas of the world, places where anything can, and usually does, go wrong. Even in Monterrey, for example, Cemex copes with unpredictable weather and traffic conditions, spontaneous labor disruptions, building permit snafus, and arbitrary government inspections of construction sites. In addition, more than half of all orders are changed or canceled by customers, usually at the last minute. Considering that a load of concrete is never more than 90 minutes from spoiling, these chaotic conditions mean high costs, complex scheduling, and frustration for employees, managers, and customers. As competition in the industry increased, Cemex managers began looking for ways to stand out from the crowd. One idea was a guaranteed delivery time, but despite the efforts of employees, the best Cemex could do was promise delivery within a three-hour window. To make matters worse, the construction business itself was becoming increasingly complex and competitive, leading to even more disruptions and cancellations. Builders were sometimes lucky to get their orders delivered on the right day, let along at the right hour. Cemex managers began to consider that the company needed a whole new approach to doing business—one that accepted rather than resisted the natural chaos of the marketplace. That would mean massive changes in operations, as well as finding ways to get dispatchers and drivers (who had an average of six years of formal education) to think like entrepreneurs.[1]

## Take A Moment

If you were a manager at Cemex, what changes would you implement to help the organization thrive in the face of constant chaos? What advice would you give managers concerning their management approach and the kind of company they might create?

Cemex is faced with a situation similar to many companies. The methods and patterns that kept the organization successful in the past no longer seem enough to keep it thriving in today's turbulent environment. Unexpected market forces or other changes in the environment can devastate a company. Major airlines in the United States are being hammered by new low-cost carriers like JetBlue and AirTran. As of September 2003, cut-rate airlines had grabbed 22 percent of U.S. market share, up from 16 percent two years earlier. Consider that while the big carriers lost customers—and money—in 2002, JetBlue's passenger traffic increased dramatically and the start-up had profits of $55 million on revenues of $635 million.[2] As another example, widespread financial and ethical scandals in the early 2000s have affected even the most unlikely of companies. Lutheran Health Network, which runs six hospitals in and around Fort Wayne, Indiana, now spends around $250,000 more per year to make sure the organization has documentation that they are complying with health care regulators and other oversight boards.[3] Confronted by ever-shifting conditions, managers have to make continual changes in their organizations, and sometimes create a new kind of company, as at Cemex, one with which they have little experience or skill.

As we discussed in Chapter 1, we are currently shifting to a new kind of workplace and a new approach to management. Managers today face the ultimate paradox: (1) Keep everything running efficiently and profitably, while, at the same time, (2) change everything.[4] It is no longer enough just to learn how to measure and control things. Success accrues to those who learn how to be leaders, to initiate change, and to participate in and even create organizations with fewer managers and less hierarchy that can change quickly.

Management philosophies and organizational forms change over time to meet new needs. The workplace of today is very different from what it was 50 years ago—indeed, from what it was even 10 years ago. Yet there are ideas and practices from the past that are still highly relevant and applicable to management today. Many students wonder why history matters to managers. A historical perspective provides a broader way of thinking, a way of searching for patterns and determining whether they recur across time periods. For example, certain management techniques that seem modern, such as employee stock-ownership programs, have repeatedly gained and lost popularity since the early twentieth century because of historical forces.[5] William Cooper Procter, grandson of the co-founder of Procter & Gamble, introduced a profit-sharing plan in 1887, and expanded it by tying it to stock ownership a few years later. Sam Walton opened Wal-Mart's financial records, including salaries, to all employees in the 1960s, long before business magazines were touting the value of *open-book management*.[6]

A study of the past contributes to understanding both the present and the future. It is a way of learning from others' mistakes so as not to repeat them; learning from others' successes so as to repeat them in the appropriate situation; and most of all, learning to understand why things happen to improve our organizations in the future. This chapter provides an overview of the ideas, theories, and management philosophies that have contributed to making the workplace what it is today. We will examine several management approaches that have been popular and successful throughout the twentieth century. The final section of the chapter will look at recent trends and current approaches that build on this foundation of management understanding. This foundation illustrates that the value of studying management lies not in learning current facts and research but in developing a perspective that will facilitate the broad, long-term view needed for management success.

# Management and Organization

A historical perspective on management provides a context or environment in which to interpret current opportunities and problems. However, studying history does not mean merely arranging events in chronological order; it means developing an understanding of the impact of societal forces on organizations. Studying history is a way to achieve strategic thinking, see the big picture, and improve conceptual skills. We will start by examining how social, political, and economic forces have influenced organizations and the practice of management.[7]

**Social forces** refer to those aspects of a culture that guide and influence relationships among people. What do people value? What do people need? What are the standards of behavior among people? These forces shape what is known as the *social contract*, which refers to the unwritten, common rules and perceptions about relationships among people and between employees and management.

**social forces**
The aspects of a culture that guide and influence relationships among people—their values, needs, and standards of behavior.

A significant social force today is the changing attitudes, ideas, and values of Generation X and Generation Y employees. Generation X workers, those now in their thirties, have had a profound impact on the workplace, and Generation Y may have an even greater one. These young workers, the most educated generation in the history of the United States, grew up technologically adept and globally conscious. Some trends sparked by Generation X and Y workers are completely reshaping the social contract.[8] Career life cycles are getting shorter, with workers typically changing jobs every few years and changing careers several times during their lifetime. Some consultants predict that the traditional 20-year career-building cycle will transform into a 20-month skills-building process.[9] Young workers also expect to have access to cutting-edge technology, opportunities to learn and further their careers and personal goals, and the power to make substantive decisions and changes in the workplace. Finally, there is a growing focus on work/life balance, reflected in trends such as telecommuting, flextime, shared jobs, and organization-sponsored sabbaticals.

**Political forces** refer to the influence of political and legal institutions on people and organizations. Political forces include basic assumptions underlying the political system, such as the desirability of self-government, property rights, contract rights, the definition of justice, and the determination of innocence or guilt of a crime. The spread of capitalism throughout the world has dramatically altered the business landscape. The dominance of the free-market system and growing interdependencies among the world's countries require organizations to operate differently and managers to think in new ways. At the same time, strong anti-American sentiments in many parts of the world create challenges for U.S. companies and managers. Another potent political force is the empowerment of citizens throughout the world. Power is being diffused both within and among countries as never before.[10] People are demanding empowerment, participation, and responsibility in all areas of their lives, including their work.

**political forces**
The influence of political and legal institutions on people and organizations.

**Economic forces** pertain to the availability, production, and distribution of resources in a society. Governments, military agencies, churches, schools, and business organizations in every society require resources to achieve their goals, and economic forces influence the allocation of scarce resources. The economy of the United States and other developed countries is shifting dramatically, with the sources of wealth, the fundamentals of distribution, and the nature of economic decision making undergoing significant changes.[11] The emerging new economy is based largely on ideas, information, and knowledge rather than material resources. Supply chains and distribution of resources have been revolutionized by digital

**economic forces**
Forces that affect the availability, production, and distribution of a society's resources among competing users.

technology. Surplus inventories, which once could trigger recessions, are declining or completely disappearing. Another economic trend is the booming importance of small and mid-sized businesses, including start-ups, which early in the twenty-first century grew at three times the rate of the national economy. "I call it 'the invisible economy,' yet it is *the* economy," says David Birch of Cognetics Inc., a Cambridge, Massachusetts, firm that tracks business formation.[12]

A massive shift in the economy is not without its upheavals, of course. In the early 2000s, years of seemingly endless growth ground to a halt as stock prices fell, particularly for dot-com and technology companies. Numerous Internet-based companies went out of business, and organizations throughout the United States and Canada began laying off hundreds of thousands of workers. However, this economic downturn may also be a stimulus for even greater technological innovation and small business vitality. Read the Unlocking Creative Solutions Through Technology box for an interesting angle on today's shifting economy

Management practices and perspectives vary in response to these social, political, and economic forces in the larger society. During difficult times, managers look for ideas to help them cope with environmental turbulence and keep their organizations vital. A survey by Bain & Company, for example, found a dramatic increase in 2002 in the variety of management ideas and techniques used by managers in the companies surveyed. With a tough economy and rocky stock market, lingering anxieties over war and terrorism, and the public suspicion and skepticism resulting from corporate scandals, executives were searching for any management tool—new or old—that could help them get the most out of limited resources.[13] This search for guidance is reflected in a recent proliferation of books, scholarly articles, and conferences dedicated to examining management fashions and trends.[14] Exhibit 2.1 illustrates the evolution of significant management perspectives over time, each of which will be examined in the remainder of this chapter. The timeline reflects the dominant time period for each approach, but elements of each are still used in today's organizations.

## Exhibit 2.1

### Management Perspectives over Time

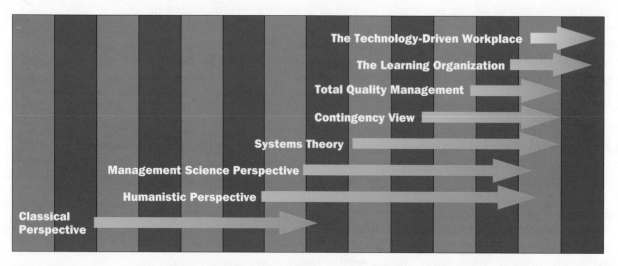

# Unlocking Creative Solutions Through Technology

## Of Railroads and Web Sites

About 150 years ago, the railroad revolution transformed the economy. Today, the Internet revolution is doing the same thing. We all know that history doesn't really repeat itself, but there are historical patterns that help us make sense of the present and predict what the future might be like.

The railroads and the Internet serve the same basic economic function: connecting buyers and sellers. And while few seem to know how to make the Internet economically profitable, the same thing could have been said about the railroad in its infancy. Yet the railroad's ability to move freight quickly and cheaply changed the world, and the Internet's ability to move information quickly and cheaply promises to do the same thing today. And whereas the railroads created the first national market, the Internet is creating the first truly global one. The railroad made it possible for companies such as Sears Roebuck, Montgomery Ward, and Woolworth to lower their prices and expand their operations nationally through catalog retailing, forcing small local retailers to compete in new ways. Similarly, successful Internet retailers such as Amazon.com are challenging bricks-and-mortar companies to rethink how they interact with suppliers and customers.

But nobody said changing the world was easy, and the early twenty first-century turbulence in the technology sector is clearly an indication. Stock prices took a sharp plunge, many of the thousands of entrepreneurs who rushed in with dreams of getting rich on the Internet fell by the wayside, and numerous dot-com companies went out of business. Over a two-year period (1999–2000), the number of Internet IPOs (initial public offerings) grew at amazing speed, and crashed just as quickly. If the history of the railroad is any indication, this is merely the shake-out to be expected from such a major economic transformation, and new leaders will step in to revise, strengthen, and perfect the new business models. For example, a few small Web-only retailers, like Blue Nile, which sells jewelry, and eBags, Inc., a luggage retailer, have thrived over the long term, demonstrating that careful management can make the difference in cyberspace just as it does in the physical world.

In the nineteenth century, railroad stocks soared and plunged as practical realities warred with potential profits and the hopes of investors fought with their fears. The railroad vastly overbuilt in the decades after the Civil War, and in the 1880s and 1890s, more than two-thirds of the railroad tracks in the United States passed through receivership and were reorganized by the big Wall Street banks. Savvy entrepreneurs who had stood on the sidelines took advantage of the shake-out in the railroad industry to build stronger companies and make themselves rich. For example, Cornelius (Commodore) Vanderbilt never built a railroad, but rather, bought badly run small, local railway lines, merged them into efficient operations, and managed them expertly, thereby creating the largest fortune of the railroad era. Similarly, the world of Internet commerce may be undergoing consolidation and focusing as today's best e-commerce leaders step in and make changes that will lead to a stronger, more stable future for the companies that survive.

SOURCES: Nick Wingfield, "Internet 2.0: E-tailing Comes of Age," *The Wall Street Journal* (December 8, 2003), B1; John Steele Gordon, "The Golden Spike," *Forbes ASAP* (February 21, 2000), 118–122; and Lee Gomes, "Fix It and They Will Come: E-commerce Isn't Dead. Just Broken," *The Wall Street Journal* (February 12, 2001), R4.

## Classical Perspective

The practice of management can be traced to 3000 B.C. to the first government organizations developed by the Sumerians and Egyptians, but the formal study of management is relatively recent.[15] The early study of management as we know it today began with what is now called the **classical perspective**.

The classical perspective on management emerged during the nineteenth and early twentieth centuries. The factory system that began to appear in the 1800s posed challenges that earlier organizations had not encountered. Problems arose in tooling the plants, organizing managerial structure, training employees (many of

**classical perspective**
A management perspective that emerged during the nineteenth and early twentieth centuries that emphasized a rational, scientific approach to the study of management and sought to make organizations efficient operating machines.

*Frederick Winslow Taylor (1856–1915) Taylor's theory that labor productivity could be improved by scientifically determined management practices earned him the status of "father of scientific management."*

**scientific management**
A subfield of the classical management perspective that emphasized scientifically determined changes in management practices as the solution to improving labor productivity.

*Lillian M. Gilbreth (1878–1972) Frank B. Gilbreth (1868–1924) Shown here using a "motion study" device, this husband-and-wife team contributed to the principles of scientific management. His development of* **time and motion studies** *and her work in* **industrial psychology** *pioneered many of today's management and human resource techniques.*

them non-English-speaking immigrants), scheduling complex manufacturing operations, and dealing with increased labor dissatisfaction and resulting strikes.

These myriad new problems and the development of large, complex organizations demanded a new approach to coordination and control, and a "new subspecies of economic man—the salaried manager"[16]—was born. Between 1880 and 1920, the number of professional managers in the United States grew from 161,000 to more than a million.[17] These professional managers began developing and testing solutions to the mounting challenges of organizing, coordinating, and controlling large numbers of people and increasing worker productivity. Thus began the evolution of modern management with the classical perspective.

This perspective contains three subfields, each with a slightly different emphasis: scientific management, bureaucratic organizations, and administrative principles.[18]

## Scientific Management

Organizations' somewhat limited success in achieving improvements in labor productivity led a young engineer to suggest that the problem lay more in poor management practices than in labor. Frederick Winslow Taylor (1856–1915) insisted that management itself would have to change and, further, that the manner of change could be determined only by scientific study; hence, the label *scientific management* emerged. Taylor suggested that decisions based on rules of thumb and tradition be replaced with precise procedures developed after careful study of individual situations.[19]

Taylor's philosophy is encapsulated in his statement, "In the past the man has been first. In the future, the system must be first."[20] The **scientific management** approach is illustrated by the unloading of iron from rail cars and reloading finished steel for the Bethlehem Steel plant in 1898. Taylor calculated that with correct movements, tools, and sequencing, each man was capable of loading 47.5 tons per day instead of the typical 12.5 tons. He also worked out an incentive system that paid each man $1.85 a day for meeting the new standard, an increase from the previous rate of $1.15. Productivity at Bethlehem Steel shot up overnight.

Although known as the *father of scientific management*, Taylor was not alone in this area. Henry Gantt, an associate of Taylor's, developed the *Gantt Chart*—a bar graph that measures planned and completed work along each stage of production by time elapsed. Two other important pioneers in this area were the husband-and-wife team of Frank B. and Lillian M. Gilbreth. Frank B. Gilbreth (1868–1924) pioneered *time and motion study* and arrived at many of his management techniques independently of Taylor. He stressed efficiency and was known for his quest for the one best way to do work. Although Gilbreth is known for his early work with bricklayers, his work had great impact on medical surgery by drastically reducing the time patients spent on the operating table. Surgeons were able to save countless lives through the application of time and motion study. Lillian M. Gilbreth (1878–1972) was more interested in the human aspect of work. When her husband died at the age of 56, she had 12 children ages 2 to 19. The undaunted "first lady of management" went right on with her work. She presented a paper in place of her late husband, continued their seminars and consulting, lectured, and eventually became a professor at Purdue University.[21] She pioneered

COURTESY OF FORD MOTOR COMPANY

in the field of industrial psychology and made substantial contributions to human resource management.

The basic ideas of scientific management are shown in Exhibit 2.2. To use this approach, managers should develop standard methods for doing each job, select workers with the appropriate abilities, train workers in the standard methods, support workers and eliminate interruptions, and provide wage incentives.

The ideas of scientific management that began with Taylor dramatically increased productivity across all industries, and they are still important today. Indeed, the concept of arranging work based on careful analysis of tasks for maximum productivity is deeply embedded in our organizations.[22] However, because

## Characteristics of Scientific Management

Exhibit 2.2

**General Approach**
- Developed standard method for performing each job.
- Selected workers with appropriate abilities for each job.
- Trained workers in standard methods.
- Supported workers by planning their work and eliminating interruptions.
- Provided wage incentives to workers for increased output.

**Contributions**
- Demonstrated the importance of compensation for performance.
- Initiated the careful study of tasks and jobs.
- Demonstrated the importance of personnel selection and training.

**Criticisms**
- Did not appreciate the social context of work and higher needs of workers.
- Did not acknowledge variance among individuals.
- Tended to regard workers as uninformed and ignored their ideas and suggestions.

scientific management ignored the social context and workers' needs, it led to increased conflict and sometimes violent clashes between managers and employees. Under this system, workers often felt exploited. This was in sharp contrast to the harmony and cooperation that Taylor and his followers had envisioned.

## Bureaucratic Organizations

A systematic approach developed in Europe that looked at the organization as a whole is the bureaucratic organizations approach, a subfield within the classical perspective. Max Weber (1864–1920), a German theorist, introduced most of the concepts on bureaucratic organizations.[23]

COURTESY OF GERMAN INFORMATION CENTER

**CONCEPT CONNECTION**

*Max Weber (1864–1920)*
*The German theorist's concepts on **bureaucratic organizations** have contributed to the efficiency of many of today's corporations.*

**bureaucratic organizations**
A subfield of the classical management perspective that emphasized management on an impersonal, rational basis through such elements as clearly defined authority and responsibility, formal recordkeeping, and separation of management and ownership.

During the late 1800s, many European organizations were managed on a personal, familylike basis. Employees were loyal to a single individual rather than to the organization or its mission. The dysfunctional consequence of this management practice was that resources were used to realize individual desires rather than organizational goals. Employees in effect owned the organization and used resources for their own gain rather than to serve customers. Weber envisioned organizations that would be managed on an impersonal, rational basis. This form of organization was called a *bureaucracy*. Exhibit 2.3 summarizes the six characteristics of bureaucracy as specified by Weber.

Weber believed that an organization based on rational authority would be more efficient and adaptable to change because continuity is related to formal structure and positions rather than to a particular person, who may leave or die. To Weber, rationality in organizations meant employee selection and advancement based not on whom you know, but rather on competence and technical qualifications, which are assessed by examination or according to training and experience. The organization relies on rules and written records for continuity. In addition, rules and procedures are impersonal and applied uniformly to all employees. There is a clear division of labor and clear definitions of authority and responsibility, legitimized as official duties. Positions are organized in a hierarchy, with each position under the authority of a higher one. The manager depends not on his or her personality for successfully giving orders but on the legal power invested in the managerial position.

*Take A Moment*

*Go to the ethical dilemma on page 67 that pertains to problems of bureaucracy.*

The term *bureaucracy* has taken on a negative meaning in today's organizations and is associated with endless rules and red tape. We have all been frustrated by waiting in long lines or following seemingly silly procedures. However, rules and other bureaucratic procedures provide a standard way of dealing with employees. Everyone gets equal treatment, and everyone knows what the rules are. This has enabled many organizations to become extremely efficient. Consider United Parcel Service (UPS), sometimes called *Big Brown*.

**UNITED PARCEL SERVICE**
http://www.ups.com

United Parcel Service took on the U.S. Postal Service at its own game—and won. UPS specializes in the delivery of small packages, delivering more than 13 million every business day. In addition, UPS is gaining market share in air service, logistics, and information services. Television commercials asking, "What can Brown do for you today?" signify the company's expanding global information services. Why has Big Brown been so successful? One important factor is the concept of bureaucracy. UPS is bound up in rules and regulations. It teaches drivers an astounding 340 steps for how to correctly deliver a

Exhibit 2.3

## Characteristics of Weberian Bureaucracy

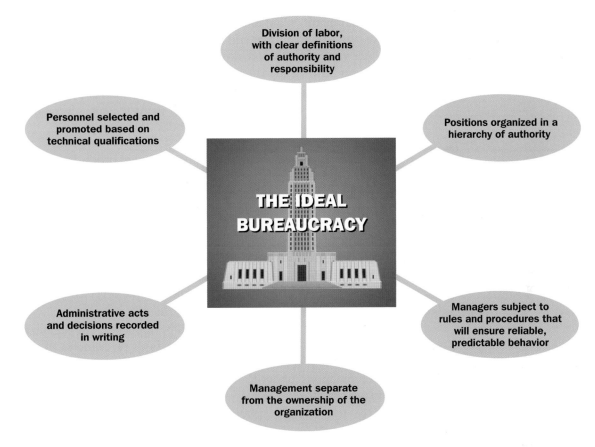

**SOURCE:** Adapted from Max Weber, *The Theory of Social and Economic Organizations*, ed. and trans. A.M. Henderson and Talcott Parsons (New York: Free Press, 1947), 328–337.

package—such as how to load the truck, how to fasten their seat belts, how to walk, and how to carry their keys. There are safety rules for drivers, loaders, clerks, and managers. Strict dress codes are enforced—clean uniforms (called *browns*), every day, black or brown polished shoes with non-slip soles, no beards, no hair below the collar, and so on. Supervisors conduct three-minute inspections of drivers each day. The company also has rules specifying cleanliness standards for buildings, trucks, and other properties. No eating or drinking is permitted at employee desks. Every manager is given bound copies of policy books and is expected to use them regularly.

UPS has a well-defined division of labor. Each plant consists of specialized drivers, loaders, clerks, washers, sorters, and maintenance personnel. UPS thrives on written records, and has been a leader in using new technology to enhance reliability and efficiency. Drivers use a computerized clipboard to track everything from miles per gallon to data on parcel delivery. All drivers have daily worksheets that specify performance goals and work output.

Technical qualification is the criterion for hiring and promotion. The UPS policy book says the leader is expected to have the knowledge and capacity to justify the position of leadership. Favoritism is forbidden. The bureaucratic model works just fine at UPS, "the tightest ship in the shipping business."[24]

## Administrative Principles

Another major subfield within the classical perspective is known as the administrative principles approach. Whereas scientific management focused on the productivity of the individual worker, the **administrative principles** approach focused on the

**administrative principles**
A subfield of the classical management perspective that focused on the total organization rather than the individual worker, delineating the management functions of planning, organizing, commanding, coordinating, and controlling.

COURTESY OF RONALD G. GREENWOOD

## CONCEPT CONNECTION

*Mary Parker Follett (1868–1933)*
*Follett was a major contributor to the **administrative principles** approach to management. Her emphasis on worker participation and shared goals among managers was embraced by many businesspeople of the day and has been recently "rediscovered" by corporate America.*

FROM NATIONAL ARCHIVES

## CONCEPT CONNECTION

*This 1914 photograph shows the initiation of a new arrival at a Nebraska planting camp. This initiation was not part of the formal rules and illustrates the significance of the **informal organization** described by Barnard. Social values and behaviors were powerful forces that could help or hurt the planting organization depending on how they were managed.*

total organization. The contributors to this approach included Henri Fayol, Mary Parker Follett, and Chester I. Barnard.

Henri Fayol (1841–1925) was a French mining engineer who worked his way up to become head of a major mining group known as Comambault. Comambault survives today as part of Le Creusot-Loire, the largest mining and metallurgical group in central France. In his later years, Fayol wrote down his concepts on administration, based largely on his own management experiences.[25]

In his most significant work, *General and Industrial Management*, Fayol discussed 14 general principles of management, several of which are part of management philosophy today. For example:

- *Unity of command.* Each subordinate receives orders from one—and only one—superior.
- *Division of work.* Managerial and technical work are amenable to specialization to produce more and better work with the same amount of effort.
- *Unity of direction.* Similar activities in an organization should be grouped together under one manager.
- *Scalar chain.* A chain of authority extends from the top to the bottom of the organization and should include every employee.

Fayol felt that these principles could be applied in any organizational setting. He also identified five basic functions or elements of management: *planning, organizing, commanding, coordinating,* and *controlling.* These functions underlie much of the general approach to today's management theory.

Mary Parker Follett (1868–1933) was trained in philosophy and political science at what today is Radcliffe College. She applied herself in many fields, including social psychology and management. She wrote of the importance of common superordinate goals for reducing conflict in organizations.[26] Her work was popular with businesspeople of her day but was often overlooked by management scholars.[27] Follett's ideas served as a contrast to scientific management and are reemerging as applicable for modern managers dealing with rapid changes in today's global environment. Her approach to leadership stressed the importance of people rather than engineering techniques. She offered the pithy admonition,"Don't hug your blueprints," and analyzed the dynamics of management-organization interactions. Follett addressed issues that are timely today, such as ethics, power, and how to lead in a way that encourages employees to give their best. The concepts of *empowerment*, facilitating rather than controlling employees, and allowing employees to act depending on the authority of the situation opened new areas for theoretical study by Chester Barnard and others.[28]

Chester I. Barnard (1886–1961) studied economics at Harvard but failed to receive a degree because he lacked a course in laboratory science. He went to work in the statistical department of AT&T and in 1927 became president of New Jersey Bell. One of Barnard's significant contributions was the concept of the informal organization. The *informal organization* occurs in all formal organizations and includes cliques and naturally occurring social groupings. Barnard argued that organizations are not machines and informal relationships are powerful forces that can help the organization if properly managed. Another significant contribution was the *acceptance theory of authority*, which states that people have free will and can choose whether to follow management orders. People typically follow orders because they perceive positive benefit to themselves, but they do have a choice. Managers should treat employees properly because their acceptance of authority may be critical to organization success in important situations.[29]

The overall classical perspective as an approach to management was very powerful and gave companies fundamental new skills for establishing high productivity and effective treatment of employees. Indeed, America surged ahead of the world in management techniques, and other countries, especially Japan, borrowed heavily from American ideas.

# Humanistic Perspective

Mary Parker Follett and Chester Barnard were early advocates of a more **humanistic perspective** on management that emphasized the importance of understanding human behaviors, needs, and attitudes in the workplace as well as social interactions and group processes.[30] We will discuss three subfields based on the humanistic perspective: the human relations movement, the human resources perspective, and the behavioral sciences approach.

**humanistic perspective**
A management perspective that emerged around the late nineteenth century that emphasized understanding human behavior, needs, and attitudes in the workplace.

## The Human Relations Movement

America has always espoused the spirit of human equality. However, this spirit has not always been translated into practice when it comes to power sharing between managers and workers. The human relations school of thought considers that truly effective control comes from within the individual worker rather than from strict, authoritarian control.[31] This school of thought recognized and directly responded to social pressures for enlightened treatment of employees. The early work on industrial psychology and personnel selection received little attention because of the prominence of scientific management. Then a series of studies at a Chicago electric company, which came to be known as the **Hawthorne studies**, changed all that.

**Hawthorne studies**
A series of experiments on worker productivity begun in 1924 at the Hawthorne plant of Western Electric Company in Illinois; attributed employees' increased output to managers' better treatment of them during the study.

FROM WESTERN ELECTRIC PHOTOGRAPHIC SERVICES

### CONCEPT CONNECTION

*This is the Relay Room of the Western Electric Hawthorne, Illinois, plant in 1927. Six women worked in this relay assembly test room during the controversial experiments on employee productivity. Professors Mayo and Roethlisberger evaluated conditions such as rest breaks and workday length, physical health, amount of sleep, and diet. Experimental changes were fully discussed with the women and were abandoned if they disapproved. Gradually the researchers began to realize they had created a change in supervisory style and **human relations**, which they believed was the true cause of the increased productivity.*

Beginning about 1895, a struggle developed between manufacturers of gas and electric lighting fixtures for control of the residential and industrial market.[32] By 1909 electric lighting had begun to win, but the increasingly efficient electric fixtures used less total power. The electric companies began a campaign to convince industrial users that they needed more light to get more productivity. When advertising did not work, the industry began using experimental tests to demonstrate their argument. Managers were skeptical about the results, so the Committee on Industrial Lighting (CIL) was set up to run the tests. To further add to the tests' credibility, Thomas Edison was made honorary chairman of the CIL. In one test location—the Hawthorne plant of the Western Electric Company—some interesting events occurred.

The major part of this work involved four experimental and three control groups. In all, five different tests were conducted. These pointed to the importance of factors *other* than illumination in affecting productivity. To more carefully examine these factors, numerous other experiments were conducted.[33] The results of the most famous study, the first Relay Assembly Test Room (RATR) experiment, were extremely controversial. Under the guidance of two Harvard professors, Elton Mayo and Fritz Roethlisberger, the RATR studies lasted nearly six years (May 10, 1927, to May 4, 1933) and involved 24 separate experimental periods. So many factors were changed and so many unforeseen factors uncontrolled that scholars disagree on the factors that truly contributed to the general increase in performance over that time period. Most early interpretations, however, agreed on one thing: Money was not the cause of the increased output.[34] It was believed that the factor that best explained increased output was *human relations*. Employees performed better when managers treated them in a positive manner. However, recent reanalyses of the experiments have revealed that a number of factors were different for the workers involved, and some suggest that money may well have been the single most important factor.[35] An interview with one of the original participants revealed that just getting into the experimental group had meant a huge increase in income.[36]

These new data clearly show that money mattered a great deal at Hawthorne. In addition, worker productivity increased partly as a result of the increased feelings of importance and group pride employees felt by virtue of being selected for this important project.[37] One unintended contribution of the experiments was a rethinking of field research practices. Researchers and scholars realized that the researcher can influence the outcome of an experiment by being too closely involved with research subjects. This has come to be known as the *Hawthorne effect* in research methodology. Subjects behaved differently because of the active participation of researchers in the Hawthorne experiments.[38]

From a historical perspective, whether the studies were academically sound is of less importance than the fact that they stimulated an increased interest in looking at employees as more than extensions of production machinery. The interpretation that employees' output increased when managers treated them in a positive manner started a revolution in worker treatment for improving organizational productivity. Despite flawed methodology or inaccurate conclusions, the findings provided the impetus for the **human relations movement**. IBM was one of the earliest proponents of a human relations approach, as described in the Unlocking Creative Solutions Through People box. This approach shaped management theory and practice for well over a quarter-century, and the belief that human relations is the best approach for increasing productivity persists today.

**human relations movement**
A movement in management thinking and practice that emphasized satisfaction of employees' basic needs as the key to increased worker productivity.

## The Human Resources Perspective

The human relations movement initially espoused a *dairy farm* view of management—contented cows give more milk, so satisfied workers will give more work. Gradually,

# Unlocking Creative Solutions Through People

## Watson Opens the Door at IBM—and Finds Happier Employees

During the early 1900s, managers in most manufacturing companies were focused on reducing jobs to repetitive, standardized tasks, following the scientific management approach advocated by Frederick Taylor and others. However, the ideals that Thomas Watson Sr. planted at IBM were based on a different approach, and they eventually helped transform the company into a corporate giant.

In 1914, Watson joined a failing conglomerate that primarily made scales, coffee grinders, cheese slicers, and time clocks. The *Computing–Tabulating–Recording* component of the conglomerate grew quickly and soon overtook the other businesses. The name was changed to International Business Machines in 1924. Rather than putting the production system first, as Taylor advised, Watson vowed to make people the cornerstone of his corporate culture. He abolished piecework, spruced up factories, paid above-average wages, and borrowed money to fund in-house education programs. Foremost among his innovations was an open-door policy that encouraged any employee to take a complaint directly to Watson himself. He virtually guaranteed lifetime employment (even during the Depression) so workers would feel free to speak their minds. In the early years of Watson's tenure with IBM, when the company didn't have funds for generous benefit plans, Watson sponsored company picnics, complete with bands, to build spirit and keep workers motivated. As the company prospered, he passed the good times on. A group life insurance plan was launched in 1934, with survivor benefits and paid vacations added soon afterward.

The human relations approach to management was continued by Thomas Watson Jr., who took over as CEO in 1956 and first pushed the company into computers. Leading IBM through one of the longest and most spectacular periods of growth in business history, the younger Watson was known as a hard charger and a tough boss. However, he maintained his father's emphasis on treating employees fairly. IBM became famous for putting all employees on salary and for its extremely generous compensation and benefit plans, as well as the continued guarantee of lifetime employment. Watson liberally distributed stock options to his executives, but stopped taking them himself as early as 1957, saying, "We didn't want to look like pigs." There are many factors involved in IBM's successful history. However, the early emphasis on treating employees well helped put the company on the map. Watson's belief that a focus on people and meeting the needs of employees was the key to increased productivity and performance was ahead of its time.

**SOURCES:** "IBM: The Open Door," vignette in Matthew Boyle, "How the Workplace Was Won," *Fortune* (January 22, 2001), 139; and Thomas A. Stewart, Alex Taylor III, Peter Petre, and Brent Schlender, "The Businessman of the Century," *Fortune* (November 22, 1999), 108–128.

views with deeper content began to emerge. The **human resources perspective** maintained an interest in worker participation and considerate leadership but shifted the emphasis to consider the daily tasks that people perform. The human resources perspective combines prescriptions for design of job tasks with theories of motivation.[39] In the human resources view, jobs should be designed so that tasks are not perceived as dehumanizing or demeaning but instead allow workers to use their full potential. Two of the best-known contributors to the human resources perspective were Abraham Maslow and Douglas McGregor.

Abraham Maslow (1908–1970), a practicing psychologist, observed that his patients' problems usually stemmed from an inability to satisfy their needs. Thus, he generalized his work and suggested a hierarchy of needs. Maslow's hierarchy started with physiological needs and progressed to safety, belongingness, esteem, and, finally, self-actualization needs. Chapter 19 discusses his ideas in more detail.

Douglas McGregor (1906–1964) had become frustrated with the early simplistic human relations notions while president of Antioch College in Ohio. He challenged both the classical perspective and the early human relations assumptions about human behavior. Based on his experiences as a manager and consultant, his training as a psychologist, and the work of Maslow, McGregor formulated his Theory X and

**human resources perspective**

A management perspective that suggests jobs should be designed to meet higher-level needs by allowing workers to use their full potential.

Theory Y, which are explained in Exhibit 2.4.[40] McGregor believed that the classical perspective was based on Theory X assumptions about workers. He also felt that a slightly modified version of Theory X fit early human relations ideas. In other words, human relations ideas did not go far enough. McGregor proposed Theory Y as a more realistic view of workers for guiding management thinking.

*Take A Moment*     *Go to the experiential exercise on page 66.*

The point of Theory Y is that organizations can take advantage of the imagination and intellect of all their employees. Employees will exercise self-control and will contribute to organizational goals when given the opportunity. A few companies today still use Theory X management, but many are trying Theory Y techniques. Consider how Signet Painting Inc. taps into the full potential of every worker by operating from Theory Y assumptions.

**SIGNET PAINTING INC.**
http://www.
signetpainting.com

A painting contractor might seem an unlikely place to look for modern management techniques, but Signet Painting is on the cutting edge in creating a work environment that affords workers self-esteem and significance as well as a paycheck. Twin brothers Larry and Garry Gehrke first started searching for a new approach to managing workers when the company grew so large they couldn't personally be involved in every project. They began by giving crew leaders the power and authority to make decisions on a job, such as reordering supplies without supervisor approval.

The Gehrkes found a number of ways to involve workers and give them opportunities to share their best knowledge and skills. One approach is a policy committee made up of volunteers who meet to brainstorm solutions to problems they encounter in the field. Managers also strive to incorporate employees' interests and past work experience into their jobs so that each person has the opportunity to make a unique contribution. "Each person wants to feel like they have the knowledge of what they're doing . . .," says foreman Derrick Borsheim. "I ask my crew questions like, 'What do you think? What should I do?' And I use their ideas."

Chief Operating Officer Julie Gehrke says that when the management team gave employees in the field more power and authority to make decisions and control their own jobs, it totally changed people's workplace identity. Managers set clear boundaries, rules, and systems, and then trust workers to carry out their responsibilities professionally and reliably. The application of Theory Y assumptions at Signet Painting has given employees a new sense of pride and ownership in their work. Gehrke says, "When I come into the office on Monday morning and hear one of our painters giving an orientation to a new hire and expounding on what a great company this is to work for, I feel triumphant."[41]

## The Behavioral Sciences Approach

**behavioral sciences approach**
A subfield of the humanistic management perspective that applies social science in an organizational context, drawing from economics, psychology, sociology, and other disciplines.

The **behavioral sciences approach** develops theories about human behavior based on scientific methods and study. Behavioral science draws from sociology, psychology, anthropology, economics, and other disciplines to understand employee behavior and interaction in an organizational setting. The approach can be seen in practically every organization. When General Electric conducts research to determine the best set of tests, interviews, and employee profiles to use when selecting new employees, it is employing behavioral science techniques. When Circuit City electronics stores train new managers in the techniques of employee motivation, most of the theories and findings are rooted in behavioral science research.

One specific set of management techniques based in the behavioral sciences approach is *organization development* (OD). In the 1970s, organization development evolved as a separate field that applied the behavioral sciences to improve the organization's health and effectiveness through its ability to cope with change,

Exhibit 2.4

**Theory X and Theory Y**

| **Assumptions of Theory X** |
| --- |

- The average human being has an inherent dislike of work and will avoid it if possible.
- Because of the human characteristic of dislike for work, most people must be coerced, controlled, directed, or threatened with punishment to get them to put forth adequate effort toward the achievement of organizational objectives.
- The average human being prefers to be directed, wishes to avoid responsibility, has relatively little ambition, and wants security above all.

| **Assumptions of Theory Y** |
| --- |

- The expenditure of physical and mental effort in work is as natural as play or rest. The average human being does not inherently dislike work.
- External control and the threat of punishment are not the only means for bringing about effort toward organizational objectives. A person will exercise self-direction and self-control in the service of objectives to which he or she is committed.
- The average human being learns, under proper conditions, not only to accept but to seek responsibility.
- The capacity to exercise a relatively high degree of imagination, ingenuity, and creativity in the solution of organizational problems is widely, not narrowly, distributed in the population.
- Under the conditions of modern industrial life, the intellectual potentialities of the average human being are only partially utilized.

**SOURCE:** Douglas McGregor, *The Human Side of Enterprise* (New York: McGraw-Hill, 1960), 33–48.

improve internal relationships, and increase problem-solving capabilities.[42] The techniques and concepts of organization development have since been broadened and expanded to cope with the increasing complexity of organizations and the environment, and OD is still a vital approach for managers. OD will be discussed in detail in Chapter 11. Other concepts that grew out of the behavioral sciences approach include matrix organizations, self-managed teams, ideas about corporate culture, and management by wandering around. Indeed, the behavioral sciences approach has influenced the majority of tools, techniques, and approaches that managers have applied to organizations since the 1970s. In recent years, behavioral sciences and OD techniques have been applied to help managers build learning organizations.

All of the remaining chapters of this book contain research findings and management applications that can be attributed to the behavioral sciences approach. This chapter's Shoptalk box illustrates a number of management innovations that have become popular over the past 50 years. Note the trend of new management concepts from the behavioral sciences, increasing about 1970 and then again from 1980 to the present. The rapid pace of change and the increased pressure of global competition have spurred even greater interest in improved behavioral approaches to management.

# Management Science Perspective

World War II caused many management changes. The massive and complicated problems associated with modern global warfare presented managerial decision makers

## Turbulent Times

# manager's Shoptalk

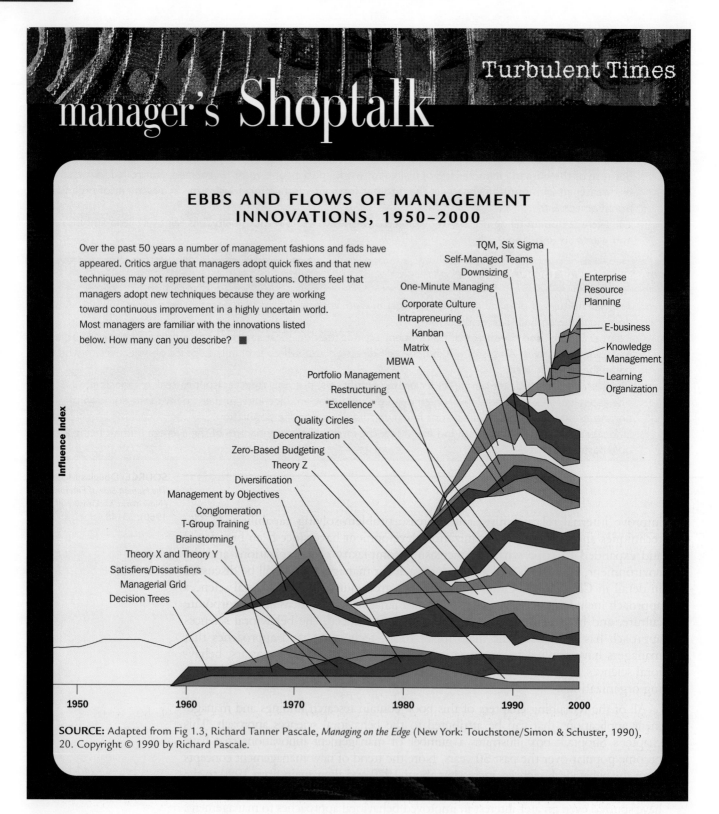

## EBBS AND FLOWS OF MANAGEMENT INNOVATIONS, 1950–2000

Over the past 50 years a number of management fashions and fads have appeared. Critics argue that managers adopt quick fixes and that new techniques may not represent permanent solutions. Others feel that managers adopt new techniques because they are working toward continuous improvement in a highly uncertain world. Most managers are familiar with the innovations listed below. How many can you describe? ■

**Influence Index**

TQM, Six Sigma
Self-Managed Teams
Downsizing
One-Minute Managing
Corporate Culture
Intrapreneuring
Kanban
Matrix
MBWA
Portfolio Management
Restructuring
"Excellence"
Quality Circles
Decentralization
Zero-Based Budgeting
Theory Z
Diversification
Management by Objectives
Conglomeration
T-Group Training
Brainstorming
Theory X and Theory Y
Satisfiers/Dissatisfiers
Managerial Grid
Decision Trees

Enterprise Resource Planning
E-business
Knowledge Management
Learning Organization

1950     1960     1970     1980     1990     2000

**SOURCE:** Adapted from Fig 1.3, Richard Tanner Pascale, *Managing on the Edge* (New York: Touchstone/Simon & Schuster, 1990), 20. Copyright © 1990 by Richard Pascale.

**management science perspective**
A management perspective that emerged after World War II and applied mathematics, statistics, and other quantitative techniques to managerial problems.

with the need for more sophisticated tools than ever before. The **management science perspective** emerged to address those problems. This view is distinguished for its application of mathematics, statistics, and other quantitative techniques to management decision making and problem solving. During World War II, groups of mathematicians, physicists, and other scientists were formed to solve military problems. Because those problems frequently involved moving massive amounts of materials and large numbers of people quickly and efficiently, the techniques had obvious applications to large-scale business firms.[43]

*Operations research* grew directly out of the World War II groups (called *operational research teams* in Great Britain and *operations research teams* in the United States).[44] It consists of mathematical model building and other applications of quantitative techniques to managerial problems.

*Operations management* refers to the field of management that specializes in the physical production of goods or services. Operations management specialists use quantitative techniques to solve manufacturing problems. Some of the commonly used methods are forecasting, inventory modeling, linear and nonlinear programming, queuing theory, scheduling, simulation, and break-even analysis.

*Information technology (IT)* is the most recent subfield of the management science perspective, which is often reflected in management information systems. These systems are designed to provide relevant information to managers in a timely and cost-efficient manner. More recently, information technology within organizations has evolved to include intranets and extranets, as well as various software programs that help managers estimate costs, plan and track production, manage projects, allocate resources, or schedule employees. When Weyerhaeuser Company's door factory implemented an intranet combined with software to track inventory, calculate estimates, schedule production, and automate ordertaking, it was applying management science to cut both manufacturing costs and production time.[45] Most of today's organizations have departments of information technology specialists to help them apply management science techniques to complex organizational problems.

# Recent Historical Trends

Management is, by nature, complex and dynamic. Elements of each of the perspectives we have discussed are still in use today. The most prevalent is the humanistic perspective, but even it has been undergoing change in recent years. Three recent trends that grew out of the humanistic perspective are systems theory, the contingency view, and total quality management.

## Systems Theory

A **system** is a set of interrelated parts that function as a whole to achieve a common purpose.[46] A system functions by acquiring inputs from the external environment, transforming them in some way, and discharging outputs back to the environment. Exhibit 2.5 shows the basic **systems theory** of organizations. Here there are five components: inputs, a transformation process, outputs, feedback, and the environment. *Inputs* are the material, human, financial, or information resources used to produce goods or services. The *transformation process* is management's use of production technology to change the inputs into outputs. *Outputs* include the organization's products and services. *Feedback* is knowledge of the results that influence the selection of inputs during the next cycle of the process. The *environment* surrounding the organization includes the social, political, and economic forces noted earlier in this chapter.

Some ideas in systems theory have had substantial impact on management thinking. These include open and closed systems, entropy, synergy, and subsystem interdependencies.[47]

**Open systems** must interact with the environment to survive; **closed systems** need not. In the classical and management science perspectives, organizations were frequently thought of as closed systems. In the management science perspective,

**system**
A set of interrelated parts that function as a whole to achieve a common purpose.

**systems theory**
An extension of the humanistic perspective that describes organizations as open systems that are characterized by entropy, synergy, and subsystem interdependence.

**open system**
A system that interacts with the external environment.

**closed system**
A system that does not interact with the external environment.

Exhibit **2.5**

## The Systems View of Organizations

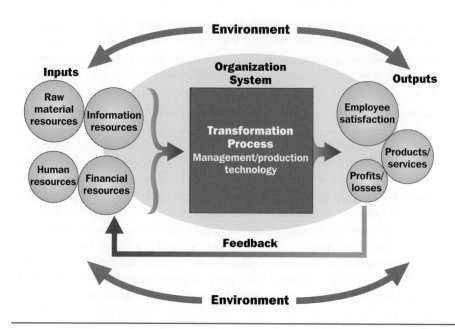

closed system assumptions—the absence of external disturbances—are sometimes used to simplify problems for quantitative analysis. In reality, however, all organizations are open systems, and the cost of ignoring the environment may be failure.

**Entropy** is a universal property of systems and refers to their tendency to run down and die. If a system does not receive fresh inputs and energy from its environment, it will eventually cease to exist. Organizations must monitor their environments, adjust to changes, and continuously bring in new inputs in order to survive and prosper. Managers try to design the organization/environment interfaces to reduce entropy.

**Synergy** means that the whole is greater than the sum of its parts. When an organization is formed, something new comes into the world. Management, coordination, and production that did not exist before are now present. Organizational units working together can accomplish more than those same units working alone. The sales department depends on production, and vice versa.

**Subsystems** are parts of a system that depend on one another. Changes in one part of the organization affect other parts. The organization must be managed as a coordinated whole. Managers who understand subsystem interdependence are reluctant to make changes that do not recognize subsystem impact on the organization as a whole. For example, at Buckman Laboratories International, the successful implementation of a new knowledge-sharing network required changes in organizational structure, job design, work processes, and cultural values.[48] Buckman's vertical hierarchy was dismantled and replaced by coordinated teams focused on horizontal work processes. Cultural values had to be shifted to emphasize collaboration and sharing rather than hoarding information. A change of this nature might take quite some time because of the interconnection of the organization's subsystems.

## Contingency View

A second contemporary extension to management thinking is the **contingency view**. The classical perspective assumed a *universalist* view. Management concepts were

**entropy**
The tendency for a system to run down and die.

**synergy**
The concept that the whole is greater than the sum of its parts.

**subsystems**
Parts of a system that depend on one another for their functioning.

**contingency view**
An extension of the humanistic perspective in which the successful resolution of organizational problems is thought to depend on managers' identification of key variations in the situation at hand.

thought to be universal; that is, whatever worked—leader style, bureaucratic structure—in one organization would work in another. In business education, however, an alternative view exists. This is the *case* view, in which each situation is believed to be unique. There are no universal principles to be found, and one learns about management by experiencing a large number of case problem situations. Managers face the task of determining what methods will work in every new situation.

To integrate these views the contingency view has emerged, as illustrated in Exhibit 2.6.[49] Here neither of the other views is seen as entirely correct. Instead, certain contingencies, or variables, exist for helping management identify and understand situations. The contingency view means that a manager's response depends on identifying key contingencies in an organizational situation. For example, a consultant might mistakenly recommend the same *management-by-objectives* (MBO) system for a manufacturing firm that was successful in a school system. The contingency view tells us that what works in one setting might not work in another. Management's job is to search for important contingencies. When managers learn to identify important patterns and characteristics of their organizations, they can then fit solutions to those characteristics.

Important contingencies that managers must understand include industry, technology, the environment, and international cultures. Management practice in a rapidly changing industry, for example, will be very different from that in a stable one.

## Total Quality Management

The quality movement in Japan emerged partly as a result of American influence after World War II. The ideas of W. Edwards Deming, known as the "father of the quality movement," were initially scoffed at in America, but the Japanese embraced his theories and modified them to help rebuild their industries into world powers.[50] Japanese companies achieved a significant departure from the American model by gradually shifting from an inspection-oriented approach to quality control toward an approach emphasizing employee involvement in the prevention of quality problems.[51]

During the 1980s and into the 1990s, **total quality management (TQM)**, which focuses on managing the total organization to deliver quality to customers, was at the forefront in helping managers deal with global competition. The approach infuses quality values throughout every activity within a company, with front-line workers intimately involved in the process. Four significant elements of quality management are employee involvement, focus on the customer, benchmarking, and continuous improvement.

**total quality management**
A concept that focuses on managing the total organization to deliver quality to customers. Four significant elements of TQM are employee involvement, focus on the customer, benchmarking, and continuous improvement.

Exhibit 2.6

**Contingency View of Management**

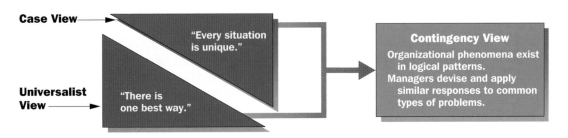

*Employee involvement* means that TQM requires companywide participation in quality control. All employees are *focused on the customer*; TQM companies find out what customers want and try to meet their needs and expectations. *Benchmarking* refers to a process whereby companies find out how others do something better than they do and then try to imitate or improve on it. *Continuous improvement* is the implementation of small, incremental improvements in all areas of the organization on an ongoing basis. TQM is not a quick fix, but companies such as Motorola, Procter & Gamble, and DuPont have achieved astonishing results in efficiency, quality, and customer satisfaction through total quality management.[52] TQM is still an important part of today's organizations, and many companies pursue challenging quality goals to demonstrate their commitment to improving quality. For example, *Six Sigma* is a highly ambitious quality standard popularized by Motorola that specifies a goal of no more than 3.4 defects per million parts. Numerous companies, including DuPont, Texas Instruments, General Electric, and Nokia, pursue Six Sigma quality standards. Quality goals and initiatives will be discussed in detail in Chapter 14.

# New Management Thinking for Turbulent Times

All of the ideas and approaches discussed so far in this chapter go into the mix that makes up modern management. A recent book on management thinking indicates dozens of ideas and techniques in current use that can trace their roots to these historical perspectives.[53] In addition, new concepts have emerged to address management challenges in today's turbulent world. Organizations are experimenting with new ways of managing that more adequately respond to the demands of today's environment and customers. Two current directions in management thinking are the shift to a learning organization and managing the technology-driven workplace.

## The Learning Organization

One of the toughest challenges for managers today is to get people focused on adaptive change to meet the demands of a turbulent and rapidly changing environment. Many problems have no ready-made solutions and require that people throughout the company think in new ways and learn new values and attitudes.[54] This requires a new approach to management and a new kind of organization. Managers began thinking about the concept of the learning organization after the publication of Peter Senge's book, *The Fifth Discipline: The Art and Practice of Learning Organizations*.[55] Senge described the kind of changes managers needed to undergo to help their organizations adapt to an increasingly chaotic world. These ideas gradually evolved to describe characteristics of the organization itself. There is no single view of what the learning organization looks like. The learning organization is an attitude or philosophy about what an organization can become.

**learning organization**
An organization in which everyone is engaged in identifying and solving problems, enabling the organization to continuously experiment, improve, and increase its capability.

The learning organization can be defined as one in which everyone is engaged in identifying and solving problems, enabling the organization to continuously experiment, change, and improve, thus increasing its capacity to grow, learn, and achieve its purpose. The essential idea is problem solving, in contrast to the traditional organization designed for efficiency. In the learning organization all employees look for problems, such as understanding special customer needs. Employees also solve problems, which means putting things together in unique ways to meet a customer's needs.

To develop a learning organization, managers make changes in all the subsystems of the organization. Three important adjustments to promote continuous learning are shifting to a team-based structure, empowering employees, and sharing information. These three characteristics are illustrated in Exhibit 2.7 and each is described here.

## Team-Based Structure

An important value in a learning organization is collaboration and communication across departmental and hierarchical boundaries. Self-directed teams are the basic building block of the structure. These teams are made up of employees with different skills who share or rotate jobs to produce an entire product or service. Traditional management tasks are pushed down to lower levels of the organization, with teams often taking responsibility for training, safety, scheduling, and decisions about work methods, pay and reward systems, and coordination with other teams. Although team leadership is critical, in learning organizations the traditional boss is practically eliminated. People on the team are given the skills, information, tools, motivation, and authority to make decisions central to the team's performance and to respond creatively and flexibly to new challenges or opportunities that arise.

## Employee Empowerment

*Empowerment* means unleashing the power and creativity of employees by giving them the freedom, resources, information, and skills to make decisions and perform effectively. Traditional management tries to limit employees, while empowerment expands their behavior. Empowerment may be reflected in self-directed work teams, quality circles, job enrichment, and employee participation groups as well as through decision-making authority, training, and information so that people can perform jobs without close supervision.

In learning organizations, people are a manager's primary source of strength, not a cost to be minimized. Companies that adopt this perspective believe in treating employees well by providing competitive wages and good working conditions, as well as by investing time and money in training programs and opportunities for personal and professional development. In addition, they often provide a sense of employee ownership by sharing gains in productivity and profits.[56]

Exhibit 2.7

**Elements of a Learning Organization**

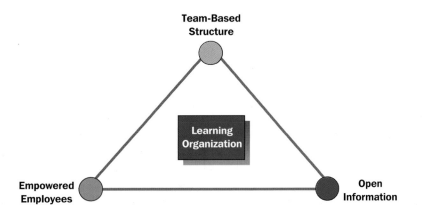

Team-Based Structure

Learning Organization

Empowered Employees

Open Information

## Open Information

A learning organization is flooded with information. To identify needs and solve problems, people have to be aware of what's going on. They must understand the whole organization as well as their part in it. Formal data about budgets, profits, and departmental expenses are available to everyone. "If you really want to respect individuals," says Solectron Corp.'s Winston Chen, "you've got to let them know how they're doing—and let them know soon enough so they can do something about it."[57] Managers know that providing too much information is better than providing too little. In addition, managers encourage people throughout the organization to share information. For example, at Viant Inc., which helps companies build and maintain Web-based businesses, people are rewarded for their willingness to absorb and share knowledge. Rather than encouraging consultants to hoard specialized knowledge, CEO Bob Gett says, "We value you more for how much information you've given to the guy next to you."[58]

## Managing the Technology-Driven Workplace

The shift to the learning organization goes hand-in-hand with the current transition to a technology-driven workplace. The physical world that Frederick Taylor and other proponents of scientific management measured determines less and less of what is valued in organizations and society. Our lives and organizations have been engulfed by information technology. Ideas, information, and relationships are becoming more important than production machinery, physical products, and structured jobs.[59] Many employees perform much of their work on computers and may work in virtual teams, connected electronically to colleagues around the world. Even in factories that produce physical goods, machines have taken over much of the routine and uniform work, freeing workers to use more of their minds and abilities. Managers and employees in today's companies focus on opportunities rather than efficiencies, which requires that they be flexible, creative, and unconstrained by rigid rules and structured tasks.

### The Shifting World of E-Business

**e-business**
Work an organization does by using electronic linkages.

Today, much business takes place by digital processes over a computer network rather than in physical space. **E-business** refers to the work an organization does by using electronic linkages (including the Internet) with customers, partners, suppliers, employees, or other key constituents. For example, organizations that use the Internet or other electronic linkages to communicate with employees or customers are engaged in e-business.

**e-commerce**
Business exchanges or transactions that occur electronically.

**E-commerce** is a narrower term referring specifically to business exchanges or transactions that occur electronically. E-commerce replaces or enhances the exchange of money and products with the exchange of data and information from one computer to another. Three types of e-commerce—*business-to-consumer*, *business-to-business*, and *consumer-to-consumer*—are illustrated in Exhibit 2.8. Companies such as Gateway, Amazon.com, 800-Flowers, Expedia.com, and Progressive are engaged in what is referred to as *business-to-consumer e-commerce (B2C)*, because they sell products and services to consumers over the Internet. Although this is probably the most visible expression of e-commerce to the public, the fastest growing area of e-commerce is *business-to-business e-commerce (B2B)*, which refers to electronic transactions between organizations. Today, much B2B e-commerce takes place over the Internet.[60] Large organizations such as Wal-Mart, General Electric, Carrier Corp., General Motors, and Ford Motor Company buy and sell billions of dollars worth of goods and services a year via either public or private Internet linkages.[61] For example, General Motors sells about 300,000 previously owned vehicles a year online through SmartAuction. Ford purchases a large portion of the steel it uses to build cars through e-Steel.[62]

Exhibit 2.8

**Three Types of E-commerce**

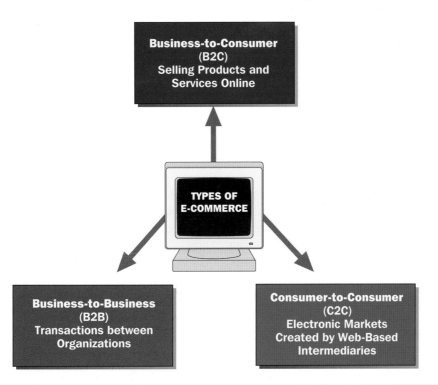

Some companies have taken e-commerce to very high levels to achieve amazing performance. Dell Computer pioneered the use of end-to-end digital supply-chain networks to keep in touch with customers, take orders, buy components from suppliers, coordinate with manufacturing partners, and ship customized products directly to consumers. This trend is affecting every industry, prompting a group of consultants at a Harvard University conference to conclude that businesses today must either "Dell or be Delled."[63] These advances mean managers not only need to be technologically savvy, but they become responsible for managing a web of relationships that reaches far beyond the boundaries of the physical organization, building flexible e-links between a company and its employees, suppliers, partners, and customers.[64]

The third area of e-commerce, *consumer-to-consumer (C2C)*, is made possible when an Internet-based business acts as an intermediary between and among consumers. One of the best-known examples of C2C e-commerce is Web-based auctions such as those made possible by eBay. Internet auctions have created a large electronic marketplace where consumers can buy and sell directly with one another, often handling practically the entire transaction via the Web. In 2003, an estimated 30 million people bought and sold more than $20 billion in merchandise over eBay.[65] Another growing area of C2C commerce is peer-to-peer file-sharing networks. Companies such as Kazaa and Gnutella provide the technology for swapping music files, video clips, software, and other files. Online music sharing, in particular, has zoomed in popularity, and although music companies and record retailers are currently engaged in a heated battle with file-sharing services, these companies are likely here to stay.[66]

## Technology in the Workplace

New electronic technologies also shape the organization and how it is managed. A century ago, Frederick Taylor described the kind of worker needed in the iron industry:

"Now one of the first requirements for a man who is fit to handle pig iron as a regular occupation is that he shall be so stupid and so phlegmatic that he more nearly resembles in his mental makeup the ox than any other type."[67] The philosophy of scientific management was that managers structured and controlled jobs so carefully that thinking on the part of employees wasn't required—indeed, it was usually discouraged. How different things are today! Many organizations depend on employees' minds more than their physical bodies. In companies where the power of an idea determines success, managers' primary goal is to tap into the creativity and knowledge of every employee.

Technology provides the architecture that supports and reinforces this new workplace. For example, one approach to information management is **enterprise resource planning (ERP)** systems, which weave together all of a company's major business functions, such as order processing, product design, purchasing, inventory, manufacturing, distribution, human resources, receipt of payments, and forecasting of future demand.[68] ERP supports a companywide management system in which everyone, from the CEO down to a machine operator on the factory floor, has instant access to critical information. People can see the big picture and act quickly, based on up-to-the-minute information. Thus, ERP also supports management attempts to harness and leverage organizational *knowledge*.

Peter Drucker coined the term *knowledge work* more than 40 years ago,[69] but it is only in recent years that managers have genuinely recognized knowledge as an important organizational resource that should be managed just as they manage cash flow or raw materials. **Knowledge management** refers to the efforts to systematically find, organize, and make available a company's intellectual capital and to foster a culture of continuous learning and knowledge sharing so that a company's activities build on what is already known.[70] Information technology plays an important role by enabling the storage and dissemination of data and information across the organization, but technology is only one part of a larger management system.[71] A complete knowledge management system includes not only the technology for capturing and storing knowledge for easy access, but also new management values that support risk taking, learning, and collaboration. Rather than seeing employees as factors of production and looking for ways to use human and material resources for greatest efficiency, today's most successful managers cherish people for their ability to think, create, share knowledge, and build relationships.

---

**enterprise resource planning (ERP)**
Systems that unite a company's major business functions—order processing, product design, purchasing, inventory, and so on.

**knowledge management**
The efforts to systematically find, organize, and make available a company's intellectual capital and to foster a culture of continuous learning and knowledge sharing.

## Manager's Solution

This chapter has examined the historical background leading up to new approaches to managing learning organizations and the digital workplace. An understanding of the evolution of management helps current and future managers understand where we are now and continue to progress toward better management.

The three major perspectives on management that have evolved since the late 1800s are the classical perspective, the humanistic perspective, and the management science perspective. Each perspective has several specialized subfields. Recent extensions include systems theory, the contingency view, and total quality management. The most recent thinking about organizations has been brought about by today's turbulent times and the shift to a new workplace described in Chapter 1. Many managers are redesigning their companies toward the learning organization, which fully engages all employees in identifying and solving problems. The learning organization is characterized by a team-based structure, empowered employees, and open information. The learning organization represents a substantial departure from the traditional management hierarchy.

The shift to a learning organization goes hand-in-hand with today's transition to a technology-driven workplace. Ideas, information, and relationships are becoming more important than production machinery and physical assets, which requires new approaches to management. E-business is burgeoning as more economic activity takes place over digital computer networks rather than in physical space. Two specific management tools that support the digital workplace are enterprise resource planning and knowledge management. Both require managers to think in new ways about the role of employees in the organization. Managers value employees for their ability to think, build relationships, and share knowledge, which is quite different from the scientific management perspective of a century ago.

One century-old company that is thriving as a technology-driven learning organization is Cementos Mexicanos (Cemex), described at the beginning of the chapter. To help the organization compete in a turbulent environment, managers looked for both technological and management innovations. A core element of the new approach is the company's complex information technology infrastructure, which includes a global positioning satellite system and on-board computers in all delivery trucks that are continuously fed with streams of day-to-day data on customer orders, production schedules, traffic problems, weather conditions, and so forth. Even more important are changes in how managers and employees think about and do their work. All drivers and dispatchers attended weekly secondary education classes for two years. Regular training in quality, customer service, and computer skills continues, with Cemex devoting at least eight percent of total work time to employee training and development. Strict and demanding work rules have been abolished so that workers have more discretion and responsibility for identifying and solving problems.

As a result, Cemex trucks now operate as self-organizing business units, run by well-trained employees who think like businesspeople. The three-hour delivery window has been reduced to 20 minutes, and managers believe a goal of 10 minutes is within reach. According to Francisco Perez, operations manager at Cemex in Guadalajara, "They used to think of themselves as drivers. But anyone can deliver concrete. Now our people know that they're delivering a service that the competition cannot deliver." Cemex has transformed the industry by combining extensive networking technology with a new management approach that taps into the mindpower of everyone in the company. People at Cemex are constantly learning—on the job, in training classes, and through visits to other organizations. As a result, the company has a startling capacity to anticipate customer needs, solve problems, and innovate quickly.[72]

# Discussion Questions

1. Why is it important to understand the different perspectives and approaches to management theory that have evolved throughout the history of organizations?

2. How do societal forces influence the practice and theory of management? Do you think management techniques are a response to these forces?

3. A management professor once said that for successful management, studying the present was most important, studying the past was next, and studying the future was least important. Do you agree? Why?

4. Which of the six characteristics of learning organizations do you find most appealing? Which would be hardest for you to adopt?

5. Some experts believe that leadership is more important than ever in a learning organization. Do you agree? Explain.

6. What is the behavioral sciences approach? How does it differ from earlier approaches to management?

7. Explain the basic idea underlying the contingency view and provide an example.

8. Contrast open and closed systems. Can you give an example of each? Can a closed system survive?

9. Why can an event such as the Hawthorne studies be a major turning point in the history of management even if the idea is later shown to be in error? Discuss.

10. Identify the major components of systems theory. Is this perspective primarily internal or external?

11. Do you think management theory will ever be as precise as theories in the fields of physics, chemistry, or experimental psychology? Why or why not?

# Management in Practice: Experiential Exercise

## Tolerance for Ambiguity Scale

Please read each of the following statements carefully. Then rate each of them in terms of the extent to which you either agree or disagree with the statement using the following scale:

| Completely Disagree | Neither Agree nor Disagree | Completely Agree |
|---|---|---|
| 1    2 | 3    4    5 | 6    7 |

Place the number that best describes your degree of agreement or disagreement in the blank to the left of each statement.

____ 1. An expert who doesn't come up with a definite answer probably doesn't know too much.

____ 2. I would like to live in a foreign country for a while.

____ 3. The sooner we all acquire similar values and ideals the better.

____ 4. A good teacher is one who makes you wonder about your way of looking at things.

____ 5. I like parties where I know most of the people more than ones where all or most of the people are complete strangers.

____ 6. Teachers or supervisors who hand out vague assignments give a chance for one to show initiative and originality.

____ 7. A person who leads an even, regular life, in which few surprises or unexpected happenings arise, really has a lot to be grateful for.

____ 8. Many of our most important decisions are based upon insufficient information.

____ 9. There is really no such thing as a problem that can't be solved.

____ 10. People who fit their lives to a schedule probably miss most of the joy of living.

____ 11. A good job is one where what is to be done and how it is to be done are always clear.

____ 12. It is more fun to tackle a complicated problem than to solve a simple one.

____ 13. In the long run, it is possible to get more done by tackling small, simple problems rather than large and complicated ones.

____ 14. Often, the most interesting and stimulating people are those who don't mind being different and original.

____ 15. What we are used to is always preferable to what is unfamiliar.

## Scoring:

For odd-numbered questions, add the total points.

For even-numbered questions, use reverse scoring (7 minus the score), and add the total points.

Your score is the total of the even- and odd-numbered questions.

This survey asks 15 questions about personal and work situations with ambiguity. You were asked to rate each situation on a scale of 1 to 7. A perfectly tolerant person would score 15 and a perfectly intolerant person 105. Scores ranging from 20 to 80 have been reported, with a mean of 45. Company managers had an average score of about 45, and nonprofit managers had an average score of about 43, although scores in both groups varied widely.

Typically, people who are highly tolerant of ambiguity (very low score) will be comfortable in organizations characterized by rapid change, unclear authority, empowerment, and movement toward a learning organization. People with low tolerance for ambiguity (high score) are comfortable in more stable, well-defined situations. However, individuals can grow in the opposite direction of their scores if they so choose.

**Source:** Paul C. Nutt, "The Tolerance for Ambiguity and Decision Making," The Ohio State University College of Business Working Paper Series, WP88–291, March 1988. Adapted from Stanley Budner, "Intolerance of Ambiguity as a Personality Variable," *Journal of Personality*, 30:1 (March 1962), table 1, p. 34. Copyright Duke University Press, 1962. Reprinted with permission.

# Management in Practice: Ethical Dilemma

## The Supervisor

Karen Lowry, manager of a social service agency in a mid-sized city in Illinois, loved to see her employees learn and grow to their full potential. When a rare opening for a supervising clerk occurred, Karen quickly decided to give Charlotte Hines a shot at the job. Charlotte had been with the agency for 17 years and had shown herself to be a true leader. Charlotte worked hard at being a good supervisor, just as she had always worked hard at being a top-notch clerk. She paid attention to the human aspects of employee problems and introduced modern management techniques that strengthened the entire agency.

However, the Civil Service Board decided that a promotional exam should be given to find a permanent placement for the supervising clerk position. For the sake of fairness, the exam was an open competition—anyone, even a new employee, could sign up and take it. The board wanted the candidate with the highest score to get the job but allowed Karen, as manager of the agency, to have the final say-so.

Since she had accepted the provisional opening and proven herself on the job, Charlotte was upset that the entire clerical force was deemed qualified to take the test. When the results came back, she was devastated. Charlotte placed twelfth in the field of candidates, while one of her newly hired clerks placed first. The Civil Service Board, impressed by the new clerk's high score, is urging Karen to give her the permanent supervisory job. Karen wonders if it's fair to base her decision only on the test results.

## What Do You Do?

1. Ignore the test. Charlotte has proven herself and deserves the job.
2. Give the job to the candidate with the highest score. You don't need to make enemies on the Civil Service Board, and, after all, it is an objective way to select a permanent placement.
3. Devise a more comprehensive set of selection criteria—including test results as well as supervisory experience, ability to motivate employees, and knowledge of agency procedures—that can be explained and justified to the board and to employees.

**Source:** Based on Betty Harrigan, "Career Advice," *Working Woman*, July 1986, 22–24.

# Surf the Net

1. **The Learning Organization.** The learning organization guru, Peter Senge, is a senior lecturer at the Massachusetts Institute of Technology (MIT) and director of the Center for Organizational Learning at MIT's Sloan School of Management. Choose one of his articles, such as the one entitled "Learning Organizations," located at *http://www.infed.org/thinkers/senge.htm*.

   Be prepared to report in class your findings about the concept of learning organizations.

2. **Culture.** In the April–May 1998 issue of *Fast Company*, Dave Duffield, president and CEO of PeopleSoft, stated: "Our true core competency is our culture . . . That's what attracts people and keeps them here. It also helps sell customers. Customers want to work with companies that are competent, trustworthy, and fun. Winners like winners."

   Visit *http://www.peoplesoft.com/corp/en/about/community/culture.jsp*

   After reading through the information provided about PeopleSoft's culture, select one of the following options to complete:

   OPTION 1: "I think I would fit in with the culture at PeopleSoft and would enjoy working there because of the following characteristics of its culture:"

   OPTION 2: "I don't think I would enjoying working at PeopleSoft because of the following characteristics of its culture:"

3. **Quality.** Provide information in response to the following questions: (a) What is the Malcolm Baldrige National Quality Award? (b) What criteria are used to evaluate the companies? (c) What organizations won the award last year? The sites below contain Malcolm Baldrige information.

   *http://www.quality.nist.gov/*

# Case for Critical Analysis

### SuperJuice

Luisa de la Cruz sat in her new office thinking about her company's future. After working her way up the corporate ladder for 15 years, she has just been appointed CEO of SuperJuice, a Florida-based company that makes juice and juice drinks that are marketed to high schools and restaurants throughout the Southeast. For nearly two decades, SuperJuice has been the most successful juice drink maker in the region. However, profits haven't risen for four straight years, and several new competitors continue to steal market share. In fact, one of the new companies was started by two former SuperJuice employees who left the company after top management continually rejected their ideas for new exotic drink mixes or new approaches to marketing. It made Luisa cringe to realize that the hottest selling drink flavors in Florida and several other states had been invented in SuperJuice's own labs but were now being made and sold by a competitor. Competitors were setting up drink carts at outdoor festivals and advertising with jingles and slogans that caught the imaginations of the region's youth. Even Luisa's own 17-year-old son often purchased her competitors' products, saying that "SuperJuice is for kids. This stuff rocks."

SuperJuice management has always prided itself on the company's efficient set of systems, both in the factory and at headquarters. Managers concentrated on making a high-quality product as inexpensively as possible. "SuperJuice is like a well-oiled machine," Luisa told herself with some pride. Most of the company's 200 employees had joined SuperJuice right out of high school or college and liked the way the company operated. They showed up for work on time, performed their jobs efficiently, and rarely complained. The long-standing rules and procedures, combined with an organizational culture that reflected the traditional, family-oriented background of SuperJuice's Cuban-born founder, contributed to a level of politeness and civility in the company that sometimes seemed like a throwback to the 1950s. "SuperJuice is a calm and civilized place to work in the midst of a rapidly changing, chaotic world," Luisa reflected with pleasure.

But her pleasure evaporated as she realized that the company could collapse beneath her if it didn't somehow respond to the changes in the environment. She remembered the scandal that had erupted several years ago when two new employees started "breaking the rules" and pushing for changes in the company. The two worked odd hours, played rock music, and decorated their offices with brightly colored posters, unique photographs, and fanciful "dream catchers" hung from the ceiling. Occasionally, one would tape a note to his door that read, "Gone to the movies to get my creative juices flowing!" Although both workers were highly productive, top management quickly took action to try to bring the two back in line. They worried that this kind of attitude would have a negative impact on the productivity of other employees, who were accustomed to coming to work and putting in their solid eight hours. The previous CEO really blew his stack when the two presented four new drink flavors they had concocted on the sly. He was so angry about the unauthorized use of lab time that he nearly fired both employees on the spot. Luisa remembered finding one of the employees in the lab dejectedly pouring the prototypes down the drain.

"You know you can't do anything new in this company," Luisa told her at that time. "It's just not the SuperJuice way." Since that time, SuperJuice has lost a few other young, ambitious employees who have chafed under the tight management control.

Luisa knew she was promoted because she had always followed the rules. But she also realized that continuing to follow the rules could take this company she loved right into bankruptcy. She knows the company has a lot of potential, starting with its loyal, committed workforce. But where should she begin? Can SuperJuice really change itself into a forward-thinking, creative company?

## Questions

1.  What are some of the social, political, and economic forces affecting SuperJuice and calling for a new approach to management?
2.  What do you believe Luisa needs to do first to begin a transformation at SuperJuice?
3.  How would you suggest she turn SuperJuice into a learning organization? Think about specific changes she can make to get all employees thinking of new and exciting ways to revitalize the SuperJuice product line and way of doing business.

Source: Based on Suzy Wetlaufer, "What's Stifling the Creativity at CoolBurst?" *Harvard Business Review*, September–October 1997, 36–40.

# Endnotes

1. Thomas Petzinger, Jr., *The New Pioneers: The Men and Women Who Are Transforming the Workplace and Marketplace* (New York: Simon & Schuster, 1999) 91–93, and "In Search of the New World of Work," *Fast Company* (April 1999), 214–220+; and Peter Katel, "Bordering on Chaos," *Wired* (July 1997), 98–107.

2. Melanie Trottman, "Big Airlines Cut Fares, Add Routes to Fight Newer Low-Cost Carriers," *The Wall Street Journal* (February 6, 2004), A1, A10; Arlyn Tobias Gajilan, "The Amazing JetBlue," *FSB* (May 2003), 51–60.

3. Jeffrey Zaslow, "Feeling the Shivers of Faraway Scandals in Fort Wayne, Ind.," *The Wall Street Journal* (February 6, 2004), A1, A10.

4. John Huey, "Managing in the Midst of Chaos," *Fortune* (April 5, 1993), 38–48; and Toby J. Tetenbaum, "Shifting Paradigms: From Newton to Chaos," *Organizational Dynamics* (Spring 1998), 21–32.

5. Eric Abrahamson, "Management Fashion," *Academy of Management Review* 21, no. 1 (January 1996), 254–285. Also see "75 Years of Management Ideas and Practice," a supplement to the *Harvard Business Review* (September–October 1997), for a broad overview of historical trends in management thinking.

6. "Of Water Coolers and Coffee Breaks," timeline in Matthew Boyle, "How the Workplace Was Won," *Fortune* (January 22, 2001), 139+.

7. Daniel A. Wren, *The Evolution of Management Thought*, 2d ed. (New York: Wiley, 1979), 6–8. Much of the discussion of these forces comes from Arthur M. Schlesinger, *Political and Social History of the United States, 1829–1925* (New York: Macmillan, 1925); and Homer C. Hockett, *Political and Social History of the United States, 1492–1828* (New York: Macmillan, 1925).

8. The discussion of trends is based on Cam Marston, "Managing Gen X and Gen Y," http://www.programresources.com/professional_speakers_tips/marston_managing_gen_X accessed on February 6, 2004, and Marnie E. Green, "Beware and Prepare: The Government Workforce of the Future," *Public Personnel Management* (Winter 2000), 435+.

9. Green, "The Government Workforce of the Future."

10. Robin Wright and Doyle McManus, *Flashpoints: Promise and Peril in a New World* (New York: Alfred A. Knopf, 1991).

11. This section is based heavily on Thomas Petzinger, Jr., "So Long Supply and Demand," *The Wall Street Journal* (January 1, 2000), R31.

12. Petzinger, "So Long Supply and Demand."

13. Darrell Rigby, "Management Tools Survey 2003: Usage Up as Companies Strive to Make Headway in Tough Times," *Strategy & Leadership* 31, no. 5 (2003), 4–11.

14. See Daniel James Rowley, "Resource Reviews," *Academy of Management Learning and Education* 2, no. 3 (2003), 313–321; Jane Whitney Gibson, Dana V. Tesone, and Charles W. Blackwell, "Management Fads: Here Yesterday, Gone Today?" *SAM Advanced Management Journal* (Autumn 2003), 12–17; David Collins, *Management Fads and Buzzwords: Critical-Practices Perspective*, (London, UK: Routledge, 2000); Timothy Clark, "Management Research on Fashion: A Review and Evaluation," *Human Relations* 54, no. 12 (2001), 1650–1661; Brad Jackson, *Management Gurus and Management Fashions* (London: Routledge, 2001); Patrick Thomas, *Fashions in Management Research: An Empirical Analysis* (Aldershot, UK: Ashgate, 1999).

15. Daniel A. Wren, "Management History: Issues and Ideas for Teaching and Research," *Journal of Management* 13 (1987), 339–350.

16. Business historian Alfred D. Chandler, Jr., quoted in Jerry Useem, "Entrepreneur of the Century," *Inc.* (20th Anniversary Issue, 1999), 159–174.

17. Useem, "Entrepreneur of the Century."

18. The following is based on Wren, *Evolution of Management Thought*, Chapters 4, 5; and Claude S. George, Jr., *The History of Management Thought* (Englewood Cliffs, N.J.: Prentice-Hall, 1968), Chapter 4.

19. Charles D. Wrege and Ann Marie Stoka, "Cooke Creates a Classic: The Story behind F. W. Taylor's Principles of Scientific Management," *Academy of Management Review* (October 1978), 736–749; Robert Kanigel, *The One Best Way: Frederick Winslow Taylor and the Enigma of Efficiency* (New York: Viking, 1997); and Alan Farnham, "The Man Who Changed Work Forever," *Fortune* (July 21, 1997), 114.

20. Quoted in Ann Harrington, "The Big Ideas," *Fortune* (November 22, 1999), 152–154.

21. Wren, *Evolution of Management Thought*, 171; and George, *History of Management Thought*, 103–104.

22. Geoffrey Colvin, "Managing in the Info Era," *Fortune* (March 6, 2000), F-5–F-9.

23. Max Weber, *General Economic History*, trans. Frank H. Knight (London: Allen & Unwin, 1927); Max Weber, *The Protestant Ethic and the Spirit of Capitalism*, trans. Talcott Parsons (New York: Scribner, 1930); and Max

Weber, *The Theory of Social and Economic Organizations*, ed. and trans. A. M. Henderson and Talcott Parsons (New York: Free Press, 1947).

24. Kelly Barron, "Logistics in Brown," *Forbes* (January 10, 2000), 78–83; Scott Kirsner, "Venture Vérité: United Parcel Service," *Wired* (September 1999), 83-96; "UPS," *The Atlanta Journal and Constitution* (April 26, 1992), H1; and Kathy Goode, Betty Hahn, and Cindy Seibert, "United Parcel Service: The Brown Giant" (unpublished manuscript, Texas A&M University, 1981).

25. Henri Fayol, *Industrial and General Administration*, trans. J. A. Coubrough (Geneva: International Management Institute, 1930); Henri Fayol, *General and Industrial Management*, trans. Constance Storrs (London: Pitman and Sons, 1949); and W. J. Arnold and the editors of *BusinessWeek, Milestones in Management* (New York: McGraw-Hill, vol. I, 1965; vol. II, 1966).

26. Mary Parker Follett, *The New State: Group Organization: The Solution of Popular Government* (London: Longmans, Green, 1918); and Mary Parker Follett, *Creative Experience* (London: Longmans, Green, 1924).

27. Henry C. Metcalf and Lyndall Urwick, eds., *Dynamic Administration: The Collected Papers of Mary Parker Follett* (New York: Harper & Row, 1940); Arnold, *Milestones in Management*.

28. Follett, *The New State*; Metcalf and Urwick, *Dynamic Administration* (London: Sir Isaac Pitman, 1941).

29. William B. Wolf, *How to Understand Management: An Introduction to Chester I. Barnard* (Los Angeles: Lucas Brothers, 1968); and David D. Van Fleet, "The Need-Hierarchy and Theories of Authority," *Human Relations* 9 (Spring 1982), 111–118.

30. Gregory M. Bounds, Gregory H. Dobbins, and Oscar S. Fowler, *Management: A Total Quality Perspective* (Cincinnati, Ohio: South-Western Publishing, 1995), 52–53.

31. Curt Tausky, *Work Organizations: Major Theoretical Perspectives* (Itasca, Ill.: F. E. Peacock, 1978), 42.

32. Charles D. Wrege, "Solving Mayo's Mystery: The First Complete Account of the Origin of the Hawthorne Studies—The Forgotten Contributions of Charles E. Snow and Homer Hibarger" (paper presented to the Management History Division of the Academy of Management, August 1976).

33. Ronald G. Greenwood, Alfred A. Bolton, and Regina A. Greenwood, "Hawthorne a Half Century Later: Relay Assembly Participants Remember," *Journal of Management* 9 (Fall/Winter 1983), 217–231.

34. F. J. Roethlisberger, W. J. Dickson, and H. A. Wright, *Management and the Worker* (Cambridge, Mass.: Harvard University Press, 1939).

35. H. M. Parson, "What Happened at Hawthorne?" *Science* 183 (1974), 922–932; John G. Adair, "The Hawthorne Effect: A Reconsideration of the Methodological Artifact," *Journal of Applied Psychology* 69, no. 2 (1984), 334–345; and Gordon Diaper, "The Hawthorne Effect: A Fresh Examination," *Educational Studies* 16, no. 3 (1990), 261–268.

36. Greenwood, Bolton, and Greenwood, "Hawthorne a Half Century Later," 219–221.

37. F. J. Roethlisberger and W. J. Dickson, *Management and the Worker*.

38. Ramon J. Aldag and Timothy M. Stearns, *Management*, 2d ed. (Cincinnati, Ohio: South-Western Publishing, 1991), 47–48.

39. Tausky, *Work Organizations: Major Theoretical Perspectives*, 55.

40. Douglas McGregor, *The Human Side of Enterprise* (New York: McGraw-Hill, 1960), 16–18.

41. Julie Gehrke, "Power to the Painters," *Painting and Wallcovering Contractor* (September–October 2003), 84.

42. Wendell L. French and Cecil H. Bell Jr., "A History of Organizational Development," in Wendell L. French, Cecil H. Bell Jr., and Robert A. Zawacki, *Organization Development and Transformation: Managing Effective Change* (Burr Ridge, Ill.: Irwin McGraw-Hill, 2000), 20–42.

43. Mansel G. Blackford and K. Austin Kerr, *Business Enterprise in American History* (Boston: Houghton Mifflin, 1986), Chapters 10, 11; and Alex Groner and the editors of *American Heritage and BusinessWeek, The American Heritage History of American Business and Industry* (New York: American Heritage Publishing, 1972), Chapter 9.

44. Larry M. Austin and James R. Burns, *Management Science* (New York: Macmillan, 1985).

45. Marcia Stepanek, "How an Intranet Opened Up the Door to Profits," *BusinessWeek E.Biz* (July 26, 1999), EB32–EB38.

46. Ludwig von Bertalanffy, Carl G. Hempel, Robert E. Bass, and Hans Jonas, "General Systems Theory: A New Approach to Unity of Science," *Human Biology* 23 (December 1951), 302–361; and Kenneth E. Boulding, "General Systems Theory—The Skeleton of Science," *Management Science* 2 (April 1956), 197–208.

47. Fremont E. Kast and James E. Rosenzweig, "General Systems Theory: Applications for Organization and Management," *Academy of Management Journal* (December 1972), 447–465.

48. "CIO Panel: Knowledge-Sharing Roundtable," *Information Week* Online, News in Review (April 26, 1999), *Information Week* Web site, downloaded on April 30, 1999; and Glenn Rifkin, "Nothing But 'Net,'" *Fast Company* (June–July 1996), 118–127.

49. Fred Luthans, "The Contingency Theory of Management: A Path Out of the Jungle," *Business Horizons* 16 (June 1973), 62–72; and Fremont E. Kast and James E. Rosenzweig, *Contingency Views of Organization and Management* (Chicago: Science Research Associates, 1973).

50. Samuel Greengard, "25 Visionaries Who Shaped Today's Workplace," *Workforce* (January 1997), 50–59; and Harrington, "The Big Ideas."

51. Mauro F. Guillen, "The Age of Eclecticism: Current Organizational Trends and the Evolution of Managerial Models," *Sloan Management Review* (Fall 1994), 75–86.

52. Jeremy Main, "How to Steal the Best Ideas Around," *Fortune* (October 19, 1992), 102–106.

53. Thomas H. Davenport and Laurence Prusak, with Jim Wilson, *What's the Big Idea? Creating and Capitalizing on the Best Management Thinking* (Boston, Mass.: Harvard Business School Press, 2003. Also see Theodore Kinni, "Have We Run Out of Big Ideas?" *Across the Board* (March-April 2003, 16–21.

54. Ronald A. Heifetz and Donald L. Laurie, "The Leader as Teacher: Creating the Learning Organization," *Ivey Business Journal* (January–February 2003), 1–9.

55. Peter Senge, *The Fifth Discipline: The Art and Practice of Learning Organizations* (New York: Doubleday/Currency, 1990).

56. Khoo Hsien Hui and Tan Kay Chuan, "Nine Approaches to Organizational Excellence," *Journal of Organizational Excellence* (Winter 2002), 53–65; Leon Martel, "The Principles of High Performance—And How to Apply Them," *Journal of Organizational Excellence* (Autumn 2002), 49–59; and Jeffrey Pfeffer, "Producing Sustainable Competitive Advantage through the Effective Management of People," *Academy of Management Executive* 9, no. 1 (1995), 55–69.

57. Alex Markels, "The Wisdom of Chairman Ko," *Fast Company* (November 1999), 258–276.

58. Edward O. Welles, "Mind Gains," *Inc.* (December 1999), 112–124.

59. Kevin Kelly, *New Rules for the New Economy: 10 Radical Strategies for a Connected World* (New York: Viking Penguin, 1998).

60. Nick Wingfield, "In the Beginning . . . ," *The Wall Street Journal* (May 21, 2001), R18.

61. Andy Reinhardt,"From Gearhead to Grand High Pooh-Bah," *BusinessWeek* (August 28, 2000), 129–130.

62. Julia Angwin, "Used Car Auctioneers, Dealers Meet Online," *The Wall Street Journal* (November 20, 2003), B1, B13; William J. Holstein and Edward Robinson, "The Re-Education of Jacques Nasser," *Business2.Com* (May 29, 2001), 60–73.

63. Bernard Wysocki, Jr., "Corporate Caveat: Dell or Be Delled," *The Wall Street Journal* (May 10, 1999), A1.

64. Reinhardt, "From Gearhead to Grand High Pooh-Bah."

65. Robert D. Hof, "The eBay Economy: The Company is Not Just a Wildly Successful Startup. It Has Invented a Whole New Business World," *BusinessWeek,* (August 25, 2003), 124.

66. Amber Chung, "Music Retailers Face Tough Times as File-Sharing Grows," *Taipei Times* (February 10, 2004), 11; http://www.taipeitimes.com accessed on February 10, 2004.

67. Quoted in Colvin, "Managing in the Info Era."

68. Jeffrey Zygmont, "The Ties That Bind," *Inc. Tech* no. 3, (1998), 70–84; and Nancy Ferris, "ERP: Sizzling or Stumbling?" *Government Executive* (July 1999), 99–102.

69. Harrington, "The Big Ideas." Also see Peter Drucker, *Post-Capitalist Society,* (Oxford: Butterworth Heinemann, 1993), 5.

70. Based on Andrew Mayo, "Memory Bankers," *People Management* (January 22, 1998), 34–38; William Miller, "Building the Ultimate Resource," *Management Review* (January 1999), 42–45; and Todd Datz, "How to Speak Geek," *CIO Enterprise,* Section 2 (April 15, 1999), 46–52.

71. Louisa Wah, "Behind the Buzz," *Management Review* (April 1999), 17–26.

72. Petzinger, *The New Pioneers: The Men and Women Who Are Transforming the Workplace and Marketplace,* and "In Search of the New World of Work"; Katel, "Bordering on Chaos"; and Oren Harari, "The Concrete Intangibles," *Management Reviews,* (May 1999), 30–33.

# Video Case

## Chapter 1: Le Meridien Managers Manage by Walking Around

Le Meridien is a chain of 125 luxury hotels in 55 countries around the globe. You can find Le Meridien hotels in the United States, throughout Europe, in Africa, Australia, India, Egypt, and other locations. Premium customer service is key to the success of a hotel chain, and a manager's skills can make or break a hotel. At Le Meridien Hotel in Boston, a manager's work is never done. Take the typical day of Bob van den Oord, assistant general manager of the hotel, which is part of a luxury chain owned by Great Eagle in Hong Kong and managed by Le Meridien in London. He arrives at the hotel before 8:00 A.M. and does a walk-through of the entire hotel, inspecting empty rooms, the kitchen, dining rooms, reservations desk, front lobby, and even the laundry, to be certain that everything is running smoothly. He may meet with other managers, such as the Dutch-born manager, Michiel Lugt, who runs room service and stewarding (restaurant and catering services) for the hotel, or the housekeeping or security managers if they have a specific issue to discuss. By 9:30, all managers—including Bob—are assembled for the daily operational meeting, in which everyone reports briefly on the hotel's activities for the past 24 hours. Managers for the information technology department, reservations, housekeeping, and human resource departments give thumbnail reports on problems currently needing solutions or ones that have already been dealt with—such as a brief lack of hot water in some of the building's guest rooms. By 9:45 the meeting is over and all managers return to their posts.

Bob van den Oord fulfills all the four management functions every day he's on the job. As assistant general manager, he meets with the general manager to "set the overall goals for the hotel, so I take a more strategic role and provide the tools and resources to the other managers" so they can do their jobs. He functions in an organizational role, assigning responsibility to other managers—such as the head of security—to accomplish particular tasks or assignments, such as evaluating and updating security at the hotel. He leads and motivates workers by constantly keeping in touch with them—he manages by walking around. "It's a good tool to see what's going on," he says, from the kitchen to the plants out front of the building. "Ninety-percent of problems are because of management screw-ups," he notes candidly. "I like [walking around], the staff likes it, and guests like to see management around as well." Van den Oord admits that he asks a lot of his managers, but he devotes a lot of himself to the job as well. "The hotel is a 24-hour operation," he explains. "We have to be here when

other people are having fun." Finally, he fulfills the control function by monitoring activities and making necessary corrections. His daily walk-through is a prime example of this function. "Management is about constant feedback," Van den Oord comments. "It allows people to improve their performance."

Michiel Lugt, the functional manager who runs room service—which is open 24 hours a day, 7 days a week—fully agrees with his boss's philosophy of management. He likes to lead by example and is always ready to help out when necessary, even if it means serving coffee to guests in one of the dining rooms. He believes that people skills are vitally important in the hotel industry, not only in dealing with staff but in dealing with guests as well. He remarks that, as a young manager, "Sometimes you have to manage people who are older than you are; that's a massive challenge. People should realize that experience is important." He makes a special effort to learn whatever he can from staff members who have been in the business longer than he has. "I try to be one of the gang, basically," he says of his relationship with his staff. "We have to run, and business and things have to be done, but that doesn't mean you have to be a tyrant." He encourages staff members to approach him with questions and concerns whenever possible.

Le Meridien—a single hotel in a huge organization—is a complex organization itself, hosting more than 100,000 visitors each year. On any given day, Bob van den Oord and his staff may welcome honeymooners, international tourists, business travelers, groups for conventions or conferences, and college reunions. "It's hard work, but it's fun," notes Van den Oord. Of his staff he says, "We're all in it together." That, in a nutshell, is the new paradigm of management at Le Meridien Hotel.

### Questions

1. In addition to human skills, a hotel manager needs technical skills and conceptual skills. Identify what you think some of those technical skills and conceptual skills might be, either for a general manager or for a functional manager at a hotel.
2. Would you call Le Meridien Hotel in Boston a learning organization? Why or why not?
3. Describe at least one social force, political force, and economic force that may influence Le Meridien and its management practices.

Source: Company Web site, *http://www.lemeridien-hotels.com*, accessed January 4, 2002.

# Video Case

## Chapter 2: In the Beginning: A Bite Taken from the Apple

On April Fool's Day, 1976, Apple Computer was founded by two guys who had been friends in high school, who liked to tinker with electronics, and who had dropped out of college to pursue jobs in the new computer industry in what would later be called the Silicon Valley of California. Apple was no April Fool's joke, although not many people took it seriously at first. Consumers hadn't yet grasped the idea that they could use computers for anything themselves. They saw large mainframes in secluded, air-conditioned rooms at work. But personal computers were still unheard of. Even businesses were reluctant to invest in computers for their employees; after all, they had typewriters, and calculators were available for number crunching. But Steve Jobs and Steve Wozniak had a product they thought they could sell: first the Apple I computer, and shortly thereafter the Apple II. They had created the first personal computer in Steve Jobs's garage. The face of business, and daily life, has never been the same.

The Apple computer did sell—in fact, the Apple II sold like crazy, once it gained momentum. Within three years, the Apple II had earned $139 million, representing a 700 percent growth. Consumers were snapping up Apple IIs for writing and calculating as quickly as the company could produce them. With success came further company growth, and the necessity for management. Through the first few years of Apple's existence, Steve Jobs controlled the business side of the company, taking on all of the management functions: planning, organizing, leading, and controlling. He hired a succession of presidents, financial officers, public relations people, and marketing people to handle the company's expanding business. Then there were the product design teams, midlevel managers, and ultimately, more and more investors. Although the atmosphere during the early days was radical—both employees and management liked to foster the counterculture image—as new investors began to take their seats on the board of directors, things changed. These older, more conservative directors insisted that the company be managed in a more traditional fashion. Meanwhile, only five years into the venture, Steve Wozniak was injured in a plane crash and forced to take a leave of absence. Steve Jobs became chairman of Apple at only 26 years old.

As a young manager, Jobs certainly had technical skills. After all, the Apple computer was his brainchild. Although some critics might disagree, he also had conceptual skills: he understood where his organization was and had a vision of where he wanted it to go. But Jobs has never been known for his human skills. Driven toward perfection himself, he expected perfection from his managers and employees. One former employee recalls that Jobs rejected anyone's work the first time he saw it, just on principle. He earned himself a notorious reputation as a manager, one that has followed him to this day.

In 1981, a competitor of goliath proportions emerged: IBM—the powerhouse of mainframe computing—introduced its first personal computer to the marketplace. Jobs, who was essentially an engineer, recognized that he did not have the business or management skills necessary to take his company to the next level. So he began to pursue John Sculley, who was then president of Pepsi-Cola. He lured Sculley to Apple with the language of a visionary: "If you stay at Pepsi, five years from now all you'll have accomplished is selling a lot more sugar water to kids. . . . If you come to Apple you can change the world." Sculley accepted the challenge.

As the company went public and began to compete with larger organizations like IBM, the people who had originally gone to work for Apple found themselves in a changing environment. Despite Jobs's iron grip, they viewed themselves as a young, hip, innovative group who did things their own way. Even though both Apple founders had dropped out of college, Apple workers were highly educated, creative, and technically skilled. They valued their independence, and most likely chafed under the new "business" orientation. On a larger scale, Apple was charged with changing the way the general public viewed—and ultimately valued—computers. Apple was lauded for its product innovations and creativity, and its users became devoted followers.

The economic environment, both inside and outside Apple, was ripe for success. The economic boom of the 1980s meant that people had money to spend. But it also meant that competition followed closely on Apple's heels. By the early 1980s, Apple management, including new CEO John Sculley (who was a

# Chapter 2: In the Beginning: A Bite Taken from the Apple (continued)

sharp businessman, but who didn't know much about computers), made some costly mistakes. For instance, the Lisa, which was the first mouse-controlled personal computer, was priced at $10,000, far above what the public would accept. No one bought it. And the Apple III was so filled with design flaws that the first 14,000 computers had to be recalled. That computer's image never recovered. Still, many more ups and downs lay ahead for the company as Apple continued to grow and change as an organization.

## Questions

1. From the overview presented in this case, what features of Apple's culture are similar to learning organizations? To bureaucratic organizations? What steps might Apple managers take toward creating—or strengthening—a learning organization?

2. Of the four management functions, which do you think Jobs excelled at? Which was his weakest? Why?

3. What types of roles does a person in Jobs's position at Apple need to perform? List as many informational, interpersonal, and decisional roles that you think apply and explain why you think so.

Sources: Apple Computer Inc. Web site, "Business Summary," "History," and "Steve Paul Jobs" accessed March 23, 1999, at *http://www.apple.com*; Brent Schlender and Michael Martin, "Paradise Lost," *Fortune* (February 19, 1996), accessed at *http://www.pathfinder. com. iMac.*

## Part 1: Ford Motor Company Makes History

# .....Continuing Case

The history of Ford Motor Company embodies the history of American management itself. When Henry Ford began a manufacturing revolution with his company's mass production of automobiles, much of the country was still bouncing along in horse-drawn carriages. A hundred years later, despite many ups and downs, Ford Motor Company is firmly established as the world's largest pickup truck manufacturer and the number-two maker of cars (behind General Motors). Ford has progressed from an offering of one color—black—to a wide range of makes, models, and hues from which consumers may choose, depending on their budgets, lifestyles, and moods. In addition to the autos it produces under its own name, Ford's brands now include Jaguar, Lincoln, Mercury, and Volvo, a 33 percent stake in Mazda, and BMW's Land Rover SUV, along with the Hertz rental agency. Ford has had hugely successful models, such as the Taurus, as well as duds that it would rather forget, such as the Pinto. In recent years, the company has been mired in a public relations disaster surrounding its popular SUV, the Explorer, and the vehicle's standard tires, which were manufactured by Firestone/Bridgestone. Still, the company has managed to survive by making changes in leadership, improving efficiency and effectiveness of its management and manufacturing operations, and embracing new management competencies. As you study your course of management this semester, you'll follow the rises, dips, and turns of one of America's most well-known and enduring organizations.

Fast-forward from that original assembly line spewing out those black Model Ts and Model As to the end of the twentieth century, when a whirlwind known as Jacques Nasser took over as CEO of Ford Motor Company and immediately began to change management practices that previously had included a complex bureaucracy bogged down by centralized decision making and an unwillingness to budge from the status quo.

Although Nasser didn't explicitly use the term learning organization, he set out to turn his company into one. He hired a group of skilled managers from different automakers around the world (including Volkswagen and BMW), lured a number of marketers and salespeople from consumer-goods manufacturers,

and pushed the entire Ford workforce to get as close to customers as possible to find out what people really wanted in their automobiles. He encouraged information sharing with such initiatives as a venture with MSN's CarPoint Web site that would provide data from online purchases. Ford marketers and designers would learn which models, colors, and features certain buyers preferred. And he let managers know in no uncertain terms that Ford Motor Company was now on the move—with their help as empowered workers who were accountable for their own (and their employees') performance. "You've got to earn [a promotion,]" Nasser supposedly thundered in one meeting. "The days of entitlement at Ford Motor Company are gone forever." To that end, he instituted a forced-ranking system, under which a certain number of employees would be considered underperformers and laid off each year. The system, which worked something like a grading curve, drew much criticism and was eventually abandoned.

On a grand scale, Nasser announced an organizational shakeup that meant decentralizing authority and decision-making powers, and transferring them to semiautonomous business units around the world. "Jac learned to make decisions without a lot of bureaucratic oversight from [Ford headquarters at] Dearborn," recalled Robert Lutz, Nasser's former boss. Now Nasser was promoting this kind of independent decision making throughout a new generation of Ford managers.

All of these actions were part of Nasser's strategy to transform a century-old industrial giant into a nimble, flexible company that could rapidly meet consumers' wants and needs. Designers, engineers, and marketers were required to attend seminars at a Consumer Insight Center to learn how to listen to customers and engage them in conversations designed to reveal what products and features they would most likely buy. Then they were sent in small teams out into the field for eight weeks of "customer immersion." Nasser wasn't kidding. He wanted all managers at all levels to understand their customers, inside and out.

Nasser made some radical changes at Ford Motor Company, an organization that has long been a symbol

# Part 1: Ford Motor Company Makes History (continued)

# ...Continuing Case

of American business and ingenuity. The company has been around so long that it has passed through several historical phases of management, from scientific management to today's learning organization. In 1913, one of the first moving assembly lines was installed in the company's Highland Park plant, reducing production time by 50 percent. With this new system, a Ford Model T came off the assembly line every ten seconds. Today, Ford managers rely on teams, empowerment, the Internet, and high-speed technology to produce thousands of cars a day. Ford's ability to change when the environment demands it may be the single most important factor in its long-term survival.

## Questions

1. How have the necessary skills for a successful manager changed at Ford over the decades?

2. Why was it important for Ford to become a learning organization?

3. Do you think that Jacques Nasser was an effective manager? Why or why not?

Sources: "Ford Motor Company," Hoover's Capsule, Hoover's Online (November 16, 2001), *http://www.hoovers.com*; "Profile—Ford Motor Company," Yahoo! Finance, *http://www.biz.yahoo.com*; Julie Cantwell, "Exec Changes Help Ford with Basics," *Automotive News* (November 12, 2001), *http://www.autonews. com*; Geoffrey Colvin, "We Can't All Be Above Average," *Fortune*, August 13, 2001, *http://www.fortune. com*; Kathleen Kerwin and Keith Naughton, "Remaking Ford," BusinessWeek Online (October 11, 1999), *http://www.businessweek. com*.

# The Environment of Management

Whether it's the glorious vista of a national park, the perennial blooms in a backyard patch, or the carefully manicured lines of a French garden, the landscape is an environment of unlimited possibilities. Few things are more elemental than the needs of a garden: dirt, water, sun, caring and knowledgeable hands. Yet there are turbulent forces at work, including constantly changing weather, human carelessness, and nature's own cycles.

Fires sweep through Yellowstone National Park every summer, but 1988 was a watershed year. That summer, as a years-long drought continued, lightning-fed and manmade flames converged to burn more than a third of the park. Some conservationists bemoaned the loss of old-growth trees, but the following spring, ample rain and the ash and nutrients of fallen trees led to spectacular wildflowers and a new cycle of forest growth.

Today, there is renewed emphasis on the use of controlled burns as a counterweight to years of uncontrolled overgrowth. Those who care most deeply about the environment have seen that managing the environment and those that thrive in it is vital to its continued vibrancy.

Whatever type of organization managers work in, they—like gardeners and park caretakers—must pay attention to the environment and its powerful, elemental forces. Controlled, they can work together harmoniously, harnessing their strengths to better compete, to better serve, to better produce. Uncontrolled, they become chaotic, inflicting damage to the organization.

Managers face their responsibilities within a variety of environments. The task environment—those customers and suppliers with whom relationships must be sown, rooted, and cultivated—affects how a manager plans, organizes, and implements or delegates tasks. The general environment involves weeding through, sowing, and reaping the rewards of economic upturns, political shifts, and technology breakthroughs.

Choices lie ahead: You can change the environment through controlled decisions or allow other, outside elements to influence your path as a manager.

Part 2

# Chapter 3

# The Environment
and Corporate Culture

## LEARNING OBJECTIVES

*After studying this chapter, you should be able to:*

1. Describe the general and task environments and the dimensions of each.

2. Explain the strategies managers use to help organizations adapt to an uncertain or turbulent environment.

3. Define corporate culture and give organizational examples.

4. Explain organizational symbols, stories, heroes, slogans, and ceremonies and their relationship to corporate culture.

5. Describe how corporate culture relates to the environment.

6. Define a cultural leader and explain the tools a cultural leader uses to create a high-performance culture.

IBM once ruled the technology industry, but the company was practically a has-been by the early 1990s. As the environment changed, IBM managers failed to keep pace, relying on outdated management procedures and clinging to mainframe computers. After the company lost $8 billion in one year, Louis V. Gerstner was brought in as CEO to try to save the giant corporation. He succeeded admirably, reviving IBM's reputation in computer hardware and software as well as moving it higher up the computing food chain by edging into business services. But now, a new CEO sees the limits IBM is facing as the environment for the computing industry continues to shift rapidly. Sam Palmisano, hand-picked by Gerstner as his successor, envisions less emphasis on technology and more on relationships—establishing deep connections with large corporate clients and helping them improve their planning, operations, marketing, and customer service. His "e-business on-demand strategy" calls for IBM to supply computing power to other companies as if it were water or electricity. IBM's systems will be infused with complex knowledge from a variety of industries, enabling the company to model human behavior and solve tough client problems. The new strategy puts IBM in the lead of a massive shift going on in the technology environment. However, to succeed, IBM will have to be fast, flexible, and innovative—characteristics that huge, hierarchical organizations typically don't possess. As he launches this bold and risky project, Palmisano wonders where to begin.[1]

## Take A Moment

If you were Sam Palmisano, what changes would you make to support a new strategy that requires speed, innovation, and flexibility? What values do employees need to model, and how would you instill them?

In high-tech industries, environmental conditions are volatile. You read in Chapter 1 about the problems Xerox is facing partly because managers missed cues from the environment. IBM once nearly faded into history by failing to keep pace with changes in the environment, and Sam Palmisano is trying to make sure the same thing doesn't happen again. Even in seemingly low-tech industries, shifts in the environment can wreak havoc on an organization. Dixon Ticonderoga Company makes pencils and once had a large share of the U.S. market. Today, though, more than 50 percent of the pencils sold in the United States come from overseas, compared to only 16 percent a decade ago. As another example, the Gerber baby food company has faced challenges from Greenpeace and other activist groups over the use of genetically altered grains.[2]

Government actions and red tape can also affect an organization's environment and create problems. Scandals in the mutual fund industry have prompted the SEC to propose a ban on special incentive payments to brokerage firms. The beef and dairy industries in the United States were hurt by increased rules and restrictions following the discovery of mad cow disease in Washington state. However, the organic and natural beef industry experienced an upturn, as consumers grew more cautious about where their meat comes from and how it is produced. And consider thousands of public schools that use a common land snail called *Helix aspera* as a major unit in their science curricula. The U.S. Department of Agriculture's unexpected ban on the interstate transport of the snails threw school science programs into disarray around the nation.[3]

The environment surprises many managers and leaves them unable to adapt their companies to new competition, shifting consumer interests, or new technologies. The study of management traditionally has focused on factors within the organization—a closed systems view—such as leading, motivating, and controlling employees. The classical, behavioral, and management science schools described in Chapter 2 focused on internal aspects of organizations over which managers have direct control. These views are accurate but incomplete. Globalization and worldwide societal turbulence affect companies in new ways. Even for those companies that try to operate solely on the domestic stage, events that have the greatest impact typically originate in the external environment. To be effective, managers must monitor and respond to the environment—an open systems view.

This chapter explores in detail components of the external environment and how they affect the organization. We will also examine a major part of the organization's internal environment—corporate culture. Corporate culture is shaped by the external environment and is an important part of the context within which managers do their jobs.

## The External Environment

The tremendous and far-reaching changes occurring in today's world can be understood by defining and examining components of the external environment. The external **organizational environment** includes all elements existing outside the boundary of the organization that have the potential to affect the organization.[4] The environment includes competitors, resources, technology, and economic conditions that influence the organization. It does not include those events so far removed from the organization that their impact is not perceived.

The organization's external environment can be further conceptualized as having two layers: general and task environments, as illustrated in Exhibit 3.1.[5] The

**organizational environment**
All elements existing outside the organization's boundaries that have the potential to affect the organization.

Exhibit 3.1

## Location of the Organization's General, Task, and Internal Environments

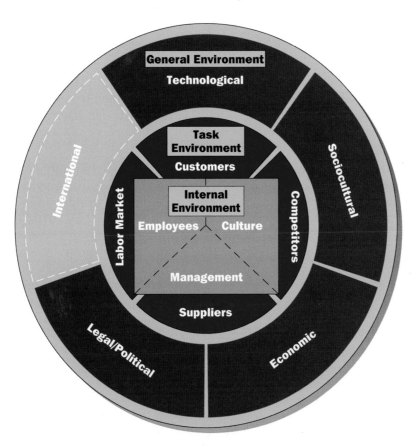

general environment is the outer layer that is widely dispersed and affects organizations indirectly. It includes social, demographic, and economic factors that influence all organizations about equally. Increases in the inflation rate or the percentage of dual-career couples in the workforce are part of the organization's general environment. These events do not directly change day-to-day operations, but they do affect all organizations eventually. The **task environment** is closer to the organization and includes the sectors that conduct day-to-day transactions with the organization and directly influence its basic operations and performance. It is generally considered to include competitors, suppliers, and customers.

The organization also has an **internal environment**, which includes the elements within the organization's boundaries. The internal environment is composed of current employees, management, and especially corporate culture, which defines employee behavior in the internal environment and how well the organization will adapt to the external environment.

Exhibit 3.1 illustrates the relationship among the general, task, and internal environments. As an open system, the organization draws resources from the external environment and releases goods and services back to it. We will now discuss the two layers of the external environment in more detail. Then we will discuss corporate culture, the key element in the internal environment. Other aspects of the internal environment, such as structure and technology, will be covered in Parts Four and Five of this book.

**general environment**
The layer of the external environment that affects the organization indirectly.

**task environment**
The layer of the external environment that directly influences the organization's operations and performance.

**internal environment**
The environment that includes the elements within the organization's boundaries.

# General Environment

The general environment represents the outer layer of the environment. These dimensions influence the organization over time but often are not involved in day-to-day transactions with it. The dimensions of the general environment include international, technological, sociocultural, economic, and legal–political.

## International

**international dimension**
Portion of the external environment that represents events originating in foreign countries as well as opportunities for U.S. companies in other countries.

The **international dimension** of the external environment represents events originating in foreign countries as well as opportunities for U.S. companies in other countries. Note in Exhibit 3.1 that the international dimension represents a context that influences all other aspects of the external environment. The international environment provides new competitors, customers, and suppliers and shapes social, technological, and economic trends, as well.

Today, every company has to compete on a global basis. High-quality, low-priced automobiles from Japan and Korea have permanently changed the American automobile industry. Toyota recently overtook Ford to become the world's second largest automaker, and managers plan to take the company to Number 1 by 2010.[6] Foreign companies like Toyota, Sony, and Nokia have made huge jumps in recent years on *Fortune* magazine's list of the World's Most Admired Companies. Nokia is the world's top maker of cell phones, and Korea's Samsung Corp. is rapidly closing in on U.S.-based Motorola for the Number 2 spot.[7] For many U.S. companies, such as Starbucks and Wal-Mart, domestic markets have become saturated and their only potential for growth lies overseas. E-commerce organizations, too, are making international expansion a priority. The United States' share of worldwide e-commerce is falling as foreign companies set up their own e-commerce ventures.[8] When operating globally, managers have to consider legal, political, sociocultural, and economic factors not only in their home countries but in various other countries as well. For example, a drop in the U.S. dollar's foreign exchange rate lowers the price of U.S. products overseas, increasing export competitiveness. Many companies have had to cut prices to remain competitive in the new global economy.

The global environment represents an ever-changing and uneven playing field compared with the domestic environment. Managers who are used to thinking only about the domestic environment must learn new rules to cope with goods, services, and ideas circulating around the globe. Chapter 4 describes how today's businesses are operating in an increasingly borderless world and examines in detail how managing in a global environment differs from the management of domestic operations. Perhaps the hardest lesson for managers in the United States to learn is that they do not always know best. U.S. decision makers know little about issues and competition in foreign countries. In addition, one recent study found that only 28 percent of surveyed executives from the United States think multicultural experience is important.[9] U.S. arrogance is a shortcut to failure. To counter this, Pall Corporation keeps a team of Ph.D.s traveling around the world gathering current information on markets and issues.[10]

## Technological

**technological dimension**
The dimension of the general environment that includes scientific and technological advancements in the industry and society at large.

The **technological dimension** includes scientific and technological advancements in a specific industry as well as in society at large. In recent years, this dimension has created massive changes for organizations in all industries. Twenty years ago, many organizations didn't even use desktop computers. Today, computer networks, Internet access, videoconferencing capabilities, cell phones, PDAs, fax machines, and laptops are practically taken for granted as the minimum tools for doing business. Technological advancements that make the Internet accessible to nearly everyone have changed the nature of competition and of organizations' relationships to customers. Many companies are adopting sophisticated e-business methods that use private networks or the

© FRITZ HOFFMANN/NETWORK

*China's membership in the World Trade Organization will dramatically change the **international dimension** of the external environment. With 1.3 billion people, China is already an attractive market, but WTO membership will spur economic growth even more. For U.S. construction companies such as Caterpillar, and sales representative Anny Wong, pictured here, China is a dream market, with highways, dams, and buildings springing up everywhere. However, doing business in this new market also presents many challenges, such as setting up distribution chains, service centers, and dealer networks.*

Internet to handle practically all their operations. Communications and computing devices are getting smaller, more powerful, and more affordable. One estimate is that 70 percent of the adult U.S. population owned a mobile phone in late 2003, and the use of advanced features such as photo messaging is growing.[11]

Other technological advances will also affect organizations and managers. The decoding of the human genome could lead to revolutionary medical advances. Cloning technology and stem cell research are raising both scientific and ethical concerns. High-tech composites, embedded with sensors that enable them to think for themselves, are being used to earthquake-proof bridges and highways as well as build better airplanes and railcars.[12] Advances in *nanotechnology*, which refers to seeing and manipulating matter at the level of molecules and atoms, will enable scientists to create amazing new materials—electronic, structural, biological, and medicinal.[13] Examples already in use include "smart gels" that mold to human needs on cue, self-repairing optical coatings, and cleansers that repair a surface at the molecular level while cleaning it.

## Sociocultural

The sociocultural dimension of the general environment represents the demographic characteristics as well as the norms, customs, and values of the general population. Important sociocultural characteristics are geographical distribution and population density, age, and education levels. Today's demographic profiles are the foundation of tomorrow's workforce and consumers. Forecasters see increased globalization of both consumer markets and the labor supply, with increasing diversity both within organizations and consumer markets.[14] Consider the following key demographic trends in the United States:

**sociocultural dimension**
The dimension of the general environment representing the demographic characteristics, norms, customs, and values of the population within which the organization operates.

1. The United States is experiencing the largest influx of immigrants in more than a century. By 2050, non-Hispanic whites will make up only about half of the population, down from 74 percent in 1995 and 69 percent in 2004. Hispanics are expected to make up about a quarter of the U.S. population.[15]
2. The huge post–World War II baby-boom generation is aging and losing its interest in high-cost goods. Meanwhile, their sons and daughters, sometimes called Generation Y, rival the baby boomers in size and will soon rival them in buying power.

© MEREDITH HEUER

*American consumers' growing taste for international foods reflects a change in the **sociocultural dimension** of the environment. Interest in Italian cuisine, for example, has been growing rapidly. Gourmet pasta maker Monterey Pasta is one of the fastest-growing companies in the United States and in 2004 announced new low-carb products and its seventh consecutive profitable year.*

3. The fastest-growing type of living arrangement is single-father households, which rose 62 percent in 10 years, even though two-parent and single-mother households are still much more numerous.[16]

4. In an unprecedented demographic shift, married couple households have slipped from 80 percent in the 1950s to just over 50 percent in 2003. Couples with kids total just 25 percent, with the number projected to drop to 20 percent by 2010. By that year, it is expected that 30 percent of homes will be inhabited by someone who lives alone.[17]

The sociocultural dimension also includes societal norms and values. As this book is being written, the low-carb craze has replaced the low-fat concerns of previous years. From pre-teens to grandparents, people are piling on the bacon and eggs, pork chops and cheese sticks and avoiding carbohydrates like the plague. A market research firm in Chicago estimated that more than 10 million people are following a low-carb regimen. The trend got hot fast, and some analysts predict it will cool just as quickly, but restaurants are altering their menus and supermarkets are devoting shelf space to a growing array of low-carb products.[18] Even the Girl Scouts are affected. In the 2004 Girl Scout cookie season, sales were down an average of 10 percent nationwide.

Other sociocultural trends also affect organizations. A groundswell of interest in spirituality and personal development in the United States since the mid-1990s has led to a proliferation of books and other materials related to religion and spiritual growth.[19] Handgun manufacturers have been tugged back and forth as public acceptance and support of guns in the home fell in the wake of tragic school shootings, and then surged following the September 11, 2001, terrorist attacks.

## Economic

**economic dimension**
The dimension of the general environment representing the overall economic health of the country or region in which the organization operates.

The **economic dimension** represents the general economic health of the country or region in which the organization operates. Consumer purchasing power, the unemployment rate, and interest rates are part of an organization's economic environment. Because organizations today are operating in a global environment, the economic dimension has become exceedingly complex and creates enormous uncertainty for managers. The economies of countries are more closely tied together now. For example, an early 2000s economic recession and the decline of consumer confidence in the United States has affected economies and organizations around the world. Similarly, economic problems in Asia and Europe have had a tremendous impact on companies and the stock market in the United States.

One significant recent trend in the economic environment is the frequency of mergers and acquisitions. Citibank and Travelers merged to form Citigroup, IBM purchased PricewaterhouseCoopers Consulting, and Cingular is acquiring AT&T Wireless. In the toy industry, the three largest toy makers—Hasbro, Mattel, and Tyco—gobbled up at least a dozen smaller competitors within a few years. At the same time, however, there is a tremendous vitality in the small business sector of the economy. Entrepreneurial start-ups are a significant aspect of today's U.S. economy and will be discussed in Chapter 6.

PHOTO COURTESY OF PPL CORPORATION

**CONCEPT CONNECTION**

*PPL Corporation controls more than 12,000 megawatts of generating capacity in the United States and sells energy in key U.S. markets. The company utilizes advances in the **technological dimension** of its environment to understand the complexities of today's ever-changing energy market. In the photo, members of PPL's risk management office, which reports directly to CEO William Hecht, analyze data to improve decision making, while controlling risk. Such high-tech analysis is essential to keeping the company competitive in the electricity market.*

## Legal–Political

The **legal–political dimension** includes government regulations at the local, state, and federal levels, as well as political activities designed to influence company behavior. The U.S. political system encourages capitalism, and the government tries not to overregulate business. However, government laws do specify rules of the game. The federal government influences organizations through the Occupational Safety and Health Administration (OSHA), Environmental Protection Agency (EPA), fair trade practices, libel statutes allowing lawsuits against business, consumer protection legislation, product safety requirements, import and export restrictions, and information and labeling requirements. The Federal Communications Commission, which regulates broadcast television to limit potentially offensive material, has been striving to extend its regulatory authority to the cable networks. Incidents such as Bono's use of a four-letter word at the 2003 Golden Globe Awards and the outrage over Janet Jackson's "wardrobe malfunction" at the 2004 Super Bowl have triggered increased attention to what is shown on television.[20] Many organizations also have to contend with government and legal issues in other countries. For example, the European Union (EU) has recently adopted new environmental and consumer protection rules that are costing American companies hundreds of millions of dollars a year. Companies like Hewlett–Packard, Ford Motor Company, and General Electric have to pick up the bill for recycling the products they sell in the EU.[21]

Managers must recognize a variety of **pressure groups** that work within the legal–political framework to influence companies to behave in socially responsible ways. Automobile manufacturers, toy makers, and airlines have been targeted by Ralph Nader's Center for Responsive Law. Tobacco companies today are certainly feeling the far-reaching power of antismoking groups. Middle-aged activists who once protested the Vietnam War have gone to battle to keep Wal-Mart from "destroying the quality of small-town life." Some groups have also attacked the giant retailer on environmental issues, which likely will be one of the strongest pressure points in coming years.[22] Two of the hottest current issues for pressure groups that are also related to environmental concerns are biotechnology and world trade. Environmental and human rights protesters have disrupted World Trade Organization meetings and meetings of the World Bank and the International Monetary Fund to protest a system of worldwide integration that has food, goods, people, and capital freely moving across borders. This current international issue will be discussed in more detail in Chapter 4.

**legal–political dimension**
The dimension of the general environment that includes federal, state, and local government regulations and political activities designed to influence company behavior.

**pressure group**
An interest group that works within the legal–political framework to influence companies to behave in socially responsible ways.

## Task Environment

As described earlier, the task environment includes those sectors that have a direct working relationship with the organization, among them customers, competitors, suppliers, and the labor market.

### Customers

Those people and organizations in the environment who acquire goods or services from the organization are **customers**. As recipients of the organization's output, customers are important because they determine the organization's success. Patients are the customers of hospitals, students the customers of schools, and travelers the customers of airlines. Toy companies have to stay in close touch with the whims of young customers and their parents. Mattel is hoping that by snapping up rights to make toys tied to Yu-Gi-Oh!, a popular Japanese monster-themed show, and SpongeBob SquarePants, it can create products that will fly off the shelves rather than sit in warehouses. Mattel is also bringing out a toy that can pick up digital signals from the new Warner Bros. *Batman* cartoon shows running on cable networks, meaning a toy Batmobile will zoom across the floor at the exact moment the cartoon car shows up on the television screen.[23]

A big concern for managers today is that the Internet has given increased power to customers and enabled them to directly impact the organization. For example, gripe sites such as *http://walmartsucks.com*, where customers and sales associates cyber-vent about the nation's largest retailer, and *http://untied.com*, where United Airlines employees and disgruntled fliers rail against the air carrier, can quickly damage a company's reputation and sales. "In this new information environment," says Kyle Shannon, CEO of e-commerce consultancy Agency.com, "you've got to assume everyone knows everything."[24]

### Competitors

Other organizations in the same industry or type of business that provide goods or services to the same set of customers are referred to as **competitors**. Each industry is characterized by specific competitive issues. The recording industry differs from the steel industry and the pharmaceutical industry.

Competitive wars are being waged worldwide in all industries. Coke and Pepsi continue to battle it out for the soft-drink market. UPS and FedEx are fighting the overnight delivery wars. Home Depot and Lowe's are brawling in the retail home improvement market, trying to out-do one another in terms of price, service, and selection.[25] This chapter's Unlocking Creative Solutions Through Technology box describes how retailer Target has achieved a competitive edge with strategic use of the Internet. In the travel and tourism industry, Internet companies like Expedia.com and Hotels.com have hurt the big hotel chains. These chains are fighting back by undercutting the brokers' prices on the hotels' own Web sites. In addition, five of the largest chains have banded together to create Travelweb.com, which is aimed directly at the online brokers.[26]

### Suppliers

The raw materials the organization uses to produce its output are provided by **suppliers**. A steel mill requires iron ore, machines, and financial resources. A small, private university may utilize hundreds of suppliers for paper, pencils, cafeteria food, computers, trucks, fuel, electricity, and textbooks. Companies from toolmakers to construction firms and auto manufacturers were hurt recently by an unanticipated jump in the price of steel. Just as they were starting to see an upturn in their business, the cost of raw materials from suppliers jumped 30 percent in a two-month period.[27] Many companies are using fewer suppliers and trying to build good relationships

# Unlocking Creative Solutions Through Technology

## Target Is Right On in Internet Retailing

Target has fewer than half the number of retail stores as Wal-Mart, but on the Internet, the smaller retailer gets almost as much business as the giant. Managers at Target have succeeded online better than those of any other mass retailer.

Target.com sells items that are too big to stock in retail stores, such as Little Tikes kiddie furniture. In addition, Target test-markets new products on the Web before committing to shelf space for them in the stores. One example is the $200 Graco jogging stroller, which debuted on Target.com in the spring of 2002. When it rapidly became the best-selling stroller online, Target managers added it to the product lineup for bricks-and-mortar stores.

The biggest success for Target.com, however, has been the "Web as gift-shop" approach. The site has sold thousands of "Student Survival Kits," such as the Movie Night package that contains a bucket of popcorn, candy, soda, and a blank VCR tape, and just as many "Cold Comfort" get-well boxes containing medicine along with a cuddly teddy bear. The site's bridal and baby registries are hot destinations, and these areas account for about 22 percent of the site's total sales.

Target.com is also helping to get more customers into the retail stores. One technique is to use the Target Visa smart card, which contains a microchip, as a repository of customer information, helping Target keep in closer touch with customer needs. Customers can also download personalized coupons from the Web site onto their smart cards. But there's only one place they can use the coupons—at their nearest Target store.

**SOURCE**: Chana R. Schoenberger, "Bull's Eye," *Forbes* (September 2, 2002): 76.

with them so that they will receive high-quality parts at lower prices. The relationship between manufacturers and suppliers has traditionally been an adversarial one, but many companies are finding that cooperation is the key to saving money, maintaining quality, and speeding products to market.

## Labor Market

The **labor market** represents people in the environment who can be hired to work for the organization. Every organization needs a supply of trained, qualified personnel. Unions, employee associations, and the availability of certain classes of employees can influence the organization's labor market. Labor market forces affecting organizations right now include (1) the growing need for computer-literate information technology workers; (2) the necessity for continuous investment in human resources through recruitment, education, and training to meet the competitive demands of the borderless world; and (3) the effects of international trading blocs, automation, outsourcing, and shifting facility location upon labor dislocations, creating unused labor pools in some areas and labor shortages in others.

Changes in these various sectors of the environment can create tremendous challenges, especially for organizations operating in complex, rapidly changing industries. Nortel Networks, a Canadian company with multiple U.S. offices, is an example of an organization operating in a highly complex environment.

**labor market**
The people available for hire by the organization.

The external environment for Nortel Networks (formerly Northern Telecom) is illustrated in Exhibit 3.2. The Canadian-based company began in 1895 as a manufacturer of telephones and has reinvented itself many times to keep up with changes in the environment. Since the late 1990s, the company has been undergoing another re-invention, transforming itself into a major player in wireless technology and equipment for connecting businesses

NORTEL
NETWORKS
http://www.nortel.com

Exhibit 3.2

## The External Environment of Nortel Networks

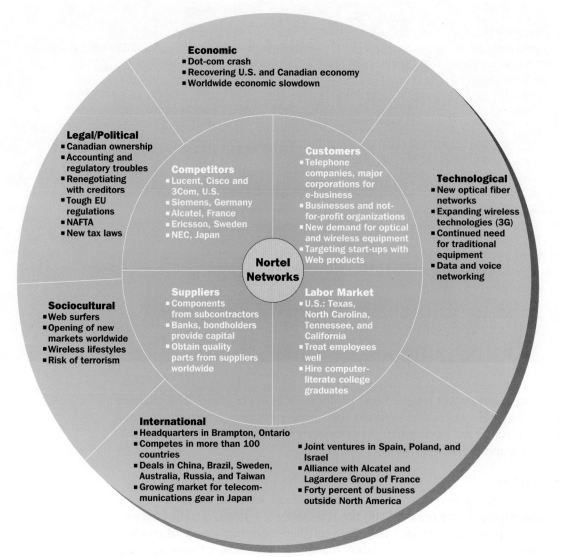

**SOURCES:** W. C. Symonds, J. B. Levine, N. Gross, and P. Coy, "High-Tech Star: Northern Telecom Is Challenging Even AT&T," *BusinessWeek*, July 27, 1992, 54–58; I. Austen, "Hooked on the Net," *Canadian Business*, June 26–July 10, 1998, 95–103; J. Weber with A. Reinhardt and P. Burrows, "Racing Ahead at Nortel," *BusinessWeek*, November 8, 1999, 93–99; "Nortel's Waffling Continues: First Job Cuts, Then Product Lines, and Now the CEO," *Telephony*, May 21, 2001, 12; and M. Heinzl, "Nortel's Profits of 499 Million Exceeds Forecast," *The Wall Street Journal*, January 30, 2004, B4.

and individuals to the Internet. When John Roth took over as CEO in 1997, the company was about to be run over by rivals such as Cisco Systems that were focused on Internet gear. Roth knew he needed to do something bold to respond to changes in the technological environment. A name change to Nortel Networks symbolized and reinforced the company's new goal of providing unified network solutions to customers worldwide.

One response to the competitive environment was to spend billions to acquire data and voice networking companies, including Bay Networks (which makes Internet and data equipment), Cambrian Systems (a hot maker of optical technology), Periphonics (maker of voice-response systems), and Clarify (customer management software). These companies brought Nortel top-notch technology to help the company, as Roth put it, "move at Net speed." Nortel began snatching customers away from rivals Cisco and Lucent Technologies. In addition, even during rough economic times, Nortel kept spending nearly 20 percent of its revenues on research and development to keep pace with changing technology.

Internationally, Nortel has made impressive inroads in Taiwan, China, Brazil, Mexico, Colombia, Japan, and Sweden, among other countries. It has also won customers by recognizing the continuing need for traditional equipment and offering hybrid gear that combines old telephone technology with new Internet features, allowing companies to transition from the old to the new. Bold new technologies for Nortel include optical systems that move voice and data at the speed of light and third-generation wireless networks (3G), which zap data and video from phone to phone. Nortel is considered a leader in wireless gear and recently won contracts from Verizon Communications and Orange SA, a unit of France Telecom, to supply equipment that sends phone calls as packets of digital data like that used over the Internet.

Companies moving in a Net speed environment risk a very hard landing, and during the economic slump of the early 2000s, Nortel's business was devastated. The company cut two-thirds of its workforce and closed dozens of plants and offices. In late 2002, Nortel's stock was trading for less than a dollar. Two years later, though, positive changes in the telecom industry and the economic environment had Nortel back on an uphill swing. The stock rebounded with news of the Verizon deal and current CEO Frank Dunn's announcement of a fourth quarter 2003 profit of $499 million. Nortel was once again recognized as an industry leader.[28]

# The Organization–Environment Relationship

Why do organizations care so much about factors in the external environment? The reason is that the environment creates uncertainty for organization managers, and they must respond by designing the organization to adapt to the environment.

## Environmental Uncertainty

Organizations must manage environmental uncertainty to be effective. *Uncertainty* means that managers do not have sufficient information about environmental factors to understand and predict environmental needs and changes.[29] As indicated in Exhibit 3.3, environmental characteristics that influence uncertainty are the number of factors that affect the organization and the extent to which those factors change. A large multinational like Nortel Networks has thousands of factors in the external environment creating uncertainty for managers. When external factors change rapidly, the organization experiences very high uncertainty; examples are telecommunications and aerospace firms, computer and electronics companies, and e-commerce organizations that sell products and services over the Internet. Companies have to make an effort to adapt to the rapid changes in the environment. When an organization deals with only a few external factors and these factors are relatively stable, such as for soft-drink bottlers or food processors, managers experience low uncertainty and can devote less attention to external issues.

## Adapting to the Environment

If an organization faces increased uncertainty with respect to competition, customers, suppliers, or government regulation, managers can use several strategies to adapt to these changes, including boundary-spanning roles, interorganizational partnerships, and mergers or joint ventures.

### Boundary-Spanning Roles

Departments and boundary-spanning roles link and coordinate the organization with key elements in the external environment. Boundary spanners serve two purposes for

**boundary-spanning roles**
Roles assumed by people and/or departments that link and coordinate the organization with key elements in the external environment.

# Exhibit 3.3

## The External Environment and Uncertainty

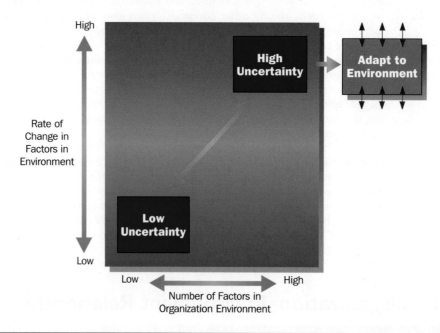

the organization: They detect and process information about changes in the environment, and they represent the organization's interest to the environment.[30] Employees in engineering or research and development scan for new technological developments, innovations, and raw materials. People in departments such as marketing and purchasing span the boundary to work with customers and suppliers, both face-to-face and through market research. Some organizations are staying in touch with customers through the Internet, such as by monitoring gripe sites, communicating with customers on company Web sites, and contracting with market-research firms such as Look-Look that use the Web to monitor rapidly changing marketplace trends.[31]

A growing area in boundary spanning is *competitive intelligence (CI)*, which refers to activities to get as much information as possible about one's rivals. Membership in the Society of Competitive Intelligence Professionals more than doubled between 1997 and 2001, and colleges are introducing master's degree programs in CI.[32] Competitive intelligence specialists use Web sites, commercial databases, financial reports, market activity, news clippings, trade publications, personal contacts, and numerous other sources to scan an organization's environment and spot potential threats or opportunities.[33] Visa has an employee who searches the Web for two hours each day for insights on MasterCard and other competitors. Harley-Davidson hires an outside research firm to search through massive amounts of data and reveal patterns that help decipher and predict competitors' actions.[34]

Managers need good information about their competitors, customers, and other elements of the environment to make good decisions. In today's turbulent environment, the most successful companies involve everyone in boundary-spanning activities. People at the grass-roots level, for instance, are often able to see and interpret significant changes sooner than managers who are more removed from the day-to-day work.[35] However, top executives, too, need to stay in tune with the environment. Tom Stemberg, CEO of Staples, visits a competitor's store once a week and shares what he learns with others on the management team.[36]

*Take A Moment*    *Go to the ethical dilemma on page 109.*

## Interorganizational Partnerships

One popular strategy for adapting to the environment is reducing boundaries and increasing collaboration with other organizations. North American companies have typically worked alone, competing with one another, but an uncertain, interconnected, global environment has changed all that. Companies are joining together to become more effective and to share scarce resources. Sony, Toshiba, and IBM are collaborating to produce a new, tiny computer chip. Kroger, Albertsons, and Safeway banded together to negotiate with labor unions.[37] Head-to-head competition among independent firms is giving way to networks of alliances that compete for business on a global basis. For example, the aerospace industry is controlled by two networks—those of Boeing and Airbus, each of which is made up of more than 100 partner organizations.[38]

Managers have shifted from an adversarial orientation to a partnership orientation, as summarized in Exhibit 3.4. The new paradigm is based on trust and the ability of partners to work out equitable solutions to conflicts so that everyone profits from the relationship. Managers work to reduce costs and add value to both sides, rather than trying to get all the benefits for their own company. The new model is also characterized by a high level of information sharing, including e-business linkages for automatic ordering, payments, and other transactions. In addition, there is a lot of person-to-person interaction to provide corrective feedback and solve problems. People from other companies may be onsite or participate in virtual teams to enable close coordination. Partners are frequently involved in one another's product design and production, and they are committed for the long term. It is not unusual for business partners to help one another, even outside of what is specified in the contract.[39] The Manager's Shoptalk further

© COURTESY OF CAMPBELL SOUP

**CONCEPT CONNECTION**

*A consumer focus group in Mexico evaluates Campbell's soups, reviewing qualities such as packaging, preparation, appearance, and taste. The passage of NAFTA broadened market opportunities in Mexico, where nearly 9 billion servings of soup are consumed each year. Marketing executives act as **boundary spanners** to test reactions and assess whether products meet local needs. Boundary spanning provided competitive intelligence that Mexican consumers like convenient dry-soup varieties as well as condensed and ready-to-serve soups.*

Exhibit 3.4

## The Shift to a Partnership Paradigm

| From Adversarial Orientation ⟶ | To Partnership Orientation |
|---|---|
| • Suspicion, competition, arm's length | • Trust, value added to both sides |
| • Price, efficiency, own profits | • Equity, fair dealing, everyone profits |
| • Information and feedback limited | • E-business links to share information and conduct digital transactions |
| • Lawsuits to resolve conflict | • Close coordination; virtual teams and people onsite |
| • Minimal involvement and up-front investment | • Involvement in partner's product design and production |
| • Short-term contracts | • Long-term contracts |
| • Contracts limit the relationship | • Business assistance goes beyond the contract |

# manager's Shoptalk

## Turbulent Times

### *The New Golden Rule: Cooperate!*

**News flash:** Companies all over the world are sleeping with the enemy. A decade ago, many managers would have considered it heresy to collaborate with competitors, but today they are finding that collaboration is necessary to compete in a rapidly changing environment. Worldwide, research and development budgets are shrinking even as technological complexity grows by leaps and bounds. Collaboration in product development is sweeping every field from autos to aircraft to biotechnology.

Suppliers are also a part of this new collaborative business model. Speed is essential in today's economy, which requires a seamless integration between a company and its suppliers. Volkswagen, Europe's biggest automaker, has stretched the supplier relationship to new limits at its revolutionary plant in Brazil. Twelve international suppliers work directly in Volkswagen's factory, making their own components and then fastening them together into finished trucks and buses. Although few have stretched the supplier relationship as far as VW, other auto companies, including Ford, DaimlerChrysler, and General Motors, are also experimenting with this *modular approach*, in which suppliers provide premade chunks of a vehicle that can be quickly assembled into a finished car or truck by a handful of workers. Manufacturers win with lower costs, while suppliers gain in higher volume, and transaction costs go down for everyone. In the quest for speed and efficiency, collaboration is a trend that is likely to go even further in coming years.

Here are a few tips from the experts about what makes a collaborative relationship successful:

- **Enter the relationship with a spirit of true partnership.** An arm's-length, semiadversarial, no-trust, "dump-them-tomorrow-if-we-get-a-better-deal" mindset guarantees failure. Successful partnerships are based on openness, trust, and long-term commitment.
- **When choosing partners, pay attention to culture and values.** Too often, managers perform due diligence on matters such as markets, products, and technologies, but overlook the "softer" side of partnerships. When it comes right down to it, incompatibility of culture and values can doom a partnership faster than anything else.
- **Clarify what each partner is expected to give and to get from the relationship.** This includes defining those who will lead the project, how decisions will be made, review and oversight responsibilities, and who has final authority regarding any negotiations, contract approvals, and so forth.
- **Put together the right team, including top management.** Top management support and active involvement is crucial for the success of the partnership In addition, team members should represent all functions, levels, and areas of expertise. The most successful alliance managers are those with open minds, strong relationship skills, and a desire for learning.
- **Put it in writing.** An open, trusting relationship does not mean there should not be a legal contract and clear, written guidelines for how the partnership will conduct business. A legal contract prevents misunderstandings and provides continuity through changes in personnel and management. However, experts warn that you can kill a partnership by turning to the contract at the first hint of any conflict. Partners should learn to resolve disagreements in a collaborative, no-blame manner.

---

SOURCES: Based on information in Lynn A. Isabella, "Managing an Alliance Is Nothing Like Business as Usual," *Organizational Dynamics 15*, no. 1 (2002): 47–59; Oren Harari, "The Logistics of Success," *Management Review* (June 1999): 24–26; Gail Dutton, "The New Consortiums," *Management Review* (January 1999): 46–50; Lee Berton, "Shall We Dance?" *CFO* (January 1998): 28–35; David Woodruff with Ian Katz and Keith Naughton, "VW's Factory of the Future," *BusinessWeek* (October 7, 1996): 52–56; and Philip Siekman, "Building 'Em Better in Brazil," *Fortune* (September 6, 1999): 246(c)–246(v).

examines the new partnership orientation and offers some guidelines for building successful partnerships.

### Mergers and Joint Ventures

A step beyond strategic partnerships is for companies to become involved in mergers or joint ventures to reduce environmental uncertainty. A frenzy of merger and acquisition activity both in the United States and internationally in recent years is an attempt by organizations to cope with the tremendous volatility of the environment.[40] A **merger** occurs when two or more organizations combine to become one. For example, Wells Fargo merged with Norwest Corp. to form the nation's fourth largest banking corporation.

A **joint venture** involves a strategic alliance or program by two or more organizations. This typically occurs when a project is too complex, expensive, or uncertain for one firm to handle alone. Oprah Winfrey's Harpo Inc. formed a joint venture with Hearst Magazines to launch *O, The Oprah Magazine*.[41] Despite her popularity and success with her television show, Winfrey recognized the complexity and uncertainty involved in starting a new magazine when so many were going out of business. The combined resources and management talents of the partners contributed to the most successful startup ever in the magazine publishing industry. Joint ventures are on the rise as companies strive to keep pace with rapid technological change and compete in the global economy. Barnes & Noble formed a joint venture with Germany's Bertelsmann AG to establish Barnesandnoble.com. MTV Networks has established joint ventures with companies in Brazil, Australia, and other countries to expand its global presence.[42] Many small businesses are also turning to joint ventures with large firms or with international partners. A larger partner can provide sales staff, distribution channels, financial resources, or a research staff. Small businesses seldom have the expertise to deal internationally, so a company such as Nypro, Inc., a plastic injection-molding manufacturer in Clinton, Massachusetts, joins with overseas experts who are familiar with the local rules. Nypro now does business in four countries.[43]

**merger**
The combining of two or more organizations into one.

**joint venture**
A strategic alliance or program by two or more organizations.

# The Internal Environment: Corporate Culture

The internal environment within which managers work includes corporate culture, production technology, organization structure, and physical facilities. Of these, corporate culture has surfaced as extremely important to competitive advantage. The internal culture must fit the needs of the external environment and company strategy. When this fit occurs, highly committed employees create a high-performance organization that is tough to beat.[44]

The concept of culture has been of growing concern to managers since the 1980s, as turbulence in the external environment has grown, often requiring new values and attitudes. Organizational culture has been defined and studied in many and varied ways. For the purposes of this chapter, we define **culture** as the set of key values, beliefs, understandings, and norms shared by members of an organization.[45] The concept of culture helps managers understand the hidden, complex aspects of organizational life. Culture is a pattern of shared values and assumptions about how things are done within the organization. This pattern is learned by members as they cope with external and internal problems and taught to new members as the correct way to perceive, think, and feel. Culture can be analyzed at three levels, as illustrated in Exhibit 3.5, with each level becoming less obvious.[46] At the surface level are visible artifacts, which include such things as manner of dress, patterns of behavior,

**culture**
The set of key values, beliefs, understandings, and norms that members of an organization share.

*With a moptop of blond hair and a love for turning cartwheels, Betsey Johnson's whimsical personality reflects her company's unique **corporate culture**. That culture provides the organization with the design sensibilities necessary to keep up with changing fashion trends. Its lacy, embroidered dresses are a big hit with prom-goers, and are sold at high-end department stores like Saks Fifth Avenue and Nordstrom. The Betsey Johnson clothing label has become a retail fashion empire with $50 million in revenue last year and 45 boutiques in the United States, Canada, and Britain.*

physical symbols, organizational ceremonies, and office layout. Visible artifacts are all the things one can see, hear, and observe by watching members of the organization. At a deeper level are the expressed values and beliefs, which are not observable but can be discerned from how people explain and justify what they do. These are values that members of the organization hold at a conscious level. They can be interpreted from the stories, language, and symbols organization members use to represent them. Some values become so deeply embedded in a culture that members are no longer consciously aware of them. These basic, underlying assumptions and beliefs are the essence of culture and subconsciously guide behavior and decisions. In some organizations, a basic assumption might be that people are essentially lazy and will shirk their duties whenever possible; thus, employees are closely supervised and given little freedom, and colleagues are frequently suspicious of one another. More enlightened organizations operate on the basic assumption that people want to do a good job; in these organizations, employees are given more freedom and responsibility, and colleagues trust one another and work cooperatively.

The fundamental values that characterize an organization's culture can be understood through the visible manifestations of symbols, stories, heroes, slogans, and ceremonies.

## Symbols

**symbol**
An object, act, or event that conveys meaning to others.

A **symbol** is an object, act, or event that conveys meaning to others. Symbols can be considered a rich, non-verbal language that vibrantly conveys the organization's important values concerning how people relate to one another and interact with the

Exhibit 3.5

**Levels of Corporate Culture**

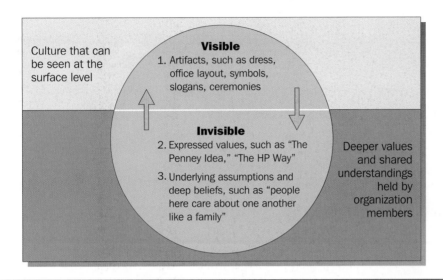

environment.[47] For example, managers at a New York–based start-up that provides Internet solutions to local television broadcasters wanted a way to symbolize the company's unofficial mantra of "drilling down to solve problems." They bought a dented old drill for $2 and dubbed it The Team Drill. Each month, the drill is presented to a different employee in recognition of exceptional work, and the employee personalizes the drill in some way before passing it on to the next winner.[48]

Steelcase Corp. built a new, pyramid-shaped corporate development center to symbolize new cultural values of collaboration, teamwork, and innovation. Whereas designers, engineers, and marketers had previously been located in different buildings, they're now all housed in the pyramid. The six-floor building features an open atrium from ground floor to ceiling, with a giant pendulum to remind people of constant change. Open areas and thought stations with white boards encourage brainstorming and the exchange of ideas.[49]

## Stories

A **story** is a narrative based on true events that is repeated frequently and shared among organizational employees. Stories are told to new employees to keep the organization's primary values alive. One of Nordstrom's primary means of emphasizing the importance of customer service is through corporate storytelling. An example is the story about a sales representative who took back a customer's two-year-old blouse with no questions asked.[50] A frequently told story at UPS concerns an employee who, without authorization, ordered an extra Boeing 737 to ensure timely delivery of a load of Christmas packages that had been left behind in the holiday rush. As the story goes, rather than punishing the worker, UPS rewarded his initiative. By telling this story, UPS workers communicate that the company stands behind its commitment to worker autonomy and customer service.[51]

**story**
A narrative based on true events that is repeated frequently and shared among organizational employees.

## Heroes

A **hero** is a figure who exemplifies the deeds, character, and attributes of a strong culture. Heroes are role models for employees to follow. Sometimes heroes are real, such as the female security supervisor who once challenged IBM's chairman because

**hero**
A figure who exemplifies the deeds, character, and attributes of a strong corporate culture.

*The AFLAC Duck, which appears in innovative commercials, is the major reason for AFLAC's brand awareness and name recognition. The AFLAC duck started as an advertising campaign for AFLAC Incorporated, an insurance company that sells its products in the United States and Japan. But the duck has been transformed into a* **symbol** *of the company's commitment to being a good corporate citizen. The company sponsors the AFLAC Cancer Center and Blood Disorders Service, which is part of Children's Healthcare of Atlanta. Employees support the center through volunteering, fundraising, and personal donations. Plush toy ducks are used to soothe children undergoing treatment at the center, and proceeds from the sales of the plush ducks on the AFLAC Web site go to the cancer center.*

IMAGE COURTESY OF AFLAC INCORPORATED

he wasn't carrying the appropriate clearance identification to enter a security area.[52] Other times they are symbolic, such as the mythical sales representative at Robinson Jewelers who delivered a wedding ring directly to the church because the ring had been ordered late. The deeds of heroes are out of the ordinary, but not so far out as to be unattainable by other employees. Heroes show how to do the right thing in the organization. Companies with strong cultures take advantage of achievements to define heroes who uphold key values.

At 3M Corp., top managers keep alive the heroes who developed projects that were killed by top management. One hero was a vice president who was fired earlier in his career for persisting with a new product even after his boss had told him, "That's a stupid idea. Stop!" After the worker was fired, he would not leave. He stayed in an unused office, working without a salary on the new product idea. Eventually he was rehired, the idea succeeded, and he was promoted to vice president. The lesson of this hero as a major element in 3M's culture is to persist at what you believe in.[53]

## Slogans

**slogan**
A phrase or sentence that succinctly expresses a key corporate value.

A **slogan** is a phrase or sentence that succinctly expresses a key corporate value. Many companies use a slogan or saying to convey special meaning to employees. H. Ross Perot of Electronic Data Systems established the philosophy of hiring the best people he could find and noted how difficult it was to find them. His motto was, "Eagles don't flock. You gather them one at a time." Averitt Express uses the slogan "Our driving force is people" on its trucks to express its commitment to treating employees and customers well. Cultural values can also be discerned in written public statements, such as corporate mission statements or other formal statements that express the core values of the organization. The mission statement for Hallmark Cards, for example, emphasizes values of excellence, ethical and moral conduct in all relationships, business innovation, and corporate social responsibility.[54]

## Ceremonies

A **ceremony** is a planned activity that makes up a special event and is conducted for the benefit of an audience. Managers hold ceremonies to provide dramatic examples of company values. Ceremonies are special occasions that reinforce valued accomplishments, create a bond among people by allowing them to share an important event, and anoint and celebrate heroes.[55]

The value of a ceremony can be illustrated by the presentation of a major award. Mary Kay Cosmetics Company holds elaborate awards ceremonies, presenting gold and diamond pins, furs, and luxury cars to high-achieving sales consultants. The setting is typically an auditorium, in front of a large, cheering audience, and everyone dresses in glamorous evening clothes. The most successful consultants are introduced by film clips, like the kind used to present award nominees in the entertainment industry. These ceremonies recognize and celebrate high-performing employees and emphasize the rewards for performance.[56] A company can also bestow an award secretly by mailing it to the employee's home or, if a check, by depositing it in a bank. But such procedures would not make the bestowal of rewards a significant organizational event and would be less meaningful to the employee.

In summary, organizational culture represents the values, norms, understandings, and basic assumptions that employees share, and these values are signified by symbols, stories, heroes, slogans, and ceremonies. Managers help define important symbols, stories, and heroes to shape the culture.

**ceremony**
A planned activity that makes up a special event and is conducted for the benefit of an audience.

# Environment and Culture

A big influence on internal corporate culture is the external environment. Cultures can vary widely across organizations; however, organizations within the same industry often reveal similar cultural characteristics because they are operating in similar environments.[57] The internal culture should embody what it takes to succeed in the environment. If the external environment requires extraordinary customer service, the culture should encourage good service; if it calls for careful technical decision making, cultural values should reinforce managerial decision making.

*Go to the experiential exercise on page 108 that pertains to corporate cultures.*

*Take A Moment*

## Adaptive Cultures

Research at Harvard on 207 U.S. firms illustrated the critical relationship between corporate culture and the external environment. The study found that a strong corporate culture alone did not ensure business success unless the culture encouraged healthy adaptation to the external environment. As illustrated in Exhibit 3.6, adaptive corporate cultures have different values and behavior from unadaptive corporate cultures. In adaptive cultures, managers are concerned about customers and those internal people and processes that bring about useful change. In the unadaptive corporate cultures, managers are concerned about themselves, and their values tend to discourage risk taking and change. Thus a strong culture alone is not enough, because an unhealthy culture may encourage the organization to march resolutely in the wrong direction. Healthy cultures help companies adapt to the environment.[58]

## Types of Cultures

In considering what cultural values are important for the organization, managers consider the external environment as well as the company's strategy and goals. Studies

Exhibit 3.6

## Environmentally Adaptive versus Unadaptive Corporate Cultures

|  | Adaptive Corporate Cultures | Unadaptive Corporate Cultures |
|---|---|---|
| **Visible Behavior** | Managers pay close attention to all their constituencies, especially customers, and initiate change when needed to serve their legitimate interests, even if it entails taking some risks. | Managers tend to behave somewhat insularly, politically, and bureaucratically. As a result, they do not change their strategies quickly to adjust to or take advantage of changes in their business environments. |
| **Expressed Values** | Managers care deeply about customers, stockholders, and employees. They also strongly value people and processes that can create useful change (e.g., leadership initiatives up and down the management hierarchy). | Managers care mainly about themselves, their immediate work group, or some product (or technology) associated with that work group. They value the orderly and risk-reducing management process much more highly than leadership initiatives. |

**SOURCE:** John P. Kotter and James L. Heskett, *Corporate Culture and Performance* (New York: The Free Press, 1992), 51.

**adaptability culture**
A culture characterized by values that support the company's ability to interpret and translate signals from the environment into new behavior responses.

NOKIA
http://www.nokia.com

have suggested that the right fit between culture, strategy, and the environment is associated with four categories or types of culture, as illustrated in Exhibit 3.7. These categories are based on two dimensions: (1) the extent to which the external environment requires flexibility or stability; and (2) the extent to which a company's strategic focus is internal or external. The four categories associated with these differences are adaptability, achievement, involvement, and consistency.[59]

The **adaptability culture** emerges in an environment that requires fast response and high-risk decision making. Managers encourage values that support the company's ability to rapidly detect, interpret, and translate signals from the environment into new behavior responses. Employees have autonomy to make decisions and act freely to meet new needs, and responsiveness to customers is highly valued. Managers also actively create change by encouraging and rewarding creativity, experimentation, and risk taking. One good example of an adaptability culture is Nokia.

Nokia has been the world's leading maker of cell phone handsets since 1998. One reason is that innovation and adaptability are built into the corporate culture. Nokia's top goal is to keep churning out new products, because what's hot in this industry one day is stone cold a few months later.

The Nokia Mobile Phones unit (NMP) launched 15 new products in 2001, doubled it to 30 in 2002, and was on track to meet or exceed that in 2003. The company has been first to market with a number of hot innovations. When it came out with the first phone to feature a built-in camera, for example, it had the market to itself for nearly six months because competitors weren't prepared. Another first was a phone with a fold-out keyboard to use for e-mail.

Nokia managers encourage "uninhibited dabbling," whereby people feel free to try crazy ideas and never shirk from making mistakes. To spur creativity and fresh thinking, people are rotated to different jobs and divisions—a lawyer might be shifted to running a division or a network engineer moved to handset design. The company also keeps divisions and teams small and gives them the power to implement their ideas. Friendly internal

Exhibit 3.7

## Four Types of Corporate Cultures

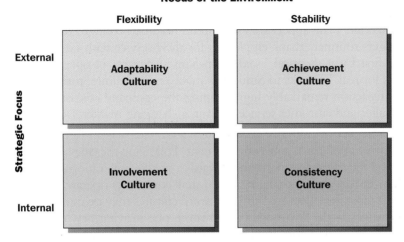

**Needs of the Environment**

SOURCES: Based on D. R. Denison and A. K. Mishra, "Toward a Theory of Organizational Culture and Effectiveness," *Organization Science* 6, no. 2 (March–April 1995): 204–223; R. Hooijberg and F. Petrock, "On Cultural Change:Using the Competing Values Framework to Help Leaders Execute a Transformational Strategy," *Human Resource Management* 32, no.1 (1993): 29–50; and R.E. Quinn, *Beyond Rational Management: Mastering the Paradoxes and Competing Demands of High Performance* (San Francisco: Jossey-Bass, 1988).

competitions celebrate individual creativity, such as photo contests where employees take pictures of their vacation homes or favorite pets with Nokia camera phones.

Nokia faces challenges as the mobile phone market matures, and market share has been dropping as consumers turn to less expensive, mid-range cell phone models from Samsung and Motorola. The history of Nokia indicates that it isn't afraid to take a dramatic turn if the environment demands it: In its lifetime, Nokia has gone from manufacturing paper to making rubber boots, then raincoats, hunting rifles, and consumer electronics, before concentrating on cellular phones.[60]

Most companies in the electronics industry, as well as those involved in e-commerce, cosmetics, and fashion, also use an adaptability culture because they must move quickly to respond to rapid changes in the environment.

The **achievement culture** is suited to organizations that are concerned with serving specific customers in the external environment but without the intense need for flexibility and rapid change. This is a results-oriented culture that values competitiveness, aggressiveness, personal initiative, and willingness to work long and hard to achieve results. An emphasis on winning and achieving specific ambitious goals is the glue that holds the organization together.[61] Siebel Systems, which sells complex software systems, has thrived on an achievement culture. Professionalism and aggressiveness are core values. Employees are forbidden to eat at their desks or to decorate with more than one or two personal photographs. People who succeed at Siebel are focused, competitive, and driven to win. Those who perform and meet stringent goals are handsomely rewarded; those who don't are fired.[62]

The **involvement culture** has an internal focus on the involvement and participation of employees to rapidly meet changing needs from the environment. This culture places high value on meeting the needs of employees, and the organization may be characterized by a caring, family-like atmosphere. Managers emphasize values such as cooperation, consideration of both employees and customers, and avoiding status

**achievement culture**
A results-oriented culture that values competitiveness, personal initiative, and achievement.

**involvement culture**
A culture that places high value on meeting the needs of employees and values cooperation and equality.

differences. One company that illustrates an involvement culture is J. M. Smucker & Co., which in 2004 became the first manufacturer to earn the top spot on *Fortune* magazine's list of "The 100 Best Companies to Work For." Co-CEOs Tim and Richard Smucker, known to employees as "the boys," have continued their father's emphasis on treating people well. Their code of conduct for managers is to listen with full attention, always look for the good in others, have a sense of humor, and say "thank you" for a job well done. Plant supervisors sometimes hold barbeques to celebrate reaching goals; managers routinely thank employees for their service with gift certificates and lunches. "At first I was skeptical," said Brian Kinsey, director of operations. "But this family feel is for real." Thanks to Smucker's involvement culture, turnover is low and employee satisfaction remarkably high, helping the company consistently meet productivity, quality, and customer service goals in a changing marketplace.[63]

**consistency culture**
A culture that values and rewards a methodical, rational, orderly way of doing things.

The final category of culture, the **consistency culture**, has an internal focus and a consistency orientation for a stable environment. Following the rules and being thrifty are valued, and the culture supports and rewards a methodical, rational, orderly way of doing things. In today's fast-changing world, few companies operate in a stable environment, and most managers are shifting toward cultures that are more flexible and in tune with changes in the environment. However, one thriving new company, Pacific Edge Software, has successfully implemented elements of a consistency culture, ensuring that all its projects are on time and on budget. The husband-and-wife team of Lisa Hjorten and Scott Fuller implanted a culture of order, discipline, and control from the moment they founded the company. The emphasis on order and focus means employees can generally go home by 6:00 P.M. rather than working all night to finish an important project. Hjorten insists that the company's culture isn't rigid or uptight, just *careful*. Although sometimes being careful means being slow, so far Pacific Edge has managed to keep pace with the demands of the external environment.[64]

Each of these four categories of culture can be successful. In addition, organizations usually have values that fall into more than one category. The relative emphasis on various cultural values depends on the needs of the environment and the organization's focus. Managers are responsible for instilling the cultural values the organization needs to be successful in its environment.

# Shaping Corporate Culture for Innovative Response

Research conducted by a Stanford University professor indicates that the one factor that increases a company's value the most is people and how they are treated.[65] In addition, a business magazine survey found that CEOs cite organizational culture as their most important mechanism for attracting, motivating, and retaining talented employees, a capability they consider the single best predictor of overall organizational excellence.[66] Corporate culture plays a key role in creating an organizational climate that enables learning and innovative responses to threats from the external environment, challenging new opportunities, or organizational crises. However, managers can't focus all their attention on values; they also need a commitment to solid business performance.

## Managing the High-Performance Culture

Companies that succeed in a turbulent world are those that pay attention both to cultural values and to business performance. Cultural values can energize and motivate employees by appealing to higher ideals and unifying people around shared goals. In addition, values boost performance by shaping and guiding employee behavior, so that everyone's actions are aligned with strategic priorities.[67] Exhibit 3.8 illustrates four organizational outcomes based on the relative attention managers pay to cultural values and business performance.[68] A company in Quadrant A pays little attention to either values or business results and is unlikely to survive for long. Managers in Quadrant B organizations are highly focused on creating a strong culture, but they don't tie organizational values directly to goals and desired business results. A strong, cohesive culture can be positive for a company, especially in terms of employee morale and satisfaction. However, if the culture isn't connected to business performance, it isn't likely to benefit the organization during hard times. For example, Levi Strauss has always been highly focused on values, even tying part of managers' pay to how well they toe the values line. The problem is that top executives lost sight of the business performance side of the issue; that is, they stopped thinking about what it took to make blue jeans profitably.[69]

Quadrant C represents organizations that are focused primarily on bottom-line results and pay little attention to organizational values. This may be profitable in the short run, but the success is difficult to sustain over the long term because the "glue" that holds the organization together—that is, shared values—is missing. Think about the numerous get-rich-quick goals of dot-com entrepreneurs. Thousands of companies sprang up in the 1990s that were aimed primarily at fast growth and quick profits, with little effort to build a solid organization based on long-term mission and values. When the crash came, these companies failed. Those that survived were typically companies that had instilled cultural values that helped them weather the storm. Giants eBay and Amazon have both paid careful attention to organizational values, as have smaller e-commerce companies like Canada's Mediagrif Interactive Technologies, an online B2B brokerage that allows businesses to meet online and trade their goods.[70]

Exhibit 3.8

## Combining Culture and Performance

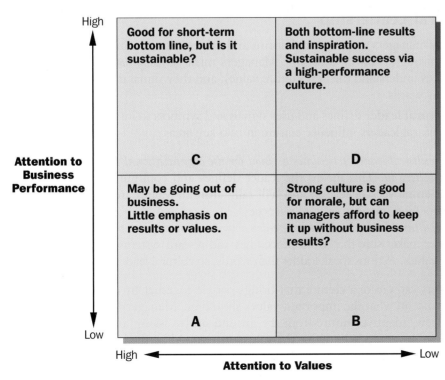

**SOURCE:** Adapted from Jeff Rosenthal and Mary Ann Masarech, "High-Performance Cultures: How Values Can Drive Business Results," *Journal of Organizational Excellence* (Spring 2003), 3–18.

Finally, companies in Quadrant D put high emphasis on both culture and solid business performance as drivers of organizational success. Managers in these organizations align values with the company's day-to-day operations—hiring practices, performance management, budgeting, criteria for promotions and rewards, and so forth. Quadrant D represents the high-performance culture, a culture that: (1) is based on a solid organizational mission or purpose, (2) embodies shared adaptive values that guide decisions and business practices, and (3) encourages individual employee ownership of both bottom-line results and the organization's cultural backbone.[71] An example from Nordstrom, which has strong values of outstanding customer service, provides an illustration. A sales associate had shown a woman nine pairs of shoes, but the store didn't have the right combination of style, size, and color the woman wanted. As she was leaving, another sales associate approached her and offered to see if he could find the shoes at another store. He informed her that he had located them at a competitor's store (Macy's) and would have the shoes shipped directly to her home. Nordstrom's would pick up the overnight shipping charge. Later, this associate reprimanded his peer for failing to try harder. "You really let us down," he said.[72] Nordstrom is a Quadrant D organization, where employees are strongly committed to the cultural values that drive the organization's success and are willing to challenge one another when they fail to honor them. This chapter's Unlocking Creative Solutions Through People box describes Wal-Mart's high-performance culture.

One of the most important things managers do is create and influence organizational culture to meet strategic goals, because culture has a significant impact on performance. In *Corporate Culture and Performance*, Kotter and Heskett provided evidence that companies that intentionally managed cultural values outperformed similar companies that did not. Jim Collins also found culture to be a key factor in his studies of successful companies compared to ones that have not done so well.[73] Caterpillar Inc. developed its Cultural Assessment Process (CAP) to measure and manage culture's contributions to organizational effectiveness. The process gave top executives hard data documenting millions of dollars in savings attributed directly to cultural factors.[74]

## Cultural Leadership

One way managers shape cultural norms and values to build a high-performance culture is through *cultural leadership*. Managers must *overcommunicate* to ensure that employees understand the new culture values, and they signal these values in actions as well as words.

**cultural leader**
A manager who uses signals and symbols to influence corporate culture.

A **cultural leader** defines and uses signals and symbols to influence corporate culture. Cultural leaders influence culture in two key areas:

1. *The cultural leader articulates a vision for the organizational culture that employees can believe in.* This means the leader defines and communicates central values that employees believe in and will rally around. Values are tied to a clear and compelling mission, or core purpose
2. *The cultural leader heeds the day-to-day activities that reinforce the cultural vision.* The leader makes sure that work procedures and reward systems match and reinforce the values. Actions speak louder than words, so cultural leaders "walk their talk."[75]

Leaders can create a culture that brings people together by ensuring that people have a voice in what the important values should be. Managers at United Stationers built a new, adaptive culture from the ground up by asking all 6,000 globally dispersed employees to help define the values that would be the building blocks of the culture.[76] Other companies, though, have found small teams and focus groups that include people from all functions and levels of the company to be more effective than trying to include everyone. Tony Wild, CEO of the pharmaceutical company

# Unlocking Creative Solutions Through People

## Wal-Mart Takes Care of Business—And Culture

Whether it's with a corny company cheer that includes an infamous rear-end wriggle know as the "squiggly," with posters on the break room walls, or through computer-based training sessions, managers at retail giant Wal-Mart are continually reinforcing the company's core values of respect for the individual, excellence, and customer service. Wal-Mart has built a high-performance culture that produces a company of disciplined employees who use disciplined thought and exercise disciplined action. People who don't share the company's values usually don't stay long because they feel like outcasts among the "Walmartians."

Wal-Mart integrates the efficiencies and competitiveness of a huge corporation with the homespun values of Main Street America. Every time a top manager visits a store, he or she leads employees in the Wal-Mart cheer: "Give me a W! Give me an A! Give me an L! Give me a squiggly! Give me an M! Give me an A! Give me an R! Give me a T! What's that spell? Wal-Mart! What's that spell? Wal-Mart! Who's No. 1? The customer!" Wal-Mart's aim is to have a company full of people who never rest on their laurels but continually strive to improve operations, customer service and satisfaction, and the company itself.

Wal-Mart is now the largest company in the world, but executives remain concerned about the future, always talking about what it would take to be more successful, always implementing changes toward that goal. Yet a main ingredient in Wal-Mart's success is its ability to change without sacrificing the sense of purpose and core values the company was founded on. Founder Sam Walton made a deal with employees: They would work hard for him and he would be fair to them. Walton's pact with his workers promised that cost cutting, efficiency, and everyday low prices would exist alongside a moral center. Training programs, hiring and promotion practices, and other procedures were built around that pact and the core values of respect, service, and excellence. The Wal-Mart Associates' handbook has a quote that runs in large type across the top of a page: "The undeniable cornerstone of Wal-Mart's success can be traced back to our strong belief in the dignity of each individual."

Wal-Mart's culture is feeling some strains in light of a recent gender discrimination suit, ongoing attempts to unionize, protests against building supercenters in some towns, and charges that Wal-Mart's low prices are hurting American manufacturers. Just the sheer size of the company, with more than a million employees, is challenging managers' ability to maintain the storied culture. However, executives are striving to make changes that reinforce the core values at the same time they move the company forward to address new challenges and responsibilities.

**SOURCES**: Patrick M. Lencioni, "Making Your Values Mean Something," *Harvard Business Review* (July 2002): 113–117; Mark Gimein, "Sam Walton Made Us A Promise," *Fortune* (March 18, 2002): 120–127; Jim Collins, "Bigger Better Faster," *Fast Company* (June 2003): 75–78; Cora Daniels, "Women Vs. Wal-Mart," *Fortune* (June 21, 2003): 78–82.

MedPoint, put together a team of trusted managers and surveyed key employees who exemplified the qualities managers wanted to see embodied in the culture.[77]

Managers widely communicate the cultural values through words and actions. Values statements that aren't reinforced by management behavior are meaningless or even harmful for employees and the organization. Consider Enron, whose values statement included things like communication, respect, and integrity. Managers' actions at the corporation clearly belied those stated values.[78] For values to guide the organization, managers have to model them every day. "I have the values in my office in a prominent place where I can see them from my desk, and I try to use them as a guidepost for all my decisions," says Christopher Rice, president and CEO of BlessingWhite, an international training and consulting firm. "I have a group of employees who know [the values] cold and they tell me every time I violate one. This is good behavior!"[79] At MTW Corp., managers work with every new employee to create an "expectations agreement," an ever-evolving document that ensures that actions and work procedures that reinforce the company's cultural values will be adhered to by both managers and workers.[80] Top executives at Weirton Steel act as cultural leaders by participating in every team training session to symbolize their commitment to a team-based culture—a significant commitment in an 8,000-employee organization.[81] Cultural leaders also uphold their commitment to values during difficult times or crises. Xilinx, a Silicon Valley semiconductor manufacturer, is based on a culture of respect and adhered to a strict no-layoffs policy throughout the technology downturn by negotiating with workers to take pay cuts. Significantly, top leaders took the hardest hit, with the CEO cutting his salary by 20 percent.[82] Maintaining consistency with the cultural values helps organizations weather the storm and come out stronger on the other side.

Creating and maintaining a high-performance culture is not easy in today's turbulent environment and changing workplace, but through their words—and particularly their actions—cultural leaders let everyone in the organization know what really counts.

## Manager's Solution

This chapter discussed several important ideas about internal and external organizational environments. Events in the external environment are considered important influences on organizational behavior and performance. The external environment consists of two layers: the task environment and the general environment. The task environment includes customers, competitors, suppliers, and the labor market. The general environment includes technological, sociocultural, economic, legal-political, and international dimensions. Management techniques for helping the organization adapt to the environment include boundary-spanning roles, interorganizational partnerships, and mergers and joint ventures.

A major internal element for helping organizations adapt to the environment is culture. Corporate culture is a major element of the internal organizational environment and includes the key values, beliefs, understandings, and norms that organization members share. Organizational activities that illustrate corporate culture include symbols, stories, heroes, slogans, and ceremonies. For the organization to be effective, corporate culture should be aligned with organizational strategy and the needs of the external environment.

Four types of culture are adaptability, achievement, involvement, and consistency. Strong cultures are effective when they enable an organization to meet strategic goals and adapt to changes in the external environment. Culture is important because it can have a significant impact on organizational performance. Managers emphasize both values and business results to create a high-performance culture, enabling the organization to consistently achieve solid business performance through the actions of motivated employees who are aligned with the mission and goals of the company. Managers create and sustain adaptive high-performance cultures through cultural leadership. They define and articulate important values that are tied to a clear and compelling mission, and they widely communicate and uphold the values through their words and particularly their actions. Work procedures, budgeting, decision making, reward systems, and other day-to-day activities are aligned with the cultural values.

At IBM, a new CEO is shifting values toward an adaptability culture to support a new strategy that requires flexibility, speed, and innovation. Sam Palmisano believes culture is the key to transforming IBM for a new era. To create the new culture, Palmisano got IBM's nearly 320,000 employees involved, setting up online forums where people could voice their ideas. The CEO was adamant about involving employees so they would be owners of the new culture. The key themes that emerged were customer relationships, innovation, and trust. Palmisano has made a number of moves to signal the new cultural values. When he asked the board to cut his 2003 bonus in half and set the money aside to be split among IBM's 20 top executives based on their performance as a team, Palmisano made a powerful statement that egalitarianism and teamwork is the new way of doing business at Big Blue. "Creativity . . . does not come from one individual," he said. "Creativity in an organization starts where the action is—either in the laboratory, or in R&D sites, at a customer place, in manufacturing."

Palmisano dismantled the 92-year-old executive committee that had previously ruled the company and formed three cross-functional and cross-hierarchical teams for strategy, operations, and technology. "Heads are spinning," said one vice president. "He's reaching six levels down and asking questions." Listening to both employees and customers is a priority. After Palmisano announced the e-business-on-demand strategy, he scheduled a two-day session to discuss how to tackle it. The CEO listened for a while, then cut the meeting short, telling people to go out and talk to customers and find out what their biggest problems were and how IBM could help to solve them. Teams of employees will work across functional boundaries and with customers to find out what clients want and produce it fast. The company will spend $100 million on training managers to lead rather than control employees so that people have more freedom and power to do their jobs. Teams are also hard at work on revising performance evaluations, career paths, training programs, reward systems, and other practices to be in line with the new values.[83] Culture change of the magnitude Palmisano is attempting at IBM is not easy, and it may take years for the new values to become firmly rooted. However, Palmisano believes instilling new cultural values tied to the organization's strategy and goals can ensure IBM's long-term prosperity.

## Discussion Questions

1. Some scientists predict major changes in the earth's climate, including a temperature rise of 8°F over the next 60 years. Should any companies be paying attention to this long-range environmental trend? Explain.

2. Would the task environment for a bank contain the same elements as that for a government welfare agency? Discuss.

3. What forces influence organizational uncertainty? Would such forces typically originate in the task environment or the general environment?

4. *In Search of Excellence*, by Thomas Peters and Robert Waterman, argued that customers were the most important element in the external environment. Are there company situations for which this may not be true?

5. Caterpillar Corporation was thriving until the mid-1980s, when low oil prices, high interest rates, a worldwide recession, a soaring U.S.

dollar, and Japanese competition stunned the giant equipment builder. Discuss the type of response Caterpillar's management might take.

6. Define corporate culture and explain its importance for managers.

7. Why are symbols important to a corporate culture? Do stories, heroes, slogans, and ceremonies also have symbolic value? Discuss.

8. Describe the cultural values of a company for which you have worked. Did those values fit the needs of the external environment? Of employees?

9. What type of environmental situation is associated with a baseball team culture? How does this culture differ from the academy culture?

10. Do you think a corporate culture with strong values is better for organizational effectiveness than a culture with weak values? Are there times when a strong culture might reduce effectiveness? Discuss.

# Management in Practice: Experiential Exercise

## What is a Strong Corporate Culture?

Think about an organization with which you are familiar, such as your school or a company for which you have worked. Answer the questions below based on whether you agree that they describe the organization.

**Disagree Strongly          Agree Strongly**

1          2          3          4          5

1.  Virtually all managers and most employees can describe the company's values, purpose, and customer importance.

    1          2          3          4          5

2.  There is clarity among organization members about how their jobs contribute to organizational goals.

    1          2          3          4          5

3.  It is very seldom that a manager will act in a way contrary to the company's espoused values.

    1          2          3          4          5

4.  Warmth and support of other employees is a valued norm, even across departments.

    1          2          3          4          5

5.  The company and its managers value what's best for the company over the long term more than short-term results.

    1          2          3          4          5

6.  Leaders make it a point to develop and mentor others.

    1          2          3          4          5

7.  Recruiting is taken very seriously, with multiple interviews in an effort to find traits that fit the culture.

    1          2          3          4          5

8.  Recruits are given negative as well as positive information about the company so they can freely choose whether to join.

    1          2          3          4          5

9.  Employees are expected to acquire real knowledge and mastery—not political alliances—before they can be promoted.

    1          2          3          4          5

10. Company values emphasize what the company must do well to succeed in a changing environment.

    1          2          3          4          5

11. Conformity to company mission and values is more important than conformity to procedures and dress.

    1          2          3          4          5

12. You have heard stories about the company's leaders or "heroes" who helped make the company great.

    1          2          3          4          5

13. Ceremonies and special events are used to recognize and reward individuals who contribute to the company in significant ways.

    1          2          3          4          5

## Total Score _____

Compute your score. If your total score is 52 or above, your organization has a strong culture, similar to a Procter & Gamble or Hewlett-Packard. A score from 26 to 51 suggests a culture of medium strength, which is positive for the organization, such as for American Airlines, Coca-Cola, and Citibank. A score of 25 or below indicates a weak culture, which is probably not helping the company adapt to the external environment or meet the needs of organization members. Discuss the pros and cons of a strong culture. Does a strong culture mean everyone has to be alike?

Source: Adapted from Richard Pascale, "The Paradox of 'Corporate Culture': Reconciling Ourselves to Socialization," *California Management Review 27,* no. 2 (1985); and David A. Kolb, Joyce S. Osland, and Irwin M. Rubin, *Organizational Behavior: An Experiential Approach,* 6th ed. (Englewood Cliffs, N.J.: Prentice-Hall, 1995), 346–347.

# Management in Practice: Ethical Dilemma

## Watching Out for Larry

It was the end of the fourth quarter, and Holly Vasquez was completing the profitability statement for her division's regional manager. She was disturbed to see that, for the first time during her tenure as a sales manager for Wallog Computers, her group was not in the top 10 percent of the region. She had watched sales slip during the past year but hoped the fourth quarter might save their numbers. The company was under pressure from stockholders to increase sales. Vasquez was afraid that Wallog would be cutting staff and altering the "people culture" that had kept her there for the past ten years.

As she entered the individual results in the spreadsheet, she saw her main problem: Larry Norris. After 27 years with the company, Norris had more career sales than anyone in the region, but, for the past 3 years, he had not even met his quota. Unlike some of her newer salespeople, Norris was uninformed on new products, and his old-style selling techniques didn't seem to be working. Vasquez had suggested he consult with the "new guys" on technical information and new sales techniques, but Norris was stubborn.

Vasquez knew she had the performance information to move him out of his position, but there was nowhere for him to go at Wallog. At 56, he was too young for retirement but too old to find a job elsewhere at his current salary. Not only was Larry Norris a friend, but also he was well liked in her department, and Vasquez wondered what effect his replacement would have on morale. She didn't want to fire him, but she couldn't risk her team's standing or her own reputation by protecting him anymore.

## What Do You Do?

1. Fire Larry Norris with two-weeks' notice, a generous severance package, and all the help you can provide him in his job hunt.
2. Give him an ultimatum to meet his sales quota or else, and let him find the way. It is his responsibility to stay current and meet his quota.
3. Assign him to study the new products and the sales techniques of the top salespeople—then hope he improves and the others don't slip.

# Surf the Net

1. **Sociocultural dimension of general environment.** As stated in this chapter, "Important sociocultural characteristics are geographical distribution and population density, age, and education levels. Today's demographic profiles are the foundation of tomorrow's workforce and consumers." Examine the demographic information available at *http://www.census.gov/*.

   For example, among the wealth of information available at this site is a collection of statistics on social and economic conditions in the United States called the Statistical Abstract of the United States *http://www.census.gov/statab/www/brief.html.*

   Find six statistics assigned by your instructor or chosen by you, and be prepared to share your

   findings in the oral or written format assigned by your instructor.

2. **Competitors.** A sector of the task environment is competitors. Select an industry you're interested in researching and write a 1 to 2 page paper about the industry describing who the major players are and identifying competitive information that would be useful for businesses operating in that industry. Try Web sites such as those that follow to gather your information.

   *http://www.fuld.com/i3/index.html*
   *http://www.companiesonline.com/*
   *http://www.companysleuth.com/*
   *http://www.corporateinformation.com/*
   *http://www.businessdirectory.com/*

3. **Culture communicated through stories.** David M. Armstrong, CEO of Armstrong International, Inc., has authored three books for the purpose of communicating Armstrong's culture—its key values, beliefs, understandings, and norms shared by members of his organization—by storytelling. His books are entitled *Managing by Storying Around; How to Turn Your Company's Parables into Profit*; and *Once Told, They're Gold*. Go to the Web site listed below and read the stories or watch the video clips that illustrate sample stories from each of his three books. If you choose a video, you will need the Quicktime movie player installed on your computer; the player is available to download from the Armstrong Web site.
*http://www.armintl.com/stories/david-bio.html*

# Case for Critical Analysis

## Society of Equals

Ted Shelby doesn't make very many mistakes, but . . .

"Hey Stanley," says Ted Shelby, leaning in through the door, "you got a minute? I've just restructured my office. Come on and take a look. I've been implementing some great new concepts!"

Stanley is always interested in Ted Shelby's new ideas, for if there is anyone Stanley wants to do as well as, it is Edward W. Shelby IV. Stanley follows Ted back to his office and stops, nonplussed.

Restructured is right! Gone are Ted's size B (Junior Exec.) walnut veneer desk and furniture, and his telephone table. In fact, the room is practically empty save for a large, round, stark white cafeteria table and the half-dozen padded vinyl swivel chairs that surround it.

"Isn't it a beauty! As far as I know, I'm the first executive in the plant to innovate this. The shape is the crucial factor here—no front or rear, no status problems. We can all sit there and communicate more effectively."

We? Communicate? Effectively? Well, it seems that Ted has been attending a series of Executive Development Seminars given by Dr. Faust. The theme of the seminars was—you guessed it—"participative management." Edward W. Shelby IV has always liked to think of himself as a truly democratic person.

"You see, Stanley," says Ted, managing his best sincere/intense attitude, "the main thing wrong with current mainstream management practice is that the principal communication channel is down-the-line oriented. We on the top send our messages down to you people, but we neglect the feedback potential. But just because we have more status and responsibility doesn't mean that we are necessarily (Stanley duly noted the word, "necessarily") better than the people below us. So, as I see the situation, what is needed is a two-way communication network: down-the-line and up-the-line."

"That's what the cafeteria table is for?" Stanley says.

"Yes!" says Ted. "We management people don't have all the answers, and I don't know why I never realized it before that seminar. Why . . . let's take an extreme example . . . the folks who run those machines out there. I'll bet that any one of them knows a thing or two that I've never thought of. So I've transformed my office into a full-feedback communication net."

"That certainly is an innovation around here," says Stanley.

A few days later Stanley passed by Ted Shelby's office and was surprised that Ted's desk, furniture, and telephone table were back where they used to be.

Stanley, curious about the unrestructuring, went to Bonnie for enlightenment. "What," he asked, "happened to Shelby's round table?"

"That table we were supposed to sit around and input things?" she said. "All I know is, about two days after he had it put in, Mr. Drake came walking through here. He looked in that office, and then he sort of stopped and went back—and he looked in there for a long time. Then he came over to me, and you know how his face sort of gets red when he's really mad? Well, this time he was so mad that his face was absolutely white. And when he talked to me, I don't think he actually opened his mouth; and I could barely hear him, he was talking so low. And he said, 'Have that removed. Now. Have Mr. Shelby's furniture put back in his office. Have Mr. Shelby see me.'"

My, my. You would think Ted would have known better, wouldn't you? But then, by now you should have a pretty firm idea of just why it is those offices are set up as they are.

## Questions

1.  How would you characterize the culture in this company? What are the dominant values?
2.  Why did Ted Shelby's change experiment fail? To what extent did Ted use the appropriate

change tools to increase employee communication and participation?
3.  What would you recommend Ted do to change his relationship with subordinates? Is it possible for a manager to change cultural values if the rest of the organization, especially top management, does not agree?

Source: R. Richard Ritti and G. Ray Funkhouser, *The Ropes to Skip & The Ropes to Know,* 3d. ed. (New York: Wiley, 1987), 176–177. Reprinted by permission of John Wiley & Sons, Inc.

# Endnotes

1.  Steve Lohr, "Big Blue's Big Bet: Less Tech, More Touch," *The New York Times* (January 25, 2004): Section 3, 1; Spencer E. Ante, "The New Blue: Lou Gerstner Saved Big Blue. Now It's Up to New CEO Sam Palmisano to Restore It to Greatness," *BusinessWeek* (March 17, 2003): 80; and Kevin Maney, "Homebred CEO Summons IBM's Past, Present, Future," *USA Today* (November 19, 2003): *http://www.usatoday.com/tech/techinvestor/2003-11-19-palmisano-cover_x.htm* accessed on November 22, 2003.
2.  Ann Carns, "Point Taken: Hit Hard by Imports, American Pencil Icon Tries to Get a Grip," *The Wall Street Journal* (November 24, 1999): A1, A6; Lucette Lagnado, "Strained Peace: Gerber Baby Food, Grilled by Greenpeace, Plans Swift Overhaul," *The Wall Street Journal* (July 30, 1999): A1, A6; and "Group Sows Seeds of Revolt Against Genetically Altered Foods in U.S.," *The Wall Street Journal* (October 12, 1999): B1, B4.
3.  Christopher Joyce, reporter, transcript of "Analysis: International Panel Says U.S. Department of Agriculture Should Take Further Steps to Protect the U.S. From Mad Cow Disease," *NPR: All Things Considered* (February 5, 2004): 1; Sue Kirchhoff, "Natural Beef Industry Might See Boost from Mad Cow Fears," *USA Today* (January 12, 2004): *http://www.usatoday.com/money/industries/food/2004-01-12-organic_x.htm*; June Kronholz, "Kindergarten Crisis: By Federal Order, Snail Races Are Over," *The Wall Street Journal* (February 11, 2004): A1.
4.  This section is based on Richard L. Daft, *Organization Theory and Design*, 8th ed. (Cincinnati, Ohio: South-Western, 2004): 136–140.
5.  L.J. Bourgeois, "Strategy and Environment: A Conceptual Integration," *Academy of Management Review* 5 (1980): 25–39.
6.  "Toyota Shoots for No. 1," *Ward's Auto World* (December 1, 2003).
7.  Paola Hjelt, "The World's Most Admired Companies," *Fortune* (March 3, 2003): 81; David Pringle, Jesse Drucker, and Evan Ramstad, "World Circuit: Cellphone Makers Pay a Heavy Toll for Missing Fads," *The Wall Street Journal* (October 30, 2003): A1.
8.  Jim Rose and Salim Teja, "The Americans Are Coming!" *Business 2.0* (May 2000): 215.
9.  Robert Rosen, with Patricia Digh, Marshall Singer, and Carl Phillips, *Global Literacies: Lessons on Business Leadership and National Cultures,* (New York: Simon and Schuster, 2000).
10. Richard I. Kirkland, Jr., "Entering a New Age of Boundless Competition," *Fortune* (March 14, 1988): 40–48; and Kenichi Ohmae, "Managing in a Borderless World," *Harvard Business Review* (May–June 1989): 152–161.
11. James Myring, "Mobile Saturation Leads to Higher Churn," *New Media Age* (October 2, 2003): 15; and Pringle, et al., "World Circuit."
12. Gene Bylinsky, "Mutant Materials," *Fortune* (October 13, 1997): 140–147.
13. John Teresko, "The Next Material World," *Industry Week* (April 2003): 41–47.
14. William B. Johnston, "Global Work Force 2000: The New World Labor Market," *Harvard Business Review* (March–April 1991): 115–127.

15. U.S. Census Bureau statistics reported in "Minorities Should Be Very Close to Majority by 2050, Census Projection Says," AP Story in *Johnson City Press* (March 18, 2004): 5A; and Peter Coy, "The Creative Economy," *BusinessWeek* (August 28, 2000): 76–82.

16. U.S. Census, http://www.census.gov/.

17. Michelle Conlin, "UnMarried America," *BusinessWeek* (October 20, 2003): 106–116.

18. Julie Dunn, "Restaurant Chains, Too, Watch Their Carbs," *The New York Times* (January 4, 2004): Section 3; and Brian Grow with Gerry Khermouch, "The Low-Carb Food Fight Ahead," *BusinessWeek* (December 22, 2003): 48.

19. Marc Gunter, "God & Business," *Fortune* (July 9, 2001): 58–80.

20. Anne Marie Squeo and Joe Flint, "FCC Tells Cable Industry to Clean Up Content—Or Else," *The Wall Street Journal* (February 11, 2004): B1; Damien Cave, "Fighting for Free Speech," *Rolling Stone* (May 27, 2004): 13.

21. Samuel Loewenberg, "Europe Gets Tougher on U.S. Companies," *The New York Times* (April 20, 2003): Section 3, 6.

22. Linda Himelstein and Laura Zinn, with Maria Mallory, John Carey, Richard S. Dunham, and Joan O'C. Hamilton, "Tobacco: Does It Have a Future?" *BusinessWeek* (July 4, 1994): 24–29; Bob Ortega, "Aging Activists Turn, Turn, Turn Attention to Wal-Mart Protests," *The Wall Street Journal* (October 11, 1994): A1, A8;

23. Chistopher Palmeri, "Mattel's New Toy Story," *BusinessWeek* (November 18, 2002): 72–74; Queena Sook Kim and Merissa Marr, "Holy Bat-Ray! New Batman Toys Get Signals from Your TV," *The Wall Street Journal* (February 11, 2004): B1.

24. John Simons, "Stop Moaning About Gripe Sites and Log On," *Fortune* (April 2, 2001): 181–182.

25. Rick Brooks, "Home Depot Turns Copycat in Its Efforts to Stoke New Growth," *The Wall Street Journal* (November 21, 2000): A1; Dan Sewell, "Home Depot, Lowe's Building Up Competition," *Lexington Herald-Leader*: Business Profile supplement (December 8, 1997): 3.

26. Julia Angwin and Motoko Rich, "Inn Fighting: Big Hotel Chains Are Striking Back Against Web Sites," *The Wall Street Journal* (March 14, 2003): A1.

27. Paul Glader, "Steel-Price Rise Crimps Profits, Adds Uncertainty," *The Wall Street Journal* (February 23, 2004): A1.

28. Bernard Simon, "A Bright New Day for the Telecom Industry, If the Public Will Go Along," *The New York Times* (January 12, 2004): C3; Mark Heinzl, "Nortel's Profit of $499 Million Exceeds Forecast," *The Wall Street Journal* (January 30, 2004): B4; Joseph Weber with Andy Reinhardt and Peter Burrows, "Racing Ahead at Nortel," *BusinessWeek* (November 8, 1999): 93–99; Ian Austen, "Hooked on the Net," *Canadian Business* (June 26–July 10, 1998): 95–103; "Nortel's Waffling Continues; First Job Cuts, Then Product Lines, and Now the CEO. What's Next?" *Telephony* (May 21, 2001): 12.

29. Robert B. Duncan, "Characteristics of Organizational Environment and Perceived Environmental Uncertainty," *Administrative Science Quarterly 17* (1972): 313–327; and Daft, *Organization Theory and Design*.

30. David B. Jemison, "The Importance of Boundary Spanning Roles in Strategic Decision-Making," *Journal of Management Studies 21* (1984): 131–152; and Marc J. Dollinger, "Environmental Boundary Spanning and Information Processing Effects on Organizational Performance," *Academy of Management Journal 27* (1984): 351–368.

31. Sarah Moore, "On Your Markets," *Working Woman* (February 2001): 26; and John Simons, "Stop Moaning about Gripe Sites and Log On," *Fortune* (April 2, 2001): 181–182.

32. Pia Nordlinger, "Know Your Enemy," *Working Woman* (May 2001): 16.

33. Gary Abramson, "All Along the Watchtower." *CIO Enterprise*, Section 2 (July 15, 1999): 24–34.

34. Kim Girard, "Snooping on a Shoestring," *Business 2.0* (May 2003): 64–66.

35. Edwin M. Epstein, "How to Learn from the Environment about the Environment—A Prerequisite for Organizational Well-Being," *Journal of General Management 29*, no. 1 (Autumn 2003): 68–80.

36. Mark McNeilly, "Gathering Information for Strategic Decisions, Routinely," *Strategy & Leadership 30*, no 5 (2002): 29–34.

37. A discussion of the Sony-Toshiba-IBM alliance was heard by the author on NPR's *Morning Edition*; information on Kroger, Albertson's, and Safeway from an Associated Press story, "Strike Increases Pressure on Safeway CEO," in *Johnson City Press* (February 1, 2004): 7D.

38. Lynn A. Isabella, "Managing an Alliance is Nothing Like Business as Usual," *Organizational Dynamics 31*, no. 1 (2002): 47–59; Cyrus F. Freidheim, Jr. *The Trillion-Dollar Enterprise: How the Alliance Revolution Will Transform Global Business* (New York: Perseus Books, 1998).

39. Stephan M. Wagner and Roman Boutellier, "Capabilities for Managing a Portfolio of Supplier Relationships," *Business Horizons* (November-December 2002): 79–88; Peter Smith Ring and Andrew H. Van de Ven, "Developmental Processes of Corporate Interorganizational Relationships," *Academy of Management Review 19* (1994): 90–118;

Myron Magnet, "The New Golden Rule of Business," *Fortune* (February 21, 1994): 60–64; and Peter Grittner, "Four Elements of Successful Sourcing Strategies," *Management Review* (October 1996): 41–45.

40. Richard L. Daft, "After the Deal: The Art of Fusing Diverse Corporate Cultures Into One," paper presented at the Conference on International Corporate Restructuring, Institute of Business Research and Education, Korea University, Seoul, Korea (June 16, 1998).

41. Patricia Sellers, "The Business of Being Oprah," *Fortune* (April 1, 2002): 50–64.

42. Warren St. John, "Barnes & Noble's Epiphany," *Wired* (June 1999): 132–144; Ron Grover and Richard Siklos, "When Old Foes Need Each Other," *BusinessWeek*, Special Report: Corporate Finance (October 25, 1999): 114, 118.

43. James E. Svatko, "Joint Ventures," *Small Business Reports* (December 1988): 65–70; and Joshua Hyatt, "The Partnership Route," *Inc.* (December 1988): 145–148.

44. Yoash Wiener, "Forms of Value Systems: A Focus on Organizational Effectiveness and Culture Change and Maintenance," *Academy of Management Review 13* (1988): 534–545; V. Lynne Meek, "Organizational Culture: Origins and Weaknesses," *Organization Studies* 9 (1988): 453–473; John J. Sherwood, "Creating Work Cultures with Competitive Advantage," *Organizational Dynamics* (Winter 1988): 5–27; and Andrew D. Brown and Ken Starkey, "The Effect of Organizational Culture on Communication and Information," *Journal of Management Studies 31*, no. 6 (November 1994): 807–828.

45. Joanne Martin, *Organizational Culture: Mapping the Terrain* (Thousand Oaks, Calif.: Sage Publications, 2002); Ralph H. Kilmann, Mary J. Saxton, and Roy Serpa, "Issues in Understanding and Changing Culture," *California Management Review* 28 (Winter 1986): 87–94; and Linda Smircich, "Concepts of Culture and Organizational Analysis," *Administrative Science Quarterly* 28 (1983): 339–358.

46. Based on Edgar H. Schein, *Organizational Culture and Leadership*, 2d ed. (San Francisco: Jossey-Bass, 1992): 3–27.

47. Michael G. Pratt and Anat Rafaeli, "Symbols as a Language of Organizational Relationships," *Research in Organizational Behavior*, 23 (2001): 93–132.

48. Christine Canabou, "Here's the Drill," *Fast Company* (February 2001): 58.

49. James M. Higgins and Craig McAllaster, "Want Innovation? Then Use Cultural Artifacts That Support It," *Organizational Dynamics* 31, no. 1 (2002), 74–84.

50. Patrick M. Lencioni, "Make Your Values Mean Something," *Harvard Business Review* (July 2002): 113–117.

51. Robert E. Quinn and Gretchen M. Spreitzer, "The Road to Empowerment: Seven Questions Every Leader Should Consider," *Organizational Dynamics* (Autumn 1997): 37–49.

52. Martin, *Organizational Culture*: 71–72.

53. Terrence E. Deal and Allan A. Kennedy, *Corporate Cultures: The Rites and Rituals of Corporate Life* (Reading, Mass.: AddisonWesley, 1982).

54. Patricia Jones and Larry Kahaner, *Say It and Live It: 50 Corporate Mission Statements That Hit the Mark* (New York: Currency Doubleday, 1995).

55. Harrison M. Trice and Janice M. Beyer, "Studying Organizational Cultures through Rites and Ceremonials," *Academy of Management Review 9* (1984): 653–669.

56. Alan Farnham, "Mary Kay's Lessons in Leadership," *Fortune* (September 20, 1993): 68–77.

57. Jennifer A. Chatman and Karen A. Jehn, "Assessing the Relationship Between Industry Characteristics and Organizational Culture: How Different Can You Be?" *Academy of Management Journal* 37, no. 3 (1994): 522–553.

58. John P. Kotter and James L. Heskett, *Corporate Culture and Performance* (New York: The Free Press, 1992).

59. This discussion is based on Paul McDonald and Jeffrey Gandz, "Getting Value from Shared Values," *Organizational Dynamics* 21, no. 3 (Winter 1992): 64–76; Daniel R. Denison and Aneil K. Mishra, "Toward a Theory of Organizational Culture and Effectiveness," *Organization Science* 6, no. 2 (March–April 1995): 204–223; and Richard L. Daft, *The Leadership Experience* 3rd ed. (Cincinnati, OH: South-Western, 2005): 570–573.

60. Ian Wylie, "Calling for a Renewable Future," *Fast Company* (May 2003): 46–48; Paul Kaihla, "Nokia's Hit Factory," *Business 2.0* (August 2002): 66–70; and David Pringle, "Wrong Number: How Nokia Chased Top End of Market, Got Hit in Middle," *The Wall Street Journal* (June 1, 2004): A1, A11.

61. Robert Hooijberg and Frank Petrock, "On Cultural Change: Using the Competing Values Framework to Help Leaders Execute a Transformational Strategy," *Human Resource Management* 32, no. 1 (1993): 29–50.

62. Lencioni, "Make Your Values Mean Something"; and Melanie Warner, "Confessions of a Control Freak," *Fortune* (September 4, 2000): 130–140.

63. Julia Boorstin, "Secret Recipe: J. M. Smucker," *Fortune* (January 12, 2004): 58–59.

64. Rekha Balu, "Pacific Edge Projects Itself," *Fast Company* (October 2000): 371–381.

65. Jeffrey Pfeffer, *The Human Equation: Building Profits by Putting People First* (Boston, Mass.: Harvard Business School Press, 1998).

66. Jeremy Kahn, "What Makes a Company Great?" *Fortune* (October 26, 1998): 218; James C. Collins

and Jerry I. Porras, *Built to Last: Successful Habits of Visionary Companies* (New York: HarperCollins, 1994); and James C. Collins, "Change is Good—But First Know What Should Never Change," *Fortune* (May 29, 1995): 141.

67. Jennifer A. Chatman and Sandra Eunyoung Cha, "Leading by Leveraging Culture," *California Management Review* 45, no. 4 (Summer 2003): 20–34.

68. This section is based on Jeff Rosenthal and Mary Ann Masarech, "High Peformance Cultures: How Values Can Drive Business Results," *Journal of Organizational Excellence* (Spring 2003): 3–18.

69. Rosenthal and Masarech, "High-Performance Cultures."

70. Katherine Mieszkowski, "Community Standards," *Fast Company* (September 2000): 368; Rosabeth Moss Kanter, "A More Perfect Union," *Inc.* (February 2001): 92-98; Raizel Robin, "Net Gains" segment of "E-Biz That Works," *Canadian Business* (October 14–October 26, 2003): 107.

71. Rosenthal and Masarech, "High-Performance Cultures."

72. Chatman and Cha, "Leading by Leveraging Culture."

73. John P. Kotter and James L. Heskett, *Corporate Culture and Performance* (New York: The Free Press, 1992); Jim Collins, *Good to Great: Why Some Companies Make the Leap . . . and Others Don't* (New York: HarperBusiness, 2001); James C. Collins and Jerry I. Porras, *Built to Last: Successful Habits of Visionary Companies* (New York: HarperBusiness, 1994); and James C. Collins, "Change Is Good—But First Know What Should Never Change," *Fortune* (May 29, 1995): 141. Also see J. M. Kouzes and B. Z. Posner, *The Leadership Challenge: How to Keep Getting Extraordinary Things Done in Organizations,* 3d ed. (San Francisco: Jossey-Bass, 2002).

74. Micah R. Kee, "Corporate Culture Makes a Fiscal Difference," *Industrial Management* (November–December 2003): 16–20.

75. Rosenthal and Masarech, "High-Performance Cultures;" Lencioni, "Make Your Values Mean Something;" and Thomas J. Peters and Robert H. Waterman, Jr., *In Search of Excellence* (New York: Warner, 1988).

76. Jenny C. McCune, "Exporting Corporate Culture," *Management Review* (December 1999): 52–56.

77. Lencioni, "Make Your Values Mean Something."

78. Lencioni, "Make Your Values Mean Something."

79. Rosenthal and Masarech, "High-Performance Cultures."

80. Jill Rosenfeld, "MTW Puts People First," *Fast Company* (December 1999): 86–88.

81. Excerpt from Peter B. Grazier, "Before It's Too Late: Employee Involvement . . . An Idea Whose Time Has Come," *Pete's Corner* by Peter B. Grazier, *http://www.teambuilding.com.*

82. Robert Levering and Milton Moskowitz, "The 100 Best Companies to Work For," *Fortune* (January 20, 2003): 127–152.

83. Lohr, "Big Blue's Big Bet," Ante, "The New Blue," and Maney, "Homebred CEO Summons IBM's Past, Present, Future."

# Chapter 4

# Managing in a Global Environment

## LEARNING OBJECTIVES

*After studying this chapter, you should be able to:*

1. Describe the emerging borderless world.

2. Define international management and explain how it differs from the management of domestic business operations.

3. Indicate how dissimilarities in the economic, sociocultural, and legal-political environments throughout the world can affect business operations.

4. Describe market entry strategies that businesses use to develop foreign markets.

5. Describe the characteristics of a multinational corporation.

6. Explain the challenges of managing in a global environment.

116

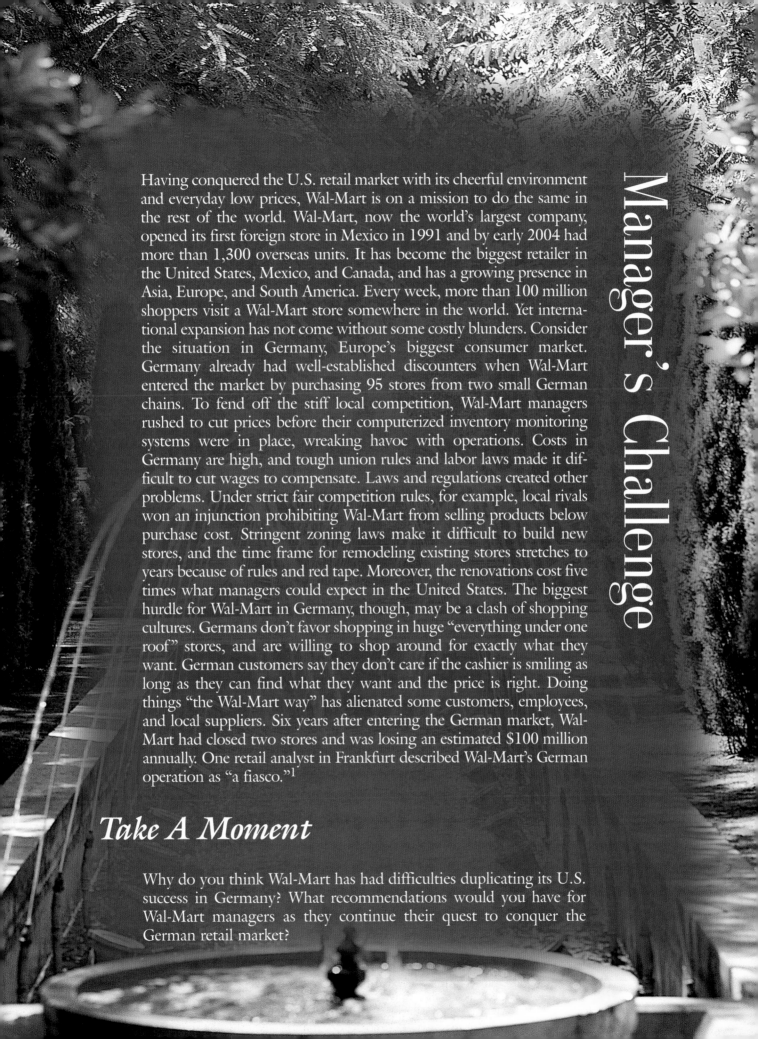

Having conquered the U.S. retail market with its cheerful environment and everyday low prices, Wal-Mart is on a mission to do the same in the rest of the world. Wal-Mart, now the world's largest company, opened its first foreign store in Mexico in 1991 and by early 2004 had more than 1,300 overseas units. It has become the biggest retailer in the United States, Mexico, and Canada, and has a growing presence in Asia, Europe, and South America. Every week, more than 100 million shoppers visit a Wal-Mart store somewhere in the world. Yet international expansion has not come without some costly blunders. Consider the situation in Germany, Europe's biggest consumer market. Germany already had well-established discounters when Wal-Mart entered the market by purchasing 95 stores from two small German chains. To fend off the stiff local competition, Wal-Mart managers rushed to cut prices before their computerized inventory monitoring systems were in place, wreaking havoc with operations. Costs in Germany are high, and tough union rules and labor laws made it difficult to cut wages to compensate. Laws and regulations created other problems. Under strict fair competition rules, for example, local rivals won an injunction prohibiting Wal-Mart from selling products below purchase cost. Stringent zoning laws make it difficult to build new stores, and the time frame for remodeling existing stores stretches to years because of rules and red tape. Moreover, the renovations cost five times what managers could expect in the United States. The biggest hurdle for Wal-Mart in Germany, though, may be a clash of shopping cultures. Germans don't favor shopping in huge "everything under one roof" stores, and are willing to shop around for exactly what they want. German customers say they don't care if the cashier is smiling as long as they can find what they want and the price is right. Doing things "the Wal-Mart way" has alienated some customers, employees, and local suppliers. Six years after entering the German market, Wal-Mart had closed two stores and was losing an estimated $100 million annually. One retail analyst in Frankfurt described Wal-Mart's German operation as "a fiasco."[1]

## Take A Moment

Why do you think Wal-Mart has had difficulties duplicating its U.S. success in Germany? What recommendations would you have for Wal-Mart managers as they continue their quest to conquer the German retail market?

Wal-Mart has deep pockets and can afford to lose money while it builds its international business. However, the organization is facing enormous challenges, not only in Germany but also in South America and Japan, where the company's way of doing business is clashing with cultural values. Other large, successful U.S. businesses, including FedEx and Nike, also have found that "the rest of the world is not the United States of America," as one FedEx competitor put it. All of these companies recognize that international expansion is necessary, despite the risks. Companies such as McDonald's, IBM, Coca-Cola, Kellogg, Texas Instruments, and Gillette rely on international business for a substantial portion of their sales and profits. Internet-based companies headquartered in the United States, such as Amazon, Yahoo, eBay, and America Online, are also rapidly expanding internationally and finding that, even on the Web, going global is fraught with difficulties. These and other online companies have encountered problems ranging from cultural blunders to violations of foreign laws. All organizations face special problems in trying to tailor their products and business management to the unique needs of foreign countries—but if they succeed, the whole world is their marketplace.

How important is international business to the study of management? *If you are not thinking international, you are not thinking business management.* It's that serious. As you read this page, ideas, takeover plans, capital investments, business strategies, products, and services are traveling around the planet by telephone, computer, fax, and overnight mail. Isolation from global events is no longer possible. The future of our businesses and our societies will be determined by global rather than local relationships.[2]

Rapid advances in technology and communications have made the international dimension an important part of the external environment discussed in Chapter 3. Companies can locate different parts of the organization wherever it makes the most business sense—top leadership in one place, technical brainpower and production in other locales. Virtual connections enable close, rapid coordination and communication among people working in different parts of the world, so it is no longer necessary to keep all operations in one place. Samsung, the Korean electronics giant, moved its semiconductor-making facilities to the Silicon Valley to be closer to the best scientific brains in the industry. Canada's Nortel Networks selected a location in the southwest of England as its world manufacturing center for a new fixed-access radio product. Siemens of Germany has moved its electronic ultrasound division to the United States, while the U.S. company DuPont shifted its electronic operations headquarters to Japan.[3]

If you think you are isolated from global influence, think again. Even if you do not budge from your hometown, your company may be purchased tomorrow by the English, Japanese, or Germans. People in the United States working for Ben & Jerry's Ice Cream, RCA, Dr. Pepper, Greyhound Bus Lines, and the Bic Pen Company already work for foreign bosses.

All this means that the environment for companies is becoming extremely complex and extremely competitive. Less-developed countries are challenging mature countries in a number of industries. India has become a major player in software development, for example. China already manufactures many of the world's computers and cellular phones and is rapidly staking a claim in the business of chip making. As many as 19 advanced new semiconductor plants were in or nearing operation by 2004.[4]

This chapter introduces basic concepts about the global environment and international management. First, we consider the difficulty managers have operating in an increasingly borderless world. We will address challenges—economic, legal-political, and sociocultural—facing companies within the global business environment. Then we will discuss multinational corporations and touch upon the various types of strategies and techniques needed for entering and succeeding in foreign markets.

# A Borderless World

Why do companies such as Wal-Mart, FedEx, and America Online want to pursue a global strategy, despite failures and losses? They recognize that business is becoming a unified, global field as trade barriers fall, communication becomes faster and cheaper, and consumer tastes in everything from clothing to cellular phones converge. Thomas Middelhoff of Germany's Bertelsmann AG, which purchased U.S. publisher Random House, put it this way: "There are no German and American companies. There are only successful and unsuccessful companies."[5]

Companies that think globally have a competitive edge. Consider Gayle Warwick Linens, whose luxury linens are woven in Europe, embroidered in Vietnam, and sold primarily in Britain and the United States. A French company handles logistics. Gayle Warwick and her one employee in London spend their time managing a web of global relationships.[6] Hong Kong's Johnson Electric Holdings Ltd.'s factories and research labs are thousands of miles away from a leading automaker. Yet the company has cornered the market for electric gizmos in U.S. automobiles by using information technology. Via videoconferencing, Johnson design teams meet "face-to-face" for two hours each morning with their customers in the United States and Europe. The company's processes and procedures are so streamlined that Johnson can take a concept and deliver a prototype to the United States in only a few weeks.[7]

In addition, domestic markets are saturated for many companies. The only potential for significant growth lies overseas. Kimberly-Clark and Procter & Gamble, which spent years slugging it out in the flat U.S. diaper market, are targeting new markets such as China, India, Israel, Russia, and Brazil. The demand for steel in China, India, and Brazil together is expected to grow 10 percent annually in the coming years—three times the U.S. rate, providing opportunities for companies such as Nucor and North Star Steel.[8] For online companies, too, going global is a key to growth as a growing percentage of Internet users are outside the United States. Western Europe and Japan together account for a huge share of the world's e-commerce revenue.[9]

The reality of today's borderless companies also means consumers can no longer tell from which country they're buying. U.S.-based Ford Motor Company owns Sweden's Volvo, while Chrysler, still considered an American brand, is owned by Germany's DaimlerChrysler and builds its PT Cruiser in Mexico. Toyota is a Japanese company, but it has manufactured more than 10 million vehicles in North American factories.

© MUNSHI AHMED

## CONCEPT CONNECTION

*Today's companies compete in a **borderless world**. Procter & Gamble sales in Southeast Asia make up a rapidly growing percentage of the company's worldwide sales. These shoppers are purchasing P&G's diaper products, Pampers, in Malaysia.*

Corporations can participate in the international arena on a variety of levels. The process of globalization typically passes through four distinct stages, as illustrated in Exhibit 4.1.

1. In the *domestic stage*, market potential is limited to the home country, with all production and marketing facilities located at home. Managers may be aware of the global environment and may want to consider foreign involvement.
2. In the *international stage*, exports increase, and the company usually adopts a *multidomestic* approach, meaning that competition is handled for each country independently. Product design, marketing, and advertising is adapted to the specific needs of each country, requiring a high level of sensitivity to local values and interests. Typically, these companies use an international division to deal with the marketing of products in several countries individually.
3. In the *multinational stage*, the company has marketing and production facilities located in many countries, with more than one-third of its sales outside the home country. These companies adopt a *globalization* approach, meaning they focus on delivering a similar product to multiple countries. Product design, marketing, and advertising strategies are standardized throughout the world. A good example of a company at the multinational stage is Coca-Cola. The United States toymaker Mattel is shifting from the international stage to the multinational stage because of changes in toy-buying patterns.

**MATTEL**
http://www.mattel.com

For many years, Mattel has been making toys based on the premise that kids in different countries have different interests and want different playthings. Mattel would produce a wide variety of toys and other gear in a variety of styles. The Barbie dolls sold in Japan, for example, had Asian features, black hair, and Japanese-inspired clothing.

Through research and focus groups, however, Mattel managers learned that blond-haired, blue-eyes Barbies sold just as well in Tokyo or Madrid as they did in Kansas City, USA. The worldwide expansion of cable and satellite television has combined with movies and the Internet to create *global kids*, who share similar values and interests because they're exposed to the same cultural icons. The shift began with the global deluge of toys, games, and gadgets associated with the release of the first

Exhibit 4.1

## Four Stages of Globalization

| | 1. Domestic | 2. International | 3. Multinational | 4. Global |
|---|---|---|---|---|
| **Strategic Orientation** | Domestically oriented | Export-oriented, multidomestic | Multinational | Global |
| **Stage of Development** | Initial foreign involvement | Competitive positioning | Explosion of international operations | Global |
| **Cultural Sensitivity** | Of little importance | Very important | Somewhat important | Critically important |
| **Manager Assumptions** | "One best way" | "Many good ways" | "The least-cost way" | "Many good ways" |

**SOURCE:** Based on Nancy J. Adler, *International Dimensions of Organizational Behavior*, 4th ed. (Cincinnati, Ohio: South-Western, 2002), 8–9.

*Harry Potter* movie, because J. K. Rowling's book series already had a global audience. Mattel managers started thinking about the possibilities for global launches of other toys.

As it shifts to a multinational approach, Mattel has consolidated its national subsidiaries into a single international organization. Rather than designing, marketing, and launching products separately for different regions, Mattel now thinks internationally right from the moment a new toy is conceived. The top goal is to come up with toys that have universal appeal and then coordinate marketing and product launches around the world. Although some toys, games, and animated figures don't translate well cross-culturally, Mattel has decreased the toys it makes for local markets to only 20 percent.[10]

4.  Finally, the *global* (or *stateless*) *stage* of corporate international development transcends any single home country. These corporations operate in true global fashion, making sales and acquiring resources in whatever country offers the best opportunities and lowest cost. At this stage, ownership, control, and top management tend to be dispersed among several nationalities.[11]

Today, the number of global or stateless corporations is increasing and the awareness of national borders decreasing, as reflected by the frequency of foreign participation at the management level. Rising managers are expected to know a second or third language and to have international experience. The need for global managers is intense. Corporations around the world want the brightest and best candidates for global management, and young managers who want their careers to move forward recognize the importance of global experience. According to Harvard Business School professor Christopher Bartlett, author of *Managing Across Borders*, people should try to get global exposure when they are young in order to start building skills and networks that will grow throughout their careers.[12] Consider the makeup of today's global companies. Nestlé (Switzerland) personifies the stateless corporation with 98 percent of sales and 96 percent of employees outside the home country. Nestlé's CEO is Austrian-born Peter Brabeck-Letmathe, and half of the company's general managers are non-Swiss. The CEO puts strong faith in regional managers who are native to the region and know the local culture. With 8,000 brands, Nestlé is the largest food company in the world.[13]

# The International Business Environment

**International management** is the management of business operations conducted in more than one country. The fundamental tasks of business management, including the financing, production, and distribution of products and services, do not change in any substantive way when a firm is transacting business across international borders. The basic management functions of planning, organizing, leading, and controlling are the same whether a company operates domestically or internationally. However, managers will experience greater difficulties and risks when performing these management functions on an international scale. For example:

**international management**
The management of business operations conducted in more than one country.

*   When U.S. chicken entrepreneur Frank Purdue translated a successful advertising slogan into Spanish, "It takes a tough man to make a tender chicken" came out as "It takes a virile man to make a chicken affectionate."[14]
*   It took McDonald's more than a year to figure out that Hindus in India do not eat beef. The company's sales took off only after McDonald's started making burgers sold in India out of lamb.[15]
*   In Africa, the labels on bottles show pictures of what is inside so illiterate shoppers can know what they're buying. When a baby-food company showed a picture of an infant on its label, the product didn't sell very well.[16]

## CONCEPT CONNECTION

*ExxonMobil operates in an **international business environment** with a presence in more than 200 countries and territories. Protecting the safety and health of employees while producing energy and chemical products all over the world is a constant challenge to managers. To reach their goal of no injuries, illnesses, or operational incidents, they developed the Operations Integrity Management System to provide a consistent and disciplined framework across ExxonMobil's diverse operations worldwide. Aboard the tanker* Raven *in the Mediterranean, two workers inspect equipment to forestall safety and environmental incidents.*

- United Airlines discovered that even colors can doom a product. The airline handed out white carnations when it started flying from Hong Kong, only to discover that to many Asians such flowers represent death and bad luck.[17]

Some of these examples might seem humorous, but there's nothing funny about them to managers trying to operate in a competitive global environment. Companies seeking to expand their international presence on the Internet also can run into cross-cultural problems, as discussed in the Unlocking Creative Solutions Through Technology box. What should managers of emerging global companies look for to avoid obvious international mistakes? When they are comparing one country with another, the economic, legal-political, and sociocultural sectors present the greatest difficulties. Key factors to understand in the international environment are summarized in Exhibit 4.2.

# The Economic Environment

The economic environment represents the economic conditions in the country where the international organization operates. This part of the environment includes such factors as economic development; infrastructure; resource and product markets; and exchange rates, each of which is discussed in the following sections. In addition, factors such as inflation, interest rates, and economic growth are also part of the international economic environment.

Exhibit 4.2

## Key Factors in the International Environment

**Economic**
- Economic development
- Infrastructure
- Resource and product markets
- Per capita income
- Exchange rates
- Economic conditions

**Legal-Political**
- Political risk
- Government takeovers
- Tariffs, quotas, taxes
- Terrorism, political instability
- Laws, regulations

**Organization**

**Sociocultural**
- Social values, beliefs
- Language
- Religion (objects, taboos, holidays)
- Kinship patterns
- Formal education, literacy
- Time orientation

## Economic Development

Economic development differs widely among the countries and regions of the world. Countries can be categorized as either *developing* or *developed*. Developing countries are referred to as *less-developed countries (LDCs)*. The criterion traditionally used to classify countries as developed or developing is *per capita income*, which is the income generated by the nation's production of goods and services divided by total population. The developing countries have low per capita incomes. LDCs generally are located in Asia, Africa, and South America. Developed countries are generally located in North America, Europe, and Japan.

Most international business firms are headquartered in the wealthier, economically advanced countries. However, smart companies are investing heavily in Asia, Eastern Europe, and Latin America.[18] For example, the number of Internet users and the rate of e-commerce in Latin America is rapidly growing.[19] Computer companies have launched online stores for Latin American customers to buy computers over the Internet. America Online sees Latin America as crucial to expanding its global presence, even though Universo Online International (UOL), based in Brazil, got a tremendous head start over AOL.[20] These companies face risks and challenges today, but they stand to reap huge benefits in the future.

## Infrastructure

A country's physical facilities that support economic activities make up its **infrastructure**, which includes transportation facilities such as airports, highways, and railroads; energy-producing facilities such as utilities and power plants; and communication

**infrastructure**
A country's physical facilities that support economic activities.

# Unlocking Creative Solutions Through Technology

## Virtual Reality: Negotiating the Cross-Cultural Web

With worldwide acceptance of the Internet blossoming, going global has the green light. But technological and cultural issues are so tightly interwoven that there are a multitude of new ways to offend or alienate customers in other nations. For instance, certain gestures, colors, and phrases don't translate well or are considered offensive. A thumb's up sign means approval or encouragement to Americans and many Europeans, but the gesture is considered an obscenity in Greece. Purple is a sign of royalty in some parts of the world, but in others it is associated with death. Credit cards are the backbone of e-commerce in the United States, but they are still a rarity in many countries, causing all sorts of payment problems. And consumers in Germany view credit as a crutch for people who cannot control their finances.

Managers should also consider that many online shoppers want to buy from sites that cater to their native language—for example, research has found that Japanese managers are much more likely to conduct an online transaction when addressed in Japanese. Unfortunately, although just 6 percent of the world's people speak English as a first language, a majority of e-commerce sites are written in English. In the early 2000s,

less than half of U.S. companies had even attempted to pattern their Web sites to the culture or language of foreign users. Some companies are taking the lead in overcoming global challenges on the Internet. The Walt Disney Internet Group now has nearly two dozen Web sites tailored to individual countries, and foreign users account for 42 percent of the audience for the group's sites. The National Basketball Association (NBA) has nine versions of NBA.com aimed at foreign markets, including Brazil, China, and Taiwan. The National Football League (NFL) is also way ahead of most businesses in creating Web sites that serve foreign audiences in their native languages. The NFL's new Chinese site features commentary by Chad Lewis, a Philadelphia Eagles tight end who speaks Mandarin as a result of missionary work he did in Taiwan.

Businesses have been slow to build foreign language Web sites because they require significant investment with no guarantee of returns. However, overseas markets are experiencing tremendous Internet growth. In mid-2003, for example, China had 68 million Internet users, which represented a 15 percent increase in six months. The virtual reality for managers is that they have to shape their Web sites if they want to reach this growing international market.

SOURCES: Bob Tedeschi, "American Web Sites Speak the Language of Overseas Users," *The New York Times* (January 12, 2004), http://www.nytimes.com/2004/01/12/business/12ecom.html; Steve Ulfelder, "All the Web's a Stage," *CIO* (October 1, 2000), 133–142; Daniel Pearl, "Lost in the Translation," *The Wall Street Journal* (February 12, 2001), R12, R14; and Adam Lincoln, "Lost in Translation," *eCFO* (Spring, 2001), 38–43.

facilities such as telephone lines and radio stations. Companies operating in LDCs must contend with lower levels of technology and perplexing logistical, distribution, and communication problems. Undeveloped infrastructures represent opportunities for some firms, such as United Technologies Corporation, based in Hartford, Connecticut, whose businesses include jet engines, air conditioning and heating systems, and elevators. As countries such as China, Russia, and Vietnam open their markets, new buildings need elevators and air and heat systems; opening remote regions for commerce requires more jet engines and helicopters.[21] Cellular telephone companies have found tremendous opportunities in LDCs, where land lines are still limited. In Latin America, for example, the number of mobile phone lines skyrocketed from 100,000 in 1990 to 38 million by 1999, and estimates are that the number will jump to 170 million by 2008.[22]

## Resource and Product Markets

When operating in another country, company managers must evaluate the market demand for their products. If market demand is high, managers may choose to export products to that country. To develop plants, however, resource markets for providing

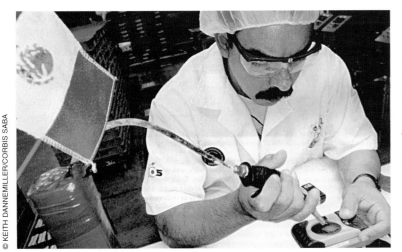

**CONCEPT CONNECTION**

*A solid **infrastructure**, including decent highways, a Pacific port, and nonstop air service to the United States, helps make Guadalajara a favorite factory town for U.S. companies such as IBM, Hewlett-Packard, and Siemens. Guadalajara and surrounding areas in the Mexican state of Jalisco boast the world's largest concentration of electronic contract manufacturers. Factories are bright, shining, and sophisticated, and the annual worker turnover rate is less than 5 percent. Single-use Kodaks, like the one being manufactured in the photo, are made with film coated in Rochester, New York, but assembled and packaged in Mexico.*

needed raw materials and labor must also be available. For example, the greatest challenge for McDonald's, which sells Big Macs on every continent except Antarctica, is to obtain supplies of everything from potatoes to hamburger buns to plastic straws. At McDonald's in Cracow, the burgers come from a Polish plant, partly owned by Chicago-based OSI Industries; the onions come from Fresno, California; the buns come from a production and distribution center near Moscow; and the potatoes come from a plant in Aldrup, Germany. McDonald's tries to contract with local suppliers when possible. In Thailand, McDonald's helped farmers cultivate Idaho russet potatoes of sufficient quality to produce their golden french fries.[23]

## Exchange Rates

*Exchange rate* is the rate at which one country's currency is exchanged for another country's. Volatility in exchange rates has become a major concern for companies doing business internationally.[24] Changes in the exchange rate can have major implications for the profitability of international operations that exchange millions of dollars into other currencies every day.[25] For example, assume that the U.S. dollar is exchanged for 0.8 euros. If the dollar increases in value to 0.9 euros, U.S. goods will be more expensive in France because it will take more euros to buy a dollar's worth of U.S. goods. It will be more difficult to export U.S. goods to France, and profits will be slim. If the dollar drops to a value of 0.7 euros, by contrast, U.S. goods will be cheaper in France and can be exported at a profit.

# The Legal-Political Environment

Businesses must deal with unfamiliar political systems when they go international, as well as with more government supervision and regulation. Government officials and the general public often view foreign companies as outsiders or even intruders and are suspicious of their impact on economic independence and political sovereignty. Some of the major legal–political concerns affecting international business are political risk, political instability, and laws and regulations.

## Political Risk and Instability

A company's **political risk** is defined as its risk of loss of assets, earning power, or managerial control due to politically based events or actions by host governments.[26]

**political risk**
A company's risk of loss of assets, earning power, or managerial control due to politically based events or actions by host governments.

Political risk includes government takeovers of property and acts of violence directed against a firm's properties or employees. In Mexico, business executives and their families are a prime target for gangs of kidnappers, many of which are reportedly led by state and local police. The daughter of the local head of a Japanese tire company, for example, was kidnaped in 2000 and the company paid a $1 million ransom. Estimates are that big companies in Mexico typically spend between 5 and 15 percent of their annual budgets on security.[27] Companies operating in other countries also formulate special plans and programs to guard against unexpected losses. Executives at Tricon, which owns KFC and Pizza Hut restaurants, monitor events through an international security service to stay on top of potential hot spots.[28] Some companies buy political risk insurance, and political risk analysis has emerged as a critical component of environmental assessment for multinational organizations.[29] To reduce uncertainty, organizations sometimes also rely on the *Index of Economic Freedom*, which ranks countries according to the impact political intervention has on business decisions, and the *Corruption Perception Index*, which assesses 91 countries according to the level of perceived corruption in government and public administration.[30]

**political instability**
Events such as riots, revolutions, or government upheavals that affect the operations of an international company.

Another frequently cited problem for international companies is **political instability**, which includes riots, revolutions, civil disorders, and frequent changes in government. In recent decades, civil wars and large-scale violence have occurred in Haiti, Indonesia, Malaysia, Thailand, Sri Lanka (Ceylon), and Myanmar (Burma). Companies moving into former Soviet republics face continued instability because of changing government personnel and political philosophies. The Middle East in early 2004 is an area of extreme instability as the United States pursues a difficult and protracted reconstruction following the Iraqi war. U.S. firms or companies linked to the United States often are subject to major threats in countries characterized by political instability. For example, on the first Muslim holy day after the U.S. began bombings in Afghanistan, thousands of demonstrators in Pakistan set fire to a KFC restaurant as a symbol of America.[31]

Although most companies would prefer to do business in stable countries, some of the greatest growth opportunities lie in areas characterized by instability. The greatest threat of violence is in countries experiencing political, ethnic, or religious upheaval. In China, for example, political winds have shifted rapidly, and often dangerously. Yet it is the largest potential market in the world for the goods and services of developed countries.

© CHRIS BROWN, POLARIS

**CONCEPT CONNECTION**

*Despite the **political risk**, **political instability**, and the local **laws and regulations** of countries such as Morocco, The Coca-Cola Company earns about 80 percent of its profits from markets outside North America. The soft-drink company suffered in global markets after complaints of tainted products from Belgium bottling plants. Managers are busily trying to rebuild relationships because of the importance of international sales.*

## Laws and Regulations

Government laws and regulations differ from country to country and make doing business a true challenge for international firms. Host governments have myriad laws concerning libel statutes, consumer protection, information and labeling, employment and safety, and wages. International companies must learn these rules and regulations and abide by them. In addition, the Internet has increased the impact of foreign laws on U.S. companies because it expands the potential for doing business on a global basis. Land's End, the Dodgeville, Wisconsin, mail-order retailer, ran afoul of Germany's laws banning lifetime guarantees, rebates, and other forms of sales promotion.[32] First Net Card, started in 1999 to provide credit for online transactions to anyone in the world, found the complication of dealing with international credit and banking laws mind-boggling. After two years and a mountain of legal research, the company was licensed to provide credit only in the United States, Canada, and Britain.[33]

# The Sociocultural Environment

A nation's culture includes the shared knowledge, beliefs, and values, as well as the common modes of behavior and ways of thinking, among members of a society. Cultural factors can be more perplexing than political and economic factors when working or living in a foreign country.

## Social Values

Culture is intangible, pervasive, and difficult for outsiders to learn. One way managers can comprehend local cultures and deal with them effectively is to understand differences in social values.

### Hofstede's Value Dimensions
Research done by Geert Hofstede on 116,000 IBM employees in 40 countries identified four dimensions of national value systems that influence organizational and employee working relationships.[34] Examples of how countries rate on the four dimensions are shown in Exhibit 4.3.

1. *Power distance.* High **power distance** means that people accept inequality in power among institutions, organizations, and people. Low power distance means that people expect equality in power. Countries that value high power distance

**power distance**
The degree to which people accept inequality in power among institutions, organizations, and people.

Exhibit 4.3

## Rank Orderings of Ten Countries along Four Dimensions of National Value Systems

| Country | Power Distance[a] | Uncertainty Avoidance[b] | Individualism[c] | Masculinity[d] |
|---|---|---|---|---|
| Australia | 7 | 7 | 2 | 5 |
| Costa Rica | 8 (tie) | 2 (tie) | 10 | 9 |
| France | 3 | 2 (tie) | 4 | 7 |
| West Germany | 8 (tie) | 5 | 5 | 3 |
| India | 2 | 9 | 6 | 6 |
| Japan | 5 | 1 | 7 | 1 |
| Mexico | 1 | 4 | 8 | 2 |
| Sweden | 10 | 10 | 3 | 10 |
| Thailand | 4 | 6 | 9 | 8 |
| United States | 6 | 8 | 1 | 4 |

[a]1 = highest power distance
10 = lowest power distance
[b]1 = highest uncertainty avoidance
10 = lowest uncertainty avoidance

[c]1 = highest individualism
10 = lowest individualism
[d]1 = highest masculinity
10 = lowest masculinity

**SOURCE:** From Dorothy Marcic, *Organizational Behavior and Cases*, 4th ed. (St. Paul, Minn.: West, 1995). Based on Geert Hofstede, *Culture's Consequences* (London: Sage Publications, 1984); and *Cultures and Organizations: Software of the Mind* (New York: McGraw-Hill, 1991).

**uncertainty avoidance**
A value characterized by people's intolerance for uncertainty and ambiguity and resulting support for beliefs that promise certainty and conformity.

**individualism**
A preference for a loosely knit social framework in which individuals are expected to take care of themselves.

**collectivism**
A preference for a tightly knit social framework in which individuals look after one another and organizations protect their members' interests.

**masculinity**
A cultural preference for achievement, heroism, assertiveness, work centrality, and material success.

**femininity**
A cultural preference for relationships, cooperation, group decision making, and quality of life.

are Malaysia, the Philippines, and Panama. Countries that value low power distance are Denmark, Austria, and Israel.

2. *Uncertainty avoidance.* High **uncertainty avoidance** means that members of a society feel uncomfortable with uncertainty and ambiguity and thus support beliefs that promise certainty and conformity. Low uncertainty avoidance means that people have high tolerance for the unstructured, the unclear, and the unpredictable. High uncertainty avoidance countries include Greece, Portugal, and Uruguay. Countries with low uncertainty avoidance values are Singapore and Jamaica.

3. *Individualism and collectivism.* **Individualism** reflects a value for a loosely knit social framework in which individuals are expected to take care of themselves. **Collectivism** means a preference for a tightly knit social framework in which individuals look after one another and organizations protect their members' interests. Countries with individualist values include the United States, Canada, Great Britain, and Australia. Countries with collectivist values are Guatemala, Ecuador, and China.

4. *Masculinity/femininity.* **Masculinity** stands for preference for achievement, heroism, assertiveness, work centrality (with resultant high stress), and material success. **Femininity** reflects the values of relationships, cooperation, group decision making, and quality of life. Societies with strong masculine values are Japan, Austria, Mexico, and Germany. Countries with feminine values are Sweden, Norway, Denmark, and France. Both men and women subscribe to the dominant value in masculine and feminine cultures.

Hofstede and his colleagues later identified a fifth dimension, long-term orientation versus short-term orientation. The **long-term orientation**, found in China and other Asian countries, includes a greater concern for the future and highly values thrift and perseverance. A **short-term orientation**, found in Russia and West Africa, is more concerned with the past and the present and places a high value on tradition and meeting social obligations.[35] Researchers have continued to explore and expand on Hofstede's findings. For example, in the last 25 years, more than 1,400 articles and numerous books have been published on individualism and collectivism alone.[36]

*Take A Moment*

*Go to the ethical dilemma on page 147.*

**long-term orientation**
A greater concern for the future and high value on thrift and perseverance.

**short-term orientation**
A concern with the past and present and a high value on meeting social obligations.

## Globe Project Value Dimensions

Recent research by the GLOBE Project extends Hofstede's assessment and offers a broader understanding for today's managers. The GLOBE (Global Leadership and Organizational Behavior Effectiveness) project used data collected from 18,000 managers in 62 countries to identify nine dimensions that explain cultural differences, including those identified by Hofstede.[37]

1. *Assertiveness.* A high value on assertiveness means a society encourages toughness, assertiveness, and competitiveness. Low assertiveness means that people value tenderness and concern for others over being competitive.

2. *Future orientation.* Similar to Hofstede's time orientation, this refers to the extent to which a society encourages and rewards planning for the future over short-term results and quick gratification.

3. *Uncertainty avoidance.* As with Hofstede's study, this is the degree to which members of a society feel uncomfortable with uncertainty and ambiguity.

4. *Gender differentiation.* This dimension refers to the extent to which a society maximizes gender role differences. In countries with low gender differentiation, such as Denmark, women typically have a higher status and stronger role in decision making. Countries with high gender differentiation accord men higher social, political, and economic status.

5. *Power distance.* This dimension is the same as Hofstede's and refers to the degree to which people expect and accept equality or inequality in relationships and institutions.
6. *Societal collectivism.* This term is defined as the degree to which practices in institutions such as schools, businesses, and other social organizations encourage a tightly-knit collectivist society, in which people are an important part of a group, or a highly individualistic society.
7. *Individual collectivism.* Rather than looking at how societal organizations favor individualism versus collectivism, this dimension looks at the degree to which individuals take pride in being members of a family, close circle of friends, team, or organization.
8. *Performance orientation.* A society with a high performance orientation places high emphasis on performance and rewards people for performance improvements and excellence. A low performance orientation means people pay less attention to performance and more attention to loyalty, belonging, and background.
9. *Humane orientation.* The final dimension refers to the degree to which a society encourages and rewards people for being fair, altruistic, generous, and caring. A country high on humane orientation places high value on helping others and being kind. A country low on this orientation expects people to take care of themselves. Self-enhancement and gratification is of high importance.

Exhibit 4.4 gives examples of how some countries rank on several of the GLOBE dimensions. These dimensions give managers an added tool for identifying and managing cultural differences. While Hofstede's dimensions are still valid, the GLOBE research provides a more comprehensive view of cultural similarities and differences.

Social values have great influence on organizational functioning and management styles. Consider the difficulty that managers have had implementing self-directed

## Exhibit 4.4

### Examples of Country Rankings on Selected GLOBE Value Dimensions

| Dimension | Low | Medium | High |
|---|---|---|---|
| Assertiveness | Sweden Switzerland Japan | Egypt Iceland France | Spain United States Germany (former East) |
| Future Orientation | Russia Italy Kuwait | Slovenia Australia India | Denmark Canada Singapore |
| Gender Differentiation | Sweden Denmark Poland | Italy Brazil Netherlands | South Korea Egypt China |
| Performance Orientation | Russia Greece Venezuela | Israel England Japan | United States Taiwan Hong Kong |
| Humane Orientation | Germany France Singapore | New Zealand Sweden United States | Indonesia Egypt Iceland |

**SOURCE:** Mansour Javidan and Robert J. House, "Cultural Acumen for the Global Manager: Lessons from Project GLOBE," *Organizational Dynamics* 29, no. 4 (2001), 289–305.

work teams in Mexico. As shown in Exhibit 4.3, Mexico is characterized by very high power distance and a relatively low tolerance for uncertainty, characteristics that often conflict with the American concept of teamwork, which emphasizes shared power and authority, with team members working on a variety of problems without formal guidelines, rules, and structure. Many workers in Mexico, as well as in France and Mediterranean countries, expect organizations to be hierarchical. In Russia, people are good at working in groups and like competing as a team rather than on an individual basis. Organizations in Germany and other central European countries typically strive to be impersonal, well-oiled machines. Effective management styles differ in each country, depending on cultural characteristics.[38]

## Other Cultural Characteristics

Other cultural characteristics that influence international organizations are language, religion, attitudes, social organization, and education. Some countries, such as India, are characterized by *linguistic pluralism*, meaning that several languages exist there. Other countries rely heavily on spoken versus written language. Religion includes sacred objects, philosophical attitudes toward life, taboos, and rituals. Attitudes toward achievement, work, and people can all affect organizational productivity. For example, a recent study found that the prevalent American attitude that treats employees as a resource to be used (an *instrumental* attitude toward people) can be a strong impediment to business success in countries where people are valued as an end in themselves rather than as a means to an end (a *humanistic* attitude). U.S. companies sometimes use instrumental human resource policies that conflict with local humanistic values.[39]

**ethnocentrism**
A cultural attitude marked by the tendency to regard one's own culture as superior to others.

**Ethnocentrism**, which refers to a natural tendency of people to regard their own culture as superior and to downgrade or dismiss other cultural values, can be found in all countries. Strong ethnocentric attitudes within a country make it difficult for foreign firms to operate there. Other factors include social organization, such as status systems, kinship and families, social institutions, and opportunities for social mobility. Education influences the literacy level, the availability of qualified employees, and the predominance of primary or secondary degrees.

American managers are regularly accused of an ethnocentric attitude that assumes the American way is the best way. At an executive training seminar at IMD, a business school in Lausanne, Switzerland, managers from Europe expressed a mixture of admiration and disdain for U.S. managers. "They admire the financial results," says J. Peter Killing, an IMD professor, "but when they meet managers from the United States they see that even these educated, affluent Americans don't speak any language besides English, don't know how or when to eat and drink properly, and don't know anything about European history, let alone geography."[40] Take the quiz in this chapter's Manager's Shoptalk box to see how much you know about cross-cultural communication and etiquette.

As business grows increasingly global, U.S. managers are learning that cultural differences cannot be ignored if international operations are to succeed. For example, Coke withdrew its two-liter bottle from the Spanish market after discovering that compartments of Spanish refrigerators were too small for it. Wal-Mart goofed by stocking footballs in Brazil, a country where soccer rules.[41] Companies can improve their success by paying attention to culture. Consider how addressing cultural differences helped McDonald's thrive in France even as the corporation's U.S. business stalled.

**McDONALD'S FRANCE**
http://www.
mcdonalds.fr

In January of 2003, McDonald's posted its first ever quarterly loss (for October–December 2002) and announced the closing of 175 outlets worldwide. Yet, during that same time period, a new McDonald's restaurant was opening in France every six days.

Managers who responded to cultural and social differences rather than trying to transfer the American fast-food concept wholesale have McDonald's French subsidiary booming. Consumers in France were initially resentful of the U.S.-based chain, and one anti-globalization activist was hailed as a national hero for razing a partially built restaurant. Denis Hennequin, the French subsidiary's CEO, responded by running a series of edgy advertisements depicting fat, ignorant Americans who couldn't understand why McDonald's France used locally produced food that wasn't genetically modified. Hennequin believed a sense of humor was the best way to address the French opposition to bio-engineered food and their distrust of all things American.

Hennequin has followed a clever strategy for giving McDonald's France its own identity and boosting the chain's attractiveness to customers. Rather than building red and yellow boxes, leaders are adapting restaurant designs to fit with the local architecture and remodeling existing outlets to include features such as hardwood floors, wood-beam ceilings, comfortable armchairs, and music videos. Rather than streamlining the menu, they've added items such as espresso, brioche, and more upscale sandwiches, including a hot ham and cheese sandwich dubbed the Croque McDo. The upscale styling doesn't come cheap, but the Gallic twists have helped sales soar. Unlike in the United States, where customers want quick service and cheap, tasty eats, the French want higher-quality food and a friendly atmosphere that encourages them to linger. The average McDonald's customer in France spends $9 per visit, compared to an average of $4 per visit in the United States.[42]

Recognizing and managing cultural differences can help organizations like McDonald's be more competitive and successful. However, differences in cultural and social values can create significant barriers to successful communication and collaboration for all companies operating internationally.

# International Trade Alliances

One of the most visible changes in the international business environment in recent years has been the development of regional trading alliances and international trade agreements. These developments are significantly shaping global trade.

## GATT and the World Trade Organization

The General Agreement on Tariffs and Trade (GATT), signed by 23 nations in 1947, started as a set of rules to ensure nondiscrimination, clear procedures, the negotiation of disputes, and the participation of lesser-developed countries in international trade. GATT and its successor, the World Trade Organization (WTO), primarily use tariff concessions as a tool to increase trade. Member countries agree to limit the level of tariffs they will impose on imports from other members. The **most favored nation** clause calls for each member country to grant to every other member country the most favorable treatment it accords to any country with respect to imports and exports.[43]

GATT sponsored eight rounds of international trade negotiations aimed at reducing trade restrictions. The 1986 to 1994 Uruguay Round (the first to be named for a developing country) involved 125 countries and cut more tariffs than ever before. The Round's multilateral trade agreement, which took effect January 1, 1995, was the most comprehensive pact since the original 1947 agreement. It boldly moved the world closer to global free trade by calling for the establishment of the WTO. The WTO represents the maturation of GATT into a permanent global institution that can monitor international trade and has legal authority to arbitrate disputes on some 400 trade issues. As of June, 2004, 147 countries were members of the WTO.[44]

**most favored nation**
A term describing a GATT clause that calls for member countries to grant other member countries the most favorable treatment they accord any country concerning imports and exports.

# manager's Shoptalk

### How Well Do You Play the Culture Game?

How good are you at understanding cross-cultural differences in communication and etiquette? For fun, see how many of the following questions you can answer correctly. The answers appear at the end.

1. You want to do business with a Greek company, but the representative insists on examining every detail of your proposal for several hours. This time-consuming detail means that the Greek representative:

   a. doesn't trust the accuracy of your proposal

   b. is being polite, and really doesn't want to go ahead with the deal

   c. is signaling you to consider a more reasonable offer, but doesn't want to ask directly

   d. is uncomfortable with detailed proposals and would prefer a simple handshake

   e. is showing good manners and respect to you and your proposal

2. Male guests in many Latin American countries often give their visitors an *abrazzo* when greeting them. An *abrazzo* is:

   a. a light kiss on the nose

   b. a special gift, usually wine or food

   c. clapping hands in the air as the visitor approaches

   d. a strong embrace, or kiss with hand on shoulder

   e. a firm two-handed handshake, lasting almost one minute.

3. Japanese clients visit you at your office for a major meeting. Where should the top Japanese official be seated?

   a. closest to the door

   b. as close to the middle of the room as is possible

   c. anywhere in the room; seating location isn't important to Japanese business people

   d. somewhere away from the door with a piece of artwork behind him or her

   e. always beside rather than facing the host

4. One of the most universal gestures is:

   a. a pat on the back (congratulations)

   b. a smile (happiness or politeness)

   c. scratching your chin (thinking)

   d. closing your eyes (boredom)

   e. arm up, shaking back and forth (waving)

5. While visiting a German client, you make a compliment about the client's beautiful pen set. What will probably happen?

   a. the client will insist very strongly that you take it

   b. the client will tell you where to buy such a pen set at a good price

   c. the client will accept the compliment and get on with business

   d. the client will probably get upset that you aren't paying attention to the business at hand

   e. the client will totally ignore the comment

6. Managers from which country are least likely to tolerate someone being 5 minutes late for an appointment?

   a. United States

   b. Australia

   c. Brazil

   d. Sweden

   e. Saudi Arabia

7. In which of the following countries are office arrangements NOT usually an indicator of the person's status?

   a. United Kingdom

   b. Germany

   c. Saudi Arabia

   d. China

   e. United States

8. In many Asian cultures, a direct order such as "Get me the Amex report" is most likely to be given by:

   a. senior management to most subordinates

   b. a junior employee to a peer

# manager's Shoptalk

**Turbulent Times**

## How Well Do You Play the Culture Game? (continued)

   c.  senior management only to very junior employees

   d.  junior employees to outsiders

   e.  none of the above

9. In the United States, scratching one's head usually means that the person is confused or skeptical. In Russia, it means:

   a.  "You're crazy!"

   b.  "I am listening carefully."

   c.  "I want to get to know you better."

   d.  "I'm confused or skeptical."

   e.  None of the above

10. A polite way to give your business card to a Japanese business person is:

   a.  casually, after several hours of getting to know the person

   b.  when first meeting, presenting your card with both hands

   c.  at the very end of the first meeting

   d.  casually during the meeting, with the information down to show humility

   e.  never; it is considered rude in Japan to give business cards

SOURCES: Steven L. McShane and Mary Ann Von Glinow, *Organizational Behavior: Emerging Realities for the Workplace Revolution,* 3d ed. (New York: McGraw-Hill/Irwin, 2004). "Cross-Cultural Communication Game" developed by Steven L. McShane, based on material in R. Axtell, *Gestures: The Do's and Taboos of Body Language Around the World* (New York: Wiley, 1991); R. Mead, *Cross-Cultural Management Communication* (Chichester, UK: Wiley, 1990), chapter 7; and J.V. Thill and C. L. Bovée, *Excellence in Business Communication* (New York: McGraw-Hill, 1995), chapter 17.

© McShane

**Answers**

1 e; 2 d; 3 d; 4 b; 5 c; 6 d; 7 c; 8 c; 9 d; 10 b

The goal of the WTO is to guide—and sometime urge—the nations of the world toward free trade and open markets.[45] The WTO encompasses the GATT and all its agreements, as well as various other agreements related to trade in services and intellectual property issues in world trade. As a permanent membership organization, the WTO is bringing greater trade liberalization in goods, information, technological developments, and services; stronger enforcement of rules and regulations; and greater power to resolve disputes. However, the power of the WTO is partly responsible for a growing backlash against global trade. An increasing number of individuals and public interest groups are protesting that global trade locks poor people into poverty and harms wages, jobs, and the environment.

## European Union

Formed in 1957 to improve economic and social conditions among its members, the European Economic Community, now called the European Union (EU), has grown to the 25-nation alliance illustrated in Exhibit 4.5. The biggest expansion came in 2004, when the EU welcomed ten new members from southern and eastern Europe: Cyprus, the Czech Republic, Estonia, Hungary, Latvia, Lithuania, Malta, Poland, Slovakia, and Slovenia. In addition, Bulgaria, Romania and Turkey

# Exhibit 4.5

## The Nations of the European Union

**European Union Countries**
**Joined EU in 2004**
**In negotiations to join**

have opened membership negotiations. A treaty signed in early 2003 formalized new rules and policies to ensure that the EU can continue to function efficiently with 25 or more members.[46]

In the early 1980s, Europeans initiated steps to create a powerful single market system called *Europe '92.* The initiative called for the creation of open markets for Europe's millions of consumers, allowing people, goods, and services to move freely. Europe '92 consisted of 282 directives proposing dramatic reform and deregulation in such areas as banking, insurance, health, safety standards, airlines, telecommunications, auto sales, social policy, and monetary union. Common policies for member countries have continued to evolve in light of changing social and economic circumstances. For example, the EU now deals with issues such as citizens' rights, job creation, and how to make globalization work for everyone. In addition, the need to protect the natural environment is a consideration in all EU policies.

Initially opposed and later embraced by European industry, the increased competition and economies of scale within Europe is enabling companies to grow large and efficient, becoming more competitive in U.S. and other world markets. Some observers fear that the EU will become a trade barrier, creating a *fortress Europe* that will be difficult to penetrate by companies in other nations. Indeed, an

EU directive adopting strict privacy protection laws has some U.S. officials worried about the alliance's power over U.S. companies wanting to do international business over the Internet.[47] The EU has also recently enacted laws that dramatically broaden its power concerning mergers and antitrust issues. For example, officials now have the power to seal off corporate offices for unspecified time periods to search for relevant documents.[48]

Another aspect of significance to countries operating globally is the EU's monetary revolution and the introduction of the **euro**. In January 2002, the **euro**, a single European currency, replaced national currencies in 12 member countries and unified a huge marketplace, creating a competitive economy second only to the United States.[49] Belgium, Germany, Greece, France, Spain, Italy, Ireland, the Netherlands, Austria, Finland, Portugal, and Luxembourg traded their deutschemarks, francs, lira, and other currencies to adopt the euro, a currency with a single exchange rate. The United Kingdom has thus far refused to accept the euro, in part because of a sense of nationalism, but many believe that the United Kingdom and new EU members will eventually adopt the currency. The implications of a single European currency are enormous, within as well as outside Europe. As it potentially replaces up to 25 European domestic currencies, the euro will affect legal contracts, financial management, sales and marketing tactics, manufacturing, distribution, payroll, pensions, training, taxes, and information management systems. Every corporation that does business in or with EU countries will feel the impact.[50] In addition, economic union is likely to speed deregulation, which has already reordered Europe's corporate and competitive landscape.

**euro**
A single European currency that replaced the currencies of 12 European nations.

## North American Free Trade Agreement (NAFTA)

The North American Free Trade Agreement, which went into effect on January 1, 1994, merged the United States, Canada, and Mexico into a megamarket with more than 421 million consumers. The agreement breaks down tariffs and trade restrictions on most agricultural and manufactured products over a 15-year period. The treaty built on the 1989 U.S.–Canada agreement and was intended to spur growth and investment, increase exports, and expand jobs in all three nations.[51]

The negotiations resulted in agreements in a number of key areas:

- *Agriculture.* Immediate removal of tariffs on half of U.S. farm exports to Mexico, with phasing out of remaining tariffs over 15 years.
- *Autos.* Immediate 50 percent cut of Mexican tariffs on autos, reaching zero in 10 years. Mandatory 62.5 percent North American content on cars and trucks to qualify for duty-free status.
- *Transport.* U.S. trucking of international cargo allowed in Mexican border area by mid-1990s and throughout Mexico by the end of the decade.
- *Intellectual property.* Mexico's protection for pharmaceutical patents boosted to international standards and North American copyrights safeguarded.

In the past decade, U.S. trade with Mexico increased more than threefold, while trade with Canada also rose dramatically.[52] NAFTA has spurred the entry of small businesses into the global arena. Jeff Victor, general manager of Treatment Products, Ltd., which makes car cleaners and waxes, credits NAFTA for his surging export volume. Prior to the pact, Mexican tariffs as high as 20 percent made it impossible for the Chicago-based company to expand its presence south of the border.[53]

On the tenth anniversary of the agreement in January 2004, opinions over the benefits of NAFTA appeared to be as divided as they were when talks began, with some people calling it a spectacular success and others referring to it as a dismal failure.[54] Although NAFTA has not lived up to its grand expectations, experts stress that it has increased trade, investment, and income and continues to enable companies in all three countries to compete more effectively with rival Asian and European firms.[55]

## Other Trade Alliances

The creation of trading blocs is an increasingly important aspect of international business. The Association of Southeast Asian Nations (ASEAN) is a trading alliance of 10 Southeast Asian nations, including Cambodia, Vietnam, Singapore, Malaysia, and the Philippines, as illustrated in Exhibit 4.6. This region will likely be one of the fastest-growing economic regions of the world, and the ASEAN could eventually be as powerful as the EU and NAFTA. A free trade block known as Mercosur encompasses Argentina, Brazil, Bolivia, Chile, Paraguay, and Uruguay. And more than 30 countries in Central and South America and the Caribbean region are negotiating to establish a Free Trade Area of the Americas (FTAA), expected to be operational by 2005.[56] These agreements entail a new future for international companies, and both corporations and managers will be affected by these important trends.

## The Globalization Backlash

As the world becomes increasingly interconnected, a backlash over globalization is occurring. Perhaps the first highly visible antiglobalization protest occurred at the meeting of the World Trade Organization (WTO) in Seattle, Washington, in the fall of 1999, where business and political leaders were caught off guard by the strong sentiments. Since then, protesters have converged on both the International Monetary Fund (IMF) and the World Bank. These three organizations are sometimes referred to as *The Iron Triangle* of globalization.

## Exhibit 4.6

### ASEAN Members

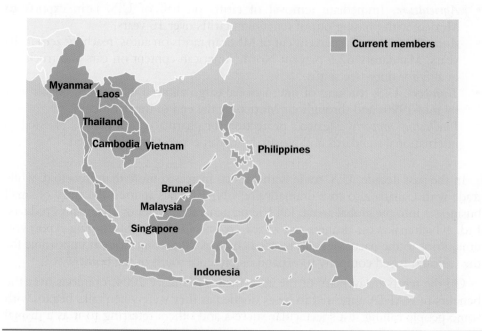

**SOURCE:** Based on J. McClenahen and T. Clark, "ASEAN at Work," *IW.* May 19, 1997, p. 42.

A primary concern is the loss of jobs as companies export work to countries with lower wages.[57] Consider, for example, that a 26-year-old engineer in Bangalore, India, designs next-generation mobile phone chips at a Texas Instruments research center for a salary of $10,000 a year. Boeing has used aeronautical specialists in Russia to design luggage bins and wing parts for planes. They make around $650 a month, compared to a counterpart in the United States making $6,000. IBM has plans to shift thousands of high-paying programming jobs to cheap-labor sites in China, India, and Brazil.[58] The transfer of jobs such as making shoes, clothing, and toys began two decades ago. Today, services and knowledge work are rapidly moving to developing countries. Outsourcing of white-collar jobs to India has exploded, with a 60 percent jump in 2003 compared to the year before. An analyst at Forrester Research Inc. predicts that at least 3.3 million mostly white-collar jobs and $136 billion in wages will shift from the United States to low-wage countries by 2015.[59]

Activists charge that globalization not only hurts people who lose their jobs in the United States, but also contributes to worldwide environmental destruction and locks poor people in developing nations into a web of poverty and suffering.[60] Political leaders have struggled to assure the public of the advantages of globalization and free trade,[61] with President George Bush recently admonishing those who oppose globalization as "no friends to the poor." Business leaders, meanwhile, insist that the economic benefits flow back to the U.S. economy in the form of lower prices, expanded markets, and increased profits that can fund innovation.[62] Yet the antiglobalization fervor is just getting hotter—and is not likely to dissipate anytime soon. Managers who once saw antiglobalists as a fringe group are starting to pay attention to the growing concerns. In the end, it is not whether globalization is good or bad, but how business and government can work together to ensure that the advantages of a global world are fully and fairly shared.

# Getting Started Internationally

Small and medium-sized companies have a couple of ways to become involved internationally. One is to seek cheaper sources of supply offshore, which is called *outsourcing*. Another is to develop markets for finished products outside their home countries, which may include exporting, licensing, and direct investing. These are called market entry strategies because they represent alternative ways to sell products and services in foreign markets. Most firms begin with exporting and work up to direct investment. Exhibit 4.7 shows the strategies companies can use to enter foreign markets.

**market entry strategy**
An organizational strategy for entering a foreign market.

## Outsourcing

Global outsourcing, sometimes called *global sourcing*, means engaging in the international division of labor so that manufacturing can be done in countries with the cheapest sources of labor and supplies. A company may take away a contract from a domestic supplier and place it with a company in the Far East, 8,000 miles away. Many manufacturers in Asia and Latin America are now wired into the Internet to help them compete in an e-business world. Large companies outsource to companies all over Asia, and they like the convenience, speed, and efficiency of handling business by electronic transactions. Singapore-based Advanced Manufacturing Online uses a system that enables both suppliers and clients to send orders and solicit price quotes over the Web.[63]

**global outsourcing**
Engaging in the international division of labor so as to obtain the cheapest sources of labor and supplies regardless of country; also called *global sourcing*.

A unique variation of global outsourcing is the *maquiladora* industry along the Texas–Mexico border. In the beginning, twin plants were set up, with the U.S. plant

Exhibit 4.7

## Strategies for Entering International Markets

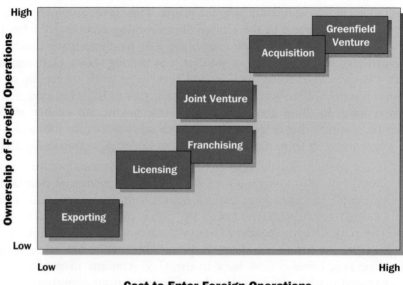

manufacturing components with sophisticated machinery and the Mexican plant assembling components using cheap labor. With increasing sophistication in Mexico, new factories with high-tech equipment are being built farther south of the border, with assembled products imported into the United States at highly competitive prices. General Electric, for example, employs more than 30,000 people in appliance factories in Mexico, and is now shifting some of its engineering work to that country, as well as to India, Brazil, and Turkey. Service companies are taking advantage of the *maquiladora* concept as well. U.S. data-processing companies use high-speed data lines to ship document images to Mexico and India, where 45,000 workers do everything from processing airline tickets to screening credit-card applications. British banks have transferred back-office operations to companies in China and India, as well.[64] As we discussed earlier, high-level knowledge work is also increasingly being outsourced to lower-wage countries.

## Exporting

**exporting**
An entry strategy in which the organization maintains its production facilities within its home country and transfers its products for sale in foreign countries.

With **exporting**, the corporation maintains its production facilities within the home nation and transfers its products for sale in foreign countries.[65] Exporting enables a country to market its products in other countries at modest resource cost and with limited risk. Exporting does entail numerous problems based on physical distances, government regulations, foreign currencies, and cultural differences, but it is less expensive than committing the firm's own capital to building plants in host countries. For example, a high-tech equipment supplier called Gerber Scientific Inc. prefers not to get involved directly in foreign country operations. Because machinery and machine tools are hot areas of export, executives are happy to ship overseas. Small- to mid-size U.S. companies are benefiting from increased exporting. Multiplex Co., a St. Louis manufacturer of beverage-dispensing equipment for fast-food service, exports about 40 percent of its products. National Graphics, a specialty coater of papers and films, ships 60 percent of its products overseas, and National's CEO believes exports helped to save the company.[66]

PHOTO BY © TIMOTHY ARCHIBALD 2003

A form of exporting to less-developed countries is called **countertrade**, which is the barter of products for products rather than the sale of products for currency. Many less-developed countries have products to exchange but have no foreign currency. An estimated 20 percent of world trade is countertrade.

**countertrade**
The barter of products for other products rather than their sale for currency.

## Licensing

The next stage in pursuing international markets is licensing and franchising, which are similar approaches. With **licensing**, a corporation (the licensor) in one country makes certain resources available to companies in another country (the licensee). These resources include technology, managerial skills, and/or patent and trademark rights. They enable the licensee to produce and market a product similar to what the licensor has been producing. This arrangement gives the licensor an opportunity to participate in the production and sale of products outside its home country at relatively low cost. Hasbro has used licensing agreements with companies in several Latin American countries and Japan. Hasbro builds brand identity and consumer awareness by contracting with toy companies in other countries to manufacture products locally. Heineken, which has been called the world's first truly global brand of beer, usually begins by exporting to help boost familiarity with its product; if the market looks enticing enough, Heineken then licenses its brands to a local brewer.

**licensing**
An entry strategy in which an organization in one country makes certain resources available to companies in another in order to participate in the production and sale of its products abroad.

**Franchising** is a special form of licensing that occurs when the franchisee buys a complete package of materials and services, including equipment, products, product ingredients, trademark and trade name rights, managerial advice, and a standardized operating system. Whereas with licensing, a licensee generally keeps its own company name and operating systems, a franchise takes the name and systems of the franchisor. For example, Anheuser-Busch licenses the right to brew and distribute Budweiser beer to several breweries, including Labatt in Canada and Kirin in Japan, but these breweries retain their own company names, identities, and autonomy. On the other hand, a Burger King franchise anywhere in the world is a Burger King, and managers use standard procedures designed by the franchisor. The fast-food chains are some of the best-known franchisors. KFC, Burger King, Wendy's, and

**franchising**
A form of licensing in which an organization provides its foreign franchisees with a complete package of materials and services.

McDonald's outlets are found in almost every large city in the world. The story is often told of the Japanese child visiting Los Angeles who excitedly pointed out to his parents, "They have McDonald's in America."

Licensing and franchising offer a business firm relatively easy access to international markets at low cost, but they limit its participation in and control over the development of those markets.

## Direct Investing

A higher level of involvement in international trade is direct investment in manufacturing facilities in a foreign country. **Direct investing** means that the company is involved in managing the productive assets, which distinguishes it from other entry strategies that permit less managerial control.

Currently, the most popular type of direct investment is to engage in strategic alliances and partnerships. In a **joint venture**, a company shares costs and risks with another firm, typically in the host country, to develop new products, build a manufacturing facility, or set up a sales and distribution network.[67] A partnership is often the fastest, cheapest, and least risky way to get into the global game. Entrepreneurial companies such as Molex, a manufacturer of connectors, and Nypro, a maker of industrial components, have used partnerships to gain overseas access to several countries. Auburn Farms, a Sacramento, California, manufacturer of all-natural snack foods, formed a joint venture with South Africa's Beacon Sweets & Chocolates. Nestlé and L'Oreal engaged in a joint venture to produce the nutritional supplement Inneov, which is designed to improve the health of skin.[68] Internet companies have also used joint ventures as a way to expand. AOL created a joint venture with Venezuela's Cisneros Group to smooth its entry into Latin America.[69]

The other choice is to have a **wholly owned foreign affiliate**, over which the company has complete control. Direct *acquisition* of an affiliate may provide cost savings over exporting by shortening distribution channels and reducing storage and transportation costs. Local managers also have heightened awareness of economic, cultural, and political conditions. For example, General Electric purchased Hungarian bulbmaker Tungsram in 1990, and quality was so good that GE eventually shifted all European light-bulb production there.[70]

The most costly and risky direct investment is called a **greenfield venture**, which means a company builds a subsidiary from scratch in a foreign country. The

**direct investing**
An entry strategy in which the organization is involved in managing its production facilities in a foreign country.

**joint venture**
A variation of direct investment in which an organization shares costs and risks with another firm to build a manufacturing facility, develop new products, or set up a sales and distribution network.

**wholly owned foreign affiliate**
A foreign subsidiary over which an organization has complete control.

**greenfield venture**
The most risky type of direct investment, whereby a company builds a subsidiary from scratch in a foreign country.

### CONCEPT CONNECTION

*Wal-Mart, the world's largest retailer, has built a solid international presence by using a market entry strategy of* **direct investment***, including joint ventures, acquisitions, and building new operations. Although Wal-Mart's international record is full of merchandising missteps and management upheaval, the company is gradually becoming a more savvy global player. It is now the biggest retailer in Canada and Mexico, and ended its fiscal year January 31, 2004, with $47.6 billion in net international sales—18.6 percent of its total $256 billion in sales. The company has more than 1,300 stores in nine countries, including the German store in the photo, which Wal-Mart bought as part of Germany's Wertkauf hypermarket chain.*

© SPALEK/BILDERBERG

advantage is that the subsidiary is exactly what the company wants and has the potential to be highly profitable. The disadvantage is that the company has to acquire all market knowledge, materials, people, and know-how in a different culture, and mistakes are possible. An example of a greenfield venture is the Mercedes-Benz plant in Vance, Alabama. This was the first time the company had built a plant outside Germany. The venture was high risk because the new plant was building a new product (sport-utility vehicle) with a new workforce, to be sold in a foreign country.[71]

# Multinational Corporations

The size and volume of international business are so large that they are hard to comprehend. The revenue of General Electric is comparable to the *gross national income* (GNI) of South Africa. The GNI (formerly referred to as *gross national product*, or GNP) of Toyota is comparable to the size of Iran's GNI, and that of Philip Morris to the GNI of Malaysia.[72]

As discussed earlier in this chapter, a large volume of international business is being carried out in a seemingly borderless world by very large international businesses that can be thought of as *global corporations, stateless corporations,* or *transnational corporations.* In the business world, these large international firms typically are called *multinational corporations (MNCs)*, which have been the subject of enormous attention. MNCs can move a wealth of assets from country to country and influence national economies, politics, and cultures.

Although there is no precise definition, a **multinational corporation (MNC)** typically receives more than 25 percent of its total sales revenues from operations outside the parent's home country. MNCs also have the following distinctive managerial characteristics:

1. An MNC is managed as an integrated worldwide business system. This means that foreign affiliates act in close alliance and cooperation with one another. Capital, technology, and people are transferred among country affiliates. The MNC can acquire materials and manufacture parts wherever in the world it is most advantageous to do so.
2. An MNC is ultimately controlled by a single management authority that makes key strategic decisions relating to the parent and all affiliates. Although some headquarters are *binational*, such as the Royal Dutch/Shell Group, some centralization of management is required to maintain worldwide integration and profit maximization for the enterprise as a whole.
3. MNC top managers are presumed to exercise a global perspective. They regard the entire world as one market for strategic decisions, resource acquisition, location of production, advertising, and marketing efficiency.

In a few cases, the MNC management philosophy may differ from that just described. For example, some researchers have distinguished among *ethnocentric companies*, which place emphasis on their home countries, *polycentric companies*, which are oriented toward the markets of individual foreign host countries, and *geocentric companies*, which are truly world oriented and favor no specific country.[73] The truly global companies that transcend national boundaries are growing in number. These companies no longer see themselves as American, Chinese, or German; they are totally globally operating and serve a global market.

**multinational corporation (MNC)**
An organization that receives more than 25 percent of its total sales revenues from operations outside the parent company's home country; also called *global corporation* or *transnational corporation.*

# Managing in a Global Environment

Managing in a foreign country is particularly challenging. Managers working in foreign countries often face tremendous personal difficulties. In addition, they must be sensitive to cultural subtleties and understand that the ways to provide proper leadership, decision making, motivation, and control vary in different cultures. A clue to the complexity of working internationally comes from a study of the factors that contribute to global manager failures. Based on extensive interviews with global managers, researchers found that personal traits, the specific cultural context, or management mistakes made by the organization could all contribute to failure in an international assignment.[74]

## Personal Challenges for Global Managers

When managing in a foreign country, the need for personal learning and growth is critical. Managers will be most successful in foreign assignments if they are culturally flexible and easily adapt to new situations and ways of doing things. A tendency to be ethnocentric—to believe that your own country's cultural values and ways of doing things are superior—is a natural human condition. One study found that the best global managers come from countries where people have grown up learning how to understand, empathize, and work with others who are different from themselves. For example, Singaporeans consistently hear English and Chinese spoken side by side. The Dutch have to learn English, German, and French, as well as Dutch, to interact and trade with their economically dominant neighbors. English Canadians must not only be well-versed in American culture and politics, but they also have to consider the views and ideas of French Canadians, who, in turn, must learn to think like North Americans, member of a global French community, Canadians, and Quebecois.[75] People who have grown up without this kind of diversity typically have more difficulties with foreign assignments, but managers from any country can learn to break down their prejudices and appreciate other viewpoints. Although they may never come to understand the local culture like a native, they can be sensitive to cultural differences and understand that other ways of thinking and doing are also valid.

Most managers in foreign assignments face a period of homesickness, loneliness, and culture shock from being suddenly immersed in a culture with completely different languages, foods, values, beliefs, and ways of doing things. **Culture shock** refers to the frustration and anxiety that result from constantly being subjected to strange and unfamiliar cues about what to do and how to do it. Even simple, daily events can become sources of stress.[76] In addition, managers in foreign countries may have to cope with political issues, government corruption, threats of violence, and other contextual factors without the kind of support systems they would have in their home country.[77]

Preparing managers to work in foreign cultures is essential. Some companies try to give future managers exposure to foreign cultures early in their careers, when people are typically more open and adaptable. American Express Company's Travel-Related Services unit gives American business-school students summer jobs in which they work outside the United States for up to 10 weeks. Colgate-Palmolive selects 15 recent graduates each year and then provides up to 24 months of training prior to multiple overseas job stints.[78]

**culture shock**
Feelings of confusion, disorientation, and anxiety that result from being immersed in a foreign culture.

*Take A Moment*    *Go to the experiential exercise on page 146 that pertains to your global management potential.*

# Managing Cross-Culturally

Which two of the following three items go together: a panda, a banana, and a monkey? If you said a monkey and a banana, you answered like a majority of Asians; if you said a panda and a monkey, you answered like a majority of people in Western Europe and the United States. Where Westerners see distinct categories (animals), Asians see relationships (monkeys eat bananas).[79] Although this is not a definitive test, it serves to illustrate an important fact for managers. There are cultural differences in how people think and see the world, and these differences affect working relationships. To be effective on an international level, managers need to interpret the culture of the country and organization in which they are working and develop the sensitivity required to avoid making costly cultural blunders.[80]

"Americans tend to think everyone's the same," says Steven Jones of East–West Business Strategies in San Francisco. "It's a dangerous assumption."[81] One way managers prepare for foreign assignments is to understand how the country differs in terms of the Hofstede and GLOBE project discussed earlier in this chapter. These values greatly influence how a manager should interact with subordinates and colleagues in the new assignment. For example, the United States scores extremely high on individualism, and a U.S. manager working in a country such as Japan, which scores very high on collectivism, will have to modify his or her approach to leading and controlling in order to be successful. The following examples illustrate how cultural differences can be significant for expatriate managers.

## Leading

In relationship-oriented societies which rank high on collectivism, such as those in Asia, the Arab world, and Latin America, leaders should use a warm, personalized approach with employees. One of the greatest difficulties U.S. leaders have had doing business in China, for example, is failing to recognize that to the Chinese any relationship is a personal relationship.[82] Managers are expected to have periodic social visits with workers, inquiring about morale and health. Leaders should be especially careful about criticizing others. To Asians, Africans, Arabs, and Latin Americans, the loss of self-respect brings dishonor to themselves and their families. One researcher tells of a Dutch doctor managing a company clinic who had what he considered a "frank discussion" with a Chinese subordinate. The subordinate, who perceived the doctor as a father figure, took the criticism as a "savage indictment" and committed suicide.[83] Though this is an extreme example, the principle of *saving face* is highly important in some cultures.

## Decision Making

In the United States, mid-level managers may discuss a problem and give the boss a recommendation. On the other hand, managers in Iran, which reflects South Asian cultural values, expect the boss to make a decision and issue specific instructions.[84] In Mexico, employees often don't understand participatory decision making. Mexico ranks extremely high on power distance, and many workers expect managers to exercise their power in making decisions and issuing orders. American managers working in Mexico have been advised to rarely explain a decision, lest workers perceive this as a sign of weakness.[85] In contrast, managers in many Arab and African nations are expected to use consultative decision making in the extreme.

## Motivating

Motivation must fit the incentives within the culture. A recent study, for example, confirmed that intrinsic factors such as challenge, recognition, and the work itself are less effective in countries that value high power distance. It may be that workers in

# Unlocking Creative Solutions Through People

### At Microsoft UK, Work-Life Balance Pays Off

How does a company where people work long, hard hours win an award for work-life balance? It seems a paradox, but employees voted Microsoft UK the best company to work for in the UK partly because of its attention to work-life balance issues.

Steve Harvey, Microsoft UK's director of people and culture, says employees choose to work long and hard because they love technology. However, they have the flexibility to work when and where they need to. If employees want to work Sunday and go golfing on Monday, they're empowered to do so. People have laptops and broadband Internet access at home so they can work flexibly. As long as employees get their work done, no one questions them. This trust and openness is a cornerstone of Microsoft UK's culture, and a big part of the reason 89 percent of employees surveyed by the *Sunday Times* said they "love working there." Microsoft UK also incorporates other benefits, such as subsidized gym memberships, free private healthcare for life partners and families, and wellness clinics, that help employees have better, more well-rounded lives.

Harvey says people who don't fit into Microsoft's technology-loving culture quickly become isolated and leave. But the company is committed to finding and keeping the best and the brightest, which is why two of Harvey's staff members work on an initiative called *great company*. The theme runs through Harvey's entire people and culture strategy. The goal is to make sure employees understand what Microsoft stands for, where it is going, and what its long-term strategies mean at the grassroots level. Another component is an extraordinary openness and honesty. Every new employee is told, "If you see something and think it's stupid, tell me and we'll get rid of it. And what you've seen in best practice elsewhere, share it." Employees respond because they know it's not just talk; managers live up to the promise. When the company tried to take away fuel cards and get people to charge fuel to their Amex cards, negative feedback was so strong that the policy was scrapped within half an hour.

Microsoft's attention to people and culture pays off. The attrition rate of hard-to-find technical employees is at 2 percent. An astounding 93 percent of employees say they "feel proud to work for the company." Moreover, they strongly believe the company they work for "makes a positive difference to the world." With that kind of commitment, employees will keep Microsoft humming for a long time.

SOURCE: Joy Persaud, "Keep the Faithful," *People Management* (June 2003), 37–38.

these cultures perceive manager recognition and support as manipulative and therefore demotivating.[86] In places like the United States and the United Kingdom, by contrast, intrinsic factors can be highly motivating. The British outpost of global giant Microsoft incorporates intrinsic factors to keep people inspired and engaged, as described in the Unlocking Creative Solutions Through People box. In Japan, which highly values collectivism, employees are motivated to satisfy the company. A financial bonus for star performance would be humiliating to employees from Japan, China, or Ecuador. An American executive in Japan offered a holiday trip to the top salesperson, but employees were not interested. After he realized that Japanese are motivated in groups, he changed the reward to a trip for everyone if together they achieved the sales target. They did. Managers in Latin America, Africa, and the Middle East improve motivation by showing respect for employees as individuals with needs and interests outside of work.[87]

## Controlling

When things go wrong, managers in foreign countries often are unable to get rid of employees who do not work out. Consider the following research finding: When asked what to do about an employee whose work had been subpar for a year after 15 years of exemplary performance, 75 percent of Americans and Canadians said fire her; only 20 percent of Singaporeans and Koreans chose that solution.[88] In Europe,

Mexico, and Indonesia, as well, to hire and fire based on performance seems unnaturally brutal. In addition, workers in some countries are protected by strong labor laws and union rules.

In foreign cultures, managers also should not control the wrong things. A Sears manager in Hong Kong insisted that employees come to work on time instead of 15 minutes late. The employees did exactly as they were told, but they also left on time instead of working into the evening as they had previously. A lot of work was left unfinished. The manager eventually told the employees to go back to their old ways. His attempt at control had a negative effect.

This chapter has emphasized the growing importance of an international perspective on management. Successful companies are expanding their business overseas and successfully competing with foreign companies on their home turf. Major alternatives for serving foreign markets are exporting, licensing, franchising, and direct investing through joint ventures or wholly owned subsidiaries. Business in the global arena involves special risks and difficulties because of complicated economic, legal-political, and sociocultural forces. Moreover, the global environment changes rapidly, as illustrated by the emergence of the World Trade Organization, the European Union, the North American Free Trade Agreement, and other emerging trade alliances. The expansion of free-trade policies has sparked a globalization backlash among people who are fearful of losing their jobs and economic security, as well as those who believe economic globalization hurts poor people worldwide.

Much of the growth in international business has been carried out by large businesses called MNCs. These large companies exist in an almost borderless world, encouraging the free flow of ideas, products, manufacturing, and marketing among countries to achieve the greatest efficiencies. Managers in MNCs as well as those in much smaller companies doing business internationally face many challenges. Managers often experience culture shock when transferred to foreign countries. They must learn to be sensitive to cultural differences and tailor their management style to the culture. Social and cultural values differ widely across cultures, and these influence appropriate patterns of leadership, decision making, motivation, and managerial control.

International markets provide many opportunities but are also fraught with difficulty, as Wal-Mart, described at the beginning of this chapter, discovered. The company first began expanding internationally nearly 15 years ago and has learned a great deal about doing business in foreign countries. However, its success in some markets led it to underestimate the potential difficulties it would face when entering Germany. Managers are having to step back and reevaluate the competition, the cultural clashes, and the regulatory hurdles they face. They believe the company's troubles there can be overcome with time and experience. The German situation may have taught Wal-Mart executives to take a more cautious approach as the company moves into Japan. In that country, where Wal-Mart faces tremendous cultural, societal, and organizational obstacles, managers see a slow, step-by-step process as the best route toward eventual success. Wal-Mart chose to work with a local partner, Seiyu, whose name still remains on stores. The American giant is staying in the shadows for now, focusing on getting all its systems in place and training local managers. It goofed in Germany by rushing to overhaul stores and lower prices before basic operational systems were ready. The Japanese managers are helping Wal-Mart understand and respond to local needs, and the subtle, patient approach is also enabling executives to learn through trial and error.[89] For a large, rich company like Wal-Mart, managers can afford to lose money internationally as the price of learning. Smaller organizations have to be even more cautious and well-prepared when entering the global marketplace.

*Manager's Solution*

# Discussion Questions

1. Why do you think international businesses traditionally prefer to operate in industrialized countries? Discuss.
2. What considerations in recent years have led international businesses to expand their activities into less-developed countries?
3. What policies or actions would you recommend to an entrepreneurial business wanting to do business in Europe?
4. What steps could a company take to avoid making product design and marketing mistakes when introducing new products into a foreign country?
5. Compare the advantages associated with the foreign-market entry strategies of exporting, licensing, and wholly owned subsidiaries.
6. Should a multinational corporation operate as an integrated, worldwide business system, or would it be more effective to let each subsidiary operate autonomously?
7. What does it mean to say that the world is becoming "borderless"? That large companies are "stateless"?
8. What might managers do to avoid making mistakes concerning control and decision making when operating in a foreign culture?
9. What is meant by the cultural values of individualism and masculinity/femininity? How might these values affect organization design and management processes?
10. How do you think trade alliances such as NAFTA and the EU may affect you as a future manager?

# Management in Practice: Experiential Exercise

**Test your Global Potential**

A global environment requires that American managers learn to deal effectively with people in other countries. The assumption that foreign business leaders behave and negotiate in the same manner as Americans is false. How well prepared are you to live with globalization? Consider the following.

**Definitely No**          **Definitely Yes**
    1        2        3        4        5

**Are you guilty of**

1. Impatience? Do you think "Time is money" or "Let's get to the point"?

    1        2        3        4        5

2. Having a short attention span, bad listening habits, or being uncomfortable with silence?

    1        2        3        4        5

3. Being somewhat argumentative, sometimes to the point of belligerence?

    1        2        3        4        5

4. Ignorance about the world beyond your borders?    1        2        3        4        5

5. Weakness in foreign languages?

    1        2        3        4        5

6. Placing emphasis on short-term success?

    1        2        3        4        5

7. Believing that advance preparations are less important than negotiations themselves?

    1        2        3        4        5

8. Being legalistic? Of believing "A deal is a deal," regardless of changing circumstances?

    1        2        3        4        5

9.  Having little interest in seminars on the subject of globalization, failing to browse through libraries or magazines on international topics, not interacting with foreign students or employees?

    1     2     3     4     5

## Total Score _____

If you scored less than 27, congratulations. You have the temperament and interest to do well in a global company. If you scored more than 27, it's time to consider a change. Regardless of your score, go back over each item and make a plan of action to correct deficiencies indicated by answers of 4 or 5 to any question.

Source: Reprinted by permission of the publisher from Cynthia Barmun and Netasha Wolninsky, "Why Americans Fail at Overseas Negotiations," *Management Review* (October 1989), 55–57, © 1989 American Management Association, New York. All rights reserved.

# Management in Practice: Ethical Dilemma

## Quality or Closing

On the way home from the launch party celebrating Plaxcor Metals' entrance into the international arena, Donald Fields should have been smiling. He was part of the team that had closed the deal to sell component parts to Asian Business Machine, after his company had spent millions trying to break into this lucrative market. There were several more deals riding on the successful outcome of the first international venture.

The expansion into new markets was critical to Plaxcor's survival. As President Leslie Hanson had put it, "If we aren't global within five years, we may as well close up shop." Fields was tense because of news he learned tonight: intense bidding for the first sale and several last-minute changes requested by the customer had forced Plaxcor to heavily modify its production process. The production manager had confided that "the product is a mess but still better than most of the competition." He went on to assure him that, although well below normal standards, the variability would "probably not cause any problems" and could be worked out after a few more orders.

Fields had spent the last few months selling Plaxcor on its quality reputation. He knew they could probably get by with the first runs and meet the opening deadline. He was afraid that telling the customer of the potential problems or extending the deadline would risk not only this deal but pending projects as well. But he knew if problems arose with the products, Plaxcor's future in the Asian market would be bleak. Donald Fields wasn't sure Plaxcor could afford to gamble its entrance in the international market on a substandard product.

## What Do You Do?

1.  Ask the customer for an extension of the deadline, and bring the products up to standard.
2.  Gamble on the first runs, and hope the products don't fail.
3.  Inform the customer of the problem, and let the customer make the decision.

# Surf the Net

1. **Languages on the Web.** According to a recent Fortune Global 500 listing Hewlett-Packard was ranked as the 47th largest company in the world based on sales revenues. Visit Hewlett-Packard's home page at *http://www.hp.com* to see how this multinational company provides information for its many customers throughout the world. Check out the links to its pages for countries in the Americas, Asia, and Europe. Compare how other Global 500 companies in the computers and office equipment industry provide access to information for their non-English-speaking customers, for example, IBM *http://www.ibm.com* and Fujitsu *http://www.fujitsu.com*. Choose the Web site you thought was most effective in providing multi-language access and explain your choice.

2. **Exchange Rates.** Visit a Web site, such as the CNN Financial Network at *http://cnnfn.com/markets/currencies* to find currency exchange rates. If the Web site provides a currency converter, determine how much $100 in U.S. currency is worth in each of the following currencies:

   Chilean Peso
   Japanese Yen
   Euro
   United Kingdom Pound

   If no currency converter is available, simply list the exchange rate per U.S. dollar for each of the above currencies.

3. **The Multinational Corporation.** To become more knowledgeable about the largest companies in the world, check out the Fortune Global 500 listing available at *http://pathfinder.com/fortune/global500/500list.html*. Answer the following questions: (a) What countries are represented in the top ten? (b) Which country has the most companies represented in the top ten? (c) Select three industries of interest to you, and identify the top three companies and their home countries in each industry. (d) After looking over the information available at this Web site, identify one fact that was particularly interesting to you.

# Case for Critical Analysis

## Unocal Corporation

Unocal Corporation seems an unlikely candidate for a high-risk global rampage. Consumers everywhere recognize the ubiquitous 76 logo of this quintessential California oil company. They know it as the nation's 11th largest petroleum retailer, with a prestigious downtown headquarters and important role as a Los Angeles civic booster. Casting aside its reputation as a conservative company with tightly defined domestic markets and focused petroleum interests in California, Unocal has rapidly transformed itself into an international company with major investments in some of the world's least-developed economies. It has also become a prominent topic among political activists, human-rights groups, and foreign policy teams. Some observers say that Unocal will become a casualty of its high-risk policies.

In 1995, immediately after becoming chairman of Unocal, Roger Beach began to sell off domestic retail assets and eliminate exploration and refining activities in the United States. Resources shifted to unlikely places where few other major oil producers had risked operations—places such as Myanmar, Turkmenistan, Uzbekistan, and the strife-ridden Balkans. Beach turned up the heat on company investments in Indonesian oil fields, launched full-service energy subsidiaries through government alliances in Thailand, broadened holdings in Malaysia, and began negotiations for an integrated refining and retailing enterprise in Pakistan. Nearly 40 percent of Unocal's exploration and extraction budget was thrown into these emerging markets, much of it pinpointed for very high risk locations in the former Soviet republics and the Persian subcontinent.

Why take these risks? Beach answers that Unocal, unable to compete head-to-head with the oil industry giants for capital markets, decided to create an extremely attractive strategic package of full-service energy production in countries grasping to develop infrastructure. "What every government likes about Unocal's strategy is one stop shopping; one group able to take the whole project from development to the marketing end," Beach said. "We have become partners in their development and as important to them as they are to us." The Unocal strategy defies normal industry trends based on distributing huge capital investments to tie up oil reserves and mineral rights, then cutting deals for operations. Instead, Unocal comes in the front door with packaged energy services ranging from turning the first spade of dirt on exploration to delivering power to the end user, and that proposal includes oil, gas, or electric power generation.

Beach sees far less risk than industry analysts perceive in the emerging markets. The dangers of war, political upheaval, and currency fluctuations are clear and present, yet the company says it has hedged against these threats by diversifying investments. By 2000, it intends to have nearly 80 percent of its exploration and production capabilities in these underdeveloped areas, and by the end of 1996, it had almost totally abandoned domestic exploration, having sold off nearly $3 billion in assets and oil-field holdings in California. However, according to Beach, success will depend on creating a globally managed company capable of understanding and participating in foreign market environments. Consequently, in 1996, he initiated a major transformation in Unocal's management systems, beginnning by relocating its headquarters from its stately downtown offices to a small, highly efficient suite near the Los Angeles International Airport. Midlevel managers were either repositioned in regional offices, such as Singapore, Istanbul, or Jakarta, or they left the company. The executive core, which had been distinctly Los Angeleno in character, gained a multicultural character, representing Eastern European and Asian group alliances. Subsidiaries in Jakarta, Thailand and Myanmar took on local names and corporate identities, shedding their American profiles, and Unocal's many foriegn alliances have made it part of the communities in which it operates.

In Thailand, Unocal has worked on the country's privatization plan to convert its Petroleum Authority of Thailand (PTT) operations into privately owned and operated international oil services. Unocal and the PTT have begun to build pipelines in the Gulf of Thailand linking Unocal's hydrocarbon fields in the nation's rugged peninsula, and a joint venture in Malaysia has begun to open regional energy markets from Myanmar to the Phillipines. Surface evaluations have hailed this consortium as a master stroke of strategy; however, related activities have exposed Unocal to strong criticism. Unocal became the largest single U.S. investor in Myanmar as part of the expansion, but Myanmar's military government has languished in political and economic isolation as a result of U.S legislation aimed at boycotting the country for its unacceptable human-rights practices. Political activists in more than a dozen U.S. states have won passage of legislation barring imports from Myanmar and outlawing private investments there by U.S. firms. Municipal governments in five states have passed boycott laws, as well, and Unocal, together with PepsiCo and several other American companies operating in Myanmar, have become major targets for international pressure groups. PepsiCo bowed to the pressure and recently moved out of Myanmar, but Unocal has flatly refused to budge.

The company's insistence on remaining in Myanmar, however, is not a vote in support of the country's human-rights record. Indeed, Unocal would find it difficult to withdraw, because it has formed an equity agreement with the giant French petrochemical company Total, which also has substantial pipeline investments with Unocal in the Persian Gulf and southern Asia. Unocal's contracts with Total make it a de facto partner of the French government. Moreover, Unocal has invested in public and private interests in Myanmar that spread to five other major Southeast Asian states. But a Unocal representative cites the importance of the company's role in helping the nation's development. "To withdraw and isolate Myanmar would have no effect. Questionable human-rights leadership and political practices would continue and perhaps proliferate," she said. "On the other hand, our strength and the fact that we can provide meaningful jobs and ethical international business, encourages changes for the good. Even if every American firm vacated, firms from other nations would welcome the chance to develop Myanmar without American competition."

That position doesn't relieve the political or financial risk to Unocal. Ethics and U.S. policies aside, Myanmar lacks a strong track record for keeping its promises. As a closed military state, self-isolated for ideological reasons since the end of World War II, it has few friends anywhere in the world. For years, it was linked to the Soviet Union for aid and military support, and Myanmar backed insurgent forces in several neighboring civil conflicts. These situations did not endear the government to potential regional economic allies. However, the country is strategically positioned within the Southeast Asian theater, and it has attracted consideration, with much controversy, for membership in ASEAN.

Unocal holds a rather exposed position in the country, as it does in Uzbekistan, Turkmenistan, and the Balkans. An American company without the legal or political support of its home government can expect little help should the host government decide to freeze its assets, bar currency repatriation, or resort to outright expropriation. Meanwhile, Unocal has tied up several billion dollars in the region while maintaining no safety net at home. Indeed, it faces potentially costly threats from home, and if the company is pushed to the wall by legislation, the chairman says, he will take Unocal out of U.S. control.

## Questions

1.  What market entry strategies has Unocal used, based on the activities described in the case?

Would you classify Unocal as a multinational corporation (MNC)? Why or why not?

2.  Identify and discuss the various types of risks faced by Unocal in emerging markets (consider the economic, legal-political, and sociocultural environment). Which risks seem most threatening to the company?

3.  What do you think of the Unocal representative's statement that "to withdraw and isolate Myanmar would have no effect" regarding that country's poor human-rights record? Do you believe U.S. companies should stay in such countries in the hope of improving the ethical climate? Discuss.

Source: "Unocal Corporation," from *International Management: Text and Cases*, 143–145, David H. Holt, Copyright © 1998 by Harcourt, Inc., reprinted by permission of the publisher.

# Endnotes

1.  Richard Ernsberger Jr., "Wal-Mart World; Can the Arkansas Giant Export Its Price-Cutting Culture Around the World?" *Newsweek* (May 20, 2002), 50; Isabelle de Pommereau, "Wal-Mart Lesson: Smiling Service Won't Win Germans; The Retailer Closed Two Stores in Germany," *The Christian Science Monitor* (October 17, 2002), 7; Ann Zimmerman and Martin Fackler, "Pacific Aisles; Wal-Mart's Foray Into Japan Spurs A Retail Upheaval," *The Wall Street Journal* (September 19, 2003), A1; and http://www.walmartstores.com accessed on February 13, 2004.

2.  David Kirkpatrick, "One World—For Better or Worse," *Fortune* (November 26, 2001), 74–75.

3.  Nilly Ostro-Landau and Hugh D. Menzies, "The New World Economic Order," in *International Business 97/98, Annual Editions*, Fred Maidment, ed. (Guilford, Conn.: Dushkin Publishing Group, 1997), 24–30; and Murray Weidenbaum, "American Isolationism versus the Global Economy," in *International Business 97/98, Annual Editions*, Fred Maidment, ed. (Guilford Conn.: Dushkin Publishing Group, 1997), 12–15.

4.  Jason Dean, "Upgrade Plan: Long a Low-Tech Player, China Sets Its Sights on Chip Making," *The Wall Street Journal* (February 17, 2004), A1.

5.  Joseph B. White, "There Are No German or U.S. Companies, Only Successful Ones," *The Wall Street Journal* (May 7, 1998), A1.

6.  Jane L. Levere, "A Small Company, A Global Approach," *The New York Times* (January 1, 2004), http://www.nytimes.com/2004

7.  Pete Engardio, with Robert D. Hof, Elisabeth Malkin, Neil Gross, and Karen Lowry Miller, "High-Tech Jobs All Over the Map," *BusinessWeek/21st Century Capitalism* (November 18, 1994), 112–117.

8.  Raju Narisetti and Jonathan Friedland, "Diaper Wars of P&G and Kimberly-Clark Now Heat Up in Brazil," *The Wall Street Journal* (June 4, 1997), and Stephen Baker, "The Bridges Steel is Building," *BusinessWeek* (June 2, 1997), 39.

9.  Figures provided by CXO Media, reported in Steve Ulfelder, "All the Web's a Stage," *CIO* (October 1, 2000), 133–142.

10. Lisa Bannon and Charles Vitzthum, "Small World: Mattel Hits Big by Marketing Same Toys around the Globe," *The Wall Street Journal* (April 29, 2003), A1, A12.

11. Nancy J. Adler, *International Dimensions of Organizational Behavior*, 4th ed. (Cincinnati, Ohio: South-Western, 2002), 8–9; William Holstein, Stanley Reed, Jonathan

Kapstein, Todd Vogel, and Joseph Weber, "The Stateless Corporation," *BusinessWeek* (May 14, 1990), 98–105; and Richard L. Daft, *Organization Theory and Design* (Cincinnati, Ohio: South-Western 2005).

12. Christopher Bartlett, *Managing Across Borders*, 2d ed. (Boston, MA: Harvard Business School Press, 1998); Eric Matson, "How to Globalize Yourself," *Fast Company* (April–May 1997), 133–139; and Gunnar Beeth, "Multicultural Managers Wanted," *Management Review* (May 1997), 17–21.

13. Holstein et al., "The Stateless Corporation"; Carol Matlack, "Nestlé Is Starting to Slim Down at Last," *BusinessWeek* (October 27, 2003), 56; Carla Rapoport, "Nestlé's Brand Building Machine," *Fortune* (September 19, 1994), 147–156; and Karl Moore, "Great Global Managers," *Across the Board* (May–June 2003), 40–43.

14. Cited in Gary Ferraro, *Cultural Anthropology: An Applied Perspective*, 3d ed. (Belmont, Calif.: West/Wadsworth, 1998), 68.

15. Jim Holt, "Gone Global?" *Management Review* (March 2000), 13.

16. Ibid.

17. "Slogans Often Lose Something in Translation," *The New Mexican* (July 3, 1994), F1, F2.

18. Louis S. Richman, "Global Growth is on a Tear," in *International Business 97/98, Annual Editions*, Fred Maidment, ed., (Guilford, Conn.: Dushkin Publishing Group, 1997), 6–11.

19. International Data Corporation, reported in Ian Katz and Elisabeth Malkin, "Battle for the Latin American Net," *BusinessWeek* (November 1, 1999), 194–200.

20. Katz and Malkin, "Battle for the Latin American Net"; Pamela Drukerman and Nick Wingfield, "Lost in Translation: AOL's Big Assault on Latin America Hits Snags in Brazil," *The Wall Street Journal*, (July 11, 2000), A1.

21. Amal Kumar Jaj, "United Technologies Looks Far from Home for Growth," *The Wall Street Journal* (May 26, 1994), B4.

22. Marcelo Jelen, "Latin America: Cell Phones—From Status Symbol to Everyman's Tool," *Global Information Network* (December 10, 2003), 1.

23. Kathleen Deveny, "McWorld?" *BusinessWeek* (October 13, 1986), 78–86; and Andrew E. Serwer, "McDonald's Conquers the World," *Fortune* (October 17, 1994), 103–116.

24. David W. Conklin, "Analyzing and Managing Country Risks," *Ivey Business Journal* (January–February 2002), 37–41.

25. Bruce Kogut, "Designing Global Strategies: Profiting from Operational Flexibility," *Sloan Management Review* 27 (Fall 1985), 27–38.

26. Mark Fitzpatrick, "The Definition and Assessment of Political Risk in International Business: A Review of the Literature," *Academy of Management Review* 8 (1983), 249–254.

27. Kevin Sullivan, "Kidnapping Is Growth Industry in Mexico; Businessmen Targeted in Climate of Routine Ransoms, Police Corruption," *The Washington Post* (September 17, 2002), A1.

28. Brian O'Keefe, "Global Brands," *Fortune* (November 26, 2001), 102–110.

29. Conklin, "Analyzing and Managing Country Risks," Nicolas Checa, John Maguire, and Jonathan Barney, "The New World Disorder," *Harvard Business Review* (August 2003), 71–79.

30. See Conklin, "Analyzing and Managing Country Risks."

31. O'Keefe, "Global Brands."

32. Brandon Mitchener, "Border Crossings," *The Wall Street Journal* (November 22, 1999), R41.

33. Barbara Whitaker, "The Web Makes Going Global Easy, Until You Try to Do It," *The New York Times* (September 2000), 20.

34. Geert Hofstede, "The Interaction between National and Organizational Value Systems," *Journal of Management Studies* 22 (1985), 347–357; and Geert Hofstede, "The Cultural Relativity of the Quality of Life Concept," *Academy of Management Review* 9 (1984), 389–398.

35. Geert Hofstede, "Cultural Constraints in Management Theory," *Academy of Management Executive* 7 (1993), 81–94; and G. Hofstede and M. H. Bond, "The Confucian Connection: From Cultural Roots to Economic Growth," *Organizational Dynamics* 16 (1988), 4–21.

36. "Retrospective: *Culture's Consequences*," a collection of articles focusing on Hofstede's work, appeared in *The Academy of Management Executive* 18, no. 1 (February 2004), 72–93. See also Michele J. Gelfand, D. P. S. Bhawuk, Lisa H. Nishii, and David J. Bechtold, "Individualism and Collectivism," in R. J. House, et al., eds., *Culture, Leadership and Organizations: The Globe Study of 62 Societies* (Thousand Oaks, CA: Sage, 2004).

37. This discussion is based on Mansour Javidan and Robert J. House, "Cultural Acumen for the Global Manager: Lessons from Project GLOBE," *Organizational Dynamics* 29, no. 4 (2001), 289–305; and R. J. House, M. Javidan, Paul Hanges, and Peter Dorfman, "Understanding Cultures and Implicit Leadership Theories Across the Globe: An Introduction to Project GLOBE," *Journal of World Business* 37 (2002), 3–10.

38. Chantell E. Nicholls, Henry W. Lane, and Mauricio Brehm Brechu, "Taking Self-Managed Teams to Mexico," *Academy of Management Executive* 13, no. 2 (1999), 15–27; Carl F. Fey and Daniel R. Denison, "Organizational Culture and Effectiveness: Can American Theory Be Applied in Russia?" *Organization Science* 14, no. 6 (November–December 2003),

686–706; Ellen F. Jackofsky, John W. Slocum, Jr., and Sara J. McQuaid, "Cultural Values and the CEO: Alluring Companions?" Academy of Management Executive 2 (1988), 39–49.

39. Terence Jackson, "The Management of People Across Cultures: Valuing People Differently," *Human Resource Management* 41, no. 4 (Winter 2002), 455–475.

40. Carol Hymowitz, "Companies Go Global, But Many Managers Just Don't Travel Well," (In the Lead column) *The Wall Street Journal* (August 15, 2000), B1.

41. Orla Sheehan, "Managing a Multinational Corporation: Tomorrow's Decision Makers Speak Out," *Fortune* (August 24, 1992), 233; Jonathan Friedland and Louise Lee, "The Wal-Mart Way Sometimes Gets Lost in Translation Overseas," *The Wall Street Journal* (October 8, 1997), A1, A12.

42. Carol Matlack with Pallave Gogoi, "What's This? The French Love McDonald's?" *Business Week* (January 13, 2003), 50; and Shirley Leung, "'McHaute Cuisine' Armchairs, TVs, and Expresso—Is It McDonald's?" *The Wall Street Journal* (August 30, 2002), A1, A6.

43. Michael R. Czinkota, Ilkka A. Ronkainen, Michael H. Moffett, and Eugene O. Moynihan, *Global Business* (Fort Worth, Tex.: The Dryden Press, 1995), 151; and Robert D. Gatewood, Robert R. Taylor, and O. C. Ferrell, *Management* (Burr Ridge, Ill.: Irwin, 1995), 131–132.

44. "For Richer, for Poorer," *The Economist* (December 1993), 66; Richard Harmsen, "The Uruguay Round: A Boon for the World Economy," *Finance & Development* (March 1995), 24–26; Salil S. Pitroda, "From GATT to WTO: The Institutionalization of World Trade," *Harvard International Review* (Spring 1995), 46–47 and 66–67; and David H. Holt, *International Management: Text and Cases* (Fort Worth: Dryden, 1998). *Also see* http://www.wto.org, accessed on February 16, 2004.

45. This discussion of WTO is based on William J. Kehoe, "GATT and WTO Facilitating Global Trade," *Journal of Global Business* (Spring 1998), 67–76.

46. "The History of the European Union," http://www.europa.eu.int/abc/history/index_en.htm, accessed on February 16, 2004.

47. Alan Charles Raul, "World to America: Zip It!" *e-Company Now* (July 2001), 26–29.

48. James Kanter, "EU Watchdog Gets More Teeth: New Powers to Enforce Competition Are Set to Go Into Effect," *The Wall Street Journal* (January 23, 2004), A10.

49. Justin Fox, "Introducing the Euro," *Fortune* (December 19, 2001), 229–236.

50. Lynda Radosevich, "New Money," *CIO Enterprise*, Section 2 (April 15, 1998), 54–58.

51. Barbara Rudolph, "Megamarket," *Time* (August 10, 1992), 43–44.

52. Tapan Munroe, "NAFTA Still a Work in Progress," *Knight Ridder/Tribune News Service* (January 9,

2004), http://www.contracostatimes.com; and J. S. McClenahan, "NAFTA Works," *IW* (January 10, 2000), 5–6.

53. Amy Barrett, "It's a Small (Business) World," *Business Week* (April 17, 1995), 96–101.

54. Eric Alterman, "A Spectacular Success?" *The Nation* (February 2, 2004), 10; Jeff Faux, "NAFTA at 10: Where Do We Go From Here?" *The Nation* (February 2, 2004), 11; Geri Smith and Cristina Lindblad, "Mexico: Was NAFTA Worth It? A Tale of What Free Trade Can and Cannot Do," *Business Week* (December 22, 2003) 66; Jeffrey Sparshott, "NAFTA Gets Mixed Reviews," *The Washington Times* (December 18, 2003), C10; and Munroe, "NAFTA Is Still Work in Progress."

55. Munroe, "NAFTA Is Still Work In Progress;" Jeffrey Sparshott, "NAFTA Gets Mixed Reviews," *The Washington Times* (December 18, 2003), C10; Amy Borrus, "A Free-Trade Milestone, with Many More Miles to Go," *Business Week* (August 24, 1992), 30–31.

56. C. Sims, "Chile Will Enter a Big South American Free-Trade Bloc," *The New York Times* (June 26, 1996), C2; "NAFTA: Five-Year Anniversary," *Latin Trade* (January 1999), 44–45; and Stephen P. Robbins and Mary Coulter, *Management*, 7th ed. (Upper Saddle River, NJ: Prentice-Hall, 2002), 92.

57. This review is based on Jyoti Thottam, "Is Your Job Going Abroad?" *Time* (March 1, 2004), 26–36; and Pete Engardio, Aaron Bernstein, and Manjeet Kripalani, "Is Your Job Next?" *Business Week* (February 3, 2003), 50–60.

58. Reported in "IBM Data Give Rare Look at Sensitive 'Offshoring' Plans," *CNNMoney* (January 19, 2004), http://www.money.cnn.com accessed on January 19, 2004.

59. Thottam, "Is Your Job Going Abroad?"

60. Jerry Useem, "There's Something Happening Here," *Fortune* (May 15, 2000); Paul Magnusson, "Meet Free Traders' Worst Nightmare," *Business Week* (March 20, 2000), 113–118; Elisabeth Malkin, "Backlash," *Business Week* (April 24, 2000), 38–44.

61. See, for example, Alan Greenspan, "International Trade: Globalization vs. Protectionism," address printed in *Vital Speeches of the Day* (April 15, 2001) 386–388.

62. Michael Schroeder and Timothy Aeppel, "Skilled Workers Sway Politicians with Fervor Against Free Trade," *The Wall Street Journal* (December 10, 2003), A1, A11.

63. Jonathan Moore with Bruce Einhorn, "A Business-to-Business E-Boom," *Business Week* (October 25, 1999), 62.

64. Malkin, "Backlash"; Engardio et al., "Is Your Job Next?"

65. Jean Kerr, "Export Strategies," *Small Business Reports* (May 1989), 20–25.

66. Robert S. Greenberger, "As U.S. Exports Rise, More Workers Benefit," *The Wall Street Journal* (September 10, 1997), A1.

67. Kathryn Rudie Harrigan, "Managing Joint Ventures," *Management Review* (February 1987), 24–41; and Therese R. Revesz and Mimi Cauley de Da La Sierra, "Competitive Alliances: Forging Ties Abroad," *Management Review* (March 1987), 57–59.

68. "Importing Can Help a Firm Expand and Diversify," *Nation's Business* (January 1995), 11; Matlack, "Nestlé Is Starting to Slim Down."

69. Katz and Malkin, "Battle for the Latin American Net."

70. Karen Lowry Miller, with Bill Javetski, Peggy Simpson, and Tim Smart, "Europe: The Push East," *BusinessWeek* (November 7, 1994), 48–49.

71. David Woodruff, with Karen Lowry Miller, "Mercedes' Maverick in Alabama," *BusinessWeek* (September 11, 1995), 64–65; and Michael A. Hitt, R. Duane Ireland, and Robert E. Hoskisson, *Strategic Management: Competitiveness and Globalization* (St. Paul, Minn.: West, 1995).

72. Company sales figures are from data reported in "The Global Giants," *The Wall Street Journal* (October 14, 2002), R10, R11. GNI data are from the World Development Indicators database, World Bank, August 2002, http://www.worldbank.org/data/ accessed on November 15, 2002.

73. Howard V. Perlmutter, "The Tortuous Evolution of the Multinational Corporation," *Columbia Journal of World Business* (January–February 1969), 9–18; and Youram Wind, Susan P. Douglas, and Howard V. Perlmutter, "Guidelines for Developing International Marketing Strategies," *Journal of Marketing* (April 1973), 14–23.

74. Morgan W. McCall Jr. and George P. Hollenbeck, "Global Fatalities: When International Executives Derail," *Ivey Business Journal* (May–June 2002), 75–78.

75. Karl Moore, "Great Global Managers," *Across the Board* (May–June 2003), 40–43.

76. James L. Gibson, John M. Ivancevich, and James H. Donnelly, Jr., *Organizations*, 8th ed. (Burr Ridge, Ill.: Irwin, 1994), 83.

77. McCall and Hollenbeck, "Global Fatalities."

78. Joann S. Lublin, "Younger Managers Learn Global Skills," *The Wall Street Journal* (March 31, 1992), B1.

79. Richard E. Nisbett, *The Geography of Thought: How Asians and Westerners Think Differently . . . and Why* (New York: The Free Press, 2003), reported in Sharon Begley, "East Vs. West: One Sees the Big Picture, The Other is Focused" (Science Journal column), *The Wall Street Journal* (March 28, 2003), B1.

80. Robert T. Moran and John R. Riesenberger, *The Global Challenge* (London: McGraw-Hill, 1994), 251–262.

81. Patricia M. Carey, "Culture Club," *Working Woman* (July/August 1999), 71–72.

82. Valerie Frazee, "Keeping Up on Chinese Culture," *Global Workforce* (October 1996), 16–17; and Jack Scarborough, "Comparing Chinese and Western Cultural Roots: Why 'East Is East and . . .'" *Business Horizons* (November/December 1998), 15–24.

83. Fons Trompenaars, *Riding the Waves of Culture: Understanding Diversity in Global Business* (Burr Ridge, Ill.: Irwin, 1994).

84. Mansour Javidan and Ali Dastmalchian, "Culture and Leadership In Iran: The Land of Individual Achievers, Strong Family Ties, and Powerful Elite," *Academy of Management Executive* 17, no. 4 (2003), 127–142.

85. Randall S. Schuler, Susan E. Jackson, Ellen Jackofsky, and John W. Slocum, Jr., "Managing Human Resources in Mexico: A Cultural Understanding," *Business Horizons* (May–June 1996), 55–61.

86. Xu Huang and Evert Van De Vliert, "Where Intrinsic Job Satisfaction Fails to Work: National Moderators of Intrinsic Motivation," *Journal of Organizational Behavior* 24 (2003), 159–179.

87. Shari Caudron, "Lessons from HR Overseas," *Personnel Journal* (February 1995), 88.

88. Reported in Begley, "East Vs. West."

89. Ken Belson, "Wal-Mart Hopes It Won't Be Lost in Translation," *The New York Times* (December 14, 2003), 1; Ann Zimmerman and Martin Fackler, "Pacific Aisles: Wal-Mart's Foray Into Japan Spurs a Retail Upheaval," *The Wall Street Journal* (September 19, 2003), A1, A6.

# Chapter 5

# Ethics and Social Responsibility

## LEARNING OBJECTIVES

*After studying this chapter, you should be able to:*

1. Define ethics and explain how ethical behavior relates to behavior governed by law and free choice.

2. Explain the utilitarian, individualism, moral-rights, and justice approaches for evaluating ethical behavior.

3. Describe how both individual and organizational factors shape ethical decision making.

4. Define corporate social responsibility and how to evaluate it along economic, legal, ethical, and discretionary criteria.

5. Describe four organizational approaches to environmental responsibility, and explain the philosophy of sustainability.

6. Discuss how ethical organizations are created through ethical leadership and organizational structures and systems.

7. Identify important stakeholders for an organization and discuss how managers balance the interests of various stakeholders.

In the early 1990s, Jeffrey Swartz, chief operating officer (now CEO) of Timberland Co. began transforming Timberland into a company known as much for philanthropy as it is for its boots. But Swartz found himself in a quandary when one of the company's bankers implied that the focus on philanthropy was hurting the company and its stakeholders. Swartz's transformation began when City Year, a nonprofit agency involved in community projects such as violence prevention and AIDs education, asked for boots for its workers. Swartz convinced other Timberland executives to answer the call. Over time, Timberland provided free boots and uniforms for about 10,000 people. Visiting some of the community projects, Swartz was deeply moved by what volunteers were accomplishing. "I saw what real power was that day," Swartz recalls. "I didn't realize how hungry I was for that kind of purpose." Timberland began shutting down operations one day each year so the company's thousands of employees could get paid to take part in a variety of company-sponsored philanthropic projects—building homeless shelters or cleaning up playgrounds. The company also started giving employees 16 hours of paid leave annually to volunteer at charities of their choosing. But the emphasis on social responsibility doesn't come cheap. The all-day event alone costs about $2 million a year in lost sales, project expenses, and wages for employees. When Timberland's profits were soaring, that seemed fine, but then the company hit a rough patch. It reported its first operating loss since going public, laid off some employees, and shipped some work overseas to cut costs. One of Timberland's bankers bluntly told Swartz that the company needed to "cut this civic stuff out and get back to business." Swartz began wondering if the banker was right. Maybe managers were failing the organization and its stakeholders by plowing too many resources into philanthropic activities.[1]

## Take A Moment

If you were in this position, would you cut out the charity work and focus everything on returning Timberland to profitability? If charity begins at home, is Timberland being ethical by spending money for philanthropic activities at the same time it is shipping jobs overseas and laying off workers?

The situation at Timberland illustrates how difficult ethical issues can be and symbolizes the growing importance of discussing ethics and social responsibility. Managers often face situations where it is difficult to determine what is right. Thus, ethics has always been a concern for managers. However, in recent years, widespread moral lapses and corporate financial scandals have brought the topic to the forefront. Corporations are rushing to adopt codes of ethics, strengthen ethical and legal safeguards, and develop socially responsible policies. Every decade sees its share of corporate, political, and social villains, but the pervasiveness of ethical lapses in the early 2000s was astounding. It began with Enron, America's seventh-largest corporation in mid-2000. The once-mighty company was essentially destroyed by a combination of deceit, arrogance, shady financial dealings, and inappropriate accounting practices that inflated earnings and hid debt. Soon, the names of other once-revered companies became synonymous with greed, dishonesty, and financial chicanery: Arthur Andersen, Adelphia, WorldCom, Tyco, HealthSouth. A poll taken in the fall of 2002 found that 79 percent of respondents believe questionable business practices are widespread. Fewer than one-third said they think most CEOs are honest.[2] Moreover, more than 20 percent of U.S. employees surveyed report having first-hand knowledge of managers making false or misleading promises to customers, discriminating in hiring or promotions, and violating employees' rights.[3]

However, there is also positive news to report. The actor Paul Newman and his friend A. E. Hotchner started a company, Newman's Own, that makes salad dressings, spaghetti sauce, and other foods and gives all the profits to charity. Boston's Bain & Co. set up a nonprofit called Bridgespan Group that gives charitable organizations world-class consulting advice at steep discounts. And Computer Associates each year pairs 75 employee volunteers with 75 employees from major customers to build playgrounds in needy areas.[4] A number of companies have begun tying managers' pay to ethical factors such as how well they treat employees or how effectively they live up to the stated corporate values.

This chapter expands on the ideas about environment, corporate culture, and the international environment discussed in Chapters 3 and 4. We will first focus on the topic of ethical values, which builds on the idea of corporate culture. Then we will examine corporate relationships to the external environment as reflected in social responsibility. Ethics and social responsibility are hot topics in corporate America. This chapter discusses fundamental approaches that help managers think through ethical issues. Understanding ethical approaches helps managers build a solid foundation on which to base future decision making.

# What Is Managerial Ethics?

**ethics**
The code of moral principles and values that govern the behaviors of a person or group with respect to what is right or wrong.

Ethics is difficult to define in a precise way. In a general sense, **ethics** is the code of moral principles and values that governs the behaviors of a person or group with respect to what is right or wrong. Ethics sets standards as to what is good or bad in conduct and decision making.[5] Ethics deals with internal values that are a part of corporate culture and shapes decisions concerning social responsibility with respect to the external environment. An ethical issue is present in a situation when the actions of a person or organization may harm or benefit others.[6]

Ethics can be more clearly understood when compared with behaviors governed by laws and by free choice. Exhibit 5.1 illustrates that human behavior falls into three categories. The first is codified law, in which values and standards are written into the legal system and enforceable in the courts. In this area, lawmakers have ruled that people and corporations must behave in a certain way, such as obtaining

Exhibit 5.1

Three Domains of Human Action

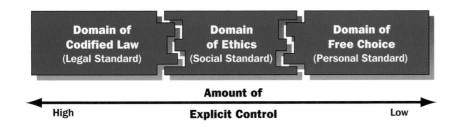

licenses for cars or paying corporate taxes. The courts alleged that Enron executives broke the law, for example, by manipulating financial results, such as using off-balance-sheet partnerships to improperly create income and hide debt.[7] The domain of free choice is at the opposite end of the scale and pertains to behavior about which the law has no say and for which an individual or organization enjoys complete freedom. A manager's choice of where to eat lunch or a music company's choice of the number of CDs to release are examples of free choice.

Between these domains lies the area of ethics. This domain has no specific laws, yet it does have standards of conduct based on shared principles and values about moral conduct that guide an individual or company. Executives at Enron, for example, did not break any specific laws by encouraging employees to buy more shares of stock even when they believed the company was in financial trouble and the price of the shares was likely to decline. However, this behavior was a clear violation of the executives' ethical responsibilities to employees.[8] These managers were acting based on their own interests rather than their duties to employees and other stakeholders. In the domain of free choice, obedience is strictly to oneself. In the domain of codified law, obedience is to laws prescribed by the legal system. In the domain of ethical behavior, obedience is to unenforceable norms and standards about which the individual or company is aware. An ethically acceptable decision is both legally and morally acceptable to the larger community.

Many companies and individuals get into trouble with the simplified view that choices are governed by either law or free choice. It leads people to mistakenly assume that if it's not illegal, it must be ethical, as if there were no third domain.[9] A better option is to recognize the domain of ethics and accept moral values as a powerful force for good that can regulate behaviors both inside and outside corporations. As principles of ethics and social responsibility are more widely recognized, companies can use codes of ethics and their corporate cultures to govern behavior, thereby eliminating the need for additional laws and avoiding the problems of unfettered choice.

Because ethical standards are not codified, disagreements and dilemmas about proper behavior often occur. Ethics is always about making decisions, and some issues are difficult to resolve. An **ethical dilemma** arises in a situation concerning right or wrong when values are in conflict.[10] Right and wrong cannot be clearly identified.

The individual who must make an ethical choice in an organization is the *moral agent*.[11] Consider the dilemmas facing a moral agent in the following situations:

- A top employee at your small company tells you he needs some time off because he has AIDS. You know the employee needs the job as well as the health insurance benefits. Providing health insurance has already stretched the company's budget, and this will send premiums through the roof. You know the federal

**ethical dilemma**
A situation that arises when all alternative choices or behaviors have been deemed undesirable because of potentially negative consequences, making it difficult to distinguish right from wrong.

courts have upheld the right of an employer to modify health plans by putting a cap on AIDS benefits. Should you investigate whether this is a legal possibility for your company?

- As a sales manager for a major pharmaceuticals company, you've been asked to promote a new drug that costs $2,500 per dose. You've read the reports saying the drug is only 1 percent more effective than an alternate drug that costs less than one-fourth as much. Can you in good conscience aggressively promote the $2,500-per-dose drug? If you don't, could lives be lost that might have been saved with that 1 percent increase in effectiveness?

- Your company is hoping to build a new overseas manufacturing plant. You could save about $5 million by not installing standard pollution control equipment that is required in the United States. The plant will employ many local workers in a poor country where jobs are scarce. Your research shows that pollutants from the factory could potentially damage the local fishing industry. Yet building the factory with the pollution control equipment will likely make the plant too expensive to build.[12]

- You are the accounting manager of a division that is $15,000 below profit targets. Approximately $20,000 of office supplies were delivered on December 21. The accounting rule is to pay expenses when incurred. The division general manager asks you not to record the invoice until February.

- You have been collaborating with a fellow manager on an important project. One afternoon, you walk into his office a bit earlier than scheduled and see sexually explicit images on his computer monitor. The company has a zero-tolerance sexual harassment policy, as well as strict guidelines regarding personal use of the Internet. However, your colleague was in his own office and not bothering anyone else.[13]

These are the kinds of dilemmas and issues with which managers must deal that fall squarely in the domain of ethics. Now let's turn to approaches to ethical decision making that provide criteria for understanding and resolving these difficult issues.

**CONCEPT CONNECTION**

*Discovered in 1998, human embryonic stem cells have the potential to revolutionize medical practice and improve the quality and length of life, but they present an **ethical dilemma** for many people. Embryonic stem cells come from in vitro fertilization clinics, and human fetal stem cells are drawn from aborted fetuses, putting researchers in the middle of America's reproductive rights debate. Federal funding for human fetal-cell research was banned from 1987 to 1993, and a five-year ban on federal funding of human embryonic-cell research was lifted only recently. Because his son was diagnosed with a brain tumor, Richard Garr, CEO of NeuralStem Biopharmaceuticals, is diligent with his company's research. He hopes that stem cells will be able to replace neurons lost to otherwise incurable brain disorders.*

# Criteria for Ethical Decision Making

Most ethical dilemmas involve a conflict between the needs of the part and the whole—the individual versus the organization or the organization versus society as a whole. For example, should a company install mandatory alcohol and drug testing for employees, which might benefit the organization as a whole but reduce the individual freedom of employees? Or should products that fail to meet tough FDA standards be exported to other countries where government standards are lower, benefiting the company but being potentially harmful to world citizens? Sometimes ethical decisions entail a conflict between two groups. For example, should the potential for local health problems resulting from a company's effluents take precedence over the jobs it creates as the town's leading employer?

Managers faced with these kinds of tough ethical choices often benefit from a normative strategy—one based on norms and values—to guide their decision making. Normative ethics uses several approaches to describe values for guiding ethical decision making. Four of these that are relevant to managers are the utilitarian approach, individualism approach, moral-rights approach, and justice approach.[14]

## Utilitarian Approach

The **utilitarian approach**, espoused by the nineteenth-century philosophers Jeremy Bentham and John Stuart Mill, holds that moral behavior produces the greatest good for the greatest number. Under this approach, a decision maker is expected to consider the effect of each decision alternative on all parties and select the one that optimizes the satisfaction for the greatest number of people. Because actual computations can be very complex, simplifying them is considered appropriate. For example, a simple economic frame of reference could be used by calculating dollar costs and dollar benefits. Also, a decision could be made that considers only the people who are directly affected by the decision, not those who are indirectly affected. The utilitarian ethic is cited as the basis for the recent trend among companies to police employee personal habits such as alcohol and tobacco consumption on the job, and in some cases after hours as well, because such behavior affects the entire workplace. Similarly, many companies argue that monitoring how employees spend their time on the Internet is necessary to maintain the company's ethical climate and workplace productivity. If employees are viewing pornographic sites, visiting racist chat rooms, or spending hours shopping or day-trading online, the entire organization ultimately suffers.[15]

The utilitarian ethic was the basis for the state of Oregon's decision to extend Medicaid to 400,000 previously ineligible recipients by refusing to pay for high-cost, high-risk procedures such as liver transplants and bone-marrow transplants. Although a few people needing these procedures have died because the state would not pay, many people have benefitted from medical services they would otherwise have had to go without.[16] Critics claim that the Oregon decision does not fully take into account the concept of justice toward the unfortunate victims of life-threatening diseases.[17] The justice approach will be discussed later in this section.

**utilitarian approach**
The ethical concept that moral behaviors produce the greatest good for the greatest number.

## Individualism Approach

The **individualism approach** contends that acts are moral when they promote the individual's best long-term interests. Individual self-direction is paramount, and external forces that restrict self-direction should be severely limited.[18] Individuals calculate the best long-term advantage to themselves as a measure of a decision's

**individualism approach**
The ethical concept that acts are moral when they promote the individual's best long-term interests, which ultimately leads to the greater good.

goodness. The action that is intended to produce a greater ratio of good to bad for the individual compared with other alternatives is the right one to perform. In theory, with everyone pursuing self-direction, the greater good is ultimately served because people learn to accommodate each other in their own long-term interest. *Individualism* is believed to lead to honesty and integrity because that works best in the long run. Lying and cheating for immediate self-interest just causes business associates to lie and cheat in return. Thus, individualism ultimately leads to behavior toward others that fits standards of behavior people want toward themselves.[19] One value of understanding this approach is to recognize short-term variations if they are proposed. People might argue for short-term self-interest based on individualism, but that misses the point. Because individualism is easily misinterpreted to support immediate self-gain, it is not popular in the highly organized and group-oriented society of today. Dozens of disgraced top executives from WorldCom, Enron, Tyco, and other companies demonstrate the flaws of the individualism approach. This approach is closest to the domain of free choice described in Exhibit 5.1.

## Moral-Rights Approach

**moral-rights approach**
The ethical concept that moral decisions are those that best maintain the rights of those people affected by them.

The **moral-rights approach** asserts that human beings have fundamental rights and liberties that cannot be taken away by an individual's decision. Thus, an ethically correct decision is one that best maintains the rights of those people affected by it.

Six moral rights should be considered during decision making:

1. *The right of free consent.* Individuals are to be treated only as they knowingly and freely consent to be treated.
2. *The right to privacy.* Individuals can choose to do as they please away from work and have control of information about their private life.
3. *The right of freedom of conscience.* Individuals may refrain from carrying out any order that violates their moral or religious norms.
4. *The right of free speech.* Individuals may criticize truthfully the ethics or legality of actions of others.
5. *The right to due process.* Individuals have a right to an impartial hearing and fair treatment.
6. *The right to life and safety.* Individuals have a right to live without endangerment or violation of their health and safety.

To make ethical decisions, managers need to avoid interfering with the fundamental rights of others. For example, a decision to eavesdrop on employees violates the right to privacy. Sexual harassment is unethical because it violates the right to freedom of conscience. The right of free speech would support whistle-blowers who call attention to illegal or inappropriate actions within a company.

## Justice Approach

**justice approach**
The ethical concept that moral decisions must be based on standards of equity, fairness, and impartiality.

**distributive justice**
The concept that different treatment of people should not be based on arbitrary characteristics. In the case of substantive differences, people should be treated differently in proportion to the differences among them.

The **justice approach** holds that moral decisions must be based on standards of equity, fairness, and impartiality. Three types of justice are of concern to managers. **Distributive justice** requires that different treatment of people not be based on arbitrary characteristics. Individuals who are similar in respects relevant to a decision should be treated similarly. Thus, men and women should not receive different salaries if they are performing the same job. However, people who differ in a substantive way, such as job skills or job responsibility, can be treated differently in proportion to the differences in skills or responsibility among them. This difference should have a clear relationship to organizational goals and tasks.

Procedural justice requires that rules be administered fairly. Rules should be clearly stated and be consistently and impartially enforced. **Compensatory justice** argues that individuals should be compensated for the cost of their injuries by the party responsible. Moreover, individuals should not be held responsible for matters over which they have no control.

The justice approach is closest to the thinking underlying the domain of law in Exhibit 5.1, because it assumes that justice is applied through rules and regulations. This theory does not require complex calculations such as those demanded by a utilitarian approach, nor does it justify self-interest as the individualism approach does. Managers are expected to define attributes on which different treatment of employees is acceptable. Questions such as how minority workers should be compensated for past discrimination are extremely difficult. However, this approach does justify as ethical behavior efforts to correct past wrongs, playing fair under the rules, and insisting on job-relevant differences as the basis for different levels of pay or promotion opportunities. Most of the laws guiding human resource management (Chapter 12) are based on the justice approach.

Understanding these various approaches is only a first step; managers still have to consider how to apply them. The approaches offer general principles that managers can recognize as useful in making ethical decisions. This chapter's Manager's Shoptalk lists some further guidelines that can help managers make ethical decisions.

**procedural justice**
The concept that rules should be clearly stated and consistently and impartially enforced.

**compensatory justice**
The concept that individuals should be compensated for the cost of their injuries by the party responsible and also that individuals should not be held responsible for matters over which they have no control.

# Factors Affecting Ethical Choices

When managers are accused of lying, cheating, or stealing, the blame is usually placed on the individual or on the company situation. Most people believe that individuals make ethical choices because of individual integrity, which is true, but it is not the whole story. Ethical or unethical business practices usually reflect the values, attitudes, beliefs, and behavior patterns of the organizational culture; thus, ethics is as much an organizational as a personal issue.[20] Let's examine how both the manager and the organization shape ethical decision making.[21]

## The Manager

Managers bring specific personality and behavioral traits to the job. Personal needs, family influence, and religious background all shape a manager's value system. Specific personality characteristics, such as ego strength, self-confidence, and a strong sense of independence, may enable managers to make ethical decisions.

One important personal trait is the stage of moral development.[22] A simplified version of one model of personal moral development is shown in Exhibit 5.2. At the *preconventional level*, individuals are concerned with external rewards and punishments and obey authority to avoid detrimental personal consequences. In an organizational context, this level may be associated with managers who use an autocratic or coercive leadership style, with employees oriented toward dependable accomplishment of specific tasks. At level two, called the *conventional level*, people learn to conform to the expectations of good behavior as defined by colleagues, family, friends, and society. Meeting social and interpersonal obligations is important. Work group collaboration is the preferred manner for accomplishment of organizational goals, and managers use a leadership style that encourages interpersonal relationships and cooperation. At the *postconventional*, or *principled* level, individuals are guided by an internal set of values and standards and will even disobey rules or laws that violate these principles. Internal values become

# manager's Shoptalk

## Turbulent Times

### Guidelines for Ethical Decision Making

If a *60 Minutes* crew were waiting on your doorstep one morning, would you feel comfortable justifying your actions to the camera? One young manager, when confronted with ethical dilemmas, gives them the *60 Minutes* test. Others say they use such criteria as whether they would be proud to tell their parents or grandparents about their decisions, or whether they could sleep well at night and face themselves in the mirror in the morning. Managers often rely on their own personal integrity in making ethical decisions. But knowing what to do is not always easy. As a future manager, you will almost surely face ethical dilemmas one day. The following guidelines will not tell you exactly what to do, but, taken in the context of the text discussion, they will help you evaluate the situation more clearly by examining your own values and those of your organization. The answers to these questions will force you to think hard about the social and ethical consequences of your behavior.

1. Is the problem/dilemma really what it appears to be? If you are not sure, *find out*.
2. Is the action you are considering legal? Ethical? If you are not sure, *find out*.
3. Do you understand the position of those who oppose the action you are considering? Is it reasonable?

4. Whom does the action benefit? Harm? How much? How long?
5. Would you be willing to allow everyone to do what you are considering doing?
6. Have you sought the opinion of others who are knowledgeable and objective regarding the subject?
7. Would your action be embarrassing to you if it were made known to your family, friends, coworkers, or superiors?
8. Even if you are sure the decision is reasonable and that you could defend it to others, does your gut instinct tell you it is the wrong thing to do?

There are no correct answers to these questions in an absolute sense. Yet, if you determine that an action is potentially harmful to someone or would be embarrassing to you, or if you do not know the ethical or legal consequences, these guidelines will help you clarify whether the action is socially responsible.

SOURCES: Anthony M. Pagano and Jo Ann Verdin, *The External Environment of Business* (New York: Wiley, 1988), Chapter 5; Joseph L. Badaracco, Jr., and Allen P. Webb, "Business Ethics: A View from the Trenches," *California Management Review* 37, no. 2 (Winter 1995), 8–28; and Sherry Baker, "Ethical Judgment," *Executive Excellence* (March 1992), 7–8.

more important than the expectations of significant others. For example, when the *USS Indianapolis* sank after being torpedoed during World War II, one Navy pilot disobeyed orders and risked his life to save men who were being picked off by sharks. The pilot was operating from the highest level of moral development in attempting the rescue despite a direct order from superiors. When managers operate from this highest level of development, they use transformative or servant leadership, focusing on the needs of followers and encouraging others to think for themselves and to engage in higher levels of moral reasoning. Employees are empowered and given opportunities for constructive participation in governance of the organization.

The great majority of managers operate at level two. A few have not advanced beyond level one. Only about 20 percent of American adults reach the level-three stage of moral development. People at level three are able to act in an independent, ethical manner regardless of expectations from others inside or outside the

# Exhibit 5.2

## Three Levels of Personal Moral Development

**Level 3: Postconventional**

Follows self-chosen principles of justice and right. Aware that people hold different values and seeks creative solutions to ethical dilemmas. Balances concern for individual with concern for common good.

**Level 2: Conventional**

Lives up to expectations of others. Fulfills duties and obligations of social system. Upholds laws.

**Level 1: Preconventional**

Follows rules to avoid punishment. Acts in own interest. Obedience for its own sake.

| | | |
|---|---|---|
| **Leadership Style:** Autocratic/coercive | Guiding/encouraging, team oriented | Transforming, or servant leadership |
| **Employee Behavior:** Task accomplishment | Work group collaboration | Empowered employees, full participation |

organization. Managers at level three of moral development will make ethical decisions whatever the organizational consequences for them.

One interesting study indicates that most researchers have failed to account for the different ways in which women view social reality and develop psychologically and have thus consistently classified women as being stuck at lower levels of development. Researcher Carol Gilligan has suggested that the moral domain be enlarged to include responsibility and care in relationships. Women may, in general, perceive moral complexities more astutely than men and make moral

**SOURCES:** Based on L. Kohlberg, "Moral Stages and Moralization: The Cognitive-Developmental Approach," in *Moral Development and Behavior: Theory, Research, and Social Issues,* ed. T. Lickona (New York: Holt, Rinehart, and Winston, 1976), 31–53; and Jill W. Graham, "Leadership, Moral Development and Citizenship Behavior," *Business Ethics Quarterly* 5, no. 1 (January 1995), 43–54.

© MICHAEL LEWIS

## CONCEPT CONNECTION

*Julius Walls, Jr., chief executive of Greyston Bakery, demonstrates the* **postconventional level of moral development**. *Greyston makes gourmet brownies, cakes, and tarts. Walls hires employees off the street, first come, first served, because he thinks everyone deserves a chance at a job. He also helps workers with problems whether or not they're job related. Greyston serves the poor by feeding the rich. Much of its $4 million in annual sales are generated by selling bits of brownies to Ben & Jerry's for its chocolate fudge brownie ice cream and frozen yogurt, and the company donates all profits to the needy.*

decisions based not on a set of absolute rights and wrongs but on principles of not causing harm to others.[23]

One reason higher levels of ethical conduct are increasingly important is the impact of globalization. Globalization has made ethical issues even more complicated for today's managers.[24] American managers working in foreign countries need sensitivity and an openness to other systems, as well as the fortitude to resolve difficult issues. For example, although tolerance for bribery is waning, a recent survey revealed disturbing results. Transparency International, an international organization that monitors corruption, publishes an annual report ranking countries according to how many bribes are offered by their international businesses. Exhibit 5.3 shows results of the organization's most recent available report. International businesses based in countries like Russia, China, Taiwan, and South Korea were found to be using bribes "on an exceptional and intolerable scale." However, multinational firms in the United States, Japan, France, and Spain also revealed a relatively high propensity to pay bribes overseas.[25]

## The Organization

Rarely can ethical or unethical corporate actions be attributed solely to the personal values of a single manager. The values adopted within the organization are highly important, especially when we understand that most people are at the level-two stage of moral development, which means they believe their duty is to fulfill obligations and expectations of others. Consider, for example, accounting managers at WorldCom, which disintegrated in an $11 billion fraud scandal.

**WORLDCOM**
http://www.mci.com

> WorldCom started out as a small long-distance company and rapidly became a dazzling star during the late 1990s Wall Street telecom boom. Just as rapidly, it all came crashing down as one executive after another was hauled away on conspiracy and securities fraud charges.
>
> For Betty Vinson and Troy Normand, the first signs of serious trouble came in mid-2000. With the telecom industry in a slump, top executives were scrambling to meet Wall Street's expectations for the quarter. Vinson and Normand's boss, Buford Yates, called the two into his office and broke the news. CEO Bernard Ebbers and Chief Financial Officer Scott Sullivan had asked that they make some highly questionable accounting adjustments—to the tune of $828 million—that would reduce expenses and boost the company's earnings for the quarter. Although the managers were initially shocked by the request and resisted, they eventually agreed to go along. Despite the misgivings they and Yates all felt, the accountants continued to make increasingly irregular adjustments over the course of six quarters, clinging to a hope that each one would be the last.
>
> Top executives persuaded these managers, who were all known as hardworking, dedicated employees, that their gimmicks would help pull WorldCom out of its troubles and get everything back to normal. A colleague of Vinson's says she felt that she needed to go along with her bosses' requests despite her own concerns. To assuage her guilt, the colleague says, Vinson rationalized that CFO Sullivan had been hailed as one of the country's top chief financial officers. Therefore, if he thought the transfers and other gimmicks were all right, she wasn't one to question it.
>
> When WorldCom's problems exploded into public view, Yates, Normand, and Vinson found themselves in the middle of the largest fraud case in corporate history. All three eventually pled guilty to conspiracy and securities fraud, which will likely result in jail time.[26]

Vinson, Normand, and Yates were not unscrupulous people. All three had misgivings about what they were doing, but they continued to go along with their superiors' requests. All ethical decisions are made within the context of our interactions with other people, and the social networks within an organization play an important

Exhibit 5.3

## The Transparency International Bribe Payers Index 2002

A score of 10 represents zero propensity to pay bribes, while a score of 0 reflects very high levels of bribery.

| Rank | | Score | Rank | | Score |
|------|--|-------|------|--|-------|
| 1 | Australia | 8.5 | 12 | France | 5.5 |
| 2 | Sweden | 8.4 | 13 | United States | 5.3 |
| 2 (tie) | Switzerland | 8.4 | 13 (tie) | Japan | 5.3 |
| 4 | Austria | 8.2 | 15 | Malaysia | 4.3 |
| 5 | Canada | 8.1 | 15 (tie) | Hong Kong | 4.3 |
| 6 | Netherlands | 7.8 | 17 | Italy | 4.1 |
| 6 (tie) | Belgium | 7.8 | 18 | South Korea | 3.9 |
| 8 | United Kingdom | 6.9 | 19 | Taiwan | 3.8 |
| 9 | Singapore | 6.3 | 20 | People's Republic of China | 3.5 |
| 9 (tie) | Germany | 6.3 | 21 | Russia | 3.2 |
| 11 | Spain | 5.8 | | | |

**SOURCE:** Transparency International, *http://www.transparency.org.*

role in guiding other people's actions. For most of us, doing something we know is wrong becomes easier when "everyone else is doing it." In organizations, the norms and values of the team, department, or organization as a whole have a profound influence on ethical behavior. Research has verified that these values strongly influence employee actions and decision making.[27] In particular, corporate culture, as described in Chapter 3, lets employees know what beliefs and behaviors the company supports and those it will not tolerate. If unethical behavior is tolerated or even encouraged, it becomes routine. For example, an investigation of thefts and kickbacks in the oil business found that the cause was the historical acceptance of thefts and kickbacks. Employees were socialized into those values and adopted them as appropriate. In many companies, employees believe that if they do not go along, their jobs will be in jeopardy or they will not fit in.[28]

*Go to the experiential exercise on page 183 that pertains to ethical work environments.*

*Take A Moment*

Culture can be examined to see the kinds of ethical signals given to employees. Exhibit 5.4 indicates questions to ask to understand the cultural system. High ethical standards can be affirmed and communicated through public awards and ceremonies. Heroes provide role models that can either support or refute ethical decision making. Culture is not the only aspect of an organization that influences ethics, but it is a major force because it defines company values. Other aspects of the organization, such as explicit rules and policies, the reward system, the extent to which the company cares for its people, the selection system, emphasis on legal and professional standards, and leadership and decision processes, can also have an impact on ethical values and manager decision making.[29]

## What Is Social Responsibility?

Now let's turn to the issue of social responsibility. In one sense, the concept of corporate social responsibility, like ethics, is easy to understand: It means distinguishing right from wrong and doing right. It means being a good corporate citizen.

Exhibit 5.4

## Questions for Analyzing a Company's Cultural Impact on Ethics

1. Identify the organization's heroes. What values do they represent? Given an ambiguous ethical dilemma, what decision would they make and why?
2. What are some important organizational rituals? How do they encourage or discourage ethical behavior? Who gets the awards, people of integrity or individuals who use unethical methods to attain success?
3. What are the ethical messages sent to new entrants into the organization—must they obey authority at all costs, or is questioning authority acceptable or even desirable?
4. Does analysis of organizational stories and myths reveal individuals who stand up for what's right, or is conformity the valued characteristic? Do people get fired or promoted in these stories?
5. Does language exist for discussing ethical concerns? Is this language routinely incorporated and encouraged in business decision making?
6. What informal socialization processes exist, and what norms for ethical/unethical behavior do they promote?

**SOURCE**: Linda Klebe Treviño, "A Cultural Perspective on Changing and Developing Organizational Ethics," in *Research in Organizational Change and Development*, ed. R. Woodman and W. Pasmore (Greenwich, Conn.: JAI Press, 1990), 4.

**social responsibility**
The obligation of organization management to make decisions and take actions that will enhance the welfare and interests of society as well as the organization.

The formal definition of **social responsibility** is management's obligation to make choices and take actions that will contribute to the welfare and interests of society as well as the organization.[30]

As straightforward as this definition seems, social responsibility can be a difficult concept to grasp, because different people have different beliefs as to which actions improve society's welfare.[31] To make matters worse, social responsibility covers a range of issues, many of which are ambiguous with respect to right or wrong. For example, if a bank deposits the money from a trust fund into a low-interest account for 90 days, from which it makes a substantial profit, is it being a responsible corporate citizen? How about two companies engaging in intense competition? Is it socially responsible for the stronger corporation to drive the weaker one into bankruptcy or a forced merger? Or consider companies such as Chiquita, Kmart, or Global Crossing, all of which declared bankruptcy—which is perfectly legal—to avoid mounting financial obligations to suppliers, labor unions, or competitors. These examples contain moral, legal, and economic considerations that make socially responsible behavior hard to define. A company's environmental impact must also be taken into consideration.

# Organizational Stakeholders

**stakeholder**
Any group within or outside the organization that has a stake in the organization's performance.

One reason for the difficulty understanding social responsibility is that managers must confront the question, "Responsibility to whom?" Recall from Chapter 3 that the organization's environment consists of several sectors in both the task and general environment. From a social responsibility perspective, enlightened organizations view the internal and external environment as a variety of stakeholders.

A **stakeholder** is any group within or outside the organization that has a stake in the organization's performance. Each stakeholder has a different criterion of responsiveness, because it has a different interest in the organization.[32] For example, Wal-Mart uses aggressive bargaining tactics with suppliers so that it is able to provide low prices for customers. Some stakeholders see this as responsible corporate behavior because it benefits customers and forces suppliers to be more efficient. Others, however, argue that the aggressive tactics are unethical and socially irresponsible because they force U.S. manufacturers to lay off workers, close factories, and outsource from low-wage countries. For instance, Wal-Mart now purchases nearly 10 percent of all Chinese imports to the United States. One supplier said clothing is being sold so cheaply at Wal-Mart that many U.S. companies could not compete even if they paid their employees nothing.[33]

The organization's performance affects stakeholders, but stakeholders can also have a tremendous effect on the organization's performance and success. Consider the case of Monsanto, a leading competitor in the life sciences industry.

Over the past decade or so, Monsanto has been transformed from a chemicals firm into a biotechnology company. The organization has a vast array of stakeholders around the world, including customers, investors, suppliers, partners, health and agricultural organizations, regulatory agencies, research institutes, and governments.

Monsanto has experienced some big problems in recent years because of its failure to satisfy various stakeholder groups. For example, the company's genetic seed business has been the target of controversy and protest. Small farmers were concerned about new dependencies that might arise for them with using the new seeds. European consumers rebelled against a perceived imposition of unlabeled, genetically-modified food ingredients. Research institutes and other organizations took offense at what they perceived as Monsanto's arrogant approach to the new business. Activist groups accused the company of creating "Frankenstein foods." Partly as a result of these public sentiments, Monsanto has had trouble getting regulatory approval for its genetically-modified organisms, including seeds for wheat, corn, soy, and other crops. Investor confidence in the company waned too and the stock took a downhill slide.

In light of these stakeholder issues, CEO Hendrik Verfaillie offered an apology to some stakeholders at a 2001 *Farm Journal* Conference in Washington, D.C., saying that Monsanto "was so blinded by its enthusiasm for this great new technology that it missed the concerns the technology raised for many people." Verfaillie has also announced a five-part pledge that aims to restore positive stakeholder relationships. Each of the five commitments requires an ongoing dialogue between Monsanto managers and various stakeholder constituencies. If they cannot effectively manage critical stakeholder relationships, Monsanto is not likely to survive as a business.[34]

MONSANTO
**http://monsanto.com**

Exhibit 5.5 illustrates important stakeholders for Monsanto. Most organizations are similarly influenced by a variety of stakeholder groups. Investors and shareholders, employees, customers, and suppliers are considered primary stakeholders, without whom the organization cannot survive. Investors, shareholders, and suppliers' interests are served by managerial efficiency—that is, use of resources to achieve profits. Employees expect work satisfaction, pay, and good supervision. Customers are concerned with decisions about the quality, safety, and availability of goods and services. When any primary stakeholder group becomes seriously dissatisfied, the organization's viability is threatened.[35]

Other important stakeholders are the government and the community. Most corporations exist only under the proper charter and licenses and operate within the limits of safety laws, environmental protection requirements, antitrust regulations, and other laws and regulations in the government sector. The community includes local government, the natural and physical environments, and the quality of life provided for residents. Special-interest groups, still another stakeholder, may include trade associations, political action committees, professional associations, and consumerists. Social activists have discovered the power of the Internet for organizing

# Exhibit 5.5

## Major Stakeholders Relevant to Monsanto Company

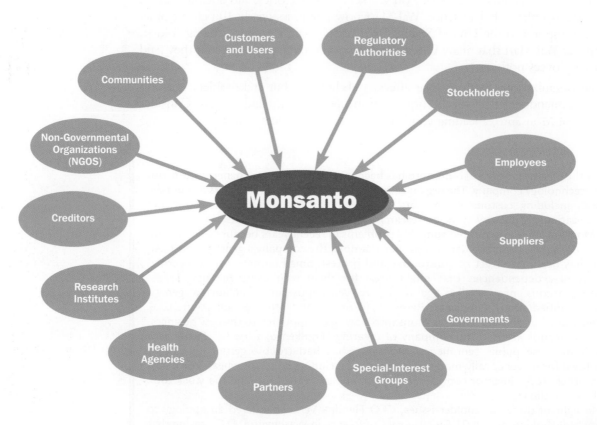

**SOURCES:** Based on information in D. Wheeler, B. Colbert, and R. E. Freeman, "Focusing on Value: Reconciling Corporate Social Responsibility, Sustainability, and a Stakeholder Approach in a Networked World," *Journal of General Management* 28, no. 3 (Spring 2003). 1–28; and J. E. Post, L. E. Preston, and S. Sachs, "Managing the Extended Enterprise: The New Stakeholder View," *California Management Review* 45, no. 1 (Fall 2002), 6–28.

stakeholders and pressuring corporations to honor their ethical, human rights, and environmental responsibilities. One organization, the As You Sow foundation, uses the Internet to mobilize investors and shareholders to push for social reforms, as described in the Unlocking Creative Solutions Through Technology box.

Socially responsible organizations consider the effects of their actions on all stakeholder groups and may also invest in a number of philanthropic causes that benefit stakeholders. Bristol-Myers Squibb, for example, provides funding for health clinics in areas of Texas, California, and Florida to hire *promotoras de salud,* or peer health educators, to help fight type 2 diabetes in the Hispanic population. Typically Hispanic women who themselves have diabetes, the *promotoras de salud* are trained to work full-time as accessible community resources. By answering questions, assuring compliance with medications, and providing nutritional advice, they help patients control their disease and provide needed support for overworked and overstressed nurses who don't have the time or Spanish language skills to address all the concerns of their many patients.[36]

Today, special-interest groups continue to be one of the largest stakeholder concerns that companies face. Environmental responsibility has become a primary issue as both business and the public acknowledge the damage that has been done to our natural environment.

# Unlocking Creative Solutions Through Technology

## Using the Web to Promote Social Responsibility

The Internet has become a crucial weapon in the fight to make corporations more socially responsible. For example, social activists have long used shareholder pressure as an important means of promoting their goals. Now, with the ability to rapidly spread information on the Web, nonprofit organizations such as the As You Sow Foundation can quickly rally shareholders and mount campaigns against corporate practices they consider irresponsible.

As You Sow (AYS) is a not-for-profit organization with a mission to promote corporate responsibility and "hold corporations accountable for complying with consumer, workplace, and environmental laws." It does so by engaging in dialogue with corporations concerning social responsibility issues and by organizing shareholder campaigns when companies balk at voluntary efforts. As You Sow works closely with other activist organizations such as the Interfaith Center on Corporate Responsibility (ICCR), a group of Protestant,

Catholic, and Jewish institutional investors that pioneered shareholder activism in the 1970s, and the Shareholder Action Network, an information, networking, and resource center that AYS helped to found. One shareholder campaign resulted in Home Depot agreeing to phase out the sale of old-growth timber, for example.

As You Sow is currently involved in dialogues with companies like Wal-Mart, Nike, McDonald's, and the Walt Disney Company concerning labor and human rights abuses in contract supplier plants. A current shareholder campaign against genetically altered foods, targeting companies such as DuPont, Hershey, Kellogg, and Sysco, has become the fastest-growing shareholder movement in history. Project director Tracey Rembert explains the value of using the Internet for social activism: "It used to be you'd call 20 people you know on the telephone and ask them to write a letter. . . . Now you can bring together many more people with just one e-mail. You can accomplish in one year what it might have taken 10 years of pickets and protests in the streets to accomplish."

**SOURCE:** Mark Schapiro, "All Over the Board," *grok* (February–March 2001), 110–112; and *http://www.asyousow.org* accessed on February 27, 2004.

# The Ethic of Sustainability and the Natural Environment

When the first Earth Day celebration was held in 1970, most managers considered environmentalists to be an extremist fringe group and felt little need to respond to environmental concerns.[37] Today environmental issues have become a hot topic among business leaders, and managers and organizations in all industries are jumping on the environmental bandwagon.

One model uses the phrase *shades of green* to evaluate a company's commitment to environmental responsibility.[38] The various shades, which represent a company's approach to addressing environmental concerns, are illustrated in Exhibit 5.6. With a *legal approach,* the organization does just what is necessary to satisfy legal requirements. In general, managers and the company show little concern for environmental issues. For example, Willamette Industries of Portland, Oregon, agreed to install $7.4 million worth of pollution control equipment in its 13 factories to comply with Environmental Protection Agency requirements. The move came only after Willamette was fined a whopping $11.2 million for violating emissions standards.[39] The next shade, the *market approach,* represents a growing awareness of and sensitivity to environmental concerns, primarily to satisfy customers. A company might provide environmentally friendly products because customers want them, for instance, not necessarily because of strong management commitment to the environment.

Exhibit 5.6

### The Shades of Corporate Green

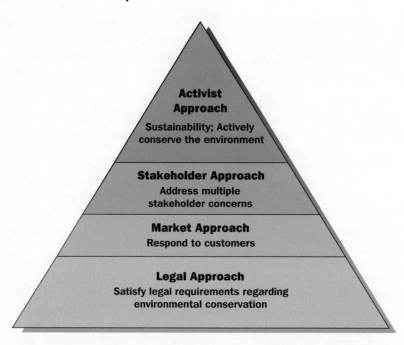

**Activist Approach**

Sustainability; Actively conserve the environment

**Stakeholder Approach**

Address multiple stakeholder concerns

**Market Approach**

Respond to customers

**Legal Approach**

Satisfy legal requirements regarding environmental conservation

**SOURCE:** Based on R.E. Freeman, J. Pierce, and R. Dodd, *Shades of Green: Ethics and the Environment* (New York: Oxford University Press, 1995).

© AP/WIDE WORLD PHOTOS

### CONCEPT CONNECTION

*Recently, Roxanne Quimby sold 80% of her company, Burt's Bees, a leading natural personal care brand, to a private-equity firm for more than $175 million. She plans to donate half the proceeds to a land trust to establish a national park in northern Maine, demonstrating her commitment to the **natural environment** and the ethic of **sustainability**.*

A further step is to respond to multiple demands from the environment. The *stakeholder approach* means that companies attempt to answer the environmental concerns of various stakeholder groups, such as customers, the local community, business partners, and special interest groups. Ontario Power Generation, Shell, and Alcan Aluminum are among the large companies that are partnering with Environmental Defense to reduce greenhouse gases.[40] The move comes in response to growing concerns among customers, communities where the companies operate, and environmental groups, as well as a recognition that emissions are likely to be regulated by government actions.

Finally, at the highest level of green, organizations take an *activist approach* to environmental issues by actively searching for ways to conserve the Earth's resources. A growing number of companies around the world are embracing a revolutionary idea called *sustainability* or *sustainable development*. **Sustainability** refers to economic development that generates wealth and meets the needs of the current generation while saving the environment so future generations can meet their needs as well.[41] With a philosophy of sustainability, managers weave environmental and social concerns into every strategic decision, revise policies and procedures to support sustainability efforts, and measure their progress toward sustainability goals.

U.S. organizations as diverse as DuPont, McDonald's, and UPS are grappling with issues related to sustainability. McDonald's, for example, buys some of its energy from renewable sources, has stopped buying poultry treated with antibiotics, and offers incentives to suppliers that support sustainable practices.[42] UPS released its first Corporate Sustainability Report in 2002, outlining how the company balances economic concerns with social responsibility and environmental stewardship.[43] The UPS fleet, for instance, includes around 2,000 alternative fuel vehicles, which emit 35 percent less pollution that standard diesel engines. The company is investing $600 million on new package flow technologies that optimize how UPS delivers packages to both improve service and reduce miles driven.[44] DuPont has developed biodegradable materials for plastic silverware, a stretchable fabric called Sorona that is made partially from corn, and a housing insulation wrap that saves far more energy than is required to produce it. The company's new mission is to eventually manage a collection of businesses that can go on forever without depleting any natural resources.[45]

Despite these impressive advances, few U.S. firms have fully embraced the principles of sustainability, as reflected in a resistance to adopting ISO 14001 standards.[46] ISO 14001 is an international environmental management system that aims to boost the sustainability agenda. To become ISO 14001 compliant, firms develop policies, procedures, and systems that will continually reduce the organization's impact on the natural environment. Sustainability argues that organizations can find innovative ways to create wealth at the same time they are preserving natural resources. ZipCar, for example, rents cars by the hour, 24 hours a day, with no paperwork. By reducing private car usage, ZipCar contributes to reduced emissions and reduced load on the nation's transit infrastructure.[47]

**sustainability**
Economic development that meets the needs of the current population while preserving the environment for the needs of future generations.

# Evaluating Corporate Social Performance

A model for evaluating corporate social performance is presented in Exhibit 5.7. The model indicates that total corporate social responsibility can be subdivided into four primary criteria—economic, legal, ethical, and discretionary responsibilities.[48] These four criteria fit together to form the whole of a company's social responsiveness. Managers and organizations are typically involved in several issues at the same time, and a company's ethical and discretionary responsibilities are increasingly considered as important as economic and legal issues Social responsibility has become an important topic on the corporate agenda in the light of corporate scandals, concerns about globalization, and a growing mistrust of business.[49]

Note the similarity between the categories in Exhibit 5.7 and those in Exhibit 5.1. In both cases, ethical issues are located between the areas of legal and freely discretionary responsibilities. Exhibit 5.7 also has an economic category, because profits are a major reason for corporations' existence.

© DAVID J. PHILLIP—AP/WIDE WORLD PHOTOS

**CONCEPT CONNECTION**

*For businesses, the first criterion of corporate social responsibility is **economic responsibility**. Recently, companies such as Enron, Lucent, and Nortel have failed to carry out their economic responsibility, especially when the value of the company stock plummeted. Not only did Enron employees such as those in the photo lose their jobs, but some lose most of their 401(k) retirement plans. One 61-year-old administrative assistant, who had dutifully placed 15 percent of her salary into a 401(k) plan, invested the entire amount in the company's rapidly climbing stock. She amassed close to $500,000, only to be forced out of work with a 401(k) worth only $22,000 when Enron collapsed.*

## Economic Responsibilities

The first criterion of social responsibility is *economic responsibility*. The business institution is, above all, the basic economic unit of society. Its responsibility is to produce the goods and services that society wants and to maximize profits for its owners and shareholders. Economic responsibility, carried to the extreme, is called the *profit-maximizing view*, advocated by Nobel economist Milton Friedman. This view argues that the corporation should be operated on a profit-oriented basis, with its sole mission to increase its profits so long as it stays within the rules of the game.[50]

The purely profit-maximizing view is no longer considered an adequate criterion of performance in Canada, the United States, and Europe. This approach means that economic gain is the only social responsibility and can lead companies into trouble.

Exhibit 5.7

## Criteria of Corporate Social Performance

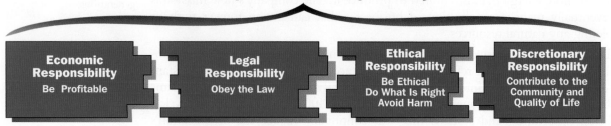

**Total Corporate Social Responsibility**

| Economic Responsibility | Legal Responsibility | Ethical Responsibility | Discretionary Responsibility |
|---|---|---|---|
| Be Profitable | Obey the Law | Be Ethical<br>Do What Is Right<br>Avoid Harm | Contribute to the Community and Quality of Life |

**SOURCES:** Based on Archie B. Carroll, "A Three-Dimensional Conceptual Model of Corporate Performance," *Academy of Management Review* 4 (1979), 499; A.B. Carroll, "The Pyramid of Corporate Social Responsibility: Toward the Moral Management of Corporate Stakeholders," *Business Horizons* 34 (July–August 1991), 42; and Mark S. Schwartz and Archie B. Carroll, "Corporate Social Responsibility: A Three-Domain Approach," *Business Ethics Quarterly* 13, no. 4 (2003), 503–530.

## Legal Responsibilities

All modern societies lay down ground rules, laws, and regulations that businesses are expected to follow. *Legal responsibility* defines what society deems as important with respect to appropriate corporate behavior.[51] Businesses are expected to fulfill their economic goals within the legal framework. Legal requirements are imposed by local town councils, state legislators, and federal regulatory agencies.

Organizations that knowingly break the law are poor performers in this category. Intentionally manufacturing defective goods or billing a client for work not done is illegal. Tenet Healthcare paid $54 million to settle a federal lawsuit charging that one of their hospitals was cheating Medicare by performing unnecessary cardiac procedures.[52] Managers at numerous other companies have also learned that organizations ultimately pay for ignoring their legal responsibilities. An example of the punishment given to one company that broke the law is described in the press release shown in Exhibit 5.8.

## Ethical Responsibilities

*Ethical responsibility* includes behaviors that are not necessarily codified into law and may not serve the corporation's direct economic interests. As described earlier in this chapter, to be *ethical*, organization decision makers should act with equity, fairness, and impartiality, respect the rights of individuals, and provide different treatment of individuals only when relevant to the organization's goals and tasks.[53] *Unethical* behavior occurs when decisions enable an individual or company to gain at the expense of other people or society as a whole. For example, at *The New York Times,* there are indications that managers suspected star reporter Jayson Blair was fabricating research on top news stories, but they ignored the signals partly to protect the paper's reputation and partly because they were concerned about questioning a rising young African American reporter. Their head-in-the-sand approach ultimately backfired when the deception became known and the paper published a lengthy story admitting how Blair had systematically fabricated or plagiarized as many as three dozen stories.[54]

*Take A Moment*    *Go to the ethical dilemma on page 183 that pertains to legal and ethical responsibilities.*

Exhibit 5.8

## One Company's Punishment for Breaking the Law

United States
Environmental Protection Agency

### Headquarters Press Release
**Washington, DC**

**Date Published:** 07/12/2001

**Title:** WASHINGTON STATE/ALASKA COMPANY SENTENCED IN ASBESTOS CASE

**FOR RELEASE: THURSDAY, JULY 12, 2001
WASHINGTON STATE/ALASKA COMPANY SENTENCED IN
ASBESTOS CASE**

Luke C. Hester 202-564-7818 / hester.luke@epa.gov

On June 27, Great Pacific Seafood, a Washington State corporation operating in Alaska, and its General Manager, Roger D. Stiles, were sentenced for violations of the Clean Air Act. Great Pacific Seafood was sentenced to serve five years probation, pay a $75,000 fine, pay $7,000 in restitution, publish a public apology statement in the local newspaper and adopt an environmental management program. Stiles was sentenced to pay a $5,000 fine, perform 120 hours of community service, and serve two to three years probation. Great Pacific Seafood and Stiles pleaded guilty to having five of its employees directly or indirectly exposed to asbestos fibers without the proper training, equipment or protective clothing. The hazardous nature of abatement was never disclosed to two of the employees. Failure to follow asbestos work practices can expose workers to the inhalation of airborne asbestos fibers which can cause lung cancer, a lung disease known as "asbestosis" and mesothelioma, a cancer of the chest and abdominal cavities. This case was investigated by the EPA Criminal Investigation Division, the FBI and the Alaska State Occupational Safety and Health Administration. Technical assistance was provided by the EPA Office of Air Quality. The case was prosecuted by the U.S. Attorney's Office in Anchorage.

R-105 ###

## Discretionary Responsibilities

**discretionary responsibility**
Organizational responsibility that is voluntary and guided by the organization's desire to make social contributions not mandated by economics, law, or ethics.

Discretionary responsibility is purely voluntary and is guided by a company's desire to make social contributions not mandated by economics, law, or ethics. Discretionary activities include generous philanthropic contributions that offer no payback to the company and are not expected. An example of discretionary behavior occurred when General Mills spent $2.5 million and donated thousands of hours of employee time to help rid a neighborhood of crime and drugs. Known as the *Hawthorne Huddle,* General Mills executives worked with law enforcement, politicians, community leaders, and residents to clean up the Minneapolis neighborhood. Today, Hawthorne homicides have dropped 32 percent and robberies 52 percent. Crack houses have been bulldozed to make way for a new elementary school, and low-income families are buying and fixing up homes with General Mills' grants. The company has been a leader in fulfilling discretionary responsibilities since the late 1800s, when it built an orphanage that continues today as a child guidance center.[55] Discretionary responsibility is the highest criterion of social responsibility, because it goes beyond societal expectations to contribute to the community's welfare.

*The Home Depot, Inc. is dedicated to "creating safe play areas in our communities." The world's largest home improvement retailer demonstrates its commitment to* **discretionary responsibility** *with its largest non-profit partner, KaBOOM! Through the KaBOOM! program, Home Depot recently built 52 playgrounds, bringing the total playgrounds built to 152 since 1996.*

THE HOME DEPOT, INC./JAMES HAYES, PHOTOGRAPHER

# Managing Company Ethics and Social Responsibility

Many managers are concerned with improving the ethical climate and social responsiveness of their companies. As one expert on the topic of ethics said, "Management is responsible for creating and sustaining conditions in which people are likely to behave themselves."[56] Managers must take active steps to ensure that the company stays on an ethical footing. As we discussed earlier in this chapter, ethical business practices depend on both individual managers and the organization's values, policies, and practices. Exhibit 5.9 illustrates the three pillars that support an ethical organization.[57]

## Ethical Individuals

Managers who are essentially ethical individuals make up the first pillar. These individuals possess honesty and integrity, which is reflected in their behavior and decisions. People inside and outside the organization trust them because they can be relied upon to follow the standards of fairness, treat people right, and be ethical in their dealings with others. Ethical individuals strive for a high level of moral development, as discussed earlier in the chapter.

However, being a moral person and making ethical decisions is not enough. Ethical managers also encourage the moral development of others.[58] They find ways to focus the entire organization's attention on ethical values and create an organizational environment that encourages, guides, and supports the ethical behavior of all employees. Two additional pillars are needed to provide a strong foundation for an ethical organization: ethical leadership and organizational structures and systems.

Exhibit 5.9

## The Three Pillars of an Ethical Organization

**The Ethical Organization**

**Ethical Individuals**
- Act with Integrity
- Behave honesty
- Inspire trust
- Treat people right
- Play fair
- Have high level of moral development

**Ethical Leadership**
- Be a role model
- Uphold ethical values in organization
- Communicate about ethics and values
- Reward ethical behavior
- Swiftly discipline unethical behavior

**Structures and Systems**
- Corporate culture
- Code of ethics
- Ethics committee
- Chief ethics officer
- Ethics training
- Whistle-blowing mechanisms

**SOURCE:** Adapted from Linda Klebe Treviño, Laura Pincus Hartman, and Michael Brown, "Moral Person and Moral Manager," *California Management Review* 42, no. 4 (Summer 2000), 128–142.

## Ethical Leadership

In a study of ethics policy and practice in successful, ethical companies no point emerged more clearly than the crucial role of leadership.[59] Employees are acutely aware of their bosses' ethical lapses, and the company grapevine quickly communicates situations in which top managers choose an expedient action over an ethical one.[60] The primary way in which leaders set the tone for an organization's ethics is through their own behavior. In addition, leaders make a commitment to ethical values and help others throughout the organization embody and reflect those values.[61]

If people don't hear about values from top leadership, they get the idea that ethical values are not important in the organization. Peter Holt, CEO of the Holt Companies, sees himself as the company's chief ethics officer. Ethical values are woven into the organizational culture, and Holt continually works to renew the values and signal his total commitment to them. Most importantly, he visits each of the firm's locations twice a year to meet with employees, answer questions, and talk about the importance of each employee upholding Holt's core values every day in every action. Holt's evaluation and reward systems are also tied to how well managers and employees live the values in their everyday actions.[62] Using performance reviews and rewards effectively is a powerful way for managers to signal that ethics counts. Consistently rewarding ethical behavior and disciplining unethical conduct at all levels of the company is a critical component of providing ethical leadership.[63]

## Organizational Structures and Systems

The third pillar of ethical organizations is the set of tools that managers use to shape values and promote ethical behavior throughout the organization. Three of these tools are codes of ethics, ethical structures, and mechanisms for supporting whistle-blowers.

## Code of Ethics

**code of ethics**

A formal statement of the organization's values regarding ethics and social issues.

A **code of ethics** is a formal statement of the company's values concerning ethics and social issues; it communicates to employees what the company stands for. Codes of ethics tend to exist in two types: principle-based statements and policy-based statements. *Principle-based statements* are designed to affect corporate culture; they define fundamental values and contain general language about company responsibilities, quality of products, and treatment of employees. General statements of principle are often called *corporate credos*. One good example is Johnson & Johnson's "The Credo."[64]

*Policy-based statements* generally outline the procedures to be used in specific ethical situations. These situations include marketing practice, conflicts of interest, observance of laws, proprietary information, political gifts, and equal opportunities. Examples of policy-based statements are Boeing's "Business Conduct Guidelines," Chemical Bank's "Code of Ethics," GTE's "Code of Business Ethics" and "Anti-Trust and Conflict of Interest Guidelines," and Norton's "Norton Policy on Business Ethics."[65]

Codes of ethics state the values or behaviors that are expected and those that will not be tolerated, backed up by management's action. A survey of *Fortune* 1,000 companies found that 98 percent address issues of ethics and business conduct in formal corporate documents, and 78 percent of those have separate codes of ethics that are widely distributed.[66] When top management supports and enforces these codes, including rewards for compliance and discipline for violation, ethics codes can uplift a company's ethical climate.[67] The code of ethics for *The Milwaukee Journal Sentinel* gives employees some guidelines for dealing with ethical questions.

**THE MILWAUKEE JOURNAL SENTINEL**
**http://www.jc.com**

In recent years, a spotlight has been cast on newspaper publishers and other media outlets in the wake of charges of plagiarism and other ethical violations. As a result, many companies are putting renewed emphasis on journalistic standards of integrity.

Executives at Journal Communications, the parent company of *The Milwaukee Journal Sentinel*, hope the company's clear and comprehensive code of ethics will reinforce the public's trust as well as prevent ethical misconduct. This excerpt from the opening sections of the code outlines some broad provisions for what the company stands for:

"Journal Communications and its subsidiaries operate in a complex and changing society. The actions of the company's employees, officers and directors clearly affect other members of that society. Therefore, every employee has an obligation to conduct the day-to-day business of the company in conformity with the highest ethical standards and in accordance with the various laws and regulations that govern modern business operations. . . .

Journal Communications' ethical standards embrace not only the letter of the law, but also the spirit of the law. To that end, we must apply plain old-fashioned honesty and decency to every aspect of our job. We must never sacrifice ethics for expedience. Broadly put, we should treat others fairly and with respect.

If faced with an ethical question, we should ask:
- Is this action legal?
- Does it comply with company policies and/or good business conduct?
- Is it something I would not want my supervisors, fellow employees, subordinates or family to know about?
- Is it something I would not want the general public to know about?

We must not condone illegal or unethical behavior . . . by failing to report it, regardless of an employee's level of authority. . . . The company will protect us if we bring unethical activity to its attention."

Journal's code of ethics also includes statements concerning respect for people, respect for the company, conflicts of interest, unfair competition, relationships with customers, suppliers, and news sources, confidential information, and accepting gifts and favors.[68]

By giving people some guidelines for confronting ethical questions and promising protection from recriminations for people who report wrongdoing, Journal's code of ethics gives all employees the responsibility and the right to maintain the organization's ethical climate.

## Ethical Structures

Ethical structures represent the various systems, positions, and programs a company can undertake to implement ethical behavior. An **ethics committee** is a group of executives appointed to oversee company ethics. The committee provides rulings on questionable ethical issues. The ethics committee assumes responsibility for disciplining wrongdoers, which is essential if the organization is to directly influence employee behavior. For example, Motorola has an Ethics Compliance Committee that is charged with interpreting, clarifying, and communicating the company's code of ethics and with adjudicating suspected code violations. Many companies, such as Sears, Northrop Grumman, and Columbia/HCA Healthcare, have set up ethics offices with full-time staff to ensure that ethical standards are an integral part of company operations. These offices are headed by a **chief ethics officer**, a company executive who oversees all aspects of ethics and legal compliance, including establishing and broadly communicating standards, ethics training, dealing with exceptions or problems, and advising senior managers in the ethical and compliance aspects of decisions.[69] The title of *chief ethics officer* was almost unheard of a decade ago, but there is a growing demand for these ethics specialists because of highly publicized ethical and legal problems faced by companies in recent years. The Ethics Officer Association, a trade group, reports that membership has soared to more than 955 companies, up from only 12 in 1992.[70] Most ethics offices also work as counseling centers to help employees resolve difficult ethical issues. A toll-free confidential hotline allows employees to report questionable behavior as well as seek guidance concerning ethical dilemmas.

**Ethics training** programs also help employees deal with ethical questions and translate the values stated in a code of ethics into everyday behavior.[71] Training programs are an important supplement to a written code of ethics. Boeing and Verizon require all employees to go through ethics training each year; at Boeing, senior managers get at least five hours annually. At McMurray Publishing Company in Phoenix, all employees attend a *weekly* meeting on workplace ethics, where they discuss how to handle ethical dilemmas and how to resolve conflicting values.[72]

A strong ethics program is important, but it is no guarantee against lapses. Enron could boast of a well-developed ethics program, but managers failed to live up to it. Enron's problems sent a warning to other managers and organizations. It is not enough to *have* an impressive ethics program. The ethics program must be merged with day-to-day operations, encouraging ethical decisions to be made throughout the company.

## Whistle-Blowing

Employee disclosure of illegal, immoral, or illegitimate practices on the employer's part is called **whistle-blowing**.[73] No organization can rely exclusively on codes of conduct and ethical structures to prevent all unethical behavior. Holding organizations accountable depends to some degree on individuals who are willing to blow the whistle if they detect illegal, dangerous, or unethical activities. Whistle-blowers often report wrongdoing to outsiders, such as regulatory agencies, senators, or newspaper reporters. One HealthSouth bookkeeper tried to blow the whistle by posting his concerns on a Yahoo! forum, but no one took the tip seriously.[74] Some firms have instituted innovative programs and confidential hotlines to encourage and support internal whistle-blowing. For this to be an effective ethical safeguard, however, companies must view whistle-blowing as a benefit to the company and make dedicated efforts to protect whistle-blowers.[75]

**ethics committee**
A group of executives assigned to oversee the organization's ethics by ruling on questionable issues and disciplining violators.

**chief ethics officer**
A company executive who oversees ethics and legal compliance.

**ethics training**
Training programs to help employees deal with ethical questions and values.

**whistle-blowing**
The disclosure by an employee of illegal, immoral, or illegitimate practices by the organization.

When there are no effective protective measures, whistle-blowers suffer. Although whistle-blowing has become widespread in recent years, it is still risky for employees, who can lose their jobs, be ostracized by coworkers, or be transferred to lower-level positions. When Colleen Rowley of the Federal Bureau of Investigation (FBI) wrote a 13-page memo to FBI director Robert Mueller about agency failures and lapses that may have contributed to the September 11, 2001, terrorist attacks, she was well aware of the risks. "Due to the frankness with which I have expressed myself . . . ," Rowley wrote, "I hope my continued employment with the FBI is not somehow placed in jeopardy." Fearing recriminations and suspecting that the FBI would suppress her allegations, Rowley also sent a copy of the memo to the Senate Intelligence Committee.[76]

There are laws protecting both government and private whistle-blowers from recrimination. However, many managers still look upon whistle-blowers as disgruntled employees who aren't good team players. To maintain high ethical standards, organizations need people who are willing to point out wrongdoing. Managers can be trained to view whistle-blowing as a benefit rather than a threat, and systems can be set up to effectively protect employees who report illegal or unethical activities.

# Ethical Challenges in Turbulent Times

The problem of lax ethical standards in business is nothing new, but in recent years it seems to have escalated. In addition, public reaction has been swift and unforgiving. Any ethical misstep can cost a company its reputation and hurt its profitability and performance. Consider Martha Stewart. Within months after she was charged with insider trading, her company's market capitalization plummeted $400 million. After a jury found her guilty in early 2004, some were concerned about whether the company could even survive. Companies like Nike and Gap have been hurt by accusations of exploitative labor practices in Third World factories. Oil companies have been targeted for allegedly abusing the environment and contributing to a host of social ills in developing nations, while pharmaceutical firms have been accused of hurting the world's poor by pricing drugs out of their reach. Some have also been accused of withholding information about their products. Organizational stakeholders including employees, shareholders, governments, and the general community are taking a keen interest in how companies conduct their business.

One reason for the proliferation of ethical lapses is the turbulence of our times. Things are moving so fast that managers who aren't firmly grounded in ethical values can find themselves making poor choices simply because they don't have the time to carefully weigh the situation and exercise considered judgment. When organizations operate in highly competitive industries, rapidly changing markets, and complex cultural and social environments, a strong corporate culture that emphasizes ethical behavior becomes even more important because it guides people to do the right thing even in the face of confusion and change.[77]

The combination of a turbulent domestic environment, the globalization of business, and increasing public scrutiny has convinced many managers to pay close attention to ethics and social responsibility as a business issue.[78] New global standards are emerging that raise the public's expectations about corporate responsibility to environmental and social ills. For example, in 1999, the United Nations General Assembly completed a Global Compact that outlines global ethical principles in the areas of human rights, labor standards, and the environment.[79] At the same time, varied stakeholders are pushing new reporting initiatives connected to the sustainability movement that emphasize the *triple bottom line* of economic, social, and environmental performance.

## Economic Performance

The relationship of a corporation's ethics and social responsibility to its financial performance concerns both managers and management scholars and has generated a lively debate.[80] One concern of managers is whether good citizenship will hurt performance—after all, ethics programs cost money. A number of studies have been undertaken to determine whether heightened ethical and social responsiveness increases or decreases financial performance. Studies have provided varying results but generally have found that there is a small positive relationship between social responsibility and financial performance.[81] For example, a recent study of the financial performance of large U.S. corporations considered "best corporate citizens" found that they have both superior reputations and superior financial performance.[82] Similarly Governance Metrics International, an independent corporate governance ratings agency in New York, found that the stocks of companies run on more selfless principles perform better than those run in a self-serving manner. Top-ranked companies such as Pfizer, Johnson Controls, and Sunoco also outperformed lower-ranking companies in measures like return on assets, return on investment, and return on capital.[83] Although results from these studies are not proof, they do provide an indication that use of resources for ethics and social responsibility does not hurt companies.[84]

Companies are also making an effort to measure the nonfinancial factors that create value. Researchers have found, for example, that people prefer to work for companies that demonstrate a high level of ethics and social responsibility, so these organizations can attract and retain high-quality employees.[85] Customers pay attention too. A study by Walker Research indicates that, price and quality being equal, two-thirds of customers say they would switch brands to do business with a company that is ethical and socially responsible.[86] Enlightened companies realize that integrity and trust are essential elements in sustaining successful and profitable business relationships with an increasingly connected web of employees, customers, suppliers, and partners. Although doing the right thing might not always be profitable in the short run, it develops a level of trust that money cannot buy and that will ultimately benefit the company. Many companies are becoming more socially responsible because they believe it provides a competitive advantage.[87]

## Social Entrepreneurship

Some organizations are taking social responsibility to the extreme, building whole companies that combine good business with good citizenship. Maria Otero is CEO of

© PROTECTIVE LIFE CORPORATION

**A corporate strategy anyone can understand.**

It's worked for Protective for almost one hundred years. Offer great products at highly competitive prices and provide the kind of attentive, personal service we'd hope to get from others. Sound too simple? Maybe, but it's helped us become one of the fastest growing companies in the life insurance industry. Isn't it reassuring to know that, "Doing the right thing is smart business"?

**Protective** *Doing the right thing is smart business.®*

▶ www.Protective.com

Life Insurance • Annuities • Retirement Savings • Asset Protection Products

Protective Life Corporation, PO Box 2606, Birmingham, AL 35202
PLC-1692 (8-03)

**CONCEPT CONNECTION**

*Protective Life Corporation shows its commitment to ethics through its corporate strategy: "Offer great products at highly competitive prices and provide the kind of attentive, personal service we'd hope to get from others." Managers at Protective believe being* **ethical and socially responsible** *has had a positive influence on the company's* **economic performance***. Protective's ethical stance has helped the company become one of the fastest growing in the life insurance industry.*

ACCIÓN International, a leader in the *microfinance* industry. ACCIÓN partners with existing banks to give tiny loans that are used to start tiny businesses in poor countries. For example, a Bolivian woman used a $100 loan to start a bread-making business using the mud oven in her one-room home. Six years later, she borrowed $2,800 to expand to five mud ovens and a backyard storefront.[88] Or consider Mitch Tobol. Tobol runs a full-service marketing agency in Port Washington, New York, that serves clients such as Weight Watchers International and Long Island Savings Bank. However, he and a friend also started an organization called Sparks, a sort of social club for learning disabled teens and adults.[89] The Sparks program serves 20 members, taking them to sporting events, dinners, and the theater, giving them opportunities to build strong social bonds and do the kinds of things most have never had a chance to do. This chapter's Unlocking Creative Solutions Through People box describes another cutting edge organization that combines good business with good citizenship.

**social entrepreneurs**
Entrepreneurial leaders who are committed to both good business and changing the world for the better.

A new breed of entrepreneur has emerged—the **social entrepreneur**. Social entrepreneurs are leaders who are committed to both good business and changing the world for the better. Social entrepreneurs have a primary goal of improving society rather than maximizing profits, but they also demand high performance standards and accountability for results. One writer referred to the breed as a cross between Richard Branson (high-powered CEO of Virgin Airlines) and Mother Teresa.[90] Social entrepreneurship is not new, but the phenomenon has blossomed over the past 15 years or so, and the organizations being created defy the traditional boundaries between business and welfare.[91] For example, David Green, founder of Project-Impact, helped start a factory in India that makes inexpensive plastic lenses used in cataract surgery. The factory provides lenses, some at no cost, for 200,000 poor Indians a year. It also makes money—30 percent profit margins in 2003—and has captured 10 percent of the global market for intraocular lenses. Green has expanded his approach to other parts of the world, as well as the United States, and is adding hearing aids to the product mix.[92] The organizations created by social entrepreneurs may or may not make a profit, but the bottom line for these companies is always social betterment rather than economic return.

Not every organization wants to become this closely involved in solving the world's social problems. However, companies that make an unwavering commitment to maintaining high standards of ethics and social responsibility will lead the way toward a brighter future for both business and society.

## Manager's Solution

Ethics and social responsibility are hot topics for today's managers. The ethical domain of behavior pertains to values of right and wrong. Ethical decisions and behavior are typically guided by a value system. Four value-based approaches that serve as criteria for ethical decision making are utilitarian, individualism, moral-rights, and justice. For an individual manager, the ability to make correct ethical choices will depend on both individual and organizational characteristics. An important individual characteristic is level of moral development. Corporate culture is an organizational characteristic that influences ethical behavior. Strong ethical cultures become more important in turbulent environments because they help people make the right choices in the face of confusion and rapid change.

Corporate social responsibility concerns a company's values toward society. How can organizations be good corporate citizens? The model for evaluating social performance uses four criteria: economic, legal, ethical, and discretionary. Evaluating corporate social behavior often requires assessing its impact on organizational stakeholders. One issue of growing concern is environmental responsibility. Organizations may take a legal, market, stakeholder, or activist approach to

# Unlocking Creative Solutions Through People

## Rubicon Does Good Deeds—and Good Business

The Rubicon Bakery has a goal of making the best cake in the business. And many people say the Rubicon Turtle Cake, with its light creamy caramel, hints of rich chocolate and a pecan crunch, meets the challenge. The Rubicon grosses $300,000 in its busiest month, and many customers don't know and don't care who makes the cakes, breads, or other goodies they enjoy.

But for Rick Aubry, executive director of Rubicon Programs, it's not all about business. Rubicon employs a unique team of bakers—formerly homeless, often mentally-ill people or recovering addicts from the San Francisco Bay Area of California. They come to Rubicon looking for a new start, and they find it. Rubicon starts them on easy tasks like peeling apples or washing utensils. Gradually they learn more complex jobs—and in the process relearn what it means to feel a sense of accomplishment and pride. The bakery is one of two businesses run by Rubicon. The other is a landscaping unit that does

$4 million a year in services from cutting grass to installing complex irrigation systems. Both businesses pay their employees a decent wage and bring in money to help support other Rubicon programs such as a career counseling center, money management classes, and substance abuse counseling. The career center provided job training for 800 people in 2003 and placed 400 in new jobs. Rubicon tracks results relentlessly, both in terms of business operations and social accomplishments.

Rubicon Programs has been in business to fulfill its social mission for more than 30 years. The organization was a pioneer in the strategy of putting social service clients to work in businesses that serve the mission at the same time they generate revenue that can support other funding sources. Together, the business operations account for about half of Rubicon's budget. By putting people to work, Aubry believes Rubicon helps them "move out of poverty and disenfranchisement, and back into the community with skills."

**SOURCE**: Alison Overholt, "Rubicon Programs Inc.," segment in "Social Capitalists: The Top 20 Groups That Are Changing the World," *Fast Company* (January 2004), 45-57.

addressing environmental concerns. Sustainability is a growing movement that emphasizes economic development that meets the needs of today while preserving resources for the future.

Ethical organizations are supported by three pillars: ethical individuals, ethical leadership, and organizational structures and systems, including codes of ethics, ethics committees, chief ethics officers, training programs, and mechanisms to protect whistle-blowers. Companies that are ethical and socially responsible perform as well as—and often better than—those that are not socially responsible. Social entrepreneurship is burgeoning as new leaders create innovative organizations that blur the boundaries between business and welfare. These organizations may or may not make a profit, but the overriding goal is to improve society.

Our management challenge at the beginning of the chapter illustrates how difficult issues of ethics and social responsibility can be. Timberland decided to continue its commitment to social causes. In fact, later the same year Swartz was faced with this dilemma, the company doubled the number of hours it underwrote for employees to do community service. That number has now increased to a full 40-hour week, plus the company offers paid sabbaticals for people to work six months full-time in community nonprofits. This commitment to *discretionary responsibility* has contributed to exceptional loyalty among many employees, because people feel good about the work they do. One vice president says she has turned down lucrative offers from other companies because at Timberland she doesn't feel like she has to check her values at the door. Timberland consistently ranks in *Fortune* magazine's survey of the 100 Best Companies to Work For, and more than 50 percent of Timberland's employees say the focus on community service is the main reason they work there. However, some people felt that

Timberland should have cut out the charity activities to focus on meeting its *economic responsibilities* when the company hit difficult times. In addition, some felt that the company was failing to meet its *ethical responsibilities* by spending money on community service when it was laying people off and shipping jobs overseas. Some employees bluntly asked, "Doesn't charity begin at home?" Swartz said. He believed, however, that cutting out community service would damage morale and lower commitment without solving the financial problems. Fortunately, Timberland rebounded from its difficulties and continued to grow. However, managers will continue to face challenges concerning how to best meet their responsibilities to all stakeholders.[93]

# Discussion Questions

1. Dr. Martin Luther King, Jr., said, "As long as there is poverty in the world, I can never be rich . . . . As long as diseases are rampant, I can never be healthy. . . . I can never be what I ought to be until you are what you ought to be." Discuss this quote with respect to the material in this chapter. Would this be true for corporations, too?

2. Environmentalists are trying to pass laws for oil spills that would remove all liability limits for the oil companies. This would punish corporations financially. Is this the best way to influence companies to be socially responsible?

3. Compare and contrast the utilitarian approach with the moral-rights approach to ethical decision making. Which do you believe is the best for managers to follow? Why?

4. Imagine yourself in a situation of being encouraged to inflate your expense account. Do you think your choice would be most affected by your individual moral development or by the cultural values of the company for which you worked? Explain.

5. Is it socially responsible for organizations to undertake political activity or join with others in a trade association to influence the government? Discuss.

6. The criteria of corporate social responsibility suggest that economic responsibilities are of the greatest magnitude, followed by legal, ethical, and discretionary responsibilities. How do these four types of responsibility relate to corporate responses to social demands? Discuss.

7. From where do managers derive ethical values? What can managers do to help define ethical standards for the corporation?

8. Have you ever experienced an ethical dilemma? Evaluate the dilemma with respect to its impact on other people.

9. Lincoln Electric considers customers and employees to be more important stakeholders than shareholders. Is it appropriate for management to define some stakeholders as more important than others? Should all stakeholders be considered equal?

10. Do you think a code of ethics combined with an ethics committee would be more effective than leadership for implementing ethical behavior? Discuss.

# Management in Practice: Experiential Exercise

## Ethical Work Climates

Answer the following questions by circling the number that best describes an organization for which you have worked.

| Disagree | | | | Agree |
|---|---|---|---|---|
| 1 | 2 | 3 | 4 | 5 |

1. What is the best for everyone in the company is the major consideration here.
   1     2     3     4     5

2. Our major concern is always what is best for the other person. 1   2   3   4   5

3. People are expected to comply with the law and professional standards over and above other considerations. 1   2   3   4   5

4. In this company, the first consideration is whether a decision violates any law.
   1     2     3     4     5

5. It is very important to follow the company's rules and procedures here.
   1     2     3     4     5

6. People in this company strictly obey the company policies.
   1     2     3     4     5

7. In this company, people are mostly out for themselves. 1   2   3   4   5

8. People are expected to do anything to further the company's interests, regardless of the consequences. 1   2   3   4   5

9. In this company, people are guided by their own personal ethics.
   1     2     3     4     5

10. Each person in this company decides for himself or herself what is right and wrong.
    1     2     3     4     5

**Total Score** _____

Add up your score. These questions measure the dimensions of an organization's ethical climate. Questions 1 and 2 measure caring for people, questions 3 and 4 measure lawfulness, questions 5 and 6 measure rules adherence, questions 7 and 8 measure emphasis on financial and company performance, and questions 9 and 10 measure individual independence. Questions 7 and 8 are reverse scored (1 = 5, 2 = 4, 3 = 3, 4 = 2, 5 = 1). A total score above 40 indicates a very positive ethical climate. A score from 30 to 40 indicates above-average ethical climate. A score from 20 to 30 indicates a below-average ethical climate, and a score below 20 indicates a very poor ethical climate.

Go back over the questions and think about changes that you could have made to improve the ethical climate in the organization. Discuss with other students what you could do as a manager to improve ethics in future companies you work for.

Source: Based on Bart Victor and John B. Cullen, "The Organizational Bases of Ethical Work Climates," *Administrative Science Quarterly* 33 (1988), 101–125.

# Management in Practice: Ethical Dilemma

## What is Right?

It is often hard for a manager to determine what is "right" and even more difficult to put ethical behavior into practice. A manager's ethical orientation often brings him or her into conflict with people, policies, customers, or bosses. Consider the following dilemmas. How would you handle them?

1. A well-liked member of your staff with an excellent record confides to you that he has Acquired Immune Deficiency Syndrome (AIDS). Although his illness has not affected his performance, you're concerned about his future health and about the reactions of his coworkers. You
   a. tell him to keep you informed about his health and say nothing to his coworkers.

b. arrange for him to transfer to an area of the organization where he can work alone.
c. hold a staff meeting to inform his coworkers and ask them how they feel about his continued presence on your team.
d. consult your human resources officer on how to proceed.

2. During a reorganization, you're told to reduce staff in the department you manage. After analyzing staffing requirements, you realize the job would be a lot easier if two professionals, who both are over age 60, would retire. You
a. say nothing and determine layoffs based purely on performance and length of service.
b. schedule a meeting with both employees and ask if they'd consider early retirement.
c. schedule a meeting with all staff and ask if anyone is interested in severance or early retirement.
d. lay off the older workers.

3. One of your colleagues has recently experienced two personal tragedies—her husband filed for divorce and her mother died. Although you feel genuine sympathy for her, her work is suffering. A report you completed, based on inaccurate data she provided, has been criticized by management. Your manager asks you for an explanation. You
a. apologize for the inaccuracies and correct the data.
b. tell your manager that the data supplied by your colleague was the source of the problem.
c. say your colleague has a problem and needs support.
d. tell your manager that because of your work load, you didn't have time to check the figures in the report.

4. Your firm recently hired a new manager who is at the same level you are. You do not like the man personally and consider him a rival professionally. You run into a friend who knows your rival well. You discover this man did not attend Harvard as he stated on his resume and in fact has not graduated from any college. You know his supposed Harvard background was instrumental in getting him hired. You
a. expose the lie to your superiors.
b. without naming names, consult your human resources officer on how to proceed.
c. say nothing. The company obviously failed to check him out, and the lie probably will surface on its own.

d. confront the man with the information and let him decide what to do.

5. During a changeover in the accounting department, you discover your company has been routinely overcharging members of the public for services provided to them. Your superiors say repayment of charges would wreak havoc on company profits. Your company is federally regulated, and the oversight commission has not noticed the mistake. Your bosses say the problem will never come to light and they will take steps to correct the problem so it never happens again. You
a. contact the oversight commission.
b. take the matter public, anonymously or otherwise.
c. say nothing. It is now in the hands of the bosses.
d. work with the bosses on a plan to recognize the company's error and set up a schedule of rebates that would not unduly penalize the company.

6. In this morning's mail, you received plans and samples for a promising new product from a competitor's disgruntled employee. You
a. throw the plans away.
b. send the samples to your research department for analysis.
c. notify your competitor about what is going on.
d. call the FBI.

## Questions

1. Use the guidelines described in Manager's Shoptalk: "Guidelines for Ethical Decision Making" to determine the appropriate behavior in these cases. Do you have all the information you need to make an ethical decision? How would family or friends react to each alternative if you were in these situations?
2. Which approach to ethical decision making—utilitarian, individualism, justice, or moral-rights—seems most appropriate for handling these situations?

Sources: Game developed by Katherine Nelson, "Board Games," *Owen Manager*, spring 1990, 14–16; Craig Dreilinger and Dan Rice, "Office Ethics," *Working Woman*, December 1991, 35–39; and Kevin Kelly and Joseph Weber, "When a Rival's Trade Secret Crosses Your Desk . . . ," *Business Week*, May 20, 1991, 48.

# Surf the Net

1. **Social Responsibility.** The Global Business Responsibility Resource Center at *http://www.bsr. org/resourcecenter/* states its mission is "to provide businesses with the information they need to understand and implement more responsible policies and practices, and to promote increased knowledge and collaboration among companies and between business and other sectors." Its goal is "to help companies achieve sustained commercial success in ways that honor high ethical standards and benefit people, communities, and the environment." After registering (free), select a topic and print out a report to submit to your instructor.

2. **Code of Ethics.** Use your search engine to find the codes of ethics for three organizations. One site that contains 850+ codes of ethics is *http:// csep.iit.edu/departments/csep/publicwww/codes/*. Compare the three codes to determine the similarities and differences among them in terms of focus, approach, language, and emphases. Provide

possible reasons for the similarities and differences you cited. How might you benefit as an employee working for an organization with a code of ethics compared to working for an organization without a code of ethics?

3. **Ethical Structures.** Lockheed Martin is one of the world's leading diversified technology companies. Government and commercial customers around the world purchase its advanced technology systems, products, and services. Its core businesses span aeronautics, electronics, energy, information and services, space, systems integration, and telecommunications. Lockheed Martin provides an excellent example of an organization with a variety of systems, positions, and programs to implement ethical behavior among its employees. Visit the Ethics section in About Us available at *http://www.lockheedmartin.com*. Write a summary of the ethical structures at Lockheed Martin.

# Case for Critical Analysis

### Colt 45 and the Ad Hoc Group Against Crime

The Ad Hoc Group Against Crime, a Kansas City organization, recently accepted a contribution from Colt 45—the group will get a 25-cent donation for every case of Colt 45 malt liquor sold through participating vendors. In accepting the money, Ad Hoc opened itself to an ethical dilemma that has hounded minority interest groups for decades. Violent crime hits many minority communities hard, and numerous studies have linked crime to alcohol consumption. Studies have also shown that although African Americans have higher rates of abstinence than whites, they still have higher death rates tied to alcohol abuse.

Ad Hoc's president, Alvin Brooks, says the group doesn't see this as encouraging sales of Colt 45. "We are saying to the alcohol companies: 'If you are taking something away from the community, you are going to have to give something back.'" Brooks also

notes that Ad Hoc is not in a financial position to turn away viable fund-raising opportunities. Other minority interest groups have long accepted alcohol and tobacco funds for the same reason, and over the years a loyalty has developed—a loyalty that the alcohol and tobacco companies began actively courting decades ago. Studies have shown that billboards advertising tobacco products are placed in black communities four to five times more often than in predominantly white communities and that the number of liquor outlets in proportion to the population is much higher in inner-city neighborhoods.

A spokesperson for Colt 45 said the fund-raiser is simply a way for retailers to show their support for the community. In general, large alcohol and tobacco companies are reluctant to discuss their funding of minority causes. A Philip Morris representative, commenting that the contributions are important in keeping communities economically able to buy products, said, "Their vibrancy is our vibrancy."

## Questions

1. Are companies such as Colt 45 and Philip Morris acting in an ethical and socially responsible way? What criteria of social responsibility are these companies following?

2. Is the Ad Hoc Group Against Crime being socially responsible by accepting this money?

3. Can you think of more socially responsible ways Colt 45 might contribute to minority communities?

Should this group take a symbolic stand against alcohol?

Source: Based on Mary Sanchez, "When Charity Taps 'Vice' for Money," *The Tennessean*, August 6, 1995, 2D.

## Endnotes

1. Christopher Marquis, "Doing Well and Doing Good," *The New York Times* (July 3, 2003), Section 3, 2; and Joseph Pereira, "Career Journal: Doing Good and Doing Well at Timberland," *The Wall Street Journal* (September 9, 2003), B1.

2. Bethany McLean, "Why Enron Went Bust," *Fortune* (December 24, 2001), 58–68; survey results reported in Patricia Wallington, "Honestly?!" *CIO*, March 15, 2003, 41–42.

3. Data from KPMG, reported in Muel Kaptein, "The Diamond of Managerial Integrity," *European Management Journal* 21, no. 1 (2003), 99–108.

4. Jon Gertner, "Newman's Own: Two Friends and a Canoe Paddle," *The New York Times* (November 16, 2003), BU4; Michelle Conlin and Jessi Hempel, with Joshua Tanzer and David Polek, "Philanthropy 2003: The Corporate Donors," *BusinessWeek* (December 1, 2003), 92–96.

5. Gordon F. Shea, *Practical Ethics* (New York: American Management Association, 1988); and Linda K. Treviño, "Ethical Decision Making in Organizations; A Person-Situation Interactionist Model," *Academy of Management Review* 11 (1986), 601–617.

6. Thomas M. Jones, "Ethical Decision Making by Individuals in Organizations: An Issue-Contingent Model," *Academy of Management Review* 16(1991), 366–395.

7. John R. Emshwiller and Alexei Barrionuevo, "U.S. Prosecutors File Indictment Against Skilling," *The Wall Street Journal* (February 20, 2004), A1, A13.

8. See Clinton W. McLemore, *Street-Smart Ethics: Succeeding in Business Without Selling Your Soul* (Louisville, Ky.: Westminster John Knox Press, 2003) for a cogent discussion of some ethical and legal issues associated with Enron's collapse.

9. Rushworth M. Kidder, "The Three Great Domains of Human Action," *Christian Science Monitor* (January 30, 1990).

10. Linda K. Treviño and Katherine A. Nelson, *Managing Business Ethics: Straight Talk About How to Do It Right* (New York: John Wiley & Sons, Inc. 1995), 4.

11. Jones, "Ethical Decision Making by Individuals in Organizations.

12. Based on information in Constance E. Bagley, "The Ethical Leader's Decision Tree," *Harvard Business Review* (February 2003), 18–19.

13. Based on information in Vadim Liberman, "Scoring on the Job," *Across the Board* (November–December 2003), 46–50.

14. This discussion is based on Gerald F. Cavanagh, Dennis J. Moberg, and Manuel Velasquez, "The Ethics of Organizational Politics," *Academy of Management Review* 6 (1981), 363–374; Justin G. Longenecker, Joseph A. McKinney, and Carlos W. Moore, "Egoism and Independence: Entrepreneurial Ethics," *Organizational Dynamics* (Winter 1988), 64–72; Carolyn Wiley, "The ABCs of Business Ethics: Definitions, Philosophies, and Implementation," *IM* (February 1995), 22–27; and Mark Mallinger, "Decisive Decision Making: An Exercise Using Ethical Frameworks," *Journal of Management Education* (August 1997), 411–417.

15. Michael J. McCarthy, "Now the Boss Knows Where You're Clicking," and "Virtual Morality: A New Workplace Quandary," *The Wall Street Journal* (October 21, 1999), B1, B4; and Jeffrey L. Seglin, "Who's Snooping on You?" *Business 2.0* (August 8, 2000), 202–203.

16. Ron Winslow, "Rationing Care," *The Wall Street Journal* (November 13, 1989), R24.

17. Alan Wong and Eugene Beckman, "An Applied Ethical Analysis System in Business," *Journal of Business Ethics* 11 (1992), 173–178.

18. John Kekes, "Self-Direction: The Core of Ethical Individualism," *Organizations and Ethical Individualism*, ed. Konstanian Kolenda (New York: Praeger, 1988), 1–18.

19. Tad Tulega, *Beyond the Bottom Line* (New York: Penguin Books, 1987).

20. Lynn Sharp Paine, "Managing for Organizational Integrity," *Harvard Business Review* (March–April 1994), 106–117.

21. This discussion is based on Treviño, "Ethical Decision Making in Organizations."

22. L. Kohlberg, "Moral Stages and Moralization: The Cognitive-Developmental Approach," in *Moral Development and Behavior: Theory, Research, and Social Issues,* ed. T. Lickona (New York: Holt, Rinehart & Winston, 1976) 31–83; L. Kohlberg, "Stage and Sequence: The Cognitive-Developmental Approach to Socialization," in *Handbook of Socialization Theory and Research,* ed. D. A. Goslin (Chicago: Rand McNally, 1969); and Jill W. Graham, "Leadership, Moral Development, and Citizenship Behavior," *Business Ethics Quarterly* 5, no. 1 (January 1995), 43–54.

23. Carol Gilligan, *In a Different Voice: Psychological Theory and Women's Development* (Cambridge, Mass.: Harvard University Press, 1982).

24. See Thomas Donaldson and Thomas W. Dunfee, "When Ethics Travel: The Promise and Peril of Global Business Ethics," *California Management Review* 41, No. 4 (Summer 1999), 45–63.

25. Transparency International, "Transparency International Releases New Bribe Payers Index," http://www.transparency.org accessed on February 24, 2004.

26. Susan Pulliam, "Over the Line: A Staffer Ordered to Commit Fraud Balked, Then Caved," *The Wall Street Journal* (June 23, 2003), A1.

27. Duane M. Covrig, "The Organizational Context of Moral Dilemmas: The Role of Moral Leadership in Administration in Making and Breaking Dilemmas," *The Journal of Leadership Studies* 7, no. 1 (2000), 40–59; and James Weber, "Influences Upon Organizational Ethical Subclimates: A Multi-Departmental Analysis of a Single Firm," *Organizational Science* 6, no. 5 (September–October 1995), 509–523.

28. Linda Klebe Treviño, "A Cultural Perspective on Changing and Developing Organizational Ethics," in *Research and Organizational Change and Development,* ed. R. Woodman and W. Pasmore (Greenwich, Conn.: JAI Press, 1990), 4.

29. *Ibid*; John B. Cullen, Bart Victor, and Carroll Stephens, "An Ethical Weather Report: Assessing the Organization's Ethical Climate," *Organizational Dynamics* (Autumn 1989), 50–62; and Bart Victor and John B. Cullen, "The Organizational Bases of Ethical Work Climates," *Administrative Science Quarterly* 33 (1988), 101–125.

30. Eugene W. Szwajkowski, "The Myths and Realities of Research on Organizational Misconduct," in *Research in Corporate Social Performance and Policy,* ed. James E. Post (Greenwich, Conn.: JAI Press, 1986), 9:103–122; and Keith Davis, William C. Frederick, and Robert L. Blostrom, *Business and Society: Concepts and Policy Issues* (New York: McGraw-Hill, 1979).

31. Douglas S. Sherwin, "The Ethical Roots of the Business System," *Harvard Business Review* 61 (November–December 1983), 183–192.

32. Nancy C. Roberts and Paula J. King, "The Stakeholder Audit Goes Public," *Organizational Dynamics* (Winter 1989), 63–79; Thomas Donaldson and Lee E. Preston, "The Stakeholder Theory of the Corporation: Concepts, Evidence, and Implications," *Academy of Management Review* 20, no. 1 (1995), 65–91; and Jeffrey S. Harrison and Caron H. St. John, "Managing and Partnering with External Stakeholders," *Academy of Management Executive* 10, no. 2 (1996), 46–60.

33. Charles Fishman, "The Wal-Mart You Don't Know—Why Low Prices Have a High Cost," *Fast Company* (December 2003), 68–80.

34. David Wheeler, Barry Colbert, and R. Edward Freeman, "Focusing on Value: Reconciling Corporate Social Responsibility, Sustainability, and a Stakeholder Approach in a Networked World," *Journal of General Management* 28, no. 3 (Spring 2003), 1–28; and James E. Post, Lee E. Preston, and Sybille Sachs, "Managing the Extended Enterprise: The New Stakeholder View," *California Management Review* 45, no. 1 (Fall 2002), 6–28.

35. Max B. E. Clarkson, "A Stakeholder Framework for Analyzing and Evaluating Corporate Social Performance," *Academy of Management Review* 20, no. 1 (1995), 92–117.

36. "The World We Serve," *Bristol-Myers Squibb 2002 Annual Report,* Bristol-Myers Squibb Company.

37. Mark A. Cohen, "Management and the Environment," *The Owen Manager* 15, no. 1 (1993), 2–6.

38. R. E. Freeman, J. Pierce, and R. Dodd, *Shades of Green: Business Ethics and the Environment* (New York: Oxford University Press, 1995).

39. Greg Toppo, "Company Agrees to Pay Record Pollution Fine," Associated Press, *Johnson City Press* (July 21, 2000), 9.

40. Andrew C. Revkin, "7 Companies Agree to Cut Gas Emissions," *The New York Times* (October 18, 2000), C1, C6.

41. This definition is based on Marc J. Epstein and Marie-Josée Roy, "Improving Sustainability Performance: Specifying, Implementing and Measuring Key Principles," *Journal of General Management* 29, no. 1 (Autumn 2003), 15–31, World Commission on Economic Development, *Our Common Future*

(Oxford: Oxford University Press, 1987), and Marc Gunther, "Tree Huggers, Soy Lovers, and Profits," *Fortune* (June 23, 2003), 98–104.

42. Gunther, "Tree Huggers, Soy Lovers, and Profits."

43. *Operating in Unison: UPS 2002 Corporate Sustainability Report,* UPS Corporate, Atlanta, Georgia.

44. Brian Deagon, "New Technology Could Boost Efficiency and Green Image for UPS," *Investor's Business Daily* (December 10, 2003); and Charles Haddad with Christine Tierney, "FedEx and Brown Are Going Green," *BusinessWeek* (August 11, 2003), 60.

45. Gunther, "Tree Huggers, Soy Lovers, and Profits."

46. The discussion of ISO 14001 is based on Pratima Bansal, "The Corporate Challenges of Sustainable Development," *Academy of Management Executive* 16, no. 2 (2002), 122–131.

47. Karina Funk, "Sustainability and Performance," *MIT Sloan Management Review* (Winter 2003), 65–70; and "The Fast 50: Trendsetters," *Fast Company* (March 2002).

48. Mark S. Schwartz and Archie B. Carroll, "Corporate Social Responsibility: A Three-Domain Approach," *Business Ethics Quarterly* 13, no. 4 (2003), 503–530; and Archie B. Carroll, "A Three-Dimensional Conceptual Model of Corporate Performance," *Academy of Management Review* 4 (1979), 497–505. For a discussion of various models for evaluating corporate social performance, also see Diane L. Swanson, "Addressing a Theoretical Problem by Reorienting the Corporate Social Performance Model," *Academy of Management Review* 20, no. 1 (1995), 43–64.

49. N. Craig Smith, "Corporate Social Responsibility: Whether or How?" *California Management Review* 45, no. 4 (Summer 2003), 52–76.

50. Milton Friedman, *Capitalism and Freedom* (Chicago: University of Chicago Press, 1962), 133; and Milton Friedman and Rose Friedman, *Free to Choose* (New York: Harcourt Brace Jovanovich, 1979).

51. Eugene W. Szwajkowski, "Organizational Illegality: Theoretical Integration and Illustrative Application," *Academy of Management Review* 10 (1985), 558–567.

52. Kurt Eichenwald, "U.S. Awards Tenet Whistle-Blowers $8.1 Million," *The New York Times* (January 8, 2004), http://www.nytimes.com.

53. David J. Fritzsche and Helmut Becker, "Linking Management Behavior to Ethical Philosophy—An Empirical Investigation," *Academy of Management Journal* 27 (1984), 165–175.

54. Sydney Finkelstein, "Jayson Blair, Meet Nicholas Leeson," (Manager's Journal column), *The Wall Street Journal,* May 20, 2003, B2; Matthew Rose and Laurie P. Cohen, "Man in the News: Amid Turmoil, Top Editors Resign at *New York Times,*" *The Wall Street Journal* (June 6, 2003), A1.

55. Conlin, et al., "Philanthropy 2003: The Corporate Donors."

56. Saul W. Gellerman, "Managing Ethics from the Top Down," *Sloan Management Review* (Winter 1989), 73–79.

57. This discussion is based on Linda Klebe Treviño, Laura Pincus Hartman, and Michael Brown, "Moral Person and Moral Manager: How Executives Develop a Reputation for Ethical Leadership," *California Management Review* 42, no. 4 (Summer 2000), 128–142.

58. Muel Kaptein, "The Diamond of Managerial Integrity," *European Management Journal* 21, no. 1 (2003), 99–108.

59. Business Roundtable Institute for Corporate Ethics, http://www.corporate-ethics.org and "Corporate Ethics: A Prime Business Asset," *The Business Roundtable,* 200 Park Avenue, Suite 2222, New York, New York, 10166, February 1988.

60. Michael Barrier, "Doing the Right Thing," *Nation's Business* (March 1998), 33–38; Joseph L. Badaracco, Jr., and Allen P. Webb, "Business Ethics: A View from the Trenches," *California Management Review* 37, no. 2 (Winter 1995), 8–28.

61. Linda Klebe Treviño, Gary R. Weaver, David G. Gibson, and Barbara Ley Toffler, "Managing Ethics and Legal Compliance: What Works and What Hurts?" *California Management Review* 41, no. 2 (Winter 1999), 131–151.

62. Linda Klebe Treviño and Katherine A. Nelson, *Managing Business Ethics: Straight Talk About How to Do It Right,* 2nd ed. (New York: John Wiley & Sons, 1999), 274–283.

63. Treviño, Hartman, and Brown, "Moral Person and Moral Manager."

64. "Corporate Ethics."

65. Ibid.

66. Treviño et al., "Managing Ethics and Legal Compliance."

67. Carolyn Wiley, "The ABC's of Business Ethics: Definitions, Philosophies, and Implementation," *IM* (January–February 1995), 22–27; Badaracco and Webb, "Business Ethics: a View from the Trenches"; and Ronald B. Morgan, "Self- and Co-Worker Perceptions of Ethics and Their Relationships to Leadership and Salary," *Academy of Management Journal* 36, no. 1 (February 1993), 200–214.

68. Journal Communications—Code of Ethics, from Codes of Ethics Online, The Center for the Study of Ethics in the Professions, Illinois Institute of Technology, http://www.iit.edu/departments/csep/PublicWWW/codes/index.html

69. Alan Yuspeh, "Do the Right Thing," *CIO* (August 1, 2000), 56–58.

70. The Ethics Officers Association, http://www.eoa.org, accessed on February 25, 2004.

71. Beverly Geber, "The Right and Wrong of Ethics Offices," *Training* (October 1995), 102–118.

72. Amy Zipkin, "Getting Religion on Corporate Ethics," *The New York Times*, (October 18, 2000), C1.

73. Marcia Parmarlee Miceli and Janet P. Near, "The Relationship among Beliefs, Organizational Positions, and Whistle-Blowing Status: A Discriminant Analysis," *Academy of Management Journal* 27 (1984), 687–705.

74. Carrick Mollenkamp, "Missed Signal: Accountant Tried in Vain to Expose HealthSouth Fraud," *The Wall Street Journal* (May 20, 2003), A1.

75. Eugene Garaventa, "*An Enemy of the People* by Henrik Ibsen: The Politics of Whistle-Blowing," *Journal of Management Inquiry* 3, no. 4 (December 1994), 369–374; Marcia P. Miceli and Janet P. Near, "Whistleblowing: Reaping the Benefits," *Academy of Management Executive* 8, no. 3 (1994), 65–74.

76. Steven L. Schooner, "Badge of Courage," *Government Executive* (August 2002), 65.

77. Jerry G. Kreuze, Zahida Luqmani, and Mushtaq Luqmani, "Shades of Gray," *Internal Auditor* (April 2001), 48.

78. Sandra A. Waddock, Charles Bodwell, and Samuel B. Graves, "Responsibility: The New Business Imperative," *Academy of Management Executive* 16, no. 2 (2002), 132–148.

79. The Global Compact Web site http://www.unglobalcompact.org, accessed on July 18, 2001; and Zipkin, "Getting Religion on Corporate Ethics."

80. Homer H. Johnson, "Does It Pay to Be Good? Social Responsibility and Financial Performance" *Business Horizons* (November–December 2003), 34–40; Jennifer J. Griffin and John F. Mahon, "The Corporate Social Performance and Corporate Financial Performance Debate: Twenty-Five Years of Incomparable Research," *Business and Society* 36, no. 1 (March 1997), 5–31; Bernadette M. Ruf, Krishnamurty Muralidar, Robert M. Brown, Jay J. Janney, and Karen Paul, "An Empirical Investigation of the Relationship between Change in Corporate Social Performance and Financial Performance: A Stakeholder Theory Perspetive," *Journal of Business Ethics* 32, no. 2 (July 2001), 143; Philip L. Cochran and Robert A. Wood, "Corporate Social Responsibility and Financial Performance," *Academy of Management Journal* 27 (1984), 42–56.

81. Curtis C. Verschoor and Elizabeth A. Murphy, "The Financial Performance of Large U. S. Firms and Those with Global Prominence: How Do the Best Corporate Citizens Rate?" *Business and Society Review* 107, no. 3 (Fall 2002), 371–381; Johnson, "Does It Pay to Be Good?"; Dale Kurschner, "5 Ways Ethical Business Creates Fatter Profits," *Business Ethics* (March–April 1996), 20–23. Also see studies reported in Lori Ioannou, "Corporate America's Social Conscience," *Fortune* (May 26, 2003), S1–S10.

82. Verschoor and Murphy, "The Financial Performance of Large U.S. Firms."

83. Gretchen Morgenson, "Shares of Corporate Nice Guys Can Finish First," *New York Times* (April 27, 2003), Section 3, 1.

84. Jean B. McGuire, Alison Sundgren, and Thomas Schneeweis, "Corporate Social Responsibility and Firm Financial Performance," *Academy of Management Journal* 31 (1988), 854–872; and Louisa Wah, "Treading the Sacred Ground," *Management Review* (July–August 1998), 18–22.

85. Daniel W. Greening and Daniel B. Turban, "Corporate Social Performance as a Competitive Advantage in Attracting a Quality Workforce," *Business and Society* 39, no. 3 (September 2000), 254.

86. "The Socially Correct Corporate Business," segment in Leslie Holstrom and Simon Brady, "The Changing Face of Global Business," special advertising section, *Fortune* (July 24, 2000), S1–S38.

87. Based on survey results from PriceWaterhouseCoopers, *2002 Sustainability Survey Report,* reported in Ioannou, "Corporate America's Social Conscience."

88. Cheryl Dahle, "Social Capitalists: The Top 20 Groups That Are Changing the World," *Fast Company* (January 2004), 45–57.

89. Tricia Tunstall, "Giving Beyond Their Means," *FSB* (December 2003–January 2004), 109–112.

90. Albert R. Hunt, "Social Entrepreneurs: Compassionate and Tough-Minded," *The Wall Street Journal* (July 13, 2000), A27; David Puttnam, "Hearts Before Pockets," *The New Statesman* (February 9, 2004), 26.

91. David Bornstein, *How to Change the World: Social Entrepreneurs and the Power of New Ideas* (Oxford and New York: Oxford University Press, 2004).

92. Brian Dumaine, "See Me, Hear Me," segment in "Two Ways to Help the Third World," *Fortune* (October 27, 2003), 187–196.

93. Marquis, "Doing Well and Doing Good," and Pereira, "Career Journal: Doing Good and Doing Well at Timberland."

# Managing Small Business Start-Ups

## LEARNING OBJECTIVES

*After studying this chapter, you should be able to*

1. Describe the importance of entrepreneurship to the U.S. economy.

2. Define the personality characteristics of a typical entrepreneur.

3. Describe the planning necessary to undertake a new business venture.

4. Explain the steps involved in launching a high-tech start-up.

5. Describe the five stages of growth for an entrepreneurial company.

6. Explain how the management functions of planning, organizing, leading, and controlling apply to a growing entrepreneurial company.

Reese Terry was working at Intermedics, a Texas medical products company, when a neurophysiologist friend showed him a primitive medical device, a vagus-nerve stimulator that seemed to halt seizures in dogs. Intrigued by the possibilities for human epilepsy patients, Terry presented the idea to Intermedics, but results of their studies were mixed. The company dropped the project. So, when Terry found himself out of a job a couple of years later due to a corporate restructuring, he decided to pursue the vagus-nerve stimulator on his own, starting a company he named Cyberonics Inc. With a carefully thought-out business plan and a story of how the device could improve the lives of thousands of epilepsy patients, Terry managed to raise $1 million in start-up costs from three venture capital firms. Thrilled to be off and running, he rented offices in a strip mall, hired an assistant, and contracted with medical device consultants. Then reality sank in. Terry was convinced that the vagus-nerve stimulator was a great idea, and no one else was picking up on it. However, he also realized that conceiving and designing a medical device, earning FDA approval, and persuading doctors to use it is one of the riskiest and most expensive ventures in the business world. His $1 million in start-up funds would not likely be enough to get the first device actually implanted into a human body. How could a small company with two employees get such a sophisticated device built and tested, raise more money, and navigate the arduous FDA approval process? Even if it could, would typically conservative neurologists be willing to use the device?[1]

## Take A Moment

What advice would you give Reese Terry about getting his new company started? Do you think one person with a good idea can create a successful business in a high-cost, high-risk industry like medical devices?

Many people dream of starting their own business. Some, like Reese Terry, decide to go into business for themselves after they get laid off from big companies, or when they come up with a great idea. Others simply pursue a longtime desire to work for themselves. Interest in entrepreneurship and small business is at an all-time high. At college campuses across the United States, ambitious courses, programs, and centers teach the fundamentals of starting a small business. Entrepreneurs have access to business incubators, support networks, and online training courses. The enormous growth of franchising gives beginners an escorted route into a new business. In addition, the Internet has opened up a new avenue for small business formation. Since the 1970s, the number of businesses in the U.S. economy has been growing faster than the labor force, and the annual number of business launches continues to increase.[2]

However, running a small business is difficult and risky. The Small Business Administration reports that about 34 percent of businesses with fewer than 500 employees close within two years of opening and 50 percent fold after three years.[3] For high-tech businesses such as Cyberonics, the failure rate is even higher. Businesses that survive continue to face tremendous challenges, yet despite the risks, people are entering the world of entrepreneurship at an unprecedented rate.

## What Is Entrepreneurship?

**entrepreneurship**
The process of initiating a business venture, organizing the necessary resources, and assuming the associated risks and rewards.

**entrepreneur**
Someone who recognizes a viable idea for a business product or service and carries it out.

**Entrepreneurship** is the process of initiating a business venture, organizing the necessary resources, and assuming the associated risks and rewards.[4] An **entrepreneur** is someone who engages in entrepreneurship. An entrepreneur recognizes a viable idea for a business product or service and carries it out. This means finding and assembling necessary resources—money, people, machinery, location—to undertake the business venture. Entrepreneurs also assume the risks and reap the rewards of the business. They assume the financial and legal risks of ownership and receive the business's profits.

A good example of entrepreneurship is the team of Shoshanna Berger and Grace Hawthorne, who launched *ReadyMade*, a magazine that brings irreverence and humor to home improvement, with $150,000 borrowed from family and friends. It's an industry in which 60 percent of start-ups fail, but Berger and Hawthorne remain optimistic and upbeat. *ReadyMade* mixes serious articles with zany stories about making fruit bowls out of melted Motley Crue LPs and off-beat lifestyle advice such as "How to Be a Rock Star Without Leaving the House." Since its launch in 2002, *ReadyMade* has become hugely popular with young, hip readers, but it continues to struggle financially. Berger and Hawthorne spotted an underserved niche in a dynamic segment of the magazine publishing industry and are willing to take the risks to get the new magazine started.[5]

Successful entrepreneurs have many different motivations, and they measure rewards in different ways. One study classified small business owners in five different categories, as illustrated in Exhibit 6.1. Some people are *idealists*, who like the idea of working on something that is new, creative, or personally meaningful. *Optimizers* are rewarded by the personal satisfaction of being business owners. Entrepreneurs in the *sustainer* category like the chance to balance work and personal life and often don't want the business to grow too large, while *hard workers* enjoy putting in the long hours and dedication to build a larger, more profitable business. The *juggler* category includes entrepreneurs who like the chance a small business gives them to handle everything themselves. These are high-energy people who thrive on the pressure of paying bills, meeting deadlines, and making payroll.[6]

Exhibit 6.1

## Five Types of Small Business Owners

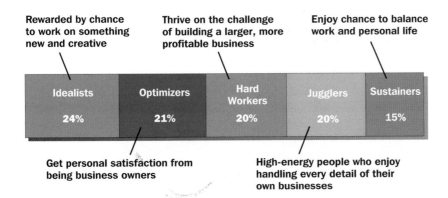

Rewarded by chance to work on something new and creative

Thrive on the challenge of building a larger, more profitable business

Enjoy chance to balance work and personal life

| Idealists | Optimizers | Hard Workers | Jugglers | Sustainers |
|---|---|---|---|---|
| 24% | 21% | 20% | 20% | 15% |

Get personal satisfaction from being business owners

High-energy people who enjoy handling every detail of their own businesses

**SOURCE:** Study conducted by Yankelovich Partners, reported in Mark Henricks, "Type-Cast," *Entrepreneur* (March 2000), 14–16.

Denver Hopkins started his business, ThoughtFarm, so he could have more time for his hobby of spelunking. The technology consulting company was immediately successful, and Hopkins found himself putting in longer and longer hours, hiring more people, and going deep into debt to finance growth. He was miserable. His motivation had been as a *sustainer*, but he found himself playing the *juggler*. Within a few years, business began to decline, and Hopkins eventually returned to working on a laptop in the park, attending conferences to absorb technology trends, and working at a slower pace with a few clients.[7] This chapter's Unlocking Creative Solutions Through People box describes two small business owners who fit in the *idealist* category.

Sometimes people start new businesses when they lose their jobs due to corporate downsizing. The major layoffs in the early 2000s provided just the push some latent entrepreneurs needed to strike out on their own. "I don't think I would have had the nerve to have left on my own," said Robin Gorman Newman, who lost her job as vice president of a public relations firm due to a restructuring. Now Newman runs her own PR business, RGN Communications, and has also fashioned a whole new career as the *Love Coach*, a separate business that offers counseling to singles.[8] Many experts actually believe an economic downturn is the best time to start a small business. For one thing, a downturn opens up lots of opportunities because people are looking for lower costs and better ways of doing things. The economic climate also enables the new business to hire good people, forces the entrepreneur to keep costs in line, and provides the time needed to build something of lasting value rather than struggling to keep pace with rapid growth.[9]

Many people also regard entrepreneurship as a better use of their time, talent, and energy. Women and minorities, who have sometimes found their opportunities limited in the corporate world, are often seeing entrepreneurship as the only way to go. Consider that the number of female-owned businesses grew 11 percent from 1997 to 2002, versus 6 percent for all privately owned U.S. firms.[10] Hispanic and African American entrepreneurship is also on the rise. For example, the National Federation of Women Business Owners reports that Hispanic women are starting companies at four times the national growth rate. "The [corporate] work environment is not friendly to Latinas," says Alma Morales Fiojas, CEO of Mana, a National Latina Organization. "Sometimes the best avenue . . . is to go into your own business, where there is more flexibility and you can accomplish more."[11]

# Unlocking Creative Solutions Through People

## Rejuvenating a Stale Business

Ari Weinzweig and Paul Saginaw started Zingerman's Delicatessen in 1982 because they wanted to sell the finest artisanal food products and the best sandwiches in the world. Within a decade, they'd achieved their goal. Zingerman's, in Ann Arbor, Michigan, became world famous, attracting tourists and celebrities and written about warmly in *The New York Times, Esquire, Bon Appetit,* and many other publications.

But then things at the deli began to go stale. Zingerman's still had its reputation for serving great food in a warm-hearted, fun-loving atmosphere, but the business was stagnating. The deli no longer offered challenges and opportunities for growth to experienced professionals. When one manager with an MBA from Columbia University decided to start her own bakery to supply breads and pastries for the deli, Weinzweig and Saginaw had an idea. Why not trust their people to start a whole community of small businesses, all bearing the Zingerman's name but each having its own specialty and identity? Each business would have a managing partner who would be an owner of the business. Although partnership was open to outsiders, the main goal was to give Zingerman's people a chance to put their own entrepreneurial dreams into action.

Thus was born Zingerman's Community of Businesses (ZCoB), with a vision of starting 12 to 15 separate businesses by 2009. The first was Zingerman's Bakehouse, owned by the former deli pastry manager Amy Emberling. Then came ZingTrain, to provide training to all ZCoB managers and staff as well as to other companies that wanted to learn the Zingerman's secrets to success. Zingerman's Mail Order and Zingermans.com ship artisan food products around the world. A creamery business produces handcrafted cheese and dairy products for the deli and other customers. Other businesses up and running to date include a catering service and Zingerman's Roadhouse, which features American regional cooking. A central administrative unit, ZingNet, provides marketing, finance, and human resources services for all the businesses. The new businesses have brought new opportunities, along with an entrepreneurial energy, passion, and excitement, which is attracting high-powered MBAs who are fed up with corporate life.

Regular partners meetings and other mechanisms have helped build a strong common culture, and ZCoB has maintained the close ties to the local community that the deli was known for. Company managers are actively involved in community life, and ZCoB donates a percentage of profits to charitable causes, prompting 13 local nonprofits to erect a giant plaque saying, "Thank you for feeding, sheltering, educating, uplifting, and inspiring an entire community." Mutual trust and respect are the values on which ZCoB operates. As new challenges arise, Weinzweig and Saginaw feel confident those values will help the partners meet them. "You have to operate in a world of integrity," Zingerman's Amy Emberling says. "There's a lot of integrity in this company at all levels—from the financial statements to the croissants."

SOURCE: Bo Burlingham, "The Coolest Small Company in America," *Inc.* (January 2003), 65–74.

## Entrepreneurship and the Environment

Not so long ago, scholars and policy makers were worrying about the potential of small business to survive. The turbulence in the technology sector and the demise of many dot-com start-ups heightened concerns about whether small companies can compete with big business. However, entrepreneurship and small business, including high-tech start-ups, are vital, dynamic, and increasingly important parts of the U.S. economy. Small businesses grew from 19 million in 1992 to 23 million in 2002.[12] These firms account for a tremendous portion of the goods and services provided. Another interesting finding is that there are approximately 10 million Americans who make their living as *solo professionals*, often working out of their homes providing services to other companies.[13] Entrepreneurship in other countries is also booming, and a list of the most entrepreneurial countries in 2002–2003 is intriguing. A project monitoring entrepreneurial activity around the world found that 29.3 percent of adults age 18 to 64 in Uganda, for example, are either starting up or managing new enterprises. The percentage in Venezuela is 27.3 percent, and in Thailand, 18.9 percent. India, Korea, Brazil, Mexico, and China all had higher rates of entrepreneurial activity than the United States rate of 11.3 percent.[14] Japan has instituted a new law that makes it possible to start a business with capital of just one yen.[15] Structural reforms in Russia have spurred a jump in small business formation in that country and one economic study predicts a doubling of small business as a part of Russia's gross domestic product between the years of 2004 and 2009.[16]

## Entrepreneurship Today

There are a number of reasons small business is such a dynamic part of today's economy. These include economic changes, globalization and increased competition, advancing technology, and new market niches.[17]

### Economic Changes

Today's economy is fertile soil for entrepreneurs. The economy changes constantly, providing opportunities for new businesses. For example, the demand for services is booming, and 97 percent of service firms are small, with fewer than 100 employees. Since government deregulation removed restrictions that inhibited small business formation in the trucking industry, thousands of small trucking companies have been started. In addition, long-distance freight trucking has become the biggest industry for one-person businesses, accounting for about $12.5 billion.[18] The trend toward outsourcing work to companies that can do it cheaper has also given entrepreneurs new openings. Ogio, a small company based in Bluffdale, Utah, engineers and manufactures innovative golf bags for Callaway, helping the smaller firm's sales skyrocket from $8 million to $47 million in five years.[19]

© DOUG FOGELSON

**CONCEPT CONNECTION**

*Entrepreneur Greg Wittstock fits into the **idealist** category. The 33 year-old founder of Aquascape, a pond-building business, is known as "the Pond guy," a name he trademarked. When Wittstock started the business in 1990, he was a student at Ohio State University, motivated by working on a new, creative, and personally meaningful business. His idealism turned into a success story; today, Aquascape has 130 employees, 35,000 customers, and $44 million in annual sales.*

### Globalization and Increased Competition

Even the largest of companies can no longer dominate their industry in a fast-changing global marketplace. Globalization demands entrepreneurial behavior—companies have to find ways to do things faster, better, and less expensively. Large companies are cutting costs by outsourcing work to smaller businesses or freelancers and selling off extraneous operations. Globalization and increased competition also give an advantage to the flexibility and fast response that small business can offer rather than to huge companies with economies of scale.

### Technology

Rapid advances and dropping prices in computer technology have spawned whole new industries, as well as entirely new methods of producing goods and delivering services. Unlike technological advances of the past, these are within the reach of companies of all sizes. The explosive growth of the Internet has created tremendous opportunities for entrepreneurs. For every story of a failed dot-com business, there are any number of small companies using the Web to sell products and services, to improve productivity, communications, and customer service, or to obtain information and market their services. Intranets.com (previously named Intranetics), for example, found new uses for its Web-based data- and document-management systems, such as helping NASA keep track of data after the 2003 Columbia space shuttle explosion.[20] Restaurant.com almost went belly-up as an all purpose dining portal offering full menus, video tours, and a reservations feature. Restaurants that paid to be on the site didn't see concrete evidence that the effort brought them more customers. However, when CEO Scott Lutwak retooled the site to be a marketer of gift certificates for frugal diners, the concept took off like a rocket.[21] Thos. Moser Cabinetmakers, a Maine-based business that makes and sells handcrafted furniture, uses the Web as an online catalog, enabling the small company to reach people it could never reach before the advent of the Internet—and that's led to lots of new buyers.[22]

Other technological advances also provide opportunities for small business. Biotechnology, aided by recent work in genomics, is a growing field for small businesses. Five Prime Therapeutics, for example, developed a protein-screening process that can accelerate the development of hit drugs for diseases like cancer, Type 2 diabetes, and rheumatoid arthritis.[23] Research into microelectromechanical systems (MEMS), tiny machines used in numerous applications from biotechnology and telecommunications to the auto industry, is being conducted primarily by small companies.

© ROBERT GALLAGHER

## CONCEPT CONNECTION

***Technological advances*** *provide new opportunities for entrepreneurs like Kevin Nakao, founder of MusicBlitz Inc. (http://www.musicblitz.com). Nakao was formerly general manager for music content company Launch.com and developed its first Web strategy. Nakao learned from his experience at Launch.com and founded MusicBlitz with goals of keeping employee turnover to a minimum, grounding financial expectations in reality, and blending online and offline operations. The obstacles of running a dot-com still exist, but the company meets them by keeping staff small and minimizing operating costs.*

### New Opportunities and Market Niches

Today's entrepreneurs are taking advantage of the opportunity to meet changing needs in the marketplace. Tapping into the growing *sustainability* movement, as discussed in Chapter 5, Ron Warnecke founded NitroCision, a company that mops up radioactive and industrial waste without the use of chemicals. Second-grade teacher Victoria Knight-McDowell is cashing in with Airborne, an herbal cold remedy now being sold in drugstore chains such as Rite-Aid and CVS.[24] Dany Levy, a 31-year-old journalist-turned-entrepreneur, found a market niche with her DailyCandy Internet company.

**DAILYCANDY**

http://www.
dailycandy.com

In a fast moving world it's easy to get left behind. Who wants to be talking about a hot new trend that everyone else knows has already gone cold? To avoid that dreaded fate, nearly 100,000 people log on each day for their morning dose of DailyCandy—a short, entertaining look at what's hot *at this very moment*.

Dany Levy got the idea for DailyCandy when she subscribed to TheStreet.com's newsletter to learn about Wall Street in preparation for applying to business school. She thought it would be fantastic to have the same type of format for lifestyles—something that would weed through all the miscellany and offer a quick glimpse of something really new and cool—a hopping new restaurant or the latest must-have digital camera. Levy set up a desk in the office of a friend and used her business school money to start DailyCandy. She sent sample e-mails that were formatted to be easily digestible and pleasing to the eye to all her friends and asked them to spread them on. Levy had 700 subscribers to the daily e-mails before she ever officially launched DailyCandy.

The company, which relies on advertising revenue, became profitable within a year and a half. It now has a full-time staff of eight, plus several commission-based salespeople. A horde of freelancers helps keep DailyCandy up to the minute. Levy is also growing the brand by finding new niches. DailyCandy Everywhere, for example, lets people know about really chic products that can be bought on the Internet. DailyCandy Kids targets parents of children up to the age of 12—an audience that is typically super busy but desperately in need of knowing what's the next cool thing.[25]

## Definition of Small Business

The full definition of *small business* used by the Small Business Administration (SBA) is detailed and complex. One could spend hours reading through the numerous Web pages that explain the definition on the SBA's Web site. In general, a small business is considered to be "one that is independently owned and operated and which is not dominant in its field of operation."[26] Most people think of a business as small if it has fewer than 500 employees, but the SBA further defines it by industry. Exhibit 6.2 gives a few examples of how the SBA defines small business for a sample of industries. It also illustrates general types of businesses most entrepreneurs start— retail, manufacturing, and service. Additional types of small businesses are construction, communications, finance, and real estate.

## Impact of Entrepreneurial Companies

The impact of entrepreneurial companies on our economy is astonishing. According to the Internal Revenue Service, only about 16,000 businesses in the United States employ more than 500 people, and the majority employ fewer than 100. In addition, the 5.7 million U.S. businesses that have fewer than 100 employees generate 40 percent of the nation's output.[27] Small business formation is also at an all-time high. Approximately 600,000 new businesses are started in the United States each year, and the status of the SBA administrator was elevated to a cabinet-level position in recognition of the importance of small business in the U.S. economy.[28]

Traditionally, new entrepreneurs frequently start businesses in the areas of business services and restaurants. Today, inspired by the growth of companies such as eBay and Amazon.com, entrepreneurs are still flocking to the Internet to start new

Exhibit 6.2

### Examples of SBA Definitions of Small Business

| Manufacturing | |
|---|---|
| Soft-drink manufacturing | Number of employees does not exceed 500 |
| Electronic computer manufacturing | Number of employees does not exceed 1,000 |
| Prerecorded CD, tape, and record producing | Number of employees does not exceed 750 |
| **Retail (Store and Non-store)** | |
| Sporting goods stores | Average annual receipts do not exceed $6.0 million |
| Electronic auctions | Average annual receipts do not exceed $21.0 million |
| Vending machine operators | Average annual receipts do not exceed $6.0 million |
| **Miscellaneous Internet Services** | |
| Internet service providers | Average annual receipts do not exceed $21.0 million |
| Web search portals | Average annual receipts do not exceed $6.0 million |
| Internet publishing and broadcasting | Number of employees does not exceed 500 |

businesses. Demographic and lifestyle trends have created new opportunities in areas such as environmental services, computer maintenance, children's markets, fitness, and home health care. Entrepreneurship and small business in the United States is an engine for job creation and innovation.

## Job Creation

Researchers disagree over what percentage of new jobs is created by small business. Research indicates that the *age* of a company, more than its size, determines the number of jobs it creates. That is, virtually *all* of the net new jobs in recent years have come from new companies, which includes not only small companies but also new branches of huge, multinational organizations.[29] However, small companies still are thought to create a large percentage of new jobs in the United States. According to the Small Business Administration, the nation's 23 million small businesses created two million jobs between October 2000 and March of 2004.[30] Jobs created by small businesses give the United States an economic vitality no other country can claim. However, as we discussed earlier, other countries are finding new ways to encourage entrepreneurial economic activity.

## Innovation

According to Cognetics, Inc., a research firm run by David Birch that traces the employment and sales records of some 9 million companies, new and smaller firms have been responsible for 55 percent of the innovations in 362 different industries and 95 percent of all radical innovations. In addition, fast-growing businesses, which Birch calls *gazelles*, produce twice as many product innovations per employee as do larger firms. Among the notable products for which small businesses can be credited are WD-40, the jet engine, and the shopping cart. Virtually every new business represents an innovation of some sort, whether a new product or service, how the product is delivered, or how it is made.[31] In addition, many of today's new products from giant corporations were originated by small companies. Consider the popular Crest Spin Brush from Procter & Gamble. The product was originally created by a tiny start-up. P&G bought the company and brought in the entrepreneurial leaders to head up the new division.[32] Entrepreneurial innovation often spurs larger companies to try new things. P&G is paying close attention to another small start-up that could threaten the giant corporation's sales of Dawn dishwashing liquid.

**METHOD**
http://www.
methodhome.com

Two twenty-something entrepreneurs are cleaning up with their new approach to cleaning products. During the dot-com boom of the 1990s, Eric Ryan and Adam Lowry wanted to start a business. But instead of going on the Internet, they went to the grocery store, scanning the shelves for a product in need of a makeover—and they found it in the cleaning products aisle.

Ryan and Lowry began mixing up cleaning solutions in their kitchen to develop a line of nontoxic cleaning products. What differentiates Method from other naturally derived cleaners is the cool packaging, affordable prices, and fresh scents like lavender, mandarin, and cucumber. Method has brought cutting-edge style to a mass-market product. Consider the hot-selling dish soap, which comes in bright colors like lime green or mandarin orange inside a sleek, stylish bottle that's so appealing you'd never want to hide it under the sink. It's designed to sit upside down on the sink, allowing for a time-saving squirt from the bottom. A unique valve design keeps the liquid from oozing out until you squeeze it. The bottles began flying off the shelves almost as soon as they were stocked. Method realized that the designer dish soap was doing something almost unheard of in the cleaning products business: inspiring impulse buys.

Method, now with 18 employees in San Francisco, has expanded to numerous other cleaning products and is selling in stores like Target, Albertson's, Safeway, and other national chains. The entrepreneurs worry that big companies will launch copycat versions, and P&G admits that it is keeping an eye on the start-up. However, Method has built a loyal following of customers who appreciate the fresh approach to age-old products.[33]

Method is an excellent example of how entrepreneurs and small companies bring fresh new ideas to stale industries. Small-business innovation keeps U.S. companies competitive, which is especially important in today's global marketplace.

# Who Are Entrepreneurs?

The heroes of American business—Fred Smith, Spike Lee, Henry Ford, Sam Walton, Mary Kay Ash, Bill Gates, Michael Dell—are almost always entrepreneurs. Entrepreneurs start with a vision. Often they are unhappy with their current jobs and see an opportunity to bring together the resources needed for a new venture. However, the image of entrepreneurs as bold pioneers probably is overly romantic. A survey of the CEOs of the nation's fastest-growing small firms found that these entrepreneurs could be best characterized as hardworking and practical, with great familiarity with their market and industry.[34] For example, Nancy Rodriguez was a veteran R&D manager at Swift Foods before she started Food Marketing Support Services. Rodriguez started the firm in the mid-1980s when Swift and other big food companies were cutting staff and R&D budgets. Large companies can now take a rough new product idea to Food Marketing, which fully develops the concept, creates prototypes, does taste-testing, and so forth. American Pop Corn, which makes Jolly Time Pop Corn, allocated 100 percent of its new-product-development dollars to the 20-person firm, which does about $5 million in business a year.[35]

© MARC LONGWOOD

*Entrepreneurs Chet and Terrie Van Scyoc spotted an **opportunity** to profit from shoppertainment, a new trend in today's retailing environment that blends entertainment with tried-and-true merchandising techniques. Shoppertainment helped the Scyocs build their Sacramento, California hobby store, R/C Country Hobbies, to revenues of approximately $1.2 million. R/C Country Hobbies sells remote-control planes and cars, model-building kits, and other toys to customers who can test collector trains on display or ask an employee to build a model so they can see and feel it. They can even fly model airplanes using a computer program that simulates the event. "This is something our biggest competitors, mail-order catalogs, can't give them," says Terrie.*

## Diversity of Entrepreneurs

Entrepreneurs often have backgrounds and demographic characteristics that distinguish them from other people. Entrepreneurs are more likely to be the first born within their families, and their parents are more likely to have been entrepreneurs. Children of immigrants also are more likely to be entrepreneurs.[36] Consider Hector Barreto Jr., whose parents were both Mexican immigrants and ran several successful businesses in Kansas City, Missouri, including a restaurant, an import-export business, and a construction firm. After a four-year stint as an area manager for Miller

Brewing Company, Hector moved to California and started Barreto Financial Services. Later, he started another firm to provide technical assistance to small businesses. Barreto's next step was into the head office of the Small Business Administration, where he became the first entrepreneur to lead the government agency.[37]

Entrepreneurship offers opportunities for individuals who may feel blocked in established corporations. Women-owned and minority-owned businesses may be the emerging growth companies of the next decade. Between the years of 1997 and 2002, the number of companies owned 50 percent or more by women jumped 11 percent, to 10.1 million, nearly twice the rate of all privately-owned firms. Annual revenues of female-owned firms during the same period increased 32 percent to more than $2.3 trillion.[38] Statistics for minorities are also impressive. The number of new firms launched by minorities is growing about 17 percent a year, with African-American businesses growing the fastest. African American males between the ages of 25 and 35 start more businesses than any other group in the country. Moreover, the face of entrepreneurship for the future will be increasingly diverse. When Junior Achievement (an organization that educates young people about business) conducted a poll of teenagers ages 13 to 18, it found a much greater interest among minorities than whites in starting a business, as shown in Exhibit 6.3.[39]

The types of businesses launched by minority entrepreneurs are also increasingly sophisticated. The traditional minority-owned mom-and-pop retail store or restaurant is being replaced by firms in industries such as financial services, insurance, and media. For example, Pat Winans, an African American who grew up in a Chicago ghetto, started Magna Securities, a successful institutional brokerage firm in New York City, with just $5,000. Ed Chin, a third-generation Chinese American, founded AIS Corporation to offer small and mid-sized companies the kind of sophisticated insurance packages usually available only to large companies. Chin originally found a niche by catering to the Asian marketplace, but word-of-mouth has helped his company expand beyond that limited market.[40]

# Exhibit 6.3

## A Glimpse of Tomorrow's Entrepreneurs

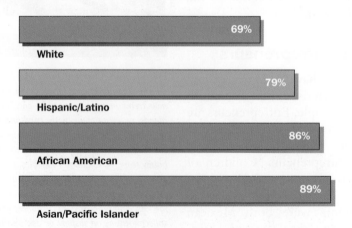

**White**  69%

**Hispanic/Latino**  79%

**African American**  86%

**Asian/Pacific Islander**  89%

**Percentage of teenagers polled by Junior Achievement who said they want to start their own business**

**SOURCE:** Junior Achievement Survey results reported in Cora Daniels, "Minority Rule," *FSB* (December 2003–January 2004), 65–66.

## Personality Traits

A number of studies have investigated the personality characteristics of entrepreneurs and how they differ from successful managers in established organizations. Some suggest that entrepreneurs in general want something different from life than do traditional managers. Entrepreneurs seem to place high importance on being free to achieve and maximize their potential. Some 40 traits have been identified as associated with entrepreneurship, but 6 have special importance.[41] These characteristics are illustrated in Exhibit 6.4.

### Internal Locus of Control

The task of starting and running a new business requires the belief that you can make things come out the way you want. The entrepreneur not only has a vision but also must be able to plan to achieve that vision and believe it will happen. An **internal locus of control** is the belief by individuals that their future is within their control and that external forces will have little influence. For entrepreneurs, reaching the future is seen as being in the hands of the individual. Many people, however, feel that the world is highly uncertain and that they are unable to make things come out the way they want. An **external locus of control** is the belief by individuals that their future is not within their control but rather is influenced by external forces. Entrepreneurs are individuals who are convinced they can make the difference between success and failure; hence, they are motivated to take the steps needed to achieve the goal of setting up and running a new business.

### High Energy Level

A business start-up requires great effort. Most entrepreneurs report struggle and hardship. They persist and work incredibly hard despite traumas and obstacles. A survey of business owners reported that half worked 60 hours or more per week. Another reported that entrepreneurs worked long hours, but that beyond 70 hours little benefit was gained. The data in Exhibit 6.5 show findings from a survey conducted by the National Federation of Independent Business. New business owners work long hours, with only 23 percent working fewer than 50 hours, which is close to a normal workweek for managers in established businesses.

### Need to Achieve

Another human quality closely linked to entrepreneurship is the **need to achieve**, which means that people are motivated to excel and pick situations in which success is likely.[42] People who have high achievement needs like to set their own goals,

**internal locus of control**
The belief by individuals that their future is within their control and that external forces will have little influence.

**external locus of control**
The belief by individuals that their future is not within their control but rather is influenced by external forces.

**need to achieve**
A human quality linked to entrepreneurship in which people are motivated to excel and pick situations in which success is likely.

Exhibit 6.4

### Characteristics of Entrepreneurs

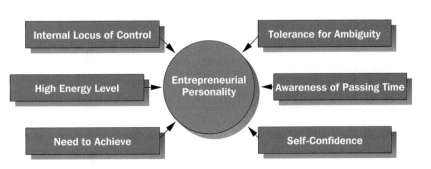

**SOURCE:** Adapted from Charles R. Kuehl and Peggy A. Lambing, *Small Business: Planning and Management* (Ft. Worth: The Dryden Press, 1994), 45.

# Exhibit 6.5

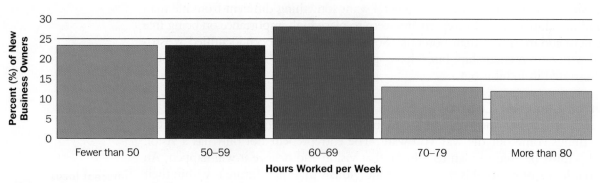

### Reported Hours per Week Worked by Owners of New Businesses

**SOURCE:** National Federation of Independent Business. Reported in Mark Robichaux, "Business First, Family Second," *The Wall Street Journal* (May 12, 1989), B1.

which are moderately difficult. Easy goals present no challenge; unrealistically difficult goals cannot be achieved. Intermediate goals are challenging and provide great satisfaction when achieved. High achievers also like to pursue goals for which they can obtain feedback about their success.

## Self-Confidence
People who start and run a business must act decisively. They need confidence about their ability to master the day-to-day tasks of the business. They must feel sure about their ability to win customers, handle the technical details, and keep the business moving. Entrepreneurs also have a general feeling of confidence that they can deal with anything in the future; complex, unanticipated problems can be handled as they arise.

*Take A Moment*

*Go to the experiential exercise on page 220 that pertains to your entrepreneurial potential.*

## Awareness of Passing Time
Entrepreneurs tend to be impatient; they feel a sense of urgency. They want things to progress as if there is no tomorrow. They want things moving immediately and seldom procrastinate. Entrepreneurs seize the moment.

## Tolerance for Ambiguity

**tolerance for ambiguity**
The psychological characteristic that allows a person to be untroubled by disorder and uncertainty.

Many people need work situations characterized by clear structure, specific instructions, and complete information. Tolerance for ambiguity is the psychological characteristic that allows a person to be untroubled by disorder and uncertainty. This is an important trait, because few situations present more uncertainty than starting a new business. Decisions are made without clear understanding of options or certainty about which option will succeed.

Taiwanese immigrants Janie and Victor Tsao illustrate many of the personality traits of successful entrepreneurs.

LINKSYS
http://www.linksys.com

Janie and Victor Tsao emigrated from Taiwan to California in the early 1980s and began working in the burgeoning field of information technology. However, they both had dreams of running their own business and were determined to be independent before they reached the age of 40. Aware of time passing by, the two founded the company that would become Linksys in 1988 when Victor was 37 and Janie 35. At first, Victor kept his full-time job while Janie got the business started.

Originally, the company was named DEW International and helped connect American technology companies with manufacturers in Taiwan that could make their products cheaply. One of the manufacturers told the Tsaos about his idea for a cable that would connect multiple PCs to multiple printers, even at distances up to 100 feet (at the time, printer cables could extend only about 15 feet before the data started to degrade). The Tsaos renamed the company Linksys, marketed the Multishare print server, and gradually expanded into all sorts of networking products, including wireless in recent years.

Victor quit his job and began regularly working 100-hour weeks at Linksys. He'd work with U.S. operations during the day and Taiwanese manufacturers at night. Janie was putting in long hours as well, primarily on the sales and marketing side. Her determination and self-confidence helped her face some tough situations and come out ahead. When she had trouble getting a hearing from Best Buy, for example, she followed the Best Buy CEO to his hotel room during a trade show. He ended up placing an order for just under $2 million of gear.

The Tsaos were always willing to work hard and make sacrifices for the business. Victor never took a salary until 1994; the family lived on Janie's salary of $2,000 a month. Their belief that they could succeed and their ability to cope with uncertainty helped the Tsaos weather the hard times. When revenues hit $430 million in 2002 and Linksys had an early lead in Wi-Fi, Victor decided he could cut back to working only 70 hours a week. By late 2003, Linksys owned 49 percent of the networking market, with a goal of 70 percent by 2005. During 2003, as well, Cisco bought the company for $500 million in stock, agreeing to let the company remain as a standalone unit under the leadership of the Tsaos.[43]

Both Janie and Victor Tsao possess some degree of each of the six personality traits of entrepreneurs: an internal locus of control, a high energy level, a need to achieve, self-confidence, awareness of passing time, and tolerance for ambiguity. These personality traits and the demographic characteristics discussed earlier offer an insightful but imprecise picture of the entrepreneur. Successful entrepreneurs come in all ages, from all backgrounds, and may have a combination of personality traits. No one should be discouraged from starting a business because he or she doesn't fit a specific profile. One review of small business suggests that the three most important traits of successful entrepreneurs in today's turbulent environment are realism, flexibility, and passion. Even the most realistic entrepreneurs tend to underestimate the difficulties of building a business, so they need flexibility and a passion for their idea to survive the hurdles.[44]

# Starting an Entrepreneurial Firm

The first step in pursuing an entrepreneurial dream is to start with a viable idea and plan like crazy. Once someone has a new idea in mind, a business plan must be drawn and decisions must be made about legal structure, financing, and basic tactics, such as whether to start the business from scratch and whether to pursue international opportunities from the start.

## New-Business Idea

To some people, the idea for a new business is the easy part. They do not even consider entrepreneurship until they are inspired by an exciting idea. Other people decide they want to run their own business and set about looking for an idea or opportunity. Exhibit 6.6 shows the most important reasons that people start a new business and the source of new-business ideas. Note that 37 percent of business founders got their idea from an in-depth understanding of the industry, primarily because of past job experience. Interestingly, almost as many—36 percent—spotted a market niche that wasn't being filled.[45]

## Exhibit 6.6

### Sources of Entrepreneurial Motivation and New-Business Ideas

**Reasons for Starting a Business**

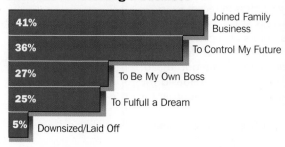

41%  Joined Family Business
36%  To Control My Future
27%  To Be My Own Boss
25%  To Fulfull a Dream
5%   Downsized/Laid Off

**Source of New-Business Ideas**

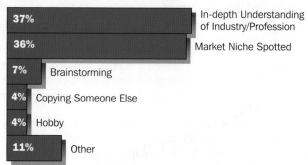

37%  In-depth Understanding of Industry/Profession
36%  Market Niche Spotted
7%   Brainstorming
4%   Copying Someone Else
4%   Hobby
11%  Other

**SOURCES:** "The Rewards," *Inc.* State of Small Business, 2001 (May 29, 2001), 50-51; and Leslie Brokaw, "How to Start an *Inc.* 500 Company," *Inc.* 500 (1994), 51-65.

The trick for entrepreneurs is to blend their own skills and experience with a need in the marketplace. Acting strictly on one's own skills may produce something no one wants to buy. On the other hand, finding a market niche that one does not have the ability to fill does not work either. Both personal skill and market need typically must be present.

## The Business Plan

**business plan**
A document specifying the business details prepared by an entrepreneur prior to opening a new business.

Once an entrepreneur is inspired by a new-business idea, careful planning is crucial. A **business plan** is a document specifying the business details prepared by an entrepreneur prior to opening a new business. Planning forces the entrepreneur to carefully think through all of the issues and problems associated with starting and developing the business. Most entrepreneurs have to borrow money, and a business plan is absolutely critical for persuading lenders and investors to participate in the business. Studies have shown that small businesses with a carefully thought out, written business plan are much more likely to succeed than those without one.[46]

The details of a business plan may vary, but successful business plans generally share several characteristics:[47]

- Demonstrate a clear, compelling vision that creates an air of excitement.
- Provide clear and realistic financial projections.
- Give detailed information about the target market.
- Include detailed information about the industry and competitors.
- Provide evidence of an effective entrepreneurial management team.
- Pay attention to good formatting and clear writing.
- Keep the plan short—no more than 50 pages long.
- Highlight critical risks that may threaten business success.
- Spell out the sources and uses of start-up funds and operating funds.
- Capture the reader's interest with a killer summary.

The business plan should indicate where the product or service fits into the overall industry and should draw on concepts that will be discussed throughout this book. For example, Chapter 8 will describe competitive strategies that entrepreneurs can use. Detailed suggestions for writing a business plan are provided in the Manager's Shoptalk box.

PHOTOGRAPHY © 2003 HENRY LEUTWYLER

## Legal Form

Before entrepreneurs have founded a business, and perhaps again as it expands, they must choose an appropriate legal structure for the company. The three basic choices are proprietorship, partnership, or corporation.

### Sole Proprietorship

A **sole proprietorship** is defined as an unincorporated business owned by an individual for profit. Proprietorships make up 70 percent of all businesses in the United States. This form is popular because it is easy to start and has few legal requirements. A proprietor has total ownership and control of the company and can make all decisions without consulting anyone. However, this type of organization also has drawbacks. The owner has unlimited liability for the business, meaning that if someone sues, the owner's personal as well as business assets are at risk. Also, financing can be harder to obtain because business success rests on one person's shoulders.

**sole proprietorship**
An unincorporated business owned by an individual for profit.

### Partnership

A **partnership** is an unincorporated business owned by two or more people. Partnerships, like proprietorships, are relatively easy to start. Two friends may reach an agreement to start a graphic arts company. To avoid misunderstandings and to make sure the business is well planned, it is wise to draw up and sign a formal partnership agreement with the help of an attorney. The agreement specifies how partners are to share responsibility and resources and how they will contribute their expertise. The disadvantages of partnerships are the unlimited liability of the partners and the disagreements that almost always occur among strong-minded people. A poll by *Inc.* magazine illustrated the volatility of partnerships. Fifty-nine percent of respondents considered partnerships a bad business move, citing reasons such as partner problems and conflicts. Partnerships often dissolve within five years. Respondents who liked partnerships pointed to the equality of partners (sharing of workload and emotional and financial burdens) as the key to a successful partnership.[48]

**partnership**
An unincorporated business owned by two or more people.

# manager's Shoptalk

## Helpful Hints for Writing the Business Plan

### The Summary

- Make it no more than three pages.
- Summarize the what, how, why, where, and so on.
- Complete this part *after* the finished business plan has been written.

This is the most crucial part of your plan because it must capture the reader's interest.

### The Business Description Segment

- List the name of the business.
- Provide a background of the industry with history of the company (if any).
- Describe clearly the potential of the new venture.
- Spell out any unique or distinctive features of the venture should be spelled out.

### The Marketing Segment

- Convince investors that sales projections and competition can be met.
- Use and disclose market studies.
- Identify target market, market position, and market share.
- Evaluate *all* competition and specifically cover why and how you will be better than the competitors.
- Identify all market sources and assistance used for this segment.
- Demonstrate pricing strategy, since your price must penetrate and maintain a market share to *produce profits*. Thus the lowest price is *not* necessarily the "best" price.
- Identify your advertising plans with cost estimates to validate the proposed strategy.

### The Research, Design, and Development Segment

- Cover the *extent* of and *costs involved* in needed research, testing, or development.
- Explain carefully what has been accomplished *already* (prototype, lab testing, early development).

- Mention any research or technical assistance provided for you.

### The Manufacturing Segment

- Provide the advantages of your location (zoning, tax laws, wage rates).
- List the production needs in terms of facilities (plant, storage, office space) and equipment (machinery, furnishings, supplies).
- Describe the access to transportation (for shipping and receiving).
- Explain proximity to your suppliers.
- Mention the availability of labor in your location.
- Provide estimates of manufacturing costs—be careful; too many entrepreneurs underestimate their costs.

### The Management Segment

- Provide résumés of all key people in the management of the venture.
- Carefully describe the legal structure of the venture (sole proprietorship, partnership, or corporation).
- Cover the added assistance (if any) of advisers, consultants, and directors.
- Provide information on how everyone is to be compensated (how much, also).

### The Critical-Risks Segment

- Discuss potential risks *before* investors point them out. Some examples follow:
  - Price cutting by competitors
  - Potentially unfavorable industry-wide trends
  - Design or manufacturing costs in excess of estimates
  - Sales projections not achieved
  - Product development schedule not met
  - Difficulties or long lead times encountered in the procurement of parts or raw materials
  - Larger-than-expected innovation and development costs to stay competitive
- Name alternative courses of action.

## manager's Shoptalk

### Turbulent Times

**The Financial Segment**

- Provide statements.
- Describe the needed sources for your funds and the uses you intend for the money.
- Provide a budget.
- Create stages of financing for the purpose of allowing evaluation by investors at various points.

**The Milestone Schedule Segment**

- Provide a timetable or chart to demonstrate when each phase of the venture is to be completed. This shows the relationship of events and provides a deadline for accomplishment.

SOURCE: Donald F. Kuratko, Ray V. Montagno, and Frank J. Sabatine, *The Entrepreneurial Decision* (Muncie, Ind.: The Midwest Entrepreneurial Education Center, Ball State University, 1997), 45–46. Reprinted with permission.

## Corporation

A **corporation** is an artificial entity created by the state and existing apart from its owners. As a separate legal entity, the corporation is liable for its actions and must pay taxes on its income. Unlike other forms of ownership, the corporation has a legal life of its own; it continues to exist regardless of whether the owners live or die. And the corporation, not the owners, is sued in the case of liability. Thus, continuity and limits on owners' liability are two principal advantages of forming a corporation. For example, a physician can form a corporation so that liability for malpractice will not affect his or her personal assets. The major disadvantage of the corporation is that it is expensive and complex to do the paperwork required to incorporate the business and to keep the records required by law. When proprietorships and partnerships are successful and grow large, they often incorporate to limit liability and to raise funds through the sale of stock to investors.

**corporation**
An artificial entity created by the state and existing apart from its owners.

## Financial Resources

A crucial concern for entrepreneurs is the financing of the business. An investment usually is required to acquire labor and raw materials and perhaps a building and equipment. The financing decision initially involves two options—whether to obtain loans that must be repaid (debt financing) or whether to share ownership (equity financing). A survey of successful growth businesses asked, "How much money was needed to launch the company?" Approximately one-third were started on less than $10,000, one-third needed from $10,000 to $50,000, and one-third needed more than $50,000. The primary source of this money was the entrepreneurs' own resources, but they often had to mortgage their homes, depend on credit cards, borrow money from the bank, or give part of the business to a venture capitalist.[49]

## Debt Financing

Borrowing money that has to be repaid at a later date in order to start a business is debt financing. One common source of **debt financing** for a start-up is to borrow from family and friends. Another common source is a bank loan. Banks provide

**debt financing**
Borrowing money that has to be repaid at a later date in order to start a business.

some 25 percent of all financing for small business. Sometimes entrepreneurs can obtain money from a finance company, wealthy individuals, or potential customers.

Another form of loan financing is provided by the Small Business Administration (SBA). Staples, which started with one office supply store in Brighton, Massachusetts, in 1986, got its start toward rapid growth with the assistance of SBA financing. Today, Staples is the country's largest operator of office superstores, with more than 1,500 stores and 58,000 employees worldwide.[50] The SBA supplies direct loans to some entrepreneurs who are unable to get bank financing because they are considered high risk. The SBA is especially helpful for people without substantial assets, providing an opportunity for single parents, minority group members, and others with a good idea. According to SBA chief Hector Barreto, in 2003 the SBA guaranteed a record 74,000 loans totaling $11.2 billion, "with double-digit increases in the percentage of loans to women, Hispanics, African Americans, and Asian Americans."[51]

### Equity Financing

**equity financing**
Financing that consists of funds that are invested in exchange for ownership in the company.

**venture capital firm**
A group of companies or individuals that invests money in new or expanding businesses for ownership and potential profits.

Any money invested by owners or by those who purchase stock in a corporation is considered equity funds. **Equity financing** consists of funds that are invested in exchange for ownership in the company.

A **venture capital firm** is a group of companies or individuals that invests money in new or expanding businesses for ownership and potential profits. This is a potential form of capital for businesses with high earning and growth possibilities. Venture capitalists are particularly interested in high-tech businesses such as software, biotechnology, and telecommunications because they have the potential for very high rates of return on investment. In 2003, most venture capital money went to these three categories.[52] Venture capitalists also usually provide assistance, advice, and information to help the entrepreneur prosper. A growing number of minority-owned venture capital firms, such as Provender Capital, founded by African American entrepreneur Fred Terrell, are ensuring that minorities have a fair shot at acquiring equity financing.[53]

### Tactics

There are several ways an aspiring entrepreneur can become a business owner. These include starting a new business from scratch, buying an existing business, or starting a franchise. Another popular entrepreneurial tactic is to participate in a business incubator.

### Start a New Business

One of the most common ways to become an entrepreneur is to start a new business from scratch. This is exciting because the entrepreneur sees a need for a product or service that has not been filled before and then sees the idea or dream become a reality. Jennifer and Brian Maxwell, both long-distance runners, founded PowerBar Inc. to give athletes a snack bar that would provide quick energy but be easy to digest. Jennifer, who studied nutrition and food science at the University of California, hit on the idea after

© GRANT KESSLER

**CONCEPT CONNECTION**

*A major concern for entrepreneurs is securing funds through **debt financing** or **equity financing**. For example, to grow Heartwise, her healthy-fast-food business, into a nationwide food chain, Rosemary Deahl must first obtain significant funding from bank loans and **venture capitalists**. Angel investors and noted Chicago restaurant consultants liked her concept of a restaurant serving high-quality, healthy fast food, but they questioned its national appeal. Finding money can be tough going, and venture capitalists could take more than 51 percent of ownership, leading to a loss of control for the entrepreneur.*

Brian told her of losing the London Marathon largely because of a case of stomach cramps.[54] The advantage of starting a business is the ability to develop and design the business in the entrepreneur's own way. The entrepreneur is solely responsible for its success. A potential disadvantage is the long time it can take to get the business off the ground and make it profitable. The uphill battle is caused by the lack of established clientele and the many mistakes made by someone new to the business. Moreover, no matter how much planning is done, a start-up is risky; there is no guarantee that the new idea will work.

## Buy an Existing Business

Because of the long start-up time and the inevitable mistakes, some entrepreneurs prefer to reduce risk by purchasing an existing business. This offers the advantage of a shorter time to get started and an existing track record. The entrepreneur may get a bargain price if the owner wishes to retire or has other family considerations. Moreover, a new business may overwhelm an entrepreneur with the amount of work to be done and procedures to be determined. An established business already has filing systems, a payroll tax system, and other operating procedures. Potential disadvantages are the need to pay for goodwill that the owner believes exists and the possible existence of ill will toward the business. In addition, the company may have bad habits and procedures or outdated technology, which may be why the business is for sale.

## Buy a Franchise

Franchising is perhaps the most rapidly growing path to entrepreneurship. The International Franchise Association reports that the country's 320,000 franchise outlets account for about $1 trillion in annual sales.[55] According to some estimates, 1 out of every 12 businesses in the United States is franchised, and a franchise opens every eight minutes of every business day.[56] **Franchising** is an arrangement by which the owner of a product or service allows others to purchase the right to distribute the product or service with help from the owner. The franchisee invests his or her money and owns the business but does not have to develop a new product, create a new company, or test the market. Franchises exist for weight-loss clinics, pet-sitting services, sports photography, bakeries, janitorial services, auto repair shops, real estate offices, and numerous other types of businesses, in addition to the traditional fast food outlets. Exhibit 6.7 lists five of the trendiest new franchise concepts, according to *The Wall Street Journal*. The exhibit lists the type of business, the number of franchisees as of late 2003, and the initial costs. Initial franchise fees

**franchising**
An arrangement by which the owner of a product or service allows others to purchase the right to distribute the product or service with help from the owner.

Exhibit 6.7

### Five Hot Franchise Concepts for Today

| Franchise | Type of Business | Number of Outlets | Initial Costs |
| --- | --- | --- | --- |
| Curves for Women | Exercise, weight loss centers | 5,646 | $30,625, not including real estate |
| Cruise Planners | Selling ocean cruises | 389 | $2,095 – $18,600 |
| Buffalo Wild Wings Grill & Bar | Sports bar | 145 | $969,500+ |
| Jani-King | Building cleaning, maintenance | 7,843 | $11,300 – $34,100 |
| Comfort Keepers | Nonmedical home care for seniors | 386 | $39,700 – $65,100 |

**SOURCE:** Richard Gibson, "Small Business (A Special Report); Where the Buzz Is: Five of the Hottest Franchise Concepts Out There—and Their Chances of Becoming the Next Big Thing," *The Wall Street Journal* (December 15, 2003), R7.

can range from $1,000 to $200,000, and that doesn't count the other start-up costs the entrepreneur will have to cover. A study by an economics professor found that the typical franchise costs $94,886 to open.[57] For a casual restaurant such as Buffalo Wild Wings Grill & Bar, listed in the exhibit, the cost is much higher, $969,500 and up, depending on the restaurant location.

The powerful advantage of a franchise is that management help is provided by the owner. For example, Subway, the second fastest growing franchise in the country, does not want a franchisee to fail. Subway has regional development agents who do the research to find good locations for Subway's sandwich outlets. The Subway franchisor also provides two weeks of training at company headquarters and ongoing operational and marketing support.[58] Franchisors provide an established name and national advertising to stimulate demand for the product or service. Potential disadvantages are the lack of control that occurs when franchisors want every business managed in exactly the same way. In some cases, franchisors require that franchise owners use certain contractors or suppliers that might cost more than others would. In addition, franchises can be very expensive, and the high start-up costs are followed with monthly payments to the franchisor that can run from 2 percent to 15 percent of gross sales.

Entrepreneurs who are considering buying a franchise should investigate the company thoroughly. The prospective franchisee is legally entitled to a copy of franchisor disclosure statements, which include information on 20 topics, including litigation and bankruptcy history, identities of the directors and executive officers, financial information, identification of any products the franchisee is required to buy, and from whom those purchases must be made. The entrepreneur also should talk with as many franchise owners as possible, since they are among the best sources of information about how the company really operates.[59] Exhibit 6.8 lists some specific questions entrepreneurs should ask about themselves and the company when considering buying a franchise. Answering such questions can improve the chances for a successful career as a franchisee.

**business incubator**
An innovation that provides shared office space, management support services, and management advice to entrepreneurs.

## Participate in a Business Incubator

An attractive innovation for entrepreneurs who want to start a business from scratch is to join a business incubator. The **business incubator** provides shared office space,

Exhibit 6.8

### Sample Questions for Choosing a Franchise

| Questions about the Entrepreneur | Questions about the Franchiser | Before Signing the Dotted Line |
|---|---|---|
| 1. Will I enjoy the day-to-day work of the business? <br> 2. Do my background, experience, and goals make this a good choice for me? <br> 3. Am I willing to work within the rules and guidelines established by the franchisor? | 1. What assistance does the company provide in terms of selection of location, set-up costs, and securing credit; day-to-day technical assistance; marketing; and ongoing training and development? <br> 2. How long does it take the typical franchise owner to start making a profit? <br> 3. How many franchises changed ownership within the past year, and why? | 1. Do I understand the risks associated with this business, and am I willing to assume them? <br> 2. Have I had an advisor review the disclosure documents and franchise agreement? <br> 3. Do I understand the contract? |

**SOURCES:** Based on Thomas Love, "The Perfect Franchisee," *Nation's Business* (April 1998), 59–65; and Roberta Maynard, "Choosing a Franchise," *Nation's Business* (October 1996), 56–63.

management support services, and management advice to entrepreneurs. By sharing office space with other entrepreneurs, managers share information about local business, financial aid, and market opportunities.

This innovation arose about two decades ago to nurture start-up companies. Business incubators have become a significant segment of the small business economy: the number of incubators nationwide jumped from 385 in 1990 to about 1,000 in 2001.[60] During the dot-com boom, there was a tremendous jump in the number of for-profit incubators, but many of them went out of business as the boom went bust.[61] The incubators that are thriving are primarily not-for-profits and those that cater to niches or focus on helping women or minority entrepreneurs. These include incubators run by government agencies and universities to boost the viability of small business and spur job creation. The value of an incubator is the expertise of an in-house mentor, who serves as adviser, role model, and cheerleader. Incubators give budding entrepreneurs a chance to network and learn from one another.[62] Incubators are also an important part of the international entrepreneurial landscape. For example, Harmony is a global network support system for business incubators. Harmony was started in 1998 with partners in Germany, France, Spain, Finland, Switzerland, Australia, Japan, and the United States, to provide training and support for both new and established incubators worldwide, enabling them to better serve clients and improve the success of small businesses.[63]

# Launching a High-Tech Start-Up

High-technology start-ups represent a special case of entrepreneurship because costs and risks are typically extremely high. After the crash of the dot-coms and the sharp decline in technology stocks in the early 2000s, people became leery of anything high-tech. Venture capital declined significantly every year between 2000 and 2003, bottoming out at $12.9 billion during the first nine months of 2003.[64] However, recent years have seen a revival of high-technology startups. Companies launched during the economic slowdown encompass a range of high-tech industries, from biotechnology to wireless networks. In addition, Internet companies are making a comeback as entrepreneurs have learned from past mistakes and found innovative ways to succeed online. Just as with other small companies, many of the high-tech companies being started now will fail, but many others will go on to become highly successful businesses. Small business formation is the primary process by which an economy recreates and reinvents itself,[65] and the turbulence in the high-tech sector is evidence of a shifting but thriving U.S. economy.

High-tech start-ups face many of the same challenges as other small businesses. However, they may also face some unique issues and problems. In this section, we will examine what's involved in launching a high-tech start-up, based on what is known about these companies so far.

## Starting with the Idea

As with any small company, an entrepreneur has to have a viable idea for the business, and one that is appropriate to the fast-changing world of technology. Dan Avida and Serge Plotkin hope they have an idea that will create a thriving business. Their company, Decru, provides a fast and easy way for companies to make all their network data accessible to authorized employees, customers, and business partners, but keep it safe from unauthorized users. Decru's custom-made processor encrypts and decrypts at lightning speed, which gives it an edge over competitors.[66]

However, research has found that the chances are only six in one million that an idea for a high-tech business eventually turns into a successful public company.[67] Entrepreneurs have to get out into the marketplace and talk to potential customers to learn whether their idea is something that can meet current and future needs.[68] Start-ups have the advantage of being nimble, but the idea itself must be flexible enough to allow rapid adaptation as the environment changes.

## Writing the Business Plan

With the lightning-fast pace of the high-technology environment, a traditional business plan is usually obsolete by the time it is written. High-tech entrepreneurs have to create a compelling story about why their idea is the seed of the next success. The entrepreneur has to convince venture capitalists and potential employees to join in a risky adventure that has huge potential but few guarantees. Venture capitalists say they prefer short business plans because they have so many to read. Therefore, the entrepreneur has to keep the story crisp and compelling. The plan should cover eight basic points:

1. A description of the business and why it is unique
2. A profile of potential customers and market needs
3. The key ingredient of the business that will attract millions of customers
4. Why customers will buy from this company rather than competitors
5. What the company has accomplished so far, including partnerships or early customer relationships
6. The entrepreneur's background and role in the company
7. Specific data about where the company is located, key management people, and contact information
8. Essential information about funding received so far, funding and staffing needs, and expectations for growth of the business over the next year.[69]

Note that many of these topics are also covered by a traditional business plan as described in the Shoptalk box earlier in this chapter. The key for the high-tech start-up is to condense the essential information into a vivid, compelling story that can be told quickly and adapted quickly as the environment changes.

## Getting Initial Financing

A vivid story, told with passion and enthusiasm, is crucial to obtaining needed up-front financing. As with other small business start-ups, the entrepreneur relies on numerous sources, including family, friends, personal savings, and credit. However, high-tech start-ups often need a large amount of funding just to get started. One estimate is that a high-tech business needs from $50,000 to $500,000 just to get through the first six months–and that's with the founders drawing no salary.[70] Forrester Research estimates that the total cost to get a business up and running on the Internet ranges from $2 million to $40 million.[71] One typical source of first funds is through **angel financing**. Angels are wealthy individuals, typically with business experience and contacts, who believe in the idea for the start-up and are willing to invest their personal funds to help the business get started. This first round of financing is extremely important. It can enable the entrepreneur to quit another job to devote time to building a foundation for the new company, filing for necessary permits or patents, hiring technical consultants, marketing the new product or service, and so forth. Significantly, angels also provide advice and assistance as the entrepreneur is developing the company. The entrepreneur wants angels who can make business contacts, help find talented employees, and serve as all-around advisors.

**angel financing**
Financing provided by a wealthy individual who believes in the idea for a start-up and provides personal funds and advice to help the business get started.

## Building and Testing the Product or Service

Once an entrepreneur has up-front financing, it is time to build and test the product. This stage may include hiring employees and consultants, buying or building the technological infrastructure, and perhaps securing office space or other needed facilities. Start-ups should also begin securing top-flight legal and financial assistance. The time to begin working with lawyers and bankers is early in the process, not after the company runs into trouble, needs specific legal or financial advice, or is ready to go public. Most experts agree, however, that the most critical hires in the early phases of the company are the technology experts, such as engineers, scientists, or computer systems architects, who can bring the entrepreneur's dream to life. An indispensable part of this stage is making sure the idea and the basic technology to support it actually work.

*Reliability* is crucial in the world of high technology. The entrepreneur has to find out as early as possible whether the product idea will work, through feasibility studies, testing, and demonstrations. Thanks to extensive testing, Brett Galloway's Airespace, a company that makes switches and other gear for wireless local area networks, pulled in more than double the revenue he expected in the first three months. One key to Airespace's success is the simplicity, flexibility, and reliability of the products. They mesh well with existing wired networks and customers don't have to be technology experts to use them.[72]

## Launching the Company

The launch phase is when the company's products and services are officially made available to the public. Marketing is the most important focus at this stage of development. High-tech start-ups cannot afford to take years to build a brand; they have to make a name for themselves virtually overnight.[73] A catchy logo and visually appealing company materials are important in creating the "look" of the company. The name, if not yet selected, should be chosen with care or modified to give the company a distinctive personality that sticks in the mind of customers. For example, Ask.com, a Web site devoted to answering questions on just about anything, revised its brand name to Ask Jeeves, which proved to be a stroke of marketing genius.[74] Hiring a competent public relations firm at this stage can help to create a buzz about the new company in the business community, which helps attract future investors as well as get the word out to customers.

## Securing Additional Financing

Almost every high-tech start-up eventually has to secure further funding to support growth and expansion. The entrepreneur has to make sure salaries are paid, infrastructure is maintained, marketing efforts are continued, distribution channels are set up, and so forth. In addition, as the company grows, it might need to add more staff, expand office space, or purchase new hardware, software, and other equipment to support growth. The most obvious source of funding at this stage is *venture capital*. As described earlier, venture capitalist firms are groups of companies or individuals that invest money in exchange for a stake in the company. For example, venture capitalist firms Alloy Ventures and Lightspeed Venture Partners provided the funding for development of Apptera, an off-the-shelf software application that uses voice recognition and transaction processing to provide a virtual phone-based customer-service representative.[75] Many start-ups form a board of directors at this stage to lend a sense of stability and permanence to the new company, which can help allay investors' fears. A board of directors helps the company stay focused on the core issues that will lead to success.[76]

*Go to the ethical dilemma on page 221.*

*Take A Moment*

## Developing Partnerships

Another role the board often plays is to help a start-up create alliances with other companies, which are critical to helping the business grow. Partnerships for high-tech startups are generally of two types.[77] A start-up that primarily needs exposure and marketing assistance will partner with a larger, well-established company that can help the smaller firm gain rapid market awareness. The second type involves partnering with a company that assists in actual operations such as customer service, logistics, or warehousing and shipping, and involves electronic linkages between the partners. The company might outsource some functions to focus on core strategic issues.

## Going Public

The final step in the start-up process is often the initial public offering (IPO), in which stock in the new company is sold to the public. The dream for many entrepreneurs is to grow fast, go public, and become a corporation rather than remain a sole proprietorship or partnership, as described earlier in this chapter. Mediagrif Interactive Technologies, Inc., an online business-to-business brokerage based in Montreal, for example, went public just four years after its launch. The company is becoming the dominant player in business-to-business transactions, giving eBay a run for its money in that niche.[78] During this stage, the entrepreneur begins interviewing bankers who are interested in leading the IPO and puts together a team of bankers, lawyers, and other advisors who can steer the company through the process. The money generated from public investors can help grow the business further and help it become firmly established in its market.

A good example of a company that has gone through these steps for launching a high-tech business and that was expected to initiate an IPO is Google, the provider of the most popular search engine on the Web. Google is described in this chapter's Unlocking Creative Solutions Through Technology box.

# Managing a Growing Business

Once an entrepreneurial business is up and running, how does the owner manage it? Often the traits of self-confidence, creativity, and internal locus of control lead to financial and personal grief as the enterprise grows. A hands-on entrepreneur who gave birth to the organization loves perfecting every detail. But after the start-up, continued growth requires a shift in management style. Those who fail to adjust to a growing business can be the cause of the problems rather than the solution.[79] In this section, we will look at the stages through which entrepreneurial companies move and then consider how managers should carry out their planning, organizing, leading, and controlling.

## Stages of Growth

Entrepreneurial businesses go through distinct stages of growth, with each stage requiring different management skills. The five stages are illustrated in Exhibit 6.9.

1. *Start-up.* In this stage, the main problems are producing the product or service and obtaining customers. Several key issues facing managers are: Can we get enough customers? Will we survive? Do we have enough money? Burt's Bees was in the start-up stage when Roxanne Quimby was hand-making candles and personal care products from the beeswax of Burt Shavitz's bees and selling them at crafts fairs in Maine.

# Unlocking Creative Solutions Through Technology

## Getting Google Right

Larry Page and Sergey Brin met in 1995 while they were doctoral candidates at Stanford University, where they were both interested in Internet search as an interesting problem in organizing very large datasets. After coming up with a search formula that they thought was better than anything available, they tried to sell the technology to established companies, but had no takers. So, in the summer of 1998 the two put their academic careers on hold to bet everything on the Internet search engine they named Google (*http://www.google.com*). An angel investor wrote a check for $100,000 to Google Inc. before the company even had a bank account. By the summer of 1999, Google had raised almost $30 million from individual investors and venture capital firms.

Page and Brin knew the best way to improve their product would be through various testing stages, with continuous testing, feedback, and refining. The Stanford University community proved to be the perfect testing ground in which Google could evolve. Through this testing, testing, and re-testing, Page and Brin were assured that the basic technology was solid enough to put before a wider public. However, they also wanted to do a further testing phase with the public before launching the official site. This phase gave much needed elbow room because it warned visitors that Google's technology was a work in progress. Putting the search engine before the public forced Google to grow with the Web and meet the needs of actual users. An added benefit was that it earned the company a loyal following among users who appreciated the chance to shape how the site would work. Google relied almost entirely on word-of-mouth advertising. Early users had such a good experience that they told others, helping Google's traffic grow from the thousands to the millions by the time the official site was launched in September 1999.

One key to Google's success is its focus on innovation. Engineers work in teams of three, with leadership rotating among team members. Everyone is aimed toward the goal of delivering exactly what the user is looking for, every time, and deliver it fast. It's an impossible task, but that doesn't stop Google from trying. Teams have the authority to make changes that improve the quality of the user experience and get rid of anything that gets in the way. Users remain a key element of Google's innovation. Ten full-time employees read and respond to e-mails from users, enabling people to feel like an important part of the Google community as well as helping Google improve.

The organic approach to innovation has served Google well. The unique understanding of users and the loyalty and trust it inspires has enabled Google to grow rapidly. Google can now be queried in 36 languages, and, according to the company processes more than 150 million searches a day (some estimates are much higher). To help keep the company on track during its rapid growth, the founders brought in a seasoned manager as chief executive, while they concentrated on improving their search formulas.

Google's next step was to go public. Google completed an initial public offering (IPO) in August of 2004. Shares immediately jumped 27 percent from the initial-offer price, giving the company a market value of nearly $30 billion.

**SOURCES:** Quentin Hardy, "All Eyes on Google," *Forbes* (May 26, 2003), 100-110; Keith H. Hammonds, "How Google Grows . . . and Grows . . . and Grows," *Fast Company* (April 2003), 74+; Larry Page and Sergey Brin, "Merits of a Beta Launch," *Business 2.0* (March 2000), 180; "When Larry Met Sergey," *http://www.up-mag.com/themag/feature1htm*, accessed on July 31, 2001; and John Markoff, "Audit Results Move Google A Step Closer to Offering," *The New York Times* (January 27, 2004), C1.

2. *Survival.* At this stage, the business has demonstrated that it is a workable business entity. It is producing a product or service and has sufficient customers. Concerns here have to do with finances—generating sufficient cash flow to run the business and making sure revenues exceed expenses. The organization will grow in size and profitability during this period. Burt's Bees reached $3 million in sales by 1993, and Quimby moved the business from Maine to North Carolina to take advantage of state policies that helped her keep costs in line.

3. *Success.* At this point, the company is solidly based and profitable. Systems and procedures are in place to allow the owner to slow down if desired. The owner can stay involved or consider turning the business over to professional managers.

Exhibit 6.9

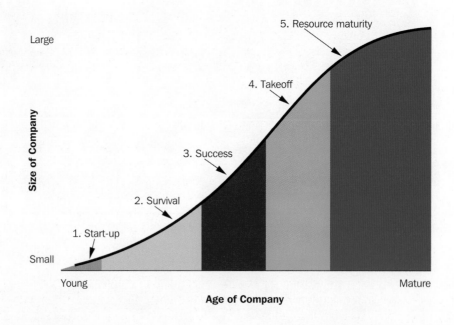

## Five Stages of Growth for an Entrepreneurial Company

*Five Stages of Growth for an Entrepreneurial Company*

Large

Size of Company

5. Resource maturity

4. Takeoff

3. Success

2. Survival

1. Start-up

Small

Young                                                  Mature

**Age of Company**

**SOURCE:** Based on Neil C. Churchill and Virginia L. Lewis, "The Five Stages of Small Business Growth," *Harvard Business Review* (May–June 1993), 30–50.

Quimby chose to stay closely involved with Burt's Bees, admitting that she's a bit of a control freak about the business.

4. *Takeoff.* Here the key problem is how to grow rapidly and finance that growth. The owner must learn to delegate, and the company must find sufficient capital to invest in major growth. This is a pivotal period in an entrepreneurial company's life. Properly managed, the company can become a big business. However, another problem for companies at this stage is how to maintain the advantages of "smallness" as the company grows. In 2003, Quimby sold 80 percent of Burt's Bees to AEA Investors, a private equity firm, for more than $175 million. She will continue as CEO and focus on continuing to grow the business.

5. *Resource maturity.* At this stage, the company has made substantial financial gains, but it may start to lose the advantages of small size, including flexibility and the entrepreneurial spirit. A company in this stage has the staff and financial resources to begin acting like a mature company with detailed planning and control systems.

## Planning

In the early start-up stage, formal planning tends to be nonexistent except for the business plan described earlier in this chapter. The primary goal is simply to remain alive. As the organization grows, formal planning usually is not instituted until around the success stage. Recall from Chapter 1 that planning means defining goals and deciding on the tasks and use of resources needed to attain them. Chapters 7, 8, and 9 will describe how entrepreneurs can define goals and implement strategies and plans to meet them. It is important that entrepreneurs view their original business plan as a living document that evolves as the company grows or the market changes.

One planning concern for today's small businesses is the need to be Web-savvy. For many small companies today, their Web operations are just as critical as traditional warehouse management or customer service operations. For example, Peter Monticup has been operating retail stores selling magic tricks, videos, and memorabilia for more than 30 years. In 1995, Monticup's wife suggested they explore the Web as a way to promote their latest store. That exploration turned into a full-fledged online store, MagicTricks.com. Online sales grew so fast that Monticup eventually closed his retail outlets and moved the entire operation online.[80] Even for companies that use the Web less extensively, the growing importance of e-business means entrepreneurs have to plan and allocate resources for Internet operations from the beginning and grow those plans as the company grows. Of the small companies that have Web sites, more than half say the site has broken even or paid for itself in greater efficiency, improved customer relationships, or increased business.[81]

## Organizing

In the first two stages of growth, the organization's structure is typically very informal with all employees reporting to the owner. At about stage 3—success—functional managers often are hired to take over duties performed by the owner. A functional organization structure will begin to evolve with managers in charge of finance, manufacturing, and marketing. Another organizational approach is to use outsourcing—having some functional activities handled by outside contractors. For example, Method, described earlier in this chapter, contracted with an industrial designer for the unique dish soap bottle and uses contract manufacturers in every region of the country to rapidly make products and get them to stores.[82] During the latter stages of entrepreneurial growth, managers must learn to delegate and decentralize authority. If the business has multiple product lines, the owner may consider creating teams or divisions responsible for each line. The organization must hire competent managers and have sufficient management talent to handle fast growth and eliminate problems caused by increasing size.

As an organization grows, it might also be characterized by greater use of rules, procedures, and written job descriptions. For example, Tara Cronbaugh started a small coffeehouse in a college town, but its success quickly led to the opening of three additional houses. With the rapid growth, Cronbaugh found that she needed a way to ensure consistency across operations. She put together an operations manual with detailed rules, procedures, and job descriptions so managers and employees at each coffeehouse would be following the same pattern.[83] Chapters 10 through 13 will discuss organizing in detail.

## Leading

The driving force in the early stages of development is the leader's vision. This vision, combined with the leader's personality, shapes corporate culture. The leader can signal cultural values of service, efficiency, quality, or ethics. Often entrepreneurs do not have good people skills but do have excellent task skills in either manufacturing or marketing. By the success stage of growth, the owner must either learn to motivate employees or bring in managers who can. Rapid takeoff is not likely to happen without employee cooperation. Stepping from the self-absorption of the early days of a company to the more active communication necessary for growth can be tricky for entrepreneurs. The president of Foreign Candy Company of Hull, Iowa, saw his company grow rapidly when he concentrated more on employee needs and less on financial results. He made an effort to communicate with employees, conducted surveys to learn how they were feeling about the company, and found ways to involve them in decision making. His shift in leadership style allowed the company to enter the takeoff stage with the right corporate culture and employee attitudes to sustain rapid growth.

Leadership also is important because many small firms have a hard time hiring qualified employees. Labor shortages often hurt small firms that grow rapidly. A healthy corporate culture can help attract and retain good people.[84] You will learn more about leadership in Chapters 17 through 21.

### CONCEPT CONNECTION

*Tennis star Venus Williams is a seasoned athlete with a plan for retirement. Williams, along with a friend who has 25 years of interior design experience, is currently in the **start-up stage** of her business, V Starr Interiors. Their plan is that when Williams, who is now 23 years old, retires from tennis, she will leverage her wealth, name recognition, and connections and devote herself full-time to the firm. Presently, V Starr Interiors has four employees, six accounts, and projected sales of $1,000,000. The start-up's main goal is to take advantage of the Florida housing market boom, where single homes approved for construction increased by nearly 32 percent in the last five years.*

## Controlling

Financial control is important in each stage of the entrepreneurial firm's growth. In the initial stages, control is exercised by simple accounting records and by personal supervision. By stage 3—success—operational budgets are in place, and the owner should start implementing more structured control systems. During the takeoff stage, the company will need to make greater use of budgets and standard cost systems and use computer systems to provide statistical reports. These control techniques will become more sophisticated during the resource maturity stage.

As Amazon.com has grown and expanded internationally, entrepreneur and CEO Jeff Bezos has found a need for increasingly sophisticated control mechanisms. Bezos hired a computer systems expert to develop a system to track and control all of the company's operations.[85] Control will be discussed further in Chapters 14 through 16.

## Manager's Solution

This chapter explored entrepreneurship and small-business management. Entrepreneurs start new businesses, and entrepreneurship plays an important role in the economy by stimulating job creation, innovation, and opportunities for minorities and women. An entrepreneurial personality includes the traits of internal locus of control, high energy level, need to achieve, tolerance for ambiguity, awareness of passing time, and self-confidence.

Starting an entrepreneurial firm requires a new-business idea. At that point a comprehensive business plan should be developed and decisions made about legal structure and financing. Tactical decisions for the new venture include whether to start, buy, or franchise, and whether to participate in a business incubator.

A special kind of small business is the high-tech start-up. These companies face the same challenges as other small businesses, but high-tech entrepreneurs also encounter some unique issues. High-tech start-ups typically follow eight steps: (1) formulating the idea and concept for the company; (2) developing a business plan and a "story" to sell the idea; (3) securing up-front financing; (4) building and testing the product and service; (5) officially launching the company; (6) obtaining additional financing; (7) developing partnerships with other organizations; and (8) perhaps taking the company public through an initial public offering.

After a business is started, it generally proceeds through five stages of growth—start-up, survival, success, takeoff, and resource maturity. The management functions of planning, organizing, leading, and controlling should be tailored to each stage of growth.

Cyberonics, described in the chapter opening, is a good example of a high-tech start-up. In the opening, the company had reached step three: Reese Terry had developed a great idea, created a compelling business plan, and successfully raised $1 million in start-up funds to create Cyberonics in 1987. That's where things got tricky. Terry managed to find a handful of doctors who were willing to test the device in their patients—and it worked. These tests were good enough to help Cyberonics get a second round of financing for $2 million, enabling Terry to bring in an outside CEO, hire a vice president of clinical studies and regulatory affairs to help win FDA approval, and grow to about 50 employees. But it wasn't nearly enough to get the product on the market. Cyberonics' first two applications to the FDA were rejected because of limited clinical studies, both the CEO and vice-president left the company, and Cyberonics shrunk from 50 employees down to about 35. "It was the lowest point of my career," Terry says, but he stuck with it. Eventually, one of the venture capitalists serving on the Cyberonics board came on as CEO to help the troubled company scrounge enough money to win FDA approval. St. Jude Medical, a large Minneapolis medical device maker, invested $12 million, which was important not just for the money but for the credibility the partnership gave the smaller company. When Cyberonics went back to the FDA for the third time, the panel unanimously approved the vagus-nerve stimulator device for epilepsy. Overall, the process had taken 10 years and $50 million. Despite its troubles and many disappointments, Cyberonics managed to go public and now employs 450 people and has annual sales of around $110 million. Cyberonics vagus-nerve stimulator devices are now implanted in 22,000 people, helping them live higher-quality lives. The company will face new challenges—for one thing, it is unlikely to survive for long on only one product. However, founder Terry and CEO Skip Cummins are committed to making the business a long-term success. "If you don't have passion and you're not committed," says Cummins, "don't waste your time."[86]

# Discussion Questions

1. Dan McKinnon started an airline with one airplane. To do so required filing more than 10,000 pages of manuals, ordering 50,000 luggage tags, buying more than $500 million in insurance, and spending more than $300,000 to train employees. A single inspection test cost $18,000. Evaluate whether you think this is a good entrepreneurial opportunity, and discuss why you think Dan McKinnon undertook it.

2. What do you think are the most important contributions of small business to our economy?

3. Why would small-business ownership have great appeal to immigrants, women, and minorities?

4. Consider the six personality characteristics of entrepreneurs. Which two traits do you think are most like those of managers in large companies? Which two are least like those of managers in large companies?

5. Why is purchasing an existing business or franchise less risky than starting a new business?

6. If you were to start a new business, would you have to search for an idea, or do you already have an idea to try? Explain.

7. Many entrepreneurs say they did little planning, perhaps scratching notes on a legal pad. How is it possible for them to succeed?

8. What is the difference between debt financing and equity financing? What are common sources of each type?

9. How does an entrepreneurial firm in the existence stage differ from one in the success stage?

10. How do the management functions of organizing and controlling differ for the existence and success stages?

11. Explain the difference between entrepreneurship and intrapreneurship. Why would entrepreneurs want intrapreneurship within their companies? Would an entrepreneur's personality tend to inhibit intrapreneurship? Discuss.

# Management in Practice: Experiential Exercise

## What Is Your Entrepreneurial Quotient?

The following questions are from a test developed by John R. Braun, psychology professor at the University of Bridgeport in Connecticut, and the Northwestern Mutual Life Insurance Company, based in Milwaukee. Simply answer yes or no to each question.

1. Are you a first-generation American?

2. Were you an honor student?

3. Did you enjoy group functions in schools—clubs, team sports, even double dates?

4. As a youngster, did you prefer to be alone frequently?

5. As a child, did you have a paper route, a lemonade stand, or some other small enterprise?

6. Were you a stubborn child?

7. Were you a cautious youngster, the last in the neighborhood to try diving off the highboard?

8. Do you worry about what others think of you?

9. Are you in a rut, tired of the same routine day in and day out?

10. Would you be willing to dip deeply into your "nest egg"—and possibly lose all you invested—to go it alone?

11. If your new business should fail, would you get to work immediately on another?

12. Are you an optimist?

### Answers:

1. Yes = 1, No = minus 1.
2. Yes = minus 4, No = 4.
3. Yes = minus 1, No = 1.
4. Yes = 1, No = minus 1.
5. Yes = 2, No = minus 2.
6. Yes = 1, No = minus 1.
7. Yes = minus 4, No = 4. If you were a particularly daring child, add another 4 points.
8. Yes = minus 1, No = 1.
9. Yes = 2, No = minus 2.
10. Yes = 2, No = minus 2.
11. Yes = 4, No = minus 4.
12. Yes = 2, No = minus 2.

Now calculate your total score. If you tallied 20 or more points, you have a strong entrepreneurial quotient. The score of 0 to 19 suggests that you have entrepreneurial possibilities. If you scored between 0 and minus 10, your chance of successfully starting an entrepreneurial business is marginal. A score below minus 11 suggests you are not the entrepreneurial type.

Go back over each question, thinking about changes you might make to become more or less entrepreneurial, depending on your career interests.

Source: Peter Lohr, "Should You Be in Business for Yourself?" *Readers Digest*, July 1989, 49-52.

# Management in Practice: Ethical Dilemma

## To Grow or Not to Grow?

Chuck Campbell is the founder of Expeditions Unlimited, a specialty travel service that researches and arranges trips to unlikely places. He is famous for his unconventional approach to business in everything from his trademark blue jeans and ball caps as working attire to his personal relationships with all clients. He is the type of entrepreneur who makes deep commitments to his employees, with generous educational allowances, family leaves, and profit sharing for all of his staff. The office atmosphere is casual but professional. People dress any way they choose and music plays continually, but everyone works long hours, and customer satisfaction is the ultimate goal. For example, a 24-hour answering service relays messages to agents at home if their clients have emergencies during a booked trip.

Five years ago, Campbell consented to acquiring a computer system when his agents insisted it would help them in their jobs, but he doesn't use it. He pays two receptionists to work full-time, rather than have an automated phone system with voice mail. He believes his clients should be able to talk to a person whenever they call. The company has grown steadily, and he knows that at least two of his senior employees are ready to start branches on their own. They want his consent and his supervision, but Campbell isn't sure he wants or can handle such a radical expansion. He knows he'll need to compromise his level of contact with clients and embrace the new technology to make it work, and he's not sure that he will still enjoy his job after the transition. He also worries that the unique nature of this highly personal business may change with the growth. Campbell says employee satisfaction and growth are important. Does his commitment to employee development demand he expose his business and his personal job satisfaction to the risk of new business arrangements?

### What Do You Do?

1. Refuse to expand your business. Stay within your comfort zone, but give your blessings to the senior employees who want to quit and start their own travel service in other cities.
2. Expand the business in its present location: delegate the bulk of the company and expedition management to the senior agents, with the rest doing the research and arrangements. Step back into a supervisory and client contact position only. Agents receive more responsibility, and you stay in control.
3. Train the senior agents to open branches under your corporate identity, trusting that your long association will insure that they run the branches with the corporate values you instilled. Then let go and give them only as much supervision as you can comfortably afford to give.

# Surf the Net

1. **Entrepreneurship.** Go to the "Quiz for Small Business Success" available at the U.S. Small Business Administration Web site (*http://www.sba.gov/BI/quiz.html*). Assume the role of a small business owner (if you are not one already) and complete the quiz and score your results. Write a paragraph summarizing how your score was interpreted according to the Success Quotient Table. Also, include in your summary whether you think a quiz such as this can be helpful to someone interested in pursuing small business ownership.

2. **Venture capital firms.** Assume you are seeking financing for an entrepreneurial venture and need to check the availability of possible funding in your situation. Visit America's Business Funding Directory at *http://www.businessfinance.com*. According to the information applicants provide for the search, list the criteria venture capitalists consider when evaluating your capital request. After reviewing the procedure for using this Web site to locate funding sources, examine the tools, references, and resources also available at this site that can help you grow and keep your business strong.

3.  **Franchise opportunities.** You will be able to find a great deal of information about franchising opportunities available for entrepreneurs. Use your Internet search engine to locate a site such as "The Franchise Handbook: On-Line" at *http://www.franchise1.com/* or "Business Opportunities Handbook: On-Line" at *http:// www. ezines.com.* Select three franchise opportunities that interest you and prepare a table where you will compare information related to each franchise. Across the top of the page list the franchises you've selected; in the left column list information categories provided below. You may add to these categories by using some of the questions from Exhibit 6.7, "Sample Questions for Choosing a Franchise." Fill in the columns with the information related to each franchise.

Franchising since

Number of franchised units

Number of company-owned units

Franchise fee

Capital requirements

Training and support provided

# Case for Critical Analysis

### I Do Its

Robi Fugate of Birmingham, Alabama, first thought of the idea for her kids' clothing line when she noticed some toddlers whose mismatched duds told her they'd picked out their own outfits. Fugate spotted a niche for a children's clothing line that would allow kids to dress themselves without help—a line of totally coordinated pieces with no defined fronts or backs and no zippers or buttons to fool with. Right then and there she came up with the name "I Do Its," because, she reasoned, "that's what kids say when you try to dress them." However, it was seven years before Fugate got up the courage to leave her $32,000-a-year job managing department store counters for Clinique. She was "scared she'd be chewed up and spit out" in the fashion world, but Fugate felt that too many years had already slipped by and that the time was right for her to start the business. Newly divorced and the mother of an infant, Fugate recruited a partner to invest $120,000, and I Do Its was born.

Fugate commissioned the North River Apparel factory in Berry, Alabama, to manufacture the clothing and contracted with representatives at Cyrilla & Co., an agency whose Atlanta showroom sells to stores from Virginia to Florida, to market the first year's line. I Do Its pulled in $32,000 in sales its first year, and sales quadrupled the following year. More sales representatives signed up in Dallas, Chicago, Los Angeles, and New York, and independent children's stores from around the country began placing orders. Then Fugate suffered the business' first crisis when she didn't have enough cash to deliver the orders. Larry Johnson, owner of North River Apparel, came to the rescue, offering Fugate a line of credit that would be paid off with a 50 percent share of I Do Its' profits. But the problems were just beginning.

Fugate has had a difficult time growing the business because she can't afford a major advertising campaign. Although she's managed to get some free publicity from the *Birmingham Post-Herald* and Parenting Life, a local television show, Fugate knows she needs more than local publicity to make I Do Its a success. In addition, she's having a hard time getting retailers to sell her clothing line the way she wants it sold: as matching outfits. She has even visited some stores and found that they had no idea the purpose of the clothing was to allow kids to dress themselves. Although she will ship I Do Its only in matching sets, many stores separate the pieces and mix them in with other labels, making it extremely difficult for parents to put together ensembles, and leaving the stores with mismatched items that have to be marked down at the end of the season.

After three years in business, the I Do Its clothing line is still struggling to catch on. However, despite her frustrations, Fugate believes in her idea and knows the company can be successful. She is particularly excited about launching a catalog next year for disabled kids, as she believes they are natural customers for the I Do Its line. She has also recently invested a modest amount in advertising and is considering how she can get sales reps to promote the I Do Its philosophy so that stores will sell the clothing in sets. I Do Its has many hurdles to cross, but Fugate believes a good idea and a lot of hard work can lead to success.

**Questions**

1. Of the six personality traits of typical entrepreneurs, which seem most present in Robi Fugate? Which trait do you think is most important for solving the problem of getting stores to sell the clothing in matching sets?

2. Discuss how Fugate should carry out her organizing, leading, and controlling to manage the business for success.

3. Do you believe Fugate will eventually succeed with I Do Its? Why?

Source: Based on: Amanda Walmac, "Getting the Word Out," *Working Woman,* September 1998, 42, 44.

# Endnotes

1. Scott Kirsner, "Fantastic Voyage," *Fast Company* (April 2004), 54+.
2. John Case, "Where We Are Now," *Inc.,* State of Small Business 2001 (May 29, 2001), 18–19.
3. Reported in Laura Randall, "Lessons Learned the Hardest Way, By Going Belly-Up," *The New York Times* (February 24, 2004), G8.
4. Donald F. Kuratko and Richard M. Hodgetts, *Entrepreneurship: A Contemporary Approach,* 4th ed. (Fort Worth: The Dryden Press, 1998), 30.
5. Tahl Ras, "This Hip House," *Inc.* (October 2002), 34–36; and http://www.readymademag.com accessed on March 12, 2004.
6. Study conducted by Yankelovich Partners, reported in Mark Henricks, "Type-Cast," *Entrepreneur* (March 2000), 14–16.
7. Jill Hecht Maxwell, "Seduced and Abandoned (and Grateful, Too)," *Inc.* (January 2003), 56–58.
8. Christina Le Beau, "Kick in the Pants," *The Wall Street Journal* (May 14, 2001), R8.
9. Norm Brodsky, "Street Smarts: Opportunity Knocks," *Inc.* (February 2002), 44–46; and Hilary Stout, "Start Low," *The Wall Street Journal* (May 14, 2001), R8.
10. Center for Women's Business Research, reported in Jim Hopkins, "Female-Owned Companies Flourish," *USA Today* (May 6, 2003), Section B, 1.
11. Kathleen Collins, "¡La Vida Próspera! Latin-Owned Businesses Explode," *Working Woman* (October 2000), 13.
12. Office of Advocacy of the U.S. Small Business Administration, reported in T. Shawn Taylor, "Kitchen Table CEOs," *Essence* (March 2004), 112.
13. Based on information in "Market Share," *Inc.,* State of Small Business 2001 (May 29, 2001), 25–26; and

"The Soloists," *Inc.,* State of Small Business 2001 (May 29, 2001), 37–39.
14. "2003 Global Entrepreneurship Monitor," based on interviews in 40 countries in 2002 and 2003, as reported in "Uganda, Entrepreneur's Paradise," *Fast Company* (May 2004), 46.
15. "One-Yen Wonders," *The Economist* (June 28, 2003), 66.
16. Ovetta Wiggins, "Report: Small Business Set to Double By 2009," *The Moscow Times,* http://www.themoscowtimes.com/ as reported on The America's Intelligence Wire, March 2, 2004.
17. This section based on John Case, "The Wonderland Economy," *The State of Small Business* (1995), 14–29; and Richard L. Daft, *Management,* 3d ed. (Fort Worth, Texas: The Dryden Press, 1992).
18. U. S. Census Bureau, 1997 Economic Census: Non-employer Statistics, reported in "The Soloists," *Inc.* State of Small Business 2001 (May 29, 2001), 37–39.
19. Susan Greco and Elaine Appleton Grant, "Innovation, Part III: Creation Nation," *Inc.* (October 2002), 72–80.
20. Elizabeth Olson, "Dot-Com Survivor Hits on Right Plan," *The New York Times* (February 5, 2004), C6.
21. "The Deal Monger," segment in Mark Athitakis, "How to Make Money on the Net," *Business 2.0* (May 2003), 83–90.
22. George Mannes, "Don't Give Up on the Web," *Fortune* Small Business section, *Fortune* (March 5, 2001), 184 [B]–184[L].
23. Brian Caulfield, Michael V. Copeland, Bridget Finn, David Howard, Kevin Kelleher, Matthew Maier, Om Malik, Jordan Robertson, and Owen Thomas, "12 Hot Startups," *Business 2.0* (January–February 2004), 93–97.

24. Caulfield, et al., "12 Hot Startups"; "Cold Cash: Second-Grade Teacher Victoria Knight-McDowell's Herbal Potion Turns Ka-choos into Ka-ching," *People Weekly* (March 15, 2004), 139.

25. Dany Levy, as told to Bobbie Gossage, "How I Did It," *Inc.* (February 2004), 60–62.

26. Small Business Administration Web site, http://www.sba.gov

27. Bill Meyers, "Worker Shortage Forces Small Businesses into Creative Hiring," *USA Today* (October 30, 1998) 1B, 2B.

28. Barbara Benham, "Big Government, Small Business," *Working Woman* (February 2001), 24.

29. Research and statistics reported in "The Job Factory," *Inc.,* State of Small Business 2001 (May 29, 2001) 40–43.

30. Reported in Elizabeth Olson, "From One Business to 23 Million," *The New York Times* (March 7, 2004), Section 3, 2.

31. Kuratko and Hodgetts, *Entrepreneurship: A Contemporary Approach*, 4th ed., 11; and "100 Ideas for New Businesses," *Venture* (November 1988), 35–74.

32. Robert Berner, "Why P&G's Smile Is So Bright," *BusinessWeek* (August 12, 2002), 58–60.

33. Bridget Finn, "Selling Cool in a Bottle—of Dish Soap," *Business 2.0* (December 2003), 72–74.

34. John Case, "The Origins of Entrepreneurship," *Inc.* (June 1989), 51–53.

35. Greco and Grant, "Innovation, Part III: Creation Nation."

36. Robert D. Hisrich, "Entrepreneurship-Intrapreneurship," *American Psychologist* (February 1990), 209–222.

37. Olson, "From One Business to 23 Million."

38. Center for Women's Business Research statistics, reported in Jim Hopkins, "Female-Owned Companies Flourish," *USA Today* (May 6, 2003), 1B.

39. Statistics reported in Cora Daniels, "Minority Rule," *FSB* (December 2003–January 2004), 65–66, and David J. Dent, "The Next Black Power Movement," *FSB* (May 2003), 10–13.

40. Ellyn Spragins, "Pat Winans" profile, and Cora Daniels, "Ed Chin" profile, in "The New Color of Money," *FSB* (December 2003–January 2004), 74–87.

41. This discussion is based on Charles R. Kuehl and Peggy A. Lambing, *Small Business: Planning and Management*, 3d ed. (Ft. Worth: The Dryden Press, 1994).

42. David C. McClelland, *The Achieving Society* (New York: Van Nostrand, 1961).

43. Ian Mount, "Be Fast, Be Frugal, Be Right," *Inc.* (January 2004), 64–70.

44. Paulette Thomas, "Entrepreneurs' Biggest Problems— And How They Solve Them" *The Wall Street Journal* (March 17, 2003), R1.

45. Leslie Brokaw, "How to Start an *Inc.* 500 Company," *Inc.* 500 (1994), 51–65.

46. Paul Reynolds, "The Truth about Start-Ups," *Inc.* (February 1995), 23; Brian O'Reilly, "The New Face of Small Businesses," *Fortune* (May 2, 1994) 82–88.

47. Based on Ellyn E. Spragins, "How to Write a Business Plan That Will Get You in the Door," *Small Business Success* (*Inc.* 2001); Linda Elkins, "Tips for Preparing a Business Plan," *Nation's Business* (June 1996), 60R–61R; Carolyn M. Brown, "The Do's and Don'ts of Writing a Winning Business Plan," *Black Enterprise* (April 1996), 114–116; and Kuratko and Hodgetts, *Entrepreneurship*, 4th ed., 295–397. For a clear, thorough step-by-step guide to writing an effective business plan, see Linda Pinson and Jerry Jinnett, *Anatomy of a Business Plan*, 5th ed. (Virginia Beach, Va: Dearborn, 2001).

48. The INC. FAXPOLL, *Inc.* (February 1992), 24.

49. "Venture Capitalists' Criteria" *Management Review* (November 1985), 7–8.

50. "Staples Makes Big Business From Helping Small Businesses," *SBA Success Stories, http://www.sba.gov/successstories.html* accessed on March 12, 2004.

51. Olson, "From One Business to 23 Million."

52. "Where the Venture Money is Going," *Business 2.0* (January–February 2004), 98.

53. Dent, "The Next Black Power Movement."

54. Jennifer Maxwell profile in Betsy Wiesendanger, "Labors of Love," *Working Woman* (May 1999), 43–56.

55. Reported in Sheryl Nance-Nash, "More Are Betting the Franchise," *The New York Times* (February 29, 2004), Section 14 LI, 6.

56. Echo Montgomery Garrett, "The Twenty-First-Century Franchise," *Inc.* (January 1995), 79–88; Lisa Benavides, "Linking Up with a Chain," *The Tennessean* (April 6, 1999), 1E.

57. Henry Weil, "Business in a Box," *Working Woman* (September 1999), 59–64.

58. Quinne Bryant, "Who Owns 20+ Subway Franchises?" *The Business Journal of Tri-Cities Tennessee/Virginia* (August 2003), 42–43.

59. Anne Field, "Your Ticket to a New Career? Franchising Can Put Your Skills to Work in Your Own Business," in *Business Week Investor: Small Business* section, *BusinessWeek* (May 12, 2003), 100+, and Roberta Maynard, "Choosing a Franchise," *Nation's Business* (October 1996), 56–63.

60. Dale Buss, "Bringing New Firms Out of Their Shell," *Nation's Business* (March 1997), 48–50; and Amy Oringel, "Sowing Success," *Working Woman* (May 2001), 72.

61. Harvard Business School statistics, reported in Kimberly Weisul, "Incubators Lay an Egg," *Business Week Frontier* (October 9, 2000), F14.

62. Oringel, "Sowing Success."

63. Peter Balan, University of South Australia, "Harmony: A Global Network Support System for Incubators," and "Harmony: A Network System to Support Innovation Commercialisation," http://business2.unisa.edu.au/cde/docs/HarmonyOverviewAndBenefits%2025Feb02.pdf

64. Thomson Venture Economics, reported in Caulfield, et al., "12 Hot Startups."

65. John Case, "Who's Looking at Start-Ups?" *Inc.*, State of Small Business 2001 (May 29, 2001) 60.

66. Caulfield et al., "12 Hot Startups."

67. Reported in "Did You Know?" sidebar in J. Neil Weintraut, "Told Any Good Stories Lately?" *Business 2.0* (March 2000), 139–140.

68. Duncan MacVicar, "Ten Steps to a High-Tech Start-Up," *The Industrial Physicist* (October 1999), 27–31.

69. J. Neil Weintraut, "Told Any Good Stories Lately?" *Business 2.0* (March 2000), 139–140.

70. MacVicar, "Ten Steps to a High-Tech Start-Up."

71. Reported in H. M. Dietel, P. J. Dietel, and K. Steinbuhler, *e-Business and e-Commerce for Managers* (Upper Saddle River, NJ: Prentice Hall, 2001), 58.

72. Stephanie N. Mehta, "Airespace" profile in "Surprise! The Startups Are Back," *Fortune* (November 24, 2003), 203–214.

73. This section is based on Glen Rifkin and Ken Lambert, "Marketing Your Startup," *Business 2.0* (March 2000), 181–184.

74. Clay Timon, "10 Steps for Naming," *Business 2.0* (March 2000). 151–152.

75. Caulfield et al, "12 Hot Startups."

76. Bruce Golden, "Forming a Board," *Fast Company* (March 2000), 171.

77. Wendy Lea, "Dancing with a Partner," *Fast Company* (March 2000), 159–161.

78. Raizel Robin, "Net Gains," E-Biz That Works section, *Canadian Business* (October 14, 2003), 107.

79. Carrie Dolan, "Entrepreneurs Often Fail as Managers," *The Wall Street Journal* (May 15, 1989), B1.

80. Leigh Buchanan, "Working Wonders on the Web," *Inc.* (November 2003), 76–84, 104.

81. Mannes, "Don't Give Up on the Web."

82. Finn, "Selling Cool in a Bottle."

83. Amanda Walmac, "Full of Beans," *Working Woman* (February 1999), 38–40.

84. Udayan Gupta and Jeffery A. Tannenbaum, "Labor Shortages Force Changes at Small Firms," *The Wall Street Journal* (May 22, 1989), B1, B2; "Harnessing Employee Productivity," *Small Business Report* (November 1987), 46–49; and Molly Kilmas, "How to Recruit a Smart Team," *Nation's Business* (May 1995), 26–27.

85. Saul Hansell, "Listen Up! It's Time for a Profit: A Front Row Seat as Amazon Gets Serious," *The New York Times* (May 20, 2001), Section 3, 1.

86. Kirsner, "Fantastic Voyage."

# Chapter 3: Fallon Worldwide: Can Its Corporate Culture Be a Soul Survivor?

When a corporate giant takes over a smaller firm, the question everyone asks is, What will happen to the culture of the small company? Will the quirks, the flexibility, and the creativity of the small fish be swallowed by the larger fish? When Paris-based Publicis Group SA announced its acquisition of Minneapolis-based advertising agency Fallon Worldwide, the worry was on every manager's, staffer's, and client's mind. "One of my greatest fears was that our people would think we sold out," recalls Pat Fallon, founder and chairman of the company. "People were worried that we would become more corporate and less like the home they knew. And if people feel as if a bond has been broken, then everything is up for grabs." Fallon Worldwide had always been known for its high-energy, creative culture. People who worked there loved the atmosphere. Clients enjoyed Fallon's cozy, quirky, sometimes outrageous spirit. "It was a time of uncertainty," says Anne Bologna, planning director of Fallon's Minneapolis office. "There was this sense that we no longer had the freedom to be entrepreneurs." So Bologna made a call to action throughout the agency for new ideas. What began as hallway chatfests turned into a full-scale company initiative bent on preserving Fallon's culture.

"People wanted proof that the soul of the company wasn't going to change," recalls Rob White, co-president of Fallon. "We had to show them that the acquisition [by Publicis] was a strategic move to help us achieve very ambitious goals that we probably couldn't achieve on our own." That was the catch: Fallon founders had to find a way to mesh the driving force of their company—its high level of energy, its creative spirit—with an external environment that included a sluggish economy, fierce competitors, and a new boss. "Staying energized is the only way to survive," insists Anne Bologna. "In a down economy, creativity as currency is needed more than ever." So, if Fallon could enhance its already-existing culture, the company might not just survive but actually thrive under the umbrella of Publicis. During the year after Bologna's initial call for new ideas, the agency launched Fallonet, an intranet that allows the free-flow of ideas, humor, and challenges. Fallon also established an interactive consulting group as a full-fledged company division.

One employee who took Anne Bologna's directive seriously was John King, a young media planner. He proposed a new program called Dream Catchers, in which Fallon would assist employees in funding their own "impossible" dreams, thus fueling their creativity. Employees who wanted to participate simply decided how much they wanted to deduct from their paychecks on a regular basis to set aside for their "dream" sabbatical. Fallon then matched their deductions up to $2,500. Once an employee had been with the company three years, he or she could take a two-week, paid sabbatical—in addition to vacation time—to pursue a dream. One staffer used the sabbatical to visit the Van Gogh Museum in Amsterdam while another ran with the bulls in Pamplona. "Dream Catchers gives you license to be selfish if you want to be," says program designer King. "So many people get caught up in day-to-day living and put their dreams on hold indefinitely. The program is supposed to be a kick in the [butt]." A company whose internal culture promotes creativity in a variety of ways is likely to see the impact in its products and services. Since Fallon instituted its new initiatives, the agency has won new clients as well as several prestigious advertising awards for its work.

Today, despite a tight labor market and a slow economy, Fallon has billings of more than $800 million per year and a client list that reads like a Who's Who of corporate giants: BMW of North America, Citibank, EDS, Holiday Inn, Nikon, Nordstrom, Nuveen Investments, PBS, Ralston Purina, Starbucks Coffee Company, Timex, and United Airlines, to name a few. In selecting Fallon, United's director of Worldwide Marketing Communications, Jerry Dow, indicated the importance of Fallon's innovative culture to the decision. "In the end, Fallon showed United that the agency best understood the airline's brand vision, and had the tools to develop and deliver a hard-hitting, integrated global message and global brand platform."

There's no doubt that Fallon faces some tough challenges as it continues to try to integrate with Publicis without losing its own identity, trudges through an economic downturn, and looks for ways to keep employees energized, happy, and productive. But company founder Pat Fallon remains optimistic. "It

## Chapter 3: Fallon Worldwide: Can Its Corporate Culture Be a Soul Survivor? (continued)

comes down to one thing," he says. "Do you or don't you live by your values? Even in this tough economic climate, we can never invest enough in our people if we want them to do the best work of their lives." Pat Fallon intends his agency to be a soul survivor.

### Questions

1.  Imagine that you are a member of Fallon's staff. Write a brief paragraph proposing your own idea for sparking creativity at Fallon.
2.  Why is maintaining Fallon's corporate culture so important?

3.  How is Fallon's corporate culture linked to its external environment?

Sources: "Forecasters Predict Drop in Ad Spending," *The New York Times*, December 3, 2001, *http://college3nytimes.com*; Christine Canabou, "Free to Innovate," *Fast Company,* November 2001, *http://www.fastcompany.com*; "United Selects Fallon Worldwide to Manage Its North American and International Advertising," United Airlines press release, January 22, 2001, *http://www. ual.com*.

# Video Case

## Chapter 4: Fallon Worldwide—Its Name Spells Global

Even before the Minneapolis-based advertising agency Fallon Worldwide was acquired by France's Publicis, Pat Fallon was on the hunt for alliances he could make with other companies around the world. Managing the global environment is more important than ever for companies as technology expands boundaries or eliminates them altogether. In early 1999, Pat Fallon met Robert Senior in London for a cup of tea. Fallon was searching for his first foreign partners in Britain. Fallon Worldwide (then called Fallon McElligott) had already established its reputation for passion and independence. Senior and his colleagues were quick to jump on board. In less than a year, the Fallon London office had a dozen top clients and billings of $40 million. What made the international alliance work? Shared values, reported Britain's Senior. "Passion for great advertising is part of Pat Fallon's DNA," he enthused. "Part of exporting the Fallon brand is to find folks who share that ambition. You need those people who are going to get out there and push harder. You can try to dress up people in a set of beliefs and values, but it's much more potent if it is fueled from within."

Julie Thompson, Fallon's director of communications said at the time, "It all comes down to relationships. We searched for two years to find our partners in London. We are very, very careful to find people of like mind. It has been a longtime goal of the partners to expand globally, but it will be a measured, well-planned expansion."

One aspect of global expansion is overcoming cultural and language barriers. As Fallon began to make plans for alliances farther afield, Julie Thompson explained how the agency would address this issue. "We suspect the models will vary in every city. Our values do seem to translate across the continents, but we'll ward off [language and other barriers to understanding] by partnering with local talent who can help us crack that code." Industry expert David Tree, who helped Young and Rubicam, Inc. open branches in Paris, Oslo, Tokyo, and Hong Kong, agreed with Fallon's approach. "There are certain cultural givens, certain global truths," he noted. "Every kid around the world wants a Coke. But there are cultural nuances that you would never understand like a national. The creative expertise you must leave up to the locals."

About a year after the London deal took place, Publicis acquired Fallon and the global focus intensified. Clients had been pressing the advertising industry in general to service them on a global basis; the only way Fallon could do that, reasoned its founders, was to partner with a larger organization. From the start, Publicis and Fallon intended to expand to up to a dozen other locations outside the United States. The company also faced the issue of e-commerce, which was mushrooming around the world. "It will take a new kind of branding communications company to succeed in the emerging worldwide digital economy, and with Publicis' support, we intend to be that company," said Pat Fallon of the merger and expansion plans. A year after the Publicis deal was finalized, Fallon Worldwide's expansion was well under way. The company announced the formation of three new "creativity centers" located on two continents, with six internationally known partners. Fallon would open agencies in Sao Paulo, Singapore, and Hong Kong. This strategy was formulated not only to overcome cultural, economic, and legal-political barriers in each region but also to maintain the flexible, innovative reputation that Fallon had built its business on. "The traditional agency network model is about distribution, which is fine for certain marketers," explained Pat Fallon. "But we believe there are clients who will get excited by the idea of a lean, agile network built around the power of creativity, not mass."

Fallon Worldwide chose the locations for the creativity centers carefully so that they would cover certain economic regions, giving multinational clients access to these markets without simply blanketing the globe with tiny agency outposts. Selecting partners to manage the centers would be crucial to the success of the entire endeavor. "Our philosophy is to find the best people in the world and give them a once-in-a-lifetime opportunity under a great brand name with collaborative support and resources from the other partners," remarked John Gerzema, Fallon's managing partner for international expansion. "Our network will be highly intimate—with people who know each other, respect each other, and share a passion for work that drives business results." These international partners share both risks and rewards based on an agreement that includes shared ownership and accountability.

Each of Fallon's top managers around the world has a global perspective on culture and on business. For instance, Calvin Soh, a creative partner for Fallon Singapore and Fallon Hong Kong, has worked in both New York and Singapore in the past. "As Asians, we found that Fallon's Midwestern values of humility, hard work, respect, and integrity weren't very different from ours. Particularly enlightening was Fallon's belief that to excel in Asia, you need to develop local talent and expose them to the world. For us, Fallon felt right." Fallon hopes to find such partners—and clients—the world over.

## Questions

1. Do you think Fallon's approach to global expansion by establishing regional creativity centers will be an effective one? Why or why not?
2. How might ASEAN affect Fallon's business in Asia?
3. What are some of the personal challenges that Fallon's global managers might face?

Sources: Sandy Hunter, "Fallon Worldwide Expands," *Boards Magazine*, November 1, 2001, http://www.boardsmag.com; "Fallon Expands Global Network," *Business Wire*, October 9, 2001, http://www.hoovnews.hoovers.com; Jennifer Franklin, "Fallon's British Invasion," City Business, July 30, 1999, http://www.twincities.bcentral.com; Christine Whitehouse, "The New Ad Ventures," *Time Europe*, April 3, 2000, http://www.time.com; "Publicis Scoops Up Fallon McElligott to Forge New Global Branding Network," *Media*, March 3, 2000, http://www.media.com; "Publicis Boosts Midwest Clout with Fallon Buy," *Chicago Tribune*, February 3, 2000, http://cgi.chicago.tribune.com.

# Video Case

## Chapter 5: Timberland Walks the Walk of Social Responsibility

The Timberland Company designs, manufactures, and sells premium boots, casual shoes, hiking boots, and boat shoes, as well as high-performance outdoor clothing and accessories. The New Hampshire based company builds its products to last—"to withstand the elements of nature," as the company's Web site states. But Timberland is striving to build something more permanent than just high-quality footwear and clothing. It's trying to make the world a better, safer place to live and work—one person and one community at a time.

Along with the customers who buy its high-quality products, Timberland considers its other stakeholders in its business dealings. First, it recognizes its responsibility to be profitable for investors and employees. With yearly revenues of nearly $1.1 billion, the company recently reported 20 consecutive quarters of record revenue and improved earnings. Even in the face of an economic downturn, which hit retail establishments hard, CEO Jeffrey Swartz said, "Timberland delivered record revenues for 2001 in a difficult environment" that included higher leather costs, increased competition, and softer U.S. sales. But he is not deterred from his goal of making Timberland a leading global lifestyle brand.

Timberland also considers its employee stakeholders as critical to its success. The company was again listed in *Fortune* magazine's list of best companies to work for, ranked at number 65. The company is committed to diversity in its workforce, with 29 percent of its employees being minorities and nearly half women. The company provides 22 hours of professional training per year to employees to improve their skills. Timberland is also concerned about its global manufacturing workforce. With repeated news reports about exploitation of foreign workers at other companies, Timberland instituted a year-long audit of all its manufacturing facilities and some of its licensee's facilities, including tanneries and other major suppliers. It hired Verit, a nonprofit nongovernmental organization, to check working conditions such as health and safety, air quality, noise, and lighting. The company also monitors its Asian factories every eight to twelve weeks to ensure that workers are paid decent wages, provided periodic work breaks, and not required to work excessive overtime. It considers its commitment an ongoing process, requiring continual checks and improvements.

Companies often profess their belief in good corporate citizenship to their communities, but Timberland is an organization that literally considers what it is like to walk in someone else's shoes. From the CEO to office workers to sales associates on the floor, Timberland encourages all its employees to become involved in their communities. Through its long-standing Path of Service program, the company gives full-time employees 40 hours of paid time off for community volunteer service during regular working hours. The company also recently instituted a paid sabbatical program, allowing four employees each year to contribute their professional skills to nonprofit organizations for up to six months. And, it has long been involved in City Year, a national youth service organization for young people aged 17 to 24 years who serve different communities for a full year. The company serves as a City Year National Leadership Sponsor, and CEO Swartz chairs the City Year board. In addition to these efforts, the company partners with many other service organizations, working on activities as wide ranging as prevention of child hunger, skills training, eliminating exploitative working conditions, and closing the technology gap between organizations. The company's Web site also provides a link to SERVnet, an online news and events site listing needed community service projects.

Finally, Timberland considers the impact on the environment that its activities may have. It created an Environmental Affairs department to reduce the harmful effects of its production on the environment. The company is committed to recycling leather scraps and minimizing its use of toxic compounds and nonrenewable resources, as well as reducing carbon dioxide emissions to help curb global warming. Using innovative methods to reduce its energy consumption and conserve other resources, Timberland includes skylights at its sites to reduce power consumption and constructs some of its retail stores with furnishings and fixtures made from recycled materials such as salvaged wood and bricks. Its shoe boxes are made entirely from recycled products and printed with environmentally friendly vegetable dyes.

Through its daily efforts to improve its operations while offering products with proven workmanship, Timberland certainly walks the walk when it comes to ethical and socially responsible behavior. Perhaps one incident can best capture Timberland's commitment to its communities: On September 11, 2001, CEO Swartz and more than 100 other employees were volunteering at a school in the Bronx, New York City. After the World Trade Center's collapse of the towers was reported, the Timberland employees were advised to evacuate the city. Instead, they chose to stay and finish their job of repairing windows, painting hallways, and doing various cleaning and repair jobs. No wonder *Fortune* magazine says of Timberland, "No one takes social responsibility more seriously."

## Questions

1. Consider the three stages of ethical development. If Timberland were an individual, what level of moral development do you think the company has attained? Explain.
2. How much does Timberland's organizational culture influence its employees' socially responsible behavior?
3. Name some ways that Timberland demonstrates a high level of discretionary responsibility in its social performance. Would you like to work at Timberland?

Sources: Timberland company Web site, *http://www.timberland.com*, accessed March 29, 2002; "Best Companies to Work for," *Fortune*, *http://www.fortune.com*, accessed March 26, 2002; Marjorie Kelly, "Capitalism Has Its Shining Side," the Corporate Social Responsibility Newswire, *http://www.csrwire.com*, accessed March 26, 2002.

# Video Case

## Chapter 6: The Geek Squad: Providing Service that Makes You Smile

Computers and technology seem to be everywhere these days. From the office desktop to home Internet surfing to e-mail on cell phones, the computer chip has invaded our lives. But the simple fact is that most of us don't have a clue how any of that technology actually works—or even worse, why it doesn't work. Enter the Geek Squad, a computer-repair, technical assistance, and maintenance service based in Minneapolis, Los Angeles, Chicago, and San Francisco. The Geek Squad offers computer service—with a twist.

Founded by twenty-something Robert Stephens in the mid-1990s, the company has "special agents" who wear white shirts, clip-on ties, too-short pants, and pocket protectors. They drive to their on-site repairs, or "crime scenes," in Geekmobiles—black and white VW Beetles, renovated ice cream trucks, and even an old police squad car emblazoned with the Geek Squad logo. Stephens, who calls himself the Chief Inspector, got the idea for his company when he over-

heard two people in a grocery store checkout line discussing whether they were going to upgrade the RAM on their computer hard drives at home. At that time, the Internet was just beginning to take off. Stephens says of his vision, "That's a fundamental social shift that occurred—that you have normal people talking computers. I thought, 'This is going to blow big.'" So Stephens saw his window of opportunity, quit his computer programming job at the University of Minnesota, and started his company with $200 and a good dose of humor.

From its humble beginnings, the Geek Squad grew under Stephens's guidance (the company motto is "Creativity in the Absence of Capital") and through his personal connections. A lucky break came when a movie was being filmed in Minneapolis, and the crew's computers crashed. The Geek Squad repaired the damage. Soon, the company was known as "computer people for the movie industry in the Twin

# Chapter 6:   The Geek Squad: Providing Service that Makes You Smile (continued)

Cities," recalls Stephens. The company repaired computers for *Grumpy Old Men* and a *Mighty Ducks* hockey movie. The company also began to help rock bands with their computers. Over the years, they've helped U2, the Rolling Stones, Ice Cube, and Jonny Lang, among others. "You wouldn't think rock stars use computers," says Stephens. "But rock stars use laptops on the road, so actually they're the most finicky, demanding people. They're great practice for us." An added bonus for employees is getting great seats at concerts.

With customers' increasing dissatisfaction with the computer support provided by large hardware and software companies, the Geek Squad has found its niche by offering personalized carry-in, on-site, and emergency service 24 hours a day, seven days a week. The company prices its services by the job, not the hour, so customers know up front what the cost of the service will be. And the company will quote the cost of the service over the phone. Geek Squad employees maintain and repair everything from IBM-compatible and Macintosh hardware and software, to networks, printers, and even cell phones and personal digital assistants. They also give their customers set time frames for when a problem will be fixed.

Once a sole proprietorship owned by Stephens, the Geek Squad has now become a corporation with several million dollars in annual sales. The Geek Squad qualifies as a small business, currently employing fewer than 100 employees. Throughout the company's growth, Stephens has managed to maintain the fun work atmosphere for his employees, and he relies on their imaginations to play the role of computer nerd for sometimes tense customers. The company dubs its carry-in service "counter intelligence." Flashing their badges before they begin work, employees quickly calm the fears and gain the trust of anxious customers, and the invoices they present carry the words, "Pay up, sucka!" All of this humor helps create not only fun for employees but goodwill for the company and referrals for future business.

Stephens has received offers to buy the company, but he says he isn't interested in selling. He takes those offers as evidence that he has created something unique and useful. In fact, Stephens has even extended his business by writing a book called *The Geek Squad Guide to Solving Any Computer Glitch* with coauthor Dale Burg, published by Simon and Schuster. The book is a compilation of useful tips, written in normal language that any nontechie can understand. Of his business, Stephens says, "I'm just having a lot of fun. I'm energized by that. For me, the Geek Squad is an artistic experiment."

## Questions

1. Review the six types of business owners in Exhibit 6.1. Which type do you think Robert Stephens is?
2. How did Stephens come up with his business idea for the Geek Squad? What qualities have helped make the company a success?
3. At what stage of growth do you think the Geek Squad is currently? Explain.

Sources: The Geek Squad company Web site, *http://www.geeksquad. com*, accessed March 28, 2002; Bob Weinstein, "Company Builds on 'Geek' Image," *Chicago Sun-Times*, April 30, 2000, *http://www. suntimes. com*; "Geek Squad's Robert Stephens—No Geek at Marketing," *Minnesota Entrepreneurs' Inc. Newsletter*, February 2000, *http:// www.mn-entrepreneurs.org*; Jamie Allen, "'Geek Squad Guide' Offers Unique Computer Help," CNN, September 3, 1999, *http://www.cnn. com*.

# .....Continuing Case

Henry Ford was an entrepreneur whose company became an American icon over the course of a century. He never could have guessed that by late 2001, CEO Jac Nasser, the aggressive, embattled Australian businessman who had been in Ford's driver's seat for only three years, would be standing by the side of the road, briefcase in hand. Nasser had shaken up Ford's stodgy, bureaucratic corporate culture and attempted to lead the organization through the worst crisis of its history—the Firestone tire debacle—but the company had suffered too many blows during his reign. During this period, Ford and its managers faced enormous challenges involving ethics, social responsibility, a change in culture, and a competitive, constantly changing environment both in the United States and abroad. Ultimately, Nasser was asked to step aside.

In August 2000, Ford's world blew apart as it became apparent that some of its standard tires, those manufactured by Bridgestone/Firestone and installed on Ford's top-selling Explorer SUV, were doing exactly that: the treads were separating from the tire's core, leading to injurious and fatal crashes. Although Nasser chose to endure public scrutiny and Bridgestone/Firestone's Japanese leaders remained in relative seclusion, neither company immediately took responsibility. Instead, they engaged in finger pointing, damaging a relationship that had gone back as far as Henry Ford and Harvey Firestone. Firestone recalled the six million tires it believed were faulty but meanwhile accused Ford of poor automobile design. Ford announced that it would replace all 13 million of the Wilderness AT tires that were on its Explorers, even those that were presumed safe. Then Firestone severed its relationship with Ford. The recall program took so long that consumers and dealers became frustrated and fearful of the consequences—and increasingly distrustful of both companies. Ford and Firestone officials were called to testify before Congress. Meanwhile, as more accidents were investigated and analyzed, the death toll associated with the faulty tires rose to more than two hundred. Who was right, Ford or Firestone? Did Ford handle the situation ethically? Much has been written about the debacle, and the answers most likely will not come for many years.

Meanwhile, Ford's general and task environments were continually changing. General Motors revamped its truck lineup, and Toyota opened up the throttle on its SUVs with its new Highlander and Sequoia models. Ford's quality was suffering, increasing the cost of its warranties and decreasing consumers' confidence in its products. Also, Ford had purchased several European brands, including Volvo and BMW Land Rover, and the economic downturn in Europe was of concern. Ford, along with other car manufacturers, tried to attract new buyers with innovative features and design. "It is a reflection of the market softening generally," explained Ford Europe's chairman and chief executive, David Thursfield. "We have to bring out more new innovative products to give the market a boost. That is what we are certainly doing at Ford." And the slowdown of the American economy, along with the $3 billion price tag attached to the tire recall, forced Ford to offer early retirement packages to nearly 5,000 managers in order to cut costs. Finally, relationships with dealers and suppliers, who continued to struggle with the tire recall, needed to be repaired. In this midst of all the turmoil, Ford's board of directors announced that Jac Nasser would be leaving the company and that Bill Ford, Jr. would be taking over. Ford, in his mid-forties, is the first Ford family member to be CEO of the company since Henry Ford II resigned in 1979.

Bill Ford, known for his commitment to environmental issues, immediately pledged to make Ford Motor Company a leader in environmental protection as part of a company turnaround plan. A visit to the company's Web site reveals a whole host of environmentally friendly initiatives—not all introduced by Bill Ford, but indicative of the company's push toward social responsibility. For instance, Ford has teamed up with Environmental Defense to "provide automotive shoppers with comprehensive information about the environmental impact of automobiles sold in North America." Environmental Defense is a group that sponsors "For My World," a Web site that allows visitors to learn about the "Green Score" of particular vehicles. In addition, Ford is experimenting with water-based paints for its vehicles and working on ways to tackle pollution-producing manufacturing processes as well as traffic congestion.

Of course, these measures deal with only one facet of the overall environment in which Ford conducts its business. Bill Ford and his team of managers need to deal with quality issues, resolve the Firestone tire situation, and get new, more exciting autos into the pipeline. As he took the wheel of his family's company, Ford was closemouthed about his strategy for guiding the company into the future. "Everything is up for review—every asset, every piece of geography," he said. "We continue to review our mix of businesses." In November 2001, Ford announced that its Australian subsidiary would begin designing and manufacturing a new vehicle for the local Australian market, creating as many as 10,000 jobs there. Code-named Raptor, the new model would be poised to take on new cars introduced in Australia by General Motors. Despite the many roadblocks, Ford was showing signs of rolling forward again.

## Questions

1. Add to your knowledge of the Firestone tire debacle by researching it on the Internet or at the library. Then prepare for a class discussion or written summary on whether or not you believe Ford acted ethically throughout the crisis and why.

2. Visit the Ford Web site and click on several of the company's pages dealing with socially responsible initiatives—the environment, education, and so forth. Then discuss the role you think these initiatives play in Ford's overall corporate culture.

3. Ford Motor Company was founded by an entrepreneur and was once a small business. Name three ways in which you think Ford has contributed to the American economy and culture over the last century.

Sources: Ford Motor Company Web site, *http://www.ford.com*, accessed January 8, 2002; Tim Burt, "Thursfield Champions Ford of Europe," *Financial Times*, November 28, 2001, *http://news.ft.com*; Virginia Marsh, "Ford Launch Could Create 10,000 Jobs in Australia," *Financial Times*, November 15, 2001, *http://news.ft.com*; Kathleen Kerwin and Joann Muller, "Bill Ford Takes the Wheel," *BusinessWeek Online*, November 1, 2001, *http://www.businesseek.com*; Charles Child and Mary Connelly, "Nasser Out; Bill Ford Takes Over," *Automotive News*, October 29, 2001, *http://www.autonews.com*; "Ford Concern on Europe Downturn," *BBC News*, September 10, 2001, *http://news.bbc.co.uk*; Jamie Butters, "Job Cuts at Ford Likely to Increase," Auto.com, August 10, 2001, *http://www.auto.com*; "Tire Trouble: The Ford-Firestone Blowout," *Forbes*, June 20, 2001, *http://www.forbes.com*.

DEMOLITION PLAN /
FLOOR TWO

TITLE

Job No.:

Drawn By:

SHEET

A-2

# Planning

"Make no little plans."—Architect Daniel Burnham

Buildings, symbols of a nation's cultural authority, tell us much about a people. The ancient Greeks produced simple, balanced buildings that defined their disciplined approach to life. Today's buildings reach for the sky, glass reflections of one another and of modern life's aspirations.

Architects are artists who create buildings. Like managers, but unlike other artists, they must sell their ideas before they can produce their work. Behind the scenes, they are making decisions, strategizing, and planning. Must the building fit into an existing environment? What materials are most suitable? How much money is available? What environmental conditions are paramount? What are the client's needs? All of these decisions are part of an overall strategy designed to create a lasting, functional, well-designed building.

As in management, it is a team effort to ensure the success of an architectural project. An architect, like a manager, must recognize needs and solve problems, choose where to build, and sift among alternative solutions to ever-evolving problems. Managers also do much of their work behind the scenes, making decisions, formulating strategies, and setting plans of action into motion.

Hand-drawn renderings of proposed buildings have been replaced through technological progress; today, high-resolution digital images make an imagined building seem real and allow one architect to do a job that once took ten professionals. That singular job, however important, is just that— one part of the plan. For any architectural project to succeed, many factors must be considered and many people involved. All the pieces must fall into place and rest on a firm foundation.

Managers also recognize that it takes a strong foundation to support the work of an organization. Like architects, managers make the decisions and formulate the strategies and plans that determine whether an organization reaches its goals and achieves its vision. Successful management, just like successful construction, requires solid planning and continual communication.

Part 3

# Managerial Planning and Goal Setting

## LEARNING OBJECTIVES

*After studying this chapter, you should be able to*

1. Define goals and plans and explain the relationship between them.

2. Explain the concept of organizational mission and how it influences goal setting and planning.

3. Describe the types of goals an organization should have and why they resemble a hierarchy.

4. Define the characteristics of effective goals.

5. Describe the four essential steps in the MBO process.

6. Explain the difference between single-use plans and standing plans.

7. Describe and explain the importance of the three stages of crisis management planning.

8. Discuss how planning in a turbulent environment differs from traditional approaches to planning.

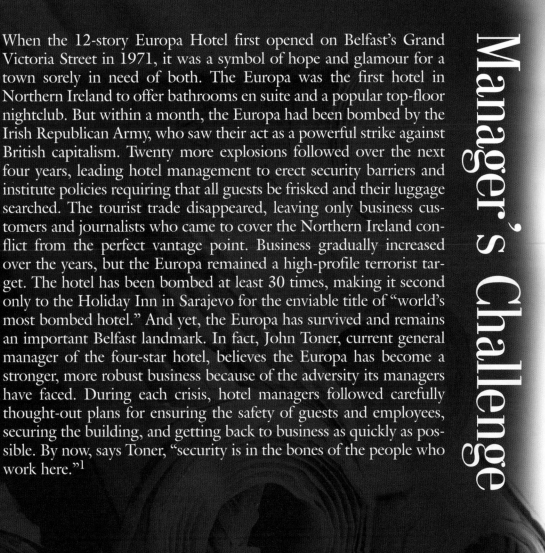

When the 12-story Europa Hotel first opened on Belfast's Grand Victoria Street in 1971, it was a symbol of hope and glamour for a town sorely in need of both. The Europa was the first hotel in Northern Ireland to offer bathrooms en suite and a popular top-floor nightclub. But within a month, the Europa had been bombed by the Irish Republican Army, who saw their act as a powerful strike against British capitalism. Twenty more explosions followed over the next four years, leading hotel management to erect security barriers and institute policies requiring that all guests be frisked and their luggage searched. The tourist trade disappeared, leaving only business customers and journalists who came to cover the Northern Ireland conflict from the perfect vantage point. Business gradually increased over the years, but the Europa remained a high-profile terrorist target. The hotel has been bombed at least 30 times, making it second only to the Holiday Inn in Sarajevo for the enviable title of "world's most bombed hotel." And yet, the Europa has survived and remains an important Belfast landmark. In fact, John Toner, current general manager of the four-star hotel, believes the Europa has become a stronger, more robust business because of the adversity its managers have faced. During each crisis, hotel managers followed carefully thought-out plans for ensuring the safety of guests and employees, securing the building, and getting back to business as quickly as possible. By now, says Toner, "security is in the bones of the people who work here."[1]

## Take A Moment

How do you think the Europa Hotel survived, and even thrived, in spite of 30 years of bombings that have disrupted business and wrecked managers' plans? What would you do as a manager to prepare your organization to cope with unexpected problems and crises?

One of the primary responsibilities of managers is to decide where the organization should go in the future and how to get it there. But how do managers plan for the future in a constantly changing environment? As we discussed in Chapter 1 of this textbook, most organizations are facing turbulence and growing uncertainty. The economic, political, and social turmoil of recent years has left many managers wondering how to cope and has sparked a renewed interest in organizational planning, particularly planning for unexpected problems and events.

In some organizations, typically small ones, planning is informal. In others, managers follow a well-defined planning framework. The company establishes a basic mission and develops formal goals and strategic plans for carrying it out. Companies such as Royal Dutch/Shell, IBM, and United Way undertake a strategic planning exercise each year—reviewing their missions, goals, and plans to meet environmental changes or the expectations of important stakeholders such as the community, owners, or stockholders. Many of these companies also develop *contingency plans* for unexpected circumstances and disaster recovery plans for what the organization would do in the event of a major disaster such as a hurricane, earthquake, or terrorist attack.

Of the four management functions—planning, organizing, leading, and controlling—described in Chapter 1, planning is considered the most fundamental. Everything else stems from planning. Yet planning also is the most controversial management function. Planning cannot read an uncertain future. Planning cannot tame a turbulent environment. A statement by General Colin Powell, former U.S. Secretary of State, offers a warning for managers: "No battle plan survives contact with the enemy."[2]

In this chapter, we will explore the process of planning and consider how managers develop effective plans that can grow and change to meet new conditions. Special attention is given to goal setting, for that is where planning starts. Then, we discuss the various types of plans that managers use to help the organization achieve those goals, with special attention paid to crisis management planning. Finally, we will examine new approaches to planning that emphasize the involvement of employees, customers, partners, and other stakeholders in strategic thinking and execution. Chapter 8 will look at strategic planning in depth and examine a number of strategic options managers can use in a competitive environment. In Chapter 9, we look at management decision making. Proper decision-making techniques are crucial to selecting the organization's goals, plans, and strategic options.

# Overview of Goals and Plans

**goal**
A desired future state that the organization attempts to realize.

**plan**
A blueprint specifying the resource allocations, schedules, and other actions necessary for attaining goals.

**planning**
The act of determining the organization's goals and the means for achieving them.

Goals and plans have become general concepts in our society. A goal is a desired future state that the organization attempts to realize.[3] Goals are important because organizations exist for a purpose and goals define and state that purpose. A plan is a blueprint for goal achievement and specifies the necessary resource allocations, schedules, tasks, and other actions. Goals specify future ends; plans specify today's means. The word **planning** usually incorporates both ideas; it means determining the organization's goals and defining the means for achieving them.[4]

Exhibit 7.1 illustrates the levels of goals and plans in an organization. The planning process starts with a formal mission that defines the basic purpose of the organization, especially for external audiences. The mission is the basis for the strategic (company) level of goals and plans, which in turn shapes the tactical (divisional) level and the operational (departmental) level.[5] Top managers are typically responsible for

Exhibit 7.1

**Levels of Goals/Plans and Their Importance**

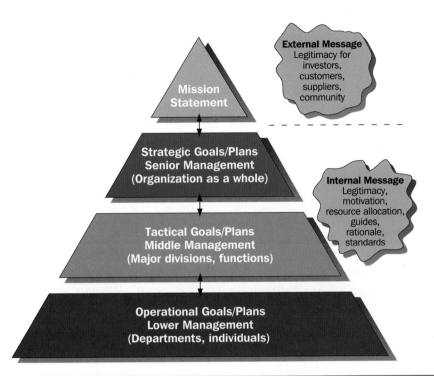

establishing *strategic* goals and plans that reflect a commitment to both organizational efficiency and effectiveness, as described in Chapter 1. *Tactical* goals and plans are the responsibility of middle managers, such as the heads of major divisions or functional units. A division manager will formulate tactical plans that focus on the major actions the division must take to fulfill its part in the strategic plan set by top management. *Operational* plans identify the specific procedures or processes needed at lower levels of the organization, such as individual departments and employees. Front-line managers and supervisors develop operational plans that focus on specific tasks and processes and that help to meet tactical and strategic goals. Planning at each level supports the other levels.

# Purposes of Goals and Plans

The complexity of today's environment and uncertainty about the future overwhelm many managers and cause them to focus on operational issues and short-term results rather than long-term goals and plans. However, planning generally positively affects a company's performance.[6] In addition to improving financial and operational performance, developing explicit goals and plans at each level illustrated in Exhibit 7.1 is important because of the external and internal messages they send. These messages go to both external and internal audiences and provide important benefits for the organization:[7]

* *Legitimacy.* An organization's mission describes what the organization stands for and its reason for existence. It symbolizes legitimacy to external audiences such

COURTESY OF THE VALSPAR CORPORATION

## CONCEPT CONNECTION

*A company's* **mission** *describes what the organization stands for and its reason for existence. Valspar Corporation, a manufacturer of industrial coatings, relies on its employees to meet customer needs. It states its mission broadly for internal and external audiences: "To be the recognized leader in the coatings industry—by meeting customer requirements, current and future; by believing in our employees and empowering them to maximize productivity; and by creating exceptional value for our shareholders." Recently, the company recorded its 26th straight year of record sales and earnings.*

as investors, customers, and suppliers. The mission helps them and the local community look on the company in a favorable light and, hence, accept its existence. A strong mission also has an impact on employees, enabling them to become committed to the organization because they can identify with its overall purpose and reason for existence. One of the traits often cited by employees in *Fortune* magazine's list of the "100 Best Companies to Work For in America" is a sense of purpose and meaning.[8] For example, at Medtronic, a medical products company, employees are inspired by the mission to "alleviate pain, restore health, and extend life."[9]

- *Source of motivation and commitment.* Goals and plans facilitate employees' identification with the organization and help motivate them by reducing uncertainty and clarifying what they should accomplish. At Boeing, the manufacturing department has a goal of moving a plane, once the wings and landing gear are attached, along the assembly line and out the door in only five days. Managers are revising processes and procedures, mechanics are coming up with innovative machine adjustments, and assembly line workers are trying new techniques to meet this ambitious goal.[10] Lack of a clear goal can damage employee motivation and commitment because people don't understand what they are working toward. Whereas a goal provides the "why" of an organization or subunit's existence, a plan tells the "how." A plan lets employees know what actions to undertake to achieve the goal.

- *Resource allocation.* Goals help managers decide where they need to allocate resources, such as employees, money, and equipment. For example, DuPont has a goal of generating 25 percent of revenues from renewable resources by 2010 (up from 14 percent in 2003). This goal lets managers know they need to use resources to develop renewable and biodegradable materials, acquire businesses that produce products with renewable resources, and buy equipment that reduces waste, emissions, and energy usage. As another example, due to new goals of fighting domestic terrorism, the Federal Bureau of Investigation (FBI) has pulled more than 600 agents off their regular beats and reassigned them to terrorist-related cases. The FBI is also allocating resources to rebuild an archaic computer network, open foreign offices, and form terrorism task forces.[11]

- *Guides to action.* Goals and plans provide a sense of direction. They focus attention on specific targets and direct employee efforts toward important outcomes. Hartford Technology Services Co., for example, set goals to establish a customer profile database, survey customer satisfaction, and secure service agreements with ten new customers.[12]

- *Rationale for decisions.* Through goal setting and planning, managers learn what the organization is trying to accomplish. They can make decisions to ensure that internal policies, roles, performance, structure, products, and expenditures will be made in accordance with desired outcomes. Decisions throughout the organization will be in alignment with the plan.

- *Standard of performance.* Because goals define desired outcomes for the organization, they also serve as performance criteria. They provide a standard of assessment. If an organization wishes to grow by 15 percent, and actual growth is 17 percent, managers will have exceeded their prescribed standard.

The following example illustrates how goals and plans serve these important purposes.

Chevrolet may have ruled the roads back in the 1960s and 1970s, but in recent years its sales have lagged. In late 2003, General Motors managers announced that the company will launch 10 new Chevrolet vehicles over 20 months to reach its goal of boosting U.S. sales to 3 million vehicles a year, a level Chevy hasn't achieved since 1979. That's a 15 percent increase over 2003 levels, an ambitious target that requires everyone in the company to focus on the goal.

Employees throughout the company are striving to meet lower-level targets that will help the company achieve its overall objective. Dealers, too, are motivated by the stretch goals laid out in a plan called "Road to 3 Million." Managers are pumping resources into design and engineering, advertising, and dealer incentives. Dealers can win trips and other prizes if they hit their targets. A new, edgy multimillion-dollar ad campaign, taglined, "An American Revolution," focuses on the cars and trucks but tries to give potential customers a feeling of freedom and "attitude." Managers and employees are also looking for alternative ways to reach new markets. Every decision at Chevrolet today is made with the goal of selling 3 million vehicles a year in mind.

Managers will use the goal as a standard of performance. Some doubt that Chevrolet can reach the target during the first year, but managers will evaluate how well the company performed and perhaps revise plans to help meet the goal of selling 3 million vehicles a year.[13]

GENERAL MOTORS–
CHEVROLET
DIVISION
http://www.
chevrolet.com

Chevrolet and General Motors managers recognize the importance of a clear goal and carefully thought out plans to help achieve it. The overall planning process prevents managers from thinking merely in terms of day-to-day activities. When organizations drift away from goals and plans, they typically get into trouble.

# Goals in Organizations

Setting goals starts with top managers. The overall planning process begins with a mission statement and strategic goals for the organization as a whole.

## Organizational Mission

At the top of the goal hierarchy is the **mission**—the organization's reason for existence. The mission describes the organization's values, aspirations, and reason for being. A well-defined mission is the basis for development of all subsequent goals and plans. Without a clear mission, goals and plans may be developed haphazardly and not take the organization in the direction it needs to go.

**mission**
The organization's reason for existence.

The formal **mission statement** is a broadly stated definition of purpose that distinguishes the organization from others of a similar type. A well-designed mission statement can enhance employee motivation and organizational performance.[14] The content of a mission statement often focuses on the market and customers and identifies desired fields of endeavor. Some mission statements describe company characteristics such as corporate values, product quality, location of facilities, and attitude toward employees. Mission statements often reveal the company's philosophy as well as purpose. One example is the mission statement for Bristol-Myers Squibb Company, presented in Exhibit 7.2. Such short, straightforward mission statements describe basic business activities and purposes, as well as the values that guide the company. Another example of this type of mission statement is that of State Farm Insurance:

**mission statement**
A broadly stated definition of the organization's basic business scope and operations that distinguishes it from similar types of organizations.

*State Farm's mission is to help people manage the risks of everyday life, recover from the unexpected, and realize their dreams.*

Exhibit **7.2**

**Mission Statement for Bristol-Myers Squibb**

# The Bristol-Myers Squibb Pledge

Our company's mission is to extend and enhance human life by providing the highest-quality pharmaceutical and related health care products.

*We pledge—to our patients and customers, to our employees and partners, to our shareholders and neighbors, and to the world we serve— to act on our belief that the priceless ingredient of every product is the honor and integrity of its maker.*

 Bristol-Myers Squibb Company

---

*We are people who make it our business to be like a good neighbor; who built a premier company by selling and keeping promises through out marketing partnership; who bring diverse talents and experiences to our work of serving the State Farm customer. Our success is built on a foundation of shared values—quality service and relationships, mutual trust, integrity, and financial strength.[15]*

Because of mission statements such as those of Bristol-Myers Squibb and State Farm, employees as well as customers, suppliers, and stockholders know the company's stated purpose and values.

## Goals and Plans

**strategic goals**
Broad statements of where the organization wants to be in the future; pertain to the organization as a whole rather than to specific divisions or departments.

Broad statements describing where the organization wants to be in the future are called **strategic goals.** They pertain to the organization as a whole rather than to specific divisions or departments. Strategic goals are often called *official goals,* because they are the stated intentions of what the organization wants to achieve. For example, five years after he started Physician Sales and Service, Pat Kelly set a strategic goal for PSS to become the first national physician supply chain, a goal he soon reached. Now, Kelly wants the company to become a global distributor of medical products.[16] A strategic goal for the new chief executive of the New York Stock Exchange is to restore the credibility of the exchange with government regulators and the public.

**strategic plans**
The action steps by which an organization intends to attain strategic goals.

**Strategic plans** define the action steps by which the company intends to attain strategic goals. The strategic plan is the blueprint that defines the organizational activities and resource allocations—in the form of cash, personnel, space, and facilities— required for meeting these targets. Strategic planning tends to be long term and may define organizational action steps from two to five years in the future. The purpose of strategic plans is to turn organizational goals into realities within that time period.

As an example, a small company wanted to improve its market share from 15 percent to 20 percent over the next three years. This strategic goal was pursued through the following strategic plans: (1) allocate resources for the development of new, competitive products with high growth potential; (2) improve production methods to achieve higher output at lower costs; and (3) conduct research to develop alternative uses for current products and services.[17]

The results that major divisions and departments within the organization intend to achieve are defined as **tactical goals**. These goals apply to middle management and describe what major subunits must do in order for the organization to achieve its overall goals.

**Tactical plans** are designed to help execute major strategic plans and to accomplish a specific part of the company's strategy.[18] Tactical plans typically have a shorter time horizon than strategic plans—over the next year or so. The word *tactical* originally comes from the military. This chapter's Unlocking Creative Solutions Through Technology box describes how the U.S. military is using an experimental software application to support tactical planning. In a business or nonprofit organization, tactical plans define what major departments and organizational subunits will do to implement the organization's strategic plan. For example, the overall strategic plan of a large florist might involve becoming the Number 1 telephone and Internet-based purveyor of flowers, which requires high-volume sales during peak seasons such as Valentine's Day and Mother's Day. Human resource managers will develop tactical plans to ensure that the company has the dedicated order takers and customer service representatives it needs during these critical periods. Tactical plans might include cross-training employees so they can switch to different jobs as departmental needs change, allowing order takers to transfer to jobs at headquarters during off-peak times to prevent burnout, and using regular order takers to train and supervise temporary workers during peak seasons.[19] These actions help top managers implement their overall strategic plan. Normally, it is the middle manager's job to take the broad strategic plan and identify specific tactical plans.

The results expected from departments, work groups, and individuals are the **operational goals**. They are precise and measurable. "Process 150 sales applications each week," "achieve 90 percent of deliveries on time," "reduce overtime by 10 percent next month," and "develop two new elective courses in accounting" are examples of operational goals. At the Internal Revenue Service (IRS), one operational goal is to give accurate responses to 85 percent of taxpayer questions.[20]

**Operational plans** are developed at the lower levels of the organization to specify action steps toward achieving operational goals and to support tactical plans. The operational plan is the department manager's tool for daily and weekly operations. Goals are stated in quantitative terms, and the department plan describes how goals will be achieved. Operational planning specifies plans for supervisors, department managers, and individual employees.

Schedules are an important component of operational planning. Schedules define precise time frames for the completion of each operational goal required for the organization's tactical and strategic goals. Operational planning also must be coordinated with the budget, because resources must be allocated for desired activities. For example, Apogee Enterprises, a window and glass fabricator with 150 small divisions, is fanatical about operational planning and budgeting.

© RICH FRISHMAN/FRISHPHOTO.COM

**CONCEPT CONNECTION**

Boeing's **strategic goal** *is to remain an aerospace industry giant despite a drop in air travel after the September 11th terrorist attacks and the resulting decrease in demand for airplanes. With current fuel bills skyrocketing due to the price of oil, airlines are more pressed than ever to control costs. To help airlines meet their challenges, Boeing's **strategic plan** includes the design and manufacture of a completely new, fuel-efficient airplane—the 7E7 Dreamliner. The success of the Dreamliner is reversing Boeing's recent layoff trend. With current orders for 200 jets from buyers around the globe, Boeing plans to increase employment by 2,000 to 3,000 jobs in one year. The new jets should be in service in 2008, with a price tag of about $125 million each.*

**tactical goals**
Goals that define the outcomes that major divisions and departments must achieve in order for the organization to reach its overall goals.

**tactical plans**
Plans designed to help execute major strategic plans and to accomplish a specific part of the company's strategy.

**operational goals**
Specific, measurable results expected from departments, work groups, and individuals within the organization.

# Unlocking Creative Solutions Through Technology

### United States Joint Forces Command

"Collateral damage"—when innocent civilians or friendly troops are killed—is one of the most heartbreaking results of any war. Needless to say, no battle commander wants to injure or kill innocent civilians or friendly troops. Now, technology may provide a way to reduce the likelihood.

A new software application, called Joint Time Sensitive Targeting Manager (JTSTM), was used in Iraq for the first time in live operations. With this system, ground, air, and maritime commanders logged onto the JTSTM network can all see a common picture of the battlefield. Using chat rooms, e-mail, and instant messaging, battle planners collaboratively figure out the situation and assess options. "The software was specifically designed to force commanders to look at a target before it can be executed," said Lt. Col. Mark Werth, head of the joint fires initiative at the U.S. Joint Forces Command. A wide range of people can see the same picture, maximizing the chance that someone can pinpoint a risky mission, such as whether the target is too close to friendly forces or civilians.

Typically, in battle situations, the Air Force might be chasing a target on the ground without the Army or special operations forces having any notion about what is occurring. With JTSTM, every group is aware of what every other group of services is doing. The program provides a seamless, horizontal knowledge base that improves fire mission coordination. The joint fires initiative is evolving to apply to any targeting mission, not just those that pop up on short notice. JTSTM is one of the software applications developed under the Automated Deep Operations Coordination System (ADOCS), funded by the Defense Department. ADOCS taps into various databases, such as the Global Command and Control System (location of friendly forces), and the Joint Targeting Toolkit (restricted target list and no-strike target list) to provide users with one-stop shopping for assessing and coordinating tactical battle plans.

The process of using this sophisticated technology was first tested in a war-fighting experiment in 2002, and its use in real-life operations in Iraq was far from smooth. However, the U.S. Joint Forces Command believes the technology will be a key factor in improving coordination and avoiding friendly fire in future conflicts. The initiative will continue to evolve and is expected to be integrated into military service programs by 2006.

**SOURCE:** Sandra I. Erwin, "Experimental Battle-Planning Software Rushed to Iraq," *National Defense* (October 2003), 22.

---

**operational plans**
Plans developed at the organization's lower levels that specify action steps toward achieving operational goals and that support tactical planning activities.

Committees are set up to review and challenge budgets, profit plans, and proposed expenditures. Assigning the dollars makes the operational plan work for everything from hiring new salespeople to increasing travel expenses.

## Hierarchy of Goals

Effectively designed organizational goals fit into a hierarchy; that is, the achievement of goals at low levels permits the attainment of high-level goals. This is called a *means-ends chain* because low-level goals lead to accomplishment of high-level goals. Operational goals lead to the achievement of tactical goals, which, in turn, lead to the attainment of strategic goals. Strategic goals are traditionally considered the responsibility of top management, tactical goals that of middle management, and operational goals that of first-line supervisors and workers. However, the shrinking of middle management combined with a new emphasis on employee empowerment have led to a greater involvement of all employees in goal setting and planning at each level.

An example of a goal hierarchy is illustrated in Exhibit 7.3. Note how the strategic goal of "excellent service to customers" translates into "Open one new sales office" and "Respond to customer inquiries within two hours" at lower management levels.

Exhibit 7.3

## Hierarchy of Goals for a Manufacturing Organization

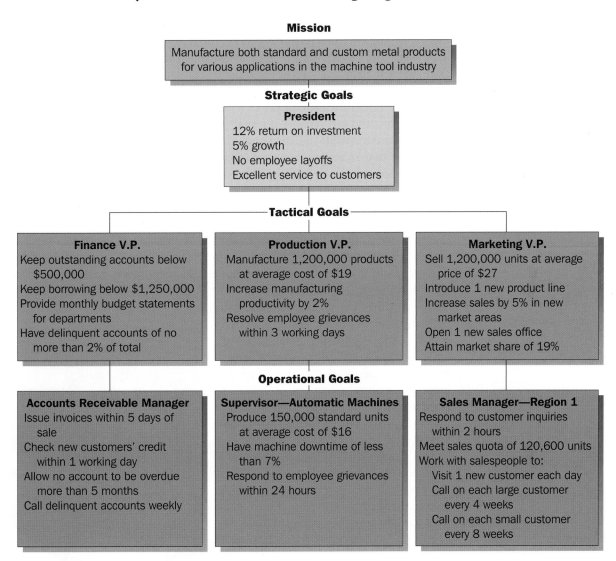

**Mission**

Manufacture both standard and custom metal products for various applications in the machine tool industry

**Strategic Goals**

**President**
12% return on investment
5% growth
No employee layoffs
Excellent service to customers

**Tactical Goals**

**Finance V.P.**
Keep outstanding accounts below $500,000
Keep borrowing below $1,250,000
Provide monthly budget statements for departments
Have delinquent accounts of no more than 2% of total

**Production V.P.**
Manufacture 1,200,000 products at average cost of $19
Increase manufacturing productivity by 2%
Resolve employee grievances within 3 working days

**Marketing V.P.**
Sell 1,200,000 units at average price of $27
Introduce 1 new product line
Increase sales by 5% in new market areas
Open 1 new sales office
Attain market share of 19%

**Operational Goals**

**Accounts Receivable Manager**
Issue invoices within 5 days of sale
Check new customers' credit within 1 working day
Allow no account to be overdue more than 5 months
Call delinquent accounts weekly

**Supervisor—Automatic Machines**
Produce 150,000 standard units at average cost of $16
Have machine downtime of less than 7%
Respond to employee grievances within 24 hours

**Sales Manager—Region 1**
Respond to customer inquiries within 2 hours
Meet sales quota of 120,600 units
Work with salespeople to:
  Visit 1 new customer each day
  Call on each large customer every 4 weeks
  Call on each small customer every 8 weeks

# Criteria for Effective Goals

To ensure goal-setting benefits for the organization, certain characteristics and guidelines should be adopted. The characteristics of both goals and the goal-setting process are listed in Exhibit 7.4. These characteristics pertain to organizational goals at the strategic, tactical, and operational levels:

- *Specific and measurable.* When possible, goals should be expressed in quantitative terms, such as increasing profits by 2 percent, decreasing scrap by 1 percent, or increasing average teacher effectiveness ratings from 3.5 to 3.7. A team at Sealed Air Corporation, a manufacturer of packaging materials, was motivated by a goal to reduce by two hours the average time needed to change machine settings.[21] Not all goals can be expressed in numerical terms, but vague goals have

Exhibit 7.4

## Characteristics of Effective Goal Setting

### Goal Characteristics

- Specific and measurable
- Cover key result areas
- Challenging but realistic
- Defined time period
- Linked to rewards

little motivating power for employees. By necessity, goals are qualitative as well as quantitative, especially at the top of the organization. The important point is that the goals be precisely defined and allow for measurable progress.

- *Cover key result areas.* Goals cannot be set for every aspect of employee behavior or organizational performance; if they were, their sheer number would render them meaningless. Instead, managers should identify a few key result areas—perhaps up to four or five for any organizational department or job. Key result areas are those activities that contribute most to company performance.[22] Most companies use a balanced approach to goal setting. For example, Northern States Power Co. tracks measurements in four key areas: financial performance, customer service and satisfaction, internal processes, and innovation and learning.[23]

- *Challenging but realistic.* Goals should be challenging but not unreasonably difficult. One new manager discovered that his staff would have to work 100-hour weeks to accomplish everything expected of them. When goals are unrealistic, they set employees up for failure and lead to decreasing employee morale.[24] However, if goals are too easy, employees may not feel motivated. *Stretch goals* are extremely ambitious but realistic goals that challenge employees to meet high standards. One example comes from 3M, where top managers set a goal that 30 percent of sales must come from products introduced in the past four years; the old standard was 25 percent. Setting ambitious goals helps to keep 3M churning out innovative new products—more than 500 in one recent year alone—and has entrenched the company as a leader in some of today's most dynamic markets.[25] The key to effective stretch goals is ensuring that goals are set within the existing resource base, not beyond departments' time, equipment, or financial resources.

- *Defined time period.* Goals should specify the time period over which they will be achieved. A time period is a deadline stating the date on which goal attainment will be measured. A goal of implementing a new customer relationship management system, for instance, might have a deadline such as June 30, 2005. If a strategic goal involves a two-to-three-year time horizon, specific dates for achieving parts of it can be set up. For example, strategic sales goals could be established on a three-year time horizon, with a $100 million target in year one, a $129 million target in year two, and a $165 million target in year three.

- *Linked to rewards.* The ultimate impact of goals depends on the extent to which salary increases, promotions, and awards are based on goal achievement. People who attain goals should be rewarded. Rewards give meaning and significance to goals and help commit employees to achieving goals. Failure to attain goals often is due to factors outside employees' control. For example, failure to achieve a financial goal may

© STEVE NEIDORF

### CONCEPT CONNECTION

*3M marketers carefully planned the global launch of Scotch-Brite Never Rust soap pads to maximize sales of the new product. Innovation is the cornerstone of 3M's culture, and the company's **challenging but realistic goals** have 3M employees turning new ideas into new products faster than ever before. The new goal of achieving 30 percent of sales from products introduced in the past four years was quickly met, thanks to the successful launch of new products such as the soap pads.*

be associated with a drop in market demand due to industry recession; thus, an employee could not be expected to reach it. A reward might still be appropriate if the employee partially achieved goals under difficult circumstances.[26]

# Planning Types

Managers use strategic, tactical, and operational goals to direct employees and resources toward achieving specific outcomes that enable the organization to perform efficiently and effectively. Managers use a number of planning approaches. Among the most popular are management by objectives, single-use plans, standing plans, and contingency plans.

## Management by Objectives

Management by objectives (MBO) is a method whereby managers and employees define goals for every department, project, and person and use them to monitor subsequent performance.[27] A model of the essential steps of the MBO process is presented in Exhibit 7.5. Four major activities must occur in order for MBO to be successful:[28]

**management by objectives**
A method of management whereby managers and employees define goals for every department, project, and person and use them to monitor subsequent performance.

1. *Set goals.* This is the most difficult step in MBO. Setting goals involves employees at all levels and looks beyond day-to-day activities to answer the question "What are we trying to accomplish?" A good goal should be concrete and realistic, provide a specific target and time frame, and assign responsibility. Goals may be quantitative or qualitative. Quantitative goals are described in numerical terms, such as "Salesperson Jones will obtain 16 new accounts in December." Qualitative goals use statements such as "Marketing will reduce complaints by improving customer service next year." Goals should be jointly derived. Mutual agreement between employee and supervisor creates the

Exhibit **7.5**

**Model of the MBO Process**

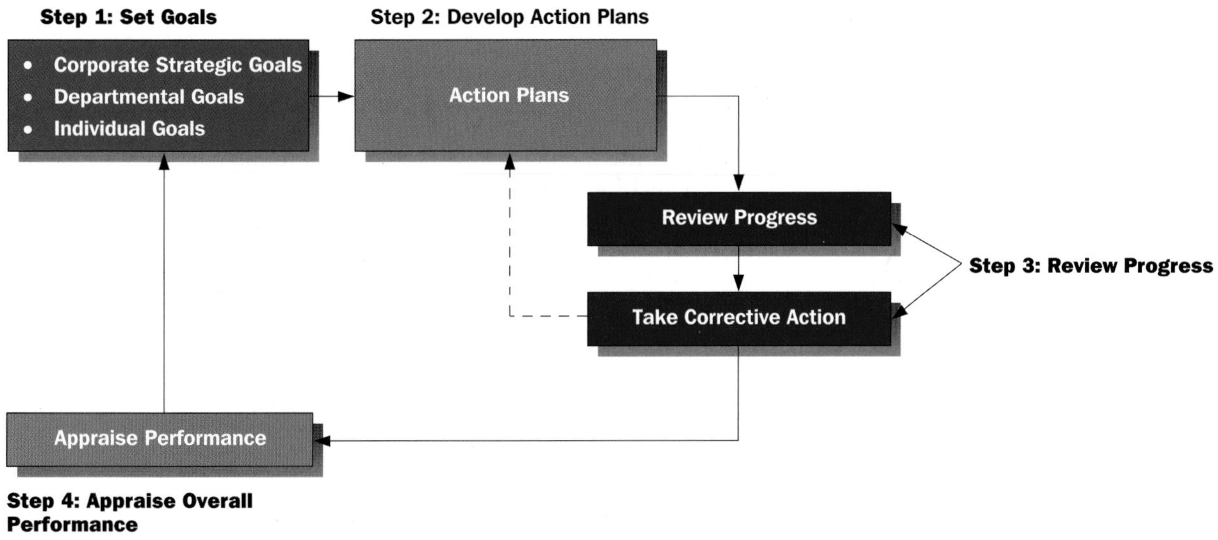

**Step 1: Set Goals**
- Corporate Strategic Goals
- Departmental Goals
- Individual Goals

**Step 2: Develop Action Plans**
Action Plans

Review Progress

Take Corrective Action

**Step 3: Review Progress**

Appraise Performance

**Step 4: Appraise Overall Performance**

strongest commitment to achieving goals. In the case of teams, all team members may participate in setting goals.

2. *Develop action plans.* An *action plan* defines the course of action needed to achieve the stated goals. Action plans are made for both individuals and departments.

3. *Review progress.* A periodic progress review is important to ensure that action plans are working. These reviews can occur informally between managers and subordinates, where the organization may wish to conduct three-, six-, or nine-month reviews during the year. This periodic checkup allows managers and employees to see whether they are on target or whether corrective action is necessary. Managers and employees should not be locked into predefined behavior and must be willing to take whatever steps are necessary to produce meaningful results. The point of MBO is to achieve goals. The action plan can be changed whenever goals are not being met.

4. *Appraise overall performance.* The final step in MBO is to carefully evaluate whether annual goals have been achieved for both individuals and departments. Success or failure to achieve goals can become part of the performance appraisal system and the designation of salary increases and other rewards. The appraisal of departmental and overall corporate performance shapes goals for the next year. The MBO cycle repeats itself on an annual basis.

The specific application of MBO must fit the needs of each company. For example, Siemens used MBO to improve its overall financial performance.

SIEMENS
http://www.siemens.com

Siemens of Germany, which makes everything from mobile phones to gas-turbine generators to light bulbs, has always had great engineers bent on producing products of the highest quality. But in recent years, managers have learned that competing with the likes of U.S.-based General Electric and Sweden's Nokia takes more than quality—it also requires speed to market, relentless innovation, and ruthless attention to costs. Between 1996 and 1998, profits sank by two-thirds and company shares fell even faster. CEO Heinrich von Pierer developed a plan for getting Siemens back on track, with a specific goal (MBO Step 1) of strengthening the overall business to be in financial shape for listing on a U.S. stock exchange within three years.

Managers developed an action plan (MBO Step 2) that included: (1) cutting the time it takes to develop and produce new products; (2) selling or closing poor-performing units and strengthening remaining businesses through acquisitions to achieve world leadership; (3) setting tough profit targets for managers and tying pay to performance; and (4) converting accounting practices to report results according to U.S. accounting standards. Managers of the various business divisions then developed action plans for employees in their own units. Progress was reviewed (MBO Step 3) at quarterly meetings where managers from the 14 business units reported on their advancements directly to von Pierer.

Managers were required to explain if benchmarks weren't met and how shortcomings would be corrected. At the end of each year of the turnaround plan, an overall performance appraisal was held for each business and the corporation as a whole (MBO Step 4). Managers who met goals were rewarded; those who had consistently failed to meet them were let go, with the poorest performers going first.

Since the plan was implemented, Siemens has dramatically improved its speed and overall financial performance. For example, mobile phones that once took a painstaking 13 hours each to produce are now sliding off the assembly line in five minutes. Many of Siemens' businesses have been transformed from money losers to profit drivers, and the stock performance has taken a sharp upturn. Siemens is on track to begin reporting results according to U.S. principles and listing on the U.S. stock exchange. The MBO system helped to energize manager and employee actions companywide toward goals deemed critical by top management.[29]

Many companies, including Intel, Tenneco, Black & Decker, and DuPont, have adopted MBO, and most managers think MBO is an effective management tool.[30] Managers believe they are better oriented toward goal achievement when MBO is used. In recent years, the U.S. Congress has required that federal agencies use a type of MBO system to help focus government employees on achieving specific outcomes, rather than focusing only on activities and work processes.[31] Like any system, MBO achieves benefits when used properly but results in problems when used improperly. Benefits and problems are summarized in Exhibit 7.6.

The benefits of the MBO process can be many. Corporate goals are more likely to be achieved when they focus manager and employee efforts. Using a performance measurement system, such as MBO, helps employees see how their jobs and performance contribute to the business, giving them a sense of ownership and commitment.[32] Performance is improved when employees are committed to attaining the goal, are motivated because they help decide what is expected, and are free to be resourceful. Goals at lower levels are aligned with and enable the attainment of goals at top management levels.

Problems with MBO occur when the company faces rapid change. The environment and internal activities must have some stability for performance to be measured and compared against goals. When new goals must be set every few months, there is no time for action plans and appraisal to take effect. Also, poor employer-employee relations reduce effectiveness because there is an element of distrust between managers and workers. Sometimes goal "displacement" occurs if employees focus exclusively on their operational goals to the detriment of other teams or departments. Overemphasis on operational goals can harm the attainment of overall goals. Another problem arises in mechanistic organizations characterized by rigidly defined tasks and rules that may not be compatible with MBO's emphasis on mutual determination of goals by employee and supervisor. In addition, when participation is discouraged, employees will lack the training and values to jointly set goals with employers. Finally, if MBO becomes a process of filling out annual paperwork rather than energizing employees to achieve goals, it becomes an empty exercise. Once the paperwork is completed, employees forget about the goals, perhaps even resenting the paperwork in the first place.

## Exhibit 7.6

### MBO Benefits and Problems

| Benefits of MBO | Problems with MBO |
|---|---|
| 1. Manager and employee efforts are focused on activities that will lead to goal attainment. | 1. Constant change prevents MBO from taking hold. |
| 2. Performance can be improved at all company levels. | 2. An environment of poor employer-employee relations reduces MBO effectiveness. |
| 3. Employees are motivated. | 3. Strategic goals may be displaced by operational goals. |
| 4. Departmental and individual goals are aligned with company goals. | 4. Mechanistic organizations and values that discourage participation can harm the MBO process. |
| | 5. Too much paperwork saps MBO energy. |

## Single-Use and Standing Plans

**single-use plans**
Plans that are developed to achieve a set of goals that are unlikely to be repeated in the future.

**standing plans**
Ongoing plans that are used to provide guidance for tasks performed repeatedly within the organization.

Single-use plans are developed to achieve a set of goals that are not likely to be repeated in the future. Standing plans are ongoing plans that are used to provide guidance for tasks performed repeatedly within the organization. Exhibit 7.7 outlines the major types of single-use and standing plans. Single-use plans typically include both programs and projects. The primary standing plans are organizational policies, rules, and procedures. Standing plans generally pertain to such matters as employee illness, absences, smoking, discipline, hiring, and dismissal. Many companies are discovering a need to develop standing plans regarding the use of e-mail, as discussed in the Manager's Shoptalk box.

*Take A Moment*     *Go to the experiential exercise on page 260 that pertains to developing standing plans.*

## Contingency Plans

When organizations are operating in a highly uncertain environment or dealing with long time horizons, sometimes planning can seem like a waste of time. In fact, strict

Exhibit 7.7

### Major Types of Single-Use and Standing Plans

| Single-Use Plans | Standing Plans |
|---|---|
| **Program**<br>• Plans for attaining a one-time organizational goal<br>• Major undertaking that may take several years to complete<br>• Large in scope; may be associated with several projects<br>  **Examples:** Building a new headquarters<br>  Converting all paper files to digital | **Policy**<br>• Broad in scope—general guide to action<br>• Based on organization's overall goals/strategic plan<br>• Defines boundaries within which to make decisions<br>  **Examples:** Sexual harassment policies<br>  Internet and e-mail usage policies |
| **Project**<br>• Also a set of plans for attaining a one-time goal<br>• Smaller in scope and complexity than a program; shorter in horizon<br>• Often one part of a larger program<br>  **Example:** Renovating the office<br>  Setting up a company intranet | **Rule**<br>• Narrow in scope<br>• Describes how a specific action is to be performed<br>• May apply to specific setting<br>  **Example:** No eating rule in areas of company where employees are visible to the public<br><br>**Procedure**<br>• Sometimes called a standard operating procedure<br>• Defines a precise series of steps to attain certain goals<br>  **Examples:** Procedures for issuing refunds<br>  Procedures for handling employee grievances |

# manager's Shoptalk

Turbulent Times

## *Regulating E-mail in the Workplace*

Top executives around the globe are discovering that casual e-mail messages can come back to haunt them—in court. The American Management Association (AMA) surveyed 1,100 companies and found that 14 percent of them had been ordered to disclose e-mail messages. In 2002, eight brokerage firms were fined $8 million for not keeping and producing e-mail in accordance with SEC guidelines. Some companies have had to pay millions to settle sexual harassment lawsuits arising from inappropriate e-mail.

As with any powerful tool, e-mail has the potential to be hazardous, backfiring not only on the employee but on the organization as well. One study found that "potentially dangerous or nonproductive" messages account for fully 31 percent of all company e-mail. Experts say a formal written policy is the best way for companies to protect themselves, and they offer some tips for managers on developing effective policies governing the use of e-mail.

- *Make clear that all e-mail and its contents are the property of the company.* Many experts recommend warning employees that the company reserves the right to read any messages transmitted over its system. "Employees need to understand that a company can access employees' e-mail at any time without advance notice or consent," says lawyer Pam Reeves. This helps to discourage frivolous e-mails or those that might be considered crude and offensive.
- *Tie the policy to the company's sexual harassment policy or other policies governing employee behavior on* 

*the job.* In almost all sexual harassment cases, judges have ruled that the use of e-mail was considered part of the workplace environment.

- *Establish clear guidelines on matters such as the use of e-mail for jokes and other non-work related communications, the sending of confidential messages, and how to handle junk e-mail.* At Prudential Insurance, for example, employees are prohibited from using company e-mail to share jokes, photographs, or any kind of nonbusiness information.
- *Establish guidelines for deleting or retaining messages.* Retention periods of 30 to 90 days for routine messages is typical. Most organizations also set up a centralized archive for retaining essential e-mail messages.
- *Consider having policies pop up on users' screens when they log on.* It is especially important to remind employees that e-mail belongs to the employer and may be monitored.

Even deleted e-mails can usually be tracked down by a computer-forensics expert. An effective policy is the best step companies can take to manage the potential risks of e-mail abuse.

SOURCES: "E-mail: The DNA of Office Crimes," *Electric Perspectives* 28, no. 5 (September–October 2003), 4; Marcia Stepanek with Steve Hamm, "When the Devil Is in the E-mails," *BusinessWeek* (June 8, 1998), 72–74; Joseph McCafferty, "The Phantom Menace," *CFO* (June 1999), 89–91; and "Many Company Internet and Email Policies Are Worth Revising," *The Kiplinger Letter* (February 21, 2003), 1.

---

plans may even hinder rather than help an organization's performance in the face of rapid technological, social, economic, or other environmental change. In these cases, managers can develop multiple future alternatives to help them form more flexible plans. **Contingency plans** define company responses to be taken in the case of emergencies, setbacks, or unexpected conditions. To develop contingency plans, managers identify important factors in the environment, such as possible economic downturns, declining markets, increases in cost of supplies, new technological developments, or safety accidents. Managers then forecast a range of alternative responses to the most likely high-impact contingencies, focusing on the worst case.[33] For example, if sales fall 20 percent and prices drop 8 percent, what will the company do? Managers can develop contingency plans that might include layoffs, emergency

**contingency plans**
Plans that define company responses to specific situations, such as emergencies, setbacks, or unexpected conditions.

A desert flare marks the area where geologists discovered Libya's rich Zilten oilfield in the 1950s. At their peak in 1970, Libyan oil fields operated by Occidental Petroleum were producing 660,000 barrels a day, more than the company's total oil production in 2003. Today, with economic sanctions against Libya lifted by the U.S. government, big oil companies like Occidental, Chevron Texaco, and Exxon Mobil are again ready to do business with Libya's National Oil Corporation. Yet, the current environment of terrorist threats and general uncertainty means managers have to be prepared for whatever might happen. They are busy developing **contingency plans** to define how their companies will respond in case of unexpected setbacks associated with renewed Libyan operations. Companies are willing to take the risks because the potential rewards are huge.

budgets, new sales efforts, or new markets. As another example, top managers at Duke Energy Corp., which invested heavily in building new power plants to meet increasing demand, developed contingency plans for what the company would do if U.S. economic growth slowed to 1 percent a year, leaving the company with too much capacity amid weakening prices.[34]

# Planning in a Turbulent Environment

Today, contingency planning has taken on a whole new urgency. As Leah Modigliani, a portfolio strategist at Morgan Stanley put it, "On September 10 [2001], our worst case was a global recession."[35] For U.S. firms, in particular, the events of September 11, 2001 marked a turning point, when the turbulence and uncertainty of today's world became frighteningly clear. Since then, managers have renewed their emphasis on bracing for unexpected—even unimaginable—events. Two recent extensions of contingency planning are *building scenarios* and *crisis management planning*.

## Building Scenarios

**scenario building**
Looking at trends and discontinuities and imagining possible alternative futures to build a framework within which unexpected future events can be managed.

One way managers cope with greater uncertainty is with a forecasting technique known as scenario building. **Scenario building** involves looking at current trends and discontinuities and visualizing future possibilities. Rather than looking only at history and thinking about what has been, managers think about what *could be*. Managers can't predict the future, but they can rehearse a framework within which future events can be managed.[36] With scenario building, a broad base of managers mentally rehearse different scenarios based on anticipating varied changes that could impact the organization. Scenarios are like stories that offer alternative vivid pictures of what the future will look like and how managers will respond. Typically, two to five scenarios are developed for each set of factors, ranging from the most optimistic to the most pessimistic view.[37] Scenario building forces managers to mentally rehearse what they would do if their best-laid plans collapse.

Royal Dutch/Shell has long used scenario building to help managers navigate the turbulence and uncertainty of the oil industry. One scenario Shell managers rehearsed in 1970, for example, focused on an imagined accident in Saudi Arabia that severed an oil pipeline, which in turn decreased supply. The market reacted by increasing oil prices, which allowed OPEC nations to pump less oil and make more money. This story caused managers to reexamine the standard assumptions about oil price and supply and imagine what would happen and how they would respond if OPEC increased prices. By rehearsing this scenario, Shell's managers were much more prepared than the competition when OPEC announced its first oil embargo in October, 1973. This speedy response to a massive shift in the environment enabled Shell to move within two years from being the world's eighth largest oil company to being number two.[38]

## Crisis Management Planning

Managers can't always anticipate future events and build scenarios to cope with them. In addition, some unexpected events are so sudden and devastating that they require immediate response. Consider events such as the November 12, 2001, crash of American Airlines Flight 587 in a New York neighborhood already devastated by terrorist attacks, the 1993 deaths due to e-coli bacteria from Jack-in-the-Box hamburgers, or the 2003 crash of the Columbia space shuttle. Companies also face many smaller crises that call for rapid response, such as the conviction of Martha Stewart, chairman of Martha Stewart Living Omnimedia, on charges of insider trading, allegations of tainted Coca-Cola in Belgium, or charges that Tyson Foods hired illegal immigrants to work in its processing plants. Crises have become integral features of our organizations.[39] For managers to respond appropriately, they need carefully thought-out and coordinated plans. Although crises may vary, a good crisis management plan can be used to respond to any disaster at any time of the day or night. In addition, crisis management planning reduces the incidence of trouble, much like putting a good lock on a door reduces burglaries.[40]

Exhibit 7.8 outlines the three essential stages of crisis management.[41] The prevention stage involves activities managers undertake to try to prevent crises from occurring and to detect warning signs of potential crises. The preparation stage includes all the detailed planning to handle a crises when it occurs. Containment focuses on the organization's response to an actual crisis and any follow-up concerns.

## Exhibit 7.8

### Three Stages of Crisis Management

**Prevention**
- Build relationships.
- Detect signals from environment.

**Preparation**
- Designate crisis management team and spokesperson.
- Create detailed crisis management plan.
- Set up effective communications system.

**Containment**
- Rapid response: Activate the crisis management plan.
- Get the awful truth out.
- Meet safety and emotional needs.
- Return to business.

**SOURCE:** Based on information in W. Timothy Coombs, *Ongoing Crisis Communication: Planning, Managing, and Responding* (Thousand Oaks, Calif.: Sage Publications, 1999).

© ROBYN BECK/GETTY IMAGES

## CONCEPT CONNECTION

*Why would the U.S. Department of Agriculture want to scan a cow's eye? Because it is part of the* **prevention stage** *of their* **Crisis Management Plan** *(CMP) for dealing with Mad Cow or Foot-and-Mouth-Disease. The pattern of veins in each cow's retina is unique, and Optibrand Ltd. of Fort Collins, Colorado, has invented a device that farmers can use to scan their cows' retinas. This allows tracking of the animal through every step of the beef production process and helps the USDA meet its CMP goal of tracing the source of any disease—within two days of an outbreak. Since radio frequency identification tags, as in the photo, are subject to damage and tampering, retinal scanning coupled with implantable computer chips may provide the fastest and most reliable form of prevention and containment of these diseases.*

### Prevention

Although unexpected events and disasters will happen, managers should do everything they can to prevent crises. A critical part of the prevention stage is building trusting relationships with key stakeholders such as employees, customers, suppliers, governments, unions, and the community. By developing favorable relationships, managers can often prevent crises from happening and respond more effectively to those that cannot be avoided. For example, organizations that have open, trusting relationships with employees and unions may avoid crippling labor strikes.

Good communication also helps managers identify problems early so they do not turn into major issues. Nike had early warning from distributors in the Middle East that its flame logo on a basketball shoe looked like the word Allah in Arabic script and would be considered offensive to Muslims. Although the company made some minor changes, managers failed to take the warning seriously. Eventually, Nike had to recall nearly 40,000 pairs of the shoes and issue an apology to Muslims.[42] Similarly, Coca-Cola suffered a major crisis in Europe because it failed to respond quickly to reports of "foul-smelling" Coke in Belgium. Former CEO Douglas Daft observed that every problem the company has faced in recent years "can be traced to a singular cause: We neglected our relationships."[43]

### Preparation

Three steps in the preparation stage are designating a crisis management team and spokesperson, creating a detailed crisis management plan, and setting up an effective communications system. Some companies are setting up crisis management offices, with high-level leaders who report directly to the CEO.[44] Although these offices are in charge of crisis management, it is important that people throughout the company be involved. The crisis management team, for example, is a cross-functional group of people who are designated to swing into action if a crisis occurs. They are closely involved in creating the crisis management plan, and they'll be called upon to implement the plan if a disaster hits. The U.S. Office of Personnel Management in Washington, D.C., has nearly 200 people assigned and trained to take immediate action if a disaster occurs, including 8 employees assigned to each of 10 floors to handle an evacuation.[45] The organization should also designate a spokesperson who will be the voice of the company during the crisis.[46] The spokesperson in many cases is the top leader of the organization. However, organizations typically assign more than one spokesperson so that someone else will be prepared if the top leader is not available.

The crisis management plan (CMP) is a detailed, written plan that specifies the steps to be taken, and by whom, if a crisis occurs. The CMP should include plans for dealing with various types of crises, such as natural disasters like fires or earthquakes, normal accidents like economic crises or industrial accidents, and abnormal events such as product tampering or acts of terrorism.[47] The plan should include details for ensuring the well-being of employees and customers, procedures for back-up and recovery of computer systems and protecting proprietary information, details on where people should go if they need to be evacuated, plans for alternative work sites if needed, and guidelines for handling media and other outside communications. Morgan Stanley Dean Witter, the World Trade Center's largest tenant with 3,700 employees, adopted a crisis management plan for abnormal events after bomb threats during the Persian Gulf War in 1991. Top managers credit its detailed evacuation procedures for saving the lives of all but six employees during the September 11, 2001 attack. "Everybody knew about the . . . plan," said a spokesman. "We met constantly to talk about it."[48] A key point is that a crisis management plan should be a living, changing document that is regularly reviewed, practiced, and updated as needed.

A major part of the CMP is a communications plan that designates a crisis command center and sets up a complete communications and messaging system. The command center serves as a place for the crisis management team to meet, gather data and monitor incoming information, and disseminate information to the media, employees, and the public. All employees should have multiple ways to get in touch with the organization and report their whereabouts and status after a disaster.

### Containment

Some crises are inevitable no matter how well prepared an organization is. When crisis hits, a rapid response is crucial. The team should be able to immediately implement the crisis management plan, so training and practice are important. In addition, the organization should "get the awful truth out" to employees and the public as soon as possible.[49] This is the stage where it becomes critical for the organization to speak with one voice so people do not get conflicting stories about what's going on and what the organization is doing about it. Consider what happened when doctors at Duke University Hospital made one of the worst mistakes in medical history—transplanting the wrong heart and lungs into 17-year-old Jessica Santillan, who later died. Although the story was already out, it took nine days for Duke leaders to admit the hospital's mistake. By that time, rumors and misinformation were rampant, further damaging the hospital's reputation and prolonging its recovery from the crisis.[50]

After ensuring people's physical safety in a crisis, the next focus should be on responding to the emotional needs of employees, customers, and the public. Giving facts and statistics to try to downplay the disaster always backfires because it does not meet people's emotional need to feel that someone cares about them and what the disaster has meant to their lives. After a crisis as devastating as the 2001 terrorist attacks or the Columbine school shootings, companies may provide counseling and other services to help people cope.

Organizations also strive to give people a sense of security and hope by getting back to business quickly. Companies that cannot get up and running within 10 days after any major crisis are not likely to stay in business.[51] People want to feel that they are going to have a job and be able to take care of their families. Taking steps to protect people from danger during future disasters is important at this stage also. In this sense, crisis management planning comes full circle, because managers use the crisis to bolster their prevention abilities and be better prepared in the future. A crisis is an important time for companies to strengthen their stakeholder relationships. By being open and honest about the crisis and putting people first, organizations build stronger bonds with employees, customers and other stakeholders, and gain a reputation as a trustworthy company.

*Go to the ethical dilemma on page 261 that pertains to crisis management.*            *Take A Moment*

# Planning for High Performance

The purpose of planning and goal setting is to help the organization achieve high performance. Overall organizational performance depends on achieving outcomes identified by the planning process. The process of planning is changing to be more in

## CONCEPT CONNECTION

*When Robert L. Nardelli took the helm at Home Depot, Inc., the company was in a dreadful slump as a result of an expansion spree by previous management that left the Atlanta-based retailer struggling to manage a bunch of new stores. Nardelli came in with a new **vision** and **framework for planning and goalsetting** that focused managers on modernizing aging stores, centralizing purchasing, and updating antiquated computer systems. After a few tough years, Home Depot began to pull out of the downturn, with profits jumping 17% on an 11% sales rise. Nardelli knows that good planning starts and stops at the top. The strong support and commitment of top managers is critical as Home Depot continues to face challenges from arch-rival Lowe's.*

tune with a rapidly changing environment. Traditionally, strategy and planning have been the domain of top managers. Today, though, managers involve people throughout the organization, which can spur higher performance because people understand the goals and plans and buy into them. We will first discuss traditional, top-down approaches to planning and then examine some of the newer approaches that emphasize bottom-up planning and the involvement of stakeholders in the planning process.

## Traditional Approaches to Planning

**central planning department**
A group of planning specialists who develop plans for the organization as a whole and its major divisions and departments and typically report directly to the president or CEO.

Traditionally, corporate planning has been done entirely by top executives, by consulting firms, or, most commonly, by central planning departments. **Central planning departments** are groups of planning specialists who report directly to the CEO or president. This approach was popular during the 1970s. Planning specialists were hired to gather data and develop detailed strategic plans for the corporation as a whole. This planning approach was top down because goals and plans were assigned to major divisions and departments from the planning department after approval by the president. This approach worked well in many applications.

Although traditional approaches to planning still are popular with some companies, formal planning increasingly is being criticized as inappropriate for today's fast-paced environment. Central planning departments may be out of touch with the constantly changing realities faced by front-line employees, which may leave employees struggling to follow a plan that no longer fits the environment and customer needs. In addition, formal plans dictated by top managers and central planning departments inhibit creativity and learning because employees have less incentive to think for themselves and come up with new ideas. Many of today's managers are taking a different approach in order to spur high performance in a difficult environment.

## High-Performance Approaches to Planning

**decentralized planning**
Managers work with planning experts to develop their own goals and plans.

A new approach to planning is to involve everyone in the organization, and sometimes outside stakeholders as well, in the planning process. The evolution to a new approach began with a shift to decentralized planning, which means that planning experts work with managers in major divisions or departments to develop their own goals and plans. This enables managers throughout the company to come up with their own creative solutions to problems and become more committed to following through on the plans. As the environment became even more volatile, top executives saw the benefits of pushing decentralized planning even further, by having planning experts work directly with line managers and front-line employees to develop dynamic plans that meet fast-changing needs.

In a complex and competitive business environment, strategic thinking and execution become the expectation of every employee.[52] For an example of a company that is finding hidden sources of ideas and innovation by involving all its workers in planning, consider Springfield Remanufacturing, described in the Unlocking Creative Solutions Through People box.

Planning comes alive when employees are involved in setting goals and determining the means to reach them. Here are some guidelines for planning in the new workplace.

## Start with a Strong Mission and Vision

Planning for high performance requires flexibility. Employees may have to adapt plans to meet new needs and respond to changes in the environment. During times of turbulence or uncertainty, a powerful sense of purpose (mission) and direction for the future (vision) becomes even more important. Without a strong mission and vision to guide employee thinking and behavior, the resources of a fast-moving company such as some of today's high-tech businesses, can quickly become uncoordinated, with employees pursuing radically different plans and activities. A compelling mission and vision can also serve to increase employee commitment and motivation, which are critical to helping organizations compete in a fast-shifting environment.[53]

## Set Stretch Goals for Excellence

Stretch goals are highly ambitious goals that are so clear, compelling, and imaginative that they fire up employees and engender excellence. As we discussed earlier in the chapter, an important criterion for effective goals is that they be challenging yet

# Unlocking Creative Solutions Through People

### SRC Holdings Corporation: Changing Lives by Changing Business

Jack Stack and 12 other former International Harvester managers started Springfield Remanufacturing Corporation on a shoestring in 1983. The company still exists, but today it is part of SRC Holdings Corporation, a group of 22 semiautonomous companies located in the Springfield, Missouri area. Stack, CEO of SRC Holdings, has built this amazingly successful corporation by tapping into people's universal desire to win. Stack's philosophy is that "the best, most efficient, most profitable way to operate a business is to give everybody a voice in how the company is run and a stake in the financial outcome, good or bad."

SRC involves everyone in the planning process and uses a bonus system based on hitting the plan's targets. Top managers meet with middle managers, supervisors, and front-line employees throughout their divisions to develop and sell their long-range plans. If a manager's plan is beyond the plant's capacity, the workers feel free to suggest workable alternatives. By the time managers present their plans to the top brass, everyone in the various divisions has had a say and has thus developed a sense of ownership in the plan.

All SRC businesses make their operating and financial performance numbers freely available so employees can compare performance to the plan. People "huddle" at least weekly around mural-sized charts in the employee cafeteria to talk about the numbers and what needs to be done to meet the targets. Employees take the company's success personally because they all own shares in the company through employee stock ownership plans (ESOPs). SRC has invested heavily in financial education for all workers so that everyone understands what is at stake and what is to be gained. "What we're doing," Stack says, "is showing people how to get through life without fear. Once people understand what it takes to be a businessperson, not just a cog in the system but someone on the brighter side of capitalism, then their lives can change forever."

**SOURCES:** Jay Finegan, "Everything According to Plan," *Inc.* (March 1995), 78–85; Art Kleiner, "Jack Stack's Story is an Open Book," *Strategy & Business* (Third Quarter 2001), 76–85; Jack Stack and Bo Burlingham, *A Stake in the Outcome: Building a Culture of Ownership for the Long-Term Success of Your Business* (New York: Currency, 2002); and Bo Burlingham, "Jack Stack: We Love Him for Going Naked," *Inc.*, 25th Anniversary Issue (April 2004), 134+.

realistic. In today's workplace, stretch goals are extremely important because things are moving so fast. A company that focuses on gradual, incremental improvements in products, processes, or systems will get left behind. Managers can use stretch goals to compel employees to think in new ways that can lead to bold, innovative breakthroughs. Motorola used stretch goals to achieve six sigma quality, as described in Chapter 2, which has now become the standard for numerous companies. Managers first set a goal of a tenfold increase in quality over a two-year period. After this goal was met, they set a new stretch goal of a hundredfold improvement over a four-year period.[54]

### Create a Culture that Encourages Learning

Today's best managers create a culture that celebrates diversity, encourages initiative, and supports continuous experimentation and learning. Managers advocate individual lifelong learning, and they invest in education and training to keep people's minds and skills sharp.[55] An important value in these organizations is questioning the status quo. Tomorrow's opportunities might come from very different directions than the basis of today's success. For example, soft-drink makers missed out on huge opportunities for new drinks such as flavored waters, sports drinks, and New Age beverages because they were focused on continuing the status quo rather than experimenting with new products.[56] Managers sometimes have to change plans at the drop of a hat, which requires a mindset that embraces ambiguity, risk taking, making mistakes, and learning.

### Embrace Event-Driven Planning

In fast-shifting environments, managers have to be in tune with what is happening right now, rather than focusing only on long-range goals and plans. Long-range strategic planning is not abandoned, but it is accompanied by event-driven planning, which responds to the current reality of what the environment and the marketplace demands.[57] Exhibit 7.9 compares traditional calendar-driven planning to event-driven planning. **Event-driven planning** is a continuous, sequential process rather than a staid planning document. It is evolutionary and interactive, taking advantage of unforeseen events to shift the company as needed to improve performance. Event-driven planning allows for flexibility to adapt to market forces or other shifts in the environment, rather than being tied to a plan that no longer works. For example, Redix International, a software development firm, has a long-term plan for items it wants to incorporate into the software. However, the plan is modified at least four or five times a year. The shifts in direction are based on weekly discussions President and CEO Randall King has with key Redix managers, where they examine what demands from clients indicate about where the marketplace is going.[58]

**event-driven planning**
Evolutionary planning that responds to the current reality of what the environment and the marketplace demands.

## Exhibit 7.9

SOURCE: Chuck Martin, "How to Plan for the Short Term," book excerpt from Chuck Martin, *Managing for the Short Term* (New York: Doubleday, 2002), in *CIO* (September 15, 2002), 90–97.

### Comparing Two Planning Styles

| Calendar-Driven Planning | Event-Driven Planning |
|---|---|
| Is based on time | Is based on events—small and large |
| Produces a document | Produces a sequential process |
| Is declared | Is evolutionary and interactive |
| Focuses on goals | Focuses on process |
| Creates obstacles to change once set | Allows for continuous change |
| Creates strategy implementers | Creates organizationwide strategists |

## Use Temporary Task Forces

A **planning task force** is a temporary group of managers and employees who take responsibility for developing a strategic plan. Many of today's companies use interdepartmental task forces to help establish goals and make plans for achieving them. The task force often includes outside stakeholders as well, such as customers, suppliers, strategic partners, investors, or even members of the general community. Today's companies are highly focused on satisfying the needs and interests of all stakeholder groups, so they bring these stakeholders into the planning and goal-setting process.[59] LendLease, an Australian real estate and financial services company, for example, involves numerous stakeholders, including community advocates and potential customers, in the planning process for every new project it undertakes.[60]

**planning task force**

A group of managers and employees who develop a strategic plan.

## Planning Still Starts and Stops at the Top

Top managers create a mission and vision that is worthy of employees' best efforts and provides a framework for planning and goal setting. Even though planning is decentralized, top managers must show support and commitment to the planning process. Top managers also accept responsibility when planning and goal setting are ineffective, rather than blaming the failure on lower-level managers or employees.

---

*Manager's Solution*

This chapter focused on organizational planning. Organizational planning involves defining goals and developing a plan with which to achieve them. An organization exists for a single, overriding purpose known as its *mission*—the basis for strategic goals and plans. Goals within the organization are defined in a hierarchical fashion, beginning with strategic goals followed by tactical and operational goals. Plans are defined similarly, with strategic, tactical, and operational plans used to achieve the goals. Other goal concepts include characteristics of effective goals and goal-setting behavior.

Several types of plans were described, including strategic, tactical, operational, single-use, standing, and contingency plans, as well as management by objectives. Two extensions of contingency planning are scenario building and crisis management planning. Scenarios are alternative vivid pictures of what the future might be like. They provide a framework for managers to cope with unexpected or unpredictable events. Crisis management planning involves the stages of prevention, preparation, and containment. The Europa Hotel, described at the beginning of the chapter, provides an excellent example of crisis management planning. The Europa, like most major hotels, has long had clear procedures for evacuation and dealing with disasters, and the hotel has a good record of getting people out fast. Amazingly, no one has ever been killed by a bomb at the Europa. Because the Europa has had so much experience dealing with crises, managers and employees have become ever alert to even the smallest signals that something is amiss, so they have been able to take quick action and prevent even greater damage or loss of life. The Europa is highly skilled at handling the containment stage of crisis. After one bomb that ripped a huge hole in the side of the hotel and injured 13 people, everyone was back to work as usual by lunchtime. Hotel manager John Toner uses every crisis as a way to learn more, be better prepared, and make the company better and stronger. He believes the tendency to immediately look for ways to cut costs and lay people off following a crisis is dangerous. "I don't look for cost savings. I don't look at the bottom line—it'll look after itself," he says. Instead, Toner focuses on taking care of employees and guests and finding ways to make the business better. Because of that attention, hotel staff and guests have remained resolutely loyal to the Europa.[61]

In the past, planning was almost always done entirely by top managers, by consultants, or by central planning departments. During turbulent times, planning is decentralized and people throughout the organization are involved in establishing dynamic plans that can meet fast-changing needs from the environment. Some guidelines for planning in a turbulent environment include starting with a powerful mission and vision, setting stretch goals for excellence, creating a culture that encourages learning, embracing event-based planning, and using temporary task forces that may include outside stakeholders. Planning is evolutionary and plans are continually adapted to meet new needs and changing markets. However, top managers are still responsible for providing a guiding mission and vision for the future and creating a solid framework for planning and goal setting.

# Discussion Questions

1. What types of planning would have helped Exxon respond more quickly to the oil spill from the Exxon Valdez near Alaska?

2. Write a brief mission statement for a local business. Can the purpose and values of a small organization be captured in a written statement?

3. What strategies could the college or university at which you are taking this management course adopt to compete for students in the marketplace? Would these strategies depend on the school's goals?

4. If you were a top manager of a medium-sized real estate sales agency, would you use MBO? If so, give examples of goals you might set for managers and sales agents.

5. A new business venture has to develop a comprehensive business plan to borrow money to get started. Companies such as Federal Express, NIKE, and Rolm Corporation say they did not follow the original plan very closely. Does that mean that developing the plan was a waste of time for these eventually successful companies?

6. A famous management theorist proposed that the time horizons for all strategic plans are becoming shorter because of the rapid changes in organizations' external environments. Do you agree? Would the planning time horizon for IBM or Ford Motor Company be shorter than it was 20 years ago?

7. What are the characteristics of effective goals? Would it be better to have no goals at all than to have goals that do not meet these criteria?

8. What are the advantages and disadvantages of having a central planning department to do an organization's planning compared with having decentralized planning groups provide planning support to line managers?

9. Assume Southern University decides to (1) raise its admission standards and (2) initiate a business fair to which local townspeople will be invited. What types of plans would it use to carry out these two activities?

# Management in Practice: Experiential Exercise

**Company Crime Wave**

Senior managers in your organization are concerned about internal theft. Your department has been assigned the task of writing an ethics policy that defines employee theft and prescribes penalties. Stealing goods is easily classified as theft, but other activities are more ambiguous. Before writing the policy, go through the following list and decide which behaviors should be defined as stealing and whether penalties should apply. Discuss the items with your department members until agreement is reached. Classify each item as an example of (1) theft, (2) acceptable behavior, or (3) in between with respect to written policy. Is it theft when an employee

- Gets paid for overtime not worked?
- Takes a longer lunch or coffee break than authorized?
- Punches a time card for another?
- Comes in late or leaves early?
- Fakes injury to receive workers' compensation?
- Takes care of personal business on company time?
- Occasionally uses company copying machines or makes long-distance telephone calls for personal purposes?

- Takes a few stamps, pens, or other supplies for personal use?
- Takes money from the petty cash drawer?
- Uses company vehicles or tools for own purposes but returns them?
- Damages merchandise so a cohort can purchase it at a discount?
- Accepts a gift from a supplier?

Now consider those items rated "in between." Do these items represent ethical issues as defined in Chapter 5? How should these items be handled in the company's written policy?

# Management in Practice: Ethical Dilemma

### Repair or Replace?

After only a few months in sales at ComputerSource, a full-service computer business, Sam Nolan realized there were serious problems in the software department. Most of the complaints from customers were related to the incorrect selection or installation of the software needed to meet their needs. He discussed the problem with his sales manager, who was part-owner and partner with the head of service for ComputerSource. They both were aware of the problem, but they were facing an industry-wide shortage of qualified software engineers.

Nolan received an urgent call from Katherine Perry, operations manager for Ross & Lindsey, a fast-growing financial management firm that was becoming one of his best accounts. She was calling to report that they were having daily network problems that were interfering with her staff's productivity and morale. She needed an immediate solution to the problem. Like many firms, Ross & Lindsey had a hodge-podge of computer equipment and software on their network. They had bought from a series of vendors, with a patchwork approach to problems.

Nolan realized it would take an expert software engineer days or weeks of work to fix all the bugs in their existing system, which ComputerSource could not afford. A costlier alternative was to recommend a system upgrade, replacing the older hardware and loading a newer software version on the entire network. Perry had already confided that she had pushed her bosses as far as they wanted to go on computer expenditures this year, but Nolan knew she was desperate. He didn't want to risk losing her business, but he didn't trust the software engineers to fix the problems. He was also pretty sure Perry would face the same dilemma at any computer retailer in town.

### What Do You Do?

1. Gamble on the service department to fix their existing system, within the limits of their budget and their frustration. If it doesn't work, it is their problem.
2. Recommend a system upgrade to correct the problem, even though it will cost the clients more than they want to pay and may jeopardize future sales.
3. Confide in the clients about your perception of the problem, give them the chance to make an informed choice, and risk having them take their business elsewhere.

# Surf the Net

1. **Organizational Mission.** As stated in the text, one of the top three traits employees cited in *Fortune* magazine's study of the "100 Best Companies to Work for in America" was a sense of purpose that employees could believe in and relate to. Find three examples of mission statements that you can contribute during a class discussion of mission. If corporate missions are available at a company's Web site, you can usually find them under the "About" option. For example at TDIndustries' home page, click on "About TDIndustries." Listed below are companies that appeared in the top ten of the January 11, 1999, edition of *Fortune's* "100 Best Companies to Work for in America." You may prefer to find mission statements for other organizations in which you have an interest.
   *http://www.tdindustries.com/* (TDIndustries— ranked #2)
   *http://www.hp.com/* (Hewlett-Packard— ranked #10)
   *www.synovus.com/* (Synovus Financial— ranked #1)

2. **Schedules.** Managers must plan for their personal schedules, as well as oversee planning for their areas of responsibility. Among the personal scheduling tools available on the Internet are online calendars. Try one of the following such tools and write a review concerning its effectiveness and usefulness. Your review should include a brief description of how the online calendar works, its main features, and the advantages and disadvantages of using such a planning tool.
   *http://e-meetings.mci.com/e-SchedulingTools/index.php.*
   *http://www.free-downloads.net/sub_category/ Scheduling_Tools*

3. **Shewhart Cycle.** Use a search engine to find information for a report on Walter A. Shewhart and the Shewhart Cycle. In your report, provide a brief biographical sketch of Shewhart as well as information to supplement what the text provides on his continuous improvement model. Two possible sites are listed below.
   *http://www.groups.dcs.st-and.ac.uk/~history/ Mathematicians/Shewhart.html*
   *http://www.asq.org/join/about/history/shewhart.html*

# Case for Critical Analysis

## H.I.D.

Dave Collins, president of H.I.D., sat down at the conference table with his management team members, Karen Setz, Tony Briggs, Dave King, and Art Johnson. H.I.D. owns ten Holiday Inns in Georgia, eight hotels of different types in Canada, and one property in the Caribbean. It also owns two Quality Inns in Georgia. Dave Collins and his managers got together to define their mission and goals and to set strategic plans. As they began their strategic planning session, the consultant they had hired suggested that each describe what he or she wanted for the company's domestic operations in the next ten years—how many hotels it should own, where to locate them, and who the target market was. Another question he asked them to consider was what the driving force of the company should be—that is, the single characteristic that would separate H.I.D. from other companies.

The team members wrote their answers on flip-charts, and the consultant summarized the results. Dave Collins's goal included 50 hotels in ten years, with the number increasing to 26 or 27 in five years. All the other members saw no more than 20 hotels in ten years and a maximum of 15 or 16 within five years. Clearly there was disagreement among the top managers about long-term goals and the desirable growth rate.

With the consultant's direction, the team members began to critique their growth targets. Dave King, director of operations and development, observed, "We just can't build that many hotels in that time period, certainly not given our current staffing, or any reasonable staffing we could afford. I don't see how we could achieve that goal." Art Johnson, the accountant, agreed. Karen Setz then asked, "Could we build them all in Georgia? You know we've centered on the medium-priced hotel in smaller towns. Do we need to move to bigger towns now, such as Jacksonville, or add another to the one we have in Atlanta?" Dave Collins responded, "We have an opportunity out in California, we may have one in New Jersey, and we are looking at the possibility of going to Jacksonville."

The consultant attempted to refocus the discussion: "Well, how does this all fit with your mission? Where are you willing to locate geographically? Most of your operation is in Georgia. Can you adequately support a national building effort?"

Tony Briggs responded, "Well, you know we have always looked at the smaller-town hotels as being our niche, although we deviated from that for the hotel in Atlanta. But we generally stay in smaller towns where we don't have much competition. Now we are talking about an expensive hotel in California."

Dave Collins suggested, "Maybe it's time we changed our target market, changed our pricing strategy, and went for larger hotels in urban areas across the whole country. Maybe we need to change a lot of factors about our company."

## Questions

1. What is H.I.D.'s mission at present? How may this mission change?
2. What do you think H.I.D.'s mission, strategic goals, and strategic plans are likely to be at the end of this planning session? Why?
3. What goal-setting behavior is being used here to reach agreement among H.I.D.'s managers? Do managers typically disagree about the direction of their organization?

Source: This case was provided by James Higgins.

# Endnotes

1. Ian Wylie, "He's Belfast's Security Blanket," *Fast Company* (December 2001), 54–58.
2. Quoted in Oren Harari, "Good/Bad News about Strategy," *Management Review* (July 1995), 29–31.
3. Amitai Etzioni, *Modern Organizations* (Englewood Cliffs, N.J.: Prentice-Hall, 1984), 6.
4. Ibid.
5. Max D. Richards, *Setting Strategic Goals and Objectives,* 2d ed. (St. Paul, Minn.: West, 1986).
6. C. Chet Miller and Laura B. Cardinal, "Strategic Planning and Firm Performance: A Synthesis of More than Two Decades of Research," *Academy of Management Journal* 37, no. 6 (1994), 1649–1685.
7. This discussion is based on Richard L. Daft and Richard M. Steers, *Organizations: A Micro/Macro Approach* (Glenview, Ill.: Scott, Foresman, 1986), 319–321; Herbert A. Simon, "On the Concept of Organizational Goals," *Administrative Science Quarterly* 9 (1964), 1–22; and Charles B. Saunders and Francis D. Tuggel, "Corporate Goals," *Journal of General Management* 5 (1980), 3–13.
8. See "2004 Special Report: The 100 Best Companies to Work For," *Fortune* (January 12, 2004), 56–80; and Kevin E. Joyce, "Lessons for Employers from *Fortune's* 100 Best," *Business Horizons* (March-April 2003), 77–84.
9. David Whitford, "A Human Place to Work," *Fortune* (January 8, 2001), 108–121.
10. J. Lynn Lunsford, "Lean Times: With Airbus on Its Tail, Boeing Is Rethinking How It Builds Planes," *The Wall Street Journal* (September 5, 2001), A1, A16.
11. Marc Gunther, "Tree Huggers, Soy Lovers, and Profits," *Fortune* (June 23, 2003), 98–104; Gary Fields and John R. Wilke, "The Ex-Files: FBI's New Focus Places Big Burden on Local Police," *The Wall Street Journal* (June 30, 2003), A1, A12.
12. David Pearson, "Breaking Away," *CIO,* Section 1 (May 1, 1998), 34–46.
13. Lee Hawkins Jr. "GM Seeks Chevrolet Revival: 'Restocked' Showroom Will Feature 10 New Models," *The Wall Street Journal* (December 19, 2003), B4; Ellen Piligian, "Chevrolet Greets the New Year with an Ambitious Campaign to Introduce 10 Vehicles in 20 Months," *The New York Times* (December 19, 2003), C6; and Dave Guilford and K. C. Crain, "Chevy Dealers Get Incentives to Sell 3 Million," *Automotive News* (February 9, 2004), 63.
14. Mary Klemm, Stuart Sanderson, and George Luffman, "Mission Statements: Selling Corporate Values to Employees," *Long-Range Planning* 24, no. 3 (1991), 73–78; John A. Pearce II and Fred David, "Corporate Mission Statements: The Bottom Line," *Academy of Management Executive* (1987), 109–116; Jerome H. Want, "Corporate Mission: The Intangible Contributor to Performance," *Management Review* (August 1986),

46–50; and Forest R. David and Fred R. David, "It's Time to Redraft Your Mission Statement," *Journal of Business Strategy* (January-February 2003), 11-14.

15. "Tennessee News and Notes from State Farm," State Farm Mutual Automobile Insurance Company, 2004.

16. Charles A. O'Reilly III and Jeffrey Pfeffer, "Star Makers," (book excerpt from *From Hidden Value: How Great Companies Achieve Extraordinary Results with Ordinary People* (Boston, Mass.: Harvard University Press, 2000), in CIO (September 15, 2000), 226–246.

17. "Strategic Planning: Part 2," *Small Business Report* (March 1983), 28–32.

18. Paul Meising and Joseph Wolfe, "The Art and Science of Planning at the Business Unit Level," *Management Science* 31 (1985), 773–781.

19. Based in part on information about 1-800-Flowers, in Jenny C. McCune, "On the Train Gang," *Management Review* (October 1994), 57–60.

20. "Study: IRS Employees Often Steer Taxpayers Wrong on Law Questions," Associated Press story in *Johnson City Press* (September 4, 2003), 4A.

21. Mark Fischetti, "Team Doctors, Report to ER!" *Fast Company* (February/March 1998), 170–177.

22. John O. Alexander, "Toward Real Performance: The Circuit-Breaker Technique," *Supervisory Management* (April 1989), 5–12.

23. Mark J. Fritsch, "Balanced Scorecard Helps Northern States Power's Quality Academy Achieve Extraordinary Performance," *Corporate University Review* (September–October 1997), 22.

24. Joy Riggs, "Empowering Workers by Setting Goals," *Nation's Business* (January 1995), 6.

25. Joel Hoekstra, "3M's Global Grip," *WorldTraveler* (May 2000), 31–34; and Thomas A. Stewart, "3M Fights Back," *Fortune* (February 5, 1996), 94–99.

26. Edwin A. Locke, Gary P. Latham, and Miriam Erez, "The Determinants of Goal Commitment," *Academy of Management Review* 13 (1988), 23–39.

27. George S. Odiorne, "MBO: A Backward Glance," *Business Horizons* 21 (October 1978), 14–24.

28. Jan P. Muczyk and Bernard C. Reimann, "MBO as a Complement to Effective Leadership," *The Academy of Management Executive* 3 (1989), 131–138; and W. Giegold, *Objective Setting and the MBO Process*, vol. 2 (New York: McGraw-Hill, 1978).

29. Jack Ewing, "Siemens Climbs Back," *BusinessWeek* (June 5, 2000), 79–82.

30. John Ivancevich, J. Timothy McMahon, J. William Streidl, and Andrew D. Szilagyi, "Goal Setting: The Tenneco Approach to Personnel Development and Management Effectiveness," *Organizational Dynamics* (Winter 1978), 48–80.

31. Brigitte W. Schay, Mary Ellen Beach, Jacqueline A. Caldwell, and Christelle LaPolice, "Using Standardized Outcome Measures in the Federal Government," *Human Resource Management* 41, no. 3 (Fall 2002), 355–368.

32. Eileen M. Van Aken and Garry D. Coleman, "Building Better Measurement," *Industrial Management* (July–August 2002), 28–33.

33. Curtis W. Roney, "Planning for Strategic Contingencies," *Business Horizons* (March–April 2003), 35–42; and "Corporate Planning: Drafting a Blueprint for Success," *Small Business Report* (August 1987), 40–44.

34. Bernard Wysocki Jr., "Soft Landing or Hard? Firm Tests Strategy on 3 Views of Future," *The Wall Street Journal* (July 7, 2000), A1, A6.

35. Saul Hansell and Joseph B. Treaster, "The Job of Imagining the Unimaginable, and Bracing For It," *The New York Times* (October 20, 2001), C1.

36. Syed H. Akhter, "Strategic Planning, Hypercompetition, and Knowledge Management," *Business Horizons* (January–February 2003), 19–24; and Steven Schnaars and Paschalina Ziamou, "The Essentials of Scenario Writing," *Business Horizons* (July–August 2001), 25–31.

37. Schnaars and Ziamou, "The Essentials of Scenario Writing."

38. Ian Wylie, "There Is No Alternative To . . . ," *Fast Company* (July 2002), 106–110.

39. Ian Mitroff with Gus Anagnos, *Managing Crises Before They Happen* (New York: AMACOM, 2001).

40. Ian Mitroff and Murat C. Alpaslan, "Preparing for Evil," *Harvard Business Review* (April 2003), 109–115.

41. This discussion is based largely on W. Timothy Coombs, *Ongoing Crisis Communication: Planning, Managing, and Responding* (Thousand Oaks, California: Sage Publications, 1999).

42. Ibid., 28–29.

43. Ian I. Mitroff, "Crisis Leadership," *Executive Excellence* (August 2001), 19; Andy Bowen, "Crisis Procedures that Stand the Test of Time," *Public Relations Tactics* (August 2001), 16.

44. Mitroff and Alpaslan, "Preparing for Evil."

45. Kirstin Downey Grimsley, "Many Firms Lack Plans for Disaster," *The Washington Post* (October 3, 2001), E1.

46. Christine Pearson, "A Blueprint for Crisis Management," *Ivey Business Journal* (January–February 2002), 69–73.

47. See Mitroff and Alpaslan, "Preparing for Evil," for a discussion of the "wheel of crises" outlining the many different kinds of crises organizations may face.

48. Grimsley, "Many Firms Lack Plans for Disaster"; "Girding Against New Risks: Global Executives Are

Working to Better Protect Their Employees and Businesses from Calamity," *Time* (October 8, 2001), B8+.

49. Mitroff, "Crisis Leadership." Also see Loretta Ucelli, "The CEO's 'How To' Guide to Crisis Communications," *Strategy & Leadership* 30, no. 2 (2002), 21–24, and Paul Argenti, "Crisis Communication: Lessons from 9/11," *Harvard Business Review* (December 2002), 103–109, for tips on crisis communication.

50. Allison Fass, "Duking It Out," *Forbes* (June 9, 2003), 74–76.

51. "Girding Against New Risks."

52. Harari, "Good News/Bad News about Strategy."

53. This discussion of the importance vision and mission is based on Khoo Hsien Hui and Tan Kay Chuan, "Nine Approaches to Organizational Excellence," *Journal of Organizational Excellence* (Winter 2002), 53–65; Gerald E. Ledford, Jr., Jon R. Wendenhof, and James T. Strahley, "Realizing a Corporate Philosophy," *Organizational Dynamics* (Winter 1995), 5–18; James C. Collins, "Building Companies to Last," *The State of Small Business* (1995), 83–86; James C. Collins and Jerry I. Porras, "Building a Visionary Company," *California*

*Management Review* 37, no. 2 (Winter 1995), 80–100; and James C. Collins and Jerry I. Porras, "The Ultimate Vision," *Across the Board* (January 1995), 19–23.

54. See Kenneth R. Thompson, Wayne A. Hockwarter, and Nicholas J. Mathys, "Stretch Targets: What Makes Them Effective?" *Academy of Management Executive* 11, no. 3 (August 1997), 48.

55. Leon Martel, "The Principles of High Performance—and How to Apply Them," *Journal of Organizational Excellence* (Autumn 2002), 49–59.

56. Gary Hamel, "Avoiding the Guillotine," *Fortune* (April 2, 2001), 139–144.

57. This discussion is based on Chuck Martin, "How to Plan for the Short Term," Book excerpt from Chuck Martin, *Managing for the Short Term* (New York: Doubleday, 2002), in *CIO* (September 15, 2002), 90–97.

58. Martin, "How to Plan for the Short Term."

59. Jeffrey A. Schmidt, "Corporate Excellence in the New Millennium," *Journal of Business Strategy* (November–December 1999), 39–43.

60. Polly LaBarre, "The Company Without Limits," *Fast Company* (September 1999), 160–186.

61. Wylie, "He's Belfast's Security Blanket."

# Strategy Formulation and Implementation

## LEARNING OBJECTIVES

1. Define the components of strategic management.

2. Describe the strategic planning process and SWOT analysis.

3. Understand grand strategies for domestic and international operations

4. Define corporate-level strategies and explain the portfolio approach.

5. Describe business-level strategies, including Porter's competitive forces and strategies and partnership strategies.

6. Explain the major considerations in formulating functional strategies.

7. Discuss the organizational dimensions used for implementing strategy.

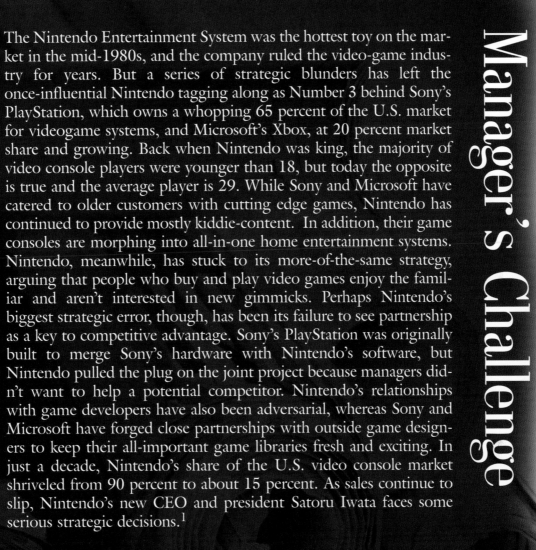

The Nintendo Entertainment System was the hottest toy on the market in the mid-1980s, and the company ruled the video-game industry for years. But a series of strategic blunders has left the once-influential Nintendo tagging along as Number 3 behind Sony's PlayStation, which owns a whopping 65 percent of the U.S. market for videogame systems, and Microsoft's Xbox, at 20 percent market share and growing. Back when Nintendo was king, the majority of video console players were younger than 18, but today the opposite is true and the average player is 29. While Sony and Microsoft have catered to older customers with cutting edge games, Nintendo has continued to provide mostly kiddie-content. In addition, their game consoles are morphing into all-in-one home entertainment systems. Nintendo, meanwhile, has stuck to its more-of-the-same strategy, arguing that people who buy and play video games enjoy the familiar and aren't interested in new gimmicks. Perhaps Nintendo's biggest strategic error, though, has been its failure to see partnership as a key to competitive advantage. Sony's PlayStation was originally built to merge Sony's hardware with Nintendo's software, but Nintendo pulled the plug on the joint project because managers didn't want to help a potential competitor. Nintendo's relationships with game developers have also been adversarial, whereas Sony and Microsoft have forged close partnerships with outside game designers to keep their all-important game libraries fresh and exciting. In just a decade, Nintendo's share of the U.S. video console market shriveled from 90 percent to about 15 percent. As sales continue to slip, Nintendo's new CEO and president Satoru Iwata faces some serious strategic decisions.[1]

## Take A Moment

If you were the CEO of Nintendo, would you continue to focus exclusively on games or compete head on with Sony and Microsoft in the battle for broader home entertainment? What strategies might you adopt to help Nintendo regain a competitive edge in the console industry?

The story of Nintendo's decline and the rise of Sony's PlayStation illustrates the importance of strategic planning. Managers at Sony formulated and implemented strategies that have made PlayStation the player to beat in the video console business, while Nintendo managers failed to respond to increased competition and changing customer expectations. Satoru Iwata is analyzing the situation and considering strategies that can ignite growth and revive the declining company.

Every company is concerned with strategy. Japan's Fuji Photo Film Company developed a strategy of being a low-cost provider to compete with Kodak. Fuji's relentless internal cost-cutting enabled the company to offer customers lower prices and gradually gain market share over the giant U.S. firm. McDonald's devised a new strategy of downsizing its menu items in response to changes in the environment. Supersize french fries and soft drinks were eliminated to counter public accusations that the fast-food icon was responsible for Americans' expanding waistlines and growing health problems. In the auto industry, PSA Peugeot Citroën SA adopted a strategy of being a fierce product innovator, coming out with 25 new models between 1999 and 2002.[2] Strategic blunders can hurt a company. Consider Mattel, which has suffered in recent years by losing sight of its core business and trying to compete as a maker of computer games.[3]

Managers at Mattel, McDonald's Fuji, and Peugeot are all involved in strategic management. They are finding ways to respond to competitors, cope with difficult environmental changes, meet changing customer needs, and effectively use available resources. Research has shown that strategic thinking and planning positively affects a firm's performance and financial success.[4] Strategic planning has taken on new importance in today's world of globalization, deregulation, advancing technology, and changing demographics and lifestyles. Managers are responsible for positioning their organizations for success in a world that is constantly changing. Today's top companies thrive by changing the rules of an industry to their advantage or by creating entirely new industries.[5] For example, when Lindsay Owens-Jones was running L'Oreal's U.S. division in the early 1980s, he was told by colleagues that European brands like Lancôme could never compete with established U.S. brands. Owens-Jones refused to accept that, and his strategic decisions changed the whole face of U.S. cosmetics counters. Today, as CEO, Owens-Jones is aggressively promoting L'Oreal's brands globally, gaining huge market share in Asia, Africa, and other parts of the world.[6]

In this chapter, we focus on the topic of strategic management. First we define components of strategic management and then discuss a model of the strategic management process. Next we examine several models of strategy formulation. Finally, we discuss the tools managers use to implement their strategic plans.

# Thinking Strategically

**strategic management**
The set of decisions and actions used to formulate and implement strategies that will provide a competitively superior fit between the organization and its environment so as to achieve organizational goals.

Chapter 7 provided an overview of the types of goals and plans that organizations use. In this chapter, we will explore **strategic management**, which is considered one specific type of planning. Strategic planning in for-profit business organizations typically pertains to competitive actions in the marketplace. In not-for-profit organizations such as the Red Cross, strategic planning pertains to events in the external environment. The final responsibility for strategy rests with top managers and the chief executive. For an organization to succeed, the CEO must be actively involved in making the tough choices and trade-offs that define and support strategy.[7] However, senior executives at such companies as General Electric, 3M, and Johnson & Johnson want middle- and low-level managers to think strategically.

Some companies also are finding ways to get front-line workers involved in strategic thinking and planning. Strategic thinking means to take the long-term view and to see the big picture, including the organization and the competitive environment, and to consider how they fit together. Understanding the strategy concept, the levels of strategy, and strategy formulation versus implementation is an important start toward strategic thinking.

## What Is Strategic Management?

Strategic management is the set of decisions and actions used to formulate and implement strategies that will provide a competitively superior fit between the organization and its environment so as to achieve organizational goals.[8] Managers ask questions such as, "What changes and trends are occurring in the competitive environment? Who are our customers? What products or services should we offer? How can we offer those products and services most efficiently?" Answers to these questions help managers make choices about how to position their organizations in the environment with respect to rival companies.[9] Superior organizational performance is not a matter of luck. It is determined by the choices that managers make. Top executives use strategic management to define an overall direction for the organization, which is the firm's grand strategy.

### CONCEPT CONNECTION

*Rivalry between hotels in Las Vegas is fierce! To compete, Mirage Hotel opened Cravings, a new $12 million buffet restaurant. Gone are the low-priced steam-warmed vats of lasagna; dinner is now $20.50 per person. Food is cooked fresh at individual stations, served up on small, stylish plates, and can be made to order. This restaurant transformation, designed by renowned designer Adam Tihany, is a part of the Mirage's **grand strategy of growth**. In the photo are chefs at the Cravings sweets station. The success of Mirage's plan to attract new customers was reflected recently by comments from two patrons, who drove over an hour to dine at Cravings, "I've eaten in so many buffets but I've never seen anything as beautiful as this."*

## Grand Strategy

**Grand strategy** is the general plan of major action by which a firm intends to achieve its long-term goals.[10] Grand strategies fall into three general categories: growth, stability, and retrenchment. A separate grand strategy can also be defined for global operations.

*Go to the ethical dilemma on page 298 that pertains to corporate grand strategy.*

*Take A Moment*

### Growth
*Growth* can be promoted internally by investing in expansion or externally by acquiring additional business divisions. Internal growth can include development of new or changed products, such as Frito Lay's introduction of baked Doritos, or expansion of current products into new markets, such as Avon's selling of products in mall kiosks. External growth typically involves *diversification*, which means the acquisition of businesses that are related to current product lines or that take the corporation into new areas. The number of companies choosing to grow through mergers and acquisitions in recent years has been astounding, as organizations strive to acquire the size and resources to compete on a global scale, to invest in new technology, and to control distribution channels and guarantee access to markets. For example, Citibank and Travelers merged to form Citigroup, which has now acquired Sears' credit card portfolio to become the nation's largest private label credit card issuer. Boeing Co. acquired McDonnell Douglas, to move more aggressively into defense contracting, and Hughes Electronics Corp.'s Space & Communications Division to tap into growth opportunities in space travel.[11] This chapter's Unlocking Creative Solutions Through Technology box describes how eBay is pursuing a growth strategy.

**grand strategy**
The general plan of major action by which an organization intends to achieve its long-term goals.

# Unlocking Creative Solutions Through Technology

## EBay: Building on Success

At a time when almost every Internet and technology company was handing out pink slips, the scene was quite different within the walls of San Jose, California-based eBay. In fact, the online auction company kept adding to its workforce during the downturn. EBay, which began as a site for selling collectibles and attic trash, is pursuing a growth strategy, successfully molding itself into a new kind of enterprise—a whole online community where 30 million people buy and sell more than $20 billion in merchandise, everything from computers to cosmetics. More used cars sell on eBay than the No. 1 U.S. auto dealer. The company has its own police force to patrol listings for fraud, an educational system that holds classes around the country to teach people how to buy and sell on the site, and even something like its own bank.

There are several elements to CEO Meg Whitman's strategic plan for growth. First, to branch out from its auction format, the company purchased Half.com, a site where new and used items can be listed at a fixed price. Then it added the "Buy It Now" feature, which allows users to acquire an item immediately, omitting the time-consuming auction process altogether. At least 35 percent of all items listed by sellers on eBay now offer that option, which speeds up the rate of trading on the site. To get its online car market going, eBay bought a collector-car auction company, Kruse International, and partnered with AutoTrader.com to list its classifieds. The company also acquired payment processor PayPal, which enables people to make electronic payments to sellers who don't have a merchant credit-card account. EBay is also on a global expansion binge, acquiring trading sites in Canada, Britain, Germany, Korea, and China since 2000.

Another growth strategy has been to allow businesses such as JCPenney, IBM, and Sears to set up virtual storefronts. EBay expected to attract around 2,000 businesses, but nearly 10 times that number wanted a piece of the action, recognizing the inexpensive potential for reaching millions of consumers. The most recent element of eBay's growth plan is selling information. Companies such as PGA of America and Intuit use eBay data to show the market value of items or help taxpayers estimate the value of charitable donations on their IRS forms. With auctions closing every minute on eBay's site, the company can provide real-time market information. Although managers don't expect this new part of the business to be an instant moneymaker, selling data will likely become an important part of eBay's business in future years.

As one manager of a struggling dot-com said, "eBay is what all of us wanted our Internet businesses to be." As eBay continues its astounding growth, no one seems to know just how far it can go. "We don't actually control this," Whitman admits. "We have a unique partner—millions of people."

**SOURCES:** Robert D. Hof, "The eBay Economy," *BusinessWeek* (August 25, 2003), 124+; Nick Wingfield, "At eBay, Even Sales Prices Are For Sale," *The Wall Street Journal* (December 8, 2003), B1, B7; and Miguel Helft, "What Makes eBay Unstoppable?" *The Industry Standard* (August 6-13, 2001), 32–37.

## Stability

*Stability*, sometimes called a *pause strategy*, means that the organization wants to remain the same size or grow slowly and in a controlled fashion. The corporation wants to stay in its current business, such as Allied Tire Stores, whose motto is, "We just sell tires." After organizations have undergone a turbulent period of rapid growth, executives often focus on a stability strategy to integrate strategic business units and ensure that the organization is working efficiently. Mattel is currently pursuing a stability strategy to recover from former CEO Jill Barad's years of big acquisitions and new businesses. The current top executive is seeking only modest new ventures to get Mattel on a slower-growth, more stable course.[12]

## Retrenchment

*Retrenchment* means that the organization goes through a period of forced decline by either shrinking current business units or selling off or liquidating entire businesses.

The organization may have experienced a precipitous drop in demand for its products or services, prompting managers to order across-the-board cuts in personnel and expenditures. For example, in the early 2000s, Nortel Networks, described in Chapter 3, laid off more than 40,000 employees, shut down several divisions, and closed dozens of plants and offices to cope with reduced demand. Gaylord Entertainment, a Nashville-based entertainment company that traces its roots to the Grand Ole Opry, had counted on digital entertainment as a growth business, but just two years later managers closed the Gaylord Digital subsidiary, cut jobs, and put the company's Web business up for sale. Top executives felt that a period of retrenchment was necessary to strengthen profitability across the company.[13]

*Liquidation* means selling off a business unit for the cash value of the assets, thus terminating its existence. An example is the liquidation of Minnie Pearl Fried Chicken. *Divestiture* involves the selling off of businesses that no longer seem central to the corporation. JCPenney recently sold its Eckerd chain of drugstores to focus on the corporation's core business of department stores and Internet and catalog sales. Studies show that between 33 percent and 50 percent of all acquisitions are later divested. When Figgies International Inc. sold 15 of its 22 business divisions, including crown jewel Rawlings Sporting Goods, and when Italy's Fiat sold its aerospace unit, both corporations were going through periods of retrenchment, also called *downsizing*.[14]

## Global Strategy

In addition to the three preceding alternatives—growth, stability, and retrenchment—companies may pursue a separate grand strategy as the focus of global business. In today's global corporations, senior executives try to formulate coherent strategies to provide synergy among worldwide operations for the purpose of fulfilling common goals. A systematic strategic planning process for deciding on the appropriate strategic alternative should be used. The grand strategy of growth is a major motivation for both small and large businesses going international. Each country or region represents a new market with the promise of increased sales and profits.

In the international arena, companies face a strategic dilemma between global integration and national responsiveness. The various global strategies are shown in Exhibit 8.1. As we discussed in Chapter 4, the first step toward a greater international presence is when companies begin exporting domestically produced products to selected countries. Because the organization is domestically focused, with only a few exports, managers have little need to pay attention to issues of either local responsiveness or global integration. Organizations that pursue further international expansion must decide whether they want each global affiliate to act autonomously or whether activities should be standardized and centralized across countries. This choice leads managers to select a basic grand strategy alternative such as globalization versus multidomestic strategy. Some corporations may seek to achieve both global integration and national responsiveness by using a transnational strategy.

### Globalization

When an organization chooses a strategy of **globalization**, it means that its product design and advertising strategies are standardized throughout the world.[15] This approach is based on the assumption that a single global market exists for many consumer and industrial products. The theory is that people everywhere want to buy the same products and live the same way. People everywhere want to drink Coca-Cola and eat McDonald's hamburgers.[16] A globalization strategy can help an organization reap efficiencies by standardizing product design and manufacturing,

**globalization**
The standardization of product design and advertising strategies throughout the world.

# Exhibit 8.1

## Global Corporate Strategies

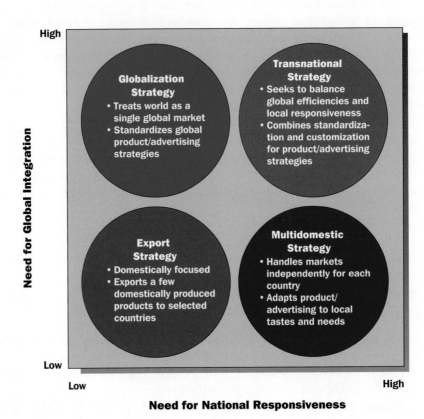

High

**Need for Global Integration**

**Globalization Strategy**
• Treats world as a single global market
• Standardizes global product/advertising strategies

**Transnational Strategy**
• Seeks to balance global efficiencies and local responsiveness
• Combines standardization and customization for product/advertising strategies

**Export Strategy**
• Domestically focused
• Exports a few domestically produced products to selected countries

**Multidomestic Strategy**
• Handles markets independently for each country
• Adapts product/advertising to local tastes and needs

Low

Low                                          High

**Need for National Responsiveness**

**SOURCES:** Based on Michael A. Hitt, R. Duane Ireland, and Robert E. Hoskisson, *Strategic Management: Competitiveness and Globalization* (St. Paul, Minn.; West, 1995), 239; and Thomas M. Begley and David P. Boyd, "The Need for a Corporate Global Mindset," *MIT Sloan Management Review* (Winter 2003), 25–32.

using common suppliers, introducing products around the world faster, coordinating prices, and eliminating overlapping facilities. Ford Motor Company's Ford 2000 initiative built a single global automotive operation. By sharing technology, design, suppliers, and manufacturing standards worldwide, Ford saved $5 billion during the first three years.[17] Similarly, Gillette Company, which makes grooming products such as the Mach3 for men and the Venus razor for women, has large production facilities that use common suppliers and processes to manufacture products whose technical specifications are standardized around the world.[18]

Globalization enables marketing departments alone to save millions of dollars. Colgate-Palmolive Company sells Colgate toothpaste in more than 40 countries. For every country where the same commercial runs, it saves $1 million to $2 million in production costs alone. More millions have been saved by standardizing the look and packaging of brands.[19]

## Multidomestic Strategy

**multidomestic strategy**
The modification of product design and advertising strategies to suit the specific needs of individual countries.

When an organization chooses a **multidomestic strategy**, it means that competition in each country is handled independently of industry competition in other countries. Thus, a multinational company is present in many countries, but it encourages marketing, advertising, and product design to be modified and adapted to the specific needs of each country.[20] Many companies reject the idea of a single global market. They have found that the French do not drink orange juice for breakfast, that laundry detergent is used to wash dishes in parts of Mexico, and that people in the Middle East prefer toothpaste that tastes spicy. Service companies also

**CONCEPT CONNECTION**

*These KitKat candy bars, being stocked by a salesperson in a Malaysian shop, are manufactured with locally grown cocoa beans—at a price 30 percent below imports. Nestlé, the world's biggest branded food company, rejects the idea of a single global market, opting for a **multidomestic strategy** that handles competition in each country independently. The Switzerland-based powerhouse is charging across the developing world by hiring people in the region, manipulating ingredients or technology for local conditions, and slapping on one of the company's 8,000 brand names. Of those 8,000 worldwide brands, only 750 are registered in more than one country.*

have to carefully consider their global strategy. The 7-Eleven convenience store chain uses a multidomestic strategy because the product mix, advertising approach, and payment methods need to be tailored to the preferences, values, and government regulations in different parts of the world. For example, credit card use is rare in Japan and Germany. In Japan, customers like to use convenience stores to pay utility and other bills. 7-Eleven Japan also set up a way for people to pick up and pay for purchases made over the Internet at their local 7-Elevens.[21]

## Transnational Strategy

A **transnational strategy** seeks to achieve both global integration and national responsiveness.[22] A true transnational strategy is difficult to achieve, because one goal requires close global coordination while the other goal requires local flexibility. However, many industries are finding that, although increased competition means they must achieve global efficiency, growing pressure to meet local needs demands national responsiveness.[23] One company that effectively uses a transnational strategy is Caterpillar, Inc., a heavy equipment manufacturer. Caterpillar achieves global efficiencies by designing its products to use many identical components and centralizing manufacturing of components in a few large-scale facilities. However, assembly plants located in each of Caterpillar's major markets add certain product features tailored to meet local needs.[24]

Although most multinational companies want to achieve some degree of global integration to hold costs down, even global products may require some customization to meet government regulations in various countries or some tailoring to fit consumer preferences. In addition, some products are better suited for standardization than others. Most large multinational corporations with diverse products and services will attempt to use a partial multidomestic strategy for some product or service lines and global strategies for others. Coordinating global integration with a responsiveness to the heterogeneity of international markets is a difficult balancing act for managers, but is increasingly important in today's global business world.

## Purpose of Strategy

Within the overall grand strategy of an organization, executives define an explicit **strategy**, which is the plan of action that describes resource allocation and activities for dealing with the environment, achieving a competitive advantage, and attaining

**transnational strategy**
A strategy that combines global coordination to attain efficiency with flexibility to meet specific needs in various countries.

**strategy**
The plan of action that prescribes resource allocation and other activities for dealing with the environment, achieving a competitive advantage, and attaining organizational goals.

the organization's goals. **Competitive advantage** refers to what sets the organization apart from others and provides it with a distinctive edge for meeting customer needs in the marketplace. The essence of formulating strategy is choosing how the organization will be different.[25] Managers make decisions about whether the company will perform different activities or will execute similar activities differently than competitors do. Strategy necessarily changes over time to fit environmental conditions, but to remain competitive, companies develop strategies that focus on core competencies, develop synergy, and create value for customers.

## Core Competence

A company's **core competence** is something the organization does especially well in comparison to its competitors. A core competence represents a competitive advantage because the company acquires expertise that competitors do not have. A core competence may be in the area of superior research and development, expert technological know-how, process efficiency, or exceptional customer service.[26] At Amgen, a pharmaceutical company, strategy focuses on the company's core competence of high-quality scientific research. Rather than starting with a specific disease and working backward, Amgen takes brilliant science and finds unique uses for it.[27] The Home Depot thrives because of a strategy focused on superior customer service. Managers stress to all employees that listening to customers and helping them solve their do-it-yourself worries takes precedence over just making a sale.[28] In each case, leaders identified what their company does particularly well and built strategy around it. Dell Computer has succeeded with its core competencies of speed and cost efficiency.

Dell Computer is constantly changing, adapting, and finding new ways to master its environment, but one thing hasn't changed since the days Michael Dell first began building computers in his dorm room: the focus on speed and low cost. A major factor in Dell's success is that it has retained a clear image of what it does best. The company spent years developing a core competence in low cost and speedy delivery by squeezing time lags and inefficiencies out of the manufacturing and assembly process, then extending the same brutal standards to the supply chain. Good relationships with a few key suppliers and precise coordination mean that Dell can sometimes receive parts in minutes rather than days.

Consider how the system works at the Topfer Manufacturing Center, the newest of Dell's seven plants. Inside the cavernous factory, located near Dell's headquarters in Round Rock, Texas, parts storage takes up about the space of an average bedroom. The factory is a blur of activity. Boxes of microchips and electronic components skitter by on double-decker conveyor belts. Assembly workers use an integrated computer system that practically hands them the right part—whether it be any of a dozen different microprocessors or a combination of software—at just the right time. The system not only cuts costs, but also saves time by decreasing the number of worker touches per machine. On a typical day, 25,000 finished computers head off toward happy customers. Dell's system offers completely transparent information about sales, orders, shipments, and other data to employees, customers, and suppliers. Precise coordination, aided by sophisticated supply-chain software, means Dell can keep just two hours' worth of parts inventory and replenish only what it needs throughout the day. The just-in-time system works so smoothly that nearly 85 percent of orders are built, customized, and shipped within eight hours.

Dell's fixation with speed and thrift is being challenged as the company moves into new areas of business, such as storage systems, networking gear, and information services. However, founder and chairman Michael Dell believes the core competencies that made Dell a star in PCs and servers can also make the company a winner as it seizes new opportunities. To anyone who doubts that Dell can compete in new markets, he says, "Bring them on. We're coming right at them." [29]

## Synergy

When organizational parts interact to produce a joint effect that is greater than the sum of the parts acting alone, **synergy** occurs. The organization may attain a special advantage with respect to cost, market power, technology, or management skill. When properly managed, synergy can create additional value with existing resources, providing a big boost to the bottom line.[30] FedEx hopes to achieve synergy with its recent acquisition of Kinko's Inc. Kinko's document delivery and office services complement FedEx's package delivery and give FedEx a greater presence among small and mid-sized businesses, a market it has long coveted. By providing full-service counters in Kinko's stores, FedEx also has the potential to double its locations over the next few years, particularly overseas, where Kinko's has centers in eight countries.[31]

Synergy can also be obtained by good relations with suppliers, as at Dell Computer, or by strong alliances among companies. Sweden's appliance giant Electrolux partnered with Ericsson, the Swedish telecommunications giant, in a joint venture called *e2 Home* to create a new way to make and sell appliances. Together, Electrolux and Ericsson are offering products such as the Screenfridge, a refrigerator with Internet connections that enables users to check traffic conditions, order take-out, or buy groceries, and an experimental *pay-per-use* washing machine. Neither company could have offered these revolutionary products on its own. "The technology was there, the appliances were there, but we needed a way to connect those two elements—to add value for consumers," said Per Grunewald, e2 Home's president.[32]

> **synergy**
> The condition that exists when the organization's parts interact to produce a joint effect that is greater than the sum of the parts acting alone.

## Value Creation

Delivering value to the customer is at the heart of strategy. Value can be defined as the combination of benefits received and costs paid by the customer. Managers help their companies create value by devising strategies that exploit core competencies and attain synergy. The cable company Charter Communications is attempting to provide better value to customers to counter charges of excessive prices and to compete with the growing clout of satellite television companies. New *cable value packages* offer a combination of basic cable, digital premium channels, and high-speed Internet for a reduced cost. Laura Alber, president of Pottery Barn, uses the company's thick bath towels to illustrate the value Pottery Barn strives to deliver to customers: "For us, this represents a combination of design, quality, and price," Alber says. "If this were $60, you'd still like it. But at $24, you go, 'This is incredible.'"[33]

# Levels of Strategy

Another aspect of strategic management concerns the organizational level to which strategic issues apply. Strategic managers normally think in terms of three levels of strategy—corporate, business, and functional—as illustrated in Exhibit 8.2.[34]

## Corporate-Level Strategy

The question *"What business are we in?"* is the cornerstone of corporate-level strategy. **Corporate-level strategy** pertains to the organization as a whole and the combination of business units and product lines that make up the corporate entity. Strategic actions at this level usually relate to the acquisition of new businesses; additions or divestments of business units, plants, or product lines; and joint ventures with other corporations in new areas. An example of corporate-level strategy is Italy's Fiat Group, which is reversing a decade-long diversification trend to focus on reviving the auto business. After a record loss of

> **corporate-level strategy**
> The level of strategy concerned with the question "What business are we in?" Pertains to the organization as a whole and the combination of business units and product lines that make it up.

Exhibit 8.2

## Three Levels of Strategy in Organizations

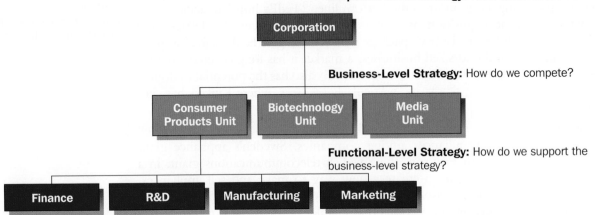

**Corporate-Level Strategy:** What business are we in?

Corporation

**Business-Level Strategy:** How do we compete?

Consumer Products Unit | Biotechnology Unit | Media Unit

**Functional-Level Strategy:** How do we support the business-level strategy?

Finance | R&D | Manufacturing | Marketing

COURTESY OF MERCK & CO., INC.

### CONCEPT CONNECTION

*Merck has a **business-level strategy** of competing through product innovation. Merck researchers such as Amy Cheung and Thomas Rano, using advanced technology, are producing more new compounds in less time than has ever been possible. Merck spends more than $2 billion on research and development and uses every means possible to reduce by months the drug discovery, development, and application processes. Merck maintains a competitive edge by having innovative products in many therapeutic categories for human and animal health.*

$4.5 billion in 2002, managers made a strategic choice to get out of other businesses and focus everything on reviving the auto division. In addition to selling off units such as insurer Toro Assicurazioni and the Fiat aerospace unit, Fiat is increasing R&D spending for new auto models, including new Alfa Romeos for the U.S. market, expanding its dealer network, and negotiating a joint venture with General Motors to build the next-generation Fiat Punto on a joint platform with GM's Corsa. The joint venture could mean savings of $1 billion for each partner in 2005 and a potential for future platform sharing.[35]

### Business-Level Strategy

The question *"How do we compete?"* is the focus of business-level strategy. **Business-level strategy** pertains to each business unit or product line. It focuses on how the business unit competes within its industry for customers. Many companies have opened e-commerce units as a part of business-level strategy. For example, Hallmark's Web site is a marketing vehicle for the company's products and retail stores, as well as a place to sell gifts and flowers online.[36]

Strategic decisions at the business level concern amount of advertising, direction and extent of research and development, product changes, new-product development, equipment and facilities, and expansion or contraction of product lines. Consider how top managers at JCPenney hope to revive the department store's image and sales with a new business-level strategy.

Will Sharon Stone and Britney Spears soon be shopping at JCPenney? If they want to keep wearing Bisou Bisou, a line of sexy clothes formerly sold in chic boutiques, they will. Since JCPenney signed an exclusive deal with designer Michele Bohbot and her marketing husband Marc, it will be the nation's only distributor of the trendy Bisou Bisou line.

JCPenney's CEO Allen Questrom, the first outsider head in the company's 101-year history, likes fashion—and he believes his customer do, too, even if they can't afford to shop at Saks. The Bisou Bisou deal rocked the fashion world, but Questrom is just getting started. He wants to shift the product mix at Penney's department stores to cater more toward 25-to 35-year old women, a group that spends almost $15 billion a year on clothes. JCPenney is in talks with several other major designers for exclusive lines and has also recruited new designers to freshen its private label brands. Questrom hired trend watcher David Hacker to keep tabs on what's hot and what's not. Hacker watches MTV in his office, sends designers to Avril Lavigne concerts, and jets off to Europe to scan the fashion runways to make sure JCPenney is ready to stock the next hot color or trendy style.

Other parts of the new business-level strategy include a makeover of Penney's stodgy-looking department stores and a renewed emphasis on marketing. Michael Cape, the new, young director of visual merchandise and store design, says that less than 10 percent of the stores are currently where he'd like them to be. His job is to make sure the store's visual appearance reflects that "this is not your granny's store anymore."[37]

JCPENNEY
http://jcpenney.com

JCPenney's new business-level strategy is getting the company noticed. Magazines such as *Cosmopolitan* and *In Style* have featured Penney's affordable merchandise alongside designer labels, and fashion shows at JCPenney stores have attracted large audiences. Questrom and other top managers believe the strategy will help them find a profitable niche squeezed somewhere between Wal-Mart's low prices and the trendiness of more expensive retailers.

**business-level strategy**
The level of strategy concerned with the question "How do we compete?" Pertains to each business unit or product line within the organization.

### Functional-Level Strategy

The question *"How do we support the business-level competitive strategy?"* is the concern of **functional-level strategy**. It pertains to the major functional departments within the business unit. Functional strategies involve all of the major functions, including finance, research and development, marketing, and manufacturing. The functional-level strategy for JCPenney's marketing department, for example, is to create a cutting-edge advertising campaign that will appeal to younger consumers and present the company as a chic place to shop. Another example of functional-level strategy is Procter & Gamble's research and development department, which invests heavily in developing new formulations of popular products. This strategy helps P&G stay competitive in the slow-growing consumer products industry by bringing out fresh versions of old favorites, such as Tide Free, Tide WearCare, and TideKick.[38]

**functional-level strategy**
The level of strategy concerned with the question "How do we support the business-level strategy?" Pertains to all of the organization's major departments.

# The Strategic Management Process

The overall strategic management process is illustrated in Exhibit 8.3. It begins when executives evaluate their current position with respect to mission, goals, and strategies. They then scan the organization's internal and external environments and identify strategic factors that might require change. Internal or external events might indicate a need to redefine the mission or goals or to formulate a new strategy at either the corporate, business, or functional level. The final stage in the strategic management process is implementation of the new strategy.

Exhibit 8.3

## The Strategic Management Process

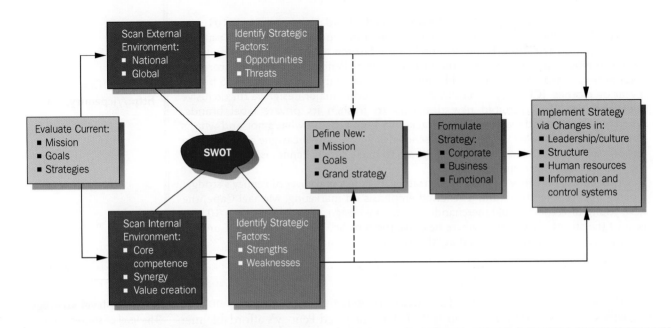

## Strategy Formulation versus Implementation

**strategy formulation**
The stage of strategic management that involves the planning and decision making that lead to the establishment of the organization's goals and of a specific strategic plan.

Strategy formulation includes the planning and decision making that lead to the establishment of the firm's goals and the development of a specific strategic plan.[39] **Strategy formulation** may include assessing the external environment and internal problems and integrating the results into goals and strategy. This is in contrast to **strategy implementation**, which is the use of managerial and organizational tools to direct resources toward accomplishing strategic results.[40] Strategy implementation is the administration and execution of the strategic plan. Managers may use persuasion, new equipment, changes in organization structure, or a revised reward system to ensure that employees and resources are used to make formulated strategy a reality.

*Take A Moment*

*Go to the experiential exercise on page 297 that pertains to strategy formulation and implementation.*

## Situation Analysis

**strategy implementation**
The stage of strategic management that involves the use of managerial and organizational tools to direct resources toward achieving strategic outcomes.

**situation analysis**
Analysis of the strengths, weaknesses, opportunities, and threats (SWOT) that affect organizational performance.

Formulating strategy often begins with an assessment of the internal and external factors that will affect the organization's competitive situation. **Situation analysis** typically includes a search for SWOT—strengths, weaknesses, opportunities, and threats that affect organizational performance. Situation analysis is important to all companies but is crucial to those considering globalization because of the diverse environments in which they will operate. External information about opportunities and threats may be obtained from a variety of sources, including customers, government reports, professional journals, suppliers, bankers, friends in other organizations, consultants, or association meetings. Many firms hire special scanning organizations to provide them with newspaper clippings, Internet research, and analyses of relevant domestic and global trends. In addition, many companies are hiring competitive intelligence professionals to scope out competitors, as we discussed in Chapter 3.

Executives acquire information about internal strengths and weaknesses from a variety of reports, including budgets, financial ratios, profit and loss statements, and surveys of employee attitudes and satisfaction. Managers spend 80 percent of their time giving and receiving information. Through frequent face-to-face discussions and meetings with people at all levels of the hierarchy, executives build an understanding of the company's internal strengths and weaknesses.

## Internal Strengths and Weaknesses

*Strengths* are positive internal characteristics that the organization can exploit to achieve its strategic performance goals. *Weaknesses* are internal characteristics that might inhibit or restrict the organization's performance. Some examples of what executives evaluate to interpret strengths and weaknesses are given in Exhibit 8.4. The information sought typically pertains to specific functions such as marketing, finance, production, and R&D. Internal analysis also examines overall organization structure, management competence and quality, and human resource characteristics. Based on their understanding of these areas, managers can determine their strengths or weaknesses vis-à-vis other companies.

## External Opportunities and Threats

*Threats* are characteristics of the external environment that may prevent the organization from achieving its strategic goals. *Opportunities* are characteristics of the external environment that have the potential to help the organization achieve or exceed its strategic goals. Executives evaluate the external environment with information about the nine sectors described in Chapter 3. The task environment sectors are the most relevant to strategic behavior and include the behavior of competitors, customers, suppliers, and the

© ATEF HASSAN/CORBIS

**CONCEPT CONNECTION**

*The effects of this oil fire in Iraq are being felt thousands of miles away—in the executive suites at companies such as United Airlines, the number 2 air carrier in the United States. Uncertainty about oil supplies is a significant **external threat** to the nation's airlines. Other threats United faces as it struggles to recover from bankruptcy are customers' continuing fear of terrorism and stiff competition from low-cost carriers like Jet Blue.*

## Exhibit 8.4

### Checklist for Analyzing Organizational Strengths and Weaknesses

| Management and Organization | Marketing | Human Resources |
|---|---|---|
| Management quality | Distribution channels | Employee experience, education |
| Staff quality | Market share | |
| Degree of Centralization | Advertising efficiency | Union status |
| Organization charts | Customer satisfaction | Turnover, absenteeism |
| Planning, information, control systems | Product quality | Work satisfaction |
| | Service reputation | Grievances |
| | Sales force turnover | |

| Finance | Production | Research and Development |
|---|---|---|
| Profit margin | Plant location | Basic applied research |
| Debt-equity ratio | Machinery obsolescence | Laboratory capabilities |
| Inventory ratio | Purchasing system | Research programs |
| Return on investment | Quality control | New-product innovations |
| Credit rating | Productivity/efficiency | Technology innovations |

labor supply. The general environment contains those sectors that have an indirect influence on the organization but nevertheless must be understood and incorporated into strategic behavior. The general environment includes technological developments, the economy, legal-political and international events, and sociocultural changes. Additional areas that might reveal opportunities or threats include pressure groups, interest groups, creditors, natural resources, and potentially competitive industries.

The *Milwaukee Journal Sentinel* used SWOT analysis to formulate a strategy to compete with new rivals in a low-growth metropolitan area hard hit by the manufacturing recession.[41] Careful analysis of strengths, weaknesses, threats, and opportunities forced managers to recognize that the newspaper needed to develop a strategy that enabled it to both run extremely efficient operations as well as find ways to truly distinguish the paper from any other source of news and information in Milwaukee. As a result, the *Journal Sentinel* has become a stronger, more flexible organization and the paper and its associated Web sites are clearly the leading source of news and information in the region. Quality, reader satisfaction, and profitability all improved as a result of the new strategy.

Kraft Foods provides another example of how situation analysis can be used to help executives formulate the correct strategy.

**KRAFT FOODS**
http://www.kraft.com

Kraft has some of the most recognizable brand names in the grocery store, but the giant food company has been facing some difficult challenges in recent years. To get things back on track, managers are evaluating the company by looking at strengths, weaknesses, opportunities, and threats (SWOT).

Kraft's greatest *strengths* are its powerful brands, its positive reputation, its track record as an innovator, and a well-funded R&D budget. Its biggest *weaknesses* include the loss of top management talent in recent years, a sluggish response to environmental changes, and declining market share and profits.

Several major *threats* have been building for a couple of years. The first is that less-expensive, private-label brands are successfully stealing market share from Kraft's core brands such as Kraft Singles cheese slices, Maxwell House coffee, Oscar Mayer cold cuts, and Ritz crackers. At the same time, other major food companies have been quicker to respond to growing consumer demands for less fattening, more healthful food choices. PepsiCo, for example, began cutting trans-fats from Doritos, Tostitos, and Cheetos, and saw sales increase by 28 percent. A third threat to Kraft is that more people are eating ready-made lunches rather than consuming home-prepared lunch foods such as sandwiches made of cheese and cold cuts. Kraft managers recognize *opportunities* in the environment, as well, however. Trends show that Americans are looking for more snack foods and comfort foods, which presents a golden opportunity for Kraft, whose name for many Americans is almost synonymous with comfort food.

What does SWOT analysis suggest for Kraft's future strategy? Kraft managers will try to capitalize on the company's strengths by investing research dollars to develop healthier snack and pre-packaged lunch foods, such as lower-fat versions of its popular "Lunchables." To bolster core brands, Kraft has pumped an additional $200 million into its multi-billion dollar marketing and advertising budget. Managers are also exploring new vending opportunities for giant Kraft-branded machines that churn out ready-made food at movie-theaters, shopping malls, and other public venues.[42]

# Formulating Corporate-Level Strategy

**portfolio strategy**
The organization's mix of SBUs and product lines that fit together in such a way as to provide the corporation with synergy and competitive advantage.

## Portfolio Strategy

**Portfolio strategy** pertains to the mix of business units and product lines that fit together in a logical way to provide synergy and competitive advantage for the corporation. For example, an individual might wish to diversify in an investment portfolio with some high-risk stocks, some low-risk stocks, some growth stocks, and perhaps a few income bonds. In much the same way, corporations like to have a balanced mix of business divisions called **strategic business units (SBUs)**. An SBU has a unique business mission, product line, competitors, and markets relative to other SBUs in the corporation.[43] Executives in charge of the entire corporation generally define the grand strategy and then bring together a portfolio of strategic business units to carry it out. Managers don't like to become too dependent on one business. For example, at United Technologies Corp. (UTC), the aerospace-related business units are struggling through one of the worst slumps in history. However, UTC's Otis Elevator division is keeping the corporation's sales and profits strong. Otis has a commanding share of the worldwide market for new elevators and escalators. In addition, the unit provides a steady revenue stream from elevator maintenance, repair, and upgrade. The elevators in the Waldorf-Astoria, for example, were installed in 1931 and have been steadily upgraded by Otis ever since.[44] One useful way to think about portfolio strategy is the BCG matrix.

**strategic business unit (SBU)**
A division of the organization that has a unique business mission, product line, competitors, and markets relative to other SBUs in the same corporation.

## The BCG Matrix

The BCG (for Boston Consulting Group) matrix is illustrated in Exhibit 8.5. The **BCG matrix** organizes businesses along two dimensions—business growth rate and market share.[45] *Business growth rate* pertains to how rapidly the entire industry is increasing. *Market share* defines whether a business unit has a larger or smaller share than competitors. The combinations of high and low market share and high and low business growth provide four categories for a corporate portfolio.

The *star* has a large market share in a rapidly growing industry. The star is important because it has additional growth potential, and profits should be plowed into

**BCG matrix**
A concept developed by the Boston Consulting Group that evaluates SBUs with respect to the dimensions of business growth rate and market share.

Exhibit 8.5

**The BCG Matrix**

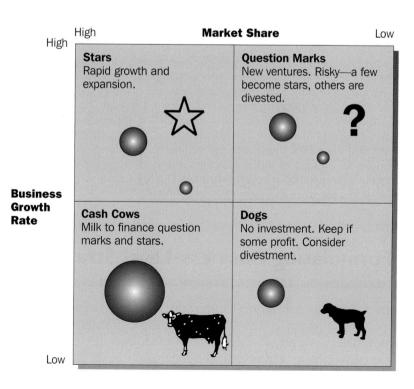

this business as investment for future growth and profits. The star is visible and attractive and will generate profits and a positive cash flow even as the industry matures and market growth slows.

The *cash cow* exists in a mature, slow-growth industry but is a dominant business in the industry, with a large market share. Because heavy investments in advertising and plant expansion are no longer required, the corporation earns a positive cash flow. It can milk the cash cow to invest in other, riskier businesses.

The *question mark* exists in a new, rapidly growing industry, but has only a small market share. The question mark business is risky: it could become a star, or it could fail. The corporation can invest the cash earned from cash cows in question marks with the goal of nurturing them into future stars.

The *dog* is a poor performer. It has only a small share of a slow-growth market. The dog provides little profit for the corporation and may be targeted for divestment or liquidation if turnaround is not possible.

The circles in Exhibit 8.5 represent the business portfolio for a hypothetical corporation. Circle size represents the relative size of each business in the company's portfolio. Most organizations, such as Gillette, have businesses in more than one quadrant, thereby representing different market shares and growth rates.

GILLETTE
COMPANY
http://www.gillette.com

The most famous cash cow in Gillette's portfolio is the shaving division, which accounts for more than half of the company's profits and holds a large share of a stable market. Gillette's razors and blades hold a commanding 74 percent share of the worldwide market. The oral care division has star status, and Gillette is pumping money into development of new electric toothbrushes and other products. Oral-B toothbrushes, dental floss, and other dental care items will soon be joined by tooth whitening products once Gillette's purchase of the Rembrandt line is completed.

The Duracell division is still a question mark, although sales in early 2004 were growing. When Gillette purchased the division in 1996, it hoped Duracell would be a vehicle for rapid growth, becoming a star and eventually as big a cash cow as razors and blades. However, the heavy investment in batteries has not yet paid off. Rivals Energizer and Rayovac have pummeled Duracell's new high-priced, long-lasting batteries with price cuts and special promotions. Until recently, Duracell has been a serious drain on company profits.

Gillette's personal care division is also a question mark. A line of women's toiletries aimed at the European market failed, and products such as Right Guard and Soft & Dri deodorant have enjoyed only cyclical success. A new line of men's toiletries, including a gel-based deodorant, a gel shaving cream, and a new body wash, has had only limited success. Some critics believe the division is a dog, but Gillette is still trying to come up with some new products to save it from the fate of the Cricket disposable lighter several years ago. Bic dominated the disposable lighter line so completely that Gillette had to recognize Cricket as a dog and put it out of its misery through liquidation. Gillette is investing heavily in its question marks, particularly Duracell, to ensure that its portfolio will continue to include stars and cash cows in the future.[46]

# Formulating Business-Level Strategy

Now we turn to strategy formulation within the strategic business unit, in which the concern is how to compete. The same three generic strategies—growth, stability, and retrenchment—apply at the business level, but they are accomplished through competitive actions rather than the acquisition or divestment of business divisions. One model for formulating strategy is Porter's competitive strategies, which provides a framework for business unit competitive action.

## Porter's Competitive Forces and Strategies

Michael E. Porter studied a number of business organizations and proposed that business-level strategies are the result of five competitive forces in the company's environment.[47] More recently, Porter has examined the impact of the Internet on business-level strategy.[48] New Web-based technology is influencing industries in both positive and negative ways, and understanding this impact is essential for managers to accurately analyze their competitive environments and design appropriate strategic actions.

### Five Competitive Forces

Exhibit 8.6 illustrates the competitive forces that exist in a company's environment and indicates some ways Internet technology is affecting each area. These forces help determine a company's position vis-à-vis competitors in the industry environment.

1. *Potential new entrants.* Capital requirements and economies of scale are examples of two potential barriers to entry that can keep out new competitors. It is far more costly to enter the automobile industry, for instance, than to start a specialized mail-order business. In general, Internet technology has made it much easier for new companies to enter an industry by curtailing the need for such

---

## Exhibit 8.6

### Porter's Five Forces Affecting Industry Competition

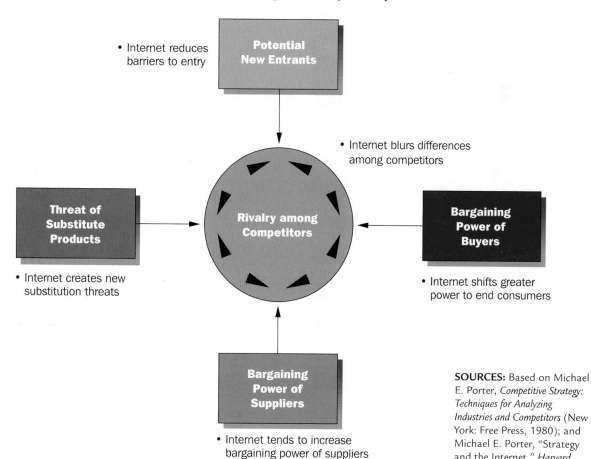

- Internet reduces barriers to entry
- Internet blurs differences among competitors
- Internet creates new substitution threats
- Internet shifts greater power to end consumers
- Internet tends to increase bargaining power of suppliers

**SOURCES:** Based on Michael E. Porter, *Competitive Strategy: Techniques for Analyzing Industries and Competitors* (New York: Free Press, 1980); and Michael E. Porter, "Strategy and the Internet," *Harvard Business Review* (March, 2001) 63–78.

organizational elements as an established sales force, physical assets such as buildings and machinery, or access to existing supplier and sales channels.

2. *Bargaining power of buyers.* Informed customers become empowered customers. The Internet provides easy access to a wide array of information about products, services, and competitors, thereby greatly increasing the bargaining power of end consumers. For example, a customer shopping for a car can gather extensive information about various options, such as wholesale prices for new cars or average value for used vehicles, detailed specifications, repair records, and even whether a used car has ever been involved in an accident.

3. Bargaining power of suppliers. The concentration of suppliers and the availability of substitute suppliers are significant factors in determining supplier power. The sole supplier of engines to a manufacturer of small airplanes will have great power, for example. The impact of the Internet in this area can be both positive and negative. That is, procurement over the Web tends to give a company greater power over suppliers, but the Web also gives suppliers access to a greater number of customers, as well as the ability to reach end users. Overall, the Internet tends to raise the bargaining power of suppliers.

4. *Threat of substitute products.* The power of alternatives and substitutes for a company's product may be affected by changes in cost or in trends such as increased health consciousness that will deflect buyer loyalty. Companies in the sugar industry suffered from the growth of sugar substitutes; manufacturers of aerosol spray cans lost business as environmentally conscious consumers chose other products. The Internet has created a greater threat of new substitutes by enabling new approaches to meeting customer needs. For example, traditional travel agencies have been hurt by the offering of low-cost airline tickets over the Internet.

5. *Rivalry among competitors.* As illustrated in Exhibit 8.6, rivalry among competitors is influenced by the preceding four forces, as well as by cost and product differentiation. With the leveling force of the Internet and information technology, it has become more difficult for many companies to find ways to distinguish themselves from their competitors, so rivalry has intensified.

LET'S SHOW THE WORLD WHAT MAKES US DIFFERENT.
Let's give our handling a name. Let's call it go-kart-like. Let's call it hairpin-ready. Let's call it turndiculous. Let's call it "whiptastic." Let's trademark it pronto. Let's stick it on the boot. Let's whip it. Let's whip it good. LET'S MOTOR.

COURTESY OF CRISPIN PORTER + BOGUSKY

**CONCEPT CONNECTION**

The MINI's trademarked term "Whiptastic Handling" is one of the ways the company distinguishes itself in the automobile industry. MINI, a division of BMW of North America, is thriving with its **differentiation strategy.** The company trademarked the Whiptastic name to emphasize that driving a MINI Cooper is unlike anything else. Customers seem to agree; sales are zooming.

Porter referred to the "advertising slugfest" when describing the scrambling and jockeying for position that often occurs among fierce rivals within an industry. Famous examples include the competitive rivalry between Pepsi and Coke, between UPS and FedEx, and between The Home Depot and Lowe's. The rivalry between Gillette, described earlier, and Schick, the No. 2 maker of razors, may soon be just as heated. Although Gillette is still way ahead, the introduction of the Schick Quattro and a massive advertising campaign helped Schick's sales grow 149 percent in 2004, while Gillette's razor sales slipped.[49] IBM and Oracle Corp. are currently involved in a fight for the No. 1 spot in the $50 billion corporate-software market. IBM rented a billboard near Oracle's headquarters proclaiming a "search for intelligent software." A few days later, Oracle fired the next shot with a competing billboard retorting, "Then you've come to the right place."[50]

## Competitive Strategies

In finding its competitive edge within these five forces, Porter suggests that a company can adopt one of three strategies: differentiation, cost leadership, and focus. Companies can use the Internet to support and strengthen the strategic approach they choose. The organizational characteristics typically associated with each strategy are summarized in Exhibit 8.7.

1. *Differentiation.* The **differentiation** strategy involves an attempt to distinguish the firm's products or services from others in the industry. The organization may use advertising, distinctive product features, exceptional service, or new technology to achieve a product perceived as unique. The differentiation strategy can be profitable because customers are loyal and will pay high prices for the product. Examples of products that have benefited from a differentiation strategy include Mercedes-Benz automobiles, Maytag appliances, and Tommy Hilfiger clothing, all of which are perceived as distinctive in their markets. Service companies can also use a differentiation strategy. For example, Washington Mutual Inc. has grown rapidly in the consumer banking industry by using a differentiation strategy. When the company moved into Chicago, it opened 28 branches on a single day, flooded the market with quirky advertising, and sent out employees with pizza delivery people, offering prospective customers "free pizza from the home of free banking."[51] The Harleysville Group uses its corporate culture to differentiate itself in the insurance industry, as described in this chapter's Unlocking Creative Solutions Through People box.

**differentiation**
A type of competitive strategy with which the organization seeks to distinguish its products or services from that of competitors.

Exhibit **8.7**

## Organizational Characteristics of Porter's Competitive Strategies

| Strategy | Organizational Characteristics |
|---|---|
| **Differentiation** | Acts in a flexible, loosely knit way, with strong coordination among departments<br>Strong capability in basic rewards<br>Creative flair, thinks "out of the box"<br>Strong marketing abilities<br>Rewards employee innovation<br>Corporate reputation for quality or technological leadership |
| **Cost Leadership** | Strong central authority; tight cost controls<br>Maintains standard operating procedures<br>Easy-to-use manufacturing technologies<br>Highly efficient procurement and distribution systems<br>Close supervision, finite employee empowerment |
| **Focus** | Frequent, detailed control reports<br>May use combination of above policies directed at particular strategic target<br>Values and rewards flexibility and customer intimacy<br>Measures cost of providing service and maintaining customer loyalty<br>Pushes empowerment to employees with customer contact |

**SOURCES:** Based on Michael E. Porter, *Competitive Strategy: Techniques for Analyzing Industries and Competitors* (New York: The Free Press: 1980); Michael Treacy and Fred Wiersema, "How Market Leaders Keep Their Edge," *Fortune*, February 6, 1995, 88–98; and Michael A. Hitt, R. Duane Ireland, and Robert E. Hoskisson, *Strategic Management* (St. Paul, Minn.: West, 1995), 100–113.

# Unlocking Creative Solutions Through People

## Happy Employees Want to Stay at the Harleysville Group

The Harleysville Group is not your average, run-of-the-mill insurance company, and employees as well as customers know it. At Harleysville, managers strive to provide their employees with an appealing atmosphere and plenty of perks. The goal is to create a work environment that makes people want to stay. They must be doing things right, because the Harleysville Group boasts a 95 percent retention rate over the past several years. That translates into experienced, knowledgeable employees who can provide top-quality service. Customers who have grown tired of working with companies where the staff is constantly changing can appreciate the difference that comes from working with people who are happy and knowledgeable.

Harleysville does plenty to keep employees happy. Besides an impressive vacation plan, extensive medical benefits, a cafeteria that serves freshly made food, and snack carts that go about the building selling coffee and pastries, the company also provides on-site ATMs and a clothes-cleaning service that includes pick-up and delivery. A massage therapist comes in once a week, and employees pay $10 for a 15-minute session, far below the market rate. The CEO pays for a 15-minute session each week and often gives it away to an employee as a way to say thanks for some extra effort. Two other, highly important perks are the company's project bonuses and matching 401(k) investments. It is not unusual for the company to hand out checks for $1,500 or $2,000 to reward people for excellent work on a team project. For the 401(k) plan, Harleysville will match an employee's contribution anywhere from 25 percent to 100 percent, depending on company performance. In the last four years, the company has matched contributions one-to-one. For example, if an employee put in $5,000, the company would add that amount.

Other perks are aimed at increasing employees' knowledge and career skills. Tech-savvy workers are critical to the Harleysville Group, so the company spends more than $600,000 every year in technical training for the IS department alone. And that doesn't include the corporate funding for employees who are taking college courses and working toward higher degrees. To make it even easier, the company brings community college professors to the company campus so employees can take some courses without having to travel at the end of their work day.

Harleysville refuses to pay sky-high salaries, but the extensive benefits and the people-friendly work environment help the company stand out in the insurance industry. Inevitably, some employees do leave, but it usually isn't for a $5,000 raise, notes CEO Wayne Ratz. "It's more for an extravagant opportunity or for a lifestyle change."

SOURCE: Erik Sherman, "Happy in Harleysville," *CIO* (October 15, 2000), 84–86.

Companies that pursue a differentiation strategy typically need strong marketing abilities, a creative flair, and a reputation for leadership.[52] A differentiation strategy can reduce rivalry with competitors if buyers are loyal to a company's brand. Successful differentiation can also reduce the bargaining power of large buyers because other products are less attractive, and this also helps the firm fight off threats of substitute products. In addition, differentiation erects entry barriers in the form of customer loyalty that a new entrant into the market would have difficulty overcoming. Consider the example of online company eBay, described earlier in the chapter. Rather than cutting prices when Amazon.com and other rivals entered the online auction business, eBay continued to focus on building a distinctive community, offering customers services and experiences they could not get on other sites. Customers stayed loyal to eBay rather than switch to low-cost rivals.

**cost leadership**
A type of competitive strategy with which the organization aggressively seeks efficient facilities, cuts costs, and employs tight cost controls to be more efficient than competitors.

2. *Cost leadership.* With a **cost leadership** strategy, the organization aggressively seeks efficient facilities, pursues cost reductions, and uses tight cost controls to produce products more efficiently than competitors. A low-cost position means that the company can undercut competitors' prices and still offer comparable quality and earn a reasonable profit. Comfort Inn and Motel 6 are low-priced

alternatives to Holiday Inn and Ramada Inn. Enterprise Rent-a-Car is a low-priced alternative to Hertz.

Being a low-cost producer provides a successful strategy to defend against the five competitive forces in Exhibit 8.6. For example, the most efficient, low-cost company is in the best position to succeed in a price war while still making a profit. Low-cost leader Dell Computer declared a brutal price war just as the PC industry entered its worst slump ever. The result? Dell racked up $361 million in profits while the rest of the industry reported losses of $1.1 billion. Likewise, the low-cost producer is protected from powerful customers and suppliers, because customers cannot find lower prices elsewhere, and other buyers would have less slack for price negotiation with suppliers. If substitute products or potential new entrants occur, the low-cost producer is better positioned than higher-cost rivals to prevent loss of market share. The low price acts as a barrier against new entrants and substitute products.[53]

3. *Focus.* With a **focus** strategy, the organization concentrates on a specific regional market or buyer group. The company will use either a differentiation or low-cost approach, but only for a narrow target market. Low-cost leader Southwest Airlines, for example, was founded in 1971 to serve only three cities—Dallas, Houston, and San Antonio—and didn't fly outside of Texas for the first eight years of its history. Managers aimed for controlled growth, gradually moving into new geographic areas where Southwest could provide short-haul service from city to city. By using a focus strategy, Southwest was able to grow rapidly and expand to other markets. It is now second only to Delta in domestic passenger share, even though it continues to operate primarily as a short-haul carrier.[54] Edward Jones Investments, a St. Louis-based brokerage house, uses a focused differentiation strategy, building its business in rural and small town America and providing clients with conservative, long-term investment advice. According to management consultant Peter Drucker, the safety-first orientation means Edward Jones delivers a product "that no Wall Street house has ever sold before: peace of mind."[55]

**focus**
A type of competitive strategy that emphasizes concentration on a specific regional market or buyer group.

Managers think carefully about which strategy will provide their company with its competitive advantage. Gibson Guitar Corp., famous in the music world for its innovative, high-quality products, found that switching to a low-cost strategy to compete against Japanese rivals such as Yamaha and Ibanez actually hurt the company. When managers realized people wanted Gibson products because of their reputation, not their price, they went back to a differentiation strategy and invested in new technology and marketing.[56] In his studies, Porter found that some businesses did not consciously adopt one of these three strategies and were stuck with no strategic advantage. Without a strategic advantage, businesses earned below-average profits compared with those that used differentiation, cost leadership, or focus strategies. Similarly, a recent five-year study of management practices in hundreds of businesses, referred to as the *Evergreen Project,* found that a clear strategic direction was a key factor that distinguished winners from losers.[57]

In addition, because the Internet is having such a profound impact on the competitive environment in all industries, it is more important than ever that companies distinguish themselves through careful strategic positioning in the marketplace.[58] The Internet tends to erode both cost-leadership and differentiation advantages by providing new tools for managing costs and giving consumers greater access to comparison shopping. However, managers can find ways to incorporate the Internet into their strategic approaches in a way that provides unique value to customers in an efficient way. Sears, for example, uses the Web to showcase it's line of Kenmore appliances, building the brand's reputation by providing detailed information in a relatively inexpensive way.[59]

**CONCEPT CONNECTION**

*The Walt Disney company has long been a believer in **partnership strategies**. Thanks to acquisitions, Disney is made up of numerous businesses such as a movie studio, the ABC Network, ESPN, the Disney Channel, other cable channels, and their popular theme parks. In 1996 Disney acquired CapCities ABC, and in 2001 they bought the Fox Family Channel for $5.2 billion.*

# Partnership Strategies

So far, we have been discussing strategies that are based on how to compete with other companies. An alternative approach to strategy emphasizes collaboration. In some situations, companies can achieve competitive advantage by cooperating with other firms rather than competing. Partnership strategies are becoming increasingly popular as firms in all industries join with other organizations to promote innovation, expand markets, and pursue joint goals. Partnering was once a strategy adopted primarily by small firms that needed greater marketing muscle or international access. Today, however, it has become a way of life for most companies, large and small. The question is no longer whether to collaborate, but rather where, how much, and with whom to collaborate.[60] Competition and cooperation often exist at the same time. Time Warner Cable, for instance, abruptly dropped Disney's ABC network in several major cities because of a dispute over fees for the Disney Channel. The companies engaged in all-out war that included front-page headlines and intervention of the Federal Communications Commission. This conflict, however, masked a simple fact: the two companies can't live without each other. Disney and Time Warner are wedded to one another in separate business deals around the world. Disney's ABC network, for example, is a major buyer of shows produced by Warner Brothers, while Time Warner's WB network carries Disney-produced programs. The two organizations will never let competition in one area upset their larger cooperation on a global scale.[61]

The Internet is both driving and supporting the move toward partnership thinking. The ability to rapidly and smoothly conduct transactions, communicate information, exchange ideas, and collaborate on complex projects via the Internet means that companies such as Citigroup, Dow Chemical, and Herman Miller have been able to enter entirely new businesses by partnering in business areas that were previously unimaginable.[62] Many companies, including Target, Circuit City, Land's End, and Golfsmith International, are gaining a stronger online presence by partnering with Amazon.com. Amazon maintains the site and processes orders, while the retailers fill the orders from their own warehouses. The arrangement gives Amazon a new source of revenue and frees the retailers to focus on their bricks-and-mortar business while also gaining new customers online.[63]

Mutual dependencies and partnerships have become a fact of life, but the degree of collaboration varies. Organizations can choose to build cooperative relationships in many ways, such as through preferred suppliers, strategic business partnering, joint ventures, or mergers and acquisitions. Exhibit 8.8 illustrates these major types of strategic business relationships according to the degree of collaboration involved. With preferred supplier relationships, a company such as Wal-Mart, for example, develops a special relationship with a key supplier such as Procter & Gamble that eliminates middlemen by sharing complete information and reducing the costs of salespeople and distributors. Preferred supplier arrangements provide long-term security for both organizations, but the level of collaboration is relatively low. Strategic business partnering requires a higher level of collaboration. Five of the largest hotel chains—Marriott International, Hilton Hotels Corp., Six Continents, Hyatt Corp., and Starwood Hotels and Resorts Worldwide Inc.—have partnered to create their own Web site, Travelweb.com, to combat the growing power of middlemen such as Expedia and Hotels.com. According to one senior vice president, the hotels felt a

Exhibit 8.8

## A Continuum of Partnership Strategies

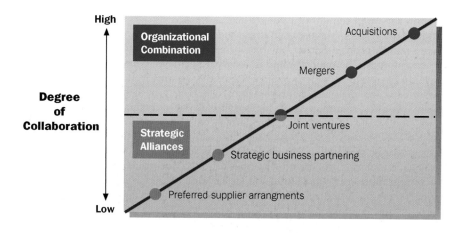

SOURCE: Adapted from Roberta Maynard, "Striking the Right Match," *Nation's Business* (May 1996), 18–28.

need to "take back our room product, and . . . sell it the way we want to sell it and maximize our revenues. At the same time, some chains are striving to build more beneficial partnerships with the third-party brokers.[64]

A still higher degree of collaboration is reflected in joint ventures, which are separate entities created with two or more active firms as sponsors. For example, MTV Networks was originally created as a joint venture of Warner Communications and American Express in the late 1970s. In a joint venture, organizations share the risks and costs associated with the new venture. It is estimated that the rate of joint venture formation between U.S. and international companies has been growing by 27 percent annually since 1985.[65]

Mergers and acquisitions represent the ultimate step in collaborative relationships. U.S. business has been in the midst of a tremendous merger and acquisition boom. IBM acquired PricewaterhouseCoopers, the U.S. pharmaceuticals company Upjohn merged with Sweden's Pharmacia, Cingular acquired AT&T Wireless, Comcast Corp. bought AT&T's Broadband division, Norwest merged with Wells Fargo, and Yahoo! Inc. is buying France's comparison-shopping service Kelkoo SA.

Using these various partnership strategies, today's companies simultaneously embrace competition *and* cooperation. Few companies can go it alone under a constant onslaught of international competition, changing technology, and new regulations. Consider how Motorola's approach to strategy has changed in today's turbulent environment.

Motorola's $8 billion business in semiconductor products shriveled to less than $5 billion in less than a year when a combination of new competition, new technologies, and shifting market conditions totally transformed the industry. Revenues dropped 37 percent virtually overnight. Rather than taking a standard response by cutting costs, laying off workers, and tinkering with operational details, Motorola managers decided to take an entirely new approach to strategy.

Motorola has always been highly competitive and determined to go it alone, but the new environment demanded a strategy that relies more on partnership. Every few years, engineers figure out how to build bigger silicon wafers that will yield more chips, lowering the per-chip cost. Managers realized that to build a new factory capable of producing the current 12-inch wafer would cost at least $2.5 billion, and it

MOTOROLA
**http://www. motorola.com**

would have to operate at near-maximum capacity to justify the investment. Motorola's output simply wasn't big enough to make that approach feasible. At the same time, big-wafer factories that have sprung up in China, Singapore, and Taiwan enjoy tremendous advantages because of lower labor costs and government support. These factories produce chips for anyone with a design, lowering the traditional barriers to entry for small semiconductor makers.

Faced with these facts, Motorola changed the strategy for how it does business. Only a few years ago, Motorola felt that it had to own all its manufacturing facilities and hoard its technology. The new strategy is: "If we don't have to own it, let's not own it. (And if we do have to own it, let's reduce the risk by sharing it.)" By 2003, Motorola's 18 wafer-making facilities had been reduced to 8. Thirty percent of its chip revenue came from products made, tested, or assembled by contractors such as Taiwan Semiconductor Manufacturing. The company is collaborating in a joint venture with Philips and STMicroelectronics on new semiconductor designs and processes.

Another strategic shift is that Motorola no longer keeps all its own technology secret, for use only in the company's own cell phones. Today, Motorola licenses its technology to partners around the world. As of 2003, ten phone makers had taken advantage of the new partnerships. Motorola executives know they're enabling smaller competitors to get into the business faster, but they know that if they don't do it, someone else will. They believe that in the current business environment, collaboration is the only strategy to help the organization survive and eventually thrive.[66]

Motorola managers realized the company could no longer compete in the way it always had. Faced with a radically new environment, they created a new approach to strategy that emphasizes partnership and sharing rather than independence and proprietary technology. Today, most businesses choose a combination of competitive and partnership strategies that add to their overall sustainable advantage.[67]

# Formulating Functional-Level Strategy

Functional-level strategies are the action plans adopted by major departments to support the execution of business-level strategy. Major organizational functions include marketing, production, finance, human resources, and research and development. Senior managers in these departments adopt strategies that are coordinated with the business-level strategy to achieve the organization's strategic goals.[68]

For example, consider a company that has adopted a differentiation strategy and is introducing new products that are expected to experience rapid growth. The human resources department should adopt a strategy appropriate for growth, which would mean recruiting additional personnel and training middle managers for movement into new positions. The marketing department should undertake test marketing, aggressive advertising campaigns, and consumer product trials. The finance department should adopt plans to borrow money, handle large cash investments, and authorize construction of new production facilities.

A company with mature products or a low-cost strategy will have different functional strategies. The human resources department should develop strategies for retaining and developing a stable work force, including transfers, advancements, and incentives for efficiency and safety. Marketing should stress brand loyalty and the development of established, reliable distribution channels. Production should maintain long production runs, routinization, and cost reduction. Finance should focus on net cash flows and positive cash balances.

# Strategy Implementation and Control

The final step in the strategic management process is implementation—how strategy is put into action. Some people argue that strategy implementation is the most difficult and important part of strategic management.[69] No matter how creative the formulated strategy, the organization will not benefit if it is not skillfully implemented. In today's competitive environment, there is an increasing recognition of the need for more dynamic approaches to implementing strategies.[70] Strategy is not a static, analytical process; it requires vision, intuition, and employee participation. Many organizations are abandoning central planning departments, and strategy is becoming an everyday part of the job for workers at all levels. Strategy implementation involves using several tools—parts of the firm that can be adjusted to put strategy into action—as illustrated in Exhibit 8.9. Once a new strategy is selected, it is implemented through changes in leadership, structure, information and control systems, and human resources.[71] For strategy to be implemented successfully, all aspects of the organization need to be in congruence with the strategy. Implementation involves regularly making difficult decisions about doing things in a way that supports rather than undermines the organization's chosen strategy. Remaining chapters of this book examine in detail topics such as leadership, organizational structure, information and control systems, and human resource management. The Manager's Shoptalk box gives some further tips for implementing strategy.

Exhibit 8.9

## Tools for Putting Strategy into Action

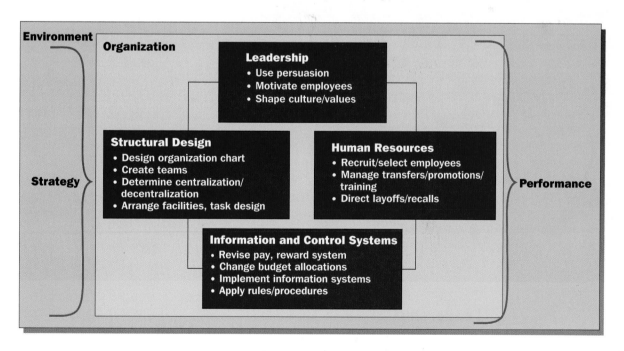

**SOURCE:** Adapted from Jay R. Galbraith and Robert K. Kazanjian, *Strategy Implementation: Structure, Systems, and Process,* 2d ed. (St. Paul, Minn.: West, 1986), 115. Used with permission.

# manager's Shoptalk

### Tips for Effective Strategy Implementation

Managers need to be aware of what goes on at the front lines of the organization to be sure their strategies can and will be translated into action. Strategy gives a company a competitive edge only if it is skillfully executed through the decisions of front-line managers and employees. Here are a few clues for creating an environment that is conducive to effective implementation.

1. *Build commitment to the strategy.* People throughout the organization have to buy into the new strategy. Managers make a deliberate and concentrated effort to bring front-line employees into the loop so they understand the new direction and have a chance to participate in decisions about how it will be implemented. When Saab managers wanted to shift their strategy, they met with front-line employees and dealers to explain the new direction and ask for suggestions and recommendations on how to put it into action. Clear, measurable goals and rewards that are tied to implementation efforts are also important for gaining commitment.

2. *Pay attention to culture.* Culture drives strategy, and without the appropriate cultural values, employees' behavior will be out of sync with the company's desired positioning in the marketplace. For example, Air Canada's CEO made a sincere commitment to making the airline the country's customer service leader. However, employee behavior didn't change because the old culture values supported doing things the way they had always been done.

3. *Take advantage of employees' knowledge and skills.* Managers need to get to know their employees on a personal basis so they understand how people can contribute to implementing the strategy. Most people want to be recognized and want to be valuable members of the organization. People throughout the organization have unused talents and skills that might be crucial for the success of a new strategy. In addition, managers can be sure people get training so they are capable of furthering the organization's new direction.

4. *Communicate, communicate, communicate.* Top managers have to continually communicate, through words and actions, their firm commitment to the strategy. In addition, managers have to keep tabs on how things are going, identify problems, and keep people informed about how the organization is progressing. Managers must break down barriers to effective communication across functional and hierarchical boundaries, often bringing customers into the communication loop as well. Information systems should provide accurate and timely information to the people who need it for decision making.

Implementing strategy is a complex job that requires everyone in the company to be aligned with the new direction and working to make it happen. These tips, combined with the information in the text, can help managers meet the challenge of putting strategy into action.

SOURCES: Brooke Dobni, "Creating a Strategy Implementation Environment," *Business Horizons* (March–April 2003), 43–46; and Thomas W. Porter and Stephen C. Harper, "Tactical Implementation: The Devil Is In the Details," *Business Horizons* (January–February 2003), 53–60.

## Leadership

The primary key to successful strategy implementation is leadership. *Leadership* is the ability to influence people to adopt the new behaviors needed for strategy implementation. An important part of implementing strategy is building consensus. People throughout the organization must believe in the new strategy and have a strong commitment to achieving the vision and goals. Leadership means using persuasion, motivating employees, and shaping culture and values to support the new strategy.

Managers can make speeches to employees, build coalitions of people who support the new strategic direction, and persuade middle managers to go along with their vision for the company. At IBM, for example, profiled at the beginning of Chapter 3, CEO Sam Palmisano is using leadership to get people throughout the organization aligned with the new e-business on demand strategy. He dismantled the executive committee that previously presided over strategic initiatives and replaced it with committees made up of people from all over the company who will now have a voice in strategy formulation and implementation. He's investing tons of money to teach managers at all levels how to lead rather than control their staff. And he is talking to people all over the company, appealing to their sense of pride and getting them fired up about making IBM great once more by uniting behind the on-demand vision.[72] With a clear sense of direction and a shared purpose, employees feel motivated, challenged, and empowered to pursue new strategic goals. Another way leaders build consensus and commitment is through broad participation. When people participate in strategy formulation, implementation is easier because managers and employees already understand the reasons for the new strategy and feel more committed to it.

## Structural Design

*Structural design* typically begins with the organization chart. It pertains to managers' responsibilities, their degree of authority, and the consolidation of facilities, departments, and divisions. Structure also pertains to such matters as centralization versus decentralization, the design of job tasks, and the organization's production technology. Structure will be discussed in detail in Chapter 10.

In many cases, implementing a new strategy requires making changes in organizational structure, such as adding or changing positions, reorganizing to teams, redesigning jobs, or shifting managers' responsibility and accountability. At IBM, the entire company is being reorganized into teams that will work directly with customers; Palmisano believes that breaking down functional and hierarchical boundaries is the only way IBM can find out what customers want and deliver it fast. In addition, practically every job in the giant corporation is being redefined to support the new strategy. Another example is the Ralston Foods' cereal plant in Sparks, Nevada, where managers wanted to reduce costs and improve efficiency to pursue a low-cost leadership strategy. They revised task design by combining several packing positions into one job and cross-training employees to operate all of the packing line's equipment. This reduced the number of workers needed during peak times and avoided leaving some workers idle during slow periods. The structural changes cut overall plant costs and manufacturing expenses, while significantly increasing the factory's productivity and yield, thus helping to implement the new strategy.[73]

## Information and Control Systems

*Information and control systems* include reward systems, pay incentives, budgets for allocating resources, information technology systems, and the organization's rules, policies, and procedures. Changes in these systems represent major tools for putting strategy into action. For example, managers can reassign resources from research and development to marketing if a new strategy requires increased advertising but no product innovations. Managers and employees must also be rewarded for adhering to the new strategy and making it a success.[74]

At ConAgra, maker of Healthy Choice and Banquet brands, top executives instituted top-down cost controls in the corporation's operating units and developed new systems for pooling resources to reduce purchasing, warehousing, and transportation costs. To ensure that managers embraced the new strategy of cooperation and efficiency, leaders tied 25 percent of their bonuses directly to savings targets.

Division heads saved $100 million in the first fiscal year. Top leaders also made changes in information systems by introducing a computerized network to track how much suppliers charge each ConAgra unit.[75]

Retailers such as Wal-Mart and Dollar General have made masterful use of sophisticated information technology to support a low-cost strategy by accelerating checkout, managing inventory, and controlling distribution. Kmart, by contrast, has been poor on implementation because of weak information and control systems that leave unpopular merchandise languishing on store shelves and hot items frequently out of stock.[76] New information technology can also be used to support differentiation strategies, such as by enabling collaborative design of new products or customizing products and services to exact customer specification. To build its new 7E7 Dreamliner, its first new commercial aircraft in 14 years, Boeing is using collaboration software that lets designers, suppliers, and manufacturers around the world collaborate on everything from wings to seat-back trays. Boeing hopes the new approach will revive its reputation as a leader in aircraft design, as well as make the entire process more efficient, helping the company compete more effectively with Airbus.[77]

## Human Resources

The organization's *human resources* are its employees. The human resource function recruits, selects, trains, transfers, promotes, and lays off employees to achieve strategic goals. For example, training employees can help them understand the purpose and importance of a new strategy or help them develop the necessary specific skills and behaviors. New strategies involve change, which naturally generates some resistance. Sometimes employees may have to be let go and replaced. One newspaper shifted its strategy from an evening to a morning paper to compete with a large newspaper from a nearby city. The new strategy required a change from working days to working from 1 P.M. to about midnight or so, fostering resentment and resistance among department heads. In order to implement it, 80 percent of the department heads had to be let go because they refused to cooperate. New people were recruited and placed in those positions, and the morning newspaper strategy was a resounding success.[78]

## Implementation during Turbulent Times

The challenges of implementing strategy have escalated with the increased complexity and turbulence in today's business environment. Many managers feel confident that they have found the right strategy to provide a competitive advantage, but they are less optimistic about their ability to implement it. Three issues that are particularly critical for implementing strategy during turbulent times are a global mindset, paying close attention to corporate culture, and embracing the Internet and other information technologies.

### Global Mindset

To implement strategies on a global scale, managers need to adopt a global mindset and be aware of varying implementation issues. Flexibility and openness emerge as mandatory leadership skills. Structural issues are more complex, as managers struggle to find the right mix to achieve the desired level of global integration and local responsiveness, as we discussed earlier. Information, control, and reward systems have to fit the values and incentives within the local cultures. Finally, the recruitment, training, transfer, promotion, and layoff of international human resources create an array of problems not confronted in North America. To be effective internationally, managers have to apply a global perspective to strategy implementation. For example, one well-respected multinational formed a task force of U.S. employees to review and revise work-force policies in connection with a new strategy. Employees from different levels and functional areas met for months and sent out employee surveys to all

U.S.-based facilities to get wider input. The final draft was reviewed and approved by top executives. They were surprised when the streamlined work-force manual, which reduced the number of policies from 120 to 10 core ones, was met with resistance and even hostility by the overseas units. Managers lack of a global mindset had led them to assume incorrectly that the international units would accept whatever was handed down from U.S. headquarters. Another multinational that used a worldwide task force for a similar process had much greater success with implementation.[79]

## Corporate Culture

At the same time managers need a global mindset, they also have to create and maintain a cohesive corporate culture that supports strategy. *Culture* is the link between strategy and performance outcomes, and different culture styles are better suited to different strategic directions.[80] Recall our discussion of different types of culture and the high-performance culture from Chapter 3. A study of the world's most admired companies, as reported annually in *Fortune* magazine, found that managers in these organizations pay close attention to culture and to the values that contribute to strategic success.[81] Managers want to develop a culture that it oriented toward performance—that encourages in everyone the behaviors and attitudes needed to meet the company's strategic goals and holds everyone responsible for success.[82] One big problem Boeing has had in recent years is a shift in cultural values that has hampered the company from implementing its strategy. CEO Philip Condit, who resigned abruptly under complaints of mismanagement and allegations of improper conduct, failed to pay attention to the culture Boeing needed to retain its position as a technology leader. As the culture grew weaker under Condit's leadership, Boeing fell behind in both technology and efficiency, enabling European rival Airbus to take the lead, delivering more new planes than Boeing for the first time in 2003.[83]

## Information Technology

A final concern for managers implementing strategy during turbulent times is to incorporate the Internet and other information technology. Dell pioneered the use of an online system to let customers configure computers to their exact specifications and submit the order over the Web, saving the cost of salespeople. Online mass customization is now used by many firms to decrease costs while enhancing their product mix and building their brand reputation.[84] Another company that successfully uses the Internet to implement strategy is retailer Target, which uses its Web site to sell items not available in stores, keep in touch with customer needs, and target customers with coupons that lure them into retail stores.[85] Target's Web strategy was discussed in more detail in Chapter 3's Unlocking Creative Solutions Through Technology box.

This chapter described important concepts of strategic management. Strategic management begins with an evaluation of the organization's current mission, goals, and strategy. This evaluation is followed by situation analysis (called SWOT analysis), which examines opportunities and threats in the external environment as well as strengths and weaknesses within the organization. Situation analysis leads to the formulation of explicit strategies, which indicate how the company intends to achieve a competitive advantage. Managers formulate strategies that focus on core competencies, develop synergy, and create value.

Strategy formulation takes place at three levels: corporate, business, and functional. Corporate grand strategies include growth, stability, retrenchment, and global. One framework for accomplishing them is the BCG matrix. An approach to business-level strategy is Porter's competitive forces and strategies. The Internet is having a profound impact on the competitive environment, and managers should consider this when analyzing the five competitive forces and formulating business strategies. An alternative

*Manager's Solution*

approach to strategic thought emphasizes cooperation rather than competition. Partnership strategies include preferred supplier arrangements, strategic business partnering, joint ventures, and mergers and acquisitions. Most of today's companies choose a mix of competitive and partnership strategies. Once business strategies have been formulated, functional strategies for supporting them can be developed.

Even the most creative strategies have no value if they cannot be translated into action. Implementation is the most important and most difficult part of strategy. Managers implement strategy by aligning all parts of the organization to be in congruence with the new strategy. Four areas that managers focus on for strategy implementation are leadership, structural design, information and control systems, and human resources. Three additional issues for managers in today's turbulent and complex environment are adopting a global mindset, paying close attention to corporate culture, and embracing use of the Internet in implementation.

Returning to the opening problem at Nintendo, CEO and president Satoru Iwata is still evaluating strengths, weaknesses, threats, and opportunities to see how Nintendo should position itself for the long-term future. In the short term, a functional level strategy of enhanced advertising and price cuts helped Nintendo increase its sales during the critical holiday sales period. Sony and Xbox both took a big hit from Nintendo's price cuts by failing to do enough marketing. In addition, Nintendo plans to bring out its next generation console ahead of Sony's and Microsoft's, giving the company a competitive edge. For the long range, Iwata so far is sticking to a focused differentiation strategy rather than trying to compete as an all-in-one entertainment company. His strategy calls for focusing all the company's energies on building great games, but his new mantra is "5-year-olds to 95-year-olds." To build a wider customer base, Iwata is investing heavily in internal game development, building a new R&D facility, and adding 50 new developers to design entertainment for all ages. He's also working hard to mend fences with third-party game publishers and partner with them on game design, something unheard of in Nintendo's past. The new inclination toward partnership may be carried even further if Iwata decides his company can't survive on games alone. He has hinted that he wouldn't mind making Nintendo's technology available for incorporating into other kinds of hardware, perhaps even building a joint venture with a major electronics power such as Panasonic, which already sells a device that combines a DVD player with a Nintendo GameCube. Some observers believe such a move is the best approach for the ailing company, but Iwata still believes that if Nintendo builds great games, it can thrive as a niche player in the entertainment industry. There is also a possibility that the all-in-one strategies of Sony and Microsoft will backfire, leading to higher prices that consumers just aren't willing to pay.[86]

# Discussion Questions

1. Assume you are the general manager of a large hotel and have formulated a strategy of renting banquet facilities to corporations for big events. At a monthly management meeting, your sales manager informed the head of food operations that a big reception in one week will require converting a large hall from a meeting room to a banquet facility in only 60 minutes—a difficult but doable operation that will require precise planning and extra help. The food operations manager is furious about not being informed earlier. What is wrong here?

2. Which is more important—strategy formulation or strategy implementation? Do they depend on each other? Is it possible for strategy implementation to occur first?

3. If an organization has hired strategic management professionals to help top managers, during which part of the strategic management process would they play the largest role?
4. Perform a situation (SWOT) analysis for the university you attend. Do you think university administrators consider these factors when devising their strategy?
5. What is meant by the core competence and synergy components of strategy? Give examples.
6. Using Porter's competitive strategies, how would you describe the strategies of Wal-Mart, Bloomingdale's, and Kmart? Do any of these companies also use cooperative strategies? Discuss.
7. Walt Disney Company has four major strategic business units: movies (including Miramax and Touchstone), theme parks, consumer products, and television (ABC and cable). Place each of these SBUs on the BCG matrix based on your knowledge of them.
8. As administrator for a medium-sized hospital, you and the board of directors have decided to change to a drug dependency hospital from a short-term, acute-care facility. Which organizational dimensions would you use to implement this strategy?
9. How would functional strategies in marketing, research and development, and production departments differ if a business changed from a differentiation to a low-cost strategy?

# Management in Practice: Experiential Exercise

**Developing Strategy for a Small Business**

Instructions: Your instructor may ask you to do this exercise individually or as part of a group. Select a local business with which you (or group members) are familiar. Complete the following activities.

**Activity 1    Perform a SWOT analysis for the business.**
Strengths: _____
_____
_____
_____
_____

Opportunities: _____
_____
_____
_____
_____

Weaknesses: _____
_____
_____
_____
_____

Threats: _____
_____
_____
_____
_____

**Activity 2**  Write a statement of the business's current strategy.
**Activity 3**  Decide on a goal you would like the business to achieve in two years, and write a statement of proposed strategy for achieving that goal.
**Activity 4**  Write a statement describing how the proposed strategy will be implemented.
**Activity 5**  What have you learned from this exercise?

# Management in Practice: Ethical Dilemma

## A Great Deal for Whom?

It seemed like a great deal for Kevin Haley, the retired president of a small accounting firm, when he took the job. To sit on the board of Keldine Technologies, all he had to do was listen to some general talk about the company at bi-monthly meetings, vote on operations issues, and collect a nice fee. He didn't worry about his lack of expertise in the company's business of manufacturing transistors, because "nothing ever changed at Keldine."

That was two years ago. Now Keldine Technologies, with 250 employees and ten years in business, was faced with a buyout offer from Graham Industries. Chairman of the Board at Keldine, Greg Bingham, called the deal a "no-brainer." Graham Industries' offer of $65 a share was high, a great deal for shareholders. The problem for Haley was that he knew Graham Industries was close to bankruptcy, and that it was probably only buying Keldine to leverage some of its debt and hold off creditors. The odds were that both companies would be wiped out within a year if the sale went through. As news of a buyout offer spread, Keldine stock had changed hands rapidly, and speculators in the shareholder ranks were pressuring for a sale. Bingham asserted, "Our mission is to create as much value for shareholders as possible."

He also assured the board that the executives were protected by contingency compensation packages in the event of a "downturn for Keldine." But Haley was torn. The deal was a short-term moneymaker but almost guaranteed disaster for the company's future and the majority of its employees. Haley's commitment to shareholders seemed compromised by the presence of speculators in their ranks. He questioned whether the interests of loyal, long-time employees weren't a higher priority than those of speculators.

## What Do You Do?

1. Vote to accept the offer of Graham Industries and assure a short-term profit for the shareholders and executives. They are your first responsibility.
2. Reject the buyout bid. Providing Keldine a future, even if uncertain because of its resistance to change, is more important than accepting what may be the best offer ever received.
3. Pass, and hope a board majority prevails without your vote. You aren't qualified to make a decision on this anyway.

Source: Based on Doug Wallace, "When the Sharks Are Circling," *What Would You Do? Business Ethics,* vol. I (September–October 1991), 42–44.

# Surf the Net

1. **Growth through Mergers and Acquisitions.** Use the Internet to identify mergers and acquisitions announced within the past month. One search option is to use Northern Light at *http://www.northernlight.com*, select "Current News," and type in under "Search for:" "mergers and acquisitions." For each merger or acquisition you identify, give the companies involved, identify the industry, and provide any other interesting information related to the merger or acquisition.
2. **Competitive Intelligence.** The Internet Intelligence Index *http://www.fuld.com/i3/index. html* is designed to help users gather competitive intelligence information. It contains links to nearly 600 intelligence-related Internet sites, covering everything from macro-economic data to individual patent and stock quote information. Select an industry from the Internet Intelligence Index Web site, such as Apparel,

Financial Services, Pharmaceutical/Biotechnology, Travel and Transportation, or one assigned by your instructor. Based on your research of your industry, prepare a written report in which you identify opportunities and threats to existing firms in that industry.
3. **Competitive Strategies.** Compare the Web sites of companies in the same industry that have adopted different strategies—either differentiation, cost leadership, or focus. For example, you could compare Motel 6 *http://www.motel6. com* with Holiday Inn *http://holiday-inn.com* and write a list of Web-site indicators of their respective strategies. Other possible comparisons are Enterprise Rent-A-Car *http://www.enterprise.com/* and Hertz *http://www.hertz.com/* or Nordstrom *http://www.nordstrom.com* and Kmart *http://www. kmart.com/*.

# Case for Critical Analysis

### Starbucks Coffee

Beginning with nine Seattle stores in 1987, Starbucks CEO Howard Schultz has exported the company's chic cafés throughout the country. Service is anything but fast, and the price of a cup of coffee could make the Dunkin' Donuts crowd faint, but each week almost two million Americans hit Starbucks to sip skinny lattes or no-whip mochas.

Despite a slowdown in sales from established stores, Starbucks is pursuing rapid expansion. It made its first acquisition in 1994, buying The Coffee Connection Inc., a 23-store Boston rival. With more than 400 stores in place, Schultz plans to open 200 more within a year and has announced plans to team up with foreign partners to open stores in Asia and Europe. In addition, Starbucks has entered into a venture with PepsiCo to develop a new bottled coffee drink. Schultz's strategies are risky, but some analysts think Starbucks has the flexibility and management strength to succeed.

Many of Starbucks's managers have years of experience from such companies as Burger King, Taco Bell, Wendy's, and Blockbuster. Schultz believes a CEO should "hire people smarter than you are and get out of their way." Equally crucial to Starbucks's success are the "baristas" who prepare coffee drinks. Starbucks recruits its workers from colleges and community groups and gives them 24 hours' training in coffeemaking and lore—a key to creating the company's hip image and quality service. To maintain quality control, Starbucks roasts all its coffee in-house. The company also has turned down lucrative alternatives such as franchising and supermarket distribution.

A computer network links the expanding Starbucks empire, and Schultz hired a top information-technology specialist from McDonald's to design a point-of-sale system to enable managers to track sales. Every night, computers from all 400-plus stores send information to headquarters in Seattle so that executives can spot regional buying trends.

For Schultz, a man who has already changed America's coffee-drinking habits, the risks Starbucks is taking are just another challenge.

### Questions

1. Which of Porter's competitive strategies is Starbucks using?
2. Discuss how Schultz is using leadership, structure, information and control systems, and human resources to implement strategy at Starbucks.
3. What challenges may Schultz face in trying to expand Starbucks internationally?

Sources: Dori Jones Yang, "The Starbucks Enterprise Shifts into Warp Speed," *BusinessWeek*, October 24, 1994, 76; and Michael Treacy, "You Need a Value Discipline—But Which One?" *Fortune*, April 17, 1995, 195.

# Endnotes

1. Geoff Keighley, "Is Nintendo Playing the Wrong Game?" *Business 2.0* (August 2003), 111–115; Mike Musgrove, "Not-So-Super Mario; Stodgy Nintendo Is Falling Behind in the Game Wars," *The Washington Post* (December 25, 2003), E1.

2. Edward W. Desmond, "What's Ailing Kodak? Fuji," *Fortune* (October 27, 1997), 185–192; William Grimes, "Supersize, We Knew Thee Too Well," *The New York Times* (March 7, 2004), Section 4, 2; Neal E. Boudette, "Road Less Traveled; Peugeot's Formula for Success: Steering Clear of Megamergers," *The Wall Street Journal* (August 4, 2003), A1, A6.

3. Christopher Palmeri, "Mattel: Up the Hill Minus Jill," *BusinessWeek* (April 9, 2001), 53–54.

4. Chet Miller and Laura B. Cardinal, "Strategic Planning and Firm Performance: A Synthesis of More than Two Decades of Research," *Academy of Management Journal* 37, no. 6 (1994), 1649–1665.

5. Gary Hamel, "Killer Strategies," *Fortune* (June 23, 1997), 70–84; and Costantinos Markides, "Strategic Innovation," *Sloan Management Review* (Spring 1997), 9–23.

6. Richard Tomlinson, "L'Oreal's Global Makeover," *Fortune* (September 30, 2002), 141–146.

7. Keith H. Hammonds, "Michael Porter's Big Ideas," *Fast Company* (March 2001), 150–156.

8. John E. Prescott, "Environments as Moderators of the Relationship between Strategy and Performance," *Academy of Management Journal* 29 (1986), 329–346; John A. Pearce II and Richard B. Robinson, Jr., *Strategic Management: Strategy, Formulation, and Implementation,* 2d ed. (Homewood, Ill.: Irwin, 1985); and David J. Teece, "Economic Analysis and Strategic Management," *California Management Review* 26 (Spring 1984), 87–110.

9. Markides, "Strategic Innovation."

10. Kotha Suresh and Daniel Orna, "Generic Manufacturing Strategies: A Conceptual Synthesis," *Strategic Management Journal* 10 (1989), 211–231; and John A. Pearce II, "Selecting among Alternative Grand Strategies," *California Management Review* (Spring 1982), 23–31.

11. "Citigroup Buys Sears Credit Card Portfolio," *New York Times News Service;* Stanley Holmes, "Boeing: What Really Happened?" *BusinessWeek* (December 15, 2003), 33–38.

12. Palmeri, "Mattel: Up the Hill Minus Jill."

13. Laura Landro, "Entertainment Giants Face Pressure to Cut Costs, Get in Focus," *The Wall Street Journal* (February 11, 1997), A1, A10.

14. Zachary Schiller, "Figgies Turns Over a New Leaf," *BusinessWeek* (February 27, 1995), 94–96; and Gail Edmondson, "Fiat's Last Stand," *BusinessWeek* (April 21, 2003), 79–80.

15. Kenichi Ohmae, "Managing in a Borderless World," *Harvard Business Review* (May–June 1990), 152–161.

16. Theodore Levitt, "The Globalization of Markets," *Harvard Business Review* (May–June 1983), 92–102.

17. Cesare R. Mainardi, Martin Salva, and Muir Sanderson, "Label of Origin: Made on Earth," *Strategy & Business,* Issue 15 (Second Quarter, 1999), 42–53; Joann S. Lublin, "Place vs. Product: It's Tough to Choose a Management Model," *The Wall Street Journal* (June 27, 2001), A1, A4.

18. Mainardi, Salva, and Sanderson, "Label of Origin."

19. Joanne Lipman, "Marketers Turn Sour on Global Sales Pitch Harvard Guru Makes," *The Wall Street Journal* (May 12, 1988), 1, 8.

20. Michael E. Porter, "Changing Patterns of International Competition," *California Management Review* 28 (Winter 1986), 40.

21. Mohanbir Sawhney and Sumant Mandal, "What Kind of Global Organization Should You Build?" *Business 2.0* (May 2000), 213.

22. Based on Michael A. Hitt, R. Duane Ireland, and Robert E. Hoskisson, *Strategic Management: Competitiveness and Globalization* (St. Paul, Minn.: West, 1995), 238.

23. Anil K. Gupta and Vijay Govindarajan, "Converting Global Presence into Global Competitive Advantage," *Academy of Management Executive* 15, No. 2 (2001), 45–56.

24. Thomas S. Bateman and Carl P. Zeithaml, *Management: Function and Strategy,* 2d ed. (Homewood, Ill.: Irwin, 1993), 231.

25. Michael E. Porter, "What is Strategy?" *Harvard Business Review* (November–December 1996), 61–78.

26. Arthur A. Thompson, Jr., and A. J. Strickland III, *Strategic Management: Concepts and Cases,* 6th ed. (Homewood, Ill.: Irwin, 1992); and Briance Mascarenhas, Alok Baveja, and Mamnoon Jamil, "Dynamics of Core Competencies in Leading Multinational Companies," *California Management Review* 40, no. 4 (Summer 1998), 117–132.

27. Ronald B. Lieber, "Smart Science," *Fortune* (June 23, 1997), 73.

28. Paul Roberts, "Live! From Your Office! It's . . ." *Fast Company* (October 1999), 151–170.

29. Kathryn Jones, "The Dell Way," *Business 2.0* (February 2003), 61–66; Betsy Morris, "Can Michael Dell

Escape The Box?" *Fortune* (October 16, 2000), 93–110; and Stewart Deck, "Fine Line," *CIO* (February 1, 2000), 88–92.

30. Michael Goold and Andrew Campbell, "Desperately Seeking Synergy," *Harvard Business Review* (September–October 1998), 131–143.

31. Chris Woodyard, "FedEx Ponies Up $2.4B for Kinko's," *USA Today* (December 30, 2003), accessed at http://www.usatoday.com/money/industries/2003-12-30-fdx-kinkos_x.htm on January 2, 2004; and Claudia H. Deutsch, "FedEx Moves to Expand with Purchase of Kinko's," *The New York Times* (December 31, 2003), C1.

32. Cathy Olofson, "No Place Like Home," *Fast Company* (July 2000), 328–329.

33. Linda Tischler, "How Pottery Barn Wins with Style," *Fast Company* (June 2003), 106.

34. Milton Leontiades, *Strategies for Diversification and Change* (Boston: Little, Brown, 1980), 63; and Dan E. Schendel and Charles W. Hofer, eds., *Strategic Management: A New View of Business Policy and Planning* (Boston: Little, Brown, 1979), 11–14.

35. Gail Edmondson, "Fiat's Last Stand," *BusinessWeek* (April 21, 2003), 79–80.

36. Susan Orenstein, "Roses Are Red, Violets Are Blue, Hallmark's Online, But What Can It Do?" *The Industry Standard* (November 27–December 4, 2000).

37. Cora Daniels, "J.C. Penney Dresses Up," *Fortune* (June 9, 2003), 127–130.

38. Katrina Brooker, "A Game of Inches," *Fortune* (February 5, 2001), 98–100.

39. Milton Leontiades, "The Confusing Words of Business Policy," *Academy of Management Review* 7 (1982), 45–48.

40. Lawrence G. Hrebiniak and William F. Joyce, *Implementing Strategy* (New York: Macmillan, 1984).

41. John Sterling, "Strategy Development for the Real World," *Strategy & Leadership* 30, no. 1 (2002), 10–17.

42. Pallavi Gogoi, "The Heat in Kraft's Kitchen; Cheap Rivals and Demands for Leaner Fare Close In," *BusinessWeek* (August 4, 2003), 82; and Shelly Branch, "Critical Curds; At Kraft, Making Cheese 'Fun' Is Serious Business," *The Wall Street Journal* (May 31, 2002), A1, A6.

43. Frederick W. Gluck, "A Fresh Look at Strategic Management," *Journal of Business Strategy* 6 (Fall 1985), 4–19.

44. J. Lynn Lunsford, "Going Up; United Technologies' Formula: A Powerful Lift from Elevators," *The Wall Street Journal* (July 2, 2003), A1, A6.

45. Thompson and Strickland, *Strategic Management*; and William L. Shanklin and John K. Ryans, Jr., "Is the International Cash Cow Really a Prize Heifer?" *Business Horizons* 24 (1981), 10–16.

46. "For Mighty Gillette, These Are the Faces of War," *The New York Times* (October 12, 2003); Charles Forelle, "Gillette Posts 6% Rise in Profit But Warns of Challenges Ahead," *The Wall Street Journal* (January 30, 2004), B3; William Symonds, "Can Gillette Regain Its Edge?" *BusinessWeek* (January 26, 2004), 46; William C. Symonds, with Carol Matlack, "Gillette's Edge," *BusinessWeek* (January 19, 1998), 70–77; William C. Symonds, "Would You Spend $1.50 for a Razor Blade?" *BusinessWeek* (April 27, 1998), 46; Barbara Carton, "Gillette Looks Beyond Whiskers to Big Hair and Stretchy Floss," *The Wall Street Journal* (December 14, 1994), B1, B4; and William C. Symonds, "Can Gillette Regain Its Voltage?" *BusinessWeek* (October 16, 2000), 102–104.

47. Michael E. Porter, *Competitive Strategy* (New York: Free Press, 1980), 36–46; Danny Miller, "Relating Porter's Business Strategies to Environment and Structure: Analysis and Performance Implementations," *Academy of Management Journal* 31 (1988), 280–308; and Michael E. Porter, "From Competitive Advantage to Corporate Strategy," *Harvard Business Review* (May–June 1987), 43–59.

48. Michael E. Porter, "Strategy and the Internet," *Harvard Business Review* (March 2001), 63–78.

49. Symonds, "Can Gillette Regain Its Edge?"

50. Jim Kerstetter and Spencer E. Ante, "IBM vs. Oracle: It Could Get Bloody," *BusinessWeek* (May 28, 2001), 65–66.

51. Joseph T. Hallinan, "Service Charge: As Banks Elbow for Consumers, Washington Mutual Thrives," *The Wall Street Journal* (November 6, 2003), A1.

52. Thomas L. Wheelen and J. David Hunger, *Strategic Management and Business Policy* (Reading, Mass.: Addison-Wesley, 1989).

53. Andrew Park and Peter Burrows, "Dell, the Conqueror," *BusinessWeek* (September 24, 2001), 92–102; and Thompson and Strickland, Strategic Management.

54. "We Weren't Just Airborne Yesterday; A Brief History of Southwest Airlines," http://www.southwest.com/about_swa/airborne.html accessed on March 29, 2004; Micheline Maynard, "Are Peanuts No Longer Enough?" *The New York Times* (March 7, 2004), Section 3, 1; and Wendy Zellner with Michael Arndt, "Holding Steady," *BusinessWeek* (February 3, 2003), 66–68.

55. Richard Teitelbaum, "The Wal-Mart of Wall Street," *Fortune* (October 13, 1997), 128–130.

56. Joshua Rosenbaum, "Guitar Maker Looks for a New Key," *The Wall Street Journal* (February 11, 1998), B1, B5.

57. Nitin Nohria, William Joyce, and Bruce Roberson, "What Really Works," *Harvard Business Review* (July 2003), 43–52.

58. Porter, "Strategy and the Internet"; Hammonds, "Michael Porter's Big Ideas"; and G. T. Lumpkin, Scott B. Droege, and Gregory G. Dess, "E-Commerce Strategies: Achieving Sustainable Competitive Advantage and Avoiding Pitfalls," *Organizational Dynamics* 30, no 4 (2002), 325–340.

59. Lumpkin, et al., "E-Commerce Strategies."

60. Based on John Burton, "Composite Strategy: The Combination of Collaboration and Competition," *Journal of General Management* 21, No. 1 (Autumn 1995), 1–23; and Roberta Maynard, "Striking the Right Match," *Nation's Business* (May 1996), 18–28.

61. Joe Flint, "Disney-Time Warner Cable Dispute Turns Many TV Screens Black," *The Wall Street Journal* (May 2, 2000), B1, B4; and Bruce Orwall, Joe Flint, and Martin Peers, "Sparring Partners—Moral of Disney's War Against Time Warner: Don't Dis Distribution," *The Wall Street Journal* (May 3, 2000), A1, A12.

62. Don Tapscott, "Rethinking Strategy in a Networked World," *Strategy & Business,* Issue 24 (Third Quarter 2001), 34–41.

63. Nick Wingfield, "New Chapter; A Web Giant Tries to Boost Profits by Taking on Tenants," *The Wall Street Journal* (September 24, 2003), A1, A10.

64 Julia Angwin and Motoka Rich, "Inn Fighting; Big Hotel Chains Are Striking Back Against Web Sites," *The Wall Street Journal* (March 14, 2003), A1, A7.

65. David Lei, "Strategies for Global Competition," *Long-Range Planning* 22 (1989) 102–109.

66. Keith H. Hammonds, "Motorola Bets on Its Chips," *Fast Company* (March 2003), 42–44.

67. Burton, "Composite Strategy: The Combination of Collaboration and Competition."

68. Harold W. Fox, "A Framework for Functional Coordination," *Atlanta Economic Review* (now *Business Magazine*) (November–December 1973).

69. L. J. Bourgeois III and David R. Brodwin, "Strategic Implementation: Five Approaches to an Elusive Phenomenon," *Strategic Management Journal* 5 (1984), 241–264; Anil K. Gupta and V. Govindarajan, "Business Unit Strategy, Managerial Characteristics, and Business Unit Effectiveness at Strategy Implementation," *Academy of Management Journal* (1984), 25–41; and Jeffrey G. Covin, Dennis P. Slevin, and Randall L. Schultz, "Implementing Strategic Missions: Effective Strategic, Structural, and Tactical Choices," *Journal of Management Studies* 31, no. 4 (1994), 481–505.

70. Rainer Feurer and Kazem Chaharbaghi, "Dynamic Strategy Formulation and Alignment," *Journal of General Management* 20, no. 3 (Spring 1995), 76–90; and Henry Mintzberg, *The Rise and Fall of Strategic Planning* (Toronto: Maxwell Macmillan Canada, 1994).

71. Jay R. Galbraith and Robert K. Kazanjian, *Strategy Implementation: Structure, Systems and Process,* 2d ed. (St. Paul, Minn.: West, 1986); and Paul C. Nutt, "Selecting Tactics to Implement Strategic Plans," *Strategic Management Journal* 10 (1989), 145–161.

72. Spencer E. Ante, "The New Blue," *BusinessWeek* (March 17, 2003), 80–88.

73. Glenn L. Dalton, "The Collective Stretch," *Management Review* (December 1998), 54–59.

74. Gupta and Govindarajan, "Business Unit Strategy"; and Bourgeois and Brodwin, "Strategic Implementation."

75. Greg Burns, "How a New Boss Got ConAgra Cooking Again," *BusinessWeek* (July 25, 1994), 72–73.

76. Nohria, et al., "What Really Works."

77. Beth Bacheldor, "Boeing's Flight Plan" *Information Week* (February 16, 2004), 20–21.

78. James E. Skivington and Richard L. Daft, "A Study of Organizational 'Framework' and 'Process' Modalities for the Implementation of Business-Level Strategies" (unpublished manuscript, Texas A&M University, 1987).

79. Thomas M. Begley and David P. Boyd, "The Need for a Corporate Global Mind-Set," *MIT Sloan Management Review* (Winter 2003), 25–32.

80. Abby Ghobadian and Nicholas O'Regan, "The Link Between Culture, Strategy, and Performance in Manufacturing SMEs," *Journal of General Management* 28, no. 1 (Autumn 2002), 16–34.

81. Melvyn J. Stark, "Five Years of Insight Into the World's Most Admired Companies," *Journal of Organizational Excellence* (Winter 2002), 3–12.

82. Nitin Nohria, William Joyce, and Bruce Roberson, "What Really Works," *Harvard Business Review* (July 2003), 43–52; and Jeff Rosenthal and Mary Ann Masarech, "High Performance Cultures: How Values Can Drive Business Results," *Journal of Organizational Excellence* (Spring 2003), 3–18.

83. Stanley H. Holmes, "Boeing: What Really Happened?" *BusinessWeek* (December 15, 2003), 33-38; and; Jerry Useem, "Boeing to Pieces," *Fortune* (December 29, 2003), 41.

84. Lumpkin, et al. "E-Commerce Strategies."

85. Chana R. Schoenberger, "Bull's Eye," *Forbes* (September 2, 2002), 76.

86. Keighley, "Is Nintendo Playing the Wrong Game?"; Musgrove, "Not-So-Super Mario,"; and Laurie J. Flynn, "Deep Price Cuts Help Nintendo Climb to No. 2 in Game Sales," *The New York Times* (January 26, 2004), C2.

# Managerial Decision Making

## LEARNING OBJECTIVES

*After studying this chapter, you should be able to:*

1. Explain why decision making is an important component of good management.

2. Explain the difference between programmed and nonprogrammed decisions and the decision characteristics of risk, uncertainty, and ambiguity.

3. Describe the classical, administrative, and political models of decision making and their applications.

4. Identify the six steps used in managerial decision making.

5. Explain four personal decision styles used by managers.

6. Discuss the advantages and disadvantages of participative decision making.

7. Identify techniques for improving decision making in today's turbulent environment.

After suffering through a 15-year slide, sales of Tupperware shot up in the early 2000s, helped along by management decisions to set up booths in shopping malls and push sales over the Internet, in addition to the traditional Tupperware parties. The icon of 1950s suburban America looked poised to keep growing, winning over a whole new generation to its unique food storage products and kitchen gadgets. Overseas, in places like China, Indonesia, and India, sales were booming. Managers knew, though, that Tupperware was facing some stiff competition from companies that were coming out with products that promised to do the same job at lower prices. To fight back, they decided to supplement home parties—the source of 90 percent of Tupperware's U.S. revenues—by placing Tupperware products in Target stores and recruiting volunteer salespeople to demonstrate the merchandise. It seemed to solve a vexing problem—how to sell products face-to-face in an age when people have little time and patience for a home sales pitch. But the decision turned out to be a disaster. Some Target stores and shoppers didn't know how to deal with the influx of Tupperware salespeople, who ended up feeling slighted. Many salespeople stopped volunteering for store duty. Others—some with great sales records—quit Tupperware entirely. Interest in home parties dwindled, decreasing sales and cutting down on opportunities for recruiting new salespeople. Tupperware's sales in North America fell to a three-year low and profits plummeted 47 percent.[1]

## Take A Moment

Why did this decision go wrong? If you were a member of the management team at Tupperware, what new decisions would you make to remedy this disaster? What alternatives would you consider for getting Tupperware back on track?

The story of Tupperware illustrates how difficult decision making can be. Top executives at Tupperware have made many good decisions over the years, helping the company maintain its clout despite changing times. When the company hit a tough spot in the 1980s, for example, it regained its footing by creating "Rush Hour" and "Office" parties to reach increasingly busy women. The decision to sell through mall kiosks and the Internet has also paid off. However, the rapid push into retail stores was a dismal failure, and Tupperware pulled its products from Target shelves within a year. Managers now face some difficult decisions that will affect the future of their business. Every organization grows, prospers, or fails as a result of decisions by its managers.

Managers often are referred to as *decision makers*. Although many of their important decisions are strategic, managers also make decisions about every other aspect of an organization, including structure, control systems, responses to the environment, and human resources. Managers scout for problems, make decisions for solving them, and monitor the consequences to see whether additional decisions are required. Good decision making is a vital part of good management, because decisions determine how the organization solves its problems, allocates resources, and accomplishes its goals.

The business world is full of evidence of both good and bad decisions. For example, Nokia became a $10 billion leader in the cell phone industry because managers at the company decided to sell off unrelated businesses such as paper, tires, and aluminum and concentrate the company's resources on electronics.[2] Cadillac managers ditched stuffy golf and yachting sponsorships and instead tied in with Hollywood movies like *The Matrix: Reloaded* and *Bad Boys II*. The decision boosted sales by 43 percent, and the brand was on track in late 2003 toward a level of sales not seen since 1994.[3] On the other hand, Boeing's decision to step up airplane production at the same time the factory was switching to a new automated manufacturing system was a fiasco. The massive assembly lines nearly broke down and the plant had to stop two lines so workers could catch up, costing the company $2.6 billion. Or, consider the decision of Timex managers to replace the classic tag line, "It takes a licking and keeps on ticking," with the bland "Life is ticking." The desire to modernize their company's image led Timex managers to ditch one of the most recognizable advertising slogans in the world in favor of a lame and rather depressing new one.[4] Decision making is not easy. It must be done amid ever-changing factors, unclear information, and conflicting points of view.

Chapters 7 and 8 described strategic planning. This chapter explores the decision process that underlies strategic planning. Plans and strategies are arrived at through decision making; the better the decision making, the better the strategic planning. First we will examine decision characteristics. Then we will look at decision-making models and the steps executives should take when making important decisions. We will also examine participative decision making and discuss techniques for improving decision making in today's organizations.

# Types of Decisions and Problems

**decision**
A choice made from available alternatives.

**decision making**
The process of identifying problems and opportunities and then resolving them.

A **decision** is a choice made from available alternatives. For example, an accounting manager's selection among Colin, Tasha, and Jennifer for the position of junior auditor is a decision. Many people assume that making a choice is the major part of decision making, but it is only a part.

**Decision making** is the process of identifying problems and opportunities and then resolving them. Decision making involves effort both before and after the actual choice. Thus, the decision as to whether to select Colin, Tasha, or Jennifer requires the accounting manager to ascertain whether a new junior auditor is needed, determine the availability of potential job candidates, interview candidates to acquire necessary information, select one candidate, and follow up with the socialization of the new employee into the organization to ensure the decision's success.

## Programmed and Nonprogrammed Decisions

Management decisions typically fall into one of two categories: programmed and nonprogrammed. **Programmed decisions** involve situations that have occurred often enough to enable decision rules to be developed and applied in the future.[5] Programmed decisions are made in response to recurring organizational problems. The decision to reorder paper and other office supplies when inventories drop to a certain level is a programmed decision. Other programmed decisions concern the types of skills required to fill certain jobs, the reorder point for manufacturing inventory, exception reporting for expenditures 10 percent or more over budget, and selection of freight routes for product deliveries. Once managers formulate decision rules, subordinates and others can make the decision, freeing managers for other tasks.

> **programmed decision**
> A decision made in response to a situation that has occurred often enough to enable decision rules to be developed and applied in the future.

Nonprogrammed decisions are made in response to situations that are unique, are poorly defined and largely unstructured, and have important consequences for the organization. Many nonprogrammed decisions involve strategic planning, because uncertainty is great and decisions are complex. Decisions to build a new factory, develop a new product or service, enter a new geographical market, or relocate headquarters to another city are all nonprogrammed decisions. One good example of a nonprogrammed decision is NBC Entertainment's search for a new sitcom. With *Friends* ending its ten-season run and *Frasier* running out of steam, president Jeffrey Zucker and other managers know the network desperately needs a new hit. But the process of finding a hit sitcom is complex, not subject to rational analysis and decision rules. The stakes are high both in terms of money and the network's image.[6] Another example of a nonprogrammed decision was when Ronald Zarella, president of General Motors North American operations, shelved plans to introduce a new design for the company's best-selling car, the Chevrolet Cavalier. He delayed building new factories and invested the millions of dollars saved in getting innovative new models of trucks and sport-utility vehicles on the market quickly. Zarrella and his top executives had to analyze complex problems, evaluate alternatives, and make a decision about the best way to reverse GM's declining market share.[7]

> **nonprogrammed decision**
> A decision made in response to a situation that is unique, is poorly defined and largely unstructured, and has important consequences for the organization.

*Go to the ethical dilemma on page 332.*

*Take A Moment*

## Certainty, Risk, Uncertainty, and Ambiguity

One primary difference between programmed and nonprogrammed decisions relates to the degree of certainty or uncertainty that managers deal with in making the decision. In a perfect world, managers would have all the information necessary for making decisions. In reality, however, some things are unknowable; thus, some decisions will fail to solve the problem or attain the desired outcome. Managers try to obtain information about decision alternatives that will reduce decision uncertainty. Every decision situation can be organized on a scale according to the availability of information and the possibility of failure. The four positions on the scale are certainty, risk, uncertainty, and ambiguity, as illustrated in Exhibit 9.1. Whereas programmed decisions can be made in situations involving certainty, many situations that managers deal with every day involve at least some degree of uncertainty and require nonprogrammed decision making.

Exhibit 9.1

## Conditions that Affect the Possibility of Decision Failure

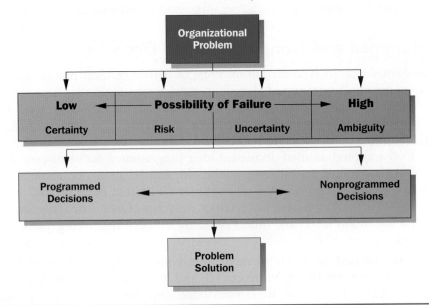

**Certainty**

**Certainty** means that all the information the decision maker needs is fully available.[8] Managers have information on operating conditions, resource costs or constraints, and each course of action and possible outcome. For example, if a company considers a $10,000 investment in new equipment that it knows for certain will yield $4,000 in cost savings per year over the next five years, managers can calculate a before-tax rate of return of about 40 percent. If managers compare this investment with one that will yield only $3,000 per year in cost savings, they can confidently select the 40 percent return. However, few decisions are certain in the real world. Most contain risk or uncertainty.

**Risk**

**Risk** means that a decision has clear-cut goals and that good information is available, but the future outcomes associated with each alternative are subject to chance. However, enough information is available to allow the probability of a successful outcome for each alternative to be estimated.[9] Statistical analysis might be used to

### CONCEPT CONNECTION

*Federal Express took a big **risk** when it decided to become an integral part of the movie* Cast Away. *Product integration goes beyond displaying a product in the background of a movie scene—with integration, products actually become part of the script. FedEx had to weigh the downside of linking its services with an unrelated and volatile film industry against the positive exposure it could possibly gain by being associated with celebrity star Tom Hanks and a blockbuster movie.*

calculate the probabilities of success or failure. The measure of risk captures the possibility that future events will render the alternative unsuccessful. For example, to make restaurant location decisions, McDonald's can analyze potential customer demographics, traffic patterns, supply logistics, and the local competition and come up with reasonably good forecasts of how successful a restaurant will be in each possible location.[10] General Electric Aircraft Engines (GEAE) took a risk on the development of regional jet engines, the engines that power smaller planes with seating for up to 100 and ranges of up to 1,500 miles. Based on trends in the environment, GEAE's managers predicted that use of regional jets would grow, so they invested more than $1 billion in new engine technology at a time when no one else was paying attention to the regional jet market. The decision paid off as full-service carriers have declined and smaller regional and low-fare airlines have grown. Between 1993 and 2003, the number of regional jets in service increased from 85 to 1,300 and the number is expected to grow. GEAC finds itself in an enviable position, with a virtual lock on one of the few growing market segments in commercial aviation.[11]

## Uncertainty

**Uncertainty** means that managers know which goals they wish to achieve, but information about alternatives and future events is incomplete. Managers do not have enough information to be clear about alternatives or to estimate their risk. Factors that may affect a decision, such as price, production costs, volume, or future interest rates are difficult to analyze and predict. Managers may have to make assumptions from which to forge the decision even though it will be wrong if the assumptions are incorrect. Managers may have to come up with creative approaches to alternatives and use personal judgment to determine which alternative is best.

**uncertainty**
Managers know which goals they wish to achieve, but information about alternatives and future events is incomplete.

John Reed, the interim chairman and CEO of the New York Stock Exchange, faced tremendous uncertainty as he struggled to restore credibility and morale following the forced resignation of Chairman Richard Grasso in late 2003. With so many constituents and diverse interests, just defining the issues was a challenge. Decisions included what kinds of corporate governance reforms to recommend, how to conduct a probe into alleged illegal trading activity of NYSE specialist firms, and whether to alter the open outcry/auction model, where every trade passes through at least one live trader on the NYSE floor.[12] Decisions such as these have no clearcut solutions and require that managers rely on creativity, judgment, intuition, and experience to craft a response.

Many decisions made under uncertainty do not produce the desired results, but managers face uncertainty every day. They find creative ways to cope with uncertainty in order to make more effective decisions.

## Ambiguity

**Ambiguity** is by far the most difficult decision situation. Ambiguity means that the goals to be achieved or the problem to be solved is unclear, alternatives are difficult to define, and information about outcomes is unavailable.[13] Ambiguity is what students would feel if an instructor created student groups, told each group to complete a project, but gave the groups no topic, direction, or guidelines whatsoever. Ambiguity has been called a *wicked decision problem*. Managers have a difficult time coming to grips with the issues. Wicked problems are associated with manager conflicts over goals and decision alternatives, rapidly changing circumstances, fuzzy information, and unclear linkages among decision elements.[14] Sometimes managers will come up with a "solution" only to realize that they hadn't clearly defined the real problem to begin with.[15] A recent example of a wicked decision problem was when managers at Ford Motor Company and Firestone confronted the problem of tires used on the Ford Explorer coming apart on the road, causing deadly blow-outs and rollovers. Just defining the problem and whether the tire itself or the design of the Explorer was at fault was the

**ambiguity**
The goals to be achieved or the problem to be solved is unclear, alternatives are difficult to define, and information about outcomes is unavailable.

first hurdle. Information was fuzzy and fast-changing, and managers were in conflict over how to handle the problem. Neither side has dealt with this decision situation very effectively, and the reputations of both companies have suffered as a result. Fortunately, most decisions are not characterized by ambiguity. But when they are, managers must conjure up goals and develop reasonable scenarios for decision alternatives in the absence of information.

# Decision-Making Models

The approach managers use to make decisions usually falls into one of three types—the classical model, the administrative model, or the political model. The choice of model depends on the manager's personal preference, whether the decision is programmed or nonprogrammed, and the extent to which the decision is characterized by risk, uncertainty, or ambiguity.

## Classical Model

**classical model**
A decision-making model based on the assumption that managers should make logical decisions that will be in the organization's best economic interests.

The **classical model** of decision making is based on economic assumptions. This model has arisen within the management literature because managers are expected to make decisions that are economically sensible and in the organization's best economic interests. The four assumptions underlying this model are as follows:

1. The decision maker operates to accomplish goals that are known and agreed upon. Problems are precisely formulated and defined.
2. The decision maker strives for conditions of certainty, gathering complete information. All alternatives and the potential results of each are calculated.
3. Criteria for evaluating alternatives are known. The decision maker selects the alternative that will maximize the economic return to the organization.
4. The decision maker is rational and uses logic to assign values, order preferences, evaluate alternatives, and make the decision that will maximize the attainment of organizational goals.

**normative**
An approach that defines how a decision maker should make decisions and provides guidelines for reaching an ideal outcome for the organization.

The classical model of decision making is considered to be **normative**, which means it defines how a decision maker *should* make decisions. It does not describe how managers actually make decisions so much as it provides guidelines on how to reach an ideal outcome for the organization. The value of the classical model has been its ability to help decision makers be more rational. Many managers rely solely on intuition and personal preferences for making decisions.[16] For example, during this era of rising medical costs, decisions in hospitals and medical centers about who gets scarce resources such as expensive procedures and drugs are usually made on an ad hoc basis. Administrators at the University of Texas Medical Branch, however, are using the classical model to provide some clear guidelines and rules that can be consistently applied. A committee of administrators, doctors and mid-level staffers codified a top-to-bottom system for allocating medical services. Patients without insurance must pay up front to see a doctor. Strict rules bar expensive drugs being given to patients who can't pay for them. Screeners see patients as soon as they come in and follow clear, rational procedures for determining who is eligible for what services. A special fund can pay for drugs that are off-limits to poor patients, but approval has to come from the chief medical director, who often uses cost-benefit analysis to make her decisions. The hospital's rationing system is controversial. However, top managers argue that it helps the institution impartially care for the poor at the same time it adheres to rational budget restrictions needed to keep the institution financially solid.[17]

# Unlocking Creative Solutions Through Technology

## Southwest Uses Technology to Keep a Hawk's Eye on Costs

The airline industry has been in the worst slump in history and the three largest carriers lost a total of $5.8 billion in 2003. But Southwest Airlines is still going strong, despite the industry downturn, rising fuel prices, difficult union negotiations, and a crop of new low-fare competitors. Southwest's 2003 profits totaled $442 million, more than all the other U.S. airlines combined. Southwest's wacky, people-oriented culture has often been cited as a key factor in the company's success. But managers point out that keeping a hawk's eye on costs is just as much a part of the culture as silliness and fun.

One way managers keep a lid on costs is by applying technology to support decision making. Consider the use of a new breed of simulation software to help make decisions about the airline's freight operations. BiosGroup, a joint venture between Santa Fe Institute biologist Stuart Kauffman and the consulting firm Cap Gemini Ernst & Young, uses adaptive, agent-based computer modeling to help companies like Southwest and Procter & Gamble solve complex business problems. For the Southwest project, the computer simulation model represented individual baggage handlers and other employees; the model was created to see how thousands of individual day-to-day decisions and interactions determined the behavior of the airline's overall freight operation.

A BiosGroup team spent many hours interviewing all the employees whose jobs related to freight handling. Then, they programmed the computer to simulate the people in the freight house who accepted a customer's package, those who figured out which flight the package should go on, those on the ramp who were loading the planes, and so forth. When the computer ran a simulation of a week's worth of freight operations, various aspects of operations were measured—such as how many times employees had to load and unload cargo or how often freight had to be stored overnight. The simulation indicated that, rather than unloading cargo from incoming flights and putting it on the next direct flight to its destination, Southwest would be better off to just let the freight take the long way around. Paradoxically, this approach turned out to usually get the freight to its destination faster and saved the time and cost of unloading and reloading.

Southwest managers lost no time in implementing the decision to change the freight handling system. By applying technology to find a more efficient way of doing things, Southwest is saving an estimated $10 million over 5 years. Now that's one way to become the most profitable airline in the country.

**SOURCES:** Mitchell Waldrop, "Chaos, Inc.," *Red Herring* (January 2003), 38–40; and Andy Serwer, "Southwest Airlines: The Hottest Thing in the Sky," *Fortune* (March 8, 2004), 86–106.

In many respects, the classical model represents an "ideal" model of decision making that is often unattainable by real people in real organizations. It is most valuable when applied to programmed decisions and to decisions characterized by certainty or risk, because relevant information is available and probabilities can be calculated. For example, new analytical software programs automate many programmed decisions, such as freezing the account of a customer who has failed to make payments.[18] GE Energy Rentals uses a system that captures financial and organizational information about customers to help managers evaluate risks and make credit decisions. The system has enabled the division to reduce costs, increase processing time, and improve cash flow. In the retail industry, software programs analyze current and historical sales data to help companies such as Home Depot and Gap decide when, where, and how much to mark down prices.[19] This chapter's Unlocking Creative Solutions Through Technology box describes how Southwest Airlines uses quantitative models to help keep costs low and retain its position as the low-cost leader. The growth of quantitative decision techniques that use computers has expanded the use of the classical approach. Quantitative techniques include such things as decision trees, payoff matrices, break-even analysis, linear programming, forecasting, and operations research models. The NBC television network uses a computer-based system to create optimum advertising schedules.

For television viewers, news and entertainment is the primary function of the NBC network. But for NBC managers, one of the biggest concerns is optimizing the advertising schedule. Each year, managers have to develop a detailed advertising plan and a schedule that meets advertisers' desires in terms of cost, target audience, program mix, and other factors. At the same time, the schedule has to get the most revenues for the available amount of inventory (advertising slots).

Creating an advertising plan and schedule can be extremely complex, with numerous decision constraints and variables, such as product conflict restraints, airtime availability restraints, client requirements, or management restrictions. NBC offices use a computerized system that quickly and efficiently makes optimal use of advertising slots. When an advertiser makes a request, planners enter all the information into the system, including the budgeted amount the customer is willing to pay for a total package of commercials, the number of people the advertiser wants to reach, the targeted demographic characteristics, how the budget is to be distributed over four quarters of the year, the number of weeks in the program year, the unit lengths of commercials, the specific shows the advertiser is interested in, and so forth. Management ranks the shows and weeks of the year by their importance, and these data are also entered into the system, along with the availability of advertising slots during each week and other constraints. The system formulates an advertising plan that uses the least amount of premium inventory subject to meeting client requirements.

By using the classical approach, NBC generates optimal plans that meet the advertiser's needs while at the same time saving millions of dollars of premium inventory, which can be used to lure new advertisers who will pay high fees to advertise on the hottest shows.[20]

NATIONAL
BROADCASTING
COMPANY (NBC)
http://www.nbc.com

## Administrative Model

**administrative model**
A decision-making model that describes how managers actually make decisions in situations characterized by nonprogrammed decisions, uncertainty, and ambiguity.

The **administrative model** of decision making describes how managers actually make decisions in difficult situations, such as those characterized by nonprogrammed decisions, uncertainty, and ambiguity. Many management decisions are not sufficiently programmable to lend themselves to any degree of quantification. Managers are unable to make economically rational decisions even if they want to.[21]

### Bounded Rationality and Satisficing

The administrative model of decision making is based on the work of Herbert A. Simon. Simon proposed two concepts that were instrumental in shaping the administrative model: bounded rationality and satisficing. **Bounded rationality** means that people have limits, or boundaries, on how rational they can be. The organization is incredibly complex, and managers have the time and ability to process only a limited amount of information with which to make decisions.[22] Because managers do not have the time or cognitive ability to process complete information about complex decisions, they must satisfice. **Satisficing** means that decision makers choose the first solution alternative that satisfies minimal decision criteria. Rather than pursuing all alternatives to identify the single solution that will maximize economic returns, managers will opt for the first solution that appears to solve the problem, even if better solutions are presumed to exist. The decision maker cannot justify the time and expense of obtaining complete information.[23]

**bounded rationality**
The concept that people have the time and cognitive ability to process only a limited amount of information on which to base decisions.

**satisficing**
To choose the first solution alternative that satisfies minimal decision criteria regardless of whether better solutions are presumed to exist.

An example of both bounded rationality and satisficing occurs when a junior executive on a business trip spills coffee on her blouse just before an important meeting. She will run to a nearby clothing store and buy the first satisfactory replacement she finds. Having neither the time nor the opportunity to explore all the blouses in town, she satisfices by choosing a blouse that will solve the immediate problem. In a similar fashion, managers generate alternatives for complex problems only until they find one they believe will work. For example, several years ago then-Disney chairman Ray Watson and chief operating officer Ron Miller attempted to thwart takeover attempts, but they had limited options. They satisficed with a quick decision to acquire Arivda Realty and

Gibson Court Company. The acquisition of these companies had the potential to solve the problem at hand; thus, they looked no further for possibly better alternatives.[24]

The administrative model relies on assumptions different from those of the classical model and focuses on organizational factors that influence individual decisions. It is more realistic than the classical model for complex, nonprogrammed decisions. According to the administrative model:

1. Decision goals often are vague, conflicting, and lack consensus among managers. Managers often are unaware of problems or opportunities that exist in the organization.
2. Rational procedures are not always used, and, when they are, they are confined to a simplistic view of the problem that does not capture the complexity of real organizational events.
3. Managers' searches for alternatives are limited because of human, information, and resource constraints.
4. Most managers settle for a satisficing rather than a maximizing solution. This is partly because they have limited information and partly because they have only vague criteria for what constitutes a maximizing solution.

The administrative model is considered to be **descriptive**, meaning that it describes how managers actually make decisions in complex situations rather than dictating how they *should* make decisions according to a theoretical ideal. The administrative model recognizes the human and environmental limitations that affect the degree to which managers can pursue a rational decision-making process. For example, interviews with CEOs in high-tech industries found that they strived to use some type of rational process in making decisions, but the way they actually decided things was through a complex interaction with other managers, subordinates, environmental factors, and organizational events.[25]

**descriptive**
An approach that describes how managers actually make decisions rather than how they should.

## Intuition

Another aspect of administrative decision making is intuition. **Intuition** represents a quick apprehension of a decision situation based on past experience but without conscious thought.[26] Intuitive decision making is not arbitrary or irrational, because it is based on years of practice and hands-on experience that enable managers to quickly identify solutions without going through painstaking computations. In today's fast-paced, turbulent business environment, intuition plays an increasingly important role in decision making. A study of 60 business professionals from a variety of industries, for example, found that nearly half said they relied on intuition often in making decisions in the workplace, while another 30 percent reported using intuition sometimes.[27]

**intuition**
The immediate comprehension of a decision situation based on past experience but without conscious thought.

Cognitive psychologist Gary Klein has studied how people make good decisions using their intuition under extreme time pressure and uncertainty.[28] Klein has found that intuition begins with *recognition*. When people build a depth of experience and knowledge in a particular area, the right decision often comes quickly and effortlessly as a recognition of information that has been largely forgotten by the conscious mind. For example, firefighters make decisions by recognizing what is typical or abnormal about a fire, based on their experience. Similarly, in the business world, managers are continuously perceiving and processing information that they may not consciously be aware of, and their base of knowledge and experience helps them make decisions that may be characterized by uncertainty and ambiguity. Research by a growing number of psychologists and neuroscientists has affirmed the power of our unconscious minds in making decisions. Studies of intuition indicate that the unconscious mind has cognitive abilities that sometimes surpass those of the conscious mind.[29]

© STAN GODLEWSKI

**CONCEPT CONNECTION**

*"It's a major gut story," Bruce Goldsmith says about his decision to open a retail store right in the warehouse of his family's mail-order coffee business. Since Baronet Coffee, Inc.'s warehouse is in an industrial area with little foot traffic, most employees thought the idea was a little wacky, but Goldsmith's **intuition** told him it was the right thing to do. His years of experience observing customers and a few assumptions about human nature gave him a hunch that people would like the idea of picking up their coffee directly from the source. The hunch was right, and Baronet's retail sales quadrupled Goldsmith's original projections.*

**coalition**
An informal alliance among managers who support a specific goal.

The entertainment industry provides many good examples of intuition because of the complex and uncertain nature of picking hit shows. For example, when Sherry Lansing of Paramount Pictures decided to do the movie *Forrest Gump*, few people expected it to be successful. "It was a film about a guy on a bench," Lansing said. "It was one of the riskiest films ever made." But Lansing's intuition told her Tom Hanks sitting on a bench and explaining how "life is like a box of chocolates" would work, and the film reaped $329 million at the box office. Another example comes from the Fox television network, where prime time ratings were dismal until Steven Chao came up with *America's Most Wanted* and *Cops*. Initially, everyone hated the idea of these raw, crime-oriented shows, but Chao and his boss Barry Diller stuck with their gut feelings and pushed the projects.[30]

## Political Model

The third model of decision making is useful for making nonprogrammed decisions when conditions are uncertain, information is limited, and there is disagreement among managers about what goals to pursue or what course of action to take. Most organizational decisions involve many managers who are pursuing different goals, and they have to talk with one another to share information and reach an agreement. Managers often engage in coalition building for making complex organizational decisions. A **coalition** is an informal alliance among managers who support a specific goal. *Coalition building* is the process of forming alliances among managers. In other words, a manager who supports a specific alternative, such as increasing the corporation's growth by acquiring another company, talks informally to other executives and tries to persuade them to support the decision. When the outcomes are not predictable, managers gain support through discussion, negotiation, and bargaining. Without a coalition, a powerful individual or group could derail the decision-making process. Coalition building gives several managers an opportunity to contribute to decision making, enhancing their commitment to the alternative that is ultimately adopted.[31]

The political model closely resembles the real environment in which most managers and decision makers operate. Decisions are complex and involve many people, information is often ambiguous, and disagreement and conflict over problems and solutions are normal. There are four basic assumptions of the political model:

1.  Organizations are made up of groups with diverse interests, goals, and values. Managers disagree about problem priorities and may not understand or share the goals and interests of other managers.
2.  Information is ambiguous and incomplete. The attempt to be rational is limited by the complexity of many problems as well as personal and organizational constraints.
3.  Managers do not have the time, resources, or mental capacity to identify all dimensions of the problem and process all relevant information. Managers talk to each other and exchange viewpoints to gather information and reduce ambiguity.
4.  Managers engage in the push and pull of debate to decide goals and discuss alternatives. Decisions are the result of bargaining and discussion among coalition members.

To support a U.S.-led campaign against terrorism and a war in Iraq, President George W. Bush has tried to take a lesson from his father, who was known as a consummate coalition-builder. The elder Bush always sought a broad-based coalition at the start of any important decision process, such as that regarding the 1990 Persian

Gulf War. The younger president has been criticized for pushing his own priorities and opinions too aggressively and is trying to engage in stronger coalition building for making decisions concerning overseas campaigns. The inability of leaders to build coalitions often makes it difficult or impossible for managers to get their decisions implemented. Hershell Ezrin resigned as CEO of Canada's Speedy Muffler King because he was unable to build a coalition of managers who supported his decisions for change at the troubled company. Many senior-level executives resented Ezrin's appointment and refused to go along with his ideas for reviving the company.[32]

The key dimensions of the classical, administrative, and political models are listed in Exhibit 9.2. Recent research into decision-making procedures has found rational, classical procedures to be associated with high performance for organizations in stable environments. However, administrative and political decision-making procedures and intuition have been associated with high performance in unstable environments in which decisions must be made rapidly and under more difficult conditions.[33]

# Decision-Making Steps

Whether a decision is programmed or nonprogrammed and regardless of managers' choice of the classical, administrative, or political model of decision making, six steps typically are associated with effective decision processes. These are summarized in Exhibit 9.3.

## Recognition of Decision Requirement

Managers confront a decision requirement in the form of either a problem or an opportunity. A **problem** occurs when organizational accomplishment is less than established goals. Some aspect of performance is unsatisfactory. An **opportunity** exists when managers see potential accomplishment that exceeds specified current goals. Managers see the possibility of enhancing performance beyond current levels.

Awareness of a problem or opportunity is the first step in the decision sequence and requires surveillance of the internal and external environment for issues that merit executive attention.[34] This resembles the military concept of gathering intelligence. Managers scan the world around them to determine whether the organization is satisfactorily progressing toward its goals.

Some information comes from periodic financial reports, performance reports, and other sources that are designed to discover problems before they become too

**problem**
A situation in which organizational accomplishments have failed to meet established goals.

**opportunity**
A situation in which managers see potential organizational accomplishments that exceed current goals.

Exhibit 9.2

## Characteristics of Classical, Administrative, and Political Decision-Making Models

| Classical Model | Administrative Model | Political Model |
|---|---|---|
| Clear-cut problem and goals | Vague problem and goals | Pluralistic; conflicting goals |
| Condition of certainty | Condition of uncertainty | Condition of uncertainty/ambiguity |
| Full information about alternatives and their outcomes | Limited information about alternatives and their outcomes | Inconsistent viewpoints; ambiguous information |
| Rational choice by individual for maximizing outcomes | Satisficing choice for resolving problem using intuition | Bargaining and discussion among coalition members |

Exhibit 9.3

## Six Steps in the Managerial Decision-Making Process

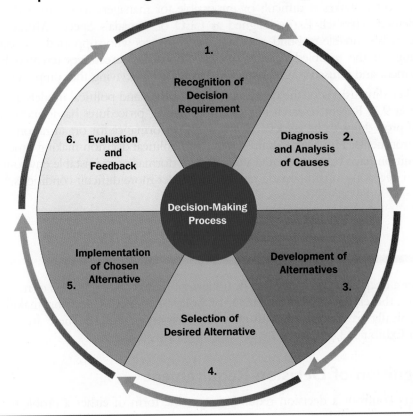

serious. For example, sharply declining sales figures in the Oldsmobile and Buick divisions of General Motors signaled a problem that needed to be addressed. Managers could see that Oldsmobile and Buick had been on a downhill slide for years as the loyal buyers of these brands were aging and the cars failed to appeal to younger buyers.[35] Recognition of the problem led managers to focus on decisions about the fate of these two divisions in their overall efforts to lead GM out of the downturn. Managers also take advantage of informal sources. They talk to other managers, gather opinions on how things are going, and seek advice on which problems should be tackled or which opportunities embraced.[36]

Recognizing decision requirements is difficult, because it often means integrating bits and pieces of information in novel ways.

## Diagnosis and Analysis of Causes

**diagnosis**
The step in the decision-making process in which managers analyze underlying causal factors associated with the decision situation.

Once a problem or opportunity has come to a manager's attention, the understanding of the situation should be refined. **Diagnosis** is the step in the decision-making process in which managers analyze underlying causal factors associated with the decision situation. Managers make a mistake here if they jump right into generating alternatives without first exploring the cause of the problem more deeply.

Kepner and Tregoe, who have conducted extensive studies of manager decision making, recommend that managers ask a series of questions to specify underlying causes, including the following:

- What is the state of disequilibrium affecting us?
- When did it occur?

- Where did it occur?
- How did it occur?
- To whom did it occur?
- What is the urgency of the problem?
- What is the interconnectedness of events?
- What result came from which activity?[37]

Such questions help specify what actually happened and why. Managers at McDonald's are struggling to diagnose the underlying factors in the company's recent troubles. The problem is an urgent one, as the stock price fell 60 percent in three years, sales and profits are declining, and quality and service lag behind those of rival fast food restaurants. Managers are examining the multitude of problems facing the fast food giant, tracing the pattern of the decline, and looking at the interconnectedness of issues such as changing eating habits, a struggling economy, increased competition, poor headquarters planning, weak control systems, and a decline in training and evaluation for franchisees.[38]

## Development of Alternatives

Once the problem or opportunity has been recognized and analyzed, decision makers begin to consider taking action. The next stage is to generate possible alternative solutions that will respond to the needs of the situation and correct the underlying causes. One study found that limiting the search for alternatives is a primary cause of decision failure in organizations.[39]

For a programmed decision, feasible alternatives are easy to identify and in fact usually are already available within the organization's rules and procedures. Nonprogrammed decisions, however, require developing new courses of action that will meet the company's needs. For decisions made under conditions of high uncertainty, managers may develop only one or two custom solutions that will satisfice for handling the problem.

Decision alternatives can be thought of as the tools for reducing the difference between the organization's current and desired performance. At McDonald's, executives are considering alternatives such as using mystery shoppers and unannounced inspections to improve quality and service, motivating demoralized franchisees to get them to invest in new equipment and programs, taking R&D out of the test kitchen and encouraging franchisees to help come up with successful new menu items, and closing some stores to avoid cannibalizing its own sales.[40]

## Selection of Desired Alternative

Once feasible alternatives have been developed, one must be selected. The decision choice is the selection of the most promising of several alternative courses of action. The best alternative is one in which the solution best fits the overall goals and values of the organization and achieves the desired results using the fewest resources.[41] The manager tries to select the choice with the least amount of risk and uncertainty. Because some risk is inherent for most nonprogrammed decisions, managers try to gauge prospects for success. Under conditions of uncertainty, they might have to rely on their intuition and experience to estimate whether a given course of action is likely to succeed. Basing choices on overall goals and values can also effectively guide selection of alternatives. For example, stockbroker Edward Jones was hit hard by the gloomy stock market and the declining economy in late 2001. To make decisions about how to cope, managers relied on the company's values and goals of treating employees right and

**CONCEPT CONNECTION**

*Jon Bon Jovi is a rock star and entrepreneur, who co-owns the Philadelphia Soul, an expansion team of the Arena Football League (AFL). Bon Jovi and his partner, businessman Craig Spencer, spotted an* **opportunity** *to capitalize on Bon Jovi's personality and fame, as well as his savvy marketing skills, by acquiring the franchise. Bon Jovi personally made decisions such as naming the team the Soul (because "anybody can have soul," he says) and creating a mascot (the Soul Man), and he is actively involved in decisions regarding everything from advertising budgets to where to place the autograph tables after a game. Today, the Soul leads the AFL in ticket sales, advertising sales, and merchandising revenue.*

© DON MURRAY/GETTY IMAGES

building long-term relationships. Not a single employee was laid off (the company hasn't laid off an employee in 34 years), and although bonuses were reduced, the company issued them a week early to help employees hurt by the trading decline. Edward Jones' values-based decision making helped win the company the Number 1 spot two years in a row on *Fortune* magazine's list of best companies to work for.[42]

Making choices depends on managers' personality factors and willingness to accept risk and uncertainty. For example, **risk propensity** is the willingness to undertake risk with the opportunity of gaining an increased payoff. The level of risk a manager is willing to accept will influence the analysis of cost and benefits to be derived from any decision. Consider the situations in Exhibit 9.4. In each situation, which alternative would you choose? A person with a low risk propensity would tend to take assured moderate returns by going for a tie score, building a domestic plant, or pursuing a career as a physician. A risk taker would go for the victory, build a plant in a foreign country, or embark on an acting career. This chapter's Manager's Shoptalk box describes biases to avoid when selecting the desired alternative.

## Implementation of Chosen Alternative

The **implementation** stage involves the use of managerial, administrative, and persuasive abilities to ensure that the chosen alternative is carried out. This is similar to the idea of strategic implementation described in Chapter 8. The ultimate success of the chosen alternative depends on whether it can be translated into action.[43] Sometimes an alternative never becomes reality because managers lack the resources or energy needed to make things happen. Implementation may require discussion with people affected by the decision. Communication, motivation, and leadership skills must be used to see that the decision is carried out. When employees see that managers follow up on their decisions by tracking implementation success, they are more committed to positive action.[44]

At General Motors, CEO Rick Wagoner has hired new top executives, including Bob Lutz, former product development chief at Chrysler, who share his vision and can help implement his decisions for livening up GM's product portfolio. For example, as vice president for product development, Lutz is personally making sure designers and engineers pay attention to all the small details that determine a new model's appeal—everything from how the stereo knob feels when you turn it to the width of the gaps where the car hood meets the headlights. By communicating with people on the front lines Lutz is helping to implement small decisions every day aimed at helping to revamp the passenger car product line and revive the image of GM's brands.[45]

If managers lack the ability or desire to implement decisions, the chosen alternative cannot be carried out to benefit the organization.

## Evaluation and Feedback

In the evaluation stage of the decision process, decision makers gather information that tells them how well the decision was implemented and whether it was effective in

**risk propensity**
The willingness to undertake risk with the opportunity of gaining an increased payoff.

**implementation**
The step in the decision-making process that involves using managerial, administrative, and persuasive abilities to translate the chosen alternative into action.

**CONCEPT CONNECTION**

*UPS knows many businesses have a low* **risk propensity** *when it comes to matters affecting their cash flow, so it spotted a business opportunity. The company's UPS Capital Insurance division reduces customers' risk of delayed payments through a variety of trade insurance policies. This advertisement for* Exchange Collect *promises peace of mind for companies dealing with international customers or suppliers. The service works like a secure international C.O.D., with UPS securing payment on behalf of the customer before delivering goods. For UPS customers, the results is improved cash flow and less risk.*

Exhibit 9.4

## Decision Alternatives with Different Levels of Risk

### For each of the following decisions, which alternative would you choose?

1   In the final seconds of a game with the college's traditional rival, the coach of a college football team may choose a play that has a 95 percent chance of producing a tie score or one with a 30 percent chance of leading to victory or to sure defeat if it fails.

2   The president of a Canadian company must decide whether to build a new plant within Canada that has a 90 percent chance of producing a modest return on investment or to build it in a foreign country with an unstable political history. The latter alternative has a 40 percent chance of failing, but the returns would be enormous if it succeeded.

3   A college senior with considerable acting talent must choose a career. She has the opportunity to go on to medical school and become a physician, a career in which she is 80 percent likely to succeed. She would rather be an actress but realizes that the opportunity for success is only 20 percent.

---

achieving its goals. For example, Tandy executives evaluated their decision to open computer centers for businesses and feedback revealed poor sales performance. Feedback indicated that implementation was unsuccessful, and computer centers were closed so Tandy could focus on its successful Radio Shack retail stores.

Feedback is important because decision making is a continuous, never-ending process. Decision making is not completed when an executive or board of directors votes yes or no. Feedback provides decision makers with information that can precipitate a new decision cycle. The decision may fail, thus generating a new analysis of the problem, evaluation of alternatives, and selection of a new alternative. Many big problems are solved by trying several alternatives in sequence, each providing modest improvement. Feedback is the part of monitoring that assesses whether a new decision needs to be made.

To illustrate the overall decision-making process, including evaluation and feedback, we can look at the decision to introduce a new deodorant at Tom's of Maine.

---

Tom's of Maine, known for its all-natural personal hygiene products, saw an opportunity to expand its line with a new natural deodorant. However, the opportunity quickly became a problem when the deodorant worked only half of the time with half of the customers who used it, and its all-recyclable plastic dials were prone to breakage.

The problem of the failed deodorant led founder Tom Chappell and other managers to analyze and diagnose what went wrong. They finally determined that the company's product development process had run amok. The same group of merry product developers was responsible from conception to launch of the product. They were so attached to the product that they failed to test it properly or consider potential problems, becoming instead "a mutual admiration society." Managers considered several alternatives for solving the problem. The decision to publicly admit the problem and recall the deodorant was an easy one for Chappell, who runs his company on principles of fairness and honesty. Not only did the company apologize to its customers, but it also listened to their complaints and suggestions. Chappell himself helped answer calls and letters. Even though the recall cost the company $400,000 and led to a stream of negative publicity, it ultimately helped the company improve relationships with customers.

**TOM'S OF MAINE**
http://www.
tomsofmaine.com

# manager's Shoptalk

## Decision Biases to Avoid

At a time when decision making is so important, many managers do not know how to make a good choice among alternatives. They might rely on computer analyses or personal intuition without realizing that their own cognitive biases affect their judgment. Many errors in judgment originate in the human mind's limited capacity and in the natural biases most managers display during decision making. Awareness of the six biases below can help managers make more enlightened choices:

1. *Being influenced by initial impressions.* When considering decisions, the mind often gives disproportionate weight to the first information it receives. These initial impressions, statistics, or estimates act as an anchor to our subsequent thoughts and judgments. Anchors can be as simple as a random comment by a colleague or a statistic read in a newspaper. Past events and trends also act as anchors. For example, in business, managers frequently look at the previous year's sales when estimating sales for the coming year. Giving too much weight to the past can lead to poor forecasts and misguided decisions.

2. *Justifying past decisions.* Many people fall into the trap of making choices that justify their past decisions, even if those decisions no longer seem valid. For example, managers may invest tremendous time and energy into improving the performance of a problem employee whom they now realize should never have been hired in the first place. Another example is when a manager continues to pour money into a failing project, hoping to turn things around. People don't like to make mistakes, so they continue to make flawed decisions in an effort to correct the past.

3. *Seeing what you want to see.* People frequently look for information that supports their existing instinct or point of view and avoid information that contradicts it. This bias affects where managers look for information, as well as how they interpret the information they find. People tend to give too much weight to

supporting information and too little to information that conflicts with their established viewpoints. It is important for managers to be honest with themselves about their motives and to examine all the evidence with equal rigor. Having a devil's advocate to argue against a decision can also help avoid this decision trap.

4. *Perpetuating the status quo.* Managers may base decisions on what has worked in the past and fail to explore new options, dig for additional information, or investigate new technologies. For example, DuPont clung to its cash cow, nylon, despite growing evidence in the scientific community that a new product, polyester, was superior for tire cords. Celanese, a relatively small competitor, blew DuPont out of the water by exploiting this new evidence, quickly capturing 75 percent of the tire market.

5. *Being influenced by problem framing.* The decision response of a manager can be influenced by the mere wording of a problem. For example, consider a manager faced with a decision about salvaging the cargo of three barges that sank off the coast of Alaska. If managers are given the option of approving (A) a plan that has a 100 percent chance of saving the cargo of one of the three barges, worth $200,000, or (B) a plan that has a one-third chance of saving the cargo of all three barges, worth $600,000 and a two-thirds chance of saving nothing, most managers choose option A. The same problem with a negative frame would give managers a choice of selecting (C) a plan that has a 100 percent chance of losing two of the three cargoes, worth $400,000, or (D) a plan that has a two-thirds chance of losing all three cargoes but a one-third chance of losing no cargo. With this framing, most managers choose option D. Because both problems are identical, the decision choice depends strictly on how the problem is framed.

6. *Overconfidence.* Most people overestimate their ability to predict uncertain outcomes. Before making a decision, managers have unrealistic expectations of their ability to

# manager's Shoptalk

understand the risk and make the right choice. Overconfidence is greatest when answering questions of moderate to extreme difficulty. For example, when people are asked to define quantities about which they have little direct knowledge ("What was Wal-Mart's 2003 revenue?" "What was the market value of Microsoft as of March 14, 2004?"), they overestimate their accuracy. Evidence of overconfidence is illustrated in cases in which subjects were so certain of an answer that they assigned odds of 1,000 to 1 of being correct but in fact were correct only about 85 percent of the time. When uncertainty is high, managers may unrealistically expect that they can successfully predict outcomes and hence select the wrong alternative.

SOURCES: Based on John Hammond, Ralph L. Keeney, and Howard Raiffa, "The Hidden Traps in Decision Making," *Harvard Business Review* (September–October 1998), 47–58; Oren Harari, "The Thomas Lawson Syndrome," *Management Review* (February 1994), 58–61; Dan Ariely, "Q&A: Why Good CIOs Make Bad Decisions," *CIO* (May 1, 2003), 83–87; Leigh Buchanan, "How To Take Risks In a Time of Anxiety," *Inc.* (May 2003), 76–81; and Max H. Bazerman, *Judgment in Managerial Decision Making*, 5th ed. (New York: John Wiley & Sons, 2002).

Evaluation and feedback also led Tom's of Maine to set up *acorn groups*, from which it hopes mighty oaks of successful products will grow. Acorn groups are cross-departmental teams that will shepherd new products from beginning to end. The cross-functional teams are a mechanism for catching problems—and new opportunities—that ordinarily would be missed. They pass on their ideas and findings to senior managers and the product-development team.

Tom's was able to turn a problem into an opportunity, thanks to evaluation and feedback. Not only did the disaster ultimately help the company solidify relationships with customers, but it also led to a formal mechanism for learning and sharing ideas—something the company did not have before.[46]

Tom's of Maine's decision illustrates all the decision steps, and the process ultimately ended in success. Strategic decisions always contain some risk, but feedback and follow-up decisions can help get companies back on track. By learning from their decision mistakes, managers and companies can turn problems into opportunities.

## Personal Decision Framework

Imagine you were a manager at Tom's of Maine, General Motors, a local movie theater, or the public library. How would you go about making important decisions that might shape the future of your department or company? So far we have discussed a number of factors that affect how managers make decisions. For example, decisions may be programmed or nonprogrammed, situations are characterized by various levels of uncertainty, and managers may use the classical, administrative, or political model of decision making. In addition, there are six recognized steps to take in the decision-making process.

**decision styles**
Differences among people with respect to how they perceive problems and make decisions.

However, not all managers go about making decisions in the same way. In fact, there are significant differences in the ways individual managers may approach problems and make decisions concerning them. These differences can be explained by the concept of personal **decision styles**. Exhibit 9.5 illustrates the role of personal style in the decision-making process. Personal decision style refers to differences among people with respect to how they perceive problems and make decisions. Research has identified four major decision styles: directive, analytical, conceptual, and behavioral.[47]

1. The *directive style* is used by people who prefer simple, clear-cut solutions to problems. Managers who use this style often make decisions quickly because they do not like to deal with a lot of information and may consider only one or two alternatives. People who prefer the directive style generally are efficient and rational and prefer to rely on existing rules or procedures for making decisions.
2. Managers with an *analytical style* like to consider complex solutions based on as much data as they can gather. These individuals carefully consider alternatives and often base their decisions on objective, rational data from management control systems and other sources. They search for the best possible decision based on the information available.
3. People who tend toward a *conceptual style* also like to consider a broad amount of information. However, they are more socially oriented than those with an analytical style and like to talk to others about the problem and possible alternatives for solving it. Managers using a conceptual style consider many broad alternatives, rely on information from both people and systems, and like to solve problems creatively.
4. The *behavioral style* is often the style adopted by managers having a deep concern for others as individuals. Managers using this style like to talk to people one-on-one and understand their feelings about the problem and the effect of a given decision upon them. People with a behavioral style usually are concerned with the personal development of others and may make decisions that help others achieve their goals.

*Take A Moment*

*Go to the experiential exercise on page 331 that pertains to evaluating your personal decision style.*

Most managers have a dominant decision style. For example, Jeff Zucker at NBC Entertainment uses a primarily conceptual style, which makes him well suited to the industry. He consults with dozens of programmers about possible new shows and likes to consider many broad alternatives before making decisions.[48] However, managers frequently use several different styles or a combination of styles in making the varied decisions they confront daily. A manager might use a directive style for deciding on which printing company to use for new business cards, yet shift to a more conceptual style when handling an interdepartmental conflict. The most effective managers are able to shift among styles as needed to meet the situation. Being aware

Exhibit 9.5

**Personal Decision Framework**

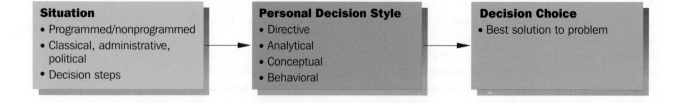

| Situation | Personal Decision Style | Decision Choice |
|---|---|---|
| • Programmed/nonprogrammed<br>• Classical, administrative, political<br>• Decision steps | • Directive<br>• Analytical<br>• Conceptual<br>• Behavioral | • Best solution to problem |

of one's dominant decision style can help a manager avoid making critical mistakes when his or her usual style may be inappropriate to the problem at hand.

# Increasing Participation in Decision Making

Managers do make some decisions as individuals, but decision makers more often are part of a group. Indeed, major decisions in the business world rarely are made entirely by an individual. Effective decision making often depends on whether managers involve the right people in the right ways in helping to solve problems. One model that provides guidance for practicing managers was originally developed by Victor Vroom and Arthur Jago.[49]

## The Vroom-Jago Model

The **Vroom-Jago model** helps a manager gauge the appropriate amount of participation by subordinates in making a specific decision. The model has three major components: leader participation styles, a set of diagnostic questions with which to analyze a decision situation, and a series of decision rules.

**Vroom-Jago model**
A model designed to help managers gauge the amount of subordinate participation in decision making.

### Leader Participation Styles

The model employs five levels of subordinate participation in decision making, ranging from highly autocratic (leader decides alone) to highly democratic (leader delegates to group), as illustrated in Exhibit 9.6.[50] The exhibit shows five decision styles, starting with the leader making the decision alone (Decide); presenting the problem to subordinates individually for their suggestions and then making the decision (Consult Individually); presenting the problem to subordinates as a group, collectively obtaining their ideas and suggestions, then making the decision (Consult Group); sharing the problem with subordinates as a group and acting as a facilitator to help the group arrive at a decision (Facilitate); or delegating the problem and permitting the group to make the decision within prescribed limits (Delegate).

### Diagnostic Questions

How does a manager decide which of the five decision styles to use? The appropriate degree of decision participation depends on a number of situational factors, such as the required level of decision quality, the level of leader or subordinate expertise, and the importance of having subordinates commit to the decision. Leaders can analyze the appropriate degree of participation by answering seven diagnostic questions.

1. *Decision significance: How significant is this decision for the project or organization?* If the quality of the decision is highly important to the success of the project or organization, the leader has to be actively involved.
2. *Importance of commitment: How important is subordinate commitment to carrying out the decision?* If implementation requires a high level of commitment to the decision, leaders should involve subordinates in the decision process.
3. *Leader expertise: What is the level of the leader's expertise in relation to the problem?* If the leader does not have a high amount of information, knowledge, or expertise, the leader should involve subordinates to obtain it.
4. *Likelihood of commitment: If the leader were to make the decision alone, would subordinates have high or low commitment to the decision?* If subordinates typically go along with whatever the leader decides, their involvement in the decision-making process will be less important.

# Exhibit 9.6

## Five Leader Participation Styles

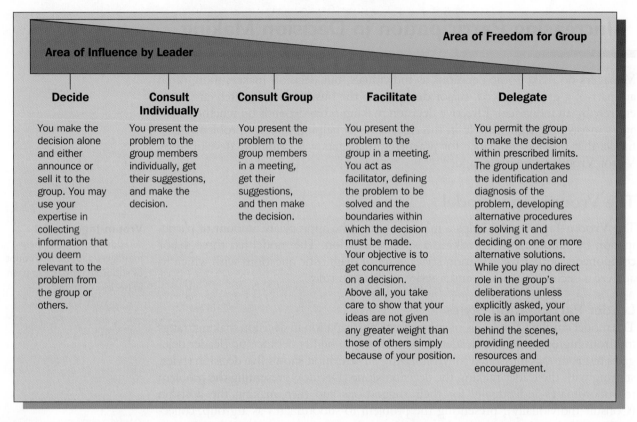

| Decide | Consult Individually | Consult Group | Facilitate | Delegate |
|---|---|---|---|---|
| You make the decision alone and either announce or sell it to the group. You may use your expertise in collecting information that you deem relevant to the problem from the group or others. | You present the problem to the group members individually, get their suggestions, and make the decision. | You present the problem to the group members in a meeting, get their suggestions, and then make the decision. | You present the problem to the group in a meeting. You act as facilitator, defining the problem to be solved and the boundaries within which the decision must be made. Your objective is to get concurrence on a decision. Above all, you take care to show that your ideas are not given any greater weight than those of others simply because of your position. | You permit the group to make the decision within prescribed limits. The group undertakes the identification and diagnosis of the problem, developing alternative procedures for solving it and deciding on one or more alternative solutions. While you play no direct role in the group's deliberations unless explicitly asked, your role is an important one behind the scenes, providing needed resources and encouragement. |

**SOURCE:** Victor H. Vroom, "Leadership and the Decision Making Process," *Organizational Dynamics* 28 no. 4 (Spring 2000), 82–94. This is Vroom's adaptation of Tannenbaum and Schmidt's Taxonomy. Used with permission.

5.  *Group support for goals: What is the degree of subordinate support for the team's or organization's objectives at stake in this decision?* If subordinates have low support for the goals of the organization, the leader should not allow the group to make the decision alone.

6.  *Group expertise: What is the level of group members' knowledge and expertise in relation to the problem?* If subordinates have a high level of expertise in relation to the problem, more responsibility for the decision can be delegated to them.

7.  *Team competence: How skilled and committed are group members to working together as a team to solve problems?* When subordinates have high skills and high desire to work together cooperatively to solve problems, more responsibility for decision making can be delegated to them.

These questions seem detailed, but considering these seven situational factors can quickly narrow the options and point to the appropriate level of group participation in decision making.

## Selecting a Decision Style

The decision matrix in Exhibit 9.7 allows a manager to adopt a participation style by answering the diagnostic questions in sequence. The manager enters the matrix at the left-hand side, at Problem Statement, and considers the seven situational questions in sequence from left to right, answering high (H) or low (L) to each one and avoiding crossing any horizontal lines. The first question would be: *How significant is this decision for the project or organization?* If the answer is High, the leader proceeds to importance of commitment: *How important is subordinate commitment to carrying*

Exhibit 9.7

## Vroom-Jago Decision Model for Determining an Appropriate Decision-Making Style—Group Problems

**Instructions:** The matrix operates like a funnel. You start at the left with a specific decision problem in mind. The column headings denote situational factors that may or may not be present in that problem. You progress by selecting High or Low (H or L) for each relevant situational factor. Proceed down the funnel, judging only those situational factors for which a judgment is required, until you reach the recommended process.

| Decision Significance? | Importance of Commitment? | Leader Expertise? | Likelihood of Commitment? | Group Support? | Group Expertise? | Team Competence? | |
|---|---|---|---|---|---|---|---|
| H | H | H | | H | – | – | – | Decide |
| | | | | | H | H | Delegate |
| | | | L | H | | L | |
| | | | | | L | – | Consult (Group) |
| | | | | L | – | – | |
| | | L | | | H | H | Facilitate |
| | | | H | H | | L | |
| | | | | | L | – | Consult (Individually) |
| | | | | L | – | – | |
| | | | | | H | H | Facilitate |
| | | | L | H | | L | |
| | | | | | L | – | Consult (Group) |
| | | | | L | – | – | |
| | L | H | – | – | – | – | Decide |
| | | L | | | H | H | Facilitate |
| | | | – | H | | L | |
| | | | | | L | – | Consult (Individually) |
| | | | | L | – | – | |
| L | H | – | | H | – | – | Decide |
| | | | L | – | | H | Delegate |
| | | | | | | L | Facilitate |
| | L | – | – | – | – | – | Decide |

*(Row label on left side, vertically: PROBLEM STATEMENT)*

**SOURCE:** Victor H. Vroom "Leadership and the Decision-Making Process," *Organizational Dynamics* 28, no. 4 (Spring 2000), 82–94. Used with permission.

*out the decision?* An answer of High leads to a question about leader expertise: *What is the level of the leader's expertise in relation to the problem?* If the leader's knowledge and expertise is High, the leader next considers likelihood of commitment: *If the leader were to make the decision alone, how likely is it that subordinates would be committed to the decision?* If there is a high likelihood that subordinates would be committed, the decision matrix leads directly to the Decide style of decision making, in which the leader makes the decision alone and presents it to the group.

The Vroom-Jago model has been criticized as being less than perfect,[51] but it is useful to managers, and the body of supportive research is growing.[52] Managers can use the model to make timely, high-quality decisions. Consider the application of the model to the following hypothetical problem.

When Madison Manufacturing won a coveted contract from a large auto manufacturer to produce an engine to power their flagship sports car, Dave Robbins was thrilled to be selected as project manager. This project has dramatically enhanced the reputation of Madison, and Robbins and his team of engineers have taken great pride in their

**MADISON MANUFACTURING**
http://www.madison manufacturing.com

work. However, their enthusiasm was dashed by a recent report of serious engine problems in cars delivered to customers. Taking quick action, the auto manufacturer suspended sales of the sports car, halted current production, and notified owners of the current model not to drive the car. Everyone involved knows this is a disaster. Unless the engine problem is solved quickly, Madison Manufacturing could be exposed to extended litigation. In addition, Madison's valued relationship with one of the world's largest auto manufacturers would likely be lost forever.

As the project manager, Robbins has spent two weeks in the field inspecting the seized engines and the auto plant where they were installed. Based on this extensive research, Robbins has some pretty good ideas about what is causing the problem, but he knows there are members of his team who may have stronger expertise for solving it. In addition, while he has been in the field, other team members have been carefully evaluating the operations and practices in Madison's plant where the engine is manufactured. Therefore, Robbins chooses to get the team together and discuss the problem before making his final decision. The group meets for several hours, discussing the problem in detail and sharing their varied perspectives, including the information Robbins and team members have gathered. Following the group session, Robbins makes his decision, which will be presented at the team meeting the following morning, after which testing and correction of the engine problem will begin.[53]

The Vroom-Jago model in Exhibit 9.7 shows that Robbins used the correct decision style. Moving from left to right in Exhibit 9.7, the questions and answers are as follows: *How significant is the decision?* Definitely high. The company's future might be at stake. *How important is subordinate commitment to the decision?* Also high. The team members must support and implement Robbins's solution. *What is the level of Robbins's information and expertise?* Probably low. Even though he has spent several weeks researching the seized engines, other team members have additional information and expertise that needs to be considered. *If Robbins makes the decision on his own, would team members have high or low commitment to it?* The answer to this question is probably also low. Even though team members respect Robbins, they take pride in their work as a team and know Robbins does not have complete information. This leads to the question, *What is the degree of subordinate support for the team's or organization's objectives at stake in this decision?* Definitely high. This leads to the question, *What is the level of group members' knowledge and expertise in relation to the problem?* The answer to this question is low, which leads to the Consult Group decision style, as described earlier in Exhibit 9.6. Thus, Robbins used the style that would be recommended by the Vroom-Jago model.

In many situations, several decision styles might be equally acceptable. However, smart managers are encouraging greater employee participation in solving problems whenever possible. The use of new knowledge management technologies allows for accessing the ideas and knowledge of a much broader group of people, both inside and outside the organization.[54] Broad participation often leads to better decisions. Involving others in decision making also contributes to individual and organizational learning, which is critical for rapid decision making in today's turbulent environment.

## New Decision Approaches for Turbulent Times

The ability to make fast, widely supported, high-quality decisions on a frequent basis is a critical skill in today's fast-moving organizations.[55] In many industries, the rate of competitive and technological change is so extreme that opportunities are fleeting, clear and complete information is seldom available, and the cost of a slow decision means lost business or even company failure. Does this mean managers in today's workplace should make the majority of decisions on their own? No. The rapid pace of today's business environment calls for just the opposite—that is, for people throughout the organization to be involved in decision making and have the

# Unlocking Creative Solutions Through People

### Atlas Container: The Power of Shared Decision Making

How do you take a nickel-and-dime, down-and-dirty business like box manufacturing and turn it into a fast-growing, exciting place to work? Paul and Peter Centenari did it by having their employees decide on just about everything, including how the company would spend its money.

The Centenaris were young, starry-eyed Harvard Business School graduates when they began looking for a low-tech business that could use some new life. They found it at Atlas Container, but their early days were rough. What they bought as a profitable, debt-free little company was suddenly on the verge of bankruptcy. The brothers thought of selling out, but then they had another idea: Let's set some ambitious goals—build a big company by acquiring competitors and keep swiping market share from the stodgy manufacturers who rule this low-margin industry. To do that, the Centenaris needed a fresh approach—one that involved everyone in the company. To do that meant opening the books so people had access to the information they needed, providing plenty of training and education opportunities, letting people participate in the decisions that would affect their jobs, and giving employees a stake in the business.

Today, Atlas is definitely a different kind of box manufacturer. For one thing, there's a big room called the Learning Center where employees can take company-sponsored classes or pursue self-directed learning. Managers hold regular employee meetings where they review sales, costs, profits, and other data about the business. Employees, not hoards of supervisors, make decisions about how to run the plant. Employees at Atlas have voted on such matters as disciplinary policies, whether to keep managers in their jobs, and which supplier to use for a new component for the corrugating machine. The Centenaris honored the employees' choice for the new $1 million piece of equipment, even though they both preferred another vendor. Installing and learning to operate the new equipment was accomplished in three days, when it might easily have taken a week. The employees saw it as "their" machine, so they had a lot invested in making the process run smoothly.

In addition, when everyone is involved in making tough decisions, everyone is paying attention to details. "It isn't just about being nice," Paul Centenari says. "The open books and democracy are ways to shape a company that can do things that its competitors can't." Despite the hot, dirty work, Atlas plants practically hum with the energy and enthusiasm of employees who feel like an important part of the business.

**SOURCE:** John Case, "The Power of Listening," *Inc.* (March 2003), 77-85.

information, skills, and freedom they need to respond immediately to problems and questions. Managers at Atlas Container discovered the power of involving everyone in decision making, as described in the Unlocking Creative Solutions Through People box. In today's fast-moving businesses, people often have to act first and analyze later.[56] Top managers do not have the time to evaluate options for every decision, conduct research, develop alternatives, and tell people what to do and how to do it. When speed matters, a slow decision may be as ineffective as the wrong decision, and companies can learn to make decisions fast. Effective decision making under turbulent conditions relies on the following guidelines.

## Start with Brainstorming

One of the best known techniques for rapidly generating creative alternatives is **brainstorming**. Brainstorming uses a face-to-face interactive group to spontaneously suggest a wide range of alternatives for decision making. The keys to effective brainstorming are that people can build on one another's ideas; all ideas are acceptable, no matter how crazy they seem; and criticism and evaluation are not allowed. The goal is to generate as many ideas as possible. Brainstorming has been found to be highly effective for generating a wide range of alternate solutions to a problem, but it does have some drawbacks. For one thing, people in a group often want to conform to what others are saying, a problem sometimes referred to as *groupthink*. Others may be concerned about

**brainstorming**
A technique that uses a face-to-face group to spontaneously suggest a broad range of alternatives for decision making.

© ROBERTO CARRA

### CONCEPT CONNECTION

*At design firm IDEO, one of today's most innovative companies, people follow a five-step process for "creating experiences, not just products" for companies like Intel, Nestlé, Lufthansa, and Samsung. One important step is **brainstorming**, where people come up with as many ideas as possible for meeting client needs. Brainstorming sessions at IDEO have been described as "managed chaos," where as many as 100 ideas are generated in a one-hour session. Managers encourage wild ideas and rapid-fire thinking, and there are strict rules against interrupting colleagues or showing disrespect and judgment of others' ideas.*

**electronic brainstorming**
Bringing people together in an interactive group over a computer network to suggest alternatives; sometimes called brainwriting.

pleasing the boss or impressing colleagues. In addition, many creative people simply have social inhibitions that limit their participation in a group session or make it difficult to come up with ideas in a group setting. In fact, one study found that when four people are asked to "brainstorm" individually, they typically come up with twice as many ideas as a group of four brainstorming together.

One recent approach, electronic brainstorming, takes advantage of the group approach while overcoming some disadvantages. **Electronic brainstorming**, sometimes called *brainwriting*, brings people together in an interactive group over a computer network.[57] One member writes an idea, another reads it and adds other ideas, and so on. Recent studies show that electronic brainstorming generates about 40 percent more ideas than individuals brainstorming alone, and 25 to 200 percent more ideas than regular brainstorming groups, depending on group size.[58] Why? Because the process is anonymous, the sky's the limit in terms of what people feel free to say. People can write down their ideas immediately, avoiding the possibility that a good idea might slip away while the person is waiting for a chance to speak in a face-to-face group. Social inhibitions and concerns are avoided, which typically allows for a broader range of participation. Another advantage is that electronic brainstorming can potentially be done with groups made up of employees from around the world, further increasing the diversity of alternatives.

### Learn, Don't Punish

Decisions made under conditions of uncertainty and time pressure produce many errors, but smart managers are willing to take the risk in the spirit of trial and error. If a chosen decision alternative fails, the organization can learn from it and try another alternative that better fits the situation. Each failure provides new information and learning. People throughout the organization are encouraged to engage in *experimentation*, which means taking risks and learning from their mistakes. Good managers know that every time a person makes a decision, whether it turns out to have positive or negative consequences, it helps the employee learn and be a better decision maker the next time around. By making mistakes, people gain valuable experience and knowledge to perform more effectively in the future.

When people are afraid to make mistakes, the company is stuck. For example, when Robert Crandall led American Airlines, he built a culture in which any problem that caused a flight delay was followed by finding someone to blame. People became so scared of making a mistake that whenever something went wrong, no one was willing to jump in and try to fix the problem. In contrast, Southwest Airlines uses what it calls *team delay*, which means a flight delay is everyone's problem. This puts the emphasis on fixing the problem rather than on finding an individual to blame.[59] In a turbulent environment, managers do not use mistakes and failure to create a climate of fear. Instead, they encourage people to take risks and move ahead with the decision process, despite the potential for errors.

### Know When to Bail

Even though managers encourage risk taking and learning from mistakes, they also aren't hesitant to pull the plug on something that is not working. Research has found that organizations often continue to invest time and money in a solution despite strong evidence that it is not appropriate. This tendency is referred to as **escalating commitment**. Managers might block or distort negative information because they don't want to be responsible for a bad decision, or they might simply refuse to accept that their solution is wrong. In today's successful companies, people don't get so attached to their own ideas that they're unwilling to recognize when to move on. According to Stanford University professor Robert Sutton, the key to successful creative decision making is to "fail early, fail often, and pull the plug early."[60]

### Practice the Five Whys

One way to encourage good decision making under high uncertainty is to get people to think more broadly and deeply about problems rather than going with a superficial understanding and a first response. However, this doesn't mean people have to spend hours analyzing a problem and gathering research. One simple procedure adopted by a number of leading companies is known as the five whys.[61] For every problem, employees learn to ask "Why?" not just once, but five times. The first *why* generally produces a superficial explanation for the problem, and each subsequent *why* probes deeper into the causes of the problem and potential solutions. The point of the *five whys* is to improve how people think about problems and generate alternatives for solving them.

### Engage in Rigorous Debate

An important key to better decision making under conditions of uncertainty is to encourage a rigorous debate of the issue at hand.[62] Good managers recognize that constructive conflict based on divergent points of view can bring a problem into focus, clarify people's ideas, stimulate creative thinking, create a broader understanding of issues and alternatives, and improve decision quality.[63] Chuck Knight, the former CEO of Emerson Electric, always sparked heated debates during strategic planning meetings. Knight believed rigorous debate gave people a clearer picture of the competitive landscape and forced managers to look at all sides of an issue, helping them reach better decisions.[64]

© DEX IMAGES/CORBIS

**CONCEPT CONNECTION**

*The current scores for the worldwide market share of video games are Sony's PlayStation 2: 69%, Nintendo's GameCube: 16%, and Microsoft's Xbox, 15%. Microsoft plans to change all that by getting a big jump on the competition. Managers have made a series of decisions that shaved a full year off development time for the next version of Xbox. That means the company can bring out hot new games ahead of Sony and Nintendo—a tremendous advantage in a business where content is king. Microsoft operates in a highly turbulent industry and managers have to make difficult decisions incredibly fast. Top leaders encourage experimentation and risk-taking to improve decision making that keeps Microsoft on the cutting edge. Some decisions fail, but Microsoft learns from the failure and tries a new alternative, in line with the **learn, don't punish** philosophy.*

There are several ways to stimulate rigorous debate. One way is by ensuring that the group is diverse in terms of age and gender, functional area of expertise, hierarchical level, and experience with the business. Some groups assign a **devil's advocate**, who has the role of challenging the assumptions and assertions made by the group.[65] The devil's advocate may force the group to rethink its approach to the problem and avoid reaching premature conclusions. Jeffrey McKeever, CEO of MicroAge, often plays the devil's advocate, changing his position in the middle of a debate to ensure that other executives don't just go along with his opinions.[66] Another approach is to have group members develop as many alternatives as they can as quickly as they can.[67] This allows the team to work with multiple alternatives and encourages people to advocate ideas they might not prefer simply to encourage debate. Still another way to encourage constructive conflict is to use a technique called **point-counterpoint**, which breaks a decision-making group into two subgroups and assigns them different, often competing responsibilities.[68] The groups then develop and exchange proposals and discuss and debate the various options until they arrive at a common set of understandings and recommendations.

**escalating commitment**
Continuing to invest time and resources in a failing decision.

**devil's advocate**
A decision-making technique in which an individual is assigned the role of challenging the assumptions and assertions made by the group to prevent premature consensus.

**point-counterpoint**
A decision-making technique in which people are assigned to express competing points of view.

Decision making in today's high-speed, complex environment is one of the most important—and most challenging—responsibilities for managers. By using brainstorming, learning from mistakes rather than assigning blame, knowing when to bail, practicing the *five whys*, and engaging in rigorous debate, managers can improve the quality and effectiveness of their organizational decisions.

## Manager's Solution

This chapter made several important points about the process of organizational decision making. The study of decision making is important because it describes how managers make successful strategic and operational decisions. Managers must confront many types of decisions, including programmed and nonprogrammed, and these decisions differ according to the amount of risk, uncertainty, and ambiguity in the environment.

Three decision-making approaches were described: the classical model, the administrative model, and the political model. The classical model explains how managers should make decisions so as to maximize economic efficiency. The administrative model describes how managers actually make nonprogrammed, uncertain decisions with skills that include intuition. The political model relates to making nonprogrammed decisions when conditions are uncertain, information is limited and ambiguous, and there is conflict among managers about what goals to pursue or what course of action to take. Managers have to engage in discussion and coalition building to reach agreement for decisions.

Decision making should involve six basic steps: problem recognition, diagnosis of causes, development of alternatives, choice of an alternative, implementation of the alternative, and feedback and evaluation. At Tupperware, described in the opening case, feedback and evaluation revealed that the decision to sell Tupperware in Target stores was not successful, so a new decision cycle has begun. Problem recognition is easy: sales and profits are on a downhill slide. In diagnosing the causes, managers determined that the shift in how the company does business has left salespeople feeling slighted. Their earnings have decreased because of dwindling parties and recruiting opportunities, further damaging morale and motivation. Some of the highest performers have already left. In addition, the image of Tupperware as stuck in the 1950s is not helping to lure modern women who could help the company rebound. Managers have considered alternatives and are now implementing three of their choices. One decision was to update the product line to stay ahead of new competitors, such as adding a new Chef Series line of stainless steel pans and knives. Managers are also reinventing the Tupperware party, making it a more sophisticated social event where guests can drink wine and sample easy-to-make dishes prepared with Tupperware gadgets and served straight out of Tupperware pans and bowls. The company plans to implement a new compensation structure that will enable Tupperware salespeople to earn much more, which managers hope will lure back some of their lost salespeople as well as appeal to new ones. Managers will gather information to see how well these new decisions are implemented and whether they are successful. So far, limited feedback indicates that the updated "Taste of Tupperware" party is effective. When people get to try a variety of gadgets, they tend to buy more. The new format is now ready to roll out across the United States with celebrity chefs doing demonstrations in various venues.[69]

Another factor affecting decision making is the manager's personal decision style. The four major decision styles are directive, analytical, conceptual, and behavioral. The chapter also explained the Vroom-Jago model, which managers can use to determine when a decision calls for group participation. Involving others in decision making contributes to individual and organizational learning, which is critical during turbulent times and in high-tech industries. Decisions often have to be made quickly and with limited information. Managers can use the following guidelines: start with brainstorming; learn, don't punish; know when to bail; practice the five whys; and engage in rigorous debate. These techniques improve the quality and effectiveness of decision making in today's turbulent business environment.

# Discussion Questions

1. You are a busy partner in a legal firm, and an experienced secretary complains of continued headaches, drowsiness, dry throat, and occasional spells of fatigue and flu. She tells you she believes air quality in the building is bad and would like something done. How would you respond?

2. Why is decision making considered a fundamental part of management effectiveness?

3. Explain the difference between risk and ambiguity. How might decision making differ for each situation?

4. Analyze three decisions you made over the past six months. Which of these were programmed and which were nonprogrammed?

5. Why are many decisions made by groups rather than by individuals?

6. The Vroom-Jago model describes five decision styles. How should a manager go about choosing which style to use?

7. What are the major differences between the administrative and political models of decision making?

8. What is meant by *satisficing* and *bounded rationality*? Why do managers not strive to find the economically best solution for many organizational decisions?

9. What techniques could you use to improve your own creativity and effectiveness in decision making?

10. Which of the six steps in the decision-making process do you think is most likely to be ignored by a manager? Explain.

# Management in Practice: Experiential Exercise

### What's Your Personal Decision Style?

Read each of the following questions and circle the answer that best describes you. Think about how you typically act in a work or school situation and mark the answer that first comes to your mind. There are no right or wrong answers.

1. In performing my job or class work, I look for:
   a. practical results
   b. the best solution
   c. creative approaches or ideas
   d. good working conditions

2. I enjoy jobs that:
   a. are technical and well-defined
   b. have a lot of variety
   c. allow me to be independent and creative
   d. involve working closely with others

3. The people I most enjoy working with are:
   a. energetic and ambitious
   b. capable and organized
   c. open to new ideas
   d. agreeable and trusting

4. When I have a problem, I usually:
   a. rely on what has worked in the past
   b. apply careful analysis
   c. consider a variety of creative approaches
   d. seek consensus with others

5. I am especially good at:
   a. remembering dates and facts
   b. solving complex problems
   c. seeing many possible solutions
   d. getting along with others

6. When I don't have much time, I:
   a. make decisions and act quickly
   b. follow established plans or priorities
   c. take my time and refuse to be pressured
   d. ask others for guidance and support

7. In social situations, I generally:
   a. talk to others
   b. think about what's being discussed
   c. observe
   d. listen to the conversation

8. Other people consider me:
   a. aggressive
   b. disciplined
   c. creative
   d. supportive

9. What I dislike most is:
   a. not being in control
   b. doing boring work
   c. following rules
   d. being rejected by others

10. The decisions I make are usually:
   a. direct and practical
   b. systematic or abstract
   c. broad and flexible
   d. sensitive to others' needs

**Scoring:** Count the number of *a* answers. This is your *directive* score:

Count the number of *b* answers for your *analytical* score:

The number of *c* answers is your *conceptual* score:

The number of *d* answers is your *behavioral* score:

What is your dominant decision style? Are you surprised, or does this reflect the style you thought you used most often?

**Source:** Adapted from Alan J. Rowe and Richard O. Mason, *Managing with Style: A Guide to Understanding, Assessing, and Improving Decision Making* (San Francisco: Jossey-Bass, 1987), 40–41.

# Management in Practice: Ethical Dilemma

### The Unhealthy Hospital

When Bruce Reid was hired as Blake Memorial Hospital's new CEO, the mandate had been clear: Improve the quality of care, and set the financial house in order.

As Reid struggled to finalize his budget for approval at next week's board meeting, his attention kept returning to one issue—the future of six off-site clinics. The clinics had been set up six years earlier to provide primary health care to the community's poorer neighborhoods. Although they provided a valuable service, they also diverted funds away from Blake's in-house services, many of which were underfunded. Cutting hospital personnel and freezing salaries could affect Blake's quality of care, which was already slipping. Eliminating the clinics, on the other hand, would save $256,000 without compromising Blake's internal operations.

However, there would be political consequences. Clara Bryant, the recently appointed commissioner of health services, repeatedly argued that the clinics were an essential service for the poor. Closing the clinics could jeopardize Blake's access to city funds. Dr. Susan Russell, the hospital's director of clinics, was equally vocal about Blake's responsibility to the community, although Dr. Winston Lee, chief of surgery, argued forcefully for closing the off-site clinics and having shuttle buses bring patients to the hospital weekly. Dr. Russell argued for an entirely new way of delivering health care—"A hospital is not a building," she said, "it's a service. And wherever the service is needed, that is where the hospital should be." In Blake's case, that meant funding more clinics. Russell wanted to create a network of neighborhood-based centers for all the surrounding neighborhoods, poor and middle income. Besides improving health care, the network would act as an in-patient referral system for hospital services. Reid considered the proposal: If a clinic network could tap the paying public and generate more in-patient business, it might be worth looking into. Blake's rival hospital, located on the affluent side of town, certainly wasn't doing anything that creative.

**What Do You Do?**

1. Close the clinics and save a quick $256,000, then move on to tackle the greater problems that threaten Blake's long-term future.
2. Gradually abandon the neighborhood altogether and open free-standing clinics in more affluent suburbs, at the same time opening a minihospital in the poor neighborhood for critical care.
3. Tighten up internal efficiency to deal with immediate financial problems. Keep the clinics open for now, bring Clara Bryant into the decision-making process, and begin working with community groups to explore unmet health-care needs and develop innovative options for meeting them.

Source: Based on Anthony R. Kovner, "The Case of the Unhealthy Hospital," *Harvard Business Review*, September–October 1991, 12–25.

# Surf the Net

1. **Creativity.** Using your creative abilities in identifying solutions to problems can be a major asset in the decision-making process. Use your search engine to find Web sites related to creativity, such as the following: *http://www.tiac.net/users/seeker/brainlinks.html*.

   Prepare a summary of your findings and present a 3- to 5-minute report to your classmates sumarizing the most useful and interesting ideas you found that relate to creativity in the problem-solving/decision-making process.

2. **Decision Making.** Use one of the sites listed or conduct your own Web search for information on management decision making. Identify the most informative site on the subject and submit to your instructor the Web address, along with a summary of the information you found that would prove helpful to anyone making management decisions.

   *http://home.ubalt.edu/ntsbarsh/opre640/opre640.htm*
   *http://www.mapnp.org/library/prsn_prd/decision.htm*
   *http://horizon.unc.edu/courses/papers/Anticipatory Management.asp*
   *http://faculty.fuqua.duke.edu/daweb/lexicon.htm*

3. **Participative Decision Making.** Gather information from the Internet suitable to share in a small-group discussion on participative decision making. This exercise provides an opportunity for you to try "Google." Go to *http://www.google.com* and type in "participative decision making." Select information from the links that "Google" provides and be prepared to discuss your findings in class. One particularly interesting article on participative decision making is available at *http://niusi.edreform.net/subject/participativedecisionmaking*

# Case for Critical Analysis

## Greyhound Lines Inc.

Everyone agreed that Greyhound Lines had problems. The company was operating on paper-thin margins and could not afford to dispatch nearly empty vehicles or have buses and drivers on call to meet surges in demand. In the terminals, employees could be observed making fun of passengers, ignoring them, and handling their baggage haphazardly. To reduce operating costs and improve customer service, Greyhound's top executives put together a reorganization plan that called for massive cuts in personnel, routes, and services, along with the computerization of everything from passenger reservations to fleet scheduling.

However, middle managers disagreed with the plan. Many felt that huge workforce reductions would only exacerbate the company's real problem regarding customer services. Managers in computer programming urged a delay in introducing the computerized reservations system, called Trips, to work out bugs in the highly complex software. The human resources department pointed out that terminal workers often had less than a high school education and would need extensive training before they could be expected to use the system effectively. Terminal managers warned that many of Greyhound's low-income passengers didn't have credit cards or even telephones to use Trips. Despite the disagreements, executives rolled out the new system, emphasizing that the data they had studied showed that Trips would improve customer service, make ticket buying more convenient, and allow customers to reserve space on specific trips. A nightmare resulted. The time Greyhound operators

spent responding to phone calls dramatically increased. Many callers couldn't even get through because of problems in the new switching mechanism. Most passengers arrived to buy their tickets and get on the bus just like they always had, but the computers were so swamped that it sometimes took 45 seconds to respond to a single keystroke and five minutes to print a ticket. The system crashed so often that agents frequently had to hand-write tickets. Customers stood in long lines, were separated from their luggage, missed connections, and were left to sleep in terminals overnight. Discourtesy to customers increased as a downsized workforce struggled to cope with a system they were ill-trained to operate. Ridership plunged sharply, and regional rivals continued to pick off Greyhound's dissatisfied customers.

### Questions

1. Was the decision facing Greyhound executives programmed or nonprogrammed?
2. Do you think Greyhound should have used the classical, administrative, or political model to make its decision? Which do you believe it used? Discuss.
3. Analyze the Greyhound case in terms of the six steps in the managerial decision-making process. Do you think top executives paid adequate attention to all six steps? If you were a Greyhound executive, what would you do now and why?

Source: Robert Tomsho, "How Greyhound Lines Re-Engineered Itself Right Into a Deep Hole," *The Wall Street Journal,* October 30, 1994, A1.

# Endnotes

1. Rick Brooks, "Sealing Their Fate: A Deal with Target Put Lid on Revival at Tupperware," *The Wall Street Journal* (February 18, 2004), A1, A9.

2. Linda Yates and Peter Skarzynski, "How Do Companies Get to the Future First?" *Management Review* (January 1999), 16–22.

3. Michael V. Copeland and Owen Thomas, "Hits (& Misses)," *Business 2.0* (January–February 2004), 126.

4. Stanley Holmes, "Boeing: What Really Happened?" *BusinessWeek* (December 15, 2003), 33–38; Adam Horowitz, Mark Athitakis, Mark Lasswell, and Owen Thomas, "101 Dumbest Moments in Business," *Business 2.0* (January–February 2004),72–81.

5. Herbert A. Simon, *The New Science of Management Decision* (Englewood Cliffs, N.J.: Prentice-Hall, 1977), 47.

6. Marc Gunther, "Jeff Zucker Faces Life Without Friends," *Fortune* (May 12, 2003), 94–98.

7. Gregory L. White, "Why GM Rewound Its Product Strategy, Delaying New Cavalier," *The Wall Street Journal* (July 30, 1999), A1, A6.

8. Samuel Eilon, "Structuring Unstructured Decisions," *Omega* 13 (1985), 369–377; and Max H. Bazerman, *Judgment in Managerial Decision Making* (New York: Wiley, 1986).

9. James G. March and Zur Shapira, "Managerial Perspectives on Risk and Risk Taking," *Management Science* 33 (1987), 1404–1418; and Inga Skromme Baird and Howard Thomas, "Toward a Contingency Model of Strategic Risk Taking," *Academy of Management Review* 10 (1985), 230–243.

10. Hugh Courtney, "Decision-Driven Scenarios for Assessing Four Levels of Uncertainty," *Strategy & Leadership* 31, no. 1 (2003), 14–22.

11. Stanley Holmes, "GE: Little Engines that Could," *BusinessWeek* (January 20, 2003), 62–63.

12. Susanne Craig, Mitchell Pacelle, and Kate Kelly, "NYSE Is Likely to Delay Governance Report," *The Wall Street Journal* (September 23, 2003).

13. Michael Masuch and Perry LaPotin, "Beyond Garbage Cans: An AI Model of Organizational Choice," *Administrative Science Quarterly* 34 (1989), 38–67; and Richard L. Daft and Robert H. Lengel, "Organizational Information Requirements, Media Richness and Structural Design," *Management Science* 32 (1986), 554–571.

14. David M. Schweiger, William R. Sandberg, and James W. Ragan, "Group Approaches for Improving Strategic Decision Making: A Comparative Analysis of Dialectical Inquiry, Devil's Advocacy, and Consensus," *Academy of Management Journal* 29 (1986), 51–71; and Richard O. Mason and Ian I. Mitroff, *Challenging Strategic Planning Assumptions* (New York: Wiley Interscience, 1981).

15. Michael Pacanowsky, "Team Tools for Wicked Problems," *Organizational Dynamics* 23, no. 3 (Winter 1995), 36–51.

16. Boris Blai, Jr., "Eight Steps to Successful Problem Solving," *Supervisory Management* (January 1986), 7–9; and Earnest R. Archer, "How to Make a Business Decision: An Analysis of Theory and Practice," *Management Review* 69 (February 1980), 54–61.

17. Bernard Wysocki Jr., "The Rules: At One Hospital, A Stark Solution for Allocating Care," *The Wall Street Journal* (September 23, 2003), A1, A21.

18. Stacie McCullough, "On the Front Lines," Section 1, *CIO*, (October 15, 1999), 78–81.

19. Srinivas Bollapragada, Prasanthi Ganti, Mark Osborn, James Quaile, and Kannan Ramanathan, "GE's Energy Rentals Business Automates Its Credit Assessment Process," *Interfaces* 33, no. 5 (September–October 2003), 45–56; Julie Schlosser, "Markdown Lowdown," *Fortune* (January 12, 2004), 40.

20. Srinivas Bollapragada, Hong Cheng, Mary Phillips, Marc Garbinas, Michael Scholes, Tim Gibbs, and Mark Humphreville, "NBC's Optimization Systems Increase Revenues and Productivity," *Interfaces* 32, no. 1 (January–February 2002), 47–60.

21. Herbert A. Simon, *The New Science of Management Decision* (New York: Harper & Row, 1960), 5–6; and Amitai Etzioni, "Humble Decision Making," *Harvard Business Review* (July–August 1989), 122–126.

22. James G. March and Herbert A. Simon, *Organizations* (New York: Wiley, 1958).

23. Herbert A. Simon, *Models of Man* (New York: Wiley, 1957), 196–205; and Herbert A. Simon, *Administrative Behavior*, 2d ed. (New York: Free Press, 1957).

24. John Taylor, "Project Fantasy: A Behind-the-Scenes Account of Disney's Desperate Battle against the Raiders," *Manhattan* (November 1984).

25. George T. Doran and Jack Gunn, "Decision Making in High-Tech Firms: Perspectives of Three Executives," *Business Horizons* (November–December 2002), 7–16.

26. Weston H. Agor, "The Logic of Intuition: How Top Executives Make Important Decisions," *Organizational Dynamics* 14 (Winter 1986), 5–18; and Herbert A. Simon, "Making Management Decisions: The Role of Intuition and Emotion," *Academy of Management Executive* 1 (1987), 57–64.

27. Lisa A. Burke and Monica K. Miller, "Taking the Mystery Out of Intuitive Decision Making," *Academy of Management Executive* 13, no. 4 (1999), 91–99.

28. Reported in Bill Breen, "What's Your Intuition?" *Fast Company* (September 2000), 290–300.

29. Sharon Begley, "Follow Your Intuition: The Unconscious You May Be the Wiser Half," *The Wall Street Journal* (August 30, 2002), B1.

30. Geraldine Fabrikant, "The Paramount Team Puts Profit Over Splash," *The New York Times* (June 30, 2002), Section 3.1; Chris Smith, "Chao, Baby," *New York* (October 18, 1993), 66–75; and "Chao in Charge," *Cablevision* (November 29, 1999), 24.

31. William B. Stevenson, Jon L. Pierce, and Lyman W. Porter, "The Concept of 'Coalition' in Organization Theory and Research," *Academy of Management Review* 10 (1985), 256–268.

32. Jonathan Harris, "Why Speedy Got Stuck in Reverse," *Canadian Business* (September 26, 1997), 87–88.

33. James W. Fredrickson, "Effects of Decision Motive and Organizational Performance Level on Strategic Decision Processes," *Academy of Management Journal* 28 (1985), 821–843; James W. Fredrickson, "The Comprehensiveness of Strategic Decision Processes: Extension, Observations, Future Directions," *Academy of Management Journal* 27 (1984), 445–466; James W. Dean, Jr., and Mark P. Sharfman, "Procedural Rationality in the Strategic Decision-Making Process," *Journal of Management Studies* 30, no. 4 (July 1993), 587–610; Nandini Rajagopalan, Abdul M. A. Rasheed, and Deepak K. Datta, "Strategic Decision Processes: Critical Review and Future Directions," *Journal of Management* 19, no. 2 (1993), 349–384; and Paul J. H. Schoemaker, "Strategic Decisions in Organizations: Rational and Behavioral Views," *Journal of Management Studies* 30, no. 1 (January 1993), 107–129.

34. Marjorie A. Lyles and Howard Thomas, "Strategic Problem Formulation: Biases and Assumptions Embedded in Alternative Decision-Making Models," *Journal of Management Studies* 25 (1988), 131–145; and Susan E. Jackson and Jane E. Dutton, "Discerning Threats and Opportunities," *Administrative Science Quarterly* 33 (1988), 370–387.

35. Anita Lienert, "Can Liz Wetzel's Baby Save Buick?" *Working Woman* (May 2001), 33–36, 78.

36. Richard L. Daft, Juhani Sormumen, and Don Parks, "Chief Executive Scanning, Environmental Characteristics, and Company Performance: An Empirical Study" (unpublished manuscript, Texas A&M University, 1988).

37. C. Kepner and B. Tregoe, *The Rational Manager* (New York: McGraw-Hill, 1965).

38. Pallavi Gogoi and Michael Arndt, "Hamburger Hell," *BusinessWeek* (March 3, 2003), 104–108.

39. Paul C. Nutt, "Surprising But True: Half the Decisions in Organizations Fail," *Academy of Management Executive* 13, no. 4 (1999), 75–90.

40. Gogoi and Arndt, "Hamburger Hell."

41. Peter Mayer, "A Surprisingly Simple Way to Make Better Decisions," *Executive Female* (March–April 1995), 13–14; and Ralph L. Keeney, "Creativity in Decision-Making with Value-Focused Thinking," *Sloan Management Review* (Summer 1994), 33–41.

42. Robert Levering and Milton Moskowitz, "The 100 Best Companies to Work For: The Best in the Worst of Times," *Fortune* (February 4, 2002), 60

43. Mark McNeilly, "Gathering Information for Strategic Decisions, Routinely," *Strategy & Leadership* 30, no. 5 (2002), 29–34.

44. Ibid

45. Danny Hakim, "GM Executive Preaches: Sweat the Smallest Details," *The New York Times* (January 5, 2004), Section C, 1.

46. Jenny C. McCune, "Making Lemonade," *Management Review*, (June 1997), 49–53, 51.

47. Based on A. J. Rowe, J. D. Boulgaides, and M. R. McGrath, *Managerial Decision Making* (Chicago: Science Research Associates, 1984); and Alan J. Rowe and Richard O. Mason, *Managing with Style: A Guide to Understanding, Assessing, and Improving Your Decision Making* (San Francisco: Jossey-Bass, 1987).

48. Gunther, "Jeff Zucker Faces Life Without *Friends*."

49. V. H. Vroom and Arthur G. Jago, *The New Leadership: Managing Participation in Organizations* (Englewood Cliffs, N.J.: Prentice-Hall, 1988).

50. Victor H. Vroom, "Leadership and the Decision-Making Process," *Organizational Dynamics* 28, no. 4 (Spring 2000), 82–94.

51. R. H. G. Field, "A Test of the Vroom-Yetton Normative Model of Leadership," *Journal of Applied Psychology* (October 1982), 523–532; and R. H. G. Field, "A Critique of the Vroom-Yetton Contingency Model of Leadership Behavior," *Academy of Management Review* 4 (1979), 249–257.

52. Vroom, "Leadership and the Decision Making Process"; Jennifer T. Ettling and Arthur G. Jago, "Participation under Conditions of Conflict: More on the Validity of the Vroom-Yetton Model," *Journal of Management Studies* 25 (1988), 73–83; Madeline E. Heilman, Harvey A. Hornstein, Jack H. Cage, and Judith K. Herschlag, "Reactions to Prescribed Leader Behavior as a Function of Role Perspective: The Case of the Vroom-Yetton Model," *Journal of Applied Psychology* (February 1984), 50–60; and Arthur G. Jago and Victor H. Vroom, "Some Differences in the

Incidence and Evaluation of Participative Leader Behavior," Journal of Applied Psychology (December 1982), 776–783.

53. Based on a decision problem presented in Victor H. Vroom, "Leadership and the Decision-Making Process," *Organizational Dynamics* 28, no. 4 (Spring, 2000): 82–94.

54. Nathaniel Foote, Eric Matson, Leigh Weiss, and Etienne Wenger, "Leveraging Group Knowledge for High-Performance Decision-Making," *Organizational Dynamics* 31, no. 3 (2002), 280–295.

55. Kathleen M. Eisenhardt, "Strategy as Strategic Decision Making," *Sloan Management Review* (Spring, 1999), 65–72.

56. See Katherine Mieszkowski, "Digital Competition," *Fast Company* (December 1999), 155–162; Thomas A. Stewart, "Three Rules for Managing in the Real-Time Economy," *Fortune* (May 1, 2000), 333–334; and Geoffrey Colvin, "How to Be a Great eCEO," *Fortune* (May 24, 1999), 104–110.

57. R. B. Gallupe, W. H. Cooper, M. L. Grise, and L. M. Bastianutti, "Blocking Electronic Brainstorms," *Journal of Applied Psychology* 79 (1994), 77–86; R. B. Gallupe and W. H. Cooper, "Brainstorming Electronically," *Sloan Management Review* (Fall 1993), 27–36; and Alison Stein Wellner, "A Perfect Brainstorm," *Inc.* (October 2003), 31–35.

58. Wellner, "A Perfect Brainstorm"; Gallupe and Cooker, "Brainstorming Electronically."

59. Michael V. Copeland, "Mistakes Happen," *Red Herring* (May 2000), 346–354.

60. Ibid.

61. Joshua Klayman, Richard P. Larrick, and Chip Heath, "Organizational Repairs," *Across the Board* (February 2000), 26–31.

62. Michael A. Roberto, "Making Difficult Decisions in Turbulent Times," *Ivey Business Journal* (May-June 2003), 1–7.

63. Eisenhardt, "Strategy as Strategic Decision Making"; and David A. Garvin and Michael A. Roberto, "What You Don't Know About Making Decisions," *Harvard Business Review* (September 2001), 108–116.

64. Roberto, "Making Difficult Decisions in Turbulent Times."

65. David M. Schweiger and William R. Sandberg, "The Utilization of Individual Capabilities in Group Approaches to Strategic Decision-Making," *Strategic Management Journal* 10 (1989), 31–43; and "The Devil's Advocate," *Small Business Report* (December 1987), 38–41.

66. Doran and Gunn, "Decision Making in High-Tech Firms."

67. Eisenhardt, "Strategy as Strategic Decision Making.

68. Garvin and Roberto, "What You Don't Know About Making Decisions."

69. Brooks, "Sealing Their Fate."

John and Kim Puckett love the outdoors. They also love coffee. About a decade ago, they were hiking Sable Mountain in Alaska. When they reached the summit, they were inspired not only by the scenery surrounding them but also by the sight of a distant herd of caribou galloping through the valley below. No, the Pucketts didn't suddenly pull a coffeemaker out of a backpack and start brewing coffee on the mountaintop, but when they got home after their mountain trip, they wanted to find a way to re-create the sights and sounds of the Alaskan wilderness, preserving some of the feelings they had experienced. They wanted to establish a place where people could gather to share good and simple things: casual conversation with friends, time for the daily newspaper, a tasty cup of coffee, "an escape from the daily grind." They also wanted to start their own business. So they opened their first coffee shop in Minneapolis, in December of 1992.

Today, Caribou Coffee is the nation's second largest specialty coffee company, with 160 stores and 2,000 employees across eight states. The Pucketts have remained true to their original vision of bringing the wilderness home: each store is built and decorated to look like an Alaskan lodge, with knotty-pine cabinets, a rustic fireplace, and comfortable seating. "We still strive to make the Caribou experience adventurous, rewarding, and fun," says the company's Web site. "Our mission is to be the best neighborhood gathering place; fast and friendly service is at the heart of this goal."

A clear mission is the soul of an organization, but achievable goals and good planning are its heart and lungs. Caribou Coffee integrates all three, but its development and growth have not been without struggle. The Pucketts perfected the company's rustic image and style. With the help of Barry Judge, vice president of marketing, and the Carmichael Lynch advertising agency in Minneapolis, Caribou came up with buzzwords to capture the Caribou experience: "Outdoorsy. Leave smiling. Hand-made. Down to earth. Clever. Transformational."

People near Caribou shops immediately became loyal customers. They seemed to prefer Caribou's brew to that of its largest competitor, Starbucks. (In fact, Caribou debuted certain flavors and brewing methods that Starbucks followed later.) Quality, service, satisfied customers—all were goals that Caribou could achieve. But the company had problems with setting more specific goals and planning for growth. For one thing, Caribou lacked the funds for the kind of expansion that the Pucketts envisioned. For another, their expansion from Minneapolis to other locations was driven by the competition—they simply went where Starbucks wasn't, instead of establishing growth goals independently. By 1997, Caribou Coffee had 123 stores, with only Starbucks ahead of it. Caribou company president Jay Willoughby declared, "Our intent is to be a national player." But Starbucks had more than 2,000 stores, including nearly 190 overseas: Caribou wasn't even close. That doesn't mean being number two is necessarily bad. In fact, said Alan Hickok, an industry analyst, "In markets where [Caribou] competes head-to-head with Starbucks, they've done just fine . . . There's no consumer category, with the exception of Microsoft, where consumers have been satisfied with having just one choice. Absolutely, there's room for a No. 2."

Caribou still wanted to grow, but they were having trouble coming up with a clear plan and the money to back it. Enter Don Dempsey, former head of McDonald's China division. Dempsey joined Caribou as its new CEO in 1999. Why would he make the leap from a giant like McDonald's to the small beans of Caribou Coffee? "When you're running an international company for McDonald's, you really have a lot of autonomy," he explained. "I wanted to take what I had learned at a large company and apply it to a small one." When one newswriter asked Dempsey about his goal for the company, he answered that he wanted to "reliably and consistently grow profits." But he needed a plan, and he needed a way to raise the money to achieve his overall goal.

Dempsey recalls that when he needed more money to fund a project at McDonald's, he just called up the CEO and asked for it. Funding wasn't so easy for Caribou. Eventually, though, the Crescent Capital group of Atlanta agreed to purchase a percentage of the company, which would pump the needed growth dollars into the organization. Dempsey outlined a plan for expansion: stick with locations in which Caribou already had stores and strengthen the Caribou brand within those locations. Caribou's largest market is its hometown of Minneapolis-St. Paul, but other markets include Columbus and Cleveland, Ohio; Raleigh and Charlotte, North Carolina; Atlanta; Detroit; Chicago; and Washington, D.C. "We have to increase penetration

# Chapter 7: Caribou Coffee Has a Mission (continued)

and increase brand awareness in order to improve our economics," Dempsey said. Meanwhile, Caribou would continue to brew a good cup of coffee in a place where people can get away from the daily grind.

## Questions

1. Write what you think would be an effective, updated mission statement for Caribou Coffee.
2. What is the relationship between Dempsey's goal and his plan for sticking with existing markets?
3. How important is the Pucketts' original vision to the company's identity today? Explain your answer.

Sources: Company Web site, *http://www.cariboucoffee.com*, accessed February 21, 2002; Jessica Griffith, "Caribou Coffee Brewing a Caffeine-Fueled Expansion," *Finance and Commerce*, December 26, 2001, *http://www.finance-commerce.com*; Eleni Chamis, "Sale Stalling Coffee Chain's Local Growth," *Washington Business Journal*, October 27, 2000, *http://washington.bizjournals.com*; Jim McCartney, "Caribou Coffee Taking on King of the Hill," *Shopping Centers Today*, May 1, 1999, *http://www.icsc.org*.

# Video Case

# Chapter 8: Caribou Coffee's Strategy: Worth More than Beans

Picture drinking your daily cuppa joe in an Alaskan lodge. You have plenty of time to chat with friends, scan the daily paper, and imagine that when you step outside you'll have a sweeping view of Denali itself, with a few stray caribou grazing its foothills. That's what the folks at Caribou Coffee want you to feel, whether you're in Minneapolis, Atlanta, or Washington, D.C. The rustic image conveyed by Caribou's 160 coffee shops is a major part of the company's strategy, which is to create a comfortable, attractive, unique atmosphere in which customers can relax and enjoy their coffee.

But the company's grand strategy is growth. At first, founders John and Kim Puckett followed a strategy of placing Caribou shops wherever their major competitor, Starbucks, didn't have shops. But that growth strategy lacked cohesiveness and planning. The company also tried to grow too fast, a pitfall of many young firms. "There's a lot of instability with rapid growth," says Jay Willoughby, a restaurant executive whom the Pucketts hired to be president of their company in 1997, five years after they opened their first shop in Minneapolis. Willoughby determined that before Caribou grew any more, it had to become more stable financially, without sacrificing value to its customers. In other words, every cup of coffee served by Caribou staff, from Kenya AA to Fireside Blend, had to be fresh, hot, and full of flavor. It also had to come at a reasonable price. To offer value and still make a profit, Willoughby had to make sure that the company's warehouse and field operations were functioning efficiently and cost effectively so that all coffee goods moved through the system quickly, remaining fresh. Only then would a grand strategy of growth make sense.

In 1999, Don Dempsey joined Caribou as its new CEO. After 20 years with McDonald's, Dempsey was ready for a new challenge. Like Willoughby, he examined the company's previous expansion strategy. "Their strategy was to go where Starbucks wasn't, and that was a flawed strategy," noted Dempsey. "They had a half-dozen stores here and a half-dozen there, but no strong brand awareness in any one market. Then, they ran out of money." First Dempsey had to come up with more backing for the company, then create a strategy of controlled growth. He found the backing he needed in the form of Crescent Capital of Atlanta, which agreed to purchase a portion of the company for $80 million, giving Caribou the funding it needed for growth. Dempsey has so far resisted

# Chapter 8: Caribou Coffee's Strategy: Worth More than Beans (continued)

franchising as a source of income or expansion, however. All Caribou stores are company owned. "Our stores run pretty well, and I like getting all of the profit from the stores," he explains. Also, the recapitalization from Crescent has given the company enough money to carry through its growth plans without franchising or making an offer of public stock. "I'd love to have a nice, big private company," Dempsey admits.

It was important to accomplish controlled growth while maintaining Caribou's woodsy, rustic, comfortable style. Everyone involved with Caribou—from its founders to its loyal customers—already knew that the Caribou shops performed well against Starbucks. In fact, claims Dempsey, "You can put us right next to a Starbucks. But our place cannot be less convenient or attractive than the Starbucks." Industry analyst Alan Hickok agrees with Dempsey. "Even in my little suburb, there are three Caribous within a couple of miles and a couple of Starbucks, and they are all doing quite well. Dempsey is a smart guy, and he knows exactly what he is doing." Minneapolis investor Jim Jundt concurs with Dempsey's strategic management. "He is using a strategy that has succeeded for him in the past," Jundt says.

Where can you go for a cup of Caribou? If you live in a few Midwestern states or Georgia, North Carolina, or Washington, D.C., you're in luck. If not, you can order coffee beans and other products through Caribou's catalog or online. If you visit the Web site, you can find out how much caffeine is in a cup of coffee, why you should use an oxygen-bleached filter, and why it's a bad idea to microwave a cooled cup of premium coffee. But you don't have to be a coffee aficionado to appreciate the aroma of success that seems to be wafting around Caribou Coffee. Don Dempsey had never sipped a cup of gourmet coffee before he came to Caribou. "I recently had some of the coffee I used to drink, and I was astounded at how bad it was," he recalls. "Once you've had good coffee . . . you can't go back."

## Questions

1. Why was it important for Caribou to achieve stability before proceeding with further growth?
2. How would you define Caribou's core competence?
3. Identify two of Caribou's internal strengths and two internal weaknesses.

Sources: Company Web site, *http://www.cariboucoffee.com*, accessed February 21, 2002; Jessica Griffith, "Caribou Coffee Brewing a Caffeine-Fueled Expansion," *Finance and Commerce*, December 26, 2001, *http://www.finance-commerce.com*; Ashley Gibson, "The Uptown Coffee Buzz: More Starbucks, Caribous," *The Business Journal*, October 27, 2000, *http://charlotte.bizjournals.com*; Eleni Chamis, "Sale Stalling Coffee Chain's Local Growth," *Washington Business Journal*, October 27, 2000, *http://washington.bizjournals.com*; Jim McCartney, "Caribou Coffee Taking on King of the Hill," *Shopping Centers Today*, May 1, 1999, *http://www.icsc.org*.

# Video Case

## Chapter 9: Machado and Silvetti: A Business Based on Decisions

When was the last time you designed a building? Maybe you cut a door in a large cardboard box when you were a child, painted on windows and crawled inside your new "house" with a couple of friends. Maybe you were one of those lucky kids who actually had a tree fort. Or perhaps an ambitious school teacher assigned you a project that involved planning and constructing an imaginary structure. Regardless of how simple or complex your building project was, it involved many decisions, from materials to dimensions. Harvard professors Rodolfo Machado and Jorge Silvetti, who also head up their own architectural firm, are examples of advanced design and architecture decision makers. In fact, almost everyone who works at Machado and Silvetti Associates makes decisions—whether programmed or nonprogrammed.

Machado and Silvetti Associates, based in Boston, specializes in creating housing and other structures for colleges and universities, as well as public buildings such as a branch of the Boston Public Library. The firm has an impressive roster of clients, including the J. Paul Getty Trust, the Utah Museum of Fine Arts, the Federal Reserve Bank of Boston, and the City of Vienna. Like most architectural firms, Machado and Silvetti is essentially organized around its projects, so that professionals such as associate Michael Yusem, a project manager, can focus on all the decisions related to a certain assignment. Since every project is different, many of these decisions are nonprogrammed, and much effort goes into reducing both uncertainty and risk. For instance, once initial design choices are made and a budget approved by a client, Yusem and his colleagues need to figure out how to deliver the design requirements within the budget, or risk losing money. Then come the building details, all of which must satisfy the customer while producing revenue for the firm. As the team develops a new graduate housing facility for a Boston-based university, they must consider the needs of future residents, the overall look or image of the complex, as well as the choice of quality materials including carpet, tiles, flooring, bathroom fixtures, and appliances. They need to determine the number and size of the rooms. They must be certain that the facility complies with local building and environmental codes. They must select and coordinate subcontractors for various phases of the project. And they must deliver the project on a schedule. All of this coordination is just for one of the firm's projects.

Across the country, another Machado and Silvetti team has undertaken the renovation of the Getty Villa, which is part of the J. Paul Getty Museum in southern California. The mission for the Getty Villa is entirely different from their graduate housing project—its residents are works of art from the museum's Antiquities Collection, which contains roughly 50,000 objects ranging from statues to ancient tools. In this case, the design team had to come up with a plan that incorporated the classical inspiration of the works themselves with the surrounding buildings of the museum. To achieve this, they chose pattern mosaic and terrazzo floors, coffered ceilings, and colorful plaster walls, with detailing in wood and bronze. The team also considered the modern needs of visitors and museum caretakers. In doing so, they added skylights and reopened some of the old windows to bring in natural light for better viewing, and added a variety of other modern amenities for comfort. Each of these decisions involved development of and selection among alternatives, along with feedback from the client. And all of the decisions had to contribute somehow to the mission of the project as a whole.

Machado and Silvetti enjoys a top-notch reputation around the world for its designs, both with clients and critics. "The new branch of the Boston Public Library in Allston is a delight: an airy, spacious place where the breeze seems to flow through uninterrupted . . . . This is the best new public building in Boston in years," writes architecture critic Robert Campbell of *The Boston Globe*. When the firm won the First Award in Architecture from the American Academy of Arts and Letters, the awards committee wrote, "In a series of boldly conceived and brilliantly executed urban projects completed over the past two decades Rodolfo Machado and Jorge Silvetti have pursued an extended and vigorous program of research through design. Their investigations . . . have been uncompromisingly dedicated to envisioning a meaningful architecture of the public realm." And it's all done one brick—and one decision—at a time.

# Chapter 9: Machado and Silvetti: A Business Based on Decisions (continued)

## Questions

1. How might project managers at Machado and Silvetti use the classical model of decision making to make a decision about what type of windows to install in a building?
2. What might be the consequences of using satisficing in a project like the Getty Villa or the graduate housing facility?
3. How might project managers at Machado and Silvetti use decision making to enhance performance beyond its current levels?

Sources: Company Web site, *http://www.machado-silvetti.com*, accessed February 5, 2002; Alex Ulam, "Harvard Inc.," *Metropolis Magazine*, February 2001, *http://www.metropolismag.com*; "The New Getty Villa," Getty Museum Web Site, 2000, *http://www.getty.edu*.

# ..Continuing Case

The story of Bill Ford and Jac Nasser is not only the story of two leaders but also the story of two strategies marked by differing management styles, differing goals, and perhaps even differing views of the company's mission. When Jac Nasser came to the top position at Ford, he had already worked for the company for thirty years. No one would argue that his sometimes harsh, autocratic decision-making style made him less than popular among Ford workers, managers, and media members. But Nasser arrived at the top in the late 1990s with bold plans to turn an aging, stumbling company into a streamlined, flexible contender in the auto industry. Ford's ventures into the financial services and defense industries in the 1980s had turned out to be disastrous. Nasser pledged that his new mission for the company, "to be the world's leading consumer company for automotive services and products," would be backed by solid strategic planning. "It's a world going through tremendous change," said Nasser early in his reign, "not just through economic events, but largely through technology. We're trying not to be left behind." So Nasser set a goal of hiring 20 percent new managers while also developing leaders from within the company. He also emphasized team building. He began to acquire other brands, in the United States and abroad, including Land Rover, Jaguar, and a chain of British auto-service centers called Kwik-Fit. He vowed to turn Ford's less profitable car lines around (the company was much stronger in the truck and SUV business): "In the past, we tried to do too much in the car business and dispersed our resources. Now we're simplifying the product line. And we're separating the models that remain and giving them better brand identities." He planned to jump into e-business with all four wheels. "Technology and networks in particular determine the shape of everything else," Nasser remarked. He began with a joint venture with Microsoft's CarPoint, which allowed consumers to build cars to order online (the site also provided Ford with data about car buyers).

How did Nasser's planning work out? Within a couple of years, Wall Street named Ford the most profitable and best-managed automaker of the Big Three (the other two are General Motors and DaimlerChrysler). Then came the Firestone tire recall, quality problems that began to surface, a sluggish economy, and other woes. Nasser's grand Internet plans didn't work out as he had hoped—the information technology department simply wasn't ready. In the summer of 2001, Ford's board of directors voted to give company chairman Bill Ford "a greater strategic role" in the company. In other words, Ford and Nasser would share power and responsibilities that would "focus on policy, strategy, key issues affecting the future direction of the company and other major business issues." For several months, the two men remained diplomatic in public, but there was no mistaking their differing management styles, visions for the company, or proposed strategies. Eventually, Nasser was voted out. Bill Ford had a huge task ahead of him.

First, Bill Ford created a triumvirate—a team of three top executives—to formulate a new vision and strategies for the company. He named Carl E. Reichardt vice-chairman and Nick Scheele chief operating officer. Scheele came from Ford's Jaguar division and Reichardt, former head of a bank, from the board of directors. "I expect the three of us will have an easygoing relationship," noted Ford. Scheele began his term with a "back to basics" slogan that indicated the company's new strategy would focus on its core business: making and selling cars and trucks. Then came the massive restructuring plan, whose goal was to cut $3 billion to $5 billion in costs. Most experts believe that Nasser would have favored downsizing in order to meet Ford's shrinking share in the marketplace, but Bill Ford would likely favor other strategies. Still, he warned in an early press release that the company would have to take "tough action" to reverse its losses. "It is not going to surprise anyone that there will be some pretty dramatic changes," noted Greg Melich of Morgan Stanley Dean Witter. "The one area where you can do more quickly is in the managerial and administrative areas, whereas restructuring the manufacturing side is much more difficult." However, it was clear that there was surplus manufacturing capacity in North America that needed to be addressed. And before Nasser's departure, the company was considering laying off as much as 20 percent of its U.S. white-collar staff, or more than 8,000 salaried workers, as part of a strategic overhaul. Also, the company proposed delaying the release of certain new auto models, including the Ford Ranger. Another part of the plan involved using more shared parts to cut manufacturing costs, even in Ford's premium car lines such as Volvo and Jaguar. A "strategy board" was developed specifically to formulate plans for the Premier Automotive Group (PAG), which would open the door for more than shared parts—perhaps shared engineering, sales, and purchasing teams—while maintaining the individual identities of the brands. "We have developed a structure which will allow us to more effectively support all our PAG brands," announced Wolfgang Reitzle, chairman of the PAG. "Individually, the companies do not have the critical mass to compete on equal terms."

Finally, Bill Ford began to push for a reconciliation between his company and Firestone/Bridgestone; after all, there are Fords and Firestones in both families. Mending the relationship might indicate a return to normalcy on the road "back to the basics." What are Ford's basics? "It's not the Internet, junkyards, or auto parts," quips David E. Cole, director of the Center for Automotive Research in Ann Arbor, Michigan. "It's building cars and trucks." Now there's a plan.

## Questions

1. Based on what you've read, formulate a brief mission statement for the "new" Ford Motor Company.

2. Imagine that you are part of Bill Ford's management team. Set a stretch goal either for the company as a whole or for the Premier group strategy board that you think would realistically help the company turn around. Explain why you chose this goal.

3. Describe the differences between Jac Nasser and Bill Ford as decision makers.

Sources: John Griffiths and Tim Burt, "Moving to Drive the Premier Growth Machine Faster," *Financial Times*, November 23, 2001, *http://news.ft.com*; Tim Burt and Nikki Tait, "Ford May Axe 20 percent of U.S. White Collar Staff," *Financial Times*, November 6, 2001, *http://news.ft.com*; Kathleen Kerwin and Joann Muller, "Bill Ford Takes the Wheel," *BusinessWeek Online*, November 1, 2001, *http://www.businessweek.com*; David Ibison, "New Ford Chief Edges Closer to Truce with Bridgestone," *Financial Times*, November 1, 2001, *http://news.ft.com*; Tim Burt, "Nasser Signals Further Cuts in Ford's U.S. Production," *Financial Times*, October 25, 2001, *http://news.ft.com*; Tim Burt, "Nasser Says Ford Has the Strategy to Confound Critics," *Financial Times*, September 13, 2001, *http://news.ft.com*; Jerry Flint, "Ford: A Distracted Driver," Forbes.com, September 6, 2001, *http://www.forbes.com*; Tim Burt and Nikki Tait, "Getting Ford Around the Corner," *Financial Times*, July 30, 2001, *http://news.ft.com; Jeff Moad*, "Ford Rebuilds IT Engine," *ZDNet News*, January 28, 2001, *http://www.zdnet.com*; Amey Stone and Kathleen Kerwin, "Can Nasser Get Ford's Stock onto a Smoother Road?" *BusinessWeek Online*, October 11, 1999, *http://www.businessweek.com*; "Jac Nasser: In the Past, We Tried to Do Too Much," *BusinessWeek* Online, October 11, 1999, *http://www.businessweek.com*.

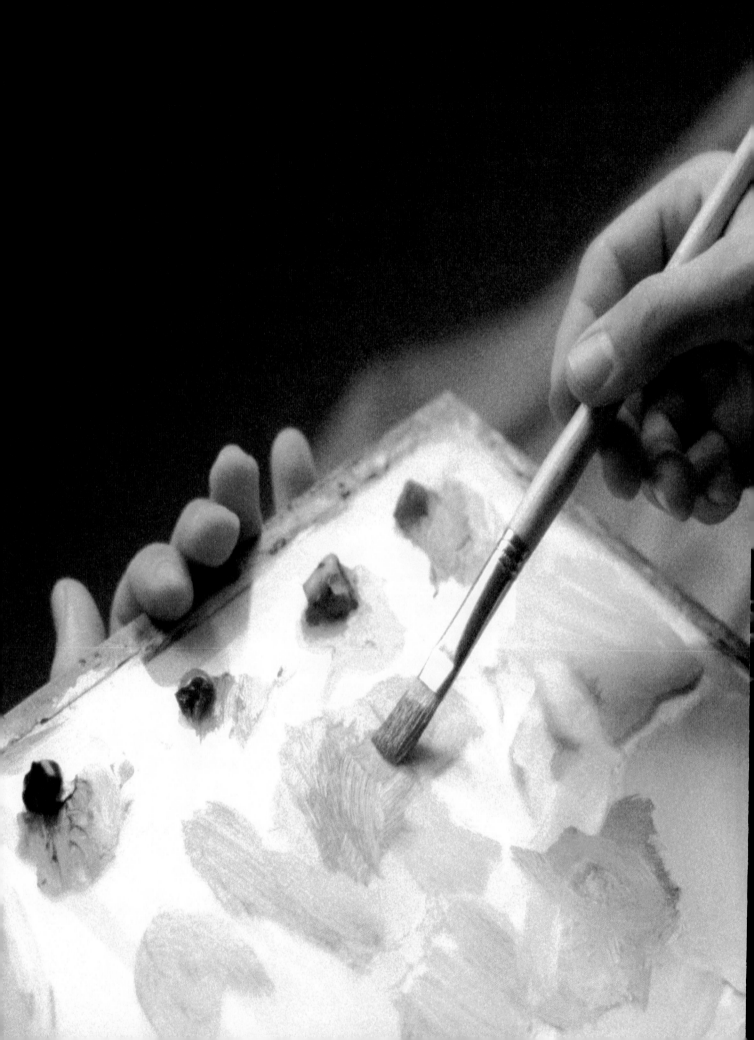

# Organizing

Look at a painting. Whether it's a centuries-old masterpiece or a modern work, you see color, texture, and shape. Look more closely, and you'll see the artist's studied technique composing and organizing the work.

Painters chart the world's turbulent history, but it all begins with a blank canvas. Will it be a landscape, a portrait, an abstract, a still life? While many different styles have evolved over the centuries—Impressionism's indistinct brush strokes of color, Cubism's angular, distorted shapes—one ideal has held fast: an artist must know the rules of composition in order to break them.

Paint is organized on canvas to convey emotion—awe, anger, comfort—or knowledge. The artist's eye organizes, but he or she begins by determining the medium and organizing materials—colors, brushes, lighting—that will best bring a personal vision to life. Paints are transferred from their blobs on a palette to their organized placement on the canvas. The artist structures the work to embody an emotion, tell a story, plant an idea, or provide beauty.

Managers also organize and deploy resources to achieve a vision and goals. Although many painters in centuries past were supported by wealthy patrons while pursuing their artistic visions, today's managers work for organizations and cannot answer only to their inner muses. They support, and must be supported by, the organization. No matter what the chain of command—whether the organization has a horizontal structure, in which managers share employees' tasks, or a vertical structure, with departmentalized top-down management—the need for coordination is paramount.

By organizing their resources, including people, technology, and institutional knowledge, and by marshaling their strengths, managers can support the organization despite economic downturns or competitive threats to achieve goals. While beauty may not be a manager's goal, organization design can be a work of art.

Part 4

# Chapter 10

# Designing Adaptive Organizations

## LEARNING OBJECTIVES

*After studying this chapter, you should be able to:*

1. Discuss the fundamental characteristics of organizing, including such concepts as work specialization, chain of command, span of management, and centralization versus decentralization.

2. Describe functional and divisional approaches to structure.

3. Explain the matrix approach to structure and its application to both domestic and international organizations.

4. Describe the contemporary team and virtual network structures and why they are being adopted by organizations.

5. Explain why organizations need coordination across departments and hierarchical levels, and describe mechanisms for achieving coordination.

6. Identify how structure can be used to achieve an organization's strategic goals.

7. Illustrate how organization structure can be designed to fit environmental uncertainty.

8. Define production technology (manufacturing, service, and digital) and explain how it influences organization structure.

The call to Carlos Ghosn came on a blustery March day in 1999. Louis Schweitzer, CEO of Renault, was asking Ghosn to take on the biggest challenge of his management career—to lead a turnaround of Japan's Nissan. Renault and Nissan had just agreed to an important strategic alliance, but its success depended on transforming Nissan into a profitable business. Ghosn had succeeded before as a turnaround artist, but Nissan was a whole different story. The once-thriving company had been struggling to turn a profit for eight years. Purchasing and manufacturing costs were high and profit margins notoriously low. The company's debt, even after the Renault investment, amounted to a staggering $11 billion. Product innovation was at a standstill, and the company was trying to compete with aging and outdated car models. When Ghosn got to Nissan, he found deeper problems, including a culture of blame where no one was willing to accept responsibility for mistakes. One reason, he discovered, was that most Nissan managers did not have clearly defined areas of responsibility and authority. Another impediment was the lack of trust, communication, and collaboration across departments. When something went wrong, sales blamed product planning, product planning blamed engineering, engineering blamed sales, sales blamed finance, and on and on—and nothing ever got solved. Ghosn knew he was facing a do-or-die situation: Either fix these fundamental problems, or Nissan would die.[1]

## Take A Moment

What advice would you give Carlos Ghosn about using structural design to help turn Nissan around? What structural changes might solve Nissan's problems with poor coordination and shatter the pervasive culture of blame?

PHOTO: CHRIS MCPHERSON

## CONCEPT CONNECTION

*Successful artist Shepard Fairey has proven himself to be an effective manager too. Fairey runs his own marketing design firm, Studio Number One, a studio to design unique graphics and logos used in untraditional advertising campaigns, and on labels for clothing, soft drinks, and other products. Fairey manages a creative team of seven full-time employees and a handful of part-timers and interns. Even in a small organization such as this, organizing is a critical part of good management. Fairey has to be sure people are assigned and coordinated to do all the various jobs necessary to satisfy clients such as Express, Levi's , and Dr Pepper/Seven Up. The right organization structure enables Studio Number One to be "fast, deadline-sensitive, and responsive."*

**organizing**
The deployment of organizational resources to achieve strategic goals.

**organization structure**
The framework in which the organization defines how tasks are divided, resources are deployed, and departments are coordinated.

The problem confronting Nissan is largely one of structural design. Carlos Ghosn wants to use elements of structure to define authority and responsibility for managers, promote accountability, and improve coordination so that Nissan can bring out new products and regain a competitive edge. Every firm wrestles with the problem of how to organize. Reorganization often is necessary to reflect a new strategy, changing market conditions, or innovative technology. In recent years, many companies, including American Express, Apple, IBM, Microsoft, and Ford Motor Co., have realigned departmental groupings, chains of command, and horizontal coordination mechanisms to attain new strategic goals. Structure is a powerful tool for reaching strategic goals, and a strategy's success often is determined by its fit with organization structure.

Many companies have found a need to make structural changes that are compatible with use of the Internet for e-business, which requires stronger horizontal coordination. For example, Brady Corporation, a Milwaukee-based manufacturer of identification and safety products, is reorganizing to increase cross-functional collaboration in connection with the rollout of a new system that links customers, distributors, and suppliers over the Internet.[2] Hewlett-Packard consolidated its 83 independently run units into four major divisions to increase internal collaboration and enhance flexibility.[3] Some companies operate as network organizations, limiting themselves to a few core activities and letting outside specialists handle the rest. Each of these organizations is using fundamental concepts of organizing. Organizing is the deployment of organizational resources to achieve strategic goals. The deployment of resources is reflected in the organization's division of labor into specific departments and jobs, formal lines of authority, and mechanisms for coordinating diverse organization tasks.

Organizing is important because it follows from strategy—the topic of Part 3. Strategy defines *what* to do; organizing defines *how* to do it. Organization structure is a tool that managers use to harness resources for getting things done. Part 4 explains the variety of organizing principles and concepts used by managers. This chapter covers fundamental concepts that apply to all organizations and departments, including organizing the vertical structure and using mechanisms for horizontal coordination. The chapter also examines how managers tailor the various elements of structural design to the organization's situation. Chapter 11 discusses how organizations can be structured to facilitate innovation and change. Chapters 12 and 13 consider how to utilize human resources to the best advantage within the organization's structure.

# Organizing the Vertical Structure

The organizing process leads to the creation of organization structure, which defines how tasks are divided and resources deployed. Organization structure is defined as

(1) the set of formal tasks assigned to individuals and departments; (2) formal reporting relationships, including lines of authority, decision responsibility, number of hierarchical levels, and span of managers' control; and (3) the design of systems to ensure effective coordination of employees across departments.[4]

The set of formal tasks and formal reporting relationships provides a framework for vertical control of the organization. The characteristics of vertical structure are portrayed in the organization chart, which is the visual representation of an organization's structure.

A sample organization chart for a water bottling plant is illustrated in Exhibit 10.1. The plant has four major departments—accounting, human resources, production, and marketing. The organization chart delineates the chain of command, indicates departmental tasks and how they fit together, and provides order and logic for the organization. Every employee has an appointed task, line of authority, and decision responsibility. The following sections discuss several important features of vertical structure in more detail.

**organization chart**
The visual representation of an organization's structure.

## Work Specialization

Organizations perform a wide variety of tasks. A fundamental principle is that work can be performed more efficiently if employees are allowed to specialize.[5] Work specialization, sometimes called *division of labor*, is the degree to which organizational tasks are subdivided into separate jobs. Work specialization in Exhibit 10.1 is illustrated by the separation of production tasks into bottling, quality control, and maintenance. Employees within each department perform only the tasks relevant to their

**work specialization**
The degree to which organizational tasks are subdivided into individual jobs; also called division of labor.

**Exhibit 10.1**

### Organization Chart for a Water Bottling Plant

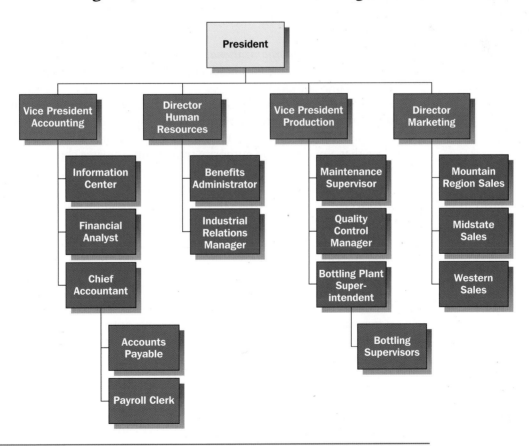

specialized function. When work specialization is extensive, employees specialize in a single task. Jobs tend to be small, but they can be performed efficiently. Work specialization is readily visible on an automobile assembly line where each employee performs the same task over and over again. It would not be efficient to have a single employee build the entire automobile, or even perform a large number of unrelated jobs.

Despite the apparent advantages of specialization, many organizations are moving away from this principle. With too much specialization, employees are isolated and do only a single, boring job. Many companies are enlarging jobs to provide greater challenges or assigning teams so that employees can rotate among the several jobs performed by the team.

## Chain of Command

**chain of command**
An unbroken line of authority that links all individuals in the organization and specifies who reports to whom.

The chain of command is an unbroken line of authority that links all persons in an organization and shows who reports to whom. It is associated with two underlying principles. *Unity of command* means that each employee is held accountable to only one supervisor. The *scalar principle* refers to a clearly defined line of authority in the organization that includes all employees. Authority and responsibility for different tasks should be distinct. All persons in the organization should know to whom they report as well as the successive management levels all the way to the top. In Exhibit 10.1, the payroll clerk reports to the chief accountant, who in turn reports to the vice president, who in turn reports to the company president.

### Authority, Responsibility, and Delegation

**authority**
The formal and legitimate right of a manager to make decisions, issue orders, and allocate resources to achieve organizationally desired outcomes.

The chain of command illustrates the authority structure of the organization. Authority is the formal and legitimate right of a manager to make decisions, issue orders, and allocate resources to achieve organizationally desired outcomes. Authority is distinguished by three characteristics:[6]

1. *Authority is vested in organizational positions, not people.* Managers have authority because of the positions they hold, and other people in the same positions would have the same authority.
2. *Authority is accepted by subordinates.* Although authority flows top down through the organization's hierarchy, subordinates comply because they believe that managers have a legitimate right to issue orders. The *acceptance theory of authority* argues that a manager has authority only if subordinates choose to accept his or her commands. If subordinates refuse to obey because the order is outside their zone of acceptance, a manager's authority disappears.[7]
3. *Authority flows down the vertical hierarchy.* Positions at the top of the hierarchy are vested with more formal authority than are positions at the bottom.

**responsibility**
The duty to perform the task or activity an employee has been assigned.

Responsibility is the flip side of the authority coin. Responsibility is the duty to perform the task or activity an employee has been assigned. Typically, managers are assigned authority commensurate with responsibility. When managers have responsibility for task outcomes but little authority, the job is possible but difficult. They rely on persuasion and luck. When managers have authority exceeding responsibility, they may become tyrants, using authority toward frivolous outcomes.[8]

**accountability**
The fact that the people with authority and responsibility are subject to reporting and justifying task outcomes to those above them in the chain of command.

Accountability is the mechanism through which authority and responsibility are brought into alignment. Accountability means that the people with authority and responsibility are subject to reporting and justifying task outcomes to those above them in the chain of command.[9] For organizations to function well, everyone needs to know what they are accountable for and accept the responsibility and authority for performing it. Accountability can be built into the organization structure. For example, at Whirlpool, incentive programs tailored to different hierarchical levels provide strict accountability. Performance of all managers is monitored, and bonus payments are tied to successful outcomes.

Another concept related to authority is delegation.[10] Delegation is the process managers use to transfer authority and responsibility to positions below them in the hierarchy. Most organizations today encourage managers to delegate authority to the lowest possible level to provide maximum flexibility to meet customer needs and adapt to the environment. However, many managers find delegation difficult. For example, Microsoft's Chief Financial Officer John Conners nearly resigned because of CEO Steven Ballmer's inability to delegate. By taking it upon himself to make financial decisions, Ballmer undermined the role of Conners and his team. Ballmer is trying to learn to give up some control and delegate more so that people can do their jobs more effectively.[11] Techniques for effective delegation are discussed in the Manager's Shoptalk box.

*Go to the ethical dilemma on page 384 that pertains to issues of authority, responsibility, and delegation.*

*Go to the ethical dilemma on page 384 that pertains to issues of authority, responsibility, and delegation.*

**delegation**
The process managers use to transfer authority and responsibility to positions below them in the hierarchy.

*Take A Moment*

## Line and Staff Authority

An important distinction in many organizations is between line authority and staff authority, reflecting whether managers work in line or staff departments in the organization's structure. *Line departments* perform tasks that reflect the organization's primary goal and mission. In a software company, line departments make and sell the product. In an Internet-based company, line departments would be those that develop and manage online offerings and sales. *Staff departments* include all those that provide specialized skills in support of line departments. Staff departments have an advisory relationship with line departments and typically include marketing, labor relations, research, accounting, and human resources.

Line authority means that people in management positions have formal authority to direct and control immediate subordinates. Staff authority is narrower and includes the right to advise, recommend, and counsel in the staff specialists' area of expertise. Staff authority is a communication relationship; staff specialists advise managers in technical areas. For example, the finance department of a manufacturing firm would have staff authority to coordinate with line departments about which accounting forms to use to facilitate equipment purchases and standardize payroll services.

**line authority**
A form of authority in which individuals in management positions have the formal power to direct and control immediate subordinates.

**staff authority**
A form of authority granted to staff specialists in their area of expertise.

## Span of Management

The span of management is the number of employees reporting to a supervisor. Sometimes called the *span of control*, this characteristic of structure determines how closely a supervisor can monitor subordinates. Traditional views of organization design recommended a span of management of about seven subordinates per manager. However, many lean organizations today have spans of management as high as 30, 40, and even higher. For example, at Consolidated Diesel's team-based engine assembly plant, the span of management is 100.[12] Research over the past 40 or so years shows that span of management varies widely and that several factors influence the span.[13] Generally, when supervisors must be closely involved with subordinates, the span should be small, and when supervisors need little involvement with subordinates, it can be large. The following factors are associated with less supervisor involvement and thus larger spans of control:

**span of management**
The number of employees reporting to a supervisor; also called *span of control*.

## Turbulent Times

# manager's Shoptalk

### *How to Delegate*

The attempt by top management to decentralize decision making often gets bogged down because middle managers are unable to delegate. Managers may cling tightly to their decision-making and task responsibilities. Failure to delegate occurs for a number of reasons: Managers are most comfortable making familiar decisions; they feel they will lose personal status by delegating tasks; they believe they can do a better job themselves; or they have an aversion to risk—they will not take a chance on delegating because performance responsibility ultimately rests with them.

Yet decentralization offers an organization many advantages. Decisions are made at the right level, lower-level employees are motivated, and employees have the opportunity to develop decision-making skills. Overcoming barriers to delegation in order to gain these advantages is a major challenge. The following approach can help each manager delegate more effectively:

1. *Delegate the whole task.* A manager should delegate an entire task to one person rather than dividing it among several people. This gives the individual complete responsibility and increases his or her initiative while giving the manager some control over the results.
2. *Select the right person.* Not all employees have the same capabilities and degree of motivation. Managers must match talent to task if delegation is to be effective. They should identify subordinates who have made independent decisions in the past and have shown a desire for more responsibility.
3. *Ensure that authority equals responsibility.* Merely assigning a task is not effective delegation. Managers often load subordinates with increased responsibility but do not extend their decision-making range. In addition to having responsibility for completing a task, the worker must be given the authority to make decisions about how best to do the job.
4. *Give thorough instruction.* Successful delegation includes information on what, when, why, where, who, and how. The subordinate must clearly understand the task and the expected

results. It is a good idea to write down all provisions discussed, including required resources and when and how the results will be reported.
5. *Maintain feedback.* Feedback means keeping open lines of communication with the subordinate to answer questions and provide advice, but without exerting too much control. Open lines of communication make it easier to trust subordinates. Feedback keeps the subordinate on the right track.
6. *Evaluate and reward performance.* Once the task is completed, the manager should evaluate results, not methods. When results do not meet expectations, the manager must assess the consequences. When they do meet expectations, the manager should reward employees for a job well done with praise, financial rewards when appropriate, and delegation of future assignments.

### *Are You a Positive Delegator?*

Positive delegation is the way an organization implements decentralization. Do you help or hinder the decentralization process? If you answer yes to more than three of the following questions, you may have a problem delegating:

- I tend to be a perfectionist.
- My boss expects me to know all the details of my job.
- I don't have the time to explain clearly and concisely how a task should be accomplished.
- I often end up doing tasks myself.
- My subordinates typically are not as committed as I am.
- I get upset when other people don't do the task right.
- I really enjoy doing the details of my job to the best of my ability.
- I like to be in control of task outcomes.

SOURCES: Thomas R. Horton "Delegation and Team Building: No Solo Acts Please," *Management Review* (September 1992), 58–61; Andrew E. Schwartz, "The Why, What, and to Whom of Delegation," *Management Solutions* (June 1987), 31–38; "Delegation," *Small Business Report* (June 1986), 38–43; and Russell Wild, "Clone Yourself," *Working Woman* (May 2000), 79–80.

1. Work performed by subordinates is stable and routine.
2. Subordinates perform similar work tasks.
3. Subordinates are concentrated in a single location.
4. Subordinates are highly trained and need little direction in performing tasks.
5. Rules and procedures defining task activities are available.
6. Support systems and personnel are available for the manager.
7. Little time is required in nonsupervisory activities such as coordination with other departments or planning.
8. Managers' personal preferences and styles favor a large span.

The average span of control used in an organization determines whether the structure is tall or flat. A tall structure has an overall narrow span and more hierarchical levels. A flat structure has a wide span, is horizontally dispersed, and has fewer hierarchical levels.

The trend in recent years has been toward wider spans of control as a way to facilitate delegation.[14] For example, a study of 300 large U.S. corporations found that the average number of division heads reporting directly to the CEO tripled between the years of 1986 and 1999.[15] Exhibit 10.2 illustrates how an international metals company was reorganized. The multilevel set of managers shown in panel *a* was replaced with ten operating managers and nine staff specialists reporting directly to the CEO, as shown in panel *b*. The CEO welcomed this wide span of 19 management subordinates because it fit his style, his management team was top quality and needed little supervision, and they were all located on the same floor of an office building.

**tall structure**
A management structure characterized by an overall narrow span of management and a relatively large number of hierarchical levels.

**flat structure**
A management structure characterized by an overall broad span of control and relatively few hierarchical levels.

## Centralization and Decentralization

Centralization and decentralization pertain to the hierarchical level at which decisions are made. Centralization means that decision authority is located near the top of the organization. With decentralization, decision authority is pushed downward to lower organization levels. Organizations may have to experiment to find the correct hierarchical level at which to make decisions.

In the United States and Canada, the trend over the past 30 years has been toward greater decentralization of organizations. Decentralization is believed to relieve the burden on top managers, make greater use of employees' skills and abilities, ensure that decisions are made close to the action by well-informed people, and permit more rapid response to external changes.

However, this trend does not mean that every organization should decentralize all decisions. Managers should diagnose the organizational situation and select the decision-making level that will best meet the organization's needs. Factors that typically influence centralization versus decentralization are as follows:

1. *Greater change and uncertainty in the environment are usually associated with decentralization.* A good example of how decentralization can help cope with rapid change and uncertainty occurred following the September 11, 2001, attacks in the United States. UPS trucks, which carry 7 percent of the country's

© DENNIS KLEIMAN

**CONCEPT CONNECTION**

*Ian Adamson is a businessman and adventure racer whose team won the Eco-Challenge in Borneo, which involves 320 miles of hiking, running, swimming, biking, canoeing, and rappelling. The flat structrure of his sports team is highly efficient for meeting such challenges. It has no leader; instead, members gather on the course and make decisions collectively as quickly as possible or spontaneously defer to someone who has expert knowledge. Teammates pitch in to help one another. For a fee, Adamson's recently formed company, Colorado Adventure Training, shows managers from companies such as Starbucks how to benefit from this non-hierarchical approach.*

# Exhibit 10.2

## Reorganization to Increase Span of Management for President of an International Metals Company

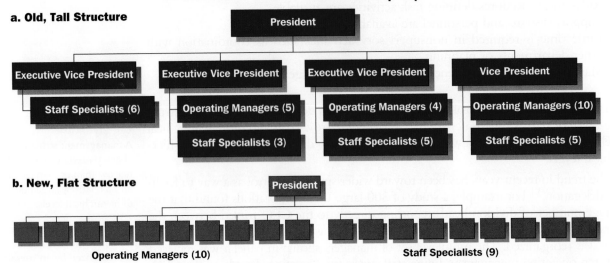

**a. Old, Tall Structure**

President

- Executive Vice President
  - Staff Specialists (6)
- Executive Vice President
  - Operating Managers (5)
  - Staff Specialists (3)
- Executive Vice President
  - Operating Managers (4)
  - Staff Specialists (5)
- Vice President
  - Operating Managers (10)
  - Staff Specialists (5)

**b. New, Flat Structure**

President

Operating Managers (10)        Staff Specialists (9)

---

**centralization**
The location of decision authority near top organizational levels.

**decentralization**
The location of decision authority near lower organizational levels.

gross domestic product on any given day, were able to keep running on time in New York, thanks largely to a decentralized management system that gives local managers authority to make key decisions.[16]

2. *The amount of centralization or decentralization should fit the firm's strategy.* For example, Johnson & Johnson gives almost complete authority to its 180 operating companies to develop and market their own products. Decentralization fits the corporate strategy of empowerment that gets each division close to customers so it can speedily adapt to their needs.[17] Taking the opposite approach, Larry Ellison at Oracle is using technology to centralize operations, cut costs, and get everyone focused, as described in the Unlocking Creative Solutions Through Technology box.

3. *In times of crisis or risk of company failure, authority may be centralized at the top.* When Honda could not get agreement among divisions about new car models, President Nobuhiko Kawamoto made the decision himself.[18]

# Departmentalization

**departmentalization**
The basis on which individuals are grouped into departments and departments into the total organization.

Another fundamental characteristic of organization structure is departmentalization, which is the basis for grouping positions into departments and departments into the total organization. Managers make choices about how to use the chain of command to group people together to perform their work. There are five approaches to structural design that reflect different uses of the chain of command in departmentalization, as illustrated in Exhibit 10.3. The functional, divisional, and matrix are traditional approaches that rely on the chain of command to define departmental groupings and reporting relationships along the hierarchy. Two contemporary approaches are the use of teams and networks, which have emerged to meet changing organizational needs in a turbulent global environment.

The basic difference among structures illustrated in Exhibit 10.3 is the way in which employees are departmentalized and to whom they report.[19] Each structural approach is described in detail in the following sections.

Exhibit 10.3

## Five Approaches to Structural Design

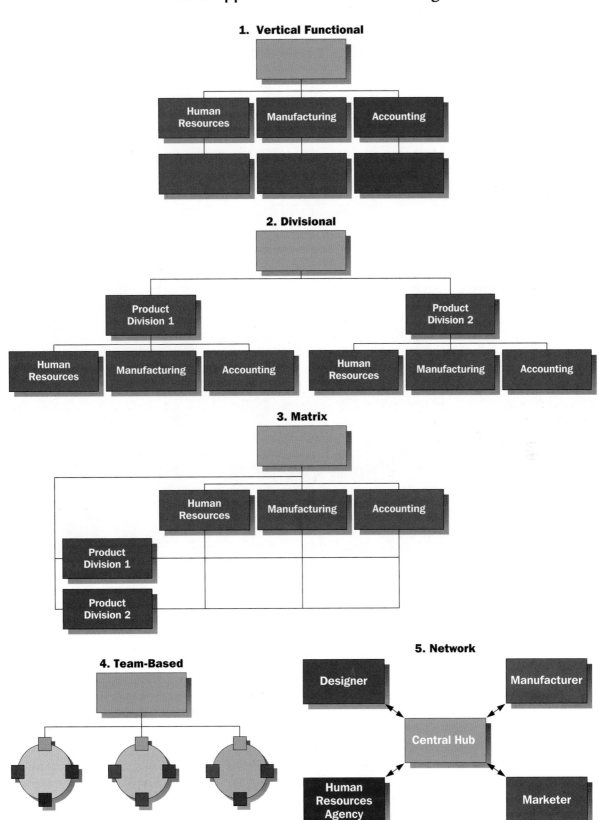

1. **Vertical Functional**

Human Resources · Manufacturing · Accounting

2. **Divisional**

Product Division 1 — Human Resources · Manufacturing · Accounting

Product Division 2 — Human Resources · Manufacturing · Accounting

3. **Matrix**

Human Resources · Manufacturing · Accounting

Product Division 1

Product Division 2

4. **Team-Based**

5. **Network**

Designer · Manufacturer · Central Hub · Human Resources Agency · Marketer

# Unlocking Creative Solutions Through Technology

### Tightening the Reins at Oracle

Much has been written about the power of the Internet to give employees more information and greater freedom. But Larry Ellison, CEO of Oracle Corporation, knows the global network also offers a major opportunity for strengthening top management command and control. By requiring employees to do their work via the Internet, Ellison can carefully track, analyze, and control the behavior of each unit, manager, and employee on a global basis.

Oracle got into trouble some years ago because sales managers were cutting back-room deals or hammering out private, individualized compensation agreements with salespeople in different countries. Today all the terms, including sales contracts and commissions, are dictated from the top and are spelled out in a global database. In addition, all deals must be reported into the database, where they can easily be tracked by Ellison back at headquarters. "I love running the business now," Ellison says. "I love getting involved in every detail. . . ." Clearly, Larry Ellison loves being in control, but he has solid business reasons for centralizing information and decision making. Several years ago, Oracle realized its future rested on building a complete suite of Internet applications that could work together on a global basis, and Ellison knew the first step would be to roll out the global system inside of Oracle itself, or as Ellison put it, to "eat our own dog food."

He first had to dismantle the separate fiefdoms that had developed inside Oracle. Each country manager had separate e-mail, human resources, and financial reporting systems, which were supported by more than 40 data centers scattered around the world. "Not only did we have 70 separate accounting systems in 70 different countries, but all of those countries hired IT departments to change them in different ways," Ellison marvels. Naturally, managers balked when the CEO decreed that there would now be only two data centers (one at headquarters and a backup center in Colorado Springs) and a single global database for each major function. To break down resistance, Ellison started by globalizing e-mail, allowing managers to see how much easier, more effective, and cheaper it was to do business. Then he gradually rolled out other global Internet-based applications.

Some managers still aren't happy about the tighter grip Ellison has over global operations, but the CEO believes it is needed to effectively manage a sprawling, global company. "Executives. We sit up here . . . and think very hard on something, tell people to do something," Ellison says. "But as these orders go out through many layers of bureaucracy, they change and change and change." Ellison believes using the Internet to centralize control and manage more "scientifically" is the best way to take Oracle to the next level.

SOURCE: G. Christian Hill, "Dog Eats Dog Food. And Damn If It Ain't Tasty," *ECompany News* (November 2000), 168–178.

## Vertical Functional Approach

### What It Is

**functional structure**
The grouping of positions into departments based on similar skills, expertise, and resource use.

Functional structure is the grouping of positions into departments based on similar skills, expertise, work activities, and resource use. A functional structure can be thought of as departmentalization by organizational resources, because each type of functional activity—accounting, human resources, engineering, manufacturing—represents specific resources for performing the organization's task. People, facilities, and other resources representing a common function are grouped into a single department.

### How It Works

Refer back to Exhibit 10.1 on page 351 for an example of a functional structure. The major departments under the president are groupings of similar expertise and resources, such as accounting, human resources, production, and marketing. Each of the functional departments is concerned with the organization as a whole. The marketing department is responsible for all sales and marketing, for example, and the accounting department handles financial issues for the entire company.

The functional structure is a strong vertical design. Information flows up and down the vertical hierarchy, and the chain of command converges at the top of the organization. In a functional structure, people within a department communicate primarily with others in the same department to coordinate work and accomplish tasks or implement decisions that are passed down the hierarchy. Managers and employees are compatible because of similar training and expertise. Typically, there are rules and procedures governing the duties and responsibilities of each employee, and employees at lower hierarchical levels accept the right of those higher in the hierarchy to make decisions and issue orders.

## Divisional Approach

### What It Is

In contrast to the functional approach, in which people are grouped by common skills and resources, the divisional structure occurs when departments are grouped together based on organizational outputs. The divisional structure is sometimes called a *product structure, program structure*, or *self-contained unit structure*. Each of these terms means essentially the same thing: Diverse departments are brought together to produce a single organizational output, whether it be a product, a program, or a service to a single customer.

Most large corporations have separate divisions that perform different tasks, use different technologies, or serve different customers. When a huge organization produces products for different markets, the divisional structure works because each division is an autonomous business. For example, Microsoft has reorganized into seven product divisions—Windows, server software, mobile software, office software, videogames, business software, and MSN Internet service. Each unit will contain the functions of a stand-alone company, doing its own product development, sales, marketing, and finance.[20]

**divisional structure**
An organization structure in which departments are grouped based on similar organizational outputs.

### How It Works

Functional and divisional structures are illustrated in Exhibit 10.4. In the divisional structure, divisions are created as self-contained units with separate functional departments for each division. For example, in Exhibit 10.4, each functional department resource needed to produce the product is assigned to each division. Whereas in a functional structure, all engineers are grouped together and work on all products, in a divisional structure separate engineering departments are created within each division. Each department is smaller and focuses on a single product line or customer segment. Departments are duplicated across product lines.

The primary difference between divisional and functional structures is that the chain of command from each function converges lower in the hierarchy. In a divisional structure, differences of opinion among research and development, marketing, manufacturing, and finance would be resolved at the divisional level rather than by the president. Thus, the divisional structure encourages decentralization. Decision making is pushed down at least one level in the hierarchy, freeing the president and other top managers for strategic planning.

### Geographic- or Customer-Based Divisions

An alternative for assigning divisional responsibility is to group company activities by geographic region or customer group. For example, The Internal Revenue Service shifted to a structure focused on four distinct taxpayer groups: individuals, small businesses, corporations, and nonprofit or government agencies.[21] A global geographic structure is illustrated in Exhibit 10.5. In this structure, all functions in a specific country or region report to the same division manager. The structure

# Exhibit 10.4

## Functional versus Divisional Structures

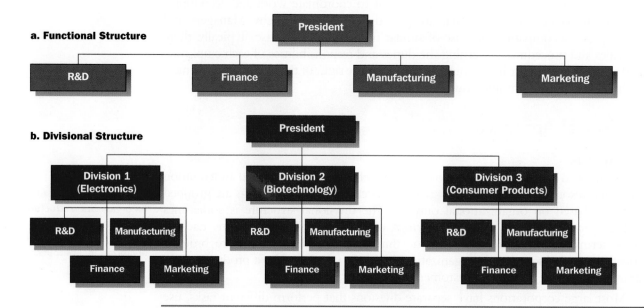

**a. Functional Structure**

President
- R&D
- Finance
- Manufacturing
- Marketing

**b. Divisional Structure**

President
- Division 1 (Electronics)
  - R&D
  - Manufacturing
  - Finance
  - Marketing
- Division 2 (Biotechnology)
  - R&D
  - Manufacturing
  - Finance
  - Marketing
- Division 3 (Consumer Products)
  - R&D
  - Manufacturing
  - Finance
  - Marketing

focuses company activities on local market conditions. For example, competitive advantage may come from the production or sale of a product adapted to a given country. Colgate-Palmolive Company is organized into regional divisions in North America, Europe, Latin America, the Far East, and the South Pacific.[22] The structure works for Colgate because personal care products often need to be tailored to cultural values and local customs.

## Matrix Approach

**matrix approach**
An organization structure that utilizes functional and divisional chains of command simultaneously in the same part of the organization.

### What It Is

The matrix approach combines aspects of both functional and divisional structures simultaneously in the same part of the organization. The matrix structure evolved as a way to improve horizontal coordination and information sharing.[23] One unique

# Exhibit 10.5

## Geographic-Based Global Organization Structure

Chief Executive Officer
- Corporate Staff
  - Western U.S. Division
  - Eastern U.S. Division
  - Latin American Division
  - Asian Division

Exhibit 10.6

## Dual-Authority Structure in a Matrix Organization

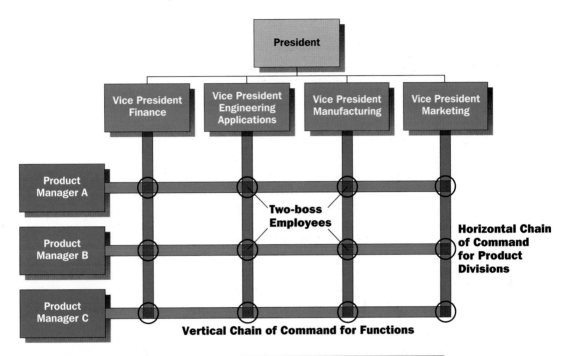

feature of the matrix is that it has dual lines of authority. In Exhibit 10.6, the functional hierarchy of authority runs vertically, and the divisional hierarchy of authority runs horizontally. While the vertical structure provides traditional control within functional departments, the horizontal structure provides coordination across departments. The matrix structure therefore provides a formal chain of command for both functional (vertical) and divisional (horizontal) relationships. As a result of this dual structure, some employees actually report to two supervisors simultaneously.

### How It Works

The dual lines of authority make the matrix unique. To see how the matrix works, consider the global matrix structure illustrated in Exhibit 10.7. The two lines of authority are geographic and product. The geographic boss in Germany coordinates all affiliates in Germany, and the plastics products boss coordinates the manufacturing and sale of plastics products around the world. Managers of local affiliate companies in Germany would report to two superiors, both the country boss and the product boss. The dual authority structure violates the unity-of-command concept described earlier in this chapter but is necessary to give equal emphasis to both functional and divisional lines of authority. Dual lines of authority can be confusing, but after managers learn to use this structure, the matrix provides excellent coordination simultaneously for each geographic region and each product line.

The success of the matrix structure depends on the abilities of people in key matrix roles. Two-boss employees, those who report to two supervisors simultaneously, must resolve conflicting demands from the matrix bosses. They must confront senior managers and reach joint decisions. They need excellent human relations skills with which to confront managers and resolve conflicts. The matrix boss is the product or functional boss, who is responsible for one side of the matrix. The top leader is responsible for the entire matrix. The top leader oversees both the product and functional chains of command. His or her responsibility is to maintain a power balance between

**two-boss employees**
Employees who report to two supervisors simultaneously.

**matrix boss**
The product or functional boss, responsible for one side of the matrix.

**top leader**
The overseer of both the product and functional chains of command, responsible for the entire matrix.

# Exhibit 10.7

## Global Matrix Structure

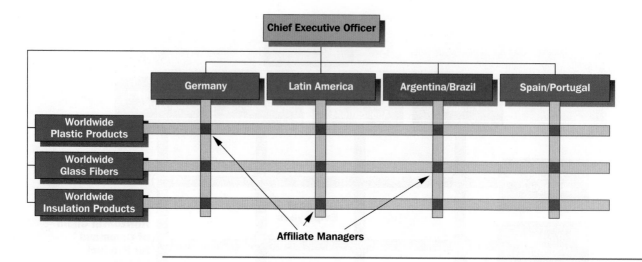

Affiliate Managers

the two sides of the matrix. If disputes arise between them, the problem will be kicked upstairs to the top leader.[24]

At General Motors' Information Systems and Services, CIO Ralph Szygenda created a matrix that helped the unit cut costs and increase effectiveness.

**GENERAL MOTORS INFORMATION SYSTEMS AND SERVICES**

http://www.general motors.com

When General Motors hired Ralph Szygenda as its first Chief Information Officer in 1996, the company didn't even *have* an information office. Because the entire information technology (IT) function had been spun off to EDS in the early 1990s, GM had no IT staff of its own. Szygenda started with a clean slate and decided to create something unique among corporate IT units—a matrix structure. Szygenda believed the matrix was the best way to cope with the massive IT problems associated with a huge enterprise like GM with several highly autonomous divisions.

Szygenda hired five divisional CIOs to be in charge of information systems and services for the various GM divisions: North America, Europe, Asia-Pacific, Latin America/Africa/Middle East, and GM Finance. At the same time, he put in place five process information officers (PIOs) to work horizontally in different processes that crossed divisional lines: product development, supply chain management, production, customer experience, and business services. Many Information Systems and Services employees thus report to both a divisional chief information officer and a process information officer (matrix bosses). Szygenda serves as the top leader, in charge of the entire matrix.

Implementing the matrix structure was not without its problems, but employees have learned to balance their overlapping responsibilities. Szygenda credits the matrix with helping to cut $1 billion out of GM's IT budget over a seven-year period. General Motors' CEO Rick Wagoner was so impressed by the success of the matrix that he set up global process leaders in other parts of the business, helping the company reap huge gains in productivity and manufacturing efficiency.[25]

## Team Approach

### What It Is

Probably the most widespread trend in departmentalization in recent years has been the implementation of team concepts. The vertical chain of command is a powerful means of control, but passing all decisions up the hierarchy takes too long and keeps responsibility at the top. The team approach gives managers a way to delegate authority, push responsibility to lower levels, and be more flexible and responsive in the competitive global environment. Chapter 21 will discuss teams in detail.

## How It Works

There are two ways to think about using teams in organizations. Cross-functional teams consist of employees from various functional departments who are responsible to meet as a team and resolve mutual problems. Team members typically still report to their functional departments, but they also report to the team, one member of whom may be the leader. Cross-functional teams are used to provide needed horizontal coordination to complement an existing divisional or functional structure. A frequent use of cross-functional teams is for change projects, such as new product or service innovation. A cross-functional team of mechanics, flight attendants, reservations agents, ramp workers, luggage attendants, and aircraft cleaners, for example, collaborated to plan and design a new low-fare airline for US Airways.[26]

The second approach is to use permanent teams, groups of employees who are brought together similar to a formal department. Each team brings together employees from all functional areas focused on a specific task or project, such as parts supply and logistics for an automobile plant. Emphasis is on horizontal communication and information sharing because representatives from all functions are coordinating their work and skills to complete a specific organizational task. Authority is pushed down to lower levels, and front-line employees are often given the freedom to make decisions and take action on their own. Team members may share or rotate team leadership. With a team-based structure, the entire organization is made up of horizontal teams that coordinate their work and work directly with customers to accomplish the organization's goals. Imagination Ltd., Britain's largest design firm, is based entirely on teamwork. Imagination puts together a diverse team at the beginning of each new project it undertakes, whether it be creating the lighting for Disney cruise ships or redesigning the packaging for Ericsson's cell-phone products. The team then works closely with the client throughout the project.[27] Imagination Ltd. has managed to make every project a smooth, seamless experience by building a culture that supports teamwork, as described in this chapter's Unlocking Creative Solutions Through People box.

COURTESY OF AVERY DENNISON CORP.

**CONCEPT CONNECTION**

*These members of the Avery Hi-Liter® EverBold™ marker team, part of the North American consumer products division at Avery Dennison Corporation, collaborated as a cross-functional team to launch a new pen-style highlighter product. Avery Dennison is a company committed to using the team-based approach to maintain and grow their market leadership. The company empowers multi-functional teams of employees to develop and launch new consumer products.*

**cross-functional teams**
A group of employees from various functional departments that meet as a team to resolve mutual problems.

**permanent teams**
A group of participants from several functions who are permanently assigned to solve ongoing problems of common interest.

**team-based structure**
Structure in which the entire organization is made up of horizontal teams that coordinate their activities and work directly with customers to accomplish the organization's goals.

## The Virtual Network Approach

### What It Is

The most recent approach to departmentalization extends the idea of horizontal coordination and collaboration beyond the boundaries of the organization. In a variety of industries, vertically integrated, hierarchical organizations are giving way to loosely interconnected groups of companies with permeable boundaries.[28] *Outsourcing*, which means farming out certain activities, such as manufacturing or credit processing, has become a significant trend. In addition, partnerships, alliances, and other complex collaborative forms are now a leading approach to accomplishing strategic goals. In the music industry, firms such as Vivendi Universal and Sony have formed networks of alliances with Internet service providers, digital retailers, software firms, and other companies to bring music to customers in new ways.[29] Some

# Unlocking Creative Solutions Through People

## Imagination Ltd.

The essence of teamwork is that people contribute selflessly, putting the good of the whole above their own individual interests. It doesn't always work that way, but Imagination Ltd. seems to have found the secret ingredient to seamless teamwork. According to Adrian Caddy, Imagination's creative director: "The culture at Imagination is this: You can articulate your ideas without fear."

Imagination Ltd. has created a company made up of teams of designers, architects, lighting experts, writers, theater people, film directors, and artists, in addition to IT specialists, marketing experts, and other functional specialties. By having employees with a wide range of skills, the company is able to put together a diverse team to provide each client with a new approach to its design problems. Imagination is deliberately nonhierarchical; only four people have formal titles, and on most project teams, no one is really in charge. Teams meet weekly, and everyone participates in every meeting from the very beginning, so there is no perception that any particular talent is primary—or secondary. Information technology

specialists, production people, and client-contact personnel are just as much a part of the team as the creative types. In addition, each person is expected to come up with ideas outside his or her area of expertise. The philosophy is that people at Imagination must be willing to *make* all kinds of suggestions and also to *take* all kinds of suggestions. So many ideas get batted around, revised, and adapted at the weekly meetings that no one can ever really claim ownership of a particular element of the project. The team also works closely with the client as a source of ideas and inspiration.

Talent and respect help to make the system work. Imagination hires its employees carefully, based not only on the quality of their work but also on their open-mindedness and curiosity about the world beyond their functional area of expertise. Then, the company makes sure everyone's work is so closely integrated that people gain an understanding and respect for what others do. "The integrated approach breeds respect for one another," says writer Chris White. "When you work alone, or in isolation within your discipline, you can get an overblown sense of your own importance to a project."

**SOURCE**: Charles Fishman, "Total Teamwork: Imagination Ltd.," *Fast Company* (April 2000), 156–168.

---

**virtual network structure**
An organization structure that disaggregates major functions to separate companies that are brokered by a small headquarters organization.

organizations take this networking approach to the extreme to create a new kind of structure. The virtual network structure means that the firm subcontracts most of its major functions to separate companies and coordinates their activities from a small headquarters organization.[30]

## How It Works

The organization may be viewed as a central hub surrounded by a network of outside specialists, as illustrated in Exhibit 10.8. Rather than being housed under one roof, services such as accounting, design, manufacturing, and distribution are outsourced to separate organizations that are connected electronically to the central office.[31] Networked computer systems, collaborative software, and the Internet enable organizations to exchange data and information so rapidly and smoothly that a loosely connected network of suppliers, manufacturers, assemblers, and distributors can look and act like one seamless company.

The idea behind networks is that a company can concentrate on what it does best and contract out other activities to companies with distinctive competence in those specific areas. This enables a company to do more with less.[32] The Birmingham, England-based company, Strida, provides an excellent example of the virtual network approach.

**STRIDA**
http://www.strida.com

How do two people run an entire company that sells thousands of high-tech folding bicycles all over the world? Steedman Bass and Bill Bennet do it with a virtual network approach that outsources design, manufacturing, customer service, logistics, accounting, and just about everything else to other organizations.

Exhibit 10.8

## Network Approach to Departmentalization

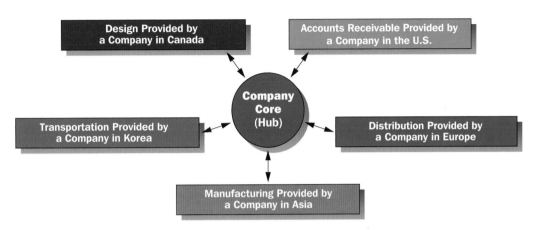

Bass, an avid cyclist, got into the bicycle business when he and his partner Bennet bought the struggling British company Strida, which was having trouble making enough quality bicycles to meet even minimum orders. The partners soon realized why Strida was struggling. The design for the folding bicycle was a clever engineering idea, but it was a manufacturing nightmare. Bass and Bennet immediately turned over production engineering and new product development to an American bicycle designer, still with intentions of building the bikes at the Birmingham factory. However, a large order from Italy sent them looking for other options. Eventually, they transferred all manufacturing to Ming Cycle Company of Taiwan, which builds the bikes with parts sourced from parts manufacturers in Taiwan and mainland China.

Finally, the last piece of the puzzle was to contract with a company in Birmingham that would take over everything else—from marketing to distribution. Bass and Bennet concentrate their energies on managing the partnerships that make the network function smoothly.[33]

With a network structure such as that used at Strida, it is difficult to answer the question, "Where is the organization?" in traditional terms. The different organizational parts may be spread all over the world. They are drawn together contractually and coordinated electronically, creating a new form of organization. Much like building blocks, parts of the network can be added or taken away to meet changing needs.[34]

A similar approach to networking is called the modular approach, in which a manufacturing company uses outside suppliers to provide entire chunks of a product, which are then assembled into a final product by a handful of workers. The Canadian firm Bombardier's new Continental business jet is made up of about a dozen huge modular components from all over the world: the engines from the United States; the nose and cockpit from Canada; the mid-fuselage from Northern Ireland; the tail from Taiwan; the wings from Japan; and so forth.[35] Automobile plants, including General Motors, Ford, Volkswagen, and DaimlerChrysler, are leaders in using the modular approach. GM has a modular factory in Brazil and is building several more. The modular approach hands off responsibility for engineering and production of entire sections of an automobile, such as the chassis or interior, to outside suppliers. Suppliers design a module, making some of the parts themselves and subcontracting others. These modules are delivered right to the assembly line, where a handful of employees bolt them together into a finished vehicle.[36]

**modular approach**
A manufacturing company uses outside suppliers to provide large components of the product, which are then assembled into a final product by a few workers.

## Advantages and Disadvantages of Each Structure

Each of these approaches to departmentalization—functional, divisional, matrix, team, and network—has strengths and weaknesses. The major advantages and disadvantages of each are listed in Exhibit 10.9.

### Functional Approach

Grouping employees by common task permits economies of scale and efficient resource use. For example, at American Airlines, all information technology (IT) people work in the same, large department. They have the expertise and skills to handle almost any IT problem for the organization. Large, functionally based departments enhance the development of in-depth skills because people work on a variety of related problems and are associated with other experts within their own

Exhibit 10.9

## Structural Advantages and Disadvantages

| Structural Approach | Advantages | Disadvantages |
|---|---|---|
| Functional | Efficient use of resources; economies of scale<br>In-depth skill specialization and development<br>Top manager direction and control | Poor communication across functional departments<br>Slow response to external changes; lagging innovation<br>Decisions concentrated at top of hierarchy, creating delay |
| Divisional | Fast response, flexibility in unstable environment<br>Fosters concern for customer needs<br>Excellent coordination across functional departments | Duplication of resources across divisions<br>Less technical depth and specialization<br>Poor coordination across divisions |
| Matrix | More efficient use of resources than single hierarchy<br>Flexibility, adaptability to changing environment<br>Interdisciplinary cooperation, expertise available to all divisions | Frustration and confusion from dual chain of command<br>High conflict between two sides of the matrix<br>Many meetings, more discussion than action |
| Team | Reduced barriers among departments, increased compromise<br>Shorter response time, quicker decisions<br>Better morale, enthusiasm from employee involvement | Dual loyalties and conflict<br>Time and resources spent on meetings<br>Unplanned decentralization |
| Virtual Network | Can draw on expertise worldwide<br>Highly flexible and responsive<br>Reduced overhead costs | Lack of control; weak boundaries<br>Greater demands on managers<br>Employee loyalty weakened |

department. Because the chain of command converges at the top, the functional structure also provides a way to centralize decision making and provide unified direction from top managers. The primary disadvantages reflect barriers that exist across departments. Because people are separated into distinct departments, communication and coordination across functions are often poor, causing a slow response to environmental changes. Innovation and change require involvement of several departments. Another problem is that decisions involving more than one department may pile up at the top of the organization and be delayed.

## Divisional Approach

By dividing employees and resources along divisional lines, the organization will be flexible and responsive to change because each unit is small and tuned in to its environment. By having employees working on a single product line, the concern for customers' needs is high. Coordination across functional departments is better because employees are grouped together in a single location and committed to one product line. Great coordination exists within divisions; however, coordination *across* divisions is often poor. Problems occurred at Hewlett-Packard, for example, when autonomous divisions went in opposite directions. The software produced in one division did not fit the hardware produced in another. Thus, the divisional structure was realigned to establish adequate coordination across divisions. Another major disadvantage is duplication of resources and the high cost of running separate divisions. Instead of a single research department in which all research people use a single facility, there may be several. The organization loses efficiency and economies of scale. In addition, because departments within each division are small, there is a lack of technical specialization, expertise, and training.

## Matrix Approach

The matrix structure is controversial because of the dual chain of command. However, the matrix can be highly effective in a complex, rapidly changing environment in which the organization needs to be flexible and adaptable.[37] The conflict and frequent meetings generated by the matrix allow new issues to be raised and resolved. The matrix structure makes efficient use of human resources because specialists can be transferred from one division to another. The major problem is the confusion and frustration caused by the dual chain of command. Matrix bosses and two-boss employees have difficulty with the dual reporting relationships. The matrix structure also can generate high conflict because it pits divisional against functional goals in a domestic structure, or product line versus country goals in a global structure. Rivalry between the two sides of the matrix can be exceedingly difficult for two-boss employees to manage. This leads to the third disadvantage: time lost to meetings and discussions devoted to resolving this conflict. Often the matrix structure leads to more discussion than action because different goals and points of view are being addressed. Managers may spend a great deal of time coordinating meetings and assignments, which takes time away from core work activities.[38]

## Team Approach

The team concept breaks down barriers across departments and improves cooperation. Team members know one another's problems and compromise rather than blindly pursue their own goals. The team concept also enables the organization to more quickly adapt to customer requests and environmental changes and speeds decision making because decisions need not go to the top of the hierarchy for approval. Another big advantage is the morale boost. Employees are enthusiastic about their involvement in bigger projects rather than narrow departmental tasks. But the team approach has disadvantages as well. Employees may be enthusiastic about team participation, but they may also experience conflicts and dual loyalties.

A cross-functional team may make different demands on members than do their department managers, and members who participate in more than one team must resolve these conflicts. A large amount of time is devoted to meetings, thus increasing coordination time. Unless the organization truly needs teams to coordinate complex projects and adapt to the environment, it will lose production efficiency with them. Finally, the team approach may cause too much decentralization. Senior department managers who traditionally made decisions might feel left out when a team moves ahead on its own. Team members often do not see the big picture of the corporation and may make decisions that are good for their group but bad for the organization as a whole.

### Virtual Network Approach

The biggest advantages to a virtual network approach are flexibility and competitiveness on a global scale. A network organization can draw on resources and expertise worldwide to achieve the best quality and price and can sell its products and services worldwide. Flexibility comes from the ability to hire whatever services are needed, and to change a few months later without constraints from owning plant, equipment, and facilities. The organization can continually redefine itself to fit new product and market opportunities. Finally, this structure is perhaps the leanest of all organization forms because little supervision is required. Large teams of staff specialists and administrators are not needed. A network organization may have only two or three levels of hierarchy, compared with ten or more in traditional organizations.[39] One of the major disadvantages is lack of hands-on control. Managers do not have all operations under one roof and must rely on contracts, coordination, negotiation, and electronic linkages to hold things together. Each partner in the network necessarily acts in its own self-interest. The weak and ambiguous boundaries create higher uncertainty and greater demands on managers for defining shared goals, coordinating activities, managing relationships, and keeping people focused and motivated.[40] Finally, in this type of organization, employee loyalty can weaken. Employees might feel they can be replaced by contract services. A cohesive corporate culture is less likely to develop, and turnover tends to be higher because emotional commitment between organization and employee is weak.

# Organizing for Horizontal Coordination

One reason for the growing use of teams and networks is that many companies are recognizing the limits of traditional vertical organization structures in today's fast-shifting environment. In general, the trend is toward breaking down barriers between departments, and many companies are moving toward horizontal structures based on work processes rather than departmental functions.[41] However, regardless of the type of structure, every organization needs mechanisms for horizontal integration and coordination. The structure of an organization is not complete without designing the horizontal as well as the vertical dimensions of structure.[42]

## The Need for Coordination

As organizations grow and evolve, two things happen. First, new positions and departments are added to deal with factors in the external environment or with new strategic needs. For example, many organizations have established Information Technology departments to cope with the proliferation of new information systems, or *chief knowledge officers* to find ways to leverage organizational knowledge in today's information-based economy. As companies add positions and departments to meet changing needs, they grow more complex, with hundreds of positions and departments performing incredibly diverse activities.

Second, senior managers have to find a way to tie all of these departments together. The formal chain of command and the supervision it provides is effective, but it is not enough. The organization needs systems to process information and enable communication among people in different departments and at different levels. Coordination refers to the quality of collaboration across departments. Without coordination, a company's left hand will not act in concert with the right hand, causing problems and conflicts. Coordination is required regardless of whether the organization has a functional, divisional, or team structure. Employees identify with their immediate department or team, taking its interest to heart, and may not want to compromise with other units for the good of the organization as a whole.

**coordination**
The quality of collaboration across departments.

Without a major effort at coordination, an organization may be like Chrysler Corporation in the 1980s when Lee Iacocca took over:

> *What I found at Chrysler were 35 vice presidents, each with his own turf. . . . I couldn't believe, for example, that the guy running engineering departments wasn't in constant touch with his counterpart in manufacturing. But that's how it was. Everybody worked independently. I took one look at that system and I almost threw up. That's when I knew I was in really deep trouble.*
>
> *I'd call in a guy from engineering, and he'd stand there dumbfounded when I'd explain to him that we had a design problem or some other hitch in the engineering-manufacturing relationship. He might have the ability to invent a brilliant piece of engineering that would save us a lot of money. He might come up with a terrific new design. There was only one problem: He didn't know that the manufacturing people couldn't build it. Why? Because he had never talked to them about it. Nobody at Chrysler seemed to understand that interaction among the different functions in a company is absolutely critical. People in engineering and manufacturing almost have to be sleeping together. These guys weren't even flirting![43]*

If one thing changed at Chrysler (now DaimlerChrysler) in the years before Iacocca retired, it was improved coordination. Cooperation among engineering, marketing, and manufacturing enabled the rapid design and production of the Chrysler PT Cruiser, for example.

The problem of coordination is amplified in the international arena, because organizational units are differentiated not only by goals and work activities but by geographical distance, time differences, cultural values, and perhaps language as well. How can managers ensure that needed coordination will take place in their company, both domestically and globally? Coordination is the outcome of information and cooperation. Managers can design systems and structures to promote horizontal coordination. For example, to support its global strategy, Whirlpool is decentralizing its operations, giving more authority and responsibility to teams of designers and engineers in developing countries like Brazil, and establishing outsourcing relationships with manufacturers in China and India.[44] Exhibit 10.10 illustrates the evolution of organizational structures, with a growing emphasis on horizontal coordination. Although the vertical functional structure is effective in stable environments, it does not provide the horizontal coordination needed in times of rapid change. Innovations such as cross functional teams, task forces, and project managers work within the vertical structure but provide a means to increase horizontal communication and cooperation. The next stage involves reengineering to structure the organization into teams working on horizontal processes. The vertical hierarchy is flattened, with perhaps only a few senior executives in traditional support functions such as finance and human resources.

# Exhibit 10.10

## Evolution of Organization Structures

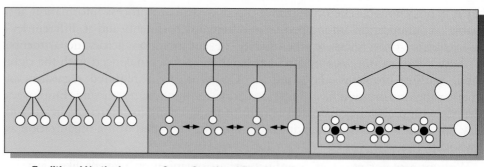

**Traditional Vertical Structure**

**Cross-functional Teams and Project Managers**

**Reengineering to Horizontal Teams**

## Task Forces, Teams, and Project Management

**task force**
A temporary team or committee formed to solve a specific short-term problem involving several departments.

A task force is a temporary team or committee designed to solve a short-term problem involving several departments.[45] Task force members represent their departments and share information that enables coordination. For example, the Shawmut National Corporation created two task forces in human resources to consolidate all employment services into a single area. The task force looked at job banks, referral programs, employment procedures, and applicant tracking systems; found ways to perform these functions for all Shawmut's divisions in one human resource department; and then disbanded.[46] In addition to creating task forces, companies also set up *cross-functional teams*, as described earlier. A cross-functional team furthers horizontal

### CONCEPT CONNECTION

*Frito-Lay, a subsidiary of PepsiCo Inc., introduced Lay's Cool Guacamole potato chips and Doritos Guacamole tortilla chips in 2003. A* task force *that included members of Adelante, the Frito-Lay network for Hispanic employees, helped develop both products. In the photo, Frito-Lay researchers and Adelante members check the quality of the new guacamole chips.*

coordination because participants from several departments meet regularly to solve ongoing problems of common interest.[47] This is similar to a task force except that it works with continuing rather than temporary problems and might exist for several years. Team members think in terms of working together for the good of the whole rather than just for their own department.

Companies also use project managers to increase coordination between functional departments. A **project manager** is a person who is responsible for coordinating the activities of several departments for the completion of a specific project.[48] Project managers are critical today because many organizations are almost constantly reinventing themselves, creating flexible structures, and working on projects with an ever-changing assortment of people and organizations.[49] Project managers might work on several different projects at one time and might have to move in and out of new projects at a moment's notice.

The distinctive feature of the project manager position is that the person is not a member of one of the departments being coordinated. Project managers are located outside of the departments and have responsibility for coordinating several departments to achieve desired project outcomes. For example, General Mills, Procter & Gamble, and General Foods all use product managers to coordinate their product lines. A manager is assigned to each line, such as Cheerios, Bisquick, and Hamburger Helper. Product managers set budget goals, marketing targets, and strategies and obtain the cooperation from advertising, production, and sales personnel needed for implementing product strategy.

In some organizations, project managers are included on the organization chart, as illustrated in Exhibit 10.11. The project manager is drawn to one side of the chart to indicate authority over the project but not over the people assigned to it. Dashed lines to the project manager indicate responsibility for coordination and communication with assigned team members, but department managers retain line authority over functional employees.

Project managers might also have titles such as product manager, integrator, program manager, or process owner. Project managers need excellent people skills. They use expertise and persuasion to achieve coordination among various departments, and their jobs involve getting people together, listening, building trust, confronting problems, and resolving conflicts and disputes in the best interest of the project and the organization. Consider the role of Hugh Hoffman at American Standard Companies.

**project manager**
A person responsible for coordinating the activities of several departments on a full-time basis for the completion of a specific project.

Exhibit 10.11

## Example of Project Manager Relationships to Other Departments

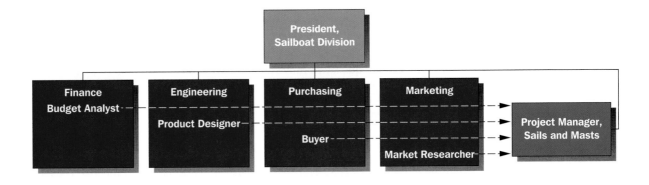

Hugh J. Hoffman began working at American Standard as a ceramic engineer in 1970. Today, he works as a full-time project manager in the company's chinaware business, which makes toilets and bidets. Hoffman, whose official title is process owner, chinaware order fulfillment, coordinates all the activities that ensure that American Standard's factories turn out the products customers order and deliver them on time. Hoffman's job requires that he think about everything that happens between the time an order comes in and the time it gets paid for, including design, manufacturing, painting, sales, shipping and receiving, and numerous other tasks. Project managers such as Hoffman have to act as if they are running their own business, setting goals and developing strategies for achieving them. It is not always easy because Hoffman works outside the boundaries and authority structure of traditional departments. His years of experience and good people skills help him motivate others and coordinate the work of many departments and geographically dispersed factories. "I move behind the scenes," Hoffman says. "I understand the workings of the company and know how to get things done."[50]

Using project managers has helped American Standard do things faster, better, and cheaper than competitors. Many organizations move to a stronger horizontal approach such as the use of permanent teams, project managers, or process owners after going through a redesign procedure called reengineering.

## Reengineering

**reengineering**
The radical redesign of business processes to achieve dramatic improvements in cost, quality, service, and speed.

**Reengineering**, sometimes called *business process reengineering*, is the radical redesign of business processes to achieve dramatic improvements in cost, quality, service, and speed.[51] Because the focus of reengineering is on process rather than function, reengineering generally leads to a shift away from a strong vertical structure to one emphasizing stronger horizontal coordination and greater flexibility in responding to changes in the environment.

Reengineering changes the way managers think about how work is done in their organizations. Rather than focusing on narrow jobs structured into distinct, functional departments, they emphasize core processes that cut horizontally across the company and involve teams of employees working to provide value directly to customers.[52] A

**process**
An organized group of related tasks and activities that work together to transform inputs into outputs and create value.

process is an organized group of related tasks and activities that work together to transform inputs into outputs and create value. Common examples of processes include new product development, order fulfillment, and customer service.[53]

Reengineering frequently involves a shift to a horizontal team-based structure, as described earlier in this chapter. All the people who work on a particular process have easy access to one another so they can easily communicate and coordinate their efforts, share knowledge, and provide value directly to customers.[54] For example, reengineering at Texas Instruments led to the formation of product development teams that became the fundamental organizational unit. Each team is made up of people drawn from engineering, marketing, and other departments, and takes full responsibility for a product from conception through launch.[55]

Reengineering can also squeeze out the dead space and time lags in work flows, as illustrated by reengineering of the travel system at the U.S. Department of Defense.

The Pentagon can act quickly to move thousands of tons of humanitarian aid material or hundreds of thousands of troops, but until recently, sending employees on routine travel has been a different story. Before Pentagon travelers could even board a bus, they had to secure numerous approvals and fill out reams of paperwork. Coming home wasn't any easier—the average traveler spent six hours preparing vouchers for reimbursement following a trip.

The Department of Defense set up a task force to reengineer the cumbersome travel system, aiming to make it cheaper, more efficient, and more customer friendly. The reengineered system reduces the steps in the pretravel process from an astounding 13 to only 4, as shown in Exhibit 10.12. Travel budgets and authority to approve travel requests and vouchers, which have traditionally rested in the budget channels of the various service commands, were transferred to local supervisors. Travelers make all their arrangements through a commercial travel office, which prepares a "should-cost" estimate for each trip. This document is all a traveler needs before, during, and after a trip: With a supervisor's signature, it becomes a travel authorization; during travel, it serves as an itinerary; after amendments to reflect variations from plans, it becomes an expense report. Other travel expenses and needed cash or travelers' checks can be charged to a government-issued travel card, with payment made directly to the travel card company through electronic funds transfer.[56]

As illustrated by this example, reengineering can lead to stunning results, but, like all business ideas, it has its drawbacks. Simply defining the organization's key business processes can be mind-boggling. AT&T's Network Systems division started with a list of 130 processes and then began working to pare them down to 13 core ones.[57] Organizations often have difficulty realigning power relationships and management processes to support work redesign, and thus do not reap the intended benefits of reengineering. According to some estimates, 70 percent of reengineering efforts fail to reach their intended goals.[58] Because reengineering is expensive, time consuming, and usually painful, it seems best suited to companies that are facing serious competitive threats.

# Factors Shaping Structure

Despite the trend toward horizontal design, vertical hierarchies continue to thrive because they often provide important benefits for organizations.[59] How do managers

## Exhibit 10.12

### Reengineering the Travel System—U.S. Department of Defense

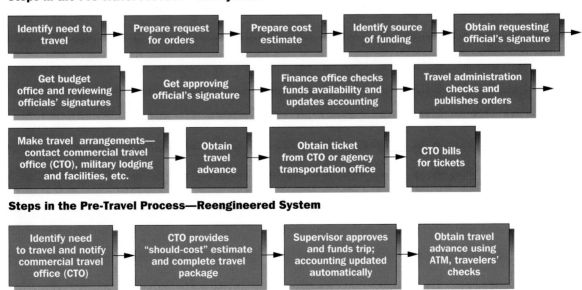

**SOURCE:** Richard Koonce, "Reengineering the Travel Game," *Government Executive* (May 1995), 28–34, 69–70.

# Exhibit 10.13

## Contingency Factors that Influence Organization Structure

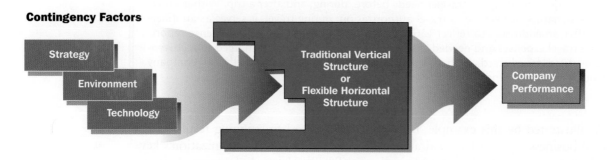

know whether to design a structure that emphasizes the formal, vertical hierarchy or one with an emphasis on horizontal communication and collaboration? The answer lies in the contingency factors that influence organization structure. Research on organization design shows that structure depends on a variety of *contingencies*, as defined in Chapter 2. The right structure is designed to "fit" the contingency factors of strategy, environment, and production technology, as illustrated in Exhibit 10.13. These three areas are changing quite dramatically for most organizations, creating a need for stronger horizontal coordination.

## Structure Follows Strategy

In Chapter 8, we discussed several strategies that business firms can adopt. Two strategies proposed by Porter are differentiation and cost leadership.[60] With a differentiation strategy, the organization attempts to develop innovative products unique to the market. With a cost leadership strategy, the organization strives for internal efficiency. The strategies of cost leadership versus differentiation typically require different structural approaches, so managers try to pick strategies and structures that are congruent.

Exhibit 10.14 shows a simplified continuum that illustrates how structural approaches are associated with strategic goals. The pure functional structure is appropriate for achieving internal efficiency goals. The vertical functional structure

# Exhibit 10.14

## Relationship of Strategic Goals to Structural Approach

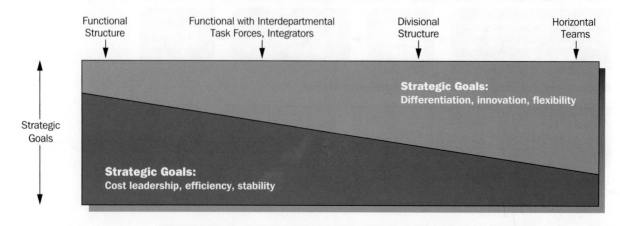

uses task specialization and a strict chain of command to gain efficient use of scarce resources, but it does not enable the organization to be flexible or innovative. In contrast, horizontal teams are appropriate when the primary goal is innovation and flexibility. Each team is small, is able to be responsive, and has the people and resources necessary for performing its task. The flexible horizontal structure enables organizations to differentiate themselves and respond quickly to the demands of a shifting environment but at the expense of efficient resource use. Changing strategies also shape structure in government organizations. Under financial pressure to cut costs and political pressure to keep customers happy, Departments of Motor Vehicles are farming out DMV business whenever possible, by building strong partnerships with other companies. For example, in many states, auto dealers register new cars on site when they are sold.[61]

Exhibit 10.14 also illustrates how other forms of structure represent intermediate steps on the organization's path to efficiency or innovation. The functional structure with cross-functional teams and project managers provides greater coordination and flexibility than the pure functional structure. The divisional structure promotes differentiation because each division can focus on specific products and customers, although divisions tend to be larger and less flexible than small teams. Exhibit 10.15 does not include all possible structures, but it illustrates how structures can be used to facilitate the strategic goals of cost leadership or differentiation.

## Structure Reflects the Environment

In Chapter 3, we discussed the nature of environmental uncertainty. Environmental uncertainty means that decision makers have difficulty acquiring good information and predicting external changes. Uncertainty occurs when the external environment is rapidly changing and complex. An uncertain environment causes three things to happen within an organization.

1. *Increased differences occur among departments.* In an uncertain environment, each major department—marketing, manufacturing, research and development— focuses on the task and environmental sectors for which it is responsible and hence distinguishes itself from the others with respect to goals, task orientation, and time horizon.[62] Departments work autonomously. These factors create barriers among departments.

## Exhibit 10.15

### Relationship between Environment and Structure

| | STRUCTURE | |
| | Vertical | Horizontal |
|---|---|---|
| **Uncertain (Unstable)** | **Incorrect Fit:** Vertical structure in uncertain environment — Mechanistic structure too tight | **Correct Fit:** Horizontal structure in uncertain environment |
| **Certain (Stable)** | **Correct Fit:** Vertical structure in certain environment | **Incorrect Fit:** Horizontal structure in certain environment — Organic structure too loose |

ENVIRONMENT

## CONCEPT CONNECTION

*Since China joined the World Trade Organization, companies such as Angang Iron and Steel have experienced greater* environmental uncertainty *that comes from participating in the global economy. Angang, one of the largest and most prestigious metal-bending companies in China, is* restructuring *to become more flexible with a trimmed, more efficient workforce. Angang has cut 30,000 people from its workforce of 165,000 at steel plants such as the one shown in the photo.*

2. *The organization needs increased coordination to keep departments working together.* Additional differences require more emphasis on horizontal coordination to link departments and overcome differences in departmental goals and orientations.
3. *The organization must adapt to change.* The organization must maintain a flexible, responsive posture toward the environment. Changes in products and technology require cooperation among departments, which means additional emphasis on coordination through the use of teams, project managers, and horizontal information processing.[63]

The terms *mechanistic* and *organic* can be used to explain structural responses to the external environment.[64] When the environment is stable, the organization uses a mechanistic system. It typically has a rigid, vertical, centralized structure, with most decisions made at the top. The organization is highly specialized and characterized by rules, procedures and a clear hierarchy of authority. In rapidly changing environments, however, the organization tends to be much looser, free-flowing, and adaptive, using an organic system. The structure is more horizontal and decision making authority is decentralized. People at lower levels have more responsibility and authority for solving problems, enabling the organization to be more fluid and adaptable to changes in the environment.[65]

*Take A Moment*    *Go to the experiential exercise on page 383 that pertains to loose versus tight organization structure.*

The contingency relationship between environmental uncertainty and structural approach is illustrated in Exhibit 10.15. When the external environment is more stable, the organization can succeed with a mechanistic structure that emphasizes vertical control. There is little need for change, flexibility, or intense coordination. The structure can emphasize specialization, centralized decision making, and wide spans of control. When environmental uncertainty is high, a flexible organic structure that emphasizes lateral relationships such as teams and horizontal projects is appropriate. Vertical structure characteristics such as specialization and centralization should be downplayed. In an uncertain environment, the organization figures things out as it goes along, departments must cooperate, and decisions should be decentralized to the teams and task forces working on specific problems. The flight deck of the *USS Dwight D. Eisenhower*, a nuclear-powered aircraft carrier, provides an excellent example of the relationship between structure and the environment.

On an aircraft carrier such as the *USS Dwight D. Eisenhower*, thousands of disastrous accidents are just waiting to happen. Launching or landing a plane from the oil-slicked deck of a nuclear-powered carrier is a tricky, finely balanced procedure. A sudden wind shift, a mechanical breakdown, or the slightest of miscommunications could spell disaster. Yet, surprisingly, flight deck operations generally run as smooth as silk, and accidents are quite rare. The reason has a lot to do with organizational structure.

At first glance, a nuclear aircraft carrier is structured in a rigid, hierarchical way—the captain issues orders to commanders, who direct lieutenants, who pass orders on to ensigns, and on down the hierarchy. There is a strict chain of command, and people are expected to follow orders promptly and without question. Manuals detail standard operating procedures for everything. But an interesting thing happens in times of high demand, such as the launching and recovery of planes during real or simulated wartime. In this different environment, the hierarchy dissolves and a loosely organized, collaborative structure in which sailors and officers work together as colleagues takes its place. People discuss and negotiate the best procedure to use, and everyone typically follows the lead of whoever has the most experience and knowledge in a particular area, no matter the person's rank or job title. During this time, no one is thinking about job descriptions, authority, or chain of command; they are just thinking about getting the job done safely. With planes landing every 60 seconds, there is no time to send messages up the chain of command and wait for decisions to come down from the top. Anyone who notices a problem is expected to respond quickly, and each member of the crew has the power—and the obligation—to shut down flight operations immediately if the circumstances warrant it.[66]

THE USS DWIGHT D. EISENHOWER
http://www02.clf.navy.mil/eisenhower/

Researchers have studied this ability to glide smoothly from a rigid, hierarchical structure to a loosely structured, horizontal one, not only on aircraft carriers but in other organizations that have to be exceptionally responsive to environmental changes—for example, air-traffic controllers or workers at nuclear power plants. The hierarchical side helps keep discipline and ensure adherence to rules that have been developed and tested over many years to cope with expected and well-understood problems and situations. However, during times of complexity and high uncertainty, the most effective structure is one that loosens the lines of command and enables people to work across departmental and hierarchical lines to anticipate and avoid problems.[67]

Not all organizations have to be as super-responsive to the environment as the *USS Dwight D. Eisenhower*, but using the correct structure for the environment is important for businesses as well. When managers use the wrong structure for the environment, reduced performance results. A rigid, vertical structure in an uncertain environment prevents the organization from adapting to change. Likewise, a loose, horizontal structure in a stable environment is inefficient. Too many resources are devoted to meetings and discussions when employees could be more productive focusing on specialized tasks.

## Structure Fits the Technology

Technology includes the knowledge, tools, techniques, and activities used to transform organizational inputs into outputs.[68] Technology includes machinery, employee skills, and work procedures. A useful way to think about technology is as production activities. The production activities may be to produce steel castings, television programs, or computer software. Technologies vary between manufacturing and service organizations. In addition, new digital technology has an impact on structure.

### Woodward's Manufacturing Technology

The most influential research into the relationship between manufacturing technology and organization structure was conducted by Joan Woodward, a British industrial sociologist.[69] She gathered data from 100 British firms to determine whether basic structural characteristics, such as administrative overhead, span of control, and centralization were different across firms. She found that manufacturing firms could be categorized according to three basic types of production technology:

**small-batch production**
A type of technology that involves the production of goods in batches of one or a few products designed to customer specification.

1. *Small-batch and unit production.* Small-batch production firms produce goods in batches of one or a few products designed to customer specification. Each customer orders a unique product. This technology also is used to make large, one-of-a-kind products, such as computer-controlled machines. Small-batch manufacturing is close to traditional skilled-craft work, because human beings are a large part of the process. Examples of items produced through small-batch manufacturing include custom clothing, special-order machine tools, space capsules, satellites, and submarines.

**mass production**
A type of technology characterized by the production of a large volume of products with the same specifications.

2. *Large-batch and mass production.* Mass production technology is distinguished by standardized production runs. A large volume of products is produced, and all customers receive the same product. Standard products go into inventory for sale as customers need them. This technology makes greater use of machines than does small-batch production. Machines are designed to do most of the physical work, and employees complement the machinery. Examples of mass production are automobile assembly lines and the large-batch techniques used to produce tobacco products and textiles.

**continuous process production**
A type of technology involving mechanization of the entire work flow and non-stop production.

3. *Continuous process production.* In continuous process production, the entire work flow is mechanized. This is the most sophisticated and complex form of production technology. Because the process runs continuously, there is no starting and stopping. Human operators are not part of actual production because machinery does all of the work. Human operators simply read dials, fix machines that break down, and manage the production process. Examples of continuous process technologies are chemical plants, distilleries, petroleum refineries, and nuclear power plants.

**technical complexity**
The degree to which complex machinery is involved in the production process to the exclusion of people.

The difference among the three manufacturing technologies is called technical complexity. Technical complexity is the degree to which machinery is involved in the production to the exclusion of people. With a complex technology, employees are hardly needed except to monitor the machines.

The structural characteristics associated with each type of manufacturing technology are illustrated in Exhibit 10.16. Note that centralization is high for mass

**CONCEPT CONNECTION**

*Employees at ConocoPhillips' Los Angeles, California, petroleum refinery at Wilmington use continuous process production to supply refined products to markets in California, Nevada, and Arizona. This sophisticated type of technology is typically associated with a small span of control, a high degree of horizontal communication, and a flexible structure to handle the complexities that arise. The ConocoPhillips global refining network has a crude oil processing capacity of 2.6 million barrels per day, including 2.2 million in the United States.*

Exhibit 10.16

## Relationship between Manufacturing Technology and Organization Structure

| | Manufacturing Technology | | |
| --- | --- | --- | --- |
| | Small Batch | Mass Production | Continuous Process |
| **Technical Complexity of Production Technology:** | Low | Medium | High |
| **Organization Structure:** | | | |
| Centralization | Low | High | Low |
| Top administrator ratio | Low | Medium | High |
| Indirect/direct labor ratio | 1/9 | 1/4 | 1/1 |
| Supervisor span of control | 23 | 48 | 15 |
| Communication: | | | |
| Written (vertical) | Low | High | Low |
| Verbal (horizontal) | High | Low | High |
| Overall structure | Organic | Mechanistic | Organic |

**SOURCE:** Based on Joan Woodward, *Industrial Organizations: Theory and Practice* (London: Oxford University Press, 1965).

production technology and low for continuous process. Unlike small-batch and continuous process, standardized mass-production machinery requires centralized decision making and well-defined rules and procedures. The administrative ratio and the percentage of indirect labor required also increase with technological complexity. Because the production process is nonroutine, closer supervision is needed. More indirect labor in the form of maintenance people is required because of the machinery's complexity; thus, the indirect/direct labor ratio is high. Span of control for first-line supervisors is greatest for mass production. On an assembly line, jobs are so routinized that a supervisor can handle an average of 48 employees. The number of employees per supervisor in small-batch and continuous process production is lower because closer supervision is needed. Overall, small-batch and continuous process firms have somewhat loose, flexible structures (organic), and mass production firms have tight vertical structures (mechanistic).

The important conclusion about manufacturing technology was described by Woodward as follows: "Different technologies impose different kinds of demands on individuals and organizations, and these demands have to be met through an appropriate structure."[70] Woodward found that the relationship between structure and technology was directly related to company performance. Low-performing firms tended to deviate from the preferred structural form, often adopting a structure appropriate for another type of technology. High-performing organizations had characteristics very similar to those listed in Exhibit 10.16.

## Service Technology

Service organizations are increasingly important in North America. For the past two decades, more people have been employed in service organizations than in manufacturing organizations. Examples of service organizations include consulting companies, law firms, brokerage houses, airlines, hotels, advertising firms, amusement parks, and educational organizations. In addition, service technology characterizes many departments in large corporations, even manufacturing firms. In a manufacturing company such as Ford Motor Company, the legal, human resources, finance, and market research departments all provide service. Thus, the structure and design of these departments reflect their own service technology rather than the manufacturing plant's technology. **Service technology** can be defined as follows:

**service technology**
Technology characterized by intangible outputs and direct contact between employees and customers.

1. *Intangible output.* The output of a service firm is intangible. Services are perishable and, unlike physical products, cannot be stored in inventory. The service is either consumed immediately or lost forever. Manufactured products are produced at one point in time and can be stored until sold at another time.
2. *Direct contact with customers.* Employees and customers interact directly to provide and purchase the service. Production and consumption are simultaneous. Service firm employees have direct contact with customers. In a manufacturing firm, technical employees are separated from customers, and hence no direct interactions occur.[71]

One distinct feature of service technology that directly influences structure is the need for employees to be close to the customer.[72] Structural characteristics are similar to those for continuous manufacturing technology, shown in Exhibit 10.16. Service firms tend to be flexible, informal, and decentralized. Horizontal communication is high because employees must share information and resources to serve customers and solve problems. Services also are dispersed; hence each unit is often small and located geographically close to customers. For example, banks, hotels, fast-food franchises, and doctors' offices disperse their facilities into regional and local offices to provide faster and better service to customers.

Some services can be broken down into explicit steps, so that employees can follow set rules and procedures. For example, McDonald's has standard procedures for serving customers and Marriott has standard procedures for cleaning hotel rooms. When services can be standardized, a tight centralized structure can be effective, but service firms in general tend to be more organic, flexible, and decentralized.

## Digital Technology

**digital technology**
Technology characterized by use of the Internet and other digital processes to conduct or support business operations.

**Digital technology** is characterized by use of the Internet and other digital processes to conduct or support business online. E-commerce organizations such as Amazon.com, which sells books and other products to consumers over the Internet, eBay, an online auction site, Google, an Internet search engine, and Priceline.com, which allows consumers to name their own prices and then negotiates electronically with its partner organizations on behalf of the consumer, are all examples of firms based on digital technology. In addition, large companies such as General Electric, Dell Computer, and Ford Motor Company are involved in business-to-business commerce, using digital technology to conduct transactions with suppliers and partners.

Like service firms, organizations based on digital technology tend to be flexible and decentralized. Horizontal communication and collaboration are typically very high, and these companies may frequently be involved in virtual network arrangements. Digital technology is driving the move toward horizontal forms that link customers, suppliers, and partners into the organizational network, with everyone working together as if they were one organization. People may use electronic connections to link themselves together into teams. For example, an employee may send an e-mail to people both within and outside the organization who can help with a particular customer problem and quickly form a virtual team to develop a solution.[73] In other words, digital technology encourages *boundarylessness*, where information and work activities flow freely among various organizational participants. Centralization is low, and employees are empowered to work in teams to meet fast-changing needs. Verbal and electronic communication is high, both up and down as well as across the organization, because up-to-the minute information is essential. In the digital world, advantage comes from seeing first and moving fastest, which requires extraordinary openness and flexibility.[74]

This chapter introduced a number of important organizing concepts. Fundamental characteristics of organization structure include work specialization, chain of command, authority and responsibility, span of management, and centralization and decentralization. These dimensions represent the vertical hierarchy and define how authority and responsibility are distributed.

Another major concept is departmentalization, which describes how organization employees are grouped. Three traditional approaches are functional, divisional, and matrix; contemporary approaches are team and virtual network structures. The functional approach groups employees by common skills and tasks. The opposite structure is divisional, which groups people by organizational output such that each division has a mix of functional skills and tasks. The matrix structure uses two chains of command simultaneously, and some employees have two bosses. The team approach uses permanent teams and cross-functional teams to achieve better coordination and employee commitment than is possible with a pure functional structure. The network approach means that a firm concentrates on what it does best and subcontracts other functions to separate organizations that are connected to the headquarters electronically. Each organization form has advantages and disadvantages and can be used by managers to meet the needs of the competitive situation. In addition, managers adjust elements of the vertical structure, such as the degree of centralization or decentralization, to meet changing needs.

As organizations grow, they add new departments, functions, and hierarchical levels. A major problem for management is how to tie the whole organization together. Horizontal coordination mechanisms provide coordination across departments and include reengineering, task forces, project managers, and horizontal teams.

Contingency factors of strategy, environment, and production technology influence the correct structural approach. When a firm's strategy is to differentiate its products or services, an organic flexible structure using teams, decentralization, and empowered employees is appropriate. A mechanistic structure is appropriate for a low-cost strategy. Similarly, the structure needs to be looser and more flexible when environmental uncertainty is high. For manufacturing firms, small batch, continuous process, and flexible manufacturing technologies tend to be structured loosely, whereas a tighter vertical structure is appropriate for mass production. Service technologies are people oriented, and firms are located geographically close to dispersed customers. In general, services have more flexible, horizontal structures, with decentralized decision making. Similarly, organizations based on new digital technology are typically horizontally structured and highly decentralized.

Returning to the opening example, Carlos Ghosn used structural changes to help revive Nissan and restore its competitive position in the auto industry. One of his first steps was to clarify managers' areas of responsibility and authority and implement mechanisms to ensure accountability. Positions were redesigned so that managers who previously acted as advisors had direct line authority and a clear understanding of how they were expected to contribute to the organization. The compensation and advancement systems were also revised. The major structural change Ghosn made was to create nine cross-functional management teams that would determine a detailed turnaround plan for the organization. Ghosn believed the team approach was the best way to get managers to see beyond the functional and regional boundaries that were hampering collaboration and new product development. Each team was made up of managers from various functional areas. For

*Manager's Solution*

example, the purchasing team consisted of members from purchasing, engineering, manufacturing, and finance. Within three months, the teams had created a detailed blueprint for Nissan's turnaround. Within three years, implementation of various aspects of the plan had returned Nissan to profitability. The cross-functional teams continue as an integral part of Nissan's management structure, helping ensure continued horizontal communication and collaboration to help the company compete in the turbulent auto industry.[75]

# Discussion Questions

1. Carnival Cruise Lines provides pleasure cruises to the masses. Carnival has several ships and works on high volume/low price rather than offering luxury cruises. What would you predict about the organization structure of a Carnival Cruise ship?

2. Why is structure different depending on whether a firm's strategy is low cost or differentiation?

3. The chapter suggested that structure should be designed to fit strategy. Some theorists argue that strategy should be designed to fit the organization's structure. With which theory do you agree? Explain.

4. Explain the three levels of departmental interdependence and give an example of each.

5. Some experts argue that interdependence within organizations is greater now than 15 years ago because of rapid changes in the global environment. If so, what does this mean for the present structure of organizations compared with that of 15 years ago?

6. Some people argue that the matrix structure should be adopted only as a last resort because the dual chains of command can create more problems than they solve. Do you agree or disagree? Why?

7. What is the network approach to structure? Is the use of authority and responsibility different compared with other forms of departmentalization? Explain.

8. Why are divisional structures frequently used in large corporations? Does it make sense for a huge corporation such as American Airlines to stay in a functional structure?

9. An international matrix structure tends to be organized by product divisions and geographic regions. Why would these two chains of command be used rather than product and function as in domestic companies? Explain.

# Management in Practice: Experiential Exercise

## Loose versus Tight Organization Structure

Interview an employee at your university, such as a department head or secretary. Have the employee answer the following thirteen questions about his or her job and organizational conditions.

|   | Disagree Strongly | | | Agree Strongly | |
|---|---|---|---|---|---|

1. Your work would be considered routine.  5  4  3  2  1

2. There is a clearly known way to do the major tasks you encounter.  5  4  3  2  1

3. Your work has high variety and frequent exceptions.  1  2  3  4  5

4. Communications from above consist of information and advice rather than instructions and directions.  1  2  3  4  5

5. You have the support of peers and supervisor to do your job well.  1  2  3  4  5

6. You seldom exchange ideas or information with people doing other kinds of jobs.  5  4  3  2  1

7. Decisions relevant to your work are made above you and passed down.  5  4  3  2  1

8. People at your level frequently have to figure out for themselves what their jobs are for the day.  1  2  3  4  5

9. Lines of authority are clear and precisely defined.  5  4  3  2  1

10. Leadership tends to be democratic rather than autocratic in style.  1  2  3  4  5

11. Job descriptions are written and up-to-date for each job.  5  4  3  2  1

12. People understand each other's jobs and often do different tasks.  1  2  3  4  5

13. A manual of policies and procedures is available to use when a problem arises.  5  4  3  2  1

**Total Score** _____

A score of 52 or above suggests that the employee is working in a "loosely structured" organization. The score reflects a flexible structure that is often associated with uncertain environments and small-batch technology. People working in this structure feel empowered. Many organizations today are moving in the direction of flexible structures and empowerment.

A score of 26 or below suggests a "tight structure." This structure utilizes traditional control and functional specialization, which often occurs in a certain environment, a stable organization, and routine or mass-production technology. People in this structure may feel controlled and constrained.

Discuss the pros and cons of loose versus tight structure. Does the structure of the employee you interviewed fit the nature of the organization's environment, strategic goals, and technology? How might you redesign the structure to make the work organization more effective?

# Management in Practice: Ethical Dilemma

### Caught in the Middle

Tom Harrington loved his job as an assistant quality control officer for Rockingham Toys. After six months of unemployment, he was anxious to make a good impression on his boss, Frank Golopolus. One of the responsibilities of his boss was ensuring that new product lines met federal safety guidelines. Rockingham had made several manufacturing changes over the past year. Golopolus and the rest of the quality control team had been working 60-hour weeks to troubleshoot the new production process.

While sorting incoming mail during the past weeks, Harrington had become aware of numerous changes in product safety guidelines that he knew would impact the new Rockingham toys. Golopolus was taking no action to implement new guidelines, and he didn't seem to understand or care about them. Harrington, who avoided the questions he received from the floor to cover for his boss, was beginning to wonder if Rockingham would have time to make changes with the Christmas season rapidly approaching.

Harrington knew it was not his job to order the changes, and he didn't want to alienate Golopolus by interfering, but he was beginning to worry what might happen if he didn't act. Rockingham had a fine product safety reputation and was rarely challenged on matters of quality. He felt loyalty to Golopolus for giving him a job, but he worried Golopolus was in over his head.

### What Do You Do?

1. Prepare a memo to Golopolus, summarizing the new safety guidelines that affect the Rockingham product line and recommending implementation.
2. Mind your own business. You do not have authority to monitor the federal regulations. Besides, you've been unemployed and need this job.
3. Send copies of the reports anonymously to the operations manager, who is Golopolus's boss.

Source: Based on Doug Wallace, "The Man Who Knew Too Much," *What Would You Do? Business Ethics,* vol. II (March–April 1993), 7–8.

# Surf the Net

1. **Examples of Organizational Structure.** Visit the Web sites for several companies to find two examples of organization charts or organizational structure descriptors that you can print out and bring to class. You and your classmates can analyze these examples to determine what approach to structure the organization has used. For example, does the chart or description illustrate the functional, divisional, matrix, contemporary team, or network approach to structure?

   Two examples are listed below. When you're looking for a company's organizational structure, you can often find it under a heading such as "Company Overview," "About Us," "Corporate Profile," or other such descriptors. Sometimes, the organizational structure is verbally described (as the US Airways example below), and other times, a literal organizational chart is provided (as the Xerox example below).
   *http://www.usairways.com/about/corporate/profile/organization/corp_organization.htm*
   *http://www.xerox.com/go/xrx/template/019d.jsp?view=Factbook&id=OrgStructure&Xcntry=USA&Xlang=en_US*

2. **Production Technology.** See how a car is manufactured at *http://www.psa-peugeot-citroen.com/en/morning.php.* The virtual visit at this site shows you the process. Next, go on a virtual tour of the X5 or Z4 manufacturing process by visiting *http://www.bmwusfactory.com/build/default.asp.* Write a brief description of what you learned about the manufacturing process.

# Case for Critical Analysis

## Malard Manufacturing Company

Malard Manufacturing Company produces control valves that regulate flows through natural gas pipelines. Malard has approximately 1,400 employees and has successfully produced a standard line of control valves that are price competitive in the industry. However, whenever the production of a new control valve is required, problems arise. Developments in electronics, metallurgy, and flow control theory require the introduction of new products every year or two. These new products have been associated with interdepartmental conflict and disagreement.

Consider the CV305, which is in process. As usual, the research and development group developed the basic design, and the engineering department converted it into a prototype control valve. Now the materials department must acquire parts for the prototype and make plans for obtaining parts needed for production runs. The production department is to manufacture and assemble the product, and marketing is responsible for sales.

Department heads believe that future work on the CV305 should be done simultaneously instead of sequentially. Marketing wants to provide input to research and development so that the design will meet customer needs. Production insists that the design fit machine limitations and be cost efficient to manufacture—indeed, it wants to speed up development of the final plans so that it can acquire tooling and be ready for standard production. Engineering, on the other hand, wants to slow down development to ensure that specifications are correct and have been thoroughly tested.

All of these controversies with the CV305 exist right now. Department managers are frustrated and becoming uncommunicative. The research and development and engineering departments are keeping their developmental plans secret, causing frustration for the other departments. Moreover, several department managers are new and inexperienced in new-product development. Ms. Crandell, the executive vice president, likes to keep tight control over the organization. Department managers must check with her before making major decisions. However, with the CV305, she has been unable to keep things running smoothly. The span of control is so large that Crandell has no time to personally shepherd the CV305 through the system.

On November 1, Crandell received a memo from the marketing department head. It said, in part,

The CV305 must go to market immediately. This is urgent. It is needed now because it provides the precision control our competitors' products already have. Three of our salespeople reported that loyal customers are about to place orders with competitors. We can keep this business if we have the CV305 ready for production in 30 days.

## Questions

1. What is the balance between vertical and horizontal structure in Malard Manufacturing? Is it appropriate that department managers always turn to the executive vice president for help rather than to one another?

2. If you were Ms. Crandell, how would you resolve this problem? What could you do to facilitate production of the CV305 over the next 30 days?

3. What structural changes would you recommend to prevent these problems in future new-product developments? Would a smaller span of control help? A project manager with responsibility for coordinating the CV305? A task force?

# Endnotes

1. Carlos Ghosn, "Saving the Business without Losing the Company," *Harvard Business Review* (January 2002), 37–45.

2. Karen Chan, "From Top to Bottom," *The Wall Street Journal* (May 21, 2001), R12.

3. Peter Burrows, "The Radical," *BusinessWeek* (February 19, 2001), 70–80.

4. John Child, *Organization: A Guide to Problems and Practice*, 2d ed. (London: Harper & Row, 1984).

5. Adam Smith, *The Wealth of Nations* (New York: Modern Library, 1937).

6. This discussion is based on Richard L. Daft, *Organization Theory and Design*, 4th ed. (St. Paul, Minn.: West, 1992), 387–388.

7. C. I. Barnard, *The Functions of the Executive* (Cambridge, Mass.: Harvard University Press, 1938).

8. Thomas A. Stewart, "CEOs See Clout Shifting," *Fortune* (November 6, 1989), 66.

9. Michael G. O'Loughlin, "What Is Bureaucratic Accountability and How Can We Measure It?" *Administration & Society* 22, no. 3 (November 1990), 275–302; and Brian Dive, "When Is An Organization Too Flat?" *Across the Board* (July–August 2003), 20–23.

10. Carrie R. Leana, "Predictors and Consequences of Delegation," *Academy of Management Journal* 29 (1986), 754–774.

11. Robert A. Guth, "Midlife Correction: Inside Microsoft, Financial Managers Win New Clout," *The Wall Street Journal* (July 23, 2003), A1, A6.

12. Curtis Sittenfeld, "Powered By the People," *Fast Company* (July–August 1999), 178–189.

13. Barbara Davison, "Management Span of Control: How Wide Is Too Wide?" *Journal of Business Strategy* 24, no. 4 (2003), 22–29; Paul D. Collins and Frank Hull, "Technology and Span of Control: Woodward Revisited," *Journal of Management Studies* 23 (March 1986), 143–164; David D. Van Fleet and Arthur G. Bedeian, "A History of the Span of Management," *Academy of Management Review* 2 (1977), 356–372; and C. W. Barkdull, "Span of Control—A Method of Evaluation," *Michigan Business Review* 15 (May 1963), 25–32.

14. Barbara Davison, "Management Span of Control"; Brian Dive, "When Is an Organization Too Flat?"; and Brian Dumaine, "What the Leaders of Tomorrow See," *Fortune* (July 3, 1989), 48–62.

15. Raghuram G. Rajan and Julie Wulf, "The Flattening Firm: Evidence From Panel Data on the Changing Nature of Corporate Hierarchies," working paper,

reported in Caroline Ellis, "The Flattening Corporation," *MIT Sloan Management Review* (Summer 2003), 5.

16. Charles Haddad, "How UPS Delivered through the Disaster," *BusinessWeek* (October 1, 2001), 66.

17. Brian O'Reilly, "J&J Is on a Roll," *Fortune* (December 26, 1994), 178–191; and Joseph Weber, "A Big Company That Works," *BusinessWeek* (May 4, 1992), 124–132.

18. Clay Chandler and Paul Ingrassia, "Just as U.S. Firms Try Japanese Management, Honda Is Centralizing," *The Wall Street Journal* (April 11, 1991), A1, A10.

19. The following discussion of structural alternatives draws heavily from Jay R. Galbraith, *Designing Complex Organizations* (Reading, Mass.: Addison-Wesley, 1973); Jay R. Galbraith, *Organization Design* (Reading, Mass.: Addison-Wesley, 1977); Jay R. Galbraith, *Designing Dynamic Organizations* (New York: AMACOM, 2002); Robert Duncan, "What Is the Right Organization Structure?" *Organizational Dynamics* (Winter 1979), 59–80; and J. McCann and Jay R. Galbraith, "Interdepartmental Relations," in *Handbook of Organizational Design*, ed. P. Nystrom and W. Starbuck (New York: Oxford University Press, 1981), 60–84.

20. Robert A. Guth, "Midlife Correction."

21. Eliza Newlin Carney, "Calm in the Storm," *Government Executive* (October 2003), 57–63; and http://www.irs.gov accessed on April 20, 2004.

22. Robert J. Kramer, *Organizing for Global Competitiveness: The Geographic Design* (New York: The Conference Board, 1993), 29–31.

23. Lawton R. Burns, "Matrix Management in Hospitals: Testing Theories of Matrix Structure and Development," *Administrative Science Quarterly* 34 (1989), 349–368; Carol Hymowitz, "Managers Suddenly Have to Answer to a Crowd of Bosses," (In the Lead column), *The Wall Street Journal* (August 12, 2003), B1.

24. Stanley M. Davis and Paul R. Lawrence, *Matrix* (Reading, Mass.: Addison-Wesley, 1977).

25. Edward Prewitt, "GM's Matrix Reloads," *CIO* (September 2003), 90–92.

26. Susan Carey, "US Air 'Peon' Team Pilots Start-Up of Low-Fare Airline," *The Wall Street Journal* (March 24, 1998), B1.

27. Charles Fishman, "Total Teamwork: Imagination Ltd.," *Fast Company* (April 2000), 156–168.

28. Melissa A. Schilling and H. Kevin Steensma, "The Use of Modular Organizational Forms: An Industry-Level Analysis," *Academy of Management Journal*, 44, no. 6 (December 2001), 1149–1169.

29. Susan G. Cohen and Don Mankin, "Complex Collaborations for the New Global Economy," *Organizational Dynamics* 31, no. 2 (2002), 117–133; David Lei and John W. Slocum Jr., "Organizational Designs to Renew Competitive Advantage," *Organizational Dynamics* 31, no. 1 (2002), 1–18.

30. Raymond E. Miles and Charles C. Snow, "The New Network Firm: A Spherical Structure Built on a Human Investment Philosophy," *Organizational Dynamics* (Spring 1995), 5–18; and Raymond E. Miles, Charles C. Snow, John A. Matthews, Grant Miles, and Henry J. Coleman, Jr., "Organizing in the Knowledge Age: Anticipating the Cellular Form," *Academy of Management Executive* 11, no. 4 (1997), 7–24.

31. Raymond E. Miles and Charles C. Snow, "Organizations: New Concepts for New Forms," *California Management Review* 28 (Spring 1986), 62–73; and "Now, The Post-Industrial Corporation," *BusinessWeek* (March 3, 1986), 64–74.

32. N. Anand, "Modular, Virtual, and Hollow Forms of Organization Design," Working paper, London Business School, 2000; Don Tapscott, "Rethinking Strategy in a Networked World," *Strategy & Business*, Issue 24 (Third Quarter 2001), 34–41.

33. Malcolm Wheatley, "Cycle Company with a Virtual Spin," *MT* (September 2003), 78–81.

34. Gregory G. Dess, Abdul M. A. Rasheed, Kevin J. McLaughlin, and Richard L. Priem, "The New Corporate Architecture," *Academy of Management Executive* 9, no. 3 (1995), 7–20.

35. Philip Siekman, "The Snap-Together Business Jet," *Fortune* (January 21, 2002), 104[A]–104[H].

36. Kathleen Kerwin, "GM: Modular Plants Won't Be a Snap," *BusinessWeek* (November 9, 1998), 168, 172.

37. Robert C. Ford and W. Alan Randolph, "Cross-Functional Structures: A Review and Integration of Matrix Organization and Project Management," *Journal of Management* 18, no. 2 (1992), 267–294; and Paula Dwyer with Pete Engardio, Zachary Schiller, and Stanley Reed, "Tearing Up Today's Organization Chart," *BusinessWeek/Twenty-First Century Capitalism*, 80–90.

38. These disadvantages are based on Michael Goold and Andrew Campbell, "Making Matrix Structures Work: Creating Clarity on Unit Roles and Responsibilities," *European Management Journal* 21, no. 3 (June 2003), 351–363; Hymowitz, "Managers Suddenly Have to Answer to a Crowd of Bosses"; and Dwyer et al., "Tearing Up Today's Organization Chart."

39. Raymond E. Miles, "Adapting to Technology and Competition: A New Industrial Relations System for the Twenty-First Century," *California Management Review* (Winter 1989), 9–28; and Miles and Snow, "The New Network Firm."

40. Dess et al., "The New Corporate Architecture"; Henry W. Chesbrough and David J. Teece, "Organizing for Innovation: When Is Virtual Virtuous?" *The Innovative Entrepreneur* (August 2002), 127–134; N. Anand, "Modular, Virtual, and Hollow Forms," and M. Lynne Markus, Brook Manville, and Carole E. Agres, "What Makes a Virtual Organization Work?" *Sloan Management Review* (Fall 2000), 13–26.

41. Laurie P. O'Leary, "Curing the Monday Blues: A U.S. Navy Guide for Structuring Cross-Functional Teams," *National Productivity Review* (Spring 1996), 43-51; and Alan Hurwitz, "Organizational Structures for the 'New World Order,'" *Business Horizons* (May–June 1996), 5–14.

42. Jay Galbraith, Diane Downey, and Amy Kates, *Designing Dynamic Organizations*, Chapter 4: Processes and Lateral Capability (New York: AMACOM, 2002).

43. Lee Iacocca with William Novak, *Iacocca: An Autobiography* (New York: Phantom Books, 1984), 152–153.

44. Miriam Jordan and Jonathan Karp, "Machines for the Masses," *The Wall Street Journal* (December 9, 2003), A1, A20.

45. William J. Altier, "Task Forces: An Effective Management Tool," *Management Review* (February 1987), 52–57.

46. "Task Forces Tackle Consolidation of Employment Services," *Shawmut News*, Shawmut National Corp. (May 3, 1989), 2.

47. Henry Mintzberg, *The Structure of Organizations* (Englewood Cliffs, N.J.: Prentice Hall, 1979).

48. Paul R. Lawrence and Jay W. Lorsch, "New Managerial Job: The Integrator," *Harvard Business Review* (November–December 1967), 142–151.

49. Ronald N. Ashkenas and Suzanne C. Francis, "Integration Managers: Special Leaders for Special Times," *Harvard Business Review* (November–December 2000), 108–116.

50. Jeffrey A. Tannenbaum, "Why Are Companies Paying Close Attention to This Toilet Maker?" (The Front Lines column), *The Wall Street Journal* (August 20, 1999), B1.

51. This discussion is based on Michael Hammer and Steven Stanton, "How Process Enterprises *Really* Work," *Harvard Business Review* (November–December 1999), 108–118; Richard L. Daft, *Organization Theory and Design*, 5th ed. (Minneapolis, Minn.: West Publishing Company, 1995), 238; Raymond L. Manganelli and Mark M. Klein, "A Framework for Reengineering," *Management Review* (June 1994), 9–16; and Barbara Ettorre, "Reengineering Tales from the Front," *Management Review* (January 1995), 13–18.

52. Hammer and Stanton, "How Process Enterprises *Really* Work."

53. Michael Hammer, definition quoted in "The Process Starts Here," *CIO* (March 1, 2000), 144–156; and David A. Garvin, "The Processes of Organization and Management," *Sloan Management Review* (Summer 1998), 33–50.

54. Frank Ostroff, *The Horizontal Organization: What the Organization of the Future Looks Like and How It Delivers Value to Customers* (New York: Oxford University Press, 1999).

55. Hammer and Stanton, "How Process Enterprises *Really* Work."

56. Richard Koonce, "Reengineering the Travel Game," *Government Executive* (May 1995), 28–34, 69–70.

57. John A. Byrne, "The Horizontal Corporation," *BusinessWeek* (December 20, 1993), 76–81.

58. Erik Brynjolfsson, Amy Austin Renshaw, and Marshall Van Alstyne, "The Matrix of Change," *Sloan Management Review* (Winter 1997), 37–54.

59. See Harold J. Leavitt, "Why Hierarchies Thrive," *Harvard Business Review* (March 2003), 96–102, for a discussion of the benefits and problems of hierarchies.

60. Michael E. Porter, *Competitive Strategy* (New York: Free Press, 1980), 36–46.

61. Pam Black, "Finally, Human Rights for Motorists," *BusinessWeek* (May 1, 1995), 45.

62. Paul R. Lawrence and Jay W. Lorsch, *Organization and Environment* (Homewood, Ill.: Irwin, 1969).

63. Robert B. Duncan, "Characteristics of Organizational Environments and Perceived Environmental Uncertainty," *Administrative Science Quarterly* 17 (1972), 313–327; W. Alan Randolph and Gregory G. Dess, "The Congruence Perspective of Organization Design: A Conceptual Model and Multivariate Research Approach," *Academy of Management Review* 9 (1984), 114–127; and Masoud Yasai-Ardekani, "Structural Adaptations to Environments," *Academy of Management Review* 11 (1986), 9–21.

64. Tom Burns and G. M. Stalker, *The Management of Innovation* (London: Tavistock, 1961).

65. John A. Coutright, Gail T. Fairhurst, and L. Edna Rogers, "Interaction Patterns in Organic and Mechanistic Systems," *Academy of Management Journal* 32 (1989), 773–802.

66. Robert Pool, "In the Zero Luck Zone," *Forbes ASAP* (November 27, 2000), 85+.

67. Ibid.

68. Denise M. Rousseau and Robert A. Cooke, "Technology and Structure: The Concrete, Abstract, and Activity Systems of Organizations," *Journal of Management* 10 (1984), 345–361; Charles Perrow, "A Framework for the Comparative Analysis of Organizations," *American Sociological Review* 32 (1967), 194–208; and Denise M. Rousseau, "Assessment of Technology in Organizations: Closed versus Open Systems Approaches," *Academy of Management Review* 4 (1979), 531–542.

69. Joan Woodward, *Industrial Organizations: Theory and Practice* (London: Oxford University Press, 1965); and Joan Woodward, Management and Technology (London: Her Majesty's Stationery Office, 1958).

70. Woodward, *Industrial Organizations*, vi.

71. Peter K. Mills and Thomas Kurk, "A Preliminary Investigation into the Influence of Customer-Firm Interface on Information Processing and Task Activity in Service Organizations," *Journal of Management* 12 (1986), 91–104; Peter K. Mills and Dennis J. Moberg, "Perspectives on the Technology of Service Operations," *Academy of Management Review* 7 (1982), 467–478; and Roger W. Schmenner, "How Can Service Businesses Survive and Prosper?" *Sloan Management Review* 27 (Spring 1986), 21–32.

72. Richard B. Chase and David A. Tansik, "The Customer Contact Model for Organization Design," *Management Science* 29 (1983), 1037–1050; and Gregory B. Northcraft and Richard B. Chase, "Managing Service Demand at the Point of Delivery," *Academy of Management Review* 10 (1985), 66–75.

73. Michael Hammer in "The Process Starts Here"; and Emelie Rutherford, "End Game," (an interview with David Weinberger, coauthor of *The Cluetrain Manifesto*), CIO (April 1, 2000), 98–104.

74. Thomas A. Stewart, "Three Rules for Managing in the Real-Time Economy," *Fortune* (May 1, 2000), 333–334.

75. Ghosn, "Saving the Business."

# Managing Change and Innovation

## LEARNING OBJECTIVES

*After studying this chapter, you should be able to:*

1. Define organizational change and explain the forces for change.

2. Describe the sequence of four change activities that must be performed in order for change to be successful.

3. Explain the techniques managers can use to facilitate the initiation of change in organizations, including idea champions, new-venture teams, idea incubators, and open innovation.

4. Define sources of resistance to change.

5. Explain force-field analysis and other implementation tactics that can be used to overcome resistance to change.

6. Discuss the differences among technology, product, structure, and culture/people changes.

7. Explain the change process—bottom up, top down, horizontal—associated with each type of change.

8. Define organizational development and large-group interventions.

When the German auto manufacturer BMW took over the British Rover group in the mid-1990s, it acquired the famed Mini, which has sold more than 5.5 million cars over 40 years of production. Top executives soon broke up the Rover group and sold it piece by piece, keeping the Mini brand with an eye toward a product overhaul. However, new managers at the Cowley manufacturing plant in Oxford, England, now realize they inherited something else besides the Mini—a poisonous culture born out of decades of apathy, labor-management conflict, and low productivity. The factory workers don't seem to feel any pride in their work or commitment to the organization's success. In fact, most of them seem to leave their minds and hearts at the gate when they come to work. What little enthusiasm they show is directed toward criticizing management failures. Top executives at BMW, a company known for its high-quality products, advanced engineering, and high performance, have clear plans for upgrading the Cowley facility, elevating manufacturing processes to world-class standards, and launching a new Mini that will take the automotive world by storm. But managers at Cowley know that unless they can first change the *us versus them* attitude of the workforce, the project is doomed to failure.[1]

## Take A Moment

How would you go about changing the toxic culture at the Cowley manufacturing plant? What techniques would you use to overcome resistance and implement the desired changes?

The BMW managers struggling with culture change at the Cowley facility in Oxford are not alone in their predicament. Every organization sometimes faces the need to change quickly and dramatically to survive in a changing environment. Sometimes, changes are brought about by forces outside the organization, such as when a powerful retailer like Wal-Mart demands annual price cuts or when a key supplier goes out of business. In China, many companies are feeling pressure from the government to increase wages to help workers cope with rising food costs. At the same time, costs of steel and other raw materials are skyrocketing.[2] These outside forces compel managers to look for greater efficiencies in operations and other changes to keep their organizations profitable. Other times managers within the company want to initiate major changes, such introducing a paperless accounting system, forming employee-participation teams, or instituting new training systems, but they don't know how to make the change successful. Organizations must embrace many types of change. Businesses must develop improved production technologies, create new products desired in the marketplace, implement new administrative systems, and upgrade employees' skills. Companies such as BMW, 3M, and Dell Computer implement all of these changes and more.

How important is organizational change? Consider this: The parents of today's college students grew up without digital cameras, e-mail, laptop computers, DVDs, Web-access cell phones, and online shopping. Companies that produce the new products and services have prospered, but many companies caught with outdated products and technologies have failed. Today's successful companies are constantly striving to come up with new products and services. For example, Johnson & Johnson Pharmaceuticals uses biosimulation software from Entelos that compiles everything that is known about a disease such as diabetes or asthma and runs extensive virtual tests of new drug candidates. With a new-drug failure rate of 50 percent even at the last stage of clinical trials, the process helps scientists cut the time and expense of early testing and focus on the most promising prospects. Engineers at automakers such as DaimlerChrysler, General Motors, and Toyota are perfecting fuel-cell power systems that could make today's internal combustion engine as obsolete as the steam locomotive.[3] Computer companies are working on developing computers that are smart enough to configure themselves, balance huge workloads, and know how to anticipate and fix problems before they happen.[4] Organizations that change successfully are both profitable and admired.

**organizational change**
The adoption of a new idea or behavior by an organization.

Organizational change is defined as the adoption of a new idea or behavior by an organization.[5] In this chapter, we will look at how organizations can be designed to respond to the environment through internal change and development. First we will examine the basic forces for organizational change. Then we will look closely at how managers facilitate two change requirements: initiation and implementation. Finally, we will discuss the four major types of change—technology, new product, structure, and culture/people—and how the organization can be designed to facilitate each.

# Turbulent Times and the Changing Workplace

Today's organizations need to continuously adapt to new situations if they are to survive and prosper. As we discussed in Chapter 2, one of the most dramatic elements of change is the shift to a technology-driven workplace in which ideas, information, and relationships are becoming critically important. Many changes are being driven by advances in information technology and the Internet. New trends such as e-business, supply chain integration, and knowledge management require profound changes in

© SHELLY HARRISON

the organization. In the previous chapter, we talked about new horizontal forms of organization that are a response to environmental turbulence and uncertainty. These new structural mechanisms break down boundaries within the organization, as well as with other companies, to promote collaboration for learning and change.

Managers also make many other organizational changes, such as changes in work procedures, administrative policies, technology, products, or corporate culture. Today's successful organizations simultaneously embrace two types of planned change: *incremental change*, which refers to organizational efforts to gradually improve basic operational and work processes in different parts of the company, and *transformational change*, which involves redesigning and renewing the entire organization.[6] Change, particularly transformational change, does not happen easily. However, managers can learn to anticipate and facilitate change to help their organizations keep pace with the rapid changes in the external environment.

# Model of Planned Organizational Change

Change can be managed. By observing external trends, patterns, and needs, managers use planned change to help the organization adapt to external problems and opportunities.[7] When organizations are caught flat-footed, failing to anticipate or respond to new needs, management is at fault.

An overall model for planned change is presented in Exhibit 11.1. Four events make up the change sequence: (1) Internal and external forces for change exist; (2) organization managers monitor these forces and become aware of a need for change; (3) the perceived need triggers the initiation of change; and (4) the change is then implemented. How each of these activities is handled depends on the organization and managers' styles.

We now turn to a brief discussion of the specific activities associated with the first two events—forces for change and the perceived need for the organization to respond.

## Forces for Change

Forces for organizational change exist both in the external environment and within the organization.

Exhibit 11.1

## Model of Change Sequence of Events

**Environmental Forces**
Monitor global competition, customers, competitors, and other factors.

**Internal Forces**
Consider plans, goals, company problems, and needs.

**Need for Change**
Evaluate problems and opportunities, and define needed changes in technology, products, structure, and culture.

**Initiate Change**
Facilitate search, creativity, idea champions, venture teams, skunkworks, and idea incubators.

**Implement Change**
Use force-field analysis, tactics for overcoming resistance.

## Environmental Forces

As described in Chapters 3 and 4, external forces originate in all environmental sectors, including customers, competitors, technology, economic forces, and the international arena. For example, changes in technology and the health care needs of customers caused Medtronic to shift how it views medical devices, from simply providing therapy to monitoring a patient's health condition. The company's cardioverter difibrillators, for example, can now send information to a secure server, allowing medical personnel to review the patient's condition in real time and see if there are any problems.[8] Yellow Freight changed how it does business when a combination of poor economic conditions and shifting customer demands led to a loss of $30 million. Yellow now bills itself as customers' one-stop source for a broad range of transportation needs. The company uses a sophisticated integrated information system to speed up order processing, manage customer relationships, monitor thousands of trucks and shipping orders, and facilitate rapid loading and unloading of trailers.[9]

## Internal Forces

Internal forces for change arise from internal activities and decisions. If top managers select a goal of rapid company growth, internal actions will have to be changed to meet that growth. New departments or technologies will be created and additional people hired to pursue growth opportunities. Demands by employees, labor unions, and production inefficiencies all can generate a force to which management must respond with change. To support growth goals at Procter & Gamble, CEO A. G. Lafley has acquired the beauty care companies Clairol and Wella, revised manufacturing systems, switched some suppliers, and put greater emphasis on partnerships, such as a joint venture with Clorox to develop Glad Press 'n' Seal food wrap.[10]

## Need for Change

As indicated in Exhibit 11.1, external or internal forces translate into a perceived need for change within the organization. Many people are not willing to change unless they perceive a problem or a crisis. For example, many U.S. companies changed how they conduct business as a result of the terrorist attacks of September 11, 2001. Top managers at E Commerce Group, a company that processes payments by phone and online, had been trying to find ways to promote teamwork and collaboration, but they kept running into resistance. However, after the hijacked planes struck the World Trade Center, across the street from E Commerce's offices, employees immediately began pitching in to help one another any way they could. "This crisis broke down the barriers," said Marc Mehl, co-founder and chief operating officer. The crisis enabled people to perceive the value of helping one another.[11]

In many cases, there is no crisis that prompts change. Most problems are subtle, so managers have to recognize and then make others aware of the need for change.[12] One way managers sense a need for change is when there is a performance gap—a disparity between existing and desired performance levels. They then try to create a sense of urgency so that others in the organization will recognize and understand the need for change. For example, the chief component-purchasing manager at Nokia noticed that order numbers for some of the computer chips it purchased from Philips Electronics weren't adding up, and he discovered that a fire at Philips' Albuquerque, New Mexico, plant had delayed production. The manager moved quickly to alert top managers, engineers, and others throughout the company that Nokia could be caught short of chips unless it took action. Within weeks, a crisis team had redesigned chips, found new suppliers, and restored the chip supply line. In contrast, managers at Ericsson, a competitor that also purchased chips from Philips, had the same information but failed to recognize or create a sense of crisis for change, which left the company millions of chips short of what it needed to produce a key product.[13]

**performance gap**
A disparity between existing and desired performance levels.

Recall from Chapter 8 the discussion of SWOT analysis. Managers are responsible for monitoring threats and opportunities in the external environment as well as strengths and weaknesses within the organization to determine whether a need for change exists.

Managers in every company must be alert to problems and opportunities, because the perceived need for change is what sets the stage for subsequent actions that create a new product or technology. Big problems are easy to spot. Sensitive monitoring systems are needed to detect gradual changes that can fool managers into thinking their company is doing fine. An organization may be in greater danger when the environment changes slowly, because managers may fail to trigger an organizational response. Failing to use planned change to meet small needs can place the organization in hot water, as illustrated in the following passage:

> *When frogs are placed in a boiling pail of water, they jump out—they don't want to boil to death. However, when frogs are placed in a cold pail of water, and the pail is placed on a stove with the heat turned very low, over time the frogs will boil to death.*[14]

# Initiating Change

After the need for change has been perceived and communicated, change must be initiated. This is a critical phase of change management—the stage where the ideas that solve perceived needs are developed. Responses that an organization can make are to search for or create a change to adopt.

## Search

Search is the process of learning about current developments inside or outside the organization that can be used to meet the perceived need for change. Search typically uncovers existing knowledge that can be applied or adopted within the organization. Managers talk to friends and colleagues, read professional reports, or hire consultants to learn about ideas used elsewhere.

**search**
The process of learning about current developments inside or outside the organization that can be used to meet a perceived need for change.

Many needs, however, cannot be resolved through existing knowledge but require that the organization develop a new response. Initiating a new response means that managers must design the organization so as to facilitate creativity of both individuals and departments, encourage innovative people to initiate new ideas, or create structural elements such as new-venture departments, skunkworks, and idea incubators.

## Creativity

**creativity**
The generation of novel ideas that might meet perceived needs or offer opportunities for the organization.

**Creativity** is the generation of novel ideas that might meet perceived needs or respond to opportunities for the organization. Creativity is the essential first step in innovation, which is vital to long-term organizational success.[15] People noted for their creativity include Edwin Land, who invented the Polaroid camera; Frederick Smith, who came up with the idea for Federal Express's overnight delivery service during an undergraduate class at Yale; and Swiss engineer George de Mestral, who created Velcro after noticing the tiny hooks on the burrs caught on his wool socks. Each of these people saw unique and creative opportunities in a familiar situation.

Each of us has the capacity to be creative. Characteristics of highly creative people are illustrated in the left-hand column of Exhibit 11.2. Creative people often are known for originality, open-mindedness, curiosity, a focused approach to problem solving, persistence, a relaxed and playful attitude, and receptivity to new ideas.[16]

Creativity can also be designed into organizations. Companies or departments within companies can be organized to be creative and initiate changes. Most companies want more highly creative employees and often seek to hire creative individuals. However, the individual is only part of the story, and everyone has some potential for creativity. Managers are responsible for creating a work environment that allows creativity to flourish.[17] The characteristics of creative organizations correspond to those of individuals, as illustrated in the right-hand column of Exhibit 11.2. Creative organizations are loosely structured. People find themselves in a situation of ambiguity, assignments are vague, territories overlap, tasks are poorly defined, and much work is done through teams.[18] Creative organizations have an internal culture of playfulness, freedom, challenge, and grass-roots participation.[19] They harness all potential sources of new ideas from within. Many participative management programs are born out of the desire to enhance creativity for initiating changes. People are not stuck in the rhythm of routine jobs.

*Take A Moment*     *Go to the experiential exercise on page 419 that pertains to creativity in organizations.*

At IDEO, the design company that came up with the idea for stand-up toothpaste tubes, Apple Computer's first mouse, and the Palm V, the mantra is "if at first the idea does not sound absurd, then there is no hope for it." Managers help stimulate

**CONCEPT CONNECTION**

*The Jack LaLanne Power Juicer is serving up vegetable and fruit juices to more than a million customers. That is great success for LaLanne, who has been in the fitness business for nearly 70 years. The key to continuing success is LaLanne's* creativity. *From his first gym opening in 1936, LaLanne has continued to come up with new ideas to build his fitness empire: a television show that aired from 1953 to 1985 and has just been resurrected on ESPN Classic; a business as a motivational speaker; and now products such as the Power Juicer that tap into a growing interest in nutrition and health. "I can't afford to die," LaLanne says. "It'll ruin my image."*

© ELAINE LALANNE/BEFIT ENTERPRISES

Exhibit 11.2

## Characteristics of Creative People and Organizations

| The Creative Individual | The Creative Organization or Department |
|---|---|
| 1. Conceptual fluency Open-mindedness | 1. Open channels of communication Contact with outside sources Overlapping territories Suggestion systems, brainstorming, group techniques |
| 2. Originality | 2. Assigning nonspecialists to problems Eccentricity allowed Hiring people who make you uncomfortable |
| 3. Less authority Independence Self-confidence | 3. Decentralization, loosely defined positions, loose control Acceptance of mistakes People encouraged to defy their bosses |
| 4. Playfulness Undisciplined exploration Curiosity | 4. Freedom to choose and pursue problems Not a tight ship, playful culture, doing the impractical Freedom to discuss ideas; long time horizon |
| 5. Persistence Commitment Focused approach | 5. Resources allocated to creative personnel and projects without immediate payoff Reward system encourages innovation Absolution of peripheral responsibilities |

**SOURCES:** Based on Gary A. Steiner, ed., *The Creative Organization* (Chicago: University of Chicago Press, 1965), 16–18; Rosabeth Moss Kanter, "The Middle Manager as Innovator," *Harvard Business Review* (July–August 1982), 104–105; James Brian Quinn, "Managing Innovation: Controlled Chaos," *Harvard Business Review* (May–June 1985), 73–84; and Robert I. Sutton, "The Weird Rules of Creativity," *Harvard Business Review* (September 2001), 94–103.

creativity by getting people to empathize with potential users of a product through a process of learn, look, ask, and try.[20] To keep creativity alive at Nokia, managers sponsor friendly internal competitions, such as a photography contest where workers take pictures of their pets or summer homes with Nokia camera phones. The photographs are shown on a slide projector in the company cafeteria as a way to further stimulate new ideas.[21] At W. L. Gore, the maker of Gore-Tex fabrics, Glide dental floss, Elixir guitar strings, and numerous other innovative products, leaders let people choose the projects they will work on, ensuring that employees (called associates) feel a passion for the work. In addition, research associates get to spend 10 percent of their work hours as dabble time, where they can explore developing their own ideas.[22]

The most creative companies embrace risk and encourage employees to experiment and make mistakes. One manager at Intel used to throw a dinner party every month for the "failure of the month," to show people that failure was an inevitable and accepted part of risk-taking.[23] Jim Read, president of the Read Corporation, says, "When my employees make mistakes trying to improve something, I give them a round of applause. No mistakes mean no new products. If they ever become afraid to make one, my company is doomed."[24]

## Idea Champions and New-Venture Teams

If creative conditions are successful, new ideas will be generated that must be carried forward for acceptance and implementation. This is where idea champions come in. The formal definition of an idea champion is a person who sees the need for and champions productive change within the organization. For example, Wendy Black of Best Western International championed the idea of coordinating the corporate mailings to the company's 2,800 hoteliers into a single packet every two weeks. Some hotels were receiving three special mailings a day from different departments. Her idea saved $600,000 a year in postage alone.[25]

*Remember*: Change does not occur by itself. Personal energy and effort are required to successfully promote a new idea. Often a new idea is rejected by management. Champions are passionately committed to a new product or idea despite rejection by others. At Kyocera Wireless, lead engineer Gary Koerper was a champion for the Smartphone, a device that combines a high-end mobile phone with a Palm digital assistant. When he could not get his company's testing department to validate the new product, he had an outside firm do the testing for him—at a cost of about $30,000—without approval from Kyocera management. Once the Smartphone was approved and went into production, demand was so great the company could barely keep up.[26]

Championing an idea successfully requires roles in organizations, as illustrated in Exhibit 11.3. Sometimes a single person may play two or more of these roles, but successful innovation in most companies involves an interplay of different people, each adopting one role. The *inventor* develops a new idea and understands its technical value but has neither the ability nor the interest to promote it for acceptance within the organization. The *champion* believes in the idea, confronts the organizational realities of costs and benefits, and gains the political and financial support needed to bring it to reality. The *sponsor* is a high-level manager who approves the idea, protects the idea, and removes major organizational barriers to acceptance. The *critic* counterbalances the zeal of the champion by challenging the concept and providing a reality test against hard-nosed criteria. The critic prevents people in the other roles from adopting a bad idea.[27]

Managers can directly influence whether champions will flourish. When Texas Instruments studied 50 of its new-product introductions, a surprising fact

Exhibit 11.3

### Four Roles in Organizational Change

| Inventor | Champion | Sponsor | Critic |
|---|---|---|---|
| Develops and understands technical aspects of idea | Believes in idea | High-level manager who removes organizational barriers | Provides reality test |
| Does not know how to win support for the idea or make a business of it | Visualizes benefits | Approves and protects idea within organization | Looks for shortcomings |
| | Confronts organizational realities of cost, benefits | | Defines hard-nosed criteria that idea must pass |
| | Obtains financial and political support | | |
| | Overcomes obstacles | | |

**SOURCES:** Based on Harold L. Angle and Andrew H. Van de Ven, "Suggestions for Managing the Innovation Journey," in *Research in the Management of Innovation: The Minnesota Studies*, ed. A.H. Van de Ven, H.L. Angle, and Marshall Scott Poole (Cambridge, Mass.: Ballinger/Harper & Row, 1989); and Jay R. Galbraith, "Designing the Innovating Organization," *Organizational Dynamics* (Winter 1982), 5–25.

emerged: Without exception, every new product that had failed had lacked a zealous champion. In contrast, most of the new products that succeeded had a champion. Texas Instruments' managers made an immediate decision: No new product would be approved unless someone championed it. Researchers have also found that the new ideas that succeed are generally those that are backed by someone who believes in the idea wholeheartedly and is determined to convince others of its value.[28]

Another way to facilitate corporate innovation is through a new-venture team. A new-venture team is a unit separate from the rest of the organization that is responsible for developing and initiating a major innovation.[29] New-venture teams give free rein to members' creativity because their separate facilities and location free them from organizational rules and procedures. These teams typically are small, loosely structured, and flexible, reflecting the characteristics of creative organizations described in Exhibit 11.2. 3M recently launched a corporate-wide initiative called 3M Acceleration, which is designed to support venture teams and speed up innovation and the commercialization of products. A person with a good idea, such as Steve Saxe, who came up with the idea for a portable digital whiteboard, can recruit people from around the company to work on the new venture team. The organization provides the space, funding, and freedom the team needs to fast-track the idea into a marketable product.[30]

One variation of a new-venture team is called a skunkworks.[31] A skunkworks is a separate small, informal, highly autonomous, and often secretive group that focuses on breakthrough ideas for the business. The original skunkworks, which still exists, was created by Lockheed Martin more than 50 years ago. The essence of a skunkworks is that highly talented people are given the time and freedom to let creativity rein.[32] The laser printer was invented by a Xerox researcher who was transferred to a skunkworks, the Xerox Palo Alto Research Center (PARC), after his ideas about using lasers were stifled within the company for being "too impractical and expensive."[33]

A related idea is the new venture fund, which provides resources from which individuals and groups can draw to develop new ideas, products, or businesses. Intel, for example, has been highly successful with Intel Capital, which provides new venture funds to both employees and outside organizations to develop promising ideas. An Intel employee came up with the idea for liquid crystal on silicon, a technology that lowers the cost of big-screen TV projection. "We took an individual who had an idea, gave him money to pursue it, and turned it into a business," said Intel CEO Craig Barrett.[34]

Another popular way to facilitate the development of new ideas in-house is the idea incubator. An idea incubator is run entirely in-house but provides a safe harbor where ideas from employees throughout the organization can be developed without interference from company bureaucracy or politics.[35] One value of an internal incubator is that an employee with a good idea has somewhere to go with it, rather than having to shop the idea all over the company and hope someone pays attention. Companies as diverse as Boeing, Adobe Systems, Ball Aerospace, United Parcel Service, and Ziff Davis are using incubators to quickly produce products and services related to the company's core business.[36]

**new-venture team**
A unit separate from the mainstream of the organization that is responsible for developing and initiating innovations.

**skunkworks**
A separate small, informal, highly autonomous, and often secretive group that focuses on breakthrough ideas for the business.

**new venture fund**
A fund providing resources from which individuals and groups can draw to develop new ideas, products, or businesses.

**idea incubator**
An in-house program that provides a safe harbor where ideas from employees throughout the organization can be developed without interference from company bureaucracy or politics.

## Open Innovation

Lack of innovation is widely recognized as one of the biggest problems facing today's businesses. Thus, many companies are undergoing a transformation in the way they find and use new ideas.[37] Traditionally, most businesses have generated their own ideas in house and then developed, manufactured, marketed, and distributed them, a closed innovation approach. Today, though, forward-looking companies are embracing open innovation. Open innovation means extending the search for and commercialization of new ideas beyond the boundaries of the organization and perhaps even beyond the boundaries of the industry.[38] For example, Procter & Gamble hits such as the Crest Spin Brush and the heartburn medicine Prilosec were created by other organizations and bought by P & G. The technology that helps P & G's Swiffer products pick up so much dust and debris came from a competitor in Japan. Procter & Gamble CEO A. G. Lafley has set a goal to get 50 percent of the company's innovation from outside the organization, up from about 35 percent in 2004.[39] Service companies are turning to open innovation as well. The Home Depot and Allstate are collaborating on an innovative project whereby insurance adjusters encourage contractors to buy materials from Home Depot, where prices are low. The arrangement reduces costs for Allstate and drives significant new business to The Home Depot.[40]

In line with the new way of thinking we discussed in Chapter 1, that sees partnership and collaboration as more important than independence and competition, the boundaries between an organization and its environment are becoming porous, so that ideas flow back and forth among different companies that engage in partnerships, joint ventures, licensing agreements and other alliances. Sometimes customers are brought into the innovation loop as well, so that their experiences spark innovations in products or services.[41] The product development process for 3M's Medical-Surgical Markets Division, for example, involves cross-functional teams that work with leading edge customers and other outsiders.[42]

**open innovation**
Extending the search for and commercialization of new ideas beyond the boundaries of the organization.

**3M MEDICAL-SURGICAL MARKETS DIVISION**
http://www.3m.com/healthcare/

To identify new customer needs and develop radical new ways of looking for product ideas, 3M's Medical-Surgical Markets Division turned to something called the *lead-user process*. Many great products are first thought of by users to meet specific needs, rather than by manufacturers. 3M's innovation process brings together teams from various functional areas within the company, who then work with outside people and companies who have leading-edge expertise in areas related to a product.

Rita Shor, a senior product specialist, and her co-leader, Susan Hiestand, put together a team of people from R&D, marketing, and manufacturing to search for a better and less expensive way to prevent the spread of infection in hospitals. The team spent the first month conducting research and interviewing specialists inside and outside the company. Then, team members worked directly with doctors, especially in developing countries where infectious diseases are still major killers and traditional products have been financially out of reach. This led to searching out people who were on the cutting edge of inexpensive infection control. One surprising source of information was veterinary hospitals. As one of the country's foremost veterinary surgeons told the team, "Our patients are covered with hair, they don't bathe, and they don't have medical insurance, so the infection controls we use can't cost much." Another source of ideas was Hollywood, where makeup artists have developed tricks for using materials that adhere well to the skin, are not irritating, and can be removed easily.

The final step was to bring all these people together in a two-and-a-half-day workshop to help the team generate concepts for new products. Although 3M naturally does not want to disclose details about the product ideas that came out of this extraordinary process, managers believe the ideas will open up major new markets for 3M.[43]

This approach to breakthrough thinking has now been used in several of 3M's 55 divisions, and many other leading companies are using similar open innovation approaches.

# Implementing Change

Creative culture, idea champions, new-venture teams, idea incubators, and open-innovation are ways to facilitate the initiation and development of new ideas. The final step to be managed in the change process is *implementation*. A new, creative idea will not benefit the organization until it is in place and being fully used. One frustration for managers is that employees often seem to resist change for no apparent reason. To effectively manage the implementation process, managers should be aware of the reasons people resist change and use techniques to enlist employee cooperation. Major, corporate-wide changes can be particularly difficult, as discussed in the Manager's Shoptalk box.

## Resistance to Change

Idea champions often discover that other employees are unenthusiastic about their new ideas. Members of a new-venture group may be surprised when managers in the regular organization do not support or approve their innovations. Managers and employees not involved in an innovation often seem to prefer the status quo. Employees appear to resist change for several reasons, and understanding them helps managers implement change more effectively.

### Self-Interest
Employees typically resist a change they believe will take away something of value. A proposed change in job design, structure, or technology may lead to a real or perceived loss of power, prestige, pay, or company benefits. The fear of personal loss is perhaps the biggest obstacle to organizational change.[44] When FedEx expanded into ground transportation to be more competitive with UPS, managers were aware that FedEx Express air service employees might feel threatened. Similarly, the recent acquisition of Kinko's requires FedEx managers to recognize that the self-interest of Kinko's employees might trigger resistance.[45]

### Lack of Understanding and Trust
Employees often distrust the intentions behind a change or do not understand the intended purpose of a change. If previous working relationships with an idea champion have been negative, resistance may occur. One manager had a habit of initiating a change in the financial reporting system about every 12 months and then losing interest and not following through. After the third time, employees no longer went along with the change because they did not trust the manager's intention to follow through to their benefit.

### Uncertainty
*Uncertainty* is the lack of information about future events. It represents a fear of the unknown. Uncertainty is especially threatening for employees who have a low tolerance for change and fear anything out of the ordinary. They do not know how a change will affect them and worry about whether they will be able to meet the demands of a new procedure or technology.[46] For example, union leaders at General Motors' Steering Gear Division in Saginaw, Michigan, resisted the introduction of employee participation programs. They were uncertain about how the program would affect their status and thus initially opposed it.

### Different Assessments and Goals
Another reason for resistance to change is that people who will be affected by an innovation may assess the situation differently from an idea champion or new-venture

# manager's Shoptalk

### Making Change Stick

Employees are not always receptive to change. A combination of factors can lead to rejection of, or even outright rebellion against, management's "new and better ideas."

Land's End, Inc., of Dodgeville, Wisconsin, began as a small mail-order business specializing in sailing gear. Employees enjoyed the family-like atmosphere and uncomplicated work environment. By the mid-1990s, the company had mushroomed into a $1 billion company with several overseas outlets and had passed giant L. L. Bean as number one in specialty catalog sales in the United States.

Such success encouraged founder and chairman Gary Comer to embark on a dramatic management experiment incorporating many of today's trends—teams, 401(k) plans, peer reviews, and the elimination of guards and time clocks. Comer brought in top talent, including former L. L. Bean executive William T. End as CEO, to implement the changes.

But employees balked. Weekly production meetings became a nuisance. "We spent so much time in meetings that we were getting away from the basic stuff of taking care of business," says one employee. Even a much-ballyhooed new mission statement seemed "pushy." One long-time employee complained that "we don't need anything hanging over our heads telling us to do something we're already doing."

Confusion and frustration reigned at Land's End and was reflected in an earnings drop of 17 percent. Eventually, End left the company, and a new CEO initiated a return to the familiar "Land's End Way" of doing things. Teams were disbanded, and many of the once-promising initiatives were shelved as workers embraced what was familiar and uncomplicated.

The inability of people to adapt to change is not new. Neither is the failure of management to sufficiently lay the groundwork to prepare employees for change. Harvard professor John P. Kotter established an eight-step plan for implementing change that can provide a greater potential for successful transformation of a company:

1. Establish a sense of urgency through careful examination of the market and identification of opportunities and potential crises.
2. Form a powerful coalition of managers able to lead the change.
3. Create a vision to direct the change and the strategies for achieving that vision.
4. Communicate the vision throughout the organization.
5. Empower others to act on the vision by removing barriers, changing systems, and encouraging risk taking.
6. Plan for visible, short-term performance improvements and create those improvements.
7. Consolidate improvements, reassess changes, and make necessary adjustments in the new programs.
8. Articulate the relationship between new behaviors and organizational success.

Major change efforts can be messy and full of surprises, but following these guidelines can break down resistance and mean the difference between success and failure.

SOURCES: Gregory A. Patterson, "Land's End Kicks Out Modern New Managers, Rejecting a Makeover," *The Wall Street Journal* (April 3, 1995), A1, A6; and John P. Kotter, "Leading Changes: Why Transformation Efforts Fail," *Harvard Business Review* (March–April 1995), 59–67.

group. Critics frequently voice legitimate disagreements over the proposed benefits of a change. Managers in each department pursue different goals, and an innovation may detract from performance and goal achievement for some departments. For example, if marketing gets the new product it wants for its customers, the cost of manufacturing may increase, and the manufacturing superintendent thus will resist. Resistance may call attention to problems with the innovation. At a consumer products company in Racine, Wisconsin, middle managers resisted the introduction of a new employee program that turned out to be a bad idea. The managers truly believed that the program would do more harm than good.[47]

These reasons for resistance are legitimate in the eyes of employees affected by the change. The best procedure for managers is not to ignore resistance but to diagnose the reasons and design strategies to gain acceptance by users.[48] Strategies for overcoming resistance to change typically involve two approaches: the analysis of resistance through the force-field technique and the use of selective implementation tactics to overcome resistance.

## Force-Field Analysis

Force-field analysis grew from the work of Kurt Lewin, who proposed that change was a result of the competition between *driving* and *restraining forces*.[49] Driving forces can be thought of as problems or opportunities that provide motivation for change within the organization. Restraining forces are the various barriers to change, such as a lack of resources, resistance from middle managers, or inadequate employee skills. When a change is introduced, management should analyze both the forces that drive change (problems and opportunities) as well as the forces that resist it (barriers to change). By selectively removing forces that restrain change, the driving forces will be strong enough to enable implementation, as illustrated by the move from A to B in Exhibit 11.4. As barriers are reduced or removed, behavior will shift to incorporate the desired changes.

Just-in-time (JIT) inventory control systems schedule materials to arrive at a company just as they are needed on the production line. In an Ohio manufacturing company, management's analysis showed that the driving forces (opportunities)

**force-field analysis**
The process of determining which forces drive and which resist a proposed change.

Exhibit 11.4

### Using Force-Field Analysis to Change from Traditional to Just-in-Time Inventory System

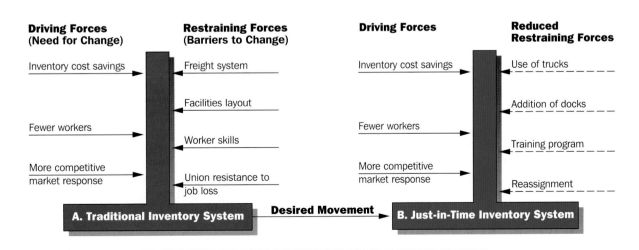

| **Driving Forces (Need for Change)** | **Restraining Forces (Barriers to Change)** | **Driving Forces** | **Reduced Restraining Forces** |
|---|---|---|---|
| Inventory cost savings | Freight system | Inventory cost savings | Use of trucks |
|  | Facilities layout |  | Addition of docks |
| Fewer workers | Worker skills | Fewer workers | Training program |
| More competitive market response | Union resistance to job loss | More competitive market response | Reassignment |

**A. Traditional Inventory System** → **Desired Movement** → **B. Just-in-Time Inventory System**

associated with the implementation of JIT were (1) the large cost savings from reduced inventories, (2) savings from needing fewer workers to handle the inventory, and (3) a quicker, more competitive market response for the company. Restraining forces (barriers) discovered by managers were (1) a freight system that was too slow to deliver inventory on time, (2) a facility layout that emphasized inventory maintenance over new deliveries, (3) worker skills inappropriate for handling rapid inventory deployment, and (4) union resistance to loss of jobs. The driving forces were not sufficient to overcome the restraining forces.

To shift the behavior to JIT, managers attacked the barriers. An analysis of the freight system showed that delivery by truck provided the flexibility and quickness needed to schedule inventory arrival at a specific time each day. The problem with facility layout was met by adding four new loading docks. Inappropriate worker skills were attacked with a training program to instruct workers in JIT methods and in assembling products with uninspected parts. Union resistance was overcome by agreeing to reassign workers no longer needed for maintaining inventory to jobs in another plant. With the restraining forces reduced, the driving forces were sufficient to allow the JIT system to be implemented.

## Implementation Tactics

The other approach to managing implementation is to adopt specific tactics to overcome employee resistance. For example, resistance to change may be overcome by educating employees or inviting them to participate in implementing the change. Researchers have studied various methods for dealing with resistance to change. The following five tactics, summarized in Exhibit 11.5, have proven successful.[50]

### Communication and Education

*Communication* and *education* are used when solid information about the change is needed by users and others who may resist implementation. Education is especially important when the change involves new technical knowledge or users are unfamiliar with the idea. Canadian Airlines International spent a year and a half preparing and training employees before changing its entire reservations, airport, cargo, and financial systems as part of a new "Service Quality" strategy. Smooth implementation resulted from this intensive training and communications effort, which involved 50,000 tasks, 12,000 people, and 26 classrooms around the world.[51] Managers should also remember that implementing change requires speaking to people's hearts (touching their feelings) as well as to their minds (communicating facts). Emotion is a key component in persuading and influencing others. People are much more likely to change their behavior when they both understand the rational reasons for doing so and see a picture of change that influences their feelings.[52]

### Participation

*Participation* involves users and potential resisters in designing the change. This approach is time consuming, but it pays off because users understand and become committed to the change. Participation also helps managers determine potential problems and understand the differences in perceptions of change among employees.[53] When General Motors tried to implement a new management appraisal system for supervisors in its Adrian, Michigan, plant, it met with immediate resistance. Rebuffed by the lack of cooperation, top managers proceeded more slowly, involving supervisors in the design of the new appraisal system. Through participation in system design, managers understood what the new approach was all about and dropped their resistance to it.

Exhibit 11.5

## Tactics for Overcoming Resistance to Change

| Approach | When to Use |
|---|---|
| Communication, education | · Change is technical.<br>· Users need accurate information and analysis to understand change. |
| Participation | · Users need to feel involved.<br>· Design requires information from others.<br>· Users have power to resist. |
| Negotiation | · Group has power over implementation.<br>· Group will lose out in the change. |
| Coercion | · A crisis exists.<br>· Initiators clearly have power.<br>· Other implementation techniques have failed. |
| Top management support | · Change involves multiple departments or reallocation of resources.<br>· Users doubt legitimacy of change. |

SOURCE: Based on J.P. Kotter and L.A. Schlesinger, "Choosing Strategies for Change," *Harvard Business Review* 57 (March–April 1979), 106–114.

### Negotiation

Negotiation is a more formal means of achieving cooperation. *Negotiation* uses formal bargaining to win acceptance and approval of a desired change. For example, if the marketing department fears losing power if a new management structure is implemented, top managers may negotiate with marketing to reach a resolution. Companies that have strong unions frequently must formally negotiate change with the unions. The change may become part of the union contract reflecting the agreement of both parties. For example, when General Motors changed the way it runs Saturn, a part of implementation involved negotiating new labor rules with the United Auto Workers union local.

### Coercion

*Coercion* means that managers use formal power to force employees to change. Resisters are told to accept the change or lose rewards or even their jobs. In most cases, this approach should not be used because employees feel like victims, are angry at change managers, and may even sabotage the changes. However, coercion may be necessary in crisis situations when a rapid response is urgent. For example, a number of top managers at Coca-Cola were reassigned or forced out after they refused to go along with a new CEO's changes for revitalizing the sluggish corporation.[54]

### Top Management Support

The visible support of top management also helps overcome resistance to change. *Top management support* symbolizes to all employees that the change is important for the organization. Top management support is especially important when a change involves multiple departments or when resources are being reallocated among departments. Fred Smith, founder of FedEx, got personally involved in communicating about the addition of ground shipping services. By giving speeches on the corporate television

## CONCEPT CONNECTION

*Herman Wright, PruCare of Austin's director of sales and marketing, shown here with his sales and service staff, knows that* **top management support** *is essential to overcoming resistance to change. In PruCare's thrust toward customer satisfaction, Wright used the* **implementation tactics** *of communication and participation. He communicated his desire to build customer relationships based on trust and then pushed responsibility down to everyone in the organization: "We stopped telling people what to do and started listening."*

network, going on road trips, and communicating via e-mail and newsletter, Smith signaled that the change was an important step for the company's future success. Without top management support, changes can get bogged down in squabbling among departments. Moreover, when change agents fail to enlist the support of top executives, these leaders can inadvertently undercut the change project by issuing contradictory orders.

The following example illustrates how smart implementation techniques can smooth the change process.

**REMPLOY LTD.**
http://www.remploy.
co.uk

Remploy, the United Kingdom's top employer of disabled people, owns 82 manufacturing sites making a diverse range of products, including car headrests, school furniture, and protective clothing for military and civil use. Top managers set some audacious growth goals—to increase staff from 12,500 to 25,000 and triple output within four years, but they knew meeting the goals would require massive changes in how work was done. To ensure success, Remploy used a team of internal consultants to identify the weakest link in a production process, fix it, and then move on to whatever emerged as the next weakest link.

The entire change process was at first frightening and confusing to Remploy's workers, 90 percent of whom have some sort of disability. However, by communicating with employees, providing training, and closely involving them in the change process, the implementation occurred smoothly. For example, at Remploy's Stirling site, top executives made sure factory manager Margaret Harrison understood the program and could communicate its importance to the plant workers. Harrison and the consultants trained people on the factory floor to look for ways to improve day-to-day work processes. "The more we involved the shopfloor people, the more they bought into it, because they were part of the decision-making process," Harrison said. As people saw their ideas implemented, they proposed even more solutions. One worker, for example, suggested sticking colored tape on the machinists' tables to ensure absolute accuracy while speeding up the process. Another group repositioned a huge overhanging machine so that shopfloor workers could see one another, communicate more easily, and pitch in to overcome any workflow slowdowns.

Communication and participation have been the key to smooth implementation of significant changes at Remploy's factories. These changes have helped Remploy achieve a 5 percent increase in its profit margin and the first growth in business in more than a decade. "If you think, 'I can do this a different way,' you approach the team leaders and tell them," machinist Helen Galloway said. "It's all teamwork. Change is frightening but, because we all have a say, we feel more confident making those changes."[55]

# Types of Planned Change

Now that we have explored how the initiation and implementation of change can be carried out, let us look at the different types of change that occur in organizations. We will address two issues: what parts of the organization can be changed and how managers can apply the initiation and implementation ideas to each type of change.

The types of organizational change are strategy, technology, products, structure, and culture/people, as illustrated in Exhibit 11.6. Organizations may innovate in one or more areas, depending on internal and external forces for change. In the rapidly changing toy and fashion industries, for example, manufacturers have to introduce new products frequently. In a mature, competitive industry, production technology changes are adopted to improve efficiency. The arrows connecting the types of change in Exhibit 11.6 show that a change in one part may affect other parts of the organization: A new product may require changes in technology, and a new technology may require new people skills or a new structure. When Boston-based New Balance installed sophisticated new technology as a way to make its U.S. athletic shoe factories more efficient, managers found that the structure had to be decentralized, employees had to be cross-trained to perform different jobs, and a more participative culture was needed. Today, New Balance, with five U.S. factories, is the industry's only company with domestic manufacturing facilities.[56] The new technology is one change that gave New Balance an edge and prevented U.S. factory shutdowns. However, related changes were required for the new technology to increase efficiency.

## Technology Changes

A technology change is related to the organization's production process—how the organization does its work. Technology changes are designed to make the production of a product or service more efficient. The adoption of automatic mail-sorting machines by the U.S. Postal Service is an example of a technology change, as is the adoption by supermarkets of computer-based self-service checkout systems. These are examples of technology change in service organizations. Manufacturing organizations also adopt many technology changes. For example, at Dana Corporation's Elizabethtown, Kentucky, plant, a new system for automatically loading steel sheets into a forming press was a technology change that saved

**technology change**
A change that pertains to the organization's production process.

## Exhibit 11.6

### Types of Organizational Change

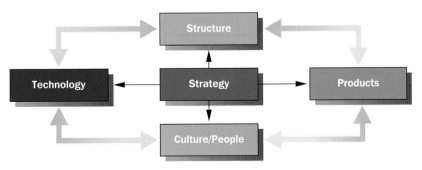

**SOURCE:** Based on Harold J. Leavitt, "Applied Organizational Change in Industry: Structural, Technical, and Human Approaches," in *New Perspectiives in Organization Research,* ed. W.W. Cooper, H.J. Leavitt, and M.W. Shelly II (New York: Wiley, 1964), 55–74.

*"Digital engineers" at Toyota can troubleshoot assembly processes and send their findings to plants around the world with engineering software that lays out data in clear three-dimensional images and allows design, development, and manufacturing engineers in different countries to inspect and work on designs at the same time. This technology change is greatly improving production efficiency at Toyota as well as other manufacturing plants, such as IBM and Pratt & Whitney Canada.*

© TOYOTA MOTOR CORPORATION

the auto parts manufacturer $250,000 a year.[57] The changes made in work processes and procedures at the Remploy factories described in the previous section are another example of technology change.

How can managers encourage technology change? The general rule is that technology change is bottom up.[58] The *bottom-up approach* means that ideas are initiated at lower organization levels and channeled upward for approval. Lower-level technical experts act as idea champions—they invent and champion technological improvements. Employees at lower levels understand the technology and have the expertise needed to propose changes. A *top-down approach* to technology change usually does not work.[59] Top managers are not close to the production process, and they lack expertise in technological developments. The spark for a creative new idea comes from people close to the technology.

Further thinking has refined these ideas with respect to proposing an innovation versus implementing the innovation.[60] A loose structure and employee freedom are great for creating and initiating ideas; however, these same conditions often make it difficult to implement a change because employees are less likely to comply. Companies often resolve this dilemma with an *ambidextrous approach*, which means incorporating structures and processes that are appropriate for both the creation and the implementation of innovations. They encourage flexibility and freedom to innovate with creative departments, new venture teams, skunkworks, and so forth, as described earlier, but use a more rigid, centralized, and standardized approach for implementing innovations. Honda, for example, uses teams of young staff members who are not entrenched in the "old way of doing things" to explore new ideas. The teams are given the authority to do whatever is needed to develop new technologies, even if it means breaking rules that are important in the larger manufacturing facility for implementing the new ideas.[61]

## New-Product Changes

**product change**
A change in the organization's product or service output.

A product change is a change in the organization's product or service output. New-product innovations have major implications for an organization, because they often are an outcome of a new strategy and may define a new market.[62] In addition, product life cycles are getting shorter, so that companies need to continuously come up with innovative ideas for new products and services that meet needs in the market-place. Product innovation is the primary way in which many organizations adapt to changes in markets, technologies, and competition.[63] Examples of new products include Apple Computer's iPod portable music player, Glad Press 'n Seal food wrap, and Toyota's Scion xB vehicle.

Product development is a risky, high-stakes game. Some experts estimate that 80 percent of new products fail upon introduction and another 10 percent disappear within five years. Despite the high failure rate, and the fact that successfully launching a new product costs $50 million or more, approximately 25,000 new products appeared in one recent year, including 5,000 new toys.[64] Many of those products will never generate an economic return.[65] Consider such flops as Procter & Gamble's Fit Produce wash, Gerber's "Singles," a line of meals for adults, or the Segway $4,000 Human Transporter scooter, a motorized two-wheeler you ride standing up. Companies that successfully develop new products usually have the following characteristics:

1.  People in marketing have a good understanding of customer needs.
2.  Technical specialists are aware of recent technological developments and make effective use of new technology.
3.  Members from key departments—research, manufacturing, marketing—cooperate in the development of the new product.[66]

These findings mean that the ideas for new products typically originate at the lower levels of the organization just as they do for technology changes. The difference is that new-product ideas flow horizontally among departments. Product innovation requires expertise from several departments simultaneously. A new-product failure is often the result of failed cooperation.[67]

## Horizontal Linkages

One approach to successful new-product innovation is called the horizontal linkage model, which is illustrated in Exhibit 11.7.[68] The model shows that research, manufacturing, and marketing must simultaneously develop new products. People from these departments meet frequently in teams and task forces to share ideas and solve problems. Research people inform marketing of new technical developments to learn whether they will be useful to customers. Marketing people pass customer complaints to research to use in the design of new products. Manufacturing informs other departments whether a product idea can be manufactured within cost limits. One example is when Hewlett-Packard's engineers wanted to do away with the on-off switch on a line of new low-cost computers. When marketing heard the idea, they immediately pointed out that the average customer would not understand how the printer could turn on and off without a manual switch and would get frustrated

**horizontal linkage model**
An approach to product change that emphasizes shared development of innovations among several departments.

Exhibit 11.7

### Horizontal Linkage Model for New-Product Innovation

## CONCEPT CONNECTION

*Baldor Electric Company is one of the leading makers of electric motors, drives, and generators. Baldor sales engineers regularly visit customers to learn how their company's products are being used. The engineers then share what they learn with Baldor's design, production, and marketing departments. By using the horizontal linkage model, the company identifies new ways to apply Baldor technology and develop products that better meet customer needs.*

looking for one.[69] When the horizontal linkage model is used, the decisions about developing a new product are joint ones.

Many of today's successful companies also include customers, strategic partners, and suppliers in the product and service development process, in line with the *open innovation* approach discussed earlier. Teams of IBM researchers, for example, regularly visit customers such as Charles Schwab, where they sit in on design meetings or brainstorming sessions, help customers solve problems, or just hang around and see how IBM's products and services could serve them better.[70]

### Fast Cycle Teams

These trends are partly in response to pressures in the environment for developing and commercializing products and services incredibly fast. Sprinting to market with a new product requires a *parallel approach*, or *simultaneous linkage* among departments. This kind of teamwork is similar to a rugby match wherein players run together, passing the ball back and forth as they move downfield.[71] Speed is emerging as a pivotal strategic weapon in the global marketplace for a wide variety of industries.[72] Some companies are using fast cycle teams to deliver products and services faster than competitors, giving them a significant strategic advantage. A fast cycle team is a multifunctional, and sometimes multinational, team that works under stringent timelines and is provided with high levels of resources and empowerment to accomplish an accelerated product development project.[73] For example, by using the Internet to collaborate on new designs with suppliers, fast cycle teams at Moen take a new kitchen or bath faucet from drawing board to store shelf in only 16 months. The time savings means engineers can work on three times as many projects and introduce up to15 new designs a year for today's fashion-conscious consumers, helping Moen move from number three in market share to a tie for number one with rival Delta Faucet Co.[74]

**fast cycle team**
A multifunctional team that is provided with high levels of resources and empowerment to accomplish an accelerated product development project.

## Structural Changes

**structural changes**
Any change in the way in which the organization is designed and managed.

Structural changes involve the hierarchy of authority, goals, structural characteristics, administrative procedures, and management systems.[75] Almost any change in how the organization is managed falls under the category of structural change. For example, in response to changes in the kind of threats and duties the United States military faces in the twenty first century, Army leaders are considering major structural changes. Their plan includes options such as altering how officers are trained; shifting resources away from high-intensity combat units to areas such as military police, engineers, and civil affairs officers; revamping the Army's intelligence systems; upgrading communications and information technology; and changing how units are organized.[76]

Other examples of structural or administrative change include shifting to a team-based structure, implementing policies regarding e-mail and Internet use, revising payroll systems, and centralizing information and accounting systems. At Nestlé USA, CEO Joe Weller has initiated a number of structural changes, as described in this chapter's Unlocking Creative Solutions Through Technology box.

Successful structural change is accomplished through a top-down approach, which is distinct from technology change (bottom up) and new products (horizontal).[77] Structural change is top down because the expertise for administrative improvements originates at the middle and upper levels of the organization. The champions for structural change are middle and top managers. Lower-level technical specialists have little interest or expertise in administrative procedures. If organization structure causes negative consequences for lower-level employees, complaints and dissatisfaction alert managers to a problem. Employee dissatisfaction is an internal force for change. The need for change is perceived by higher managers, who then take the initiative to propose and implement it.

The top-down process does not mean that coercion is the best implementation tactic. Implementation tactics include education, participation, and negotiation with employees. Unless there is an emergency, managers should not force structural change on employees. They may hit a resistance wall, and the change will fail. Consider the recent sweeping overhaul of the Internal Revenue Service (IRS), when the agency replaced its geographically-based structure with four customer-oriented operating divisions, rewrote personnel policies and job descriptions, cut several layers of management, and totally revised rules for hiring, training, evaluating, and rewarding employees. Charles Mader, a leading member of the management team in charge of the overhaul, took great pains to talk with lower-level managers and employees to explain what was happening, get their input, and enlist their participation in the changes. One of Mader's most important challenges was working with the National Treasury Employees Union and helping to move the agency and union toward a less adversarial, more collaborative relationship.[78]

*Go to the ethical dilemma on page 420 that pertains to structural change.*

*Take A Moment*

Top-down change means that initiation of the idea occurs at upper levels and is implemented downward. It does not mean that lower-level employees are not educated about the change or allowed to participate in it.

# Culture/People Changes

Changes in structure, technologies, and products or services do not happen on their own, and changes in any of these areas require changes in people as well. For example, putting together a horizontal, cross-functional team for new product development does not ensure a collaborative process unless it is accompanied by significant changes in the attitudes and beliefs of both employees and managers. Employees have to adopt new, collaborative ways of thinking and acting, while managers have to be willing to give up control and empower teams to make decisions and take action.[79]

# Unlocking Creative Solutions Through Technology

**Nestlé: Making "E-business the Way We Do Business"**

Leaders at Nestlé USA are turning to the Internet to change everything about how the giant company operates, from buying raw materials to processing purchase orders, to marketing the company's 2,000 or so products, such as Nestlé Crunch bars, Toll House cookie dough, and Lean Cuisine frozen dinners. The size and past success of the company make some people reluctant to change (the "if it ain't broke, don't fix it" mindset), but top managers are determined to gradually implement administrative and structural changes to help reach Chairman and CEO Joe Weller's goal to "make e-business the way we do business."

Change at Nestlé USA, the largest subsidiary of the world's largest food company, began literally at the top—on the twenty first floor of the company's glass-and-steel headquarters office building in Glendale, California. Top managers rolled up their Oriental rugs and moved their offices down several floors to work more closely with people in the trenches, turning the former executive suites into meeting rooms and temporary office space for telecommuters and virtual workers. Weller also implemented a number of top-down changes designed to make the company a leaner, faster organization. One was the "No meetings after 10 A.M. on Friday" rule. Weller believed people were spending so much time in meetings that they did not have time to think about strategy and long-term goals. Another

was his "Blueprint for Success" document, a two-sided sheet of paper that serves as a mission statement as well as a guide for turning Nestlé into a fast-moving, entrepreneurial company.

But the biggest change is the Internet strategy itself. Instead of creating a separate e-business division, top leaders decided to make e-business an integral part of every division and department in the company. Each operating division was assigned an "e-business catalyst" who helps managers develop business-to-consumer (B2C) and business-to-business (B2B) functions. The company's overall B2C strategy is focused on creating sites that help and inform consumers rather than push Nestlé's brands. A VeryBestBaking.com site offers recipes and cooking tips; VeryBestPets.com gives advice on grooming, health care, and nutrition for dogs and cats. The goal is that the sites will increase the percentage of consumers who have a "bonded relationship" to Nestlé products. As for B2B, the company recently launched NestléEZOrder, which will eliminate many of the 100,000 phone and fax orders the company gets each year—and the high transaction costs that go along with them.

Nestlé's USA's top managers still face challenges getting buy-in for all these structural changes from employees, but they believe with careful implementation the changes will take root and become the everyday way the company does business.

**SOURCE**: Bill Breen, "Change is Sweet," *Fast Company* (June 2001), 168–177.

**culture/people change**
A change in employees' values, norms, attitudes, beliefs, and behavior.

A culture/people change refers to a change in employees' values, norms, attitudes, beliefs, and behavior. Changes in culture and people pertain to how employees think; these are changes in mindset. *People change* pertains to just a few employees, such as when a handful of middle managers is sent to a training course to improve their leadership skills. *Culture change* pertains to the organization as a whole, such as when the IRS shifted its basic mindset from an organization focused on collection and compliance to one dedicated to informing, educating, and serving customers (taxpayers).[80] Two specific tools for changing people and culture are training and development programs and organizational development (OD).

## Training and Development

Training is one of the most frequently used approaches to changing people's mindset. A company might offer training programs to large blocks of employees on subjects such as teamwork, diversity, emotional intelligence, quality circles, communication skills, or participative management. Training and development programs aimed at changing individual behavior and interpersonal skills have become a big business for consultants, universities, and training firms.

Some companies particularly emphasize training and development for managers, with the idea that the behavior and attitudes of managers will influence people throughout the organization and lead to culture change. A number of Silicon Valley companies, including Intel, Advanced Micro Devices (AMD), and Sun Microsystems, regularly send managers to the Growth and Leadership Center (GLC), where they learn to use emotional intelligence to build better relationships. Nick Kepler, director of technology development at AMD, was surprised to learn how his emotionless approach to work was intimidating people and destroying the rapport needed to shift to a culture based on collaborative teamwork.[81]

Leading companies also want to provide training and development opportunities for everyone. An excellent example of training is First Data Corp., which uses a multifaceted, team-based approach first initiated by CFO Kim Patmore to boost morale among finance personnel.[82] First Data's "Extreme Teams" bring together employees from all hierarchical levels to organize departmental training and development programs for each of First Data's six regional finance units. One team is charged with organizing a mentoring program that pairs less-experienced personnel with seasoned managers who support and encourage them to make changes needed to further their own and the organization's well-being. Another team focuses on a program called *Fast Tracks*, an annual two-day seminar that brings people from all areas and levels of the company together to learn skills such as communication or conflict resolution.

## Organization Development

Organization development (OD) is a planned, systematic process of change that uses behavioral science knowledge and techniques to improve an organization's health and effectiveness through its ability to adapt to the environment, improve internal relationships, and increase learning and problem-solving capabilities.[83] OD focuses on the human and social aspects of the organization and works to change attitudes and relationships among employees, helping to strengthen the organization's capacity for adaptation and renewal.[84]

OD can help managers address at least three types of current problems:[85]

1. *Mergers/acquisitions.* The disappointing financial results of many mergers and acquisitions are caused by the failure of executives to determine whether the administrative style and corporate culture of the two companies fit. Executives may concentrate on potential synergies in technology, products, marketing, and control systems but fail to recognize that two firms may have widely different values, beliefs, and practices. These differences create stress and anxiety for employees, and these negative emotions affect future performance. Cultural differences should be evaluated during the acquisition process, and OD experts can be used to smooth the integration of two firms.

2. *Organizational decline/revitalization.* Organizations undergoing a period of decline and revitalization experience a variety of problems, including a low level of trust, lack of innovation, high turnover, and high levels of conflict and stress. The period of transition requires opposite behaviors, including confronting stress, creating open communication, and fostering creative innovation to emerge with high levels of productivity. OD techniques can contribute greatly to cultural revitalization by managing conflicts, fostering commitment, and facilitating communication.

3. *Conflict management.* Conflict can occur at any time and place within a healthy organization. For example, a product team for the introduction of a new software

**organization development (OD)**
The application of behavioral science techniques to improve an organization's health and effectiveness through its ability to cope with environmental changes, improve internal relationships, and increase learning and problem-solving capabilities.

*Lincoln Electric in Cleveland, Ohio, has one of the oldest and most radical pay-for-performance incentive programs in the country. The Lincoln Electric system paid employees up to 100 percent of their wages in annual performance bonuses. However, due to recent global competition and an increase in institutional shareholders, workers' bonuses have decreased while revenues reached $1 billion. Many workers are concerned about future bonus reductions. As managers struggle to meet new competitive threats, they may use organization development techniques to adapt to current conditions without sacrificing employee goodwill.*

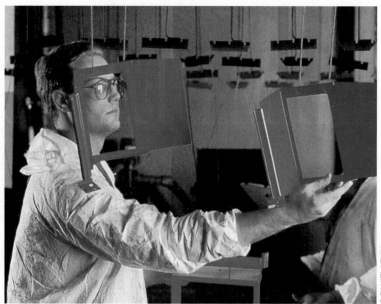

package was formed at a computer company. Made up of strong-willed individuals, the team made little progress because members could not agree on project goals. At a manufacturing firm, salespeople promised delivery dates to customers that were in conflict with shop supervisor priorities for assembling customer orders. In a publishing company, two managers disliked each other intensely. They argued at meetings, lobbied politically against each other, and hurt the achievement of both departments. Organization development efforts can help solve these kinds of conflicts, as well as conflicts that are related to growing diversity and the global nature of today's organizations.

Organization development can be used to solve the types of problems just described and many others. However, to be truly valuable to companies and employees, organization development practitioners go beyond looking at ways to solve specific problems. Instead, they become involved in broader issues that contribute to improving organizational life, such as encouraging a sense of community, pushing for an organizational climate of openness and trust, and making sure the company provides employees with opportunities for personal growth and development.[86] Specialized techniques have been developed to help meet OD goals.

## OD Activities

A number of OD activities have emerged in recent years. Three of the most popular and effective are as follows.

**team building**
A type of OD intervention that enhances the cohesiveness of departments by helping members learn to function as a team.

1. *Team-building activities.* Team building enhances the cohesiveness and success of organizational groups and teams. For example, a series of OD exercises can be used with members of cross-departmental teams to help them learn to act and function as a team. An OD expert can work with team members to increase their communication skills, facilitate their ability to confront one another, and help them accept common goals.

**survey feedback**
A type of OD intervention in which questionnaires on organizational climate and other factors are distributed among employees and their results reported back to them by a change agent.

2. *Survey-feedback activities.* Survey feedback begins with a questionnaire distributed to employees on values, climate, participation, leadership, and group cohesion within their organization. After the survey is completed, an OD consultant meets with groups of employees to provide feedback about their

responses and the problems identified. Employees are engaged in problem solving based on the data.

3. *Large-group interventions.* In recent years, there has been a growing interest in applications of OD techniques to large group settings, which are more attuned to bringing about fundamental organizational change in today's complex, fast-changing world.[87] The large-group intervention approach brings together participants from all parts of the organization—often including key stakeholders from outside the organization as well—to discuss problems or opportunities and plan for change. A large-group intervention might involve 50 to 500 people and last several days. The idea is to include everyone who has a stake in the change, gather perspectives from all parts of the system, and enable people to create a collective future through sustained, guided conversation and dialogue.

**large-group intervention**
An approach that brings together participants from all parts of the organization (and may include key outside stakeholders as well) to discuss problems or opportunities and plan for major change.

Large-group interventions reflect a significant shift in the approach to organizational change from earlier OD concepts and approaches. Exhibit 11.8 lists the primary differences between the traditional OD model and the large-scale intervention model of organizational change.[88] In the newer approach, the focus is on the entire system, which takes into account the organization's interaction with its environment. The source of information for discussion is expanded to include customers, suppliers, community members, even competitors, and this information is shared widely so that everyone has the same picture of the organization and its environment. The acceleration of change when the entire system is involved can be remarkable. In addition, learning occurs across all parts of the organization simultaneously, rather than in individuals, small groups, or business units. The result is that the large-group approach offers greater possibilities for fundamental, radical transformation of the entire culture, whereas the traditional approach creates incremental change in a few individuals or small groups at a time. General Electric's Work Out Program provides an excellent example of the large-group intervention approach.

Exhibit 11.8

## OD Approaches to Culture Change

| | Traditional Organization Development Model | Large-Group Intervention Model |
|---|---|---|
| **Focus for action:** | Specific problem or group | Entire system |
| **Information Source:** | Organization | Organization and environment |
| **Distribution:** | Limited | Widely shared |
| **Time frame:** | Gradual | Fast |
| **Learning:** | Individual, small group | Whole organization |
| **Change process:** | Incremental change | Rapid transformation |

**SOURCE:** Adapted from Barbara Benedict Bunker and Billie T. Alban, "Conclusion: What Makes Large Group Interventions Effective," *The Journal of Applied Behavioral Science* 28, no. 4 (December 1992), 579–591.

GE's Work Out began in large-scale off-site meetings facilitated by a combination of top leaders, outside consultants, and human resources specialists. In each business unit, the basic pattern was the same. Hourly and salaried workers came together from many different parts of the organization in an informal three-day meeting to discuss and solve problems. Gradually, the Work Out events began to include external stakeholders such as suppliers and customers as well as employees. Today, Work Out is not an event, but a process of how work is done and problems are solved at GE.

The format for Work Out includes seven steps:

1. Choose a work process or problem for discussion.
2. Select an appropriate cross-functional team, to include external stakeholders.
3. Assign a "champion" to follow through on recommendations.
4. Meet for several days and come up with recommendations to improve processes or solve problems.
5. Meet with leaders, who are asked to respond to recommendations on the spot.
6. Hold additional meetings as needed to implement the recommendations.
7. Start the process all over again with a new process or problem.

GE's Work Out process forces a rapid analysis of ideas, the creation of solutions, and the development of a plan for implementation. Over time, this large-group process creates an organizational culture where ideas are rapidly translated into action and positive business results.[89]

## GENERAL ELECTRIC
http://www.ge.com

Large-group interventions represent a significant shift in the way leaders think about change and reflect an increasing awareness of the importance of dealing with the entire system, including external stakeholders, in any significant change effort.

### OD Steps

Organization development experts acknowledge that changes in corporate culture and human behavior are tough to accomplish and require major effort. The theory underlying OD proposes three distinct stages for achieving behavioral and attitudinal change: (1) unfreezing, (2) changing, and (3) refreezing.[90] The Unlocking Creative Solutions Through People box describes how Alberto-Culver created a new employee-focused culture that helped turn the business around by following the stages of unfreezing, changing, and refreezing.

The first stage, unfreezing, means that people throughout the organization are made aware of problems and the need for change. This stage creates the motivation for people to change their attitudes and behaviors. Unfreezing may begin when managers present information that shows discrepancies between desired behaviors or performance and the current state of affairs. In addition, as we discussed earlier in the chapter, managers need to establish a sense of urgency to unfreeze people and create an openness and willingness to change. The unfreezing stage is often associated with *diagnosis*, which uses an outside expert called a *change agent*. The change agent is an OD specialist who performs a systematic diagnosis of the organization and identifies work-related problems. He or she gathers and analyzes data through personal interviews, questionnaires, and observations of meetings. The diagnosis helps determine the extent of organizational problems and helps unfreeze managers by making them aware of problems in their behavior.

The second stage, changing, occurs when individuals experiment with new behavior and learn new skills to be used in the workplace. This is sometimes known as intervention, during which the change agent implements a specific plan for training managers and employees. The changing stage might involve a number of specific steps.[91] Recall the eight steps for leading change from the Manager's Shoptalk

**unfreezing**
The stage of organization development in which participants are made aware of problems in order to increase their willingness to change their behavior.

**change agent**
An OD specialist who contracts with an organization to facilitate change.

**changing**
The intervention stage of organization development in which individuals experiment with new workplace behavior.

# Unlocking Creative Solutions Through People

## Alberto-Culver Gets a Cultural Makeover

"Do we make people happy and then the business gets better; or do we fix the business, which will make people happier?" That's the question top executives were asking Carol Lavin Bernick, president of Alberto-Culver North America. It became clear to Bernick that the company was facing a cultural crisis. For years, Alberto-Culver had suffered from general overall employee dissatisfaction, a turnover rate that was double the national average, deflated sales and slipping margins on their most popular brands, and an organization that was not equal to the challenge of an emerging competitive environment. Bernick wanted to make culture change a priority, but she had to find a way to get everyone throughout the organization committed to change.

She began the change process with a companywide meeting aimed at letting everyone know where the company stood and where it needed to go in the future (unfreezing). Before the meeting began, Bernick scattered pennies around the floor and observed employees as they entered the room—no one attempted to pick up a cent. "Can anyone name our best-selling product?" she asked. "V05 shampoo!" came the resounding response. "Look around you on the floor, and if you see a penny, pick it up," Bernick continued. "That penny represents our total profit on a bottle of Alberto V05 shampoo." Employees were already aware of many problems in the business, but this was an eye-opener. Thus began the process of creating a culture of honesty and shared ownership, where employees think like business people and act like team players.

The next stage (changing) involved creating a specific plan for change. One step was to develop a list of ten cultural imperatives: honesty, ownership, trust, customer orientation, commitment, fun, innovation, risk taking, speed and urgency, and teamwork. Another was to create a specific role called the *growth development leader* (GDL). Each handpicked GDL mentors about a dozen people, helping to bring about culture change at the individual and small-group level. GDLs work to build team spirit and help people understand how their work fits into the big picture. One specific task is helping to spell out *Individual Economic Values*, or IEVs, short statements that describe how each individual contributes to the organization's productivity and profitability. With the IEVs, managers have given employees greater freedom and power to drive the success of the company. Growth development leaders also get intimately involved in people's lives and careers. For example, they help people set personal and professional goals that achieve the right balance for the individual, reinforcing the idea that Alberto-Culver is a company that respects and values its employees as individuals with lives outside of work.

Finally, Bernick needed to find ways to make the changes stick (refreezing). At every opportunity, managers reinforce the central cultural tenet that individuals can make a difference, and that companies don't succeed—people do. Managers regularly measure individual and organizational progress against the cultural goals. "I'm a firm believer that you change what you measure," says Bernick. "Once a year, we do an all-employee survey to assess our progress against cultural goals and to gather feedback." Managers also celebrate every success and reward people for exhibiting the attitudes and behaviors that fit the new culture, such as through stock options, Business Builder Awards, and People's Choice Awards. "If you want something to grow," claims Bernick, "pour champagne on it."

**SOURCE**: Carol Lavin Bernick, "When Your Culture Needs a Makeover," *Harvard Business Review* (June 2001), 53–61.

box earlier in this chapter. For example, managers put together a coalition of people with the will and power to guide the change, create a vision for change that everyone can believe in, and widely communicate the vision and plans for change throughout the company. In addition, successful change involves using emotion as well as logic to persuade people and empowering employees to act on the plan and accomplish the desired changes.

The third stage, refreezing, occurs when individuals acquire new attitudes or values and are rewarded for them by the organization. The impact of new behaviors is evaluated and reinforced. The change agent supplies new data that show positive changes in performance. Managers may provide updated data to employees that demonstrate positive changes in individual and organizational performance. Top executives celebrate successes and reward positive behavioral changes. This is the stage where changes

**refreezing**
The reinforcement stage of organization development in which individuals acquire a desired new skill or attitude and are rewarded for it by the organization.

are institutionalized in the organizational culture, so that employees begin to view the changes as a normal, integral part of how the organization operates. Employees may also participate in refresher courses to maintain and reinforce the new behaviors.

## Manager's Solution

Change is inevitable in organizations. This chapter discussed the techniques available for managing the change process. Managers should think of change as having four elements—the forces for change, the perceived need for change, the initiation of change, and the implementation of change. Forces for change can originate either within or outside the firm, and managers are responsible for monitoring events that may require a planned organizational response. Techniques for initiating changes include designing the organization for creativity, encouraging change agents, establishing new-venture teams and idea incubators, and using open innovation. The final step is implementation. Managers should be prepared to encounter resistance to change. Some typical reasons for resistance include self-interest, lack of trust, uncertainty, and conflicting goals. Force field analysis is one technique for diagnosing barriers, which often can be removed. Managers also should draw on the implementation tactics of communication, participation, negotiation, coercion, or top management support.

This chapter also discussed specific types of change. Technology changes are accomplished through a bottom-up approach that utilizes experts close to the technology. Successful new-product introduction requires horizontal linkage among marketing, research and development, manufacturing, and perhaps other departments or customers, partners, and suppliers. Structural changes tend to be initiated in a top-down fashion, because upper managers are the administrative experts and champion these ideas for approval and implementation. Culture/people change pertains to the skills, behaviors, and attitudes of employees. Training and organization development are important approaches to change people's mindset and corporate culture. The OD process entails three steps—unfreezing (diagnosis of the problem), the actual change (intervention), and refreezing (reinforcement of new attitudes and behaviors). Popular OD techniques include team building, survey feedback, and large-group interventions.

Managers at BMW's Cowley, Oxford, plant, described at the beginning of the chapter, were facing the need for a major cultural overhaul. They began by shifting the plant to a self-directed team-based structure and training employees to work as part of a team. Team-building sessions, cross-training, and coaching by external consultants helped people make the transition from working on a traditional assembly line to working in teams of 8 to 15 members who rotate jobs and solve production problems. One person within each team is designated to be responsible for continuous team development, with a reduction in other day-to-day duties. The next aspect of the Wings (Working in Groups) change program was to involve employees directly in determining other changes the factory could make to improve effectiveness. Every two weeks, each of the three shifts shuts down production for a 45-minute period to discuss ideas for technology changes. As managers implemented the ideas, more and more employees began to participate. BMW also instituted a "Back to the Track" scheme that puts managers and directors on the production lines working side-by-side with plant workers. Employees saw first-hand that they—not managers–were the ones with expertise and knowledge for solving production problems. The approach helped bridge the gulf between management and labor and enhanced the empowerment process. Within three years, BMW had implemented more than 8,000 ideas from employees. Production targets were exceeded by more than 60 percent, contributing to significant cost savings. Plant workers now feel like an important part of the business rather than like pieces of production equipment.[92]

# Discussion Questions

1. A manager of an international chemical company said that very few new products in her company were successful. What would you advise the manager to do to help increase the company's success rate?

2. What are internal and external forces for change? Which force do you think is the major cause of organizational change?

3. Carefully planned change often is assumed to be effective. Do you think unplanned change can sometimes be beneficial to an organization? Discuss.

4. Why do organizations experience resistance to change? What techniques can managers use to overcome resistance?

5. Explain force field analysis. Analyze the driving and restraining forces for a change with which you have been associated.

6. Define the roles associated with an idea champion. Why are idea champions so essential to the initiation of change?

7. To what extent would changes in technology affect products and vice versa? Compare the process for changing technology and that for product change.

8. Given that structural change is often made top down, should coercive implementation techniques be used?

9. Do the underlying values of organizational development differ from assumptions associated with other types of change? Discuss.

10. How do large-group interventions differ from OD techniques such as team-building and survey feedback?

# Management in Practice: Experiential Exercise

**Is Your Company Creative?**

An effective way to assess the creative climate of an organization for which you have worked is to fill out the questionnaire below. Answer each question based on your work experience in that firm. Discuss the results with members of your group, and talk about whether changing the firm along the dimensions in the questions would make it more creative.

Instructions: Answer each of the following questions using the five-point scale. (Note there is no rating of 4):0, we never do this; 1, we rarely do this; 2, we sometimes do this; 3, we frequently do this; and 5, we always do this.)

\_\_\_ We are encouraged to seek help anywhere inside or outside the organization with new ideas for our work unit.

\_\_\_ Assistance is provided to develop ideas into proposals for management review.

\_\_\_ Our performance reviews encourage risky, creative efforts, ideas, and actions.

\_\_\_ We are encouraged to fill our minds with new information by attending professional meetings and trade fairs, visiting customers, and so on.

\_\_\_ Our meetings are designed to allow people to free-wheel, brainstorm, and generate ideas.

\_\_\_ All members contribute ideas during meetings.

\_\_\_ During meetings, there is much spontaneity and humor.

\_\_\_ We discuss how company structure and our actions help or spoil creativity within our work unit.

___ During meetings, the chair is rotated among members.

___ Everyone in the work unit receives training in creativity techniques and maintaining a creative climate.

To measure how effectively your organization fosters creativity, use the following scale:

Highly effective: 35–50
Moderately effective: 20–34
Moderately ineffective: 10–19
Ineffective: 0–9

Source: Adapted from Edward Glassman, *Creativity Handbook: Idea Triggers and Sparks That Work* (Chapel Hill, N.C.: LCS Press, 1990). Used by permission. (919/967–2015)

# Management in Practice: Ethical Dilemma

## Research for Sale

Lucinda Jackson walked slowly back to R&D Laboratory 4 at Reed Pharmaceuticals. She was stunned. Top management was planning to sell her entire team project to Trichem Industries in an effort to raise the capital Reed needed to buy a small, competing drug company. Two years ago, when she was named project administrator for the cancer treatment program, Jackson was assured that the program was the highest priority at Reed. She was allowed to recruit the best and the brightest in the research center in their hunt for an effective drug to treat lung cancer. There had been press releases and personal appearances at stockholder meetings.

When she first approached a colleague, Len Rosen, to become head chemist on the project, he asked her whether Reed was in cancer research for the long haul or if they were just grabbing headlines. Based on what she had been told by the vice president in charge of R&D, Jackson assured him that their project was protected for as long as it took. Now, a short two years later, she learned that not only was Reed backing out but also that the project was being sold as a package to an out-of-state firm. There were no jobs at Reed being offered as alternatives for the team. They were only guaranteed jobs if they moved with the project to Trichem.

Jackson felt betrayed, but she knew it was nothing compared to what the other team members would feel. Rosen was a ten-year veteran at Reed, and his wife and family had deep roots in the local community. A move would be devastating to them. Jackson had a few friends in top management, but she didn't know if any would back her if she fought the planned sale.

## What Do You Do?

1. Approach top management with the alternative of selling the project and sending the team temporarily to train staff at Trichem but allowing them to return to different projects at Reed after the transition. After all, they promised a commitment to the project.
2. Wait for the announcement of the sale of the project and then try to secure as much support as possible for the staff and families in their relocation: moving expense reimbursement, job placement for spouses, etc.
3. Tell a few people, such as Rosen, and then combine forces with them and threaten to quit if the project is sold. Make attempts to scuttle the sale to Trichem before it happens, and perhaps even leak the news to the press. Perhaps the threat of negative publicity will cause top management to reconsider.

Source: Adapted from Doug Wallace, "Promises Made, Promises Broken," *What Would You Do? Business Ethics 1* (March–April 1990), 16–18. Reprinted with permission from Business Ethics, P.O. Box 8439, Minneapolis, MN 55408, (612) 879-0695.

# Surf the Net

1. **The Learning Organization.** Released in March 1999, the learning organization guru, Peter Senge, authored *The Dance of Change: The Challenges of Sustaining Momentum in Learning Organizations*. Use your search engine to find a book review of this work and write a summary of your findings. One place to find book reviews is *http://www.amazon.com*.

2. **New-Venture Team.** Xerox Corporation's Palo Alto Research Center (PARC) was mentioned in the text as an example of an organization with new-venture teams. Visit PARC at *http://www.parc.xerox.com/parc-go.html* to find answers to the following questions: (a) What are the strategic themes of PARC's research agenda? (b) Which one of PARC's inventions (available under the "History" section) do you think is most useful, and why? (c) Which one of the current PARC projects did you find most intriguing, and why?

3. **Survey feedback.** One of the OD activities mentioned in the chapter is survey feedback. One leading company in the field of employee attitude surveys is Stanard and Associates, Chicago, Illinois. Go to their Web site at *http://stanard.com* to learn more about the attitude survey instrument and to respond to the survey questions online so you can see how the procedure would work in an organizational setting. If your instructor asks you to do so, you may also want to print out the sample survey to refer to during the classroom discussion on this topic.

# Case for Critical Analysis

## Southern Discomfort

Jim Malesckowski remembers the call of two weeks ago as if he just put down the telephone receiver. "I just read your analysis and I want you to get down to Mexico right away," Jack Ripon, his boss and chief executive officer, had blurted in his ear. "You know we can't make the plant in Oconomo work anymore—the costs are just too high. So go down there, check out what our operational costs would be if we move, and report back to me in a week."

At that moment, Jim felt as if a shiv had been stuck in his side, just below the rib cage. As president of the Wisconsin Specialty Products Division of Lamprey, Inc., he knew quite well the challenge of dealing with high-cost labor in a third-generation, unionized U.S. manufacturing plant. And although he had done the analysis that led to his boss's knee-jerk response, the call still stunned him. There were 520 people who made a living at Lamprey's Oconomo facility, and if it closed, most of them wouldn't have a journeyman's prayer of finding another job in the town of 9,000 people.

Instead of the $16-per-hour average wage paid at the Oconomo plant, the wages paid to the Mexican workers—who lived in a town without sanitation and with an unbelievably toxic effluent from industrial pollution—would amount to about $1.60 an hour on average. That's a savings of nearly $15 million a year for Lamprey, to be offset in part by increased costs for training, transportation, and other matters.

After two days of talking with Mexican government representatives and managers of other companies in the town, Jim had enough information to develop a set of comparative figures of production and shipping costs. On the way home, he started to outline the report, knowing full well that unless some miracle occurred, he would be ushering in a blizzard of pink slips for people he had come to appreciate.

The plant in Oconomo had been in operation since 1921, making special apparel for persons suffering injuries and other medical conditions. Jim had often talked with employees who would recount stories about their fathers or grandfathers working in the same Lamprey company plant—the last of the original manufacturing operations in town.

But friendship aside, competitors had already edged past Lamprey in terms of price and were dangerously close to overtaking it in product quality.

Although both Jim and the plant manager had tried to convince the union to accept lower wages, union leaders resisted. In fact, on one occasion when Jim and the plant manager tried to discuss a cell manufacturing approach, which would cross-train employees to perform up to three different jobs, local union leaders could barely restrain their anger. Yet probing beyond the fray, Jim sensed the fear that lurked under the union reps' gruff exterior. He sensed their vulnerability, but could not break through the reactionary bark that protected it.

A week has passed and Jim just submitted his report to his boss. Although he didn't specifically bring up the point, it was apparent that Lamprey could put its investment dollars in a bank and receive a better return than what its Oconomo operation is currently producing.

Tomorrow, he'll discuss the report with the CEO. Jim doesn't want to be responsible for the plant's dismantling, an act he personally believes would be wrong as long as there's a chance its costs can be lowered. "But Ripon's right," he says to himself. "The costs are too high, the union's unwilling to cooperate, and the company needs to make a better return on its investment if it's to continue at all. It sounds right but feels wrong. What should I do?"

## Questions

1. Assume you want to lead the change to save the Oconomo plant. Describe how you would proceed, using the four stages of the change process described in the chapter—forces, need, initiation, and implementation.

2. What is the primary type of change needed—technology, product, structure, or people/culture? To what extent will the primary change have secondary effects on other types of change at the Oconomo factory?

3. What techniques would you use to overcome union resistance and implement change?

Source: Doug Wallace, "What Would You Do?" *Business Ethics*, March/April 1996, 52–53. Reprinted with permission.

# Endnotes

1. Jon Watkins, "A Mini Adventure," *People Management* (November 6, 2003), 30–32.

2. Keith Bracsher, "Newest Export Out of China: Inflation Fears," *The New York Times* (April 16, 2004), http://www.nytimes.com.

3. Scott Kirsner, "5 Technologies That Will Change the World," *Fast Company* (September 2003), 93–98; Stuart F. Brown, "The Automaker's Big-Time Bet on Fuel Cells," *Fortune* (March 30, 1998), 122(B)–122(D).

4. Kirsner, "5 Technologies that Will Change the World."

5. Richard L. Daft, "Bureaucratic vs. Nonbureaucratic Structure in the Process of Innovation and Change," in *Perspectives in Organizational Sociology: Theory and Research*, ed. Samuel B. Bacharach (Greenwich, Conn.: JAI Press, 1982), 129–166.

6. Tom Broersma, "In Search of the Future," *Training and Development* (January 1995), 38–43.

7. Andre L. Delbecq and Peter K. Mills, "Managerial Practices that Enhance Innovation," *Organizational Dynamics* 14 (Summer 1985), 24–34.

8. Interview with Art Collins in Ellen Florian, "CEO Voices: 'I Have a Cast-Iron Stomach,'" Special Insert: CEOs on Innovation, *Fortune* (March 8, 2004).

9. Chuck Salter, "On the Road Again," *Fast Company*, (January 2002), 50–58.

10. Interview with A. G. Lafley in Ellen Florian, "CEO Voices"; and Patricia Sellers, "Teaching an Old Dog New Tricks," *Fortune* (May 31, 2004), 166–180.

11. Carol Hymowitz, "Managing in a Crisis Can Bring Better Ways to Conduct Business," (In the Lead column) *The Wall Street Journal* (October 23, 2001), B1.

12. John P. Kotter, *Leading Change* (Boston: Harvard University Press, 1996), 20–25; and "Leading Change: Why Transformation Efforts Fail," *Harvard Business Review* (March–April, 1995), 59–67.

13. Almar Latour, "Trial by Fire: A Blaze in Albuquerque Sets Off Major Crisis for Cell-Phone Giants," *The Wall Street Journal* (January 29, 2001), A1, A8.

14. Attributed to Gregory Bateson in Andrew H. Van de Ven, "Central Problems in the Management of Innovation," *Management Science* 32 (1986), 595.

15. Teresa M. Amabile, "Motivating Creativity in Organizations: On Doing What You Love and Loving What You Do," *California Management Review* 40, no. 1 (Fall 1997), 39–58; Brian Leavy, "Creativity: The New Imperative," *Journal of General Management* 28, no. 1 (Autumn 2002), 70–85; and Timothy A. Matherly and Ronald E. Goldsmith, "The Two Faces of Creativity," *Business Horizons* (September/October 1985), 8.

16. Gordon Vessels, "The Creative Process: An Open-Systems Conceptualization," *Journal of Creative Behavior* 16 (1982), 185–196.

17. Robert J. Sternberg, Linda A. O'Hara, and Todd I. Lubart, "Creativity as Investment," *California Management Review* 40, no. 1 (Fall 1997), 8–21; Teresa M. Amabile, "Motivating Creativity in Organizations"; Leavy, "Creativity: The New Imperative"; and Ken Lizotte, "A Creative State of Mind," *Management Review* (May 1998), 15–17.

18. James Brian Quinn, "Managing Innovation: Controlled Chaos," *Harvard Business Review* 63 (May–June 1985), 73–84; Howard H. Stevenson and David E. Gumpert, "The Heart of Entrepreneurship," *Harvard Business Review* 63 (March–April 1985), 85–94; and Marsha Sinetar, "Entrepreneurs, Chaos, and Creativity—Can Creative People Really Survive Large Company Structure?" *Sloan Management Review* 6 (Winter 1985), 57–62.

19. Cynthia Browne, "Jest for Success," *Moonbeams* (August 1989), 3–5; and Rosabeth Moss Kanter, *The Change Masters* (New York: Simon and Schuster, 1983).

20. S. Thomke and A. Nimgade, "IDEO Product Development", Case #9-600-143, Harvard Business School, 2000, reported in Leavy, "Creativity: The New Imperative"; Daniel H. Pink, "Out of the Box," *Fast Company* (October 2003), 104–106.

21. Ian Wylie, "Calling for a Renewable Future," *Fast Company* (May 2003), 46–48.

22. Ann Harrington, "Who's Afraid of a New Product?" *Fortune* (November 10, 2003), 189–192.

23. Harold J. Leavitt, "Why Hierarchies Thrive," *Harvard Business Review* (March 2003), 96–102.

24. "Hands On: A Manager's Notebook," *Inc.* (January 1989), 106.

25. Katy Koontz, "How to Stand Out from the Crowd," *Working Woman* (January 1988), 74–76.

26. George Anders, "Hard Cell," *Fast Company* (May 2001), 108–122.

27. Harold L. Angle and Andrew H. Van de Ven, "Suggestions for Managing the Innovation Journey," in *Research in the Management of Innovation: The Minnesota Studies,* ed. A. H. Van de Ven, H. L. Angle, and Marshall Scott Poole (Cambridge, Mass.: Ballinger/Harper & Row, 1989).

28. Robert I. Sutton, "The Weird Rules of Creativity," *Harvard Business Review* (September 2001), 94–103.

29. C. K. Bart, "New Venture Units: Use Them Wisely to Manage Innovation," *Sloan Management Review* (Summer 1988), 35–43; Michael Tushman and David Nadler, "Organizing for Innovation," *California Management Review* 28 (Spring 1986), 74–92; Peter F. Drucker, *Innovation and Entrepreneurship* (New York: Harper & Row, 1985); and Henry W. Chesbrough, "Making Sense of Corporate Venture Capital, *Harvard Business Review* (March 2002), http://www.hbsp.harvard.edu

30. Christine Canabou, "Fast Ideas for Slow Times," *Fast Company* (May 3002), 52.

31. Christopher Hoenig, "Skunk Works Secrets," *CIO* (July 1, 2000), 74–76; and Tom Peters and Nancy Austin, *A Passion for Excellence: The Leadership Difference* (New York: Random House, 1985).

32. Hoenig, "Skunk Works Secrets."

33. Sutton, "The Weird Rules of Creativity."

34. Interview with Craig Barrett in Ellen Florian, "CEO Voices: 'I Have a Cast-Iron Stomach,'" Special Insert: CEOs on Innovation, *Fortune* (March 8, 2004); and Sherry Eng, "Hatching Schemes," *The Industry Standard* (November 27–December 4, 2000), 174–175.

35. Eng, "Hatching Schemes."

36. Ibid.

37. Henry Chesbrough, "The Logic of Open Innovation: Managing Intellectual Property," *Califoenia Management Review* 45, no. 3 (Spring 2003), 33–58.

38. This discussion is based on Henry Chesbrough, "The Era of Open Innovation," *MIT Sloan Management Review* (Spring 2003), 35–41; and Amy Muller and Liisa Välikangas, "Extending the Boundary of Corporate Innovation," *Strategy & Leadership* 30, no. 3 (2002), 4–9.

39. Chesbrough, "The Era of Open Innovation"; Robert Berner, "Why P&G's Smile Is So Bright," *BusinessWeek* (August 12, 2002), 58–60; Interview with A. G. Lafley in Ellen Florian, "CEO Voices: 'I Have a Cast Iron Stomach'"; and Sellers, "P&G: Teaching an Old Dog."

40. Muller and Välikangas, "Extending the Boundary of Corporate Innovation."

41. C. K. Prahalad and Venkatram Ramaswamy, "The New Frontier of Experience Innovation," *MIT Sloan Management Review* (Summer 2003), 12–18.

42. Eric von Hippel, Stefan Thomke, and Mary Sonnack, "Creating Breakthroughs at 3M," *Harvard Business Review* (September–October 1999), 47–57.

43. Ibid.

44. J. P. Kotter and L. A. Schlesinger, "Choosing Strategies for Change," *Harvard Business Review* 57 (March–April 1979), 106–114.

45. Interview with Fred Smith in Ellen Florian, "CEO Voices."

46. G. Zaltman and Robert B. Duncan, *Strategies for Planned Change* (New York: Wiley Interscience, 1977).

47. Leonard M. Apcar, "Middle Managers and Supervisors Resist Moves to More Participatory Management," *The Wall Street Journal* (September 16, 1985), 25.

48. Dorothy Leonard-Barton and Isabelle Deschamps, "Managerial Influence in the Implementation of New Technology," *Management Science* 34 (1988), 1252–1265.

49. Kurt Lewin, *Field Theory in Social Science: Selected Theoretical Papers* (New York: Harper & Brothers, 1951).

50. Paul C. Nutt, "Tactics of Implementation," *Academy of Management Journal* 29 (1986), 230–261; Kotter and Schlesinger, "Choosing Strategies"; R. L. Daft and S. Becker, *Innovation in Organizations: Innovation Adoption in School Organizations* (New York: Elsevier, 1978); and R. Beckhard, *Organization Development: Strategies and Models* (Reading, Mass.: Addison-Wesley, 1969).

51. Rob Muller, "Training for Change," *Canadian Business Review* (Spring 1995), 16–19.

52. Gerard H. Seijts and Grace O'Farrell, "Engage the Heart: Appealing to the Emotions Facilitates Change," *Ivey Business Journal* (January–February 2003), 1–5; John P. Kottter and Dan S. Cohen, *The Heart of Change: Real-Life Stories of How People Change Their Organizations* (Boston, Mass.: Harvard Business School Press, 2002); and Shaul Fox and Yair Amichai-Hamburger, "The Power of Emotional Appeals in Promoting Organizational Change Programs," *Academy of Management Executive* 15, no. 4 (2001), 84–95.

53. Taggart F. Frost, "Creating a Teamwork-Based Culture within a Manufacturing Setting," *IM* (May–June 1994), 17–20.

54. Dean Foust with Gerry Khermouch, "Repairing the Coke Machine," *BusinessWeek* (March 19, 2001), 86–88.

55. Joy Persaud, "Strongest Links," *People Management* (May 29, 2003), 40–41.

56. Jerry Harkavy, "Footwear Maker Stays Step Ahead to Keep 'Made-in-USA' on Shoes," Associated Press story in *Johnson City Press* (March 3, 2002), 27; and http://www.newbalance.com accessed on April 15, 2004.

57. Richard Teitelbaum, "How to Harness Gray Matter," *Fortune* (June 9, 1997), 168.

58. R.L. Daft, *Organization Theory and Design,* 8th ed. (Cincinnati, OH: South-Western, 2004, Chapter 11; and Tom Burns and G. M. Stalker, *The Management of Innovation* (London: Tavistock Publications, 1961).

59. Richard L. Daft, "A Dual-Core Model of Organizational Innovation," *Academy of Management Journal* 21 (1978), 193–210; and Kanter, *The Change Masters*.

60. Michael L. Tushman and Charles A. O'Reilly III, "Building Ambidextrous Organizations: Forming Your Own 'Skunk Works,'" *Health Forum Journal* 42, no. 2 (March–April 1999), 20–23.

61. James B. Treece, "Improving the Soul of an Old Machine," *BusinessWeek* (October 25, 1993), 134–136.

62. Harold J. Leavitt, "Applied Organizational Change in Industry: Structural, Technical, and Human Approaches," in *New Perspectives in Organization Research*, ed. W. W. Cooper, H. J. Leavitt, and M. W. Shelly II (New York: Wiley, 1964), 55–74.

63. Glenn Rifkin, "Competing through Innovation: The Case of Broderbund," *Strategy & Business* 11 (Second Quarter, 1998), 48–58; and Deborah Dougherty and Cynthia Hardy, "Sustained Product Innovation in Large, Mature Organizations: Overcoming Innovation-to-Organization Problems," *Academy of Management Journal* 39, no. 5 (1996), 1120–1153.

64. Cliff Edwards, "Many Products Have Gone the Way of the Edsel," *Johnson City Press* (May 23, 1999), 28; Robert McMath, *What Were They Thinking? Marketing Lessons I've Learned from Over 80,000 New Product Innovations and Idiocies* (New York: Times Business, 1998); and Paul Lukas, "The Ghastliest Product Launches," *Fortune* (March 16, 1998), 44.

65. Melissa A. Schilling and Charles W. L. Hill, "Managing the New Product Development Process," *Academy of Management Executive* 12, no. 3 (1998), 67–81.

66. Andrew H. Van de Ven, "Central Problems in the Management of Innovation," *Management Science* 32 (1986), 590–607; Daft, *Organization Theory*; and Science Policy Research Unit, University of Sussex, *Success and Failure in Industrial Innovation* (London: Centre for the Study of Industrial Innovation, 1972).

67. William L. Shanklin and John K. Ryans, Jr., "Organizing for High-Tech Marketing," *Harvard Business Review* 62 (November–December 1984), 164–171; and Arnold O. Putnam, "A Redesign for Engineering," *Harvard Business Review* 63 (May–June 1985), 139–144.

68. Daft, *Organization Theory*.

69. Noshua Watson, "What's Wrong With This Printer?" *Fortune* (February 17, 2003), 120[C]–120[H].

70. Brent Schlender, "How Big Blue Is Turning Geeks Into Gold," *Fortune* (June 9, 2003), 133–140.

71. Brian Dumaine, "How Managers Can Succeed through Speed," *Fortune* (February 13, 1989), 54–59; and George Stalk, Jr., "Time—The Next Source of Competitive Advantage," *Harvard Business Review* (July–August 1988), 41–51.

72. John A. Pearce II, "Speed Merchants," *Organizational Dynamics* 30, no. 3 (2002), 191–205.

73. V. K. Narayanan, Frank L. Douglas, Brock Guernsey, and John Charnes, "How Top Management Steers Fast Cycle Teams to Success," *Strategy & Leadership* 30, no. 3 (2002), 19–27.

74. Faith Keenan, "Opening the Spigot," *BusinessWeek E.biz* (June 4, 2001), EB17–EB20.

75. Fariborz Damanpour, "The Adoption of Technological, Administrative, and Ancillary Innovations: Impact of Organizational Factors," *Journal of Management* 13 (1987), 675–688.

76. Greg Jaffe, "New Formation: A Maverick's Plan to Revamp Army Is Taking Shape," *The Wall Street Journal* (December 12, 2003), A1.

77. Daft, "Bureaucratic vs. Nonbureaucratic Structure."

78. Eliza Newlin Carney, "Calm in the Storm," *Government Executive* (October 2003), 57–63.

79. Avan R. Jassawalla and Hemant C. Sashittal, "Building Collaborative New Product Processes: Why Instituting Teams Is Not Enough," *SAM Advanced Management Journal* (Winter 2002), 27–36.

80. E. H. Schein, "Organizational Culture," *American Psychologist* 45 (February 1990), 109–119; Eliza Newlin Carey, "Calm in the Storm,"

81. Michelle Conlin, "Tough Love for Techie Souls," *BusinessWeek* (November 29, 1999), 164–170.

82. Alix Nyberg, "Kim Patmore," profile in "The Class of 2000," *CFO* (October 2000), 81–82.

83. M. Sashkin and W. W. Burke, "Organization Development in the 1980s," *General Management 13* (1987), 393–417; and Richard Beckhard, "What Is Organization Development?" in *Organization Development and Transformation: Managing Effective Change,* Wendell L. French, Cecil H. Bell, Jr., and Robert A. Zawacki, eds., (Burr Ridge, Ill.: Irwin McGraw Hill, 2000), 16–19.

84. Wendell L. French and Cecil H. Bell, Jr., "A History of Organization Development," in French, Bell, and Zawacki, *Organization Development and Transformation,* 20–42; and Christopher G. Worley and Ann E. Feyerherm, "Reflections on the Future of Organization Development," *The Journal of Applied Behavioral Science* 39, no. 1 (March 2003), 97–115.

85. Paul F. Buller, "For Successful Strategic Change: Blend OD Practices with Strategic Management," *Organizational Dynamics* (Winter 1988), 42–55; Robert M. Fulmer and Roderick Gilkey, "Blending Corporate Families: Management and Organization Development in a Postmerger Environment," *The Academy of Management Executive* 2 (1988), 275–283; and Worley and Feyerherm, "Reflections on the Future of Organization Development."

86. W. Warner Burke, "The New Agenda for Organization Development," *Organizational Dynamics* (Summer 1997), 7–19.

87. This discussion is based on Kathleen D. Dannemiller and Robert W. Jacobs, "Changing the Way Organizations Change: A Revolution of Common Sense," *The Journal of Applied Behavioral Science* 28, no. 4 (December 1992), 480–498; and Barbara Benedict Bunker and Billie T. Alban, "Conclusion: What Makes Large Group Interventions Effective?" *The Journal of Applied Behavioral Science* 28, no. 4 (December 1992), 570–591.

88. Bunker and Alban, "What Makes Large Group Interventions Effective?"

89. Dave Ulrich, Steve Kerr, and Ron Ashkenas, with Debbie Burke and Patrice Murphy, *The GE Work-Out: How to Implement GE's Revolutionary Method for Busting Bureaucracy and Attacking Organizational Problems— Fast!* (New York: McGraw-Hill, 2002); J. Quinn, "What a Work-Out!" *Performance* (November 1994), 58–63; and B. B. Bunker and B. T. Alban, "Conclusion: What Makes Large Group Interventions Effective?" *The Journal of Applied Behavioral Science* 28, no. 4 (December 1992), 572–591.

90. Kurt Lewin, "Frontiers in Group Dynamics: Concepts, Method, and Reality in Social Science," *Human Relations* 1 (1947), 5–41; and E. F. Huse and T. G. Cummings, *Organization Development and Change,* 3rd ed. (St. Paul, Minn.: West, 1985).

91. Based on John Kotter's eight-step model of planned change, which is described in John Kotter, *Leading Change* (Boston: Harvard Business School Press, 1996), 20–25, and "Leading Change: Why Transformation Efforts Fail," *Harvard Business Review* (March–April, 1995), 59–67.

92. Watkins, "A Mini Adventure."

# Human Resource Management

## LEARNING OBJECTIVES

*After studying this chapter, you should be able to:*

1. Explain the role of human resource management in organizational strategic planning.

2. Describe federal legislation and societal trends that influence human resource management.

3. Explain what the changing social contract between organizations and employees means for workers and human resource managers.

4. Show how organizations determine their future staffing needs through human resource planning.

5. Describe the tools managers use to recruit and select employees.

6. Describe how organizations develop an effective workforce through training and performance appraisal.

7. Explain how organizations maintain a workforce through the administration of wages and salaries, benefits, and terminations.

Every hour or so throughout the night, big brown trucks back into the bays at UPS's distribution center in Buffalo, New York, where part-time workers load, unload, and sort packages at a rate of 1,200 boxes an hour. A typical employee handles a box every three seconds. The packages don't stop until the shift is over, and there's little time for friendly banter and chit-chat, even if you could hear over the din of the belts and ramps that carry packages through the cavernous 270,000-square-foot warehouse. It's not the easiest job in the world, and many people don't stick around for long. When Jennifer Shroeger arrived in Buffalo as the new district manager, the attrition rate of part-time workers, who account for half of Buffalo's workforce, was 50 percent a year. With people deserting at that rate, hiring and training costs were through the roof, not to mention the slow-down in operations caused by continually training new workers. Something had to be done to bring in the right employees and make them want to stay longer than a few weeks.[1]

## Take A Moment

How would you address this enormous human resources challenge? What changes in recruiting, hiring, training, and other human resource practices can help to solve Jennifer Shroeger's problem in Buffalo?

PHOTO BY MICHAEL MAUREY COURTESY OF WALGREENS CO.

## CONCEPT CONNECTION

*Walgreens Co., the leader in the chain drugstore industry in both sales and profits, recognizes the strategic role of human resource management. In its Annual Report, the company states, "Well-trained pharmacy technicians like Celeste Burgess (photo) are pivotal to both patient service and the efficient operation of Walgreens Intercom Plus workflow system. Approximately 2,000 technicians passed a national certification exam, enhancing their pay and pharmacy knowledge."*

**human resource management (HRM)**
Activities undertaken to attract, develop, and maintain an effective workforce within an organization.

The situation at UPS's Buffalo distribution center provides a dramatic example of the challenges that managers face every day. The people who make up an organization give that organization its primary source of competitive advantage, and human resource management plays a key role in finding and developing the organization's people as human resources that contribute to and directly affect company success. The term human resource management (HRM) refers to the design and application of formal systems in an organization to ensure the effective and efficient use of human talent to accomplish organizational goals.[2] This includes activities undertaken to attract, develop, and maintain an effective workforce.

Managers at Electronic Arts, the world's largest maker of computer games, include a commitment to human resources as one of the company's four worldwide goals. They have to, in a company where the creativity and mindpower of artists, designers, model makers, mathematicians, and filmmakers determines strategic success, and the war for talent is intense.[3] HRM is equally important for government and nonprofit organizations. For example, public schools in the United States are facing a severe teacher shortage, with HRM directors struggling with how to fill an estimated 2.2 million teacher vacancies over the next decade. Many are trying innovative programs such as recruiting in foreign countries, establishing relationships with leaders at top universities, and having their most motivated and enthusiastic teachers work with university students considering teaching careers.[4]

Over the past decade, human resource management has shed its old "personnel" image and gained recognition as a vital player in corporate strategy.[5] Today's best HRM departments not only support the organization's strategic objective but actively pursue an ongoing, integrated plan for furthering the organization's performance.[6] Research has found that effective human resource management has a positive impact on strategic performance, including higher employee productivity and stronger financial results.[7] Human resource personnel are considered key players on the management team. In addition, all managers need to be skilled in the basics of human resource management. Today's flatter organizations often require that managers throughout the organization play an active role in recruiting and selecting the right personnel, developing effective training programs, or creating appropriate performance appraisal systems. HRM professionals act to guide and assist line managers in managing their human resources to achieve the organization's strategic goals.

# The Strategic Role of Human Resource Management

The strategic approach to human resource management recognizes three key elements. First, as we just discussed, all managers are human resource managers. For example, at IBM every manager is expected to pay attention to the development and satisfaction of subordinates. Line managers use surveys, career planning, performance appraisal, and compensation to encourage commitment to IBM.[8] Second, employees are viewed as assets. Employees, not buildings and machinery, give a company a competitive advantage. How a company manages its workforce may be the single most important factor in sustained competitive success.[9] Third, human resource management is a matching process, integrating the organization's strategy and goals with the correct approach to managing the firm's human resources.[10] Current strategic issues of particular concern to managers include the following:

• Becoming more competitive on a global basis
• Improving quality, productivity, and customer service
• Managing mergers and acquisitions
• Applying new information technology for e-business

All of these strategic decisions determine a company's need for skills and employees.

*Go to the experiential exercise on page 457 that pertains to your potential for strategic human resource management.*

*Take A Moment*

This chapter examines the three primary goals of HRM as illustrated in Exhibit 12.1. HRM activities and goals do not take place inside a vacuum but within the context of issues and factors affecting the entire organization, such as globalization, changing technology and the shift to knowledge work, rapid shifts in markets and the external environment, societal trends, government regulations, and changes in the organization's culture, structure, strategy, and goals.

The three broad HR activities outlined in Exhibit 12.1 are to attract an effective workforce to the organization, develop the workforce to its potential, and maintain the workforce over the long term.[11] Achieving these goals requires skills in planning, recruiting, training, performance appraisal, wage and salary administration, benefit programs, and even termination. Each of the activities in Exhibit 12.1 will be discussed in this chapter.

Exhibit 12.1

**Strategic Human Resource Management**

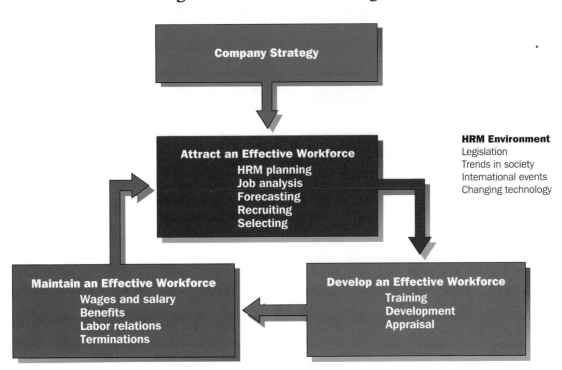

# Environmental Influences on HRM

*"Our strength is the quality of our people."*

*"Our people are our most important resource."*

These often-repeated statements by executives emphasize the importance of HRM. Human resource managers must find, recruit, train, nurture, and retain the best people.[12] Without the right people, the brightest idea or management trend—whether virtual teams, e-business, or flexible compensation—is doomed to failure. In addition, when employees don't feel valued, usually they are not willing to give their best to the company and often leave to find a more supportive work environment. For these reasons, it is important that human resource executives be involved in competitive strategy. Human resource executives also interpret federal legislation and respond to the changing nature of careers and work relationships.

## Competitive Strategy

HRM contributes directly to the bottom line through its appreciation that it is the organization's human assets—its people—that meet or fail to meet strategic goals. To keep companies competitive, HRM is changing in three primary ways: focusing on building human capital; developing global HR strategies; and using information technology.

**human capital**
The economic value of the knowledge, experience, skills, and capabilities of employees.

### Building Human Capital

Today, more than ever, strategic decisions are related to human resource considerations. In many companies, especially those that rely more on employee information, creativity, knowledge, and service rather than on production machinery, success depends on the ability to manage *human capital*.[13] Human capital refers to the economic value of the combined knowledge, experience, skills, and capabilities of employees.[14] To build human capital, HRM develops strategies for finding the best talent, enhancing their skills and knowledge with training programs and opportunities for personal and professional development, and providing compensation and benefits that enhance the sharing of knowledge and appropriately reward people for their contributions to the organization. Human resource managers also help create an environment that gives highly talented people compelling reasons to stay with the company. Judy Lyles of DET Distributing Company in Nashville, Tennessee, sees the human resource department not just as the keeper of the rules, but as the "keeper of workers' hearts—the keeper of why they want to come to work every day."[15] A related concern for managers is *social capital*, which refers to the quality of interactions among employees and whether they share a common perspective.[16] In organizations with a high degree of social capital, for example, relationships are based on honesty, trust, and respect, and people cooperate smoothly to achieve shared goals and outcomes.

© PORTER GIFFORD

**CONCEPT CONNECTION**

*Even in a "cold" job market, successful companies recognize the need to build human capital by hiring people with special knowledge, skills, or experience. For example, during a time when U.S. companies shed 415,000 jobs in one month, Bill Conner found work just one day after turning to an online job board. Conner, an executive in the telecom industry, lost his job overseeing the inspection of cell-tower parts and found a new position managing quality control for Boston's Solectria Corp., which makes parts for electric vehicles. Even as many companies have begun hiring freezes, firms such as Solectria see the economic value of snapping up highly experienced workers such as Bill Conner.*

### Globalization

Another issue for today's organizations is competing on a global basis, which brings tremendous new challenges for human resource management. Most companies are still in the early stages of developing effective HRM policies, structures, and services that respond to the current reality of globalization.[17] In a study of more than 200 global companies, including Eli Lilly, PPG Industries, and UPS, managers reported that the biggest challenge for HRM is leadership development and training for the international arena. In addition, HRM is responsible for recruitment, training, and performance management of employees who might have to work across geographical, technical, and cultural boundaries to help the organization achieve its goals. The success of global business strategies is closely tied to the effectiveness of the organization's global HR strategies.[18]

A subfield known as international human resource management (IHRM) specifically addresses the added complexity that results from coordinating and managing diverse people on a global scale.[19] Recent research in IHRM revealed that, as the world becomes increasingly interconnected, some HR practices and trends are converging. However, IHRM managers need a high degree of cultural sensitivity and the ability to tailor and communicate policies and practices for different cultures.[20] What works in one country may not translate well to another. Consider the human resources department at the UK division of Electronic Arts. In the United States, talented young people are eager to work for companies such as Electronic Arts, but bright college graduates in the UK often don't see designing computer games as a worthwhile career. Thus, the UK division's HR director has to take a different approach to recruiting, developing close relationships with specific universities and finding other innovative ways to promote the company.[21] Exhibit 12.2 lists some interesting trends related to selection, compensation, performance appraisal, and training in different countries.

**international human resource management (IHRM)**
A subfield of human resource management that addresses the complexity that results from recruiting, selecting, developing, and maintaining a diverse workforce on a global scale.

## Information Technology

Information technology is transforming human resource management and helping to meet the challenges of today's global environment. A study of the transition from

Exhibit 12.2

### Some Trends in International Human Resource Management

| | |
|---|---|
| **Selection** | • In Japan, HR managers focus on a job applicant's potential and his or her ability to get along with others.  Less emphasis is placed on job-related skills and experience.<br>• Employment tests are considered a crucial part of the selection process in Korea, whereas in Taiwan, the job interview is considered the most important criterion for selection. |
| **Compensation** | • Seniority-based pay is used to a greater extent in Asian and Latin countries.<br>• China and Taiwan have surprisingly high use of pay incentives, and are moving toward more incentives based on individual rather than group performance. |
| **Performance Appraisal** | • Across ten countries surveyed, managers consider recognizing subordinates' accomplishments, evaluating their goal achievement, planning their development, and improving their performance to be the most important reasons for performance appraisals. |
| **Training** | • In Mexico, managers consider training and development a reward to employees for good performance.<br>• HR managers in Korea incorporate team-building into nearly all training and development practices. |

**SOURCE:** Mary Ann Von Glinow, Ellen A. Drost, and Mary B. Teagarden, "Converging on IHRM Best Practices: Lessons Learned from a Globally Distributed Consortium on Theory and Practice," *Human Resource Management* 41, no. 1 (Spring 2002), 123–140.

traditional HR to e-HR found that the Internet and information technology has significantly affected every area of human resource management, from recruiting, to training, to retention strategies.[22] A human resource information system is an integrated computer system designed to provide data and information used in HR planning and decision making. The most basic use is the automation of administrative duties such as handling pay, benefits, and retirement plans, which can lead to significant cost savings. At General Motors, automating just one task—how managers authorize subordinates' pay increases—saves an estimated $650,000 a year. Allowing employees to make changes to their personal information or benefits saves further thousands.[23]

Some organizations are coming close to a paperless HRM system, which not only saves time and money but also frees staff from mundane chores so they can focus on important strategic issues, such as how to effectively evaluate and compensate virtual workers or how to meet the challenge of a coming skilled labor shortage.[24] Consider that annual labor force growth is expected to slow to 0.2 percent by 2020 and stay there for decades.[25] By simplifying the task of analyzing vast amounts of data, human resource information systems can dramatically improve the effectiveness of long-term planning to meet this and other HR challenges. This chapter's Unlocking Creative Solutions Through Technology box describes the benefits of an Internet-based HR system for PSS/World Medical, a global distributor of medical supplies and equipment based in Jacksonville, Florida.

## Federal Legislation

Over the past 40 years, a number of federal laws have been passed to ensure equal employment opportunity (EEO). Some of the most significant legislation and executive orders are summarized in Exhibit 12.3. The point of the laws is to stop discriminatory practices that are unfair to specific groups and to define enforcement agencies for these laws. EEO legislation attempts to balance the pay given to men and women; provide employment opportunities without regard to race, religion, national origin, and gender; ensure fair treatment for employees of all ages; and avoid discrimination against disabled individuals.

The Equal Employment Opportunity Commission (EEOC) created by the Civil Rights Act of 1964 initiates investigations in response to complaints concerning discrimination. The EEOC is the major agency involved with employment discrimination. Discrimination occurs when some applicants are hired or promoted based on criteria that are not job relevant. For example, refusing to hire a black applicant for a job he is qualified to fill or paying a woman a lower wage than a man for the same work are discriminatory acts. When discrimination is found, remedies include providing back pay and taking affirmative action. Affirmative action requires that an employer take positive steps to guarantee equal employment opportunities for people within protected groups. An affirmative action plan is a formal document that can be reviewed by employees and enforcement agencies. The goal of organizational affirmative action is to reduce or eliminate internal inequities among affected employee groups.

Failure to comply with equal employment opportunity legislation can result in substantial fines and penalties for employers. Suits for discriminatory practices can cover a broad range of employee complaints. One issue of growing concern is *sexual harassment*, which is also a violation of Title VII of the Civil Rights Act. The EEOC guidelines specify that behavior such as unwelcome advances, requests for sexual favors, and other verbal and physical conduct of a sexual nature becomes sexual harassment when submission to the conduct is tied to continued employment or advancement or when the behavior creates an intimidating, hostile, or offensive work environment.[26] Sexual harassment will be discussed in detail in Chapter 13.

**human resource information system**
An integrated computer system designed to provide data and information used in HR planning and decision making.

**discrimination**
The hiring or promoting of applicants based on criteria that are not job relevant.

**affirmative action**
A policy requiring employers to take positive steps to guarantee equal employment opportunities for people within protected groups.

Exhibit 12.3

## Major Federal Laws Related to Human Resource Management

| Federal Law | Year | Provisions |
|---|---|---|
| **Equal Opportunity/Discrimination Laws** | | |
| Civil Rights Act | 1991 | Provides for possible compensatory and punitive damages plus traditional back pay for cases of intentional discrimination brought under title VII of the 1964 Civil Rights Act. Shifts the burden of proof to the employer. |
| Americans with Disabilities Act | 1990 | Prohibits discrimination against qualified individuals by employers on the basis of disability and demands that "reasonable accommodations" be provided for the disabled to allow performance of duties. |
| Vocational Rehabilitation Act | 1973 | Prohibits discrimination based on physical or mental disability and requires that employees be informed about affirmative action plans. |
| Age Discrimination in Employment Act (ADEA) | 1967 (amended 1978, 1986) | Prohibits age discrimination and restricts mandatory retirement. |
| Civil Rights Act, Title VII | 1964 | Prohibits discrimination in employment on the basis of race, religion, color, sex, or national origin. |
| **Compensation/Benefits Laws** | | |
| Health Insurance Portability and Accountability Act (HIPPA) | 1996 | Allows employees to switch health insurance plans when changing jobs and get the new coverage regardless of preexisting health conditions; prohibits group plans from dropping a sick employee. |
| Family and Medical Leave Act | 1993 | Requires employers to provide up to 12 weeks unpaid leave for childbirth, adoption, or family emergencies. |
| Equal Pay Act | 1963 | Prohibits sex differences in pay for substantially equal work. |
| **Health/Safety Laws** | | |
| Consolidated Omnibus Budget Reconciliation Act (COBRA) | 1985 | Requires continued health insurance coverage (paid by employee) following termination. |
| Occupational Safety and Health Act (OSHA) | 1970 | Establishes mandatory safety and health standards in organizations. |

# Unlocking Creative Solutions Through Technology

**Internet-Based System Puts the People Back in HR**

Jeff Anthony, senior vice president for corporate development at PSS/World Medical, had a mess on his hands. He'd been tapped to "fix" the company's human resource management department, which was 100 percent paper-driven and nearly 100 percent out of control. The company grew from $35 million in business in 1993 to about $2 billion in 2001. The rapid growth threw the HR department into chaos. An internal audit found that the company had overpaid $180,000 in administrative fees to a medical insurer because it listed the wrong number of employees. Some employees were getting their paychecks weeks late and sometimes via overnight mail. People were quitting at a rate of 50 percent a year. One year, PSS paid out $600,000 in unused vacation time to departing employees because it lacked a system to track that information.

The HR function was drowning in nearly 80,000 pieces of paperwork a year. Anthony decided automation was the only way to go. He selected a system from Employease, a developer of Internet-based HR services. PSS immediately saw savings in paper costs and man-agers' time, not to mention the reduction in errors. Employees use a self-service system to manage benefits, cutting the time it once took to process enrollment from weeks to hours. Employment is verified in 30 seconds. Paychecks roll out on time, and new employee enrollments proceed smoothly. When employees leave, the system automatically calculates what they are owed in terms of pay, benefits, and unused vacation time.

However, the most important benefit Anthony sees is that the automated system has freed HR staff from the deluge of paper and allowed them to be involved in offline projects that focus on employees. The combination of more focus on people and the smoother HR processes has contributed to a decrease in turnover to 8 percent a year. HR personnel now spend their time and energy helping PSS find the right people, providing them with training and career development opportunities, and creating an environment where people want to stay and succeed. Anthony believes the right use of technology has put the emphasis in HR back where it should be. "The key word to my department is *human–human* resources," he says.

SOURCES: Jennifer Jaroneczyk, "Internet-Based HR," *Internet World* (November 2001), 18; and Peter Krass, "Precious Resources," *CFO-IT* (Summer 2003), 38–45.

Exhibit 12.3 also lists the major federal laws related to compensation and benefits and health and safety issues. The scope of human resource legislation is increasing at federal, state, and municipal levels. The working rights and conditions of women, minorities, older employees, and the disabled will likely receive increasing legislative attention in the future.

## The Changing Nature of Careers

Another current issue is the changing nature of careers. HRM can benefit employees and organizations by responding to recent changes in the relationship between employers and employees and new ways of working, such as telecommuting, job sharing, and virtual teams.

### The Changing Social Contract

In the old social contract between organization and employee, the employee could contribute ability, education, loyalty, and commitment and expect, in return that the company would provide wages and benefits, work, advancement, and training throughout the employee's working life. But volatile changes in the environment have disrupted this contract. Many organizations have been downsized, eliminating many employees. Employees who are left may feel little stability. In a fast-moving company, a person is hired and assigned to a project. The project changes over time, as do the person's tasks. Then the person is assigned to another project and then to still another. These new projects require working with different groups and leaders and schedules, and people may be working in a virtual environment, where they rarely see their colleagues face to face.[27] Careers no longer progress up a vertical hierarchy but move across jobs horizontally. In many of today's companies, everyone is expected to be a self-motivated worker who has excellent interpersonal relationships and is continuously acquiring new skills.

Exhibit 12.4 lists some elements of the new social contract. The new contract is based on the concept of employability rather than lifetime employment. Individuals manage their own careers; the organization no longer takes care of them or guarantees employment. Companies agree to pay somewhat higher wages and invest in creative training and development opportunities so that people will be more employable when the company no longer needs their services. Employees take more responsibility and control in their jobs, becoming partners in business improvement rather than cogs in a machine. In return, the organization provides challenging work assignments as well as information and resources to enable people to continually learn new skills. The new contract can provide many opportunities for employees to be more involved and express new aspects of themselves.

However, many employees are not prepared for new levels of cooperation or responsibility on the job. Employment insecurity is stressful for most employees, and it is harder than it was in the past to gain an employee's full commitment and enthusiasm. In addition, one study found that while most workers today feel they are contributing to their companies' success, they are increasingly skeptical that their hard work is being fully recognized.[28] Some companies are finding it difficult to keep good workers because employee trust has been destroyed. An important challenge for HRM is revising performance evaluation, training, career development, compensation, and reward practices to address the changing way of working. In addition, smart organizations contribute to employees' long-term success by offering career information and assessment, combined with career coaching, to help people determine new career directions.[29] This helps to preserve trust and enhance the

Exhibit 12.4

### The Changing Social Contract

| | New Contract | Old Contract |
|---|---|---|
| Employee | • Employability, personal responsibility<br>• Partner in business improvement<br>• Learning | • Job security<br>• A cog in the machine<br>• Knowing |
| Employer | • Continuous learning, lateral career movement, incentive compensation<br>• Creative development opportunities<br>• Challenging assignments<br>• Information and resources | • Traditional compensation package<br>• Standard training programs<br>• Routine jobs<br>• Limited information |

**SOURCES:** Based on Louisa Wah, "The New Workplace Paradox," *Management Review* (January 1998), 7; and Douglas T. Hall and Jonathan E. Moss, "The New Protean Career Contract: Helping Organizations and Employees Adapt," *Organizational Dynamics* (Winter, 1998), 22–37.

organization's social capital. Even when employees are let go or voluntarily leave, they often maintain feelings of goodwill toward the company.

## HR Issues in the New Workplace

The rapid change and turbulence in today's business environment bring significant new challenges for human resource management. As we have just discussed, one important issue is responding to the increasing use of teams and project management. In addition, HRM must devise policies to address the needs of temporary employees and virtual workers, effectively manage downsizing, and acknowledge growing employee demands for work–life balance.

### Teams and Projects

The advent of *teams* and *project management* is a major trend in today's workplace. People who used to work alone on the shop floor, in the advertising department, or in middle management are now thrown into teams and succeed as part of a group. Each member of the team acts like a manager, becoming responsible for quality standards, scheduling, and even hiring and firing other team members. With the emphasis on projects, the distinctions between job categories and descriptions are collapsing. Many of today's workers straddle functional and departmental boundaries and handle multiple tasks and responsibilities.[30]

### Temporary Employees

In the opening years of the twenty-first century, the largest employer in the United States was a temporary employment agency, Manpower Inc.[31] Temporary agencies such as Manpower grew rapidly during the 1990s, and by 2001, more than 3.3 million workers were in temporary firm placements. People in these temporary jobs do everything from data entry to becoming the interim CEO. Although in the past, most temporary workers were in clerical and manufacturing positions, in recent years demand has grown for professionals, particularly financial analysts, information technology specialists, accountants, product managers, and operations experts.[32] Contingent workers are people who work for an organization, but not on a permanent or full-time basis. This might include temporary placements, contracted professionals, leased employees, or part-time workers. One estimate is that contingent workers make up at least 25 percent of the U.S. workforce.[33] The use of contingent workers means reduced payroll and benefit costs, as well as increased flexibility for both employers and employees.

**contingent workers**
People who work for an organization, but not on a permanent or full-time basis, including temporary placements, contracted professionals, or leased employees.

### Technology

Related trends are virtual teams and telecommuting. Some virtual teams are made up entirely of people who are hired on a project-by-project basis. Team members are geographically or organizationally dispersed and rarely meet face to face, doing their work instead through advanced information technologies and collaborative software. Telecommuting means using computers and telecommunications equipment to do work without going to an office. TeleService Resources has more than 25 telephone agents who work entirely from home, using state-of-the-art call-center technology that provides seamless interaction with TSR's Dallas–Fort Worth call center.[34] Millions of people in the United States and Europe telecommute on a regular or occasional basis.[35] Wireless Internet devices, laptops, cell phones, and fax machines make it possible for people to work just about anywhere. There's a growth of what is called *extreme telecommuting*, which means that people live and work in countries far away from the organization's physical location. For example, Paolo Concini works from his home in Bali, Indonesia, even though his company's offices are located in China and Europe.[36]

**virtual team**
A team made up of members who are geographically or organizationally dispersed, rarely meet face to face, and do their work using advanced information technologies.

**telecommuting**
Using computers and telecommunications equipment to perform work from home or another remote location.

## Work-Life Balance

Telecommuting is one way organizations are helping employees lead more balanced lives. By working part of the time from home, for example, parents can avoid some of the conflicts they often feel with coordinating their work and family responsibilities. *Flexible scheduling* for regular employees is also important in today's workplace. Approximately 27 percent of the workforce has flexible hours. When and where an employee does the job is becoming less important.[37] In addition, broad work–life balance initiatives have become a critical retention strategy. Managers are recognizing that people have personal needs that may require special attention. Some HR responses include benefits such as on-site gym facilities and childcare, assistance with arranging child- and eldercare, and paid leaves or sabbaticals. In some industries, the war for talent is intense, and companies can't afford to lose experienced and knowledgeable employees. Many European companies are miles ahead of U.S. firms in supporting work–life balance, as illustrated by the example in this chapter's Unlocking Creative Solutions Through People box.

## Downsizing

In some cases, organizations have more people than they need and have to let some employees go. **Downsizing** refers to an intentional, planned reduction in the size of a company's workforce. Some researchers have found that massive downsizing has often not achieved the intended benefits and in some cases has significantly harmed the organization.[38] Unless HRM departments manage the downsizing process, layoffs can lead to decreased morale and performance. Managers can smooth the downsizing process by regularly communicating with employees and providing them with as much information as possible, providing assistance to workers who will lose their jobs, and using training and development to help address the emotional needs of remaining employees and enable them to cope with new or additional responsibilities.[39]

These issues present many challenges for organizations and human resource management, such as new ways of recruiting and compensation that address the interests and needs of contingent and virtual workers, new training methods that help people work cross-functionally, or new ways to retain valuable employees. All of these concerns are taken into consideration as human resource managers work toward the three primary HR goals described earlier: attracting, developing, and maintaining an effective workforce.

INC. MAGAZINE, AUGUST 2004, P83

### CONCEPT CONNECTION

*This employee is working in the wiring room at Cobalt Boats, whose high-performance craft are widely admired as the Steinways of the runabout class. Cobalt builds its boat in Neodesha, Kansas, a town of 2,800 in the middle of the prairie, about as far from a lapping tide as one can get in America. But the location has a tremendous advantage—it enables Cobalt to attract an effective workforce, mostly second- and third-generation farmers who can no longer make a living from farming alone. These farm-toughened employees have a can-do attitude and an owner's mindset that matches perfectly with Cobalt's emphasis on individual initiative, ingenuity, and responsibility. Cobalt truly values its employees as "the finest boat builders in the world."*

**downsizing**
Intentional, planned reduction in the size of a company's workforce.

# Attracting an Effective Workforce

The first goal of HRM is to attract individuals who show signs of becoming valued, productive, and satisfied employees. The first step in attracting an effective workforce involves human resource planning, in which managers or HRM professionals predict the need for new employees based on the types of vacancies that

# Unlocking Creative Solutions Through People

## Norsk Hydro: Working Better by Working Less

Norwegians have always had a very different attitude than Americans about the meaning of work and its place in one's life. Their view is rooted in the notion of balance, and the idea that working less often means working better. As one of Norway's dominant institutions, Norsk Hydro has long been involved in innovative work approaches that enable employees to live a balanced life. Hydro operates in 70 countries and employs 39,000 people in businesses ranging from salmon farming, to fertilizers, to oil and metal. But despite its diverse businesses, the core values of the company haven't changed in its 95 years of operation. "What is deep in the culture of Hydro is to think in the long term, to think more holistically—to think about the connections between employees, the company, and society," says Roald Nomme, a consultant and former Hydro manager.

Today, Hydro is expanding its thinking about those connections further than ever before in a project called Hydroflex, which offers employees varying combinations of flexible hours, teamwork, home offices, new technology, and redesigned office space. For example, Atle Tærum, chief agronomist at Norsk Hydro, spends two days a week at home, where he tends to his farm and cares for his children. With his cell phone constantly within reach, Tærum may be consulting with customers from Africa or the Middle East while he's plowing a field or chaperoning his son's kindergarten class. Before the flexible arrangement, Tærum says he was tired and unhappy most of the time. "Now I can manage my day and my life a bit better. I think I'm doing a better job for Hydro." Another employee, Unni Foss, who works as a graphic artist at Hydro Media, was able to work at home full time during the months before her father's death, to be with him and help her mother. The arrangement allowed her to keep a job and salary she needed and enabled Hydro to get good work from a talented worker. "We used to focus on how many hours people were in the office," says Ole Johan Sagafos, the head of Hydro Media. "Now we focus on results. It doesn't really matter to me what my colleagues are doing as long as they deliver the results on time."

Hydro sees its work–life balance initiatives as critical strategic elements for remaining competitive. Offering people flexibility in terms of how, where, and when they work attracts better workers and makes them more productive. In addition, the initiatives promote flexibility and diversity of thinking that is critical for success in today's fast-paced world. Ragnhild Sohlberg, vice president of external relations and special projects, uses the analogy of an experienced farmer who knows better than to plant, harvest, plow, and reseed the same field season after season—he knows that the soil needs a period of time to rest and rejuvenate. Modern corporations, though, think nothing of working their most talented people ceaselessly until they burn out and leave. "And all their experience goes with them," she says. "It's lost. That practice is not good business."

**SOURCE:** Charles Fishman, "The Way to Enough," *Fast Company* (July–August 1999), 160–174.

---

exist, as illustrated in Exhibit 12.5. The second step is to use recruiting procedures to communicate with potential applicants. The third step is to select from the applicants those persons believed to be the best potential contributors to the organization. Finally, the new employee is welcomed into the organization.

**matching model**
An employee selection approach in which the organization and the applicant attempt to match each other's needs, interests, and values.

Underlying the organization's effort to attract employees is a matching model. With the matching model, the organization and the individual attempt to match the needs, interests, and values that they offer each other.[40] HRM professionals attempt to identify a correct match. For example, a small software developer might require long hours from creative, technically skilled employees. In return, it can offer freedom from bureaucracy, tolerance of idiosyncrasies, and potentially high pay. A large manufacturer can offer employment security and stability, but it might have more rules and regulations and require greater skills for "getting approval from the higher-ups." The individual who would thrive working for the software developer might feel stymied and unhappy working for a large manufacturer. Both the company and the employee are interested in finding a good match. A new approach, called *job sculpting*, attempts to match people to jobs that enable them to fulfill deeply embedded life interests.[41] This often requires that HR managers play

Exhibit 12.5

**Attracting an Effective Workforce**

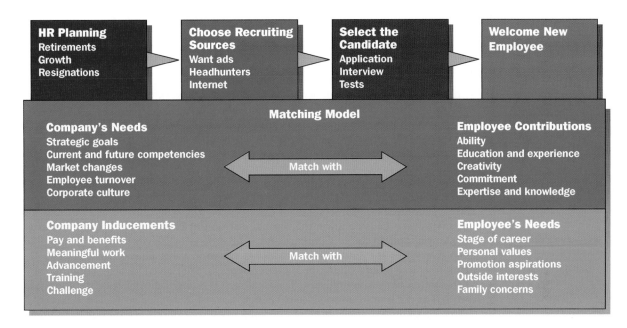

detective to find out what really makes a person happy. The idea is that people can fulfill deep-seated needs and interests on the job, which will induce them to stay with the organization.

## Human Resource Planning

Human resource planning is the forecasting of human resource needs and the projected matching of individuals with expected vacancies. Human resource planning begins with several questions:

- What new technologies are emerging, and how will these affect the work system?
- What is the volume of the business likely to be in the next five to ten years?
- What is the turnover rate, and how much, if any, is avoidable?

The responses to these questions are used to formulate specific questions pertaining to HR activities, such as the following:

- How many senior managers will we need during this time period?
- What types of engineers will we need, and how many?
- Are persons with adequate computer skills available for meeting our projected needs?
- How many administrative personnel—technicians, IT specialists—will we need to support the additional managers and engineers?
- Can we use temporary, contingent, or virtual workers to handle some tasks?[42]

Answers to these questions help define the direction for the organization's HRM strategy. For example, if forecasting suggests that there will be a strong need for more technically trained individuals, the organization can (1) define the jobs and skills needed in some detail, (2) hire and train recruiters to look for the specified

**human resource planning**
The forecasting of human resource needs and the projected matching of individuals with expected vacancies.

skills, and (3) provide new training for existing employees. By anticipating future HRM needs, the organization can prepare itself to meet competitive challenges more effectively than organizations that react to problems only as they arise.

One of the most successful applications of human resource planning is the Tennessee Valley Authority's development of an eight-step system.

**TVA**

http://www.tva.com

> In the confusion and uncertainty following a period of reorganization and downsizing, a crucial role for HRM is balancing the need for future workforce planning with the creation of a climate of stability for the remaining workers. TVA created an eight-step plan that assesses future HR needs and formulates actions to meet those needs. The first step is laying the groundwork for later implementation of the program by creating planning and oversight teams within each business unit. Step two involves assessing processes and functions that can be benchmarked. Step three involves projecting the skills and employee numbers (demand data) that will be necessary to reach goals within each business unit. Once these numbers are in place, step four involves projecting the current employee numbers (supply data) over the planning horizon without new hires and taking into consideration the normal attrition of staff through death, retirement, resignation, and so forth. Comparison of the difference between supply and demand (step five) gives the future gap or surplus situation. This knowledge enables HR to develop strategies and operational plans (step six). Step seven involves communicating of the action plan to employees. The final step is to periodically evaluate and update the plan as the organization's needs change.
>
> In a small organization, developing demand and supply data could be handled with a pad and a calculator. However, TVA uses a sophisticated automated system to update and revise the plan as needed to meet new competitive situations. Determining skills-gap and surplus information (step five) helped TVA develop a workforce plan to implement cross-organizational placement and retraining as alternatives to further employee cutbacks in the individual business units, thereby providing a greater sense of stability for workers. If needs change and TVA faces a demand for additional employees, this process will enable the company to recruit workers with the skills needed to help meet organizational goals.[43]

## Recruiting

**recruiting**
The activities or practices that define the desired characteristics of applicants for specific jobs.

Recruiting is defined as "activities or practices that define the characteristics of applicants to whom selection procedures are ultimately applied."[44] Although we frequently think of campus recruiting as a typical recruiting activity, many organizations use *internal recruiting*, or *promote-from-within* policies, to fill their high-level positions.[45] At Mellon Bank, for example, current employees are given preference when a position opens. Internal recruiting has several advantages: It is less costly than an external search, and it generates higher employee commitment, development, and satisfaction because it offers opportunities for career advancement to employees rather than outsiders.

Frequently, however, *external recruiting*—recruiting newcomers from outside the organization—is advantageous. Applicants are provided by a variety of outside sources including advertising, state employment services, private employment agencies (*headhunters*), job fairs, and employee referrals.

### Assessing Organizational Needs

**job analysis**
The systematic process of gathering and interpreting information about the essential duties, tasks, and responsibilities of a job.

An important step in recruiting is to get a clear picture of what kinds of people the organization needs. Basic building blocks of human resource management include job analysis, job descriptions, and job specifications. Job analysis is a systematic process of gathering and interpreting information about the essential duties, tasks, and responsibilities of a job, as well as about the context within which the job is performed.[46] To perform job analysis, managers or specialists ask about work activities and work flow, the degree of supervision given and received in the job, knowledge and skills needed, performance standards, working conditions, and so forth. The manager then prepares a written job description, which is a clear and concise summary of the specific tasks, duties, and responsibilities, and job specification, which outlines the knowledge, skills, education, physical abilities, and other characteristics needed to adequately perform the job.

Job analysis helps organizations recruit the right kind of people and match them to appropriate jobs. For example, to enhance internal recruiting, Sara Lee Corporation identified six functional areas and 24 significant skills that it wants its finance executives to develop, as illustrated in Exhibit 12.6. Managers are tracked on their development and moved into other positions to help them acquire the needed skills.[47]

## Realistic Job Previews

Job analysis also helps enhance recruiting effectiveness by enabling the creation of realistic job previews. A realistic job preview gives applicants all pertinent and realistic information—positive and negative—about the job and the organization.[48] RJPs enhance employee satisfaction and reduce turnover, because they facilitate matching individuals, jobs, and organizations. Individuals have a better basis on which to determine their suitability to the organization and "self-select" into or out of positions based on full information.

## Legal Considerations

Organizations must ensure that their recruiting practices conform to the law. As discussed earlier in this chapter, equal employment opportunity (EEO) laws stipulate that recruiting and hiring decisions cannot discriminate on the basis of race, national origin, religion, or gender. The Americans with Disabilities Act underscored the

**job description**
A concise summary of the specific tasks and responsibilities of a particular job.

**job specification**
An outline of the knowledge, skills, education, and physical abilities needed to adequately perform a job.

**realistic job preview**
A recruiting approach that gives applicants all pertinent and realistic information about the job and the organization.

## Exhibit 12.6

### Sara Lee's Required Skills for Finance Executives

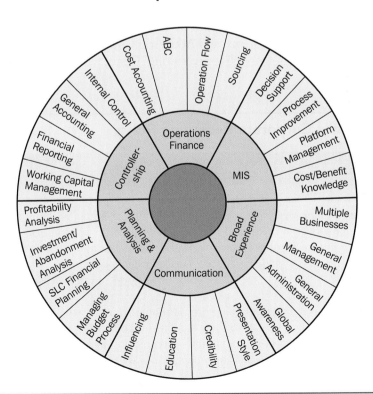

**SOURCE:** Victoria Griffith, "When Only Internal Expertise Will Do," *CFO* (October 1998), 95–96, 102.

## CONCEPT CONNECTION

*This ad from* Black Enterprise *magazine enhances external recruiting by giving potential applicants a realistic job preview. The applicant must possess critical skills such as speaking a foreign language, have a four-year college degree plus three years of professional work experience, be willing to live anywhere on assignment, be between the ages of 23 and 36, and be able to pass "a rigorous physical fitness test." If you possess these requirements, you can even apply online at http://www.fbijobs.com.*

need for well-written job descriptions and specifications that accurately reflect the mental and physical dimensions of jobs. *Affirmative action* refers to the use of goals, timetables, or other methods in recruiting to promote the hiring, development, and retention of *protected groups*—persons historically underrepresented in the workplace. For example, a city might establish a goal of recruiting one black firefighter for every white firefighter until the proportion of black firefighters is commensurate with the black population in the community.

Most large companies try to comply with affirmative action and EEO guidelines. Prudential Insurance Company's policy is presented in Exhibit 12.7. Prudential actively recruits employees and takes affirmative action steps to recruit individuals from all walks of life.

### E-cruiting

One of the fastest-growing approaches to recruiting is use of the Internet, which dramatically extends an organization's recruiting reach.[49] Although traditional recruiting methods such as print advertisements and job fairs work quite well for many companies, e-cruiting, or recruiting job applicants online, offers access to a wider pool of applicants and can save time and money. In addition to posting job openings on company Web sites, many organizations use commercial recruiting sites such as Monster.com, CareerBuilder.com and hotjobs.com. where job seekers can post their résumés and companies can search for qualified applicants. Forrester Research reports that approximately 2.5 million résumés are posted online, and the number is growing.[50]

Companies as diverse as Prudential Insurance, Cisco Systems, and Atkinsson Congregational Church have used the Web for recruiting. Cisco, which gets about 66 percent

Exhibit 12.7

## Prudential's Corporate Recruiting Policy

### An Equal Opportunity Employer

Prudential recruits, hires, trains, promotes, and compensates individuals without regard to race, color, religion or creed, age, sex, marital status, national origin, ancestry, liability for service in the armed forces of the United States, status as a special disabled veteran or veteran of the Vietnam era, or physical or mental handicap.

This is official company policy because:  • we believe it is right
                                         • it makes good business sense
                                         • it is the law

We are also committed to an ongoing program of affirmative action in which members of under-represented groups are actively sought out and employed for opportunities in all parts and at all levels of the company. In employing people from all walks of life, Prudential gains access to the full experience of our diverse society.

**SOURCE:** Prudential Insurance Company

of new hires from the Web, claims that e-cruiting has cut the time it takes to fill a job from 113 days down to 45 days.[51] Costs go down, too. The Employee Management Association estimates that the cost per hire using Internet recruiting is $377, versus $3,295 per hire using print media.[52] Organizations have not given up their traditional recruiting strategies, but the Internet has given HR managers new tools for searching the world to find the best available talent. The do-it-yourself retail giant B & Q combines e-cruiting with psychometric testing to quickly eliminate unsuitable candidates and build a database of potential applicants.

B & Q, the United Kingdom's version of The Home Depot, grew in eight years from 0 to 100 warehouse stores that employ about 250 staff members. In addition, the company has numerous supercenters that employ 40-60 staff members each. B & Q is creating about 1,000 new management positions and 5,000 staff and shopfloor jobs each year through the opening of new stores. With such rapid growth comes the problem of finding good people.

B & Q uses a unique recruiting tool, online pyschometric testing. The recruiting strategy has been used for all management applicants since July of 2002 and was later extended to applicants for any position. Applicants answer a series of questions that were developed over the course of seven years by Colin Gill, chief psychologist at Psychological Solutions. Much of Gill's research was done with B & Q staff, so executives believe the instrument is a good indicator of whether a person will succeed at the company. The test is assessed immediately by complex formulae that rate an applicant's suitability for the job. For some applicants, this serves as a self-selecting mechanism because the applicant sees that he or she will not be happy working in the B & Q culture.

Top executives also like the unbiased nature of the online recruiting tool. Our image of candidates used to be founded on their [résumé]," says HR Director Mike Cutt. Now the initial screening is done blind, it is totally unbiased as to age, gender, and ethnic background. We think that's a big step forward in systematically avoiding the bias you would get in any recruitment drive."

By streamlining and eliminating bias during the initial stage of recruitment, the online recruiting system has helped B & Q dramatically improve the quality of its candidates. Cutt also thinks it has helped the company spot employee talent and potential earlier and more carefully align training and career development activities.[53]

B & Q
**http://www.diy.com**

## Other Recent Approaches to Recruiting

Organizations are also finding other ways to enhance their recruiting success. One highly effective approach is getting referrals from current employees. A company's employees often know of someone who would be qualified for a position and fit in with the organization's culture. Many organizations offer cash awards to employees who submit names of people who subsequently accept employment, because referral by current employees is one of the cheapest and most reliable methods of external recruiting.[54] The professional service firm Deloitte has shelled out more than $3.5 million in cash awards to employees who refer candidates through the "Refer Potential Movers and Shakers" program, the firm's single best source of high-talent hires.[55]

In addition, some companies turn to nontraditional sources to find dedicated employees, particularly when there is a tight labor market. Manufacturer Dee Zee, which makes aluminum truck accessories in a factory in Des Moines, Iowa, found a source of loyal, hard-working employees among refugees from Bosnia, Vietnam, and Kosovo.[56] Since 1998, Bank of America has hired and trained more than 3,000 former welfare recipients in positions that offer the potential for promotions and long-term careers. Days Inn has experimented with hiring the homeless, offering them wages plus a room for a small fee. Recruiting on a global basis is on the rise, as well. Public schools are recruiting teachers from overseas. High-tech companies are looking for qualified workers in foreign countries because they cannot find people with the right skills in the United States.[57]

## Selecting

**selection**
The process of determining the skills, abilities, and other attributes a person needs to perform a particular job.

The next step for managers is to select desired employees from the pool of recruited applicants. In the selection process, employers assess applicants' characteristics in an attempt to determine the "fit" between the job and applicant characteristics. Several selection devices are used for assessing applicant qualifications. The most frequently used are the application form, interview, employment test, and assessment center. Human resource professionals may use a combination of these devices to obtain a valid prediction of employee job performance. Validity refers to the relationship between one's score on a selection device and one's future job performance. A valid selection procedure will provide high scores that correspond to subsequent high job performance.

**validity**
The relationship between an applicant's score on a selection device and his or her future job performance.

### Application Form

**application form**
A device for collecting information about an applicant's education, previous job experience, and other background characteristics.

The application form is used to collect information about the applicant's education, previous job experience, and other background characteristics. Research in the life insurance industry shows that biographical information inventories can validly predict future job success.[58]

One pitfall to be avoided is the inclusion of questions that are irrelevant to job success. In line with affirmative action, the application form should not ask questions that will create an adverse impact on protected groups unless the questions are clearly related to the job.[59] For example, employers should not ask whether the applicant rents or owns his or her own home because (1) an applicant's response might adversely affect his or her chances at the job, (2) minorities and women may be less likely to own a home, and (3) home ownership is probably unrelated to job performance. By contrast, the CPA exam is relevant to job performance in a CPA firm; thus, it is appropriate to ask whether an applicant for employment has passed the CPA exam, even if only one-half of all female or minority applicants have done so versus nine-tenths of male applicants.

### Interview

The *interview* serves as a two-way communication channel that allows both the organization and the applicant to collect information that would otherwise be difficult to obtain. This selection technique is used in almost every job category in nearly every organization. This is another area where the organization can get into legal trouble if the interviewer asks questions that violate EEO guidelines. Exhibit 12.8 lists some examples of appropriate and inappropriate interview questions.

Although widely used, the interview is not generally a valid predictor of job performance. Studies of interviewing have suggested that people tend to make snap judgments of others within the first few seconds of meeting them and only rarely change their opinions based on anything that occurs in the interview.[60] However, the interview as a selection tool has high *face validity*. That is, it seems valid to employers, and managers prefer to hire someone only after they have been through some form of interview, preferably face-to-face. The Manager's Shoptalk offers some tips for effective interviewing and provides a humorous look at some interview blunders. Today's organizations are trying different approaches to overcome the limitations of the interview. Some put candidates through a series of interviews, each one conducted by a different person and each one probing a different aspect of the candidate. Other companies, including Virginia Power and Philip Morris USA, use *panel interviews*, in which the candidate meets with several interviewers who take turns asking questions,

Exhibit 12.8

## Employment Applications and Interviews: What Can You Ask?

| Category | Okay to Ask | Inappropriate or Illegal to Ask |
|---|---|---|
| National origin | • The applicant's name<br>• If applicant has ever worked under a different name | • The origin of applicant's name<br>• Applicant's ancestry/ethnicity |
| Race | • Nothing | • Race or color of skin |
| Disabilities | • Whether applicant has any disabilities that might inhibit performance of job | • If applicant has any physical or mental defects<br>• If applicant has ever filed workers' compensation claim |
| Age | • If applicant is over 18 | • Applicant's age<br>• When applicant graduated from high school |
| Religion | • Nothing | • Applicant's religious affiliation<br>• What religious holidays applicant observes |
| Criminal record | • If applicant has ever been convicted of a crime | • If applicant has ever been arrested |
| Marital/ family status | • Nothing | • Marital status, number of children or planned children<br>• Childcare arrangements |
| Education and Experience | • Where applicant went to school<br>• Prior work experience | • When applicant graduated<br>• Hobbies |
| Citizenship | • If applicant has a legal right to work in the United States | • If applicant is a citizen of another country |

**SOURCES**: Based on "Appropriate and Inappropriate Interview Questions," in George Bohlander, Scott Snell, and Arthur Sherman, *Managing Human Resources*, 12th ed. (Cincinnati, Ohio: South-Western, 2001), 207; and "Guidelines to Lawful and Unlawful Preemployment Inquiries," Appendix E, in Robert L. Mathis and John H. Jackson, *Human Resource Management*, 2nd ed., (Cincinnati, Ohio: South-Western, 2002), 189–190.

to increase interview validity.[61] Microsoft and other high-tech companies often use puzzle questions, riddles, or other tricky queries to assess a candidate's creativity, problem-solving skills, and ability to think under pressure. Typical questions might include: "Why are manhole covers round rather than square?" or "How would you weigh a jet plane without using a scale?"[62] The idea is that people who can successfully handle these types of questions are more adept at solving the problems high-tech companies face in today's turbulent business environment.

Some organizations also use *computer-based interviews* to complement traditional interviewing information. These typically require a candidate to answer a series of multiple-choice questions tailored to the specific job. The answers are compared to an ideal profile or to a profile developed on the basis of other candidates. Companies such as Pinkerton Security, Coopers & Lybrand, and Pic n' Pay Shoe Stores have found computer-based interviews to be valuable for searching out information regarding the applicant's honesty, work attitude, drug history, candor, dependability, and self-motivation.[63]

## Employment Test

Employment tests may include intelligence tests, aptitude and ability tests, and personality inventories, particularly those shown to be valid predictors. Many companies

**employment test**
A written or computer-based test designed to measure a particular attribute such as intelligence or aptitude.

# manager's Shoptalk

### The Right Way to Interview a Job Applicant

A so-so interview usually nets a so-so employee. Many hiring mistakes can be prevented during the interview. The following techniques will ensure a successful interview:

1. *Know what you want.* Before the interview, prepare questions based on your knowledge of the job to be filled.

2. *Prepare a road map.* Develop questions that will reveal whether the candidate has the correct background and qualifications. The questions should focus on previous experiences that are relevant to the current job.

3. *Use open-ended questions in which the right answer is not obvious.* Ask the applicant to give specific examples of previous work experiences. For example, don't ask, "Are you a hard worker?" or "Tell me about yourself." Instead ask, "Can you give me examples from your previous work history that reflect your level of motivation?" or "How did you go about getting your current job?"

4. *Do not ask questions that are irrelevant to the job.* This is particularly important when the irrelevant questions might adversely affect minorities or women.

5. *Listen; don't talk.* You should spend most of the interview listening. If you talk too much, the focus will shift to you, and you might miss important cues. One expert actually recommends stating all your questions right at the beginning of the interview. This forces you to sit back and listen and also gives you a chance to watch a candidate's behavior and body language.

6. *Allow enough time so that the interview will not be rushed.* Leave time for the candidate to ask questions about the job. The types of questions the candidate asks can be an important clue to his or her interest in the job.

7. *Avoid reliance on your memory.* Request the applicant's permission to take notes; then do so unobtrusively during the interview or immediately after.

Even a well-planned interview may be disrupted by the unexpected. Here are some of the unusual things that have happened during job interviews, based on surveys of vice-presidents and human resource directors at major U.S. corporations:

- The applicant announced she hadn't had lunch and proceeded to eat a hamburger and french fries in the interviewer's office.
- When asked if he had any questions about the job, the candidate answered, "Can I get an advance on my paycheck?"
- The applicant chewed bubble gum and constantly blew bubbles.
- The job candidate said the main thing he was looking for in a job was a quiet place where no one would bother him.
- The job applicant challenged the interviewer to arm wrestle.
- The applicant dozed off and started snoring during the interview.
- When asked how she would handle a difficult situation, the candidate replied, "I'd let you do it."

SOURCES: James M. Jenks and Brian L. P. Zevnik, "ABCs of Job Interviewing," *Harvard Business Review* (July–August 1989), 38–42; Dr. Pierre Mornell, "Zero Defect Hiring," *Inc,* (March 1998), 75–83; Martha H. Peak, "What Color Is Your Bumbershoot?" *Management Review* (October 1989), 63; and Meridith Levinson, "How to Hire So You Don't Have to Fire," *CIO* (March 1, 2004), 72–80.

today are particularly interested in personality inventories that measure such characteristics as openness to learning, initiative, responsibility, creativity, and emotional stability. Brian Kautz of Arnold Logistics has used a Web-based personality assessment called the Predictive Index (PI) to hire six people in Arnold's IT department since 2001, and all six still work at the company. The PI, originally developed in the 1950s, provides information about the working conditions that are most rewarding to an applicant and that make the person the most motivated and productive. The test is based on the notion that different types of jobs require different personality characteristics and behaviors.[64]

### Assessment Center

First developed by psychologists at AT&T, assessment centers are used to select individuals with high potential for managerial careers by such organizations as IBM, General Electric, and JCPenney.[65] Assessment centers present a series of managerial situations to groups of applicants over, say, a two- or three-day period. One technique is the *in-basket simulation*, which requires the applicant to play the role of a manager who must decide how to respond to ten memos in his or her in-basket within a two-hour period. Panels of two or three trained judges observe the applicant's decisions and assess the extent to which they reflect interpersonal, communication, and problem-solving skills.

Assessment centers have proven to be valid predictors of managerial success, and some organizations now use them for hiring front-line workers as well. Mercury Communications in England uses an assessment center to select telecommunications customer assistants. Applicants participate in simulated exercises with customers and in various other exercises designed to assess their listening skills, customer sensitivity, and ability to cope under pressure.[66] Many organizations also work with consulting companies such as Development Dimensions International, which makes extensive use of assessments to help fill jobs—whether it be a supermarket checker or a CEO—with the right people. DDI works closely with clients to determine what skills and competencies are needed for the job and designs the assessment exercises to assess those specific areas.[67]

**assessment center**
A technique for selecting individuals with high managerial potential based on their performances on a series of simulated managerial tasks.

# Developing an Effective Workforce

Following selection, the next goal of HRM is to develop employees into an effective workforce. Development includes training and performance appraisal.

## Training and Development

*Training and development* represent a planned effort by an organization to facilitate employees' learning of job-related skills and behaviors.[68] Organizations spend nearly $100 billion each year on training. Training may occur in a variety of forms. The most common method is on-the-job training. In on-the-job training (OJT), an experienced employee is asked to take a new employee "under his or her wing" and show the newcomer how to perform job duties. OJT has many advantages, such as few out-of-pocket costs for training facilities, materials, or instructor fees and easy transfer of learning back to the job. When implemented well, OJT is considered the fastest and most effective means of facilitating learning in the workplace.[69] One type of on-the-job training involves moving people to various types of jobs within the organization, where they work with experienced employees to learn different tasks. This *cross-training* may place an employee in a new position for as short a time as a

**on-the-job training (OJT)**
A type of training in which an experienced employee "adopts" a new employee to teach him or her how to perform job duties.

few hours or for as long as a year, enabling the employee to develop new skills and giving the organization greater flexibility.

Another type of on-the-job training is *mentoring*, which means a more experienced employee is paired with a newcomer or a less-experienced worker to provide guidance, support, and learning opportunities. An innovative program at General Electric has turned the mentoring relationship upside down, pairing older, senior executives with little or no computer knowledge and expertise with young, computer and Internet-savvy employees to help the old-timers learn about the world of e-business.[70]

Other frequently used training methods include the following:

- *Orientation training*, in which newcomers are introduced to the organization's culture, standards, and goals
- *Classroom training*, including lectures, films, audiovisual techniques, and simulations
- *Self-directed learning*, also called programmed instruction, which involves the use of books, manuals, or computers to provide subject matter in highly organized and logical sequences that require employees to answer a series of questions about the material
- *Computer-based training*, sometimes called *e-training*, including computer-assisted instruction, Web-based training, and teletraining. (As with self-directed learning, the employee works at his or her own pace and instruction is individualized, but the training program is interactive and more complex, nonstructured information can be communicated.)

Exhibit 12.9 shows the most frequently used types and methods of training in today's organizations.

## Corporate Universities

A recent popular approach to training and development is the corporate university. A corporate university is an in-house training and education facility that offers broad-based learning opportunities for employees—and frequently for customers, suppliers, and strategic partners as well—throughout their careers.[71] The number of corporate universities ballooned during the 1990s, with more than 2,000 in operation by 2001. With the economic decline of the early 2000s, many companies cut budgets for training, but smart managers at places like Intel, Harley-Davidson, and Capital One kept pumping money into their corporate universities to keep building human capital.[72] Perhaps the most well-known example of a corporate university is Hamburger University, McDonald's worldwide training center, which has been in existence for more than 40 years. Tens of thousands of FedEx employees, from couriers to top executives, have attended training at the company's Leadership Institute located near Memphis, Tennessee. And the U.S. Department of Defense runs Defense Acquisition University to provide ongoing training to129,000 military and civilian workers in acquisitions, technology, and logistics.[73] Although corporate universities have extended their reach with new technology that enables distance learning via videoconferencing and online education, most emphasize the importance of classroom interaction. Participants at a recent corporate university conference indicated that they try to keep electronic forms of learning to about 25 percent of their course offerings.[74]

## Promotion from Within

Another way to further employee development is through promotion from within, which can help companies retain valuable employees. This provides challenging assignments, prescribes new responsibilities, and helps employees grow by expanding

**corporate university**
An in-house training and education facility that offers broad-based learning opportunities for employees.

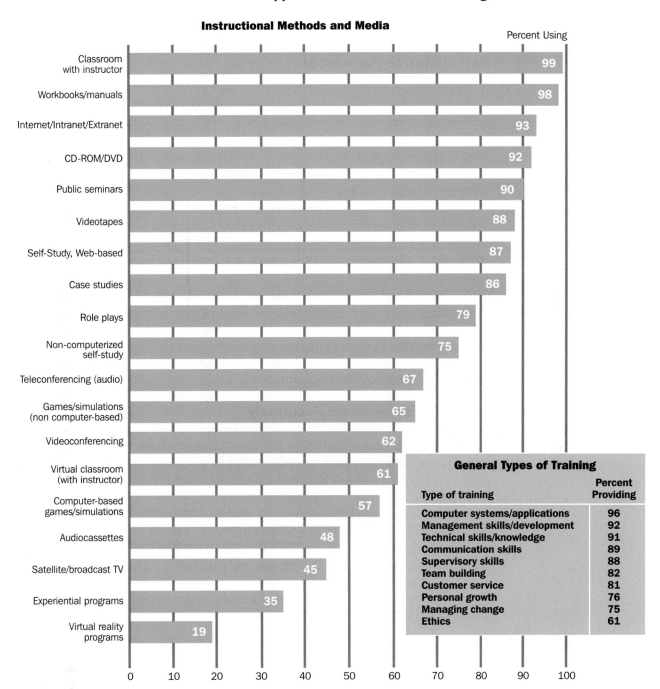

Exhibit 12.9

**Types and Methods of Training**

SOURCE: Data from Tammy Galvin, "2003 Industry Report," *Training* (October 2003): 21+. Reprinted with permission from the October 2003 issue of *Training* magazine, Copyright 2003, Bill Communications, Minneapolis, Minn. All rights reserved. Not for resale.

and developing their abilities. The Peebles Hydro Hotel in Scotland is passionate about promoting from within as a way to retain good people and give them opportunities for growth. A maid has been promoted to head housekeeper, a wine waitress to restaurant head, and a student worker to deputy manager. The hotel also provides constant training in all areas. These techniques, combined with a commitment to job flexibility, have helped the hotel retain high-quality workers at a time when others in the tourism and hospitality industry are suffering from a shortage of skilled labor. Isobelle Nairn started at Hydro 24 years ago as a receptionist and is still there, organizing 350 conferences a year as the hotel's conference coordinator. Staff members with 10, 15, or 20 years of service aren't uncommon at Hydro.[75]

## Performance Appraisal

Performance appraisal is another important technique for developing an effective workforce. Performance appraisal comprises the steps of observing and assessing employee performance, recording the assessment, and providing feedback to the employee. During performance appraisal, skillful managers give feedback and praise concerning the acceptable elements of the employee's performance. They also describe performance areas that need improvement. Employees can use this information to change their job performance.

Performance appraisal can also reward high performers with merit pay, recognition, and other rewards. However, the most recent thinking is that linking performance appraisal to rewards has unintended consequences. The idea is that performance appraisal should be ongoing, not something that is done once a year as part of a consideration of raises.

Generally, HRM professionals concentrate on two things to make performance appraisal a positive force in their organizations: (1) the accurate assessment of performance through the development and application of assessment systems such as rating scales and (2) training managers to effectively use the performance appraisal interview, so managers can provide feedback that will reinforce good performance and motivate employee development.

### Assessing Performance Accurately

To obtain an accurate performance rating, managers acknowledge that jobs are multidimensional and performance thus may be multidimensional as well. For example, a sports broadcaster may perform well on the job-knowledge dimension; that is, she or he may be able to report facts and figures about the players and describe which rule applies when there is a questionable play on the field. But the same sports broadcaster may not perform as well on another dimension, such as communication. She or he may be unable to express the information in a colorful way that interests the audience or may interrupt the other broadcasters.

If performance is to be rated accurately, the performance appraisal system should require the rater to assess each relevant performance dimension. A multidimensional form increases the usefulness of the performance appraisal and facilitates employee growth and development.

A recent trend in performance appraisal is called 360-degree feedback, a process that uses multiple raters, including self-rating, as a way to increase awareness of strengths and weaknesses and guide employee development. Members of the appraisal group may include supervisors, co-workers, and customers, as well as the individual, thus providing appraisal of the employee from a variety of perspectives.[76] One study found that 26 percent of companies used some type of multirater performance appraisal in 2000, up from 11 percent in 1995.[77]

Other alternative performance-evaluation methods have also been gaining ground. One controversial method of evaluating managers, which is nevertheless growing in popularity, is the *performance review ranking system*.[78] As most commonly used, a manager evaluates his or her direct reports relative to one another and categorizes each on a scale, such as A = outstanding performance, B = high-middle performance, or C = in need of improvement. Most companies routinely fire those

**performance appraisal**
The process of observing and evaluating an employee's performance, recording the assessment, and providing feedback to the employee.

**360-degree feedback**
A process that uses multiple raters, including self-rating, to appraise employee performance and guide development.

managers falling in the bottom 10 percent of the ranking. Capital One, Ford Motor Company, Cisco Systems, Intel, General Electric, Microsoft, and Sun Microsystems all use versions of the ranking system. Proponents say the technique provides an effective way to assess performance and offer guidance for employee development. But critics of these systems, sometimes called *rank and yank*, argue that they are based on subjective judgments, produce skewed results, and discriminate against employees who are "different" from the mainstream. A class-action lawsuit charges that Ford's ranking system discriminates against older managers. Use of the system has also triggered employee lawsuits at Conoco and Microsoft, and employment lawyers warn that other suits will follow.[79] Nevertheless, appropriate use of performance ranking has been useful for many companies. A variation of the system is helping Applebee's retain quality workers in the high-turnover restaurant business.

Most people working in fast-food and casual dining restaurants don't stay very long. Turnover of hourly employees is a perpetual problem, averaging more than 200 percent a year in the casual dining sector for the past 30 years. Applebee's managers wanted to reduce their turnover rate, but they also wanted to focus their retention efforts on the best people.

A key aspect of the new retention strategy was the Applebee's Performance Management system, called ApplePM. ApplePM took performance appraisal to the Web, making it easier for managers to complete the evaluations and—more importantly—put the results to good use. Twice a year each hourly employee conducts a self-evaluation that covers nine areas: appearance, reliability, fun (including the ability to tolerate frustration), ability, guest service, willingness to be a team player, initiative, stamina, and cooperation. The store manager does the same for each employee; then they meet, compare results, and discuss areas for improvement. But the feedback loop doesn't end there. With a few mouse clicks the manager looks at how each employee ranks with respect to all others in the restaurant, separating employees into the top 20 percent, the middle 60 percent, and the bottom 20 percent.

The system is not the basis for firing low-ranking employees, but they usually leave soon enough anyway. Its value lies in helping managers focus their retention efforts on the top 20 percent, who have management potential, and provide training and development opportunities to the middle 60 percent, who have the potential to move up the ranking. Concentrating on certain employees is paying off for Applebee's. The turnover rate dropped almost 50 percentage points within less than two years.[80]

## Performance Evaluation Errors

Although we would like to believe that every manager assesses employees' performance in a careful and bias-free manner, researchers have identified several rating problems.[81] One of the most dangerous is stereotyping, which occurs when a rater places an employee into a class or category based on one or a few traits or characteristics—for example, stereotyping an older worker as slower and more difficult to train. Another rating error is the halo effect, in which a manager gives an employee the same rating on all dimensions even if his or her performance is good on some dimensions and poor on others.

One approach to overcome performance evaluation errors is to use a behavior-based rating technique, such as the behaviorally anchored rating scale. The behaviorally anchored rating scale (BARS) is developed from critical incidents pertaining to job performance. Each job performance scale is anchored with specific behavioral statements that describe varying degrees of performance. By relating employee performance to specific incidents, raters can more accurately evaluate an employee's performance.[82]

Exhibit 12.10 illustrates the BARS method for evaluating a production line supervisor. The production supervisor's job can be broken down into several dimensions, such as equipment maintenance, employee training, or work scheduling. A

**stereotyping**
Placing an employee into a class or category based on one or a few traits or characteristics.

**halo effect**
A type of rating error that occurs when an employee receives the same rating on all dimensions regardless of his or her performance on individual ones.

**behaviorally anchored rating scale (BARS)**
A rating technique that relates an employee's performance to specific job-related incidents.

behaviorally anchored rating scale should be developed for each dimension. The dimension in Exhibit 12.10 is work scheduling. Good performance is represented by a 4 or 5 on the scale and unacceptable performance as a 1 or 2. If a production supervisor's job has eight dimensions, the total performance evaluation will be the sum of the scores for each of eight scales.

# Maintaining an Effective Workforce

Now we turn to the topic of how managers and HRM professionals maintain a workforce that has been recruited and developed. Maintenance of the current workforce involves compensation, wage and salary systems, benefits, and occasional terminations.

## Compensation

**compensation**
Monetary payments (wages, salaries) and nonmonetary goods/commodities (benefits, vacations) used to reward employees.

The term compensation refers to (1) all monetary payments and (2) all goods or commodities used in lieu of money to reward employees.[83] An organization's compensation structure includes wages and/or salaries and benefits such as health insurance, paid vacations, or employee fitness centers. Developing an effective compensation system is an important part of human resource management because it helps to attract and retain talented workers. In addition, a company's compensation system has an impact on strategic performance.[84] Human resource managers design the pay and benefits systems to fit company strategy and to provide compensation equity.

Exhibit **12.10**

### Example of a Behaviorally Anchored Rating Scale

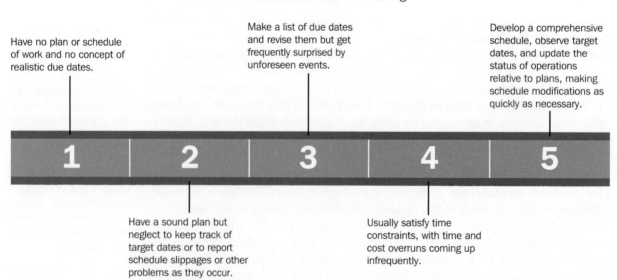

**Job:** Production Line Supervisor
**Work Dimension:** Work Scheduling

Have no plan or schedule of work and no concept of realistic due dates.

Make a list of due dates and revise them but get frequently surprised by unforeseen events.

Develop a comprehensive schedule, observe target dates, and update the status of operations relative to plans, making schedule modifications as quickly as necessary.

1     2     3     4     5

Have a sound plan but neglect to keep track of target dates or to report schedule slippages or other problems as they occur.

Usually satisfy time constraints, with time and cost overruns coming up infrequently.

**SOURCES**: Based on J. P. Campbell, M. D. Dunnette, R. D. Arvey, and L. V. Hellervik, "The Development and Evaluation of Behaviorally Based Rating Scales," *Journal of Applied Psychology* 57 (1973), 15–22; and Francine Alexander, "Performance Appraisals," *Small Business Reports* (March 1989), 20–29.

## Wage and Salary Systems

Ideally, management's strategy for the organization should be a critical determinant of the features and operations of the pay system.[85] For example, managers may have the goal of maintaining or improving profitability or market share by stimulating employee performance. Thus, they should design and use a merit pay system rather than a system based on other criteria such as seniority.

The most common approach to employee compensation is *job-based pay*, which means linking compensation to the specific tasks an employee performs. However, these systems present several problems. For one thing, job-based pay may fail to reward the type of learning behavior needed for the organization to adapt and survive in today's environment. In addition, these systems reinforce an emphasis on organizational hierarchy and centralized decision making and control, which are inconsistent with the growing emphasis on employee participation and increased responsibility.[86]

*Skill-based pay systems* are becoming increasingly popular in both large and small companies, including Sherwin-Williams, au Bon Pain, and Quaker Oats. Employees with higher skill levels receive higher pay than those with lower skill levels. At Quaker Oats pet food plant in Topeka, Kansas, for example, employees start at $8.75 per hour but can reach a top hourly rate of $14.50 when they master a series of skills.[87] Also called *competency-based pay*, skill-based pay systems encourage employees to develop their skills and competencies, thus making them more valuable to the organization as well as more employable if they leave their current jobs.

## Compensation Equity

Whether the organization uses job-based pay or skill-based pay, good managers strive to maintain a sense of fairness and equity within the pay structure and thereby fortify employee morale. Job evaluation refers to the process of determining the value or worth of jobs within an organization through an examination of job content. Job evaluation techniques enable managers to compare similar and dissimilar jobs and to determine internally equitable pay rates—that is, pay rates that employees believe are fair compared with those for other jobs in the organization.

Organizations also want to make sure their pay rates are fair compared to other companies. HRM managers may obtain wage and salary surveys that show what other organizations pay incumbents in jobs that match a sample of "key" jobs selected by the organization. These surveys are available from a number of sources, including the U.S. Bureau of Labor Statistics National Compensation Survey.

## Pay for Performance

Many of today's organizations develop compensation plans based on a *pay-for-performance standard* to raise productivity and cut labor costs in a competitive global environment. Pay-for-performance, also called *incentive pay*, means tying at least part of compensation to employee effort and performance, whether it be through merit-based pay, bonuses, team incentives, or various gainsharing or profit-sharing plans. Data show that, while growth in base wages is slowing in many industries, the use of pay-for-performance has steadily increased since the early 1990s, with approximately 70 percent of companies now offering some form of incentive pay.[88] The U.S. Congress and President Bush have recently called for implementing performance-based pay in agencies of the federal government. The seniority-based pay system used by most federal agencies has come under intense scrutiny in recent years, with critics arguing that it creates an environment where poor performers tend to stay and the best and brightest leave out of frustration. A survey conducted by the Office of Personnel Management found that only one in four federal employees believe adequate steps are taken to deal with poor performers,

**job evaluation**
The process of determining the value of jobs within an organization through an examination of job content.

**wage and salary surveys**
Surveys that show what other organizations pay incumbents in jobs that match a sample of "key" jobs selected by the organization.

**pay-for-performance**
Incentive pay that ties at least part of compensation to employee effort and performance.

and only two in five think strong performers are appropriately recognized and rewarded.[89]

With pay for performance, incentives are aligned with the behaviors needed to help the organization achieve its strategic goals. Employees have an incentive to make the company more efficient and profitable because if goals are not met, no bonuses are paid.

## Benefits

The best human resource managers know that a compensation package requires more than money. Although wage and salary is an important component, it is only a part. Equally important are the benefits offered by the organization. Benefits make up 40 percent of labor costs in the United States.[90]

Some benefits are required by law, such as Social Security, unemployment compensation, and workers' compensation. In addition, companies with 50 or more employees are required by the Family and Medical Leave Act to give up to twelve weeks of unpaid leave for such things as the birth or adoption of a child, the serious illness of a spouse or family member, or an employee's serious illness. Other types of benefits, such as health insurance, vacations, and such things as on-site day care or fitness centers are not required by law but are provided by organizations to maintain an effective workforce.

One reason that benefits make up such a large portion of the compensation package is that health-care costs have been increasing so quickly. Many organizations are requiring that employees absorb a greater share of the cost of medical benefits, such as through higher co-payments and deductibles.

Computerization has cut the time and expense of administering benefits programs tremendously. At companies such as Wells Fargo and LG&E Energy, employees access their benefits package through an intranet, creating a "self-service" benefits administration.[91] This also enables employees to change their benefits selections easily. Today's organizations realize that the "one-size-fits-all" benefits package is no longer appropriate, so they frequently offer *cafeteria-plan benefits packages* that allow employees to select the benefits of greatest value to them.[92] Other companies use surveys to determine which combination of fixed benefits is

### CONCEPT CONNECTION

*Talk about* benefits*! At ArchivesOne, a records-storage business in Waterbury, Connecticut, employees like Brian Smith (right) appreciate perks such as tuition reimbursement, professional training, and raffles of prizes like DVD players. But when CEO A.J. Wasserstein (left) loaned Smith $5,000 at 2% interest to help him buy his new home, Smith was sold on managing the company's Watertown facility. If Smith stays for five or more years, the principal will be forgiven. Wasserstein says the program helps retain valuable employees and has lowered the annual turnover rate from about 20% to 14%.*

© EVAN KAFKA

most desirable. The benefits packages provided by large companies attempt to meet the needs of all employees.

## Termination

Despite the best efforts of line managers and HRM professionals, the organization will lose employees. Some will retire, others will depart voluntarily for other jobs, and still others will be forced out through mergers and cutbacks or for poor performance.

*Go to the ethical dilemma on page 458 that pertains to termination of employees for poor performance.*

*Take A Moment*

The value of termination for maintaining an effective workforce is twofold. First, employees who are poor performers can be dismissed. Productive employees often resent disruptive, low-performing employees who are allowed to stay with the company and receive pay and benefits comparable to theirs. Second, employers can use exit interviews as a valuable HR tool, regardless of whether the employee leaves voluntarily or is forced out. An exit interview is an interview conducted with departing employees to determine why they are leaving. The value of the exit interview is to provide an excellent and inexpensive way to learn about pockets of dissatisfaction within the organization and hence reduce future turnover.

**exit interview**
An interview conducted with departing employees to determine the reasons for their termination.

When companies experience downsizing through mergers or because of global competition or a shifting economy, often a large number of managers and workers are terminated at the same time. In these cases, enlightened companies try to find a smooth transition for departing employees. For example, General Electric laid off employees in three gradual steps. It also set up a reemployment center to assist employees in finding new jobs or in learning new skills. It provided counseling in how to write a résumé and conduct a job search. Additionally, General Electric placed an advertisement in local newspapers saying that these employees were available.[93] By showing genuine concern in helping laid-off employees, a company communicates the value of human resources and helps maintain a positive corporate culture.

© ELENA DORFMAN—MATRIX

### CONCEPT CONNECTION

*Managers at Agilent Technologies, an $8.3 billion technology spin-off from Hewlett-Packard, have worked hard to gain employees' trust. When* downsizing *became necessary and managers had to terminate a large number of workers, they made the layoffs easier by showing empathy and respect for employees. As a result, after the workers at this Agilent plant in Newark, California, were told their plant was closing, they upped production higher than ever before—out of respect for their managers and concern for co-workers in other plants. Agilent's humane approach helped the company attain a spot on* Fortune *magazine's list of Best Companies to Work For even in the midst of downsizing and cost-cutting.*

Manager's Solution

This chapter described several important points about human resource management in organizations. All managers are responsible for human resources, and most organizations have a human resource department that works with line managers to ensure a productive workforce. Human resource management plays a key strategic role in today's organizations. HRM is changing in three ways to keep today's organizations competitive—focusing on human and social capital; globalizing HR systems, policies, and structures; and using information technology to help achieve strategic HR goals. The HR department must also implement procedures to reflect federal and state legislation and respond to changes in working relationships and career directions. The old social contract of the employee being loyal to the company and the company taking care of the employee until retirement no longer holds. Employees are responsible for managing their own careers. Although many people still follow a traditional management career path, others look for new opportunities as contingent workers, telecommuters, project managers, and virtual employees. Other current issues of concern to HRM are downsizing and implementing work–life balance initiatives.

The HR department strives to achieve three goals for the organization. The first goal of the human resource department is to attract an effective workforce through human resource planning, recruiting, and employee selection. The second is to develop an effective workforce. Newcomers are introduced to the organization and to their jobs through orientation and training programs. Moreover, employees are evaluated through performance appraisal programs. The third goal is to maintain an effective workforce. Human resource managers retain employees with wage and salary systems, benefits packages, and termination procedures. In many organizations, information technology is being used to more effectively meet all three of these important HR goals.

At UPS, described in the opening example, new district manager Jennifer Shroeger worked with the HRM department to solve the problem of high turnover at the Buffalo distribution center, dramatically cutting the attrition rate in the first quarter of 2002 to a low 6 percent. Managers realized that keeping more people had a lot to do with how those people were selected in the first place. Previously, UPS had basically been hiring the first applicant who walked in and was capable of handling heavy packages. Shroeger decided they needed to start asking what the applicant was looking for in the job. Many of those hired as part-timers were really looking for full-time jobs, which rarely opened up. After a few months, these people realized their chances of full-time work were slim, so they'd move on. UPS started giving realistic job previews, emphasizing not only the hard, intimidating environment of the warehouse, but also the fact that these were part-time jobs and short shifts that were never going to be anything else. The upside to this aspect of the job is that it is perfect for students, mothers, and other people who genuinely *want* to work only part-time. But hiring those people meant UPS needed to build in flexibility. Students and mothers, for example, tend to need more occasional days off or frequent changes in their schedule. Instead of just saying "we can't do that," HRM started looking for ways the company could do it. Other changes involved improved training and mentoring for new employees, handled by part-time shift supervisors who understood the problems of the work environment. The supervisors themselves also got upgraded training in communication skills, motivation, and flexibility to meet the needs of diverse workers. A final, important aspect of the new strategy was to accept that most people they hired wouldn't want to load and unload boxes for their entire careers. "Instead of worrying about them leaving, we should be taking an interest in their future," Shroeger says. "I'd like for all of those part-time workers to graduate from college and start their own businesses—and become UPS customers."[94]

# Discussion Questions

1. It is the year 2010. In your company, central planning has given way to frontline decision making, and bureaucracy has given way to teamwork. Shop floor workers use computers and robots. There is a labor shortage for many job openings, and the few applicants lack skills to work in teams, make decisions, or use sophisticated technology. As vice-president of human resource management since 1990, what did you do to prepare for this problem?

2. If you were asked to advise a private company about its equal employment opportunity responsibilities, what two points would you emphasize as most important?

3. How can the human resource activities of planning, recruiting, performance appraisal, and compensation be related to corporate strategy?

4. Think back to your own job experience. What human resource management activities described in this chapter were performed for the job you filled? Which ones were absent?

5. How might the changing social contract affect the ways human resource departments recruit, develop, and retain workers?

6. How "valid" do you think the information obtained from a personal interview versus a paper-and-pencil test versus an assessment center would be for predicting effective job performance for a college professor? An assembly-line worker in a team-oriented plant? Discuss.

7. What techniques can managers adopt to improve their recruiting and interviewing practices?

8. How does affirmative action differ from equal employment opportunity in recruiting and selection?

9. How can exit interviews be used to maintain an effective workforce?

10. Describe the procedure used to build a wage and salary structure for an organization.

# Management in Practice: Experiential Exercise

### Test Your Human Resources Knowledge

This quiz will test your knowledge of human resources issues affecting today's workplace. The quiz was designed by the Council on Education in Management, a Walnut Creek, California, firm that conducts human resources and employment law seminars nationwide.

1. If you receive an unsolicited résumé in the mail, you must keep it for two years.    T    F

2. Time-management principles are pretty much the same in any administrative job.    T    F

3. Regardless of the type of business or the various laws that may apply, there is a core of common practices for keeping personnel records and files that makes sense for almost any organization.    T    F

4. Every employer must have an affirmative action plan.    T    F

5. An employer must investigate an allegation of sexual harassment even if the victim asks to remain anonymous.    T    F

6. An employer is not obligated to pay overtime to a nonexempt employee who works more than 40 hours in a week after being asked not to put in overtime.    T    F

7. If your company is found guilty of discrimination, the Equal Employment Opportunity Commission will be more lenient if your records show that the violation was unintentional.    T    F

8. Americans with Disabilities Act regulations require companies to maintain written job descriptions.    T    F

9. Reference checking is an important procedure, despite the fact that many companies won't release this information.    T    F

10. Your employee orientation and handbook should help assure new employees that they will be a part of the team as long as they do a good job.    T    F

Answers: 1. F; 2. F; 3. T; 4. F; 5. T; 6. F; 7. F; 8. F; 9. T; 10. F.

# Management in Practice: Ethical Dilemma

## A Conflict of Responsibilities

As director of human resources, Tess Danville was asked to negotiate a severance deal with Terry Winston, the Midwest regional sales manager for Cyn-Com Systems. Winston's problems with drugs and alcohol had become severe enough to precipitate his dismissal. His customers were devoted to him, but top management was reluctant to continue gambling on his reliability. Lives depended on his work as the salesman and installer of Cyn-Com's respiratory diagnostic technology. Winston had been warned twice to clean up his act, but had never succeeded. Only his unique blend of technical knowledge and high-powered sales ability had saved him before.

But now the vice-president of sales asked Danville to offer Winston the option of resigning rather than be fired if he would sign a noncompete agreement and agree to go into rehabilitation. Cyn-Com would also extend a guarantee of confidentiality on the abuse issue and a good work reference as thanks for the millions of dollars of business that Winston had brought to Cyn-Com. Winston agreed to take the deal. After his departure, a series of near disasters was uncovered as a result of Winston's mismanagement. Some of his maneuvers to cover up his mistakes bordered on fraud.

Today Danville received a message to call the human resources director at a cardiopulmonary technology company to give a personal reference on Terry Winston. From the area code, Danville could see that he was not in violation of the noncompete agreement. She had also heard that Winston had completed a 30-day treatment program as promised. Danville knew she was expected to honor the confidentiality agreement, but she also knew that if his shady dealings had been discovered before his departure, he would have been fired without any agreement. Now she was being asked to give Winston a reference for another medical sales position.

## What Do You Do?

1. Honor the agreement, trusting Winston's rehabilitation is complete on all levels and that he is now ready for a responsible position. Give a good recommendation.

2. Contact the vice-president of sales and ask him to release you from the agreement or to give the reference himself. After all, he made the agreement. You don't want to lie.

3. Without mentioning specifics, give Winston such an unenthusiastic reference that you hope the other human resources director can read between the lines and believe that Winston will be a poor choice.

# Surf the Net

1. **Equal Employment Opportunity.** Andrea Kingston, a small business owner with 35 employees, has hired you as a human resources consultant. One area you are working on is making sure your client is in compliance with the federal laws related to her employees. The first step in the process is educating Andrea on what is required of her because her level of knowledge in this area is very minimal. Go to "Small Business Information" at the U.S. Equal Employment Opportunity Commission's home page (*http://www.eeoc.gov*) to gather information for Andrea. Write an outline of the information you will cover in that meeting.

2. **Recruiting.** Just as you get impressions about companies based on how you are treated when you visit their human resources departments to inquire about job openings or to ask for a job application form, you also get impressions based on how companies present themselves on the Internet. Go to several online human resources departments at companies you might like to work for someday, or check out those listed below, and record your impressions—things you liked and didn't like—as you conduct your online job search:
   Federal Express (*http://www.fedex.com/us/careers*)
   Intel (*http://www.intel.com*)
   Cisco Systems (*http://www.cisco.com/jobs*)

3. **Benefits.** The Employee Benefit Research Institute (EBRI) at *http://www.ebri.org* provides access to a number of sites that deal with benefits issues. Assuming the human resources consultant role described in problem 1, prepare a recommended benefits checklist for Andrea so that she can compare her current benefits package with the benefits appropriate for a small business to offer its employees.

# Case for Critical Analysis

## Waterway Industries

Waterway Industries was founded in the early 1960s as a small manufacturer of high-quality canoes. Based in Lake Placid, New York, the company quickly gained a solid reputation throughout the Northeast and began building a customer base in the Pacific Northwest as well. By the early 1980s, Waterway was comfortably ensconced in the canoe market nationwide. Although earnings growth was fairly steady up until 1990, CEO Cyrus Maher was persuaded by a friend to venture into kayaks. After Waterway began selling its own line of compact, inexpensive kayaks in 1992, Maher quickly learned that the decision was a good one. Most of Waterway's existing canoe customers placed sizable kayak orders, and a number of private-label companies also began contacting Maher about making kayaks for their companies. When Lee Carter was hired to establish a formal marketing department at Waterway, things really took off. Carter began bringing in so many large orders that the company had to contract with other manufacturers to keep up.

For the most part, Waterway's 45 or so employees adjusted well to the faster pace at the company. The expanded business didn't seem to change the company's relaxed, informal working atmosphere. Most employees were outdoor enthusiasts, and on days when the weather was good Maher knew that the building would be almost empty by 4:00 pm. He also knew, however, that employees enjoyed their jobs, got their work completed on time, and were always speaking out with new ideas and suggestions. However, Lee Carter, unlike other employees, seemed totally focused on her work. She traveled constantly and worked so hard that she barely had time to get to know the rest of the staff. She came in on weekends to catch up on paperwork. She had even missed the Waterway picnic, along with two of her direct reports, because the three were on the road trying to nail down a large order. Maher likes the dedication but wonders if this approach could eventually have a negative effect on the company's culture.

Turnover at Waterway has always been low, and Maher believes most employees are happy working at the company. However, within the past year, both of Waterway's designers have approached Maher to request salary adjustments. Each suggested they would be interested in equity in the company, whereby they would receive a share of the profits if their designs did well. Maher's response was to give the senior designer a modest pay raise and extra vacation and to increase the bonuses for both designers. Both seemed satisfied with the new arrangement. Waterway's CFO, on the other hand, recently left the company to take a position with a power boat manufacturer after Maher twice refused his request for a redesigned compensation package to include equity. Now, on a trip to the cafeteria to get a cup of coffee, Maher has just overheard Lee Carter discussing a possible job opportunity with another company. He is well aware of the lucrative packages being offered to sales and marketing managers in the sporting goods industry, and he doesn't want to lose Carter. Even though he suspects she will eventually leave the company anyway, especially if the market for kayaks falls flat, he would like to find a way to recognize her hard work and keep her at Waterway for at least a few more years.

Maher has asked you, the company's sole human resource manager, for advice about changing the company's compensation system. In the past, he has handled things informally, giving employees annual salary increases and bonuses, and dealing with employees one-on-one (as he did with the designers) when they have concerns about their current compensation. Now, Maher is wondering if his company has grown to the point where he needs to establish some kind of formal compensation system that can recognize employees who make outstanding contributions to the company's success.

## Questions

1.   What impact, positive or negative, do you think a formal compensation system might have on Waterway?

2.   What type of compensation approach would you suggest Maher implement?

3.   How can nonfinancial incentives play a role in helping Waterway retain aggressive, ambitious employees like Lee Carter?

Source: Based on Robert D. Nicoson, "Growing Pains," *Harvard Business Review*, July–August 1996, 20–36.

# Endnotes

1. Keith H. Hammonds, "Handle with Care," *Fast Company* (August 2002), 103–107.

2. Robert L. Mathis and John H. Jackson, *Human Resource Management: Essential Perspectives*, 2nd ed., (Cincinnati, Ohio: South-Western Publishing, 2002), 1.

3. Joy Persaud, "Game On," *People Management* (September 25, 2003), 40–41.

4. Jonathan Poet, "Schools Looking Overseas for Teachers," *Johnson City Press* (April 20, 2001), 6; and Jill Rosenfeld, "How's This for a Tough Assignment?" *Fast Company* (November 1999), 104–106.

5. See Jonathan Tompkins, "Strategic Human Resources Management in Government: Unresolved Issues," *Public Personnel Management* (Spring 2002), 95–110; Noel M. Tichy, Charles J. Fombrun, and Mary Anne Devanna, "Strategic Human Resource Management," *Sloan Management Review* 23 (Winter 1982) 47–61; Cynthia A. Lengnick-Hall and Mark L. Lengnick-Hall, "Strategic Human Resources Management: A Review of the Literature and a Proposed Typology," *Academy of Management Review* 13 (July 1988), 454–470; Eugene B. McGregor, *Strategic Management of Human Knowledge, Skills, and Abilities*, (San Francisco: Jossey-Bass, 1991).

6. Tompkins, "Strategic Human Resource Management in Government: Unresolved Issues."

7. Mark A. Huselid, Susan E. Jackson, and Randall S. Schuler, "Technical and Strategic Human Resource Management Effectiveness as Determinants of Firm Performance," *Academy of Management Journal* 40, no. 1 (1997), 171–188; and John T. Delaney and Mark A. Huselid, "The Impact of Human Resource Management Practices on Perceptions of Organizational Performance," *Academy of Management Journal* 39, no. 4 (1996), 949–969.

8. D. Kneale, "Working at IBM: Intense Loyalty in a Rigid Culture," *The Wall Street Journal* (April 7, 1986), 17.

9. Jeffrey Pfeffer, "Producing Sustainable Competitive Advantage through the Effective Management of People," *Academy of Management Executive* 9, no. 1 (1995), 55–72; and Harry Scarbrough, "Recipe for Success," *People Management* (January 23, 2003), 32–25.

10. James N. Baron and David M. Kreps, "Consistent Human Resource Practices," *California Management Review* 41, no. 3 (Spring 1999), 29–53.

11. Cynthia D. Fisher, "Current and Recurrent Challenges in HRM," *Journal of Management* 15 (1989), 157–180.

12. See Dave Ulrich, "A New Mandate for Human Resources," *Harvard Business Review* (January–February 1998), 124–134; Philip H. Mirvis, "Human Resource Management: Leaders, Laggards, and Followers," *Academy of Management Executive* 11, no. 2 (1997), 43–56; Richard McBain, "Attracting, Retaining, and Motivating Capable People," *Manager Update* (Winter 1999), 25–36; and Oren Harari, "Attracting the Best Minds," *Management Review* (April 1998), 23–26.

13. Floyd Kemske, "HR 2008: A Forecast Based on Our Exclusive Study," *Workforce* (January 1998), 46–60.

14. This definition and discussion is based on George Bollander, Scott Snell, and Arthur Sherman, *Managing Human Resources* 12th ed., (Cincinnati, Ohio: South-Western, 2001), 13–15; and Scarbrough, "Recipe for Success."

15. Jennifer J. Laabs, "It's OK to Focus on Heart and Soul," *Workforce* (January 1997), 60–69.

16. Mark C. Bolino, William H. Turnley, and James M. Bloodgood, "Citizenship Behavior and the Creation of Social Capital in Organizations," *Academy of Management Review* 27, no. 5 (2002), 505–522.

17. Rich Wellins and Sheila Rioux, "The Growing Pains of Globalizing HR," *Training and Development* (May 2000), 79–85.

18. Ibid.

19. Helen DeCieri, Julie Wolfram Cox, Marilyn S. Fenwick, "Think Global, Act Local: From Naive Comparison to Critical Participation in the Teaching of Strategic International Human Resource Management," *Tamara: Journal of Critical Postmodern Organization Science* 1, no. 1 (2001), 68+; S. Taylor, S. Beecher, and N. Napier, "Towards an Integrative Model of Strategic Human Resource Management *Academy of Management Review* 21 (1996), 959–985; Mary Ann Von Glinow, Ellen A. Drost, and Mary B. Teagarden, "Converging on IHRM Best Practices: Lessons Learned from a Globally Distributed Consortium on Theory and Practice," *Human Resource Management* 41, no. 1 (Spring 2002), 123–140.

20. Von Glinow, Drost, and Teagarden, "Converging on IHRM Best Practices;" and Jennifer J. Laabs, "Must-Have Global HR Competencies," *Workforce* 4, no. 2 (1999), 30–32.

21. Joy Persaud, "Game On."

22. Ellen A. Ensher, Troy R. Nielson, and Elisa Grant-Vallone, "Tales from the Hiring Line: Effects of the Internet and Technology on HR Processes," *Organizational Dynamics* 31, no. 3 (2002), 224–244.

23. Peter Krass, "Precious Resources?" *CFO-IT* (Summer 2003), 38–45.

24. Krass, "Precious Resources?"; Alison Stein Wellner, "Click Here for HR," *Business Week Frontier* (April 24, 2000), F24–F26; and Esther Shein, "Requiem for a Paperweight," *eCFO* (Winter 2000), 81–83.

25. Aaron Bernstein, "Too Many Workers? Not For Long," *BusinessWeek* (May 20, 2002), 126–130.

26. Section 1604.1 of the EEOC Guidelines based on the Civil Rights Act of 1964, Title VII.

27. Charles F. Falk and Kathleen A. Carlson, "Newer Patterns in Management for the Post–Social Contract Era," *Midwest Management Society Proceedings* (1995), 45–52.

28. Richard Pascale, "The False Security of 'Employability,'" *Fast Company* (April–May 1996), 62, 64; and Louisa Wah, "The New Workplace Paradox," *Management Review*, January 1998, 7.

29. Douglas T. Hall and Jonathan E. Moss, "The New Protean Career Contract: Helping Organizations and Employees Adapt," *Organizational Dynamics* (Winter 1998), 22–37.

30. Sean Donahue, "New Jobs for the New Economy," *Business 2.0* (July 1999), 102–109.

31. The discussion of temporary employment agencies is based on David Wessel, "Capital: Temp Workers Have a Lasting Effect," *The Wall Street Journal* (February 1, 2001), A1.

32. Brenda Paik Sunoo, "Temp Firms Turn Up the Heat on Hiring," *Workforce* (April 1999), 50–54.

33. Jaclyn Fierman, "The Contingency Workforce," *Fortune* (January 24, 1994), 30–31.

34. Nancy B. Kurland and Diane E. Bailey, "Telework: The Advantages and Challenges of Working Here, There, Anywhere, Anytime," *Organizational Dynamics* (Autumn 1999), 53–68.

35. Kevin Voigt, "For 'Extreme Telecommuters,' Remote Work Means Really Remote," *The Wall Street Journal* (January 31, 2001), B1.

36. Ibid.

37. John Challenger, "There Is No Future for the Workplace," *Public Management* (February 1999), 20–23.

38. James R. Morris, Wayne F. Cascio, and Clifford Young, "Downsizing After All These Years: Questions and Answers About Who Did It, How Many Did It, and Who Benefited From It," *Organizational Dynamics* (Winter 1999), 78–86; William McKinley, Carol M. Sanchez, and Allen G. Schick, "Organizational Downsizing: Constraining, Cloning, Learning," *Academy of Management Executive* 9, no. 3 (1995), 32–42; and Brett C. Luthans and Steven M. Sommer,

"The Impact of Downsizing on Workplace Attitudes," *Group and Organization Management* 2, no. 1 (1999), 46–70.

39. Effective downsizing techniques are discussed in detail in Bob Nelson, "The Care of the Un-Downsized," *Training and Development* (April 1997), 40–43; Shari Caudron, "Teaching Downsizing Survivors How to Thrive," *Personnel Journal* (January 1996), 38; Joel Brockner, "Managing the Effects of Layoffs on Survivors," *California Management Review* (Winter 1992), 9–28; and Kim S. Cameron, "Strategies for Successful Organizational Downsizing," *Human Resource Management* 33, no. 2 (Summer 1994), 189–211.

40. James G. March and Herbert A. Simon, *Organizations* (New York: Wiley, 1958).

41. Richard McBain, "Attracting, Retaining, and Motivating Capable People: A Key to Competitive Advantage," *Manager Update* (Winter 1999), 25–36.

42. Dennis J. Kravetz, *The Human Resources Revolution* (San Francisco, Calif.: Jossey-Bass, 1989).

43. David E. Ripley, "How to Determine Future Workforce Needs," *Personnel Journal* (January 1995), 83–89.

44. J. W. Boudreau and S. L. Rynes, "Role of Recruitment in Staffing Utility Analysis," *Journal of Applied Psychology* 70 (1985), 354–366.

45. Brian Dumaine, "The New Art of Hiring Smart," *Fortune* (August 17, 1987), 78–81.

46. This discussion is based on Mathis and Jackson, *Human Resource Management*, Chapter 4, 49–60.

47. Victoria Griffith, "When Only Internal Expertise Will Do," *CFO* (October 1998), 95–96, 102.

48. J. P. Wanous, *Organizational Entry* (Reading, Mass.: Addison-Wesley, 1980).

49. Samuel Greengard, "Technology Finally Advances HR," *Workforce* (January 2000), 38–41; and Scott Hays, "Hiring on the Web," *Workforce* (August 1999), 77–84.

50. Marlene Piturro, "The Power of E-Cruiting," *Management Review* (January 2000), 33–37.

51. Jerry Useem, "For Sale Online: You," *Fortune* (July 5, 1999), 67–78.

52. George Bohlander, Scott Snell, and Arthur Sherman, *Managing Human Resources*, 12th ed., (Cincinnati, Ohio: South-Western College Publishing, 2001), 145.

53. Elizabeth Davidson, You Can Do It . . . " *People Management* (February 20, 2003), 42–43.

54. Kathryn Tyler, "Employees Can Help Recruit New Talent," *HR Magazine* (September 1996), 57–60.

55. Carol Leonetti Dannhauser, "Putting the Ooh in Recruiting," *Working Woman* (March 2000), 32–34.

56. Ann Harrington, "Anybody Here Want a Job?" *Fortune* (May 15, 2000), 489–498.

57. "Bank of America to Hire 850 Ex-Welfare Recipients," *Johnson City Press* (January 14, 2001), 29; E. Blacharczyk, "Recruiters Challenged by Economy, Shortages, Unskilled," *HR News* (February 1990), B1; Victoria Rivkin, "Visa Relief," *Working Woman* (January 2001), 15.

58. P. W. Thayer, "Somethings Old, Somethings New," *Personnel Psychology* 30 (1977), 513–524.

59. J. Ledvinka, *Federal Regulation of Personnel and Human Resource Management* (Boston: Kent, 1982); and Civil Rights Act, Title VII, 42 U.S.C. Section 2000e *et seq.* (1964).

60. Studies reported in William Poundstone, "Impossible Questions," *Across the Board* (September–October 2003), 44–48.

61. Bohlander, Snell, and Sherman, *Managing Human Resources*, 202.

62. Poundstone, "Impossible Questions." Also see *How Would You Move Mount Fuji? Microsoft's Cult of the Puzzle—How the World's Smartest Companies Select the Most Creative Thinkers* (New York: Little Brown 2003).

63. Bohlander, Snell, and Sherman, *Managing Human Resources.*

64. Meridith Levinson, "How to Hire So You Don't Have to Fire," *CIO* (March 1, 2004), 72–80.

65. "Assessment Centers: Identifying Leadership through Testing," *Small Business Report* (June 1987), 22–24; and W. C. Byham, "Assessment Centers for Spotting Future Managers," *Harvard Business Review* (July–August 1970), 150–167.

66. Mike Thatcher, "'Front-line' Staff Selected by Assessment Center," *Personnel Management* (November 1993), 83.

67. Adam Hanft, "Smarter Hiring, the DDI Way," *Inc.* (March 2003), 92–98.

68. Bernard Keys and Joseph Wolfe, "Management Education and Development: Current Issues and Emerging Trends," *Journal of Management* 14 (1988), 205–229.

69. William J. Rothwell and H. C. Kazanas, *Improving On-The-Job Training: How to Establish and Operate a Comprehensive OJT Program* (San Francisco, CA: Jossey-Bass, 1994).

70. Matt Murray, "GE Mentoring Program Turns Underlings into Teachers of the Web," *The Wall Street Journal* (February 15, 2000), B1, B16.

71. Jeanne C. Meister, "The Brave New World of Corporate Education" *The Chronicle of Higher Education* (February 9, 2001), B10; and Meryl Davids Landau, "Corporate Universities Crack Open Their Doors," *The Journal of Business Strategy* (May–June 2000), 18–23.

72. Meister, "The Brave New World of Corporate Education"; and Edward E. Gordon, "Bridging the Gap," *Training* (September 2003), 30.

73. John Byrne, "The Search for the Young and Gifted," *BusinessWeek* (October 4, 1999), 108–116; and Joel Schettler, "Defense Acquisition University: Weapons of Mass Instruction," *Training* (February 2003), 20–27.

74. Gordon, "Bridging the Gap."

75. Jim Dow, "Spa Attraction," *People Management* (May 29, 2003), 34-35.

76. Walter W. Tornow, "Editor's Note: Introduction to Special Issue on 360-Degree Feedback," *Human Resource Management* 32, no. 2/3 (Summer/Fall 1993), 211–219; and Brian O'Reilly, "360 Feedback Can Change Your Life," *Fortune* (October 17, 1994), 93–100.

77. Kris Frieswick, "Truth & Consequences," *CFO* (June 2001), 56–63.

78. This discussion is based on Dick Grote, "Forced Ranking: Behind the Scenes," *Across the Board*, (November–December 2002), 40–45; Matthew Boyle, "Performance Reviews: Perilous Curves Ahead," *Fortune* (May 28, 2001), 187–188; Carol Hymowitz, "Ranking Systems Gain Popularity But Have Many Staffers Riled," (In the Lead column), *The Wall Street Journal* (May 15, 2001), B1; and Frieswick, "Truth & Consequences."

79. Hymowitz, "Ranking Systems Gain Popularity," and Boyle, "Performance Reviews."

80. Lou Kaucic, "Finding Your Stars," *Microsoft Executive Circle* (Summer 2003), 14.

81. V. R. Buzzotta, "Improve Your Performance Appraisals," *Management Review* (August 1988), 40–43; and H. J. Bernardin and R. W. Beatty, *Performance Appraisal: Assessing Human Behavior at Work* (Boston: Kent, 1984).

82. Ibid.

83. Richard I. Henderson, *Compensation Management: Rewarding Performance*, 4th ed. (Reston, Va.: Reston, 1985).

84. L. R. Gomez-Mejia, "Structure and Process Diversification, Compensation Strategy, and Firm Performance," *Strategic Management Journal* 13 (1992), 381–397; and E. Montemayor, "Congruence Between Pay Policy and Competitive Strategy in High-Performing Firms," *Journal of Management* 22, no. 6 (1996), 889–908.

85. Renée F. Broderick and George T. Milkovich, "Pay Planning, Organization Strategy, Structure and 'Fit': A Prescriptive Model of Pay" (paper presented at the 45th Annual Meeting of the Academy of Management, San Diego, August 1985).

86. E. E. Lawler, III, *Strategic Pay: Aligning Organizational Strategies and Pay Systems*, (San Francisco: Jossey-Bass, 1990); and R. J. Greene, "Person-Focused Pay: Should It Replace Job-Based Pay?" *Compensation and Benefits Management* 9, no. 4 (1993), 46–55.

87. L. Wiener, "No New Skills? No Raise," *U.S. News and World Report* (October 26, 1992), 78.

88. Data from Hewitt Associates, Bureau of Labor Statistics, reported in Michelle Conlin and Peter Coy, with Ann Therese Palmer, and Gabrielle Saveri, "The Wild New Workforce," *BusinessWeek* (December 6, 1999), 39–44.

89. Brian Friel, "The Rating Game," *Government Executive* (August 2003), 46–52.

90. *Employee Benefits*, 1997 (Washington, D.C.: U. S. Chamber of Commerce, 1997), 7.

91. Frank E. Kuzmits, "Communicating Benefits: A Double-Click Away," *Compensation and Benefits Review* 30, no. 5 (September–October 1998), 60–64; and Lynn Asinof, "Click and Shift: Workers Control Their Benefits Online," *The Wall Street Journal* (November 27, 1997), C1.

92. Robert S. Catapano-Friedman, "Cafeteria Plans: New Menu for the '90s," *Management Review* (November 1991), 25–29.

93. Yvette Debow, "GE: Easing the Pain of Layoffs," *Management Review* (September 1997), 15–18.

94. Hammonds, "Handle with Care."

# Chapter 13

## Meeting the Challenge of Diversity

### LEARNING OBJECTIVES

*After studying this chapter, you should be able to*

1. Explain the dimensions of employee diversity and why ethnorelativism is the appropriate attitude for today's organizations.

2. Discuss the changing workplace and how to effectively manage a culturally diverse workforce.

3. Understand the challenges minority employees face daily.

4. Explain affirmative action and why factors such as the glass ceiling have kept it from being more successful.

5. Describe how to change corporate culture, structure, and policies and how to use diversity awareness training to meet the needs of diverse employees.

6. Explain the importance of addressing sexual harassment in the workplace.

7. Define the importance of multicultural teams and employee network groups for today's globally diverse organizations.

It started in July 2001 when seven women filed suit in a California court charging that Wal-Mart systematically denies women equal pay and opportunities for promotion. It could balloon into the largest gender discrimination lawsuit in U.S. history and cost the giant corporation hundreds of millions of dollars. The women have already won a major battle when the courts required Wal-Mart to turn over workforce data from 3,400 U.S. stores, information that the company had previously closely guarded. Although Wal-Mart is vigorously denying discriminatory practices, one analysis of the data indicates that between the years of 1996 and 2001, women at Wal-Mart earned from 5 to 15 percent less than men performing the same job, even though women typically received higher performance evaluations. Another study reports that women employees wait much longer than men for their first promotion at Wal-Mart. In 1999, Wal-Mart had a lower percentage of female managers than its retail counterparts had in 1975. Lawyers are arguing that the patterns reflect discriminatory attitudes embedded in the famous Wal-Mart culture that call for strict penalties and serious reform.[1]

## Take A Moment

If you were a top manager at Wal-Mart, what steps would you take to solve this problem? What changes can make Wal-Mart a company where all employees feel valued, respected, and supported?

Wal-Mart is not the only company that has faced difficulties with issues of diversity. In recent years, high-profile racial discrimination or harassment lawsuits have been filed against Texaco, Lockheed Martin, Coca-Cola, and Boeing. Mitsubishi is still reeling from the effects of a sexual harassment lawsuit charging that managers ignored complaints that women were regularly groped on the factory floor and made to endure crude jokes and lewd photographs.[2]

Diversity in the population, the workforce, and the marketplace is a fact of life no manager can afford to ignore. In addition, diversity issues are growing more complex than they were 30 years ago. Among the groups now seeking full inclusion in the workforce are many not even considered back then, including the disabled, the obese, and non-heterosexuals. Managing diversity today entails recruiting, training, valuing, and maximizing the potential of people who reflect the broad spectrum of society in all areas—gender, race, age, disability, ethnicity, religion, sexual orientation, education, and economic level.

Many companies, including IBM, Pfizer, Allstate Insurance, and Ford Motor Company, are finding innovative ways to integrate diversity initiatives into their business. These initiatives teach current employees to value differences, direct corporate recruiting efforts, influence supplier decisions, and provide development training for women and minorities. Smart managers value diversity and enforce the value in day-to-day decision making.

Today's companies reflect the U.S. image as a melting pot, but with a difference. In the past, the United States was a place where people of different national origins, ethnicities, races, and religions came together and blended to resemble one another. Opportunities for advancement were limited to those workers who fit easily into the mainstream of the larger culture. Some immigrants chose desperate measures to fit in, such as abandoning their native languages, changing their last names, and sacrificing their own unique cultures. In essence, everyone in workplace organizations was encouraged to share similar beliefs, values, and lifestyles despite differences in gender, race, and ethnicity.[3]

Now organizations recognize that everyone is not the same and that the differences people bring to the workplace are valuable.[4] Rather than expecting all employees to adopt similar attitudes and values, managers are learning that these differences enable their companies to compete globally and to tap into rich sources of new talent. Although diversity in North America has been a reality for some time, genuine efforts to accept and *manage* diverse people began only in recent years. Exhibit 13.1 lists some interesting milestones in the history of corporate diversity.

This chapter introduces the topic of diversity, its causes and consequences. We will look at some of the challenges minorities face, ways managers deal with workforce diversity, and organizational responses to create an environment that welcomes and values diverse employees. The chapter will also look at issues of sexual harassment, global diversity, and new approaches to managing diversity in today's workplace.

# Valuing Diversity

Top managers say their companies value diversity for a number of reasons, such as to give the organization access to a broader range of opinions and viewpoints, to reflect an increasingly diverse customer base, to obtain the best talent in a competitive environment, and to demonstrate the company's commitment to "doing the right thing."[5] Moreover, a survey commissioned by *The New York Times* found that 91 percent of job seekers think diversity programs make a company a better place to work. Nearly all minority job seekers said they would prefer to work in a diverse workplace.[6]

Exhibit 13.1

## Some Milestones in the History of Corporate Diversity in the United States

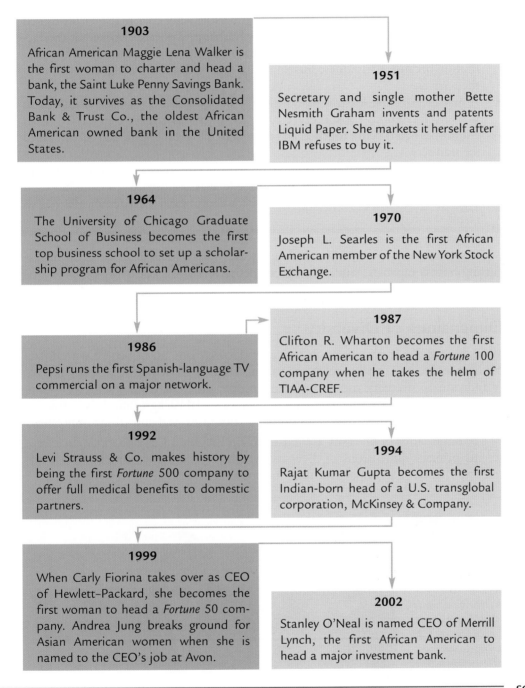

**1903**

African American Maggie Lena Walker is the first woman to charter and head a bank, the Saint Luke Penny Savings Bank. Today, it survives as the Consolidated Bank & Trust Co., the oldest African American owned bank in the United States.

**1951**

Secretary and single mother Bette Nesmith Graham invents and patents Liquid Paper. She markets it herself after IBM refuses to buy it.

**1964**

The University of Chicago Graduate School of Business becomes the first top business school to set up a scholarship program for African Americans.

**1970**

Joseph L. Searles is the first African American member of the New York Stock Exchange.

**1986**

Pepsi runs the first Spanish-language TV commercial on a major network.

**1987**

Clifton R. Wharton becomes the first African American to head a *Fortune* 100 company when he takes the helm of TIAA-CREF.

**1992**

Levi Strauss & Co. makes history by being the first *Fortune* 500 company to offer full medical benefits to domestic partners.

**1994**

Rajat Kumar Gupta becomes the first Indian-born head of a U.S. transglobal corporation, McKinsey & Company.

**1999**

When Carly Fiorina takes over as CEO of Hewlett-Packard, she becomes the first woman to head a *Fortune* 50 company. Andrea Jung breaks ground for Asian American women when she is named to the CEO's job at Avon.

**2002**

Stanley O'Neal is named CEO of Merrill Lynch, the first African American to head a major investment bank.

**SOURCE:** "Spotlight on Diversity," special advertising section, *MBA Jungle* (March–April 2003), 58–61.

However, many managers are ill-prepared to handle diversity issues. Many Americans grew up in racially unmixed neighborhoods and had little exposure to people substantially different from themselves.[7] The challenge is particularly great when working with people from other countries and cultures. For example, one recent challenge at IBM involved a new immigrant, a Muslim woman who was required to have a photo taken for a company identification badge. She protested that her religious beliefs required that, as a married woman, she wear a veil and not expose her face to men in public. A typical American manager, schooled in traditional management training, might insist that she have the photo taken or hit the door. Fortunately, IBM has a well-developed diversity program and managers worked out a satisfactory compromise.[8] Consider some other mistakes that American managers could easily make:[9]

- To reward a Vietnamese employee's high performance, her manager promoted her, placing her at the same level as her husband, who also worked at the factory. Rather than being pleased, the worker became upset and declined the promotion because Vietnamese husbands are expected to have a higher status than their wives.
- A manager, having learned that a friendly pat on the arm or back would make workers feel good, took every chance to touch his subordinates. His Asian employees hated being touched and thus started avoiding him, and several asked for transfers.
- A manager declined a gift offered by a new employee, an immigrant who wanted to show gratitude for her job. He was concerned about ethics and explained the company's policy about not accepting gifts. The employee was so insulted she quit.

These issues related to cultural diversity are difficult and real. But before discussing how companies handle them, let's define *diversity* and explore people's attitudes toward it.

## Dimensions of Diversity

**workforce diversity**
Hiring people with different human qualities or who belong to various cultural groups.

Workforce diversity means an inclusive workforce made up of people with different human qualities or who belong to various cultural groups. From the perspective of individuals, diversity means including people different from themselves along dimensions such as race, age, ethnicity, gender, or social background. It is important to remember that diversity includes everyone, not just racial and ethnic minorities.

Key dimensions of diversity are illustrated in Exhibit 13.2. The inner circle represents primary dimensions of diversity, which include inborn differences or differences that have an impact throughout one's life.[10] Primary dimensions are core

**CONCEPT CONNECTION**

*Many people are opting to stay in the workforce long past retirement age, giving managers opportunities to enhance* workforce diversity *by incorporating older employees. When CPI Aerostructures in Edgewood, New York, earned new contracts to provide spare parts to the U.S. government, CEO Edward J. Fred needed skilled mechanics ready to work. He was flooded with inquiries from retired mechanics, many well past the age of 65. Fred hired two seniors as part-time workers, and two as full-time employees. The decision gave CPI flexibility in scheduling, experienced workers to serve as teachers to younger colleagues, and a workplace culture that increased pride in the work for employees of all ages.*

Exhibit 13.2

## Primary and Secondary Dimensions of Diversity

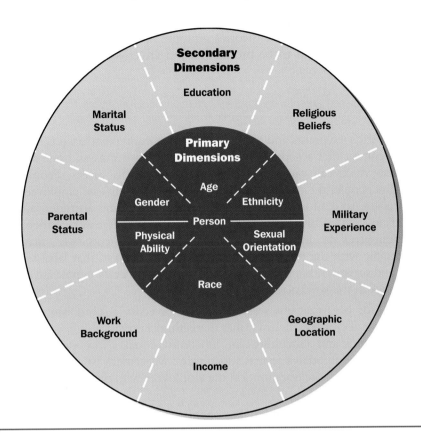

SOURCE: Adapted from Marilyn Loden and Judy B. Rosener, *Workforce America!* (Homewood, IL: Business One Irwin, 1991), 20. Used with permission.

elements through which people shape their self-image and world view. These dimensions include age, race, ethnicity, gender, mental or physical abilities, and sexual orientation

Secondary dimensions, shown in the outer ring of Exhibit 13.2, can be acquired or changed throughout one's lifetime. These dimensions tend to have less impact than those of the core but nevertheless affect a person's self-definition and world view and have an impact on how the person is viewed by others. For example, an employee living in a public housing project will certainly be perceived differently from one who lives in an affluent part of town. Married people and people with children may be perceived differently and have different attitudes from those who are single and childless. Likewise, a person's military experience, religion, native language, socioeconomic status, and educational and work background add dimensions to the way that person defines him- or herself and is defined by others. Secondary dimensions such as work style, communication style, and educational or skill level are particularly relevant in the organizational setting.[11] The challenge for today's managers is to recognize that each person can bring value and strengths to the workplace based on his or her own unique combination of diversity characteristics.

## Attitudes toward Diversity

Valuing diversity by recognizing, welcoming, and cultivating differences among people so they can develop their unique talents and be effective organizational members is difficult to achieve. Ethnocentrism is the belief that one's own group and subculture are inherently superior to other groups and cultures. Ethnocentrism makes it

**ethnocentrism**
The belief that one's own group or subculture is inherently superior to other groups or cultures.

difficult to value diversity. Viewing one's own culture as the best culture is a natural tendency among most people. Moreover, the business world still tends to reflect the values, behaviors, and assumptions based on the experiences of a rather homogeneous, white, middle-class, male workforce.[12] Indeed, most theories of management presume that workers share similar values, beliefs, motivations, and attitudes about work and life in general. These theories presume there is one set of behaviors that best help an organization to be productive and effective and therefore should be adopted by all employees.[13]

*Take A Moment*    *Go to the experiential exercise on page 492 that pertains to attitudes toward diversity.*

**monoculture**
A culture that accepts only one way of doing things and one set of values and beliefs.

Ethnocentric viewpoints and a standard set of cultural practices produce a monoculture, a culture that accepts only one way of doing things and one set of values and beliefs, which can cause problems for minority employees. People of color, women, gay people, the disabled, the elderly, and other diverse employees may feel undue pressure to conform, may be victims of stereotyping attitudes, and may be presumed deficient because they are different. White, heterosexual men, many of whom themselves do not fit the notions of the "ideal" employee, may also feel uncomfortable with the monoculture and resent stereotypes that label white males as racists and sexists. Valuing diversity means ensuring that *all* people are given equal opportunities in the workplace.[14]

**ethnorelativism**
The belief that groups and subcultures are inherently equal.

**pluralism**
The organization accommodates several subcultures, including employees who would otherwise feel isolated and ignored.

The goal for organizations seeking cultural diversity is pluralism rather than a monoculture and ethnorelativism rather than ethnocentrism. Ethnorelativism is the belief that groups and subcultures are inherently equal. Pluralism means that an organization accommodates several subcultures. Movement toward pluralism seeks to fully integrate into the organization the employees who otherwise would feel isolated and ignored.

Most organizations must undertake conscious efforts to shift from a monoculture perspective to one of pluralism. For example, a recent report from the National Bureau of Economic Research, entitled *Are Greg and Emily More Employable than Lakisha and Jamal?*, shows that employers often unconsciously discriminate against job applicants based solely on the Afrocentric or black-sounding names on their resume. In interviews prior to the research, most human resource managers surveyed said they expected only a small gap and some expected to find a pattern of reverse discrimination. The results showed instead that white-sounding names got 50 percent more callbacks than black-sounding names, even when skills and experience were equal.[15]

This type of discrimination is often not intentional but is based on deep-seated personal biases and deep-rooted organizational assumptions. Employees in a monoculture may not be aware of their biases and the negative stereotypes they apply toward people who represent diverse groups. Through effective training, employees can be helped to accept different ways of thinking and behaving, the first step away from narrow, ethnocentric thinking. Ultimately, employees are able to integrate diverse cultures, which means that judgments of appropriateness, goodness, badness, and morality are no longer applied to racial or cultural differences. These differences are experienced as essential, natural, and joyful, enabling an organization to enjoy true pluralism and take advantage of diverse human resources.[16]

One organization that is making a firm commitment to break out of monoculture thinking is Ford Motor Company. Ford sponsors ten different employee resource groups—one each for African Americans, Latinos, Middle Easterners, gays, lesbians, bisexuals, Chinese, Asian-Indians, parents, and women—which come up with recommendations for how to make Ford a better place to work for diverse employees. A Minority Dealer Operations program is aimed at increasing minority ownership,

© TERRY LORANT

*The Carol H. Williams Advertising agency reflects today's changing workplace. The staff is an intentional mix of conservative, funky, trendy, and Bohemian types who represent a cross section of cultures: African, African American, Caribbean, Asian, Italian, Hispanic, and various ethnic combinations. "They hail from Morehouse to Harvard," and are led by a black woman, Carol H. Williams (center). For clients such as General Motors, Procter & Gamble, Kmart, Coors, and Pacific Bell, the Williams mix of diversity, business savvy, and creative talent creates winning advertising campaigns, resulting in explosive growth for the agency.*

sometimes financing up to 90 percent of the cost for opening a dealership. Members of ethnic minority groups now own about 350 Ford dealerships, and women own an additional 300.[17] Since September 11, 2001, Ford has also made a strong effort to improve understanding between Arab-Americans and their colleagues. For example, at the Ford plant in Dearborn, Michigan, home of the nation's largest Arab-American community, Ford holds regular Islam 101 meetings and other programs to further understanding between Muslims and non-Muslims.[18]

# The Changing Workplace

Diversity is no longer just the right thing to do; it has become a business imperative. One reason is the dramatic change taking place in the workplace, in our society, and in the economic environment. These changes include globalization and the changing workforce and customer base.[19] Earlier chapters described the impact of global competition on business in North America. Competition is intense. At least 70 percent of all U.S. businesses are engaged directly in competition with companies overseas. Companies that succeed in this environment need to adopt radical new ways of doing business, with sensitivity toward the needs of different cultural practices. Consider the consulting firm McKinsey & Co. In the 1970s, most consultants were American, but by 1999, McKinsey's chief partner was a foreign national (Rajat Gupta from India), only 40 percent of consultants were American, and the firm's foreign-born consultants came from 40 different countries.[20] Companies that ignore diversity have a hard time competing in today's global marketplace. This chapter's Unlocking Creative Solutions Through People box describes the India division of Procter & Gamble, a huge global organization that has learned how to tap into the ideas and creativity of employees in different regions of the world.

The other dominant trend is the changing composition of the workforce and the customer base. The average worker is older now, and many more women, people of color, and immigrants are seeking job and advancement opportunities. The demographics of the U.S. population are shifting dramatically. According to the 2000 census, Hispanics, African Americans, and Asian Americans make up about 30 percent of the U.S. population. Already, nonwhite residents are the majority in 48 of the nation's 100 largest cities, as they are in New Mexico, Hawaii, the District of Columbia, and California—the largest consumer market in the country. Hispanics,

# Unlocking Creative Solutions Through People

## Procter & Gamble India

A *best employer* is an organization "that helps its employees realize their true potential . . . by creating a work environment that is fair, motivated, and transparent." Those words guided the selection of BT–Hewitt's "Best Employers in India 2003"—and Procter & Gamble came out on top. The annual survey considers factors such as senior leadership commitment to employee development, how people practices are aligned to meet employee needs, and the connection between attention to people and superior business performance.

Procter & Gamble India hires local managers but gives them plenty of opportunities for broad global exposure through diverse assignments. Country manager Shantanu Khosla explains how the system has worked for him. "I've been here 20 years and have established relationships with people from Cincinnati to Warsaw and today we see this as our competitive strength in an increasingly globalized world. . . ."

The two top priorities for senior leaders at Procter & Gamble are the company's people and its brands, and leaders have established a strong link between the two. Human resource practices are designed to align the interests of employees with the interests of the company from the beginning. A recruitment manager, for example, knows that the person he is hiring may someday be CEO. A key to building a powerful organization with truly global managers has been P & G's promote-from-within philosophy. Middle- and senior-level managers are never hired from outside. People are given plenty of opportunities for learning, as well as early responsibility to help them build management skills and global insights. Young, talented MBAs are eager to join the company because of strong people-oriented policies, opportunities for international experience, and ample room for career development and growth. Employees don't have to wait until they are older to handle important and challenging assignments. Early career responsibility builds an enthusiasm and passion in P & G managers that the competition can't beat.

The people-company connection is captured in a pamphlet called "Purpose, Values, and Principles" (the PVP), which guides everything P & G does. The PVP concludes with the lines: "Two billion times a day, P & G brands touch the lives of people round the world. P & G people work to make sure those brands live up to their promise to make life just a little bit better."

SOURCE: Priya Srinivasan, "In Touch, In the Lead," *Business Today* (September 14, 2003), 64–66; and Purva Misra and Madhavi Misra Wadhwa, "Are They Really Better? *Business Today* (September 14, 2003), 46–50.

African Americans, and Asian Americans together represent $1.5 trillion in annual purchasing power.[21] During the 1990s, the foreign-born population of the United States nearly doubled, and immigrants now make up more than 12 percent of the total U.S. workforce. By 2050, 85 percent of entrants into the workforce will likely be women and people of color. Already, white males, the majority of workers in the past, represent less than half of the workforce.[22] So far, the ability of organizations to manage diversity has not kept pace with these demographic trends, thus creating a number of significant challenges for minority workers and managers.

## Challenges Minorities Face

A one-best-way approach leads to a mindset that views difference as deficiency or dysfunction. For many career women and minorities, their experience suggests that no matter how many college degrees they earn, how many hours they work, how they dress, or how much effort and enthusiasm they invest, they are never perceived as "having the right stuff." If the standard of quality were based, for instance, on being white and male, anything else would be seen as deficient. This dilemma often is difficult for white men to understand because most of them are not intentionally racist and sexist. As one observer points out, you would need to be nonwhite to understand what it is like to have people assume a subordinate is your superior simply because he is white, or to lose a sale after the customer sees you in person and finds out you're not Caucasian.[23]

Although blatant discrimination is not as widespread as in the past, bias in the workplace often shows up in subtle ways—a lack of choice assignments; the disregard by a subordinate of a minority manager's directions; or the ignoring of comments made by women and minorities at meetings. A survey by Korn Ferry International found that 59 percent of minority managers surveyed had observed a racially motivated double standard in the delegation of assignments.[24] Their perceptions are supported by a study that showed minority managers spend more time in the "bullpen" waiting for their chance and then have to prove themselves over and over again with each new assignment. Another recent study found that white managers gave more negative performance ratings to black leaders and white subordinates and more positive ratings to white leaders and black subordinates, affirming the widespread acceptance of these employees in their stereotypical roles.[25] Minority employees typically feel that they have to put in longer hours and extra effort to achieve the same status as their white colleagues. "It's not enough to be as good as the next person," says Bruce Gordon, president of Bell Atlantic's enterprise group. "We have to be better."[26]

Another problem is that many minority workers feel they have to become bicultural in order to succeed. Biculturalism can be defined as the sociocultural skills and attitudes used by racial minorities as they move back and forth between the dominant culture and their own ethnic or racial culture.[27] Research on differences between whites and blacks has focused on issues of biculturalism and how it affects employees' access to information, level of respect and appreciation, and relation to superiors and subordinates. In general, African Americans feel less accepted in their organizations, perceive themselves to have less discretion on their jobs, receive lower ratings on job performance, experience lower levels of job satisfaction, and reach career plateaus earlier than whites. They find themselves striving to adopt behaviors and attitudes that will help them be successful in the white-dominated corporate world while at the same time maintaining their ties to the black community and culture.

**biculturalism**
The sociocultural skills and attitudes used by racial minorities as they move back and forth between the dominant culture and their own ethnic or racial culture.

The Unlocking Creative Solutions Through Technology box describes a company with a goal of helping African Americans achieve career success and stay connected to black culture and lifestyle.

Other minority groups struggle with biculturalism as well. For example, Asian Americans who aspire to management positions are often frustrated by the stereotype that they are hardworking but not executive material because they are too quiet and deferential. Assertiveness and pressing your views in a group is seen as a characteristic of leadership in American culture, but Asians typically view this behavior as inappropriate and immature.[28] Some Asian Americans feel they have a chance for career advancement only by becoming bicultural or abandoning their native cultures altogether. Hispanics, who officially passed African Americans in 2003 as the nation's largest minority group, typically live in communities with high concentrations of Hispanics and maintain their native language and traditions outside of work.[29]

## Management Challenges

What does this mean for managers who are responsible for creating a workplace that offers fulfilling work, opportunities for professional development and career advancement, and respect for all individuals? Inappropriate behavior by employees lands squarely at the door of the organization's top executives. Managers can look at different areas of the organization to see how well they are doing in creating a workplace that values and supports all people. Exhibit 13.3 illustrates some of the key areas of management challenge for dealing with a diverse workforce. Managers focus on these issues to see how well they are addressing the needs and concerns of diverse employees. One step is to ensure that their organizations' human resources systems are designed to be bias-free, dropping the perception of the middle-aged white male as the ideal employee. Consider how the FBI has expanded its recruiting efforts.

# Unlocking Creative Solutions Through Technology

## Living on BlackPlanet.com

When Omar Wasow started BlackPlanet.com in 1999, industry skeptics dismissed the site as too racially-specific and doomed to failure. It didn't take long to prove them wrong. BlackPlanet is the most heavily trafficked African American Web destination, with nearly 12 million registered members and 1.5 million different visitors in any given month. At just about any time of the day or night, more than 20,000 people are logged on. Not long ago, Media Metrix rated BlackPlanet.com as the eighth "stickiest" Web site, referring to how often people come back to the site and how long they stay.

In the past five years, African Americans have embraced the Internet at about twice the rate of the general population. BlackPlanet.com was ready, giving African Americans a place where they could be part of a thriving online community, investigate new areas of interest, explore job and education opportunities, examine paths to economic advancement, build social and romantic relationships, and obtain information related to virtually any aspect of their lives.

The essence of BlackPlanet.com's success, according to Wasow, is building connections. "We focus on the conversation," he says. "What we've done is taken the grapevine in the black community and extended it to the Internet." Wasow believes African Americans have always found ways to communicate within the black community and stay in touch with their history and culture. The Internet is just a new way for people to explore issues of common interest with others who understand their frustrations and share their experiences as African Americans. Some of the most popular aspects are the message boards, chat rooms, and community sections, where members can interact with others.

The Internet is today's fastest highway to information, entertainment, and cultural connections, and BlackPlanet.com has tapped into a deep desire among African Americans for a site that caters to their interests, preferences, and needs.

SOURCE: Ines Bebea, "Blacks and the Internet: Power Resides in Interconnectivity," *Network Journal* (October 31, 2003), 46; Lynda Richardson, "Enterpreneur Takes Black-Oriented Site Out of Red," *The New York Times* (November 27, 2002), B4; and *http://www.blackplanet.com.*

## FEDERAL BUREAU OF INVESTIGATION (FBI)

http://www.fbi.gov

How does the FBI gain credibility and obtain the information it needs to investigate and solve crimes? One way is by looking and thinking like the people in the communities where it seeks information. Not so very long ago, if you were a woman or member of a minority group, you didn't stand a chance of becoming an FBI agent. Today, though, the agency's goal is to reflect the diversity of U.S. society. Each of the FBI's 56 field offices gets a report card on how well they've done in terms of making their offices reflective of the community. Each office is responsible for bringing minorities on board and providing them with advancement opportunities.

In addition, the FBI's national recruitment office was launched specifically to develop programs for recruiting women and minorities. One innovative initiative was the EdVenture Partners Collegiate Marketing Program, which worked with two historically black universities. The program gave students college credit and funding to devise and implement a local marketing plan for the FBI. As a result of the program, the agency received 360 minority applications. "In many cases, the students' perceptions about the FBI were totally changed," says Gwen Hubbard, acting chief of the national recruitment office. "Initially, we were not viewed as an employer of choice by the diverse student populations." The EdVenture Partners program is being expanded to eight colleges and universities. Another initiative is a minority summer intern program, which started with 21 full-time student interns and is being expanded to at least 40.

These programs on the national level, along with emphasis in the field offices on reflecting the local communities, ensure that the Federal Bureau of Investigation recruits diverse candidates. Today, the FBI has thousands of female and minority agents. Top leaders are also focusing on ways to make sure those people have full opportunity to move up the ranks so that there is diversity at leadership levels as well.[30]

Exhibit 13.3

## Management Challenges for a Culturally Diverse Workforce

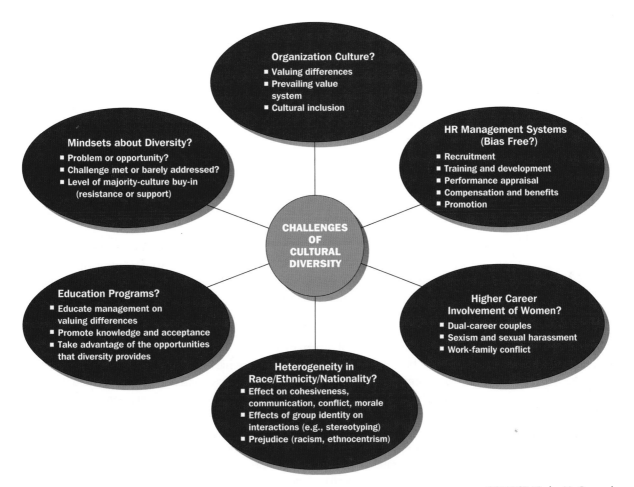

**Organization Culture?**
- Valuing differences
- Prevailing value system
- Cultural inclusion

**HR Management Systems (Bias Free?)**
- Recruitment
- Training and development
- Performance appraisal
- Compensation and benefits
- Promotion

**Mindsets about Diversity?**
- Problem or opportunity?
- Challenge met or barely addressed?
- Level of majority-culture buy-in (resistance or support)

**CHALLENGES OF CULTURAL DIVERSITY**

**Higher Career Involvement of Women?**
- Dual-career couples
- Sexism and sexual harassment
- Work-family conflict

**Education Programs?**
- Educate management on valuing differences
- Promote knowledge and acceptance
- Take advantage of the opportunities that diversity provides

**Heterogeneity in Race/Ethnicity/Nationality?**
- Effect on cohesiveness, communication, conflict, morale
- Effects of group identity on interactions (e.g., stereotyping)
- Prejudice (racism, ethnocentrism)

**SOURCE:** Taylor H. Cox and Stacy Blake, "Managing Cultural Diversity: Implications for Organizational Competitiveness," *Academy of Management Executive* 5, no. 3 (1991), 45–56.

Recruiting and career development are only one part of the human resources challenge. For example, the increased career involvement of women represents an enormous opportunity to organizations, but it also means managers must deal with issues such as work-family conflicts, dual-career couples, and sexual harassment. Providing reasonable accommodation for disabled employees requires more than putting in a handicap access ramp. Demands for equal opportunities for the physically and mentally disabled are growing, and most companies have done little to respond. "When it comes to dealing with the disabled, we are about where we were with race in the 1970s," says David Thomas, a professor of organizational behavior and human resource management at Harvard Business School.[31] For the most part, these workers are tracked into low-skill, low-pay jobs rather than being allowed to fully participate in training and educational programs available to other employees.[32]

The growing immigrant population presents other challenges. Whereas in previous generations most foreign-born immigrants came from Western Europe, 84 percent of recent immigrants come from Asia and Latin America.[33] These immigrants come to the United States with a wide range of backgrounds, often without adequate skills in using English. Organizations must face not only the issues of dealing with race, ethnicity, and nationality to provide a prejudice-free workplace, but also develop sufficient educational programs to help immigrants acquire the technical and customer service skills required in a service economy.

# Current Debates about Affirmative Action

**affirmative action**
Government mandated programs that focus on providing opportunities to women and members of minority groups who have previously experienced discrimination.

**Affirmative action** refers to government-mandated programs that focus on providing opportunities to women and members of minority groups who have previously been discriminated against. It is not the same thing as diversity, but affirmative action has facilitated greater recruitment, retention, and promotion of minorities and women. Affirmative action has made workplaces much more fair and equitable. However, recent research shows that full integration of women and racial minorities into organizations is still at least a decade away.[34] Despite affirmative action's successes, salaries and promotion opportunities for women and minorities continue to lag behind those of white males.

Affirmative action was developed in response to conditions 40 years ago. Adult white males dominated the workforce, and economic conditions were stable and improving. Because of widespread prejudice and discrimination, legal and social coercion were necessary to allow women, people of color, immigrants, and other minorities to become part of the economic system.[35]

Affirmative action is highly controversial today. The economic and social environment has changed tremendously since the 1960s. Some "minority" groups are becoming the majority in large U.S. cities. More than half the U.S. workforce consists of women and minorities, and the economic climate changes rapidly as a result of globalization. Some members of nonprotected groups argue that affirmative action is no longer needed and that it leads to *reverse discrimination*. Even the intended beneficiaries of affirmative action programs often disagree as to their value, and some believe these programs do more harm than good. One reason for this may be the *stigma of incompetence* that often is associated with affirmative action hires. One study found that both working managers and students consistently rated people portrayed as affirmative action hires as less competent and recommended lower salary increases than for those not associated with affirmative action.[36] In addition, people who perceive that they were hired because of affirmative action requirements may demonstrate negative self-perceptions and negative views of the organization, which leads to lower performance and reinforces the opinions of others that they are less competent.[37]

Recent court decisions have weakened affirmative action's clout while still upholding its value. For example, the Supreme Court recently preserved affirmative action policies as a means of achieving diversity in universities, but barred the use of point systems that might favor minority candidates.[38] Other court decisions have also limited the use of certain affirmative action practices for hiring and college admissions. In general, though, the courts support the continued use of affirmative action as a means of giving women and minority groups equal access to opportunities. In addition, according to a Gallup poll conducted to coincide with the 50th anniversary of the *Brown v. Board of Education* ruling that declared school segregation unconstitutional, 57 percent of Americans support the continued use of affirmative action.[39]

# The Glass Ceiling

**glass ceiling**
Invisible barrier that separates women and minorities from top management positions.

The **glass ceiling** is an invisible barrier that separates women and minorities from top management positions. They can look up through the ceiling and see top management, but prevailing attitudes and stereotypes are invisible obstacles to their own advancement.

In addition, women and minorities are often excluded from informal manager networks and often don't get access to the type of general and line management experience that is required for moving to the top.[40] Research has suggested the existence of *glass walls* that serve as invisible barriers to important lateral movement within the organization. Glass walls bar experience in areas such as line supervision or general management that would enable women and minorities to advance vertically.[41]

*Go to the ethical dilemma on page 494.*                          *Take A Moment*

Evidence that the glass ceiling persists is the distribution of women and minorities, who are clustered at the bottom levels of the corporate hierarchy. Among minority groups, women have made the biggest strides in recent years, but they still represent only 15.7 percent of corporate officers in America's 500 largest companies, up from 12.5 percent in 2000 and 8.7 percent in 1995.[42] Only eight *Fortune* 500 companies have female CEOs.[43] And both male and female African Americans and Hispanics continue to hold only a small percentage of all management positions in the United States.[44]

Women and minorities also make less money. As shown in Exhibit 13.4, black men earn about 22 percent less, white women 28 percent less, and Hispanic men 36 percent less than white males. Black and Hispanic women earn substantially less than white men, and these differences persist even when educational levels are the same. Recent U.S. Census Bureau figures show that college-educated black and Hispanic women earn about 46 percent less, and educated black and Hispanic men about 30 percent less, than white men with bachelor's degrees.[45]

Another sensitive issue related to the glass ceiling is homosexuals in the workplace. Many gay men and lesbians believe they will not be accepted as they are and risk losing their jobs or their chances for advancement. Gay employees of color are particularly hesitant to disclose their sexual orientation at work because by doing so they risk a double dose of discrimination.[46] Although there are some big name examples of openly gay corporate leaders, such as David Geffen, co-founder of DreamWorks SKG, and Ford Vice-Chairman Allan D. Gilmour, most managers still believe staying in the closet is the only way they can succeed at work. One director of human resources for a large Midwestern hospital says she would like to be honest about her lesbianism but knows of almost no one at her level of the corporate hierarchy who has taken that step— "It's just not done here."[47] Thus, gays and lesbians often fabricate heterosexual identities to keep their jobs or avoid running into the glass ceiling they see other employees encounter.

© ALYSON ALIANO

**CONCEPT CONNECTION**

*Colleen Barrett broke through corporate America's glass ceiling when she became president of Southwest Airlines after the retirement of Herb Kelleher. "Some CEOs will still introduce me as Herb's secretary," she says. The now highest-ranking woman in the U.S. airline industry did indeed begin her career 34 years ago as Kelleher's secretary at his San Antonio law firm. Today, Barrett just laughs when people mistake her for a secretary, but she knows there are still too many barriers to women moving into higher-level positions. As Southwest's president, Barrett oversees the airline's marketing, advertising, customer service, and human resources. She is also chiefly responsible for safeguarding Southwest's famed esprit de corps.*

## The Opt-Out Trend

Many women are never hitting the glass ceiling because they choose to get off the fast track long before it comes into view. There is currently much discussion of something referred to as the *opt-out trend*. The opt-out proponents say that greater numbers of highly-educated, professional

Exhibit 13.4

## The Wage Gap

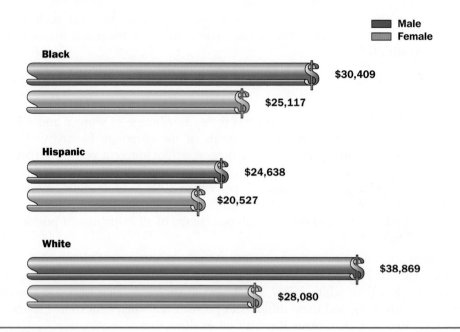

SOURCE: "2000 Median Annual Earnings by Race and Sex," reported by the National Committee on Pay Equity, *http://www.infoplease.com.*

women are deciding that corporate success isn't worth the price in terms of reduced family and personal time, greater stress, and negative health effects.[48] Women don't want corporate power and status in the same way that men do, and clawing one's way up the corporate ladder has become less appealing. For example, Brenda Barnes was on the fast track right to the top of PepsiCo, but she stepped down when the toll of the job—rising at 3:30 A.M., consistent 14-hour work days, a grueling travel schedule—began to outweigh its rewards. "When you talk about those big jobs, those CEO jobs, you just have to give them your life," Barnes says.[49] For many women, today, it's just not worth it. Some are opting-out to be stay-at-home moms, while others want to continue working but just not in the kind of fast-paced, competitive, aggressive environment that exists in most corporations. Most women, some who have studied the opt-out trend say, just don't want to work as hard and competitively as most men want to work.[50]

Critics, however, argue that this is just another way to blame women themselves for the dearth of female managers at higher levels.[51] Although many women are voluntarily leaving the fast track, there are many more who genuinely want to move up the corporate ladder but find their paths blocked. Fifty-five percent of executive women surveyed by Catalyst said they aspire to senior leadership levels.[52] In addition, a recent survey of 103 women voluntarily leaving executive jobs in *Fortune* 1000 companies found that corporate culture was cited as the Number 1 reason for leaving.[53] The greatest disadvantages of women leaders stem largely from prejudicial attitudes and a heavily male-oriented corporate culture.[54] Top-level corporate culture evolves around white, heterosexual, American males, who tend to hire and promote people who look, act, and think like them. Compatibility in thought and behavior plays an important role at higher levels of organizations. For example, in a survey of women who have managed to break through the glass ceiling, fully 96 percent said adapting to a predominantly white male culture was an important factor in their success.[55]

## The Female Advantage

Some people think women might actually be better managers, partly because of a more collaborative, less hierarchical, relationship-oriented approach that is in tune with today's global and multicultural environment.[56] As attitudes and values change with changing generations, the qualities women seem to naturally possess may lead to a gradual role reversal in organizations. For example, there's a stunning gender reversal in U. S. education, with girls taking over almost every leadership role from kindergarten to graduate school. In addition, women of all races and ethnic groups are outpacing men in earning bachelor's and master's degrees. Among 25- to 29-year-olds, 32 percent of women have college degrees, compared to 27 percent of men. Women are rapidly closing the M.D. and Ph.D. gap and make up about half of all U.S. law students. They make up half of all undergraduate business majors and about 30 percent of MBA candidates. Overall, women's participation in both the labor force and civic affairs has steadily increased since the mid-1950s, while men's participation has slowly but steadily declined.[57]

According to James Gabarino, an author and professor of human development at Cornell University, women are "better able to deliver in terms of what modern society requires of people—paying attention, abiding by rules, being verbally competent, and dealing with interpersonal relationships in offices."[58] His observation is supported by the fact that female managers are typically rated higher by subordinates on interpersonal skills as well as on factors such as task behavior, communication, ability to motivate others, and goal accomplishment.[59] Recent research found a correlation between balanced gender composition in companies (that is, roughly equal male and female representation) and higher organizational performance. Moreover, a study by Catalyst indicates that organizations with the highest percentage of women in top management financially outperform, by about 35 percent, those with the lowest percentage of women in higher-level jobs.[60] It seems that women should be marching right to the top of the corporate hierarchy, but prevailing attitudes, values, and perceptions in organizations create barriers and a glass ceiling.

# Current Responses to Diversity

Today's companies are searching for inclusive practices that go well beyond affirmative action to confront the obstacles that prevent women and minorities from advancing to senior management positions. For example, Texas Instruments CEO Thomas Engibous admits that his company needs to do a better job of placing women and minorities in key positions. "We do a good job hiring women, African Americans, and Hispanics," Engibous says. "But we have too many high-ranking women in peripheral areas. We need a better mix in the business's line management if we're going to have a woman or minority as TI's CEO someday."[61]

In addition, to prepare for and respond to an increasingly diverse business climate, managers in most companies are expanding the organization's emphasis on diversity beyond race and gender to consider such factors as ethnicity, age, physical ability, religion, and sexual orientation.

Once managers create and define a vision for a diverse workplace, they can analyze and assess the current culture and systems within the organization. Actions to develop an inclusive workplace that values and respects all people include three major steps: (1) building a corporate culture that values diversity; (2) changing structures, policies, and systems to support diversity; and (3) providing diversity awareness training.

## Changing the Corporate Culture

When the underlying culture of an organization does not change, all the other efforts to support diversity fail, as managers at Mitsubishi learned. Even though the company settled a sexual harassment suit filed by women at the Normal, Illinois, plant, established a zero tolerance policy, and fired workers who were guilty of blatant harassment, workers complained that the work environment remained deeply hostile to women and minorities. Although the incidents of harassment decreased, women and minority workers still felt threatened and powerless because the culture and environment that allowed the harassment to occur had not changed. Mitsubishi managers are still struggling with these difficult issues.[62]

Chapters 3 and 11 described approaches for changing corporate culture. Managers can start by actively using symbols for the new values, such as encouraging and celebrating the promotion of minorities and disciplining employees who display behavior that does not fit a diverse workplace. At Baxter Healthcare, CEO Harry Jansen Kraemer symbolizes the importance of balance by writing a newsletter column about his family. For women executives juggling a career and family, this sends a clear signal that personal and family issues are important and do not limit career advancement. Culture change starts at the top, and most organizations recognized as diversity leaders have CEOs and other top executives who demonstrate a strong commitment to making diversity part of the organizational mission.[63]

Managers throughout the company can be educated to help transform the culture. For one thing, they can examine the unwritten rules and assumptions. What are the myths about minorities? What are the values that exemplify the existing culture? Are unwritten rules communicated from one person to another in a way that excludes women and minorities? For example, many men may not discuss unwritten rules with women and minorities because they assume everyone is aware of them and they do not want to seem patronizing.[64]

Companies are addressing the issue of changing culture in a variety of ways. Some are using surveys, interviews, and focus groups to identify how the cultural values affect minorities and women. Others have set up structured networks of people of color, women, and other minority groups to explore the issues they face in the workplace and to recommend changes to senior management.

© SARAH A. FRIEDMAN

**CONCEPT CONNECTION**

*Denny's Restaurants, which was hit with a series of discrimination lawsuits in the early 1990s, has been changing structures and policies to promote and support diversity. The company responded to the discrimination charges with aggressive minority hiring and supplier-diversity efforts. In 2001, for the second year in a row, Denny's was awarded first place in* Fortune *magazine's list of "America's 50 Best Companies for Minorities" and it continues to rank in the top 5. Four of the company's eight board members, 45 percent of top officials and managers, and 48 percent of employees are members of minority groups.*

## Changing Structures and Policies

Many policies within organizations originally were designed to fit the stereotypical male employee. Now leading companies are changing structures and policies to facilitate and support a diverse workforce. A survey of *Fortune* 1,000 companies conducted by the Center for Creative Leadership found that 85 percent of companies surveyed have formal policies against racism and sexism, and 76 percent have structured grievance procedures and complaint review processes.[65] Companies are also developing policies to support the recruitment and career advancement of diverse employees. At least half of *Fortune* 1,000 companies have staff dedicated exclusively to encouraging diversity.

Exhibit 13.5

## The Most Common Diversity Initiatives: Percentage of *Fortune* 1,000 Respondents

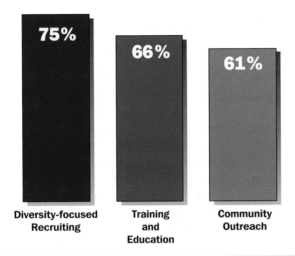

**75%** Diversity-focused Recruiting

**66%** Training and Education

**61%** Community Outreach

**SOURCE:** Data reported in "Impact of Diversity Initiatives on the Bottom Line: A SHRM Survey of the *Fortune* 1000," pp. S12–S14, in *Fortune*, special advertising section, "Keeping Your Edge: Managing a Diverse Corporate Culture," produced in association with the Society for Human Resource Management, *http://www. fortune.com/sections*.

Increasingly, organizations such as Procter & Gamble, Ernst & Young, and Allstate Insurance are tying managers' bonuses and promotions to how well they diversify the workforce. Exhibit 13.5 illustrates the most common diversity initiatives.

### Recruitment

A good way to revitalize the recruiting process is for the company to examine employee demographics, the composition of the labor pool in the area, and the composition of the customer base. Managers then can work toward a workforce composition that reflects the labor pool and the customer base. This is a key technique of the Federal Bureau of Investigation, described earlier.

For many organizations, a new approach to recruitment means making better use of formal recruiting strategies, offering internship programs to give people opportunities, and developing creative ways to draw upon previously unused labor markets. Nationwide's Scholars Program brings in Hispanic and African American college students for a three-year program that includes summer internships and year-long mentoring.[66] Marathon Ashland Petroleum has created a six-point recruiting strategy to increase diversity, including: (1) recruiting corporatewide and cross-functionally; (2) building relationships with first- and second-tiered schools to recruit minority students; (3) offering internships for racial and ethnic minorities; (4) offering minority scholarships; (5) establishing informal mentoring programs; and (6) forming affiliations with minority organizations.[67]

### Career Advancement

The successful advancement of diverse group members means that organizations must find ways to eliminate the glass ceiling. One of the most successful structures to accomplish this is the mentoring relationship. A mentor is a higher ranking, senior organizational member who is committed to providing upward mobility and support to a protégé's professional career.[68] Mentoring provides minorities and women with direct training and inside information on the norms and expectations of the organization. A mentor also acts as a friend or counselor, enabling the employee to feel more confident and capable. Leticia Aguilar manages 28 branches

**mentor**
A higher-ranking, senior organizational member who is committed to providing upward mobility and support to a protégé's professional career.

for Bank of America in greater Los Angeles, but when she started her career 32 years ago as a filing clerk, she didn't speak a word of English. Intensive night classes paid for by the company and a series of mentors helped Aguilar attain her goals for advancement.[69]

One researcher who has studied the career progress of high-potential minorities has found that those who advance the furthest all share one characteristic—a strong mentor or network of mentors who nurtured their professional development.[70] However, research also indicates that minorities, as well as women, are much less likely than men to develop mentoring relationships.[71] Women and minorities might not seek mentors because they feel that job competency should be enough to succeed, or they might feel uncomfortable seeking out a mentor when most of the senior executives are white males. Women might fear that initiating a mentoring relationship could be misunderstood as a romantic overture, whereas male mentors may think of women as mothers, wives, or sisters rather than as executive material. Cross-race mentoring relationships sometimes leave both parties uncomfortable, but the mentoring of minority employees must often be across race since there are few minorities in upper-level positions. The few minorities and women who have reached the upper ranks often are overwhelmed with mentoring requests from people like themselves, and they may feel uncomfortable in highly visible minority—minority or female—female mentoring relationships, which isolate them from the white male status quo.

The solution is for organizations to overcome some of the barriers to mentor relationships between white males and minorities. When organizations can institutionalize the value of white males actively seeking women and minority protégés, the benefits will mean that women and minorities will be steered into pivotal jobs and positions critical to advancement. Mentoring programs also are consistent with the Civil Rights Act of 1991 that requires the diversification of middle and upper management.

## Accommodating Special Needs

Many people have special needs of which top managers are unaware. For example, if a number of people entering the organization at the lower level are single parents, the company can reassess job scheduling and opportunities for child care. If a substantial labor pool is non–English-speaking, training materials and information packets can be provided in another language.

In many families today, both parents work, which means that the company can provide structures to deal with child care, maternity or paternity leave, flexible work schedules, home-based employment, and perhaps part-time employment or seasonal hours that reflect the school year. The key to attracting and keeping elderly or disabled workers may include long-term-care insurance and special health or life benefits. Alternative work scheduling also may be important for these groups of workers. Many organizations are struggling with *generational diversity*, striving to meet the needs of workers at different ages and life cycles.[72] Pitney Bowes created the Life Balance Resources program to help employees in different generations cope with life cycle issues, such as helping Generation Y workers find their first apartments or cars, assisting Generation X employees in locating child care or getting home loans, and helping baby boomers plan for retirement or find elder care for aging parents.[73]

Another issue for U.S. companies is that racial/ethnic minorities and immigrants have often had fewer educational opportunities than other groups. Some companies have worked with high schools to provide fundamental skills in literacy and math, or they provide these programs within the company to upgrade employees to appropriate educational levels. The movement toward increasing educational services for employees can be expected to increase for immigrants and the economically disadvantaged in the years to come.

Changing organizational structures and policies is important because it demonstrates a concrete commitment to supporting diversity. If managers talk about the value of a diverse workforce but do not do anything to ensure that diverse workers have opportunities and support in the workplace, employees are not likely to trust that the company truly values diversity.

## Diversity Awareness Training

Many organizations, including Monsanto, Xerox, and Mobil Oil, provide special training, called diversity awareness training, to help people become aware of their own cultural boundaries, their prejudices and stereotypes, so they can learn to work and live together. Working or living within a multicultural context requires a person to use interaction skills that transcend the skills typically effective when dealing with others from one's own in-group.[74] Diversity awareness programs help people learn how to handle conflict in a constructive manner, which tends to reduce stress and negative energy in diverse work teams.

**diversity awareness training**
Special training designed to make people aware of their own prejudices and stereotypes.

People vary in their sensitivity and openness to other cultures. Exhibit 13.6 shows a model of six stages of diversity awareness. The continuum ranges from a total lack of awareness to a complete understanding and acceptance of people's differences. This model is useful in helping diversity awareness trainers assess participants' openness to change. People at different stages might require different kinds of training. A basic aim of awareness training is to help people recognize that hidden and overt biases direct their thinking about specific individuals and groups. If people can come away from a training session recognizing that they prejudge people and that this needs to be consciously addressed in communications with and treatment of others, an important goal of diversity awareness training has been reached.

Many diversity awareness programs used today are designed to help people of varying backgrounds communicate effectively with one another and to understand the language and context used in dealing with people from other groups. The point of this training is to help people be more flexible in their communications with others, to treat each person as an individual, and not to rely on stereotypes. For example, if you were a part of such a program, it would help you develop an explicit awareness of your own cultural values, your own cultural boundaries, and your own cultural behaviors. Then you would be provided the same information about other groups, and you would be given the opportunity to learn about and communicate with people from other groups. One of the most important elements in diversity training is to bring together people of differing perspectives so that they can engage in learning new interpersonal communication skills with one another. Diversity awareness training is an important part of a cultural overhaul at Denny's Restaurants.

Things have certainly changed at Denny's Restaurants in the past decade or so. In the early 1990s, Denny's became an icon for racism in the United States when six black Secret Service officers accused servers and managers at an Annapolis, Maryland, restaurant of humiliating and discriminating against them. Other incidents of racism and discrimination soon surfaced, including managers barring black customers or asking them to prepay their dinner bills. At that time, only one of the chain's franchises was minority owned.

Today, a sweeping cultural overhaul has transformed Denny's into a model for inclusiveness. At least 45 percent of Denny's franchises are owned by minorities, 45 percent of senior executives are women or people of color, and the board is 50 percent minority. The company has ranked in the top five on *Fortune's* list of the best companies for minorities for five years in a row.

The company hasn't just opened the doors to women and minorities, but incorporated high levels of diversity awareness training to make sure inclusiveness is a primary value that is woven through everything the company does. Every single person employed by Denny's,

DENNY'S
RESTAURANTS
**http://www.dennys.com**

Exhibit 13.6

### Stages of Diversity Awareness

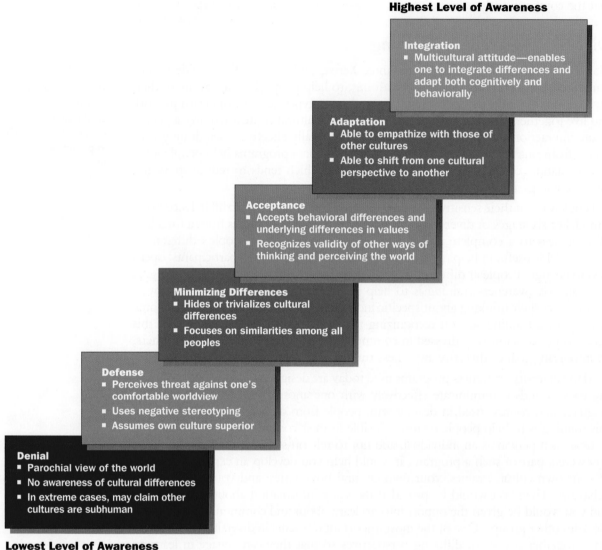

**Highest Level of Awareness**

**Integration**
- Multicultural attitude—enables one to integrate differences and adapt both cognitively and behaviorally

**Adaptation**
- Able to empathize with those of other cultures
- Able to shift from one cultural perspective to another

**Acceptance**
- Accepts behavioral differences and underlying differences in values
- Recognizes validity of other ways of thinking and perceiving the world

**Minimizing Differences**
- Hides or trivializes cultural differences
- Focuses on similarities among all peoples

**Defense**
- Perceives threat against one's comfortable worldview
- Uses negative stereotyping
- Assumes own culture superior

**Denial**
- Parochial view of the world
- No awareness of cultural differences
- In extreme cases, may claim other cultures are subhuman

**Lowest Level of Awareness**

SOURCE: Based on M. Bennett, "A Developmental Approach to Training for Intercultural Sensitivity," *International Journal of Intercultural Relations* 10 (1986), 179–196.

from servers and managers to media planners and part-time leased security guards, goes through extensive training. One aspect is how to apply cultural awareness, sensitivity, and effective conflict-resolution in a restaurant setting. Denny's spends several million dollars a year on diversity compliance and training.[75]

# Defining New Relationships in Organizations

One outcome of diversity is an increased incidence of close personal relationships in the workplace, which can have both positive and negative results for employees as well as the organization. Two issues of concern are emotional intimacy and sexual harassment.

## Emotional Intimacy

Close emotional relationships, particularly between men and women, often have been discouraged in companies for fear that they would disrupt the balance of power and threaten organizational stability.[76] This opinion grew out of the assumption that organizations are designed for rationality and efficiency, which were best achieved in a nonemotional environment.

However, a recent study of friendships in organizations sheds interesting light on this issue.[77] Managers and workers responded to a survey about emotionally intimate relationships with both male and female coworkers. Many men and women reported having close relationships with an opposite-sex coworker. Called *nonromantic love relationships*, the friendships resulted in trust, respect, constructive feedback, and support in achieving work goals. Intimate friendships did not necessarily become romantic, and they affected each person's job and career in a positive way. Rather than causing problems, nonromantic love relationships, according to the study, affected work teams in a positive manner because conflict was reduced. Indeed, men reported somewhat greater benefit than women from these relationships, perhaps because the men had fewer close relationships outside the workplace upon which to depend.

However, when such relationships *do* become romantic or sexual in nature, real problems can result. Romances that require the most attention from managers are those that arise between a supervisor and a subordinate. These relationships often lead to morale problems among other staff members, complaints of favoritism, and questions about the supervisor's intentions or judgment. Although few companies have written policies about workplace romance in general, 70 percent of companies surveyed have policies prohibiting romantic relationships between a superior and a subordinate.[78]

## Sexual Harassment

Although psychological closeness between men and women in the workplace may be a positive experience, sexual harassment is not. Sexual harassment is illegal. As a form of sexual discrimination, sexual harassment in the workplace is a violation of Title VII of the 1964 Civil Rights Act. Sexual harassment in the classroom is a violation of Title VIII of the Education Amendment of 1972. The following categorize various forms of sexual harassment as defined by one university:

- *Generalized.* This form involves sexual remarks and actions that are not intended to lead to sexual activity but that are directed toward a coworker based solely on gender and reflect on the entire group.
- *Inappropriate/offensive.* Though not sexually threatening, it causes discomfort in a coworker, whose reaction in avoiding the harasser may limit his or her freedom and ability to function in the workplace.
- *Solicitation with promise of reward.* This action treads a fine line as an attempt to "purchase" sex, with the potential for criminal prosecution.
- *Coercion with threat of punishment.* The harasser coerces a coworker into sexual activity by using the threat of power (through recommendations, grades, promotions, and so on) to jeopardize the victim's career.
- *Sexual crimes and misdemeanors.* The highest level of sexual harassment, these acts would, if reported to the police, be considered felony crimes and misdemeanors.[79]

Statistics in Canada indicate that between 40 and 70 percent of women and about 5 percent of men have been sexually harassed at work.[80] The situation in the United States is just as dire. Between 1992 and 2002, the Equal Employment Opportunity

Commission shows a 150 percent increase in the number of sexual harassment cases filed annually.[81] About 10 percent of those were filed by males. The Supreme Court has held that same-sex harassment as well as harassment of men by female coworkers is just as illegal as the harassment of women by men. In the suit that prompted the Court's decision, a male oil-rig worker claimed he was singled out by other members of the all-male crew for crude sex play, unwanted touching, and threats of rape.[82] A growing number of men are urging recognition that sexual harassment is not just a woman's problem.[83]

Because the corporate world is dominated by a male culture, however, sexual harassment affects women to a much greater extent. Companies such as Dow Chemical, Xerox, and *The New York Times* have been swift to fire employees for circulating pornographic images, surfing pornographic Web sites, or sending offensive e-mails.[84]

# Global Diversity

Globalization is a reality for today's companies. As stated in a report from the Hudson Institute, *Workforce 2020*, "The rest of the world matters to a degree that it never did in the past."[85] Even small companies that do not do business in other countries are affected by global diversity issues. However, large multinational companies that hire employees in many countries face tremendous challenges because they must apply diversity management across a broader stage than North America. For example, Citigroup has more than 260,000 employees in more than 100 countries, creating a tremendous multicultural management challenge. Managers must develop new skills and awareness to handle the unique challenges of global diversity: cross-cultural understanding, the ability to build networks, and the understanding of geopolitical forces. Two significant aspects of global diversity programs involve employee selection and training and the understanding of the communication context.

## Selection and Training

**expatriates**
Employees who live and work in a country other than their own.

Expatriates are employees who live and work in a country other than their own. Careful screening, selection, and training of employees to serve overseas increase the potential for corporate global success. Human resource managers consider

*The children in this Avezzano, Italy, school share cultures and learn firsthand the dynamics of global diversity. The school was established by Texas Instruments for the families of U.S. and Japanese employees involved in T.I.'s six-nation team building Europe's largest semiconductor. Such efforts, along with Minority Procurement programs, demonstrate T.I.'s commitment to a diverse, multinational corporate environment.*

COURTESY OF TEXAS INSTRUMENTS

# manager's Shoptalk

**Turbulent Times**

**A Guide for Expatriate Managers in America**
Although each person is different, individuals from a specific country typically share certain values and attitudes. Managers who are planning to work in a foreign country can learn about these broad value patterns to help them adjust to working and living in a foreign country. The following characteristics are some that are often used to help foreign managers understand what Americans are like.

1. Americans are very informal. They tend to treat everyone alike, even when there are significant differences in age or social status.
2. Americans are direct. They don't "beat around the bush," which means they don't talk around things but get right to the point. To some foreigners, this may seem abrupt or even rude.
3. Americans are competitive. Some foreigners might think they are aggressive or overbearing.
4. Americans are achievers. They like to keep score, whether at work or play. They emphasize accomplishments.
5. Americans are independent and individualistic. They place a high value on freedom and believe that people can control their own destinies.
6. Americans are questioners. They ask a lot of questions, even of someone they have just met. Some of these questions may seem pointless ("How ya' doin'?") or personal ("What kind of work do you do?")

7. Americans dislike silence. They would rather talk about the weather than deal with silence in a conversation.
8. Americans value punctuality. They keep appointment calendars and live according to schedules and clocks.
9. Americans value cleanliness. They may seem obsessed with bathing, eliminating body odors, and wearing clean clothes.

How many of these statements do you agree with? Discuss them with your friends and classmates, including people from different countries and members of different subcultural groups from the United States.

SOURCES: "What Are Americans Like?," Exhibit 4-6 in Stephen P. Robbins and Mary Coulter, *Management*, 8th ed. (Upper Saddle River, NJ: Pearson Prentice Hall, 2005), as adapted from M. Ernest, ed., *Predeparture Orientation Handbook: For Foreign Students and Scholars Planning to Study in the United States* (Washington, D.C.: U.S. Information Agency, Bureau of Cultural Affairs, 1984), 103–105; Amanda Bennett, "American Culture is Often a Puzzle for Foreign Managers in the U.S.," *The Wall Street Journal* (February 12, 1986), 29; "Don't Think Our Way's the Only Way," *The Pryor Report* (February 1988), 9; and B. Wattenberg, "The Attitudes Behind American Exceptionalism," *U.S. News and World Report* (August 7, 1989), 25.

global skills in the selection process. In addition, expatriates receive cross-cultural training that develops language skills and provides cultural and historical orientation.[86] The Manager's Shoptalk lists some interesting tips for foreign managers working in the United States to help them understand and relate to Americans. Do you agree that these statements provide a good introduction to American culture for a non-native?

Equally important is honest self-analysis by overseas candidates and their families. Before seeking or accepting an assignment in another country, a candidate should ask himself or herself such questions as the following:

• Is your spouse interrupting his or her own career path to support your career? Is that acceptable to both of you?
• Is family separation for long periods involved?
• Can you initiate social contacts in a foreign culture?

- Can you adjust well to different environments and changes in personal comfort or quality of living, such as the lack of television, gasoline at $5 per gallon, limited hot water, varied cuisine, and national phone strikes?
- Can you manage your future reentry into the job market by networking and maintaining contacts in your home country?[87]

Employees working overseas must adjust to all of these conditions. Managers going global might find that their own management styles need adjustment to succeed in a foreign country. One aspect of this adjustment is understanding differences in social and cultural values as identified by the Hofstede research and the Globe Project described in Chapter 4 of this text. Another important consideration is understanding the communication context of a foreign location.

## Communication Differences

People from some cultures tend to pay more attention to the social context (social setting, nonverbal behavior, social status) of their verbal communication than Americans do. For example, American managers working in China have discovered that social context is considerably more important in that culture, and they have learned to suppress their impatience and devote the time needed to establish personal and social relationships.

Exhibit 13.7 indicates how the emphasis on social context varies among countries. In a **high-context culture**, people are sensitive to circumstances surrounding social exchanges. People use communication primarily to build personal social relationships; meaning is derived from context—setting, status, nonverbal behavior— more than from explicit words; relationships and trust are more important than business; and the welfare and harmony of the group are valued. In a **low-context culture**, people use communication primarily to exchange facts and information; meaning is derived primarily from words; business transactions are more important than building relationships and trust; and individual welfare and achievement are more important than the group.[88]

To understand how differences in cultural context affect communications, consider the U.S. expression, "The squeaky wheel gets the oil." It means that the loudest person will get the most attention, and attention is assumed to be favorable. Equivalent sayings in China and Japan are "Quacking ducks get shot," and "The nail that sticks up gets hammered down," respectively. Standing out as an individual in these cultures clearly merits unfavorable attention.

**high-context culture**
A culture in which communication is used to enhance personal relationships.

**low-context culture**
A culture in which communication is used to exchange facts and information.

## Exhibit 13.7

### Arrangement of High- and Low-Context Cultures

| High Context | |
|---|---|
| | Chinese |
| | Korean |
| | Japanese |
| | Vietnamese |
| | Arab |
| | Greek |
| | Spanish |
| | Italian |
| | English |
| | North American |
| | Scandinavian |
| Low Context | Swiss |
| | German |

**SOURCES:** Edward T. Hall, *Beyond Culture* (Garden City, N.Y.: Anchor Press/Doubleday, 1976); and J. Kennedy and A. Everest, "Put Diversity in Context," *Personnel Journal* (September 1991), 50–54.

High-context cultures include Asian and Arab countries. Low-context cultures tend to be American and Northern European. Even within North America, cultural subgroups vary in the extent to which context counts, explaining why differences among groups make successful communication difficult. White females, Native Americans, and African Americans all tend to prefer higher context communication than do white males. A high-context interaction requires more time because a relationship has to be developed, and trust and friendship must be established. Furthermore, most male managers and most people doing the hiring in organizations are from low-context cultures, which conflicts with people entering the organization from a background in a higher context culture. Overcoming these differences in communication is a major goal of diversity awareness training.

# Diversity in a Turbulent World

Ninety-one percent of companies responding to a survey by the Society for Human Resource Management believe that diversity initiatives help maintain a competitive advantage. Some specific benefits include improving employee morale, decreasing interpersonal conflict, facilitating progress into new markets, and increasing the organization's creativity.[89] In addition to the ideas we have discussed, two new approaches to diversity management—multicultural teams and employee networks—have arisen in response to the rapid change and complexity of organizations in today's global environment.

## Multicultural Teams

Companies have long known that putting together teams made up of members from different functional areas results in better problem solving and decision making. Now, they are recognizing that multicultural teams—teams made up of members from diverse national, racial, ethnic, and cultural backgrounds—provide even greater potential for enhanced creativity, innovation, and value in today's global marketplace.[90] Research has found that diverse teams generate more and better alternatives to problems and produce more creative solutions than homogeneous teams.[91] A team made up of people with different perspectives, backgrounds, and cultural values creates a healthy mix of ideas and leads to greater creativity and better decisions.

**multicultural teams**
Teams made up of members from diverse national, racial, ethnic, and cultural backgrounds.

Some organizations, such as RhonePoulenc Rorer (RPR), based in Collegeville, Pennsylvania, are committed to mixing people from diverse countries and cultures, from the top to the bottom of the organization. There are 15 nationalities represented in RPR's top management teams, including a French CEO, an Austrian head of operations, an American general counsel, an Egyptian head of human resources, and an Italian director of corporate communications.[92] The technology start-up Obongo has teams made up of people from 12 countries and 18 different cultures.[93]

Multicultural teams are becoming common in both U.S. and Canadian organizations. One consultant notes that the workforce of many Canadian organizations is often jokingly referred to as the *United Nations* because companies have so many different nationalities working together on project teams.[94]

Despite their many advantages,[95] multicultural teams are more difficult to manage because of the increased potential for miscommunication and misunderstanding. Multicultural teams typically have more difficulty learning to communicate and work well together, but with effective cross-cultural training and good management, the problems seem to dissipate over time.[96] One management team videotaped its meetings so members could see how their body language reflects cultural differences.

An American manager remarked, "I couldn't believe how even my physical movements dominated the table, while Ron [a Filipino American] . . . actually worked his way off-camera within the first five minutes."[97]

## Employee Network Groups

Employee network groups are based on social identity, such as gender or race, and are organized by employees to focus on concerns of employees from that group.[98] For example, when Marita Golden was teaching at George Mason University, she often heard other African American women at the university talk about how they felt isolated and needed to get together. So, Golden started a networking group that has grown and expanded, incorporating women from other local colleges and universities as well, who get together and share their research interests, talk about career and personal development issues, and explore both positive and negative experiences of their work lives.[99] At Visteon Corp., a global automotive systems producer, the women's network group develops the leadership and technical skills of female employees, designs strategies for how members can contribute to Visteon's business and diversity goals, and works to keep top managers informed of members' contributions, concerns, and needs.[100] Whereas multicultural teams help bind diverse people together for the accomplishment of shared goals, network groups provide people with comfort and support in an often-crazy world. The idea behind network groups is that minority employees can join together across traditional organizational boundaries for mutual support and to extend member influence in the organization.

Network groups pursue a variety of activities, such as meetings to educate top managers, mentoring programs, networking events, training sessions and skills seminars, minority intern programs, and community volunteer activities. Network groups give people a chance to meet, interact with, and develop social and professional ties to others throughout the organization, which may include key decision makers. Network groups are a powerful way to reduce social isolation for women and minorities, help these employees be more effective, and enable members to achieve greater career advancement. A recent study confirms that network groups can be an important tool for helping organization's retain managerial-level minority employees.[101]

An important characteristic of network groups is that they are created informally by employees, not the organization, and membership is voluntary. However, successful organizations support and encourage network groups. Even managers who once thought of minority networks as "gripe groups" are now seeing them as essential to organizational success because they help to retain minority employees, enhance diversity efforts, and spark new ideas that can benefit the organization.[102] Although at first glance the proliferation of employee network groups seems to be in direct opposition to the trend toward multicultural teams, the two mechanisms actually work quite well together. At Kraft Foods, networks are considered critical to the success of multicultural teams because they build awareness and acceptance of cultural differences and help people feel more comfortable working together.[103]

There has been a tremendous growth of employee networks for minorities who have faced barriers to advancement in organizations, including African Americans, Hispanics, American Indians, Asian Americans, women, gays and lesbians, and disabled employees. In general, female and minority employees who participate in a network group feel more pride about their work and are more optimistic about their careers than those who do not have the support of a network.[104]

Several important ideas pertain to workforce diversity, which is the inclusion of people with different human qualities and from different cultural groups. Dimensions of diversity are both primary, such as age, gender, and race, and secondary, such as education, marital status, and income. Ethnocentric attitudes generally produce a monoculture that accepts only one way of doing things and one set of values and beliefs, thereby excluding nontraditional employees from full participation. Minority employees face several significant challenges in the workplace.

Acceptance of diversity is becoming especially important because of sociocultural changes and the changing workforce. Diversity in the workplace reflects diversity in the larger environment.

Affirmative action programs have been successful in gaining employment for women and minorities, but the glass ceiling has kept many women and minorities from obtaining top management positions. Some women are opting to get off the corporate ladder, although studies indicate that women have characteristics that may make them better managers than men in today's diverse organizations. Breaking the glass ceiling ultimately means changing the corporate culture within organizations; changing internal structures and policies toward employees, including accommodating special needs; and providing diversity awareness training to help people become aware of their own cultural boundaries and prejudices. This training also helps employees learn to communicate with people from other cultural contexts.

Wal-Mart, described in the chapter opening, is facing a potentially devastating gender-discrimination lawsuit. CEO Lee Scott has publicly vowed to work harder to equalize pay and promote more women to management positions. At the company's 2004 annual meeting, Scott announced that executives' bonuses will be cut 7.5 percent this year and 15 percent next year if Wal-Mart fails to meet its goals of promoting women and minorities in proportion to the number who apply for management positions. Scott has also set up a 140-person compliance office to ensure that the new goals are met. The diversity issues at Wal-Mart will not be resolved easily. Top executives want to revise structures, policies, and processes so they are unequivocally fair without losing the culture that makes Wal-Mart special. Some believe, however, that massive culture change is the only way to solve the deep-rooted problems that led to the lawsuit. There are indications that top Wal-Mart managers have long been aware that some of the company's policies and practices might create barriers for women and minorities. It is likely that legal action will ultimately force the company to make big changes designed to create a more inclusive work environment.[105]

Another result of increased diversity in organizations is the opportunity for emotional intimacy and friendships between men and women that are beneficial to all parties. However, while emotional connections are a positive outcome, sexual harassment has become a serious problem for today's managers. Increasing diversity also means that organizations must develop programs to deal with global as well as domestic diversity and with potential conflicts that arise.

Two recent approaches to supporting and leveraging the power of diversity in organizations are multicultural teams and employee network groups. Multicultural teams provide a broader and deeper base of experience and ideas for enhanced problem solving, creativity, and innovation. Organizations that value diversity also encourage and support network groups to enable minority organization members to reduce their social isolation, be more effective in their jobs, have a greater impact on the organization, and achieve greater opportunities for career advancement.

# Discussion Questions

1. If you were a senior manager at a company such as R. R. Donnelley, Allstate Insurance, or Texaco, how would you address the challenges faced by minority employees?

2. Some people argue that social class is a major source of cultural differences, yet social class is not listed as a primary or secondary dimension in Exhibit 14.1. Discuss reasons for this.

3. Have you been associated with an organization that made assumptions associated with a mono-culture? Describe the culture.

4. Do you think any organization can successfully resist diversity today? Discuss.

5. What is the glass ceiling, and why do you think it has proved to be such a barrier to women and minorities?

6. In preparing an organization to accept diversity, do you think it is more important to change the corporate culture or to change structures and policies? Explain.

7. If a North American corporation could choose either high-context or low-context communications, which do you think would be best for the company's long-term health? Discuss.

8. What do you think the impact on an organization would be for diversity within its own country versus international diversity? Discuss.

9. Many single people meet and date people from their work organization because the organization provides a context within which to know and trust another person. How do you think this practice affects the potential for emotional intimacy? Sexual harassment?

10. How might diversity within the organization ultimately lead to better problem solving and greater creativity?

# Management in Practice: Experiential Exercise

**How Tolerant Are You?**

For each of the following questions circle the answer that best describes you.

1. Most of your friends
   a. are very similar to you
   b. are very different from you and from each other
   c. are like you in some respects but different in others

2. When someone does something you disapprove of, you
   a. break off the relationship
   b. tell how you feel but keep in touch
   c. tell yourself it matters little and behave as you always have

3. Which virtue is most important to you?
   a. kindness
   b. objectivity
   c. obedience

4. When it comes to beliefs, you
   a. do all you can to make others see things the same way you do
   b. actively advance your point of view but stop short of argument
   c. keep your feelings to yourself

5. Would you hire a person who has had emotional problems?
   a. no
   b. yes, provided there is evidence of complete recovery
   c. yes, if the person is suitable for the job

6. Do you voluntarily read material that supports views different from your own?
   a. never
   b. sometimes
   c. often

7. You react to old people with
   a. patience
   b. annoyance
   c. sometimes a, sometimes b

8. Do you agree with the statement, "What is right and wrong depends upon the time, place, and circumstance?"
   a. strongly agree
   b. agree to a point
   c. strongly disagree

9. Would you marry someone from a different race?
   a. yes
   b. no
   c. probably not

10. If someone in your family were homosexual, you would
    a. view this as a problem and try to change the person to a heterosexual orientation
    b. accept the person as a homosexual with no change in feelings or treatment
    c. avoid or reject the person

11. You react to little children with
    a. patience
    b. annoyance
    c. sometimes a, sometimes b

12. Other people's personal habits annoy you
    a. often
    b. not at all
    c. only if extreme

13. If you stay in a household run differently from yours (cleanliness, manners, meals, and other customs), you
    a. adapt readily
    b. quickly become uncomfortable and irritated
    c. adjust for a while, but not for long

14. Which statement do you agree with most?
    a. We should avoid judging others because no one can fully understand the motives of another person.

b. People are responsible for their actions and have to accept the consequences.
c. Both motives and actions are important when considering questions of right and wrong.

Circle your score for each of the answers below and total the scores:

1. a 5 4; b 5 0; c 5 2
2. a 5 4; b 5 2; c 5 0
3. a 5 0; b 5 2; c 5 4
4. a 5 4; b 5 2; c 5 0
5. a 5 4; b 5 2; c 5 0
6. a 5 4; b 5 2; c 5 0
7. a 5 0; b 5 4; c 5 2
8. a 5 0; b 5 2; c 5 4
9. a 5 0; b 5 4; c 5 2
10. a 5 2; b 5 0; c 5 4
11. a 5 0; b 5 4; c 5 2
12. a 5 4; b 5 0; c 5 2
13. a 5 0; b 5 4; c 5 2
14. a 5 0; b 5 4; c 5 2

**Total Score:**

**0–14:** If you score 14 or below, you are a very tolerant person and dealing with diversity comes easily to you.

**15–28:** You are basically a tolerant person and others think of you as tolerant. In general, diversity presents few problems for you, but you may be broad minded in some areas and have less tolerant ideas in other areas of life, such as attitudes toward older people or male-female social roles.

**29–42:** You are less tolerant than most people and should work on developing greater tolerance of people different from you. Your low tolerance level could affect your business or personal relationships.

**43–56:** You have a very low tolerance for diversity. The only people you are likely to respect are those with beliefs similar to your own. You reflect a level of intolerance that could cause difficulties in today's multicultural business environment.

Source: Adapted from the Tolerance Scale by Maria Heiselman, Naomi Miller, and Bob Schlorman, Northern Kentucky University, 1982, in George Manning, Kent Curtis, and Steve McMillen, *Building Community: The Human Side of Work*, (Cincinnati, Ohio: Thomson Executive Press, 1996), 272–277.

# Management in Practice: Ethical Dilemma

**Promotion or Not?**

You are the president of CrownCutters, Inc. You have worked closely with Bill Smith for several years now. In many situations, he has served as your de facto right-hand person.

Due to a retirement, you have an opening in the position of executive vice president. Bill is the natural choice—and this is obvious to the other mid- and senior-level managers at CrownCutters. Bill is popular with most of the managers in the company. Of course, he also has his share of detractors.

Prior to announcing the appointment of Bill Smith, you receive a memo from Jane Jones, your controller. Jane's memo indicates that she was subjected to sporadic sexual harassment by Bill starting ten years ago when she first joined the company and was working for him. Her memo indicates that the harassment essentially stopped six years ago when she moved to a position in which Bill was no longer her superior. She requests that this information be kept totally confidential.

You have never heard of any allegations like this about Bill before.

**What Do You Do?**

1.  Move ahead with the promotion because, even if true, this is an isolated incident that is a part of Bill's past and is not his current behavior.
2.  Stop the promotion because Bill is not the type of person who should help lead the company and shape its values.
3.  Put the promotion on hold until you can discuss the situation extensively with Bill and Jane, although this means the accusation probably will become public knowledge.

Source: This case was provided by Professor David Scheffman, Owen Graduate School of Management, Vanderbilt University, Nashville, Tennessee.

# Surf the Net

1.  **The Glass Ceiling.** In order to learn more about the glass ceiling, visit *http://www.ilr.cornell. edu/library/keyWorkplaceDocuments/government/ federal/Glassceilingreport.html*. You will need to have the Acrobat Reader, available as a free download from this site, installed on your computer. Select the "Recommendations of the Glass Ceiling Commission," and answer these two questions: (a) What was the mission of the Glass Ceiling Commission? (b) What are the eight recommendations the Commission made for business?
2.  **Diversity Awareness Training.** Use a search engine keying in the words "diversity awareness training," and compare the content and focus of 3 to 4 different training programs in this area. Recommend the training program you think

    would do the best job of improving employees' diversity awareness. Sample sites are included below:
    *http://www.adl.org/blueprint.pdf*
    *http://www.ibisconsultinggroup.com*
    *http://www.hodes.com/diversitymatters/*
    *http://www.edgeohio.com*
3.  **Sexual Harassment.** Go to *http://www. harbeck.com/sexual_harassment_quiz.htm* and find the sexual harassment quiz prepared by the HarBeck Company. Take the quiz, print out a copy after you have selected your answers, and bring the completed quiz to class. Your instructor may wish to use this quiz to determine how well the class understands sexual harassment.

# Case for Critical Analysis

## Draper Manufacturing

You have just been hired as a diversity consultant by Draper Manufacturing. Ralph Draper, chairman and CEO, and other top managers feel a need to resolve some racial issues that have been growing over the past several years at their plant in Nashville, Tennessee. Draper Manufacturing is a small, family-owned company that manufactures mattresses. It employs 90 people full-time, including African Americans, Asians, and Hispanics. About 75 percent of the workforce is female. The company also occasionally hires part-time workers, most of whom are Hispanic women. Most of these part-timers are hired for periods of a few months at a time, when production is falling behind schedule.

To begin your orientation to the company, Draper has asked his production manager, Wallace Burns, to take you around the plant. As Burns points out the various areas responsible for each stage of the production process, you overhear several different languages being spoken. In the shipping and receiving department, you notice that most workers are black men. Burns confirms that 90 percent of the workers in shipping and receiving are African American and points out that the manager of that department, Adam Fox, is also African American.

Later in the afternoon you attend a regular meeting of top managers to meet everyone and get a feel for the organizational culture. Draper introduces you as a diversity consultant and notes that several of his managers have expressed concerns about festering racial tensions in the company. He notes that "Each of the minority groups sticks together. The blacks and Orientals rarely mix, and most of the Mexicans stick together and speak only in Spanish. It seems that some of our workers are just downright lazy sometimes. We keep falling behind in our production schedule and having to hire part-time workers, but then we generally have to fire two or three of those a month for goofing off on the job." He closes his introduction by saying that you have been hired to help the company solve their growing diversity problems.

Draper then turns toward the management committee's routine daily business. The others present are the general manager, human resources manager (the only woman), sales manager, quality control manager, plant manager (Wallace Burns), and shipping and receiving manager (Adam Fox, the only non-white manager). Soon an angry debate begins between Fox and the sales manager. The sales manager says that orders are not being shipped on time, and several complaints have been received about the quality of the product. Fox argues that he needs more workers in shipping and receiving to do the job right, and he adds that the quality of incoming supplies is lousy. While this debate continues, the other managers remain silent and seem quite uncomfortable. Finally, the quality control manager attempts to calm things down with a joke about his wife. Most of the men in the group laugh loudly, and the conversation shifts to other topics on the agenda.

## Questions

1.  What suggestions would you make to Draper's managers to help them move toward successfully managing diversity issues?
2.  If you were the shipping and receiving or human resources manager, how do you think you would feel about working at Draper? What are some of the challenges you might face at this company?
3.  Based on the information in the case, at what stage of diversity awareness (Exhibit 14.5) do managers at Draper Manufacturing seem to be? Discuss.

Source: Based on "Northern Industries," a case prepared by Rae Andre of Northeastern University.

# Endnotes

1. Wendy Zellner, "No Way to Treat a Lady," *BusinessWeek* (March 3, 2003), 63, 66; Ann Zimmerman, "Judge to Weigh Wal-Mart Suit for Class Action," *The Wall Street Journal* (September 23, 2003), B1; and Douglas P. Shuit, "People Problems on Every Aisle, Part 1 of 2," *Workforce Management* (February 1, 2004), 26+.

2. Kenneth Labich, "No More Crude at Texaco," *Fortune* (September 6, 1999), 205–212; and Aaron Bernstein with Michael Arndt, "Racism in the Workplace," *BusinessWeek* (July 30, 2001); Reed Abelson, "Can Respect Be Mandated? Maybe Not Here," *The New York Times* (September 10, 2000), BU1.

3. M. Fine, F. Johnson, and M. S. Ryan, "Cultural Diversity in the Workforce," *Public Personnel Management* 19 (1990), 305–319.

4. Taylor H. Cox, "Managing Cultural Diversity: Implications for Organizational Competitiveness," *Academy of Management Executive* 5, no. 3 (1991), 45–56; and Faye Rice, "How to Make Diversity Pay," *Fortune* (August 8, 1994), 78–86.

5. Roy Harris, "The Illusion of Inclusion," *CFO* (May 2001), 42–50.

6. Survey results reported in "Diversity Initiatives Shown to Be Critical to Job Seekers," *The New York Times Magazine* (September 14, 2003), 100, part of a special advertisement, "Diversity Works."

7. Lennie Copeland "Valuing Diversity, Part I: Making the Most of Cultural Differences at the Workplace," *Personnel* (June 1988), 52–60.

8. Lee Smith, "The Business Case for Diversity" in "The Diversity Factor," Special Advertising Section, *Fortune* (October 13, 2003), S1–S12.

9. Lennie Copeland, "Learning to Manage a Multicultural Workforce," *Training* (May 25, 1988), 48–56; and D. Farid Elashmawi, "Culture Clashes: Barriers to Business," *Managing Diversity* 2, no. 11 (August 1993), 1–3.

10. Marilyn Loden and Judy B. Rosener, *Workforce America!* (Homewood, Ill.: Business One Irwin, 1991); and Marilyn Loden, *Implementing Diversity* (Homewood, Ill.: Irwin, 1996).

11. Frances J. Milliken and Luis I. Martins, "Searching for Common Threads: Understanding the Multiple Effects of Diversity in Organizational Groups," *Academy of Management Review* 21, no. 2 (1996), 402–433.

12. N. Songer, "Workforce Diversity," *B&E Review* (April–June 1991), 3–6.

13. Robert Doktor, Rosalie Tung, and Mary Ann von Glinow, "Future Directions for Management Theory Development," *Academy of Management Review* 16 (1991), 362–365; and Mary Munter, "Cross-Cultural Communication for Managers," *Business Horizons* (May–June 1993), 69–78.

14. Renee Blank and Sandra Slipp, "The White Male: An Endangered Species?" *Management Review* (September 1994), 27–32; Michael S. Kimmel, "What Do Men Want?" *Harvard Business Review* (November–December 1993), 50–63; and Sharon Nelton, "Nurturing Diversity," *Nation's Business* (June 1995), 25–27.

15. Marianne Bertrand and Sendhil Mullainathan, *Are Emily and Greg More Employable than Lakisha and Jamal?* National Bureau of Economic Research report, as reported in L. A. Johnson, "What's in a Name: When Emily Gets the Job Over Lakisha," *The Tennessean* (January 4, 2004), 14A.

16. M. Bennett, "A Developmental Approach to Training for Intercultural Sensitivity," *International Journal of Intercultural Relations* 10 (1986), 179–196.

17. Reported in "The Diversity Factor," *Fortune* (October 13, 2003), S1–S12.

18. Judy C. Nixon and Judy F. West, "Growing Importance: America Addresses Work Force Diversity," *Business Forum* 25, no. 1–2 (Winter–Spring, 2000, 4–9.

19. Jason Forsythe, "Winning with Diversity," special advertising supplement to *The New York Times Magazine* (March 28, 2004), 65–72; Amy Aronson, "Getting Results: Corporate Diversity, Integration, and Market Penetration," special advertising section, *BusinessWeek* (October 20, 2003), 140–144; and Nixon and West, "America Addresses Work Force Diversity,"

20. G. Pascal Zachary, "Mighty is the Mongrel," *Fast Company* (July 2000), 270–284.

21. Elizabeth Wasserman, "A Race for Profits," *MBA Jungle* (March–April 2003), 40–41; Amy Aronson, "Getting Results."

22. Steven Greenhouse, N.Y. Times News Service, "Influx of Immigrants Having Profound Impact on Economy," *Johnson City Press* (September 4, 2000), 9; Richard W. Judy and Carol D'Amico, *Workforce 2020: Work and Workers in the 21st Century* (Indianapolis, Ind.: Hudson Institute, 1997); statistics reported in Jason Forsythe, "Diversity Works," special advertising supplement to *The New York Times Magazine* (September 14, 2003), 75–100.

23. Stephanie N. Mehta, "What Minority Employees Really Want," *Fortune* (June 10, 2000), 181–186.

24. Harris, "The Illusion of Inclusion."

25. Jennifer L. Knight, Michelle R. Hebl, Jessica B. Foster, and Laura M. Mannix, "Out of Role? Out of Luck: The Influence of Race and Leadership Status on Performance Appraisals," *The Journal of Leadership and Organizational Studies* 9, no. 3 (2003), 85–93.

26. Mehta, "What Minority Employees Really Want."

27. Robert Hooijberg and Nancy DiTomaso, "Leadership In and Of Demographically Diverse Organizations," *Leadership Quarterly* 7, no. 1 (1996): 1–19.

28. Harris, "The Illusion of Inclusion."

29. Brian Grow, "Hispanic Nation," *BusinessWeek* (March 15, 2004), 58–70.

30. "Diversity in the Federal Government," report of a roundtable discussion on "Addressing Diversity Issues in the Government," July 10, 2003, moderated by Omar Wasow, executive director of BlackPlanet.com, reported in *The New York Times Magazine* (September 14, 2003), 95–99.

31. Quoted in Lee Smith, "The Business Case for Diversity."

32. Bryan Gingrich, "Individual and Organizational Accountabilities: Reducing Stereotypes and Prejudice within the Workplace," *Diversity Factor* 8, no. 2 (Winter 2000), 14–20.

33. Copeland, "Valuing Diversity, Part I: Making the Most of Cultural Differences at the Workplace"; Judy and D'Amico, *Workforce 2020*; and S. Hutchins, Jr., "Preparing for Diversity: The Year 2000," *Quality Process* 22, no. 10 (1989), 66–68.

34. Fred L. Fry and Jennifer R. D. Burgess, "The End of the Need for Affirmative Action: Are We There Yet?" *Business Horizons* (November–December 2003), 7–16.

35. Roosevelt Thomas, Jr., "From Affirmative Action to Affirming Diversity," *Harvard Business Review* (March–April 1990), 107–117; Nicholas Lemann, "Taking Affirmative Action Apart," *The New York Times Magazine* (July 11, 1995), 36–43; and Terry H. Anderson, *The Pursuit of Fairness: A History of Affirmative Action* (New York: Oxford University Press, 2004).

36. Robert J. Grossman, "Behavior at Work," *HR Magazine* 46, no. 3 (March 2001), 50+; Madeline E. Heilman, Caryn J. Block, and Peter Stathatos, "The Affirmative Action Stigma of Incompetence: Effects of Performance Information Ambiguity," *Academy of Management Journal* 40, no. 1 (1997), 603–625.

37. Fry and Burgess, "The End of the Need for Affirmative Action"; and Erika H. James, Arthur P. Brief, Joerg Dietz, and Robin R. Cohen, "Prejudice Matters: Understanding the Reactions of Whites to Affirmative Action Programs Targeted to Benefit Blacks," *Journal of Applied Psychology* 86, no. 6 (December 2001), 1120+.

38. Greg Winter, "After Ruling, 3 Universities Maintain Diversity in Admissions," *The New York Times* (April 13, 2004), A22.

39. "Race Relations Better but Bias Persists, Poll Finds," *Jet* (May 3, 2004), 10.

40. Sheila Wellington, Marcia Brumit Kropf, and Paulette R. Gerkovich, "What's Holding Women Back?" *Harvard Business Review* (June 2003), 18–19.

41. Julie Amparano Lopez, "Study Says Women Face Glass Walls as Well as Ceilings," *The Wall Street Journal* (March 3, 1992), B1, B2; Ida L. Castro, "Q: Should Women Be Worried About the Glass Ceiling in the Workplace?" *Insight* (February 10, 1997), 24–27; Debra E. Meyerson and Joyce K. Fletcher, "A Modest Manifesto for Shattering the Glass Ceiling," *Harvard Business Review* (January–February 2000), 127–136; and Wellington, Brumit Bropf, and Gerkovich, "What's Holding Women Back?"; Finnegan, "Different Strokes."

42. Catalyst survey results reported in Forsythe, "Winning with Diversity."

43. Lisa Belkin, "The Opt-Out Revolution," *The New York Times Magazine* (October 26, 2003), 43–47, 58+.

44. Annie Finnigan, "Different Strokes," *Working Woman* (April 2001), 42–48; and Meyerson and Fletcher, "A Modest Manifesto for Shattering the Glass Ceiling".

45. 2002 U.S. Census Bureau figures, reported in "A Better Education Equals Higher Pay; Whites Fare Best," AP story, *Johnson City Press* (March 21, 2003), 9.

46. Cliff Edwards, "Coming Out in Corporate America," *BusinessWeek* (December 15, 2003), 64–72; Belle Rose Ragins, John M. Cornwell, and Janice S. Miller, Heterosexism in the Workplace: Do Race and Gender Matter?" *Group & Organization Management* 28, no. 1 (March 2003), 45–74.

47. Barbara Presley Noble, "A Quiet Liberation for Gay and Lesbian Employees," *The New York Times* (June 13, 1993), F4.

48. Belkin, "The Opt-Out Revolution."

49. Linda Tischler, "Where Are the Women?" *Fast Company* (February 2004), 52–60.

50. John Byrne, "The Price of Balance," *Fast Company* (February 2004); Tischler, "Where Are the Women?" *Fast Company* (February 2004), 52–60; Patricia Sellers, "Power: Do Women Really Want It?" *Fortune* (October 13, 2003), 80–100.

51. C. J. Prince, "Media Myths: The Truth About the Opt-Out Hype," *NAFE Magazine* (Second Quarter, 2004), 14–18; Sellers, "Power: Do Women Really Want It?"

52. Wellington et al., "What's Holding Women Back?"

53. The Leader's Edge/Executive Women Research 2002 survey, reported in "Why Women Leave," *Executive Female* (Summer 2003), 4.

54. Alice H. Eagly and Linda L. Carli, "The Female Leadership Advantage: An Evaluation of the Evidence," *The Leadership Quarterly* 14 (2003), 807–834.

55. C. Soloman, "Careers under Glass," *Personnel Journal* 69, no. 4 (1990), 96–105; and Belle Rose Ragins, Bickley Townsend, and Mary Mattis, "Gender Gap in the Executive Suite: CEOs and Female Executives Report on Breaking the Glass Ceiling," *Academy of Management Executive* 12, no. 1 (1998), 28–42.

56. Eagly and Carli, "The Female Leadership Advantage: An Evaluation of the Evidence"; Sally Helgesen, *The Female Advantage: Women's Ways of Leadership* (New York: Doubleday Currency, 1990); Rochelle Sharpe, "As Leaders, Women Rule: New Studies Find that Female Managers Outshine Their Male Counterparts in Almost Every Measure," *BusinessWeek* (November 20, 2000), 5+; and Del Jones, "2003: Year of the Woman Among the Fortune 500?" (December 30, 2003), 1B.

57. Michelle Conlin, "The New Gender Gap," *BusinessWeek* (May 26, 2003), 74–82; and "A Better Education Equals Higher Pay."

58. Quoted in Conlin, "The New Gender Gap."

59. Kathryn M. Bartol, David C. Martin, and Julie A. Kromkowski, "Leadership and the Glass Ceiling: Gender and Ethnic Group Influences on Leader Behaviors at Middle and Executive Managerial Levels," *The Journal of Leadership and Organizational Studies* 9, no. 3 (2003), 8–19; Bernard M. Bass and Bruce J. Avolio, "Shatter the Glass Ceiling: Women May Make Better Managers," *Human Resource Management* 33, no. 4 (Winter 1994), 549–560; and Rochelle Sharpe, "As Leaders, Women Rule," *BusinessWeek* (November 20, 2002), 75–84.

60. Dwight D. Frink, Robert K. Robinson, Brian Reithel, Michelle M. Arthur, Anthony P. Ammeter, Gerald R. Ferris, David M. Kaplan, and Hubert S. Morrisette, "Gender Demography and Organization Performance: A Two-Study Investigation with Convergence," *Group & Organization Management* 28, no. 1 (March 2003), 127–147; Catalyst research project cited in Jason Forsythe, "Winning with Diversity." *Also see* Jones, "2003: Year of the Woman Among the Fortune 500?"

61. Finnigan, "Different Strokes."

62. Abelson, "Can Respect Be Mandated?"

63. Jacqueline A. Gilbert and John M. Ivancevich, "Valuing Diversity: A Tale of Two Organizations," *Academy of Management Executive* 14, no. 1 (2000), 93–105; and Vanessa Weaver, "What These CEOs and Their Companies Know About Diversity," in "Winning with Diversity, *Business Week*, (September 10, 2001).

64. Copeland, "Learning to Manage a Multicultural Workforce."

65. Reported in "Strength Through Diversity for Bottom-Line Success," special advertising section, *Working Woman* (March 1999).

66. Finnigan, "Different Strokes."

67. "Diversity in an Affiliated Company," in Vanessa J. Weaver, "Winning with Diversity," special advertising section, *BusinessWeek* (September 10, 2001).

68. B. Ragins, "Barriers to Mentoring: The Female Manager's Dilemma," *Human Relations* 42, no. 1 (1989), 1–22; and Ragins et al., "Gender Gap in the Executive Suite."

69. Johathan Hickman, Christopher Tkaczyk, Ellen Florian, and Jaclyn Stemple, "50 Best Companies for Minorities," *Fortune* (July 7, 2003), 103–120.

70. David A. Thomas, "The Truth About Mentoring Minorities—Race Matters," *Harvard Business Review* (April 2001), 99–107.

71. Mary Zey, "A Mentor for All," *Personnel Journal* (January 1988), 46–51.

72. Joanne Sujansky, "Lead a Multi-Generational Workforce," *The Business Journal of Tri-Cities, Tennessee–Virginia* (February 2004), 21–23.

73. "Keeping Your Edge: Managing a Diverse Corporate Culture," special advertising section, *Fortune* (June 3, 2001).

74. J. Black and M. Mendenhall, "Cross-Cultural Training Effectiveness: A Review and a Theoretical Framework for Future Research," *Academy of Management Review* 15 (1990), 113–136.

75. Jim Adamson, "How Denny's Went from Icon of Racism to Diversity Award Winner," Journal of Organizational Excellence (Winter 2000), 55–68; Alex Lash, "Courting Diversity," *MBA Jungle* (March–April 2003), 48–49; and Jonathan Hickman, "50 Best Companies for Minorities," *Fortune* (July 7, 2003), 103–120.

76. E. G. Collins, "Managers and Lovers," *Harvard Business Review* 61 (1983), 142–153.

77. Sharon A. Lobel, Robert E. Quinn, Lynda St. Clair, and Andrea Warfield, "Love without Sex: The Impact of Psychological Intimacy between Men and Women at Work," *Organizational Dynamics* (Summer 1994), 5–16.

78. William C. Symonds with Steve Hamm and Gail DeGeorge, "Sex on the Job," *BusinessWeek* (February 16, 1998), 30–31.

79. "Sexual Harassment: Vanderbilt University Policy" (Nashville: Vanderbilt University, 1993).

80. Rachel Thompson, "Sexual Harassment: It Doesn't Go with the Territory," *Herizons* 15, no. 3 (Winter 2002), 22–26.

81. Statistics reported in Jim Mulligan and Norman Foy, "Not in My Company: Preventing Sexual Harassment," *Industrial Management* (September/October 2003), 26–29; also see *EEOC Charge Complaints* at http://www.eeoc.gov.

82. Jack Corcoran, "Of Nice and Men," *Success* (June 1998), 65–67.

83. Barbara Carton, "At Jenny Craig, Men Are Ones Who Claim Sex Discrimination," *The Wall Street Journal* (November 29, 1994), A1, A11.

84. Thompson, "Sexual Harassment: It Doesn't Go with the Territory."

85. Judy and D'Amico, *Workforce 2020*.

86. Joann S. Lublin, "Companies Use Cross-Cultural Training to Help Their Employees Adjust Abroad," *The Wall Street Journal* (August 4, 1992), B1, B9.

87. Gilbert Fuchsberg, "As Costs of Overseas Assignments Climb, Firms Select Expatriates More Carefully," *The Wall Street Journal* (January 9, 1992), B3, B4.

88. J. Kennedy and A. Everest, "Put Diversity in Context," *Personnel Journal* (September 1991), 50–54.

89. "Impact of Diversity Initiatives on the Bottom Line: A SHRM Survey of the Fortune 1000," S12–S14, in *Fortune*, special advertising section, "Keeping Your Edge: Managing a Diverse Corporate Culture," produced in association with the Society for Human Resource Management, (June 3, 2001) http://www.fortune.com/sections.

90. Joseph J. Distefano and Martha L. Maznevski, "Creating Value with Diverse Teams in Global Management," *Organizational Dynamics* 29, no. 1 (Summer 2000), 45–63; and Finnigan, "Different Strokes."

91. W. E. Watson, K. Kumar, and L. K. Michaelsen, "Cultural Diversity's Impact on Interaction Process and Performance: Comparing Homogeneous and Diverse Task Groups," *Academy of Management Journal* 36 (1993), 590–602; G. Robinson and K. Dechant, "Building a Business Case for Diversity," *Academy of Management Executive* 11, no. 3 (1997), 21–31; and D. A. Thomas and R. J. Ely, "Making Differences Matter: A New Paradigm for Managing Diversity," *Harvard Business Review* (September–October 1996), 79–90.

92. Marc Hequet, Chris Lee, Michele Picard, and David Stamps, "Teams Get Global," *Training* (December 1996), 16–17.

93. Chiori Santiago, "Culture Club," *Working Woman* (April 2001), 46–47, 78.

94. Lionel Laroche, "Teaming Up," *CMA Management* (April 2001), 22–25.

95. See Distefano and Maznevski, "Creating Value with Diverse Teams" for a discussion of the advantages of multicultural teams.

96. Watson, Kumar, and Michaelsen, "Cultural Diversity's Impact on Interaction Process and Performance."

97. Distefano and Maznevski, "Creating Value with Diverse Teams."

98. This definition and discussion is based on Raymond A. Friedman, "Employee Network Groups: Self-Help Strategy for Women and Minorities," *Performance Improvement Quarterly* 12, no. 1 (1999), 148–163.

99. Ann C. Logue, "Girl Gangs: They Got It Goin' On," *Training & Development* (January 2001), 24–28.

100. "Leveraging Diversity: Opportunities in the New Market," Part III of "Diversity: The Bottom Line," *Forbes*, special advertising section (November 13, 2000).

101. Raymond A. Friedman and Brooks Holtom, "The Effects of Network Groups on Minority Employee Turnover Intentions," *Human Resource Management* 41, no. 4 (Winter 2002), 405–421.

102. Wassserman, "A Race for Profits."

103. Finnigan, "Different Strokes."

104. Raymond A. Friedman, Melinda Kane, and Daniel B. Cornfield, "Social Support and Career Optimism: Examining the Effectiveness of Network Groups Among Black Managers," *Human Relations* 51, no. 9 (1998), 1155–1177; "Diversity in the New Millennium," special advertising supplement, *Working Woman* (March 2000).

105. Ann Zimmerman, "Wal-Mart Plans Changes to Wages, Labor Practices," *The Wall Street Journal* (June 7, 2004), B3; Cora Daniels, "Women vs. Wal-Mart," *Fortune* (July 21, 2003), 78–82; and Douglas P. Shuit, "People Problems on Every Aisle: Part 1 of 2," *Workforce Management* (February 1, 2004), 26+.

# Video Case

For about $20 a year, college students can join a club that offers all kinds of services, from online purchase of textbooks to discounts on travel. Maybe most students do not have $20 in their pockets at any given time, but that is about the price of two large pizzas, and Student Advantage is committed to providing value to its members.

Massachusetts-based Student Advantage is made up of a number of divisions, each organized around a particular focus. Perhaps the most well-known is CollegeClub.com, a Web site that provides "one-stop shopping" for financial aid information, including comparisons of different student loans and opportunities for online application; a program that allows students to use their university ID cards for off-campus purchases; online shopping for student-only values, and more. CollegeClub.com also provides marketing opportunities for companies promoting travel, events, and other services—as well as some administrative services for universities.

The SA Marketing Group, another Student Advantage division, develops and manages marketing programs for the college and youth markets on behalf of such clients as AT&T, Amtrak, New Balance, and Hotjobs.com. CarePackages.com, a third Student Advantage operation, was founded in 1999 to establish relationships with more than 25 colleges and universities and related Internet sites such as Yahoo! Greetings and FTD.com florist service. Through CarePackages.com, parents, grandparents, and just about anyone else can select and send gift packages to students as they study for exams, or to make them laugh for Halloween. (There is even a special "ScarePackage.") CarePackages.com has created such a successful relationship between consumers and retail companies that *The Wall Street Journal* rated it one of the best such sites in business. In addition, CarePackages.com's revenue-sharing partnerships have helped associations, campus organizations, other nonprofits, and business owners earn money without taking any risk.

For sports fans—and there are usually plenty of those on campus—Student Advantage's FANSonly Network provides online brand management, content delivery, consumer marketing, and business assistance to more than 120 colleges and universities around the nation. FANSonly works like a network hub for individual colleges' official athletic sites, so students and coaches can log on to get all kinds of information specific to their school and team, from scores to schedules to merchandise. Finally, Student Advantage's U-Wire division is the country's largest free newswire for college media. The site delivers student-produced news and commentary to U-Wire members, professional media outlets and syndication partners (including Yahoo! and USAToday.com).

Each of these sites is developed with the specific purpose of contributing to the company's overall mission of connecting students, universities, and businesses with each other in a positive relationship. If any site does not fit the overall mission—or actually siphons off valuable resources from the company without contributing to it—then Student Advantage lets it go, keeping only the strongest divisions. One such business unit was Voice FX, which operated Campus Direct, a service that allowed students and alumni to access grades and order transcripts over the Internet and by phone. After reviewing the unit's performance relative to Student Advantage as a whole, CEO Ray Sozzi decided to sell Voice FX. "Our focus and our future are on the core enterprises on which the company's been built—our media properties, our membership program, including SA Cash, and our expanding online and offline commerce operations," explained Sozzi. In a sluggish economy, Student Advantage would retain only its "core" or central operations, and manage these as strategically as possible.

Student Advantage is structured around the consumer needs of college students. Such a well-defined focus makes it easier to structure the organization so that each division is related to students and the universities they attend. While some critics believe that targeting college students on the Web is too limiting, founder Ray Sozzi disagrees. He does, however, believe that a Web presence must be complemented by an offline presence. "The Internet is very important to college students, but it is not the end-all, be-all medium. There are plenty of transactions that happen offline; college students still go to local stores to buy books and CDs. The most limiting thing is if you only have an offline presence. You have to establish customer loyalty, and the most effective way is through an integrated approach . . . . That's the way we run our business."

**Questions**

1. Draw a diagram of Student Advantage's divisional structure. Do you see an advantage in using this type of structure at Student Advantage? Why or why not?

2. Do you think an emphasis on centralization or decentralization would be more appropriate for helping Student Advantage achieve its goals? Discuss.

3. In what ways might Student Advantage benefit from the use of teams?

Sources: Company Web site, *http://www.studentadvantage.com*, accessed February 8, 2002; "Student Advantage Sheds Division," Boston. internet.com, November 8, 2001, *http://boston.internet.com*; Seth Fineberg, "An Interview with Ray Sozzi, CEO of Student Advantage," NewsBeat Channel 7, January 13, 2000, *http://www.channelseven.com*.

# Video Case

## Chapter 11: Machado and Silvetti: Building the Business of Building

An organization is a lot like a building: it relies on structure just to stand up. It has a foundation, some system of support, pathways between areas, and a roof for protection. The Boston-based architectural firm of Machado and Silvetti, founded by Harvard professors Rodolfo Machado and Jorge Silvetti, knows plenty about structure. Without structure, there would be no building—and no firm. Because the two founders have spent so much of their careers in an academic setting, says associate Michael Yusem, "Our office is structured very similar to a typical academic studio configuration, where projects are developed through an intensive, workshop style environment."

This studio environment means that the Machado and Silvetti firm relies heavily on teams to develop the projects for which it has become famous—a new branch of the Boston Public Library, a renovation of the Getty Villa at the J. Paul Getty Museum, the South Boston waterfront, the Rockefeller Stone Barns, and a 365-bed graduate housing dormitory for a local university. "Team structure for specific projects is usually based on a principal-in-charge, a managing associate, and a team of designers," says Michael Yusem. Although many architectural firms are similarly organized on a project basis, Machado and Silvetti has a less hierarchical, more horizontal struc-

ture than more traditional firms. "By encouraging creative input at all staff levels, the system intends to encourage commitment and dedication among team members by creating opportunities for personal input and involvement," continues Yusem.

The team structure also contributes to decision making through meetings in which team members, associates, and principals gather to review the progress on each project and discuss problems and potential solutions. "We find that this approach encourages creative problem solving and minimizes the tendency for stagnation and repetition that more traditional bureaucracies may yield," explains Yusem. It also supports the concept of the learning organization.

Coordination among team members, between teams, and with outside groups and individuals is vital to the success of a firm like Machado and Silvetti. Since the firm does not specialize in designing a particular category of structure, each project team must address different demands related to the project. Many times, the firm will call in outside consultants who have expertise that applies to a certain project, and these individuals must be coordinated with the in-house architectural design team as well as the client's staff. "Once established, the architectural and consultant team works closely with the client, user

# Chapter 11: Machado and Silvetti: Building the Business of Building (continued)

group representatives, and construction managers to provide for the design, schedule, construction and budget of the project," says Yusem. "This involves an exhaustive review of program requirements, user-group demands, as well as the appropriateness of various design solutions which are tested throughout the process." All of this spells coordination. For instance, during the graduate housing project, the interests of the university and the surrounding community—including donor groups, trustees, facilities managers, faculty, student groups, and community organizations—all had to be addressed and coordinated.

This level of coordination requires patience from Machado and Silvetti's project managers. They must make sure everyone receives relevant information and has time to understand and respond to issues, and they must be able to anticipate and resolve conflicts. The firm tries to structure its contact with its clients in much the same way it is structured internally in order to achieve this coordination. "We have found that the particular circumstances of each project and client group differ, and our ability to hand-select the appropriate design team personalities and consultant group is paramount in creating an effective project delivery system," says Michael Yusem. "In this sense, we strive to establish a similar interactive, collaborative decision-making process with our client as we do with our own internal structure." In other words, they build each museum, library wing, or housing facility as if it were their own.

## Questions

1. Can you see any possible downside to the way Machado and Silvetti is structured? If not, why not? If so, what is it?
2. If Machado and Silvetti were organized in a vertical structure, how would the approach to projects be different?
3. How important is open information to a firm like Machado and Silvetti?

Sources: Company Web site, *http://www.machado-silvetti.com*, accessed February 5, 2002; Alex Ulam, "Harvard Inc.," *Metropolis Magazine*, February 2001, *http://www.metropolismag.com*; "The New Getty Villa," Getty Museum Web Site, 2000, *http://www.getty.edu*.

# Video Case

Many organizations have taken a second look at their safety and security procedures since the terrorist attacks of September 11, 2001. Financial institutions have updated security of their computer data; hotels have examined ways to make guests safer from intruders or unauthorized visitors; and every company operating modes of travel, from airlines to bus lines, has re-evaluated ways to ensure the safety and security of its passengers and staff. Re-evaluation and resulting changes are two positive actions that have come out of a great tragedy. Peter Pan Bus Lines, based in Springfield, Massachusetts, has been in business since 1933 and has undergone plenty of changes. But its attention to the details of safety and security post-September 11 is much more focused and intense.

"It is the policy of Peter Pan Bus Lines, Inc., to promote a safe and secure environment for all of our employees and customers," writes Peter A. Picknelly, president of the company. This policy extends to all of the company's 850 employees, 3.5 million passengers, 150 coaches (buses), and routes ranging from Concord, New Hampshire, to Washington, D.C. And it encompasses the entire Peter Pan Group, which includes the bus lines, Peter Pan World Travel, several hotels, and other affiliates. Some of the changes resulting from the new safety policy involve technology; others involve changes in people or culture, such as creating a heightened alertness to safety issues. Of course, it is important for the changes to be supported by the top of the organization, as they are at Peter Pan; otherwise, they will not receive the attention and resources they need for implementation.

As Christopher Crean, director of safety for the company, and other managers reviewed the company's safety procedures, they were happy to note that Peter Pan had instituted important safety measures long before September 11. For instance, bus drivers have had on-board computers (similar to the "black boxes" on airplanes) since 1989. Recently, Crean was presented with the first Safety Leader of the Year Award by the United Motorcoach Association (UMA) for his previous six years of work in the company's safety program. Under Crean's leadership, Peter Pan had achieved the highest safety rating from the Department of Defense for three years and the highest safety rating from the Department of Transportation for five years. But September 11 threw safety and security issues into a whole new arena, so Crean and his colleagues examined the company's practices from top to bottom.

When the review was complete, they decided to implement some changes in employee training and testing, and in policies and procedures. All employees, including the president of the company, would participate in a three-and-a-half hour safety and security training program to reinforce their existing knowledge, heighten their awareness of potential dangers or threats, and teach them how to make the best decisions for their safety and that of their passengers. Meanwhile, Peter Pan would be implementing its "mystery rider" program, which operates much like the "mystery shopper" that restaurants or department stores might use. Mystery riders take Peter Pan buses several times each month and rate all aspects of service. In addition, according to Crean, all managers are required to ride a coach twice a month.

New policies and procedures for the company include the following: requiring identification of all passengers when they buy tickets, issuing company ID badges to all employees, instituting a new security plan, and implementing new security measures for the buses themselves. Some of the additions to security on the buses include interior mirrors, which allow drivers greater visibility of passengers' activities, and plastic ties placed on all luggage hatches once they have been closed so no new items may be added. In addition, Peter Pan has worked with the Springfield, Massachusetts, police—the company's home base—to make sure that its emergency action plans are up-to-date and workable.

Change isn't easy, even for a company that already has a superior track record in the area of safety and security. People need to be re-educated and motivated to implement changes on a daily basis, and sometimes it takes weeks or months for the changes to settle into place. But when change begins at the top—as it has at Peter Pan—it is very likely to succeed. Peter Pan takes security seriously on every run because every passenger's safety is important to the company.

**Questions**

1.  What characteristics of Peter Pan would identify it to you as a learning organization?

2.  What might be some sources of resistance to the changes in Peter Pan's safety and security practices?

3.  Of the implementation tactics discussed in the chapter, which seem to have been used successfully by Peter Pan?

Source: Company Web site, *http://www.peterpanbus.com*

# Video Case

## Chapter 13:  Fannie Mae Promotes a Diverse Workforce

Many companies try, with greater or lesser success, to recruit, develop, and promote a truly diverse workforce. Federal and local guidelines govern such areas as equal opportunity and affirmative action. But organizations that move beyond rules and regulations to embrace diversity as a core value can reap rewards in employee satisfaction and performance. At the Federal National Mortgage Association (Fannie Mae), which employs over 4,000 workers, diversity is a way of life. Fannie Mae's corporate culture is grounded in diversity. "In keeping with [our] values, our corporate philosophy on diversity is based on respect for one another and recognition that each person brings his or her own unique attributes to the corporation," states the company Web site. "We are committed to providing equal opportunity for all employees to reach their full potential; it is a fundamental value, and it makes good business sense. . . . We are committed to demonstrating that 'Diversity Works at Fannie Mae.'"

That said, how does Fannie Mae breathe life into its words? First, the diversity of American society as a whole is reflected at every level of the corporate structure. More than 47 percent of Fannie Mae's management group, including officers and directors, are minorities; nearly 54 percent of the company's employees are women; and 42 percent of the employees are minorities. In addition, the company is pledged to equal opportunity for workers with disabilities, older employees, and gay or lesbian workers.

"Diversity is not just an initiative at Fannie Mae; it's a principle that permeates every aspect of how we do business," explains Maria Johnson, vice president of diversity, health, and work-life. "Diversity is codified as one of the company's core commitments."

Fannie Mae also supports diversity by awarding a significant number of outsourced contracts to minority-owned businesses, a practice for which it was named among the top 30 companies for achievements in increasing supplier diversity by *Working Woman* magazine. "More than 21 percent of the company's discretionary spending in 2000 went to minority- and women-owned businesses, proof that Fannie Mae's commitment to diversity extends to all areas of the organization," says Barbara Lang, Fannie Mae's vice president of corporate services. "We require minority contractors to be included on all bids, where possible, and also encourage our majority suppliers and customers to work with capable minority vendors." In addition, Fannie Mae provides diversity training to its lender customers and hosts regular benchmarking sessions for other employers who want to learn more about how diversity can contribute to a company's success.

Fannie Mae has established specific goals to increase the ratio of minorities at upper levels, ties certain compensation to promoting diversity, and has implemented a number of programs, such as mentoring, to make certain everyone gets equal opportunity for career growth. "Company leaders are urged to

# Chapter 13: Fannie Mae Promotes a Diverse Workforce (continued)

unleash the potential of all employees, promote a spectrum of perspectives, view differences as assets rather than liabilities, and help create a diverse, talented, and committed workforce," says Maria Johnson.

Promoting diversity within the workforce at Fannie Mae is good strategy not only because a diverse workforce can bring more strength and creativity to an organization, but also because such a workforce reflects Fannie Mae's customer base. People of all backgrounds come to Fannie Mae's lenders in search of mortgage loans. In addition, Fannie Mae's philanthropic arm, the Fannie Mae Foundation, works to increase the supply of affordable housing to those who might not otherwise be able to find a home—to homeless individuals and families, immigrant communities, those in rural areas, and lower-income minority groups.

Diversity has been an integral part of Fannie Mae's corporate culture for at least 15 years, illustrating the importance of support from a company's senior managers. "Fannie Mae committed to incorporate diversity as part of its core culture back in the late 1980s," reports Maria Johnson. "Our program has been successful because top executives have had an ongoing relationship with our diversity initiatives from the onset." Because diversity programs have support at the very top of the organization, they are much more apt to be successful at lower levels. But Fannie Mae doesn't engage in these initiatives entirely out of

socially responsible motives; instead, the company believes that being socially responsible is also good business. "The company's record of 14 consecutive years of double-digit growth in operating earnings shows that a company can act responsibly and still deliver value to its shareholders," says Jamie Gorelick, vice chair of Fannie Mae. There's no arguing with success.

## Questions

1. No one is perfect, including managers and workers at Fannie Mae. What are some of the challenges that mid-level managers at Fannie Mae might face in managing a diverse group of workers?

2. Based on what you have read in this case and the previous case on Fannie Mae, what type of initiatives can you identify that should prevent women from encountering the glass ceiling at Fannie Mae?

3. Using the chart in Exhibit 14.5, try to identify—honestly—your own level of diversity awareness. Based on your evaluation, do you think you would fit in as a manager at Fannie Mae? Why or why not?

Sources: Company Web site, accessed January 17, 2002, http://www. fanniemae.com; "Fannie Mae Foundation Receives New $300 Million Contribution from Fannie Mae," company press release, January 14, 2002.

# .....Continuing Case

Most of us resist change: it is human nature to want things to stay the same, even if the conditions of our lives are less than ideal. Changes within organizations are just as difficult for managers to implement and employees to accept. Whether it is learning a new technology, increasing or decreasing staff, expanding or downsizing manufacturing capabilities, or adding or deleting products to the line, change can be stressful for everyone in the organization. Conceiving of and announcing the change may fall to upper-level executives, but implementing the change is usually the responsibility of managers, including human resource managers. When the restructuring plan put together by Bill Ford's new executive team began to unfold in late 2001 and early 2002, all of Ford Motor Company was on edge.

After announcing a series of management changes, including the retirement of the chief financial officer, the elevation of Nick Scheele to chief operating officer, and the appointment of three new group vice presidents, the team focused on massive restructuring of Ford's U.S. operations. In January 2002, the team announced that Ford would be closing key manufacturing plants in New Jersey, Missouri, Ohio, Michigan, and Ontario, citing too much capacity at those plants. In other words, the company was overproducing and did not need to build as many cars in a weak economy. In addition, Ford took several well-known but slow-selling models out of production—the Ford Escort, the Mercury Villager (a minivan), the Mercury Cougar, and the Lincoln Continental. Saying that former CEO Jac Nasser had diversified the organization too much, the new group declared that Ford was now focusing on its core business of building cars and trucks. Overall, 35,000 Ford workers (10 percent of the total global workforce) would probably lose their jobs, at least temporarily. Although this sounds grim, managers and other experts believed that these massive changes would ultimately help Ford survive a weak economy and the costs incurred by the Firestone tire debacle and ultimately lead to its growth.

A company such as Ford naturally has a huge, diverse workforce to manage. Although diversity challenges most often relate to ensuring that a variety of people have equal job opportunity, rarely do we think of older, white male employees as needing protection by the law. But that is exactly what happened at Ford, when a class-action lawsuit was filed against the company for reverse discrimination. The suit alleged that the company's performance appraisal system was targeting those workers for dismissal or early retirement. How could this happen? Under a system instituted by former CEO Jac Nasser, called the Performance Management Process, workers were given performance grades of A, B, or C. Those who received a C could lose their bonuses and raises; those who received two C grades in a row could be fired. If that sounds fair, here's the catch: Under the original plan, a quota of at least 10 percent of Ford employees were to receive C grades; later, the percentage was lowered to 5 percent. Many liken the ranking system, currently being used by a number of leading companies, to a grading curve because regardless of actual performance, a certain number of employees received high scores and a certain number received low ones. As it turned out at Ford, many of the C grades were handed out to older white males. Ford's system was eventually changed to one designating top achievers, achievers, and those requiring improvement. But within a year and a half, Ford agreed to abandon the system, which affected about 18,000 managers. As Bill Ford took over the CEO spot in late 2001, negotiations in the lawsuits continued. However, it seemed clear that both sides wanted the cases settled as amicably as possible.

Compensating nearly half a million employees in different countries is another huge challenge for human resource managers at Ford. In the fall of 2001, the combination of sluggish car sales and the Firestone recall forced the human resources department to circulate a memo announcing that about 6,000 managers would not be receiving their typical yearly bonuses. The company simply did not have the

# Part 4: Managing Organizational Changes at Ford (continued)

# ..Continuing Case

pool of cash—about $440 million—it had had in the past to pay out the bonuses. Nasser's retirement package was also tied to the company's overall financial performance, but he still received a bonus worth more than $5 million.

It is doubtful that anyone would dispute that Ford's management team has had an extremely rocky ride during the past few years. Managers at every level have faced constant challenges as their organization has struggled with massive changes. However, Ford is taking clear steps to survive and ultimately come out on top with its focus on producing new car models and perhaps even a retooled organization model.

## Questions

1. What factors in the environment do you believe have affected Ford's structure in the past? What environmental factors do you believe will affect its structure in the future?
2. What internal forces for change has Ford faced in the last five years?
3. From a human resource management perspective, why do you think Jac Nasser's performance appraisal system failed?

SOURCES: Ed Garsten, "Tentative Terms in Ford Bias Cases," *Associated Press*, (November 16, 2001), *http://www.ford.com*; "Ford Moving Closer to Settling Suits—WSJ," *Reuters Limited* (November 16, 2001); Ed Garsten, "Ford Announces Management Shuffle," *Associated Press* (November 15, 2001), *http://dailynews.yahoo.com*; August Cole, "Ford Shuffles Another Round of Execs," *CBS MarketWatch.com* (November 15, 2001), *http://www.marketwatch.com*; "Nasser's Retirement Package Tied to Ford's Performance," *Auto.com*, (November 15, 2001), *http://www.auto.com*; "Exec Changes Help Ford with Basics," *Automotive News* (November 12, 2001), *http://www.autonews.com*; Nikki Tait, "Lincoln Bears Brunt of Ford Restructuring," *Financial Times* (November 11, 2001), *http://news.ft.com*; Tim Burt and Nikki Tait, "Ford May Axe 20 Percent of White Collar Staff," *Financial Times* (November 6, 2001), *http://news.ft.com*; John Gallagher, "No Bonuses This Year for Ford's Top Bosses," *Detroit Free Press* (August 29, 2001), *http://www.freep.com*; Tim Burt and Nikki Tait, "Ford Refines Chain of Command in U.S," *Financial Times* (July 16, 2001), *http://news.ft.com*; Tim Burt, "Ford's White Knight Summoned to Aid of U.S. in Distress," *Financial Times* (July 15, 2001), *http://news.ft.com*.

# Controlling

If every picture tells a story, then every piece of marble, every lump of clay, holds within it some work of art. Hands-on art shapes, molds, pushes, and pulls. The sculptor controls the process, whether carving solid stone or pouring liquid metal, but a slip of the hand or an incline of the elbow can alter the final effect. Control is as important to artistic vision as it is to organizational success.

For a sculptor, a variety of tools, such as chisels and mallets, are required to create and control the work. A manager's tools provide similar hands-on control. Managers practice a variety of controlling measures to ensure that goods and services are high in quality, expenses lie within certain parameters, facilities are well sited, operations are efficient, and inventory is maintained at optimal levels.

A sculptor creates three-dimensional art; you can walk around it, touch it, and feel its texture. A sculpture's shape makes it interesting. Looking at a sculpture from a different angle changes its appearance completely and allows for varying interpretations of meaning and intent. Managers must also examine their task environment and project goals from every angle, obtaining feedback and data to help them guide the organization.

A sculptor chooses the medium which best suits his work. Perhaps it is marble, a popular choice that does not fracture unpredictably when struck. Although they may not have a choice of medium, managers also must assess data, analyze financial and operations information, and listen to suggestions. In much of this analysis and decision making, they are aided by information technology, used to accomplish the organization's mission and overall strategy.

Control enables a sculptor to bring his artistic vision to life for a public audience. For managers, control is more complex. Circling the task environment, and looking at it from every angle, can help them carve out their vision—and success.

# Chapter 14

# Managerial and Quality Control

## LEARNING OBJECTIVES

*After studying this chapter, you should be able to*

1. Define organizational control and explain why it is a key management function.

2. Describe differences in control focus, including feedforward, concurrent, and feedback control.

3. Explain the four steps in the control process.

4. Discuss the use of financial statements, financial analysis, and budgeting as management controls.

5. Contrast the bureaucratic and decentralized control approaches.

6. Describe the concept of total quality management and major TQM techniques.

7. Identify current trends in financial control and discuss their impact on organizations.

8. Explain the value of open-book management and the balanced scorecard approaches to control in a turbulent environment.

Ted and Norm Waitt co-founded Gateway Inc. in an Iowa farmhouse in 1985 and soon gained national acclaim with the company's quality computers and distinctive cow-spotted boxes. The company's management style also reflected the founders' cattleman heritage. CEO Ted Waitt wore his long hair in a ponytail and built the company on plain talk, loose control, and fair dealing with employees and customers. He stayed closely involved with almost all of the company's decisions, from advertising spots to corporate partnerships, and worked closely with other managers in day-to-day operations. If managers were failing to perform as expected, they often got a friendly chat from Waitt in the hallway. Decisions at Gateway were often made cowboy style, and the "shoot from the hip" approach worked. Gateway was known for innovation, being the first PC company to offer systems with color monitors as standard, the first to offer a standard three-year warranty, and the first to commercially explore convergence between the PC and television. Over the years, Gateway evolved from a PC maker to a full-service technology provider. But as the technology industry grew ever more complex and competitive, the undisciplined ways were no longer working. Costs spiraled out of control. In 2001, Gateway posted a loss of $1 billion and sales fell 37 percent. The company is still searching for its way back to profitability. Waitt knows he needs to dramatically improve efficiency or Gateway is doomed.[1]

## Take A Moment

If you were a consultant to Ted Waitt at Gateway, what advice would you give him about using control systems and strategies to improve cost efficiency and revive the organization? What is the first step you would recommend top managers take to gain better control over the company?

Control is a critical issue facing every manager in every organization. At Gateway, managers need to find new ways to cut costs, increase efficiency, and build sales, or the organization will not survive. Other organizations face similar challenges, such as improving product quality, minimizing the time needed to resupply merchandise in retail stores, decreasing the number of steps needed to process an online merchandise order, or improving the tracking procedures for overnight package delivery. Control, including quality control, also involves office productivity, such as elimination of bottlenecks and reduction in paperwork mistakes. In addition, every organization needs basic systems for allocating financial resources, developing human resources, analyzing financial performance, and evaluating overall profitability.

This chapter introduces basic mechanisms for controlling the organization. It begins by summarizing the basic structure and objectives of the control process. Then it discusses controlling financial performance, including the use of budgets and financial statements. The next sections examine the changing philosophy of control, today's approach to total quality management, and recent trends such as ISO 9000 certification, economic value-added and market value-added systems, and activity-based costing. The chapter concludes with a look at control systems for a turbulent environment, including the use of open-book management and the balanced scorecard, and control problems in the new workplace.

# The Meaning of Control

**organizational control**

The systematic process through which managers regulate organizational activities to make them consistent with expectations established in plans, targets, and standards of performance.

On a bright October day in 2003, storm clouds gathered over Wall Street. A just-issued Securities and Exchange Commission (SEC) report blasted the New York Stock Exchange for failing to adequately monitor its elite floor-trading firms, track violations, and address blatant abuses in which investors were shortchanged by millions of dollars. The criticism of the exchange's regulatory and compliance procedures was a big blow to an institution already reeling from months of difficulties, including the ouster of Chairman Dick Grasso. Poor control systems had gotten the venerable New York Stock Exchange into a public relations and political nightmare. Interim Chairman John Reed has proposed major revisions in the exchange's control systems, including committing more personnel and resources to regulation.[2]

A lack of effective control can seriously damage an organization's health and threaten its future. Consider Enron, which was held up as a model of modern management in the late 1990s but came crashing down a couple of years later.[3] There are numerous reasons for Enron's shocking collapse, including unethical managers and an arrogant, free-wheeling culture. But it ultimately comes down to a lack of control. No one was keeping track to make sure managers stayed within acceptable ethical and financial boundaries. Although chairman Kenneth Lay claimed he didn't know the financial shenanigans were going on at the company, federal investigators disagreed and indicted him on criminal charges.[4] At a minimum, Lay along with other top managers neglected their responsibilities by failing to set up and maintain adequate controls on the giant corporation.

**Organizational control** refers to the systematic process of regulating organizational activities to make

COURTESY OF HONEYWELL, INC.

### CONCEPT CONNECTION

*A new philosophy about **organizational control** involves lower-level workers in management and control decisions. At the Honeywell Industrial Automation and Control facility in Phoenix, employees' quality-control decisions cut defect rates by 70 percent, inventory by 46 percent, and customer lead times by an average of 75 percent.*

them consistent with the expectations established in plans, targets, and standards of performance. In a classic article on the control function, Douglas S. Sherwin summarizes this concept as follows: "The essence of control is action which adjusts operations to predetermined standards, and its basis is information in the hands of managers."[5] Thus, effectively controlling an organization requires information about performance standards and actual performance, as well as actions taken to correct any deviations from the standards. Managers need to decide what information is essential, how they will obtain that information (and share it with employees), and how they can and should respond to it. Having the correct data is essential. Managers have to decide which standards, measurements, and metrics are needed to effectively monitor and control the organization and set up systems for obtaining that information. For example, an important metric for a pro football or basketball team might be the number of season tickets, which reduces the organization's dependence on more labor-intensive box-office sales.[6] One issue of current concern to many managers is how to track valuable metrics for e-commerce, as discussed in this chapter's Manager's Shoptalk.

# Organizational Control Focus

Control can focus on events before, during, or after a process. For example, a local automobile dealer can focus on activities before, during, or after sales of new cars. Careful inspection of new cars and cautious selection of sales employees are ways to ensure high quality or profitable sales even before those sales take place. Monitoring how salespeople act with customers would be considered control during the sales task. Counting the number of new cars sold during the month or telephoning buyers about their satisfaction with sales transactions would constitute control after sales have occurred. These three types of control are formally called *feedforward*, *concurrent*, and *feedback,* and are illustrated in Exhibit 14.1.

Exhibit 14.1

## Organizational Control Focus

**Feedforward Control Anticipates Problems**

Examples
- Pre-employment drug testing
- Inspect raw materials
- Hire only college graduates

Focus is on **Inputs**

**Concurrent Control Solves Problems as They Happen**

Examples
- Monitoring employees
- Total quality management
- Employee self-adjustment

Focus is on **Ongoing Processes**

**Feedback Control Solves Problems After They Occur**

Examples
- Analyze sales per employee
- Final quality inspection
- Survey customers

Focus is on **Outputs**

## manager's Shoptalk

### Turbulent Times

#### E-Commerce Metrics

How do organizations know how well their Web site is doing? It is not too difficult to find out how many people visit the site and how many pages they look at. But that's only the first step toward finding out how effective the site is in terms of achieving organizational goals. Managers have been struggling to identify metrics that will help them evaluate a company's performance and compare it to others. During the dot-com heydey, measures such as *eyeballs* and *stickiness* (measuring how much attention a site gets over time) were important. Today, though, more sophisticated metrics have evolved. Although different companies will use different standards and measurements, some common e-commerce metrics have emerged:

- *Conversion rate*. Conversion means the moment a customer buys, signs up for a seminar, subscribes to a newsletter, and so on. *Cost per conversion* is a critical number to track because it tells managers how much money they are spending to get one person to buy. Companies also track the *conversion rate*, which means the ratio of buyers to visitors, and the average order size.
- *Clickstream*. Clickstream analysis is more than a metric; it is a way to analyze customer behavior by looking at where people enter a site, where they typically convert from visitors to customers, and where the site typically loses visitors. Clickstream analysis also helps companies track their *customer drop-off rate*, which means

how many customers start to purchase a product or sign up for a service but abandon it before completion.

- *Retention or customer loyalty*. Companies want people to buy again and again, so it is important to track customer retention. The online auction site eBay has a high retention rate, because the same people keep coming back to the site to buy and sell merchandise.
- *Site performance*. How well the site performs, including raw performance data on such matters as how long it takes to load a page, how easy it is to find what you're looking for, how long it takes to place an order, and so forth, is one of the most important metrics for many sites, especially B2B sites that sell to time-pressed business users.

E-commerce organizations track many other metrics. Numerous software programs are now available to help managers better measure, analyze, guide, and control e-commerce operations. These new analytical tools enable managers to get a broader, clearer picture of Web site performance and customer activity so they can cut costs and maximize efficiency.

SOURCES: Susannah Patton, "Web Metrics That Matter," *CIO* (November 15, 2002), 84–88; Jim Sterne, "Making Metrics Count," *Business2.com* (April 3, 2001), 72; and Ramin Jaleshgari, "The End of the Hit Parade," *CIO* (May 15, 2000), 183–190.

## Feedforward Control

**feedforward control**
Control that focuses on human, material, and financial resources flowing into the organization; also called *preliminary* or *preventive* control.

Control that attempts to identify and prevent deviations before they occur is called **feedforward control**. Sometimes called *preliminary* or *preventive control*, it focuses on human, material, and financial resources that flow into the organization. Its purpose is to ensure that input quality is high enough to prevent problems when the organization performs its tasks.

Feedforward controls are evident in the selection and hiring of new employees. Organizations attempt to improve the likelihood that employees will perform up to standards by identifying the necessary skills, using tests and other screening devices to hire people who have those skills, and providing necessary training to upgrade important skills. Numerous nursing homes and assisted living centers have come under fire in recent years due to lax feedforward controls, such as failing to ensure that workers have the appropriate skills or provide them with the training needed to adequately care for residents. Brookside Gables, an assisted living center in the Panhandle region of Florida, eventually closed after a resident died because caregivers didn't have basic skills in first aid and emergency procedures.[7] Another type of feedforward control is forecasting trends in the environment and managing risk. In tough economic times, for example, consulting companies such as A. T. Kearney try to stay in close touch with clients to monitor how much business and money will be coming in. The fashion company Liz Claiborne gathers information about consumer fads to determine what supplies to purchase and inventory to stock. Banks typically require extensive documentation before approving major loans to identify and manage risks.[8]

## Concurrent Control

Control that monitors ongoing employee activities to ensure they are consistent with performance standards is called **concurrent control**. Concurrent control assesses current work activities, relies on performance standards, and includes rules and regulations for guiding employee tasks and behaviors.

Many manufacturing operations include devices that measure whether the items being produced meet quality standards. Employees monitor the measurements; if they see that standards are not met in some area, they make a correction themselves or signal the appropriate person that a problem is occurring. Technology advancements are adding to the possibilities for concurrent control in services as well. For example, retail stores such as Beall's, Sunglass Hut, and Saks use cash-register-management software to monitor cashiers' activities in real time and help prevent employee theft. Trucking companies like Schneider National and Covenant use computers to track the position of their trucks and monitor the status of deliveries.[9]

Other concurrent controls involve the ways in which organizations influence employees. An organization's cultural norms and values influence employee behavior, as do the norms of an employee's peers or work group. Concurrent control also includes self-control, through which individuals impose concurrent controls on their own behavior because of personal values and attitudes.

## Feedback Control

Sometimes called *postaction* or *output control*, **feedback control** focuses on the organization's outputs—in particular, the quality of an end product or service. An example of feedback control in a manufacturing department is an intensive final inspection of a refrigerator at an assembly plant. In Kentucky, school administrators conduct feedback control by evaluating each school's performance every other year. They review reports of students' test scores as well as the school's dropout and attendance rates. The state rewards schools with rising scores and brings in consultants to work with schools whose scores have fallen.[10]

Besides producing high-quality products and services, businesses need to earn a profit, and even nonprofit organizations need to operate efficiently to carry out their missions. Therefore, many feedback controls focus on financial measurements. Budgeting, for example, is a form of feedback control because managers monitor whether they have operated within their budget targets and make adjustments accordingly.

**concurrent control**
Control that consists of monitoring ongoing activities to ensure that they are consistent with standards.

**feedback control**
Control that focuses on the organization's outputs; also called *postaction* or *output control*.

# Feedback Control Model

All well-designed control systems involve the use of feedback to determine whether performance meets established standards. In this section, we will examine the key steps in the feedback control model and then look at how the model applies to organizational budgeting.

## Steps of Feedback Control

Managers set up control systems that consist of the four key steps illustrated in Exhibit 14.2: establish standards, measure performance, compare performance to standards, and make corrections as necessary.

### Establish Standards of Performance

Within the organization's overall strategic plan, managers define goals for organizational departments in specific, operational terms that include a *standard of performance* against which to compare organizational activities. A standard of performance could include "reducing the reject rate from 15 to 3 percent," "increasing the corporation's return on investment to 7 percent," or "reducing the number of accidents to one per each 100,000 hours of labor."

Managers should carefully assess what they will measure and how they will define it. Tracking such matters as customer service, employee involvement, and turnover is an important supplement to traditional financial performance measurement, but many companies fail to adequately identify and define nonfinancial measurements.[11] To effectively evaluate and reward employees for the achievement of standards, managers need clear standards that reflect activities that contribute to the organization's overall strategy in a significant way. Standards should be defined clearly and precisely so employees know what they need to do and can determine whether their activities are on target.[12]

### Measure Actual Performance

Most organizations prepare formal reports of quantitative performance measurements that managers review daily, weekly, or monthly. These measurements should be related to the standards set in the first step of the control process. For example, if sales growth is a target, the organization should have a means of gathering and

Exhibit 14.2

## Feedback Control Model

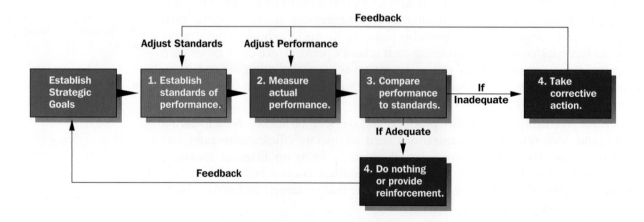

reporting sales data. If the organization has identified appropriate measurements, regular review of these reports helps managers stay aware of whether the organization is doing what it should be.

In most companies, managers do not rely exclusively on quantitative measures. They get out into the organization to see how things are going, especially for such goals as increasing employee participation or improving customer satisfaction. Managers have to observe for themselves whether employees are participating in decision making and have opportunities to add to and share their knowledge. Interaction with customers is necessary for managers to really understand whether activities are meeting customer needs.

## Compare Performance to Standards

The third step in the control process is comparing actual activities to performance standards. When managers read computer reports or walk through the plant, they identify whether actual performance meets, exceeds, or falls short of standards. Typically, performance reports simplify such comparisons by placing the performance standards for the reporting period alongside the actual performance for the same period and by computing the variance—that is, the difference between each actual amount and the associated standard. To correct the problems that most require attention, managers focus on variances.

When performance deviates from a standard, managers must interpret the deviation. They are expected to dig beneath the surface and find the cause of the problem. If the sales goal is to increase the number of sales calls by 10 percent and a salesperson achieved an increase of 8 percent, where did she fail to achieve her goal? Perhaps several businesses on her route closed, additional salespeople were assigned to her area by competitors, or she needs training in making cold sales calls more effectively. Managers should take an inquiring approach to deviations in order to gain a broad understanding of factors that influence performance. Effective management control involves subjective judgment and employee discussions, as well as objective analysis of performance data.

## Take Corrective Action

Managers also determine what changes, if any, are necessary. In a traditional top-down approach to control, managers exercise their formal authority to make necessary changes. Managers may encourage employees to work harder, redesign the production process, or fire employees. In contrast, managers using a participative control approach collaborate with employees to determine the corrective action necessary.

In some cases, managers may take corrective action to change performance standards. They may realize that standards are too high or too low if departments continually fail to meet or routinely exceed standards. If contingency factors that influence organizational performance change, performance standards may need to be altered to make them realistic and to provide continued motivation for employees.

Managers may wish to provide positive reinforcement when performance meets or exceeds targets. They may reward a department that has exceeded its planned goals or

© EVAN KAFKA

### CONCEPT CONNECTION

*When Paul Pressler became CEO of retailer Gap Inc. two years ago, he launched a makeover. By **comparing performance to standards**, Pressler could see that basic operations, marketing, and inventory were out of control. He took **corrective action** by tightening operations, increasing focus on the customer, and implementing inventory control measures that would prevent boatloads of unsold merchandise from sitting in warehouses and storerooms. To avoid panicky clearance sales, Pressler insisted that managers rely on new software that helps determine when and how much to mark down items. These control actions have resulted in increasing sales and six straight quarters of earnings growth.*

congratulate employees for a job well done. Managers should not ignore high-performing departments at the expense of taking corrective actions elsewhere. The online auction company eBay provides a good illustration of the feedback control model.

One of Meg Whitman's guiding rules is: "If you can't measure it, you can't control it." As CEO of eBay, Whitman runs a company that is obsessed with performance measurement. She personally monitors a slew of performance metrics, including standard measurements such as site visitors, new users, and time spent on the site, as well as the ratio of eBay's revenues to the value of goods traded. She recently brought in a benchmarking consultant to measure eBay against peers to see how fast it adds features to the Web site. The results showed Whitman the company has some improvement to make in that area.

Managers and employees throughout the company also monitor performance almost obsessively. Category managers, for example, have clear standards of performance for their auction categories (such as sports memorabilia; jewelry and watches; health and beauty; fashion, etc.). They are constantly measuring, tweaking, and promoting their categories to meet or outperform the targets.

Whitman believes getting a firm grip on performance measurement is essential for a company to know where to spend money, where to assign more personnel, and which projects to promote or abandon. But performance measurement isn't just about numbers. At eBay, "it's all about the customer," and gauging customer (user) satisfaction requires a mix of methods, such as surveys, monitoring eBay's discussion boards, and personal contact. Whitman gets her chance to really connect with users at the annual eBay Live conference. There, she wanders the convention-hall floor talking with anyone and everyone about their eBay experiences.

By defining standards, using a combination of measurement approaches, and comparing performance to standards, eBay managers are able to identify trouble spots and move quickly to take corrective action when and where it's needed.[13]

## Application to Budgeting

*Budgetary control*, one of the most commonly used methods of managerial control, is the process of setting targets for an organization's expenditures, monitoring results and comparing them to the budget, and making changes as needed. As a control device, budgets are reports that list planned and actual expenditures for cash, assets, raw materials, salaries, and other resources. In addition, budget reports usually list the variance between the budgeted and actual amounts for each item.

**Take A Moment**        *Go to the experiential exercise on page 538 that pertains to budgetary control.*

A budget is created for every division or department within an organization, no matter how small, so long as it performs a distinct project, program, or function. The fundamental unit of analysis for a budget control system is called a responsibility center. A responsibility center is defined as any organizational department or unit under the supervision of a single person who is responsible for its activity.[14] A three-person appliance sales office in Watertown, New York, is a responsibility center, as is a quality control department, a marketing department, and an entire refrigerator manufacturing plant. The manager of each unit has budget responsibility. Top managers use budgets for the company as a whole, and middle managers traditionally focus on the budget performance of their department or division. Budgets that managers typically use include expense budgets, revenue budgets, cash budgets, and capital budgets.

**responsibility center**
An organizational unit under the supervision of a single person who is responsible for its activity.

**expense budget**
A budget that outlines the anticipated and actual expenses for a responsibility center.

### Expense Budget

An expense budget includes anticipated and actual expenses for each responsibility center and for the total organization. An expense budget may show all types of expenses or may focus on a particular category, such as materials or research and development expenses. When actual expenses exceed budgeted amounts, the difference signals the need for managers to identify whether a problem exists and take corrective action if needed. The difference may arise from inefficiency, or expenses may be higher because the organization's sales are growing faster than anticipated. Conversely, expenses below budget may signal exceptional efficiency or failure to meet some other standards, such as a desired level of sales or quality of service. Either way, expense budgets can help identify the need for further investigation but do not substitute for it.

## Revenue Budget

A revenue budget lists forecasted and actual revenues of the organization. In general, revenues below the budgeted amount signal a need to investigate the problem to see whether the organization can improve revenues. In contrast, revenues above budget would require determining whether the organization can obtain the necessary resources to meet the higher-than-expected demand for its products. Managers then formulate action plans to correct the budget variance.

**revenue budget**
A budget that identifies the forecasted and actual revenues of the organization.

## Cash Budget

The cash budget estimates receipts and expenditures of money on a daily or weekly basis to ensure that an organization has sufficient cash to meet its obligations. The cash budget shows the level of funds flowing through the organization and the nature of cash disbursements. If the cash budget shows that the firm has more cash than necessary to meet short-term needs, the company can arrange to invest the excess to earn interest income. In contrast, if the cash budget shows a payroll expenditure of $20,000 coming at the end of the week but only $10,000 in the bank, the organization must borrow cash to meet the payroll.

**cash budget**
A budget that estimates and reports cash flows on a daily or weekly basis to ensure that the company has sufficient cash to meet its obligations.

## Capital Budget

The capital budget lists planned investments in major assets such as buildings, heavy machinery, or complex information technology systems, often involving expenditures over more than a year. Capital expenditures not only have a large impact on future expenses, they are investments designed to enhance profits. Therefore, a capital budget is necessary to plan the impact of these expenditures on cash flow and profitability. Controlling involves not only monitoring the amount of capital expenditures but evaluating whether the assumptions made about the return on the investments are holding true. Managers should evaluate whether continuing investment in particular projects is advisable, as well as whether their procedures for making capital expenditure decisions are adequate. Some companies, including Boeing, Merck, Shell, United Technologies, and Whirlpool, evaluate capital projects at several stages to determine whether they still are in line with the company's strategy.[15]

**capital budget**
A budget that plans and reports investments in major assets to be depreciated over several years.

Budgeting is an important part of organizational planning and control. Many traditional companies use top-down budgeting, which means that the budgeted amounts for the coming year are literally imposed on middle and lower-level managers.[16] These managers set departmental budget targets in accordance with overall company revenues and expenditures specified by top executives. Although there are some advantages to the top-down process, the movement toward employee empowerment, participation, and learning means that many organizations are adopting bottom-up budgeting, a process in which lower-level managers anticipate their departments' resource needs and pass them up to top management for approval.[17] At MediHealth Outsourcing, top executives give department managers the financial information for the entire company and ask them to define their own departmental budget needs. The budgets are then reviewed and approved by top management.[18]

**top-down budgeting**
A budgeting process in which middle- and lower-level managers set departmental budget targets in accordance with overall company revenues and expenditures specified by top management.

**bottom-up budgeting**
A budgeting process in which lower-level managers budget their departments' resource needs and pass them up to top management for approval.

# Financial Control

In every organization, managers need to watch how well the organization is performing financially. Not only do financial controls tell whether the organization is on sound financial footing, but they can be useful indicators of other kinds of performance problems. For example, a sales decline may signal problems with products, customer service, or sales force effectiveness.

## Financial Statements

Financial statements provide the basic information used for financial control of an organization. Two major financial statements—the balance sheet and the income statement—are the starting points for financial control.

**balance sheet**
A financial statement that shows the firm's financial position with respect to assets and liabilities at a specific point in time.

The balance sheet shows the firm's financial position with respect to assets and liabilities at a specific point in time. An example of a balance sheet is presented in Exhibit 14.3. The balance sheet provides three types of information: assets, liabilities, and owners' equity. *Assets* are what the company owns, and they include *current assets* (those that can be converted into cash in a short time period) and *fixed assets* (such as buildings and equipment that are long term in nature). *Liabilities* are the firm's debts, including both *current debt* (obligations that will be paid by the company in the near future) and *long-term debt* (obligations payable over a long period). *Owners' equity* is the difference between assets and liabilities and is the company's net worth in stock and retained earnings.

**income statement**
A financial statement that summarizes the firm's financial performance for a given time interval; sometimes called a profit-and-loss statement.

The income statement, sometimes called a profit-and-loss statement or P & L for short, summarizes the firm's financial performance for a given time interval, usually one year. A sample income statement is shown in Exhibit 14.4. Some

Exhibit 14.3

## Balance Sheet

| New Creations Landscaping Consolidated Balance Sheet December 31, 2004 | | | | | |
|---|---|---|---|---|---|
| **Assets** | | | **Liabilities and Owners' Equity** | | |
| Current assets: | | | Current liabilities: | | |
| Cash | $25,000 | | Accounts payable | $200,000 | |
| Accounts receivable | 75,000 | | Accrued expenses | 20,000 | |
| Inventory | 500,000 | | Income taxes payable | 30,000 | |
| Total current assets | | $600,000 | Total current liabilities | | $250,000 |
| Fixed assets: | | | Long-term liabilities: | | |
| Land | 250,000 | | Mortgages payable | 350,000 | |
| Buildings and fixtures | 1,000,000 | | Bonds outstanding | 250,000 | |
| Less depreciation | 200,000 | | Total long-term liabilities | | $600,000 |
| Total fixed assets | | 1,050,000 | Owners' equity: | | |
| | | | Common stock | 540,000 | |
| | | | Retained earnings | 260,000 | |
| | | | Total owners' equity | | 800,000 |
| Total assets | | $1,650,000 | Total liabilities and net worth | | $1,650,000 |

Exhibit 14.4

**Income Statement**

| New Creations Landscaping<br>Statement of Income<br>For the Year Ended December 31, 2004 | | |
|---|---:|---:|
| Gross sales | $3,100,000 | |
| Less sales returns | 200,000 | |
| Net sales | | $2,900,000 |
| Less expenses and cost of goods sold: | | |
| Cost of goods sold | 2,110,000 | |
| Depreciation | 60,000 | |
| Sales expenses | 200,000 | |
| Administrative expenses | 90,000 | 2,460,000 |
| Operating profit | | 440,000 |
| Other income | | 20,000 |
| Gross income | | 460,000 |
| Less interest expense | 80,000 | |
| Income before taxes | | 380,000 |
| Less taxes | 165,000 | |
| Net income | | $215,000 |

organizations calculate the income statement at three-month intervals during the year to see if they are on target for sales and profits. The income statement shows revenues coming into the organization from all sources and subtracts all expenses, including cost of goods sold, interest, taxes, and depreciation. The *bottom line* indicates the net income—profit or loss—for the given time period.

The owner of Aahs!, a specialty retailing chain in California, used the income statement to detect that sales and profits were dropping significantly during the summer months.[19] He immediately evaluated company activities and closed two money-losing stores. He also began a training program to teach employees how to increase sales and cut costs to improve net income. This use of the income statement follows the control model described in the previous section, beginning with setting targets, measuring actual performance, and then taking corrective action to improve performance to meet targets.

## Financial Analysis: Interpreting the Numbers

A manager needs to be able to evaluate financial reports that compare the organization's performance with earlier data or industry norms. These comparisons enable the manager to see whether the organization is improving and whether it is competitive with others in the industry. The most common financial analysis focuses on ratios, statistics that express the relationships between performance indicators such as profits and assets, sales, and inventory. Ratios are stated as a fraction or proportion; Exhibit 14.5 summarizes some financial ratios, which are measures of an organization's liquidity, activity, profitability, and leverage. These are among the most common ratios, but many measures are used. Managers decide which ratios reveal the most important relationships for their business.

Exhibit 14.5

### Common Financial Ratios

| | |
|---|---|
| **Liquidity Ratios** | |
| Current ratio | Current assets/Current liabilities |
| **Activity Ratios** | |
| Inventory turnover | Total sales/Average inventory |
| Conversion ratio | Purchase orders/Customer inquiries |
| **Profitability Ratios** | |
| Profit margin on sales | Net income/Sales |
| Gross margin | Gross income/Sales |
| Return on assets (ROA) | Net income/Total assets |
| **Leverage Ratios** | |
| Debt ratio | Total debt/Total assets |

**liquidity ratio**
A financial ratio that indicates the organization's ability to meet its current debt obligations.

**activity ratio**
A financial ratio that measures the organization's internal performance with respect to key activities defined by management.

**profitability ratio**
A financial ratio that describes the firm's profits in terms of a source of profits (for example, sales or total assets).

## Liquidity Ratios

A **liquidity ratio** indicates an organization's ability to meet its current debt obligations. For example, the *current ratio* (current assets divided by current liabilities) tells whether there are sufficient assets to convert into cash to pay off debts, if needed. If a hypothetical company, Oceanographics, Inc., has current assets of $600,000 and current liabilities of $250,000, the current ratio is 2.4, meaning it has sufficient funds to pay off immediate debts 2.4 times. This is normally considered a satisfactory margin of safety.

## Activity Ratios

An **activity ratio** measures internal performance with respect to key activities defined by management. For example, *inventory turnover* is calculated by dividing total sales by average inventory. This ratio tells how many times the inventory is used up to meet the total sales figure. If inventory sits too long, money is wasted. Dell Computer Corporation has achieved a strategic advantage by minimizing its inventory costs. Dividing Dell's annual sales by its small inventory generates an inventory turnover rate of 35.7, up from 14 in 1997.[20] Another type of activity ratio, the *conversion ratio*, is purchase orders divided by customer inquiries. This ratio is an indicator of a company's effectiveness in converting inquiries into sales. For example, if Cisco Systems moves from 26.5 to 28.2 percent conversion ratio, more of its inquiries are turned into sales, indicating better sales activity.

## Profitability Ratios

Managers analyze a company's profits by studying **profitability ratios**, which state profits relative to a source of profits, such as sales or assets. One important profitability ratio is the *profit margin on sales*, which is calculated as net income divided by sales. Similarly, *gross margin* is the gross (before-tax) profit divided by total sales. As described in the Unlocking Creative Solutions Through Technology box, the British online grocer Tesco.com is thriving, whereas U.S.-based Webvan failed, because Tesco managers paid close attention to profitability rather than adopting the "growth now, profits later" model of many early dot-com companies.

Another profitability measure is *return on total assets (ROA)*, which is a percentage representing what a company earned from its assets, computed as net income divided by total assets. ROA is a valuable yardstick for comparing a company's

# Unlocking Creative Solutions Through Technology

## Tesco.com

Tesco, Britain's number-one supermarket chain, recently achieved something extraordinary for a retailer—being named Britain's Most Admired Company. Tesco is so well-managed that it earned as much profit in one recent year as its four biggest competitors combined. One illustration of the company's solid management is the launch of Tesco.com. When top executives decided to launch a dot-com division, the main thing they focused on was ensuring profitability. Tesco implemented strict financial controls from the beginning by launching the Internet business from within the chain's current grocery stores. Managers developed and fine-tuned the formula for years, keeping a go-slow, by-the-numbers management approach that has won Tesco the title of world's biggest and most successful online grocer.

The idea of creating an electronic version of a 1950s delivery boy seemed simple, but for many online grocery businesses, such as U.S.-based Webvan, the underlying details proved more difficult. Webvan had to build its Internet business from the ground up, requiring huge investments in new buildings and infrastructure. In addition, Webvan focused too much energy on rapid growth and too little on financial control. The chart in the next column compares Tesco.com and Webvan's simplified income statements.

Tesco.com had a built-in advantage by being a part of the greater Tesco enterprise, which enabled the operation to ride on the back of its parent company, leveraging its brand, suppliers, advertising, and customer database. Tesco started by offering delivery from just one store, gradually rolling out online service to other areas. Webvan tried to do too much too soon, aiming to enter 24 U.S. markets within three years. This required building two dozen automated food distribution warehouses at a cost of about $35 million per building. After building only three warehouses, Webvan's numbers just got worse and worse, and the startup went bankrupt in July 2001. With no existing suppliers or customer base, fixed costs quickly overwhelmed Webvan's revenues. By contrast, Tesco.com didn't build anything, choosing instead to pick goods off the shelves of existing supermarkets. Using the store-based picking approach kept startup costs low—Tesco spent only $58 million on its dot-com operation during its first four years of operation. Note in the income statement that Tesco's marketing and administrative cost per order is only $5.67, compared to a cost of $133.04 per order for Webvan.

By maintaining strict control over operating costs, checking and rechecking the math to make sure the company was headed in the right direction, Tesco has slowly rolled out online service all across Britain. In addition, the company now has successful online ventures in South Korea and the United States and is likely to continue international expansion of its online business.

| | TESCO.COM | WEBVAN |
|---|---|---|
| **Average Sale** | $123.25 | $114.00 |
| **Minus:** | | |
| Cost of groceries | $85.66 | $83.00 |
| Other store costs | $15.16 | —— |
| Marketing and administration | $5.67 | $133.04 |
| Picking and delivery | $17.80 | $30.00 |
| **Plus:** | | |
| Delivery fee | $7.25 | —— |
| **Net Profit (Loss)** | $6.21 | ($132.04) |

**SOURCE**: Andy Reinhardt, "Tesco Bets Small—and Wins Big," *BusinessWeek e.biz* (October 1, 2001), EB26–EB32; and Nils Pratley, "Britain's Most Admired Companies," *Management Today* (December 2003), 35.

ability to generate earnings with other investment opportunities. In basic terms, the company should be able to earn more by using its assets to operate the business than it could by putting the same investment in the bank. Caterpillar Inc., which produces construction and mining equipment, uses return on assets as its main measure of performance. It sets ROA standards for each area of its business and uses variances from the standards to identify problems with how efficiently it is operating and whether it is fully using its assets. Since it began using ROA standards, Caterpillar has enjoyed double-digit returns.[21]

## Leverage Ratios

*Leverage* refers to funding activities with borrowed money. A company can use leverage to make its assets produce more than they could on their own. However, too much borrowing can put the organization at risk such that it will be unable to keep up with repayment of its debt. Managers therefore track their *debt ratio*, or total debt divided by total assets, to make sure it does not exceed a level they consider acceptable. Lenders may consider a company with a debt ratio above 1.0 to be a poor credit risk.

# The Changing Philosophy of Control

**bureaucratic control**
The use of rules, policies, hierarchy of authority, reward systems, and other formal devices to influence employee behavior and assess performance.

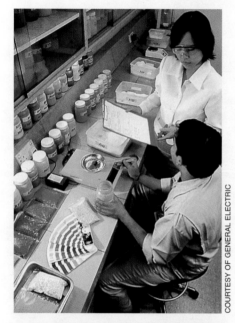

COURTESY OF GENERAL ELECTRIC

**CONCEPT CONNECTION**

*For more than a decade, managers at General Electric have been dedicated to **decentralized control** through a program called "Work Out." Work Out is an ongoing effort to achieve what former CEO Jack Welch called boundaryless behavior—behavior that "ends all barriers of rank, function, geography, and bureaucracy in an endless pursuit of the best idea." With boundaries diminished, GE launched **Six Sigma**, a disciplined methodology that focuses on quality for every process that affects the GE customer. Cindy Lee and S. Mani were part of a Six Sigma team at the color lab of the GE Plastics plant in Singapore. The team reduced the lead time for matching colors of GE resins to customer requirements by 85 percent, providing a distinct competitive advantage in the fast-paced global market for plastics.*

Managers' approach to control is changing in many of today's organizations. In connection with the shift to employee participation and empowerment, many companies are adopting a *decentralized* rather than a *bureaucratic* control process. Bureaucratic control and decentralized control represent different philosophies of corporate culture, which was discussed in Chapter 3. Most organizations display some aspects of both bureaucratic and decentralized control, but managers generally emphasize one or the other, depending on the organizational culture and their own beliefs about control.

**Bureaucratic control** involves monitoring and influencing employee behavior through extensive use of rules, policies, hierarchy of authority, written documentation, reward systems, and other formal mechanisms.[22] In contrast, decentralized control relies on cultural values, traditions, shared beliefs, and trust to foster compliance with organizational goals. Managers operate on the assumption that employees are trustworthy and willing to perform effectively without extensive rules and close supervision.

Exhibit 14.6 contrasts the use of bureaucratic and decentralized methods of control. Bureaucratic methods define explicit rules, policies, and procedures for employee behavior. Control relies on centralized authority, the formal hierarchy, and close personal supervision. Responsibility for quality control rests with quality control inspectors and supervisors rather than with employees. Job descriptions generally are specific and task related, and managers define minimal standards for acceptable employee performance. In exchange for meeting the standards, individual employees are given extrinsic rewards such as wages, benefits, and possibly promotions up the hierarchy. Employees rarely participate in the control process, with any participation being formalized through mechanisms such as grievance procedures. With bureaucratic control, the organizational culture is somewhat rigid, and managers do not consider culture a useful means of controlling employees and the organization. Technology often is used to control the flow and pace of work or to monitor employees, such as by measuring how long employees spend on phone calls or how many keystrokes they make at the computer.

Bureaucratic control techniques can enhance organizational efficiency and effectiveness. Many employees appreciate a system that clarifies what is expected of them, and they may be motivated by challenging, but achievable, goals.[23] However, although many managers effectively use bureaucratic control, too much control can backfire. Employees resent being watched too closely, and they may try to sabotage the control system. One veteran truck driver expressed his unhappiness with electronic monitoring to a *Wall Street Journal*

Exhibit 14.6

## Bureaucratic and Decentralized Methods of Control

| Bureaucratic Control | Decentralized Control |
|---|---|
| Uses detailed rules and procedures; formal control systems | Limited use of rules; relies on values, group and self-control, selection and socialization |
| Top-down authority, formal hierarchy, position power, quality control inspectors | Flexible authority, flat structure, expert power, everyone monitors quality |
| Task-related job descriptions; measurable standards define minimum performance | Results-based job descriptions; emphasis on goals to be achieved |
| Emphasis on extrinsic rewards (pay, benefits, status) | Extrinsic and intrinsic rewards (meaningful work, opportunities for growth) |
| Rewards given for meeting individual performance standards | Rewards individual and team; emphasis on equity across employees |
| Limited, formalized employee participation (e.g., grievance procedures) | Broad employee participation, including quality control, system design, and organizational governance |
| Rigid organizational culture; distrust of cultural norms as means of control | Adaptive culture; culture recognized as means for uniting individual, team, and organizational goals for overall control |

**SOURCES**: Based on Richard E. Walton, "From Control to Commitment in the Workplace," *Harvard Business Review* (March–April 1985), 76–84; and Don Hellriegel, Susan E. Jackson, and John W. Slocum, Jr., *Management*, 8th ed. (Cincinnati, Ohio: South-Western, 1999), 663.

reporter investigating the use of devices that monitor truck locations. According to the driver, "It's getting worse and worse all the time. Pretty soon they'll want to put a chip in the drivers' ears and make them robots." He added that he occasionally escapes the relentless monitoring by parking under an overpass to take a needed nap out of the range of the surveillance satellites.[24]

**Decentralized control** is based on values and assumptions that are almost opposite to those of bureaucratic control. Rules and procedures are used only when necessary. Managers rely instead on shared goals and values to control employee behavior. The organization places great emphasis on the selection and socialization of employees to ensure that workers have the appropriate values needed to influence behavior toward meeting company goals. No organization can control employees 100 percent of the time, and self-discipline and self-control are what keep workers performing their jobs up to standard. Empowerment of employees, effective socialization, and training all can contribute to internal standards that provide self-control.

With decentralized control, power is more dispersed and is based on knowledge and experience as much as position. The organizational structure is flat and horizontal, as discussed in Chapter 10, with flexible authority and teams of workers solving problems and making improvements. Everyone is involved in quality control on an ongoing basis. Job descriptions generally are results-based, with an emphasis more

**decentralized control**
The use of organizational culture, group norms, and a focus on goals, rather than rules and procedures, to foster compliance with organizational goals.

on the outcomes to be achieved than on the specific tasks to be performed. Managers use not only extrinsic rewards such as pay, but the intrinsic rewards of meaningful work and the opportunity to learn and grow. Technology is used to empower employees by giving them the information they need to make effective decisions, work together, and solve problems. People are rewarded for team and organizational success as well as their individual performance, and there is an emphasis on equity among employees. Employees participate in a wide range of areas, including setting goals, determining standards of performance, governing quality, and designing control systems.

With decentralized control, the culture is adaptive, and managers recognize the importance of organizational culture for uniting individual, team, and organizational goals for greater overall control. Ideally, with decentralized control, employees will pool their areas of expertise to arrive at procedures that are better than managers could come up with working alone.

# Total Quality Management

**total quality management (TQM)**
An organizationwide commitment to infusing quality into every activity through continuous improvement.

One popular approach based on a decentralized control philosophy is **total quality management (TQM)**, an organizationwide effort to infuse quality into every activity in a company through continuous improvement. TQM became attractive to U.S. managers in the 1980s because it had been successfully implemented by Japanese companies that were gaining market share—and an international reputation for high quality. The Japanese system was based on the work of such U.S. researchers and consultants as Deming, Juran, and Feigenbaum, whose ideas attracted U.S. executives after the methods were tested overseas.[25]

The TQM philosophy focuses on teamwork, increasing customer satisfaction, and lowering costs. Organizations implement TQM by encouraging managers and employees to collaborate across functions and departments, as well as with customers and suppliers, to identify areas for improvement, no matter how small. Each quality improvement is a step toward perfection and meeting a goal of zero defects. Quality control becomes part of the day-to-day business of every employee, rather than being assigned to specialized departments.

The implementation of total quality management is similar to that of other decentralized control methods. Feedforward controls include training employees to think in terms of prevention, not detection, of problems and giving them the responsibility and power to correct errors, expose problems, and contribute to solutions. Concurrent controls include an organizational culture and employee commitment that favor total quality and employee participation. Feedback controls include targets for employee involvement and for zero defects.

## TQM Techniques

The implementation of total quality management involves the use of many techniques, including quality circles, benchmarking, Six Sigma principles, reduced cycle time, and continuous improvement.

### Quality Circles

**quality circle**
A group of 6 to 12 volunteer employees who meet regularly to discuss and solve problems affecting the quality of their work.

One technique for implementing the decentralized approach of TQM is to use quality circles. A quality circle is a group of 6 to 12 volunteer employees who meet regularly to discuss and solve problems affecting the quality of their work.[26] At a set time during the workweek, the members of the quality circle meet, identify problems, and try to find solutions. Circle members are free to collect data and take surveys. Many companies train team members in team building, problem solving, and statistical quality control. The reason for using quality circles is to push decision making to an organization level at which recommendations can be made by the people who do the job and know it better than anyone else.

## Benchmarking

Introduced by Xerox in 1979, benchmarking is now a major TQM component. Benchmarking is defined as "the continuous process of measuring products, services, and practices against the toughest competitors or those companies recognized as industry leaders."[27] The key to successful benchmarking lies in analysis. Starting with its own mission statement, a company should honestly analyze its current procedures and determine areas for improvement. As a second step, a company *carefully* selects competitors worthy of copying. For example, Xerox studied the order fulfillment techniques of L. L. Bean and learned ways to reduce warehouse costs by 10 percent. Companies can emulate internal processes and procedures of competitors, but must take care to select companies whose methods are compatible. Once a strong, compatible program is found and analyzed, the benchmarking company can then devise a strategy for implementing a new program.

**benchmarking**
The continuous process of measuring products, services, and practices against major competitors or industry leaders.

## Six Sigma

Six Sigma quality principles were first introduced by Motorola in the 1980s and were later popularized by General Electric, where former CEO Jack Welch praised Six Sigma for quality and efficiency gains that saved the company billions of dollars. Based on the Greek letter *sigma*, which statisticians use to measure how far something deviates from perfection, Six Sigma is a highly ambitious quality standard that specifies a goal of no more than 3.4 defects per million parts. That essentially means being defect-free 99.9997 percent of the time.[28] However, Six Sigma has deviated from its precise definition to become a generic term for a quality-control approach that takes nothing for granted and emphasizes a disciplined and relentless pursuit of higher quality and lower costs. The discipline is based on a five-step methodology referred to as *DMAIC* (Define, Measure, Analyze, Improve, and Control, pronounced "de-May-ick" for short), which provides a structured way for organizations to approach and solve problems.[29]

**Six Sigma**
A quality control approach that emphasizes a relentless pursuit of higher quality and lower costs.

Effectively implementing Six Sigma requires a major commitment from top management, because Six Sigma requires widespread change throughout the organization. Hundreds of organizations have adopted some form of Six Sigma program in recent years. Highly committed companies, including ITT Industries, Motorola, General Electric, Allied Signal, ABB Ltd., and DuPont & Co., send senior managers to weeks of training to become qualified as Six Sigma "black belts." These black belts lead projects aimed at improving targeted areas of the business.[30] Although originally applied to manufacturing, Six Sigma has evolved to a process used in all industries and affecting every aspect of company operations, from human resources to customer service. Exhibit 14.7 lists some statistics that illustrate why Six Sigma is important for both manufacturing and service organizations.

## Reduced Cycle Time

Recall our discussion of *fast cycle teams* from Chapter 11. Cycle time has become a critical quality issue in today's fast-paced world. Cycle time refers to the steps taken to complete a company process, such as teaching a class, publishing a textbook, or designing a new car. The simplification of work cycles, including the dropping of barriers between work steps and among departments and the removal of worthless steps in the process, enables a TQM program to succeed. Even if an organization decides not to use quality circles or other techniques, substantial improvement is

**cycle time**
The steps taken to complete a company process.

## Exhibit 14.7

### The Importance of Quality Improvement Programs

| 99 Percent Amounts to: | Six Sigma Amounts to: |
|---|---|
| 117,000 pieces of lost first-class mail per hour | 1 piece of lost first-class mail every two hours |
| 800,000 mishandled personal checks each day | 3 mishandled checks each day |
| 23,087 defective computers shipped each month | 8 defective computers shipped each month |
| 7.2 hours per month without electricity | 9 seconds per month without electricity |

SOURCE: Based on data from Statistical Abstract for the United States, U.S. Postal Service, as reported in Tracy Mayor, "Six Sigma Comes to IT: Targeting Perfection," *CIO* (December 1, 2003), 62–70.

**continuous improvement**
The implementation of a large number of small, incremental improvements in all areas of the organization on an ongoing basis.

© JASON FULFORD

### CONCEPT CONNECTION

*Delphi Automotive Systems' injection-molding plant in Cortland, Ohio, produces a billion plastic housings a year for electrical connectors used in motor vehicles and telecom equipment. Delphi spent $14 million to renovate the building and another $30 million for production equipment, computers and software, and a network linking the factory floor with suppliers and customers. This investment in automation and e-business systems has greatly improved the plant's* **cycle time,** *enabling Delphi to churn out products faster than ever before. Even from his PC at home, plant superintendent John Stefanko can see what part a machine is currently making, whether it's taking 15, 18, or 20 seconds to do so, and how many parts it has made in the last 15 minutes.*

possible by focusing on improved responsiveness and acceleration of activities into a shorter time. Reduction in cycle time improves overall company performance as well as quality.[31]

L. L. Bean, Inc., the Freeport, Maine, mail-order firm, is a recognized leader in cycle time control. Workers used flowcharts to track their movements, pinpoint wasted motions, and completely redesign the order-fulfillment process. Today, a computerized system breaks down an order based on the geographic area of the warehouse in which items are stored. Items are placed on conveyor belts, where electronic sensors re-sort the items for individual orders. After orders are packed, they are sent to a FedEx facility on site. Improvements such as these have enabled L. L. Bean to process most orders within two hours after the order is received.[32]

### Continuous Improvement

In North America, crash programs and designs have traditionally been the preferred method of innovation. Managers measure the expected benefits of a change and favor the ideas with the biggest payoffs. In contrast, Japanese companies have realized extraordinary success from making a series of mostly small improvements. This approach, called **continuous improvement,** or *kaizen,* is the implementation of a large number of small, incremental improvements in all areas of the organization on an ongoing basis. In a successful TQM program, all employees learn that they are expected to contribute by initiating changes in their own job activities. The basic philosophy is that improving things a little bit at a time, all the time, has the highest probability of success. Innovations can start simple, and employees can build on their success in this unending process.

© STEVE JONES

## TQM Success Factors

Despite its promise, total quality management does not always work. A few firms have had disappointing results. In particular, Six Sigma principles might not be appropriate for all organizational problems, and some companies have expended tremendous energy and resources for little payoff.[33] Many contingency factors (listed in Exhibit 14.8) can influence the success of a TQM program. For example, quality circles are most beneficial when employees have challenging jobs; participation in a quality circle can contribute to productivity because it enables employees to pool their knowledge and solve interesting problems. TQM also tends to be most successful when it enriches jobs and improves employee motivation. In addition, when participating in the quality program improves workers' problem-solving skills, productivity is likely to increase. Finally, a quality program has the greatest chance of success in a corporate culture that values quality and stresses continuous improvement as a way of life. The best illustration of a successful quality program is still the Japanese car company, Toyota.

Exhibit 14.8

### Quality Program Success Factors

| Positive Factors | Negative Factors |
|---|---|
| • Tasks make high skill demands on employees | • Management expectations are unrealistically high. |
| • TQM serves to enrich jobs and motivate employees. | • Middle managers are dissatisfied about loss of authority. |
| • Problem-solving skills are improved for all employees. | • Workers are dissatisfied with other aspects of organizational life. |
| • Participation and teamwork are used to tackle significant problems. | • Union leaders are left out of QC discussions. |
| • Continuous improvement is a way of life. | • Managers wait for big, dramatic innovations. |

At many of Toyota's manufacturing plants, workers can assemble as many as eight different models on the same line. Production has been streamlined to the point where workers can build a car in just 20 hours. But speed and flexibility are only part of Toyota's success. Quality is the primary goal. Toyota has a defect rate far below that of any other Japanese or U.S. automaker

Toyota managers created the doctrine of *kaizen* or continuous improvement. Today, methodically studying problems and quickly solving them is second nature to people throughout the organization. Employees can receive cash awards for searching out glitches in production and coming up with solutions. No detail is too small. The impact of *kaizen* can be seen in the revamping of Toyota's 2004 Sienna minivan after the previous model got disappointing reviews. A lot of small changes amounted to a tremendous improvement. The engine of the Sienna is now bigger and more powerful, but it gets better gas mileage. Turning diameter was reduced by 3.2 feet, making the new model nimbler and easier to handle. The third row seats now fold flat rather than having to be removed to maximize cargo space. And, although the new model is longer and wider and has more head and leg room, the cost of the 2004 Sienna minivan is $920 less than the previous model.

Toyota has kicked its *kaizen* process into overdrive in it's quest to become the world's leading automaker (it overtook Ford to become Number 2 in 2004). Unfortunately, the rapid growth has strained Toyota's focus on quality. To stop the quality slide, Toyota is getting back to basics by launching special task forces to reinvigorate the *kaizen* concept. In the Kentucky factory, for example, a group of highly productive employees has been pulled off regular assembly to serve on a special *Kaizen* team. The team works in a barracks-like structure and spends all its time just coming up with ways to save time and money while maintaining standards of excellence.[34]

**TOYOTA**
http://www.toyota.com

Toyota has a slogan emblazoned on a giant banner than hangs in its Takaoka assembly plant just outside Nagoya, Japan: "Yoi Kangae, Yoi Shina!" It means "Good thinking means good products," and the culture of Toyota supports the belief that everyone throughout the company should continuously be thinking of ways to make products better, faster, and cheaper. Although many U.S. and European automakers have implemented elements of TQM, no company has yet come close to Toyota in its execution.

# Trends in Quality and Financial Control

Many companies are responding to changing economic realities and global competition by reassessing organizational management and processes—including control mechanisms. Some of the major trends in quality and financial control include international quality standards, economic value-added and market value-added systems, and activity-based costing.

## International Quality Standards

One impetus for total quality management in the United States is the increasing significance of the global economy. Many countries have endorsed a universal framework for quality assurance called **ISO 9000**, a set of international standards for quality management systems established by the International Organization for Standardization in 1987 and revised in late 2000.[35] Hundreds of thousands of organization in 150 countries, including the United States, have been certified to demonstrate their commitment to quality. Europe continues to lead in the total number of certifications, but the greatest number of new certifications in recent years has been in the United States. One of the more interesting organizations to recently become ISO 9000 certified was the Phoenix, Arizona, Police Department's Records and Information Bureau. In today's environment, where the credibility of

**ISO 9000**
A set of international standards for quality management, setting uniform guidelines for processes to ensure that products conform to customer requirements.

law enforcement agencies has been called into question, the Bureau wanted to make a clear statement about it's commitment to quality and accuracy of information provided to law enforcement personnel and the public.[36] ISO 9000 has become the recognized standard for evaluating and comparing companies on a global basis, and more U.S. companies are feeling the pressure to participate in order to remain competitive in international markets. In addition, many countries and companies require ISO 9000 certification before they will do business with an organization.

## New Financial Control Systems

In addition to traditional financial tools, managers in many of today's organizations are using systems such as economic value-added, market value-added, and activity-based costing to provide effective financial control.

### Economic Value-Added (EVA)

Hundreds of companies, including AT&T, Quaker Oats, the Coca-Cola Company, and Philips Petroleum Company, have set up **economic value-added (EVA)** measurement systems as a new way to gauge financial performance. EVA can be defined as a company's net (after-tax) operating profit minus the cost of capital invested in the company's tangible assets.[37] Measuring performance in terms of EVA is intended to capture all the things a company can do to add value from its activities, such as run the business more efficiently, satisfy customers, and reward shareholders. Each job, department, process, or project in the organization is measured by the value added. EVA can also help managers make more cost-effective decisions. At Boise Cascade, the vice president of IT used EVA to measure the cost of replacing the company's existing storage devices against keeping the existing storage assets that had higher maintenance costs. Using EVA demonstrated that buying new storage devices would lower annual maintenance costs significantly and easily make up for the capital expenditure.[38]

**economic value-added (EVA) system**
A control system that measures performance in terms of after-tax profits minus the cost of capital invested in tangible assets.

### Market Value-Added (MVA)

Market value-added (MVA) adds another dimension because it measures the stock market's estimate of the value of a company's past and projected capital investment projects. For example, when a company's market value (the value of all outstanding stock plus the company's debt) is greater than all the capital invested in it from shareholders, bondholders, and retained earnings, the company has a positive MVA, an indication that it has increased the value of capital entrusted to it and thus created shareholder wealth. A positive MVA usually, though not always, goes hand-in-hand with a high overall EVA measurement.[39] For example, in a recent study, General Electric had both the highest MVA and the highest EVA in its category (companies were categorized by size). Microsoft was ranked second in MVA but had a lower EVA rating than GE and many other companies. This indicates that the stock market believes Microsoft has greater opportunities for further growth, which will, in turn, increase its EVA.[40]

**market value-added (MVA) system**
A control system that measures the stock market's estimate of the value of a company's past and expected capital investment projects.

### Activity-Based Costing (ABC)

Managers measure the cost of producing goods and services so they can be sure they are selling those products for more than the cost to produce them. Traditional methods of costing assign costs to various departments or functions, such as purchasing, manufacturing, human resources, and so on. With a shift to more horizontal, flexible organizations has come a new approach called **activity-based costing (ABC)**, which allocates costs across business processes. ABC attempts to identify all the various activities needed to provide a product or service and allocate costs accordingly. For example, an activity-based costing system might list the costs associated with processing

**activity-based costing (ABC)**
A control system that identifies the various activities needed to provide a product and allocates costs accordingly.

orders for a particular product, scheduling production for that product, producing it, shipping it, and resolving problems with it. Because ABC allocates costs across business processes, it provides a more accurate picture of the cost of various products and services.[41] In addition, it enables managers to evaluate whether more costs go to activities that add value (meeting customer deadlines, achieving high quality) or to activities that do not add value (such as processing internal paperwork). They can then focus on reducing costs associated with non–value-added activities.

# Control Systems for Turbulent Times

As we have discussed throughout this text, globalization, increased competition, rapid change, and uncertainty have resulted in new organizational structures and management methods that emphasize information sharing, employee participation, learning, and teamwork. These shifts have, in turn, led to some new approaches to control. Two significant aspects of control in today's organizations are open-book management and use of the balanced scorecard.

## Open-Book Management

**open-book management**
Sharing financial information and results with all employees in the organization.

In an organizational environment that touts information sharing, teamwork, and the role of managers as facilitators, executives cannot hoard information and financial data. They must admit employees throughout the organization into the loop of financial control and responsibility to encourage active participation and commitment to goals. A growing number of managers are opting for full disclosure in the form of open-book management. **Open-book management** allows employees to see for themselves—through charts, computer printouts, meetings, and so forth—the financial condition of the company. Second, open-book management shows the individual employee how his or her job fits into the big picture and affects the financial future of the organization. Finally, open-book management ties employee rewards to the company's overall success. With training in interpreting the financial data, employees can see the interdependence and importance of each function. If they are rewarded according to performance, they become motivated to take responsibility for their entire team or function, rather than merely their individual jobs.[42] Cross-functional communication and cooperation are also enhanced.

© NOAMANI-AFT/GETTY

### CONCEPT CONNECTION

*The war in Iraq created a need for security contractors to perform many military functions outsourced by the stretched-thin Pentagon. Many of these firms are headed by former members of elite units, such as the ex-Navy SEALs in this photo, who are employees of Blackwater. Managers at these firms are typically very mission-oriented, but they may lack the management expertise to develop effective **control systems for turbulent times**. They might know everything about securing a building or guarding a top officer, but nothing at all about business ideas such as **open book management** or new **financial control systems**. As these firms branched into more varied activities and events in Iraq grew more complex and volatile, the lack of business experience led to chaos for many contractors.*

The goal of open-book management is to get every employee thinking and acting like a business owner. To get employees to think like owners, management provides them with the same information owners have: what money is coming in and where it is going. Open-book management helps employees appreciate why efficiency is important to the organization's—and their own—success. Open-book management turns traditional control on its head. This chapter's Unlocking Creative Solutions Through People box describes how Ricardo Semler runs a successful company by being an "anti-control freak" when it comes to financial data and information.

# Unlocking Creative Solutions Through People

## Semco's Open Book Policy

When Ricardo Semler took over from his father as head of the family business, Brazil's Semco, he decided to manage based on a philosophy of "giving up control" by having faith in people and respect for their ideas. At Semco, he designed a business model in which employees have no set work schedules, no dress codes, no strict rules and regulations, and no employee manuals. Workers choose their own training and nobody approves expense accounts. About 30 percent of employees even set their own pay, and everyone in the company knows everyone else's salary. All workers receive the company's financial statements and are taught how to read them through classes set up by the labor union. Two board seats are reserved for employees, and board meetings are open to all employees who want to attend. Self-managed teams have replaced the management hierarchy, and people have a chance to choose how they can best contribute to the company. Top managers are evaluated on a regular basis by employees—with the outcomes posted for all to see.

The idea that ties all this together is Semler's belief in taking top management out of running the business, which led *Fortune* magazine to give him the title of "anti-control freak." Semler believes that if an organization gives people complete freedom and full information, they will act in their own, and consequently the company's, best interests. "It is only when you rein them in, when you tell them what to do and how to think, that they become inflexible, bureaucratic, and stagnant," says Semler. Semler dislikes the American organization model, which he sees as basically a military hierarchy. Despite all the freedom, organizational control at Semco is quite strong, based not on power and authority but on organizational vision and cultural values that emphasize self-initiative, self-discipline, and full disclosure of all types of information. Employees think like business owners because they can see how their jobs and actions fit in and contribute to the organization's—and their own—success or failure.

The decentralized approach must be working. In the past ten years, Semco has quadrupled its revenues and increased its workforce from 450 to 1,300 employees. Semler believes his company's success is a powerful reminder that it is possible to have an efficient business with shared norms, values, and self-discipline replacing strict rules and controls, guided by managers who lead rather than wield their power.

**SOURCES**: A. J. Vogl, "The Anti-CEO," *Across the Board*, (May/June 2004), 30–36; Geoffrey Colvin, "The Anti-Control Freak," *Fortune* (November 26, 2001), 60, 80; and Ricardo Semler, "How We Went Digital Without a Strategy," *Harvard Business Review* (September/October 2000), 51–58

In some countries, managers have more trouble running an open-book company because prevailing attitudes and standards encourage confidentiality and even secrecy concerning financial results. Many businesspeople in countries such as China, Russia, and South Korea are not accustomed to publically disclosing financial details, which can present problems for multinational companies operating there.[43] Exhibit 14.9 lists a portion of a recent *Opacity Index*, developed by PriceWaterhouseCoopers, which indicates the degree to which various countries are open regarding economic matters. The higher the rating, the more opaque, or hidden, the economy of that country. In the partial index in Exhibit 14.9, China has the highest opacity rating at 87, and Singapore the lowest at 29. The United States has an opacity rating of 36, which is fairly low. In countries with higher ratings, financial figures are typically closely guarded and managers may be discouraged from sharing information with employees and the public. Globalization is beginning to have an impact on economic opacity in various countries by encouraging a convergence toward global accounting standards that support more accurate collection, recording, and reporting of financial information.

## The Balanced Scorecard

Another recent innovation is to integrate the various dimensions of control, combining internal financial measurements and statistical reports with a concern for markets

Exhibit 14.9

## International Opacity Index: Which countries have the most secretive economies?

| Country | Opacity Rating |
|---|---|
| China | 87 |
| Russia | 84 |
| Indonesia | 75 |
| Turkey | 74 |
| South Korea | 73 |
| Rumania | 71 |
| Poland | 64 |
| India | 64 |
| Argentina | 61 |
| Taiwan | 61 |
| Japan | 60 |
| Italy | 48 |
| Mexico | 48 |
| United Kingdom | 38 |
| United States | 36 |
| Singapore | 29 |

The higher the opacity rating, the more secretive the national economy, meaning that prevailing attitudes and standards discourage openness regarding financial results and other data.

SOURCE: The Opacity Index, *http://www.opacity-index.com* accessed on July 22, 2004.

**balanced scorecard**
A comprehensive management control system that balances traditional financial measures with measures of customer service, internal business processes, and the organization's capacity for learning and growth.

and customers as well as employees.[44] Whereas many managers once focused primarily on measuring and controlling financial performance, they are increasingly recognizing the need to measure other, intangible aspects of performance to assess the value-creating activities of the contemporary organization.[45] Many of today's companies compete primarily on the basis of ideas and relationships, which requires that managers find ways to measure intangible as well as tangible assets.

One fresh approach is the balanced scorecard. The balanced scorecard is a comprehensive management control system that balances traditional financial measures with operational measures relating to a company's critical success factors.[46] A balanced scorecard contains four major perspectives, as illustrated in Exhibit 14.10: financial performance, customer service, internal business processes, and the organization's capacity for learning and growth.[47] Within these four areas, managers identify key performance metrics the organization will track. The financial performance perspective reflects a concern that the organization's activities contribute to improving short- and long-term financial performance. It includes traditional measures such as net income and return on investment. *Customer service* indicators measure such things as how customers view the organization, as well as customer retention and satisfaction. *Business process* indicators focus on production and operating statistics, such as order fulfillment or cost per order. The final component looks at the organization's *potential for learning and growth*, focusing on how well resources and human capital are being managed for the company's future. Metrics may include such things as employee retention and the introduction of new products. The components of the scorecard are designed in an integrative manner, as illustrated in Exhibit 14.10.

Managers record, analyze, and discuss these various metrics to determine how well the organization is achieving its strategic goals. At its best, the use of the scorecard

Exhibit 14.10

## The Balanced Scorecard

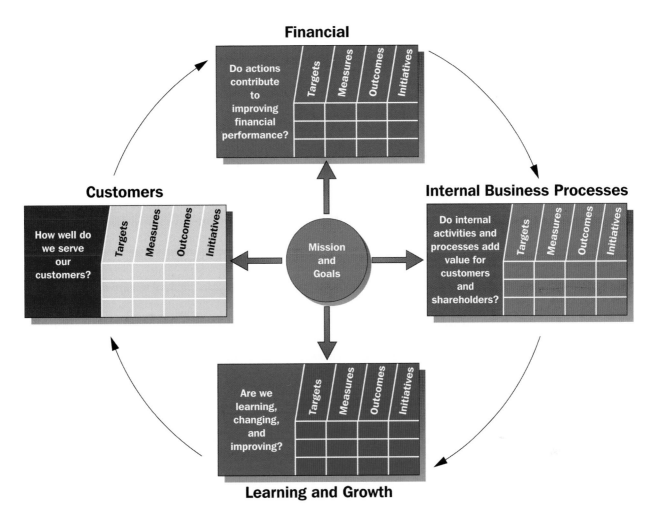

**Financial**

Do actions contribute to improving financial performance?

Targets | Measures | Outcomes | Initiatives

**Customers**

How well do we serve our customers?

Targets | Measures | Outcomes | Initiatives

**Internal Business Processes**

Do internal activities and processes add value for customers and shareholders?

Targets | Measures | Outcomes | Initiatives

Mission and Goals

**Learning and Growth**

Are we learning, changing, and improving?

Targets | Measures | Outcomes | Initiatives

**SOURCES**: Based on Robert S. Kaplan and David P. Norton, "Using the Balanced Scorecard as a Strategic Management System," *Harvard Business Review* (January– February 1996), 75–85; and Chee W. Chow, Kamal M. Haddad, and James E. Williamson, "Applying the Balanced Scorecard to Small Companies," *Management Accounting* 79, no. 2 (August 1997), 21–27.

cascades down from the top levels of the organization, so that everyone becomes involved in thinking about and discussing strategy.[48] The scorecard has become the core management control system for many organizations today, including well-known organizations such as Bell Emergis (a division of Bell Canada), ExxonMobil, Cigna Insurance, British Airways, Hilton Hotels Corp., and even some units of the United States federal government.[49] British Airways clearly ties its use of the balanced scorecard to the feedback control model we discussed early in this chapter. Scorecards are used as the agenda for monthly management meetings. Managers focus on the various elements of the scorecard to set targets, evaluate performance, and guide discussion about what further actions need to be taken.[50] As with all management systems, the balanced scorecard is not right for every organization in every situation. The simplicity of the system causes some managers to underestimate the time and commitment that is needed for the approach to become a truly useful management control system.

## New Workplace Concerns

Managers in today's organizations face some difficult control issues. The matter of control has come to the forefront in light of the failure of top executives and corporate directors to provide adequate oversight and control at companies such as Enron, HealthSouth, Adelphia, and WorldCom. Thus, there is a move toward increasing control in many organizations, particularly in terms of **corporate governance**, which refers to the system of governing an organization so that the interests of corporate owners are protected. The financial reporting systems and the roles of boards of directors are being scrutinized in organizations around the world. At the same time, top leaders are keeping a closer eye on the activities of lower-level managers and employees. In a fast-moving environment, *undercontrol* can be a problem because managers can't keep personal tabs on everything in a large, global organization. Consider, for example, that many of the CEOs who have been indicted in connection with financial misdeeds have claimed that they were unaware that the misconduct was going on. In some cases, this might be true, and it reflects a significant breakdown in control. Because managers can't personally keep tabs on every employee and every activity at all times, effective control systems are essential. Top managers are responsible for what goes on in the organization.

**corporate governance**
The system of governing an organization so the interests of corporate owners are protected.

*Take A Moment*

*Go to the ethical dilemma on page 539 that pertains to new workplace control issues.*

However, *overcontrol* can be an equally touchy situation. Managers might feel justified in monitoring e-mail and Internet use, for example, to ensure that employees are directing their behavior toward work rather than personal outcomes and alleviate concerns about potential racial or sexual harassment. Yet employees often resent and feel demeaned by close monitoring that limits their personal freedom and makes them feel as if they are constantly being watched. Excessive control of employees can lead to demotivation, low morale, lack of trust, and even hostility among workers. Managers have to find an appropriate balance, as well as develop and communicate clear policies regarding workplace monitoring. Although oversight and control are important, good organizations also depend on mutual trust and respect among managers and employees.

## Manager's Solution

This chapter introduced a number of important concepts about organizational control. Organizational control is the systematic process through which managers regulate organizational activities to meet planned goals and standards of performance. The focus of the control system may include feedforward control to prevent problems, concurrent control to monitor ongoing activities, and feedback control to evaluate past performance. Well-designed control systems include four key steps: establish standards, measure performance, compare performance to standards, and make corrections as necessary.

Budgeting is one of the most commonly used forms of managerial control. Managers might use expense budgets, revenue budgets, cash budgets, and capital budgets, for example. Other financial controls include use of the balance sheet, income statement, and financial analysis of these documents.

The philosophy of controlling has shifted to reflect changes in leadership methods. Traditional bureaucratic controls emphasize establishing rules and procedures, then monitoring employee behavior to make sure the rules and procedures are followed. With decentralized control, employees assume responsibility for monitoring their own performance.

Besides monitoring financial results, organizations control the quality of their goods and services. They might do this by adopting total quality management (TQM) techniques such as quality circles, benchmarking, Six Sigma, reduced cycle time, and continuous improvement.

Recent trends in control include the use of international quality standards, economic value-added (EVA) and market value-added (MVA) systems, and activity-based costing (ABC). Other important aspects of control in today's turbulent environment are open-book management and use of the balanced scorecard. In addition, concerns such as corporate governance and employee monitoring are significant issues for today's managers.

The story of Gateway, Inc. at the beginning of the chapter demonstrates the importance of control. The control system at Gateway, developed based on the personal preferences of co-founder and CEO Ted Waitt, was too loose for the organization as it grew large and complex. The company's losses began piling up and market share was declining. Waitt shifted toward a system emphasizing rigorous measurement and discipline to try to get Gateway back on track. At the company's new Poway, California, headquarters, a 9 foot by 12 foot screen that is visible to all employees displays a running daily score comparing sales and costs with projected targets. Specific goals for all managers and departments are clearly defined, and their performance is regularly reviewed by Gateway's top human resources executive. This new approach to performance measurement has led to the departure of several managers who consistently failed to meet goals or didn't agree with action plans for correction. After Gateway acquired eMachines, Waitt turned the CEO's job over to eMachines head Wayne Inouye, who naturally takes a more disciplined approach to measurement and control than Waitt. In addition to monitoring costs, sales, and other financial metrics, the new system includes ways to measure customer service and satisfaction. Gateway is still struggling, and it's too soon to tell if the more disciplined control approach can save the company. However, focusing on specific targets has had a significant impact. For example, the first week Gateway began tracking customer service indicators, managers were hitting their performance targets only 60 percent of the time. Within a couple of weeks, the rate had increased to 98 percent. In the second quarter of 2004, Gateway also announced a better-than-expected increase in sales, indicating that performance in that area is improving as well.[51]

# Discussion Questions

1. Why is it important for managers to understand the process of organizational control?

2. How might a public school system use feedforward control to identify the best candidates for its teaching positions?

3. How might the manager of a family-style restaurant use concurrent controls to ensure that the restaurant is providing customers with the highest quality food and service? What feedback controls could be useful?

4. What standards of performance has your professor established for this class? How will your actual performance be measured? How will your performance be compared to the standards? Do you think the standards and methods of measurement are fair? Why or why not?

5. What is the difference between budgeting and financial analysis? Why is each type of control important to a company?

6. Imagine that you are going to be the manager of a new Wal-Mart being built in your area. What items might be listed in your capital budget? What items might be listed in your expense budget?

7. In what ways could a university benefit from bureaucratic control? In what ways might it benefit from decentralized control? Overall, which approach do you think would be best at your college or university? Why?

8. If you were managing a local video rental store, which company would you choose to benchmark one aspect of your store's performance against? Why?

9. Would you like to work for a company that uses open-book management? Would you like to be a manager in the company? Why or why not?

10. Why is it important for an organization's control system to be linked to its overall strategy?

# Management in Practice: Experiential Exercise

## Is Your Budget in Control?

By the time you are in college, you are in charge of at least some of your own finances. How well you manage your personal budget may indicate how well you will manage your company's budget on the job. Respond to the following statements to evaluate your own budgeting habits. If the statement doesn't apply directly to you, respond the way you think you would behave in a similar situation.

1. I spend all my money as soon as I get it.
   Yes    No

2. At the beginning of each week (or month, or term), I write down all my fixed expenses.
   Yes    No

3. I never seem to have any money left over at the end of the week (or month).
   Yes    No

4. I pay all my expenses, but I never seem to have any money left over for fun.
   Yes    No

5. I am not putting any money away in savings right now; I'll wait until after I graduate from college.
   Yes    No

6. I can't pay all my bills.
   Yes    No

7. I have a credit card, but I pay the balance in full each month.
   Yes    No

8. I take cash advances on my credit card.
   Yes    No

9. I know how much I can spend on eating out, movies, and other entertainment each week.
   Yes    No

10. I pay cash for everything.
    Yes    No

11. When I buy something, I look for value and determine the best buy.
    Yes    No

12. I lend money to friends whenever they ask, even if it leaves me short of cash.
    Yes    No

13. I never borrow money from friends.
    Yes    No

14. I am putting aside money each month to save for something that I really need.
    Yes    No

*Yes* responses to statements 2, 9, 10, 13, and 14 point to the most disciplined budgeting habits; *yes* responses to 4, 5, 7, and 11 reveal adequate budgeting habits; *yes* responses to 1, 3, 6, 8, and 12 indicate the poorest budgeting habits. If you have answered honestly, chances are you'll have a combination of all three. Look to see where you can improve your budgeting.

# Management in Practice: Ethical Dilemma

### Go Along to Get Along?

Rhonda Gilchrist became a nurse because she wanted to help people. As the home health care industry began to take off, she was presented with what she thought she was a terrific opportunity: a start-up home health care agency offered her a position managing its staff of visiting nurses. She supported home health care because patients were treated in the relaxed, comfortable atmosphere of their homes; home visits gave patients and nurses more independence; and home visits were intended to be much cheaper than hospital stays or doctor's office visits. Therefore, Rhonda eagerly accepted the job.

Most of the patients treated by Gilchrist's nurses were elderly, with a variety of complaints ranging from diabetes to hip injuries. At first, Gilchrist encouraged her staff to make their visits efficient and productive so that patients could be weaned from care in a timely manner. She assumed this was what the head of the agency wanted. However, when she reported that one patient had recovered enough from a heart attack that he no longer needed three visits a week, the agency owner replied, "You should be looking for ways to increase the number of visits, not decrease them!" Gilchrist was shocked, but she soon understood that the only way to keep her job—and her nurses' jobs—was to go along with her company's wishes. Those extra visits, paid for by Medicare, were paying her salary.

Meanwhile, Gilchrist did some research on her own. She learned that the average home-care patient now gets 80 visits per year (nearly four times the number of a decade ago), for which Medicare pays up to $90 per visit. In 1995, Medicare spent $16 billion on home care. Although lawmakers eagerly embraced the idea of home health care in the 1980s, believing that the shift would save insurance companies,

Medicare, and even average citizens a huge sum, the savings haven't materialized. In fact, the opposite has happened. Rhonda knows home health care is extremely important to many patients, but she also realizes it is being abused by others, as well as by the agencies. As she learned in her research, people who want to start up home health agencies don't even need any type of special training. One local doctor told her in confidence that the owner of her own agency, an engineer by training, simply wanted to open his own business, so he chose between retail clothing and home health care. The latter, with its guaranteed payments from Medicare, was a sure bet.

As she drove to the office, Rhonda considered her alternatives. She knew that some of her clients no longer needed care. But she also knew that she needed a job, and most patients were lonely and looked forward to the nurses' visits. She wondered if there was a better way to control costs and deliver the best care to her patients.

### What Do You Do?

1. Go along with the status quo and forget about the abuses of the system—that's your boss's problem. Besides, Medicare has deep pockets.
2. Look for another job as soon as possible. You don't want to be associated with unethical, and potentially illegal, practices.
3. Approach the owner of the agency and suggest other ways the agency might make a profit and deliver high-quality care, such as innovative ways to attract new clients to replace those that leave the roster in better health.

Source: Based on George Anders and Laurie McGinley, "Medical Morass: How Do You Tame a Wild U.S. Program?" *The Wall Street Journal*, March 6, 1997, A1, A8.

# Surf the Net

1. **Benchmarking.** Assume your boss is interested in adding benchmarking to your company's recently-instituted TQM program and has asked you to locate benchmarking information on the Internet. He told you that at the conference he attended last week he heard about a Web site called "The Benchmark Exchange" *(http://www.benchnet.com)*. Your job is to report back to your boss with a complete report on what the Web site is all about, what the benefits of subscribing are, how much it costs to join, and the reasons for or against your company subscribing.

2. **ISO 9000.** Visit a site such as *http://praxiom.com* or find another where you can locate the following information about ISO 9000, the international standards for quality management. (a) Briefly describe the kind of company that would use each of the three sets of standards: ISO 9001, ISO 9002, and ISO 9003. (b) Select one of the guidelines sections—ISO 9000, ISO 9004, ISO 10011, or ISO 10012—and tell how many sections it has and what the section titles are. (c) At the site listed above, go to page *http://www.connect.ab.ca/~praxiom/concepts. htm*, briefly read the "Theoretical Overview of ISO 9000," and describe your impressions of the process.

3. **Economic Value Added (EVA) Systems.** Go to *http://www.sternstewart.com* to supplement the text information on EVA Systems. At this site select one of the following activities: (a) View the video under About EVA, Client Comments on EVA showing what corporate executives have to say about EVA and submit a summary of their comments; (b) Go to the "Client Stories" section and check out two companies. Submit a comparison summary of what you learned; or (c) Choose another category of information available at the site and submit a summary of your findings.

# Case for Critical Analysis

## Lincoln Electric

Imagine having a management system that is so successful people refer to it with capital letters—the Lincoln Management System—and other businesses benchmark their own systems by it. That is the situation of Ohio-based Lincoln Electric. For a number of years, other companies have tried to figure out Lincoln Electric's secret—how management coaxes maximum productivity and quality from its workers, even during difficult financial times.

Lincoln Electric is a leading manufacturer of welding products, welding equipment, and electric motors, with more than $1 billion in sales and six thousand workers worldwide. The company's products are used for cutting, manufacturing, and repairing other metal products. Although it is now a publicly traded company, members of the Lincoln family still own more than 60 percent of the stock.

Lincoln uses a diverse control approach. Tasks are rigidly defined, and individual employees must meet strict measurable standards of performance. However,

the Lincoln system succeeds largely because of an organizational culture based on openness and trust, shared control, and an egalitarian spirit. Although the line between managers and workers at Lincoln is firmly drawn, managers respect the expertise of production workers and value their contributions to many aspects of the business. The company has an open-door policy for all top executives, middle managers, and production workers, and regular face-to-face communication is encouraged. Workers are expected to challenge management if they believe practices or compensation rates are unfair. Most workers are hired right out of high school, then trained and cross-trained to perform different jobs. Some eventually are promoted to executive positions, because Lincoln believes in promoting from within. Many Lincoln workers stay with the company for life.

One of Lincoln's founders felt that organizations should be based on certain values, including honesty, trustworthiness, openness, self-management, loyalty, accountability, and cooperativeness. These values continue to form the core of Lincoln's culture, and management regularly rewards employees who manifest them. Because Lincoln so effectively socializes employees, they exercise a great degree of self-control on the job. Production workers are paid on a piece-rate system, plus merit pay based on performance. Employees also are eligible for annual bonuses which fluctuate according to the company's fortunes, and they participate in stock purchase plans. Bonuses are based on a number of factors, such as productivity, quality, dependability, and cooperation with others. Factory workers at Lincoln have been known to earn more than $100,000 a year, and the average compensation in 1996 was $62,000. However, there also are other, less tangible rewards. Pride of workmanship and feelings of involvement, contribution, and esprit de corps are intrinsic rewards that flourish at Lincoln Electric. Cross-functional teams, empowered to make decisions, take responsibility for product planning, development, and marketing. Information about the company's operations and financial performance is openly shared with workers throughout the company.

Lincoln places emphasis on anticipating and solving customer problems. Sales representatives are given the technical training they need to understand customer needs, help customers understand and use Lincoln's products, and solve problems. This customer focus is backed up by attention to the production process through the use of strict accountability standards and formal measurements for productivity, quality, and innovation for all employees. In addition, a software program called Rhythm is used to streamline the flow of goods and materials in the production process.

Lincoln's system has worked extremely well in the United States. The cultural values, open communication, and formal control and reward systems interact to align the goals of managers, workers, and the organization as well as encourage learning and growth. Now Lincoln is discovering whether its system can hold up overseas. Although most of Lincoln's profits come from domestic operations, and a foreign venture in the 1990s lost a lot of money for the company, top managers want to expand globally because foreign markets are growing much more rapidly than domestic markets. Thus far, Lincoln managers have not developed a strategic control plan for global operations, relying instead on duplicating the domestic Lincoln system.

## Questions

1. What types of control—feedforward, concurrent, or feedback—are illustrated in this case? Explain.
2. Based on what you've just read, what do you think makes the Lincoln System so successful?
3. What changes might Lincoln managers have to make to adapt their management system to overseas operations?

Source: Joseph Maciariello, "A Pattern of Success: Can This Company Be Duplicated?" *Drucker Management 1,* no. 1 (spring 1997) 7–11.

# Endnotes

1. Gary McWilliams, "Gateway Adopts Tough New Style as Sales Tumble," *The Wall Street Journal* (May 28, 2002), B1, B4; Mike Musgrove, "Gateway's Changes Yield Little Reward," *The Washington Post* (January 11, 2003), E1; and http://www.gateway.com.

2. Deborah Solomon and Susanne Craig, "Taking Stock: SEC Blasts Big Board Oversight of 'Specialist' Trading Firms," *The Wall Street Journal* (November 3, 2003), A1, A6.

3. John A. Byrne with Mike France and Wendy Zellner, "The Environment Was Ripe for Abuse," *BusinessWeek* (February 25, 2002), 118–120.

4. Susan Pulliam, "The 'It Wasn't Me' Defense; CEOs from Enron to Sotheby's Blame Scandals on Underlings; Too Busy for All The Details?" *The Wall Street Journal* (July 9, 2004), B1.

5. Douglas S. Sherwin, "The Meaning of Control," *Dunn's Business Review* (January 1956).

6. Russ Banham, "Nothin' But Net Gain," *eCFO* (Fall 2001), 32–33.

7. Kevin McCoy and Julie Appleby, "Problems with Staffing, Training Can Cost Lives," *USA Today* (May 26, 2004), http://www.usatoday.com

8. Carol Hymowitz, "As Economy Slows, Executives Learn Ways to Make Predictions," (In the Lead column), *The Wall Street Journal* (August 21, 2001), B1.

9. Jennifer S. Lee, "Tracking Sales and the Cashiers," *The New York Times* (July 11, 2001), C1, C6; Anna Wilde

Mathews, "New Gadgets Track Truckers' Every Move," *The Wall Street Journal* (July 14, 1997), B1, B10.

10. Steve Stecklow, "Kentucky's Teachers Get Bonuses, but Some Are Caught Cheating," *The Wall Street Journal* (September 2, 1997), A1, A5.

11. Richard E. Crandall, "Keys to Better Performance Measurement," *Industrial Management* (January–February 2002), 19–24; Christopher D. Ittner and David F. Larcker, "Coming Up Short on Nonfinancial Performance Measurement," *Harvard Business Review* (November 2003), 88–95.

12. Crandall, "Keys to Better Performance Measurement."

13. Adam Lashinsky, "Meg and the Machine," *Fortune* (September 1, 2003), 68–78.

14. Sumantra Ghoshal, *Strategic Control* (St. Paul, Minnesota: West, 1986), Chapter 4; and Robert N. Anthony, John Dearden, and Norton M. Bedford, *Management Control Systems*, 5th ed. (Homewood, Illinois: Irwin, 1984).

15. John A. Boquist, Todd T. Milbourn, and Anjan V. Thakor, "How Do You Win the Capital Allocation Game?" *Sloan Management Review* (Winter 1998), 59–71.

16. Anthony, Dearden, and Bedford, *Management Control Systems*.

17. Participation in budget setting is described in a number of studies, including Neil C. Churchill, "Budget Choice: Planning versus Control," *Harvard Business Review* (July–August 1984), 150–164; Peter Brownell, "Leadership Style, Budgetary Participation, and Managerial Behavior," *Accounting Organizations and Society* 8 (1983), 307–321; and Paul J. Carruth and Thurrell O. McClandon, "How Supervisors React to 'Meeting the Budget' Pressure," Management Accounting 66 (November 1984), 50–54.

18. Donna Fenn, "Personnel Best," *Inc*. (February 2000), 75–83.

19. Bruce G. Posner, "How to Stop Worrying and Love the Next Recession," *Inc*. (April 1986), 89–95.

20. Lawrence M. Fisher, "Inside Dell Computer Corporation," *Strategy and Business*, Issue 10, first quarter 1998, 68–75; and Randy Myers, "Cash Crop: The 2000 Working Capital Survey," *CFO* (August 2000), 59–69.

21. Robin Goldwyn Blumenthal, "'Tis the Gift to Be Simple," *CFO* (January 1998), 61–63.

22. William G. Ouchi, "Markets, Bureaucracies, and Clans," *Administrative Science Quarterly* 25 (1980), 129–141; and B. R. Baligia and Alfred M. Jaeger, "Multinational Corporations: Control Systems and Delegation Issues," *Journal of International Business Studies* (Fall 1984), 25–40.

23. Sherwin, "The Meaning of Control."

24. Mathews, "New Gadgets Track Truckers' Every Move," B10.

25. A. V. Feigenbaum, *Total Quality Control: Engineering and Management* (New York: McGraw-Hill, 1961); John Lorinc, "Dr. Deming's Traveling Quality Show," *Canadian Business* (September 1990), 38–42; Mary Walton, *The Deming Management Method* (New York: Dodd-Meade & Co., 1986); and J. M. Juran and Frank M. Gryna, eds., *Juran's Quality Control Handbook,* 4th ed. (New York: McGraw-Hill, 1988).

26. Edward E. Lawler III and Susan A. Mohrman, "Quality Circles after the Fad," *Harvard Business Review* (January–February 1985), 65–71; and Philip C. Thompson, *Quality Circles: How to Make Them Work in America* (New York: AMACOM, 1982).

27. Howard Rothman, "You Need Not Be Big to Benchmark," *Nation's Business* (December 1992), 64–65.

28. Tracy Mayor, "Six Sigma Comes to IT: Targeting Perfection," *CIO* (December 1, 2003), 62–70; Hal Plotkin, "Six Sigma: What It Is and How to Use It," *Harvard Management Update* (June 1999), 3–4; Tom Rancour and Mike McCracken, "Applying 6 Sigma Methods for Breakthrough Safety Performance," *Professional Safety* 45, no. 10 (October 2000), 29–32; G. Hasek, "Merger Marries Quality Efforts," *Industry Week* (August 21, 2000), 89–92; and Lee Clifford, "Why You Can Safely Ignore Six Sigma," *Fortune* (January 22, 2001), 140.

29. Dick Smith and Jerry Blakeslee "The New Strategic Six Sigma," *Training & Development* (September 2002), 45–52; Michael Hammer and Jeff Goding, "Putting Six Sigma in Perspective," *Quality* (October 2001), 58–62; and Mayor, "Six Sigma Comes to IT."

30. Plotkin, "Six Sigma: What It Is"; Timothy Aeppel, "Nicknamed 'Nag,' She's Just Doing Her Job," *The Wall Street Journal* (May 14, 2002), B1, B12; John S. McClenahen, "ITT's Value Champion," *IndustryWeek* (May 2002), 44–49.

31. Philip R. Thomas, Larry J. Gallace, and Kenneth R. Martin, *Quality Alone Is Not Enough* (AMA Management Briefing), New York: American Management Association, August 1992.

32. Kate Kane, "L. L. Bean Delivers the Goods," *Fast Company* (August/September 1997), 104–113.

33. Clifford, "Why You Can Safely Ignore Six Sigma"; and Hammer and Goding, "Putting Six Sigma in Perspective."

34. Brian Bremmer and Chester Dawson, "Can Anything Stop Toyota?" *BusinessWeek* (November 17, 2003), 114–122; and Norihiko Shirouzu and Sebastian Moffett, "Bumpy Road: As Toyota Closes In on GM, It Develops a Big Three Problem," *The Wall Street Journal* (August 4, 2004), A1.

35. Syed Hasan Jaffrey, "ISO 9001 Made Easy," *Quality Progress* 37, no. 5 (May 2004), 104; Frank C. Barnes, "ISO 9000 Myth and Reality: A Reasonable Approach to ISO 9000," *SAM Advanced Management Journal* (Spring 1998), 23–30; and Thomas H. Stevenson and Frank C. Barnes, "Fourteen Years of ISO 9000: Impact, Criticisms, Costs, and Benefits," *Business Horizons* (May–June 2001), 45–51.

36. David Amari, Don James, and Cathy Marley, "ISO 9001 Takes On a New Role—Crime Fighter," *Quality Progress* 37, no. 5 (May 2004), 57+.

37. Don L. Bohl, Fred Luthans, John W. Slocum Jr., and Richard M. Hodgetts, "Ideas That Will Shape the Future of Management Practice," *Organizational Dynamics* (Summer 1996), 7–14.

38 John Berry, "How To Apply EVA to I.T.," *CIO* (January 15, 2003) 94–98.

39. Stephen Taub, "MVPs of MVA," *CFO* (July 2003), 59–66; and K. Lehn and A. K. Makhija, "EVA and MVA as Performance Measures and Signals for Strategic Change," *Strategy & Leadership* (May–June 1996), 34–38.

40. Taub, "MVPs of MVA."

41. Sidney J. Baxendale, "Activity-Based Costing for the Small Business: A Primer," *Business Horizons* (January–February 2001), 61–68; Terence C. Pare, "A New Tool for Managing Costs," *Fortune* (June 14, 1993), 124–129; and Don L. Bohl, Fred Luthans, John W. Slocum Jr., and Richard M. Hodgetts, "Ideas that Will Shape the Future of Management Practice," *Organizational Dynamics* (Summer 1996), 7–14.

42. Perry Pascarella, "Open the Books to Unleash Your People," *Management Review* (May 1998), 58–60.

43. Mel Mandell, "Accounting Challenges Overseas," *World Trade* (December 1, 2001).

44. This discussion is based on a review of the balanced scorecard in Richard L. Daft, *Organization Theory and Design*, 7th ed. (Cincinnati, Ohio: South-Western, 2001), 300–301.

45. "On Balance," a *CFO* Interview with Robert Kaplan and David Norton, *CFO* (February 2001), 73–78; and Bill Birchard, "Intangible Assets + Hard Numbers = Soft Finance," *Fast Company* (October 1999), 316–336.

46. Robert Kaplan and David Norton, "The Balanced Scorecard: Measures that Drive Performance," *Harvard Business Review* (January–February 1992), 71–79; and Chee W. Chow, Kamal M. Haddad, and James E. Williamson, "Applying the Balanced Scorecard to Small Companies," *Management Accounting* 79, no. 2 (August 1997), 21–27.

47. Based on Kaplan and Norton, "The Balanced Scorecard"; Chow, Haddad, and Williamson, "Applying the Balanced Scorecard"; and Cathy Lazere, "All Together Now," *CFO* (February 1998), 28–36.

48. Nils-Göran Olve, Carl-Johan Petri, Jan Roy and Sofie Roy, "Twelve Years Later: Understanding and Realizing the Value of Balanced Scorecards," *Ivey Business Journal* (May–June 2004); Eric M. Olson and Stanley F. Slater, "The Balanced Scorecard, Competitive Strategy, and Performance," *Business Horizons* (May–June 2002), 11–16; and Eric Berkman, "How to Use the Balanced Scorecard," *CIO* (May 15, 2002), 93–100.

49. Ibid.; and Brigitte W. Schay, Mary Ellen Beach, Jacqueline A. Caldwell, and Christelle LaPolice, "Using Standardized Outcome Measures in the Federal Government," *Human Resource Management* 41, no. 3 (Fall 2002): 355–368.

50. Olve et al., "Twelve Years Later: Understanding and Realizing the Value of Balanced Scorecards."

51. McWilliams, "Gateway Adopts Tough New Style as Sales Tumble," Jeffrey Burt and Shelley Solheim, "Users Back Moves; PC Maker's Store Closings, New Retail Direction Supported," *eWeek* (April 12, 2004), 53; and "Gateway Inc.: Narrower Operating Loss Seen for 2nd Period as Sales Grow," *The Wall Street Journal* (June 16, 2004), A1.

# Information Technology and E-Business

## LEARNING OBJECTIVES

*After studying this chapter, you should be able to*

1. Describe the importance of information technology for organizations and the attributes of quality information.

2. Identify different types of information systems and discuss recent trends in information technology.

3. Tell how information systems support daily operations and decision making.

4. Summarize the key components of e-business and explain e-business strategies.

5. Describe enterprise resource planning and customer relationship management systems.

6. Explain the importance of knowledge management in today's organizations.

7. Identify specific management implications of information technology.

Robert Michael MacDonald and Robert Garff were partners in the Bountiful (Utah) Mazda franchise for six years before they sold the dealership to the Utah Auto Collection. But when the Auto Collection broke apart in January 2002, MacDonald decided he wanted his old dealership back. Now, he couldn't be happier than he is running the Bountiful Mazda franchise in partnership with his brother and wife. But the car selling business has changed a lot since 1998. Today, Internet-savvy buyers are causing dealers a lot of headaches. More than half of all customers have already been bargain hunting online before they ever step foot on the car lot. They show up carrying their quotes like a shield against high sales prices. Salespeople dread to see them coming because they realize the customer has the upper hand, equipped with up-to-date information on dealer invoice value, average retail price, and other data. These customers are frustrated by annoying and time-consuming questions about budget and transportation needs, where the sales staff tries to gauge how likely they are to buy and how much they're willing to pay. All these customers want is to test-drive the vehicle and seal the deal at the price they're looking for. MacDonald knows that Mazda is offering seed money and financing for a revamp of its dealerships. He wonders if there is a way to include information technology to not only please, but also profit from, the new breed of Web-savvy customer.[1]

## Take A Moment

What advice would you give Michael MacDonald and Mazda about turning the power of the Internet to their advantage? How can information technology be used to increase dealership effectiveness and improve customer relationships?

Almost every company uses some form of information technology. Indeed, the strategic use of information technology is one of the defining aspects of organizational success in today's world. A classic example is the success of Wal-Mart, which can be traced partly to the extensive use of information technology to manage every aspect of the business. Managers use information systems that rely on a massive data warehouse to make decisions about what to stock, how to price and promote it, and when to reorder or discontinue items. Handheld scanners enable managers to keep close tabs on inventory and monitor sales; at the end of each workday, orders for new merchandise are sent by computer to headquarters, where they are automatically organized and sent to regional distribution centers, which have electronic linkages with key suppliers for reordering. A recent innovation is using tiny chips with identification numbers on shipments of products, which enables close tracking of inventory all through the supply chain. As the merchandise moves from the warehouse to stores and off the shelves, electronic readers automatically track its progress and send the data to a network, where everyone can track the movement of goods. Back at headquarters, top Wal-Mart executives analyze buying patterns and other information, enabling them to spot problems or opportunities and convey the information to stores.[2] Many other companies, in industries from manufacturing to entertainment, are using information technology to get closer to customers, enter new markets, and streamline business processes.

Information technology and e-business have changed the way people and organizations work and thus present new challenges for managers. Despite the dot-com collapse of the early 2000s, the Internet continues to disrupt and transform traditional ways of doing business.[3] E-business still has a bright and bold future as it makes good on the promise of helping companies cut costs, increase efficiency, speed up innovation, and improve productivity. This chapter will explore the management of information technology and e-business. We begin by developing a basic understanding of information technology and the types of information systems frequently used in organizations. Then, the chapter will look at the growing use of the Internet and e-business, including a discussion of fundamental e-business strategies, business-to-business marketplaces, use of information technology in business operations, and the importance of knowledge management. The next section will discuss the management implications of using new information technology. Finally, we will briefly examine some recent information technology trends.

# Information Technology

**information technology**
The hardware, software, telecommunications, database management, and other technologies used to store, process, and distribute information.

An organization's **information technology** consists of the hardware, software, telecommunications, database management, and other technologies it uses to store data and make them available in the form of information for organizational decision making.

By providing managers with more information, more quickly than ever before, modern information technology improves efficiency and effectiveness at each stage of the strategic decision-making process. Whether through computer-aided manufacturing, information sharing with customers, or international inventory control, information technology aids operational processes and decision making. Consider the pharmaceutical giant Eli Lilly, which set up an online scientific forum called InnoCentive. The forum is open to anyone and is available in multiple languages. Lilly posts thorny research problems and offers cash awards to anyone who can solve them, thus increasing its knowledge and speeding innovation without expanding its R&D budget. At General Motors, CEO Rick Wagoner and other top managers keep tabs on GM operations around the world and around the clock by logging on to the corporate network from secure Wi-Fi connections at home. This up-to-the-minute information helps GM executives make better decisions "in a world where everything is moving faster."[4]

## Data versus Information

The ability to generate more information with technology presents a serious challenge to information technicians, managers, and other users of information. They must sort through overwhelming amounts of data to identify only that information necessary for a particular purpose. Data are raw facts and figures that in and of themselves may not be useful. To be useful, data must be processed into finished **information**— that is, data that have been converted into a meaningful and useful context for specific users. An increasing challenge for managers is being able to effectively identify and access useful information. For example, American Greetings Corporation, which sells greeting cards, might gather *data* about demographics in various parts of the country. These data are then translated into *information*; for example, stores in Florida require an enormous assortment of greeting cards directed at grandson, granddaughter, niece, and nephew, while stores in some other parts of the country might need a larger percentage of slightly irreverent, youth-oriented products.[5]

The magnitude of the job of transforming data into useful information is reflected in organizations' introduction of the chief information officer (CIO) position. CIOs are responsible for managing organizational databases and implementing new information technology. As they make decisions involving the adoption and management of new technologies, CIOs integrate old and new technology to support organizational decision making, operations, and communication. Effective CIOs not only manage the technology infrastructure but also focus on information design, so that managers have high-quality information to improve decision making, solve problems, and boost performance.[6] Ideally, the CIO combines a knowledge of technology with the ability to help managers identify their information needs and how the organization can use its IT capabilities to support competitive strategy. An important part of the CIO's job is establishing systems that shape disjointed data into clear, meaningful, and useful information.

USED WITH PERMISSION OF CITIBANK, A MEMBER OF CITIGROUP, INC.

**CONCEPT CONNECTION**

*You may live in the United States, but it is possible for you to access your financial information at this Citibank facility in Budapest, Hungary. Due to advances in **information technology**, the banking industry has developed complex databases to provide financial information globally, and it is estimated that by the year 2010, four to five billion people worldwide will be active users of a vast range of financial products and services. Today, Citibank's business is as much information and communication as financial services.*

**data**
Raw, unsummarized, and unanalyzed facts and figures.

**information**
Data that have been converted into a meaningful and useful context for the receiver.

## Characteristics of Useful Information

Organizations depend on high-quality information to develop strategic plans, identify problems, and interact with other organizations. Information is of high quality if it has characteristics that make it useful for these tasks. The characteristics of useful information fall into three broad categories, as illustrated in Exhibit 15.1.[7]

1. *Time.* Information should be available and provided when needed, up to date, and related to the appropriate time period (past, present, or future).
2. *Content.* Useful information is error free, suited to the user's needs, complete, concise, relevant (that is, it excludes unnecessary data), and an accurate measure of performance.
3. *Form.* The information should be provided in a form that is easy for the user to understand and that meets the user's needs for the level of detail. The presentation should be ordered and use the combination of words, numbers, and diagrams that is most helpful to the user. Also, information should be presented in a useful medium (printed documents, video display, sound).

Exhibit **15.1**

## Characteristics of High-Quality Information

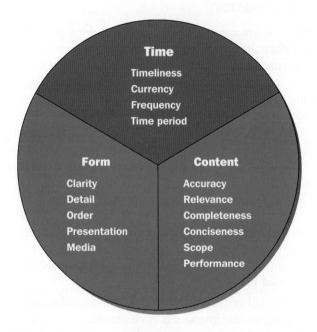

**SOURCE:** Adapted from James A. O'Brien, *Introduction to Information Systems*, 8th ed. (Burr Ridge, IL: Irwin, 1997), 284–285.

# Types of Information Systems

Most managers appreciate the value of making information readily available in some kind of formal, computer-based information system. Such a system combines hardware, software, and human resources to support organizational information and communication needs. One way to distinguish among the many types of information systems is to focus on the functions they perform and the people they serve in an organization. Two broad categories of information systems widely used today are shown in Exhibit 15.2. **Operations information systems** support information-processing needs of a business's day-to-day operations, as well as low-level operations management functions. Management information systems typically support the strategic decision-making needs of higher-level managers.

## Operations Information Systems

A variety of systems, called operations information systems, support the information-processing needs related to a business's day-to-day operations. Types of operations information systems include transaction-processing systems, process control systems, and office automation systems. Each of these supports daily operations and decisions that typically are made by nonmanagement employees or lower-level managers.

**Transaction-processing systems (TPSs)** record and process data resulting from business operations. They include information systems that record sales to customers, purchases from suppliers, inventory changes, and wages to employees. A TPS collects data from these transactions and stores them in a database. Employees use the database to produce reports and other information, such as customer statements and employee paychecks. Most of an organization's reports are generated from these databases. Transaction-processing systems identify, collect, and organize the fundamental information from which an organization operates.

**operations information system**
A computer-based information system that supports a company's day-to-day operations.

**transaction-processing system**
A type of operations information system that records and processes data resulting from routine business transactions such as sales, purchases, and payroll.

Exhibit 15.2

## Types of Information Systems

**Operations Information Systems**
- Transaction-processing systems
- Process control systems
- Office automation systems

**Management Information Systems**
- Information-reporting systems
- Decision support systems
- Executive information systems
- Groupware

While a transaction-processing system keeps track of the size, type, and financial consequences of the organization's transactions, companies also need information about the quantity and quality of their production activities. Therefore, they may use process control systems to monitor and control ongoing physical processes. For example, petroleum refineries, pulp and paper mills, food manufacturing plants, and electric power plants use **process control systems** with special sensing devices that monitor and record physical phenomena such as temperature or pressure changes. The system relays the measurements or sensor-detected data to a computer for processing; employees and operations managers can check the data to look for problems requiring action.

**Office automation systems** combine modern hardware and software such as word processors, desktop publishers, e-mail, and teleconferencing to handle the tasks of publishing and distributing information. Office automation systems also are used to transform manual accounting procedures to electronic media. Companies such as Wal-Mart, Chevron, and American Airlines send thousands of electronic payments a month to suppliers, eliminating the need for writing and mailing checks. Merrill Lynch uses office automation to electronically manage consultants' travel and entertainment expenses, cutting the time it takes to process a report and issue reimbursement from six weeks to four days and slashing the average cost of processing a report from $25 to only a few bucks.[8] These systems enable businesses to streamline office tasks, reduce errors, and improve customer service. In this way, office automation systems support the other kinds of information systems.

Operations information systems aid organizational decision makers in many ways and across various settings. For example, Enterprise Rent-a-Car's Computer Assisted Rental System (Ecars) provides front-line employees with up-to-the-minute information that enables them to provide exceptional service to each customer. The computer-based system helps Enterprise keep track of the 1.4 million transactions the company logs every hour. If a customer visits a branch office and requests a certain kind of car, the agent can immediately determine if one is available anywhere in the city. Insurance companies such as Geico can also link their claims systems directly to Enterprise's automated rental system, book a reservation, and send payments electronically, eliminating the need for paper invoices and checks.[9]

## Management Information Systems

Until the 1960s, information systems were used primarily for transaction processing, accounting, and record keeping. Then the introduction of computers using silicon chip circuitry allowed for more processing power per dollar. As computer manufacturers promoted these systems and managers began visualizing ways in which the computers could help them make important decisions, management information systems were

**process control system**
A computer system that monitors and controls ongoing physical processes, such as temperature or pressure changes.

**office automation systems**
Systems that combine modern hardware and software to handle the tasks of publishing and distributing information.

**management information system (MIS)**
A computer-based system that provides information and support for effective managerial decision making.

born. A **management information system (MIS)** is a computer-based system that provides information and support for effective managerial decision making. The basic elements of a management information system are illustrated in Exhibit 15.3. The MIS is supported by the organization's operations information systems and by organizational databases (and frequently databases of external data as well). Management information systems typically include reporting systems, decision support systems, executive information systems, and groupware, each of which will be explained in this section.

MISs typically support strategic decision-making needs of mid-level and top management. However, as technology becomes more widely accessible, more employees are wired into networks, and organizations push decision making downward in the hierarchy, these kinds of systems are seeing use at all levels of the organization.

*Take A Moment*

*Go to the experiential exercise on page 569 that pertains to how you use information for decision making.*

**information reporting system**
A system that organizes information in the form of prespecified reports that managers use in day-to-day decision making.

**decision support system (DSS)**
An interactive, computer-based system that uses decision models and specialized databases to support organization decision makers.

When a production manager needs to make a decision about production scheduling, he or she may need data on the anticipated number of orders in the coming month, inventory levels, and availability of computers and personnel. The MIS can provide these data. In fact, **information reporting systems**, the most common form of MIS, provide managers and decision makers with reports that support day-to-day decision-making needs. At Harrah's casinos, an information reporting system uses quantitative models to predict each customer's potential long-term value and enables managers to create customized marketing and rewards programs that address individual players' unique preferences. "Almost everything we do in marketing and decision making is influenced by technology," says Harrah's CEO Gary Loveman. The approach has helped Harrah's achieve 16 straight quarters of same-store sales growth, as well as the highest profit growth in the industry.[10]

**Decision support systems (DSSs)** are interactive, computer-based information systems that rely on decision models and specialized databases to support decision makers. With electronic spreadsheets and other decision support software, users can

Exhibit **15.3**

**Basic Elements of Management Information Systems**

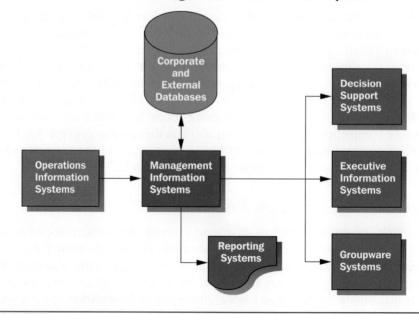

**SOURCE:** Adapted from Ralph M. Stair and George W. Reynolds, *Principles of Information Systems: A Managerial Approach*, 4th ed. (Cambridge, Mass,: Course Technology, 1999) 391.

# manager's Shoptalk

### Executive Dashboard Can Put Control at Your Fingertips

Simply collecting more data and information doesn't help managers make better decisions. What really matters is how well the organization's systems make sense of endless data and transform it into knowledge and intelligence that managers can use to make the right choices and act in a unified way.

The executive dashboard is a visual display that creates a context for information and gives top managers the big picture about where the organization stands. Much like an automobile or airplane instrument panel, the dashboard gives executives real-time information so they can determine at a glance where their company is and where it is headed.

Specifics such as how much cash is on hand, how many products are on back-order, or how product returns have affected the bottom line are all displayed in easy-to-read charts, graphs, and tables. The manager can click on any button and get to the level of detail desired regarding any particular category of information. John Garrett, co-president of Triad Distributing Northwest, Inc., a building-supplies wholesaler in Nampa, Idaho, checks his dashboard hourly. There, he gets updated snapshots of Triad's general ledger, accounts receivable, accounts payable, cash-on-hand, and inventory levels. If he sees a problem, he can take action right away to see why the numbers are off. In addition, Garrett uses the dashboard to identify and eliminate slow-moving and unprofitable products.

Many of today's managers are inundated with information. One study found that the average businessperson in the United States, Canada, and the United Kingdom sends or receives 190 messages a day. In a world of information overload, what most managers really want is information that makes their lives easier. By providing a context that makes sense out of endless data, executive dashboards can do just that.

---

SOURCES: Kevin Ferguson, "Mission Control," *Inc.* (November 2003), 27–28; and D. Keith Denton, "Focus on Data Context, Not Content," *Communications News* (December 2003), 50.

---

pose a series of what-if questions to test alternatives they are considering. Based on the assumptions used in the software or specified by the user, managers can explore various alternatives and receive tentative information to help them choose the alternative with the best outcome. Big retailers such as The Home Depot, Bloomingdale's, and Gap use decision support systems to help them gauge when to mark down prices and what items to discount, for example.[11]

**Executive information systems (EISs)** are management information systems to facilitate strategic decision making at the highest level of management. These systems are typically based on software that provides easy access to large amounts of complex data and can analyze and present the data in a timely fashion. EISs provide top management with quick access to relevant internal and external information and, if designed properly, can help them diagnose problems as well as develop solutions. Many companies use executive information systems that enable top executives to view a *dashboard* of key performance indicators at their desktops. These systems take relevant data from databases, transaction-processing systems, and information reporting systems; gauge the data against key performance metrics; and pull out the right nuggets of information to deliver to top managers for analysis and action.[12] The use of executive dashboards is further discussed in this chapter's Shoptalk box.

Modern information technology systems also recognize that many organizational and managerial activities involve groups of people working together to solve problems and meet customer needs. **Groupware** is software that works on a computer network

**executive information system (EIS)**
A management information system designed to facilitate strategic decision making at the highest levels of management by providing executives with easy access to timely and relevant information.

**groupware**
Software that works on a computer network or the Internet to facilitate information sharing, collaborative work, and group decision making.

**Internet**
A global collection of computer networks linked together for the exchange of data and information.

**World Wide Web (WWW)**
A collection of central servers for accessing information on the Internet.

**e-business**
Any business that takes place by digital processes over a computer network rather than in physical space.

**e-commerce**
Business exchanges that occur electronically.

**intranet**
An internal communications system that uses the technology and standards of the Internet but is accessible only to people within the organization.

or via the Internet to link people or workgroups across a room or around the globe. The software enables managers or team members to communicate, share information, and work simultaneously on the same document, chart, or diagram and see changes and comments as they are made by others. Sometimes called *collaborative work systems*, groupware systems allow people to interact with one another in an electronic meeting space and at the same time take advantage of computer-based support data. Groupware supports virtual and global teamwork by facilitating efficient and accurate sharing of ideas and simultaneous task execution. Team members in different geographical areas with varied expertise can work together almost as easily as if they were in the same room.

# The Internet and E-Business

In recent years, most organizations have incorporated the Internet as part of their information technology strategy.[13] The **Internet** is a global collection of computer networks linked together for the exchange of data and information. The **World Wide Web (WWW)** is a set of central servers for accessing information on the Internet. Originally developed for use by the U.S. military, the Internet, and the World Wide Web have become household words and an important part of our personal and work lives. Exhibit 15.4 shows the opening Web page for Herman Miller Inc., the first office furniture maker to design and sell a line of products over the Internet. Both business and nonprofit organizations quickly realized the potential of the Internet for expanding their operations globally, improving business processes, reaching new customers, and making the most of their resources. E-business began to boom. **E-business** can be defined as any business that takes place by digital processes over a computer network rather than in physical space. Most commonly today, it refers to electronic linkages over the Internet with customers, partners, suppliers, employees or other key constituents. **E-commerce** is a more limited term that refers specifically to business exchanges or transactions that occur electronically.

Some organizations are set up as e-businesses that are run completely over the Internet, such as eBay, Amazon.com, Expedia, and Yahoo!. These companies would not exist without the Internet. However, most established organizations, including General Electric, the City of Madison, Wisconsin, Target stores, and the U.S. Postal Service, also make extensive use of the Internet, and we will focus on these types of organizations in the remainder of this section. The goal of e-business for established organizations is to digitalize as much of the business as possible to make the organization more efficient and effective. Companies are using the Internet and the Web for everything from filing expense reports and calculating daily sales to connecting directly with suppliers for the exchange of information and ordering of parts.[14]

Exhibit 15.5 illustrates the key components of e-business for two organizations, a manufacturing company and a retail chain. First, each organization uses an **intranet**, an internal communications system that uses the technology and standards of the Internet but is accessible only to people within the company. The next component is a system that allows the separate companies to share data and information. Two options are an electronic data interchange network or an extranet.

© JONATHAN BLAIR/CORBIS

**CONCEPT CONNECTION**

*Burlington Northern Santa Fe (BNSF) railroad solved an old business problem with a new* **e-commerce** *solution. BNSF's massive locomotives eventually wear out, and disposing of them used to be a complex, time-consuming process. Company officials turned to the Web, auctioning off 47 locomotives in one afternoon, with prices averaging 11 percent above previous sales. Since then, BNSF has expanded its* **e-business** *initiatives. It recently allowed timber companies to bid on booking capacity, helping to ensure that each of its 200,000 boxcars travels fully loaded. A half-full boxcar barely breaks even. Today, many U.S. trains are running with the help of e-business—at a profit.*

Exhibit 15.4

## Opening Page of the Web Site for Herman Miller, Inc.

Exhibit 15.5

## The Key Components of E-Business for Two Traditional Organizations

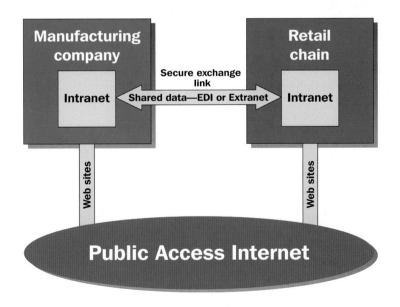

**SOURCE:** Based on Jim Turcotte, Bob Silveri, and Tom Jobson, "Are You Ready for the E-Supply Chain?", *APICS—The Performance Advantage* (August 1998), 56–59.

**electronic data interchange (EDI)**
A network that links the computer systems of buyers and sellers to allow the transmission of structured data primarily for ordering, distribution, and payables and receivables.

**extranet**
An external communications system that uses the Internet and is shared by two or more organizations.

Electronic data interchange (EDI) networks link the computer systems of buyers and sellers to allow the transmission of structured data primarily for ordering, distribution, and payables and receivables.[15] An **extranet** is an external communications system that uses the Internet and is shared by two or more organizations. With an extranet, each organization moves certain data outside of its private intranet, but makes the data available only to the other companies sharing the extranet. The final piece of the overall system is the Internet, which is accessible to the general public. Organizations make some information available to the public through their Web sites, which may include products or services offered for sale. For example, at the Web site of Herman Miller, shown earlier in Exhibit 15.4, dealers and consumers can place orders for furniture online and also check order status or make changes with just a few mouse clicks.

## E-Business Strategies

The first step toward a successful e-business is for managers to determine why they need such a business to begin with.[16] Failure to align the e-business initiative with corporate strategy can lead to e-business failure. Two basic strategic approaches for traditional organizations setting up an Internet operation are illustrated in Exhibit 15.6. Some companies embrace e-business primarily to expand into new markets and reach new customers. Others use e-business as a route to increased productivity and cost efficiency. As shown in the exhibit, these strategies are implemented either by setting up an in-house Internet division or by partnering with other organizations to handle online activities.

### Market Expansion

An Internet division allows a company to establish direct links to customers and expand into new markets. The organization can provide access around the clock to a worldwide market and thus reach new customers. Eddie Bauer estimates that more than half of the customers making purchases on its electronic storefront are new to the site, supporting the idea that e-business helps reach new customers and markets.[17]

*Take A Moment*

*Go to the ethical dilemma on page 570 that pertains to using the Internet for market expansion.*

An e-business division also enables customization of offerings at significantly lower costs than traditional distribution channels, helping a company differentiate it's products and services. The market expansion strategy is competitively sustainable because the e-business division works in conjunction with the established bricks-and-mortar company. One example is National Public Radio (NPR), which simulcasts pictures on its Web site connected to radio shows such as *Morning Edition*, serving to increase listener traffic to the show. Consider how REI, an outdoor equipment retailer, uses its online business for market expansion.

**REI**
http://www.rei.com

When REI wanted to boost its in-store sales, it turned to its Web site to do it. Customers who order online can have the item shipped free to the nearest REI retail outlet, where they pick it up and save the shipping cost.

Managers soon discovered that one out of every three people who buy something online will spend about $90 more when they come to pick up the item. People are swayed to spend more when they get into the store and see the colorful displays of bikes, climbing gear, and outdoor clothing. Another successful approach has been REI's gift registry. People can set up a gift list and friends or relatives can purchase requested items either online or at any retail channel. Once a person sets up a gift registry, REI sends notices to a designated list of recipients. The gift registry has been an effective way of expanding sales to people who don't traditionally shop at REI, and some have become new regular customers.

By integrating their online products and services with their traditional retail operations, REI has grown its sales and expanded its market reach.[18]

Exhibit 15.6

## Strategies for Engaging Clicks with Bricks

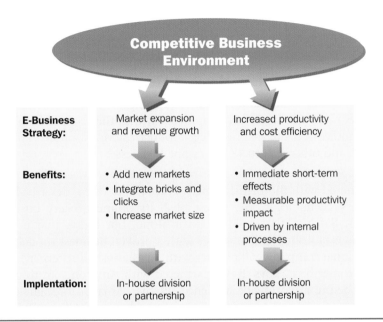

| | **Competitive Business Environment** | |
|---|---|---|
| **E-Business Strategy:** | Market expansion and revenue growth | Increased productivity and cost efficiency |
| **Benefits:** | • Add new markets<br>• Integrate bricks and clicks<br>• Increase market size | • Immediate short-term effects<br>• Measurable productivity impact<br>• Driven by internal processes |
| **Implentation:** | In-house division or partnership | In-house division or partnership |

## Productivity and Efficiency

With this approach, the e-business initiative is seen primarily as a way to improve the bottom line by increasing productivity and cutting costs. An automaker, for example, might use e-business to reduce the cost of ordering and tracking parts and supplies and to implement just-in-time manufacturing. GM is now using wireless Internet technology to increase productivity in 90 of its plants, where Wi-Fi devices are mounted on forklifts and used by assembly workers to track the movement of engine parts and car seats tagged with tiny chips that emit electronic signals.[19] This approach can have immediate short-term effects and produce measurable productivity hikes and cost savings. Productivity gains from businesses using the Internet are projected to reach $450 billion a year by 2005.[20] Even the smallest companies can realize gains. Rather than purchasing parts from a local supplier at premium rates, a small firm can access a worldwide market and find the best price, or negotiate better terms with the local supplier.[21] Service firms and government agencies can benefit too. The City of Madison, Wisconsin, found that getting all the city's agencies online significantly reduced paperwork and staff time and cost. People can log on to pay their taxes, water bills, parking tickets, and other fees. The convenience has enabled the city to collect millions in overdue parking ticket fines, increasing revenues and saving the time and expense of sending repeat notices.[22]

## Implementing E-Business Strategies

When traditional organizations such as REI, Herman Miller, or General Motors Corporation want to establish

© BLAIR CORPORATION

### CONCEPT CONNECTION

*Blair Corporation is a multi-channel direct marketer of apparel and home merchandise for value-conscious customers. In 2003, Blair launched an Internet division aimed at **market expansion**. Using a variety of tools and techniques, including virtual catalogs, Blair.com added 170,000 new-to-file customers in its first year, with an average age nearly 15 years younger than their traditional core customers: "proof of the power of this new channel."*

an Internet division, managers have to decide how best to integrate bricks and clicks—that is, how to blend their traditional operations with an Internet initiative.[23] One approach is to set up an *in-house division*. This approach offers tight integration between the online business and the organization's traditional operation. Managers create a separate department or unit within the company that functions within the structure and guidance of the traditional organization. This approach gives the new division several advantages by piggybacking on the established company, including brand recognition, purchasing leverage with suppliers, shared customer information, and marketing opportunities. Office Depot, for example, launched an online unit for market expansion as a tightly integrated in-house part of its overall operation. Managers and employees within the company are assigned to the unit to handle Web site maintenance, product offerings, order fulfillment, customer service, and other aspects of the online business.

A second approach is through *partnerships*, such as joint ventures or alliances. Safeway partnered with the British supermarket chain Tesco, described in the previous chapter's Technology box, to establish its online grocery business in the United States. Safeway first tried to go it alone, but found that it needed the expertise of an established online player with a proven business model.[24] In many cases, a traditional company will partner with an established Internet firm to reach a broader customer base. Toys 'R' Us partnered with Amazon.com to get its product offerings before a worldwide audience. Partner Amazon brought e-commerce experience and an entrepreneurial mindset, while Toys 'R' Us provided purchasing leverage and brand recognition in the toy industry. Each company can provide its core strengths—Amazon handles customer service, warehousing, order fulfillment, and maintenance of the Web site, while Toys 'R' Us does all inventory management, merchandising, purchasing, and marketing for the co-branded site.[25]

## E-Marketplaces

The biggest boom in e-commerce is in business-to-business (B2B) transactions, or buying and selling between companies. Business-to-business transactions were at $2.4 trillion and growing in 2004, according to Forrester Research Inc.[26] A significant trend is the development of **B2B marketplaces**, in which an intermediary sets up an electronic marketplace where buyers and sellers meet, acting as a hub for B2B commerce. Exhibit 15.7 illustrates a B2B marketplace, where many different sellers offer products and services to many different buyers through a *hub*, or online portal. Conducting business through a Web marketplace can mean lower transaction costs, more favorable negotiations, and productivity gains for both buyers and sellers. For example, defense contractor United Technologies buys around $450 million worth of metals, motors, and other products annually via an e-marketplace and gets prices about 15 percent less than what it once paid.[27]

Ebay, which started out as a marketplace primarily for consumers, has rapidly expanded into B2B commerce. Reliable Tools, Inc., a machine tool shop, tried listing a few items on eBay in late 1998, including items such as a $7,000, 2,300-pound milling machine. The items "sold like ice cream in August," and sales on eBay now make up about 75 percent of Reliable's overall business. Pioneers like Reliable spurred eBay to set up an industrial products markeplace, which is now on track to top $500 million in annual gross sales.[28] The success of eBay has created an entirely new kind of marketplace, where both individuals and businesses are buying and selling billions of dollars

**B2B marketplace**
An electronic marketplace set up by an intermediary where buyers and sellers meet.

### CONCEPT CONNECTION

*Many of the world's largest corporations depend on Siemens Business Services to manage their advanced information technology infrastructures. Turning to outside experts such as Siemens helps companies keep up with constantly-evolving technology as they keep their IT costs down. This advertisement promotes Siemens' SieQuence solution, which provides an integrated suite of services, from managing networks and **knowledge management systems**, to integrated **enterprise resource planning** and real-time management of the entire IT infrastructure. Within a year of its introduction in the United States, SieQuence was making up 30% of the company's total U.S. revenue, prompting a global launch in 2004.*

Exhibit 15.7

### B2B Marketplace Model

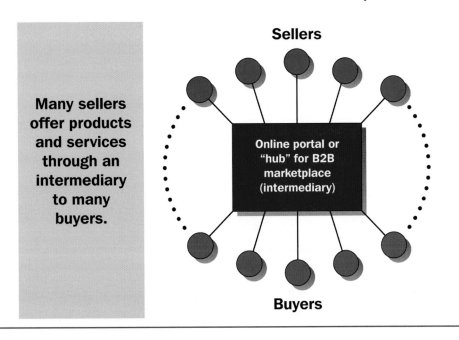

Many sellers offer products and services through an intermediary to many buyers.

**Sellers**

Online portal or "hub" for B2B marketplace (intermediary)

**Buyers**

worth of goods a year. A Canadian organization, Mediagrif Interactive Technologies, is giving eBay a run for its money in the B2B marketplace. Mediagrif focuses its efforts entirely on business-to-business exchanges in markets such as used computer parts, routers and switches, automotive parts, medical equipment, and other areas.[29]

In addition to open, public B2B marketplaces such as eBay, Mediagrif, and AutoTradeCenter, where dealers buy about 100,000 used cars a year, some companies set up private marketplaces to link with a specially invited group of suppliers and partners.[30] For example, General Motors spends billions a year on public marketplaces, but it also operates its own private marketplace, GMSupplyPower, to share proprietary information with thousands of its parts suppliers. E-marketplaces can bring efficiencies to many operations, but some companies find that they don't offer the personal touch their type of business needs, as described in this chapter's Unlocking Creative Solutions Through People box.

## Enterprise Resource Planning Systems

A key e-business component for many companies is a new approach to information management called enterprise resource planning. **Enterprise resource planning (ERP) systems** integrate and optimize all the various business processes across the entire firm.[31] The massive computing power required to run complex ERP systems once prohibited many smaller companies from using ERP. However, the top ERP vendors today host the applications themselves and offer their products through Internet portals; customers access the applications with standard browsers.

An enterprise resource planning system can become the backbone of an organization's operations. It collects, processes, and provides information about an organization's entire enterprise, including orders, product design, production, purchasing, inventory, distribution, human resources, receipt of payments, and forecasting of future demand. Such a system links these areas of activity into a network,

**enterprise resource planning (ERP) system** A networked information system that collects, processes, and provides information about an organization's entire enterprise, from identification of customer needs and receipt of orders to distribution of products and receipt of payments.

# Unlocking Creative Solutions Through People

## Grant J. Hunt Co. Likes the Personal Touch

For five generations, family-owned Grant J. Hunt Co. has reached out for new technology to speed up its food distribution business. So, when sales crews began pitching the concept of an online produce marketplace, 47-year-old Grant Hunt listened. One executive from a B2B marketplace start-up assured Hunt he could lay off half his sales staff because of the efficiencies gained. Others pointed out the potential for gaining new customers all over the world and getting higher prices by advertising produce to the highest bidder.

Yet today, Hunt's salespeople are working the way they have for years, buying and selling produce using the telephone and the fax machine. Although the B2B marketplaces put Hunt in touch with a host of potential new customers, most of them were marginal operations with shaky credit histories. In addition, Hunt was a little leery about the public nature of the exchanges, which meant that all sorts of confidential information could get out to customers and competitors. However, the biggest drawback was that the online marketplace could not provide personal attention to customers or to constantly shifting marketplace conditions. "No B-to-B site can say to a buyer at a supermarket, 'How about a special this weekend on tomatoes, because we are coming into a lot of them right now,'" Hunt points out.

The Hunt Co. has always tried to develop close, personalized relationships with its suppliers and customers, negotiating deals on an individual basis. Hunt prides himself on the fact that customers trust him to provide accurate and honest information. He or his salespeople make daily visits to large growers and the local produce markets, shaking hands and talking small talk. The rest of the time they spend glued to the telephone, matching farmers' crops with buyers such as regional supermarket chains, wholesalers, and restaurant supply outfits, often varying their prices as needed with each customer to close a deal. "The Internet is very good at taking one message and sending it out to the whole world," he says. "That's not how our world works."

Hunt found that the relationships he had developed and the processes he had in place were so efficient that he had little to gain from joining the B2B marketplace craze. In fact, over time, many of the start-ups have also realized that the produce business doesn't fit well with the online marketplace concept. BuyProduce.com, for example, has shifted its emphasis from its exchange business to helping produce companies such as Hunt improve their own in-house systems. Hunt is careful to point out that he is not anti-technology. "If they provided something that would be of real value, I would use it in a heartbeat."

SOURCE: Lee Gomes, "How Lower-Tech Gear Beat Web 'Exchanges' at Their Own Game," *The Wall Street Journal* (March 16, 2001), A11.

as illustrated in Exhibit 15.8. When a salesperson takes an order, the ERP system checks to see how the order affects inventory levels, scheduling, human resources, purchasing, and distribution. The system replicates organizational processes in software, guides employees through the processes step by step, and automates as many of them as possible. For example, the software can automatically cut an accounts payable check as soon as a clerk confirms that goods have been received in inventory, send an online purchase order immediately after a manager has authorized a purchase, or schedule production at the most appropriate plant after an order is received.[32] In addition, because the system integrates data about all aspects of operations, managers and employees at all levels can see how decisions and actions in one part of the organization affect other parts, using this information to make better decisions. Customers and suppliers are typically linked into the information exchange as well.

When carefully implemented, ERP can cut costs, shorten cycle time, enhance productivity, and improve relationships with customers and suppliers. One organization that is reaping benefits from an ERP system is Medecins du Monde (Doctors of the World).

Exhibit 15.8

## Example of ERP Applications

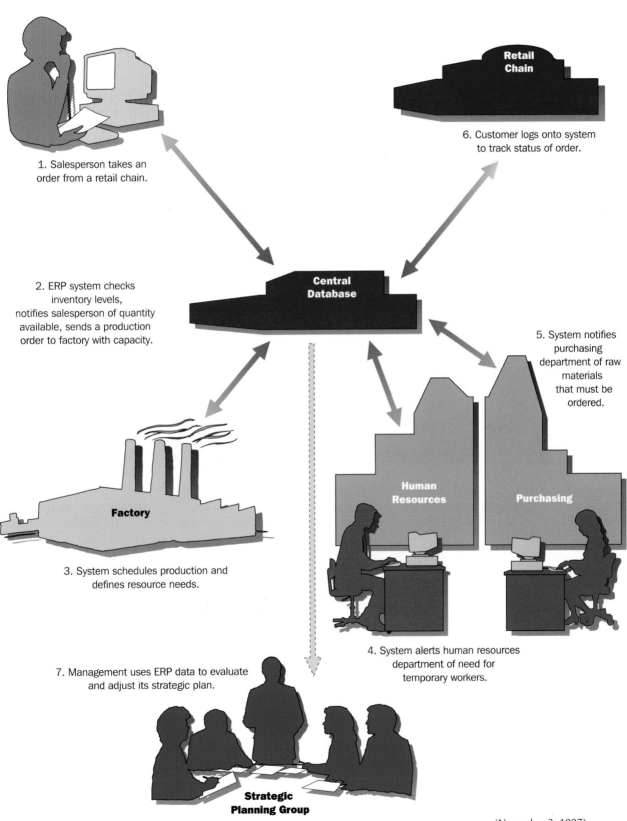

1. Salesperson takes an order from a retail chain.

2. ERP system checks inventory levels, notifies salesperson of quantity available, sends a production order to factory with capacity.

**Central Database**

**Retail Chain**

6. Customer logs onto system to track status of order.

5. System notifies purchasing department of raw materials that must be ordered.

**Factory**

3. System schedules production and defines resource needs.

**Human Resources**    **Purchasing**

4. System alerts human resources department of need for temporary workers.

7. Management uses ERP data to evaluate and adjust its strategic plan.

**Strategic Planning Group**

(November 2, 1997), 162–166.

MEDECINS
DU MONDE
http://www.
medecinsdumonde.org

When Catherine Duffau joined Medecins du Monde as chief information officer, the international aid organization had disparate systems for purchasing, finance, accounting, and communication. Trying to keep people connected and get them the information and supplies they needed to provide medical services to victims of war, famine, and drought in 59 countries was overwhelming the staff and its limited resources.

Duffau believed an ERP system would solve the problem by helping integrate functions as well as collect precise data on doctors' needs and expenses in the field. She selected a small ERP system provided by French software maker Qualiac, which was known for its ease of use, thus making it more manageable for Medecins du Monde's many volunteers.

So far, the accounting, purchasing, stock and investment records are set up and running on the system, and tests in the field have begun. When a rebellion in the Ivory Coast left thousands dead and more than a million homeless, doctors and volunteers could log onto the system and quickly see how much had already been spent and how much they had left to expand treatment when needed. Volunteers enter information into the ERP system so offices back in France can keep track of expenses, supplies, and needs.

Duffau's ultimate goal for the ERP system is information in real time. "Then we would know immediately when we had enough money to expand our missions," she says. The integration provided by ERP answers the urgent problem of connecting people who have to rely on their brains, commitment, and limited resources to solve huge human problems around the world.[33]

## Customer Relationship Management

In addition to better internal information management and information sharing with suppliers and other organizations, companies are using e-business solutions to build stronger customer relationships. One approach is **customer relationship management (CRM)** systems that help companies track customers' interactions with the firm and allow employees to call up a customer's past sales and service records, outstanding orders, or unresolved problems.[34] CRM stashes away in a database all the customer information that small-town store owners would keep in their heads—the names of all their customers, what they bought, what problems they've had with their purchases, and so forth. CRM helps to coordinate sales, marketing, and customer service departments so that all are smoothly working together to best serve customer needs. For example, when a customer places an order, the salesperson enters the order and the CRM software updates the database. Whenever the customer calls with a question or problem, CRM automatically brings up the customer's record so that the customer service or technical support representative has all pertinent information at hand and is able to provide personalized service, make additional sales pitches based on the customer's purchasing history, and update the database with information related to the call. Data from Web site customer contacts is also automatically entered into the database. Marketing can use the detailed customer information to implement tailored marketing programs. Organizations also use CRM to cut costs while improving service. Morgan Stanley uses CRM to calculate each customer's profitability and assign service levels, since the company doesn't have the staff and resources to give every customer the red carpet treatment. Stanely LoFrumento, executive director for CRM, says the program has already paid for itself in reduced costs and more targeted cross-selling efforts.[35]

Increasingly, what distinguishes an organization from its competitors are its knowledge resources, such as product ideas and the ability to identify and find solutions to customers' problems. Exhibit 15.9 lists examples of how CRM and other information technology can shorten the distance between customers and the organization, contributing to organizational success through customer loyalty, superior service, better information gathering, and organizational learning.

**customer relationship management (CRM) systems**
Systems that help companies track customers' interactions with the firm and allow employees to call up information on past transactions.

Exhibit 15.9

## Competitive Advantages Gained from Customer Relationship Management (CRM) Systems

| Competitive Advantage | Example |
|---|---|
| • **Increase in customer loyalty** | Full information about customer profile and previous requests or preferences is instantly available to sales and service representatives when a customer calls. |
| • **Superior service** | Customer representatives can provide personalized service, offer new products and services based on customer's purchasing history. |
| • **Superior information gathering and knowledge sharing** | The system is updated each time a customer contacts the organization, whether the contact is in person, by phone, or via the Web. Sales, marketing, service, and technical support have access to shared database. |
| • **Organizational learning** | Managers can analyze patterns to solve problems and anticipate new ones. |

## Knowledge Management

The Internet also plays a key role in the recent emphasis managers are putting on **knowledge management**, the efforts to systematically gather knowledge, make it widely available throughout the organization, and foster a culture of learning. Some researchers believe that intellectual capital will soon be the primary way in which businesses measure their value.[36] Therefore, managers see knowledge as an important resource to manage, just as they manage cash flow, raw materials, and other resources. An effective knowledge management system may incorporate a variety of technologies, supported by leadership that values learning, an organizational structure that supports communication and information sharing, and processes for managing change.[37] Two specific technologies that facilitate knowledge management are business intelligence software and corporate intranets or networks. The use of new business intelligence software helps organizations make sense out of huge amounts of data. These programs combine related pieces of information to create knowledge. Knowledge that can be codified, written down, and contained in databases is referred to as *explicit knowledge*. However, much organizational knowledge is unstructured and resides in people's heads. This *tacit knowledge* cannot be captured in a database, making it difficult to formalize and transmit. Intranets and knowledge sharing networks can support the spread of tacit knowledge.

**knowledge management**
The process of systematically gathering knowledge, making it widely available throughout the organization, and fostering a culture of learning.

### Business Intelligence

Today's organizations can collect and store tremendous amounts of data. Some companies use **data warehousing**, which refers to the use of a huge database that combines all of a company's data and allows business users to access the data directly, create reports, and obtain answers to what-if questions. Others have data stored in multiple sources. In addition, companies have access to numerous sources of outside data. How do managers make sense of it all? They do so through the use of business intelligence.

Business intelligence (BI) refers to the high-tech analysis of a company's data in order to make better strategic decisions.[38] Sometimes referred to as *data mining*, business intelligence means searching out and analyzing data from multiple sources across the enterprise, and sometimes from outside sources as well, to identify patterns and relationships that might be significant. Business intelligence tools to automate this process are the hottest area of software right now, with companies

**data warehousing**
The use of a huge database that combines all of a company's data and allows users to access the data directly, create reports, and obtain answers to what-if questions.

**business intelligence**
The high-tech analysis of data from multiple sources to identify patterns and relationships that might be significant.

spending $4 billion on business intelligence software in 2003. The amount is projected to double by 2006.[39] This powerful new software can manipulate trillions of pieces of data and provide managers with targeted information to help them improve efficiency, increase customer satisfaction and loyalty, and pump up sales and profits. Managers can, for example, identify sets of products that particular market segments purchase, patterns of transactions that signal possible fraud, or patterns of product performance that may indicate defects. The application of business intelligence helped managers at Staples, the office-supply chain, create a more profitable product mix in its stores. Managers had thought that devoting a large part of their floor space to desks, file cabinets, and other big-ticket items made sense. However, the BI system indicated that the overall profitability of the furniture category was actually less than that for smaller goods like paper and pens. Staples now devotes more of its floor space to such items as paper clips, highlighters, mailing labels, post-it notes, and yellow pads, helping to keep the chain's net income growing at a 12 percent compounded rate for five straight years.[40] The following example illustrates how Anheuser-Busch makes profitable use of business intelligence.

**ANHEUSER-BUSCH**
http://www.
anheuser-busch.com

> Only a few years ago, beer distributors and sales reps were turning their information in on stacks of paper invoices and sales orders. Keeping track of what products were selling and what marketing campaigns were effective was an arduous and time-consuming process. If a certain product wasn't going over well in a particular market, managers wouldn't even know it for months.
>
> But all that changed at Anheuser-Busch with the introduction of BudNet, a corporate data network through which distributors and sales reps report in excruciating detail on everything from new orders and level of sales to competitors' shelf stock and current promotional efforts. Sales reps use hand-held PDAs and laptops to enter data that are compiled and transmitted nightly to Anheuser corporate headquarters. Then, business intelligence software goes to work, helping brand managers find out what beer drinkers are buying, as well as when, where, and why. Managers use the intelligence to constantly alter marketing strategies, design promotions to target the ethnic makeup of various markets, and get an early warning when rivals may be gaining an edge. For example, by cross-analyzing company data with U.S. Census figures on the ethnic and economic makeup of neighborhoods, Anheuser can tailor marketing campaigns with local precision. It knows that Tequiza goes over well in San Antonio, but not in Peoria; that the Fourth of July is a big beer sales holiday in Atlanta but St. Patrick's Day isn't; and that beer drinkers in blue-collar neighborhoods prefer cans over bottles.
>
> Every morning, distributors log on to BudNet to access the latest intelligence and get their new marching orders for what products to promote, what displays to use, and what discounts to offer in what neighborhoods. "They're drilling down to the level of the individual store," says Joe Thompson, president of Independent Beverage Group. "They can pinpoint if customers are gay, Latino, 30-year-old college-educated conservatives."[41]

Store-level data has become the lifeblood of Anheuser-Busch's business. Since it began collecting the right data and using business intelligence to analyze it and spot trends and patterns, Anheuser-Busch has greatly expanded its market share compared to competitors. Independent wholesalers are benefitting too. The operating income for the average Anheuser wholesaler is five times greater than the average for Miller or Coors distributors. As one independent distributor's representative said about the competition, "It's no extra work to get the competitive info. . . . I think I know more about these guys' business than they do."[42]

### Intranets

**knowledge management portal**
A single point of access for employees to multiple sources of information that provides personalized access on the corporate intranet.

Many companies are building knowledge management portals on the corporate intranet to give employees an easier way to access and share information. A **knowledge management portal** is a single, personalized point of access for employees to multiple sources of information on the corporate intranet. Intranets can give employees access to explicit knowledge that may be stored in databases, but the greatest value of intranets for knowledge management is increasing the transfer of tacit knowledge. For example, Xerox tried to codify the knowledge of its service technicians and embed it in an expert decision system that was installed in the copiers. The idea was that technicians could be guided by the system and complete repairs more quickly, sometimes even off-site. However, the project failed because it did not take into account the tacit knowledge—the nuances and details—that could not be codified. After a study found that service techs shared their knowledge primarily by telling "war stories," Xerox developed an intranet system called *Eureka* to link 25,000 field service representatives. Eureka, which enables technicians to electronically share war stories and tips for repairing copiers, has cut average repair time by 50 percent.[43]

Organizations typically combine several technologies to facilitate the sharing and transfer of both tacit and explicit knowledge. For example, to spur sharing of explicit knowledge, a leading steel company set up a centralized data warehouse containing the financial and operational performance data and standards for each business unit. Managers can use business intelligence and other decision tools to identify performance gaps and make changes as needed. The company also enables tacit knowledge transfer through an intranet-based document management system, combined with Web conferencing systems, where worldwide experts can exchange ideas.[44] Similarly, when employees of Barclays Global Investors are working on proposals from large customers who require answers to hundreds of complex questions, they can access the knowledge network to re-use answers from previous similar proposals. In addition, employees set up online workspaces to tap into subject experts who can collaborate to help answer new kinds of queries and complete proposals faster.[45]

# Management Implications of Information Technology

Information technology and e-business can enable managers to be better connected with employees, the environment, and each other. In general, information technology has positive implications for the practice of management, although it can also present problems. Some specific implications of information technology for managers include improved employee effectiveness, increased efficiency, empowered employees, information overload, and enhanced collaboration.

## Improved Employee Effectiveness

Information technology can provide employees with all kinds of information about their customers, competitors, markets, and service, as well as enable them to share information or insights with colleagues. In addition, time and geographic boundaries are dissolving. A management team can work throughout the day on a project in Switzerland and, while they sleep, a team in the United States can continue where the Swiss team left off. Employees all over the world have instant access to databases at any time of the day or night and the ability to share information via an intranet. Advanced information technology allows managers and employees to work whenever and wherever they are most needed and most productive.

In general, information technology enables managers to design jobs to provide employees with more intellectual engagement and more challenging work. The availability of information technology does not guarantee increased job performance, but when implemented and used appropriately, it can have a dramatic influence

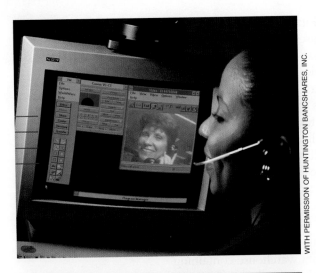

**CONCEPT CONNECTION**

*Huntington Bancshares, Inc., is using cutting-edge information technology to provide customers with the most personal kind of banking. The Personal Touch two-way video system enables this customer to apply for an Instant Access Loan from a Personal Banker, in total privacy and at the customer's convenience. Information technology is improving organizational **efficiency** and **effectiveness** throughout Huntington's subsidiaries, operating in 12 states as well as Hong Kong and the Cayman Islands. Huntington's systems reduce expenses by as much as 65 percent, at the same time improving customer service.*

on employee effectiveness. Siemens is developing a high-speed global intranet that will enable its 450,000 employees around the world to share knowledge and collaborate on projects to provide better solutions for customers. One example that has already occurred is when employees in the information and communications division collaborated with the medical division to develop products for the healthcare market.[46]

## Increased Efficiency

New information technology offers significant promise for speeding work processes, cutting costs, and increasing efficiency. For example, at IBM, automating customer service helped reduce the number of call center employees and saved $750 million in one year alone. Companies like IBM are also moving all aspects of purchasing to the Web, helping slash costs and wring deeper discounts from suppliers.

Sweeping away administrative paperwork and automating mundane tasks is another advantage of new technology. At EZRider, a Massachusetts-based retailer of snowboards, whenever a salesperson keys in a purchase, the company's computer system records the amount of the sale; at the end of the pay period, the system automatically computes the salesperson's commission in a matter of seconds.[47]

## Empowered Employees

Information technology is profoundly affecting the way organizations are structured. Through implementing IT, organizations change the locus of knowledge by providing information to people who would not otherwise receive it. Lower-level employees are increasingly challenged with more information and are expected to make decisions previously made by supervisors. Nurses, bellhops, truck drivers, utility repair workers, and warehouse staffers all need easy access to information to do their jobs well in today's fast-paced environment.[48]

These changes support the objectives of knowledge management by enabling decisions to be made by the employees who are in the best position to implement the decisions and see their effects. For example, the U.S. Army is beginning to use new information technology that pushes information about battlefield conditions, the latest intelligence on the enemy, and so forth, down the line to the lower troops. Armed with better data and trained to see patterns in the barrage of information, lieutenants in the field will be making more of the tough decisions once made by commanders.[49]

## Information Overload

One problem associated with advances in technology is that the company can become a quagmire of information, with employees so overwhelmed by the sheer volume that they are unable to sort out the valuable from the useless.[50]

In many cases, the ability to produce data and information is outstripping employees' ability to process it. One British psychologist claims to have identified a new mental disorder caused by too much information; he has termed it *Information Fatigue Syndrome*.[51] Information technology is a primary culprit in contributing to this new "disease." However, managers have the ability to alleviate the problem and improve information quality. The first step is to ensure that suppliers of information technology and CIOs work closely with employees to identify the kinds of questions they must answer and the kinds of data and information they really need. Specialists often are enamored with the volume of data a system can produce and overlook the need to provide small amounts of quality information in a timely and useful manner for decision making. Top executives should be actively involved in setting limits by focusing the organization on key strategies and on the critical questions that must be answered to pursue those strategies.[52]

## Enhanced Collaboration

Information technology enhances collaboration both within the organization and with customers, suppliers, and partners. The Internet, corporate networks, knowledge management systems, and collaborative work systems can connect employees around the world for the sharing and exchange of information and ideas. An interesting example is Petfinder.com, an online organization that was set up by a young couple in New Jersey to increase collaboration among animal shelters, humane societies, and pet rescue groups, and to connect more adoptable pets with potential adopters. Through enhanced collaboration, Petfinder.com has facilitated the placement of millions of animals that once might have faced euthanasia in shelters.[53] In businesses, one of the most effective uses of information technology for collaboration has been in the area of product development, as described in this chapter's Unlocking Creative Solutions Through Technology box. Extranets are increasingly important for linking companies with contract manufacturers and outsourcers, supporting the development of the virtual network organization we discussed in Chapter 10.

The emphasis on using information technology rather than personal travel for collaboration has increased in response to reduced travel budgets, concern over incidents such as international terrorism, and world health epidemics such as the SARS virus.[54] As we discussed in Chapters 1 and 7, a company's normal business operations may be disrupted by crises or unexpected events, and information technology plays a key role in helping to maintain essential channels of communication. The Centers for Disease Control in Atlanta, for example, sponsors PulseNet, an information network that uses collaborative information technology to help federal and state agencies stay up to date regarding food-borne disease outbreaks.[55]

# IT Trends

Information technology continues to evolve, and new concepts and applications are emerging every day. Some recent trends in information technology that are having the greatest impact are wireless applications, peer-to-peer technology, new communication tools such as blogs and wikis, and international expansion.

## Wireless Internet

A promising technology is the wireless Internet, or Wi-Fi. Early estimates of the growth of Wi-Fi proved to be grossly exaggerated, but Wi-Fi advocates continue to suggest that the technology will eventually change the way we work and play on the Web.[56] Going wireless means employees can gain access to bits of data and information over handheld devices exactly when and where they need it. With 21 million or so workers on the move on any given day, wireless technologies are becoming critical for helping people be more efficient and effective outside of the office. At Starbucks, 600 district managers access Wi-Fi in Starbucks stores, enabling them to

# Unlocking Creative Solutions Through Technology

## General Motors: On the Road to Smoother Collaboration

It used to take General Motors at least 12 weeks to complete a full mock-up of a new car design. Today, it takes just two. The complete design cycle time has been cut from 44 months to just 18. Have managers hired smarter, more creative, more efficient employees? No, they've applied information technology to help the smart, creative, and efficient employees they already had do their work faster and better.

By using collaborative product development technologies, GM employees around the world can collaborate with one another and with external auto parts suppliers in real time to share product design information. Prior to 1999, GM had no way to coordinate its complex auto designs across 14 engineering sites scattered around the world, plus the dozens of worldwide partners that design subsystems for GM. Then, managers implemented a collaboration system from EDS that lets more than 16,000 employees collaborate and keep track of parts and subassemblies. The system serves as a central clearinghouse for all design data. When changes are finalized, the system automatically updates the master design.

Now GM is kicking collaboration up another notch. By the end of 2004, employees in Asia, Europe, Latin America, and the United States are scheduled to begin working together in virtual reality studios. The computer-linked studios allow design engineers and managers to view three-dimensional, full-sized representations of vehicle designs. Designers in different parts of the world can view the same images at the same time, down to the level of surface details, and review and revise projects together.

Perhaps the biggest advantage of the enhanced collaboration is the time and the money GM saves by cutting product development time. The company has slashed about $1 billion from product development and engineering costs, and improved accuracy resulting from virtual reality collaboration is expected to save millions more each year. However, an equally important advantage is that employees around the world can have input into every new design and have the time and tools to think more creatively.

**SOURCE**: Based on Faith Keenan and Spencer E. Ante, "The New Teamwork," *BusinessWeek* e.biz (February 18, 2002), EB12–EB16; Dave Guilford, "As Clay Fades, GM Relies on Digital Imagery," *Automotive News* (April 12, 2004), 4; and Paul McDougall, "EDS Can't Afford To Be Tech Agnostic," *Information Week* (February 23, 2004), 25.

spend more time in the field and less at headquarters. A representative of enterprise software maker J. D. Edwards says two-thirds of his clients are interested in wireless versions of the company's sales-force automation software. That means salespeople can stay where they're most needed, on the road drumming up new business and keeping old business satisfied.[57] Already, Celanese Chemical's remote sales force can access real-time company information from the company's ERP system via wireless devices. One saleswoman was able to get instant confirmation on availability of a product and promise immediate shipment, helping her close a lucrative sale. "If the system saves just one order," says William Schmitt, a senior IT executive at Celanese, "it will practically pay for itself." [58]

## Peer-to-Peer File Sharing

Napster and other music-sharing services have gotten into trouble for enabling the illegal sharing and distribution of copyrighted music. However, the technology behind Napster is finding a variety of uses in legitimate business. Software can enable one person to locate and download files, such as songs, directly from another person's personal computer. This cutting-edge technology, called **peer-to-peer (P2P) file sharing**, allows PCs to communicate directly with one another over the Internet, bypassing central databases, servers, control points, and Web pages.[59] Peer-to-peer software lets any individual's computer "talk" directly to another PC without an intermediary, enhancing the opportunities for information

**peer-to-peer (P2P) file sharing**
File sharing that allows PCs to communicate directly with one another over the Internet, bypassing central databases, servers, control points, and Web pages.

sharing and collaboration. Personal computers today have enormous storage capacity. Peer-to-peer technology improves efficiency by allowing for the sharing of PC files directly between two PCs, eliminating the need for setting up and managing huge central storage systems. GlaxoSmithKline uses P2P technology to let its employees and researchers outside the company share their drug test data digitally and work collaboratively on new projects. Law firm Baker & McKenzie uses it to allow major clients to tap directly into its attorney's files stored on computers worldwide. For example, clients closing a merger can monitor the progress of the deal without attorneys having to keep files in one place or send lengthy electronic documents, improving organizational speed and efficiency.[60]

© CHARLIE SAMUELS

## Blogs and Wikis

A recent approach that is being embraced by corporate America is writing Web logs, or blogs. A **blog** is a running Web log that allows an individual to post opinions and ideas on anything from products to management.[61] Internal blogs can serve as superb horizontal and bottom-up communication tools, enabling people to get a better picture of what's going on all around the organization. Blogs contribute to collaboration and knowledge sharing as well. When IBM initiated blogging, within three months, 500 people in more than 30 countries were using it to discuss software development and other business projects. The simplicity and informality of blogs make them an easy and comfortable medium for people to communicate and share ideas. Unlike many knowledge management tools, blog software is very simple to use and fits well with employees' regular daily communications. Some companies extend the approach to external blogs, which provide a way to communicate with customers, market products, and monitor public opinion about the organization. An extension of blogs is an emerging collaboration tool referred to as *wikis*.[62] Unlike blogs, which allow individuals to just broadcast their views to an online audience, wikis are free-form, allowing visitors to edit what they find on the site or add content to it. Wikis haven't yet caught on in the corporate world, but technology watchers expect this to be a growing approach to communication, collaboration, and knowledge sharing.

**CONCEPT CONNECTION**

*The major providers of wireless phone service have introduced a new generation of mobile phones with services including **wireless Internet access** and **text messaging**. Miss Teen USA Marissa Whitley, who lives and works in New York City and takes frequent trips all over the country, uses wireless Internet services to keep in touch with friends and family. Her first text message was from her best friend: "Don't forget about me in the Big Apple." Whitley, who does not own a computer, finds text messaging and wireless Internet access "really quick and easy."*

**blog**
Web log that allows individuals to post opinions and ideas.

## Going International

When businesses were first rushing to set up Web sites, managers envisioned easily doing business all over the world. Soon, though, they awakened to the reality that national boundaries matter just as much as they ever did. The global e-market can't be approached as if it were one homogeneous piece.[63] Organizations that want to succeed with international e-business are tailoring their Web sites to address differences in language, regulations, payment systems, and consumer preferences in different parts of the world. For example, Yahoo!, Amazon, Dell Computer, Walt Disney, and the National Football League have all set up country-specific sites in the local language. The Washingtonpost.com gives its news a broader global flavor during the overnight hours when international readers frequent the site. EBay is struggling with currency issues, as it has alienated many potential users in other countries by quoting prices only in U.S. dollars. And companies with online stores are finding that they may need to offer a different product mix and discounts tailored to local preferences. The Internet is a powerful way to reach customers and partners around the world, and managers are learning to address the cross-national challenges that come with serving a worldwide market.

Information technology and e-business are changing the way people and organizations work. Organizations are evolving into information cultures in which managers and employees can share information and knowledge across boundaries of time and geography. In addition, customers, partners, and suppliers are brought into the information network.

Modern information technology gathers huge amounts of data and transforms them into useful information for decision makers. The systems that use this technology should be designed to generate information with appropriate time, content, and form attributes. Many organizations hire a chief information officer to help manage decisions regarding technology infrastructure and information design.

Information systems combine hardware, software, and human resources to organize information and make it readily available. Operations information systems, including transaction-processing systems, process control systems, and office automation systems, support daily business operations and the needs of low-level managers. Management information systems, including information reporting systems, decision support systems, and executive information systems, typically support the decision-making needs of middle- and upper-level managers. Collaborative work systems allows groups of managers or employees to share information, collaborate electronically, and have access to computer-based support data for group decision making and problem solving.

Most organizations have incorporated the Internet and e-business as part of their information technology strategy. Traditional organizations use an online division primarily for market expansion or to increase productivity and reduce costs. Two primary ways e-business strategies are implemented are through an in-house dot-com division or by partnering with other organizations for the Internet business. Companies are also benefitting from participation in electronic marketplaces, where many different sellers offer products and services to many different buyers through an online hub.

Important e-business solutions for improving business operations and customer relationships include enterprise resource planning (ERP) systems and customer relationship management (CRM) software. Knowledge management is also an important application for new technology. Key technologies for knowledge management are business intelligence software and knowledge management portals on the corporate intranet. Information technology and e-business have a number of specific implications for managers and organizations, including greater employee effectiveness, increased efficiency, empowered employees, information overload, and enhanced collaboration. Information technology continues to evolve. Some recent trends include wireless Internet applications, peer-to-peer technology, blogs and wikis, and going international.

Recall the opening case of Bountiful Mazda, which was looking for a way to use new Internet technology to increase effectiveness. Owner Michael MacDonald decided to participate in a Mazda-supported remake of its dealership (the company kicks in around $350,000 and plans to overhaul 200 dealerships by 2008). A big part of the makeover is to invite customers to do their price research on new and used cars right inside the dealership. Bountiful Mazda is now a Wi-Fi hotspot, where customers and employees can use their own wireless devices to check prices and specifications. Several computer kiosks are also scattered around the dealership. Unlike some dealers that keep their on-site PCs locked down to the maker's own website, Mazda encourages users to browse anywhere they want and even catch up on e-mail or personal business. A separate Internet café near the showroom is off-limits to sales staff members unless they're invited inside by a customer to discuss terms or draw up paperwork. Gone are the high pressure sales pitches and the "closing booths," where customers are often pressed into paying higher prices. Bountiful has a fleet of washed , waxed, and polished vehicles gassed up and ready to take for a spin the minute a customer walks on the lot. Talk comes later, with both customer and salesperson armed with on-the-spot information from the Web. The new, friendlier approach and open information via the Internet has translated into some big results. Customers tend to let their guard down in this open atmosphere, enabling the salesperson to upsell, cross-sell and accessorize. A customer who feels she's getting the lowest price on the car is often more willing to tack on a $2,800 warranty package or a $2,000 in-dash global positioning system (GPS). Overall, the Bountiful store and Mazda's five other revamped showrooms are seeing 32 percent jumps in annual sales and generating twice the profit of older dealerships.[64]

# Discussion Questions

1. Why is it important for managers to understand the difference between data and information?
2. In what ways would the role of the CIO of a hospital be important?
3. What types of information technology do you use as a student on a regular basis? How might your life be different if you did not have this technology available to you?
4. How might the organizers of an upcoming Olympics use an extranet to get all the elements of the event up and running on schedule?
5. How might groupware be useful to a worldwide restaurant chain such as McDonald's?
6. In what ways might access to an MIS change the way decisions are made at a large package-delivery company?
7. Do you think that a geographic information system would be beneficial to a large mail-order company such as L. L. Bean or Spiegel? Why or why not?
8. Why is knowledge management an important consideration in the use of information technology?
9. Do you believe information overload is a problem for today's students? For employees? Discuss.
10. How is information technology affecting the way organizations are structured and the way jobs are designed?

# Management in Practice: Experiential Exercise

**What Is Your MIS Style?**

Following are 14 statements. Circle the number that indicates how much you agree that each statement is characteristic of you. The questions refer to how you use information and make decisions.

|  | Disagree Strongly | Agree Strongly |
|---|---|---|

1. I like to wait until all relevant information is examined before deciding something.      1  2  3  4  5

2. I prefer information that can be interpreted in several ways and leads to different but acceptable solutions.      1  2  3  4  5

3. I like to keep gathering data until an excellent solution emerges.      1  2  3  4  5

4. To make decisions, I often use information that means different things to different people.      1  2  3  4  5

|  | **Disagree Strongly** | | | **Agree Strongly** | |
|---|---|---|---|---|---|
| 5. I want just enough data to make a decision quickly. | 5 | 4 | 3 | 2 | 1 |
| 6. I act on logical analysis of the situation rather than on my "gut feelings" about the best alternative. | 5 | 4 | 3 | 2 | 1 |
| 7. I seek information sources or people that will provide me with many ideas and details. | 1 | 2 | 3 | 4 | 5 |
| 8. I try to generate more than one satisfactory solution for the problem faced. | 1 | 2 | 3 | 4 | 5 |
| 9. When reading something, I confine my thoughts to what is written rather than search for additional understanding. | 5 | 4 | 3 | 2 | 1 |
| 10. When working on a project, I try to narrow, not broaden, the scope so it is clearly defined. | 5 | 4 | 3 | 2 | 1 |
| 11. I typically acquire all possible information before making a final decision. | 1 | 2 | 3 | 4 | 5 |
| 12. I like to work on something I've done before rather than take on a complicated problem. | 5 | 4 | 3 | 2 | 1 |
| 13. I prefer clear, precise data. | 5 | 4 | 3 | 2 | 1 |

14. When working on a project, I like to explore various options rather than maintain a narrow focus.   1   2   3   4   5

**Total Score** _____

Your information-processing style determines the extent to which you will benefit from computer-based information systems.

The *odd-numbered* questions pertain to the "amount of information" you like to use. A score of 28 or more suggests you prefer a large amount. A score of 14 or less indicates you like a small amount of information.

The *even-numbered* questions pertain to the "focus of information" you prefer. A score of 28 or more suggests you are comfortable with ambiguous, multi-focused information, while a score of 14 or less suggests you like clear, unifocused data.

If you are a person who likes a large amount of information and clear, focused data, you will tend to make effective use of management information systems. You could be expected to benefit greatly from an EIS or MIS in your company. If you are a person who prefers a small amount of data and data that are multifocused, you would probably not get the information you need to make decisions through formal information systems. You probably won't utilize EIS or MIS to a great extent, preferring instead to get decision data from other convenient sources, including face-to-face discussions.

Sources: This questionnaire is adapted from Richard L. Daft and Norman B. Macintosh, "A Tentative Exploration into the Amount and Equivocality of Information Processing in Organizational Work Units," *Administrative Science Quarterly 26* (1981), 207–224; and Dorothy Marcic, *Organizational Behavior: Experiences and Cases*, 4th ed. (St. Paul, Minn.: West, 1995).

# Management in Practice: Ethical Dilemma

## Manipulative or Not?

As head of the marketing department for Butter Crisp Snack Foods, fifty-five-year-old Frank Bellows has been forced to learn a lot about the Internet in recent years. Although he initially resisted the new technology, Frank has gradually come to appreciate the potential of the Internet for serving existing customers and

reaching potential new ones. In fact, he has been one of the biggest supporters of the company's increasing use of the Internet to stay in touch with customers.

However, something about this new plan just doesn't feel right. At this morning's meeting, Keith Deakins, Butter Crisp's CEO, announced that the company would soon be launching a Web site geared specifically to children. Although Deakins has the authority to approve the site on his own, he has asked all department heads to review the site and give their approval for its launch. He then turned the meeting over to the Information Technology team that developed the new site, which will offer games and interactive educational activities. The team pointed out that although it will be clear that Butter Crisp is the sponsor of the site, there will be no advertising of Butter Crisp products. So far, so good, Frank thinks. However, he knows that two of the young hot-shot employees in his department have been helping to develop the site and that they provided a list of questions that children will be asked to answer online. Just to enter the Web site, for example, a user must provide name, address, gender, e-mail address, and favorite TV show. In return, users receive "Crisp Cash," a form of virtual money that they can turn in for toys, games, Butter Crisp samples, and other prizes. After they enter the site, children can earn more Crisp Cash by providing other information about themselves and their families.

Frank watched the demonstration and agreed that the Web site does indeed have solid educational content. However, he is concerned about the tactics for gathering information from children that will almost certainly be used for marketing purposes. So far, it seems that the other department heads are solidly in favor of launching the Web site. Frank is wondering if he can sign his approval with a clear conscience. He also knows that several groups, including the national PTA and the Center for Media Education, are calling for stricter governmental controls regarding collecting information from children via the Internet.

**What Do You Do?**

1.  Stop worrying about it. There's nothing illegal about what Butter Crisp is proposing to do, and any personal information gathered will be closely guarded by the company. Children can't be harmed in any way by using the new Web site.
2.  Begin talking with other managers and try to build a coalition in support of some stricter controls, such as requiring parental permission to enter areas of the site that offer Crisp Cash in exchange for personal information.
3.  Contact the Center for Media Education and tell them you suspect Butter Crisp intends to use the Web site to conduct marketing research. The Center might be able to apply pressure that would make it uncomfortable enough for Deakins to pull the plug on the new kid's Web site.

Source: Based on Denise Gellene, "Internet Marketing to Kids Is Seen as a Web of Deceit," *Los Angeles Times*, March 29, 1996, A1, A20.

# Surf the Net

1.  **Decision Support Systems.** Visit the Web site of a company, such as SAS Institute, Inc., listed below, that creates software designed to aid in the decision-making process. If the site you visit provides information about client companies that have successfully used SAS software products, then provide a brief summary of what the company used the product for and how it helped improve the company's decision-making process. If no examples are provided, then briefly describe one SAS DSS product—its function, as well as examples of who might use the product. *http://www.sas.com*—client profiles available at *http://www.sas.com/success/index.html*.

2.  **Knowledge Management.** The WWW Virtual Library on Knowledge Management—Forums, Articles, Magazines, Events, Resources, Analyses, and News—is located at *http://www. brint.com/ km*.

Review comments of this Web site include: "Largest Collection of Knowledge Management Literature" (*The Wall Street Journal*) "Best Sources for Knowledge Management and Intellectual Capital" (*Fast Company*) "Tool for Raising Your Company's IQ" (*Forbes*) "Best Web site on the topic of Knowledge Management" (*InfoWorld*) "Wealth of Incredibly Rich, Useful and Interesting Information" (*CIO Magazine*)

Visit several sections of this virtual library to familiarize yourself with its contents, select one item you found most interesting, print it out, and bring it to class so that you may contribute your findings during a classroom discussion on knowledge management.

3.  **Data Warehousing.** Microsoft provides many resources for corporate IT professionals. The Web site at *http://www.microsoft.com/technet* is constantly

being updated to reflect the rapidly-changing needs of its users. Go to the site, look over what's available, and then use the search feature on TechNet's home page or go to *http://www. microsoft. com/technet/prodtechnol/sql/2005/evaluate/dwsqlsy.*

*mspx* to locate information on data warehousing. Access any of the articles, case studies, white papers, or Web site links available at Microsoft TechNet, and write a one- to two-page paper outlining your most significant findings.

# Case for Critical Analysis

## Clarklift/FIT

Wayne Reece, head of Clarklift/FIT, which owns several central Florida forklift dealerships, tried computers a decade ago. He didn't like them, and he didn't think he needed information technology to run his business. But as his company began to grow, he realized that he had taken on more debt than he was comfortable with, so he recruited a chief financial officer named Ken Daley. Reece also got back into the technology game, investing $100,000 in a proprietary inventory and accounting system developed by Fetner Associates. Daley began to look for better financing for the company and approached Citicorp's Global Equipment Finance Division. Surprisingly, it seemed that Citicorp was more interested in Clarklift's information technology capacity than it was in how many forklifts the company had sold. David B. Hilton explains why. "The theory goes that if you can trust the computer systems, you can trust the company's numbers."

Clarklift wanted to borrow a significant amount of money, so Citicorp sent CMS Management Services Co., an Indiana-based technology consulting firm, to evaluate Clarklift's existing systems. Hilton explains further, "If clients don't have the proper systems to automatically generate the sorts of financial reports we need on a monthly basis, this sort of loan would overwhelm them." Reece was already on the right track with the inventory and accounting system. Thus, the necessary data were there in the system; but as Reece, Daley, and CMS learned, it was difficult to turn the data into quality information. For instance, if someone wanted a list of accounts receivable that were past due, the database would output about 500 pages of indecipherable codes and numbers. "None of the answers just popped out of the computer," recalls Daley.

So Daley began using a software program called Monarch (ironically, already installed on the computer) to turn the data into information printed on

neat, readable spreadsheets. In the process, Clarklift not only qualified for a $5 million loan from Citicorp but also discovered some of its own poor business practices. For example, Reece and Daley discovered over $100,000 worth of unused parts that could be returned to manufacturers. As Clarklift's ability to turn data into quality information has increased, Reece and Daley can see at a moment's notice how the company is performing. For instance, they can see which forklifts are being rented or sold and which are not—and on which sales lots. "It only takes me a second to know who to congratulate and who needs a good talking to," says Reece. In addition, salespeople, who now carry laptops, can enter sales figures directly into a customer's file in the contract-management software program ACT!, which Reece can access at any time. When a salesperson gives a quote to a client, he or she e-mails the quote to Reece. When Reece opens the e-mail message, the quote is automatically deposited in a central database for later reference. Finally, when customers' invoices are generated each month, the computer also produces a list of those customers who are past due and even prints out appropriate collection letters—instead of 500 pages of unintelligible numbers.

## Questions

1. With its newfound reliance on information technology, do you think that Clarklift/FIT might fall into an information overload trap? Why or why not?

2. How does information technology contribute to Clarklift's knowledge management? What other strategic advantages does IT provide?

3. What steps might Clarklift/FIT take to evaluate the success of its information technology systems?

Source: Joshua Macht, "The Accidental Automator," *Inc. Tech.*, 1997, no. 2, 66–71.

# Endnotes

1. Bob Parks, "Let's Remake a Dealership," *Business 2.0* (June 2004), 65–67; Warren Brown, "Savvy Buyers Might Appreciate the Smart Approach," *The Washington Post* (April 18, 2004), G2; and Jaclyn Olsen, "Mazda to Unveil New Prototype in Bountiful," *The Enterprise* (May 13, 2002), 5.

2. Christopher Palmeri, "Believe in Yourself, Believe in the Merchandise," *Continental* (December 1997), 49–51; Timothy J. Mullaney with Heather Green, Michael Arndt, Robert D. Hof, and Linda Himelstein, "The E-Biz Surprise," *Business Week*, (May 12, 2003), 60–68.

3. Timothy J. Mullaney, "E-Biz Strikes Again," *BusinessWeek* (May 10, 2004), 80–82; and Mullaney et al., "The E-Biz Surprise."

4. Mullaney, et al., "The E-Biz Surprise."

5. Derek Slater, "Chain Commanders," *CIO Enterprise* (August 15, 1998), 29–30+.

6. Jane Linder and Drew Phelps, "Call to Action," *CIO* (April 1, 2000), 166–174.

7. James A. O'Brien, *Introduction to Information Systems*, 8th ed. (Burr Ridge, Ill.: Irwin, 1997), 284–285; and Nathaniel Foote, Eric Matson, Leigh Weiss, and Etienne Wenger, "Leveraging Group Knowledge for High-Performance Decision Making," *Organizational Dynamics* 31, no. 3 (2002): 280–295.

8. John P. Mello Jr., "Fly Me To the Web," *CFO* (March 2000), 79–84.

9. Heather Harreld, "Pick-Up Artists," *CIO* (November 1, 2000), 148–154.

10. Gary Loveman, "Diamonds in the Data Mine," *Harvard Business Review* (May 2003), 109–113; and Meridith Levinson, "Harrah's Knows What You Did Last Night," *Darwin Magazine* (May 2001), 61–68.

11. Julie Schlosser, "Markdown Lowdown," *Fortune* (January 12, 2004), 40.

12. Russ Banham, "Seeing the Big Picture: New Data Tools Are Enabling CEOs to Get a Better Handle on Performance Across Their Organizations," *Chief Executive* (November 2003), 46.

13. Jim Turcotte, Bob Silveri, and Tom Jobson, "Are You Ready for the E-Supply Chain?" *APICS–The Performance Advantage* (August 1998), 56–59.

14. Steve Hamm with David Welch, Wendy Zellner, Faith Keenan, and Peter Engardio, "E-Biz: Down but Hardly Out," *BusinessWeek* (March 26, 2001), 126–130.

15. David Drickhamer, "EDI Is Dead! Long Live EDI!," *Industry Week* (April 2003), 31–38; Ian Mount, "Why EDI Won't Die," *Business 2.0* (August 2003), 68–69; and Marie-Claude Boudreau, Karen D. Loch, Daniel Robey,

and Detmar Straud, "Going Global: Using Information Technology to Advance the Competitiveness of the Virtual Transnational Organization," *Academy of Management Executive* 12, no. 4 (1998) 120–128.

16. This discussion is based on Long W. Lam and L. Jean Harrison-Walker, "Toward an Objective-Based Typology of E-Business Models," *Business Horizons* (November–December 2003), 17–26; and Detmar Straub and Richard Klein, "E-Competitive Transformations," *Business Horizons* (May–June 2001), 3–12.

17. Straub and Klein, "E-Competitive Transformations."

18. Megan Santosus, "How REI Scaled E-Commerce Mountain," *CIO* (May 15, 2004), 52–54.

19. Mullaney et al., "The E-Biz Surprise."

20. Reported in Mullaney et al., "The E-Biz Surprise."

21. Straub and Klein, "E-Competitive Transformations."

22. Elizabeth Weinstein, "City Sites," *The Wall Street Journal* (April 28, 2003), R8.

23. This discussion of implementation approaches is based on Ranjay Gulati and Jason Garino, "Get the Right Mix of Bricks and Clicks," *Harvard Business Review* (May–June 2000), 107–114.

24. "Business: Surfing USA," *The Economist* (June 30, 2001), 58; and James R. Hagerty and James Hall, "British Supermarket Giant Cooks Up Plans to Go Global—Tesco's Move to Duplicate High Growth at Home Comes with Big Risks," *The Wall Street Journal* (July 5, 2001), A9.

25. Kris Frieswick, "You've Got to Have Friends," *CFO* (August 2001), 50–53.

26. Statistic reported in Mullaney et al., "The E-Biz Surprise." This discussion is based on Pamela Barnes-Vieyra and Cindy Claycomb, "Business-to-Business E-Commerce: Models and Managerial Decisions," *Business Horizons* (May–June 2001), 13–20.

27. Reported in Hamm et al., "E-Biz: Down but Hardly Out."

28. Robert D. Hof, "The E-Bay Economy," *BusinessWeek* (August 25, 2003), 124+.

29. Raizel Robin, "Net Gains," *Canadian Business* (October 14–October 26, 2003), 107.

30. Eric Young, "Web Marketplaces That Really Work," *Fortune/CNET Tech Review* (Winter 2001), 78–86.

31. F. C. "Ted" Weston, Jr., "ERP II: The Extended Enterprise System," *Business Horizons* (November–December 2003), 49–55; and Vincent A. Mabert, Ashok Soni, and M. A. Venkataramanan, "Enterprise Resource Planning: Common Myths Versus Evolving Reality," *Business Horizons* (May–June 2001), 69–76.

32. Derek Slater, "What Is ERP?" *CIO* Enterprise (May 15, 1999), 86.

33. Susannah Patton, "Doctors' Group Profits From ERP," *CIO* (September 1, 2003), 32.

34. Brian Caulfield, "Facing Up to CRM," *Business 2.0* (August–September 2001), 149–150; and "Customer Relationship Management: The Good. The Bad. The Future." special advertising section, *BusinessWeek* (April 28, 2003), 53–64.

35. Alix Nyberg," "Buyer Be Aware," *CFO* (July 2003), 69–72.

36. Reported in Eric Seubert, Y. Balaji, and Mahesh Makhija, "The Knowledge Imperative," *CIO Advertising Supplement* (March 15, 2001), S1–S4.

37. Ryan K. Lahti and Michael M. Beyerlein, "Knowledge Transfer and Management Consulting: A Look at 'The Firm,'" *Business Horizons* (January–February 2000), 65–74.

38. "Business Intelligence," special advertising section, *Business 2.0* (February 2003), S1–S4; and Alice Dragoon, "Business Intelligence Gets Smart," *CIO* (September 15, 2003), 84–91.

39. Julie Schlosser, "Looking for Intelligence in Ice Cream," *Fortune* (March 17, 2003), 114–120.

40. Reported in Schlosser, "Looking for Intelligence in Ice Cream."

41. Kevin Kelleher, "66,207,896 Bottles of Beer on the Wall," *Business 2.0* (January–February 2004), 47–49.

42. Ibid.

43. Morten T. Hansen, Nitin Nohria, and Thomas Tierney, "What's Your Strategy for Managing Knowledge?" *Harvard Business Review* (March–April 1999), 106–116; Louisa Wah, "Behind the Buzz," *Management Review* (April 1999), 17–26; and Jenny C. McCune, "Thirst for Knowledge," *Management Review* (April, 1999), 10–12.

44. Seubert, Balaji, and Makhija, "The Knowledge Imperative."

45. Tony Kontzer with Melanie Turek, "Learning to Share," *Information Week* (May 5, 2003), 29–37.

46. "Mandate 2003: Be Agile and Efficient," *Microsoft Executive Circle* (Spring 2003), 46–48.

47. Anthony Scaturro, "All in the Family," *Inc. Technology* no. 1, (1998), 25–26.

48. Liz Thach and Richard W. Woodman, "Organizational Change and Information Technology: Managing on the Edge of Cyberspace," *Organizational Dynamics* (Summer 1994), 30–46; and Elizabeth Horwitt, "Going Deep: Empowering Employees," *Microsoft Executive Circle* (Summer 2003), 24–26.

49. Greg Jaffe, "Tug of War: In the New Military, Technology May Alter Chain of Command," *The Wall Street Journal* (March 30, 2001), A3, A6.

50. Tonya Vinas, "Surviving Information Overload," *Industry Week* (April 2003), 24–29.

51. Joseph McCafferty, "Coping with Infoglut," *CFO* (September 1998), 101–102.

52. Leonard M. Fuld, "The Danger of Data Slam," *CIO Enterprise*, Section 2 (September 15, 1998), 28–33.

53. Janine Adams, "Want a New Pet? Check the Web," *The Christian Science Monitor* (April 28, 2004), 11.

54. Michael A. Fontaine, Salvatore Parise, and David Miller, "Collaborative Environments: An Effective Tool for Transforming Business Processes," *Ivey Business Journal* (May–June 2004).

55. Ibid.

56. Matthew Boyle, "The Really Really Messy Wi-Fi Revolution," *Fortune* (May 12, 2003), 86–92.

57. Ibid.

58. Susannah Patton, "The Wisdom of Starting Small," *CIO* (March 15, 2001), 80–86.

59. Spencer E. Ante, et al., "In Search of the Net's Next Big Thing" *BusinessWeek* (March 26, 2001), 140–141; Amy Cortese, "Peer to Peer: P2P Taps the Power of Distant Computers in a Way that Could Transform Whole Industries," *The BusinessWeek 50*, Supplement to *BusinessWeek* (Spring 2001), 194–196.

60. Mark Roberti, "Peer-to-Peer Isn't Dead," *The Industry Standard* (April 23, 2001), 58–59.

61. This discussion is based on Jena McGregor, "It's a Blog World After All," *Fast Company* (April 2004), 84–86.

62. Tony Kontzer, "Kitchen Sink: Many Collaborative Options," *Information Week* (May 5, 2003), 35; sidebar in Kontzer, "Learning to Share."

63. This discussion is based on Mauro F. Guillén, "What Is the Best Global Strategy for the Internet?" *Business Horizons* (May–June 2002), 39–46; and Bob Tedeschi, "American Web Sites Speak the Language of Overseas Users," *The New York Times* (January 12, 2004), http://www.nytimes.com

64. Parks, "Let's Remake a Dealership"; Brown, "Savvy Buyers Might Appreciate the Smart Approach"; and Olsen, "Mazda to Unveil New Prototype in Bountiful."

# Chapter 16

# Operations and Service Management

## LEARNING OBJECTIVES

*After studying this chapter, you should be able to*

1. Define *operations management* and describe its application within manufacturing and service organizations.

2. Discuss the role of operations management strategy in the company's overall competitive strategy.

3. Explain the role of e-business in today's partnership approach to supply chain management.

4. Summarize considerations in designing an operations system, including product and service design, facilities layout, and capacity planning.

5. Explain why small inventories are preferred by most organizations.

6. Discuss major techniques for the management of materials and inventory.

7. Describe what is meant by lean manufacturing.

8. Define productivity and explain why and how managers seek to improve it.

When Donal L. Robb arrived as vice president and plant manager for R. R. Donnelley's Roanoke, Virginia, printing facility, Donnelley was struggling. It had just closed five plants and laid off 3,000 employees from a total workforce of 34,000. Things weren't so bright at the Roanoke plant either. Print orders were slow, productivity was lagging, and morale was low. Uncertainty about the future and dissatisfaction with nighttime shift work had pushed employee turnover to 25 percent a year. Robb and other Donnelley top managers first reassured people that the company intended to keep the Roanoke facility open. Then, they began looking for ways to increase productivity, lower costs, and build customer satisfaction. In talking with customers, Robb has learned that the biggest problem of publishers is that they either have too much stock or none at all. The printing industry in general has lagged years behind other industries in adopting new manufacturing technology. Robb wonders if there is a way to apply new technology and management methods to meet his three primary goals of increasing productivity, lowering costs, and better serving the needs of publishers.[1]

## Take A Moment

If you were in Donal Robb's position, how would you go about improving productivity at the Roanoke plant and addressing the concerns of customers by providing the books they need when they need them? Do you think new technology is the answer to Donnelley's problems in Roanoke?

Like R. R. Donnelley, many companies with successful products have found themselves with out-of-date, inefficient operations systems that contribute to performance problems. Strategic success depends on efficient operations. Operational concerns such as updating production technology, obtaining parts and supplies, and implementing efficient delivery systems take on even greater importance in today's competitive environment where consumers often want customized products and services delivered immediately. Production costs are a major expense for organizations, especially for manufacturers. Organizations therefore try to limit costs and increase quality by improving how they obtain materials, set up production facilities, and produce goods and services. Likewise, companies are seeking a strategic advantage in the ways they deliver products and services to consumers.

In the manufacturing sector, the efficiency of Toyota's automobile production is legendary. Computer manufacturer Dell won the PC wars and is rapidly taking over in other areas by pioneering an end-to-end supply chain that integrates every step from suppliers of raw materials to end customers. But service organizations have to be concerned with productivity and efficiency as well. Wal-Mart's emergence as a retail giant is largely due to the company's use of sophisticated electronics to run a huge supply and distribution network that enables the company to keep costs and prices at rock bottom. FedEx succeeds by applying operations strategy and techniques to move more than 5 million packages a day. Manufacturing and service operations such as these are important because they signify the company's basic purpose—indeed, its reason for existence. Without the ability to produce products and services that are competitive in the global marketplace, companies cannot expect to succeed.

This chapter describes techniques for the planning and control of manufacturing and service operations. Whereas the two preceding chapters described overall control concepts, including management information systems, this chapter will focus on the management and control of production operations. First we define operations management. Then we look at how some companies bring operations into strategic decision making and provide an overview of the integrated enterprise, in which managers use electronic linkages to manage interrelated operations activities. Next, we consider specific operational design issues, such as product and service design, procurement, location planning and facilities layout, production technology, and capacity planning. We give special attention to inventory management, including a discussion of just-in-time inventory systems and logistics. Finally, we look at how managers measure and improve productivity.

# Organizations as Production Systems

**technical core**
The heart of the organization's production of its product or service.

In Chapter 1, the organization was described as a system used for transforming inputs into outputs. At the center of this transformation process is the **technical core**, which is the heart of the organization's production of its product or service.[2] In an automobile company, the technical core includes the plants that manufacture automobiles. In a university, the technical core includes the academic activities of teaching and research. Inputs into the technical core include human resources, land, equipment, buildings, and technology. Outputs from the technical core include the goods and services that are provided for customers and clients. Operations strategy and control feedback shape the quality of outputs and the efficiency of operations within the technical core.

**operations management**
The field of management that focuses on the physical production of goods or services and uses specialized techniques for solving manufacturing problems.

The topic of operations management pertains to the day-to-day management of the technical core, as illustrated in Exhibit 16.1. **Operations management** is formally defined as the field of management that specializes in the production of goods and services and uses special tools and techniques for solving production problems.

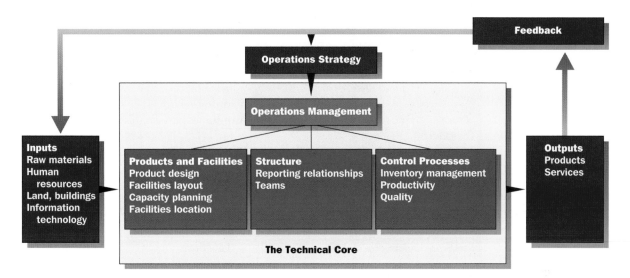

Exhibit 16.1

**The Organization as an Operations Management System**

In essence, operations managers are concerned with all the activities involved in the conversion of inputs into outputs. This includes decisions about where to locate facilities and what equipment to install in them.

However, as with all areas of management, operations management also requires the ability to lead people. For example, Toyota's operations are admired worldwide as a model of quality and efficiency, but this success is not merely a result of using the right machines or setting the right standards. U.S. automakers have had difficulty duplicating Toyota's success with *lean manufacturing* because they have focused primarily on the technical elements of the system and failed to implement the necessary cultural and leadership changes.[3] Toyota's system combines techniques, systems, and philosophy, such as commitment to employee empowerment and a creative culture. Besides installing the methodology for running an efficient assembly line, such as *just-in-time* shipments of supplies, managers must instill the necessary attitudes, such as concern for quality and a desire to innovate.

## Manufacturing and Service Operations

Although terms such as *production* and *operations* seem to imply manufacturing organizations, operations management applies to all organizations. The service sector has increased three times as fast as the manufacturing sector in the North American economy. Today more than one-half of all businesses are service organizations and two-thirds of the U.S. workforce is employed in services, such as hospitals, hotels and resorts, financial services, or telecommunications firms. Operations management tools and techniques apply to services as well as manufacturing. Exhibit 16.2 shows differences between manufacturing and service organizations.

**Manufacturing organizations** are those that produce physical goods, such as cars, books, computers, or tennis balls. In contrast, **service organizations** produce nonphysical outputs, such as medical, educational, communication, or transportation services provided for customers. Doctors, consultants, online auction companies, and the local barber all provide services. Services also include the sale of merchandise. Although merchandise is a physical good, the service company does not manufacture it but merely sells it as a service to the customer.

**manufacturing organization**
An organization that produces physical goods.

**service organization**
An organization that produces nonphysical outputs that require customer involvement and cannot be stored in inventory.

Exhibit 16.2

## Differences between Manufacturing and Service Organizations

| Manufacturing Organizations | Service Organizations |
| --- | --- |
| Produce physical goods | Produce nonphysical outputs |
| Goods inventoried for later consumption | Simultaneous production and consumption |
| Quality measured directly | Quality perceived and difficult to measure |
| Standardized output | Customized output |
| Production process removed from consumer | Consumer participates in production process |
| Facilities site moderately important to business success | Facilities site crucial to success of firm |
| Capital intensive | Labor intensive |
| *Examples:* | *Examples:* |
|     Automobile manufacturers |     Airlines |
|     Steel companies |     Hotels |
|     Soft-drink companies |     Law firms |

SOURCE: Based on Richard L. Daft, *Organization Theory and Design* (Cincinnati, Ohio: South-Western, 2005), 256; and Byron J. Finch and Richard L. Luebbe, *Operations Management* (Fort Worth, Texas: The Dryden Press, 1995), 50.

Services differ from manufactured products in two ways. First, the service customer is involved in the actual production process.[4] The patient actually visits the doctor to receive the service, and it's difficult to imagine a hairstylist providing services without direct customer contact. The same is true for airlines, restaurants, and banks. Second, manufactured goods can be placed in inventory, whereas service outputs, being intangible, cannot be stored. Manufactured products such as clothes, food, cars, and DVD players all can be put in warehouses and sold at a later date. However, a hairstylist cannot wash, cut, and style hair in advance and leave it on the shelf for the customer's arrival, nor can a doctor place examinations in inventory. The service must be created and provided for the customer exactly when he or she wants it.

Despite the differences between manufacturing and service firms, they face similar operational problems. First, each kind of organization needs to be concerned with scheduling. A medical clinic must schedule appointments so that doctors' and patients' time will be used efficiently. Second, both manufacturing and service organizations must obtain materials and supplies. Third, both types of organizations should be concerned with quality and productivity. Because many operational problems are similar, operations management tools and techniques can and should be applied to service organizations as readily as they are to manufacturing operations.

## Operations Strategy

Many operations managers are involved in day-to-day problem solving and lose sight of the fact that the best way to control operations is through strategic planning. The more operations managers become enmeshed in operational details, the less likely they are to see the big picture with respect to inventory buildups, parts shortages, and seasonal fluctuations. To manage operations effectively, managers must understand operations strategy.

**operations strategy**
The recognition of the importance of operations to the firm's success and the involvement of operations managers in the organization's strategic planning.

Operations strategy is the recognition of the important role of operations in organizational success and the involvement of operations managers in the organization's strategic planning. Superior operations effectiveness can support existing strategy and contribute to new strategic directions that can be difficult for competitors to copy.[5] When an organization's operations effectiveness is based on capabilities that are ingrained in its employees, its culture, and its operating processes, the company can be tough to beat.[6]

Exhibit 16.3 illustrates four stages in the evolution of operations strategy. Many companies are at Stage 1, in which business strategy is set without considering the capability of operations. The operations department is concerned only with labor costs and operational efficiency. For example, a major electronics instrument producer experienced a serious mismatch between strategy and the ability of operations to manufacture products. Because of fast-paced technological changes, the company was changing its products and developing new ones. The manufacturer had installed a materials-handling system in the operations department that was efficient, but it could not handle change of this magnitude. Operations managers were blamed for the company's failure to achieve strategic goals even though the operations department's capacity had never been considered during strategy formulation.

At Stage 2, the operations department sets goals according to industry practice. The organization tries to be current with respect to operations management techniques and views capital investment in plant and equipment, quality control, or inventory management as ways to be competitive.

At Stage 3, operations managers are more strategically active. Operations strategy is in concert with company strategy, and the operations department will seek new operational techniques and technologies to enhance competitiveness. For example, computer-based business operating systems and work flow automation help employees coordinate activities across functional and geographical boundaries and pinpoint bottlenecks or outdated procedures that slow production and increase costs.

At the highest level of operations strategy, Stage 4, operations managers may pursue new technologies on their own in order to do the best possible job of delivering the product or service. At Stage 4, operations can be a genuine competitive weapon.[7] Operations departments develop new strategic concepts themselves. With the use of new technologies, operations management becomes a major force in overall company strategic planning. Operations can originate new products and processes that will add to or change company strategy.

Exhibit 16.3

**Four Stages of Operations Strategy**

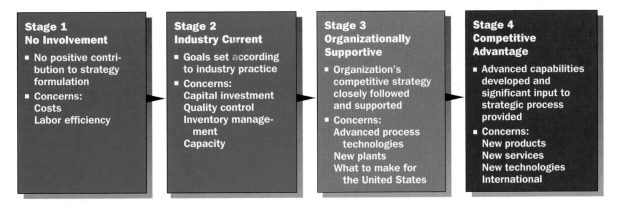

**SOURCE:** Based on R.H. Haynes and S.C Wheelwright, *Restoring Our Competitive Edge: Competing through Manufacturing* (New York: Wiley, 1984).

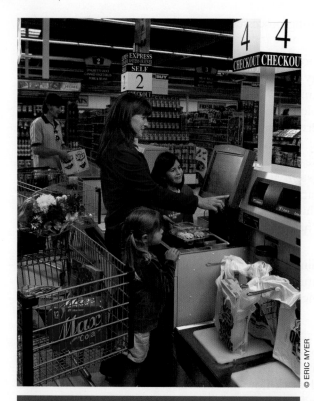

© ERIC MYER

## CONCEPT CONNECTION

*Albertson's Corporation is at **Stage 4 of operations strategy**, moving aggressively to apply leading-edge service technology to streamline operations "from factory to shelf and from field to mouth." Albertson's is an industry leader in building an **integrated supply chain** that can transmit real-time information about purchasing choices to manufacturers and distributors, enabling speed, efficiency, and flexibility to the changing needs and desires of customers. In-store systems such as self-service checkout lanes, shown in the photo, cut operating costs as well as maximize customer's shopping efficiency.*

**supply chain management**
Managing the sequence of suppliers and purchasers, covering all stages of processing from obtaining raw materials to distributing finished goods to final consumers.

A company that operates at Stage 3 or 4 will be more competitive than those that rely on marketing and financial strategies because customer orders are won through better price, quality, performance, delivery, or responsiveness to customer demand, and all these factors are affected by operations. UPS provides a good example of a company at Stage 4 of operations strategy. Operational efficiency is at the heart of UPS's business. Top operations managers recently proposed cutting one day from the average delivery time for ground packages to major metropolitan areas to fend off increased competition from FedEx and Germany's DHL Worldwide Express. The company is using new package-handling equipment, changes in package-sorting and deadlines, and a streamlined logistics system to make one of the most significant changes in UPS's 96-year history.[8]

## The Integrated Enterprise

As operations managers adopt a strategic approach, they appreciate that their operations are not independent of other activities. To operate efficiently and produce high-quality items that meet customers' needs, the organization must have reliable deliveries of high-quality, reasonably priced supplies and materials. It also requires an efficient and reliable system for distributing finished products, making them readily accessible to customers. Operations managers with a strategic focus therefore recognize that they need to manage the entire supply chain. **Supply chain management** is the term for managing the sequence of suppliers and purchasers covering all stages of processing from obtaining raw materials to distributing finished goods to final consumers.[9]

The most recent advances in supply chain management involve using Internet technologies to achieve the right balance of low inventory levels and customer responsiveness. An e-supply chain creates a seamless, integrated line that stretches from customers to suppliers, as illustrated in Exhibit 16.4, by establishing electronic linkages between the organization and these external partners for the sharing and exchange of data.[10] For example, in the exhibit, as consumers purchase products in retail stores, the data are automatically fed into the retail chain's information system via an intranet, as described in the previous chapter. In turn, the retail chain gives access to this constantly updated data to the manufacturing company through a secure extranet link. With knowledge of this demand data, the manufacturer can produce and ship the correct products when needed. As products are made, data about raw materials used in the production process, updated inventory information, and updated forecasted demand are electronically provided to the manufacturer's suppliers via an extranet, and the suppliers automatically replenish the manufacturer's raw materials inventory as needed. The integration of IBM's massive supply chains provides an illustration.

**IBM**
http://www.ibm.com

Robert W. Moffat, Jr., who runs IBM's Integrated Supply Chain division, believes the future of competition will be a battle among supply chains. In the past, every IBM division operated its own supply chain, but new CEO Sam Palmisano has asked Moffat to smash those individual systems and create a single integrated chain to handle procurement, manufacturing, logistics, and delivery across the entire corporation. It is a daunting task—IBM runs 16 manufacturing plants in 10 countries, buys materials from 33,000

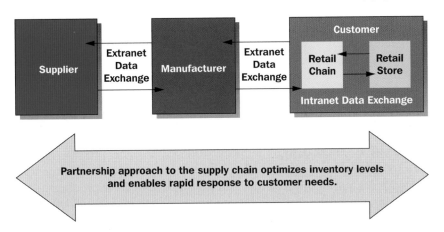

Exhibit 16.4

**The E-Supply Chain**

Partnership approach to the supply chain optimizes inventory levels and enables rapid response to customer needs.

**SOURCE:** Based on Jim Turcotte, Bob Silveri, and Tom Jobson, "Are You Ready for the E-Supply Chain?" *APICS–The Performance Advantage* (August 1998), 56–59.

suppliers, offers products available in 3 million possible variations, processes 1.7 million customer orders a year, and keeps 6.5 million records.

Moffat has made impressive steps toward a fully integrated supply chain, and in the process slashed about $3 billion in annual costs. He has centralized the procurement of supplies and cut the number of suppliers the firm uses. Products are being redesigned to use more common parts, and some manufacturing is being outsourced to lower-cost manufacturers. The suppliers IBM uses most are linked into an electronic procurement system.

Next comes the really hard work of linking everyone into a single system so that 90 percent of orders can be processed, built, shipped, and billed without any human interference. Everything will be handled electronically. Here's how Moffat sees the system working: Whenever a customer orders an IBM Thinkpad, for example, the order will flow automatically to the IBM plant in Shenzhen, China, where the product is manufactured. The laptop will be built and shipped the next day, while 60 or so suppliers will already be shipping parts to replenish the factory's depleted inventory.[11]

In a huge, complex, global organization such as IBM, building an integrated enterprise is a massive project. Operations experts, mathematicians, managers, and scientists are laying the groundwork. "What makes Dell and Wal-Mart successful?" asks IBM's Moffat. "It's the business model, and the supply chain is an enabler. . . . People realize this is the weapon of the future."[12]

At IBM, as at all companies, an important aspect of supply chain management is managing relationships with suppliers.[13] Today, IBM concentrates 80 percent of its spending on just 2 percent of its suppliers, allowing the company to build and maintain close, collaborative relationships. Enterprise integration through the use of electronic linkages can create a level of cooperation not previously imaginable. Many supplier relationships used to be based on an *arm's-length* approach, in which an organization spreads purchases among many suppliers and encourages them to compete with one another. With integration, more companies are opting for a *partnership* approach, which involves cultivating intimate relationships with a few carefully selected suppliers and collaborating closely to coordinate tasks that benefit both parties.

Electronic linkages also contribute to more rapid response to the end consumers by reducing the time it takes to move critical data through the information pipeline. Manufacturers have immediate access to sales data and can deliver new products as needed. In addition, electronic linkages enable the rapid manufacture of customized products. Ford Motor Company is currently involved in a supply-chain makeover intended to enable the company to manufacture cars on a reasonable build-to-order basis, so that customers no longer have to wait months for delivery of the car of their dreams.[14]

By integrating everyone along the entire supply chain, the idea is that every organization involved can move in lock-step to meet the customer's product and time demands.

# Designing Operations Management Systems

Every organization must design its production system. This process starts with the design of the product or service to be produced. A restaurant designs the food items on the menu. An automobile manufacturer designs the cars it produces. A management consulting firm designs the various types of services it will offer to clients. Other considerations in designing the production system include purchasing raw materials, layout of facilities, designing production technology, facilities location, and capacity planning.

## Product and Service Design

The way a product or service is designed affects its appeal for customers; it also affects how easy or expensive operations will be. Design has become a critical aspect of product development for many companies, even old-line manufacturers of products such as appliances and tools. Whirlpool's Duet line of washers and dryers, with soft curves and splashes of color, captured 19 percent of the front-loading washer market in only two years. MasterLock now changes the designs of its padlocks every year. Today, customers often think how a product looks is just as important as how it works.[15]

However, some product designs are difficult to execute properly. When Volant began making an unconventional type of skis from steel, skiers began snapping them up, delighted with their flexibility and tight grip of the snow. However, producing the skis turned out to be a nightmare, and many pairs had to be scrapped or reworked. Expenses mounted, and the company failed to meet promised delivery dates. Eventually, Volant hired Mark Soderberg, an engineer with experience at Boeing. Soderberg made a small design change that allowed more generous manufacturing tolerances (variances from the design specifications). After the tooling was adjusted to accommodate the design change, Volant began producing the modified skis—and forecast its first year of operating in the black.[16]

To prevent such problems in the first place, a growing number of businesses are using *design for manufacturability and assembly* (DFMA). In the past, many engineering designers fashioned products with disdain for how they would be produced. Elegant designs nearly always had too many parts. The watchword today is simplicity, making the product easy and inexpensive to manufacture.

Using DFMA is extremely inexpensive, but it does require a shift in how design work is done. DFMA often requires restructuring operations, creating teams of designers, manufacturers, and assemblers to work together. They collaborate on achieving four objectives of product design:

1. *Producibility.* The degree to which a product or service can actually be produced for the customer within the firm's existing operational capacity.
2. *Cost.* The sum of the materials, labor, design, transportation, and overhead expense associated with a product or service. Striving for simplicity and few parts keeps product and service designs within reasonable costs.

3. *Quality.* The excellence of the product or service—the serviceability and value that customers gain by purchasing the product. Companies are taking the time to ask questions such as "How do people use this product?" and "How can we make this product more user friendly?"
4. *Reliability.* The degree to which the customer can count on the product or service to fulfill its intended function. The product should function as designed for a reasonable length of time. Highly complex products often have lower reliability because more things can go wrong.

***Go to the ethical dilemma on page 606 that pertains to product design.***

*Take A Moment*

Ford Motor Company is taking such criteria into account in its new product development process.[17] Previously, Ford's development process was build around five teams organized by vehicle type. Each team had its own budget and often created its own highly unique body frames, suspensions, brakes, engines, and transmissions. Now, teams are based on the vehicle's basic "platform," and the goal is to share parts, systems, and engineering across all vehicles. Teams have access to information from finance, engineering, purchasing, manufacturing, and so on, so that car-development teams think in terms of cost, producibility, required resources, and quality, as well as design innovation and artistry, avoiding problems down the line.[18]

The design of services also should reflect producibility, cost, quality, and reliability. However, services have one additional design requirement: timing. *Timing* is the degree to which the provision of a service meets the customer's delivery requirements. Recall that a service cannot be stored in inventory and must be provided when the customer is present. Banking by machine, pumping your own gas, and trying on your own shoes are all ways that organizations provide timely service, which is important in today's time-pressured world. Some service firms, including banks, medical centers, and retailers, have worked with cutting-edge design firm IDEO to help them design better consumer experiences. The firm helped Warnaco, for example, design a new, customer-friendly approach to selling lingerie in department stores to combat the stiff competition from private shops.[19]

## Procurement

The purchasing of supplies, services, and raw materials for use in the production process, known as **procurement**, has increased in importance as an operations issue. On average, a manufacturing company spends 50 to 60 percent of its revenues to buy materials and supplies. For example, auto manufacturers spend about 60 percent of revenues on material purchases, food processors about 70 percent, and oil refineries about 80 percent, and the percentages keep going up.[20] Expenses for materials, supplies, and services also represent a huge expense for service companies. Having the right materials of the correct design and quality is essential to the smooth functioning of the production process.

**procurement**
Purchasing supplies, services, and raw materials for use in the production process.

The Internet and business-to-business (B2B) commerce are having a tremendous impact on procurement. Purchasing department employees can now use the Internet to search for new sources of materials, place orders, request bids via B2B marketplaces, and participate in online auctions. Employees have quick access to more information about availability and cost. They can often submit purchase orders online and track the status of orders over the Web, cutting down on operating costs and speeding up the procurement lead time.[21] For example, by eliminating purchase orders and moving procurement online where employees ordered from suppliers that offered the company a discount, DuPont cut procurement costs by $200 million in one recent year. In addition, the typical order is now processed in one day instead of five.[22] Verizon Wireless hopes to shave 5 to 10 percent off the $150 million it spends on procurement of temporary contract workers each year by using competitive bidding and contract management over the Internet.[23] Whether they're looking for paper clips, jet engines, or consultants, more and more companies are using the Internet to control and streamline the procurement process.

Burlington Northern Santa Fe Railway set up an online procurement system for supplies as a first step toward a fully Web-enabled supply chain. Employees are required to make all purchases—from pencils to computers—over the Web, where they can be easily tracked. The goal, according to vice president and chief sourcing officer for BNSF, Jeff Campbell, was to eliminate *maverick spends*—random purchases made by employees at local office supply stores. The maverick spend makes it practically impossible for procurement departments to track costs or budget and forecast accurately. Purchase orders are now submitted online, with automated approval based on certain criteria, eliminating the time-sapping manual approval process. Campbell estimates that online procurement saves 3 percent to 8 percent on all the various purchases made, because of the opportunity to negotiate discounts by purchasing in volume from a few suppliers.[24]

## Facilities Layout

Once a product or service has been designed and systems set up for procurement of materials, the next consideration is planning for the actual production through facilities layout. The four most common types of layout are process, product, cellular, and fixed-position, shown in Exhibit 16.5.

### Process Layout

**process layout**
A facilities layout in which machines that perform the same function are grouped together in one location.

As illustrated in Exhibit 16.5(a), a **process layout** is one in which all machines that perform a similar function or task are grouped together. In a machine shop, the lathes perform a similar function and are located together in one section. The grinders are in another section of the shop. Service organizations also use process layouts. In a bank, the loan officers are in one area, the tellers in another, and the managers in a third.

The advantage of the process layout is that it has the potential for economies of scale and reduced costs. For example, having all painting done in one spray-painting area means that fewer machines and people are required to paint all products for the organization. In a bank, having all tellers located in one controlled area provides increased security. Placing all operating rooms together in a hospital makes it possible to control the environment for all rooms simultaneously.

The drawback to the process layout, as illustrated in Exhibit 16.5(a), is that the actual path a product or service takes can be long and complicated. A product may need several different processes performed on it and thus must travel through many different areas before production is complete.

### Product Layout

**product layout**
A facilities layout in which machines and tasks are arranged according to the sequence of steps in the production of a single product.

Exhibit 16.5(b) illustrates a **product layout**—one in which machines and tasks are arranged according to the progressive steps in producing a single product. The automobile assembly line is a classic example, because it produces a single product starting from the raw materials to the finished output. Many fast-food restaurants use the product layout, with activities arranged in sequence to produce hamburgers or fried chicken, depending on the products available.

The product layout is efficient when the organization produces huge volumes of identical products. Note in Exhibit 16.5(b) that two lines have paint areas. This duplication of functions can be economical only if the volume is high enough to keep each paint area busy working on specialized products.

Exhibit 16.5

## Basic Production Layouts

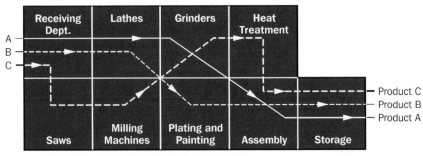

**(a) Process Layout**

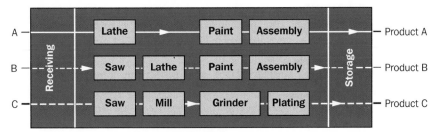

**(b) Product Layout**

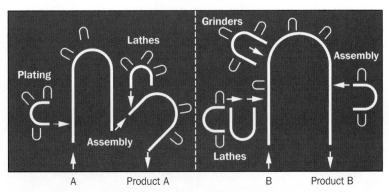

**(c) Cellular Layout**

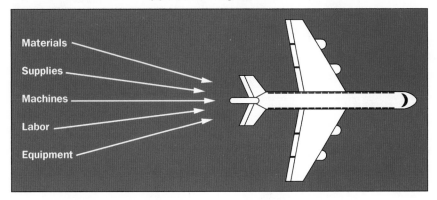

**(d) Fixed-Position Layout**

**SOURCES**: Based on J.T. Black, "Cellular Manufacturing Systems Reduce Setup Time, Make Small Lot Production Economical," *Industrial Engineering* (November 1983), 36–48; and Richard J. Schonberger, "Plant Layout Becomes Product-Oriented with Cellular, Just-in-Time Production Concepts," *Industrial Engineering* (November 1983), 66–77.

**cellular layout**
A facilities layout in which machines dedicated to sequences of production are grouped into cells in accordance with group-technology principles.

## Cellular Layout

Illustrated in Exhibit 16.5(c) is an innovative layout, called **cellular layout**, based on group-technology principles. In a manufacturing plant, all machines dedicated to sequences of operations are grouped into cells, as shown in the exhibit. In a service organization, all the people who work on a process, such as insurance claims processing, are organized into cells where they can see and easily communicate with one another. Work flows from one station to another, similar to materials movement in the manufacturing plant.[25] Grouping technology into cells provides some of the efficiencies of both process and product layouts. Even more important, the U-shaped cells in Exhibit 16.5(c) provide efficiencies in material and tool handling and inventory movement. Employees work in clusters that facilitate teamwork and joint problem solving. Staffing flexibility is enhanced because people are cross-trained so that each worker can perform all the tasks, assisting co-workers as needed.

**fixed-position layout**
A facilities layout in which the product remains in one location and the required tasks and equipment are brought to it.

## Fixed-Position Layout

As shown in Exhibit 16.5(d), the **fixed-position layout** is one in which the product remains in one location, and employees and equipment are brought to it. The fixed-position layout is used to create a product or service that is either very large or is one of a kind, such as aircraft, ships, and buildings. The product cannot be moved from function to function or along an assembly line; rather, the people, materials, and machines all come to the fixed-position site for assembly and processing. This layout is not good for high volume, but it is necessary for large, bulky products and custom orders.

As the need for speed and responsiveness has increased, some organizations have been designing facilities layout to allow for a high level of flexibility. This chapter's Shoptalk offers some tips from a German factory that is on the cutting edge of a new way of working.

### CONCEPT CONNECTION

*Last year, Boeing Corporation reported $50 billion in revenues from its commercial aircraft and growing defense businesses. Products such as Apache helicopters and Boeing 737s (shown in the photo) are too large and cumbersome to move along a traditional assembly line. Boeing typically uses a **fixed position layout**, where the product remains in one location and employees, components, and equipment are brought to it for assembly. However, to increase speed and flexibility, Boeing has also implemented a system whereby a huge 737, after the wings and landing gear are attached, is dragged toward the door at two inches a minute, with assembly workers moving along with it on a float-like apparatus. Boeing's **productivity goal** is to push a 737 out the door in only five days.*

# manager's Shoptalk

## Turbulent Times

### A German Factory Shows How to Be Fast and Flexible

Many students might think a factory that makes polymer bearings and power-supply chains is not the best place to get a view of the factory of the future, but they'd be wrong. Cologne, Germany's igus Inc. manufacturing plant represents a highly innovative approach to facilities design. The plant's flexible design enables the factory to shrink or expand at a moment's notice, keeping pace with an unpredictable market. Almost nothing is bolted down on the plant floor, so that machines, modules, and entire departments can be rearranged. Other design features, such as exposed overhead wiring and few support columns, mean the company can redesign itself as needed with little disruption to the 24-7 production flow. Over the past five years, igus has made at least 50 significant changes to the factory's configuration to accommodate strategic shifts, facilitate fast growth, or meet new customer needs.

Fast, agile organizations do not occur on their own. Managers have to make decisions that include considering the physical as well as the human environment. Frank Blase, president of igus, offers the following tips for building a nimble organization:

1. *Create a flexible environment.* A plant's space, facilities design, and layout should accommodate the business, not the other way around.

2. *Recruit carefully.* Not everyone is comfortable working in a highly flexible, fast-changing environment. Human resource managers should screen job candidates carefully and make sure they understand the nature of the workplace. At igus, candidates are given a *schnuppertag*, or sniffing-around day, to explore, observe, and ask questions.

3. *Practice being fast.* Every aspect of the company should be designed to encourage speed and agility. All igus employees are equipped with mobile phones and get around on shiny, motorized scooters. An open physical environment encourages collaboration and information transparency. Department teams conduct quick daily huddles to review what went well and what didn't the day before.

4. *Inspire your staff.* This last tip may be the most important of all. Flexibility hinges on innovation and creativity, Blase says, which depends on employees who are inspired to think differently and express their ideas and opinions. "We're trying to be a different kind of company," he adds, "and our building helps us tremendously in doing that. It creates a holistic system for how to behave."

SOURCE: Chuck Salter, "This is One Fast Factory," *Fast Company* (August 2001), 32–33.

## Technology Automation

One goal of many operations managers is to implement more sophisticated technologies for producing products and services. Extremely advanced systems that can work almost unaided by employees are being designed.

## Service Technology

Services have seen tremendous growth in automation technologies in recent years. Restaurant kitchen managers can use computer programs to calculate the exact cost and ingredient needs for each menu item, from building a cheeseburger to putting together a seafood buffet, instead of having to perform arduous and time-consuming manual calculations. In the banking industry, automatic teller machines (ATMs) and telephone and online banking allow customers to obtain a wide range of banking services at any time of day or night. Many gas stations now have pay-at-pump systems where customers insert a credit or debit card to pay for their gas without having to go inside the station. In the supermarket industry, self-service checkout technology is growing in use.

More complex technologies are also revolutionizing the service industry. The rage in retailing is *radio-frequency identification (RFID)*, a sort of high-tech barcode that is tucked inside a sticker on boxes of merchandise or individual products. The RFID tags emit signals that are read by electronic readers and provide precise, real-time information about the location of merchandise as it moves through the supply chain, from manufacture to checkout (and perhaps even beyond).[26] The biggest names in retail, including Wal-Mart, The Home Depot, Carrefour, and Tesco, are lined up to take advantage of the new technology. Yet, to allay growing concerns about the potential of RFID for compromising consumer privacy, most companies are using it just for backroom operations and distribution centers, not at the checkout. The potential of RFID for streamlining inventory management and cutting costs is enormous. Other service firms use RFID as well. New York's E-Z Pass and California's FasTrak both use RFID to speed cars through toll booths, for example.[27] The U.S. Department of Defense uses it to track some 400,000 items.[28]

Various types of advanced technology systems are continuously being integrated into today's service organizations to improve operations efficiency. Consider how Burlington Northern Santa Fe Railway is using advanced computer technology to reinvigorate the railroad business.

**BURLINGTON NORTHERN SANTA FE**

http://www.bnsf.com

Few people would think of the railroad industry as a technological marvel, but recent developments might change that. Burlington Northern, the nation's second-largest railroad, has been spending $100 million a year on new technologies for the past several years. Included in the long list of innovations are remote-controlled locomotives, wireless computers that control engine output for maximum efficiency and fuel conservation, satellite-based mapping, and sophisticated scheduling and trip-planning software.

The new technology is helping Burlington Northern and other railroads keep trains running on time, cut costs, and both combat and partner with rival trucking companies. For example, trains haul truck trailers long distances from one hub to another, where they're hooked back up to trucks and driven to their final destination. Thanks to new scheduling software, Burlington Northern feels confident enough about its ability to meet schedules that it can offer its trucking customers guaranteed arrival times. On-duty railroad crews once sat waiting for trains that were hours late, but no longer. The crew-dispatching center is run by 100 employees, rather than the 600 it once took, because every rail car is equipped with an RFID tag. Managers and employees can log onto the company Web site and track the progress of any train in the system.

Managers also keep track of performance data on every train. Every engine is hooked to a digital event recorder that monitors speed, power, throttle position, braking, and other performance metrics. The information is sent via WiFi to the network operations center (or NOC) where it is combed through to spot potential problems, reducing both costs and accidents. Also in the NOC, nine huge screens continuously track performance data for major customers like UPS and J. B. Hunt, as well as weather conditions, earthquake reports, and other data. According to Dale Demaree, an engineer foreman, technology "allows us to have the pulse of the railroad right there in that room."[29]

Although some engineers are a little uneasy about the loss of autonomy that advanced technology brings to rail service workers, most believe it saves both money and lives and might ultimately be the key to saving the railroad. The next two sections talk about the use of advanced technology in manufacturing companies. Two approaches that are revolutionizing manufacturing are flexible manufacturing systems and CAD/CAM.

## Flexible Manufacturing Systems

The use of automated production lines that can be quickly adapted to produce more than one kind of product is called a **flexible manufacturing system**.[30] The machinery uses sophisticated computer technology to coordinate and integrate the machines. Automated functions include loading, unloading, storing parts, changing tools, and machining. The computer can instruct the machines to change parts, machining, and tools when a new product must be produced. Human operators made adjustments to the computer, not the production machinery itself, dramatically cutting the time and expense of making changes. This is a breakthrough compared with the product layout, in which a single line is restricted to a single product. With a flexible manufacturing system, a single production line can be readily readapted to small batches of different products based on computer instructions. At the Nissan factory in Canton, Mississippi, for example, minivans, pickup trucks, and sport utility vehicles can all be sent down the same assembly line. Robotic arms on machines are programmed to weld in the spots needed for different vehicles. Highly automated painting machines are programmed to paint all kinds of vehicles one after another, with no down time for reconfiguration.[31]

COURTESY OF AMETEK, INC.

**CONCEPT CONNECTION**

*AMETEK is a leading manufacturer of electronic motors and electronic instruments in North America, Europe, and Asia. To achieve earnings per share growth from continuing operations, one of the company's strategies is "Operational Excellence." AMETEK states that a true test of Operational Excellence is taking the best and making it better. This was done at the AMETEK Lamb Electrical motor manufacturing plant in Racine, Wisconsin, which was redesigned to incorporate flow manufacturing techniques. The company's five-year growth strategy includes the expansion of its **flexible manufacturing systems** to achieve world-class manufacturing at all of its operations.*

## CAD/CAM

Operations management in most businesses today employs computers for the design of products, and often for their manufacture as well. **CAD** (computer-aided design) enables engineers to develop new-product designs in about half the time required with traditional methods. Computers provide a visual display for the engineer and illustrate the implications of any design change.

**CAM** (computer-aided manufacturing) uses computers to direct manufacturing processes, as in flexible manufacturing systems. Typically, the CAM system is linked to CAD, so that the product specifications drive the manufacturing specifications. The computer system thus guides and controls the manufacturing process. For example, a sportswear manufacturer can use computers to mechanize the entire sequence of manufacturing operations—pattern scaling, layout, and printing. Computer-controlled cutting tables are installed. Once the computer has mathematically defined the geometry, it guides the cutting blade, eliminating the need for paper patterns. Computer programs also can direct fabric requisitions, production orders for cutting and sewing operations, and sewing line work.

Advanced factories are using **product life-cycle management (PLM)** software, which manages a product from creation through development, manufacturing, testing, and even maintenance in the field. PLM can coordinate people and facilities around the world for the design, development, and manufacture of products as small as the roller skates produced by GID of Yorba Linda, California, or as large as Boeing's new 7E7 Dreamliner passenger jet. PLM connects design and development of new products to the design of tools, assembly lines, and even entire factories. In addition, it links employees to a digital repository of project data so that ideas and parts can be accessed and used efficiently.[32] The software can link well-known older programs, such as CAD/CAM, with newer tools that can perform tasks such as simulating an assembly line or an entire factory. The most efficient manufacturing layout can be created even as the product is being designed.

**flexible manufacturing system**
A small- or medium-sized automated production line that can be adapted to produce more than one product line.

**CAD**
A production technology in which computers perform new-product design.

**CAM**
A production technology in which computers help guide and control the manufacturing system.

**product life-cycle management**
Manufacturing software that manages a product from creation through development, manufacturing, testing, and even maintenance in the field.

Pratt & Whitney Canada has been using PLM software since 2002 and estimates that it saves $500,000 to $1 million on each new engine design. In addition, PLM has helped the company reduce scrap by 86 percent and cut rework by nearly 10 percent. Inventory turns jumped from 4 per year to 14 per year. One application of PLM at Pratt & Whitney Canada uses a visual computer-imaged manikin equipped with digital bones, joints, and ligaments to reach inside a 3-D computer image of an aircraft engine. Nicknamed George, the manikin tests to see whether a human repair person would encounter any obstructions in accessing parts of a real-life engine. If George cannot reach a part, his arm turns red, letting designers know that a change needs to be made. The 3-D design and development is also linked to manufacturing, so that manufacturing processes and machining are automatically programmed, telling production floor machines the right paths to take as they cut engine parts. PLM software is relatively new, and few factories have mastered the technology. Those that have, though, typically report profits that are 73 percent higher than other leading manufacturers.

## Facility Location

At some point, almost every organization must decide on the location of facilities. Commerce Bank needs to open a new branch office in central Ohio, Subway needs to find locations for the new restaurants it is opening every three hours in the United States, or Intel needs to find locations somewhere in the world for a new research facility and a new chip assembly and testing plant. When these decisions are made unwisely, they are expensive and troublesome for the organization.

The most common approach to selecting a site for a new location is to do a cost-benefit analysis. For example, managers at bank headquarters may identify four possible locations. The costs associated with each location are the land (purchase or lease); moving from the current facility; and construction, including zoning laws, building codes, land features, and size of the parking lot. Taxes, utilities, rents, and maintenance are other cost factors to be considered in advance. Each possible bank location also will have certain benefits. Benefits to be evaluated are accessibility of customers, location of major competitors, general quality of working conditions, and nearness to restaurants and shops, which would be desirable for both employees and customers. Once the bank managers have evaluated the worth of each benefit, they can divide total benefits by total costs for each location, then select the location with the highest ratio.

New location scouting software is helping managers turn facilities location from guesswork into a science. These programs use sophisticated number crunching tools, for example, to help fast food chains like Arby's determine the best areas for expansion. Location-scouting software is further described in this chapter's Unlocking Creative Solutions Through Technology box. However, most companies don't rely on technology alone, but also use human location scouts, who combine heaps of research with an eye for details and a honed instinct about where the business will succeed. Barbara Vinson is the top scout for Arbys, Inc.

Whenever a new franchisee for Arby's needs to locate a site, Barbara Vinson is likely to get a call. She's the top location scout for Arby's and travels about 15 days a month looking for locations.

Vinson blends technical mapping, demographic analysis, and personal observation to pick good new locations. When scouting for a new store, Vinson drives thousands of miles crisscrossing the same streets, watching traffic patterns, chatting up people in McDonald's and other competitors, and seeing where people spend their time during weekdays and weekends. She likes to locate near booming retail areas, especially Wal-Mart, because it generates traffic. However, for Arby's, which is trying to position itself as more upscale and

# Unlocking Creative Solutions Through Technology

## Retailers Use Mapping Software to Hit the Right Spot

In the early 2000s, Jo-Ann Stores, a fabric and craft retailer, was having great success with its 70 superstores. Top managers wanted to launch an expansion of the big-box concept, but they worried that the units might not make enough money to justify the expense of building them. Enter MapInfo, whose software predicted that the market would support as many as 700 superstores. The data analysis also showed that, rather than alienating loyal customers, the superstores simply got them to buy about 50 percent more.

In addition to helping companies determine whether to open stores, MapInfo's biggest benefit may be telling them the right spot to locate them. Consider The Home Depot. The company was itching to put a store in New York City, but wondered if it would work. After all, The Home Depot's best customers own large homes and yards to take care of—not the Big Apple's strong suit. When a site became available in Queens, managers didn't think the area could support a store, since it is less affluent than The Home Depot's usual

demographic, with small row houses and apartments. The company turned to MapInfo for guidance and learned that, according to data analysis, a Home Depot in Queens would do quite well. The data was right—since opening, the store has become one of The Home Depot's highest-volume outlets.

MapInfo was founded in 1986, but struggled in recent years until it got into the game of "predictive analysis," a technology that uses modeling techniques to anticipate consumer behavior. Since then, managers of retail organizations from fast food chains to clothing stores have used MapInfo for information that helps them make better decisions about where to locate stores, when to close underperforming outlets, and when expansion is cost-effective. MapInfo can predict not only which markets are best for expansion, but also how each new store will affect revenue across the entire chain.

For companies that live by the rule of "location, location, location," MapInfo can provide a tremendous advantage. As one securities analyst put it, "In an increasingly competitive world, companies take an edge wherever they can get it."

**SOURCE:** Amy Cortese, "Is Your Business in the Right Spot?" *Business 2.0* (May 2004), 76–77.

healthier than competing fast-food chains, finding the right *type* of neighborhood is important, too. Once, Vinson thought her preliminary research had pinpointed a good piece of real estate near a Sam's Club—until personal investigation revealed an all-you-can-eat pizza place nearby. Further investigation confirmed Vinson's hunch that the neighborhood was too poor for the Arby's store. Similarly, if one glance at the parking lot of a mall reveals a lot of Jaguars, Vinson moves on. "Too high end," she says. "I'm not going in."

Although Vinson appreciates the support of new analytical tools, she believes personal investigation and "gut instinct" play a big part in location selection as well. So far, her instincts are right on in picking good locations for restaurants. She picked hot spots for drive-in burger chain Sonic for years before being lured away by Arby's.[33]

Particularly for global corporations, selecting facility location is an important and complex consideration. When locating facilities in other countries, managers must take into account cost-based variables such as transportation, exchange rates, and cost of labor. In addition, the skill levels of potential workers, the development of regional infrastructure, a good quality of life, and a favorable business climate are important considerations in selecting a location overseas. For high-tech firms, proximity to world-class research institutions and access to venture capital are also essential criteria.[34]

## Capacity Planning

**Capacity planning** is the determination and adjustment of an organization's ability to produce products or services to match demand. For example, if an automaker anticipates a 15 percent increase in sales over the next year, capacity planning is the procedure whereby it will ensure that it has sufficient capacity to service that demand.

**capacity planning**
The determination and adjustment of the organization's ability to produce products and services to match customer demand.

*Harley-Davidson Motor Company is using **capacity planning** to keep pace with the growing, worldwide demand for its high-quality motorcycles. As the only major American-based motorcycle, Harley-Davidson has brand names that are among the best known in the industry. All three of the company's manufacturing facilities have been extensively redesigned and reconfigured to improve productivity, workflow, product quality, and the environment. Facilities such as this touring motorcycle assembly line in York, Pennsylvania, have put Harley-Davidson a full year ahead in its production schedule, and the company plans to have the capacity to produce 115,000 units a year.*

Organizations can do several things to increase capacity. One is to create additional shifts and hire people to work on them. A second is to ask existing people to work overtime to add to capacity. A third is to outsource or subcontract extra work to other firms. A fourth is to expand a plant and add more equipment. Each of these techniques will increase the organization's ability to meet demand without risk of major excess capacity.

The biggest problem for most organizations, however, is excess capacity. When misjudgments occur, transportation companies have oil tankers sitting empty in the harbor, oil companies have refineries sitting idle, semiconductor companies have plants shuttered, developers have office buildings half full, and the service industry may have hotels or amusement parks operating at partial capacity. Consider movie theater chains, which have grossly overbuilt in recent years, more than doubling the number of screens in the United States in a 20-year period. Some theaters show films to only one or two people at a time because of excess capacity.[35] The challenge is for managers to add capacity as needed without excess. For many of today's companies, the solution is contracting work out to other organizations. Outsourcing and new organizational forms such as the virtual network organization described in Chapter 10 enable companies to quickly ramp up production to increase capacity and dissolve partnerships when extra help is no longer needed.

# Inventory Management

**inventory**
The goods that the organization keeps on hand for use in the production process up to the point of selling the final products to customers.

**finished-goods inventory**
Inventory consisting of items that have passed through the complete production process but have yet to be sold.

**work-in-process inventory**
Inventory composed of the materials that still are moving through the stages of the production process.

A large portion of the operations manager's job consists of inventory management. Inventory is the goods the organization keeps on hand for use in the production process. Most organizations have three types of inventory: finished goods prior to shipment, work in process, and raw materials.

**Finished-goods inventory** includes items that have passed through the entire production process but have not been sold. This is highly visible inventory. The new cars parked in the storage lot of an automobile factory are finished-goods inventory, as are the hamburgers and french fries stacked under the heat lamps at a McDonald's restaurant. Finished-goods inventory is expensive, because the organization has invested labor and other costs to make the finished product.

**Work-in-process inventory** includes the materials moving through the stages of the production process that are not completed products. Work-in-process inventory in an automobile plant includes engines, wheel and tire assemblies, and dashboards waiting to be installed. In a fast-food restaurant, the french fries in the fryer and hamburgers on the grill are work-in-process inventory.

Raw materials inventory includes the basic inputs to the organization's production process. This inventory is cheapest, because the organization has not yet invested labor in it. Steel, wire, glass, and paint are raw materials inventory for an auto plant. Meat patties, buns, and raw potatoes are the raw materials inventory in a fast-food restaurant.

**raw materials inventory**
Inventory consisting of the basic inputs to the organization's production process.

## The Importance of Inventory

Inventory management is vitally important to organizations, because inventory sitting idly on the shop floor or in the warehouse costs money. Many years ago, a firm's wealth was measured by its inventory. Today inventory is recognized as an unproductive asset in cost-conscious firms. Dollars not tied up in inventory can be used in other productive ventures. Keeping inventory low is especially important for high-tech firms, because so many of their products lose value quickly, as they are replaced by more innovative and lower-cost models. For example, the value of a completed personal computer falls rapidly; even if shelf space for PCs were free, a company would lose money on its PC inventory.[36]

Managers at retail giants such as Wal-Mart, Toys 'R' Us, The Home Depot, and Best Buy understand that efficient inventory management is essential to their ability to keep prices low and attract more customers. State-of-the-art, integrated e-business systems, including the use of new wireless RFID technology as described earlier, allow tight inventory control and enable the retailers to eliminate excess inventory. Their suppliers have refined their delivery systems so that the stores receive only the products needed to meet customer purchases.

Many companies recognize the critical role of inventory management in organizational success. The Japanese analogy of rocks and water describes the current thinking about the importance of inventory.[37] As illustrated in Exhibit 16.6, the water is the inventory in the organization. The higher the water, the less managers have to worry about the rocks, which represent problems. In operations management, these problems apply to scheduling, facilities layout, product or service design, and quality. When the water level goes down, managers see the rocks and must deal with them. When inventories are reduced, the problems of a poorly designed and managed operations process also are revealed. The problems then must be solved. When inventory can be kept at an absolute minimum, operations management is considered excellent.

We now consider specific techniques for inventory management. Four important concepts are economic order quantity, material requirements planning, just-in-time inventory systems, and distribution management.

### Exhibit 16.6

### Large Inventories Hide Operations Management Problems

**SOURCE:** R.J. Schonberger, *Japanese Manufacturing Techniques: Nine Hidden Lessons in Simplicity* (New York: The Free Press, 1982).

## Economic Order Quantity

Two basic decisions that can help minimize inventory are how many raw materials to order and when to order from outside suppliers. Ordering the minimum amounts at the right time keeps the raw materials, work-in-process, and finished-goods inventories at low levels. One popular technique is economic order quantity (EOQ), which is designed to minimize the total of ordering costs and holding costs for inventory items. *Ordering costs* are the costs associated with actually placing the order, such as postage, receiving, and inspection. *Holding costs* are costs associated with keeping the item on hand, such as storage space charges, finance charges, and materials-handling expenses.

The EOQ calculation indicates the order quantity size that will minimize holding and ordering costs based on the organization's use of inventory. The EOQ formula includes ordering costs ($C$), holding costs ($H$), and annual demand ($D$). For example, consider a hospital's need to order surgical dressings. Based on hospital records, the ordering costs for surgical dressings are $15, the annual holding cost is $6, and the annual demand for dressings is 605. The following is the formula for the economic order quantity:

$$\text{EOQ} = \sqrt{\frac{2DC}{H}} = \sqrt{\frac{2(605)(15)}{6}} = 55$$

The EOQ formula tells us that the best quantity to order is 55.

The next question is when to make the order. For this decision, a different formula, called reorder point (ROP), is used. ROP is calculated by the following formula, where $D$ is the annual demand for dressings, $T$ is the time period (365 days in the year), and $L$ is the lead time, or number of days between ordering and receiving the product. In this example, we assume that it takes three days to receive the order after the hospital has placed it:

$$\text{ROP} = \frac{D}{T}(L) = \frac{605}{365}(3) = 4.97, \text{or } 5$$

The reorder point tells us that because it takes three days to receive the order, at least 5 dressings should be on hand when the order is placed. As nurses use surgical dressings, operations managers will know that when the level reaches the point of 5, the new order should be placed for a quantity of 55.

This relationship is illustrated in Exhibit 16.7. Whenever the reorder point of 5 dressings is reached, the new order is initiated, and the 55 arrive just as the inventory is depleted. In a typical hospital, however, some variability in lead time and use of surgical dressings will occur. Thus, a few extra items of inventory, called safety stock, are used to ensure that the hospital does not run out of surgical dressings. In general, companies keep more safety stock when demand for items is highly variable. When demand is easy to predict, the safety stock may be lower. However, a careful inventory manager may take into account other criteria as well. A sizable price cut or volume discount might make a large purchase economically more attractive, especially in the case of a product the company is almost certain to need in the future.[38]

## Material Requirements Planning

The EOQ formula works well when inventory items are not dependent on one another. For example, in a restaurant the demand for hamburgers is independent of the demand for milkshakes; thus, an economic order quantity is calculated for each item. A more complicated inventory problem occurs with dependent demand inventory, meaning that item demand is related to the demand for other inventory items. For example, if Ford Motor Company decides to make 100,000 cars, it will also need 400,000 tires, 400,000 rims, and 400,000 hubcaps. The demand for tires is dependent on the demand for cars.

The most common inventory control system used for handling dependent demand inventory is **material requirements planning (MRP)**. MRP is a dependent demand inventory planning and control system that schedules the exact amount of all materials required to support the desired end product. MRP is computer based and requires sophisticated calculations to coordinate information on production scheduling, inventory location, forecasting, and ordering. Unlike with EOQ, inventory levels are not based on past consumption; rather, they are based on precise estimates of future needs for production. MRP can dramatically reduce inventory costs. With MRP, managers can better control the quantity and timing of deliveries of raw materials, ensuring that the right materials arrive at approximately the right time they are needed in the production process. The computerized MRP system can slow or accelerate the inflow of materials in response to changes in the production schedule. These controls result in lower labor, materials, and overhead costs.[39]

As competitive pressures increased, MRP gradually evolved into the broader enterprise resource planning (ERP) systems described in Chapter 15.[40] MRP is focused only on manufacturing and inventory, while ERP incorporates computerized links to other business functions, such as human resources, finance, and sales, enabling managers to evaluate trade-offs such as the balance between workload and the human resources and manufacturing capacity.[41] ERP systems can integrate, track, and optimize functions across the entire organization. MRP systems are a valuable subset of ERP, enabling managers to have greater insight into operations so they can optimize the use of human and material resources.

## Just-in-Time Inventory

**Just-in-time (JIT) inventory systems** are designed to reduce the level of an organization's inventory and its associated costs, aiming to push to zero the amount of

**material requirements planning (MRP)**
A dependent demand inventory planning and control system that schedules the precise amount of all materials required to support the production of desired end products.

**just-in-time (JIT) inventory system**
An inventory control system that schedules materials to arrive precisely when they are needed on a production line.

Exhibit 16.7

### Inventory Control of Surgical Dressings by EOQ

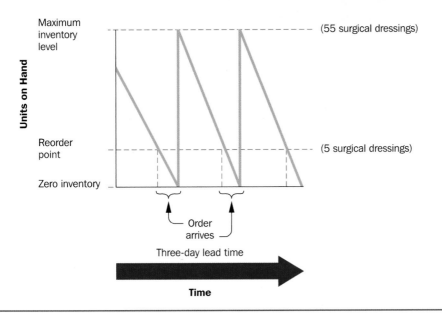

time that raw materials and finished products are sitting in the factory, being inspected, or in transit.[42] Sometimes these systems are referred to as *stockless systems*, *zero inventory systems*, or *Kanban systems*. Each system centers on the concept that suppliers deliver materials only at the exact moment needed, thereby reducing raw material inventories to zero. Moreover, work-in-process inventories are kept to a minimum because goods are produced only as needed to service the next stage of production. Finished-goods inventories are minimized by matching them exactly to sales demand. Just-in-time systems have tremendous advantages. In particular, the reduced inventory level frees productive capital for other company uses.

Recall the analogy of the rocks and the water. To reduce inventory levels to zero means that all management and coordination problems will surface and must be resolved. Scheduling must be scrupulously precise and logistics tightly coordinated. For example, follow the movement of a shipment of odometers and speedometers from a supplier in Winchester, Virginia, to the new Nissan plant in Canton, Mississippi.

| | |
|---|---|
| Thursday, 9 A.M. | An Averitt Express truck arrives at the supplier. As workers load the parts, drivers check on-board computers for destination, route, and estimated time of arrival (ETA) data. |
| Friday, 3 A.M. | The truck arrives at Canton, Mississippi, and approaches a switching yard two miles from the Nissan plant, parking in a computer-assigned spot. The driver downloads a key-shaped floppy disk from the on-board computer into Averitt's mainframe, which relays the performance report directly to Nissan. |
| Friday, 12:50 P.M. | The trailer leaves the switching yard at a designated time and arrives at a predetermined receiving dock at the Nissan plant, where workers unload the parts and send them to the production line just in time.[43] |

The coordination required by JIT demands that information be shared among everyone in the supply chain. Communication between only adjoining links in the supply chain is too slow. Rather, coordination requires a kind of information web in which members of the supply chain share information simultaneously with all other participants, often using Internet technologies and perhaps RFID.[44] For example, Dell's factory in Austin, Texas, uses online information exchange so effectively that it can order only the materials needed to keep production running for the next two hours. In addition, Web hook-ups to shipping companies mean that finished inventory can often be loaded onto trucks less than 15 hours after a customer submits an order.[45]

Just-in-time inventory systems also require excellent employee motivation and cooperation. Workers are expected to perform at their best because they are entrusted with the responsibility and authority to make the zero inventory system work. Employees must help one another when they fall behind and must be capable of doing different jobs. Workers experience the satisfaction of being in charge of the system and making useful improvements in the company's operations.[46]

DAN COHEN BUSINESSWEEK

**CONCEPT CONNECTION**

*Dell Computer is one of today's best examples of the **integrated enterprise.** Dell has squeezed every cent possible out of the cost of building and selling PCs by using the Internet to integrate the entire supply chain, from purchasing to distribution. The company's **just-in-time inventory system** is legendary. At any given moment, there's just four days of stock in Dell's warehouses, compared to 24 days for most computer makers. Last year, Dell began requiring that suppliers be wired directly to the factory floor, enabling Dell plants to keep just a few hours worth of parts on hand and replenish only what is needed throughout the day. By reducing inventory costs, the new system saved Dell $50 million in the first six months of use.*

# Logistics and Distribution Management

A critical aspect of managing inventory is efficiently moving raw materials into the facility and moving finished products out to customers. Some companies develop the necessary logistics expertise in house. Logistics refers to managing the movement of materials within the facility, the shipment of incoming materials from suppliers, and the shipment of outgoing products to customers. For example, Wal-Mart uses regional distribution centers, such as the one in New Braunfels, Texas, which has more than 1 million square feet of floor space, 96 dock doors for loading and unloading trailers, and 5.62 miles of conveyors for moving merchandise.[47] These regional centers receive incoming shipments from suppliers, receive orders from the retail stores, make up the orders, and load and ship merchandise orders to stores throughout the region. Distribution center employees coordinate the entire system and schedule inbound trucks from suppliers and company-owned trucks outbound to the retail stores. Using computers, the system can be so precisely coordinated that the stores don't need warehouses; orders of merchandise go directly from the trucks to the shelves, usually within 48 hours.

Other organizations outsource logistics to a growing number of contract logistics firms, such as Ryder Systems, Caliber Systems Inc., and Emery Global Logistics, which manage the movement of incoming materials and the shipment of outgoing products for the company. General Motors gained efficiencies by outsourcing logistics to Penske Logistics, which coordinates and consolidates shipments of supplies and materials for all of GM's U.S. assembly plants.[48]

Moving finished products out to customers is usually referred to as **distribution** or *order fulfillment*. The faster and more accurately a company can fill customer orders, the lower the costs for the organization and the greater the likelihood that the customer will return. Companies such as BarnesandNoble.com and Amazon.com are testing a new service that delivers products on the same day they're ordered to see whether same-day shipping is a desirable service to customers.[49] Read this chapter's Unlocking Creative Solutions Through People box for an interesting variation on order fulfillment. For many online companies, distribution snafus in the early days have led to greater emphasis on the nuts and bolts of order fulfillment. One approach is to rely on contract fulfillment companies such as SubmitOrder.com, which stores, packs, and ships products for a variety of companies, including MuseumCompany.com. As soon as a customer hits the "Buy" button on MuseumCompany.com's Web page, SubmitOrder spits out the customer's mailing labels, receipt, and the shelf location for each item ordered.[50] A stock *picker* takes the paperwork and starts running to select the items and send them along a conveyor belt to a *packer* who packages the items and sends them to the appropriate dock for shipping. The whole process can take less than an hour.

SubmitOrder's computers also send hourly updates to the company so managers can replenish goods as needed. Online catalogs can be automatically updated as soon as new merchandise arrives in the warehouse. Further automation will enable SubmitOrder pickers to remain in one part of the warehouse and assemble small portions of larger orders, allowing the company to send out as many as 5,000 orders an hour, shaving a little more off the delivery time for each package.

Traditional organizations are also finding new ways to deliver products faster and less expensively by using the Internet. In the latest advance in interorganizational collaboration, some companies share transportation information and resources with unrelated companies, even competitors, so they can share truck space and avoid hauling an empty trailer on a return trip. Subaru of America is talking with a rival automaker about the possibility of sharing rail and truck space so cars will get to dealers faster. Nabisco uses electronic linkages to share warehouses and trucks with companies such as Dole and Lea & Perrins, and coordinate order shipments to retailers, enabling stores to more closely match orders to consumer needs.[51]

**logistics**
The activities required to physically move materials into the company's operations facility and to move finished products to customers.

**distribution**
Moving finished products to customers; also called *order fulfillment*.

# Unlocking Creative Solutions Through People

## Remaking Logistics at a Chicago Food Bank

When former Marine Brigadier General Michael P. Mulqueen took over as head of the Greater Chicago Food Depository, he made it his mission to serve the hungry people of Chicago by applying logistical genius.

When Mulqueen arrived, the Depository had little structure and few business practices. He used retail giant Wal-Mart as a model for remaking the organization into a state-of-the art food warehouse. He started with the food supply. Food banks typically take whatever they can get, which is usually products that companies overproduce. That means they might get a lot of boxes of croutons one week, but no staples like peanut butter, macaroni, or canned tuna. Mulqueen developed strategic alliances with several companies to deliver a steady supply of needed staple products. Golden Grain Macaroni Co., for example, now sells its pasta in bulk cardboard tubes to the organization at a steep discount. The business gets a tax write-off, and volunteers at the food bank handle the scooping and packaging into smaller containers.

Mulqueen also set up a production line in the warehouse to organize and assemble the massive amounts of food the depository receives each day into packages that are precisely categorized and stacked for pick-up by local agencies that serve the poor. Fresh fruits and vegetables are loaded onto ProduceMobiles, sort of like roving farmer's markets that make the rounds of the city's shelters and housing projects. Cooked foods, such as rotisserie chickens from supermarket delis, are distributed to soup kitchens and after-school dinner programs. On a typical day, the Depository handles 3,162 pounds of dairy products, 53,763 pounds of fruits and vegetables (fresh and canned), and 18,322 pounds of meat.

The new logistics procedures strengthen volunteer commitment and performance because things run so much more smoothly. Without a corps of loyal volunteers, the depository could not accomplish its mission. Mulqueen's next revolutionary step is the establishment of Pantry University, modeled after the best corporate universities. Pantry U. will help Chicago's various agencies that serve the poor and homeless develop their own standard practices to make collecting and distributing food more efficient and effective. "Mike knows that he can do everything possible to make the depository efficient," said Gary Garland, executive director at Chicago's Lakeway Pantry. "But if the food gets dished out to substandard agencies, it won't make a difference."

**SOURCE**: Fara Warner, "The Wal-Mart of Food Banks," (Social Capital column) *Fast Company* (September 2003), 42.

# Lean Manufacturing and Productivity

Productivity is significant because it influences the well-being of the entire society as well as of individual companies. The only way to increase the output of goods and services to society is to increase organizational productivity.

## Lean Manufacturing

**lean manufacturing**
Manufacturing process using highly trained employees at every stage of the production process to cut waste and improve quality.

Lean manufacturing was pioneered by Toyota and has spread around the world. Today's organizations are trying to become more efficient, and implementing the lean manufacturing philosophy is one popular approach to doing do. **Lean manufacturing** uses highly trained employees at every stage of the production process who take a painstaking approach to details and problem solving to cut waste and improve quality and productivity.

The heart of lean manufacturing is not machines or technology, but employee involvement. Employees are trained to "think lean," and empowered to make changes to attack waste and strive for continuous improvement in all areas.[52] Toyota's system combines techniques such as just-in-time inventory, continuous-flow production, quick changeover of assembly lines, continuous improvement, and preventive maintenance with a management system that encourages employee involvement and problem solving. Any employee can stop the production line at any time to solve a problem. In addition equipment is often designed to stop automatically so that a defect can be fixed.[53]

Arvin Meritor, which makes car and truck parts, has implemented lean manufacturing to "take distance, time, and space out of work," according to Sean Wright, vice president of continuous improvement. With customers continually forcing price cuts, suppliers like Arvin Meritor have had a tough time making a profit. The company has been implementing various productivity improvements for a decade to become more efficient and offset price pressure, but many of them turned out to be temporary. That changed in 2000, when Arvin Meritor embarked on a full-out attempt to incorporate not only the tools but the philosophy of lean manufacturing. The implementation began in one plant, which served as a kind of template to spread lean manufacturing to all Arvin Meritor manufacturing facilities. Results have been impressive. Within two years, the Asheville plant where the program began had cut annual costs by 26 percent, doubled inventory turnover, and cut customer complaints in half. However, the goal of getting more and more efficient remains. "We're not done yet," said one executive. "We're going to get a lot better."[54]

**CONCEPT CONNECTION**

*For Anadarko, **productivity** is measured by the amount of oil and natural gas it can locate and extract from deep inside the earth. To measure the company's productivity, the cost of inputs (which includes exploration and drilling costs) must be measured against the value of the outputs (the oil and natural gas it can produce). Recent productivity has been very high for Anadarko, due mainly to its use of cutting-edge technology and exploration techniques. For instance, while exploring in a part of Algeria that bigger competitors had given up on, these Anadarko workers used an unorthodox imaging technique to discover a three-billion barrel field of oil.*

## Measuring Productivity

One important question when considering productivity improvements is: What is productivity, and how do managers measure it? In simple terms, **productivity** is the organization's output of goods and services divided by its inputs. This means that productivity can be improved by either increasing the amount of output using the same level of inputs or reducing the number of inputs required to produce the output. Sometimes a company can even do both. Ruggieri & Sons, for example, invested in mapping software to help it plan deliveries of heating fuel. The software plans the most efficient routes based on the locations of customers and fuel reloading terminals, as well as the amount of fuel each customer needs. When Ruggieri switched from planning routes by hand to using the software, its drivers began driving fewer miles but making 7 percent more stops each day—in others words, burning less fuel in order to sell more fuel.[55]

**productivity**
The organization's output of products and services divided by its inputs.

The accurate measure of productivity can be complex. Two approaches for measuring productivity are total factor productivity and partial productivity. **Total factor productivity** is the ratio of total outputs to the inputs from labor, capital, materials, and energy:

**total factor productivity**
The ratio of total outputs to the inputs from labor, capital, materials, and energy.

$$Total\ factor\ productivity = \frac{Output}{Labor\ +\ Capital\ +\ Materials\ +\ Energy}$$

Total factor productivity represents the best measure of how the organization is doing. Often, however, managers need to know about productivity with respect to certain inputs. **Partial productivity** is the ratio of total outputs to a major category of inputs. For example, many organizations are interested in labor productivity, which would be measured as follows:

**partial productivity**
The ratio of total outputs to the inputs from a single major input category.

$$Labor\ productivity = \frac{Output}{Labor\ dollars}$$

Calculating this formula for labor, capital, or materials provides information on whether improvements in each element are occurring. However, managers often are criticized for relying too heavily on partial productivity measures, especially direct labor.[56] Measuring direct labor misses the valuable improvements in materials, work processes, and quality. Labor productivity is easily measured, but may show an increase as a result of capital improvements. Thus, managers will misinterpret the reason for productivity increases.

## Improving Productivity

When an organization decides that improving productivity is important, there are three places to look: technological productivity, employee productivity, and managerial productivity.

*Take A Moment*

*Go to the experiential exercise on page 605 that pertains to your personal orientation toward productivity improvements.*

### Technological Productivity

Increased *technological productivity* refers to the use of more efficient machines, robots, computers, and other technologies to increase outputs. The flexible manufacturing systems, CAD-CAM, and new project life-cycle management software described earlier in this chapter are technological improvements that enhance productivity in manufacturing firms. New technology can increase productivity for service firms, as well. Schneider National, the largest trucking company in the United States, installed a computer terminal in each of its 26 maintenance centers and connected them to an intranet so that mechanics can access up-to-date diagrams and data for repairing trucks. Each mechanic can now fix 20 percent more tractors than before, enabling trucks to get back on the road faster.[57]

Outsourcing is being used by some companies to increase productivity. Companies can farm out certain activities to a specialized firm that can afford to invest in the most modern technology related to the service it provides. NationsBank, for example, arranged for Pitney Bowes Management Services (PBMS) to handle its mail services, in part because PBMS has the computer applications to more efficiently handle the task. Outsourcing frees NationsBank from having to incur the cost of new technology needed to set up a modern mailing system for its 60 mail centers spread out over 16 states and the District of Columbia.[58]

### Employee Productivity

Increased *employee productivity* means having workers produce more output in the same time period. Companies can improve employee productivity by establishing the means for existing employees to do more by working harder or by improving work processes. Employees may simply need more knowledge, more resources, or improved task or workplace design. The company may also decide to hire employees with greater expertise or to outsource certain operations to a firm with expertise in that area, as NationsBank did to obtain the knowledge of PBMS. Improving employee productivity can be a real challenge for American companies, because too often workers have an antagonistic relationship with management. Thus, increasing employee productivity often requires improving the worker-management relationship. Many of the leadership and management approaches described in this book can enhance worker productivity by motivating and inspiring employees.

### Managerial Productivity

Increased managerial productivity simply means that managers do a better job of running the business. Leading experts in productivity and quality often have stated that the real reason for productivity problems in the United States is poor management.[59] One of these authorities, W. Edwards Deming, proposed specific points for telling management how to improve productivity. These points are listed in Exhibit 16.8.

**SOURCE:** Reprinted from *Out of the Crisis*, by W. Edwards Deming by permission of MIT and The W. Edwards Deming Institute. Published by MIT, Center for Advanced Educational Services, Cambridge, MA 02139. Copyright 1986 by The W. Edwards Deming Institute.

Exhibit 16.8

## Condensation of the 14 Points for Management

1. Create constancy of purpose toward improvement of product and service, with the aim to become competitive and to stay in business, and to provide jobs.

2. Adopt the new philosophy. We are in a new economic age. Western management must awaken to the challenge, must learn its responsibilities, and take on leadership for change.

3. Cease dependence on inspection to achieve quality. Eliminate the need for inspection on a mass basis by building quality into the product in the first place.

4. End the practice of awarding business on the basis of price tag. Instead, minimize total cost. Move toward a single supplier for any one item, on a long-term relationship of loyalty and trust.

5. Improve constantly and forever the system of production and service, to improve quality and productivity, and thus constantly decrease costs.

6. Institute training on the job.

7. Institute leadership (see Point 11). The aim of supervision should be to help people and machines and gadgets do a better job. Supervision of management is in need of overhaul as well as supervision of production workers.

8. Drive out fear, so that everyone may work effectively for the company.

9. Break down barriers between departments. People in research, design, sales, and production must work as a team, to foresee problems of production and in use that may be encountered with the product or service.

10. Eliminate slogans, exhortations, and targets for the the workforce asking for zero defects and new levels of productivity. Such exhortations only create adversarial relationships, as the bulk of the causes of low quality and low productivity belong to the system and thus lie beyond the power of the workforce.

11. a. Eliminate work standards (quotas) on the factory floor. Substitute leadership.

    b. Eliminate management by objective. Eliminate management by numbers, numerical goals. Substitute leadership.

12. a. Remove barriers that rob hourly workers of their right to pride of workmanship. The responsibility of supervisors must be changed from sheer numbers to quality.

    b. Remove barriers that rob people in management and in engineering of their right to pride of workmanship. This means, *inter alia*, abolishment of the annual merit rating and of management by objective.

13. Institute a vigorous program of education and self-improvement.

14. Put everybody in the company to work to accomplish the transformation. The transformation is everybody's job.

Managerial productivity improves when managers emphasize quality over quantity, break down barriers and empower their employees, and do not overmanage using numbers. Managers can learn to use reward systems, employee involvement, team-work, and other management techniques that have been described throughout this book. However, it is important for managers to consider the linkage between these techniques and the company's strategy—not just to blindly insert a technique into the organization's activities. For example, although many managers have encouraged their employees to share knowledge, their efforts often fail because employees see no benefits and they lose interest. In contrast, knowledge management efforts succeed when managers establish a strategy-related focus for what information is to be shared, then measure the results. At General Electric, for example, employees focused on learning about how to improve response time. Management had determined that improvements in this area would significantly improve the company's performance.

When GE instituted its knowledge management system, managers looked for—and found—improvements in such performance measures as sales per employee.[60] In this, as in many other examples throughout this chapter, the difference can be attributed to better management, not to specific techniques.

**Manager's Solution**

This chapter described several points about operations management. Operations management pertains to the tools and techniques used to manage the organization's core production process. These techniques apply to both manufacturing and service organizations. Operations management has a great impact when it influences competitive strategy, applying strategic tools such as supply chain management. Areas of operations management described in the chapter include product and service design, procurement, location of facilities, facilities layout, capacity planning, and the use of new technologies.

The chapter also discussed inventory management. Three types of inventory are raw materials, work in process, and finished goods. Economic order quantity, material requirements planning, and just-in-time inventory are techniques for minimizing inventory levels. Logistics is an important part of inventory management because it manages the movement of materials within the facility, the shipment of incoming materials from suppliers, and the shipment of outgoing products to customers. Efficient and effective distribution of products to customers, sometimes called order fulfillment, is critical to organizational success.

Another important concept is that operations management can enhance organizational productivity. Many organizations are striving to become more productive and efficient through lean manufacturing. Total factor productivity is the best measurement of organizational productivity. Managers can focus on improving productivity in three areas: technological productivity, worker productivity, and managerial productivity.

R. R. Donnelley, described in the chapter opening, applied new technology to increase productivity, cut costs, and improve customer satisfaction. Traditionally, preparing text and pictures for printing had created the biggest bottlenecks for Donnelley, as it does for many printers. By making plates digitally rather than from photographic film, the Roanoke plant can now complete a job that once took hours in only 12 minutes. All-digital processing also produces cleaner and sharper plates. Managers saw a tremendous surge in productivity because the digital plates were more consistent. The plant also now handles paper more efficiently. Electronic sensors measure what paper has been consumed and monitor consistency, reporting any problems electronically to the paper mill. Computers monitor the quality of printing and automatically make adjustments as needed. At the end of the press run, printed sheets are folded and stored on reels until they are cut and bound a few hours later, with specifications set by computer. Printed books with jackets are pulled off the line at regular intervals and checked by employees to confirm quality. Finally, the books are shrink wrapped and stacked by machine and shipped immediately. The new technology has enabled Donnelley's Roanoke plant to schedule production runs so precisely that it no longer uses warehouses to store books. Books are printed on demand, providing publishers with just-in-time product when they need it. The plant produces about 75 percent of its titles in two weeks or less, compared with four to six weeks for a four-color book in a traditional printing plant. Moreover, with automation and quick, efficient press changeovers, Donnelley can profitably print as few as 50 copies of a single-color book, 2,500 copies of a four-color book, or quickly manufacture millions of copies of a blockbuster like J. K. Rowling's most recent Harry Potter saga. [61]

# Discussion Questions

1. What are the major differences between manufacturing and service organizations? Give examples of each type.
2. In what ways might a long-distance telephone company be more competitive if it operates at State 3 or Stage 4 of operations strategy?
3. What is meant by supply chain management? Does supply chain management apply to service organizations even though they do not produce physical goods? Discuss.
4. What type of production layout do you think would work best in a car dealership? What type would work best for a company that produces handmade pottery? Discuss reasons for your answers.
5. If you were asked to identify a location for a new resort catering to retirees, what steps would you take? How would you plan for the new resort's capacity?
6. What are the three types of inventory? Which of these is most likely to be affected by the just-in-time inventory system? Explain.
7. What is materials requirement planning? How does it differ from economic order quantity to reduce inventory?
8. Imagine you are the manager of a gourmet pizza restaurant. Identify one specific item or process for each of the six steps of implementing statistical quality control in your restaurant.
9. If you were a consultant to a local manufacturing plant that wants to improve productivity, what advice would you give managers?
10. Do you believe operations management can influence competitive strategy? Discuss.

# Management in Practice: Experiential Exercise

## What is Your Attitude Toward Productivity?

Complete the following questions based on how you think and act in a typical work situation. For each item circle the number that best describes you.

|  | Disagree Strongly |  |  | Agree Strongly |  |
|---|---|---|---|---|---|

1. I spend time developing new ways of approaching old problems.　　1　2　3　4　5

2. As long as things are done correctly and efficiently, I prefer not to take on the hassle of changing them.　　5　4　3　2　1

3. I always believe the "effort" to improve something should be rewarded, even if the final improvement is disappointing.　　1　2　3　4　5

4. A single change that improves things 30 percent is much better than 30 improvements of 1 percent each.　　5　4　3　2　1

5. I frequently compliment others on changes they have made.　　1　2　3　4　5

6. I let people know in a variety of ways that I like to be left alone to do my job efficiently.　　5　4　3　2　1

7. I am personally involved in several improvement projects at one time.　　1　2　3　4　5

8. I try to be a good listener and be patient with what people say, except when it is a "stupid" idea　　5　4　3　2　1

|  | **Disagree Strongly** |  |  | **Agree Strongly** |  |
|---|---|---|---|---|---|
| 9. I am always proposing unconventional techniques and ideas. | 1 | 2 | 3 | 4 | 5 |
| 10. I usually do not take risks that would create a problem for me if the idea failed. | 5 | 4 | 3 | 2 | 1 |

**Total Score** _____

This scale indicates the extent to which your orientation toward productivity is based on "efficiency" or "continuous improvement." Efficieincy sometimes can be maximized by eliminating change. This may be appropriate in a stable organization environment. Continuous improvement is an attitude that productivity can always get better and you take personal responsibility to improve it. This attitude is appropriate for a quality-conscious company experiencing frequent change.

A score of 40 or higher indicates that you take personal responsibility for improving productivity and frequently initiate change. A score of 20 or less indicates you make contributions through efficient work in a stable environment. Discuss the pros and cons of the efficiency versus continuous improvement orientations for organizations and employees.

# Management in Practice: Ethical Dilemma

### A Friend for Life?

Priscilla Dennis has always loved her job as president of Smallworld, a small company that produces and markets toys for young children. As a mother, Priscilla appreciates the care that goes into producing safe, high-quality toys. Late last year, Smallworld's designer invented a small cuddly talking bear. Called the Binky-Bear, the toy was made of soft brown simulated fur and had a tape inside that played 50 messages. To see what kind of appeal the Binky-Bear might have, Smallworld produced 50 of the toys and placed them in kindergartens and nurseries. Results were better than managers had hoped, with many of the kindergartens reporting that the toy quickly became the most popular in the school.

Based on these results, Smallworld decided to produce 1,000 of the bears, and developed a catchy marketing slogan: "A Friend for Life." The bear was marketed as a toy that children could play with for years and years, and perhaps still have around as a keepsake when they had long outgrown toys. The first batch sold out within a week, so the company scheduled another production run of 25,000. However, during the run, the production manager discovered a problem. In the excitement over the new product, the designer and managers had failed to carefully look at manufacturing considerations. It turned out that the process needed to make Binky-Bear's soft fur was much more expensive than anticipated. Using the original fur will cost the company $4.98 per bear, but the manufacturing department can produce a substitute that will cut the cost to only $2.75 per bear. However, as compared with the original fur, which should last approximately eight years, the alternate, less-expensive fur will last for only eight months.

In an emergency meeting to discuss the problem, Smallworld's managers are considering two options: absorb the extra cost, or use the cheaper substitute fur that will not last nearly as long. Many of the managers emphasize that children aren't interested in playing with toys for more than a few months—or even weeks—anyway, so substituting the less-expensive fur shouldn't be a problem. Others, including the production manager, believe the company's reputation for quality will be severely damaged. "We're going to have complaints within eight months, and we will rue the day we agreed to a cheaper substitute," the production manager said. The vice president for manufacaturing agreed, asking, "What are we going to do about our slogan—change it to 'A Friend for Eight Months'"? The marketing and sales managers forcefully argued the opposite viewpoint, pointing out that Smallworld already had a fortune tied up in the bear. "If you stop production now or continue with the expensive fur, we'll lose our shirts," the marketing manager said. "The bear looks the same. I say we substitute the cheaper fur and no one will ever know the difference."

The final decision about how to handle the problem rests with Priscilla Dennis. She knows Smallworld can't afford to absorb the extra production costs, but can it afford to lose its reputation for quality? Also, she wonders if she can look her young daughter in the eye if she goes along with what the marketing manager is suggesting.

**What Do You Do?**

1. Substitute the less expensive fur but insist on a revised marketing campaign and advise buyers about the change in the production process.

2. Substitute the less expensive fur and wait to see what happens. The company would not be doing anything illegal, and most customers probably will never notice that the fur wears out so quickly.

3. Absorb the extra production costs. It's the ethical thing to do, and besides, the company's reputation for quality is too important to risk.

Source: Based on "A Friend for Life," in Donald F. Kuratko and Richard M. Hodgetts, *Entrepreneurship: A Contemporary Approach*, 4th ed. (Fort Worth: The Dryden Press, 1998), 172–173.

# Surf the Net

1. **Supply Chain Management.** Use your search engine to locate, visit, and write a review of three supply chain management resource Web sites. For example, the Stanford Global Supply Chain Management Forum *http://www.stanford. edu/group/scforum* "is a program in partnership with industry and the School of Engineering and Graduate School of Business at Stanford University that advances the theory and practice of excellence in global supply chain management." Another resource site can be found at *http://www.createcom.com* and key in "supply chain management" in the search box. You may review any three sites you choose to explain what is available at each site and which site you would rate as most helpful to a student group preparing a classroom presentation on supply chain management.

2. **CAD/CAM.** Visit a Web site, such as the following, that provides information about CAD and CAM software applications. *http://metals.about.com/od/cadcam/*
   Prepare a list of three software products in each category. For each product listed, include as much information as you can find about it from the list that follows: (a) name, (b) manufacturer, (c) price, (d) main use, (e) review comments of the product, (f) miscellaneous information, such as a Web site address that provides downloadable demos of the product

3. **Inventory Management and MRP.** Use your search engine to find Web sites that provide information on inventory management and scheduling systems. Contribute your findings during class discussions on inventory management.

# Case for Critical Analysis

## Intel

The old adage used to be that fish, newspapers, and houseguests went stale after a day; these days, we could add computer microprocessors to the list. The management at Intel, which constantly manufactures new chips, knows this fact. In order to stay ahead of the competition, Intel has had to juggle its supply chain and its customers' just-in-time inventory demands with supreme skill.

Today, PC manufacturers such as Dell Computer Corporation specialize in build-to-order manufacturing, which means that they expect no slack in the supply chain and hold little or no inventory of finished product or even components. This means that Intel must coordinate its own supply levels, inventory, and manufacturing capacity to meet customers needs and at the same time demand the same thing from its own suppliers. "All of our [customers] are trying to operate with essentially zero inventory," explains Alan Baldwin, vice president of Intel's planning and logistics group. "They need just-in-time delivery from us and real-time feedback from the marketplace." To accomplish this, Intel set up an extranet to transmit real-time inventory levels and demand to both its suppliers and its customers. Intel also put in place an enterprise resource planning system to improve inventory control, product delivery, and business integration, with an intranet designed to accelerate procurement cycles. But before Intel could actually satisfy its customers' demands, managers had to adjust production capacity so that it could fluctuate when necessary. This meant Intel managers had to analyze suppliers' abilities to provide high-quality materials and equipment.

To help suppliers develop the materials Intel needed, Intel set up Web-based tools that allow suppliers to study new products as Intel designers work on them. Intel maintains strict requirements of its suppliers. "We say to our suppliers, we're going to help you understand our needs, and your responsibility is to keep the bins stocked," notes Mary Murphy-Hoye, manager of strategic programs. Beacause it is in Intel's best interest to have healthy suppliers, managers work with suppliers to help them improve their own inventory and demand-forecasting methods. "You're only as good as your supply chain," notes Murphy-Hoye.

Intel's focus on its supply chain has paid off. The company used to take 24 hours to confirm orders; now, deliveries can be confirmed as soon as orders are placed. Alan Baldwin asserts that customer satisfaction has increased dramatically. Intel redesigns its products constantly, overhauling the whole product line about every eighteen months, so manufacturing plants must be flexible. To be flexible, however, management has discovered that instituting identical architecture and applications support for ordering and production planning at every manufaacturing site actually speeds up the process. According to Louis Burns, Intel's vice president and director of IT, this system allows the company to make changes and upgrades much more quickly than it could if each site were operated differently. In an industry in which products become obsolete as rapidly as fish or newspapers, speed is everything.

## Questions

1. What type of facilities layout do you think would work best at Intel's plants? Why?
2. How might Intel managers use MRP II to control its resources?
3. Imagine that you are a manager at one of Intel's manufacturing plants. What steps might you take to ensure that workers are as productive as possible?

Source: Peter Fabris, "Intel Outside," *CIO*, Section 1, August 15, 1998, pp. 64–69.

## Endnotes

1. Gene Bylinsky, "Elite Factories," *Fortune* (September 1, 2003), 154[B]–154 [J].
2. James D. Thompson, *Organizations in Action* (New York: McGraw-Hill, 1967).
3. Brian Heymans, "Leading the Lean Enterprise," *Industrial Management* (September–October 2002), 28–33; and Norihiko Shirouzu, "Gadget Inspector: Why Toyota Wins Such High Marks on Quality Surveys," *The Wall Street Journal* (March 15, 2001), A1, A11.
4. Gregory B. Northcraft and Richard B. Chase, "Managing Service Demand at the Point of Delivery," *Academy of Management Review* 10 (1985), 66–75; and Richard B. Chase and David A. Tanski, "The Customer Contact Model for Organization Design," *Management Science* 29 (1983), 1037–1050.
5. Robert H. Lowson, "Strategic Operations Management—The New Competitive Advantage?" *Journal of General Management* 28, no. 1 (Autumn 2002): 36–56; and Everett E. Adam Jr. and Paul M. Swamidass, "Assessing Operations Management from a Strategic Perspective," *Journal of Management* 15 (1989), 181–203.
6. Robert H. Hayes and David M. Upton, "Operations-Based Strategy," *California Management Review* 40, no. 4 (Summer 1998), 8–25.
7. R. H. Hayes and S. C. Wheelwright, *Restoring Our Competitive Edge: Competing through Manufacturing* (New York: Wiley, 1984).
8. Rick Brooks, "Leading the News: UPS Cuts Ground Delivery Time; One-Day Reduction Aims to Repel FedEx Assault on Company's Dominance," *The Wall Street Journal* (October 6, 2003), A3.

9. Definition based on Steven A. Melnyk and David R. Denzler, *Operations Management: A Value-Driven Approach* (Burr Ridge, Ill.: Richard D. Irwin, 1996), 613.

10. Based on Jim Turcotte, Bob Silveri, and Tom Jobson, "Are You Ready for the E-Supply Chain?" *APICS–The Performance Advantage* (August 1998), 56–59.

11. Daniel Lyons, "Back on the Chain Gang," *Forbes* (October 13, 2003), 114–123.

12. Ibid.

13. F. Ian Stuart and David M. McCutcheon, "The Manager's Guide to Supply Chain Management," *Business Horizons* (March–April 2000), 35–44.

14. Russ Banham, "Caught in the Middle," *CFO* (May 2001), 69–74.

15. Jason Tanz, "From Drab to Fab," *Fortune* (December 8, 2003), 178–184.

16. Thomas Petzinger Jr., "How a Ski Maker on a Slippery Slope Regained Control," *The Wall Street Journal* (October 3, 1997), B1.

17. Norihiko Shirouzu, "Copy That; Ford's New Development Plan: Stop Reinventing the Wheel," *The Wall Street Journal* (April 16, 2003), A1, A14.

18. Ibid.

19. Bruce Nussbaum, "The Power of Design," *BusinessWeek* (May 17, 2004), 86–94.

20. Christopher Koch, "The Big Payoff," Special Section on Supply Chain Management, *CIO* (October 1, 2000), 101–112; Norman Gaither and Greg Frazier, *Operations Management*, 9th ed. (Cincinnati, Ohio: South-Western Publishing, 2002), 428–429.

21. Gaither and Frazier, *Operations Management*, 429.

22. David Rocks, "The Net as a Lifeline," *BusinessWeek e.biz* (October 29, 2001), EB16–EB28.

23. Scott Leibs, "First Pencils, Now People," *CFO* (November 2001), 91–94.

24. Christopher Koch, "Four Strategies," Special Section on Supply Chain Management, *CIO* (October 1, 2000), 116–128.

25. Nancy Lea Hyer and Karen A. Brown, "Work Cells with Staying Power: Lessons for Process-Complete Operations," *California Management Review* 46, no. 1 (Fall 2003), 27–52.

26. John Teresko, "Plant Strategies: Winning with Wireless," *Industry Week* (June 2003), 60–66; Meridith Levinson, "The RFID Imperative," *CIO* (December 1, 2003), 78–91.

27. Maryanne Murray Buechner, "Cracking the Code," *FSB: Fortune Small Business* (March 2004), 72–73.

28. Reported in Matthew Boyle, "Wal-Mart Keeps the Change," *Fortune* (November 10, 2003), 46.

29. Erick Schonfeld, "Next Stop: The 21st Century," *Business 2.0* (September 2003), 153–157.

30. Sumer C. Aggarwal, "MRP, JIT, OPT, FMS?" *Harvard Business Review* 63 (September–October 1985), 8–16; and Paul Ranky, *The Design and Operation of Flexible Manufacturing Systems* (New York: Elsevier, 1983).

31. David Welch, "How Nissan Laps Detroit," *BusinessWeek* (December 22, 2003), 58–60.

32. This discussion of product life-cycle management software is based on Gene Bylinsky, "Not Your Grandfather's Assembly Line," *Fortune* special section, "Industrial Management and Technology (June 28, 2004), http://www.fortune.com

33. Shirley Leung, "Where's the Beef? A Glutted Market Leaves Food Chains Hungry for Sites," *The Wall Street Journal* (October 1, 2003), A1, A12.

34. Alan David MacCormack, Lawrence James Newman III, and Donald B. Rosenfield, "The New Dynamics of Global Manufacturing Site Location," *Sloan Management Review* (Summer 1994), 69–80; and Chen May Yee, "Let's Make a Deal," *The Wall Street Journal* (September 25, 2000), R10.

35. Claudia Eller and James Bates, "Not All Projections Bad for Overgrown Theater Chains," *Los Angeles Times* (September 8, 2000).

36. Evan Ramstad, "Compaq Stumbles Amid New Pressures on PCs," *The Wall Street Journal* (March 9, 1998), B1, B8.

37. R. J. Schonberger, *Japanese Manufacturing Techniques: Nine Hidden Lessons in Simplicity* (New York: Free Press, 1982).

38. Cathy Lazere, "Taking Stock of Inventory: Beyond Mean and Lean," *CFO* (November 1997), 95–97.

39. Gaither and Frazier, *Operations Management*, 587.

40. F. C. "Ted" Watson, Jr., "ERP II: The Extended Enterprise System," *Business Horizons* (November–December 2003), 49–55.

41. Vincent A. Mabert, Ashok Soni, and M. A. Venkataramanan, "Enterprise Resource Planning: Common Myths Versus Evolving Reality," *Business Horizons* (May–June 2001), 69–76.

42. Luciana Beard and Stephen A. Butler, "Introducing JIT Manufacturing: It's Easier than You Think," *Business Horizons* (September–October 2000), 61–64.

43. Based on Ronald Henkoff, "Delivering the Goods," *Fortune* (November 28, 1994), 64–78.

44. Noel P. Greis and John D. Kasarda, "Enterprise Logistics in the Information Era," *California Management Review* 39(4) (Summer 1997), 55–78.

45. David Rocks, "Dell's Second Web Revolution," *BusinessWeek e.biz* (September 18, 2000), EB62–EB63.

46. "Kanban: The Just-in-Time Japanese Inventory System," *Small Business Report* (February 1984), 69–71; and Richard C. Walleigh, "What's Your Excuse for Not Using JIT?" *Harvard Business Review* 64 (March–April 1986), 38–54.

47. Gaither and Frazier, *Operations Management*, 150–151.

48. Francis J. Quinn, "Logistics' New Customer Focus," *BusinessWeek* special advertising section (March 10, 1997).

49. Nick Wingfield, "Racing Barnes & Noble for Same-Day Delivery in New York," *The Wall Street Journal* (June 3, 2004), B1.

50. Carol Vinzant, "SubmitOrder Thinks Inside the Box," *eCompany* (August 2000), 58–59; and Faith Keenan, "Logistics Gets a Little Respect," *BusinessWeek e.Biz* (November 20, 2000), EB112–EB116.

51. Faith Keenan, "Logistics Gets a Little Respect," and "One Smart Cookie," *BusinessWeek e.biz* (November 20, 2000), EB120.

52. Fara Warner, "Think Lean," *Fast Company* (February 2002), 40, 42.

53. Peter Strozniak, "Toyota Alters Face of Production," *Industry Week* (August 13, 2001), 46–48.

54. Philip Siekman, "The Struggle to Get Lean," *Fortune*, Industrial Management and Technology section, (January 12, 2004), 128[B]–128[H].

55. Emily Esterson, "First-Class Delivery," *Inc. Technology* (September 15, 1998), 89.

56. W. Bouce Chew, "No-Nonsense Guide to Measuring Productivity," *Harvard Business Review* (January–February 1988), 110–118.

57. Anna Bernasek, "Pattern for Prosperity," *Fortune* (October 2, 2000), 100–108.

58. The Outsourcing Institute, "Outsourcing: The New Midas Touch," *BusinessWeek* (December 15, 1997), special advertising section.

59. W. E. Deming, *Quality, Productivity, and Competitive Position* (Cambridge, Mass.: Center for Advanced Engineering Study, MIT, 1982); and P. B. Crosby, *Quality Is Free* (New York: McGraw-Hill, 1979).

60. Charles E. Lucier and Janet D. Torsilieri, "Why Knowledge Programs Fail: A C.E.O.'s Guide to Managing Learning," *Strategy and Business* (Fourth Quarter 1997), 14–16, 21–27.

61. Bylinsky, "Elite Factories."

# Video Case

## Chapter 14: Cannondale Has Finely Tuned Control Processes

Organizations today face the constant challenge of controlling their activities to reduce waste, shorten time frames, and maximize profits. Their very survival depends on how well they can streamline processes and produce high-quality products from the outset. The high-performance bicycle industry is no different; it is extremely competitive among the top handful of companies. Known for its innovative designs, Connecticut-based Cannondale Corporation believes in control before, during, and after its design and manufacturing processes. In fact, to remain a profitable, viable, business, the organization needs to run as a finely tuned machine, with all parts contributing to overall goals.

Creativity drives and inspires Cannondale's teams, but continual innovation also requires checks and balances to ensure quality. After new bicycle designs are created using a computer-aided design (CAD) software program, teams review them carefully. And before a bicycle design is approved for production, design engineers check its accuracy and feasibility through a proofing process, the first step in quality control. The goal of proofing is to answer the question, Can the design be built as envisioned? Once they feel confident in the new design, engineers send the CAD system's design to a rapid prototyping machine, which constructs a plastic model so that engineers can see in three dimensions what they have planned. Overseeing this design process is the research and development project manager, who keeps an eye on design timelines and prototyping schedules. John Horn, a Cannondale R&D project manager says, "Engineers are perfectionists, but the R&D project manager must make sure the product gets to market when it's needed."

Once the design engineers have perfected a design, they transmit it electronically to the production teams in Bedford, Pennsylvania. Production engineers at the factory use the computer design to develop working samples using actual materials. New designs undergo 12 to 15 different tests to ensure impact strength, durability of the materials, and performance. Testing includes actually riding the prototype, as well as destructive testing to check the design's limits.

Manufacturing processes are controlled through precision machinery and empowered teams. Cannondale uses computer-guided laser machines to cut the frame's aluminum tubes to precise dimensions.

Then the company relies on its craftsmen's experience and training. Because the strength of a bicycle frame depends on the quality of its welds, welders undergo a training and certification program to ensure that they meet quality standards. During manufacturing, any employee on the assembly line can speak up and stop production anytime to fix problems immediately. Once a frame has been constructed, Cannondale's coordinate measuring machine checks every measurement, and as a final control, a technician manually verifies the measurements. The frame is then sanded, cleaned, and hand painted, and protective finishes are applied.

Critical to bicycle design is actual testing of performance in the field. Cannondale seeks ideas from professional bicycle racers to maintain its cutting-edge designs. The company sponsors professional racing teams—two mountain bike racing teams, three road racing teams, and a triathlon team. The feedback that the racers supply is invaluable to the company's design and manufacturing processes. The company has won many quality awards through the years, among them *Bicycling* magazine's "Publisher's Award for Innovation," *VeloNews* magazine's "Technological Development of the Year Award," *Popular Science's* "Best of What's New" award, *BusinessWeek's* "Best New Products of the Year Award," *Design News* magazine's "Computer-Aided Design Award," and *Popular Mechanics'* "Design and Engineering Award."

Even with such acclaim, Cannondale is not content to rest. The company can change product lines as often as every six months to remain at the forefront of bicycle design and competitive in its market. And it has been revamping its inventory and manufacturing processes to streamline them for profitability. It recently switched its materials control computer software from a time-consuming program that took 9 hours and much manual intervention to complete to one that performed profitability analyses in $2\frac{1}{2}$ minutes. With such timely information, the company was able to review its processes and reduce its inventory stock by roughly 25 percent, which freed up money and resources to be used elsewhere—such as research and development. Cannondale's purchasing manager says that the new system has eliminated not only the time involved but many headaches as well. "Before, it took so much effort to work through

Chapter 14: Cannondale Has Finely Tuned Control Processes (continued)

the mountain of computer printouts to find what you were looking for that you just wouldn't do it." Now the company can generate that information in seconds and feed it back to critical decision makers. That kind of speed record is as critical to Cannondale as awards and races won.

**Questions**
1. Review the three types of control outlined in Exhibit 20.1 in Chapter 20. From the information provided, categorize the types of control Cannondale uses in its design and manufacturing processes as feedforward, concurrent, or feedback.

2. Would you say that Cannondale relies more on bureaucratic control or decentralized control to ensure quality?
3. Does Cannondale practice total quality management? Explain.

Sources: Interview with John Horn, Cannondale research and development project manager, April 9, 2002; Cannondale company Web site, *http://www.cannondale.com*, accessed March 22, 2002; Nick Wreden, "Doing Wheelies," *Consumer Goods*, May 2000, *http://www.consumergoods.com*; David J. Bak, "Skin and Bones, but Plenty Tough: Cannondale Combines CAD and Composites for a Breakthrough Bike," *Design News*, March 2, 1998, accessed at *http://www.findarticles.com*.

# Video Case

Chapter 15: Cannondale's Information Technology: From Office to Factory Floor—and Beyond

Information is a valuable resource for today's organizations, and information technology can tap its potential. Cannondale Corporation, the leading designer and manufacturer of high-performance aluminum bicycles and cycling accessories, believes in the strategic use of information technology. The company employs computer systems for everything from bicycle design, precision manufacturing, and quality control, to inventory and sales management. Cannondale's director of marketing and media relations, Tom Armstrong, says the goal of using information technology is to move faster than competitors. "We have tried to do that by innovating not only on the product front but in every other aspect as well. A lot of our own production engineering is about getting inside the development cycle of our competitors."

Cannondale's design engineers based in Connecticut use a computer-aided design (CAD) system called Pro/Engineer, a three-dimensional modeling program. With the program, designers can execute an idea and nearly instantly generate the measurements and parts needed for prototyping and

mold making for manufacturing. They can also automatically create many different sizes in the same model style—to fit cyclists of many different shapes and sizes. With more than 80 different bicycle models currently, the CAD system gives the company flexibility—and a competitive edge.

After a design is finalized, the CAD system relays the design electronically to the production engineers in the company's Bedford, Pennsylvania, factories. Several years ago, the company saw the promise of Internet technology and harnessed it to track its manufacturing process. It installed an intranet in its Pennsylvania manufacturing plants to reduce the complexity and costs of the manufacturing system. The company's application engineer installed Web browser software on personal computers on the factory floor and replaced the keyboards with bar-code scanners and mouses for ease of input. As employees on the assembly line finish a step, they swipe the scanner across a barcode on each bicycle. The company's managers can then capture information and track the manufacturing processes to ensure that parts and supplies are available when needed.

# Chapter 15: Cannondale's Information Technology: From Office to Factory Floor—and Beyond (continued)

Cannondale also uses the Internet's communications capability to relay product specifications to its subsidiaries in the Netherlands, Japan, and Australia, which do final product assembly and finishing for overseas products. Before the use of the Web, workers sent hard-copy drawings to the subsidiaries, and employees there placed them in binders, which had to be updated periodically. That process was time-consuming and unreliable. Now the company can instantly transmit its drawings electronically, complete with final paint colors. The result is consistency in product manufacturing, reduced time, and reduced costs.

Cannondale has focused most of its information technology system on personal computers running Windows software. This strategic decision simplifies the company's hardware and software systems and allows employees in all divisions to share the information in word processing, spreadsheet, and other programs. Cannondale recently began working with AimNet Solutions to handle its network infrastructure. AimNet will monitor the company's network and ensure it performs reliably. Cannondale's vice president of information technology, Mike Dower, explains the strategic partnership this way: "Our strategy at Cannondale has been the same since our inception. We strive to create innovative, differentiated, high-performance products. With our passion for growth, . . . we couldn't afford to be distracted from that strategy. . . . We can stay focused on creating superior products" and let AimNet oversee the network infrastructure.

Cannondale has also reconstructed its inventory and sales management systems with information technology. With its new PC-based system, the company is able to track supplies more accurately and, as a result, reduced inventory stocks by approximately one quarter. The system may eventually be used to tie Cannondale's information system with its suppliers'.

Cannondale sales representatives also gather data from retail partners about which models are selling well. They relay that information to the company's information system, and managers can switch manufacturing to needed models. This quick response to customer needs is important to Cannondale's success. The company has also begun using its corporate Web site to inform prospective customers about tailor-made bicycles. Currently, the company allows the customer to choose from over eight million possible frame and color variations available on the CAAD5 road frame. Giving customers such wide choices and ensuring the product they want is in their local store helps solidify their relationships with the company. Cannondale's Web site says, "Our focus is people—employees, customers, retailers, and our vendors—working together to accomplish our mission." And Cannondale uses sophisticated information technology systems to link those people into one big network.

## Questions

1. What types of groupware does Cannondale use?
2. How important is Cannondale's information technology to its design and manufacturing?
3. Cannondale uses information technology in many ways to streamline its business processes. What other ways could it use this technology in the future?

Sources: Cannondale company Web site, *http://www.cannondale.com*, accessed March 22, 2002; "Cannondale Signs with Genosys Technology Management," *Business Wire*, October 29, 2001; Blaise Zerega, "Cannondale Rides Web for Productivity," *InfoWorld*, November 16, 1998, *http://www.infoworld.com*; David F. Carr, "Extending an Intranet to the Factory Floor," *Internet World*, September 21, 1998, accessed at *http://www.findarticles.com*.

# Video Case

## Chapter 16: Cannondale's Consuming Passion for Perfection

You'd expect a company that produces premium bicycles to care about its manufacturing processes. After all, the company knows how gears must mesh perfectly and how lightweight and durable frames must fit their riders' bodies seamlessly to form a single unit built for speed. You'd expect the company to realize how each system must perform flawlessly. You'd expect that, and you'd be right. Cannondale Corporation pursues its mission of producing innovative, quality products with nothing short of passion.

Cannondale's manufacturing organization produces physical goods—bicycles, cycling accessories, and off-road vehicles. And its operations strategy lies at the very heart of the company—it must produce its products quickly, efficiently, and well to survive. But Cannondale has another goal in mind besides mere survival: it strives to be an innovator. That focus places additional pressure on its operations, not only to support the company but to provide a competitive advantage.

As the Internet became more widely used in the mid-1990s, Cannondale foresaw its potential for supply chain management. Rather than install complex systems, the company used the simplicity of Web technology to manage its manufacturing processes. It installed personal computers directly on the factory floor and used scanners and bar-code technology to track the stages of the manufacturing process. Workers simply swipe the scanner over a bar code attached to a bicycle frame, and the system automatically updates a database. The database serves as a gateway to the company's material requirements planning (MRP) application. The database can also be accessed by management and Cannondale's overseas subsidiaries for decision making and planning.

Cannondale revamped its inventory control system in the late 1990s to allow it more flexibility. The old system created a one-to three-week delay in analyzing design or order changes—too long a time frame for a company that can change its product line every six months. Frustrated with the system's pokiness, the company invited vendor WebPlan to demonstrate its system using actual corporate data. The new system allowed the company to do an MRP run in $2\frac{1}{2}$ minutes. Cannondale expanded the system's use to scheduling and planning in purchasing, finance, and other departments. Such efficiency allowed the company to reduce its inventory drastically and use the dollars previously tied up in inventory for other purposes, especially product design. The company is also planning to link its suppliers to the system via the Internet. As Cannondale's purchasing manager says, "If [suppliers] can see our requirements on the Internet as fast as we can, then a lot of time can be saved. Buyers and planners don't have to spend time communicating on every little detail, and parts production can begin when it's needed, not when it's communicated using a phone or fax." Integrating suppliers into the system provides a unified supply chain management system.

Cannondale's small production runs on its assembly lines allow the company to be more flexible in its manufacturing systems than other companies, which produce thousands of units at a time with robotics. Cannondale can quickly and easily change paint colors or customize decal designs to meet sales demand or customer preferences. It uses technology when appropriate for accuracy and consistency but also provides craftsmanship with skilled employees. Such flexibility enables Cannondale to ship a custom bicycle out of the factory within six weeks of a signed custom order. It can also meet its retail partners' specific demands more quickly.

Productivity is a key to Cannondale's success—through technology and its employees. From its Web-based factory floor software to its computer-aided design and manufacturing systems, the company has created a top-performing production line. With its redesigned production processes, the company expanded from manufacturing one product line of about 50 bike models to six lines with 120 models. But the constant push for design innovation and new materials keeps the company on its toes. Sophisticated bicycles must balance strength, flexibility, and weight for peak performance. Cannondale is meeting those challenges head on and aiming to change the bicycle world at the same time. As the company's Web site says, "We devise flexible manufacturing processes that enable us to deliver those innovative, quality products to the market quickly and then back them with excellent customer service." From its early beginnings in a loft above a pickle factory, Cannondale has been racing toward perfection for 30 years, and it hasn't tired yet.

# Chapter 16: Cannondale's Consuming Passion for Perfection (continued)

**Questions**

1. From this video case and those for Chapters 14 through 15, identify the inputs to Cannondale's manufacturing organization.
2. Review the basic production layouts in Exhibit 16.4. Which type of layout does Cannondale have?
3. How does Cannondale's operations support its production of high-performance bicycles?

Sources: Interview with John Horn, Cannondale research and development project manager, April 9, 2002; Nick Wreden, "Doing Wheelies," *Consumer Goods*, May 2000, *http://www.consumergoods.com*; David F. Carr, "Extending an Intranet to the Factory Floor," *Internet World*, September 21, 1998, accessed at *http://www.findarticles.com*.

## Part 5: At Ford, Quality Is Job 1—Again!

# .....Continuing Case

A few years ago, Ford ran an advertising campaign whose motto was "At Ford, Quality Is Job 1." The company boasted top quality not only in the manufacture of its trucks and cars but also in its service. In the summer of 2000, the old slogan came back to haunt the company, as it became evident that literally millions of tires—made by Firestone—on Ford's popular SUVs, including the Explorer, were separating and shredding, causing serious and even fatal accidents. Even though Ford didn't manufacture the tires, those tires were installed on Ford vehicles; and the press, general public, and even Congress had a hard time distinguishing between the two. The situation was exacerbated as Bridgestone/Firestone accused Ford of building inferior vehicles. Finger pointing between the two organizations, centered on quality issues, continued for months as the tires were recalled and replaced. A year later, the National Highway Traffic Safety Administration reported that the defective tires, not the Ford vehicles, were to blame for the crashes; but the damage was already done in the public's eyes. "I think as long as this battle is going on in the press nobody is going to win," noted Anne Sceia Klein, a public relations expert in Philadelphia. "The general public will walk away from [the Ford Explorer] if they can't sort it out."

Maintaining the quality of goods and services is a major part of the controlling function in an organization. Unfortunately, even if a quality problem is only a perceived one—or is exaggerated by publicity—damage to the organization's reputation can occur, and ultimately sales can drop. Ford faced both real and perceived quality issues in its struggle with the tire/SUV problem. Former CEO Jacques Nasser disputed Firestone's charges that the Explorer was at least partially to blame for the rollover crashes. "If you happen to be in a vehicle that had a tread separation, and that vehicle happens to be a compact SUV, you'd be much safer in an Explorer," argued Nasser. "If those Firestone tires were on other SUVs, the rollover instance would be much worse."

Some experts believe that the right information technology, which would have allowed greater knowledge sharing between Bridgestone/Firestone and Ford, and better designed production systems could have prevented the mismatch of tires and vehicles. In fact, Ford already had in place its own Best Practices Replication Process, which was designed to improve the efficiency of various parts of the manufacturing process. In 1995, Dale McKeehan, then vice president of manufacturing, called together his vehicle operations people, including the heads of body construction, painting, and final assembly and said, "Figure out a way to share best practices." Stan Kwiecien, then head of a group working on plant productivity recalls, "So we figured it out. We're engineers." Around the same time, McKeehan met with another manager, Dar Wolford, who was using early information technology to improve efficiency at Ford plants. McKeehan introduced Wolford to Kwiecien, and Ford's Best Practices Replication Process was born. Within four years, more than 2,800 proven superior practices had been shared among Ford's widespread manufacturing facilities, at a total documented value of $850 million. But knowledge sharing did not extend outside the company, so Ford and Firestone never communicated with each other about potential problems with the pairing of their two products.

Around the time of the tire recall, Ford began training managers in a program called Six Sigma, which is a system for continuous improvement in quality and efficiency to help the organization avoid manufacturing mistakes. Six Sigma uses statistical analysis to find the root of a problem that other methods can't seem to locate. For instance, the company's new Lincoln LS sedan had trouble starting on the first try. Using Six Sigma, an engineering team traced the problem to a screw that wasn't properly tightened. How did so many of these screws come off the assembly line loose? Because workers were using the wrong power tool to tighten them. Ford managers claim that Six Sigma saved the company $52 million in errors the first year, with another $300 million projected for the following year.

Feedback is a vital component of control, and recently Ford faced a hard feedback fact: although customers who participated in marketing surveys consistently said they wanted more environmentally responsible vehicles, they are unwilling to pay a higher sticker price for them. Meanwhile, Ford received feedback from the Insurance Institute for Highway Safety in the form of poor results from low-speed crash tests designed to test bumper damage. Still, the Ford Explorer remains the most popular sport utility vehicle on the market, accounting for 20 percent of Ford Motor Company's sales. And Bill Ford remains firm in his commitment to improve the overall quality of his company's vehicles, including reducing their impact on the environment. As for his competitors, Ford notes, "If we didn't provide [the SUV], someone else would, and they wouldn't provide it as responsibly as we do." Already, Ford Motor Company voluntarily builds its SUVs to emit less tailpipe pollution than allowed by law. If Bill Ford has his way, quality will indeed be job 1 at the century-old company for the next one hundred years.

## Questions

1. Do you think that Ford Motor Company would benefit from open-book management? Why or why not?
2. In what ways might Ford Motor Company further use information technology to manage knowledge and create a competitive strategy?
3. Which stage of operations strategy would you say is illustrated by Ford Motor Company in this case? Why?

Sources: Nedra Pickler, "Explorer Fender Benders Costly," Auto.com, November 30, 2002, *http://www.auto.com*; "Jacques Knifed," *The Economist*, November 3, 2001, *http://www.economist.com*; Alex Taylor III, "What's Behind Ford's Fall?" *Fortune*, October 29, 2001, *http://www.fortune.com*; Joann Muller, "Ford: Why It's Worse Than You Think," *BusinessWeek Online*, June 25, 2001, *http://www.businessweek.com*; "Ford Goes on Offensive to Explain Massive Tire Replacement Plan," *Fox News*, May 24, 2001, *http://www.foxnews.com*; Thomas A. Stewart, "Knowledge Worth $1.25 Billion," *Fortune*, November 27, 2001, *http://www.fortune.com*; Keith Bradsher, "Ford Is Conceding S.U.V. Drawbacks," *The New York Times*, May 12, 2000, *http://www.serv.com*.

# Leading

"There is music in the air, music all around us," said composer Edward Elgar.

The tune heard most often by today's managers may be the constant ring of a cell phone tying them to the organization. However, like a conductor guiding an orchestra, managers can become leaders who set the pace for an organization and lead people in a different kind of performance.

The conductor's ear hears each player, able to find the off-key note, the tinny whine, or the pure beauty of a single musician. He communicates with body language a nod, a tilt of the head, a carefully chosen wag of the finger. His baton thrusts and parries, pulling out the interpretations best suited to each performance piece. The players watch and heed, blending their talents and actions into a seamless crescendo of music and magic.

Leaders also find the off-key notes, bring people together, and inspire them to act in ways that accomplish the organization's vision. Understanding people, communicating, building teamwork, and inspiring others are the essentials of effective organizational leadership, just as a conductor must understand the players and the music, find successful ways to guide and convey direction, and unite and inspire musicians to higher levels of performance.

When the final note has sounded and applause fills the concert hall, the conductor shares the tribute with the orchestra. Yet he alone often shoulders the blame when critics decry a sloppy or uninspired performance. Leaders also take the heat when organizations fail to meet their goals and serve the interests of society. By developing leadership skills in understanding human behavior, communication, teamwork, and motivation, managers can boost an organization's chance of hitting all the right notes.

Part 6

# Dynamics of Behavior in Organizations

## LEARNING OBJECTIVES

*After studying this chapter, you should be able to*

1. Define attitudes, including their major components, and explain their relationship to personality, perception, and behavior.

2. Discuss the importance of work-related attitudes.

3. Identify major personality traits and describe how personality can influence workplace attitudes and behaviors.

4. Define the four components of emotional intelligence and explain why they are important for today's managers.

5. Explain how people learn in general and in terms of individual learning styles.

6. Discuss the effects of stress and identify ways individuals and organizations can manage stress to improve employee health, satisfaction, and productivity

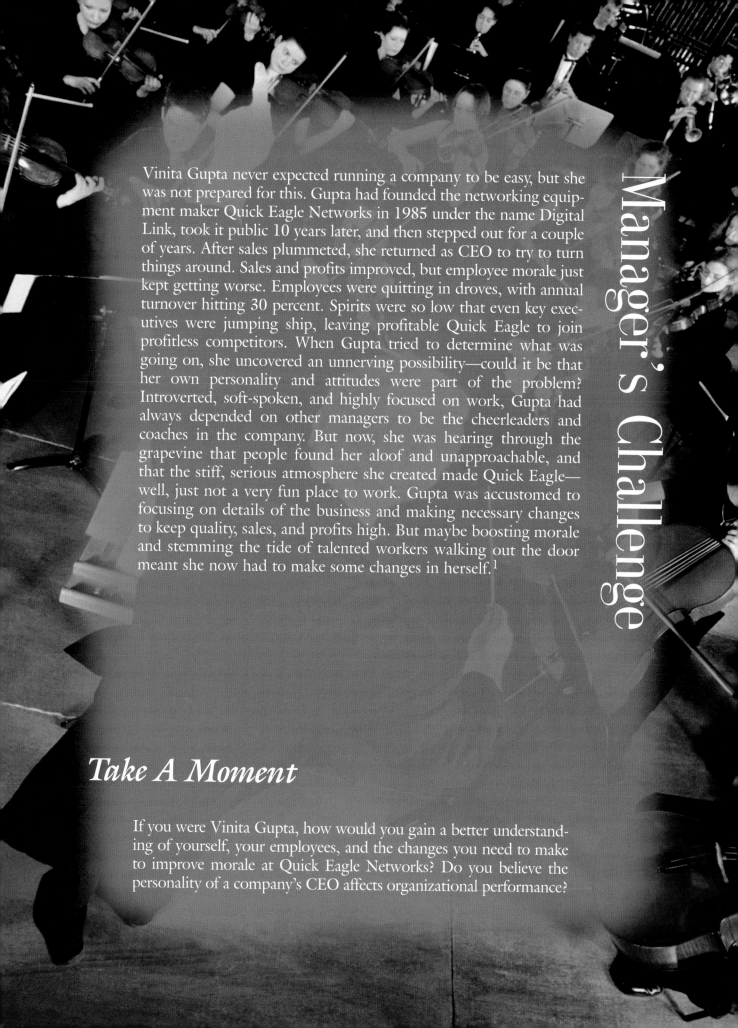

Vinita Gupta never expected running a company to be easy, but she was not prepared for this. Gupta had founded the networking equipment maker Quick Eagle Networks in 1985 under the name Digital Link, took it public 10 years later, and then stepped out for a couple of years. After sales plummeted, she returned as CEO to try to turn things around. Sales and profits improved, but employee morale just kept getting worse. Employees were quitting in droves, with annual turnover hitting 30 percent. Spirits were so low that even key executives were jumping ship, leaving profitable Quick Eagle to join profitless competitors. When Gupta tried to determine what was going on, she uncovered an unnerving possibility—could it be that her own personality and attitudes were part of the problem? Introverted, soft-spoken, and highly focused on work, Gupta had always depended on other managers to be the cheerleaders and coaches in the company. But now, she was hearing through the grapevine that people found her aloof and unapproachable, and that the stiff, serious atmosphere she created made Quick Eagle— well, just not a very fun place to work. Gupta was accustomed to focusing on details of the business and making necessary changes to keep quality, sales, and profits high. But maybe boosting morale and stemming the tide of talented workers walking out the door meant she now had to make some changes in herself.[1]

## Take A Moment

If you were Vinita Gupta, how would you gain a better understanding of yourself, your employees, and the changes you need to make to improve morale at Quick Eagle Networks? Do you believe the personality of a company's CEO affects organizational performance?

People differ in many ways. Some are quiet and shy while others are gregarious; some are thoughtful and serious while others are impulsive and fun-loving. Employees—and managers—bring their individual differences to work each day. Differences in attitudes, values, personality, and behavior influence how people interpret an assignment, whether they like to be told what to do, how they handle challenges, and how they interact with others. Managers' personalities and attitudes, as well as their ability to understand individual differences among employees, can profoundly affect the workplace and influence employee motivation, morale, and job performance. People are an organization's most valuable resource—and the source of some of managers' most difficult problems. Three basic leadership skills are at the core of identifying and solving people problems: (1) diagnosing, or gaining insight into the situation a manager is trying to influence; (2) adapting individual behavior and resources to meet the needs of the situation; and (3) communicating in a way that others can understand and accept. Thus, managers need insight about individual differences to understand what a behavioral situation is now and what it may be in the future.

To handle this responsibility, managers need to understand the principles of organizational behavior—that is, the ways individuals and groups tend to act in organizations. By increasing their knowledge of individual differences in the areas of attitudes, personality, perception, learning, and stress management, managers can understand and lead employees and colleagues through many workplace challenges. This chapter introduces basic principles of organizational behavior in each of these areas.

# Organizational Behavior

**organizational behavior**
An interdisciplinary field dedicated to the study of how individuals and groups tend to act in organizations.

**Organizational behavior**, commonly called OB, is an interdisciplinary field dedicated to the study of human attitudes, behavior, and performance in organizations. OB draws concepts from many disciplines, including psychology, sociology, cultural anthropology, industrial engineering, economics, ethics, and vocational counseling, as well as the discipline of management. The concepts and principles of organizational behavior are important to managers because in every organization human beings ultimately make the decisions that control how the organization will acquire and use resources. Those people may cooperate with, compete with, support, or undermine one another. Their beliefs and feelings about themselves, their coworkers, and the organization shape what they do and how well they do it. People can distract the organization from its strategy by engaging in conflict and misunderstandings, or they can pool their diverse talents and perspectives to accomplish much more as a group than they could ever do as individuals.

**organizational citizenship**
Work behavior that goes beyond job requirements and contributes as needed to the organization's success.

By understanding what causes people to behave as they do, managers can exercise leadership to achieve positive outcomes. They can foster behaviors such as organizational citizenship, that is, work behavior that goes beyond job requirements and contributes as needed to the organization's success. An employee demonstrates organizational citizenship by being helpful to coworkers and customers, doing extra work when necessary, and looking for ways to improve products and procedures. These behaviors enhance the organization's performance by helping to build *social capital*, as described in Chapter 12.[2] Organizational citizenship helps build positive relationships both within the organization and with customers, leading to a high level of social capital and smooth organizational functioning. Managers can encourage organizational citizenship by applying their knowledge of human behavior, such as selecting people with positive attitudes and personalities, helping them see how they can contribute, and enabling them to learn from and cope with workplace challenges.

# Attitudes

Most students have probably heard the expression that someone "has an attitude problem," which means there is some consistent quality about the person that affects his or her behavior in a negative way. An employee with an attitude problem might be hard to get along with, might constantly gripe and cause problems, and might persistently resist new ideas. We all seem to know intuitively what an attitude is, but we do not consciously think about how strongly attitudes affect behavior. Defined formally, an attitude is an evaluation—either positive or negative—that predisposes a person to act in a certain way. Understanding employee attitudes is important to managers because attitudes determine how people perceive the work environment, interact with others, and behave on the job. A person who has the attitude "I love my work; it's challenging and fun" probably will tackle work-related problems cheerfully, while one who comes to work with the attitude "I hate my job" is not likely to show much enthusiasm or commitment to solving problems. Managers strive to develop and reinforce positive attitudes among employees.

**attitude**
A cognitive and affective evaluation that predisposes a person to act in a certain way.

Managers should recognize that negative attitudes can be both the result of underlying problems in the workplace as well as a contributor to forthcoming problems.[3] For example, top executives at Federated Department Stores appointed a young, computer whiz-kid as chief operating officer for its e-commerce division. Older managers with years of experience in retailing had negative attitudes about this guy they considered still wet behind the ears, while the new COO had negative attitudes about older workers, whom he considered slow to accept new ideas or learn new methods. Soon, experienced managers started leaving the company. Federated's top leaders realized that the company needed to do a better job of handling generational diversity and help employees develop more positive attitudes.[4]

## Components of Attitudes

One important step for managers is recognizing and understanding the *components* of attitudes, which is particularly important when attempting to change attitudes.

Behavioral scientists consider attitudes to have three components: cognitions (thoughts), affect (feelings), and behavior.[5] The cognitive component of an attitude includes the beliefs, opinions, and information the person has about the object of the attitude, such as knowledge of what a job entails and opinions about personal abilities. The affective component is the person's emotions or feelings about the object of the attitude, such as enjoying or hating a job. The behavioral component of an attitude is the person's intention to behave toward the object of the attitude in a certain way. Exhibit 17.1 illustrates the three components of a positive attitude toward one's job. The cognitive element is the conscious thought that "my job is interesting and challenging." The affective element is the feeling that "I love this job." These, in turn, are related to the behavioral component—an employee might choose to arrive at work early because he or she is happy with the job.

© ERNEST WASHINGTON

**CONCEPT CONNECTION**

*Baseball legend Hank Aaron is still hitting home runs. Aaron has successfully made the transition from sports to business, and built a BMW dealership from the ground up that now ranks in the top 50% in sales for BMW of North America, with revenue growth of 54.6% last year. Aaron's **positive attitude** played a large role in his success, first as a baseball player and now as a business leader. "I believed if I could just get into something and keep it growing, I could do well. That's when I looked at myself and said I was a businessman."*

Exhibit 17.1

## Components of an Attitude

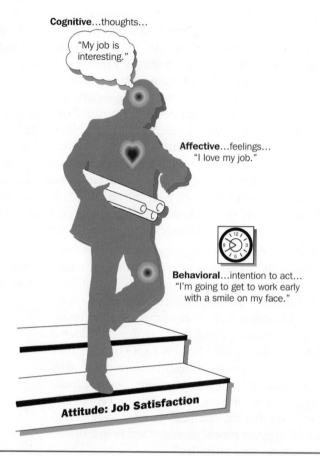

**Cognitive**...thoughts...

"My job is interesting."

**Affective**...feelings...
"I love my job."

**Behavioral**...intention to act...
"I'm going to get to work early with a smile on my face."

**Attitude: Job Satisfaction**

Often, when we think about attitudes, we focus on the cognitive component. However, it is important for managers to remember the other components as well. When people feel strongly about something, the affective component may influence them to act in a certain way, no matter what someone does to change their opinions. Recall the discussion of idea champions in Chapter 11. When someone is passionate about a new idea, he or she may go to great lengths to implement it, even when colleagues and superiors say the idea is stupid. Another example is an employee who is furious about being asked to work overtime on his birthday. The supervisor might present clear, rational reasons for the need to work over, but the employee might still act based on his anger—by failing to cooperate, lashing out at coworkers, or even quitting. In cases such as these, effective leadership includes addressing the affect (emotions) associated with the attitude. Are employees so excited that their judgment may be clouded, or so discouraged that they have given up trying? If nothing else, the manager probably needs to be aware of situations that involve strong emotions and give employees a chance to vent their feelings appropriately.

As a general rule, changing just one component—cognitions, affect, or behavior—can contribute to an overall change in attitude. Suppose a manager concludes that some employees have the attitude that the manager should make all the decisions affecting the department, but the manager prefers that employees assume more decision-making responsibility. To change the underlying attitude, the manager would consider whether to educate employees about the areas in which they can make good decisions (changing the cognitive component), build enthusiasm with pep talks about the satisfaction of employee empowerment (changing the affective component), or simply insist that employees make their own decisions (behavioral component) with the expectation that, once they experience the advantages of decision-making authority, they will begin to like it.

## High-Performance Work Attitudes

The attitudes of most interest to managers are those related to work, especially attitudes that influence how well employees perform. To lead employees effectively, managers logically seek to cultivate the kinds of attitudes that are associated with high performance. Two attitudes that might relate to high performance are satisfaction with one's job and commitment to the organization.

### Job Satisfaction

A positive attitude toward one's job is called job satisfaction. In general, people experience this attitude when their work matches their needs and interests, when working conditions and rewards (such as pay) are satisfactory, when they like their co-workers, and when they have positive relationships with supervisors. You can take the quiz in Exhibit 17.2 to better understand some of the factors that contribute to job satisfaction.

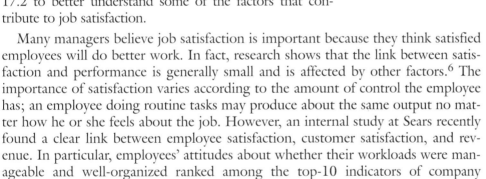

**CONCEPT CONNECTION**

*Set designer Ann Larlarb's **job satisfaction** is high. After college graduation, Larlarb arrived in London on a student visa to assist a famous set designer. Now she is in Thailand where she is apprenticing in the art workshop for a major motion picture, working 14-hour days, living out of three suitcases at a hotel, and using e-mail as her only address. But Larlarb thinks it's worth it—the exposure to new cultures has been invaluable research for her design work. She displays her attitude with a one-word comment as she pages through her journal: "Wow!"*

Many managers believe job satisfaction is important because they think satisfied employees will do better work. In fact, research shows that the link between satisfaction and performance is generally small and is affected by other factors.[6] The importance of satisfaction varies according to the amount of control the employee has; an employee doing routine tasks may produce about the same output no matter how he or she feels about the job. However, an internal study at Sears recently found a clear link between employee satisfaction, customer satisfaction, and revenue. In particular, employees' attitudes about whether their workloads were manageable and well-organized ranked among the top-10 indicators of company performance.[7]

Managers of today's knowledge workers often rely on job satisfaction to keep motivation and enthusiasm for the organization high. Organizations don't want to lose talented, highly skilled workers. In addition, most managers care about their employees and simply want them to feel good about their work—and almost everyone prefers being around people who have positive attitudes. However, a survey by International Survey Research found that Generation X employees, those who are carrying the weight of much of today's knowledge work, are the least satisfied of all demographic groups.[8] Managers play an important role in whether employees have positive or negative attitudes toward their jobs.[9] The CEO of General Mills recognizes that managers have to pay attention to their own attitudes and behaviors to influence the attitudes and performance of employees.

**job satisfaction**
A positive attitude toward one's job.

Steve Sanger, CEO of General Mills, recently told his co-workers that he was working on being a better leader by developing his coaching skills. Sanger had been reviewing his 360-degree feedback, in which people told him he needed to do a better job of coaching his direct reports. Rather than becoming defensive, Sanger adopted the attitude that he needed to improve himself in order to help others grow and improve.

GENERAL MILLS
**http://www.generalmills. com**

Exhibit 17.2

## Rate Your Job Satisfaction

Think of a job—either a current or previous job—that was important to you, and then answer the questions below with respect to how satisfied you were with that job. Please answer the six questions below with a number 1–5 that reflects the extent of your satisfaction.

| | | |
|---|---|---|
| 1 = Very dissatisfied | 3 = Neutral | 5 = Very satisfied |
| 2 = Dissatisfied | 4 = Satisfied | |

| | | | | | |
|---|---|---|---|---|---|
| 1. Overall, how satisfied are you with your job? | 1 | 2 | 3 | 4 | 5 |
| 2. How satisfied are you with the opportunities to learn new things? | 1 | 2 | 3 | 4 | 5 |
| 3. How satisfied are you with your boss? | 1 | 2 | 3 | 4 | 5 |
| 4. How satisfied are you with the people in your work group? | 1 | 2 | 3 | 4 | 5 |
| 5. How satisfied are you with the amount of pay you receive? | 1 | 2 | 3 | 4 | 5 |
| 6. How satisfied are you with the advancement you are making in the organization? | 1 | 2 | 3 | 4 | 5 |

**Scoring and Interpretation:** Add up your responses to the six questions to obtain your total score: _____. The questions represent various aspects of satisfaction that an employee may experience on a job. If your score is 24 or above, you probably feel satisfied with the job. If your score is 12 or below, you probably do not feel satisfied. What is your level of performance in your job, and is your performance related to your level of satisfaction?

**SOURCES:** These questions were adapted from Daniel R. Denison, *Corporate Culture and Organizational Effectiveness* (New York, John Wiley, 1990; and John D. Cook, Susan J. Hepworth, Toby D. Wall, and Peter B. Warr, *The Experience of Work: A Compendium and Review of 249 Measures and their Use* (San Diego, Calif. Academic Press, 1981).

When the top leader of a company displays arrogance and simply tells everyone else how they need to improve, that attitude and behavior filters down to every level of management. An "us-versus-them" mindset often develops between employees and managers and job satisfaction, motivation, and performance decline.

Steve Sanger, though, had an insight. By being open with people and admitting his own weaknesses and efforts to improve, he set an example for others to do the same. Sanger is noted for his enlightened attitudes about how to help employees be successful both at work and in their personal lives. The first step, he knows, is for a leader to be aware of how his attitudes and behaviors influence others and create either a positive or a negative organizational environment.[10]

By creating a positive environment, leaders like Steve Sanger contribute to higher job satisfaction for employees. A related attitude is organizational commitment.

### Organizational Commitment

**organizational commitment**
Loyalty to and heavy involvement in one's organization.

Organizational commitment refers to an employee's loyalty to and engagement with the organization. An employee with a high degree of organizational commitment is likely to say *we* when talking about the company. Such a person likes being a part of the organization and tries to contribute to its success. This attitude is illustrated by an incident at the A. W. Chesterton Company, a Massachusetts company that produces mechanical seals and pumps. When two Chesterton pumps that supply water on Navy ship *USS John F. Kennedy* failed on a Saturday night just before the ship's scheduled departure, Todd Robinson, the leader of the team that produces the seals, swung into action. He and his fiancèe, who also works for Chesterton, worked through the night to make new seals and deliver them to be installed before the ship left port.[11]

Most managers want to enjoy the benefits of loyal, committed employees, including low turnover and willingness to do more than the job's basic requirements. In addition, results of a recent survey of more than 650,000 employees in global organizations suggests that companies with committed employees perform better. The study found that companies with highly committed employees outperformed the industry average over a 12-month period by 6 percent, while those with low levels of commitment underperformed the average by 9 percent.[12] Alarmingly, levels of commitment in the United States are significantly lower than those in half of the world's other large economies, as illustrated in Exhibit 17.3. U.S. employees are less committed than those in Brazil, Spain, Germany, Canada, and Italy. This low level of organizational commitment puts U.S. firms at a serious disadvantage in the global marketplace.[13]

The high motivation and engagement that comes with organizational commitment is essential to the success of knowledge-based organizations that depend on employees' ideas and creativity. Trust in management's decisions and integrity is an important component of organizational commitment.[14] Unfortunately, in recent years, many employees have lost that trust, resulting in a decline in commitment.

Managers can take action to promote organizational commitment by keeping employees informed, giving them a say in decisions, providing the necessary training and other resources that enable them to succeed, treating them fairly, and offering rewards they value. For example, recent studies suggest that employee commitment in today's workplace is strongly correlated with initiatives and benefits that help people balance their work and personal lives.[15] The Unlocking Creative Solutions Through People box describes one organization that was built on the concept of fostering a good life for the people who work there.

## Conflicts among Attitudes

Sometimes a person may discover that his or her attitudes conflict with one another or are not reflected in behavior. For example, a person's high level of organizational

Exhibit 17.3

### Variations in Organizational Commitment:
### The World's Ten Largest Economies

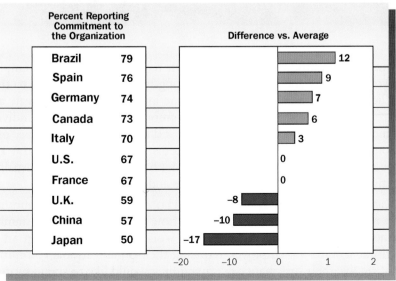

Shaded difference bar denotes a statistically significant difference

**SOURCE:** "Employee Commitment—U.S.: Leader or Follower?" International Survey Research, *http://www. isrsurveys.com* 1-800-300-0750.

# Unlocking Creative Solutions Through People

## The Rokenbok Magic

Paul Eichen wondered what a company would look like if its only aim was to promote a balanced, healthy, soulful life. Work was everything to Eichen, who had helped start a successful technology company and grow it to sales of $100 million. However, work was eating him alive, so he walked away from his lucrative, successful job and began pursuing the answer to his question.

As a boy, Eichen had loved LEGOs, model kits, and machines, a love that would prove to be his salvation for a better life. "I think people tend to know what they need to do in their lives, and they can either ignore it or get on with it," Eichen says. He knew what he needed to do—start a toy company. But even more importantly, he wanted to create a new kind of business, one in which every company-defining decision was based on the way it would make work feel for the people who worked there. When Eichen opened the doors to Rokenbok Toy Co., it wasn't in an industrial park but in a village by the beach, in an old, rehabilitated warehouse just a short walk from the sand, with ethnic restaurants and sundries emporiums, coffee shops, and used bookstores as neighbors. Having the real world surround Rokenbok held a kind of magic for Eichen and his employees, who realized that where a company is located determines not only the commute but also the richness of life outside the office.

The pattern of work at Rokenbok was also different from many companies. As long as employees did their work, they were encouraged to set their own hours, dress as they liked, tend to their health, and put their families first. One Rokenbok engineer describes playing on the living room floor with his child and company toys, piecing together problems, working as he played, playing as he worked. For most company employees, work became a source of re-connection with family, friends, and neighbors. "We're trying to make something classic, not disposable. Values that are important personally—quality, constructive fun, learning, design sophistication—are things we're trying to design right into the product, and that feels great."

Rokenbok's employees have accomplished something noteworthy: They've created an independent American toy company, establishing a product that has won toy-industry accolades and climbed from sales of $2.6 million in 1997 to $10 million in 1999. And even though Eichen believes that during the dot-com heyday every one of his managers were recruited and promised "instant millions," none of them left. "Our executives have chosen quality of life over the seductiveness of . . . wealth," says Eichen.

Eichen does not kid himself that even the most balanced workplaces can prevent life from getting a little messy, but the Rokenbok work style allows employees to have the energy and flexibility to pay attention to health, friends, family, and dreams, as well as their work "Look," Eichen says, "at a company like Rokenbok you still get to keep the good parts [of work]: intellectual stimulation, social activity, the fun of competing to win." Plus, you get to have a personal life, too. It's a winning combination.

SOURCE: Michael Hopkins, "The Pursuit of Happiness," *Inc.* (August 2000), 72–89.

**cognitive dissonance**
A condition in which two attitudes or a behavior and an attitude conflict.

commitment might conflict with a commitment to family members. If employees routinely work evenings and weekends, their long hours and dedication to the job might conflict with their belief that family ties are important. This can create a state of cognitive dissonance, a psychological discomfort that occurs when individuals recognize inconsistencies in their own attitudes and behaviors.[16] The theory of cognitive dissonance, developed by social psychologist Leon Festinger in the 1950s, says that people want to behave in accordance with their attitudes and usually will take corrective action to alleviate the dissonance and achieve balance.

In the case of working overtime, people who can control their hours might restructure responsibilities so that they have time for both work and family. In contrast, those who are unable to restructure workloads might develop an unfavorable attitude toward the employer, reducing their organizational commitment. They might resolve their dissonance by saying they would like to spend more time with their kids but their unreasonable employer demands that they work too many hours.

# Perception

Another critical aspect of understanding behavior is perception. Perception is the cognitive process people use to make sense out of the environment by selecting, organizing, and interpreting information from the environment. Attitudes affect perceptions, and vice versa. For example, a person might have developed the attitude that managers are insensitive and arrogant, based on a pattern of perceiving arrogant and insensitive behavior from managers over a period of time. If the person moves to a new job, this attitude will continue to affect the way he or she perceives superiors in the new environment, even though managers in the new workplace might take great pains to understand and respond to employees' needs.

Because of individual differences in attitudes, personality, values, interests, and so forth, people often "see" the same thing in different ways. A class that is boring to one student might be fascinating to another. One student might perceive an assignment to be challenging and stimulating, whereas another might find it a silly waste of time. Referring back to the topic of diversity discussed in Chapter 13, many African Americans perceive that blacks are regularly discriminated against, whereas many white employees perceive that blacks are given special opportunities in the workplace.[17]

We can think of perception as a step-by-step process, as shown in Exhibit 17.4. First, we observe information (sensory data) from the environment through our senses: taste, smell, hearing, sight, and touch. Next, our mind screens the data and will select only the items we will process further. Third, we organize the selected data into meaningful patterns for interpretation and response. Most differences in perception among people at work are related to how they select and organize sensory data. You can experience differences in perceptual organization by looking at the visuals in Exhibit 17.5. What do you see in part *a* of the Exhibit 17.5? Most people see this as a dog, but others see only a series of unrelated ink blots. Some people will see the figure in part *b* as a beautiful young woman while others will see an old one. Now look at part *c*. How many blocks do you see—six or seven? Some people have to turn the figure upside down before they can see seven blocks. These visuals illustrate how complex perception is.

## Perceptual Selectivity

We all are aware of our environment, but not everything in it is equally important to our perception of it. We tune in to some data (e.g., a familiar voice off in the distance) and tune out other data (e.g., paper shuffling next to us). People are bombarded by so much sensory data that it is impossible to process it all. The brain's solution is to run the data through a perceptual filter that retains some parts (selective attention) and eliminates others. Perceptual selectivity is the process by which individuals screen and select the various objects and stimuli that vie for their attention. Certain stimuli catch their attention, and others do not.

**perception**
The cognitive process people use to make sense out of the environment by selecting, organizing, and interpreting information.

**perceptual selectivity**
The process by which individuals screen and select the various stimuli that vie for their attention.

Exhibit 17.4

**The Perception Process**

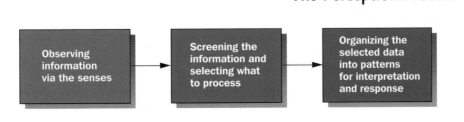

Exhibit **17.5**

**Perception—What Do You See?**

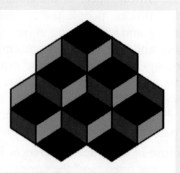

**a.** Do you see the dog?    **b.** Old woman or young woman?    **c.** How many blocks?

People typically focus on stimuli that satisfy their needs and that are consistent with their attitudes, values, and personality. For example, employees who need positive feedback to feel good about themselves might pick up on positive statements made by a supervisor but tune out most negative comments. A supervisor could use this understanding to tailor his feedback in a positive way to help the employee improve her work. The influence of needs on perception has been studied in laboratory experiments and found to have a strong impact on what people perceive.[18]

Characteristics of the stimuli itself also affect perceptual selectivity. People tend to notice stimuli that stand out against other stimuli or that are more intense than surrounding stimuli. Examples would be a loud noise in a quiet room or a bright red dress at a party where most women are wearing basic black. People also tend to notice things that are familiar to them, such as a familiar voice in a crowd, as well as things that are new or different from their previous experiences. In addition, *primacy* and *recency* are important to perceptual selectivity. People pay relatively greater attention to sensory data that occur toward the beginning of an event or toward the end. Primacy supports the old truism that first impressions really do count, whether it be on a job interview, meeting a date's parents, or participating in a new social group. Recency reflects the reality that the last impression might be a lasting impression. For example, Malaysian Airlines has discovered its value in building customer loyalty. A woman traveling with a nine-month-old might find the flight itself an exhausting blur, but one such traveler enthusiastically told people for years how Malaysian Airlines flight attendants helped her with baggage collection and ground transportation.[19]

As these examples show, perceptual selectivity is a complex filtering process. Managers can use an understanding of perceptual selectivity to obtain clues about why one person sees things differently from others, and they can apply the principles to their own communications and actions, especially when they want to attract or focus attention.

## Perceptual Distortions

**perceptual distortions**
Errors in perceptual judgment that arise from inaccuracies in any part of the perceptual process.

Once people have selected the sensory data to be perceived, they begin grouping the data into recognizable patterns. Perceptual organization is the process by which people organize or categorize stimuli according to their own frame of reference. Of particular concern in the work environment are perceptual distortions, errors in perceptual judgment that arise from inaccuracies in any part of the perceptual process.

Some types of errors are so common that managers should become familiar with them. These include stereotyping, the halo effect, projection, and perceptual defense. Managers who recognize these perceptual distortions can better adjust their perceptions to more closely match objective reality.

Stereotyping is the tendency to assign an individual to a group or broad category (e.g., female, black, elderly or male, white, disabled) and then to attribute widely held generalizations about the group to the individual. Thus, someone meets a new colleague, sees he is in a wheelchair, assigns him to the category "physically disabled," and attributes to this colleague generalizations she believes about people with disabilities, which may include a belief that he is less able than other co-workers. However, the person's inability to walk should not be seen as indicative of lesser abilities in other areas. Indeed, the assumption of limitations may not only offend him or her, it also prevents the person making the stereotypical judgment from benefiting from the many ways in which this person can contribute. Stereotyping prevents people from truly knowing those they classify in this way. In addition, negative stereotypes prevent talented people from advancing in an organization and fully contributing their talents to the organization's success.

The halo effect occurs when the perceiver develops an overall impression of a person or situation based on one characteristic, either favorable or unfavorable. In other words, a halo blinds the perceiver to other characteristics that should be used in generating a more complete assessment. The halo effect can play a significant role in performance appraisal, as we discussed in Chapter 12. For example, a person with an outstanding attendance record may be assessed as responsible, industrious, and highly productive; another person with less-than-average attendance may be assessed as a poor performer. Either assessment may be true, but it is the manager's job to be sure the assessment is based on complete information about all job-related characteristics and not just his or her preferences for good attendance.

Projection is the tendency of perceivers to see their own personal traits in other people; that is, they project their own needs, feelings, values, and attitudes into their judgment of others. A manager who is achievement oriented might assume that subordinates are as well. This might cause the manager to restructure jobs to be less routine and more challenging, without regard for employees' actual satisfaction. The best guards against errors based on projection are self-awareness and empathy.

Perceptual defense is the tendency of perceivers to protect themselves against ideas, objects, or people that are threatening. People perceive things that are satisfying and pleasant but tend to disregard things that are disturbing and unpleasant. In essence, people develop blind spots in the perceptual process so that negative sensory data do not hurt them. For example, the director of a nonprofit educational organization in Tennessee hated dealing with conflict because he had grown up with parents who constantly argued and often put him in the middle of their arguments. The director consistently overlooked discord among staff members until things would reach a boiling point. When the blow-up occurred, the director would be shocked and dismayed, because he had truly perceived that everything was going smoothly among the staff. Recognizing perceptual blind spots can help people develop a clearer picture of reality.

## Attributions

As people organize what they perceive, they often draw conclusions, such as about an object or a person. For example, stereotyping involves assigning a number of traits to a person. Among the judgments people make as part of the perceptual process are attributions. Attributions are judgments about what caused a person's behavior—something about the person or something about the situation. An

**stereotyping**
The tendency to assign an individual to a group or broad category and then attribute generalizations about the group to the individual.

**halo effect**
An overall impression of a person or situation based on one characteristic, either favorable or unfavorable.

**projection**
The tendency to see one's own personal traits in other people.

**perceptual defense**
The tendency of perceivers to protect themselves by disregarding ideas, objects, or people that are threatening to them.

**attributions**
Judgments about what caused a person's behavior—either characteristics of the person or of the situation.

*internal attribution* says characteristics of the person led to the behavior ("My boss yelled at me because he's impatient and doesn't listen"). An *external attribution* says something about the situation caused the person's behavior ("My boss yelled at me because I missed the deadline and the customer is upset"). Attributions are important because they help people decide how to handle a situation. In the case of the boss yelling, a person who blames the yelling on the boss's personality will view the boss as the problem and might cope by avoiding the boss. In contrast, someone who blames the yelling on the situation might try to help prevent such situations in the future.

Social scientists have studied the attributions people make and identified three factors that influence whether an attribution will be external or internal.[20] These three factors are illustrated in Exhibit 17.6.

1. *Distinctiveness*. Whether the behavior is unusual for that person (in contrast to a person displaying the same kind of behavior in many situations). If the behavior is distinctive, the perceiver probably will make an *external* attribution.
2. *Consistency*. Whether the person being observed has a history of behaving in the same way. People generally make *internal* attributions about consistent behavior.
3. *Consensus*. Whether other people tend to respond to similar situations in the same way. A person who has observed others handle similar situations in the same way will likely make an *external* attribution; that is, it will seem that the situation produces the type of behavior observed.

**fundamental attribution error**
The tendency to underestimate the influence of external factors on another's behavior and to overestimate the influence of internal factors.

In addition to these general rules, people tend to have biases that they apply when making attributions. When evaluating others, we tend to underestimate the influence of external factors and overestimate the influence of internal factors. This tendency is called the fundamental attribution error. Consider the case of someone

Exhibit 17.6

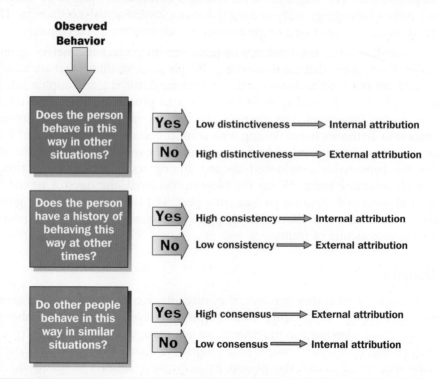

**Factors Influencing Whether Attributions Are Internal or External**

being promoted to CEO. Employees, outsiders, and the media generally focus on the characteristics of the person that allowed him or her to achieve the promotion. In reality, however, the selection of that person might have been heavily influenced by external factors, such as business conditions creating a need for someone with a strong financial or marketing background at that particular time.

Another bias that distorts attributions involves attributions we make about our own behavior. People tend to overestimate the contribution of internal factors to their successes and overestimate the contribution of external factors to their failures. This tendency, called the self-serving bias, means people give themselves too much credit for what they do well and give external forces too much blame when they fail. Thus, if your manager says you don't communicate well enough, and you think your manager doesn't listen well enough, the truth may actually lie somewhere in between.

**self-serving bias**
The tendency to overestimate the contribution of internal factors to one's successes and the contribution of external factors to one's failures.

# Personality and Behavior

Another area of particular interest to organizational behavior is personality. In the workplace, we find people whose behavior is consistently pleasant or aggressive or stubborn in a variety of situations.

An individual's personality is the set of characteristics that underlie a relatively stable pattern of behavior in response to ideas, objects, or people in the environment. Understanding personality can help managers predict how that person might act in a particular situation. Managers who appreciate the ways their employees' personalities differ have insight into what kinds of leadership behavior will be most influential.

**personality**
The set of characteristics that underlie a relatively stable pattern of behavior in response to ideas, objects, or people in the environment.

## Personality Traits

In common usage, people think of personality in terms of traits, or relatively stable characteristics of a person. Researchers have investigated whether any traits stand up to scientific scrutiny. Although investigators have examined thousands of traits over the years, their findings have been distilled into five general dimensions that describe personality. These often are called the "Big Five" personality factors, as illustrated in Exhibit 17.7.[21] Each factor may contain a wide range of specific traits. The Big Five personality factors describe an individual's extroversion, agreeableness, conscientiousness, emotional stability, and openness to experience:

**Big Five personality factors** .
Dimensions that describe an individual's extroversion, agreeableness, conscientiousness, emotional stability, and openness to experience.

1. *Extroversion.* The degree to which a person is sociable, talkative, assertive, and comfortable with interpersonal relationships.
2. *Agreeableness.* The degree to which a person is able to get along with others by being good-natured, cooperative, forgiving, understanding, and trusting.
3. *Conscientiousness.* The degree to which a person is focused on a few goals, thus behaving in ways that are responsible, dependable, persistent, and achievement oriented.
4. *Emotional stability.* The degree to which a person is calm, enthusiastic, and secure, rather than tense, nervous, depressed, moody, or insecure.
5. *Openness to experience.* The degree to which a person has a broad range of interests and is imaginative, creative, artistically sensitive, and willing to consider new ideas.

As illustrated in the exhibit, these factors represent a continuum. That is, a person may have a low, moderate, or high degree of each quality. Answer the questions in Exhibit 17.7 to see where you fall on the Big Five scale for each of the factors. A person who has an extremely high degree of agreeableness would likely be described

Exhibit 17.7

## The Big Five Personality Traits

Each individual's collection of personality traits is different; it is what makes us unique. But, although each *collection* of traits varies, we all share many common traits. The following phrases describe various traits and behaviors. Rate how accurately each statement describes you, based on a scale of 1 to 5, with 1 being very inaccurate and 5 very accurate. Describe yourself as you are now, not as you wish to be. There are no right or wrong answers.

|   | 1 | 2 | 3 | 4 | 5 |
|---|---|---|---|---|---|
| | Very Inaccurate | | | | Very Accurate |

**Extroversion**

| | 1 | 2 | 3 | 4 | 5 |
|---|---|---|---|---|---|
| I am usually the life of the party. | 1 | 2 | 3 | 4 | 5 |
| I feel comfortable around people. | 1 | 2 | 3 | 4 | 5 |
| I am talkative. | 1 | 2 | 3 | 4 | 5 |

**Agreeableness**

| | 1 | 2 | 3 | 4 | 5 |
|---|---|---|---|---|---|
| I am kind and sympathetic. | 1 | 2 | 3 | 4 | 5 |
| I have a good word for everyone. | 1 | 2 | 3 | 4 | 5 |
| I never insult people. | 1 | 2 | 3 | 4 | 5 |

**Conscientiousness**

| | 1 | 2 | 3 | 4 | 5 |
|---|---|---|---|---|---|
| I am systematic and efficient. | 1 | 2 | 3 | 4 | 5 |
| I pay attention to details. | 1 | 2 | 3 | 4 | 5 |
| I am always prepared for class. | 1 | 2 | 3 | 4 | 5 |

**Neuroticism (Low Emotional Stability)**

| | 1 | 2 | 3 | 4 | 5 |
|---|---|---|---|---|---|
| I often feel critical of myself. | 1 | 2 | 3 | 4 | 5 |
| I often envy others. | 1 | 2 | 3 | 4 | 5 |
| I am temperamental. | 1 | 2 | 3 | 4 | 5 |

**Openness to New Experiences**

| | 1 | 2 | 3 | 4 | 5 |
|---|---|---|---|---|---|
| I am imaginative. | 1 | 2 | 3 | 4 | 5 |
| I prefer to vote for liberal political candidates. | 1 | 2 | 3 | 4 | 5 |
| I really like art. | 1 | 2 | 3 | 4 | 5 |

Which are your most prominent traits? For fun and discussion, compare your responses with those of classmates.

**SOURCE:** These questions were adapted from a variety of sources.

as warm, friendly, and good natured, while one at the opposite extreme might be described as cold, rude, or hard to get along with. In general, having a moderate-to-high degree of each of the personality factors is considered desirable for a wide range of employees. In addition, certain factors may be particularly important for specific kinds of work. For example, Nancy Naatz works for Aramark, a company that caters big events and runs cafeterias for universities and corporate clients. Naatz, a district manager, needs a high degree of extroversion and agreeableness to build the relationships that are critical to her success working with clients such as Sears. These traits might not be as important for an employee who has little need to interact with others.

Many companies, including JCPenney, Toys 'R' Us, and the Union Pacific Railroad, use personality testing to hire, evaluate, or promote employees. American MultiCinema (AMC), one of the largest theater chains in the United States, looks for front-line workers with high conscientiousness and high emotional stability.[22] Marriott Hotels looks for people who score high on conscientiousness and agreeableness because they believe these individuals will provide better service to guests.[23] Companies also use personality testing for managers. Hewlett-Packard, Dell Computer, and General Electric all put candidates for top positions through testing, interviews with psychologists, or both to see if they have the "right stuff" for the job.[24] The Unlocking Creative Solutions Through Technology box describes how a young Harvard Business School graduate found Internet success with a company built around personality testing.

# Unlocking Creative Solutions Through Technology

**Tickle Lets You Get To Know All About You**

When James Currier took the Myers–Briggs Type Inventory at Harvard Business School, he not only learned his personality type but also saw his future. Currier was looking for an Internet business idea, and the interest and excitement the Myers–Briggs test generated among his classmates told him there was potential in bringing personality testing online.

Currier's company, originally called eMode.com and renamed Tickle, managed to survive the dot-com collapse and is growing and profitable today. Tickle offers a range of online tests on personality, careers, and relationships. The site makes these tests highly personal with customized results and gives people a chance to share them with each other. Some of the tests are based on standard measurements like Myers–Briggs, while others are just for fun. For example, there are quizzes to tell you what breed of dog you are or what the theme song of your life is. The dog test attracted a million users within two weeks of its introduction.

Currier's goal is to keep a good balance among science, entertainment, and commercialism. "Everyone says you can't be scientific and fun, but we think you can," he says. Test results are always phrased in a positive way. For example, someone might be told, "You are more optimistic than 15 percent of the other people who took this quiz" (the reverse side, of course, is that the person scored exceedingly high on being a pessimistic Gloomy Gus).

To grow, Currier has added a dating service as well as a social network to help people find friends based on their compatible personality types. He's thinking about getting into the market for job placements and classifieds. The links to career and personality testing could give Tickle an advantage over other job sites, for example. And Currier thinks used car buyers just might like the idea of buying from someone who scores high on honesty and integrity.

**SOURCE**: Saul Hansell, "Getting to Know Me, Getting to Know All About Me: Web Personality Tests," *The New York Times* (March 8, 2004), *http://www.nytimes.com*.

Despite growing use, there is little evidence that personality tests are a valid predictor of job success. In addition, the Big Five dimensions have been criticized because they are difficult to measure precisely. Because each dimension is made up of a number of specific traits, a person might score high on some traits but low on others. For example, considering the dimension of conscientiousness, a person might score high on a trait such as dependability, but score low on achievement orientation. Furthermore, research on the Big Five has mostly been limited to the United States, so there are dangers in applying the theory cross-culturally.

## Emotional Intelligence

In recent years, new insights into personality have been gained through research in the area of *emotional intelligence*. Emotional intelligence (EQ) includes four basic components:[25]

1. *Self-awareness.* The basis for all the other components; being aware of what you are feeling. People who are in touch with their feelings are better able to guide their own lives and actions. A high degree of self-awareness means you can accurately assess your own strengths and limitations and have a healthy sense of self-confidence.

2. *Self-management.* The ability to control disruptive or harmful emotions and balance one's moods so that worry, anxiety, fear, or anger do not cloud thinking and get in the way of what needs to be done. People who are skilled at self-management remain optimistic and hopeful despite setbacks and obstacles. This

ability is crucial for pursuing long-term goals. For example, MetLife found that applicants who failed the regular sales aptitude test but scored high on optimism made 21 percent more sales in their first year and 57 percent more in their second year than those who passed the sales test but scored high on pessimism.[26]

3. *Social awareness.* The ability to understand others and practice *empathy*, which means being able to put yourself in someone else's shoes, to recognize what others are feeling without them needing to tell you. People with social awareness are capable of understanding divergent points of view and interacting effectively with many different types of people.

4. *Relationship awareness.* The ability to connect to others, build positive relationships, respond to the emotions of others, and influence others. People with relationship awareness know how to listen and communicate clearly and they treat others with compassion and respect.

**CONCEPT CONNECTION**

*Harvard Law School's Program on Negotiation offers seminars that help small business owners develop their* **emotional intelligence** *and be more effective leaders. "People [wrongly] assume that you check your feelings at the door when you go to work," says Sheila Heen, a Harvard Law School lecturer. The program offers training in topics such as Improving Your Listening Skills, Managing Anger at Work, Managing Your Feelings, and Getting Straight on Purposes. In the photo, participants practice expressing their emotions without becoming "emotional."*

Studies have found a positive relationship between job performance and high degrees of emotional intelligence in a variety of jobs. Numerous organizations, including the U.S. Air Force and Canada Life, have used EQ tests to measure such things as self-awareness, ability to empathize, and capacity to build positive relationships.[27] EQ seems to be particularly important for jobs that require a high degree of social interaction, which includes managers, who are responsible for influencing others and building positive attitudes and relationships in the organization. Managers with low emotional intelligence can harm the organization. Consider Peter Angelos, who bought the Baltimore Orioles in 1993. Angelos' domineering approach to leadership drove away some of the team's most experienced managers and executives, leaving the Orioles weakened and demoralized.[28]

At times of great change or crisis, managers need a higher EQ level to help employees cope with the anxiety and stress they may be experiencing. In the United States, fears of terrorism, anxiety and sorrow over the war in Iraq, and continuing economic hardships for many people has made meeting the psychological and emotional needs of employees a new role for managers. This chapter's Shoptalk box outlines some elements of emotional intelligence that are particularly important in times of crisis and turmoil. It is important to remember that emotional intelligence is not an in-born personality characteristic, but something that can be learned and developed throughout one's lifetime.[29]

## Attitudes and Behaviors Influenced by Personality

An individual's personality influences a wide variety of work-related attitudes and behaviors. Among those that are of particular interest to managers are locus of control, authoritarianism, Machiavellianism, and problem-solving styles.

**locus of control**
The tendency to place the primary responsibility for one's success or failure either within oneself (internally) or on outside forces (externally).

### Locus of Control
People differ in terms of what they tend to attribute as the cause of their success or failure. Their locus of control defines whether they place the primary responsibility within themselves or on outside forces.[30] Some people believe that their actions can strongly influence what happens to them. They feel in control of their own fate. These individuals have a high *internal* locus of control. Other people believe that events in

## manager's Shoptalk

### Turbulent Times

### What's Your Crisis EQ?

Threats of terrorist attacks. Downsizing. The SARS virus. Company failures. Anthrax in the mail. Stock market crashes. Rapid technological changes. Information overload. The turbulence of today's world has left lingering psychological and emotional damage in workplaces all across the United States, as well as in the rest of the world. When even a minor crisis hits an organization, uncertainty and fear are high. Today's managers need the skills to help people deal with their emotions and return to a more normal work routine. Although managers cannot take the place of professional counselors, they can use patience, flexibility, and understanding to assist people through a crisis. Here are some important elements of crisis EQ for managers:

- Be visible and provide as much up-to-date, accurate information as possible about what's going on in the company and the industry. Rumor control is critical.
- Find simple ways to get employees together. Order pizza for the entire staff. Invite telecommuters to come in to the office so they can connect with others and have a chance to share their emotions.
- Give employees room to be human. It is natural for people to feel anger and other strong emotions, so allow those feelings to be expressed as long as they aren't directed at other employees.
- Publicize the company's charitable endeavors and make employees aware of the various opportunities both within and outside the organization to volunteer and donate to charity.
- Thank employees in person and with handwritten notes when they go above and beyond the call of duty during a difficult time.
- Recognize that routine, structured work can help people heal. Postpone major, long-term projects and decisions to the extent possible and break work into shorter, more manageable tasks. Listen to employees and determine what they need to help them return to a normal work life.
- Provide professional counseling services for people who need it. Those with a history of alcohol abuse, trouble at home, or previous mental or emotional problems are especially at risk, but anyone who has trouble gradually returning to his or her previous level of work may need outside counseling.

SOURCES: Based on Matthew Boyle, "Nothing Really Matters," *Fortune* (October 15, 2001), 261–264; and Sue Shellenbarger, "Readers Face Dilemma Over How Far to Alter Post-Attack Workplace," (Work & Family column), *The Wall Street Journal* (October 31, 2001), B1.

their lives occur because of chance, luck, or outside people and events. They feel more like pawns of their fate. These individuals have a high *external* locus of control. Many top leaders of e-commerce and high-tech organizations possess a high internal locus of control. These managers have to cope with rapid change and uncertainty associated with Internet business. They must believe that they and their employees can counter the negative impact of outside forces and events. John Chambers, CEO of Cisco Systems, is a good example. Despite a tough economy and a drastically diminished stock price, Chambers maintained his belief that Cisco can defeat any challenge thrown its way.[31] A person with a high external locus of control would likely feel overwhelmed trying to make the rapid decisions and changes needed to keep pace with the industry, particularly in the current environment of uncertainty.

Research on locus of control has shown real differences in behavior across a wide range of settings. People with an internal locus of control are easier to motivate because they believe the rewards are the result of their behavior. They are better able to handle complex information and problem solving, are more achievement oriented, but are also more independent and therefore more difficult to lead. By contrast, people with an external locus of control are harder to motivate, less involved in their jobs, more likely to blame others when faced with a poor performance evaluation, but more compliant and conforming and, therefore, easier to lead.[32]

Do you believe luck plays an important role in your life, or do you feel that you control your own fate? To find out more about your locus of control, read the instructions and complete the questionnaire in Exhibit 17.8.

## Authoritarianism

**authoritarianism**
The belief that power and status differences should exist within the organization.

Authoritarianism is the belief that power and status differences should exist within the organization.[33] Individuals high in authoritarianism tend to be concerned with power and toughness, obey recognized authority above them, stick to conventional values, critically judge others, and oppose the use of subjective feelings. The degree to which managers possess authoritarianism will influence how they wield and share power. The degree to which employees possess authoritarianism will influence how

Exhibit 17.8

### Measuring Locus of Control

**Your Locus of Control**

This questionnaire is designed to measure locus-of-control beliefs. Researchers using this questionnaire in a study of college students found a mean of 51.8 for men and 52.2 for women, with a standard deviation of 6 for each. The higher your score on this questionnaire, the more you tend to believe that you are generally responsible for what happens to you; in other words, higher scores are associated with internal locus of control. Low scores are associated with external locus of control. Scoring low indicates that you tend to believe that forces beyond your control, such as powerful other people, fate, or chance, are responsible for what happens to you.

For each of these 10 questions, indicate the extent to which you agree or disagree using the following scale:

1 = strongly disagree      4 = neither disagree nor agree        7 = strongly agree
2 = disagree               5 = slightly agree
3 = slightly disagree      6 = agree

| | |
|---|---|
| 1. When I get what I want, it is usually because I worked hard for it. | 1  2  3  4  5  6  7 |
| 2. When I make plans, I am almost certain to make them work. | 1  2  3  4  5  6  7 |
| 3. I prefer games involving some luck over games requiring pure skill. | 1  2  3  4  5  6  7 |
| 4. I can learn almost anything if I set my mind to it. | 1  2  3  4  5  6  7 |
| 5. My major accomplishments are entirely due to my hard work and ability. | 1  2  3  4  5  6  7 |
| 6. I usually don't set goals, because I have a hard time following through on them. | 1  2  3  4  5  6  7 |
| 7. Competition discourages excellence. | 1  2  3  4  5  6  7 |
| 8. Often people get ahead just by being lucky. | 1  2  3  4  5  6  7 |
| 9. On any sort of exam or competition, I like to know how well I do relative to everyone else. | 1  2  3  4  5  6  7 |
| 10. It's pointless to keep working on something that's too difficult for me. | 1  2  3  4  5  6  7 |

**Scoring and Interpretation**

To determine your score, reverse the values you selected for questions 3, 6, 7, 8, and 10 (1 = 7, 2 = 6, 3 = 5, 4 = 4, 5 = 3, 6 = 2, 7 = 1). For example, if you strongly disagree with the statement in question 3, you would have given it a value of 1. Change this value to a 7. Reverse the scores in a similar manner for questions 6, 7, 8, and 10. Now add the point values for all 10 questions together.

Your score _____

**SOURCE:** Adapted from J. M. Burger, *Personality: Theory and Research* (Belmont, Calif.: Wadsworth, 1986), 400–401, cited in D. Hellriegel, J. W. Slocun, Jr., and R. W. Woodman, *Organizational Behavior*, 6th ed. (St. Paul, Minn.: West, 1992), 97–100. Original source: "Sphere-Specific Measures of Perceived Control" by D. L. Paulhus, *Journal of Personality and Social Psychology*, 44, 1253–1265.

they react to their managers. If a manager and employees differ in their degree of authoritarianism, the manager may have difficulty leading effectively. The trend toward empowerment and shifts in expectations among younger employees for more equitable relationships have contributed to a decline in strict authoritarianism in many organizations. The shift can be seen in the National Football League, where a rising number of coaches put more emphasis on communication and building relationships than on ruling with an iron hand. Coaches Steve Mariucci (San Francisco 49ers), Tony Dungy (Indianapolis Colts), and Jeff Fisher (Tennessee Titans) are aware that today's players have different expectations than those of previous generations. "This is not old Rome with gladiators," says San Francisco's Mariucci. "This is modern day football. . . . If you cannot relate to today's player, you are through as a coach."[34]

## Machiavellianism

Another personality dimension that is helpful in understanding work behavior is Machiavellianism, which is characterized by the acquisition of power and the manipulation of other people for purely personal gain. Machiavellianism is named after Niccolo Machiavelli, a sixteenth-century author who wrote *The Prince*, a book for noblemen of the day on how to acquire and use power.[35] Psychologists have developed instruments to measure a person's Machiavellianism (Mach) orientation.[36] Research shows that high Machs are predisposed to being pragmatic, capable of lying to achieve personal goals, more likely to win in win-lose situations, and more likely to persuade than be persuaded.[37]

> **Machiavellianism**
> The tendency to direct much of one's behavior toward the acquisition of power and the manipulation of other people for personal gain.

Different situations may require people who demonstrate one or the other type of behavior. In loosely structured situations, high Machs actively take control, while low Machs accept the direction given by others. Low Machs thrive in highly structured situations, while high Machs perform in a detached, disinterested way. High Machs are particularly good in jobs that require bargaining skills or that involve substantial rewards for winning.[38]

## Problem-Solving Styles and the Myers-Briggs Type Indicator

Managers also need to understand that individuals differ in the way they solve problems and make decisions. One approach to understanding problem-solving styles grew out of the work of psychologist Carl Jung. Jung believed differences resulted from our preferences in how we go about gathering and evaluating information.[39] According to Jung, gathering information and evaluating information are separate activities. People gather information either by *sensation* or *intuition*, but not by both simultaneously. Sensation-type people would rather work with known facts and hard data and prefer routine and order in gathering information. Intuitive-type people would rather look for possibilities than work with facts and prefer solving new problems and using abstract concepts.

Evaluating information involves making judgments about the information a person has gathered. People evaluate information by *thinking* or *feeling*. These represent the extremes in orientation. Thinking-type individuals base their judgments on impersonal analysis, using reason and logic rather than personal values or emotional aspects of the situation. Feeling-type individuals base their judgments more on personal feelings such as harmony and tend to make decisions that result in approval from others.

According to Jung, only one of the four functions—sensation, intuition, thinking, or feeling—is dominant in an individual. However, the dominant function usually is backed up by one of the functions from the other set of paired opposites. Exhibit 17.9 shows the four problem-solving styles that result from these matchups, as well as occupations that people with each style tend to prefer.

Exhibit 17.9

## Four Problem-Solving Styles

| Personal Style | Action Tendencies | Likely Occupations |
|---|---|---|
| Sensation–thinking | • Emphasizes details, facts, certainty<br>• Is a decisive, applied thinker<br>• Focuses on short-term, realistic goals<br>• Develops rules and regulations for judging performance | • Accounting<br>• Production<br>• Computer programming<br>• Market research<br>• Engineering |
| Intuitive–thinking | • Prefers dealing with theoretical or technical problems<br>• Is a creative, progressive, perceptive thinker<br>• Focuses on possibilities using impersonal analysis<br>• Is able to consider a number of options and problems simultaneously | • Systems design<br>• Systems analysis<br>• Law<br>• Middle/top management<br>• Teaching business, economics |
| Sensation–feeling | • Shows concern for current, real-life human problems<br>• Is pragmatic, analytical, methodical, and conscientious<br>• Emphasizes detailed facts about people rather than tasks<br>• Focuses on structuring organizations for the benefit of people | • Directing supervisor<br>• Counseling<br>• Negotiating<br>• Selling<br>• Interviewing |
| Intuitive–feeling | • Avoids specifics<br>• Is charismatic, participative, people oriented, and helpful<br>• Focuses on general views, broad themes, and feelings<br>• Decentralizes decision making, develops few rules and regulations | • Public relations<br>• Advertising<br>• Human Resources<br>• Politics<br>• Customer service |

Two additional sets of paired opposites not directly related to problem solving are *introversion–extroversion* and *judging–perceiving*. Introverts gain energy by focusing on personal thoughts and feelings, whereas extroverts gain energy from being around others and interacting with others. On the judging versus perceiving dimension, people with a judging preference like certainty and closure and tend to make decisions quickly based on available data. Perceiving people, on the other hand, enjoy ambiguity, dislike deadlines, and may change their minds several times as they gather large amounts of data and information to make decisions.

A widely used personality test that measures how people differ on all four of Jung's sets of paired opposites is the Myers–Briggs Type Indicator (MBTI). The MBTI measures a person's preferences for introversion versus extroversion, sensation versus intuition, thinking versus feeling, and judging versus perceiving. The various combinations of these four preferences result in 16 unique personality types.

**Myers–Briggs Type Indicator (MBTI)**
Personality test that measures a person's preference for introversion vs. extroversion, sensation vs. intuition, thinking vs. feeling, and judging vs. perceiving.

*Take A Moment*

*Go to the experiential exercise on page 651.*

Each of the 16 different personality types can have positive and negative consequences for behavior. Based on the limited research, the two preferences that seem to be most strongly associated with effective management in a variety of organizations and industries are thinking and judging.[40] However, people with other preferences can also be good managers. One advantage of understanding your natural preferences is to maximize your innate strengths and abilities. Dow Chemical manager Kurt Swogger believes the MBTI can help put people in the right jobs—where they will be happiest and make the strongest contribution to the organization.

When Kurt Swogger arrived at Dow Chemical's plastics business in 1991, it took anywhere from 6 to 15 years to launch a new product—and the unit hadn't launched a single one for three years. Today, a new product launch takes just two to four years, and Swogger's R&D team has launched 13 product hits over the past decade.

How did Swogger lead such an amazing transformation? By making sure people were doing the jobs they were best suited for. The simple fact, Swogger says, "is that some [people] do development better than others. The biggest obstacle to launching great new products was not having the right people in the right jobs." Swogger began reassigning people based on his intuition and insight, distinguishing pure inventors from those who could add value later in the game and still others who were best at marketing the new products. Swogger says he was right-on about 60 percent of the time. If someone didn't work out after six months, he'd put them in another assignment.

Seeking a better way to determine people's strengths, Swogger turned to a former Dow employee, Greg Stevens, who now owns a consulting firm. Stevens and Swogger used the Myers–Briggs Type Indicator (MBTI), predicting which types would be best suited to each stage of the product development and launch cycles. After administering the test to current and former Dow plastics employees, they found some startling results. In 1991, when Swogger came on board, the match between the right personality type and the right role was only 29 percent. By 2001, thanks to Swogger's great instincts, the rate had jumped to 93 percent.

Swogger's next step is to administer the MBTI to new hires, so the job match is right to begin with. He believes the MBTI can help him assign people to jobs that match their natural abilities and interests, leading to happier employees and higher organizational performance.[41]

**DOW CHEMICAL**
http://www.dow.com

Matching the right people to the right jobs is an important responsibility for managers, whether they do it based on intuition and experience or by using personality tests such as the MBTI. Managers strive to create a good fit between the person and the job he or she is asked to do.

## Person–Job Fit

Given the wide variation among personalities and among jobs, an important responsibility of managers is to try to match employee and job characteristics so that work is done by people who are well suited to do it. This requires that managers be clear about what they expect employees to do and have a sense of the kinds of people who would succeed at various types of assignments. The extent to which a person's ability and personality match the requirements of a job is called person–job fit. When managers achieve person–job fit, employees are more likely to contribute and have higher levels of job satisfaction and commitment.[42] The importance of person–job fit became very apparent during the dot-com heydey of the late 1990s. People who had rushed to

**person–job fit**
The extent to which a person's ability and personality match the requirements of a job.

© DAVID FOSTER

Internet companies in hopes of finding a new challenge—or making a quick buck—found themselves floundering in jobs for which they were unsuited. One manager recruited by a leading executive search firm lasted less than two hours at his new job. The search firm, a division of Russell Reynolds Associates, later developed a "Web Factor" diagnostic to help determine whether people have the right personality for the Internet, including such things as a tolerance for risk and uncertainty, an obsession with learning, and a willingness to do whatever needs doing, regardless of job title.[43]

A related concern is *person–environment fit*, which looks not only at whether the person and job are suited to one another but also at how well the individual will fit in the overall organizational environment. An employee who is by nature strongly authoritarian, for example, would have a hard time in an organization such as W. L. Gore and Associates, where there are few rules, no hierarchy, no fixed or assigned authority, and no bosses. Many of today's organizations pay attention to person–environment fit from the beginning of the recruitment process. Texas Instruments' Web page includes an area called Fit Check that evaluates personality types anonymously and gives prospective job candidates a chance to evaluate for themselves whether they would be a good match with the company.[44]

# Learning

Years of schooling have conditioned many of us to think that learning is something students do in response to teachers in a classroom. With this view, in the managerial world of time deadlines and concrete action, learning seems remote—even irrelevant. However, today's successful managers need specific knowledge and skills as well as the ability to adapt to changes in the world around them. Managers have to learn.

Learning is a change in behavior or performance that occurs as the result of experience. Experience may take the form of observing others, reading or listening to sources of information, or experiencing the consequences of one's own behavior. This important way of adapting to events is linked to individual differences in attitudes, perception, and personality.

Two individuals who undergo similar experiences—for example, a business transfer to a foreign country—probably will differ in how they adapt their behaviors to (that is, learn from) the experience. In other words, each person learns in a different way.

**learning**
A change in behavior or performance that occurs as the result of experience.

© DAVID FOSTER

## CONCEPT CONNECTION

*Alasdair McLean-Foreman dropped out of Harvard University in his sophomore year to build HDO Sport, a high-tech sporting goods company he founded in his freshman dorm. But McLean-Foreman values **learning**. He has returned to the classroom, shifting day-to-day running of HDO to his staff of five. He is also on Harvard's track team and is training for the Olympic trials for his native England. "The company would be more productive if I hadn't gone back," he says. "But there is plenty of time in the future. There is no ceiling to what we can do."*

## The Learning Process

One model of the learning process, shown in Exhibit 17.10, depicts learning as a four-stage cycle.[45] First, a person encounters a concrete experience. This is followed by thinking and reflective observation, which lead to abstract conceptualization and, in turn, to active experimentation. The results of the experimentation generate new experiences, and the cycle repeats.

The Best Buy chain of consumer electronics superstores owes its birth to the learning process of its founder, Richard M. Schulze. In the 1960s, Schulze built a stereo store called Sound of Music into a chain of nine stores in and near St. Paul, Minnesota. However, a tornado destroyed his largest and most profitable store, so he held a massive clearance sale in the parking lot. So many shoppers descended on the lot that they caused traffic to back up for two miles. Reflecting on this experience, Schulze decided there was great demand for a store featuring large selection and low prices, backed by heavy advertising. He tried out his idea by launching his first Best Buy superstore. Today there are more than 700 Best Buy retail outlets as well as a thriving online division, and the chain's profits are in the billions of dollars.[46]

The arrows in the model of the learning process in Exhibit 17.10 indicate that this process is a recurring cycle. People continually test their conceptualizations and adapt them as a result of their personal reflections and observations about their experiences.

## Learning Styles

Individuals develop personal learning styles that vary in terms of how much they emphasize each stage of the learning cycle. These differences occur because the learning process is directed by individual needs and goals. For example, an engineer might place greater emphasis on abstract concepts, while a salesperson might emphasize concrete experiences. Because of these preferences, personal learning styles typically have strong and weak points.

Questionnaires can assess a person's strong and weak points as a learner by measuring the relative emphasis the person places on each of the four learning stages

Exhibit 17.10

**The Experiential Learning Cycle**

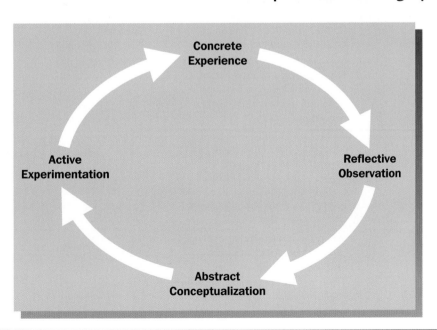

shown in Exhibit 17.10: concrete experience, reflective observation, abstract conceptualization, and active experimentation. Some people have a tendency to overemphasize one stage of the learning process, or to avoid some aspects of learning. Not many people have totally balanced profiles, but the key to effective learning is competence in each of the four stages when it is needed.

Researchers have identified four fundamental learning styles that combine elements of the four stages of the learning cycle.[47] Exhibit 17.11 summarizes the characteristics and dominant learning abilities of these four styles, labeled Diverger, Assimilator, Converger, and Accommodator. The exhibit also lists occupations that frequently attract individuals with each of the learning styles. For example, people whose dominant style is Accommodator are often drawn to sales and marketing. A good example is Gertrude Boyle, who took over Columbia Sportswear after the death of her husband. She and her son, Tim, propelled the company from sales of $13 million to $358 million over a 13 year period by observing what competitors were doing and actively experimenting to find a novel sales approach. The 74-year-old Gert Boyle decided to star in her own "Tough Mother" ads as a way to distinguish the company from competitors who advertised their products worn by fit, young models. Boyle believes in constantly pushing herself and her company, questioning everything, and trying new ideas.[48] Exhibit 17.11 lists other likely occupations for Divergers, Assimilators, Convergers, and Accommodators.

## Exhibit 17.11    Learning Style Types

| Learning Style Type | Dominant Learning Abilities | Learning Characteristics | Likely Occupations |
|---|---|---|---|
| Diverger | • Concrete experience<br>• Reflective observation | • Is good at generating ideas, seeing a situation from multiple perspectives, and being aware of meaning and value<br>• Tends to be interested in people, culture, and the arts | • Human resource management<br>• Counseling<br>• Organization development specialist |
| Assimilator | • Abstract conceptualization<br>• Reflective observation | • Is good at inductive reasoning, creating theoretical models, and combining disparate observations into an integrated explanation<br>• Tends to be less concerned with people than ideas and abstract concepts. | • Research<br>• Strategic planning |
| Converger | • Abstract conceptualization<br>• Active experimentation | • Is good at decisiveness, practical application of ideas, and hypothetical deductive reasoning<br>• Prefers dealing with technical tasks rather than interpersonal issues | • Engineering |
| Accommodator | • Concrete experience<br>• Active experimentation | • Is good at implementing decisions, carrying out plans, and getting involved in new experiences<br>• Tends to be at ease with people but may be seen as impatient or pushy | • Marketing<br>• Sales |

Through awareness of their learning styles, managers can understand how they approach problems and issues, their learning strengths and weaknesses, and how they react to employees or coworkers who have different learning styles.

## Continuous Learning

To thrive in today's turbulent business climate, individuals and organizations must be continuous learners. For individuals, continuous learning entails looking for opportunities to learn from classes, reading, and talking to others, as well as looking for the lessons in life's experiences. One manager who embodies the spirit of continuous learning is Larry Ricciardi, senior vice president and corporate counsel at IBM. Ricciardi is an avid traveler and voracious reader who likes to study art, literature, and history. In addition, Ricciardi likes to add supermarket tabloids to his daily fare of *The Wall Street Journal*. On business trips, he scouts out side trips to exotic or interesting sites so he can learn something new.[49] Ricciardi never knows when he might be able to apply a new idea or understanding to improve his life, his job, or his organization.

For organizations, continuous learning involves the processes and systems through which the organization enables its people to learn, share their growing knowledge, and apply it to their work. In an organization in which continuous learning is taking place, employees actively apply comments from customers, news about competitors, training programs, and more to increase their knowledge and improve the organization's practices. For example, at the Mayo Clinic, doctors are expected to consult with doctors in other departments, with the patient, and with anyone else inside or outside the clinic who might help with any aspect of the patient's problem.[50] The emphasis on teamwork, openness, and collaboration keeps learning strong at Mayo.

Managers can foster continuous learning by consciously stopping from time to time and asking, "What can we learn from this experience?" They can allow employees time to attend training and reflect on their experiences. Recognizing that experience can be the best teacher, managers should focus on how they and their employees can learn from mistakes, rather than fostering a climate in which employees hide mistakes because they fear being punished for them. Managers also encourage organizational learning by establishing information systems that enable people to share knowledge and learn in new ways. Information technology was discussed in detail in Chapter 15. As individuals, managers can help themselves and set an example for their employees by being continuous learners, listening to others, reading widely, and reflecting on what they observe.

# Stress and Stress Management

Just as organizations can support or discourage learning, organizational characteristics also interact with individual differences to influence other behaviors in the organization. In every organization, these characteristics include sources of stress. Formally defined, stress is an individual's physiological and emotional response to external stimuli that place physical or psychological demands on the individual and create uncertainty and lack of personal control when important outcomes are at stake.[51] These stimuli, called *stressors,* produce some combination of frustration (the inability to achieve a goal, such as the inability to meet a deadline because of inadequate resources) and anxiety (such as the fear of being disciplined for not meeting deadlines).

**stress**
A physiological and emotional response to stimuli that place physical or psychological demands on an individual.

People's responses to stressors vary according to their personalities, the resources available to help them cope, and the context in which the stress occurs. Thus, a looming deadline will feel different depending on the degree to which the individual enjoys a challenge, the willingness of coworkers to team up and help each other succeed, and family members' understanding of an employee's need to work extra hours, among other factors.

*Take A Moment*    *Go to the ethical dilemma on page 652 that pertains to organizational sources of stress.*

When the level of stress is low relative to a person's coping resources, stress can be a positive force, stimulating desirable change and achievement. However, too much stress is associated with many negative consequences, including sleep disturbances, drug and alcohol abuse, headaches, ulcers, high blood pressure, and heart disease. People who are experiencing the ill effects of too much stress may become irritable or withdraw from interactions with their co-workers, take excess time off, and have more health problems. For example, a recent study of manufacturing workers in Bangladesh found a significant connection between job stress and absenteeism. Another study of 46,000 workers in the United States found that health care costs are 147 percent higher for individuals who are stressed or depressed.[52] People suffering from stress are less productive and may leave the organization. Clearly, too much stress is harmful to employees as well as to companies.

## Type A and Type B Behavior

Researchers have observed that some people seem to be more vulnerable than others to the ill effects of stress. From studies of stress-related heart disease, they have categorized people as having behavior patterns called Type A and Type B.[53] The Type A behavior pattern includes extreme competitiveness, impatience, aggressiveness, and devotion to work. In contrast, people with a Type B behavior pattern exhibit less of these behaviors. They consequently experience less conflict with other people and a more balanced, relaxed lifestyle. Type A people tend to experience more stress-related illness than Type B people.

Most Type A individuals are high-energy people and may seek positions of power and responsibility. One example is John Haughom, senior vice president for healthcare improvement at PeaceHealth, a network of private hospitals in the Pacific Northwest. When Haughom was in charge of establishing an information network of community-wide medical records to support patient care, he typically began his day at 6 A.M. and worked until 11 P.M. His days were a blur of conference calls, meetings, and e-mail exchanges. "I could move mountains if I put my mind to it," he says. "That's what good executives do."[54]

By pacing themselves and learning control and intelligent use of their natural high-energy tendencies, Type A individuals can be powerful forces for innovation and leadership within their organizations, as John Haughom has been at PeaceHealth. However, many Type A personalities cause stress-related problems for themselves, and sometimes for those around them. Haughom eventually reached burnout. He couldn't sleep, he began snapping at colleagues, and he finally took a sabbatical and learned to lead a more balanced life.[55] Type B individuals typically live with less stress unless they are in high-stress situations. There are a number of factors that can cause stress in the workplace, even for people who are not naturally prone to high stress.

## Causes of Work Stress

Workplace stress is skyrocketing. The percentage of working Americans reporting that stress is a major problem in their lives more than doubled between 1992 and 2002. The number of people calling in sick due to stress tripled over just a four-year period. And the United States is not alone. In 2002, the European Committee officially cited stress as the second-biggest occupational health problem facing the European Union.[56]

---

**Type A behavior**
Behavior pattern characterized by extreme competitiveness, impatience, aggressiveness, and devotion to work.

**Type B behavior**
Behavior pattern that lacks Type A characteristics and includes a more balanced, relaxed lifestyle.

Most people have a general idea of what a stressful job is like: difficult, uncomfortable, exhausting, even frightening. Managers can better cope with their own stress and establish ways for the organization to help employees cope if they define the conditions that tend to produce work stress. One way to identify work stressors is to place them in four categories: demands associated with job tasks, physical conditions, roles (sets of expected behaviors), and interpersonal pressures and conflicts.

- *Task demands* are stressors arising from the tasks required of a person holding a particular job. Some kinds of decisions are inherently stressful: those made under time pressure, those that have serious consequences, and those that must be made with incomplete information. For example, emergency room doctors are under tremendous stress as a result of the task demands of their jobs. They regularly have to make quick decisions, based on limited information, that may determine whether a patient lives or dies. Almost all jobs, especially those of managers, have some level of stress associated with task demands.
- *Physical demands* are stressors associated with the setting in which an individual works. Some people must work in a poorly designed setting, such as an office with inadequate lighting or little privacy. Some employees must maneuver in a cramped workspace; some have too little or too much heat for comfort. Some workplaces even present safety and health hazards, from greasy floors to polluted air.
- *Role demands* are challenges associated with a role—that is, the set of behaviors expected of a person because of that person's position in the group. Some people encounter role ambiguity, meaning they are uncertain about what behaviors are expected of them. Role conflict occurs when an individual perceives incompatible demands from others. Managers often feel role conflict because the demands of their superiors conflict with those of the employees in their department. They may be expected to support employees and provide them with opportunities to experiment and be creative, while at the same time top executives are demanding a consistent level of output that leaves little time for creativity and experimentation.
- *Interpersonal demands* are stressors associated with relationships in the organization. Although in some cases interpersonal relationships can alleviate stress, they also can be a source of stress when the group puts pressure on an individual or when there are conflicts between individuals. Managers can resolve many conflicts using techniques that will be discussed in Chapter 21. A particularly challenging stressor is the personality clash. A personality clash occurs when two people simply cannot get along and do not see eye-to-eye on any issue. This type of conflict can be exceedingly difficult to resolve, and many managers have found that it is best to separate the two people so that they do not have to interact with one another.

Almost everyone experiences some degree of job stress associated with these various factors. For example, consider the stress caused by task demands on Verizon's call center representatives.

**CONCEPT CONNECTION**

*Sylvia Weinstock is founder of Sylvia Weinstock Cakes in New York City, known for celebrity wedding cakes, including those for Catherine Zeta-Jones and Donald Trump. With annual revenues of nearly $2 million, and 16 employees, including eight who are devoted solely to making "botanically correct" sugar flowers by hand, Weinstock loves her job, but feels the work stress of* **task demands.** *"This is an obsessive business because of the intensity and personal value that everyone places on their occasion," she says. "And I honor that. I fret. I worry. And unless I heard that the cake arrived happy, I'm checking that phone all the time."*

**role ambiguity**
Uncertainty about what behaviors are expected of a person in a particular role.

**role conflict**
Incompatible demands of different roles.

Roland G. Collins Jr. loves his job as a call center representative for Verizon Communications. He enjoys connecting with customers; he makes good money and has good benefits. But he admits that it's not the job for everyone. About a third of the 100 or so calls a representative handles each day are stressful. Besides dealing with irate customers and handling calls regarding billing or other problems, representatives have to be able to rattle off Verizon's string of products and services, including terms and rates, and try to sell

**VERIZON COMMUNICATIONS**
http://www.verizon.com

them to each and every call. It doesn't matter how angry or rude the customer on the other end of the line—pushing new services is a key requirement of the job.

What makes matters worse is that representatives often have to do all this under observation. Managers routinely sit next to a representative or listen in on a call to check whether the rep has hit on nearly 80 different points required in every customer contact. Call center reps must meet precise performance specifications, and managers defend the observation practice as a way to ensure consistency and better customer service. However, employees almost always find the experience adds to their stress level. For some employees, particularly inexperienced ones, an observation can create a panic situation, causing heart pounding and profuse sweating, which, in turn, creates even greater stress.[57]

Can you think of task, physical, role, or interpersonal demands associated with your job? Take the quick quiz in Exhibit 17.12 to assess your level of stress in your work or student life.

## Stress Management

Organizations that want to challenge their employees and stay competitive in a fast-changing environment will never be stress-free. But because many consequences of stress are negative, managers need to make stress management a priority. In Britain, lawmakers have implemented a new requirement that employers meet certain conditions that help to manage workplace stress, such as ensuring that employees are not exposed to a poor physical work environment, have the necessary skills and training to meet their job requirements, and are given a chance to offer input into the way their work is done.[58]

### Individual Stress Management

A variety of techniques help individuals manage stress. Among the most basic strategies are those that help people stay healthy: exercising regularly, getting plenty of rest, and eating a healthful diet.

In addition, most people cope with stress more effectively if they lead balanced lives and are part of a network of people who support and encourage them. Family, relationships, friendships, and memberships in nonwork groups such as community or religious organizations are helpful for stress management, as well as for other benefits. People who don't take care of themselves physically and emotionally are more susceptible to stress in their personal as well as professional lives. Managers and employees in today's hectic, competitive work environment may sometimes think of leisure activities as luxuries. The study of organizational behavior, however, offers a reminder that employees are *human* resources with human needs.

### New Workplace Responses to Stress Management

Although individuals can pursue stress management strategies on their own, today's enlightened companies support healthy habits to help employees manage stress and be more productive. Stress costs U.S. businesses billions of dollars a year in absenteeism, lower productivity, staff turnover, accidents, and higher health insurance and workers' compensation costs.[59] In the new workplace, taking care of employees has become a business as well as ethical priority.

Supporting employees can be as simple as encouraging people to take regular breaks and vacations. BellSouth, First Union, and Tribble Creative Group are among the companies that have designated areas as quiet rooms or meditation centers where employees can take short, calming breaks at any time they feel the need.[60] The time off is a valuable investment when it allows employees to approach their work with renewed energy and a fresh perspective. Companies also develop other programs aimed at helping employees reduce stress and lead healthier, more

Exhibit 17.12

### How Stressed Are You?

Respond to the following on a 1-to-5 scale, with 1 meaning Never and 5 meaning Very Often. The higher the score, the higher your stress level. If you have a high score, what will you do to cope with stress at school or work?

| | 1 | 2 | 3 | 4 | 5 | |
|---|---|---|---|---|---|---|
| | Never | | | | Very Often | |

| | 1 | 2 | 3 | 4 | 5 |
|---|---|---|---|---|---|
| 1. Conditions at work are unpleasant and sometimes unsafe. | 1 | 2 | 3 | 4 | 5 |
| 2. I feel that my job is making me physically and emotionally sick. | 1 | 2 | 3 | 4 | 5 |
| 3. I have too much work or too many unreasonable deadlines. | 1 | 2 | 3 | 4 | 5 |
| 4. I can't express my opinions or feelings about my job to my boss. | 1 | 2 | 3 | 4 | 5 |
| 5. My work interferes with my family or personal life. | 1 | 2 | 3 | 4 | 5 |
| 6. I have no control over my life at work. | 1 | 2 | 3 | 4 | 5 |
| 7. My good performance goes unrecognized and unrewarded. | 1 | 2 | 3 | 4 | 5 |
| 8. My talents are underutilized at work. | 1 | 2 | 3 | 4 | 5 |

**Add up the numbers for your Total Score**                              **Total Score:** _____

### Scoring and Interpretation

15 or lower: Low stress level.

16 to 20:    Fairly low stress. Coping should be easy, but you probably have a tough day now and then.

21 to 25:    Moderate stress. You're suffering about the same amount of pressure as most people cope with today.

26 to 30:    Severe stress. You may be coping, but you could probably benefit from stress counseling or stress management techniques.

31 to 40:    Potentially dangerous stress. Seek professional help.

**SOURCE:** This quiz appeared in Cora Daniels, "The Last Taboo," *Fortune* (October 28, 2002), 137–144, and was adapted from a stress test created by workplace research firm Marlin Company and the American Institute of Stress.

balanced lives. Some have wellness programs that provide access to nutrition counseling and exercise facilities. A worldwide study of wellness programs conducted by the Canadian government found that for each dollar spent, the company gets from $1.95 to $3.75 return payback from benefits.[61] Other organizations create broad work–life balance initiatives that may include flexible work options such as telecommuting and flexible hours, as well as benefits such as onsite daycare, fitness centers, and personal services such as pick-up and delivery of dry cleaning. *Daily flextime* is considered by many employees to be the most effective work-life practice, which means giving employees the freedom to vary their hours as needed, such as leaving early to take an elderly parent shopping or taking time off to attend a child's school play.[62]

By acknowledging the personal aspects of employees' lives, work–life practices also communicate that managers and the organization care about employees as human beings. In addition, managers' attitudes make a tremendous difference in whether employees are stressed out and unhappy or relaxed, energetic, and productive.

Manager's Solution

The principles of organizational behavior describe how people as individuals and groups behave and affect the performance of the organization as a whole. Desirable work-related attitudes include job satisfaction and organizational commitment. Attitudes affect people's perceptions and vice versa. Individuals often "see" things in different ways. The perceptual process includes perceptual selectivity and perceptual organization. Perceptual distortions, such as stereotyping, the halo effect, projection, and perceptual defense, are errors in judgment that can arise from inaccuracies in the perception process. Attributions are judgments that individuals make about whether a person's behavior was caused by internal or external factors.

Another area of interest is personality, the set of characteristics that underlie a relatively stable pattern of behavior. One way to think about personality is the Big Five personality traits of extroversion, agreeableness, conscientiousness, emotional stability, and openness to experience. Some important work-related attitudes and behaviors influenced by personality are locus of control, authoritarianism, Machiavellianism, and problem-solving styles. A widely used personality test is the Myers–Briggs Type Indicator. Managers want to find a good person–job fit by ensuring that a person's personality, attitudes, skills, abilities, and problem-solving styles match the requirements of the job and the organizational environment.

New insight into personality has been gained through research in the area of emotional intelligence (EQ). Emotional intelligence includes the components of self-awareness, self-management, social awareness, and relationship management. EQ is not an in-born personality characteristic, but can be learned and developed. Vinita Gupta, described at the beginning of this chapter, needed to strengthen her emotional intelligence, particularly in the areas of self-awareness and relationship management. Gupta hired a corporate coach to help her learn more about herself and manage the personality characteristics and behaviors that could be contributing to decreased performance and higher turnover at Quick Eagle. Gupta worked on a series of exercises to help develop greater empathy and improve her social skills, including coaching employees, being more open and less defensive, and using humor to create a lighter atmosphere. She now makes a point of greeting people upon arrival, introducing herself to employees she's never met, and having lunch with colleagues. Gupta has learned that she cannot change some of her personality characteristics—for example, she will never score high on extroversion. However, she has learned to manage her attitudes and behaviors to make Quick Eagle a more pleasant, comfortable place to work. Employees have noticed that the atmosphere is lighter, and people are no longer afraid to speak up in meetings or if they have a concern. Turnover has decreased by 20 percent from a year earlier.[63]

Even though people's personalities may be relatively stable, individuals, like Vinita Gupta, can learn new behaviors. Learning refers to a change in behavior or performance that occurs as a result of experience. The learning process goes through a four-stage cycle, and individual learning styles differ. Four learning styles are Diverger, Assimilator, Converger, and Accommodator. Rapid changes in today's marketplace create a need for ongoing learning. They may also create greater stress for many of today's workers. The causes of work stress include task demands, physical demands, role demands, and interpersonal demands. Individuals and organizations can alleviate the negative effects of stress by engaging in a variety of techniques for stress management.

# Discussion Questions

1. What are the three basic leadership skills that lie at the core of identifying and solving people problems? Why is it important for managers to develop these skills?

2. In what ways might the cognitive and affective components of attitude influence the behavior of employees who are faced with learning an entirely new set of computer-related skills in order to retain their jobs at a manufacturing facility?

3. What steps might managers at a company that is about to be merged with another company take to promote organizational commitment among employees?

4. Think about an important event in your life. Do you believe that the success or failure of the event was your responsibility (internal locus of control) or the responsibility of outside forces or people (external locus of control)? Has your belief changed since the event took place? How does your locus of control affect the way you now view the event?

5. In the Big Five personality factors, extroversion is considered a "good" quality to have. Why might introversion be an equally positive quality?

6. Review Exhibit 17.9. According to the chart, which type of problem-solving style do you prefer? Describe briefly a decision you have made using this style.

7. Why is it important for managers to achieve person-job fit when they are hiring employees?

8. How might a design manager use a combination of novelty, familiarity, and repetition in the presentation of a new product idea to the company's financial managers?

9. What characteristics of perceivers might influence the attendees of a human resources seminar on employee benefits (such as retirement planning, health care insurance, vacation, and the like)?

10. Describe a situation in which you learned how to do something—use a computer or ride a snowboard. In your description, identify the four stages of the learning cycle.

11. Do you think that a Type A person or a Type B person would be better suited to managing a health care facility? Why?

# Management in Practice: Experiential Exercise

## High Five: How Many of the "Big Five" Personality Traits Are Yours?

Each individual's collection of personality traits is different; it's what makes us unique. But, although each collection of traits varies, we all share many common traits. To find out which are your most prominent traits, mark "yes" or "no" after each of the following statements. Then, for fun, compare your responses with classmates.

1. I love meeting and talking with new people at parties. _____

2. I try not to hold grudges against others. _____

3. I am focused on graduating from college and finding a good job in my field. _____

4. I enjoy performing under pressure—for example, in a big athletic event. _____

5. When I finish school, I want to travel around the world. _____

6. Final exams don't really bother me because I prepare well for them. _____

7. I like to take part in group projects. _____

8. I don't mind giving oral presentations in class. _____

9. Just for fun, I would sign up to take a course in a discipline completely outside my field. _____

10. I work summers in order to fund as much of my own education as I can. _____

Statements 1 and 8 deal with extroversion; statements 2 and 7 deal with agreeableness; statements 3, 6, and 10 deal with conscientiousness; statements 4 and 6 deal with emotional stability; statements 5 and 9 deal with openness to new experiences.

# Management in Practice: Ethical Dilemma

## Should I Fudge the Numbers?

Sara MacIntosh recently joined MicroPhone, a large telecommunications company with headquarters in Denver, to take over the implementation of a massive customer service training project. The program was created by Kristin Cole, head of human resources and Sara's new boss. According to the grapevine, Kristin was hoping this project alone would give her the "star quality" she needed to earn a promotion she'd been longing for. Industry competition was heating up, and MicroPhone's strategy called for being the very best at customer service. That meant having the most highly trained people in the industry, especially those who would work directly with customers. Kristin had put together a crash team to develop the new training program, which called for an average of one full week of intense customer service training for each of three thousand people and had a price tag in the neighborhood of $40 million. Kristin's team, made up of several staffers who already felt overwhelmed with their day-to-day workload, rushed to put the proposal together. It was scheduled to go to the board of directors next month.

Kristin knew she needed someone well qualified and dedicated to manage and implement the project, and Sara, with eight years of experience, a long list of accomplishments, and advanced degrees in finance and organizational behavior, was perfect for the job. When Sara agreed to come aboard, Kristin expressed great relief and confidence in Sara's ability to make the program work. However, during a thorough review of the proposal, Sara discovered some assumptions built into the formulas of the proposal that raised red flags. She approached Dan Sotal, the team's

coordinator, about her concerns, but the more Dan tried to explain how the financial projections were derived, the more Sara realized that Kristin's proposal was seriously flawed. No matter how she tried to work them out, the most that could be squeezed out of the $40 million budget was 20 hours of training a week, not the 40 hours everyone expected for such a high price tag.

Sara knew that, although the proposal had been largely developed before she came on board, it would bear her signature. As she carefully described the problems with the proposal to Kristin and outlined the potentially devastating consequences, Kristin impatiently tapped her pencil on the marble tabletop. Finally, she stood up, leaned forward, and interrupted Sara, quietly saying, "Sara, make the numbers work so that it adds up to forty hours and stays within the $40 million budget." Sara glanced up and replied, "I don't think it can be done unless we either change the number of employees who are to be trained or the cost figure. . . . " Kristin's smile froze on her face and her eyes began to snap as she again interrupted. "I don't think you understand what I'm saying. We have too much at stake here. Make the previous numbers work." Stunned, Sara belatedly began to realize that Kristin was ordering her to fudge the numbers. She felt an anxiety attack coming on as she wondered what she should do.

## What Do You Do?

1. Make the previous numbers work. Kristin and the entire team have put massive amounts of time into the project and they all expect you to be a team player. You don't want to let them down.

Besides, this is a great opportunity for you in a highly visible position.

2.  Stick to your ethical principles and refuse to fudge the numbers. Tell Kristin you will work overtime to help develop an alternate proposal that stays within the budget by providing more training to employees who work directly with customers and fewer training hours for those who don't have direct customer contact.

3.  Go to the team and tell them what you've been asked to do. If they refuse to support you, threaten to reveal the true numbers to the CEO and board members.

Source: Adapted from Doug Wallace, "Fudge the Numbers or Leave," *Business Ethics*, May–June, 1996, 58–59. Adapted with permission.

# Surf the Net

1.  **Authoritarianism.** Carlson Companies, one of the largest privately held corporations in the United States, with operations in more than 140 countries and 147,000 people employed under its brands, is an example of authoritarianism. Go to the corporate Web site at *http://www.carlson. com* and find information for the following items: (a) Name two of Carlson Companies' brands. (b) Besides the fact that Curtis Carlson graduated from the University of Minnesota's School of Management, what other connection is there between the two?

2.  **Perceptual Organization.** Using the keyword "perception" in your Web browser, locate other interesting perceptual images that could supplement those in Exhibit 17.5 in this chapter. The following sites provide excellent examples. Select your favorite perceptual image; print it out, and bring it to class to contribute during a class discussion on this topic.
    *http://www.optillusions.com*
    *http://www.coolopticalillusions.com*
    *http://www.exploratorium.edu/exhibits*

    (NOTE: Many of the Exploratorium online exhibits at this site require plug-ins, such as Shockwave, RealAudio, or QuickTime)

3.  **Learning Styles.** Many approaches exist for analyzing personal learning styles. For example, at *http://honolulu.hawaii.edu/intranet/committees/ FacDevCom/guidebk/teachtip/keirsey2.htm*, you can access a learning styles instrument that will categorize you as a visual, auditory, or tactile learner. Other sites at which you can get feedback on your learning styles are *http://pss.uvm.edu/pss162/ learning_styles.html*
    *http://www.usd.edu/trio/tut/ts/style.html*
    *http://www.clat.psu.edu/gems/Other/LSI/LSI.htm*
    Choose and take an online learning styles instrument, print out the results, and submit a copy of both the instrument and the results to your instructor.

# Case for Critical Analysis

## Volkswagen's Ferdinand Piëch

While many of today's organizations are shifting toward more democratic, participative types of management, one is not: Volkswagen. In fact, Volkswagen's chief executive, Ferdinand Piëch, rules his realm with an iron hand. After a long executive career at such prestigious automakers as Audi and Porsche (Piëch's maternal grandfather was Ferdinand Porsche), Piëch took over as Volkswagen's CEO in 1993. He immediately centralized power in the organization, firing managers who questioned his ideas or who didn't follow his lead. He dove into engineering projects himself, proposing new projects, tinkering with designs. He presided over meetings with the demeanor of an autocrat, with the occasional result that "critical questions aren't asked, because people know things can rapidly get uncomfortable," notes one former executive.

Piëch had—and still has—a reason for ruling supreme over his company. He isn't satisfied that VW is Europe's leading mass-market auto manufacturer; he wants to turn it into the most powerful, most respected carmaker in the world. He won't settle for less. "We're trying to redefine the status game," explains Jens Neumann, a member of Volkswagen's management board and supporter of Piëch. After creating successes at both Porsche and Audi, such as the Quattro all-wheel drive, Piëch is intent on doing even more at VW. "He is the most brilliant and forward-looking CEO in the business today," claims an analyst for a major VW investor. Indeed, in the first five years at the wheel, Piëch turned around several languishing auto models, increased the company's lead in Europe, and created a comeback in the United States market. His most famous project perhaps is his reintroduction of the beloved VW Beetle. Despite warnings by market experts, Piëch pushed the bug ahead—redesigned so it's a little larger than its predecessor and with all the necessary technological bells and whistles—to a warm welcome from U.S. customers.

Perhaps one reason Piëch is so successful in his method of management is his extensive knowledge of and passion for the cars themselves. From his days as an automotive engineering student at Zurich's Swiss Federal Institute of Technology, through his stint at Porsche, where he helped create world-class race cars, to his development of Audi's Quattro and now the launch of the VW Beetle, Piëch has been found under the hood, tinkering. Thus, he knows his product and his customers and how to fit them together better than anyone else in the industry.

Critics charge that Piëch has too tight a hold over his company. "At VW, nothing happens without Piëch," notes a former colleague. One-person rule can result in massive mistakes. For instance, several years ago, Piëch pushed for the purchase of Rolls-Royce Motors from its parent, Vickers PLC. But in a botched deal, he lost the rights to the Rolls-Royce brand name, which actually belongs to Rolls-Royce PLC, the aerospace manufacturer. Critics also point out that Piëch's fanatical grip on VW has more to do with his personal insecurity than a philosophy of management. "He wants to prove that he has been underestimated for years," muses one former VW executive. But with Piëch in the lead, VW now is reporting over $2 billion a year in earnings, over 100 percent more than before he took the driver's seat.

## Questions

1. What personality traits do you think Ferdinand Piëch exhibits? Do you think these contribute to a good person-job fit? Why or why not?

2. Hardly anyone would argue that Piëch is an authoritarian executive. Do you sense that he is Machiavellian as well? Do you think these characteristics have a positive or negative impact on the way Volkswagen is run? Explain your answer.

3. Imagine that you are a manager at Volkswagen, and you are experiencing some cognitive dissonance about being asked to work long hours on one of Piëch's pet projects—a new car model whose success you have doubts about. How might you resolve your dissonance?

Source: David Woodruff and Keith Naughton, "Hard-Driving Boss," *BusinessWeek*, October 5, 1998, 82–87

# Endnotes

1. Julia Lawlor, "Personality 2.0," *Red Herring* (April 1, 2001), 98–103.

2. See Mark C. Bolino, William H. Turnley, and James M. Bloodgood, "Citizenship Behaviors and the Creation of Social Capital in Organizations," *Academy of Management Review 27*, no. 4 (2002), 505–522.

3. John W. Newstrom and Keith Davis, *Organizational Behavior: Human Behavior at Work,* 11th ed. (Burr Ridge, Ill.: McGraw-Hill Irwin, 2002), Chapter 9.

4. A. Feuerstein, "E-marketing Firm Lands Hotshot CEO," *San Francisco Business Times* (January 17, 2000), 1–2; and J. Kaufman, "What Happens When a 20-Something Whiz Is Suddenly the Boss," *The Wall Street Journal* (October 8, 1999), A1, A10.

5. S. J. Breckler, "Empirical Validation of Affect, Behavior, and Cognition as Distinct Components of Attitude," *Journal of Personality and Social Psychology* (May 1984), 1191–1205; and J. M. Olson and M. P. Zanna, "Attitudes and Attitude Change," *Annual Review of Psychology* 44 (1993), 117–154.

6. M. T. Iaffaldano and P. M. Muchinsky, "Job Satisfaction and Job Performance: A Meta-Analysis," *Psychological Bulletin* (March 1985), 251–273; C. Ostroff, "The Relationship between Satisfaction, Attitudes, and Performance: An Organizational Level Analysis," *Journal of Applied Psychology* (December 1992), 963–974; and M. M. Petty, G. W. McGee, and J. W. Cavender, "A Meta-Analysis of the Relationship between Individual Job Satisfaction and Individual Performance," *Academy of Management Review* (October 1984), 712–721.

7. Sue Shellenbarger, "Companies Are Finding Real Payoffs in Aiding Employee Satisfaction," (Work & Family column), *The Wall Street Journal* (October 11, 2000), B1.

8. "Worried at Work: Generation Gap in Workplace Woes," International Survey Research, http://www.isrsurveys.com accessed on May 19, 2004.

9. Tony Schwartz, "The Greatest Sources of Satisfaction in the Workplace Are Internal and Emotional," *Fast Company* (November 2000), 398–402.

10. Marshall Goldsmith, "To Help Others Develop, Start with Yourself," *Fast Company* (March, 2004), 100; and Bonnie Miller Rubin and Sharman Stein, "Think Outside the [Cereal] Box," *Working Mother* (October 2002), 60.

11. William C. Symonds, "Where Paternalism Equals Good Business," *BusinessWeek* (July 20, 1998), 16E4, 16E6.

12. "The People Factor: Global Survey Shows That an Engaged Workforce Measurably Improves the Bottom Line—and How," International Survey Research, http://www.isrsurveys.com accessed on May 19, 2004.

13. "Employee Commitment; U.S.: Leader or Follower?" International Survey Research, http://www.isrsurveys.com accessed on May 19, 2004.

14. W. Chan Kin and Renée Mauborgne, "Fair Process: Managing in the Knowledge Economy," *Harvard Business Review* (January 2003), 127–136.

15. Jennifer Laabs, "They Want More Support—Inside and Outside of Work," *Workforce* (November 1998), 54–56.

16. For a discussion of cognitive dissonance theory, see Leon A. Festinger, *Theory of Cognitive Dissonance* (Stanford, Calif.: Stanford University Press, 1957).

17. D. A. Kravitz and S. L. Klineberg, "Reactions to Two Versions of Affirmative Action Among Whites, Blacks, and Hispanics," *Journal of Applied Psychology* 85 (2000), 597–611; and Robert J. Grossman, "Race in the Workplace" *HR Magazine* (March 2000), 41–45.

18. J. A. Deutsch, W. G. Young, and T. J. Kalogeris, "The Stomach Signals Satiety," *Science* (April 1978), 22–33.

19. Richard B. Chase and Sriram Dasu, "Want to Perfect Your Company's Service? Use Behavioral Science," *Harvard Business Review* (June 2001), 79–84.

20. H. H. Kelley, "Attribution in Social Interaction," in E. Jones et al. (eds.), *Attribution: Perceiving the Causes of Behavior* (Morristown, N.J.: General Learning Press, 1972).

21. See J. M. Digman, "Personality Structure: Emergence of the Five-Factor Model," *Annual Review of Psychology* 41 (1990), 417–440; M. R. Barrick and M. K. Mount, "Autonomy as a Moderator of the Relationships Between the Big Five Personality Dimensions and Job Performance," *Journal of Applied Psychology* (February 1993), 111–118; and J. S. Wiggins and A. L. Pincus, "Personality: Structure and Assessment," *Annual Review of Psychology* 43 (1992), 473–504.

22. Michelle Leder, "Is That Your Final Answer?" *Working Woman* (December–January 2001), 18; "Can You Pass the Job Test?" *Newsweek* (May 5, 1986), 46–51.

23. Alan Farnham, "Are You Smart Enough to Keep Your Job?" *Fortune* (January 15, 1996), 34–47.

24. Cora Daniels, "Does This Man Need a Shrink?" *Fortune* (February 5, 2001), 205–208.

25. Daniel Goleman, "Leadership That Gets Results," *Harvard Business Review* (March–April 2000), 79–90; Richard E. Boyatzis and Daniel Goleman, *The Emotional Competence Inventory–University Edition*, The Hay Group, 2001; and Daniel Goleman, *Emotional*

*Intelligence: Why It Can Matter More than IQ* (New York: Bantam Books, 1995).

26. Farnham, "Are You Smart Enough to Keep Your Job?"

27. Hendrie Weisinger, *Emotional Intelligence at Work* (San Francisco, Calif.: Jossey–Bass, 2000); D. C. McClelland, "Identifying Competencies with Behavioral-Event Interviews," *Psychological Science* (Spring 1999), 331–339; Daniel Goleman, "Leadership That Gets Results," *Harvard Business Review* (March–April 2000), 78–90; D. Goleman, *Working with Emotional Intelligence* (New York: Bantam Books, 1999); and Lorie Parch, "Testing . . . 1, 2, 3," *Working Woman* (October 1997), 74–78.

28. "Dumb and Dumberer—Hall of Infamy," *MBA Jungle* (October–November 2003), 49.

29. Goleman, "Leadership That Gets Results."

30. J. B. Rotter, "Generalized Expectancies for Internal versus External Control of Reinforcement," *Psychological Monographs* 80, no. 609 (1966).

31. Andy Serwer, "There's Something about Cisco," *Fortune* (May 15, 2000); Stephanie N. Mehta, "Cisco Fractures Its Own Fairy Tale," *Fortune* (May 14, 2001), 104–112.

32. See P. E. Spector, "Behavior in Organizations as a Function of Employee's Locus of Control," *Psychological Bulletin* (May 1982), 482–497.

33. T. W. Adorno, E. Frenkel-Brunswick, D. J. Levinson, and R. N. Sanford, *The Authoritarian Personality* (New York: Harper & Row, 1950).

34. Mike Freeman, "A New Breed of Coaches Relates Better to Players," *The New York Times* (August 19, 2001), Y36.

35. Niccolo Machiavelli, *The Prince,* trans. George Bull (Middlesex: Penguin, 1961).

36. Richard Christie and Florence Geis, *Studies in Machiavellianism* (New York: Academic Press, 1970).

37. R. G. Vleeming, "Machiavellianism: A Preliminary Review," *Psychological Reports* (February 1979), 295–310.

38. Christie and Geis, *Studies in Machiavellianism.*

39. Carl Jung, *Psychological Types* (London: Routledge and Kegan Paul, 1923).

40. Mary H. McCaulley, "Research on the MBTI and Leadership: Taking the Critical First Step," Keynote Address, The Myers–Briggs Type Indicator and Leadership: An International Research Conference, January 12–14, 1994.

41. Alison Overhold, "Are You a Polyolefin Optimizer? Take This Quiz!" *Fast Company* (April 2004), 37.

42. Charles A. O'Reilly III, Jennifer Chatman, and David F. Caldwell, "People and Organizational Culture: A Profile Comparison Approach to Assessing Person-Organization Fit," *Academy of Management Journal* 34, no.3 (1991), 487–516.

43. Anna Muoio, "Should I Go .Com?" *Fast Company* (July 2000), 164–172.

44. Leder, "Is That Your Final Answer?"

45. David A. Kolb, "Management and the Learning Process," *California Management Review* 18, no. 3 (Spring 1976), 21–31.

46. De' Ann Weimer, "The Houdini of Consumer Electronics," *BusinessWeek* (June 22, 1998), 88, 92; and http://www.bestbuy.com accessed on May 19, 2004.

47. See David. A. Kolb, I. M. Rubin, and J. M. McIntyre, *Organizational Psychology: An Experimental Approach,* 3rd ed. (Englewood Cliffs, N.J.: Prentice–Hall, 1984), 27–54.

48. Stephanie Gruner, "Our Company, Ourselves," *Inc.* (April 1998), 127–128.

49. Ira Sager, "Big Blue's Blunt Bohemian," *BusinessWeek* (June 14, 1999), 107–112.

50. Paul Roberts, "The Best Interest of the Patient Is the Only Interest to be Considered," *Fast Company* (April 1999), 149–162.

51. T. A. Beehr and R. S. Bhagat, *Human Stress and Cognition in Organizations: An Integrated Perspective* (New York: Wiley, 1985); and Bruce Cryer, Rollin McCraty, and Doc Childre, "Pull the Plug on Stress," *Harvard Business Review* (July 2003), 102–107.

52. Ekramul Hoque and Mayenul Islam, "Contribution of Some Behavioural Factors to Absenteeism of Manufacturing Workers in Bangladesh," *Pakistan Journal of Psychological Research* 18, no. 3–4 (Winter 2003), 81–96; U.S. research study conducted by HERO, a not-for-profit coalition of organizations with common interests in health promotion, disease management, and health-related productivity research, and reported in Bruce Cryer, Rollin McCraty, and Doc Childre, "Pull the Plug on Stress," *Harvard Business Review* (July 2003), 102–107.

53. M. Friedman and R. Rosenman, *Type A Behavior and Your Heart* (New York: Knopf, 1974).

54. John L. Haughom, "How to Pass the Stress Test," *CIO* (May 1, 2003), 50–52; Quote from Cora Daniels, "The Last Taboo," *Fortune* (October 28, 2002), 137–144.

55. Haughom, "How to Pass the Stress Test."

56. U.S. research study results by the Nationsal Institute for Occupational Safety and Health, reported in Daniels, "The Last Taboo."

57. Kris Maher, "At Verizon Call Center, Stress Is Seldom On Hold," *The Wall Street Journal* (January 16, 2001), B1, B12.

58. Donalee Moulton, "Buckling Under the Pressure," *OH & S Canada* 19, no. 8 (December 2003), 36.

59. Claire Sykes, "Say Yes to Less Stress," *Office Solutions* (July–August 2003), 26; and Andrea Higbie, "Quick Lessons in the Fine Old Art of Unwinding," *The New York Times* (February 25, 2001), BU–10.

60. Leslie Gross Klass, "Quiet Time at Work Helps Employee Stress," *Johnson City Press* (January 28, 2001), 30.

61. Moulton, "Buckling Under the Pressure."

62. David T. Gordon, "Balancing Act," *CIO* (October 15, 2001), 58–62.

63. Lawlor, "Personality 2.0."

# Chapter 18

# Leadership

## LEARNING OBJECTIVES

*After studying this chapter, you should be able to*

1. Define leadership and explain its importance for organizations.

2. Identify personal characteristics associated with effective leaders.

3. Describe the leader behaviors of initiating structure and consideration and when they should be used.

4. Describe Hersey and Blanchard's situational theory and its application to subordinate participation.

5. Explain the path–goal model of leadership.

6. Discuss how leadership fits the organizational situation and how organizational characteristics can substitute for leadership behaviors.

7. Describe transformational leadership and when it should be used.

8. Identify the five sources of leader power and how each causes different subordinate behavior.

9. Explain innovative approaches to leadership in a turbulent environment.

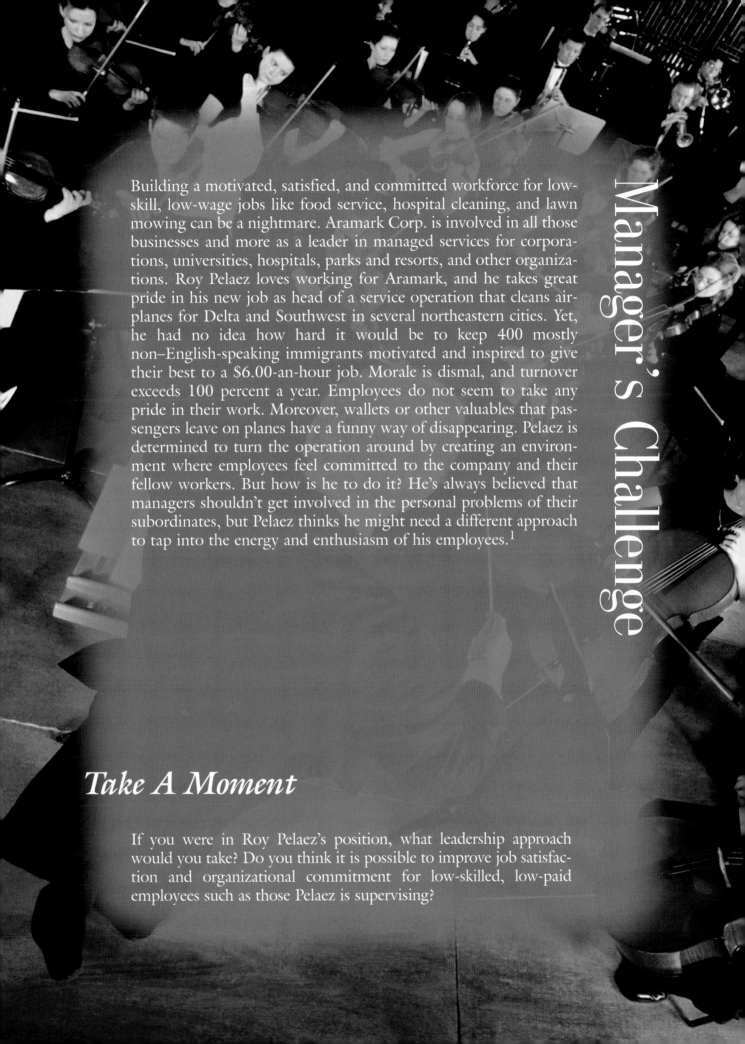

Building a motivated, satisfied, and committed workforce for low-skill, low-wage jobs like food service, hospital cleaning, and lawn mowing can be a nightmare. Aramark Corp. is involved in all those businesses and more as a leader in managed services for corporations, universities, hospitals, parks and resorts, and other organizations. Roy Pelaez loves working for Aramark, and he takes great pride in his new job as head of a service operation that cleans airplanes for Delta and Southwest in several northeastern cities. Yet, he had no idea how hard it would be to keep 400 mostly non–English-speaking immigrants motivated and inspired to give their best to a $6.00-an-hour job. Morale is dismal, and turnover exceeds 100 percent a year. Employees do not seem to take any pride in their work. Moreover, wallets or other valuables that passengers leave on planes have a funny way of disappearing. Pelaez is determined to turn the operation around by creating an environment where employees feel committed to the company and their fellow workers. But how is he to do it? He's always believed that managers shouldn't get involved in the personal problems of their subordinates, but Pelaez thinks he might need a different approach to tap into the energy and enthusiasm of his employees.[1]

## Take A Moment

If you were in Roy Pelaez's position, what leadership approach would you take? Do you think it is possible to improve job satisfaction and organizational commitment for low-skilled, low-paid employees such as those Pelaez is supervising?

In the previous chapter, we explored differences in attitudes and personality that affect behavior. The attitudes and behaviors of leaders play an important role in shaping employee attitudes, such as their job satisfaction and organizational commitment. Different leaders behave in different ways, depending on their individual differences as well as their followers' needs and the organizational situation. Many different styles of leadership can be effective. For example, contrast the styles of two leaders of software companies. Tom Siebel, CEO of Siebel Systems, is known as a disciplined and dispassionate manager who likes to maintain control over every aspect of the business. He enforces a dress code, sets tough goals and standards, and holds people strictly accountable. "We go to work to realize our professional ambitions, not to have a good time," Siebel says. Contrast Siebel's style with that of David A. Duffield, founder, chairman, and former CEO of PeopleSoft. As CEO, Duffield was known for hugging his employees, letting people bring their pets to work, providing free snacks, and signing his e-mails D.A.D.[2] Both Siebel and Duffield have been successful as leaders, although their styles are quite different.

This chapter explores one of the most widely discussed and researched topics in management—leadership. Here we will define leadership and explore the differences between leadership and management. We will examine trait, behavioral, and contingency theories of leadership effectiveness, discuss charismatic and transformational leadership, and consider how leaders use power and influence to get things done. The final section of the chapter looks at new leadership approaches for today's turbulent environment. Chapters 19 through 21 will look in detail at many of the functions of leadership, including employee motivation, communication, and encouraging teamwork.

# The Nature of Leadership

There is probably no topic more important to business success today than leadership. The concept of leadership continues to evolve as the needs of organizations change. Among all the ideas and writings about leadership, three aspects stand out—people, influence, and goals. Leadership occurs among people, involves the use of influence, and is used to attain goals.[3] *Influence* means that the relationship among people is not passive. Moreover, influence is designed to achieve some end or goal. Thus, leadership as defined here is the ability to influence people toward the attainment of goals. This definition captures the idea that leaders are involved with other people in the achievement of goals.

Leadership is reciprocal, occurring *among* people.[4] Leadership is a "people" activity, distinct from administrative paper shuffling or problem-solving activities. Leadership is dynamic and involves the use of power to get things done.

**leadership**
The ability to influence people toward the attainment of organizational goals.

# Leadership versus Management

Much has been written in recent years about the leadership role of managers. Management and leadership are both important to organizations. Effective managers have to be leaders, too, because there are distinctive qualities associated with management and leadership that provide different strengths for the organization, as illustrated in Exhibit 18.1. As shown in the exhibit, management and leadership

Exhibit 18.1

## Leader and Manager Qualities

**LEADER QUALITIES**

**SOUL**
Visionary
Passionate
Creative
Flexible
Inspiring
Innovative
Courageous
Imaginative
Experimental
Initiates change
Personal power

**MANAGER QUALITIES**

**MIND**
Rational
Consulting
Persistent
Problem solving
Tough-minded
Analytical
Structured
Deliberate
Authoritative
Stabilizing
Position power

**SOURCE:** Based on Genevieve Capowski, "Anatomy of a Leader: Where Are the Leaders of Tomorrow?" *Management Review* (March 1994) 12.

reflect two different sets of qualities and skills that frequently overlap within a single individual. A person might have more of one set of qualities than the other, but ideally a manager develops a balance of both manager and leader qualities.

A primary distinction between management and leadership is that management promotes stability, order and problem solving within the existing organizational structure and systems. Leadership promotes vision, creativity, and change. In other words, "a manager takes care of where you are; a leader take you to a new place."[5] Leadership means questioning the status quo so that outdated, unproductive, or socially irresponsible norms can be replaced to meet new challenges. Leadership cannot replace management; it should be in addition to management. Good management is needed to help the organization meet current commitments, while good leadership is needed to move the organization into the future.[6]

# Leadership Traits

Early efforts to understand leadership success focused on the leader's personal characteristics or traits. Traits are the distinguishing personal characteristics of a leader, such as intelligence, values, self-confidence, and appearance. The early research focused on leaders who had achieved a level of greatness, and hence was referred to as the *Great Man* approach. The idea was relatively simple: Find out what made these people great, and select future leaders who already exhibited the same traits or could be trained to develop them. Generally, early research found only a weak relationship between personal traits and leader success.[7]

**traits**
Distinguishing personal characteristics, such as intelligence, values, and appearance.

In recent years, there has been a resurgence of interest in examining leadership traits. In addition to personality traits, physical, social, and work-related characteristics of leaders have been studied.[8] Exhibit 18.2 summarizes the physical, social, and personal leadership characteristics that have received the greatest research support. However, these characteristics do not stand alone. The appropriateness of a trait or set of traits depends on the leadership situation. The same traits do not apply to every organization or situation. Consider the personal traits that are helping Ralph Szygenda transform General Motors into the first totally wired car company, as described in the Unlocking Creative Solutions Through Technology box.

Further studies have expanded the understanding of leadership beyond the personal traits of the individual to focus on the dynamics of the relationship between leaders and followers.

© VITO ALUIA

## CONCEPT CONNECTION

*Joanna B. Meiseles, president and founder of Snip-its Corp., a $1.5 million children's haircutting chain based in Natick, Massachusetts, demonstrates many of the **personal traits** associated with effective leadership. For example, she displayed intelligence, ability, knowledge, and judgment by knowing that to make her company successful, it had to be unique. Everything about Snip-its is tailored to children. Snip-its characters perch on a hot pink and lime green entry arch, games and stories are loaded on funky quasi-anthropomorphic computers at every cutting station, and the Magic Box dispenses a prize in exchange for a swatch of hair at the end of a visit.*

# Behavioral Approaches

The inability to define effective leadership based solely on traits led to an interest in looking at the behavior of leaders and how it might contribute to leadership success or failure. Perhaps any leader can adopt the correct behavior with appropriate training. Two basic leadership behaviors that have been identified as important for leadership are *task-oriented behavior* and *people-oriented behavior*. These two *metacategories*, or broadly defined behavior categories, have been found to be applicable to effective leadership in a variety of situations and time periods.[9] Although these are not the only important leadership behaviors, concern for tasks and concern for people must be shown at some

## Exhibit 18.2

### Personal Characteristics of Leaders

| Physical Characteristics | Personality | Work-Related Characteristics |
|---|---|---|
| Energy | Self-confidence | Achievement drive, desire to excel |
| Physical stamina | Honesty and integrity | Conscientiousness in pursuit of goals |
| | Enthusiasm | Persistence against obstacles, tenacity |
| | Desire to lead | |
| | Independence | |
| **Intelligence and Ability** | **Social Characteristics** | **Social Background** |
| Intelligence, cognitive ability | Sociability, interpersonal skills | Education |
| Knowledge | Cooperativeness | Mobility |
| Judgment, decisiveness | Ability to enlist cooperation | |
| | Tact, diplomacy | |

**SOURCES**: Based on Bernard M. Bass, *Bass & Stogdill's Handbook of Leadership: Theory, Research, and Managerial Applications*, 3rd ed. (New York: The Free Press, 1990), 80–81; and S. A. Kirkpatrick and E. A. Locke, "Leadership: Do Traits Matter?" *Academy of Management Executive* 5, no. 2 (1991), 48–60.

# Unlocking Creative Solutions Through Technology

## An E-Commerce Revolution at General Motors

When Ralph Szygenda first arrived at General Motors, the company's information technology systems were so outdated, inflexible, and poorly integrated that they were practically useless. As GM's first chief information officer, Szygenda has brought GM into the Internet Age. According to vice chairman Harry Pearce, prodding GM out of its inertia "was as tough a challenge as there was in corporate America."

Fortunately, Szygenda has always loved a challenge. "In my career, I've always tried to take on impossible jobs," he says. After nearly a decade on the job, the CIO has taken GM a long way toward his goal of creating the first totally wired car company. GM buys more IT products and services than any other company in the world. Today, employees around the globe can communicate and collaborate on projects. Before, the company's systems were so walled off from one another that the Cadillac division could not access marketing data assembled by Buick, and project engineers at headquarters in Michigan had no easy way to collaborate with their overseas colleagues. In addition, GM's site for consumers, GMBuyPower, is one of the most powerful on the Internet, offering more configuration and comparison options than either Ford's or DaimlerChrysler's, as well as the ability to find out whether the car is in dealers' stock and where. The company's GMPowerSupply site lets suppliers tap directly into GM factories to access production schedules, inventories, and so forth.

The next step for Szygenda is to tie everything together into a seamless "sense and respond" system that would make GM a superefficient information link between customers and suppliers. This integration would allow GM to build at least half of its cars to order, cut delivery times of custom vehicles from months to weeks, and slash inventory in half. In other words, Szygenda wants to do for cars what Michael Dell has done for computers. It is a tremendous undertaking, but Szygenda thrives on such monumental tasks. He is known as an overachiever who loves the sense of accomplishment that comes from completing seemingly impossible jobs. His high energy level enables him to work 70-hour weeks and take home massive amounts of work on the weekends. He is a tough boss who sets high standards and expects everyone to be as focused on meeting them as he is. However, Szygenda doesn't insist on "his way or the highway." To build his executive team, he deliberately picked strong-willed people he knew would challenge him and each other. He likes to have a lot of people looking at and debating a problem. Szygenda also is known as a consummate diplomat and a skillful negotiator, who can get things accomplished through tact and compromise. His executive team members typically see him as a demanding but supportive boss with a good sense of humor.

Szygenda believes persistence and determination are his best qualities. He will do whatever it takes to get the job done, and he has the confidence to see it through to the end. "My job," he says, "is to make sure this all comes together."

SOURCES: Alex Taylor III, "Ralph's Agenda," *eCompany* (July 2000), 96–101; Robin Gareiss, "Chief of the Year: Ralph Szygenda," *Information Week* (December 2, 2002), 34–40; and Craig Zarley, "Ralph Szygenda," *CRN* (December 15, 2003), 60.

reasonable level. Thus, many approaches to understanding leadership use these metacategories as a basis for study and comparison. Important research programs on leadership behavior were conducted at The Ohio State University, the University of Michigan, and the University of Texas.

## Ohio State Studies

Researchers at The Ohio State University surveyed leaders to study hundreds of dimensions of leader behavior.[10] They identified two major behaviors, called consideration and initiating structure.

Consideration falls in the category of people-oriented behavior, and is the extent to which the leader is mindful of subordinates, respects their ideas and feelings, and

**consideration**
The type of behavior that describes the extent to which the leader is sensitive to subordinates, respects their ideas and feelings, and establishes mutual trust.

establishes mutual trust. Considerate leaders are friendly, provide open communication, develop teamwork, and are oriented toward their subordinates' welfare.

**initiating structure**
A type of leader behavior that describes the extent to which the leader is task oriented and directs subordinate work activities toward goal attainment.

Initiating structure is the degree of task behavior, that is, the extent to which the leader is task oriented and directs subordinate work activities toward goal attainment. Leaders with this style typically give instructions, spend time planning, emphasize deadlines, and provide explicit schedules of work activities.

Consideration and initiating structure are independent of each other, which means that a leader with a high degree of consideration may be either high or low on initiating structure. A leader may have any of four styles: high initiating structure–low consideration, high initiating structure–high consideration, low initiating structure–low consideration, or low initiating structure–high consideration. The Ohio State research found that the high consideration–high initiating structure style achieved better performance and greater satisfaction than the other leader styles. The value of the high-high style is illustrated by some of today's successful pro football coaches, such as Brian Billick of the Baltimore Ravens and Herman Edwards of the New York Jets.[11] Coaches have to keep players focused on winning football games by scheduling structured practices, emphasizing careful planning, and so forth. However, today's best coaches are those who genuinely care about and show concern for their players. The Unlocking Creative Solutions Through People box profiles Bob Ladouceur, the coach of an extraordinary high school football team, who personifies the high-high leadership style.

However, new research has found that the "high-high" style is not necessarily the best. These studies indicate that effective leaders may be high on consideration and low on initiating structure or low on consideration and high on initiating structure, depending on the situation.[12]

## Michigan Studies

Studies at the University of Michigan at about the same time took a different approach by comparing the behavior of effective and ineffective supervisors.[13] The most effective supervisors were those who focused on the subordinates' human needs in order to "build effective work groups with high performance goals." The Michigan researchers used the term *employee-centered leaders* for leaders who established high performance goals and displayed supportive behavior toward subordinates. The less-effective leaders were called *job-centered leaders;* these tended to be less concerned with goal achievement and human needs in favor of meeting schedules, keeping costs low, and achieving production efficiency.

## The Leadership Grid

**leadership grid**
A two-dimensional leadership theory that measures the leader's concern for people and for production.

Blake and Mouton of the University of Texas proposed a two-dimensional leadership theory called the leadership grid that builds on the work of The Ohio State and Michigan studies.[14] The two-dimensional model and five of its seven major management styles are depicted in Exhibit 18.3. Each axis on the grid is a nine-point scale, with 1 meaning low concern and 9 high concern.

*Team management* (9,9) often is considered the most effective style and is recommended for managers because organization members work together to accomplish tasks. *Country club management* (1,9) occurs when primary emphasis is given to people rather than to work outputs. *Authority-compliance management* (9,1) occurs when efficiency in operations is the dominant orientation. *Middle-of-the-road management* (5,5) reflects a moderate amount of concern for both people and production. *Impoverished management* (1,1) means the absence of a management philosophy; managers exert little effort toward interpersonal relationships or work accomplishment. Consider these examples.

Exhibit 18.3

## The Leadership Grid® Figure

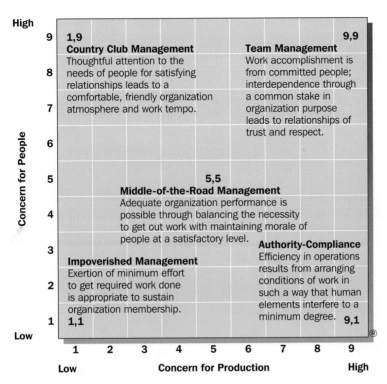

**SOURCE**: The Leadership Grid® figure, Paternalism figure and Opportunism from *Leadership Dilemmas-Grid Solutions*, by Robert R. Blake and Anne Adams McCanse (formerly the Managerial Grid by Robert R. Blake and Jane S. Mouton). Houston: Gulf Publishing Company. (Grid figure: p. 29, Paternalism figure: p. 30, Opportunism figure: p. 31). Copyright © 1991, by Blake and Mouton, and Scientific Methods, Inc. Reproduced by permission of the owners.

When Pamela Forbes Lieberman learned that her subordinates called her *the dragon lady*, she embraced the moniker and hung a watercolor of a dragon in her office. Lieberman makes no apologies for her hard-driving leadership style. Her emphasis on ambitious goals, tough standards, and bottom-line results has brought renewed health and vitality to hardware cooperative TruServ, which supplies inventory to True Value hardware stores. As soon as Lieberman became CEO, she began slashing costs and setting tough performance targets. "If [people] succeed, they will be rewarded, but if they don't, then we're going to have to look for new people sitting in their chairs," Lieberman says.

Compare Lieberman's hard-nosed approach to that of Tom Gegax, who calls himself the head coach of Tires Plus, a fast-growing chain of retail tire stores. Gegax believes that you cannot manage people like you manage fixed assets. His emphasis is on treating employees just as well as they are expected to treat their customers. Gegax personally leads classes at Tires Plus University, where employees learn not just about changing tires but about how to make their whole lives better. Gegax also makes sure stores are clean, bright, and airy, so that employees have a pleasant work environment. He believes all this translates into better service. Employees, as well as customers, like the approach. "The last thing the world needs is another chain of stores," Gegax says. "What it does need is a company with a new business model—one that embraces customers and employees as whole people."[15]

TRUSERV AND TIRES PLUS
http://www.tiresplus.com

The leadership style of Pamela Lieberman is characterized by high concern for tasks and production (task-oriented behavior) and low-to-moderate concern for people (people-oriented behavior). Tom Gegax, in contrast, is high on concern for people and

# Unlocking Creative Solutions Through People

**The De La Salle Spartans Win with Soul**

The last time the De La Salle Spartans lost a football game was December 7, 1991. Since then, coach Bob LaDouceur has led his team of players, many of whom are derided as "undersized" and "untalented," to one victory after another, year after year. Despite competing against bigger schools and tougher players, the De La Salle Spartans just keep on winning.

De La Salle is a small, private parochial school in Concord, California. Years ago, LaDouceur sized up his team of a few, small demoralized players and made a decision. He was going to teach these guys what it takes to win, and then make it a day-to-day process. LaDouceur directs close attention to the tasks needed to accomplish the goal of winning. He keeps his players on a year-round strength and conditioning program. Each practice is methodical, and LaDouceur constantly tells his players to leave every practice just a little bit better than they were when it started. He teaches players to make up for what they lack in size and talent with intelligence and wit.

However, the coach hasn't just institutionalized the process of drills, workouts, and practices. He has also institutionalized a process of building bonds and intimacy among his players. "If a team has no soul," LaDouceur says, "you're just wasting your time." Tasks are important, but for LaDouceur, people always come first. "It's not about how we're getting better physically, it's about how we're getting better as people," he says. During the off season, players go camping and rafting together and volunteer for community service. When the season starts, the team attends chapel together for readings and songs. After every practice, there's a dinner at a player's home.

Then comes what LaDouceur's considers his central task and his main goal for the team. As tensions build during the season, players are encouraged to speak their hearts, to confess their fears and shortcomings, and to talk about their commitments and expectations of themselves for the next game. On Thursday night before Friday games, LaDouceur doesn't give a typical locker room speech. He talks about the "L word." "Love. Why is that word so hard to say?" he asks his players. And then he waits—as long as it takes—until a few players overcome their embarrassment enough to say it.

**SOURCE**: Don Wallace, "The Soul of a Sports Machine," *Fast Company* (October 2003), 100–102.

moderate on concern for production. Both leaders are successful, although they display very different leadership styles, because of their different situations. The next group of theories builds on the leader-follower relationship of behavioral approaches to explore how organizational situations affect the leader's approach.

*Take A Moment*    *Go to the experiential exercise on page 687 to measure your degree of task-orientation and people-orientation.*

## Contingency Approaches

**contingency approach**
A model of leadership that describes the relationship between leadership styles and specific organizational situations.

There are several models of leadership that explain the relationship between leadership styles and specific situations. These are termed contingency approaches and include the leadership model developed by Fiedler and his associates, the situational theory of Hersey and Blanchard, the path-goal theory presented by Evans and House, and the substitutes-for-leadership concept.

### Fiedler's Contingency Theory

An early, extensive effort to combine leadership style and organizational situation into a comprehensive theory of leadership was made by Fiedler and his associates.[16]

The basic idea is simple: Match the leader's style with the situation most favorable for his or her success. By diagnosing leadership style and the organizational situation, the correct fit can be arranged.

## Leadership Style

The cornerstone of Fiedler's contingency theory is the extent to which the leader's style is relationship oriented or task oriented. A *relationship-oriented leader* is concerned with people, similar to the consideration style described earlier. A *task-oriented leader* is primarily motivated by task accomplishment, which is similar to the initiating structure style described earlier.

Leadership style was measured with a questionnaire known as the least preferred co-worker (LPC) scale. The LPC scale has a set of 16 bipolar adjectives along an 8-point scale. Examples of the bipolar adjectives used by Fiedler on the LPC scale follow:

| | | guarded |
|---|---|---|
| open | _ _ _ _ _ _ _ _ | guarded |
| quarrelsome | _ _ _ _ _ _ _ _ | harmonious |
| efficient | _ _ _ _ _ _ _ _ | inefficient |
| self-assured | _ _ _ _ _ _ _ _ | hesitant |
| gloomy | _ _ _ _ _ _ _ _ | cheerful |

**LPC scale**
A questionnaire designed to measure relationship-oriented versus task-oriented leadership style according to the leader's choice of adjectives for describing the "least preferred co-worker."

If the leader describes the least preferred co-worker using positive concepts, he or she is considered relationship oriented, that is, a leader who cares about and is sensitive to other people's feelings. Conversely, if a leader uses negative concepts to describe the least preferred coworker, he or she is considered task oriented—that is, a leader who places greater value on task activities than on people.

## Situation

Leadership situations can be analyzed in terms of three elements: the quality of leader-member relationships, task structure, and position power.[17] Each of these elements can be described as either favorable or unfavorable for the leader.

1. *Leader-member relations* refers to group atmosphere and members' attitude toward and acceptance of the leader. When subordinates trust, respect, and have confidence in the leader, leader-member relations are considered good. When subordinates distrust, do not respect, and have little confidence in the leader, leader-member relations are poor.

2. *Task structure* refers to the extent to which tasks performed by the group are defined, involve specific procedures, and have clear, explicit goals. Routine, well-defined tasks, such as those of assembly-line workers, have a high degree of structure. Creative, ill-defined tasks, such as research and development or strategic planning, have a low degree of task structure. When task structure is high, the situation is considered favorable to the leader; when low, the situation is less favorable.

3. *Position power* is the extent to which the leader has formal authority over subordinates. Position power is high when the leader has the power to plan and direct the work of subordinates, evaluate it, and reward or punish them. Position power is low when the leader has little authority over subordinates and cannot evaluate their work or reward them. When position power is high, the situation is considered favorable for the leader. When low, the situation is unfavorable.

© KEN HAWKINS

**CONCEPT CONNECTION**

*At Earnest Partners, an asset management firm in Atlanta, Georgia, the quality of **leader-member relationships** is high. CEO Paul Viera has gained the respect and trust of colleagues and followers because he has proven that he has the integrity, skills, and commitment to keep the company thriving. In 2004, Earnest had $8.2 billion in assets under management. Viera can be characterized as a **task-oriented leader** because he is focused, prepared, and competitive, and he expects others to be as well. According to Fiedler's contingency theory, Viera's style succeeds at Earnest because of positive leader-member relations, strong leader position power, and jobs that contain some degree of task structure.*

Combining the three situational characteristics yields a list of eight leadership situations, which are illustrated in Exhibit 18.4. Situation I is most favorable to the leader because leader-member relations are good, task structure is high, and leader position power is strong. Situation VIII is most unfavorable to the leader because leader-member relations are poor, task structure is low, and leader position power is weak. All other octants represent intermediate degrees of favorableness for the leader.

## Contingency Theory

When Fiedler examined the relationships among leadership style, situational favorability, and group task performance, he found the pattern shown in Exhibit 18.4. Task-oriented leaders are more effective when the situation is either highly favorable or highly unfavorable. Relationship-oriented leaders are more effective in situations of moderate favorability.

The task-oriented leader excels in the favorable situation because everyone gets along, the task is clear, and the leader has power; all that is needed is for someone to take charge and provide direction. Similarly, if the situation is highly unfavorable to the leader, a great deal of structure and task direction is needed. A strong leader defines task structure and can establish authority over subordinates. Because leader-member relations are poor anyway, a strong task orientation will make no difference in the leader's popularity.

The relationship-oriented leader performs better in situations of intermediate favorability because human relations skills are important in achieving high group performance. In these situations, the leader may be moderately well liked, have some power, and supervise jobs that contain some ambiguity. A leader with good interpersonal skills can create a positive group atmosphere that will improve relationships, clarify task structure, and establish position power.

A leader, then, needs to know two things in order to use Fiedler's contingency theory. First, the leader should know whether he or she has a relationship- or task-oriented style. Second, the leader should diagnose the situation and determine whether leader-member relations, task structure, and position power are favorable or unfavorable.

Exhibit 18.4

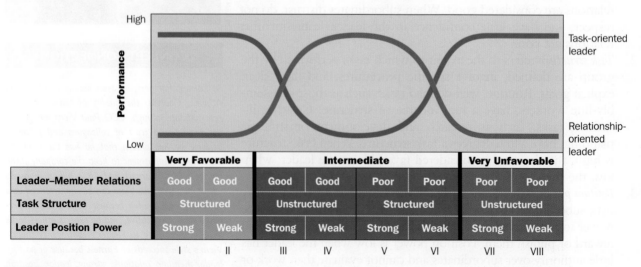

### How Leader Style Fits the Situation

| | Very Favorable | | Intermediate | | | | Very Unfavorable | |
|---|---|---|---|---|---|---|---|---|
| **Leader–Member Relations** | Good | Good | Good | Good | Poor | Poor | Poor | Poor |
| **Task Structure** | Structured | | Unstructured | | Structured | | Unstructured | |
| **Leader Position Power** | Strong | Weak | Strong | Weak | Strong | Weak | Strong | Weak |
| | I | II | III | IV | V | VI | VII | VIII |

**SOURCE**: Based on Fred E. Fiedler, "The Effects of Leadership Training and Experience: A Contingency Model Interpretation," *Administrative Science Quarterly* 17 (1972), 455.

Consider how Stanley O'Neal's style fits his current situation as CEO of Merrill Lynch.

A lot of people inside Merrill Lynch just don't like Stan O'Neal, who took over the CEO's job at the lowest point in the firm's history. They grumble that he is cold, aloof, and ruthless. O'Neal doesn't care. "People say all these things about me," O'Neal acknowledges. "But . . . I can't do anything about it. I have a job to do, and it has nothing to do with worrying about what people call me."

The job to do is saving Merrill Lynch, which only a few years ago was sliding toward irrelevance. Few believed the firm could survive its massive problems, and rumors were that it would be swallowed up by a big bank. Merrill's financial results were dismal and costs were out of control. In addition, Merrill and nine other large securities firms were forced to pay a whopping $1.4 billion in penalties to settle government charges of investor abuses. The loss of public trust, combined with a declining stock market and general economic uncertainty, was a heavy blow to the already-struggling firm.

From the beginning, O'Neal took a tough approach to cutting costs. He froze everyone's pay, cut bonuses, and did away with the free gourmet meals provided for top managers. He met with every one of his direct reports and told them they were personally accountable for the company's profitability and performance. He set brutally ambitious targets for cost-cutting and profit margins and weeded out anyone who wouldn't commit to meeting them.

By early 2004, O'Neal had slashed 24,000 jobs, closed more than 300 field offices, and demoted or fired dozens of veteran managers. He had also achieved one of the most remarkable turnarounds in recent corporate history, perhaps saving Merrill Lynch from extinction. "Stan was made CEO at the ultimate moment of truth," said the head of Merrill's retail brokerage unit. "Our world was imploding, and he had the courage to make difficult decisions."[18]

MERRILL LYNCH
http://www.ml.com

Stan O'Neal might be characterized as using a task-oriented style in an unfavorable situation. The recent environment has been as challenging as any the company has ever faced. Task structure is low, and leader-member relations are poor. Many employees oppose O'Neal's massive changes and don't like his aloof personality. When O'Neal was first promoted, his personal power with managers was low. Many didn't believe he should have gotten the top job and didn't agree with his plans for the company. Overall, the situation can be considered very unfavorable to the leader, suggesting that O'Neal's strong task-oriented style might be the best approach. Even O'Neal's critics have grudgingly admitted that he is just what Merrill Lynch needed. The company has become the leanest and most profitable on Wall Street under O'Neal's leadership. A leader using a relationship-oriented style might not be able to impose the structure and discipline needed for the organization to succeed in this difficult situation. "Ruthless," O'Neal once said, "isn't always that bad."[19]

An important contribution of Fiedler's research is that it goes beyond the notion of leadership styles to show how styles fit the situation to improve organizational effectiveness. Fitting leader style to the situation can yield big dividends in profits and efficiency.[20] On the other hand, the model has also been criticized.[21] Using the LPC score as a measure of relationship- or task-oriented behavior seems simplistic, and how the model works over time is unclear. For example, if a task-oriented leader is matched with an unfavorable situation and is successful, the organizational situation is likely to improve and become more favorable to the leader. Thus, the leader might have to adjust his or her style or go to a new situation. For example, employees at Merrill Lynch are feeling a great sense of relief and pride that the company is thriving again. As the situation continues to become more favorable, Stan O'Neal's strong task-oriented style will not be as effective.

## CONCEPT CONNECTION

*The labor, technology, and infrastructure required to get a box of bananas from the plantations of Latin America to supermarkets in the United States is truly astounding. United Fruit Company, owner of the Chiquita brand of bananas, was responsible for building many roads and train tracks, and entire villages with homes, schools, medical facilities, and factories. Consistent with the **situational theory of leadership**, leaders used a telling style to direct the activities of low-skilled workers. However, as the company's power in the region grew, critics charged that leaders sought total control of workers—as well as attempting to control the leaders of the republics where the company did business. These alleged abuses of power led to devastating results. Over the past decade, the company has lost $700 million and watched its stock price plunge from a high of $50 to a low of 48 cents.*

**situational theory**
A contingency approach to leadership that links the leader's behavioral style with the task readiness of subordinates.

# Hersey and Blanchard's Situational Theory

The situational theory of leadership is an interesting extension of the behavioral theories described earlier and summarized in the leadership grid (Exhibit 18.3). More than previous theories, Hersey and Blanchard's approach focuses a great deal of attention on the characteristics of employees in determining appropriate leadership behavior. The point of Hersey and Blanchard is that subordinates vary in readiness level. People low in task readiness, because of little ability or training, or insecurity, need a different leadership style than those who are high in readiness and have good ability, skills, confidence, and willingness to work.[22]

According to the situational theory, a leader can adopt one of four leadership styles, based on a combination of relationship (concern for people) and task (concern for production) behavior. These four styles are illustrated in Exhibit 18.5. The *telling style* reflects a high concern for tasks and a low concern for people and relationships. This is a very directive style. It involves giving explicit directions about how tasks should be accomplished. The *selling style* is based on a high concern for both people and tasks. With this approach, the leader explains decisions and gives subordinates a chance to ask questions and gain clarity and understanding about work tasks. The next leader behavior style, the *participating style*, is based on a combination of high concern for people and relationships and low concern for production tasks. The leader shares ideas with subordinates, gives them a chance to participate, and facilitates decision making. The fourth style, the *delegating style*, reflects a low concern for both relationships and tasks. This leader style provides little direction and little support because the leader turns over responsibility for decisions and their implementation to subordinates.

## Exhibit 18.5

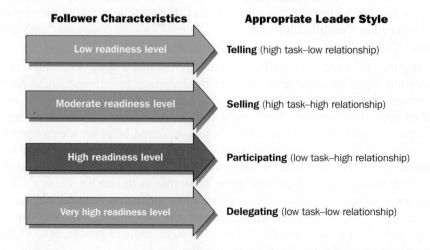

**Hersey and Blanchard's Situational Theory of Leadership**

| Follower Characteristics | Appropriate Leader Style |
|---|---|
| Low readiness level | **Telling** (high task–low relationship) |
| Moderate readiness level | **Selling** (high task–high relationship) |
| High readiness level | **Participating** (low task–high relationship) |
| Very high readiness level | **Delegating** (low task–low relationship) |

The essence of Hersey and Blanchard's situational theory is to select a leader style that is appropriate for the readiness level of subordinates—their degree of education and skills, experience, self-confidence, and work attitudes. Followers may be at low, moderate, high, or very high levels of readiness.

### Low Readiness Level

A telling style is appropriate when followers are at a low readiness level because of poor ability and skills, little experience, insecurity, or unwillingness to take responsibility for their own task behavior. When one or more subordinates exhibit very low levels of readiness, the leader is very specific, telling followers exactly what to do, how to do it, and when.

### Moderate Readiness Level

A selling style works best for followers with moderate levels of readiness. These subordinates, for example, might lack some education and experience for the job, but they demonstrate high confidence, ability, interest, and willingness to learn. The selling style involves giving direction, but it also includes seeking input from others and clarifying tasks rather than simply instructing that they be performed.

### High Readiness Level

When subordinates demonstrate a high readiness level, a participating style is effective. These subordinates might have the necessary education, experience, and skills but might be insecure in their abilities and need some guidance from the leader. The participating style enables the leader to guide followers' development and act as a resource for advice and assistance.

### Very High Readiness Level

When followers have very high levels of education, experience, and readiness to accept responsibility for their own task behavior, the delegating style can effectively be used. Because of the high readiness level of followers, the leader can delegate responsibility for decisions and their implementation to subordinates, who have the skills, abilities, and positive attitudes to follow through. The leader provides a general goal and sufficient authority to do the task as followers see fit.

In summary, the telling style is best suited for subordinates who demonstrate very low levels of readiness to take responsibility for their own task behavior, the selling and participating styles work for subordinates with moderate-to-high readiness, and the delegating style is appropriate for employees with very high readiness. This contingency model is easier to understand than Fiedler's model, but it incorporates only the characteristics of followers, not those of the situation. The leader carefully diagnoses the readiness level of followers and adopts whichever style is necessary—telling, selling, participating, or delegating. For example, Phil Hagans, who owns two McDonald's franchises in northeast Houston, uses different styles as employees grow in their readiness level. Hagans gives many young employees their first job, and he tells them every step to take during their first days, instructing them on everything from how to dress to how to clean the grill. As they grow in ability and confidence, he shifts to a selling or participating style. Hagans has had great success by carefully guiding young workers through each level of readiness.[23] A fast-food franchise leader would probably need to take a different approach with a part-time worker who was retired after 40 years in the business world.

## Path-Goal Theory

Another contingency approach to leadership is called the path-goal theory.[24] According to the path-goal theory, the leader's responsibility is to increase subordinates'

**path-goal theory**
A contingency approach to leadership specifying that the leader's responsibility is to increase subordinates' motivation by clarifying the behaviors necessary for task accomplishment and rewards.

motivation to attain personal and organizational goals. As illustrated in Exhibit 18.6, the leader increases their motivation by either (1) clarifying the subordinates' path to the rewards that are available or (2) increasing the rewards that the subordinates value and desire. Path clarification means that the leader works with subordinates to help them identify and learn the behaviors that will lead to successful task accomplishment and organizational rewards. Increasing rewards means that the leader talks with subordinates to learn which rewards are important to them—that is, whether they desire intrinsic rewards from the work itself or extrinsic rewards such as raises or promotions. The leader's job is to increase personal payoffs to subordinates for goal attainment and to make the paths to these payoffs clear and easy to travel.[25]

This model is called a contingency theory because it consists of three sets of contingencies—leader behavior and style, situational contingencies, and the use of rewards to meet subordinates' needs.[26] Whereas in the Fiedler theory described earlier the assumption would be to switch leaders as situations change, in the path–goal theory leaders switch their behaviors to match the situation.

### Leader Behavior

The path–goal theory suggests a fourfold classification of leader behaviors.[27] These classifications are the types of leader behavior the leader can adopt and include supportive, directive, achievement-oriented, and participative styles.

*Supportive leadership* involves leader behavior that shows concern for subordinates' well-being and personal needs. Leadership behavior is open, friendly, and approachable, and the leader creates a team climate and treats subordinates as equals. Supportive leadership is similar to the consideration, employee-centered, or relationship-oriented leadership described earlier.

## Exhibit 18.6

### Leader Roles in the Path–Goal Model

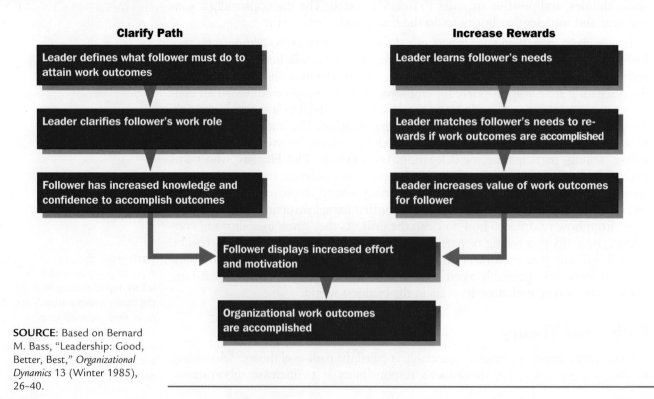

**Clarify Path**

- Leader defines what follower must do to attain work outcomes
- Leader clarifies follower's work role
- Follower has increased knowledge and confidence to accomplish outcomes

**Increase Rewards**

- Leader learns follower's needs
- Leader matches follower's needs to rewards if work outcomes are accomplished
- Leader increases value of work outcomes for follower

- Follower displays increased effort and motivation
- Organizational work outcomes are accomplished

**SOURCE**: Based on Bernard M. Bass, "Leadership: Good, Better, Best," *Organizational Dynamics* 13 (Winter 1985), 26–40.

*Directive leadership* occurs when the leader tells subordinates exactly what they are supposed to do. Leader behavior includes planning, making schedules, setting performance goals and behavior standards, and stressing adherence to rules and regulations. Directive leadership behavior is similar to the initiating-structure, job-centered, or task-oriented leadership style described earlier.

*Participative leadership* means that the leader consults with his or her subordinates about decisions. Leader behavior includes asking for opinions and suggestions, encouraging participation in decision making, and meeting with subordinates in their workplaces. The participative leader encourages group discussion and written suggestions.

*Achievement-oriented leadership* occurs when the leader sets clear and challenging goals for subordinates. Leader behavior stresses high-quality performance and improvement over current performance. Achievement-oriented leaders also show confidence in subordinates and assist them in learning how to achieve high goals.

The four types of leader behavior are not considered ingrained personality traits as in the Fiedler theory; rather, they reflect types of behavior that every leader is able to adopt, depending on the situation.

© SCOTT PETERSON/GAMMA LIAISON

## CONCEPT CONNECTION

*"Nothing can quite compare with the Marine Corps training and combat service to stretch your leadership skills,"* states Phillip Rooney, vice-chairman of the building and maintenance service company, ServiceMaster. Marines demonstrate **participative leadership**. The colonel, or Marine form of CEO, has absolute authority, but is trained in making team decisions. For example, if a group gets a humanitarian mission order, such as the one in the photo, the team rather than a single leader determines issues such as information requirements, targets, key questions, and detailed mission plans.

## Situational Contingencies

The two important situational contingencies in the path–goal theory are (1) the personal characteristics of group members and (2) the work environment. Personal characteristics of subordinates include such factors as ability, skills, needs, and motivations. For example, if employees have low ability or skill, the leader may need to provide additional training or coaching in order for workers to improve performance. If subordinates are self-centered, the leader must use rewards to motivate them. Subordinates who want clear direction and authority require a directive leader who will tell them exactly what to do. Craftworkers and professionals, however, may want more freedom and autonomy and work best under a participative leadership style.

The work environment contingencies include the degree of task structure, the nature of the formal authority system, and the work group itself. The task structure is similar to the same concept described in Fiedler's contingency theory; it includes the extent to which tasks are defined and have explicit job descriptions and work procedures. The formal authority system includes the amount of legitimate power used by managers and the extent to which policies and rules constrain employees' behavior. Work group characteristics are the educational level of subordinates and the quality of relationships among them.

## Use of Rewards

Recall that the leader's responsibility is to clarify the path to rewards for subordinates or to increase the value of rewards to enhance satisfaction and job performance. In some situations, the leader works with subordinates to help them acquire the skills and confidence needed to perform tasks and achieve rewards already available. In others, the leader may develop new rewards to meet the specific needs of a subordinate.

Exhibit 18.7 illustrates four examples of how leadership behavior is tailored to the situation. In the first situation, the subordinate lacks confidence; thus, the supportive leadership style provides the social support with which to encourage the subordinate to undertake the behavior needed to do the work and receive the rewards. In the second situation, the job is ambiguous, and the employee is not performing effectively. Directive leadership behavior is used to give instructions and clarify the

# Exhibit 18.7

## Path–Goal Situations and Preferred Leader Behaviors

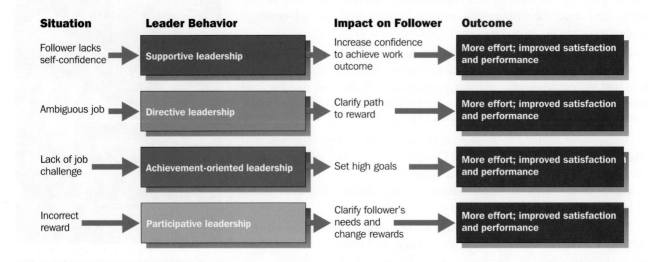

**SOURCE**: Adapted from Gary A. Yukl, *Leadership in Organizations* (Englewood Cliffs, N.J.: Prentice-Hall, 1981), 146–152.

task so that the follower will know how to accomplish it and receive rewards. In the third situation, the subordinate is unchallenged by the task; thus, an achievement-oriented behavior is used to set higher goals. This clarifies the path to rewards for the employee. In the fourth situation, an incorrect reward is given to a subordinate, and the participative leadership style is used to change this. By discussing the subordinate's needs, the leader is able to identify the correct reward for task accomplishment. In all four cases, the outcome of fitting the leadership behavior to the situation produces greater employee effort by either clarifying how subordinates can receive rewards or changing the rewards to fit their needs.

Pat Kelly, founder and CEO of PSS World Medical, a specialty marketer and distributor of medical products, hires people who exhibit a desire to win and then keeps them motivated with his achievement-oriented leadership.

**PSS WORLD MEDICAL**
http://www. pssworldmedical.com

Pat Kelly strives to hire enterprising, hard-working professionals who thrive on challenge, responsibility, and recognition. He keeps them performing at high levels by establishing ambitious goals and making sure people have the skills and resources to reach them. Kelly realizes that what gets people's juices flowing is not just reaching a new financial target, but the idea of winning. So Kelly makes sure employees have what they need to win and receive high rewards for their performance. PSS spends about 5 percent of its payroll budget each year on training, so that employees have the knowledge and skills they need to succeed. The company also emphasizes promotion from within. Moving people around to different divisions and different roles gives them opportunities for learning and advancement. If an employee does not do well in one position, PSS will help the person find another avenue to success.

Open communication plays an important role in Kelly's leadership. To meet high goals, employees have to know how they contribute and where they stand. Open book management is a cornerstone of corporate culture because Kelly believes people can succeed only when everyone knows the numbers and how they fit in. By setting high goals, providing people with the knowledge and skills to succeed, and running an open company, Kelly has created an organization full of people who think and act like CEOs. In fact, all delivery drivers have business cards with their names and "CEO" printed on them. As Kelly puts it, "When you're standing in front of the customer, you are the CEO."[28]

Kelly's achievement-oriented leadership is successful because it keeps talented, ambitious professionals challenged and motivated. Path–goal theorizing can be complex, but much of the research on it has been encouraging.[29] Using the model to specify precise relationships and make exact predictions about employee outcomes may be difficult, but the four types of leader behavior and the ideas for fitting them to situational contingencies provide a useful way for leaders to think about motivating subordinates.

## Substitutes for Leadership

The contingency leadership approaches considered so far have focused on the leaders' style, the subordinates' nature, and the situation's characteristics. The final contingency approach suggests that situational variables can be so powerful that they actually substitute for or neutralize the need for leadership.[30] This approach outlines those organizational settings in which a leadership style is unimportant or unnecessary.

Exhibit 18.8 shows the situational variables that tend to substitute for or neutralize leadership characteristics. A substitute for leadership makes the leadership style unnecessary or redundant. For example, highly professional subordinates who know how to do their tasks do not need a leader who initiates structure for them and tells them what to do. A neutralizer counteracts the leadership style and prevents the leader from displaying certain behaviors. For example, if a leader has absolutely no position power or is physically removed from subordinates, the leader's ability to give directions to subordinates is greatly reduced.

Situational variables in Exhibit 18.8 include characteristics of the group, the task, and the organization itself. For example, when subordinates are highly professional and experienced, both leadership styles are less important. The employees do not need much direction or consideration. With respect to task characteristics, highly structured tasks substitute for a task-oriented style, and a satisfying task substitutes for a people-oriented style. With respect to the organization itself, group cohesiveness substitutes for both leader styles. Formalized rules and procedures substitute for leader task orientation. Physical separation of leader and subordinate neutralizes both leadership styles.

**substitute**
A situational variable that makes a leadership style unnecessary or redundant.

**neutralizer**
A situational variable that counteracts a leadership style and prevents the leader from displaying certain behaviors.

## Exhibit 18.8

### Substitutes and Neutralizers for Leadership

| Variable | | Task-Oriented Leadership | People-Oriented Leadership |
|---|---|---|---|
| **Organizational variables** | Group cohesiveness | Substitutes for | Substitutes for |
| | Formalization | Substitutes for | No effect on |
| | Inflexibility | Neutralizes | No effect on |
| | Low position power | Neutralizes | Neutralizes |
| | Physical separation | Neutralizes | Neutralizes |
| **Task characteristics** | Highly structured task | Substitutes for | No effect on |
| | Automatic feedback | Substitutes for | No effect on |
| | Intrinsic satisfaction | No effect on | Substitutes for |
| **Group characteristics** | Professionalism | Substitutes for | Substitutes for |
| | Training/experience | Substitutes for | No effect on |

The value of the situations described in Exhibit 18.8 is that they help leaders avoid leadership overkill. Leaders should adopt a style with which to complement the organizational situation. Consider the work situation for bank tellers. A bank teller performs highly structured tasks, follows clear written rules and procedures, and has very little flexibility in terms of how to do the work. The head teller should not adopt a task-oriented style, because the organization already provides structure and direction. The head teller should concentrate on a people-oriented style. In other organizations, if group cohesiveness or previous training meet employees' social needs, the leader is free to concentrate on task-oriented behaviors. The leader can adopt a style complementary to the organizational situation to ensure that both task needs and people needs of the work group will be met.

# Leading Change

In Chapter 1, we defined management to include the functions of leading, planning, organizing, and controlling. But recent work on leadership has begun to distinguish leadership as something more: a quality that inspires and motivates people beyond their normal levels of performance. Leadership is particularly important in companies trying to meet the challenges of a turbulent environment. Leaders in many organizations have had to reconceptualize almost every aspect of how they do business to meet the needs of increasingly demanding customers, keep employees motivated and satisfied, and remain competitive in a rapidly changing global environment.

Research has found that some leadership approaches are more effective than others for bringing about change in organizations. Two types of leadership that can have a substantial impact are charismatic and transformational. These types of leadership are best understood in comparison to *transactional leadership*.[31] Transactional leaders clarify the role and task requirements of subordinates, initiate structure, provide appropriate rewards, and try to be considerate to and meet the social needs of subordinates. The transactional leader's ability to satisfy subordinates may improve productivity. Transactional leaders excel at management functions. They are hardworking, tolerant, and fair minded. They take pride in keeping things running smoothly and efficiently. Transactional leaders often stress the impersonal aspects of performance, such as plans, schedules, and budgets. They have a sense of commitment to the organization and conform to organizational norms and values. Transactional leadership is important to all organizations, but leading change requires a different approach.

## Charismatic and Visionary Leadership

Charismatic leadership goes beyond transactional leadership techniques. Charisma has been referred to as "a fire that ignites followers' energy and commitment, producing results above and beyond the call of duty."[32] The charismatic leader has the ability to inspire and motivate people to do more than they would normally do, despite obstacles and personal sacrifice. Followers transcend their own self-interests for the sake of the department or organization. The impact of charismatic leaders is normally from (1) stating a lofty vision of an imagined future that employees identify with, (2) shaping a corporate value system for which everyone stands, and (3) trusting subordinates and earning their complete trust in return.[33] Charismatic leaders tend to be less predictable than transactional leaders. They create an atmosphere of change, and they may be obsessed by visionary ideas that excite, stimulate, and drive other people to work hard.

Charismatic leaders are often skilled in the art of *visionary leadership*. Visionary leaders speak to the hearts of employees, letting them be part of something bigger

**transactional leader**
A leader who clarifies subordinates' role and task requirements, initiates structure, provides rewards, and displays consideration for subordinates.

**charismatic leader**
A leader who has the ability to motivate subordinates to transcend their expected performance.

© RYSTEDT/GETTY

than themselves. They see beyond current realities and help followers believe in a brighter future as well. A **vision** is an attractive, ideal future that is credible yet not readily attainable. In an examination of leadership lessons from one of history's most famous and most successful leaders, Alexander the Great, no factor emerges more clearly than his capacity for visionary leadership. Alexander the Great knew what he wanted to accomplish, and he was able to communicate a vision that spoke to the collective imagination of his followers.[34] His vision enabled Alexander within a period of 12 years to conquer for the Greek kingdom almost the entire known world of the time. Vision is just as powerful for less legendary leaders. Consider Michael Dell, who had a vision of conquering the personal computer market with a new build-to-order model for making and selling PCs. Twenty years ago, no one thought Dell stood a chance, but the company quickly rose to number one in PC sales. Dell's vision continues to grow and change. Today, his vision is to double sales by 2007, with half of that coming from non-PC businesses like corporate computing and services.[35]

**vision**
An attractive, ideal future that is credible yet not readily attainable.

Vision is an important component of both charismatic and transformational leadership. Charismatic leaders typically have a strong vision for the future, almost an obsession, and they can motivate others to help realize it.[36] These leaders have an emotional impact on subordinates because they strongly believe in the vision and can communicate it to others in a way that makes the vision real, personal, and meaningful to others. This chapter's Manager's Shoptalk provides a short quiz to help you determine whether you have the potential to be a charismatic leader.

Charismatic leaders include Mother Theresa, Adolf Hitler, Sam Walton, Ronald Reagan, David Koresh, Martin Luther King Jr., and Osama bin Laden. Charisma can be used for positive outcomes that benefit the group, but it can also be used for self-serving purposes that lead to deception, manipulation, and exploitation of others. When charismatic leaders respond to organizational problems in terms of the needs of the entire group rather than their own emotional needs, they can have a powerful, positive influence on organizational performance.[37]

## CONCEPT CONNECTION

*UPS has come a long way since it was founded in 1907. When the telephone threatened to kill off the company's original messenger business, founder James Casey transformed UPS into a company that delivered goods from retailers. UPS leaders have reinvented the company time after time to stay in step with the changing world. Today, under the transformational leadership of Michael L. Eskew, UPS is undergoing another makeover. Eskew is transforming the company into a logistics expert, leveraging decades of experience managing its own global delivery network to serve as traffic manager for corporate America. Logistics management—where UPS does everything from scheduling the planes, trains, and trucks on which goods move to managing companies' distribution centers and warehouses—accounted for 6 percent of UPS's total revenues last year and is a rapidly growing part of the company's business.*

**transformational leader**
A leader distinguished by a special ability to bring about innovation and change.

**WELLS FARGO & COMPANY**
http://www.wellsfargo.com

# Transformational Leaders

**Transformational leaders** are similar to charismatic leaders, but are distinguished by their special ability to bring about innovation and change by recognizing followers' needs and concerns, helping them look at old problems in new ways, and encouraging them to question the status quo. Transformational leaders inspire followers not just to believe in the leader personally, but to believe in their own potential to imagine and create a better future for the organization. Transformational leaders create significant change in both followers and the organization.[38] They have the ability to lead changes in the organization's mission, strategy, structure, and culture, as well as to promote innovation in products and technologies. Transformational leaders do not rely solely on tangible rules and incentives to control specific transactions with followers. They focus on intangible qualities such as vision, shared values, and ideas to build relationships, give larger meaning to diverse activities, and find common ground to enlist followers in the change process.[39]

A recent study confirmed that transformational leadership has a positive impact on follower development and follower performance. Moreover, transformational leadership skills can be learned and are not ingrained personality characteristics.[40] However, some personality traits may make it easier for a leader to display transformational leadership behaviors. For example, a study of transformational leadership and the Big Five model of personality discussed in the previous chapter found that the traits of extroversion and agreeableness are associated with transformational leaders.[41] This is not surprising considering that these leaders accomplish change by building networks of positive relationships.

A good example of a transformational leader is Richard Kovacevich, who steered mid-sized Norwest Corp. (now Wells Fargo & Co.) through numerous acquisitions to make it one of the largest and most powerful banking companies in the United States.

A community banker listening to Wells Fargo's Richard Kovacevich discuss the secrets of his success might think, "There's nothing his bank does that we can't do." That might be true, but Kovacevich seems to do it better than anyone. Why? It comes down to his leadership style, a style that puts accountability for success in the hands of each and every employee.

Kovacevich has inspired his followers with a vision of becoming the Wal-Mart of financial services—and the company is well on its way. The average customer buys four financial products (such as checking accounts, credit cards, home equity loans, and certificates of deposit), compared to the industry average of two. To motivate employees, Kovacevich leads with slogans such as, "Mind share plus heart share equals market share." Although some people might think it sounds hokey, Kovacevich and his employees don't care. It is the substance behind the slogans that matters. Kovacevich believes it's not what employees know that is important, but whether they care. Employees are rewarded for putting both their hearts and minds into their work. Kovacevich spends a lot of time out in the field, meeting employees, patting backs and giving pep talks. He likes to personally remind people on the front lines that they are the heart and soul of Wells Fargo, and that only through their efforts can the company succeed.

At the beginning of his speech accepting American Banker's 2003 Banker of the Year Award, Kovacevich stressed that the award was won not by him but by the 140,000 Wells Fargo employees spread throughout the nation.[42]

# manager's Shoptalk

## Turbulent Times

### Are You a Charismatic Leader?

If you were the head of a major department in a corporation, how important would each of the following activities be to you? Answer yes or no to indicate whether you would strive to perform each activity.

1. Help subordinates clarify goals and how to reach them.
2. Give people a sense of mission and overall purpose.
3. Help get jobs out on time.
4. Look for the new product or service opportunities.
5. Use policies and procedures as guides for problem solving.
6. Promote unconventional beliefs and values.
7. Give monetary rewards in exchange for high performance from subordinates.
8. Command respect from everyone in the department.
9. Work alone to accomplish important tasks.
10. Suggest new and unique ways of doing things.
11. Give credit to people who do their jobs well.
12. Inspire loyalty to yourself and to the organization.
13. Establish procedures to help the department operate smoothly.
14. Use ideas to motivate others.
15. Set reasonable limits on new approaches.
16. Demonstrate social nonconformity.

The even-numbered items represent behaviors and activities of charismatic leaders. Charismatic leaders are personally involved in shaping ideas, goals, and direction of change. They use an intuitive approach to develop fresh ideas for old problems and seek new directions for the department or organization. The odd-numbered items are considered more traditional management activities, or what would be called *transactional leadership*. Managers respond to organizational problems in an impersonal way, make rational decisions, and coordinate and facilitate the work of others. If you answered yes to more even-numbered than odd-numbered items, you may be a potential charismatic leader.

SOURCES: Based on "Have You Got It?" a quiz that appeared in Patricia Sellers, "What Exactly Is Charisma?" *Fortune* (January 15, 1996), 68–75; Bernard M. Bass, *Leadership and Performance beyond Expectations* (New York: Free Press, 1985); and Lawton R. Burns and Selwyn W. Becker, "Leadership and Managership," in *Health Care Management*, eds. S. Shortell and A. Kaluzny (New York: Wiley, 1986).

# Using Power and Influence

Recall our definition of leadership, which is the ability to influence people to achieve goals. Particularly for leaders involved in major change initiatives, the effective and appropriate use of power is crucial. One way to understand power and influence is to look at the source of power and the level of compliance and commitment it engenders within followers.

Power is the potential ability to influence the behavior of others.[43] Sometimes the terms power and influence are used synonymously, but there are distinctions between the two. Basically, influence is the effect a person's actions have on the attitudes, values, beliefs, or behavior of others. Whereas power is the capacity to cause a change in a person, influence may be thought of as the degree of actual change.

Power results from an interaction of leader and followers. Some power comes from an individual's position in the organization. Power may also come from personal

**power**
The potential ability to influence others' behavior.

**influence**
The effect a person's actions have on the attitudes, values, beliefs, or behavior of others.

sources that are not as invested in the organization, such as a leader's personal interests, goals, and values. A good example of personal power is Josh Raskin, a middle school teacher in upper Manhattan who became a mission-critical leader in the hours and days following the destruction of the World Trade Center towers in September 2001. Although he didn't have a formal position of authority, Raskin found himself in charge of coordinating a massive psych-clergy effort for crisis counseling, as well as guiding hundreds of other volunteers, based on his personal power. As he assigned a volunteer to guard a medical supply room, for example, Raskin infused the mundane chore with a higher vision and purpose by telling the young man everyone was counting on him to make sure no one stole drugs that would be desperately needed for the injured.[44]

Within organizations, there are typically five sources of power: legitimate, reward, coercive, expert, and referent.[45]

## Position Power

The traditional manager's power comes from the organization. The manager's position gives him or her the power to reward or punish subordinates in order to influence their behavior. Legitimate power, reward power, and coercive power are all forms of position power used by managers to change employee behavior.

### Legitimate Power

**legitimate power**
Power that stems from a formal management position in an organization and the authority granted to it.

Power coming from a formal management position in an organization and the authority granted to it is called legitimate power. For example, once a person has been selected as a supervisor, most workers understand that they are obligated to follow his or her direction with respect to work activities. Subordinates accept this source of power as legitimate, which is why they comply.

### Reward Power

**reward power**
Power that results from the authority to bestow rewards on other people.

Another kind of power, reward power, stems from the authority to bestow rewards on other people. Managers may have access to formal rewards, such as pay increases or promotions. They also have at their disposal such rewards as praise, attention, and recognition. Managers can use rewards to influence subordinates' behavior.

### Coercive Power

**coercive power**
Power that stems from the authority to punish or recommend punishment.

The opposite of reward power is coercive power: It refers to the authority to punish or recommend punishment. Managers have coercive power when they have the right to fire or demote employees, criticize, or withdraw pay increases. For example, if Sanjay, a salesman, does not perform as expected, his supervisor has the coercive power to criticize him, reprimand him, put a negative letter in his file, and hurt his chance for a raise.

Different types of position power elicit different responses in followers.[46] Legitimate power and reward power are most likely to generate follower compliance. *Compliance* means that workers will obey orders and carry out instructions, although they may personally disagree with them and might not be enthusiastic. Coercive power most often generates resistance. *Resistance* means that workers will deliberately try to avoid carrying out instructions or will attempt to disobey orders.

## Personal Power

In contrast to the external sources of position power, personal power most often comes from internal sources, such as a person's special knowledge or personal characteristics. Personal power is the primary tool of the leader. Subordinates follow a leader because of the respect, admiration, or caring they feel for the individual and his or her ideas. Personal power is becoming increasingly important as more businesses are run by teams of workers who are less tolerant of authoritarian management.[47] Two types of personal power are expert power and referent power.

## Expert Power

Power resulting from a leader's special knowledge or skill regarding the tasks performed by followers is referred to as expert power. When the leader is a true expert, subordinates go along with recommendations because of his or her superior knowledge. Leaders at supervisory levels often have experience in the production process that gains them promotion. At top management levels, however, leaders may lack expert power because subordinates know more about technical details than they do. One top manager who benefits from expert power is Hector de Jesus Ruiz, president and COO of Advanced Micro Devices (AMD). Ruiz has a B.S. in electrical engineering and nearly 30 years of experience in all facets of the semiconductor industry, from top to bottom. Employees respect Ruiz's technical knowledge and operational expertise as a valuable strength as AMD battles Intel in the microprocessor wars. They appreciate having someone in top management who understands the nitty gritty technical and production details that lower-level employees deal with every day.[48]

**expert power**
Power that stems from special knowledge of or skill in the tasks performed by subordinates.

## Referent Power

The last kind of power, referent power, comes from a leader's personal characteristics that command followers' identification, respect, and admiration so they wish to emulate the leader. When workers admire a supervisor because of the way she deals with them, the influence is based on referent power. Referent power does not depend on a formal title or position. Referent power is most visible in the area of charismatic leadership. In social and religious movements, for example, we often see charismatic leaders who emerge and gain a tremendous following based solely on their personal power.

**referent power**
Power that results from characteristics that command subordinates' identification with, respect and admiration for, and desire to emulate the leader.

An example of referent power in the business world is Mary Cadigan, who was called upon to lead a project to move Fannie Mae's computer data center from Washington, D.C., to a new location 25 miles away in Reston, Virginia. The job required employees to do their "day jobs" all week and then throw themselves into the massive and complicated computer center relocation over 13 consecutive weekends. Cadigan used humor, caring, and food to keep people psyched and create a sense of community and fun. Every Friday at 5 P.M., things would kick off with a meal. Snacks were served at midnight, and a full breakfast was brought out at 8 A.M. on Saturday morning. Cadigan made herself highly visible and constantly available throughout the project. She made sure the company provided whatever people needed to get the job done with as little stress and hardship as possible, such as offering hotel rooms to anyone who was too tired to drive home. In the end, she also convinced Fannie Mae to give everyone on the team a bonus. By relying on referent power, Cadigan inspired 550 employees to smoothly accomplish an extraordinary feat, transferring the data center without a single interruption to Fannie Mae's business.[49]

The follower reaction most often generated by expert power and referent power is commitment. *Commitment* means that workers will share the leader's point of view and enthusiastically carry out instructions. Needless to say, commitment is preferred to compliance or resistance. It is particularly important when change is the desired outcome of a leader's instructions, because change carries risk or uncertainty. Commitment assists the follower in overcoming fear of change.

Leaders can increase their referent power when they share power and authority with followers. A significant recent trend in corporate America is for top executives to *empower* lower employees. Empowering employees works because total power in the organization seems to increase. Everyone has more say and hence contributes more to organizational goals. The goal of senior executives in many corporations today is not simply to wield power but also to give it away to people who can get jobs done.[50]

# Post-Heroic Leadership for Turbulent Times

The concept of leadership continues to grow and change. A significant influence on leadership styles in recent times is the turbulence and uncertainty of the environment in which most organizations are operating. Ethical and economic difficulties, corporate governance concerns, globalization, changes in technology, new ways of working, shifting employee expectations, and significant social transitions have all contributed to a shift in how we think about and practice leadership.

Of particular interest for leadership during these turbulent times is a *post-heroic approach* that focuses on the subtle, unseen, and often unrewarded acts that good leaders perform every day, rather than on the grand accomplishments of celebrated business heroes.[51] During the 1980s and 1990s, leadership became equated with larger-than-life personalities, strong egos, and personal ambitions. In contrast, the post-heroic leader's major characteristic is humility. Humility means being unpretentious and modest rather than arrogant and prideful. Humble leaders don't have to be in the center of things. They quietly build a strong, enduring company by developing and supporting others rather than touting their own abilities and accomplishments.[52] Five approaches that are in tune with post-heroic leadership for turbulent times are servant leadership, Level 5 leadership, interactive leadership, e-leadership, and moral leadership.

**humility**
Being unpretentious and modest rather than arrogant and prideful.

*Take A Moment*

*Go to the ethical dilemma on page 689 that pertains to post-heroic leadership for turbulent times.*

## Servant Leadership

There have always been leaders who operate from the assumption that work exists for the development of the worker as much as the worker exists to do the work.[53] For example, a young David Packard, who co-founded Hewlett-Packard, made a spectacle of himself in 1949 by standing up in a roomful of business leaders and arguing that companies had a responsibility to recognize the dignity and worth of their employees and share the wealth with those who helped to create it.[54]

The concept of servant leadership, first described by Robert Greenleaf, is leadership upside down, because leaders transcend self-interest to serve others and the organization.[55] Servant leaders operate on two levels: for the fulfillment of their subordinates' goals and needs and for the realization of the larger purpose or mission of their organization. Servant leaders give things away—power, ideas, information, recognition, credit for accomplishments, even money. Harry Stine, founder of Stine Seed Company in Adel, Iowa, casually announced to his employees at the company's annual post-harvest luncheon that they would each receive $1,000 for each year they had worked at the company. For some loyal workers, that amounted to a $20,000 bonus.[56] Servant leaders truly value other people. They are trustworthy and they trust others. They encourage participation, share power, enhance others' self-worth, and unleash people's creativity, full commitment, and natural impulse to learn and contribute. Servant leaders can bring their followers' higher motives to the work and connect their hearts to the organizational mission and goals.

**servant leader**
A leader who works to fulfill subordinates' needs and goals as well as to achieve the organization's larger mission.

Servant leaders often work in the nonprofit world because it offers a natural way to apply their leadership drive and skills to serve others. Consider the example of Susie Scott Krabacher, a former *Playboy* Playmate who sold a thriving restaurant business and mortgaged her house to set up a network of schools and orphanages in

Haiti.[57] But servant leaders also succeed in the business world. George Merck believed the purpose of a corporation was to do something useful. At Merck & Co., he insisted that people always come before profits. By insisting on serving people rather than profits, Merck shaped a company that averaged 15 percent earnings growth for an amazing 75 years.[58]

## Level 5 Leadership

A recent five-year study conducted by Jim Collins and his research associates identified the critical importance of what Collins calls *Level 5 leadership* in transforming companies from merely good to truly great organizations.[59] As described in his book *Good to Great: Why Some Companies Make the Leap . . . and Others Don't*, Level 5 leadership refers to the highest level in a hierarchy of manager capabilities, as illustrated in Exhibit 18.9. A key characteristic of Level 5 leaders is an almost complete lack of ego. In contrast to the view of great leaders as larger-than-life personalities with strong egos and big ambitions, Level 5 leaders often seem shy and unpretentious. Although they accept full responsibility for mistakes, poor results, or failures, Level 5 leaders give credit for successes to other people. For example, Joseph F. Cullman III, former CEO of Philip Morris, staunchly refused to accept credit for the company's long-term success, citing his great colleagues, successors, and predecessors as the reason for the accomplishments.

Exhibit 18.9

### The Level 5 Leadership Hierarchy

**Level 5: The Level 5 Leader**
Builds an enduring great organization through a combination of personal humility and professional resolve.

**Level 4: The Effective Executive**
Builds widespread commitment to a clear and compelling vision; stimulates people to high performance.

**Level 3: Competent Manager**
Sets plans and organizes people for the efficient and effective pursuit of objectives.

**Level 2: Contributing Team Member**
Contributes to the achievement of team goals; works effectively with others in a group.

**Level 1: Highly Capable Individual**
Productive contributor; offers talent, knowledge, skills, and good work habits as an individual employee.

**SOURCE**: "The Level 5 Leadership Hierarchy" from *Good to Great: Why Some Companies Make the Leap . . . and Others Don't*, by Jim Collins. Reprinted by permission of HarperCollins Publishers, Inc.

Yet, despite their personal humility, Level 5 leaders have a fierce determination to do whatever it takes to produce great and lasting results for their organizations. They are extremely ambitious for their companies rather than for themselves. This becomes most evident in the area of succession planning. Level 5 leaders develop a solid corps of leaders throughout the organization, so that when they leave the company it can continue to thrive and grow even stronger. Egocentric leaders, by contrast often set their successors up for failure because it will be a testament to their own greatness if the company doesn't perform well without them. Rather than an organization built around "a genius with a thousand helpers," Level 5 leaders build an organization with many strong leaders who can step forward and continue the company's success. These leaders want everyone in the organization to develop to their fullest potential.

## Interactive Leadership

The focus on minimizing personal ambition and developing others is also a hallmark of *interactive leadership*, which has been found to be common among female leaders. Recent research indicates that women's style of leadership is particularly suited to today's organizations.[60] Using data from actual performance evaluations, one study found that when rated by peers, subordinates, and bosses, female managers score significantly higher than men on abilities such as motivating others, fostering communication, and listening.[61]

**interactive leadership**
A leadership style characterized by values such as inclusion, collaboration, relationship building, and caring.

Interactive leadership means that the leader favors a consensual and collaborative process, and influence derives from relationships rather than position power and formal authority.[62] For example, Nancy Hawthorne, former chief financial officer at Continental Cablevision Inc., felt that her role as a leader was to delegate tasks and authority to others and to help them be more effective. "I was being traffic cop and coach and facilitator," Hawthorne says. "I was always into building a department that hummed."[63] It is important to note that men can be interactive leaders as well. The characteristics associated with interactive leadership are emerging as valuable qualities for both male and female leaders in today's workplace Values associated with interactive leadership include personal humility, inclusion, relationship building, and caring.

## E-Leadership

In today's workplace, many people may work from home or other remote locations, connected to the office and one another through information technology. People from all over the world participate in virtual teams and rarely or never meet face-to-face. Leaders sometimes lead a complete project from a distance, interacting with followers solely online. This new way of working brings new challenges for leadership.[64] In a virtual environment, leaders face a constant tension in trying to balance structure and accountability with flexibility.[65] They have to provide enough structure and direction so that people have a clear understanding of what is required of them, but they also have to trust that virtual workers will perform their duties responsibly without close control and supervision. Effective e-leaders set clear goals and timelines and are very explicit about how people will communicate and coordinate their work. However, the details of day-to-day activities are left up to employees. This doesn't mean, however, that virtual workers are left on their own. Leaders take extra care to keep people informed and involved with one another and with the organization.[66]

People who excel at e-leadership tend to be open-minded and flexible, exhibit positive attitudes that focus on solutions rather than problems, and have superb communication, coaching, and relationship-building skills.[67] Good e-leaders never forget that work is accomplished through *people*, not technology. Although they must understand how to select and use technology appropriately, e-leaders emphasize human interactions as the key to success. Building trust, maintaining open lines of communication, caring about people, and being open to subtle cues from others are crucial leadership qualities in a virtual environment.[68]

## Moral Leadership

Since leadership can be used for good or evil, to help or to harm others, all leadership has a moral component. Leaders carry a tremendous responsibility to use their power wisely and ethically. Sadly, in recent years, too many have chosen to act from self-interest and greed rather than behaving in ways that serve and uplift others. The disheartening ethical climate in American business has led to a renewed interest in moral leadership. Moral leadership is about distinguishing right from wrong and choosing to do right. It means seeking the just, the honest, the good, and the decent behavior in the practice of leadership.[69] Moral leaders remember that business is about values, not just economic performance.

**moral leadership**
Distinguishing right from wrong and choosing to do right in the practice of leadership.

Distinguishing the right thing to do is not always easy, and doing it is sometimes even harder. Leaders are often faced with right-versus-right decisions, in which several responsibilities conflict with one another.[70] Commitments to superiors, for example, may mean a leader feels the need to hide unpleasant news about pending layoffs from followers. Moral leaders strive to find the moral answer or compromise, rather than taking the easy way out. Consider Katherine Graham, the long-time leader of *The Washington Post*, when she was confronted with a decision in 1971 about what to do with the Pentagon Papers, a leaked Defense Department study that showed Nixon administration deceptions about the Vietnam War. Graham admitted she was terrified—she knew she was risking the whole company on the decision, possibly inviting prosecution under the Espionage Act and jeopardizing thousands of employees' jobs. She decided to go ahead with the story, and reporters Bob Woodward and Carl Bernstein made Watergate—and *The Washington Post*—a household name.[71]

Clearly, moral leadership requires courage, the ability to step forward through fear and act on one's values and conscience. Leaders often behave unethically simply because they lack courage. Most people want to be liked, and it is easy to do the wrong thing in order to fit in or impress others. One example might be a leader who holds his tongue in order to "fit in with the guys" when colleagues are telling sexually or racially offensive jokes. Moral leaders summon the fortitude to do the right thing, even if it is unpopular. Standing up for what is right is the primary way in which leaders create an environment of honesty, trust, and integrity in the organization.

**courage**
The ability to step forward through fear and act on one's values and conscience.

This chapter covered several important ideas about leadership. The early research on leadership focused on personal traits such as intelligence, energy, and appearance. Later, research attention shifted to leadership behaviors that are appropriate to the organizational situation. Behavioral approaches dominated the early work in this area; task-oriented behavior and people-oriented behavior were suggested as essential behaviors that lead work groups toward high performance. The Ohio State and Michigan approaches and the managerial grid are in this category. Contingency approaches include Fiedler's theory, Hersey and Blanchard's situational theory, the path–goal model, and the substitutes-for-leadership concept.

Leadership concepts have evolved from the transactional approach to charismatic and transformational leadership behaviors. Charismatic leadership is the ability to articulate a vision and motivate followers to make it a reality. Transformational leadership extends charismatic qualities to guide and foster dramatic organizational

Manager's Solution

change. Leadership involves the use of power to influence others. Five types of power are legitimate, reward, coercive, expert, and referent. Leaders rely more on personal power than position power.

The concept and practice of leadership continues to grow and change. Of particular interest in today's turbulent times is a post-heroic leadership approach. Five significant leadership concepts in line with the post-heroic approach are servant leadership, Level 5 leadership, interactive leadership, e-leadership, and moral leadership. Servant leaders facilitate the growth, goals, and development of others to liberate their best qualities in pursuing the organization's mission. Level 5 leaders are characterized by personal humility combined with ambition to build a great organization that will thrive beyond the leader's direct influence. Interactive leadership emphasizes relationships and helping others develop to their highest potential, and may be particularly well-suited to today's workplace. E-leadership requires flexibility and open-mindedness, as well as the ability to build trusting, positive relationships. Moral leadership means seeking to do the honest and decent thing in the practice of leadership.

Returning to our opening example, Roy Pelaez wanted to create an organization where people cared about each other and about the customer and willingly gave their best. To do so meant breaking some "unwritten management rules" about not getting involved with followers' personal problems. Pelaez quickly realized that his subordinates (many of whom were immigrants) had very low levels of skill, ability, and confidence, along with tremendous personal needs that consumed much of their attention and motivation. In terms of the theories discussed in the chapter, Pelaez combined a *telling leadership style*, as indicated by the Hersey and Blanchard Theory for followers at a low readiness level, with a *supportive leadership approach*, as defined by the Path-Goal Theory. Pelaez had to use a telling style because if he didn't, many of his workers simply didn't know what to do. However, he also knew he needed to be supportive to help build the pride and confidence of employees.

In addition, Pelaez acted as a servant leader by being deeply committed to helping his followers grow and improve in their personal as well as their work lives, such as setting up classes for anyone interested in improving their English language skills. He instituted an Employee of the Month recognition program, which provided a reward beyond a weekly paycheck. Anyone who had perfect attendance over a six-week period or who turned in a purse or wallet with cash and credit cards got a day off without pay. Members of the "Top Crew of the Month" were rewarded with free movie passes, calling cards, or "burger bucks." These forms of recognition and reward were a real boost to workers who had received little attention and appreciation in their lives. The outcome of Pelaez's leadership was a drop in the turnover rate from 100 percent a year to 12 percent a year and an increase in revenue from $5 million to $14 million. Employees began turning in large amounts of money found on planes, returning some 250 wallets with more than $50,000 in cash to passengers who had left them on board. By genuinely caring about and giving to his employees, Pelaez tremendously increased his personal power and built a community of highly satisfied and committed employees. According to one observer, Pelaez "created a group of people who will do anything in the world for him."[72]

# Discussion Questions

1. Rob Martin became manager of a forklift assembly plant and believed in participative management, even when one supervisor used Rob's delegation to replace two competent line managers with his own friends. What would you say to Rob about his leadership style in this situation?

2. Suggest some personal traits that you believe would be useful to a leader. Are these traits more valuable in some situations than in others?

3. What is the difference between trait theories and behavioral theories of leadership?

4. Suggest the sources of power that would be available to a leader of a student government organization. To be effective, should student leaders keep power to themselves or delegate power to other students?

5. Would you prefer working for a leader who has a consideration or an initiating-structure leadership style? Discuss the reasons for your answer.

6. Consider Fiedler's theory as illustrated in Exhibit 18.4. How often do very favorable, intermediate, or very unfavorable situations occur in real life? Discuss.

7. What is transformational leadership? Differentiate between transformational leadership and transactional leadership. Give an example of each.

8. Some experts believe that leadership is more important than ever in a learning organization. Do you agree? Explain.

9. What is meant by "servant leadership"? Have you ever known a servant leader? Discuss.

10. Do you think leadership style is fixed and unchangeable for a leader or flexible and adaptable? Discuss.

11. Consider the leadership position of a senior partner in a law firm. What task, subordinate, and organizational factors might serve as substitutes for leadership in this situation?

# Management in Practice: Experiential Exercise

## T–P Leadership Questionnaire: An Assessment of Style

Some leaders deal with general directions, leaving details to subordinates. Other leaders focus on specific details with the expectation that subordinates will carry out orders. Depending on the situation, both approaches may be effective. The important issue is the ability to identify relevant dimensions of the situation and behave accordingly. Through this questionnaire, you can identify your relative emphasis on two dimensions of leadership: task orientation (T) and people orientation (P). These are not opposite approaches, and an individual can rate high or low on either or both.

*Directions:* The following items describe aspects of leadership behavior. Respond to each item according to the way you would most likely act if you were the leader of a work group. Circle whether you would most likely behave in the described way: always (A), frequently (F), occasionally (O), seldom (S), or never (N).

1. I would most likely act as the spokesperson of the group.    A   F   O   S   N

2. I would encourage overtime work.
A   F   O   S   N

3. I would allow members complete freedom in their work.    A   F   O   S   N

4. I would encourage the use of uniform procedures.    A   F   O   S   N

5. I would permit members to use their own judgment in solving problems.
A   F   O   S   N

6. I would stress being ahead of competing groups.
A   F   O   S   N

7. I would speak as a representative of the group.
A   F   O   S   N

8. I would needle members for greater effort.
A F O S N

9. I would try out my ideas in the group.
A F O S N

10. I would let members do their work the way they think best. A F O S N

11. I would be working hard for a promotion.
A F O S N

12. I would tolerate postponement and uncertainty.
A F O S N

13. I would speak for the group if there were visitors present. A F O S N

14. I would keep the work moving at a rapid pace.
A F O S N

15. I would turn the members loose on a job and let them go to it. A F O S N

16. I would settle conflicts when they occur in the group. A F O S N

17. I would get swamped by details.
A F O S N

18. I would represent the group at outside meetings. A F O S N

19. I would be reluctant to allow the members any freedom of action. A F O S N

20. I would decide what should be done and how it should be done. A F O S N

21. I would push for increased production.
A F O S N

22. I would let some members have authority which I could keep. A F O S N

23. Things would usually turn out as I had predicted. A F O S N

24. I would allow the group a high degree of initiative. A F O S N

25. I would assign group members to particular tasks. A F O S N

26. I would be willing to make changes.
A F O S N

27. I would ask the members to work harder.
A F O S N

28. I would trust the group members to exercise good judgment. A F O S N

29. I would schedule the work to be done.
A F O S N

30. I would refuse to explain my actions.
A F O S N

31. I would persuade others that my ideas are to their advantage. A F O S N

32. I would permit the group to set its own pace.
A F O S N

33. I would urge the group to beat its previous record. A F O S N

34. I would act without consulting the group.
A F O S N

35. I would ask that group members follow standard rules and regulations.
A F O S N

T _____ P_____

The T–P Leadership Questionnaire is scored as follows:

a. Circle the item number for items 8, 12, 17, 18, 19, 30, 34, and 35.
b. Write the number 1 in front of *a circled item number* if you responded S (seldom) or N (never) to that item.
c. Also write a number 1 in front of *item numbers not circled* if you responded A (always) or F (frequently).
d. Circle the number 1s that you have written in front of the following items: 3, 5, 8, 10, 15, 18, 19, 22, 24, 26, 28, 30, 32, 34, and 35.
e. *Count the circled number 1s.* This is your score for concern for people. Record the score in the blank following the letter P at the end of the questionnaire.
f. *Count uncircled number 1s.* This is your score for concern for task. Record this number in the blank following the letter T.

Source: The T–P Leadership Questionnaire was adapted by J. B. Ritchie and P. Thompson in *Organization and People* (New York: West, 1984). Copyright 1969 by the American Educational Research Association. Adapted by permission of the publisher.

# Management in Practice: Ethical Dilemma

## Does Wage Reform Start at the Top?

Paula Smith has just been offered the opportunity of a lifetime. The chairman of the board of Resitronic Corporation has just called to ask her to take the job as director of the troubled audio equipment manufacturing subsidiary. The first question Smith asked was "Will the board give me the autonomy to turn this company around?" The answer was yes. Resitronic's problems were so severe that the board was desperate for change and ready to give Smith whatever it took to save the company.

Smith knows that cost cutting is the first place she needs to focus. Labor expenses are too high, and product quality and production times are below industry standards. She sees that labor and management at Resitronic are two armed camps, but she needs cooperation at all levels to achieve a turn-around. Smith is energized. She knows she finally has the autonomy to try out her theories about an empowered workforce. Smith knows she must ask managers and workers to take a serious pay cut, with the promise of incentives to share in any improvements they might make. She also knows that every-one will be looking at her own salary as an indication of whether she walks her talk.

Smith is torn. She realizes she faces a year or two of complete hell, with long hours, little time for her family or outside interests, bitter resistance in subordinates, and no guarantees of success. Even if she comes in at the current director's salary, she will be taking a cut in pay. But if she takes a bigger cut com-ing in, with the promise of bonuses and stock options tied to her own performance, she sends a strong mes-sage to the entire subsidiary that they rise or fall together. She wonders what might happen if she fails. Many influences on the audio equipment subsidiary are beyond her control. Resitronic itself is in trouble. From her current vantage point, Smith believes she can turn things around, but what will she discover when she gets inside? What if the board undercuts her? Doesn't she owe it to herself and her family to be compensated at the highest possible level for the stress and risk they will be enduring? Can she afford to risk her own security to send a message of commit-ment to the plan she is asking others to follow?

## What Do You Do?

1. Take the same salary as the current director for one year. Circulate the information that although you are taking a cut to come to Resitronic, you are confident that you can make a difference. Build in pay incentive bonuses for the following years if the subsidiary succeeds.

2. Take a bigger cut in pay with generous incentive bonuses. Ask the board and the entire workforce to do the same. Open the books and let the whole company know exactly where they stand.

3. Ask for the same salary you are making now. You know you are going to be worth it, and you don't want to ask your family to suffer monetar-ily as well as in their quality of life during this transition.

# Surf the Net

1. **Leadership Style.** Test your leadership style with a questionnaire available at *http://www.leaderx.com*. After you complete the assessment, select the "Submit to Tabulate Your Score" button, and receive a customized report on your leader-ship style. Print out your report so that you may evaluate it. Write a one- to two-paragraph state-ment regarding what you agree/disagree with in the report, whether anything surprised you in the report, and what you've learned from the report. Submit both the printout and your com-ments to your instructor.

2. **Leadership Training.** As stated at its Web site, Ninth House Network *http://www.ninthhouse.com* is the "leading provider of leadership devel-opment delivered through blended formats." Further, Ninth House Network "improves lead-ership skills in less time and for less cost than traditional development programs." Through an innovative combination of proven training tech-

niques, captivating storytelling, and universally adopted technology, the Ninth House Network provides business skills learning in areas that corporations consider most critical to their success, including leadership, communication, the basics of good business, managing, team building and project management. Watch one of the Instant Advice videos at this Web site (video player instructions are provided at the Web site) to become familiar with this leadership training tool.

3. **Leadership Research.** The Leadership-Development.com Web site offers insight and information on leadership for executives, CEOs, and other leaders. Visit the site at *http://www.leadershipnow.com*, select a leadership topic of interest to you, and print out the information you can use during a small-group discussion of your topic.

# Case for Critical Analysis

## DGL International

When DGL International, a manufacturer of refinery equipment, brought in John Terrill to manage its Technical Services division, company executives informed him of the urgent situation. Technical Services, with 20 engineers, was the highest-paid, best-educated, and least-productive division in the company. The instructions to Terill: Turn it around. Terrill called a meeting of the engineers. He showed great concern for their personal welfare and asked point blank: "What's the problem? Why can't we produce? Why does this division have such turnover?"

Without hesitation, employees launched a hail of complaints. "I was hired as an engineer, not a pencil pusher." "We spend over half our time writing asinine reports in triplicate for top management, and no one reads the reports."

After a two-hour discussion, Terrill concluded he had to get top management off the engineers' backs. He promised the engineers, "My job is to stay out of your way so you can do your work, and I'll try to keep top management off your backs too." He called for the day's reports and issued an order effective immediately that the originals be turned in daily to his office rather than mailed to headquarters. For three weeks, technical reports piled up on his desk. By month's end, the stack was nearly three feet high. During that time no one called for the reports. When other managers entered his office and saw the stack, they usually asked, "What's all this?" Terrill answered, "Technical reports." No one asked to read them.

Finally, at month's end, a secretary from finance called and asked for the monthly travel and expense report. Terrill responded, "Meet me in the president's office tomorrow morning."

The next morning the engineers cheered as Terrill walked through the department pushing a cart loaded with the enormous stack of reports. They knew the showdown had come.

Terrill entered the president's office and placed the stack of reports on his desk. The president and the other senior executives looked bewildered.

"This," Terrill announced, "is the reason for the lack of productivity in the Technical Services division. These are the reports you people require every month. The fact that they sat on my desk all month shows that no one reads this material. I suggest that the engineers' time could be used in a more productive manner, and that one brief monthly report from my office will satisfy the needs of other departments."

## Questions

1. What leadership style did John Terrill use? What do you think was his primary source of power?
2. Based on the Hersey-Blanchard theory, should Terrill have been less participative? Should he have initiated more task structure for the engineers? Explain.
3. What leadership approach would you have taken in this situation?

# Endnotes

1. John A. Bryne, "How to Lead Now: Getting Extraordinary Performance When You Can't Pay For It," *Fast Company* (August 2003), 62–70.

2. Melanie Warner, "Confessions of a Control Freak," *Fortune* (September 4, 2000), 130–140; Ian Mount, "Underlings: That's *Mister* Conway to You. And I Am Not a People Person," *Business* 2.0 (February 2002), 53–58.

3. Gary Yukl, "Managerial Leadership: A Review of Theory and Research," *Journal of Management* 15 (1989), 251–289.

4. James M. Kouzes and Barry Z. Posner, "The Credibility Factor: What Followers Expect from Their Leaders," *Management Review* (January 1990), 29–33.

5. James E. Colvard, "Managers Vs. Leaders," *Government Executive* 35, no. 9 (July 2003): 82–84.

6. Richard L. Daft, *The Leadership Experience* 3rd ed. (Cincinnati, Ohio: South-Western, 2005), 15–22.

7. G. A. Yukl, *Leadership in Organizations* (Englewood Cliffs, N.J.: Prentice-Hall, 1981); and S. C. Kohs and K. W. Irle, "Prophesying Army Promotion," *Journal of Applied Psychology* 4 (1920), 73–87.

8. R. Albanese and D. D. Van Fleet, *Organizational Behavior: A Managerial Viewpoint* (Hinsdale, Ill.: The Dryden Press, 1983).

9. Gary Yukl, Angela Gordon, and Tom Taber, "A Hierarchical Taxonomy of Leadership Behavior: Integrating a Half Century of Behavior Research," *Journal of Leadership and Organizational Studies* 9, no. 1 (2002), 13–32.

10. C. A. Schriesheim and B. J. Bird, "Contributions of the Ohio State Studies to the Field of Leadership," *Journal of Management* 5 (1979), 135–145; and C. L. Shartle, "Early Years of the Ohio State University Leadership Studies," *Journal of Management* 5 (1979), 126–134.

11. Patrick J. Sauer, "Are You Ready for Some Football Clichés?" *Inc.* (October 2003), 96–99.

12. P. C. Nystrom, "Managers and the High-High Leader Myth," *Academy of Management Journal* 21 (1978), 325–331; and L. L. Larson, J. G. Hunt, and Richard N. Osborn, "The Great High-High Leader Behavior Myth: A Lesson from Occam's Razor," *Academy of Management Journal* 19 (1976), 628–641.

13. R. Likert, "From Production- and Employee-Centeredness to Systems 1–4," *Journal of Management* 5 (1979), 147–156.

14. Robert R. Blake and Jane S. Mouton, *The Managerial Grid III* (Houston: Gulf, 1985).

15. Jo Napolitano, "No, She Doesn't Breathe Fire," *The New York Times* (September 1, 2002), Section 3, 2; Katharine Mieszkowski, "Changing Tires, Changing the World," *Fast Company* (October 1999), 58–60.

16. Fred E. Fiedler, "Assumed Similarity Measures as Predictors of Team Effectiveness," *Journal of Abnormal and Social Psychology* 49 (1954), 381–388; F. E. Fiedler, *Leader Attitudes and Group Effectiveness* (Urbana, Ill.: University of Illinois Press, 1958); and F. E. Fiedler, *A Theory of Leadership Effectiveness* (New York: McGraw-Hill, 1967).

17. Fred E. Fiedler and M. M. Chemers, *Leadership and Effective Management* (Glenview, Ill.: Scott, Foresman, 1974).

18. David Rynecki, "Putting the Muscle Back in the Bull," *Fortune* (April 5, 2004), 162–170; and David Rynecki, "Can Stan O'Neal Save Merrill?" *Fortune* (September 20, 2002), 76–88.

19. Rynecki, "Putting the Muscle Back in the Bull."

20. Fred E. Fiedler, "Engineer the Job to Fit the Manager," *Harvard Business Review* 43 (1965), 115–122; and F. E. Fiedler, M. M. Chemers, and L. Mahar, *Improving Leadership Effectiveness: The Leader Match Concept* (New York: Wiley, 1976).

21. R. Singh, "Leadership Style and Reward Allocation: Does Least Preferred Coworker Scale Measure Tasks and Relation Orientation?" *Organizational Behavior and Human Performance* 27 (1983), 178–197; and D. Hosking, "A Critical Evaluation of Fiedler's Contingency Hypotheses," *Progress in Applied Psychology* 1 (1981), 103–154.

22. Paul Hersey and Kenneth H. Blanchard, *Management of Organizational Behavior: Utilizing Human Resources*, 4th ed. (Englewood Cliffs, N.J.: Prentice-Hall, 1982).

23. Jonathan Kaufman, "A McDonald's Owner Becomes a Role Model for Black Teenagers," *The Wall Street Journal* (August 23, 1995), A1, A6.

24. M. G. Evans, "The Effects of Supervisory Behavior on the Path-Goal Relationship," *Organizational Behavior and Human Performance* 5 (1970), 277–298; M. G. Evans, "Leadership and Motivation: A Core Concept," *Academy of Management Journal* 13 (1970), 91–102; and B. S. Georgopoulos, G. M. Mahoney, and N. W. Jones, "A Path-Goal Approach to Productivity," *Journal of Applied Psychology* 41 (1957), 345–353.

25. Robert J. House, "A Path-Goal Theory of Leader Effectiveness," *Administrative Science Quarterly* 16 (1971), 321–338.

26. M. G. Evans, "Leadership," in *Organizational Behavior*, ed. S. Kerr (Columbus, Ohio: Grid, 1974), 230–233.

27. Robert J. House and Terrence R. Mitchell, "Path-Goal Theory of Leadership," *Journal of Contemporary Business* (Autumn 1974), 81–97.

28. Charles A. O'Reilly III and Jeffrey Pfeffer, "Star Makers," book excerpt from *From Hidden Value: How Great Companies Achieve Extraordinary Results with Ordinary People* (Harvard Business School Press, 2000), published in *CIO* (September 15, 2000), 226–246.

29. Charles Greene, "Questions of Causation in the Path-Goal Theory of Leadership," *Academy of Management Journal* 22 (March 1979), 22–41; and C. A. Schriesheim and Mary Ann von Glinow, "The Path-Goal Theory of Leadership: A Theoretical and Empirical Analysis," *Academy of Management Journal* 20 (1977), 398–405.

30. S. Kerr and J. M. Jermier, "Substitutes for Leadership: Their Meaning and Measurement," *Organizational Behavior and Human Performance* 22 (1978), 375–403; and Jon P. Howell and Peter W. Dorfman, "Leadership and Substitutes for Leadership among Professional and Nonprofessional Workers," *Journal of Applied Behavioral Science* 22 (1986), 29–46.

31. The terms *transactional* and *transformational* come from James M. Burns, *Leadership* (New York: Harper & Row, 1978); and Bernard M. Bass, "Leadership: Good, Better, Best," *Organizational Dynamics* 13 (Winter 1985), 26–40.

32. Katherine J. Klein and Robert J. House, "On Fire: Charismatic Leadership and Levels of Analysis," *Leadership Quarterly* 6, no. 2 (1995), 183–198.

33. Jay A. Conger and Rabindra N. Kanungo, "Toward a Behavioral Theory of Charismatic Leadership in Organizational Settings," *Academy of Management Review* 12 (1987), 637–647; Walter Kiechel III, "A Hard Look at Executive Vision," *Fortune* (October 23, 1989), 207–211; and William L. Gardner and Bruce J. Avolio, "The Charismatic Relationship: A Dramaturgical Perspective," *Academy of Management Review* 23, no. 1 (1998), 32–58.

34. Manfred Kets de Vries, "'Doing an Alexander': Lessons on Leadership by a Master Conqueror," *European Management Journal* 21, no. 3 (2003), 370–375.

35. Steve Lohr, "On a Roll, Dell Enters Uncharted Territory," *The New York Times* (August 25, 2002), Section 3, 1; and Andrew Park with Faith Keenan and Cliff Edwards, "Whose Lunch Will Dell Eat Next?" *BusinessWeek* (August 12, 2002), 66–67.

36. Robert J. House, "Research Contrasting the Behavior and Effects of Reputed Charismatic vs. Reputed Non-Charismatic Leaders" (paper presented as part of a symposium, "Charismatic Leadership: Theory and Evidence," Academy of Management, San Diego, 1985).

37. Robert J. House and Jane M. Howell, "Personality and Charismatic Leadership," *Leadership Quarterly* 3, no. 2 (1992), 81–108; and Jennifer O'Connor, Michael D. Mumford, Timothy C. Clifton, Theodore L. Gessner, and Mary Shane Connelly, "Charismatic Leaders and Destructiveness: A Historiometric Study," *Leadership Quarterly* 6, no. 4 (1995), 529–555.

38. Bernard M. Bass, "Theory of Transformational Leadership Redux," *Leadership Quarterly* 6, no. 4 (1995), 463–478; Noel M. Tichy and Mary Anne Devanna, *The Transformational Leader* (New York: John Wiley & Sons, 1986); and Badrinarayan Shankar Pawar and Kenneth K. Eastman, "The Nature and Implications of Contextual Influences on Transformational Leadership: A Conceptual Examination," *Academy of Management Review* 22, no. 1 (1997) 80–109.

39. Richard L. Daft and Robert H. Lengel, *Fusion Leadership: Unlocking the Subtle Forces that Change People and Organizations* (San Francisco: Berrett-Koehler, 1998).

40. Taly Dvir, Dov Eden, Bruce J. Avolio, and Boas Shamir, "Impact of Transformational Leadership on Follower Development and Performance: A Field Experiment," *Academy of Management Journal* 45, no. 4 (2002), 735–744.

41. Timothy A. Judge and Joyce E. Bono, "Five-Factor Model of Personality and Transformational Leadership," *Journal of Applied Psychology* 85, no. 5 (October 2000), 751+.

42. Paul Nadler, "The Litttle Things That Help Make Wells a Giant," *American Banker* (December 10, 2003), 4; John R. Enger, "Cross-Sell Campaign," *Banking Strategies* 77, no. 6 (November–December 2001), 34; Bethany McLean, "Is This Guy the Best Banker in America?" *Fortune* (July 6, 1998), 126–128; and Jacqueline S. Gold, "Bank to the Future," *Institutional Investor* (September 2001), 54–63.

43. Henry Mintzberg, *Power In and Around Organizations* (Englewood Cliffs, N.J.: Prentice-Hall, 1983); and Jeffrey Pfeffer, *Power in Organizations* (Marshfield, Mass.: Pitman, 1981).

44. Andy Raskin, "The Accidental Leader," *Business 2.0* (November 2001), 32.

45. J. R. P. French, Jr., and B. Raven, "The Bases of Social Power," in *Group Dynamics*, ed. D. Cartwright and Alvin F. Zander (Evanston, Ill.: Row, Peterson, 1960), 607–623.

46. G. A. Yukl and T. Taber, "The Effective Use of Managerial Power," *Personnel* (March–April 1983), 37–44.

47. Jay A. Conger, "The Necessary Art of Persuasion," *Harvard Business Review* (May–June 1998), 84–95.

48. Andy Reinhardt, "Meet AMD's Rags-to-Riches Heir Apparent," *BusinessWeek* (October 2, 2000), 112–117.

49. John A. Byrne, "How to Lead Now," *Fast Company* (August 2003), 62–70.

50. Thomas A. Stewart, "New Ways to Exercise Power," *Fortune* (November 6, 1989), 52–64; and Thomas A. Stewart, "CEOs See Clout Shifting," *Fortune* (November 6, 1989), 66.

51. Joseph L. Badaracco, Jr. "A Lesson for the Times: Learning From Quiet Leaders," *Ivey Business Journal* (January–February 2003), 1–6; and Matthew Gwyther, "Back to the Wall," *Management Today* (February 2003), 58–61.

52. See James C. Collins, *From Good to Great: Why Some Companies Make the Leap . . . And Others Don't* (New York: HarperCollins 2001); Charles A. O'Reilly III and Jeffrey Pfeffer, *Hidden Value: How Great Companies Achieve Extraordinary Results with Ordinary People* (Boston, MA: Harvard Business School Press, 2000); Rakesh Khurana, "The Curse of the Superstar CEO," *Harvard Business Review* (September 2002), 60–66, excerpted from his book, *Searching for a Corporate Savior: The Irrational Quest for Charismatic CEOs* (Princeton University Press, 2002); and Joseph Badaracco, *Leading Quietly* (Boston, MA: Harvard Business School Press, 2002).

53. Daft and Lengel, *Fusion Leadership*.

54. Jim Collins, "The 10 Greatest CEOs of All Time," *Fortune* (July 21, 2003), 54–68.

55. Robert K. Greenleaf, *Servant Leadership: A Journey into the Nature of Legitimate Power and Greatness* (Mahwah, N.J.: Paulist Press, 1977).

56. Anne Fitzgerald, "Christmas Bonus Stuns Employees," *The Des Moines Register* (December 20, 2003), http://www.desmoinesregister.com

57. José de Córdoba, "Why Susie Krabacher Sold the Sushi Bar to Buy an Orphanage," *The Wall Street Journal* (March 1, 2004), A1.

58 Collins, "The 10 Greatest CEOs of All Time."

59. Jim Collins, "Level 5 Leadership: The Triumph of Humility and Fierce Resolve," *Harvard Business Review* (January 2001), 67–76; Collins, "Good to Great," *Fast Company* (October 2001), 90–104; A.J. Vogl, "Onward and Upward" (an interview with Jim Collins), *Across the Board* (September–October 2001), 29–34; and Jerry Useem, "Conquering Vertical Limits," *Fortune* (February 19, 2001), 84–96.

60. Alice H. Eagly and Linda L. Carli, "The Female Leadership Advantage: An Evaluation of the Evidence," *The Leadership Quarterly* 14 (2003), 807–834; Judy B. Rosener, *America's Competitive Secret: Utilizing Women as a Management Strategy* (New York: Oxford University Press, 1995); Rosener, "Ways Women Lead," *Harvard Business Review* (November–December 1990), 119–125; Sally Helgesen, *The Female Advantage: Women's Ways of Leadership* (New York: Currency/Doubleday, 1990); and Bernard M. Bass and Bruce J. Avolio, "Shatter the Glass Ceiling: Women May Make Better Managers," *Human Resource Management* 33, no. 4 (Winter 1994), 549–560.

61. Rochelle Sharpe, "As Leaders, Women Rule," *BusinessWeek* (November 20, 2000), 75–84.

62. Rosener, *America's Competitive Secret*. 129–135.

63. Sharpe, "As Leaders, Women Rule."

64. For an overview of issues and challenges of virtual leadership, see Bruce J. Avolio and Surinder S. Kahai, "Adding the 'E' to E-Leadership: How It May Impact Your Leadership," *Organizational Dynamics* 31, no. 4 (2003), 325–338.

65. Deborah L. Duarte and Nancy Tennant Snyder, *Mastering Virtual Teams: Strategies, Tools, and Techniques That Succeed*, (San Francisco: Jossey-Bass, 1999).

66. Avolio and Kahai, "Adding the 'E' to E-Leadership."

67. This discussion is based on Wayne F. Cascio, "Managing a Virtual Workplace," *Academy of Management Executive* 14, no. 3 (August 2000), 81–90; and Charlene Marmer Solomon, "Managing Virtual Teams," *Workforce* (June 2001), 60–65.

68. Nancy Chase, "Learning to Lead a Virtual Team," *Quality* (August 1999), 76.

69. Richard L. Daft *The Leadership Experience*, 3rd ed. Chapter 6: Courage and Moral Leadership, (Cincinnati, Ohio: South-Western, 2005).

70. Badaracco, "A Lesson for the Times: Learning From Quiet Leaders."

71. Jim Collins, The 10 Greatest CEOs of All Time."

72. Byrne, "How to Lead Now."

# Motivation

## LEARNING OBJECTIVES

*After studying this chapter, you should be able to*

1. Define *motivation* and explain the difference between current approaches and traditional approaches to motivation.

2. Identify and describe content theories of motivation based on employee needs.

3. Identify and explain process theories of motivation.

4. Describe reinforcement theory and how it can be used to motivate employees.

5. Discuss major approaches to job design and how job design influences motivation.

6. Explain how empowerment heightens employee motivation.

7. Describe ways that managers can create a sense of meaning and importance for employees at work.

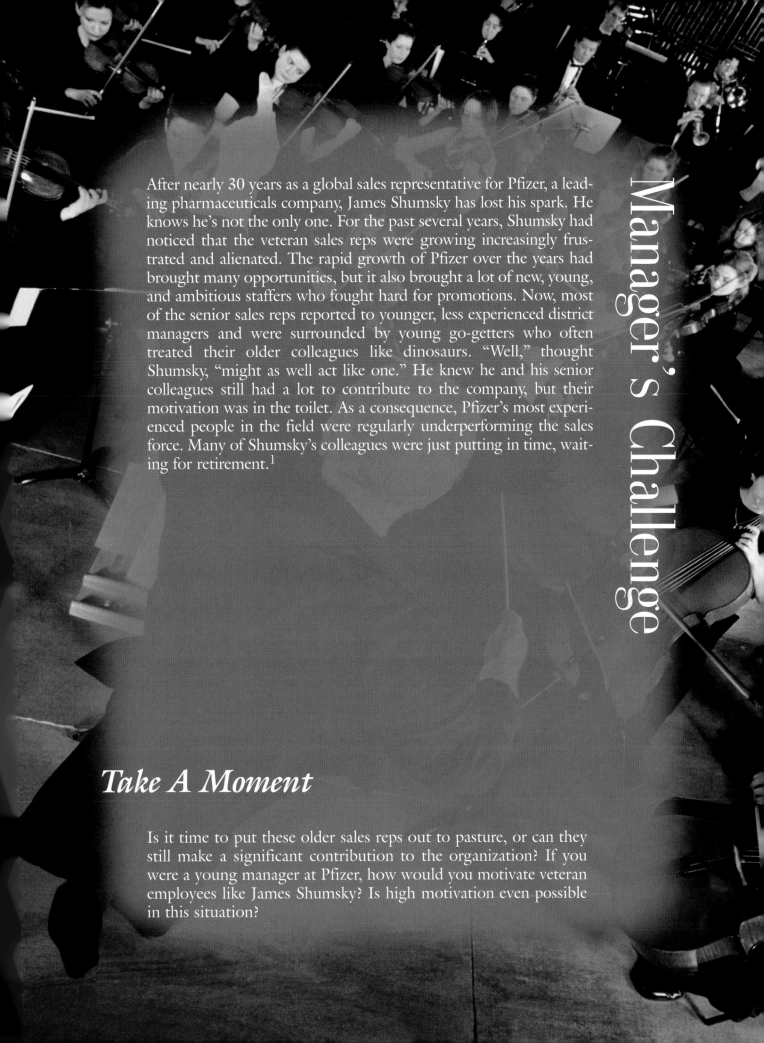

After nearly 30 years as a global sales representative for Pfizer, a leading pharmaceuticals company, James Shumsky has lost his spark. He knows he's not the only one. For the past several years, Shumsky had noticed that the veteran sales reps were growing increasingly frustrated and alienated. The rapid growth of Pfizer over the years had brought many opportunities, but it also brought a lot of new, young, and ambitious staffers who fought hard for promotions. Now, most of the senior sales reps reported to younger, less experienced district managers and were surrounded by young go-getters who often treated their older colleagues like dinosaurs. "Well," thought Shumsky, "might as well act like one." He knew he and his senior colleagues still had a lot to contribute to the company, but their motivation was in the toilet. As a consequence, Pfizer's most experienced people in the field were regularly underperforming the sales force. Many of Shumsky's colleagues were just putting in time, waiting for retirement.[1]

## Take A Moment

Is it time to put these older sales reps out to pasture, or can they still make a significant contribution to the organization? If you were a young manager at Pfizer, how would you motivate veteran employees like James Shumsky? Is high motivation even possible in this situation?

The problem for Pfizer is that experienced employees have lost their drive and are not achieving the sales targets they're capable of reaching. This can be a problem even for the most successful and admired of organizations, when experienced, valuable employees lose the motivation and commitment they once felt, causing a decline in their performance. One secret for success in organizations is motivated and enthusiastic employees. The challenge for Pfizer and other companies is to keep employee motivation consistent with organizational goals. Motivation is a challenge for managers because motivation arises from within employees and typically differs for each person. For example, Janice Rennie makes a staggering $350,000 a year selling residential real estate in Toronto; she attributes her success to the fact that she likes to listen carefully to clients and then find houses to meet their needs. Greg Storey is a skilled machinist who is challenged by writing programs for numerically controlled machines. After dropping out of college, he swept floors in a machine shop and was motivated to learn to run the machines. Frances Blais sells educational books and software. She is a top salesperson, but she doesn't care about the $50,000-plus commissions: "I'm not even thinking money when I'm selling. I'm really on a crusade to help children read well." In stark contrast, Rob Michaels gets sick to his stomach before he goes to work. Rob is a telephone salesperson who spends all day trying to get people to buy products they do not need, and the rejections are painful. His motivation is money; he earned $120,000 in the past year and cannot make nearly that much doing anything else.[2]

Rob is motivated by money, Janice by her love of listening and problem solving, Frances by the desire to help children read, and Greg by the challenge of mastering numerically controlled machinery. Each person is motivated to perform, yet each has different reasons for performing. With such diverse motivations, it is a challenge for managers to motivate employees toward common organizational goals.

This chapter reviews theories and models of employee motivation. First we will review several perspectives on motivation and cover models that describe the employee needs and processes associated with motivation. We will discuss the reinforcement perspective on motivation, and examine how *job design*—changing the structure of the work itself—can affect employee satisfaction and productivity. Finally, we will discuss the trend of *empowerment*, where authority and decision making are delegated to subordinates to increase employee motivation, and look at how managers can imbue work with a sense of meaning to inspire and motivate employees to higher performance.

# The Concept of Motivation

Most of us get up in the morning, go to school or work, and behave in ways that are predictably our own. We respond to our environment and the people in it with little thought as to why we work hard, enjoy certain classes, or find some recreational activities so much fun. Yet all these behaviors are motivated by something. Motivation refers to the forces either within or external to a person that arouse enthusiasm and persistence to pursue a certain course of action. Employee motivation affects productivity, and part of a manager's job is to channel motivation toward the accomplishment of organizational goals.[3] The study of motivation helps managers understand what prompts people to initiate action, what influences their choice of action, and why they persist in that action over time.

A simple model of human motivation is illustrated in Exhibit 19.1. People have basic *needs*, such as for food, achievement, or monetary gain, that translate into an internal tension that motivates specific behaviors with which to fulfill the need. To the extent that the behavior is successful, the person is rewarded in the sense that the need

**motivation**
The arousal, direction, and persistence of behavior.

Exhibit 19.1

## A Simple Model of Motivation

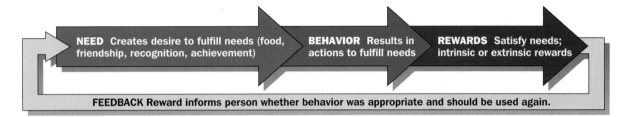

**NEED** Creates desire to fulfill needs (food, friendship, recognition, achievement)

**BEHAVIOR** Results in actions to fulfill needs

**REWARDS** Satisfy needs; intrinsic or extrinsic rewards

**FEEDBACK** Reward informs person whether behavior was appropriate and should be used again.

is satisfied. The reward also informs the person that the behavior was appropriate and can be used again in the future.

Rewards are of two types: intrinsic and extrinsic. Intrinsic rewards are the satisfactions a person receives in the process of performing a particular action. The completion of a complex task may bestow a pleasant feeling of accomplishment, or solving a problem that benefits others may fulfill a personal mission. For example, Frances Blais sells educational materials for the intrinsic reward of helping children read well. Extrinsic rewards are given by another person, typically a manager, and include promotions and pay increases. They originate externally, as a result of pleasing others. Rob Michaels, who hates his sales job, nevertheless is motivated by the extrinsic reward of high pay. Although extrinsic rewards are important, good managers strive to help people achieve intrinsic rewards, as well. Today's managers are finding that the most talented and innovative employees are rarely motivated exclusively by rewards such as money and benefits, or even praise and recognition. Instead, they seek satisfaction from the work itself.[4]

The importance of motivation as illustrated in Exhibit 19.1 is that it can lead to behaviors that reflect high performance within organizations. Studies have found that high employee motivation goes hand-in-hand with high organizational performance and profits.[5] Managers can use motivation theory to help satisfy employees' needs and simultaneously encourage high work performance. With recent massive layoffs in many U.S. organizations and a decline in trust of corporate leadership, managers are struggling to keep employees focused and motivated. Finding and keeping talented workers may be a significant challenge because of weakened trust and commitment. Managers have to find the right combination of motivational techniques and rewards to keep workers satisfied and productive in a variety of organizational situations.

**intrinsic reward**
The satisfaction received in the process of performing an action.

**extrinsic reward**
A reward given by another person.

# Foundations of Motivation

A manager's assumptions about employee motivation and use of rewards depend on his or her perspective on motivation. Four distinct perspectives on employee motivation have evolved: the traditional approach, the human relations approach, the human resource approach, and the contemporary approach.[6]

## Traditional Approach

The study of employee motivation really began with the work of Frederick W. Taylor on scientific management. Recall from Chapter 2 that scientific management pertains to the systematic analysis of an employee's job for the purpose of increasing efficiency.

Economic rewards are provided to employees for high performance. The emphasis on pay evolved into the notion of the *economic man*—people would work harder for higher pay. This approach led to the development of incentive pay systems, in which people were paid strictly on the quantity and quality of their work outputs.

## Human Relations Approach

The economic man was gradually replaced by a more sociable employee in managers' minds. Beginning with the landmark Hawthorne studies at a Western Electric plant, as described in Chapter 2, noneconomic rewards, such as congenial work groups that met social needs, seemed more important than money as a motivator of work behavior.[7] For the first time, workers were studied as people, and the concept of *social man* was born.

## Human Resource Approach

The human resource approach carries the concepts of economic man and social man further to introduce the concept of the *whole person*. Human resource theory suggests that employees are complex and motivated by many factors. For example, the work by McGregor on Theory X and Theory Y described in Chapter 2 argued that people want to do a good job and that work is as natural and healthy as play. Proponents of the human resource approach believed that earlier approaches had tried to manipulate employees through economic or social rewards. By assuming that employees are competent and able to make major contributions, managers can enhance organizational performance. The human resource approach laid the groundwork for contemporary perspectives on employee motivation.

## Contemporary Approach

The contemporary approach to employee motivation is dominated by three types of theories, each of which will be discussed in the following sections. The first are *content theories*, which stress the analysis of underlying human needs. Content theories provide insight into the needs of people in organizations and help managers understand how needs can be satisfied in the workplace. *Process theories* concern the thought processes that influence behavior. They focus on how employees seek rewards in work circumstances. *Reinforcement theories* focus on employee learning of desired work behaviors. In Exhibit 19.1, content theories focus on the concepts in the first box, process theories on those in the second, and reinforcement theories on those in the third.

© ERIC MEYER

### CONCEPT CONNECTION

*Managers at Albertson's believe that creating a work environment that is rich in opportunity, challenge, and reward **motivates employees** and is key to the company's success. By providing clear goals and objectives, performance reviews, formal and informal education programs, functional training, lateral promotions, and individual mentoring, managers help employees such as Raymond Harlan (photo), find both **intrinsic and extrinsic rewards** in their work. Harlan has been assisting shoppers and winning hearts at Albertson's Acme supermarket in Philadelphia since the store opened in 1999. "He's the 'Mayor of Acme,'" says store director Dan Houck.*

# Content Perspectives on Motivation

**content theories**
A group of theories that emphasize the needs that motivate people.

Content theories emphasize the needs that motivate people. At any point in time, people have basic needs such as those for food, achievement, or monetary reward. These needs translate into an internal drive that motivates specific behaviors in an attempt to fulfill the needs. An individual's needs are like a hidden catalog of the things he or she wants and will work to get. To the extent that managers understand worker needs, the organization's reward systems can be designed to meet them and reinforce employees for directing energies and priorities toward attainment of organizational goals.

## Hierarchy of Needs Theory

Probably the most famous content theory was developed by Abraham Maslow.[8] Maslow's hierarchy of needs theory proposes that humans are motivated by multiple needs and that these needs exist in a hierarchical order as illustrated in Exhibit 19.2. Maslow identified five general types of motivating needs in order of ascendance:

1. *Physiological needs.* These are the most basic human physical needs, including food, water, and oxygen. In the organizational setting, these are reflected in the needs for adequate heat, air, and base salary to ensure survival.
2. *Safety needs.* These are the needs for a safe and secure physical and emotional environment and freedom from threats—that is, for freedom from violence and for an orderly society. In an organizational workplace, safety needs reflect the needs for safe jobs, fringe benefits, and job security.
3. *Belongingness needs.* These needs reflect the desire to be accepted by one's peers, have friendships, be part of a group, and be loved. In the organization, these needs influence the desire for good relationships with co-workers, participation in a work group, and a positive relationship with supervisors.
4. *Esteem needs.* These needs relate to the desire for a positive self-image and to receive attention, recognition, and appreciation from others. Within organizations, esteem needs reflect a motivation for recognition, an increase in responsibility, high status, and credit for contributions to the organization.
5. *Self-actualization needs.* These represent the need for self-fulfillment, which is the highest need category. They concern developing one's full potential, increasing one's competence, and becoming a better person. Self-actualization needs can be met in the organization by providing people with opportunities to grow, be creative, and acquire training for challenging assignments and advancement.

**hierarchy of needs theory**
A content theory that proposes that people are motivated by five categories of needs—physiological, safety, belongingness, esteem, and self-actualization—that exist in a hierarchical order.

According to Maslow's theory, low-order needs take priority—they must be satisfied before higher-order needs are activated. The needs are satisfied in sequence: Physiological needs come before safety needs, safety needs before social needs, and so on. A person desiring physical safety will devote his or her efforts to securing a safer environment and will not be concerned with esteem needs or self-actualization needs. Once a need is satisfied, it declines in importance and the next higher need is activated.

Exhibit 19.2

**Maslow's Hierarchy of Needs**

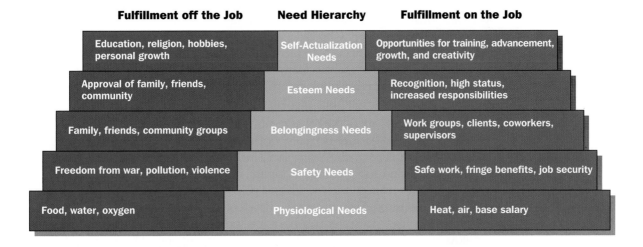

| Fulfillment off the Job | Need Hierarchy | Fulfillment on the Job |
|---|---|---|
| Education, religion, hobbies, personal growth | Self-Actualization Needs | Opportunities for training, advancement, growth, and creativity |
| Approval of family, friends, community | Esteem Needs | Recognition, high status, increased responsibilities |
| Family, friends, community groups | Belongingness Needs | Work groups, clients, coworkers, supervisors |
| Freedom from war, pollution, violence | Safety Needs | Safe work, fringe benefits, job security |
| Food, water, oxygen | Physiological Needs | Heat, air, base salary |

*Take A Moment*        *Go to the experiential exercise on page 724 that pertains to which lower- and higher-level needs motivate you.*

At All Metro Health Care in Lynbrook, New York, CEO Irving Edwards set up a special "employee service" department for his home health aides to help meet their basic needs, such as applying for food stamps and finding transportation and child care. Three employees are available solely to help workers with these issues. Once these lower-level needs are met, employees desire to have higher-level needs met in the workplace, so Irving developed programs such as an award for caregiver of the year, essay contests with prizes, and special recognition for high scoring on quarterly training exercises.[9]

## ERG Theory

**ERG theory**
A modification of the needs hierarchy theory that proposes three categories of needs: existence, relatedness, and growth.

Clayton Alderfer proposed a modification of Maslow's theory in an effort to simplify it and respond to criticisms of its lack of empirical verification.[10] His ERG theory identified three categories of needs:

1. *Existence needs.* These are the needs for physical well-being.
2. *Relatedness needs.* These pertain to the need for satisfactory relationships with others.
3. *Growth needs.* These focus on the development of human potential and the desire for personal growth and increased competence.

**frustration-regression principle**
The idea that failure to meet a high-order need may cause a regression to an already satisfied lower-order need.

The ERG model and Maslow's need hierarchy are similar because both are in hierarchical form and presume that individuals move up the hierarchy one step at a time. However, Alderfer reduced the number of need categories to three and proposed that movement up the hierarchy is more complex, reflecting a frustration-regression principle, namely, that failure to meet a high-order need may trigger a regression to an already fulfilled lower-order need. Thus, a worker who cannot fulfill a need for personal growth may revert to a lower-order need and redirect his or her efforts toward making a lot of money. The ERG model therefore is less rigid than Maslow's need hierarchy, suggesting that individuals may move down as well as up the hierarchy, depending on their ability to satisfy needs.

Need hierarchy theory helps explain why organizations find ways to recognize employees, encourage their participation in decision making, and give them opportunities to make significant contributions to the organization and society. J. M. Smucker, the 105-year-old company best known for jams and jellies, offers employees paid time off for volunteer activities, which helps people meet higher level needs and thus contributes to high employee satisfaction and motivation.[11] Sterling Bank, with headquarters in Houston, Texas, no longer uses *bank tellers*. These positions are now front-line managers who are expected to make decisions and contribute ideas for improving the business.[12] A recent survey found that employees who contribute ideas at work are more likely to feel valued, committed, and motivated. In addition, when employees' ideas are implemented and recognized, there tends to be a motivational ripple effect throughout the workforce.[13]

Many companies are finding that creating a humane work environment that allows people to achieve a balance between work and personal life is also a great high-level motivator. Flexibility in the workplace, including options such as telecommuting, flexible hours, and job sharing, is highly valued by today's employees because it enables them to manage their work and personal responsibilities. Flexibility is good for organizations too. Employees who have control over their work schedules are significantly less likely to suffer job burnout and are more highly committed to their employers, as shown in Exhibit 19.3. This idea was supported by a survey conducted at Deloitte, which found that client service professionals cited workplace flexibility as a strong reason for wanting to stay with the firm. Another study at Prudential Insurance found that work-life satisfaction and work flexibility directly correlated to job satisfaction, organizational commitment, and employee retention.[14]

Making work fun plays a role in creating this balance as well. One psychologist has recently updated Maslow's hierarchy of needs for a new generation, and he includes the need to have fun as a substantial motivator for today's employees.[15] Having fun at work relieves stress and enables people to feel more "whole," rather than feeling that their personal lives are totally separate from their work lives. A manager doesn't have to be like Herb Kelleher, the retired CEO of Southwest Airlines, who called himself the "High Priest of Ha Ha" and dressed up like the Easter Bunny and Elvis Presley to amuse employees. Something as simple as a choice of language can create a lighter, more fun environment. Research suggests the use of phrases such as "Play around with this . . . Explore the possibility of . . . Have fun with . . . Don't worry about little mistakes . . . View this as a game . . ." and so forth can effectively build elements of fun and playfulness into a workplace.[16]

## Two-Factor Theory

Frederick Herzberg developed another popular theory of motivation called the *two-factor theory*.[17] Herzberg interviewed hundreds of workers about times when they were highly motivated to work and other times when they were dissatisfied and unmotivated at work. His findings suggested that the work characteristics associated with dissatisfaction were quite different from those pertaining to satisfaction, which prompted the notion that two factors influence work motivation.

The two-factor theory is illustrated in Exhibit 19.4. The center of the scale is neutral, meaning that workers are neither satisfied nor dissatisfied. Herzberg believed

Exhibit 19.3

## The Motivational Benefits of Job Flexibility

Commitment Score          Burnout Score

- Employees who have control over their work schedules
- Employees who lack control over their work schedules

**SOURCE:** WFD Consulting data, as reported in Karol Rose, "Work-Life Effectiveness," special advertising supplement, *Fortune* (September 29, 2003), S1–S17.

**hygiene factors**
Factors that involve the presence or absence of job dissatisfiers, including working conditions, pay, company policies, and interpersonal relationships.

**motivators**
Factors that influence job satisfaction based on fulfillment of high-level needs such as achievement, recognition, responsibility, and opportunity for growth.

that two entirely separate dimensions contribute to an employee's behavior at work. The first, called hygiene factors, involves the presence or absence of job dissatisfiers, such as working conditions, pay, company policies, and interpersonal relationships. When hygiene factors are poor, work is dissatisfying. However, good hygiene factors simply remove the dissatisfaction; they do not in themselves cause people to become highly satisfied and motivated in their work.

The second set of factors does influence job satisfaction. Motivators focus on high-level needs and include achievement, recognition, responsibility, and opportunity for growth. Herzberg believed that when motivators are absent, workers are neutral toward work, but when motivators are present, workers are highly motivated and satisfied. Thus, hygiene factors and motivators represent two distinct factors that influence motivation. Hygiene factors work only in the area of dissatisfaction. Unsafe working conditions or a noisy work environment will cause people to be dissatisfied, but their correction will not lead to a high level of motivation and satisfaction. Motivators such as challenge, responsibility, and recognition must be in place before employees will be highly motivated to excel at their work.

The implication of the two-factor theory for managers is clear. On one hand, providing hygiene factors will eliminate employee dissatisfaction but will not motivate workers to high achievement levels. On the other hand, recognition, challenge, and opportunities for personal growth are powerful motivators and will promote high satisfaction and performance. The manager's role is to remove dissatisfiers—that is, to provide hygiene factors sufficient to meet basic needs—and then use motivators to meet higher-level needs and propel employees toward greater achievement and satisfaction. Consider how Vision Service Plan (VSP), the nation's largest provider of eyecare benefits, uses both hygiene factors and motivators.

Exhibit 19.4

**Herzberg's Two-Factor Theory**

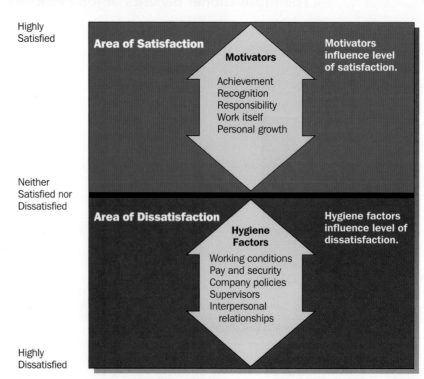

Based in Sacramento, California, VSP has seen its workforce nearly triple over the past decade. Despite the challenges of rapid growth, employee satisfaction levels have continued to climb, reaching a high of 98 percent.

VSP doesn't offer outrageous salaries and stock options, but it does make sure people are paid fairly and provided with the benefits they need to live comfortably. For example, the company offers a full benefits package to all domestic partners, gives parental leave and adoption assistance, and allows employees to "gift" their accrued sick leave to fellow employees with long-term illnesses. Flexible scheduling enables employees to work when they're most productive and balance their home and work commitments.

But what contributes most to high motivation and satisfaction at VSP is making employees feel valued and important. The process starts the minute someone is hired. Managers use a New Employee Checklist of things that should be ready and waiting for the new hire upon arrival. Having such basics as a computer, voice mail and e-mail accounts, a nameplate, and business cards helps the newcomer feel like a member of the team. Supervisors also give each new employee a picture frame with a note from the company CEO encouraging them to use it to display the important people in their lives. A formal career development program gives all employees opportunities to examine their personal priorities, develop their skills, and discuss their career objectives. If someone wants a new job in the company that he or she is not qualified for, VSC sets up an individualized training program to help bridge the gaps.

Open communication is another high-level motivator. Issues are raised, debated, and dealt with openly, and people have all the information they need to do their best work. CEO Roger Levine personally answers e-mails from any employee, randomly sits with employees in the company cafeteria, and holds biannual employee meetings where he shares all company information and allows employees to ask any question on the spot. This openness is intrinsically motivating to employees, who appreciate the higher level of responsibility and the trust it implies.[18]

**VISION SERVICE PLAN (VSP)**
http://www.vsp.com

By incorporating both hygiene factors and motivators, managers at VSC have created an environment where employees are highly motivated and want to stay. The company regularly shows up on *Fortune* magazine's list of the 100 Best Companies to Work For.

## Acquired Needs Theory

The final content theory was developed by David McClelland. The *acquired needs theory* proposes that certain types of needs are acquired during the individual's lifetime. In other words, people are not born with these needs but may learn them through their life experiences.[19] The three needs most frequently studied are these:

1. *Need for achievement.* The desire to accomplish something difficult, attain a high standard of success, master complex tasks, and surpass others.
2. *Need for affiliation.* The desire to form close personal relationships, avoid conflict, and establish warm friendships.
3. *Need for power.* The desire to influence or control others, be responsible for others, and have authority over others.

Early life experiences determine whether people acquire these needs. If children are encouraged to do things for themselves and receive reinforcement, they will acquire a need to achieve. If they are reinforced for forming warm human relationships, they will develop a need for affiliation. If they get satisfaction from controlling others, they will acquire a need for power. For example, Jack Welch, former CEO of General Electric, has credited his mother for his ambition and achievement drive. Welch's mother was determined that he be successful, so she constantly encouraged and pushed him to do better in school.[20]

© PETER YANG

**CONCEPT CONNECTION**

*Guerra DeBerry Coody, a full-service marketing firm based in San Antonio, reflects a high level of positive* hygiene factors, *provided in part by its on-site childcare facility. According to partner Tess Coody, "We were always family focused, and we wanted to create a work environment that championed that ethic." Video writer and producer Michelle Brown, who checks on her son Noah each afternoon during naptime, has had other offers, but can't imagine leaving her job. "What we have here is really special. There is a quality of life here that no other place can offer."*

For more than 20 years, McClelland studied human needs and their implications for management. People with a high need for achievement are frequently entrepreneurs. They like to do something better than competitors and take sensible business risks. On the other hand, people who have a high need for affiliation are successful integrators, whose job is to coordinate the work of several departments in an organization.[21] Integrators include brand managers and project managers who must have excellent people skills. People high in need for affiliation are able to establish positive working relationships with others.

A high need for power often is associated with successful attainment of top levels in the organizational hierarchy. For example, McClelland studied managers at AT&T for 16 years and found that those with a high need for power were more likely to follow a path of continued promotion over time. More than half of the employees at the top levels had a high need for power. In contrast, managers with a high need for achievement but a low need for power tended to peak earlier in their careers and at a lower level. The reason is that achievement needs can be met through the task itself, but power needs can be met only by ascending to a level at which a person has power over others.

In summary, content theories focus on people's underlying needs and label those particular needs that motivate behavior. The hierarchy of needs theory, the ERG theory, the two-factor theory, and the acquired needs theory all help managers understand what motivates people. In this way, managers can design work to meet needs and hence elicit appropriate and successful work behaviors.

# Process Perspectives on Motivation

**process theories**
A group of theories that explain how employees select behaviors with which to meet their needs and determine whether their choices were successful.

Process theories explain how workers select behavioral actions to meet their needs and determine whether their choices were successful. There are two basic process theories: equity theory and expectancy theory.

## Equity Theory

**equity theory**
A process theory that focuses on individuals' perceptions of how fairly they are treated relative to others.

Equity theory focuses on individuals' perceptions of how fairly they are treated compared with others. Developed by J. Stacy Adams, equity theory proposes that people are motivated to seek social equity in the rewards they expect for performance.[22]

According to equity theory, if people perceive their compensation as equal to what others receive for similar contributions, they will believe that their treatment is fair and equitable. People evaluate equity by a ratio of inputs to outcomes. Inputs to a job include education, experience, effort, and ability. Outcomes from a job include pay, recognition, benefits, and promotions. The input-to-outcome ratio may be compared to another person in the work group or to a perceived group average. A state of equity exists whenever the ratio of one person's outcomes to inputs equals the ratio of another's outcomes to inputs. Equity theory partly explains the success of a new motivational program at Google, as described in the Unlocking Creative Solutions Through Technology Box.

**equity**
A situation that exists when the ratio of one person's outcomes to inputs equals that of another's.

Inequity occurs when the input/outcome ratios are out of balance, such as when a person with a high level of education or experience receives the same salary as a new, less-educated employee. Perceived inequity also occurs in the other direction. Thus, if an employee discovers she is making more money than other people who contribute the same inputs to the company, she may feel the need to correct the inequity by working harder, getting more education, or considering lower pay. Studies of the brain have shown that people get less satisfaction from money they receive without

# Unlocking Creative Solutions Through Technology

## Simplicity Is the Key to Motivation at Google

Just as simplicity is the cornerstone of success for Google's search engine, it is also the key to powerful motivation.

Larry Page and Sergey Brin, co-founders of Google, wrote a software program that automatically e-mails engineers every week asking them what they have been working on for the week, their accomplishments and problems. Then, the program puts all the answers together into a document that everyone can read. Anyone who doesn't respond gets put at the top of the list so everyone will know he or she didn't answer.

The simple idea turned out to have an unexpectedly strong impact on engineers' motivation. For one thing, it gives people a chance to share with others what they are doing and talk about their successes and challenges. Engineers at Google are permitted to spend 20 percent of their time on projects of their own choosing, so this is a way to promote their own projects. Another motivator is that engineers want to perform as well as

or better than their colleagues. When everyone reads about what everyone else is doing, it encourages people to make sure they're pulling their fair share of the work load. In line with equity theory, no one wants to be seen as a goof-off or to feel like a loafer when they compare their activities to those of their colleagues.

Google's flexible work hours and excellent benefits are also powerful motivational tools. The company spends a lot of money on taking care of employees. Free lunches feature organic foods, vegetarian dishes, and a sandwich and salad bar. On-site laundry and dry cleaning facilities, a fitness center, and a staff masseuse are other perks. There is no dress code, dogs are allowed in the offices, and people have the flexibility to work when and how they feel most productive.

All these things go into creating a highly motivating environment at Google. However, the simple, specific technique of having people report on their activities via e-mail every week acts as a regular reminder for people to always do their best.

**SOURCE**: Larry Page, "Motivate Your Staff," segment of "How to Succeed in 2004," Business 2.0, *http://www.business2.com* and Steven Levy with Brad Stone, "All Eyes on Google," *Newsweek* (April 12, 2004), 40.

having to earn it than they do from money they work to receive.[23] Perceived inequity creates tensions within individuals that motivate them to bring equity into balance.[24]

The most common methods for reducing a perceived inequity are these:

- *Change inputs.* A person may choose to increase or decrease his or her inputs to the organization. For example, underpaid individuals may reduce their level of effort or increase their absenteeism. Overpaid people may increase effort on the job.
- *Change outcomes.* A person may change his or her outcomes. An underpaid person may request a salary increase or a bigger office. A union may try to improve wages and working conditions in order to be consistent with a comparable union whose members make more money.
- *Distort perceptions.* Research suggests that people may distort perceptions of equity if they are unable to change inputs or outcomes. They may artificially increase the status attached to their jobs or distort others' perceived rewards to bring equity into balance.
- *Leave the job.* People who feel inequitably treated may decide to leave their jobs rather than suffer the inequity of being under- or overpaid. In their new jobs, they expect to find a more favorable balance of rewards.

The implication of equity theory for managers is that employees indeed evaluate the perceived equity of their rewards compared to others'. An increase in salary or a promotion will have no motivational effect if it is perceived as inequitable relative to that of other employees. A good example of equity theory comes from the J. Peterman Company, the trendy catalog company that eventually slid into bankruptcy before being acquired by another firm. John Peterman had created a comfortable, creative culture where employees were highly motivated to work together toward common goals.

However, when the company began to grow rapidly, Peterman found himself having to hire people very quickly—and he often had to offer them higher salaries than those of his current employees to match what they were making elsewhere. In addition, when making important decisions, leaders tended to pay more attention to the ideas and thoughts of the new staff than they did the "old timers." Long-time employees felt slighted, and motivation declined significantly. Many employees began putting less energy and effort into their jobs. They were no longer willing to go the extra mile because of a perceived state of inequity.[25] Inequitable pay puts pressure on employees that is sometimes almost too great to bear. They attempt to change their work habits, try to change the system, or leave the job.[26]

Smart managers try to keep feelings of equity in balance in order to keep their workforces motivated.

## Expectancy Theory

Expectancy theory suggests that motivation depends on individuals' expectations about their ability to perform tasks and receive desired rewards. Expectancy theory is associated with the work of Victor Vroom, although a number of scholars have made contributions in this area.[27] Expectancy theory is concerned not with identifying types of needs but with the thinking process that individuals use to achieve rewards. Consider Amy Huang, a university student with a strong desire for a B in her accounting course. Amy has a C+ average and one more exam to take. Amy's motivation to study for that last exam will be influenced by (1) the expectation that hard study will lead to an A on the exam and (2) the expectation that an A on the exam will result in a B for the course. If Amy believes she cannot get an A on the exam or that receiving an A will not lead to a B for the course, she will not be motivated to study exceptionally hard.

### Elements of Expectancy Theory

Expectancy theory is based on the relationship among the individual's *effort*, the individual's *performance*, and the desirability of *outcomes* associated with high performance. These elements and the relationships among them are illustrated in Exhibit 19.5. The keys to expectancy theory are the expectancies for the relationships among effort, performance, and outcomes with the value of the outcomes to the individual.

E → P expectancy involves whether putting effort into a task will lead to high performance. For this expectancy to be high, the individual must have the ability, previous experience, and necessary machinery, tools, and opportunity to perform. For Amy Huang to get a B in the accounting course, the E → P expectancy is high if Amy truly believes that with hard work, she can get an A on the final exam. If Amy believes she has neither the ability nor the opportunity to achieve high performance, the expectancy will be low, and so will be her motivation.

P → O expectancy involves whether successful performance will lead to the desired outcome. In the case of a person who is motivated to win a job-related award, this expectancy concerns the belief that high performance will truly lead to the award. If the P → O expectancy is high, the individual will be more highly motivated. If the expectancy is that high performance will not produce the desired outcome, motivation will be lower. If an A on the final exam is likely to produce a B in the accounting course, Amy Huang's P → O expectancy will be high. Amy might talk to the professor to see whether an A will be sufficient to earn her a B in the course. If not, she will be less motivated to study hard for the final exam.

---

**expectancy theory**
A process theory that proposes that motivation depends on individuals' expectations about their ability to perform tasks and receive desired rewards.

**E → P expectancy**
Expectancy that putting effort into a given task will lead to high performance.

**P → O expectancy**
Expectancy that successful performance of a task will lead to the desired outcome.

*© BARBARA LAING*

**CONCEPT CONNECTION**

*Circuit City managers are using **expectancy theory** principles to help meet employee's needs while attaining organizational goals. By creating an incentive program that is a commission-based plan designed to provide the highest compensation to sales counselors who are committed to serving every customer, Circuit City achieves its volume and profitability objectives. The incentive program is also used in other areas such as distribution, where employees are recognized for accomplishment in safety, productivity, and attendance.*

Exhibit 19.5

## Major Elements of Expectancy Theory

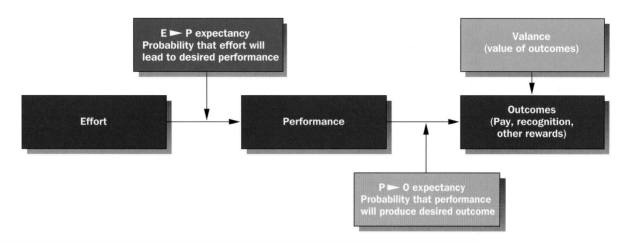

Valence is the value of outcomes, or attraction to outcomes, for the individual. If the outcomes that are available from high effort and good performance are not valued by employees, motivation will be low. Likewise, if outcomes have a high value, motivation will be higher.

**valence**
The value or attraction an individual has for an outcome.

Expectancy theory attempts not to define specific types of needs or rewards but only to establish that they exist and may be different for every individual. One employee might want to be promoted to a position of increased responsibility, and another might have high valence for good relationships with peers. Consequently, the first person will be motivated to work hard for a promotion and the second for the opportunity for a team position that will keep him or her associated with a group.

A simple sales department example will explain how the expectancy model in Exhibit 19.5 works. If Carlos, a salesperson at the Diamond Gift Shop, believes that increased selling effort will lead to higher personal sales, we can say that he has a high E → P expectancy. Moreover, if Carlos also believes that higher personal sales will lead to a promotion or pay raise, we can say that he has a high P → O expectancy. Finally, if Carlos places a high value on the promotion or pay raise, valence is high and he will have a high motivational force. On the other hand, if either the E → P or P → O expectancy is low, or if the money or promotion has low valence for Carlos, the overall motivational force will be low. For an employee to be highly motivated, all three factors in the expectancy model must be high.[28]

### Implications for Managers

The expectancy theory of motivation is similar to the path-goal theory of leadership described in Chapter 18. Both theories are personalized to subordinates' needs and goals. Managers' responsibility is to help subordinates meet their needs and at the same time attain organizational goals. Managers must try to find a match between a subordinate's skills and abilities and the job demands. To increase motivation, managers can clarify individuals' needs, define the outcomes available from the organization, and ensure that each individual has the ability and support (namely, time and equipment) needed to attain outcomes.

Some companies use expectancy theory principles by designing incentive systems that identify desired organizational outcomes and give everyone the same shot at getting the rewards. The trick is to design a system that fits with employees' abilities and needs.

## Goal Setting Theory

Recall from Chapter 7 our discussion of the importance and purposes of goals. Numerous studies have shown that people are more motivated when they have specific targets or objectives to work toward.[29] You have probably noticed in your own life that you are more motivated when you have a specific goal, such as making an A on a final exam, losing 10 pounds before spring break, or earning enough money during the summer to buy a used car.

Goal-setting theory, described by Edwin Locke and Gary Latham, proposes that specific, challenging goals increase motivation and performance when the goals are accepted by subordinates and these subordinates receive feedback to indicate their progress toward goal achievement.[30] There are four key components of goal-setting theory:

- *Goal specificity* refers to the degree to which goals are concrete and unambiguous. As we discussed in Chapter 7, specific goals such as "Visit one new customer each day," or "Sell $1,000 worth of merchandise a week" are more motivating than vague goals such as "Keep in touch with new customers" or "Increase merchandise sales."
- In terms of *goal difficulty*, hard goals are more motivating than easy ones. Easy goals provide little challenge for employees and don't require them to increase their output. Highly ambitious but achievable goals ask people to stretch their abilities.
- *Goal acceptance* means that employees have to "buy into" the goals and be committed to them. Managers often find that having people participate in setting goals is a good way to increase acceptance and commitment.
- Finally, the component of *feedback* means that people get information about how well they are doing in progressing toward goal achievement. It is important for managers to provide performance feedback on a regular, ongoing basis. However, self-feedback, where people are able to monitor their own progress toward a goal, has been found to be an even stronger motivator than external feedback.[31]

Why does goal setting increase motivation? For one thing, it enables people to focus their energies in the right direction. People know what to work toward, so they can direct their efforts toward the most important activities to accomplish the goals. Goals also energize behavior because people feel compelled to develop plans and strategies to accomplish the objective. Specific, difficult goals provide a challenge and encourage people to put forth high levels of effort.

Steve and Diane Warren, owners of Katzinger's Delicatessen in Columbus, Ohio, used elements of goal setting theory to motivate employees and dramatically reduce food costs. The Katzingers had asked their employees to find ways to cut costs and offered to share any savings with them. But nothing happened—the goal was too vague to serve as a motivator. So, the deli owners proposed an explicit, ambitious goal—to reduce food costs to below 35 percent of sales without sacrificing food quality or service. With this goal as a motivator, employees focused their efforts and met the goal. By the end of the year, food quality and service had actually improved, and food costs were cut to below 35 percent of sales, saving the Katzinger's $30,000. As a reward, half of that amount was distributed to employees for helping to meet the goal.[32]

# Reinforcement Perspective on Motivation

The reinforcement approach to employee motivation sidesteps the issues of employee needs and thinking processes described in the content and process theories.

**goal-setting theory**
A motivation theory in which specific, challenging goals increase motivation and performance when the goals are accepted by subordinates and these subordinates receive feedback to indicate their progress toward goal achievement.

© DAVID DEAL

Reinforcement theory simply looks at the relationship between behavior and its consequences. It focuses on changing or modifying the employees' on-the-job behavior through the appropriate use of immediate rewards and punishments.

## Reinforcement Tools

Behavior modification is the name given to the set of techniques by which reinforcement theory is used to modify human behavior.[33] The basic assumption underlying behavior modification is the law of effect, which states that behavior that is positively reinforced tends to be repeated, and behavior that is not reinforced tends not to be repeated. Reinforcement is defined as anything that causes a certain behavior to be repeated or inhibited. The four reinforcement tools are positive reinforcement, avoidance learning, punishment, and extinction. Each type of reinforcement is a consequence of either a pleasant or unpleasant event being applied or withdrawn following a person's behavior. The four types of reinforcement are summarized in Exhibit 19.6.

### Positive Reinforcement

*Positive reinforcement* is the administration of a pleasant and rewarding consequence following a desired behavior. A good example of positive reinforcement is immediate praise for an employee who arrives on time or does a little extra work. The pleasant consequence will increase the likelihood of the excellent work behavior occurring again. As another example, Frances Flood, CEO of Gentner Communications, a manufacturer of high-end audioconferencing equipment based in Salt Lake City, offered engineers a stake in the company's profits if they met targets for getting new products to market faster. Within two years, product development time had been slashed by 30 percent.[34] Studies have shown that positive reinforcement does help to improve performance. In addition, nonfinancial reinforcements such as positive feedback, social recognition, and attention are just as effective as financial incentives.[35]

### Avoidance Learning

*Avoidance learning* is the removal of an unpleasant consequence following a desired behavior. Avoidance learning is sometimes called *negative reinforcement*. Employees learn to do the right thing by avoiding unpleasant situations. Avoidance learning occurs when a supervisor stops criticizing or reprimanding an employee once the incorrect behavior has stopped.

**reinforcement theory**
A motivation theory based on the relationship between a given behavior and its consequences.

**behavior modification**
The set of techniques by which reinforcement theory is used to modify human behavior.

**law of effect**
The assumption that positively reinforced behavior tends to be repeated and unreinforced or negatively reinforced behavior tends to be inhibited.

**reinforcement**
Anything that causes a given behavior to be repeated or inhibited.

Exhibit 19.6

## Changing Behavior with Reinforcement

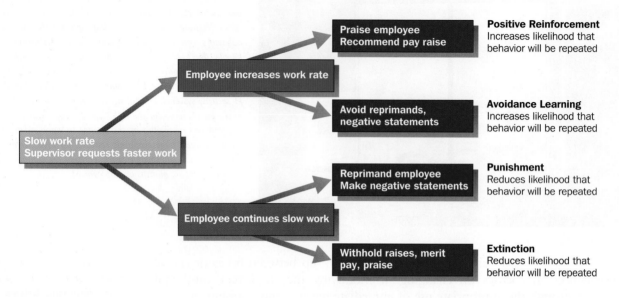

**SOURCE:** Based on Richard L. Daft and Richard M. Steers, *Organizations: A Micro/Macro Approach* (Glenview, Ill.; Scott, Foresman, 1986), 109.

## Punishment

*Punishment* is the imposition of unpleasant outcomes on an employee. Punishment typically occurs following undesirable behavior. For example, a supervisor may berate an employee for performing a task incorrectly. The supervisor expects that the negative outcome will serve as a punishment and reduce the likelihood of the behavior recurring. The use of punishment in organizations is controversial and often criticized because it fails to indicate the correct behavior. However, almost all managers report finding it necessary to occasionally impose forms of punishment ranging from verbal reprimands to employee suspensions or firings.[36]

## Extinction

*Extinction* is the withdrawal of a positive reward. Whereas with punishment, the supervisor imposes an unpleasant outcome such as a reprimand, extinction involves withholding pay raises, praise, and other positive outcomes. The idea is that behavior that is not positively reinforced will be less likely to occur in the future. For example, if a perpetually tardy employee fails to receive praise and pay raises, he or she will begin to realize that the behavior is not producing desired outcomes. The behavior will gradually disappear if it is continually nonreinforced.

Some executives use reinforcement theory very effectively to shape employees' behavior. Arunas Chesonis, CEO of PaeTec Communications, is a master motivator, relying primarily on positive reinforcement to encourage employee behavior that has enabled PaeTec to keep growing during the worst downturn in the history of the telecommunications industry. This chapter's Unlocking Creative Solutions Through People box further describes this leader's approach to motivation.

**schedule of reinforcement**
The frequency with which and intervals over which reinforcement occurs.

## Schedules of Reinforcement

A great deal of research into reinforcement theory suggests that the timing of reinforcement has an impact on the speed of employee learning. Schedules of reinforcement pertain to the frequency with which and intervals over which

# Unlocking Creative Solutions Through People

**At PaeTec Communications, It's All About Respect**
PaeTec CEO Arunas Chesonis expects employees to always put customers first. In the Network Operations Center, or NOC, irate customers reach a live human voice after the first ring. Employees in the NOC handle 4,000 problem calls a month, but they solve them so well and so cheerfully that the company has maintained a monthly customer retention rate of 99.5 percent since it was founded in 1998.

To get his people to put customers first, Chesonis puts employees first. He is known for writing short notes to employees all over the company to praise them or thank them. He sends e-mails, makes phone calls, and personally visits people in their offices to tell them how much he appreciates their efforts and accomplishments. Although the company gives financial awards for some types of exceptional service, the smaller forms of recognition seem to have the most pervasive impact. The vice president of engineering recalls Chesonis asking who had worked the hardest recently. After he got his answer, Chesonis showed up in the employee's office with a flower arrangement as tall as the employee was and said, "Marion told me how hard you worked this week."

Chesonis has incorporated other motivational ideas as well. For one thing, at PaeTec, everyone is considered equal, and everyone is a potential expert. There are no perks for anyone, from the CEO on down, and everyone gets stock options and bonuses based on the company's performance. People are expected to share knowledge and help each other out instinctively. On any given day, the expert in the problem at hand might be a customer service representative, the CEO, an engineer, or a file clerk. "One thing that endeared this place to me from the start, you could have a good idea and that good idea can become company policy," says Jason Ellston, the manager of the NOC. At PaeTec, managers automatically assume that employees on the front lines know what needs to be done better than anyone else.

People respond to this kind of respect, and they pass it on to their own subordinates and to PaeTec's customers. Some employees have taken a pay cut to come to work at PaeTec. Chesonis believes it only makes business sense to put people first and reap the rewards of having a team of motivated, committed, even devoted employees. Jason Ellston encapsulates the company's motivation philosophy in talking about a newly-hired employee who was worried about being fired when he had to take excess time off work early in his career at PaeTec. Ellston told him to take all the time he needed, and his job would be there when he got back. "Just thinking like a human being, why would you not want to extend yourself for an employee?" Ellston asks. "That guy will run through a wall for me."

**SOURCE**: David Dorsey, "Happiness Pays," *Inc.* (February 2004), 88–94.

reinforcement occurs. A reinforcement schedule can be selected to have maximum impact on employees' job behavior. There are five basic types of reinforcement schedules, which include continuous and four types of partial reinforcement.

## Continuous Reinforcement

With a continuous reinforcement schedule, every occurrence of the desired behavior is reinforced. This schedule can be very effective in the early stages of learning new types of behavior, because every attempt has a pleasant consequence.

**continuous reinforcement schedule**
A schedule in which every occurrence of the desired behavior is reinforced.

## Partial Reinforcement

However, in the real world of organizations, it is often impossible to reinforce every correct behavior. With a partial reinforcement schedule, the reinforcement is administered only after some occurrences of the correct behavior. There are four types of partial reinforcement schedules: fixed interval, fixed ratio, variable interval, and variable ratio.

**partial reinforcement schedule**
A schedule in which only some occurrences of the desired behavior are reinforced.

1. *Fixed-interval schedule.* The *fixed-interval schedule* rewards employees at specified time intervals. If an employee displays the correct behavior each day, reinforcement may occur every week. Regular paychecks or quarterly bonuses are examples of a fixed-interval reinforcement. At Leone Ackerly's Mini Maid franchise in

Marietta, Georgia, workers are rewarded with an attendance bonus each pay period if they have gone to work every day on time and in uniform.[37]

2. *Fixed-ratio schedule.* With a *fixed-ratio schedule*, reinforcement occurs after a specified number of desired responses, say, after every fifth. For example, paying a field hand $1.50 for picking 10 pounds of peppers is a fixed-ratio schedule. Most piece-rate pay systems are considered fixed-ratio schedules.

3. *Variable-interval schedule.* With a *variable-interval schedule*, reinforcement is administered at random times that cannot be predicted by the employee. An example would be a random inspection by the manufacturing superintendent of the production floor, at which time he or she commends employees on their good behavior.

4. *Variable-ratio Schedule.* The *variable-ratio schedule* is based on a random number of desired behaviors rather than on variable time periods. Reinforcement may occur sometimes after 5, 10, 15, or 20 displays of behavior. One example is random monitoring of telemarketers, who may be rewarded after a certain number of calls in which they perform the appropriate behaviors and meet call performance specifications. Employees know they may be monitored but are never sure when checks will occur and when rewards may be given.

The schedules of reinforcement available to managers are illustrated in Exhibit 19.7. Continuous reinforcement is most effective for establishing new learning, but behavior is vulnerable to extinction. Partial reinforcement schedules are more effective for maintaining behavior over extended time periods. The most powerful is the variable-ratio schedule, because employee behavior will persist for a long time due to the administration of reinforcement only after a long interval.[38]

One example of a small business that successfully uses reinforcement theory is Emerald Packaging in Union City, California.

## EMERALD PACKAGING

Emerald Packaging is a family-owned business that prints plastic bags for prepackaged salads and other vegetables. The company employs about 100 people and is the tenth largest manufacturer in Union City, California, located about 30 miles southeast of San Francisco.

Kevin Kelly, CEO of Emerald, was looking for a way to reduce accidents and improve the company's safety record. Despite all efforts, employees continued to practice unsafe work habits, leading to accidents that caused workers compensation costs to skyrocket. Kelly decided to try a positive reinforcement scheme that would reward employees for meeting safety goals.

Kelly set a goal of no more than 12 accidents for the year—half the total of the previous year—with none causing lost time. To motivate employees to achieve the goal, Kelly told employees that if they racked up no more than three injuries a quarter, he would buy them lunch, hand out company T-shirts, and raffle off $1,000. If they made it though the entire year with 12 or fewer minor accidents, the company would distribute a significant monetary reward among all employees.

The reinforcement plan worked. By the end of the year, Emerald had logged only 11 accidents, none causing lost-time injuries. Not a single employee missed work at Emerald because of injury for a full 1,252 days. Employees began policing one another, such as reprimanding one worker who was repeatedly injured while cleaning machines without his safety glasses.

In 2003, Emerald handed out a total of $50,000 to its 100 employees for their contribution to keeping injury and workers' comp costs low and giving the company one of the best safety records in the industry.[39]

This type of reinforcement worked so well at Emerald that Kelly later developed reinforcement programs for quality and waste reduction. Reinforcement also works at such organizations as Campbell Soup Co., Emery Air Freight, Michigan

Bell, and PSS World Medical, because managers reward appropriate behavior. They tell employees what they can do to receive reinforcement, tell them what they are doing wrong, distribute rewards equitably, tailor rewards to behaviors, and keep in mind that failure to reward deserving behavior has an equally powerful impact on employees.

Reward and punishment motivational practices dominate organizations, with as many as 94 percent of companies in the United States reporting that they use practices that reward performance or merit with pay.[40] In addition, a recent report by human resources consulting firm Towers Perrin indicates that incentive systems that reward employees with bonuses or other rewards for meeting certain goals are becoming increasingly popular. However, less than one-third of the companies reported seeing any noticeable impact of incentive pay on business results.[41] Despite the testimonies of numerous organizations that enjoy successful incentive programs, there is growing criticism of these carrot-and-stick methods, as discussed in the Manager's Shoptalk.

# Job Design for Motivation

A *job* in an organization is a unit of work that a single employee is responsible for performing. A job could include writing tickets for parking violators in New York City or doing long-range planning for the Discovery cable television channel. Jobs are important because performance of their components may provide rewards that meet employees' needs. An assembly-line worker may install the same bolt over and over, whereas an emergency room physician may provide each trauma victim with a unique treatment package. Managers need to know what aspects of a job provide motivation as well as how to compensate for routine tasks that have little inherent satisfaction. Job design is the application of motivational theories to the structure of work for improving productivity and satisfaction. Approaches to job design are generally classified as job simplification, job rotation, job enlargement, and job enrichment.

**job design**
The application of motivational theories to the structure of work for improving productivity and satisfaction.

## Exhibit 19.7

### Schedules of Reinforcement

| Schedule of Reinforcement | Nature of Reinforcement | Effect on Behavior When Applied | Effect on Behavior When Withdrawn | Example |
|---|---|---|---|---|
| **Continuous** | Reward given after each desired behavior | Leads to fast learning of new behavior | Rapid extinction | Praise |
| **Fixed-Interval** | Reward given at fixed time intervals | Leads to average and irregular performance | Rapid extinction | Weekly paycheck |
| **Fixed-ratio** | Reward given at fixed amounts of output | Quickly leads to very high and stable performance | Rapid extinction | Piece-rate pay system |
| **Variable-Interval** | Reward given at variable times | Leads to moderately high and stable performance | Slow extinction | Performance appraisal and awards given at random times each month |
| **Variable-ratio** | Reward given at variable amounts of output | Leads to very high performance | Slow extinction | Sales bonus tied to number of sales calls, with random checks |

Turbulent Times

# manager's Shoptalk

### The Carrot-and-Stick Controversy

Everybody thought Rob Rodin was crazy when he decided to wipe out all individual incentives for his sales force at Marshall Industries, a large distributor of electronic components based in El Monte, California. He did away with all bonuses, commissions, vacations, and other awards and rewards. All salespeople would receive a base salary plus the opportunity for profit sharing, which would be the same percent of salary for everyone, based on the entire company's performance. Six years later, Rodin says productivity per person has tripled at the company, but still he gets questions and criticism about his decision.

Rodin is standing right in the middle of a big controversy in modern management. Do financial and other rewards really motivate the kind of behavior organizations want and need? A growing number of critics say no, arguing that carrot-and-stick approaches are a holdover from the Industrial Age and are inappropriate and ineffective in today's economy. Today's workplace demands innovation and creativity from everyone—behaviors that rarely are inspired by money or other financial incentives. Reasons for criticism of carrot-and-stick approaches include the following:

1. *Extrinsic rewards diminish intrinsic rewards.* When people are motivated to seek an extrinsic reward, whether it be a bonus, an award, or the approval of a supervisor, generally they focus on the reward rather than on the work they do to achieve it. Thus, the intrinsic satisfaction people receive from performing their jobs actually declines. When people lack intrinsic rewards in their work, their performance stays just adequate to achieve the reward offered. In the worst case, employees may cover up mistakes or cheat in order to achieve the reward. One study found that teachers who were rewarded for increasing test scores frequently used various forms of cheating, for example.

2. *Extrinsic rewards are temporary.* Offering outside incentives may ensure short-term success, but not long-term high performance. When employees are focused only on the reward, they lose interest in their work. Without personal interest, the potential for exploration, creativity, and innovation disappears. Although the current deadline or goal may be met, better ways of working and serving customers will not be discovered and the company's long-term success will be affected.

3. *Extrinsic rewards assume people are driven by lower-level needs.* Rewards such as bonuses, pay increases, and even praise presume that the primary reason people initiate and persist in behavior is to satisfy lower-level needs. However, behavior also is based on yearnings for self-expression, and on feelings of self-esteem and self-worth. Typical individual incentive programs don't reflect and encourage the myriad behaviors that are motivated by people's need to express themselves and realize their higher needs for growth and fulfillment.

As Rob Rodin discovered at Marshall Industries, today's organizations need employees who are motivated to think, experiment, and continuously search for ways to solve new problems. Alfie Kohn, one of the most vocal critics of carrot-and-stick approaches, offers the following advice to managers regarding how to pay employees: "Pay well, pay fairly, and then do everything you can to get money off people's minds." Indeed there is some evidence that money is not primarily what people work for. Managers should understand the limits of extrinsic motivators and work to satisfy employees' higher, as well as lower, needs. To be motivated, employees need jobs that offer self-satisfaction in addition to a yearly pay raise.

SOURCES: Alfie Kohn, "Incentives Can Be Bad for Business," *Inc.* (January 1998), 93–94; A.J. Vogl, "Carrots, Sticks, and Self-Deception" (an interview with Alfie Kohn), *Across the Board* (January 1994), 39–44; Geoffrey Colvin, "What Money Makes You Do," *Fortune* (August 17, 1998), 213–214; and Jeffrey Pfeffer, "Sins of Commission," *Business 2.0* (May 2004), 56.

## Job Simplification

**Job simplification** pursues task efficiency by reducing the number of tasks one person must do. Job simplification is based on principles drawn from scientific management and industrial engineering. Tasks are designed to be simple, repetitive, and standardized. As complexity is stripped from a job, the worker has more time to concentrate on doing more of the same routine task. Workers with low skill levels can perform the job, and the organization achieves a high level of efficiency. Indeed, workers are interchangeable, because they need little training or skill and exercise little judgment. As a motivational technique, however, job simplification has failed. People dislike routine and boring jobs and react in a number of negative ways, including sabotage, absenteeism, and unionization. Job simplification is compared with job rotation and job enlargement in Exhibit 19.8.

**job simplification**
A job design whose purpose is to improve task efficiency by reducing the number of tasks a single person must do.

## Job Rotation

**Job rotation** systematically moves employees from one job to another, thereby increasing the number of different tasks an employee performs without increasing the complexity of any one job. For example, an autoworker might install windshields one week and front bumpers the next. Job rotation still takes advantage of engineering efficiencies, but it provides variety and stimulation for employees. Although employees might find the new job interesting at first, the novelty soon wears off as the repetitive work is mastered.

Companies such as The Home Depot, Motorola, 1-800-Flowers, and Dayton Hudson have built on the notion of job rotation to train a flexible workforce. As companies break away from ossified job categories, workers can perform several jobs, thereby reducing labor costs and giving employees opportunities to develop new skills. At The Home Depot, for example, workers scattered throughout the company's vast chain of stores can get a taste of the corporate climate by working at in-store support centers, while associate managers can dirty their hands out on the sales floor.[42] Job rotation also gives companies greater flexibility. One production worker might shift among the jobs of drill operator, punch operator, and assembler, depending on the company's need at the moment. Some unions have resisted the idea, but many now go along, realizing that it helps the company be more competitive.[43]

**job rotation**
A job design that systematically moves employees from one job to another to provide them with variety and stimulation.

## Job Enlargement

**Job enlargement** combines a series of tasks into one new, broader job. This is a response to the dissatisfaction of employees with oversimplified jobs. Instead of only one job, an employee may be responsible for three or four and will have more time

**job enlargement**
A job design that combines a series of tasks into one new, broader job to give employees variety and challenge.

Exhibit 19.8

**Types of Job Design**

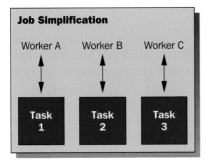

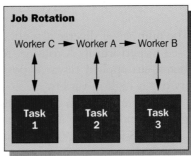

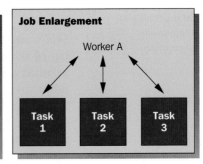

**CONCEPT CONNECTION**

*At the Frito-Lay plant in Lubbock, Texas, Julia Garcia used to just pack bags of chips into cardboard cartons. Today, she's interviewing new hires, refusing products that don't meet quality standards, and sending home excess workers if machines shut down. Hourly workers have been enjoying the benefits of job enlargement and job enrichment since Frito-Lay introduced work teams six years ago. Garcia's 11-member potato chip team is responsible for everything from potato processing to equipment maintenance.*

**job enrichment**
A job design that incorporates achievement, recognition, and other high-level motivators into the work.

**work redesign**
The altering of jobs to increase both the quality of employees' work experience and their productivity.

**job characteristics model**
A model of job design that comprises core job dimensions, critical psychological states, and employee growth-need strength.

to do them. Job enlargement provides job variety and a greater challenge for employees. At Maytag, jobs were enlarged when work was redesigned such that workers assembled an entire water pump rather than doing each part as it reached them on the assembly line. Similarly, rather than just changing the oil at a Precision Tune location, a mechanic changes the oil, greases the car, airs the tires, checks fluid levels, battery, air filter, and so forth. Then, the same employee is responsible for consulting with the customer about routine maintenance or any problems he or she sees with the vehicle.

## Job Enrichment

Recall the discussion of Maslow's need hierarchy and Herzberg's two-factor theory. Rather than just changing the number and frequency of tasks a worker performs, job enrichment incorporates high-level motivators into the work, including job responsibility, recognition, and opportunities for growth, learning, and achievement. In an enriched job, employees have control over the resources necessary for performing it, make decisions on how to do the work, experience personal growth, and set their own work pace.

Many companies have undertaken job enrichment programs to increase employees' motivation and job satisfaction. At Ralcorp's cereal manufacturing plant in Sparks, Nevada, for example, managers enriched jobs by combining several packing positions into a single job and cross-training employees to operate all of the packing line's equipment. In addition, assembly line employees screen, interview, and train all new hires. They are responsible for managing the production flow to and from their upstream and downstream partners, making daily decisions that affect their work, managing quality, and contributing to continuous improvement. Enriched jobs have improved employee motivation and satisfaction, and the company has benefited from higher long-term productivity, reduced costs, and happier, more motivated employees.[44]

## Job Characteristics Model

One significant approach to job design is the job characteristics model developed by Richard Hackman and Greg Oldham.[45] Hackman and Oldham's research concerned work redesign, which is defined as altering jobs to increase both the quality of employees' work experience and their productivity. Hackman and Oldham's research into the design of hundreds of jobs yielded the job characteristics model, which is illustrated in Exhibit 19.9. The model consists of three major parts: core job dimensions, critical psychological states, and employee growth-need strength.

### Core Job Dimensions
Hackman and Oldham identified five dimensions that determine a job's motivational potential:

1. *Skill variety.* The number of diverse activities that compose a job and the number of skills used to perform it. A routine, repetitious, assembly line job is low in variety, whereas an applied research position that entails working on new problems every day is high in variety.
2. *Task identity.* The degree to which an employee performs a total job with a recognizable beginning and ending. A chef who prepares an entire meal has more task identity than a worker on a cafeteria line who ladles mashed potatoes.

Exhibit 19.9

## The Job Characteristics Model

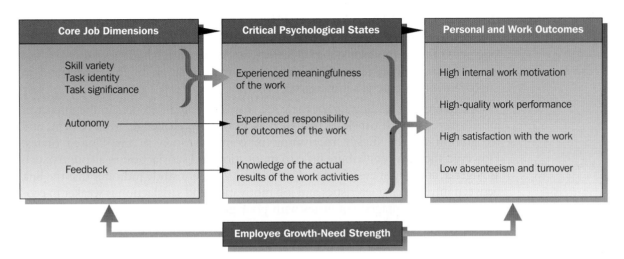

SOURCE: Adapted from J. Richard Hackman and G.R. Oldham, "Motivation through the Design of Work: Test of a Theory," *Organizational Behavior and Human Performance* 16 (1976), 256.

3. *Task significance.* The degree to which the job is perceived as important and having impact on the company or consumers. People who distribute penicillin and other medical supplies during times of emergencies would feel they have significant jobs.
4. *Autonomy.* The degree to which the worker has freedom, discretion, and self-determination in planning and carrying out tasks. A house painter can determine how to paint the house; a paint sprayer on an assembly line has little autonomy.
5. *Feedback.* The extent to which doing the job provides information back to the employee about his or her performance. Jobs vary in their ability to let workers see the outcomes of their efforts. A football coach knows whether the team won or lost, but a basic research scientist may have to wait years to learn whether a research project was successful.

The job characteristics model says that the more these five core characteristics can be designed into the job, the more the employees will be motivated and the higher will be performance, quality, and satisfaction.

### Critical Psychological States
The model posits that core job dimensions are more rewarding when individuals experience three psychological states in response to job design. In Exhibit 19.9, skill variety, task identity, and task significance tend to influence the employee's psychological state of *experienced meaningfulness of work*. The work itself is satisfying and provides intrinsic rewards for the worker. The job characteristic of autonomy influences the worker's *experienced responsibility*. The job characteristic of feedback provides the worker with *knowledge of actual results*. The employee thus knows how he or she is doing and can change work performance to increase desired outcomes.

### Personal and Work Outcomes
The impact of the five job characteristics on the psychological states of experienced meaningfulness, responsibility, and knowledge of actual results leads to the personal and work outcomes of high work motivation, high work performance, high satisfaction, and low absenteeism and turnover.

### Employee Growth-Need Strength

The final component of the job characteristics model is called *employee growth-need strength*, which means that people have different needs for growth and development. If a person wants to satisfy low-level needs, such as safety and belongingness, the job characteristics model has less effect. When a person has a high need for growth and development, including the desire for personal challenge, achievement, and challenging work, the model is especially effective. People with a high need to grow and expand their abilities respond favorably to the application of the model and to improvements in core job dimensions.

One interesting finding is that there are cross-cultural differences in the impact of job characteristics. Intrinsic factors such as autonomy, challenge, achievement, and recognition can be highly motivating in countries such as the United States. However, they may contribute little to motivation and satisfaction in a country such as Nigeria, and might even lead to *demotivation*. A recent study indicates that the link between intrinsic characteristics and job motivation and satisfaction is weaker in economically disadvantaged countries with poor governmental social welfare systems, and in high power distance countries, as defined in Chapter 4.[46] Thus, the job characteristics model would be expected to be less effective in these countries.

# Motivational Ideas for Turbulent Times

Despite the controversy over carrot-and-stick motivational practices discussed in the Shoptalk box earlier in this chapter, organizations are increasingly using various types of incentive compensation as a way to motivate employees to higher levels of performance. Exhibit 19.10 summarizes several methods of incentive pay.

*Take A Moment*     *Go to the ethical dilemma on page 725 that pertains to the use of incentive compensation as a motivational tool.*

Variable compensation and forms of "at risk" pay are key motivational tools and are becoming more common than fixed salaries at many companies. These programs can be effective if they are used appropriately and combined with motivational ideas that also provide employees with intrinsic rewards and meet higher-level needs. Effective organizations do not use incentive plans as the sole basis of motivation.

In addition, many organizations give employees a voice in how pay and incentive systems are designed, which increases motivation by increasing employees' sense of involvement and control.[47] At Premium Standard Farms' pork-processing plant, for example, managers hired a consultant to help slaughterhouse workers design and implement an incentive program. Annual payouts to employees in one recent year were around $1,000 per employee. More important, though, is that workers feel a greater sense of dignity and purpose in their jobs, which has helped to reduce turnover significantly. As one employee put it, "Now I have the feeling that this is my company, too."[48] The most effective motivational programs typically involve much more than money or other external rewards. Two recent motivational trends are empowering employees and framing work to have greater meaning.

## Empowering People to Meet Higher Needs

**empowerment**
The delegation of power or authority to subordinates.

One significant way managers can meet higher motivational needs is to shift power down from the top of the organization and share it with subordinates to enable them to achieve goals. Empowerment is power sharing, the delegation of power

Exhibit 19.10

## New Motivational Compensation Programs

| Program | Purpose |
|---|---|
| **Pay for performance** | Rewards individual employees in proportion to their performance contributions. Also called *merit pay*. |
| **Gain sharing** | Rewards all employees and managers within a business unit when predetermined performance targets are met. Encourages teamwork. |
| **Employee Stock Ownership Plan (ESOP)** | Gives employees part ownership of the organization, enabling them to share in improved profit performance. |
| **Lump-sum bonuses** | Rewards employees with a one-time cash payment based on performance |
| **Pay for knowledge** | Links employee salary with the number of task skills acquired. Workers are motivated to learn the skills for many jobs, thus increasing company flexibility and efficiency. |
| **Flexible work schedule** | *Flextime* allows workers to set their own hours. *Job sharing* allows two or more part-time workers to jointly cover one job. *Telecommuting*, sometimes called *flex-place*, allows employees to work from home or an alternative workplace. |
| **Team-based compensation** | Rewards employees for behavior and activities that benefit the team, such as cooperation, listening, and empowering others. |
| **Lifestyle awards** | Rewards employees for meeting ambitious goals with luxury items, such as high-definition televisions, tickets to big-name sporting events, and exotic travel. |

or authority to subordinates in an organization.[49] Increasing employee power heightens motivation for task accomplishment because people improve their own effectiveness, choosing how to do a task and using their creativity.[50] Most people come into an organization with the desire to do a good job, and empowerment releases the motivation that is already there. Research indicates that most people have a need for *self-efficacy*, which is the capacity to produce results or outcomes, to feel that they are effective.[51] By meeting higher-level needs, empowerment can provide powerful motivation.

Empowering employees involves giving them four elements that enable them to act more freely to accomplish their jobs: information, knowledge, power, and rewards.[52]

1. *Employees receive information about company performance.* In companies where employees are fully empowered, such as Semco, a Brazilian manufacturing company, all employees have access to all financial and operational information.
2. *Employees have knowledge and skills to contribute to company goals.* Companies use training programs to help employees acquire the knowledge and skills they need to contribute to organizational performance. For example, when DMC, which makes pet supplies, gave employee teams the authority and responsibility for assembly-line shutdowns, it provided extensive training on how to diagnose and

interpret line malfunctions, as well as the costs related to shut-down and start-up. Employees worked through several case studies to practice decision making related to line shut-downs.[53]

3. *Employees have the power to make substantive decisions.* Workers have the authority to directly influence work procedures and organizational performance, often through quality circles or self-directed work teams. Semco pushes empowerment to the limits by allowing its employees to choose what they do, how they do it, and even how they get compensated for it. Employees set their own pay by choosing from a list of 11 different pay options, such as set salary or a combination of salary and incentives.[54]

4. *Employees are rewarded based on company performance.* Organizations that empower workers often reward them based on the results shown in the company's bottom line. For example, at Semco, in addition to employee-determined compensation, a company profit-sharing plan gives each employee an even share of 23 percent of his or her department's profits each quarter.[55] Organizations may also use other motivational compensation programs described in Exhibit 19.10 to tie employee efforts to company performance.

Many of today's organizations are implementing empowerment programs, but they are empowering workers to varying degrees. At some companies, empowerment means encouraging workers' ideas while managers retain final authority for decisions; at others it means giving employees almost complete freedom and power to make decisions and exercise initiative and imagination.[56] Current methods of empowerment fall along a continuum, as illustrated in Exhibit 19.11. The continuum runs from a situation in which front-line workers have almost no discretion, such as on a traditional assembly line, to full empowerment, where workers even participate in formulating organizational strategy. Studies indicate that higher-level empowerment programs are still relatively rare.[57] One U.S. company that has developed a high-level empowerment program is Delta Air Lines.

**DELTA AIR LINES**
http://www.delta.com

Delta, like all the major airlines, has experienced tremendous uncertainty and turmoil since the events of September 11, 2001, caused the airline industry to change forever. Every big airline has suffered a dramatic drop in passenger traffic and revenue and been forced to substantially reduce capacity and cut costs. The difference at Delta from the other major carriers is that employees throughout the company have had a big voice in how the airline responded to current challenges.

Delta Air Lines has developed one of the most advanced and comprehensive empowerment programs in the country, ensuring that employees share in information, decision making, risks, and rewards. One element is the Delta Board Council (DBC), made up of seven peer-selected employees representing the seven major employee divisions. The DBC serves as the "eyes, ears, and voice of Delta people from the boardroom to the breakroom." These seven employees serve full-time for two years and provide employee input at the top executive and board of directors level on the entire range of business issues. The Board was actively involved in selecting Delta's current CEO, Leo Mullin, for instance, and worked with top managers to make sure employees' concerns and suggestions were addressed in a recent compensation review.

Other elements of Delta's empowerment program include division-level employee councils, continuous improvement teams, and local-level employee councils. At each level, employees are provided with the information they need to fully contribute to decision making.[58]

This example touches on a few of the elements of Delta's empowerment program, which operates on various levels throughout the organization. Taken together, these elements ensure that employees have input and decision making power related to both everyday operational issues and higher-level strategic decisions.

Exhibit 19.11

**A Continuum of Empowerment**

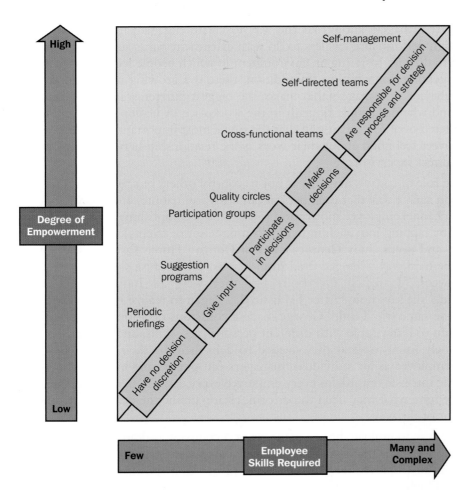

**SOURCES:** Based on Robert C. Ford and Myron D. Fottler, "Empowerment: A Matter of Degree," *Academy of Management Executive 9*, no 3 (1995), 21–31; Lawrence Holpp, "Applied Empowerment," *Training* (February 1994), 39–44; and David P. McCaffrey, Sue R. Faerman, and David W. Hart, "The Appeal and Difficulties of Participative Systems," *Organization Science 6*, no. 6 (November–December 1995), 603–627.

## Giving Meaning to Work

Another way to meet higher-level motivational needs and help people get intrinsic rewards from their work is to instill a sense of importance and meaningfulness. Consider that people who work for a social cause or mission are often more highly motivated. David Maxwell understood this when he was brought in to save the troubled mortgage lender Fannie Mae in the early 1980s. At the time, Fannie Mae was losing $1 million a day. Maxwell began a transformation by instilling employees with a sense of importance for the job he was asking them to do. Maxwell helped employees understand that if Fannie Mae did it's job well, people who had traditionally been excluded from home ownership, such as immigrants and minorities, could more easily claim their piece of the American dream. Many employees poured their hearts and souls into saving the organization because they looked at it as a way to strengthen America's social fabric.[59]

Another example is Les Schwab, founder of Les Schwab Tire Centers. Schwab has created an organization where employees feel like partners united toward a goal of making people's lives easier. Stores fix flats for free, and some have been known to install tires hours before opening time for an emergency trip. Employees frequently stop to help stranded motorists. Schwab rewards people with a generous profit-sharing plan for everyone and promotes store managers solely from within. However, these external rewards only supplement, not create, the high motivation Schwab's employees feel.[60]

Smart managers know that the way to create engaged, motivated employees and high performance has less to do with extrinsic rewards such as pay and much more to do with fostering an environment in which people feel that they are making a genuine contribution. In addition, there is a growing recognition that it is the behavior of managers that makes the biggest difference in employee motivation and whether people flourish in the workplace. A Gallup Organization study conducted over 25 years found that the single most important variable in whether employees feel good about their work is the relationship between employees and their direct supervisors.[61]

The role of today's manager is not to control others but to organize the workplace in such a way that each person can learn, contribute, and grow. Good managers channel employee motivation toward the accomplishment of organizational goals by tapping into each individual's unique set of talents, skills, interests, attitudes, and needs. Judy George, CEO of Domain Home Fashions learned to do this the hard way—she got fired from her last job because she didn't engage her employees. "I treated everybody like they were all Judy Georges running around," she says now. "After I was fired, I began to realize not everybody operated the same way I did." George made a conscious decision when she founded Domain to hire people with different personalities, skills, and interests, and then genuinely listen to what they needed to help them be their best.[62] By treating each employee as an individual, managers can put people in the right jobs and provide intrinsic rewards to every employee every day. Then, managers make sure people have what they need to perform, clearly define the desired outcomes, and get out of the way.

One way to evaluate how a manager or a company is doing in meeting higher-level needs is a metric developed by the Gallup researchers called the Q12. When a majority of employees can answer these 12 questions positively, the organization enjoys a highly motivated and productive workforce:

1. Do I know what is expected of me at work?
2. Do I have the materials and equipment that I need in order to do my work right?
3. At work, do I have the opportunity to do what I do best every day?
4. In the past seven days, have I received recognition or praise for doing good work?
5. Does my supervisor, or someone at work, seem to care about me as a person?
6. Is there someone at work who encourages my development?
7. At work, do my opinions seem to count?
8. Does the mission or purpose of my company make me feel that my job is important?
9. Are my co-workers committed to doing quality work?
10. Do I have a best friend at work?
11. In the past six months, has someone at work talked to me about my progress?
12. This past year, have I had opportunities to learn and grow?[63]

Results of the Gallup study show that organizations where employees give high marks on the Q12 have less turnover, are more productive and profitable, and enjoy greater employee and customer loyalty.[64] When employees are more engaged and motivated, they—and their organizations—thrive.

Manager's Solution

This chapter introduced a number of important ideas about the motivation of people in organizations. Rewards are of two types: intrinsic rewards that result from the satisfactions a person receives in the process of performing a job, and extrinsic rewards such as promotions that are given by another person. Managers work to help employees receive both intrinsic and extrinsic rewards from their jobs. The content theories of motivation focus on the nature of underlying employee needs. Maslow's hierarchy of needs, Alderfer's ERG theory, Herzberg's two-factor theory, and McClelland's acquired needs theory all suggest that people are motivated to meet a range of needs. Process theories examine how people go about selecting rewards with which to meet needs. Equity theory says that people compare their contributions and outcomes with others' and are motivated to maintain a feeling of equity. Expectancy theory suggests that people calculate the probability of achieving certain outcomes. Managers can increase motivation by treating employees fairly and by clarifying employee paths toward meeting their needs. Goal setting theory indicates that employees are more motivated if they have clear, specific goals and receive regular feedback concerning their progress toward meeting goals. Still another motivational approach is reinforcement theory, which says that employees learn to behave in certain ways based on the use of reinforcements.

The application of motivational ideas is illustrated in job design and other motivational programs. Job design approaches include job simplification, job rotation, job enlargement, job enrichment, and the job characteristics model. Managers can change the structure of work to meet employees' high-level needs. The recent trend toward empowerment motivates by giving employees more information and authority to make decisions in their work while connecting compensation to the results. Managers can instill employees with a sense of importance and meaningfulness to help them reap intrinsic rewards and meet higher level needs for esteem and self-fulfillment. Managers create the environment that determines employee motivation. One way to measure the factors that determine whether people have high levels of engagement and motivation is the Q12, a list of 12 questions about the day-to-day realities of a person's job.

A highly successful application of motivational ideas occurred for veteran salespeople at Pfizer, described in the opening example. Top managers realized these senior employees no longer felt like an important part of the organization. Their first step was to create a program originally called "The Second Wind," which set up self-reinforcing peer groups of four to seven senior sales reps, who kept in close touch via phone, e-mail, and personal contact. The teams compete with one another and with the rest of the sales force to meet specific sales goals. The most important part of the program was asking the veteran sales reps to give talks to groups of new management trainees and to speak and lead sessions at conferences of district managers, helping to fulfill higher-level esteem and self-actualization needs. The older reps were also assigned mentoring relationships with younger staffers. Soon some amazing things started happening. The sales of the older sales representatives took off like a rocket. Many times, these employees far exceeded their sales quotas and were recognized as leading the nation in the sales of certain drugs. Rick Burch, senior vice president, saw the program as a way to engage the older employees by recognizing and helping them to see their value to the company, thus allowing them to reap intrinsic as well as extrinsic rewards. He renamed the program the Master's Group, after the famous golf tournament. The 700 or so nationwide participants meet annually, most of them wearing company-provided green jackets that resemble those awarded at the prestigious Master's Tournament. "It was like recharging a battery," said veteran rep James Shumsky. "A lot of energy and enthusiasm came out. What makes it go is . . . that senior people are now respected for what they bring to meetings, and their mentoring is invaluable."[65]

# Discussion Questions

1. Low-paid service workers represent a motivational problem for many companies. Consider the ill-trained and poorly motivated X-ray machine operators trying to detect weapons in airports. How might these people be motivated to reduce boredom and increase their vigilance?

2. One small company recognizes an employee of the month, who is given a parking spot next to the president's space near the front door. What theories would explain the positive motivation associated with this policy?

3. Campbell Soup Company reduces accidents with a lottery. Each worker who works 30 days or more without losing a day for a job-related accident is eligible to win prizes in a raffle drawing. Why has this program been successful?

4. One executive argues that managers have too much safety because of benefit and retirement plans. He rewards his managers for taking risks and has removed many guaranteed benefits. Would this approach motivate managers? Why?

5. If an experienced secretary discovered that she made less money than a newly hired janitor, how would she react? What inputs and outcomes might she evaluate to make this comparison?

6. Would you rather work for a supervisor high in need for achievement, need for affiliation, or need for power? Why? What are the advantages and disadvantages of each?

7. A survey of teachers found that two of the most important rewards were the belief that their work was important and a feeling of accomplishment. Is this consistent with Hackman and Oldham's job characteristics model?

8. The teachers in question 7 also reported that pay and benefits were poor, yet they continued to teach. Use Herzberg's two-factor theory to explain this finding.

9. Many organizations use sales contests and motivational speakers to motivate salespeople to overcome frequent rejections and turndowns. How would these devices help motivate salespeople?

10. What characteristics of individuals determine the extent to which work redesign will have a positive impact on work satisfaction and work effectiveness?

11. Do you think an empowerment program of increased employee authority and responsibility would succeed without being tied to a motivational compensation program, such as gain sharing or ESOPs? Discuss.

# Management in Practice: Experiential Exercise

### What Motivates You?

You are to indicate how important each characteristic is to you. Answer according to your feelings about the most recent job you had or about the job you currently hold. Circle the number on the scale that represents your feeling—1 (very unimportant) to 7 (very important).

When you have completed the questionnaire, score it as follows:

Rating for question 5 = _____. Divide by 1 = _____ security.

Rating for questions 9 and 13 = _____. Divide by 2 = _____ social.

Rating for questions 1, 3, and 7 = _____. Divide by 3 = _____ esteem.

Rating for questions 4, 10, 11, and 12 = _____. Divide by 4 = _____ autonomy.

Rating for questions 2, 6, and 8 = _____. Divide by 3 = _____ self-actualization.

The instructor has national norm scores for presidents, vice-presidents, and upper middle-level, lower middle-level, and lower-level managers with which you can compare your mean importance scores. How do your scores compare with the scores of managers working in organizations?

1. The feeling of self-esteem a person gets from being in that job  1  2  3  4  5  6  7

2. The opportunity for personal growth and development in that job  1  2  3  4  5  6  7

3. The prestige of the job inside the company (that is, regard received from others in the company)  1  2  3  4  5  6  7

4. The opportunity for independent thought and action in that job  1  2  3  4  5  6  7

5. The feeling of security in that job  1  2  3  4  5  6  7

6. The feeling of self-fulfillment a person gets from being in that position (that is, the feeling of being able to use one's own unique capabilities, realizing one's potential)  1  2  3  4  5  6  7

7. The prestige of the job outside the company (that is, the regard received from others not in the company)  1  2  3  4  5  6  7

8. The feeling of worthwhile accomplishment in that job  1  2  3  4  5  6  7

9. The opportunity in that job to give help to other people  1  2  3  4  5  6  7

10. The opportunity in that job for participation in the setting of goals  1  2  3  4  5  6  7

11. The opportunity in that job for participation in the determination of methods and procedures  1  2  3  4  5  6  7

12. The authority connected with the job  1  2  3  4  5  6  7

13. The opportunity to develop close friendships in the job  1  2  3  4  5  6  7

Source: Lyman W. Porter, *Organizational Patterns of Managerial Job Attitudes* (New York: American Foundation for Management Research, 1964), 17, 19.

# Management in Practice: Ethical Dilemma

## Compensation Showdown

When Suzanne Lebeau, human resources manager, received a call from Bert Wilkes, comptroller of Farley Glass Works, she anticipated hearing good news to share with the Wage and Bonus Committee. She had already seen numbers to indicate that the year-end bonus plan, which was instituted by her committee in lieu of the traditional guaranteed raises of the past, was going to exceed expectations. It was a real relief to her, because the plan, devised by a committee representing all levels of the workforce, had taken eleven months to complete. It had also been a real boost to morale at a low point in the company's history. Workers at the glass shower production plant were bringing new effort and energy to their jobs, and Lebeau wanted to see them rewarded.

She was shocked to see Wilkes's face so grim when she arrived for her meeting. "We have a serious problem, Suzanne," Wilkes said to open the meeting. "We ran the numbers from third quarter to project our end-of-the-year figures and discovered that the executive bonus objectives, which are based on net operating profit, would not be met if we paid out the employee bonuses first. The executive bonuses are a major source of their income. We can't ask them to do without their salary to insure a bonus for the workers."

Lebeau felt her temper rising. After all their hard work, she was not going to sit by and watch the employees be disappointed because the accounting department had not structured the employee bonus plan to work with the executive plan. She was afraid they would undo all the good that the bonus plan had done in motivating the plant workers. They had kept their end of the bargain, and the company's high profits were common knowledge in the plant.

## What Do You Do?

1. Ask to appear before the executive committee to argue that the year-end bonus plan for workers be honored. Executives could defer their bonuses until the problem in the structure of the compensation plan is resolved.
2. Go along with the comptroller. It isn't fair for the executives to lose so much money. Begin to prepare the workers to not expect much this first year of the plan.
3. Go to the board of directors and ask for a compromise plan that splits the bonuses between the executives and the workers.

Source: Based on Doug Wallace, "Promises to Keep," *What Would You Do?* (reprinted from *Business Ethics*), vol. II (July–August 1993), 11–12. Reprinted with permission from *Business Ethics Magazine*, P.O. Box 8439, Minneapolis, MN 55408 (612) 879-0695.

# Surf the Net

1. **Motivation**. Go to *http://www.accel-team.com* and print out the "Employee Motivation" article. Think of personal or work-related examples that illustrate the points being made. If you disagree with any of the points, be prepared to give your reasons during a class discussion on motivation.
2. **Employee Rewards and Recognition.** Bob Nelson, author of two best-selling books on motivation, *1001 Ways to Reward Employees* and *1001 Ways to Energize Employees* provides many excellent resources at his Web site (*http://www.nelson-motivation.com*). Check out the Recommended Sites page under Recognition Resources. After checking out several sites, write a one- to two-page summary of what you learned about rewarding and recognizing employees that you believe would be most useful for managers.
3. **Motivational Compensation Programs.** The Beyster Institute provides a quiz that allows you to test your knowledge of employee ownership as a means of motivating employees at *http://beyster.ucsd.edu/about_employee_ownership/employee_ownership_quiz.cfm*. After completing and scoring the quiz, explore the links provided to learn more about employee ownership. In addition, check out the links on the Beyster home page that provide articles, case studies, and research on entrepreneurship and employee ownership topics.

# Case for Critical Analysis

## Bloomingdale's

Bloomingdale's is at the forefront of a quiet revolution sweeping department store retailing. Thousands of hourly sales employees are being converted to commission pay. Bloomingdale's hopes to use commissions to motivate employees to work harder, to attract better salespeople, and to enable them to earn more money. For example, under the old plan, a Bloomingdale's salesclerk in women's wear would earn about $16,000 a year, based on $7 per hour and 0.5 percent commission on $500,000 sales. Under the new plan, the annual pay would be $25,000 based on 5 percent commission on $500,000 sales.

John Palmerio, who works in the men's shoe salon, is enthusiastic about the changeover. His pay has increased an average of $175 per week. But in women's lingerie, employees are less enthusiastic. A target of $1,600 in sales per week is difficult to achieve but is necessary for salespeople to earn their previous salary and even to keep their jobs. In previous years, the practice of commission pay was limited to big-ticket items such as furniture, appliances, and men's suits, where extra sales skill pays off. The move into small-item purchases may not work as well, but Bloomingdale's and other stores are trying anyway.

One question is whether Bloomingdale's can create more customer-oriented salespeople when they work on commission. They may be reluctant to handle complaints, make returns, and clean shelves, preferring instead to chase customers. Moreover, it cost Bloomingdale's about $1 million per store to install the commission system because of training programs, computer changes, and increased pay in many departments. If the overall impact on service is negative, the increased efficiency may not seem worthwhile.

## Questions

1. What theories about motivation underlie the switch from salary to commission pay?
2. Are high-level needs met under the commission system?
3. As a customer, would you prefer to shop where employees are motivated to make commissions?

Sources: Based on Francine Schwadel, "Chain Finds Incentives a Hard Sell," *The Wall Street Journal*, July 5, 1990, B4; and Amy Dunkin, "Now Salespeople Really Must Sell for Their Supper," *Business Week*, July 31, 1989, 50–52.

# Endnotes

1. John A. Byrne, "How to Lead Now: Getting Extraordinary Performance When You Can't Pay For It," *Fast Company* (August 2003), 62–70.
2. David Silburt, "Secrets of the Super Sellers," *Canadian Business* (January 1987), 54–59; "Meet the Savvy Supersalesmen," *Fortune* (February 4, 1985), 56–62; Michael Brody, "Meet Today's Young American Worker," *Fortune* (November 11, 1985), 90–98; and Tom Richman, "Meet the Masters. They Could Sell You Anything . . . ," *Inc.* (March 1985), 79–86.
3. Richard M. Steers and Lyman W. Porter, eds., *Motivation and Work Behavior,* 3d ed. (New York: McGraw-Hill, 1983); Don Hellriegel, John W. Slocum, Jr., and Richard W. Woodman, *Organizational Behavior,* 7th ed. (St. Paul, Minn.: West, 1995), 170; and Jerry L. Gray and Frederick A. Starke, *Organizational Behavior: Concepts and Applications,* 4th ed. (New York: Macmillan, 1988), 104–105.
4. Carol Hymowitz, "Readers Tell Tales of Success and Failure Using Rating Systems," (In the Lead column), *The Wall Street Journal* (May 29, 2001), B1.
5. See Linda Grant, "Happy Workers, High Returns," *Fortune* (January 12, 1998), 81; Elizabeth J. Hawk and Garrett J. Sheridan, "The Right Stuff," *Management Review* (June 1999), 43–48; Michael West and Malcolm Patterson, "Profitable Personnel," *People Management* (January 8, 1998), 28–31; Anne Fisher, "Why Passion Pays," *FSB* (September 2002), 58; and Curt Coffman and Gabriel Gonzalez-Molina, *Follow This Path: How the World's Great Organizations Drive Growth By Unleashing Human Potential* (New York: Warner Books, 2002).
6. Steers and Porter, *Motivation.*
7. J. F. Rothlisberger and W. J. Dickson, *Management and the Worker* (Cambridge, Mass.: Harvard University Press, 1939).
8. Abraham F. Maslow, "A Theory of Human Motivation," *Psychological Review* 50 (1943), 370–396.
9. Roberta Maynard, "How to Motivate Low-Wage Workers," *Nation's Business* (May 1997), 35–39.
10. Clayton Alderfer, *Existence, Relatedness and Growth* (New York: Free Press, 1972).
11. Robert Levering and Milton Moskowitz, "100 Best Companies to Work For," *Fortune* (January 20, 2003), 127–152.
12. Robert Levering and Milton Moskowitz, "2004 Special Report: The 100 Best Companies To Work For," *Fortune* (January 12, 2004), 56–78.
13. Jeff Barbian, "C'mon, Get Happy," *Training* (January 2001), 92–96.
14. Karol Rose, "Work-Life Effectiveness," special advertising supplement, *Fortune* (September 29, 2003), S1–S17.
15. W. Glaser, *The Control Theory Manager* (New York: HarperBusiness, 1994); and John W. Newstrom, "Making Work Fun: An Important Role for Managers," *SAM Advanced Management Journal* (Winter 2002), 4–8, 21.
16. Newstrom, "Making Work Fun."
17. Frederick Herzberg, "One More Time: How Do You Motivate Employees?" Best of HBR, *Harvard Business Review* (January 2003), 87–96.
18. Elaine Leuchars, Shauna Harrington, and Carrie Erickson, "Putting People First: How VSP Achieves High Employee Satisfaction Year After Year," *Journal of Organizational Excellence* (Spring 2003), 33–41;

Levering and Moskowitz, "The 100 Best Companies to Work For 2004."

19. David C. McClelland, *Human Motivation* (Glenview, Ill.: Scott, Foresman, 1985).

20. Carol Hymowitz, "For Many Executives, Leadership Lessons Started with Mom," (In the Lead column), *The Wall Street Journal* (May 16, 2000), B1.

21. David C. McClelland, "The Two Faces of Power," in *Organizational Psychology,* ed. D.A. Colb, I.M. Rubin, and J.M. McIntyre (Englewood Cliffs, N.J.: Prentice-Hall, 1971), 73–86.

22. J. Stacy Adams, "Injustice in Social Exchange," in *Advances in Experimental Social Psychology,* 2d ed., ed. L. Berkowitz (New York: Academic Press, 1965); and J. Stacy Adams, "Toward an Understanding of Inequity," *Journal of Abnormal and Social Psychology* (November 1963), 422–436.

23. "Study: The Brain Prefers Working Over Getting Money For Nothing," *TheJournalNews.com* (May 14, 2004), http://www.thejournalnews.com/newsroom/051404/d01a/4moneyfornothing.html

24. Ray V. Montagno, "The Effects of Comparison to Others and Primary Experience on Responses to Task Design," *Academy of Management Journal* 28 (1985), 491–498; and Robert P. Vecchio, "Predicting Worker Performance in Inequitable Settings," *Academy of Management Review* 7 (1982), 103–110.

25. John Peterman, "The Rise and Fall of the J. Peterman Company," *Harvard Business Review* (September–October 1999), 59–66.

26. James E. Martin and Melanie M. Peterson, "Two-Tier Wage Structures: Implications for Equity Theory," *Academy of Management Journal* 30 (1987), 297–315.

27. Victor H. Vroom, *Work and Motivation* (New York: Wiley, 1964); B. S. Georgopoulos, G. M. Mahoney, and N. Jones, "A Path-Goal Approach to Productivity," *Journal of Applied Psychology* 41 (1957), 345–353; and E. E. Lawler III, *Pay and Organizational Effectiveness: A Psychological View* (New York: McGraw-Hill, 1981).

28. Richard L. Daft and Richard M. Steers, *Organizations: A Micro/Macro Approach* (Glenview, Ill.: Scott, Foresman, 1986).

29. See Edwin A. Locke and Gary P. Latham, "Building a Practically Useful Theory of Goal Setting and Task Motivation: A 35-Year Odyssey", *The American Psychologist* 57, no. 9 (September 2002), 705+; Gary P. Latham and Edwin A. Locke, "Self-Regulation through Goal Setting", *Organizational Behavior and Human Decision Processes* 50, no. 2 (1991), 212+; G. P. Latham and G. H. Seijts, "The Effects of Proximal and Distal Goals on Performance of a Moderately Complex Task," *Journal of Organizational Behavior* 20, no. 4 (1999), 421+; P. C. Early, T. Connolly, and G. Ekegren, "Goals, Strategy Development, and Task Performance: Some Limits on the Efficacy of Goal Setting," *Journal of Applied Psychology* 74 (1989), 24–33; E. A. Locke, "Toward a Theory of Task Motivation and Incentives," *Organizational Behavior and Human Performance* 3 (1968), 157-189; Gerard H. Seijts, Ree M. Meertens, and Gerjo Kok, "The Effects of Task Importance and Publicness on the Relation Between Goal Difficulty and Performance," *Canadian Journal of Behavioural Science* 29, no. 1 (1997), 54+.

30. Locke and Latham, "Building a Practically Useful Theory of Goal Setting and Task Motivation."

31. J. M. Ivancevich and J. T. McMahon, "The Effects of Goal Setting, External Feedback, and Self-Generated Feedback on Outcome Variables: A Field Experiment," *Academy of Management Journal* (June 1982), 359+; G. P. Latham and E. A. Locke, "Self-Regulation Through Goal Setting," *Organizational Behavior and Human Decision Processes* 50, no. 2 (1991), 212+.

32. Mike Hofman, "Everyone's a Cost Cutter," *Inc.* (July 1998), 117; and Abby Livingston, "Gain-Sharing Encourages Productivity," *Nation's Business* (January 1998), 21–22.

33. Alexander D. Stajkovic and Fred Luthans, "A Meta-Analysis of the Effects of Organizational Behavior Modification on Task Performance, 1975–95," *Academy of Management Journal* (October 1997), 1122–1149; H. Richlin, *Modern Behaviorism* (San Francisco: Freeman, 1970); and B. F. Skinner, *Science and Human Behavior* (New York: Macmillan, 1953).

34. Lea Goldman, "Over the Top," *Forbes* (October 29, 2001), 146–147.

35. Stajkovic and Luthans, "A Meta-Analysis of the Effects of Organizational Behavior Modification on Task Performance, 1975–95," and Fred Luthans and Alexander D. Stajkovic, "Reinforce for Performance: The Need to Go Beyond Pay and Even Rewards," *Academy of Management Executive* 13, no. 2 (1999), 49–57.

36. Kenneth D. Butterfield and Linda Klebe Treviño, "Punishment from the Manager's Perspective: A Grounded Investigation and Inductive Model," *Academy of Management Journal* 39, no. 6 (December 1996), 1479–1512; and Andrea Casey, "Voices from the Firing Line: Managers Discuss Punishment in the Workplace," *Academy of Management Executive* 11, no. 3 (1997), 93–94.

37. Roberta Maynard, "How to Motivate Low-Wage Workers."

38. L. M. Sarri and G. P. Latham, "Employee Reaction to Continuous and Variable Ratio Reinforcement Schedules Involving a Monetary Incentive," *Journal of Applied Psychology* 67 (1982), 506–508; and R. D. Pritchard, J. Hollenback, and P. J. DeLeo, "The Effects of Continuous and Partial Schedules of Reinforcement

on Effort, Performance, and Satisfaction," *Organizational Behavior and Human Performance* 25 (1980), 336–353.

39. Kevin Kelly, "Getting What You Pay For," *FSB* (March 2003), 24.

40. A. J. Vogl, "Carrots, Sticks, and Self-Deception" (an interview with Alfie Kohn), *Across the Board* (January 1994), 39–44.

41. Hilary Rosenberg, "Building a Better Carrot," *CFO* (June 2001), 64–70.

42. Barbian, "C'mon, Get Happy."

43. Norm Alster, "What Flexible Workers Can Do," *Fortune* (February 13, 1989), 62–66.

44. Glenn L. Dalton, "The Collective Stretch," *Management Review* (December 1998), 54–59.

45. J. Richard Hackman and Greg R. Oldham, *Work Redesign* (Reading, Mass.: Addison-Wesley, 1980); and J. Richard Hackman and Greg Oldham, "Motivation through the Design of Work: Test of a Theory," *Organizational Behavior and Human Performance* 16 (1976), 250–279.

46. Xu Huang and Evert Van de Vliert, "Where Intrinsic Job Satisfaction Fails to Work: National Moderators of Intrinsic Motivation," *Journal of Organizational Behavior* 24 (2003), 157–179.

47. Ann Podolske, "Giving Employees a Voice in Pay Structures," *Business Ethics* (March–April 1998), 12.

48. Rekha Balu, "Bonuses Aren't Just For the Bosses," *Fast Company* (December 2000), 74–76.

49. Edwin P. Hollander and Lynn R. Offermann, "Power and Leadership in Organizations," *American Psychologist* 45 (February 1990), 179–189.

50. Jay A. Conger and Rabindra N. Kanungo, "The Empowerment Process: Integrating Theory and Practice," *Academy of Management Review* 13 (1988), 471–482.

51. Jay A. Conger and Rabindra N. Kanungo, "The Empowerment Process: Integrating Theory and Practice," *Academy of Management Review* 13 (1998), 471–482.

52. David E. Bowen and Edward E. Lawler III, "The Empowerment of Service Workers: What, Why, How, and When," *Sloan Management Review* (Spring 1992),

31–39; and Ray W. Coye and James A. Belohav, "An Exploratory Analysis of Employee Participation," *Group and Organization Management* 20, no. 1, (March 1995), 4–17.

53. Russ Forrester, "Empowerment: Rejuvenating a Potent Idea," *Academy of Management Executive* 14, no. 3 (2000), 67–80.

54. Ricardo Semler, "How We Went Digital Without a Strategy," *Harvard Business Review* (September–October 2000), 51–58.

55. Podolske, "Giving Employees a Voice in Pay Structures."

56. This discussion is based on Robert C. Ford and Myron D. Fottler, "Empowerment: A Matter of Degree," *Academy of Management Executive* 9, no. 3 (1995), 21–31.

57. Bruce E. Kaufman, "High-Level Employee Involvement at Delta Air Lines," *Human Resource Management* 42, no. 2 (Summer 2003), 175–190.

58. Ibid.

59. Jim Collins, "The 10 Greatest CEOs of All Time," *Fortune* (July 21, 2003), 54–68.

60. Cheryl Dahle, "Four Tires, Free Beef," *Fast Company* (September 2003), 36.

61. This discussion is based on Tony Schwartz, "The Greatest Sources of Satisfaction in the Workplace are Internal and Emotional," *Fast Company* (November 2000), 398–402; and Marcus Buckingham and Curt Coffman, *First, Break All the Rules: What the World's Greatest Managers Do Differently* (New York: Simon and Schuster, 1999).

62. Margaret Littman, "Best Bosses Tell All," *Working Woman* (October 2000), 48–56.

63. The Gallup Organization, Princeton, NJ. All rights reserved. Used with permission.

64. Curt Coffman and Gabriel Gonzalez-Molina, *Follow This Path: How the World's Greatest Organizations Drive Growth by Unleashing Human Potential* (New York: Warner Books, 2002), as reported in Anne Fisher, "Why Passion Pays," *FSB* (September 2002), 58.

65. Byrne, "How to Lead Now."

# Communication

## LEARNING OBJECTIVES

*After studying this chapter, you should be able to*

1. Explain why communication is essential for effective management and describe how nonverbal behavior and listening affect communication among people.

2. Explain how managers use communication to persuade and influence others.

3. Describe the concept of channel richness, and explain how communication channels influence the quality of communication.

4. Explain the difference between formal and informal organizational communications and the importance of each for organization management.

5. Identify how structure influences team communication outcomes.

6. Explain why open communication, dialogue, and feedback are essential approaches to communication in a turbulent environment.

7. Identify the skills managers need for communicating during a crisis situation.

8. Describe barriers to organizational communication, and suggest ways to avoid or overcome them.

Patrick Charmel is facing one of the most difficult decisions of his career as president and CEO of Griffin Hospital, located in Derby, Connecticut. When a 94-year-old patient had checked into the hospital complaining of flu-like symptoms, no one was particularly alarmed. After all, elderly people get sick a lot, and it had been a bad year for flu. Within a short time, though, doctors advised Charmel that they suspected the patient, Ollie Lundgren, was suffering from anthrax poisoning. Quick as a blink, the word was put out to the state health department, the governor, the FBI, the Centers for Disease Control and Prevention, and other state and federal agencies involved in fighting America's new war against terrorism. The governor and the FBI have asked Charmel to keep quiet—even to his own employees—and pretend that this is a normal case of flu until a final analysis confirms the diagnosis and federal agencies can plan a news conference. They argue that putting out the news now would just start a panic and do no one any good.[1]

## Take A Moment

If you were in Patrick Charmel's position, what would you do? Do employees really need to know that anthrax is suspected at this point? Is there any reason to alert the public and perhaps raise unnecessary fears?

Patrick Charmel believes in open communication, but he's got some pretty heavy advisors telling him to keep quiet. It is a dilemma that could confront any manager in today's turbulent environment, where crisis communication is at the top of everyone's needed-skills list. Derby, Connecticut, is a place where no one would ever expect an anthrax scare, and Charmel never expected to find himself in such a fix.

Effective communication, both within the organization and with people outside the company, is a major challenge and responsibility for managers. In today's uncertain and intensely competitive environment, managers at many companies are trying to improve their communications knowledge and skills. To break down communication barriers at Guidant Corporation, now owned by pharmaceutical giant Eli Lilly, CEO Ginger Graham assigned each top manager a coach from lower levels of the organization. The coaches were trained to ask questions and gather information from people throughout the company about the manager's openness and communication skills. With the support of top management, this reverse mentoring program helped to close a communication gap at Guidant.[2] Michael J. Critelli, chairman and CEO of Pitney Bowes, has more than 150 one-hour "skip-level" meetings a year, where he meets with managers from lower levels of the company to learn about what's going on from their point of view. In addition, Critelli takes advantage of opportunities for impromptu conversations with employees during lunch in the cafeteria or in his visits to field offices.[3]

To stay connected with employees and customers and shape company direction, managers must excel at personal communications. Nonmanagers often are amazed at how much energy successful executives put into communication. Consider the comment about Robert Strauss, former chairman of the Democratic National Committee and former ambassador to Russia:

> One of his friends says, "His network is everywhere. It ranges from bookies to bank presidents. . . . "
>   He seems to find time to make innumerable phone calls to "keep in touch"; he cultivates secretaries as well as senators; he will befriend a middle-level White House aide whom other important officials won't bother with. Every few months, he sends candy to the White House switchboard operators.[4]

This chapter explains why executives such as Robert Strauss, Michael Critelli, and Ginger Graham are effective communicators. First, we will see how managers' jobs require communication and describe a model of the communication process. Next, we will consider the interpersonal aspects of communication, including communication channels, persuasion, listening skills, and nonverbal communication that affect managers' ability to communicate. Then, we will look at the organization as a whole and consider formal upward, downward, and horizontal communications as well as personal networks and informal communications. We will discuss the importance of keeping multiple channels of communication open and examine how managers can effectively communicate during times of turbulence, uncertainty, and crisis. Finally, we will examine barriers to communication and how managers can overcome them.

# Communication and the Manager's Job

How important is communication? Consider this: Managers spend at least 80 percent of every working day in direct communication with others. In other words, 48 minutes of every hour is spent in meetings, on the telephone, communicating online, or talking informally while walking around. The other 20 percent of a typical manager's time is spent doing desk work, most of which is also communication in the form of reading and writing.[5]

Exhibit 20.1 illustrates the crucial role of managers as communication champions. Managers gather important information from both inside and outside the organization and then distribute appropriate information to others who need it. Managers' communication is *purpose-directed*, in that it directs everyone's attention toward the vision, values, and desired goals of the team or organization and influences people to act in a way to achieve the goals. Managers facilitate *strategic conversations* by using open communication, actively listening to others, applying the practice of dialogue, and using feedback for learning and change. Strategic conversation refers to people talking across boundaries and hierarchical levels about the team or organization's vision, critical strategic themes, and the values that help achieve important goals.[6] For example, at Royal Philips Electronics, president Gerald Kleisterlee defined four strategic technology themes that he believes should define Philips's future in the industry: display, storage, connectivity, and digital video processing. These themes intentionally cross technology boundaries, which requires that people communicate and collaborate across departments and divisions to accomplish goals.[7] Effective managers use many communication methods, including selecting rich channels of communication, facilitating upward, downward, and horizontal communication, understanding and using nonverbal communication, and building informal communication networks that cross organization boundaries.

One good example of a manager as communication champion is David Neeleman, CEO of the fast-growing low-fare airline, JetBlue. Neeleman demonstrates a genuine commitment to communication by regularly going on flights to talk with customers and employees, as described in the Unlocking Creative Solutions Through People box.

**strategic conversation**
Dialogue across boundaries and hierarchical levels about the team or organization's vision, critical strategic themes, and the values that help achieve important goals.

Exhibit 20.1

**The Manager as Communication Champion**

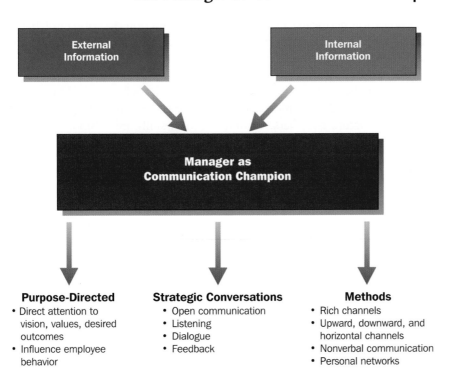

**SOURCES:** Adapted from Henry Mintzberg, *The Nature of Managerial Work* (New York; Harper and Row, 1973); and Richard L. Daft, *The Leadership Experience,* 3rd ed. (Cincinnati, OH: South-Western, 2005), 346.

# Unlocking Creative Solutions Through People

### JetBlue CEO Walks His Talk—Up and Down the Airplane Aisles

On a recent flight from New York to California, passengers on JetBlue had an unusual experience—being served by the company's CEO, Dave Neeleman. Neeleman cheerfully joined other flight attendants in passing out snacks—even though it took him hours to get through the plane because he stopped to chat with anyone who wanted to talk.

As it turns out, this wasn't so unusual at all. Neeleman tries to come on flights and talk to customers at least once a month. He says it's where he gets his best ideas for JetBlue. As JetBlue grows, Neeleman is making a conscious effort to make sure he doesn't lose contact with the people who made the company a success. As he slowly makes his way through the plane, Neeleman listens to complaints, answers questions, and even helps passengers network with other people on the plane who share their interests.

Serving as a flight attendant also strengthens communication with employees, who say they bump into Neeleman all the time in their jobs. His actions serve as a symbolic, nonverbal communication to employees of the importance of customer service. People see him going out of his way to help customers and they feel inspired to do the same. They see him putting in overtime when he could easily stay in his office and go home at the end of the day, and they think of him as one of the team. As a result, a high level of trust, respect, and goodwill exists between employees and managers at JetBlue, as well as between the company and its customers.

Another advantage of Neeleman's efforts is that it facilitates and improves upward communication. Not only do employees like the chance to talk with Neeleman informally, the CEO also gets to see first hand what employees go through and how management's actions affect them. Employees feel that Neeleman understands what's happening on the front lines because he's been there.

**SOURCE**: Norm Brodsky, "Learning From JetBlue" *Inc.* (March 2004), 59–60.

Communication permeates every management function described in Chapter 1.[8] For example, when managers perform the planning function, they gather information; write letters, memos, and reports; and meet with other managers to formulate the plan. When managers lead, they communicate to share a vision of what the organization can be and motivate employees to help achieve it. When managers organize, they gather information about the state of the organization and communicate a new structure to others. Communication skills are a fundamental part of every managerial activity.

## What Is Communication?

A professor at Harvard once asked a class to define communication by drawing pictures. Most students drew a manager speaking or typing on a computer keyboard. Some placed "speech balloons" next to their characters; others showed pages flying from a laser printer. "No," the professor told the class, "none of you has captured the essence of communication." He went on to explain that communication means "to share"—not "to speak" or "to write."

**communication**
The process by which information is exchanged and understood by two or more people, usually with the intent to motivate or influence behavior.

Communication thus can be defined as the process by which information is exchanged and understood by two or more people, usually with the intent to motivate or influence behavior. Communication is not just sending information. Honoring this distinction between *sharing* and *proclaiming* is crucial for successful management. A manager who does not listen is like a used-car salesperson who claims, "I sold a car—they just did not buy it." Management communication is a two-way street that includes listening and other forms of feedback. Effective communication, in the words of one expert, is as follows:

*When two people interact, they put themselves into each other's shoes, try to perceive the world as the other person perceives it, try to predict how the other will respond. Interaction involves reciprocal role-taking, the mutual employment of empathetic skills. The goal of interaction is the merger of self and other, a complete ability to anticipate, predict, and behave in accordance with the joint needs of self and other.[9]*

It is the desire to share understanding that motivates executives to visit employees on the shop floor, hold small, informal meetings, or eat with employees in the company cafeteria. The things managers learn from direct communication with employees shape their understanding of the organization.

## The Communication Process

Many people think communication is simple. After all, we communicate every day without even thinking about it. However, communication usually is complex, and the opportunities for sending or receiving the wrong messages are innumerable. No doubt, you have heard someone say, "But that's not what I meant!" Have you ever received directions you thought were clear and yet still got lost? How often have you wasted time on misunderstood instructions?

To more fully understand the complexity of the communication process, note the key elements outlined in Exhibit 20.2. Two common elements in every communication situation are the sender and the receiver. The *sender* is anyone who wishes to convey an idea or concept to others, to seek information, or to express a thought or emotion. The *receiver* is the person to whom the message is sent. The sender encodes the idea by selecting symbols with which to compose a message. The message is the tangible formulation of the idea that is sent to the receiver. The message is sent through a channel, which is the communication carrier. The channel can be a formal report, a telephone call or e-mail message, or a face-to-face meeting. The receiver decodes the symbols to interpret the meaning of the message. Encoding and decoding are potential sources for communication errors, because knowledge, attitudes, and background act as filters and create *noise* when translating from symbols to meaning. Finally, feedback occurs when the receiver responds to the sender's communication with a return message. Without feedback, the communication is *one-way*; with feedback, it is *two-way*. Feedback is a powerful aid to communication effectiveness, because it enables the sender to determine whether the receiver correctly interpreted the message.

**encode**
To select symbols with which to compose a message.

**message**
The tangible formulation of an idea to be sent to a receiver.

**channel**
The carrier of a communication.

**decode**
To translate the symbols used in a message for the purpose of interpreting its meaning.

**feedback**
A response by the receiver to the sender's communication.

Exhibit 20.2

### A Model of the Communication Process

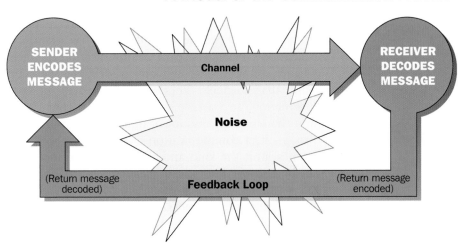

Managers who are effective communicators understand and use the circular nature of communication. Consider Nortel Networks' *Virtual Leadership Academy*, a monthly televised program hosted by Dan Hunt, president of Nortel's Caribbean and Latin American operations, and Emma Carrasco, vice president of marketing and communications. Hunt and Carrasco use a talk-show format to get people talking. Employees from about 40 different countries watch the show from their regional offices and call in their questions and comments. "We're always looking for ways to break down barriers," says Carrasco. "People watch talk shows in every country, and they've learned that it's okay to say what's on their minds."[10] The television program is the channel through which Hunt and Carrasco send their encoded message. Employees decode and interpret the message and encode their feedback, which is sent through the channel of the telephone hookup. The communications circuit is complete.

# Communicating among People

The communication model in Exhibit 20.2 illustrates the components that must be mastered for effective communication. Communications can break down if sender and receiver do not encode or decode language in the same way.[11] We all know how difficult it is to communicate with someone who does not speak our language, and managers in U.S. organizations today are often trying to communicate with people who speak many different native languages and have limited English skills. However, communication breakdowns can also occur between people who speak the same language.

Many factors can lead to a breakdown in communications. For example, the selection of communication channel can determine whether the message is distorted by noise and interference. The listening skills of both parties and attention to nonverbal behavior can determine whether a message is truly shared. Thus, for managers to be effective communicators, they must understand how factors such as communication channels, nonverbal behavior, and listening all work to enhance or detract from communication.

**channel richness**
The amount of information that can be transmitted during a communication episode.

## CONCEPT CONNECTION

*Equipped with laptops, pagers, and cell phones, Intel employees can now communicate and collaborate on group projects from anywhere in the world. These forms of communication lack the channel richness found in face-to-face discussions. However, new technology such as instant messaging, groupware, and wireless Internet applications enable these devices to facilitate rapid feedback, thus increasing their value for organizational communication.*

## Communication Channels

Managers have a choice of many channels through which to communicate to other managers or employees. A manager may discuss a problem face-to-face, make a telephone call, use instant messaging, send an e-mail, write a memo or letter, or put an item in a newsletter, depending on the nature of the message. Research has attempted to explain how managers select communication channels to enhance communication effectiveness.[12] The research has found that channels differ in their capacity to convey information. Just as a pipeline's physical characteristics limit the kind and amount of liquid that can be pumped through it, a communication channel's physical characteristics limit the kind and amount of information that can be conveyed among managers. The channels available to managers can be classified into a hierarchy based on information richness. Channel richness is the amount of information that can be transmitted during a communication episode. The hierarchy of channel richness is illustrated in Exhibit 20.3.

Exhibit 20.3

## The Pyramid of Channel Richness

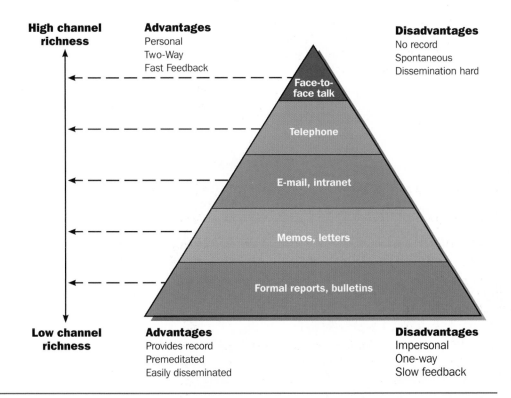

**High channel richness**

**Advantages**
Personal
Two-Way
Fast Feedback

**Disadvantages**
No record
Spontaneous
Dissemination hard

Face-to-face talk

Telephone

E-mail, intranet

Memos, letters

Formal reports, bulletins

**Low channel richness**

**Advantages**
Provides record
Premeditated
Easily disseminated

**Disadvantages**
Impersonal
One-way
Slow feedback

The capacity of an information channel is influenced by three characteristics: (1) the ability to handle multiple cues simultaneously; (2) the ability to facilitate rapid, two-way feedback; and (3) the ability to establish a personal focus for the communication. Face-to-face discussion is the richest medium, because it permits direct experience, multiple information cues, immediate feedback, and personal focus. Face-to-face discussions facilitate the assimilation of broad cues and deep, emotional understanding of the situation. Telephone conversations are next in the richness hierarchy. Although eye contact, posture, and other body language cues are missing, the human voice can still carry a tremendous amount of emotional information.

Electronic messaging, such as e-mail and instant messaging, is increasingly being used for messages that were once handled via the telephone. A survey by researchers at The Ohio State University found that about half the respondents reported making fewer telephone calls since they began using e-mail. However, respondents also said they preferred the telephone or face-to-face conversation for communicating difficult news, giving advice, or expressing affection.[13] Because e-mail messages lack both visual and verbal cues and don't allow for interaction and feedback, messages can sometimes be misunderstood. Using e-mail to discuss disputes, for example, can lead to an escalation rather than a resolution of conflict.[14] This chapter's Shoptalk box offers some tips for effectively using electronic mail.

Instant messaging alleviates the problem of miscommunication to some extent by allowing for immediate feedback. Instant messaging (IM) allows users to see who is connected to a network and share short-hand messages or documents with them instantly A growing number of managers and organizations are using IM, indicating that it helps people get responses faster and collaborate more smoothly.[15] In March 2003, 84 percent of companies surveyed in North America reported using IM, and

**instant messaging (IM)**
Electronic communication that allows users to see who is connected to a network and share information instantly.

## manager's Shoptalk

### Turbulent Times

### Make Your E-Mails Count

Electronic communication has many advantages, but the quick and easy nature of e-mail increases the potential for communication errors. Managers can learn to benefit from the tremendous efficiencies of e-mail while preventing its unintended problems. Here are some Dos and Don'ts for effectively using electronic mail.

### Do

- Keep e-mail messages short and to the point. Use the subject line to convey key, precise information. Bullet points make messages easier to read.
- Remember your manners. Use salutations and proper forms of closing. Turn on your grammar and spell-checker.
- Use e-mail to set up meetings, recap spoken conversations, or follow up on information already discussed.
- Use the "out of office" feature to let people know when you are traveling.
- Respond to e-mail messages as quickly as possible, preferably by the end of the same day.
- Slow down and take the time to read your message a couple of times before hitting the "Send" button.

### Don't

- Use e-mail to mock the boss or lambaste a colleague.
- Treat e-mail casually. Never write anything in an e-mail you wouldn't want to see published in a newspaper or broadcast on *60 Minutes*.
- Hire and fire via e-mail. Important, personal, and difficult messages should always be conveyed in person or at least by telephone.
- Use profanity. It always looks bad in print, and there are plenty of other ways to get your point across.
- Copy to the world. Smart managers use group mail only sparingly.
- Use e-mail to start or perpetuate a feud. E-mail should never be used to convey feelings of anger. Take the old fashioned approach and chew people out only in person.

SOURCES: Based on Andrea C. Poe, "Don't Touch That 'Send' Button," *HR Magazine* (July 2001), 74-80; Michael Goldberg, "The Essentials of E-Mail," *CIO* (June 1, 2003), 24; and Jared Sandberg, "Workplace E-Mail Can Turn Radioactive in Clumsy Hands," *The Wall Street Journal* (February 12, 2003), B1.

one market research firm predicts 300 million business users worldwide by the end of 2005.[16] Organizations are also using interactive meetings over the Internet, sometimes adding video capabilities to provide visual cues and greater channel richness.

One psychiatrist argues that the growing use of technology for communicating has created hidden problems for both individuals and organizations by depriving people of the "human moments" that are needed to energize people, inspire creativity, and support emotional well-being.[17] People need to interact with others in physical space to build the connections that create great organizations. However, some research indicates that electronic messaging can enable reasonably rich communication if the technology is used appropriately.[18]

Still lower on the hierarchy of channel richness are written letters and memos. These can be personally focused, but they convey only the cues written on paper and are slow to provide feedback. Impersonal written media, including fliers, bulletins, and standard computer reports, are the lowest in richness. These channels are not focused on a single receiver, use limited information cues, and do not permit feedback.

It is important for managers to understand that each communication channel has advantages and disadvantages, and that each can be an effective means of communication in the appropriate circumstances.[19] Channel selection depends on whether the message is routine or nonroutine. *Nonroutine messages* typically are ambiguous, concern novel events, and impose great potential for misunderstanding. They often are characterized by time pressure and surprise. Managers can communicate nonroutine messages effectively only by selecting rich channels. Routine messages are simple and straightforward. They convey data or statistics or simply put into words what managers already agree on and understand. Routine messages can be efficiently communicated through a channel lower in richness. Written communications also should be used when the audience is widely dispersed or when the communication is official and a permanent record is required.[20]

Consider law enforcement personnel trying to work out a press release concerning the sniper shootings in the Washington, D.C., area in the fall of 2002. An immediate response is critical. This type of nonroutine communication forces a rich information exchange. The group will meet face to face, brainstorm ideas, and provide rapid feedback to resolve disagreement and convey the correct information. If, in contrast, an agency director is preparing a press release about a routine matter such as a policy change or new K9 training, less information capacity is needed. The director and public relations people might begin developing the press release with an exchange of memos, telephone calls, and e-mail messages.

The key is to select a channel to fit the message. During a major acquisition, one firm decided to send top executives to all major work sites of the acquired company, where 75 percent of the workers met the managers in person, heard about their plans for the company, and had a chance to ask questions. The results were well worth the time and expense of the personal, face-to-face meetings because the acquired workforce saw their new managers as understanding, open, and willing to listen.[21] Communicating their nonroutine message about the acquisition in person prevented damaging rumors and misunderstandings. The choice of a communication channel can also convey a symbolic meaning to the receiver; in a sense, the medium becomes the message. The firm's decision to communicate face to face with the acquired workforce signaled to employees that managers cared about them as individuals.

## Communicating to Persuade and Influence Others

Communication is not just for conveying information, but to persuade and influence people. Although communication skills have always been important to managers, the ability to persuade and influence others is even more critical today. Businesses are run largely by cross-functional teams who are actively involved in making decisions. Issuing directives is no longer an appropriate or effective way to get things done.[22]

To persuade and influence, managers have to communicate frequently and easily with others. Yet some people find interpersonal communication experiences unrewarding or difficult and thus tend to avoid situations where communication is required. The term communication apprehension describes this avoidance behavior, and is defined as "an individual's level of fear or anxiety associated with either real or anticipated communication." With training and practice, managers can overcome their communication apprehension and become more effective communicators.

**communication apprehension**
An individual's level of fear or anxiety associated with interpersonal communications.

*Go to the experiential exercise on page 759.*

*Take A Moment*

One important way managers influence others is by using symbols, metaphors, and stories to deliver their messages. Stories tap into people's imaginations and emotions, helping managers make sense of a fast-changing environment in ways that people can understand and share. When Hubertus von Grünberg was CEO of

Germany's Continental AG, he used storytelling to set the company on a path toward transformation. Von Grünberg knew Continental, today the world's fourth largest tire company, could never compete as a global player without building alliances and partnerships with other companies, a strategy that went against Continental's self-reliant culture. Rather than using facts and figures to persuade others of the need for new partnership strategies, von Grünberg told a story illustrating Continental's ever-smaller place in a rapidly changing industry. It worked. Managers throughout the company were inspired to begin discussing how Continental could increase its global power by sharing its innovation and expertise and in turn learning from others.[23]

If we think back to our early school years, we may remember that the most effective lessons often were couched in stories. Presenting hard facts and figures rarely has the same power. Evidence of the compatibility of stories with human thinking was demonstrated by a study at Stanford Business School.[24] The point was to convince MBA students that a company practiced a policy of avoiding layoffs. For some students, only a story was used. For others, statistical data were provided that showed little turnover compared to competitors. For other students, statistics and stories were combined, and yet other students were shown the company's official policy statements. Of all these approaches, the students presented with a vivid story alone were most convinced that the company truly practiced a policy of avoiding layoffs. Managers can learn to use elements of storytelling to enhance their communication.[25] Stories need not be long, complex, or carefully constructed. A story can be a joke, an analogy, or a verbal snapshot of something from the manager's own past experiences.[26]

## Nonverbal Communication

Managers also use symbols to communicate what is important. Managers are watched, and their behavior, appearance, actions, and attitudes are symbolic of what they value and expect of others.

Most of us have heard the saying that "actions speak louder than words." Indeed, we communicate without words all the time, whether we realize it or not. Nonverbal communication refers to messages sent through human actions and behaviors rather than through words.[27] Most managers are astonished to learn that words themselves carry little meaning. Major parts of the shared understanding from communication come from the nonverbal messages of facial expression, voice, mannerisms, posture, and dress.

**nonverbal communication**
A communication transmitted through actions and behaviors rather than through words.

Nonverbal communication occurs mostly face to face. One researcher found three sources of communication cues during face-to-face communication: the *verbal*, which are the actual spoken words; the *vocal*, which include the pitch, tone, and timbre of a person's voice; and *facial expressions*. According to this study, the relative weights of these three factors in message interpretation are as follows: verbal impact, 7 percent; vocal impact, 38 percent; and facial impact, 55 percent.[28] To some extent, we are all natural *face readers*. Managers can hone this skill, learning to consciously read facial expressions and improve their ability to connect with and influence followers.[29]

This research strongly implies that "it's not what you say but how you say it." Nonverbal messages and body language often convey our real thoughts and feelings with greater force than do our most carefully selected words. Thus, while the conscious mind may be formulating vocal messages such as "I'm happy," or "Congratulations on your promotion," body language may be signaling true feelings through blushing, perspiring, glancing, crying, or avoiding eye contact. When the verbal and nonverbal messages are contradictory, the receiver will usually give more weight to behavioral actions than to verbal messages.[30]

A manager's office also sends powerful nonverbal cues. For example, what do the following seating arrangements mean? (1) The supervisor stays behind her desk, and you sit in a straight chair on the opposite side. (2) The two of you sit in straight chairs away from her desk, perhaps at a table. (3) The two of you sit in a seating arrangement consisting of a sofa and easy chair. To most people, the first arrangement indicates, "I'm the boss here," or "I'm in authority." The second arrangement indicates, "This is serious business." The third indicates a more casual and friendly, "Let's get to know each other."[31] Nonverbal messages can be a powerful asset to communication if they complement and support verbal messages. Managers should pay close attention to nonverbal behavior when communicating. They can learn to coordinate their verbal and nonverbal messages and at the same time be sensitive to what their peers, subordinates, and supervisors are saying nonverbally.

## Listening

One of the most important tools of manager communication is listening, both to employees and customers. Most managers now recognize that important information flows from the bottom up, not the top down, and managers had better be tuned in.[32] In the communication model in Exhibit 20.2, the listener is responsible for message reception, which is a vital link in the communication process. Listening involves the skill of grasping both facts and feelings to interpret a message's genuine meaning. Only then can the manager provide the appropriate response. Listening requires attention, energy, and skill. Although about 75 percent of effective communication is listening, most people spend only 30 to 40 percent of their time listening, which leads to many communication errors.[33] One of the secrets of highly successful salespeople is that they spend 60 to 70 percent of a sales call letting the customer talk.[34] However, listening involves much more than just not talking. Many people do not know how to listen effectively. They concentrate on formulating what they are going to say next rather than on what is being said to them. Our listening efficiency, as measured by the amount of material understood and remembered by subjects 48 hours after listening to a ten-minute message, is, on average, no better than 25 percent.[35]

What constitutes good listening? Exhibit 20.4 gives ten keys to effective listening and illustrates a number of ways to distinguish a bad from a good listener. A good listener finds areas of interest, is flexible, works hard at listening, and uses thought speed to mentally summarize, weigh, and anticipate what the speaker says. Good listening means shifting from thinking about self to empathizing with the other person and thus requires a high degree of emotional intelligence, as described in Chapter 17. Dr. Robert Buckman, a cancer specialist who teaches other doctors, as well as businesspeople, how to break bad news, emphasizes the importance of listening: "The trust that you build just by letting someone say what they feel is incredible."[36] Few things are as maddening to people as not being listened to.

Some organizations have created a culture that emphasizes active manager listening. Procter & Gamble learned how listening to employees translates into business success.

© KYOKO HAMADA

### CONCEPT CONNECTION

*About a year ago, Hillary Johnson became the editor of a small newspaper in California. Describing her new responsibilities, Johnson emphasizes the importance of **listening**. "Whenever someone walks into my office with a knitted brow and an open mouth, I say, preemptively, 'Would you like a cup of tea?' Whatever the answer, this creates a pause and sets the tone for the discussion to follow." Johnson is convinced that listening to employees, although time consuming, is essential to her success as a manager.*

**listening**
The skill of receiving messages to accurately grasp facts and feelings to interpret the genuine meaning.

# Exhibit 20.4

## Ten Keys to Effective Listening

| Keys | Poor Listener | Good Listener |
|---|---|---|
| 1. Listen actively. | Is passive, laid back | Asks questions, paraphrases what is said |
| 2. Find areas of interest. | Tunes out dry subjects | Looks for opportunities, new learning |
| 3. Resist distractions. | Is easily distracted | Fights or avoids distraction, tolerates bad habits, knows how to concentrate |
| 4. Capitalize on the fact that thought is faster. | Tends to daydream with slow speakers | Challenges, anticipates, mentally summarizes; weighs the evidence; listens between the lines to tone of voice |
| 5. Be responsive. | Is minimally involved | Nods, shows interest, give and take, positive feedback |
| 6. Judge content, not delivery. | Tunes out if delivery is poor | Judges content; skips over delivery errors |
| 7. Hold one's fire. | Has preconceptions, starts to argue | Does not judge until comprehension is complete |
| 8. Listen for ideas. | Listens for facts | Listens to central themes |
| 9. Work at listening. | Shows no energy output; faked attention | Works hard, exhibits active body state, eye contact |
| 10. Exercise one's mind. | Resists difficult material in favor of light, recreational material | Uses heavier material as exercise for the mind |

**SOURCES:** Adapted from Sherman K. Okum, "How to Be a Better Listener," *Nation's Business* (August 1975), 62; and Philip Morgan and Kent Baker, "Building a Professional Image: Improving Listening Behavior," *Supervisory Management* (November 1985), 34–38.

## PROCTER AND GAMBLE

http://www.pg.com

Procter & Gamble is one of the best companies in the world at listening to customers. Despite that, when CEO A.G. Lafley took over in 2000, he discovered that half of P & G's brands were losing market share. Moreover, the morale of marketing employees was so low that reviving customer loyalty seemed like the least of P & G's problems.

It was a wake-up call to Procter & Gamble's top executives: Listening begins at home. Managers decided to apply P & G famed market research techniques to find out why marketing employees were unhappy and what the company could do to change it. The first stage of the research was to shadow ten marketing employees for a full day, just to see the challenges they faced. One-on-one interviews were held with P & G marketing directors, brand managers, and assistant brand managers. This feedback enabled researchers to develop an employee survey questionnaire, which people could submit anonymously to a secure server at the University of Cincinnati.

Managers were amazed by the degree of openness and sincerity shown by employees in the surveys and interviews. Most people were just glad somebody was finally asking about their thoughts, feelings, and opinions. Management's willingness to hear the bad news was equally critical to the success of the project.

Listening to employees set P & G on a new path. Morale improved, the marketing department was completely transformed, and market share started going up. Most importantly, the project set the stage for a new era of listening at P & G. Managers continue to emphasize the importance of listening to both internal as well as external customers. "Gaining the hearts and minds of every employee . . . is no small challenge, and it's one that managers have to wrestle with every day to succeed," says P & G's global marketing officer James Stengel. "That's what we do with our customers—and now we're making sure we do it with our own employees."[37]

# Organizational Communication

Another aspect of management communication concerns the organization as a whole. Organizationwide communications typically flow in three directions—downward, upward, and horizontally. Managers are responsible for establishing and maintaining formal channels of communication in these three directions. Managers also use informal channels, which means they get out of their offices and mingle with employees.

## Formal Communication Channels

Formal communication channels are those that flow within the chain of command or task responsibility defined by the organization. The three formal channels and the types of information conveyed in each are illustrated in Exhibit 20.5.[38] Downward and upward communication are the primary forms of communication used in most traditional, vertically organized companies. However, many of today's organizations emphasize horizontal communication, with people continuously sharing information across departments and levels.

Electronic communication such as e-mail and instant messaging have made it easier than ever for information to flow in all directions. For example, the U.S. Army is using technology to rapidly transmit communications about weather conditions, the latest intelligence on the enemy, and so forth to lieutenants on the battlefield. Similarly, the Navy uses instant messaging to communicate within ships, across Navy divisions, and even back to the Pentagon in Washington. "Instant messaging has allowed us to keep our crew members on the same page at the same time," says Lt. Cmdr. Mike Houston, who oversees the Navy's communications program. "Lives are at stake in real time, and we're seeing a new level of communication and readiness."[39]

### Downward Communication

The most familiar and obvious flow of formal communication, downward communication, refers to the messages and information sent from top management to subordinates in a downward direction.

**formal communication channel**
A communication channel that flows within the chain of command or task responsibility defined by the organization.

**downward communication**
Messages sent from top management down to subordinates.

## Exhibit 20.5

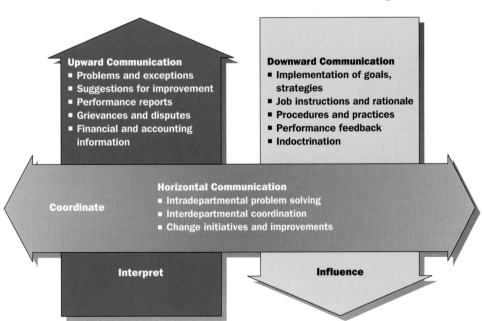

**Downward, Upward, and Horizontal Communication in Organizations**

**Upward Communication**
- Problems and exceptions
- Suggestions for improvement
- Performance reports
- Grievances and disputes
- Financial and accounting information

**Downward Communication**
- Implementation of goals, strategies
- Job instructions and rationale
- Procedures and practices
- Performance feedback
- Indoctrination

**Horizontal Communication**
- Intradepartmental problem solving
- Interdepartmental coordination
- Change initiatives and improvements

Coordinate

Interpret     Influence

**SOURCE:** Adapted from Richard L. Daft and Richard M. Steers, *Organizations: A Micro/Macro Approach*, 538. Copyright © 1986 by Scott, Foresman and Company. Used with permission.

Managers can communicate downward to employees in many ways. Some of the most common are through speeches, messages in company newsletters, e-mail, information leaflets tucked into pay envelopes, material on bulletin boards, and policy and procedures manuals. Managers sometimes use creative approaches to downward communication to make sure employees get the message. Mike Olson, plant manager at Ryerson Midwest Coil Processing, noticed that workers were dropping expensive power tools, so he hung price tags on the tools to show the replacement cost. Employees solved the problem by finding a way to hook up the tools so they wouldn't be dropped. Olson's symbolic communication created a climate of working together for solutions.[40]

Managers also have to decide what to communicate about. It is impossible for managers to communicate with employees about everything that goes on in the organization, so they have to make choices about the important information to communicate.[41] Recall our discussion of purpose-directed communication from early in this chapter. Downward communication usually encompasses these five topics:

1. *Implementation of goals and strategies.* Communicating new strategies and goals provides information about specific targets and expected behaviors. It gives direction for lower levels of the organization. *Example:* "The new quality campaign is for real. We must improve product quality if we are to survive."
2. *Job instructions and rationale.* These are directives on how to do a specific task and how the job relates to other organizational activities. *Example:* "Purchasing should order the bricks now so the work crew can begin construction of the building in two weeks."
3. *Procedures and practices.* These are messages defining the organization's policies, rules, regulations, benefits, and structural arrangements. *Example:* "After your first 90 days of employment, you are eligible to enroll in our company-sponsored savings plan."
4. *Performance feedback.* These messages appraise how well individuals and departments are doing their jobs. *Example:* "Joe, your work on the computer network has greatly improved the efficiency of our ordering process."
5. *Indoctrination.* These messages are designed to motivate employees to adopt the company's mission and cultural values and to participate in special ceremonies, such as picnics and United Way campaigns. *Example:* "The company thinks of its employees as family and would like to invite everyone to attend the annual picnic and fair on March 3."

The major problem with downward communication is *drop off*, the distortion or loss of message content. Although formal communications are a powerful way to reach all employees, much information gets lost—25 percent or so each time a message is passed from one person to the next. In addition, the message can be distorted if it travels a great distance from its originating source to the ultimate receiver. A tragic example is the following historical example:

> *A reporter was present at a hamlet burned down by the U.S. Army 1st Air Cavalry Division in 1967. Investigations showed that the order from the Division headquarters to the brigade was: "On no occasion must hamlets be burned down."*
>
> *The brigade radioed the battalion: "Do not burn down any hamlets unless you are absolutely convinced that the Viet Cong are in them."*
>
> *The battalion radioed the infantry company at the scene: "If you think there are any Viet Cong in the hamlet, burn it down."*
>
> *The company commander ordered his troops: "Burn down that hamlet."*[42]

Information drop off cannot be completely avoided, but the techniques described in the previous sections can reduce it substantially. Using the right communication channel, consistency between verbal and nonverbal messages, and active listening can maintain communication accuracy as it moves down the organization.

## Upward Communication

Formal upward communication includes messages that flow from the lower to the higher levels in the organization's hierarchy. Most organizations take pains to build in healthy channels for upward communication. Employees need to air grievances, report progress, and provide feedback on management initiatives. Coupling a healthy flow of upward and downward communication ensures that the communication circuit between managers and employees is complete.[43] Five types of information communicated upward are the following:

**upward communication** Messages transmitted from the lower to the higher levels in the organization's hierarchy.

1. *Problems and exceptions.* These messages describe serious problems with and exceptions to routine performance in order to make senior managers aware of difficulties. *Example:* "The printer has been out of operation for two days, and it will be at least a week before a new one arrives."
2. *Suggestions for improvement.* These messages are ideas for improving task-related procedures to increase quality or efficiency. *Example:* "I think we should eliminate step 2 in the audit procedure because it takes a lot of time and produces no results."
3. *Performance reports.* These messages include periodic reports that inform management how individuals and departments are performing. *Example:* "We completed the audit report for Smith & Smith on schedule but are one week behind on the Jackson report."
4. *Grievances and disputes.* These messages are employee complaints and conflicts that travel up the hierarchy for a hearing and possible resolution. *Example:* "The manager of operations research cannot get the cooperation of the Lincoln plant for the study of machine utilization."
5. *Financial and accounting information.* These messages pertain to costs, accounts receivable, sales volume, anticipated profits, return on investment, and other matters of interest to senior managers. *Example:* "Costs are 2 percent over budget, but sales are 10 percent ahead of target, so the profit picture for the third quarter is excellent."

Many organizations make a great effort to facilitate upward communication. Mechanisms include suggestion boxes, employee surveys, open-door policies, management information system reports, and face-to-face conversations between workers and executives. Consider how one entrepreneur keeps the upward communication flowing.

Pat Croce is currently involved in the development of Pirate Soul, "the ultimate pirate museum," in Key West. But he has several other businesses going, too. Like many entrepreneurs, Croce spends a lot of time on the road, traveling from his home office in Philadelphia all across the country.

To make sure he stays in touch with what's going on in his various businesses, Croce implemented a key communication tool he calls the Five-Fifteen. Each Friday, all employees and managers take 15 minutes to write brief progress reports and forward them to their immediate supervisors. Within a few days, all the information trickles up to Croce in a sort of "corporate Cliff Notes" version. The idea is that the reports take Croce only five minutes to read (hence the name Five-Fifteen). Croce says the Five-Fifteens have enabled him to keep in touch with the little details that make a big difference in the success of his businesses.

Employees typically look at the Five-Fifteens as a chance to be heard, while Croce looks at them as a way to keep his finger on the pulse of each business. In addition, the reports give him a chance to compliment and thank people for their accomplishments and offer questions or suggestions in areas that need improvement.[44]

**PAT CROCE, ENTREPRENEUR**
http://www.croceonthemove.com

# Unlocking Creative Solutions Through Technology

### Amazon.com Keeps Track of Employees' "Pulse Rate"

How do managers at Amazon.com keep in touch with employees' opinions and feelings about company decisions? By taking the organization's collective pulse twice a week.

Amazon works with eePulse, an Ann Arbor, Michigan–based applications service provider, to electronically poll employees biweekly on their opinions and attitudes about various developments within the company. The electronic survey and communications tool uses a question format and asks employees to rate their "pulse," or energy level. Responses range from "not doing much, not having fun" to "overwhelmed by work and need help." Employees also have an opportunity for open comments about their work environment. These quick e-mail surveys, which take about two minutes to complete, provide feedback on a regular basis, enabling managers to collect information and assess how things are going in real time. "Changes happen very quickly here," says one

manager. "By polling people this way, by e-mail, it's consistent and fast and provides the data we need." Employees are encouraged to talk to their managers about any specific concerns, and managers are trained to effectively use the eePulse and follow up on potential problems, such as low pulse rates or an employee whose pulse is about to go through the roof from overwork.

Whereas managers loved the new communications tool from the beginning, employees took a little longer to warm up to it. With typical management surveys, employees rarely see changes after results are compiled and publicized, and Amazon's workers expected this was just another useless poll. However, after numerous months in which Amazon's managers consistently reported back results to the employees and made sincere efforts to address concerns, attitudes toward eePulse have changed. Some people even enjoy regularly keeping tabs on the survey results and finding out what their co-workers are saying about their jobs and the company.

**Source**: Teresa Welbourne, "New ASP Takes Workforce's 'Pulse,'" *The New Corporate University Review* (July–August 2000), 20–21.

In today's fast-paced world, many managers find it hard to maintain constant communication. Ideas such as the Five-Fifteen help keep information flowing upward so managers get feedback from lower levels. This chapter's Unlocking Creative Solutions Through Technology box describes an idea that Amazon.com uses to find out what's on employees' minds.

Despite these efforts, however, barriers to accurate upward communication exist. Managers may resist hearing about employee problems, or employees might not trust managers sufficiently to push information upward.[45] Innovative companies search for ways to ensure that information gets to top managers without distortion. One creative approach is found at Golden Corral, a restaurant chain with headquarters in Raleigh, North Carolina. Top managers spend at least one weekend a year in the trenches—cutting steaks, rolling silverware, setting tables, and taking out the trash. By understanding the daily routines and challenges of waiters, chefs, and other employees at their restaurants, Golden Corral executives increase their awareness of how management actions affect others.[46]

## Horizontal Communication

**horizontal communication**
The lateral or diagonal exchange of messages among peers or co-workers.

**Horizontal communication** is the lateral or diagonal exchange of messages among peers or co-workers. It may occur within or across departments. The purpose of horizontal communication is not only to inform but also to request support and coordinate activities. Horizontal communication falls into one of three categories:

1. *Intradepartmental problem solving.* These messages take place among members of the same department and concern task accomplishment. *Example:* "Kelly, can you help us figure out how to complete this medical expense report form?"

**CONCEPT CONNECTION**

*Valassis Communication, Inc.'s "On the M.O.V.E." committee (which stands for Motivate Our Valassis Employees) researches and implements programs such as flexible hours, job sharing, and suggestion review systems, as well as plans a variety of "lighten up" events that contribute to high employee morale and a strong corporate culture. Valassis formed the committee to improve **horizontal communication** and create positive energy across the entire organization. It is one of many techniques VCI uses to stimulate new ideas, promote teamwork, and encourage ongoing communication.*

2. *Interdepartmental coordination.* Interdepartmental messages facilitate the accomplishment of joint projects or tasks. *Example:* "Bob, please contact marketing and production and arrange a meeting to discuss the specifications for the new subassembly. It looks like we might not be able to meet their requirements."

3. *Change initiatives and improvements.* These messages are designed to share information among teams and departments that can help the organization change, grow, and improve. *Example:* "We are streamlining the company travel procedures and would like to discuss them with your department."

Horizontal communication is particularly important in learning organizations, where teams of workers are continuously solving problems and searching for new ways of doing things. Recall from Chapter 10 that many organizations build in horizontal communications in the form of task forces, committees, or even a matrix structure to encourage coordination. At Chicago's Northwestern Memorial Hospital, two doctors created a horizontal task force to solve a serious patient health problem.

---

We've all heard of it happening—a patient checks into the hospital for a routine procedure and ends up getting sicker instead of better. Hospital-borne infections afflict about 2 million patients—and kill nearly 100,000—each year. Greater antibiotic use causes the germs to develop greater resistance. The infection epidemic is growing worse worldwide, but a task force at Northwestern Memorial Hospital has reversed the trend by breaking down communication barriers.

When a cancer patient became Northwestern's first victim of a new strain of deadly bacteria, infectious-disease specialists Lance Peterson and Gary Noskin realized it would take everyone's help to defeat the insidious enemy. As infection spread throughout the hospital, they launched a regular Monday morning meeting to plot countermoves. Although some physicians and staff members were offended at having their procedures questioned, the goal of preventing needless deaths overrode their concerns. Absolute candor was the rule at the Monday morning meetings, which involved not only doctors and nurses, but also lab technicians, pharmacists, computer technicians, and admissions representatives. One pharmacist, for example, recognized that antibiotics act as fertilizer for many bacteria, which encouraged physicians to decrease their use of antibiotics in favor of alternative treatments. Computer representatives and admissions people got together to develop software to identify which returning patients might pose a threat for bringing infection back into the hospital. Eventually, the task force even included maintenance staff when studies showed that a shortage of sinks was inhibiting hand-washing.

Increasing horizontal communication paid off at Northwestern, saving millions in annual medical costs and at least a few lives. Over three years, Northwestern's rate of hospital-borne infections plunged 22 percent. In a recent fiscal year, such infections totaled 5.1 per 1,000 patients, roughly half the national average.[47]

**NORTHWESTERN MEMORIAL HOSPITAL**
http://www.nmh.org

## Team Communication Channels

A special type of horizontal communication is communicating in teams. Teams are the basic building block of many organizations. Team members work together to accomplish tasks, and the team's communication structure influences both team performance and employee satisfaction.

Research into team communication has focused on two characteristics: the extent to which team communications are centralized and the nature of the team's task.[48] The relationship between these characteristics is illustrated in Exhibit 20.6. In a centralized network, team members must communicate through one individual to solve problems or make decisions. In a decentralized network, individuals can communicate freely with other team members. Members process information equally among themselves until all agree on a decision.[49]

In laboratory experiments, centralized communication networks achieved faster solutions for simple problems. Members could simply pass relevant information to a central person for a decision. Decentralized communications were slower for simple problems because information was passed among individuals until someone finally put the pieces together and solved the problem. However, for more complex problems, the decentralized communication network was faster. Because all necessary information was not restricted to one person, a pooling of information through widespread communications provided greater input into the decision. Similarly, the accuracy of problem solving was related to problem complexity. The centralized networks made fewer errors on simple problems but more errors on complex ones. Decentralized networks were less accurate for simple problems but more accurate for complex ones.[50]

The implication for organizations is as follows: In a highly competitive global environment, organizations typically use teams to deal with complex problems. When team activities are complex and difficult, all members should share information in a decentralized structure to solve problems. Teams need a free flow of communication in all directions.[51] At start-up Alteon Web Systems (now owned by Nortel Networks), teams learned to make important decisions in a single meeting. Each person would collect as much information as possible to support his or her

### centralized network
A team communication structure in which team members communicate through a single individual to solve problems or make decisions.

### decentralized network
A team communication structure in which team members freely communicate with one another and arrive at decisions together.

---

Exhibit 20.6

### Effectiveness of Team Communication Networks

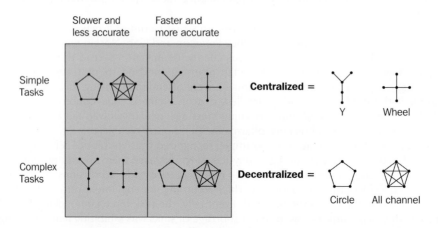

**SOURCES:** Adapted from A. Bavelas and D. Barrett, "An Experimental Approach to Organization Communication," *Personnel* 27 (1951), 366–371; M.E. Shaw, *Group Dynamics: The Psychology of Small Group Behavior* (New York: McGraw-Hill, 1976); and E.M. Rogers and R.A. Rogers, *Communication in Organizations* (New York: Free Press, 1976).

proposed ideas or solutions and then share it with the team. Constructive conflict was encouraged, with one team member acting as a referee to help the team arrive at the best decision based on the information available.[52] Teams that perform routine tasks spend less time processing information, and thus communications can be centralized. Data can be channeled to a supervisor for decisions, freeing workers to spend a greater percentage of time on task activities.

## Personal Communication Channels

Personal communication channels exist outside the formally authorized channels. These are informal communications that coexist with formal channels but may skip hierarchical levels, cutting across vertical chains of command to connect virtually anyone in the organization. In most organizations, these informal channels are the primary way information spreads and work gets accomplished. Three important types of personal communication channels are *personal networks*, *management by wandering around*, and the *grapevine*.

### Developing Personal Communication Networks

Personal networking refers to the acquisition and cultivation of personal relationships that cross departmental, hierarchical, and even organizational boundaries.[53] Smart managers consciously develop personal communication networks and encourage others to do so. In a communication network, people share information across boundaries and reach out to anyone who can further the goals of the team and organization. Exhibit 20.7 illustrates a communication network. Some people are central to the network while others play only a peripheral role. The key is that relationships are built across functional and hierarchical boundaries.

The value of personal networks for managers is that people who have more contacts have greater influence in the organization and get more accomplished. For example, in exhibit 20.7, Sharon has a well-developed personal communication network, sharing information and assistance with many people across the marketing, manufacturing, and engineering departments. Contrast Sharon's contacts with those of Mike or Jasmine. Who do you think is likely to have greater access to resources

**personal communication channels**
Communication channels that exist outside the formally authorized channels and do not adhere to the organization's hierarchy of authority.

**personal networking**
The acquisition and cultivation of personal relationships that cross departmental, hierarchical, and even organizational boundaries.

## Exhibit 20.7

### An Organizational Communication Network

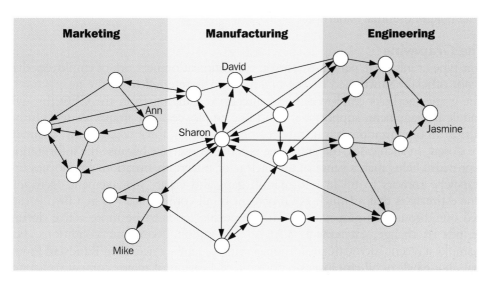

and more influence in the organization? Here are a few tips from one expert net-worker for building a personal communication network:[54]

1.  *Build it before you need it.* Smart managers don't wait until they need something to start building a network of personal relationships—by then, it's too late. Instead, they show genuine interest in others and develop honest connections.
2.  *Never eat lunch alone.* People who excel at networking make an effort to be visible and connect with as many people as possible. Master networkers keep their social as well as business conference and event calendars full.
3.  *Make it win–win.* Successful networking isn't just about getting what *you* want; it's also about making sure other people in the network get what *they* want.
4.  *Focus on diversity.* The broader your base of contacts, the broader your range of influence. Build connections with people from as many different areas of interest as possible (both within and outside of the organization).

Most of us know from personal experience that "who you know" sometimes counts for more than what you know. By cultivating a broad network of contacts, managers can significantly extend their influence and accomplish greater results.

## Management by Wandering Around

**management by wandering around (MBWA)**
A communication technique in which managers interact directly with workers to exchange information.

The communication technique known as management by wandering around (MBWA) was made famous by the books *In Search of Excellence* and *A Passion for Excellence*.[55] These books describe executives who talk directly with employees to learn what is going on. MBWA works for managers at all levels. They mingle and develop positive relationships with employees and learn directly from them about their department, division, or organization. For example, the president of ARCO had a habit of visiting a district field office. Rather than schedule a big strategic meeting with the district supervisor, he would come in unannounced and chat with the lowest-level employees. In any organization, both upward and downward communications are enhanced with MBWA. Managers have a chance to describe key ideas and values to employees and, in turn, learn about the problems and issues confronting employees.

When managers fail to take advantage of MBWA, they become aloof and isolated from employees. For example, Peter Anderson, president of Ztel, Inc., a maker of television switching systems, preferred not to personally communicate with employees. He managed at arm's length. As one manager said, "I don't know how many times I asked Peter to come to the lab, but he stayed in his office. He wasn't that visible to the troops." This formal, impersonal management style contributed to Ztel's troubles and eventual bankruptcy.[56]

## The Grapevine

**grapevine**
An informal, person-to-person communication network of employees that is not officially sanctioned by the organization.

One type of informal, person-to-person communication network of employees that is not officially sanctioned by the organization is referred to as the grapevine.[57] The grapevine links employees in all directions, ranging from the CEO through middle management, support staff, and line employees. The grapevine will always exist in an organization, but it can become a dominant force when formal channels are closed. In such cases, the grapevine is actually a service because the information it provides helps makes sense of an unclear or uncertain situation. Employees use grapevine rumors to fill in information gaps and clarify management decisions. One estimate is that as much as 70 percent of all communication in a firm is carried out through its grapevine.[58] The grapevine tends to be more active during periods of change, excitement, anxiety, and sagging economic conditions. For example, a recent survey by professional employment services firm Randstad found that about half of all employees reported first hearing of major company changes through the grapevine.[59] Consider what happened at Jel, Inc., an auto supply firm that was under great pressure from Ford and GM to increase quality. Management changes to improve quality—learning statistical process control, introducing a new compensation system, buying a fancy new screw machine from Germany—all started out as rumors, circulating days ahead of the actual announcements, and were generally accurate.[60]

Surprising aspects of the grapevine are its accuracy and its relevance to the organization. About 80 percent of grapevine communications pertain to business-related topics rather than personal, vicious gossip. Moreover, from 70 to 90 percent of the details passed through a grapevine are accurate.[61] Many managers would like the grapevine to be destroyed because they consider its rumors to be untrue, malicious, and harmful. Typically, this is not the case; however, managers should be aware that almost five of every six important messages are carried to some extent by the grapevine rather than through official channels. In a survey of 22,000 shift workers in varied industries, 55 percent said they get most of their information via the grapevine.[62] Smart managers understand the company's grapevine. They recognize who's connected to whom and which employees are key players in the informal spread of information. In all cases, but particularly in times of crisis, executives need to manage communications effectively so that the grapevine is not the only source of information.[63]

# Communicating during Turbulent Times

During turbulent times, communication becomes even more important. To build trust and promote learning and problem solving, managers incorporate ideas such as open communication, dialogue, and feedback and learning. In addition, they develop their crisis communication skills for communicating with both employees and the public in exceptionally challenging or frightening circumstances.

## Open Communication

A recent trend that reflects managers' increased emphasis on empowering employees, building trust and commitment, and enhancing collaboration is open communication. Open communication means sharing all types of information throughout the company, across functional and hierarchical levels. Many companies, such as Springfield Remanufacturing Corporation, AmeriSteel, and Whole Foods Markets, are opening the financial books to workers at all levels and training employees to understand how and why the company operates as it does. At Wabash National Corporation, one of the nation's leading truck-trailer manufacturers, employees complete several hours of business training and attend regular meetings on the shop floor to review the company's financial performance.[64]

Open communication runs counter to the traditional flow of selective information downward from supervisors to subordinates. By breaking down conventional hierarchical barriers to communication, the organization can gain the benefit of all employees' ideas. The same ideas batted back and forth among a few managers do not lead to effective learning or to a network of relationships that keep companies thriving. New voices and conversations involving a broad spectrum of people revitalize and enhance organizational communication.[65] Open communication also builds trust and a commitment to common goals, which is essential in organizations that depend on collaboration and knowledge-sharing to accomplish their purpose. Fifty percent of executives surveyed report that open communication is a key to building trust in the organization.[66]

**open communication**
Sharing all types of information throughout the company, across functional and hierarchical levels.

## Dialogue

**dialogue**
A group communication process aimed at creating a culture based on collaboration, fluidity, trust, and commitment to shared goals.

Another popular means of fostering trust and collaboration in organizations is through dialogue. The "roots of dialogue" are *dia* and *logos*, which can be thought of as *stream of meaning*. Dialogue is a group communication process in which people together create a stream of shared meaning that enables them to understand each other and share a view of the world.[67] People may start out at polar opposites, but by talking openly, they discover common ground, common issues, and shared goals on which they can build a better future.

A useful way to describe dialogue is to contrast it with discussion (see Exhibit 20.8). The intent of discussion, generally, is to deliver one's point of view and persuade others to adopt it. A discussion is often resolved by logic or "beating down" opponents. Dialogue, by contrast, asks that participants suspend their attachments to a particular viewpoint so that a deeper level of listening, synthesis, and meaning can evolve from the group. A dialogue's focus is to reveal feelings and build common ground. Both forms of communication—dialogue and discussion—can result in change. However, the result of discussion is limited to the topic being deliberated, whereas the result of dialogue is characterized by group unity, shared meaning, and transformed mindsets. As new and deeper solutions are developed, a trusting relationship is built among team members.[68]

Exhibit **20.8**

### Dialogue and Discussion: The Differences

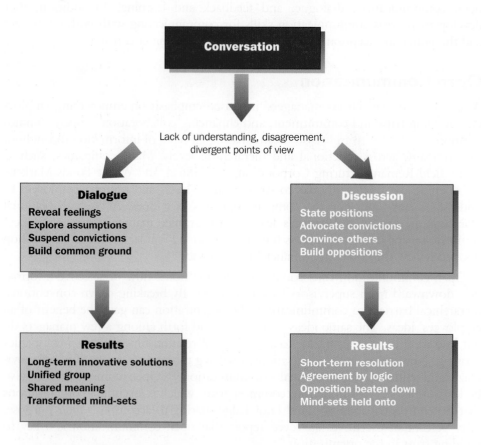

**SOURCE:** Adapted from Edgar Schein, "On Dialogue, Culture, and Organizational Learning," *Organizational Dynamics* (Autumn 1993), 46.

## Crisis Communication

Over the past few years, the sheer number and scope of crises has made communication a more demanding job for managers. Organizations face small crises every day, such as charges of racial discrimination, a factory fire, or a flu epidemic. Moreover, acts of intentional evil, such as bombings or kidnappings, continue to increase, causing serious repercussions for people and organizations.[69] Managers can develop four primary skills for communicating in a crisis.[70]

- *Maintain your focus.* Good crisis communicators don't allow themselves to be overwhelmed by the situation. Calmness and listening become more important than ever. Managers also learn to tailor their communications to reflect hope and optimism at the same time they acknowledge the current difficulties.
- *Be visible.* Many managers underestimate just how important their presence is during a crisis.[71] As we discussed in Chapter 1, people need to feel that someone is in control. A manager's job is to step out immediately, both to reassure employees and respond to public concerns. Face-to-face communication with employees is crucial for letting people know that managers care about them and what they're going through.
- *Get the awful truth out.*[72] Effective managers gather as much information as they can, do their best to determine the facts, and tell the truth to employees and the public as soon as possible. Getting the truth out quickly prevents rumors and misunderstandings.
- *Communicate a vision for the future.* People need to feel that they have something to work for and look forward to. Moments of crisis present opportunities for managers to communication a vision of a better future and unite people toward common goals.

## Feedback and Learning

Feedback occurs when managers use evaluation and communication to help individuals and the organization learn and improve. It enables managers to determine whether they have been successful in communicating with others. Recall from Exhibit 20.2 that feedback is an important part of the communication process. However, despite its importance, feedback is often neglected. Giving and receiving feedback is typically difficult for both managers and employees. Yet, by avoiding feedback, people miss a valuable opportunity to help one another learn, develop, and improve.[73] At General Electric, managers are evaluated partly on their ability to give and receive effective feedback.[74]

Successful managers focus their feedback to help develop the capacities of subordinates and to teach the organization how to better reach its goals. Feedback is an important means by which individuals and organizations learn from their mistakes and improve their work. When managers enlist the whole organization in reviewing the outcomes of activities, they can quickly learn what works and what doesn't and use that information to improve the organization. Consider how the U.S. Army's feedback system promotes whole-system learning.

At the National Training Center just south of Death Valley, U.S. Army troops engage in a simulated battle: The "enemy" has sent unmanned aerial vehicles (UAVs) to gather targeting data. When the troops fire on the UAVs, they reveal their location to attack helicopters hovering just behind a nearby ridge. After the exercise, unit members and their superiors hold an *after-action review* to review battle plans, discuss what worked and what didn't, and talk about how to do things better. General William Hertzog suggests that inexpensive decoy UAVs might be just the thing to make a distracted enemy reveal its location. The observation became a "lesson learned" for the entire army, and UAVs became an important part of battle operations in Iraq.

**U.S. ARMY**
http://www.army.mil

Many researchers attribute the transformation of the army from a demoralized, dysfunctional organization following the Vietnam War into an elite force capable of effectively accomplishing Operation Iraqi Freedom to this unique feedback and learning system. In the U.S. Army, after-action reviews take just 15 minutes, and they occur after every identifiable event—large or small, simulated or real. The review involves asking four simple questions: What was supposed to happen? What actually happened? What accounts for any difference? What can we learn? It is a process of identifying mistakes, of innovating, and of continually learning from experience.

The lessons are based not only on simulated battles, but also on real-life experiences of soldiers in the field. The Center for Army Lessons Learned (CALL) sends experts into the field to observe after-action reviews, interview soldiers, and compile intelligence reports. Leaders in all army divisions are currently engaged in a detailed analysis of lessons learned during Operation Iraqi Freedom and Operation Enduring Freedom. The lessons will be used to train soldiers and develop action plans for resolving problems in future conflicts. For example, many of the problems and issues from a similar process following Operation Desert Storm had been resolved by the time of Operation Iraqi Freedom. A primary focus for current leaders is to improve training regarding the difficult shift from offensive operations to humanitarian and relief efforts.[75]

In this example, the organization is learning by communicating feedback about the consequences of field operations and simulated battles. Compiling what is learned and using communication feedback create an improved organization. After-action reviews are also used in corporate America. Steelcase Inc., an office furniture manufacturer, and BP are among the companies adapting the army's system to create a process of continuous learning and improvement. BP credits the feedback system for $700 million in cost savings and other gains.[76]

# Managing Organizational Communication

Many of the ideas described in this chapter pertain to barriers to communication and how to overcome them. Exhibit 20.9 lists some of the major barriers to communication, along with some techniques for overcoming them.

Exhibit 20.9

**Communication Barriers and Ways to Overcome Them**

| Barriers | How to Overcome |
|---|---|
| **Individual** | |
| Interpersonal dynamics | Active listening |
| Channels and media | Selection of appropriate channel |
| Semantics | Knowledge of other's perspective |
| Inconsistent cues | MBWA |
| | |
| **Organizational** | |
| Status and power differences | Climate of trust, Dialogue |
| Departmental needs and goals | Development and use of formal channels |
| Lack of formal channels | Encouragement of multiple channels, formal and informal |
| Communication network unsuited to task | Changing organization or group structure to fit communication needs |
| Poor coordination | Feedback and learning |

# Barriers to Communication

Barriers can be categorized as those that exist at the individual level and those that exist at the organizational level.

## Individual Barriers

First, there are *interpersonal barriers*; these include problems with emotions and perceptions held by employees. For example, rigid perceptual labeling or stereotyping prevents people from modifying or altering their opinions. If a person's mind is made up before the communication starts, communication will fail. Moreover, people with different backgrounds or knowledge may interpret a communication in different ways.

Second, *selecting the wrong channel* or *medium* for sending a communication can be a problem. For example, when a message is emotional, it is better to transmit it face to face rather than in writing. E-mail can be particularly risky for discussing difficult issues. On the other hand, e-mail is highly efficient for routine messages but lacks the capacity for rapid feedback and multiple cues needed for difficult messages.

Third, *semantics* often causes communication problems. Semantics pertains to the meaning of words and the way they are used. A word such as *effectiveness* may mean achieving high production to a factory superintendent and employee satisfaction to a human resources staff specialist. Many common words have an average of 28 definitions; thus, communicators must take care to select the words that will accurately encode ideas.[77] Language differences can also be a barrier in today's organizations. At Semifreddi's, an artisan bread bakery in Emeryville, California, CEO Tom Frainier had to hire translators to help him communicate effectively with his employees, most of whom came from Mexico, Laos, China, Peru, Cambodia, Yemen, and Vietnam.[78]

© AP HONOT BY PAVEL RAHMAN

**CONCEPT CONNECTION**

*The "telephone ladies" of Bangladesh, an impoverished South Asian nation where the average person lives on a dollar a day, provide a significant **communication** service for farmers, fishermen, and small business owners. The country has only about 3 telephone lines per 1,000 people, making it difficult for people to **give and receive feedback** from customers and colleagues. About 41,000 women have purchased cellular phones with no-collateral loans from Grameen Bank, the pioneer of the microfinance industry. The telephone ladies offer phone services in about half the villages, earning around $50 a month while helping farmers and fishermen close deals, check competitors' prices, and stay in touch with colleagues and family.*

*Go to the ethical dilemma on page 760 that pertains to individual barriers to communication.*

*Take A Moment*

Fourth, sending *inconsistent cues* between verbal and nonverbal communications will confuse the receiver. If one's facial expression does not reflect one's words, the communication will contain noise and uncertainty. The tone of voice and body language should be consistent with the words, and actions should not contradict words.

**semantics**
The meaning of words and the way they are used.

## Organizational Barriers

Organizational barriers pertain to factors for the organization as a whole. First is the problem of *status and power differences*. Low-power people may be reluctant to pass bad news up the hierarchy, thus giving the wrong impression to upper levels.[79] High-power people may not pay attention or may think that low-status people have little to contribute.

Second, *differences across departments in terms of needs and goals* interfere with communications. Each department perceives problems in its own terms. The production department is concerned with production efficiency whereas the marketing department's goal is to get the product to the customer in a hurry.

Third, the *absence of formal channels* reduces communication effectiveness. Organizations must provide adequate upward, downward, and horizontal communication in the form of employee surveys, open-door policies, newsletters, memos, task forces, and liaison personnel. Without these formal channels, the organization cannot communicate as a whole.

Fourth, the *communication flow* may not fit the team's or organization's task. If a centralized communication structure is used for nonroutine tasks, there will not be enough information circulated to solve problems. The organization, department, or team is most efficient when the amount of communication flowing among employees fits the task.

A final problem is *poor coordination*, so that different parts of the organization are working in isolation without knowing and understanding what other parts are doing. Top executives are out of touch with lower levels, or departments and divisions are poorly coordinated so that people do not understand how the system works together as a whole.

## Overcoming Communication Barriers

Managers can design the organization so as to encourage positive, effective communication. Designing involves both individual skills and organizational actions.

### Individual Skills

Perhaps the most important individual skill is *active listening*. Active listening means asking questions, showing interest, and occasionally paraphrasing what the speaker has said to ensure that one is interpreting accurately. Active listening also means providing feedback to the sender to complete the communication loop.

Second, individuals should select the *appropriate channel* for the message. A complicated message should be sent through a rich channel, such as face-to-face discussion or telephone. Routine messages and data can be sent through memos, letters, or e-mail, because there is little chance of misunderstanding.

Third, senders and receivers should make a special effort to understand each other's perspective. Managers can sensitize themselves to the information receiver so that they will be better able to target the message, detect bias, and clarify missed interpretations. By communicators understanding others' perspectives, semantics can be clarified, perceptions understood, and objectivity maintained.

The fourth individual skill is *management by wandering around*. Managers must be willing to get out of the office and check communications with others. Glenn Tilton, the CEO of United Airlines, takes every opportunity to introduce himself to employees and customers and find out what's on their minds. He logs more airplane time than many of his company's pilots, visits passenger lounges, and chats with employees on concourses, galleys and airport terminals.[80] Through direct observation and face-to-face meetings, managers develop an understanding of the organization and are able to communicate important ideas and values directly to others.

### Organizational Actions

Perhaps the most important thing managers can do for the organization is to create a *climate of trust and openness*. Open communication and dialogue can encourage people to communicate honestly with one another. Subordinates will feel free to transmit negative as well as positive messages without fear of retribution. Efforts to develop interpersonal skills among employees can also foster openness, honesty, and trust.

**CONCEPT CONNECTION**

*The scoreboard at Colonial Mills, Inc., a $7 million specialty-rug manufacturer in Pawtucket, Rhode Island, overcomes communication barriers by helping all employees get involved in business targets and results. The board stretches 30 feet and covers most of the lunchroom wall. A big gold rocket ship in the middle shows the year-to-date company profit. Columns for winding, braiding, and other production departments show monthly output—cans filled, square feet braided, etc.—all compared with the company's plan. The Colonial Mills scoreboard is a unique communication channel that encourages upward, downward, and horizontal communication. "Our targets aren't the powers-that-be coming down and saying 'This shall be the number,'" says Colonial Mills CEO Don Scarlata. "They're numbers everybody has discussed and signed off on."*

Second, managers should develop and use *formal information channels* in all directions. Scandinavian Design uses two newsletters to reach employees. GM's Packard Electric plant is designed to share all pertinent information—financial, future plans, quality, performance—with employees. Dana Corporation has developed innovative programs such as the "Here's a Thought" board—called a HAT rack—to get ideas and feedback from workers. Other techniques include direct mail, bulletin boards, and employee surveys.

Third, managers should encourage the use of *multiple channels*, including both formal and informal communications. Multiple communication channels include written directives, face-to-face discussions, MBWA, and the grapevine. For example, managers at GM's Packard Electric plant use multimedia, including a monthly newspaper, frequent meetings of employee teams, and an electronic news display in the cafeteria. Sending messages through multiple channels increases the likelihood that they will be properly received.

Fourth, the structure should *fit communication needs*. An organization can be designed to use teams, task forces, project managers, or a matrix structure as needed to facilitate the horizontal flow of information for coordination and problem solving. Structure should also reflect information needs. When team or department tasks are difficult, a decentralized structure should be implemented to encourage discussion and participation.

A system of organizational *feedback and learning* can help to overcome problems of poor coordination. Harrah's created a *Communication Team* as part of its structure at the Casino/Holiday Inn in Las Vegas. The team includes one member from each department. This cross-functional team deals with urgent company problems and helps people think beyond the scope of their own departments to communicate with anyone and everyone to solve those problems.

## Manager's Solution

This chapter described several important points about communicating in organizations. Communication takes up at least 80 percent of a manager's time. Managers' communication is purpose-directed, in that it unites people around a shared vision and goals and directs attention to the values and behaviors that achieve goals. Communication is a process of encoding an idea into a message, which is sent through a channel and decoded by a receiver. Communication among people can be affected by communication channels, nonverbal communication, and listening skills. An important aspect of management communication is persuasion. The ability to persuade others to behave in ways that help accomplish the vision and goals is crucial to good management. Managers frequently use symbols, stories, and metaphors to persuade and influence others.

At the organizational level, managers are concerned with managing formal communications in a downward, upward, and horizontal direction. Informal communications also are important, especially management by wandering around, developing personal networks, and the grapevine. Moreover, research shows that communication structures in teams and departments should reflect the underlying tasks. Open communication, dialogue, feedback, and learning are important communication mechanisms during times of turbulence and uncertainty. In addition, today's managers have to develop effective crisis communication skills. Four important skills for communicating in a crisis are to remain calm and focused, be visible, "get the awful truth out," and communicate a vision for a brighter future.

Patrick Charmel, CEO of Griffin Hospital, described in the chapter opening, showed his commitment to open and honest communication when the FBI asked him to keep quiet about a possible case of anthrax poisoning at the Derby,

Connecticut, hospital. Charmel proved himself to be a master of communicating in a crisis. His primary concern was for the safety of his employees and of the larger community. He immediately scheduled informational meetings with employees throughout the hospital to let them know about the possible case of anthrax and review guidelines and procedures for handling such a crisis. Prior to making the information public, Charmel gathered as much information and data as he could and sought the counsel of trusted advisors. Ultimately, he decided honesty was the best policy. Rather than shunning publicity, Charmel welcomed reporters. Along with members of his management team and several physicians, Charmel kept the media and the public up to date on what was happening with the case throughout the night and into the next day, when the diagnosis was confirmed and Mrs. Lundgren died. Most news stories related to anthrax poisonings in organizations such as the U.S. Postal Service, newsrooms, and the U.S. Congress focused on the failure of these organizations to adequately deal with the crisis. The news stories of Griffin Hospital, instead, looked to the hope and strength that comes from putting people first and meeting challenges with honesty and openness. "Our concern," said Charmel, "was for the patient, the employees who work here, and the health of our community."[81]

The final part of this chapter described several individual and organizational barriers to communication. These barriers can be overcome by active listening, selecting appropriate channels, engaging in MBWA, using dialogue, developing a climate of trust, using formal channels, designing the correct structure to fit communication needs, and using feedback for learning.

# Discussion Questions

1. ATI Medical, Inc., has a "no-memo" policy. The 300 employees must interact directly for all communications. What impact do you think this policy would have on the organization?

2. Describe the elements of the communication process. Give an example of each part of the model as it exists in the classroom during communication between teacher and students.

3. Why do you think stories are more effective than hard facts and figures in persuading others?

4. Should the grapevine be eliminated? How might managers control information that is processed through the grapevine?

5. What do you think are the major barriers to upward communication in organizations? Discuss.

6. What is the relationship between group communication and group task? For example, how should communications differ in a strategic planning group and a group of employees who stock shelves in a grocery store?

7. Some senior managers believe they should rely on written information and computer reports because these yield more accurate data than do face-to-face communications. Do you agree?

8. Why is management by wandering around considered effective communication? Consider channel richness and nonverbal communications in formulating your answer.

9. Is speaking accurately or listening actively the more important communication skill for managers? Discuss.

10. Assume that you have been asked to design a training program to help managers become better communicators. What would you include in the program?

# Management in Practice: Experiential Exercise

**Listening Self-Assessment**

**Instructions:** Choose one response for each of the items below. Base your choice on what you usually do, not on what you think a person should do.

1. When you are going to lunch with a friend, you:
   a. Focus your attention on the menu and then on the service provided
   b. Ask about events in your friend's life and pay attention to what's said
   c. Exchange summaries of what is happening to each of you while focusing attention on the meal

2. When someone talks nonstop, you:
   a. Ask questions at an appropriate time in an attempt to help the person focus on the issue
   b. Make an excuse to end the conversation
   c. Try to be patient and understand what you are being told

3. If a group member complains about a fellow employee who, you believe, is disrupting the group, you:
   a. Pay attention and withhold your opinions
   b. Share your own experiences and feelings about that employee
   c. Acknowledge the group member's feelings and ask the group member what options he or she has

4. If someone is critical of you, you:
   a. Try not to react or get upset
   b. Automatically become curious and attempt to learn more
   c. Listen attentively and then back up your position

5. You are having a very busy day and someone tells you to change the way you are completing a task. You believe the person is wrong, so you:
   a. Thank her or him for the input and keep doing what you were doing
   b. Try to find out why she or he thinks you should change
   c. Acknowledge that the other may be right, tell her or him you are very busy, and agree to follow up later

6. When you are ready to respond to someone else, you:
   a. Sometimes will interrupt the person if you believe it is necessary
   b. Almost always speak before the other is completely finished talking
   c. Rarely offer your response until you believe the other has finished

7. After a big argument with someone you have to work with every day, you:
   a. Settle yourself and then try to understand the other's point of view before stating your side again
   b. Just try to go forward and let bygones be bygones
   c. Continue to press your position

8. A colleague calls to tell you that he is upset about getting assigned to a new job. You decide to:
   a. Ask him if he can think of options to help him deal with the situation
   b. Assure him that he is good at what he does and that these things have a way of working out for the best
   c. Let him know you have heard how badly he feels

9. If a friend always complains about her problems but never asks about yours, you:
   a. Try to identify areas of common interest
   b. Remain understanding and attentive, even if it becomes tedious
   c. Support her complaints and mention your own complaints

10. The best way to remain calm in an argument is to:
    a. Continue to repeat your position in a firm but even manner
    b. Repeat what you believe is the other person's position
    c. Tell the other person that you are willing to discuss the matter again when you are both calmer

## Score each item of your Listening Self-Assessment

1.  (a)  0        (b)  10        (c)  5
2.  (a)  10        (b)  0        (c)  5
3.  (a)  5        (b)  0        (c)  5
4.  (a)  5        (b)  10        (c)  0
5.  (a)  0        (b)  10        (c)  5
6.  (a)  5        (b)  0        (c)  10
7.  (a)  10        (b)  5        (c)  0
8.  (a)  5        (b)  5        (c)  10
9.  (a)  0        (b)  10        (c)  5
10.  (a)  0        (b)  10        (c)  5

## Add up your total score

**80–100**    **You are an active, excellent listener.** You achieve a good balance between listening and asking questions, and you strive to understand others.

**50–75**    **You are an adequate-to-good listener.** You listen well, although you may sometimes react too quickly to others before they are finished speaking.

**25–45**    **You have some listening skills but need to improve them.** You may often become impatient when trying to listen to others, hoping they will finish talking so you can talk.

**0–20**    **You listen to others very infrequently.** You may prefer to do all of the talking and experience extreme frustration while waiting for others to make their point.

Source: Richard G. Weaver and John D. Farrell, *Managers As Facilitators: A Practical Guide to Getting Work Done in a Changing Workplace* (San Francisco: Berrett-Koehler Publishers, 1997), 134–136. Used with permission.

# Management in Practice: Ethical Dilemma

### The Voice of Authority

When Gehan Rasinghe was hired as an account assistant at Werner and Thompson, a business and financial management firm, he was very relieved. He was overqualified for the job with his degree in accounting, but the combination of his accented English and his quiet manner had prevented him from securing any other position. Beatrice Werner, one of the managing partners of the firm, was impressed by his educational credentials and his courtly manner. She assured him he had advancement potential with the firm, but the account assistant position was the only one available. After months of rejections in his job hunt, Rasinghe accepted the position. He was committed to making his new job work at all costs.

Account Manager Cathy Putnam was Rasinghe's immediate superior. Putnam spoke with a heavy Boston accent, speaking at a lightning pace to match her enormous workload. She indicated to Rasinghe that he would need to get up to speed as quickly as possible to succeed in working with her. It was soon apparent that Putnam and Rasinghe were at odds. She resented having to repeat directions more than once to teach him his responsibilities. He also seemed resistant to making the many phone calls asking for copies of invoices, disputing charges on credit cards, and following up with clients' staff to get the information necessary to do his job. His accounting work was impeccable, but the public contact part of his job was in bad shape. Even his quiet answer of "No problem" to all her requests was starting to wear thin on Putnam. Before giving Rasinghe his three-month review, Putnam appealed to Beatrice Werner for help. Putnam was frustrated at their communication problems and didn't know what to do.

Werner had seen the problem coming. Although she had found Rasinghe's bank reconciliations and financial report preparations to be first-rate, she knew that phone work and client contact were a big part of any job in the firm. But as the daughter of German immigrants, Werner also knew that language and cultural barriers could be overcome with persistence and patience. Diversity was one of her ideals for her company, and it was not always easy to achieve. She felt sure that Rasinghe could become an asset to the firm in time. She worried that the time it would take was more than they could afford to give him.

**What Do You Do?**

1. Give Rasinghe his notice, with the understanding that a job that is primarily paperwork would be a better fit for him. Make the break now rather than later.
2. Place him with an account manager who has more time to help him develop his assertiveness and telephone skills and appreciates his knowledge of accounting.
3. Create a new position for him, where he could do the reports and reconciliations for several account managers, while their assistants concentrated on the public contact work. He would have little chance of future promotion, however.

# Surf the Net

1. **E-mail.** E-mail is a common communication channel used in organizations. The Internet provides much advice on how to effectively use e-mail. Visit one of the sites below and prepare a two- to three-paragraph summary of the ideas that you found most helpful to you in improving your skill at using this communication channel.
   *http://www.webfoot.com/advice/email.top.html*
   *http://www.emailreplies.com/Index.html*
   *http://email.about.com*
2. **Group Presentations.** Another common communication channel, particularly for managers, is speaking before groups both inside and outside the organization. Go to *http://www. presentationhelper.co.uk/presentation_business. htm* for presentation tips and ideas. Prepare and read a report, highlighting the most valuable idea you received from this site. Submit the printout to your instructor.
3. **Listening.** A communication skill development area from which nearly everyone can benefit is improving listening skills. Use your search engine to find helpful information on being a better listener (one example is provided below). After reading through the materials you locate, select one specific area that you will work to improve. Use every listening opportunity you have for the next 24 hours to apply what you have learned. Then write a two- to three-paragraph summary of what you practiced to become a better listener and the results you experienced. *http://www.thepargroup.com/ articles.html*.

# Case for Critical Analysis

### Inter-City Manufacturing, Inc.

The president of Inter-City Manufacturing Inc., Rich Langston, wanted to facilitate upward communication. He believed an open-door policy was a good place to start. He announced that his own door was open to all employees and encouraged senior managers to do the same. He felt this would give him a way to get early warning signals that would not be filtered or redirected through the formal chain of command. Langston found that many employees who used the open-door policy had been with the company for years and were comfortable talking to the president. Sometimes messages came through about inadequate policies and procedures. Langston would raise these issues and explain any changes at the next senior managers' meeting.

The most difficult complaints to handle were those from people who were not getting along with their bosses. One employee, Leroy, complained bitterly that his manager had overcommitted the department and put everyone under too much pressure. Leroy argued that long hours and low morale were major problems. But he would not allow Rich Langston to bring the manager into the discussion nor to seek out other employees to confirm the complaint. Although Langston suspected that Leroy might be right, he could not let the matter sit and blurted out, "Have you considered leaving the company?" This made Leroy realize that a meeting with his immediate boss was unavoidable.

Before the three-party meeting, Langston contacted Leroy's manager and explained what was going on. He insisted that the manager come to the meeting willing to listen and without hostility toward Leroy. During the meeting, Leroy's manager listened actively and displayed no ill will. He learned the problem from Leroy's perspective and realized he was over his head in his new job. After the meeting, the manager said he was relieved. He had been promoted into the job from a technical position just a few months

earlier and had no management or planning experience. He welcomed Rich Langston's offer to help him do a better job of planning.

## Questions

1. What techniques increased Rich Langston's communication effectiveness? Discuss.
2. Do you think that an open-door policy was the right way to improve upward communications? What other techniques would you suggest?
3. What problems do you think an open-door policy creates? Do you think many employees are reluctant to use it? Why?

Source: Based on Everett T. Suters, "Hazards of an Open-Door Policy," *Inc.*, January 1987, 99–102.

# Endnotes

1. Chris Serv, "Straight Talk," *Hospitals and Health Networks* (September 2002), 26+.
2. Ginger Graham, "If You Want Honesty, Break Some Rules," *Harvard Business Review* (April 2002), 42–47.
3. Michael J. Critelli, "How to Subvert Hierarchy: CEOs Must 'Skip Levels' To Manage More Effectively," *Chief Executive* (January–February 2004), 12.
4. Elizabeth B. Drew, "Profile: Robert Strauss," *The New Yorker* (May 7, 1979), 55–70.
5. Henry Mintzberg, *The Nature of Managerial Work* (New York: Harper & Row, 1973).
6. Phillip G. Clampitt, Laurey Berk, and M. Lee Williams, "Leaders as Strategic Communicators," *Ivey Business Journal* (May–June 2002), 51–55.
7. Ian Wylie, "Can Philips Learn to Walk the Talk?" *Fast Company* (January 2003), 44–45.
8. Fred Luthans and Janet K. Larsen, "How Managers Really Communicate," *Human Relations* 39 (1986), 161–178; and Larry E. Penley and Brian Hawkins, "Studying Interpersonal Communication in Organizations: A Leadership Application," *Academy of Management Journal* 28 (1985), 309–326.
9. D. K. Berlo, *The Process of Communication* (New York: Holt, Rinehart and Winston, 1960), 24.
10. Paul Roberts, "Live! From Your Office! It's . . . ," *Fast Company* (October 1999), 150–170.
11. Bruce K. Blaylock, "Cognitive Style and the Usefulness of Information," *Decision Sciences* 15 (Winter 1984), 74–91.

12. Robert H. Lengel and Richard L. Daft, "The Selection of Communication Media as an Executive Skill," *Academy of Management Executive* 2 (August 1988), 225–232; Richard L. Daft and Robert H. Lengel, "Organizational Information Requirements, Media Richness and Structural Design," *Managerial Science* 32 (May 1986), 554–572; and Jane Webster and Linda Klebe Treviño, "Rational and Social Theories as Complementary Explanations of Communication Media Choices: Two Policy-Capturing Studies," *Academy of Management Journal* 38, no. 6 (1995), 1544–1572.
13. Research reported in "E-mail Can't Mimic Phone Calls," *Johnson City Press* (September 17, 2000), 31.
14. Raymond E. Friedman and Steven C. Currall, "E-Mail Escalation: Dispute Exacerbating Elements of Electronic Communication, http://www.mba.vanderbilt.edu/ray.friedman/pdf/emailescalation.pdf; and Lauren Keller Johnson, "Does E-Mail Escalate Conflict?" *MIT Sloan Management Review* (Fall 2002), 14–15.
15. Scott Kirsner, "IM Is Here. RU Prepared?" *Darwin Magazine* (February 2002), 22–24.
16. Daniel Nasaw, "Instant Messages Are Popping Up All Over," *The Wall Street Journal* (June 12, 2003), B4; William H. Bulkeley, "Instant Message Goes Corporate; 'You Can't Hide,'" *The Wall Street Journal* (September 4, 2002), B1.
17. Edward M. Hallowell, "The Human Moment at Work," *Harvard Business Review* (January–February 1999), 58–66.

18. John R. Carlson and Robert W. Smud, "Channel Expansion Theory and the Experiential Nature of Media Richness Perceptions," *Academy of Management Journal* 42, no. 2 (1999), 153–170; R. Rice and G. Love, "Electronic Emotion," *Communication Research* 14 (1987), 85–108.

19. Ronald E. Rice, "Task Analyzability, Use of New Media, and Effectiveness: A Multi-Site Exploration of Media Richness," *Organizational Science* 3, no. 4 (November 1992), 475–500; and M. Lynne Markus, "Electronic Mail as the Medium of Managerial Choice," *Organizational Science* 5, no. 4 (November 1994), 502–527.

20. Richard L. Daft, Robert H. Lengel, and Linda Klebe Treviño, "Message Equivocality, Media Selection and Manager Performance: Implication for Information Systems," *MIS Quarterly* 11 (1987), 355–368.

21. Mary Young and James E. Post, "Managing to Communicate, Communicating to Manage: How Leading Companies Communicate with Employees," *Organizational Dynamics* (Summer 1993), 31–43.

22. Jay A. Conger, "The Necessary Art of Persuasion," *Harvard Business Review* (May–June 1998), 84–95.

23. Douglas A. Ready, "How Storytelling Builds Next-Generation Leaders," *MIT Sloan Management Review* (Summer 2002), 63–69.

24. J. Martin and M. Powers, "Organizational Stories: More Vivid and Persuasive than Quantitative Data," in B. M. Staw, ed., *Psychological Foundations of Organizational Behavior* (Glenview, Illinois: Scott Foresman, 1982), 161–168.

25. Bronwyn Fryer, "Storytelling that Moves People: A Conversation with Screenwriting Coach Robert McKee," *Harvard Business Review* (June 2003), 51–55.

26. Bill Birchard, "Once Upon a Time," *Strategy & Business* Issue 27 (Second Quarter, 2002), 99–104; and Laura Shin, "You Can Be a Great Storyteller," *USA Weekend* (January 16–18, 2004), 14.

27. I. Thomas Sheppard, "Silent Signals," *Supervisory Management* (March 1986), 31–33.

28. Albert Mehrabian, *Silent Messages* (Belmont, Calif.: Wadsworth, 1971); and Albert Mehrabian, "Communicating without Words," *Psychology Today* (September 1968), 53–55.

29. Mac Fulfer, "Nonverbal Communication: How To Read What's Plain as the Nose . . . Or Eyelid . . . Or Chin . . . On Their Faces," *Journal of Organizational Excellence* (Spring 2001), 19–27.

30. Sheppard, "Silent Signals."

31. Arthur H. Bell, *The Complete Manager's Guide to Interviewing* (Homewood, Ill.: Richard D. Irwin, 1989).

32. C. Glenn Pearce, "Doing Something about Your Listening Ability," *Supervisory Management* (March 1989), 29–34; and Tom Peters, "Learning to Listen," *Hyatt Magazine* (Spring 1988), 16–21.

33. M. P. Nichols, *The Lost Art of Listening* (New York: Guilford Publishing, 1995).

34. "Benchmarking the Sales Function," a report based on a study of 100 salespeople from small, medium, and large businesses, conducted by Ron Volper Group Inc. Sales Consulting and Training, White Plains, NY (1996), as reported in "Nine Habits of Highly Successful Salespeople," *Inc. Small Business Success* insert.

35. Gerald M. Goldhaber, *Organizational Communication*, 4th ed. (Dubuque, Iowa: Wm. C. Brown, 1980), 189.

36. Curtis Sittenfeld, "Good Ways To Deliver Bad News," *Fast Company* (April 1999), 58, 60.

37. James R. Stengel, Andrea L. Dixon, and Chris T. Allen, "Listening Begins at Home," *Harvard Business Review* (November 2003), 106–116.

38. Richard L. Daft and Richard M. Steers, *Organizations: A Micro/Macro Approach* (New York: Harper Collins, 1986); and Daniel Katz and Robert Kahn, *The Social Psychology of Organizations*, 2d ed. (New York: Wiley, 1978).

39. Greg Jaffe, "Tug of War: In the New Military, Technology May Alter Chain of Command," *The Wall Street Journal* (March 30, 2001), A3; and Aaron Pressman, "Business Gets the Message," *The Industry Standard* (February 26, 2001), 58–59.

40. Roberta Maynard, "It Can Pay to Show Employees the Big Picture," *Nation's Business* (December 1994), 10.

41. Phillip G. Clampitt, Robert J. DeKoch, and Thomas Cashman, "A Strategy for Communicating about Uncertainty," *Academy of Management Executive* 14, no. 4 (2000), 41–57.

42. J. G. Miller, "Living Systems: The Organization," *Behavioral Science* 17 (1972), 69.

43. Michael J. Glauser, "Upward Information Flow in Organizations: Review and Conceptual Analysis," *Human Relations* 37 (1984), 613–643; and "Upward/Downward Communication: Critical Information Channels," *Small Business Report* (October 1985), 85–88.

44. Pat Croce, "Catching the 5:15: A Simple Reporting System Can Help You Keep Tabs on Your Business," *FSB* (March 2004), 34.

45. Mary P. Rowe and Michael Baker, "Are You Hearing Enough Employee Concerns?" *Harvard Business Review* 62 (May–June 1984), 127–135; W. H. Read, "Upward Communication in Industrial Hierarchies," *Human Relations* 15 (February 1962), 3–15; and Daft and Steers, *Organizations*.

46. Barbara Ettorre, "The Unvarnished Truth," *Management Review* (June 1997), 54–57; and Roberta Maynard, "Back to Basics, From the Top," *Nation's Business* (December 1996), 38–39.

47. Thomas Petzinger, "A Hospital Applies Teamwork to Thwart An Insidious Enemy," *The Wall Street Journal* (May 8, 1998), B1.

48. E. M. Rogers and R. A. Rogers, *Communication in Organizations* (New York: Free Press, 1976); and A. Bavelas and D. Barrett, "An Experimental Approach to Organization Communication," *Personnel* 27 (1951), 366–371.

49. This discussion is based on Daft and Steers, *Organizations*.

50. Bavelas and Barrett, "An Experimental Approach"; and M. E. Shaw, *Group Dynamics: The Psychology of Small Group Behavior* (New York: McGraw-Hill, 1976).

51. Richard L. Daft and Norman B. Macintosh, "A Tentative Exploration into the Amount and Equivocality of Information Processing in Organizational Work Units," *Administrative Science Quarterly* 26 (1981), 207–224.

52. Cathy Olofson, "So Many Decisions, So Little Time," *Fast Company* (October 1999), 62.

53. This discussion of informal networks is based on Rob Cross, Nitin Nohria, and Andrew Parker, "Six Myths About Informal Networks," *MIT Sloan Management Review* (Spring 2002), 67–75; and Rob Cross and Laurence Prusak, "The People Who Make Organizations Go—or Stop," *Harvard Business Review* (June 2002): 105–112.

54. Tahl Raz, "The 10 Secrets of a Master Networker," *Inc.* (January 2003).

55. Thomas J. Peters and Robert H. Waterman Jr., *In Search of Excellence* (New York: Harper & Row, 1982); and Tom Peters and Nancy Austin, *A Passion for Excellence: The Leadership Difference* (New York: Random House, 1985).

56. Lois Therrien, "How Ztel Went from Riches to Rags," *BusinessWeek* (June 17, 1985), 97–100.

57. Keith Davis and John W. Newstrom, *Human Behavior at Work: Organizational Behavior*, 7th ed. (New York: McGraw-Hill, 1985).

58. Suzanne M. Crampton, John W. Hodge, and Jitendra M. Mishra, "The Informal Communication Network: Factors Influencing Grapevine Activity," *Public Personnel Management* 27, no. 4 (Winter, 1998), 569–584.

59. Survey results reported in Jared Sandberg, "Ruthless Rumors and the Managers Who Enable Them," *The Wall Street Journal* (October 29, 2003), B1

60. Joshua Hyatt, "The Last Shift," *Inc.* (February 1989), 74–80.

61. Donald B. Simmons, "The Nature of the Organizational Grapevine," *Supervisory Management* (November 1985), 39–42; and Davis and Newstrom, *Human Behavior*.

62. Barbara Ettorre, "Hellooo. Anybody Listening?" *Management Review* (November 1997), 9.

63. Lisa A. Burke and Jessica Morris Wise, "The Effective Care, Handling, and Pruning of the Office Grapevine," *Business Horizons* (May–June 2003), 71–74; "They Hear It Through the Grapevine," in Michael Warshaw, "The Good Guy's Guide to Office Politics," *Fast Company* (April–May 1998), 157–178 (page 160); and Carol Hildebrand, "Mapping the Invisible Workplace," *CIO Enterprise*, Section 2 (July 15, 1998), 18–20.

64. John Case, "Opening the Books," *Harvard Business Review*, (March–April 1997), 118–127.

65. Gary Hamel, "Killer Strategies That Make Shareholders Rich," *Fortune* (June 23, 1997), 70–84.

66. "What Is Trust?" results of a survey by Manchester Consulting, reported in Jenny C. McCune, "That Elusive Thing Called Trust," *Management Review* (July–August 1998), 10–16.

67. David Bohm, *On Dialogue* (Ojai, Calif.: David Bohm Seminars, 1989).

68. This discussion is based on Glenna Gerard and Linda Teurfs, "Dialogue and Organizational Transformation," in *Community Building: Renewing Spirit and Learning in Business*, ed. Kazinierz Gozdz (New Leaders Press, 1995), 142–153; and Edgar H. Schein, "On Dialogue, Culture, and Organizational Learning," *Organizational Dynamics* (Autumn 1993), 40–51.

69. Ian I. Mitroff and Murat C. Alpaslan, "Preparing for Evil," *Harvard Business Review* (April 2003), 109–115.

70. This section is based on Leslie Wayne and Leslie Kaufman, "Leadership, Put To a New Test," *The New York Times* (September 16, 2001), Section 3, 1, 4; Ian I. Mitroff, "Crisis Leadership," *Executive Excellence* (August 2001), 19; Jerry Useem, "What It Takes," *Fortune* (November 12, 2001), 126–132; Andy Bowen, "Crisis Procedures That Stand the Test of Time," *Public Relations Tactics* (August 2001), 16; and Matthew Boyle, "Nothing Really Matters," *Fortune* (October 15, 2001), 261–264.

71. Stephen Bernhut, "Leadership, with Michael Useem" (Leader's Edge Interview), *Ivey Business Journal* (January–February 2002), 42–43.

72. Mitroff, "Crisis Leadership."

73. Jay M. Jackman and Myra H. Strober, "Fear of Feedback," *Harvard Business Review* (April 2003), 101–108.

74. Carol Hymowitz, "How to Tell Employees All the Things They Don't Want to Hear" (In the Lead column), *The Wall Street Journal* (August 22, 2000), B1.

75. Thomas E. Ricks, "Army Devises System to Decide What Does, and Does Not, Work," *The Wall Street Journal* (May 23, 1997), A1, A10; Stephanie Watts Sussman, "CALL: A Model for Effective Organizational Learning," *Strategy* (Summer 1999), 14–15; John O'Shea, "Army: The Leader as Learner-in-Chief," *The Officer* (June 2003), 31; Michael D. Maples, "Fires

First in Combat—Train the Way We Fight," *Field Artillery* (July–August 2003), 1; Thomas E. Ricks, "Intelligence Problems in Iraq Are Detailed," *The Washington Post* (October 25, 2003, A1; and Richard W. Koenig, "Forging Our Future: Using Operation Iraqi Freedom Phase IV Lessons Learned," *Engineer* (January–March 2004), 21–22.

76. Thomas A. Stewart, "Listen Up, Maggots! You *Will* Deploy a More Humane and Effective Managerial Style!" *Ecompany* (July 2001), 95.

77. James A. F. Stoner and R. Edward Freeman, *Management*, 4th ed. (Englewood Cliffs, N.J.: Prentice-Hall, 1989).

78. Mike Hofman, "Lost in the Translation," *Inc.* (May 2000), 161–162.

79. Janet Fulk and Sirish Mani, "Distortion of Communication in Hierarchical Relationships," in *Communication Yearbook*, vol. 9, ed. M. L. McLaughlin (Beverly Hills, Calif.: Sage, 1986), 483–510.

80. "CEO Stopping Descent of Airline That's In Trouble," Associated Press story, *Johnson City Press* (June 20, 2004), 7D.

81. Chris Serb, "Straight Talk."

# Chapter 21

# Teamwork

## LEARNING OBJECTIVES

*After studying this chapter, you should be able to*

1. Identify the types of teams in organizations.

2. Discuss new applications of teams to facilitate employee involvement.

3. Identify roles within teams and the type of role you could play to help a team be effective.

4. Explain the general stages of team development.

5. Identify ways in which team size and diversity of membership affects team performance.

6. Explain the concepts of team cohesiveness and team norms and their relationship to team performance.

7. Understand the causes of conflict within and among teams and how to reduce conflict.

8. Discuss the assets and liabilities of organizational teams.

Nestled in the foothills of the Appalachian Mountains, the Rowe Furniture Company of Salem, Virginia, has been cranking out sofas, loveseats, and easy chairs for more than 40 years. When Charlene Pedrolie arrived as the plant's new manufacturing chief, she found 500 people who came to work, punched their time cards, turned off their brains, and did exactly what they were told to do. The pay was good by local standards, but workers were bored and apathetic. The traditional assembly line, which required that workers perform the same tasks over and over—one person cutting, another sewing, another gluing, and so forth—had worked well for Rowe in the past, but the marketplace was undergoing a revolution. Furniture shoppers used to be content to buy what was on the showroom floor or else wait months for a custom-made product. But not any longer—customers were demanding custom-designed pieces, but they balked at the idea of waiting the standard three to six months for delivery. Managers wanted to increase sales by installing a network of showroom computers, which would allow customers to choose fabrics and furniture designs to their individual taste and zap the order directly to the Rowe plant. And, they wanted to promise delivery within a month. Plant workers snorted at the preposterous idea. How on earth were they supposed to do it? Pedrolie knew the factory needed a hyperefficient assembly process—and a management system that tapped into the minds and energy of every single worker.[1]

## Take A Moment

If you were plant manager, how would you meet this challenge? Can the formation of teams help solve the problem?

The problems facing Rowe Furniture also confront many other companies. How can they be more flexible and responsive in an increasingly competitive, fast-changing environment? One solution is the formation of teams. A quiet revolution has been taking place in organizations across the country and around the world. From the assembly line to the executive office, from large corporations such as Ford Motor Company and 3M to small businesses such as St. Louis plantscaping firm Growing Green and Radius, a Boston restaurant, teams are becoming the basic building block of organizations.

Over the past two decades, the use of teams has increased dramatically in response to new competitive pressures, the need for greater flexibility and speed, and a desire to give people more opportunities for involvement. Hecla Mining Company uses teams for company goal setting; a major telecommunications company uses teams of salespeople to deal with big customers with complex purchasing requirements; and Lassiter Middle School in Jefferson County, Kentucky, uses teams of teachers to prepare daily schedules and handle student discipline problems. Some companies are now using virtual teams composed of managers and employees working in different countries.[2] Many organizations have had great success with teams, including increased productivity, quality improvements, greater innovation, and higher employee satisfaction. FedEx, for example, cut service problems such as incorrect bills and lost packages by 13 percent by using teams. At Xerox, production plants using teams reported a 30 percent increase in productivity.[3] A study of team-based organizations in Australia supports the idea that teams provide benefits to both employees and organizations.[4]

This chapter focuses on teams and their applications within organizations. We will define various types of teams, explore their stages of development, and examine such characteristics as size, cohesiveness, diversity, and norms. We will discuss how individuals can make contributions to teams and review the benefits and costs associated with teamwork. Teams are an important aspect of organizational life, and the ability to manage them is an important component of manager and organization success.

# Teams at Work

In this section, we will first define teams and then discuss a model of team effectiveness that summarizes the important concepts.

## What Is a Team?

**team**
A unit of two or more people who interact and coordinate their work to accomplish a specific goal.

A team is a unit of two or more people who interact and coordinate their work to accomplish a specific goal.[5] This definition has three components. First, two or more people are required. Teams can be quite large, although most have fewer than 15 people. Second, people in a team have regular interaction. People who do not interact, such as when standing in line at a lunch counter or riding in an elevator, do not compose a team. Third, people in a team share a performance goal, whether it be to design a new hand-held computer, build a car, or write a textbook. Students often are assigned to teams to do classwork assignments, in which case the purpose is to perform the assignment and receive an acceptable grade.

Although a team is a group of people, the two terms are not interchangeable. An employer, a teacher, or a coach can put together a *group* of people and never build a *team*. The team concept implies a sense of shared mission and collective responsibility. Exhibit 21.1 lists the primary differences between groups and teams. One example of a true team comes from the military, where U.S. Navy surgeons, nurses,

**CONCEPT CONNECTION**

*Teams are emerging as a **powerful management tool** and are popping up in the most unexpected places, such as this manufacturing cell at TRINOVA'S Aeroquip Inoac facility in Fremont, Ohio. The facility uses more than 40 teams that cross operations and job functions, helping the company eliminate non-value-added activities, lower costs, improve customer responsiveness, and increase quality.*

anesthesiologists, and technicians make up eight-person forward surgical teams that operated for the first time ever in combat during Operation Iraqi Freedom. These teams were scattered over Iraq and were able to move to new locations in four trucks and be set up within an hour. With a goal of saving the 15 to 20 percent of wounded soldiers and civilians who will die unless they receive critical care within 24 hours, members of these teams smoothly coordinate their activities to accomplish a critical shared mission.[6] The sports world also provides many examples of the importance of teamwork. One manager learned valuable lessons about team-building by participating in the ten-month BT Global Challenge around-the-world race, as described in this chapter's Unlocking Creative Solutions Through People box.

# Exhibit 21.1

## Differences between Groups and Teams

| Group | Team |
|---|---|
| • Has a designated strong leader | • Shares or rotates leadership roles |
| • Holds individuals accountable | • Holds team accountable to each other |
| • Sets identical purpose for group and organization | • Sets specific team vision or purpose |
| • Has individual work products | • Has collective work products |
| • Runs efficient meetings | • Runs meetings that encourage open-ended discussion and problem solving |
| • Measures effectiveness indirectly by influence on business (such as financial performance) | • Measures effectiveness directly by assessing collective work |
| • Discusses, decides, delegates work to individuals | • Discusses, decides, shares work |

**SOURCE**: Adapted from Jon R. Katzenbach and Douglas K. Smith, "The Discipline of Teams," *Harvard Business Review* (March–April 1995), 111–120.

# Unlocking Creative Solutions Through People

### A High-Tech Executive Sails Away for a Lesson on Teamwork

Much of what Doug Webb knows about teamwork he learned during his 10 months as a crew member on the yacht Logica, participating in the BT Global Challenge, an around-the-world race for amateurs, many of whom have never sailed before. Competitors put to sea in boats that are identical in every way, and crews are selected by race organizers to be as equal as possible. What makes the difference is the ability to quickly turn a group of diverse individuals into a high-performance team.

One key, Webb discovered, is to make sure everyone feels equal and to help each individual contribute to his or her full potential. In business, the tendency is often to identify the least dependable or weakest members of a team and replace them, but during the BT Global Challenge, that was not possible. Therefore, it was important to identify and understand every person's motivations, interests, and capabilities and use these to benefit the common good. With effective coaching, individuals who at first seemed less competent became key team members, with the leader enabling them to fill roles where they could make a maximum contribution and avoid areas where they were likely to fail. Success breeds confidence, and as people grew in their roles, their contributions expanded. Another important aspect of building a team is communication. The Logica crew met long before the race to get to know one another and set ground rules for how they would communicate, learning to accept both positive and negative feedback. The emphasis was on the ability to have open and frank conversations without crew members feeling hurt or insecure about their performance.

During the race itself, everyone engaged in evaluating and learning from mistakes, as well as celebrating each accomplishment. Conflicts were discussed openly instead of being allowed to fester and grow. The Logica team finished fourth out of a group of 12 racing teams. But the most important win for Webb was that as he returned to his job as CFO of Logica, a leading information technology company with more than 11,000 employees in 28 countries, he took with him the lessons of teamwork he learned at sea.

**SOURCE**: Doug Webb, "Rhyme of the Ancient Manager: A High-Tech Exec Takes a New Tack," *Forbes* (September 10, 2001), 76–79.

## Model of Work Team Effectiveness

Some of the factors associated with team effectiveness are illustrated in Exhibit 21.2. Work team effectiveness is based on two outcomes—productive output and personal satisfaction.[7] *Satisfaction* pertains to the team's ability to meet the personal needs of its members and hence maintain their membership and commitment. *Productive output* pertains to the quality and quantity of task outputs as defined by team goals.

The factors that influence team effectiveness begin with the organizational context.[8] The organizational context in which the team operates is described in other chapters and includes such factors as structure, strategy, environment, culture, and reward systems. Within that context, managers define teams. Important team characteristics are the type of team, the team structure, and team composition. Managers must decide when to create permanent teams within the formal structure and when to use a temporary task team. Factors such as the diversity of the team in terms of gender and race, as well as knowledge, skills, and attitudes, can have a tremendous impact on team processes and effectiveness.[9] Team size and roles also are important. Managers always must consider whether a team is the best way to do a task. If costs outweigh benefits, managers may wish to assign an individual employee to the task.

These team characteristics influence processes internal to the team, which, in turn, affect output and satisfaction. Good team leaders understand and manage stages of team development, cohesiveness, norms, and conflict in order to establish an effective team. These processes are influenced by team and organizational characteristics and by the ability of members and leaders to direct these processes in a positive manner.

Exhibit 21.2

**Work Team Effectiveness Model**

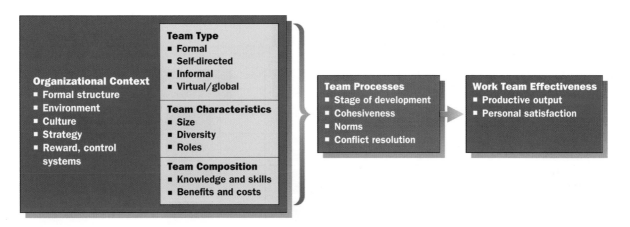

The model of team performance in Exhibit 21.2 is the basis for this chapter. In the following sections, we will examine types of organizational teams, team structure, internal processes, and team benefits and costs.

# Types of Teams

Many types of teams can exist within organizations. The easiest way to classify teams is in terms of those created as part of the organization's formal structure and those created to increase employee participation.

## Formal Teams

Formal teams are created by the organization as part of the formal organization structure. Two common types of formal teams are vertical and horizontal, which typically represent vertical and horizontal structural relationships, as described in Chapter 10. These two types of teams are illustrated in Exhibit 21.3. A third type of formal team is the special-purpose team.

**formal team**
A team created by the organization as part of the formal organization structure.

### Vertical Team

A vertical team is composed of a manager and his or her subordinates in the formal chain of command. Sometimes called a *functional team* or a *command team*, the vertical team may in some cases include three or four levels of hierarchy within a functional department. Typically, the vertical team includes a single department in an organization. The third-shift nursing team on the second floor of St. Luke's Hospital is a vertical team that includes nurses and a supervisor. A financial analysis department, a quality control department, an accounting department, and a human resource department are all command teams. Each is created by the organization to attain specific goals through members' joint activities and interactions.

**vertical team**
A formal team composed of a manager and his or her subordinates in the organization's formal chain of command.

### Horizontal Team

A horizontal team is composed of employees from about the same hierarchical level but from different areas of expertise.[10] A horizontal team is drawn from several

**horizontal team**
A formal team composed of employees from about the same hierarchical level but from different areas of expertise.

Exhibit 21.3

## Horizontal and Vertical Teams in an Organization

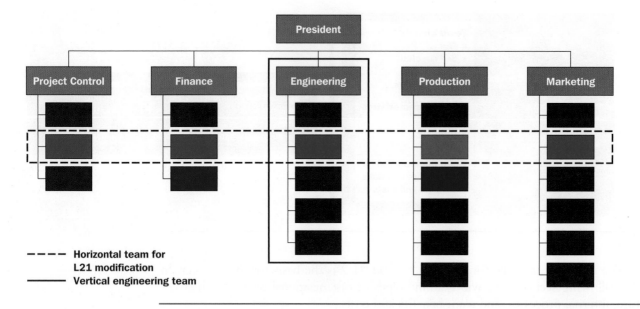

departments, is given a specific task, and may be disbanded after the task is completed. The two most common types of horizontal teams are cross-functional teams and committees.

As described in Chapter 10, a *cross-functional team* is a group of employees from different departments formed to deal with a specific activity and existing only until the task is completed. Sometimes called a *task force*, the team might be used to create a new product in a manufacturing organization or a new history curriculum in a university. Several departments are involved, and many views have to be considered, so these tasks are best served with a horizontal, cross-functional team.

**committee**
A long-lasting, sometimes permanent team in the organization structure created to deal with tasks that recur regularly.

A committee generally is long-lived and may be a permanent part of the organization's structure. Membership on a committee usually is decided by a person's title or position rather than by personal expertise. A committee often needs official representation, compared with selection for a cross-functional team, which is based on personal qualifications for solving a problem. Committees typically are formed to deal with tasks that recur regularly. For example, a grievance committee handles employee grievances; an advisory committee makes recommendations in the areas of employee compensation and work practices; a worker-management committee may be concerned with work rules, job design changes, and suggestions for work improvement.[11]

As part of the horizontal structure of the organization, cross-functional teams and committees offer several advantages: (1) They allow organization members to exchange information; (2) they generate suggestions for coordinating the organizational units that are represented; (3) they develop new ideas and solutions for existing organizational problems; and (4) they assist in the development of new organizational practices and policies.

**special-purpose team**
A team created outside the formal organization to undertake a project of special importance or creativity.

### Special-Purpose Team

Special-purpose teams, sometimes called *project teams*, are created outside the formal organization structure to undertake a project of special importance or creativity. Special-purpose teams focus on a specific purpose and expect to disband once the specific project is completed.[12] Examples include the team that developed the first IBM ThinkPad and the project team for the Chrysler PT Cruiser. A special-purpose team still is part of the formal organization and has its own reporting structure, but members perceive themselves as a separate entity.[13] Many of today's companies are using special-purpose teams to dramatically speed up development of a special product or execute a highly important project. These *fast-cycle teams*, set up to work on projects that top management deems highly important, are provided the freedom and resources to bring projects to closure quickly.[14]

## Self-Directed Teams

Employee involvement through teams is designed to increase the participation of low-level workers in decision making and the conduct of their jobs, with the goal of improving performance. Employee involvement started out simply with techniques such as information sharing with employees or asking employees for suggestions about improving the work. Gradually, companies moved toward greater autonomy for employees, which led first to problem-solving teams and then to self-directed teams.[15]

Problem-solving teams typically consist of 5 to 12 hourly employees from the same department who voluntarily meet to discuss ways of improving quality, efficiency, and the work environment. Recommendations are proposed to management for approval. Problem-solving teams usually are the first step in a company's move toward greater employee participation. The most widely known application is *quality circles*, first used by Japanese companies, in which employees focus on ways to improve quality in the production process. USX adopted this approach in several of its steel mills, recognizing that quality takes a team effort. Under the title All Product Excellence program (APEX), USX set up APEX teams of up to 12 employees who met several times a month to solve quality problems.[16]

As a company matures, problem-solving teams can gradually evolve into self-directed teams, which represent a fundamental change in how employee work is organized. Self-directed teams enable employees to feel challenged, find their work meaningful, and develop a strong sense of identity with the company.[17] Self-directed teams typically consist of 5 to 20 multiskilled workers who rotate jobs to produce an entire product or service or at least one complete aspect or portion of a product or service (e.g., engine assembly, insurance claim processing). The central idea is that the teams themselves, rather than managers or supervisors, take responsibility for their work, make decisions, monitor their own performance, and alter their work behavior as needed to solve problems, meet goals, and adapt to changing conditions.[18] Self-directed teams are permanent teams that typically include the following elements:

- The team includes employees with several skills and functions, and the combined skills are sufficient to perform a major organizational task. A team may include members from the foundry, machining, grinding, fabrication, and sales departments, with members cross-trained to perform one another's jobs. The team eliminates barriers among departments, enabling excellent coordination to produce a product or service.

© BERND AUERS

### CONCEPT CONNECTION

*James Frankel, James McLurkin, and Jennifer Smith serve on the SwarmBot team, a **special purpose team** at iRobot in Burlington, Massachusetts, that is researching how SwarmBots can benefit mankind. SwarmBots are small robots in the form of cubes with rechargeable batteries that can potentially collaborate like a colony of ants to accomplish difficult tasks, such as disposing of land mines or taking over buildings held by bad guys. The team is perfecting software that can work with as few as 10 robots or as many as 10,000, and asking the critical question: "If you could make small robots cheaply, what would you use them for?"*

**problem-solving team**
Typically 5 to 12 hourly employees from the same department who meet to discuss ways of improving quality, efficiency, and the work environment.

**self-directed team**
A team consisting of 5 to 20 multiskilled workers who rotate jobs to produce an entire product or service, often supervised by an elected member.

© MARC HAUSER

**CONCEPT CONNECTION**

*Highsmith Inc., a Fort Atkinson, Wisconsin, company, is the country's leading mail-order supplier of equipment such as book displays, audio-video tools, and educational software for schools and libraries. The company's employees work in a flat organization in which self-directed teams, along with a continuous-learning program and flextime, are manifest. According to CEO Duncan Highsmith, "We have a limited labor market, so I wanted to make the most of the people we had by helping them become decision makers, by providing them with information and the context to make good decisions." In the photo is a team of librarians (left to right, Oma Dixon, Lisa Guedea Carreño, and Genevieve Mecherly) who facilitate the culture of autonomy at Highsmith. "We're here to help people integrate information into their jobs as seamlessly as possible," says Carreño. "That way, they can keep doing their jobs."*

- The team is given access to resources such as information, equipment, machinery, and supplies needed to perform the complete task.
- The team is empowered with decision-making authority, which means that members have the freedom to select new members, solve problems, spend money, monitor results, and plan for the future.[19]

In a self-directed team, team members take over managerial duties such as scheduling or ordering materials. They work with minimum supervision, perhaps electing one of their own as supervisor, who may change each year. The most effective self-directed teams are those that are fully empowered, as described in the discussion of empowerment in Chapter 19. In addition to having increased responsibility and discretion, empowered teams are those that have a strong belief in their team's capabilities, find value and meaning in their work, and recognize the impact the team's work has on customers, other stakeholders, and organizational success.[20] Managers create the conditions that determine whether self-directed teams are empowered by giving teams true power and decision making authority, complete information, knowledge and skills, and appropriate rewards. The manager to whom the team and team leaders report, sometimes referred to as the *external leader*, has a tremendous impact on the team's success. In addition to creating conditions for empowerment, effective external leaders serve as an active link between the team and the organization, building constructive relationships and getting the team what it needs to do its best work.[21] An interesting example of the use of self-directed teams is the Orpheus Orchestra of New York City.

**ORPHEUS ORCHESTRA**

http://www. orpheusnyc.com

Most orchestras are strongly hierarchical and structured around a conductor who wields almost complete power and control. Not Orpheus, a world-renowned chamber orchestra started in the 1970s by a small group of musicians committed to democratic power sharing.

Orpheus operates completely without a conductor! Teams of musicians determine the repertoire, schedule concerts, select new musicians, interpret musical works, and handle all the other artistic and performance duties a conductor usually controls. The instrument sections constitute natural, specialized self-directed teams. Leadership rotates among different members, who are elected by their teammates.

The actual structure of teams at Orpheus is quite complex and is designed to facilitate participative leadership, avoid hierarchical control, and allow everyone to participate in decision making.[22]

The Orpheus Orchestra has found that using self-directed teams provides a number of advantages. The greater information flow and diverse artistic input contributes to a superb performance. In addition, members typically feel a high degree of commitment, and turnover is quite low. One business organization that succeeds with teamwork is Consolidated Diesel's engine factory in Whitakers, North Carolina. In its 20 or so years of operation as a team-based organization, the plant has had higher revenues, lower turnover, and significantly lower injury rates than the industry average.

In addition, while most plants average 1 supervisor for every 25 workers, Consolidated Diesel has 1 for every 100 employees because the plant workers themselves handle many supervisory duties. The difference yields a savings of about $1 million a year.[23]

## Teams in the New Workplace

Some exciting new approaches to teamwork have resulted from advances in information technology, shifting employee expectations, and the globalization of business. Two types of teams that are increasingly being used are virtual teams and global teams.

### Virtual Teams

A virtual team is made up of geographically or organizationally dispersed members who are linked primarily through advanced information and telecommunications technologies.[24] Although some virtual teams may be made up of only organizational members, virtual teams often include contingent workers, members of partner organizations, customers, suppliers, consultants, or other outsiders. Team members use e-mail, voice mail, videoconferencing, Internet and intranet technologies, and various types of collaboration software to perform their work, although they might also sometimes meet face to face. Many virtual teams are cross-functional teams that emphasize solving customer problems or completing specific projects. Others are permanent self-directed teams.

**virtual team**
A team that uses advanced information and telecommunications technologies so that geographically distant members can collaborate on projects and reach common goals.

With virtual teams, team leadership is typically shared or rotated, depending on the area of expertise needed at each stage of the project.[25] In addition, team membership in virtual teams may change fairly quickly, depending on the tasks to be performed. One of the primary advantages of virtual teams is the ability to rapidly assemble the most appropriate group of people to complete a complex project, solve a particular problem, or exploit a specific strategic opportunity. Virtual teams present unique challenges. Managers as team leaders should consider these critical issues when building virtual teams:[26]

- *Select the right team members.* The first step is creating a team of people who have the right mix of technical and interpersonal skills, task knowledge, and personalities to work in a virtual environment. Interviews with virtual team members and leaders find that the ability to communicate and a desire to work as a team are the most important personal qualities for virtual team members.[27]
- *Manage socialization.* People need to get to know one another and understand the appropriate behaviors and attitudes. Smart team leaders establish team norms and ground rules for interaction early in the team's formation.
- *Foster trust.* Trust might be the most important ingredient in a successful virtual team. Teams that exhibit high levels of trust tend to have clear roles and expectations of one another, get to know one another as individuals, and maintain positive action-oriented attitudes.
- *Effectively manage communications.* Frequent communication is essential. Team leaders need to understand when and how to use various forms of communication to best advantage. Some experts suggest regular face-to-face meetings, while others believe virtual teams can be successful even if they always interact electronically. One time when face-to-face communication might be essential is when misunderstandings, frustrations, or conflicts threaten the team's work.[28]

### Global Teams

Virtual teams are also sometimes global teams. Global teams are cross-border work teams made up of members of different nationalities whose activities span multiple countries.[29] Generally, global teams fall into two categories: intercultural teams,

**global team**
A work team made up of members of different nationalities whose activities span multiple countries; may operate as a virtual team or meet face to face.

# Unlocking Creative Solutions Through Technology

## STMicroelectronics Makes Virtual Teams Work

If you worked at STMicroelectronics, formed from the 1987 merger of two ailing European semiconductor companies—one French and one Italian—you might work side-by-side with people from London and New Dehli, Singapore and Sicily, Geneva and Madrid. STMicroelectronics is a truly global corporation and teams include people from a variety of countries. STMicro has grown to become one of the world's largest computer chip makers and continues to win new business all over the world.

But managers faced a problem when the company won a coveted order for microchips to power the brains for a navigational mapping system to be installed in new Fiats and Peugeots. Getting the order was a major coup, but filling it wasn't going to be easy. STMicro executives knew a chip project of this magnitude required collaboration among a wide range of disciplines, including chip design, engineering, fabrication, systems integration, quality control, packaging, marketing, and sales. Moreover, the people with the expertise to complete the project lived in five different countries, spanned 14 time zones, and spoke six different native languages.

The car makers needed the chips in a big hurry—if they couldn't get the navigational systems installed for the new models, they would lose sales. The time constraints on the project, as well as personal and cost factors, made it impossible to get everyone together in one location, so a virtual global team was formed to collaborate on the project using electronic communication systems and collaborative software.

Thanks to training and excellent leadership, STMicro's first major virtual team project was a success. One reason is that team leaders united everyone around a common purpose of designing and developing the new chips in time to meet the customers' needs; members were willing to sublimate their individual goals, viewpoints, and egos for the sake of achieving this ambitious goal. As the team's work progressed, members began to deeply care about each other as well as the project, even though many of them had never met face-to-face. At the end of the project, one of the team members said, "This was the best experience of my life. I learned so much."

As STMicroelectronics continues to build business and open customer support and design centers in different areas of the world, the use of virtual global teams will be an important way to accomplish organizational goals. Virtual teams enable the company to tap into knowledge around the globe to develop creative solutions to customers' problems.

**SOURCE**: Based on Jon Katzenbach and Douglas Smith, "Virtual Teaming," *Forbes* (May 21, 2001), 48–51; and Cassell Bryan-Low, "Can STMicro's Run Continue?" *The Wall Street Journal* (July 21, 2004), B8.

whose members come from different countries or cultures and meet face to face, and virtual global teams, whose members remain in separate locations around the world and conduct their work electronically.[30] For example, the research department at BT Labs has 660 researchers spread across the United Kingdom and several other countries. The researchers work in global virtual teams that investigate virtual reality, artificial intelligence, and other advanced information technologies.[31] This chapter's Unlocking Creative Solutions Through Technology box describes the use of virtual teams at STMicroelectronics.

Global teams can present enormous challenges for team leaders, who have to bridge gaps of time, distance, and culture. In some cases, members speak different languages, use different technologies, and have different beliefs about authority, time orientation, decision making, and even teamwork itself. For example, multinational organizations have found that many team phenomena are culture-specific. The acceptance and effectiveness of team-based systems can vary widely across different cultures, which makes implementing and evaluating teams quite complex.[32] Organizations using global teams invest the time and resources to adequately educate employees. They have to make sure all team members appreciate and understand cultural differences, are focused on goals, and understand their responsibilities to the team. For a global team to be effective, all team members must be willing to deviate somewhat from their own values and norms and establish new norms for the team.[33] As with virtual teams, carefully selecting team members, building trust, and sharing information are critical to success.

# Team Characteristics

The next issue of concern to managers is designing the team for greatest effectiveness. One factor is *team characteristics*, which can affect team dynamics and performance. Characteristics of particular concern are team size, diversity, and member roles.

## Size

The ideal size of work teams often is thought to be 7, although variations of from 5 to 12 typically are associated with good team performance. These teams are large enough to take advantage of diverse skills, enable members to express good and bad feelings, and aggressively solve problems. They also are small enough to permit members to feel an intimate part of the group. A recent Gallup poll in the United States found that 82 percent of employees surveyed believe that small teams are more productive.[34] In general, as a team increases in size, it becomes harder for each member to interact with and influence the others. Ray Oglethorpe, president of AOL Technologies, which makes extensive use of teams, believes keeping teams small is the key to success. "If you have more than 15 or 20 people, you're dead," he says. "The connections between team members are too hard to make."[35]

A summary of research on group size suggests the following:[36]

1. Small teams (2 to 4 members) show more agreement, ask more questions, and exchange more opinions. Members want to get along with one another. Small teams report more satisfaction and enter into more personal discussions. They tend to be informal and make few demands on team leaders.
2. Large teams (12 or more) tend to have more disagreements and differences of opinion. Subgroups often form, and conflicts among them occur, ranging from protection of "turf" to trivial matters, such as "What kind of coffee is brewing in the pot?" Demands on leaders are greater because there is more centralized decision making and less member participation. Large teams also tend to be less friendly. Turnover and absenteeism are higher in a large team, especially for blue-collar workers. Because less satisfaction is associated with specialized tasks and poor communication, team members have fewer opportunities to participate and feel like an important part of the group.

As a general rule, large teams make need satisfaction for individuals more difficult; thus, there is less reason for people to remain committed to their goals. Teams of from 5 to 12 seem to work best. If a team grows larger than 20, managers should divide it into subgroups, each with its own members and goals.

## Diversity

Since teams require a variety of skills, knowledge, and experience, it seems likely that heterogeneous teams would be more effective than homogeneous ones. In general, research supports this idea, showing that diverse teams produce more innovative solutions to problems.[37] Diversity in terms of functional area and skills, thinking styles, and personal characteristics is often a source of creativity.

**CONCEPT CONNECTION**

*This landscaping team from Christy Webber & Company is working on the Millennium Park in Chicago, which opened in 2004. Christy Webber, who owns the firm headquartered on Chicago's West Side, appreciates the value of **team diversity**. Her 100 employees are formed into teams that include both union and nonunion members and represent a mix of ethnic groups, genders, and skills. Yet, diversity can occasionally be a challenge. "Sometimes there is friction between the groups," Webber says. "It's really hard to get them to mix." Webber's excellent people skills enable her to help people work well together and gain the benefits of diverse opinions and skills.*

In addition, diversity may contribute to a healthy level of conflict that leads to better decision making.

Recent research studies have confirmed that both functional diversity and gender diversity can have a positive impact on work team performance.[38] Racial, national, and ethnic diversity can also be good for teams, but in the short term these differences might hinder team interaction and performance. Teams made up of racially and culturally diverse members tend to have more difficulty learning to work well together, but, with effective leadership, the problems fade over time.[39]

## Member Roles

For a team to be successful over the long run, it must be structured so as to both maintain its members' social well-being and accomplish its task. In successful teams, the requirements for task performance and social satisfaction are met by the emergence of two types of roles: task specialist and socioemotional.[40]

**task specialist role**
A role in which the individual devotes personal time and energy to helping the team accomplish its task.

People who play the task specialist role spend time and energy helping the team reach its goal. They often display the following behaviors:

- *Initiate ideas.* Propose new solutions to team problems.
- *Give opinions.* Offer opinions on task solutions; give candid feedback on others' suggestions.
- *Seek information.* Ask for task-relevant facts.
- *Summarize.* Relate various ideas to the problem at hand; pull ideas together into a summary perspective.
- *Energize.* Stimulate the team into action when interest drops.[41]

**socioemotional role**
A role in which the individual provides support for team members' emotional needs and social unity.

People who adopt a socioemotional role support team members' emotional needs and help strengthen the social entity. They display the following behaviors:

- *Encourage.* Are warm and receptive to others' ideas; praise and encourage others to draw forth their contributions.
- *Harmonize.* Reconcile group conflicts; help disagreeing parties reach agreement.
- *Reduce tension.* Tell jokes or in other ways draw off emotions when group atmosphere is tense.

- *Follow*.  Go along with the team; agree to other team members' ideas.
- *Compromise*.  Will shift own opinions to maintain team harmony.[42]

Exhibit 21.4 illustrates task specialist and socioemotional roles in teams. When most individuals in a team play a social role, the team is socially oriented. Members do not criticize or disagree with one another and do not forcefully offer opinions or try to accomplish team tasks, because their primary interest is to keep the team happy. Teams with mostly socioemotional roles can be very satisfying, but they also can be unproductive. At the other extreme, a team made up primarily of task specialists will tend to have a singular concern for task accomplishment. This team will be effective for a short period of time but will not be satisfying for members over the long run. Task specialists convey little emotional concern for one another, are unsupportive, and ignore team members' social and emotional needs. The task-oriented team can be humorless and unsatisfying.

As Exhibit 21.4 illustrates, some team members may play a dual role. People with dual roles both contribute to the task and meet members' emotional needs. Such people often become team leaders. A study of new-product-development teams in high-technology firms found that the most effective teams were headed by leaders who balanced the technical needs of the project with human interaction issues, thus meeting both task and socio-emotional needs.[43] Exhibit 21.4 also shows the final type of role, called the nonparticipator role, in which people contribute little to either the task or the social needs of team members. Nonparticipators typically are held in low esteem by the team.

The important thing for managers to remember is that effective teams must have people in both task specialist and socioemotional roles. Humor and social concern are as important to team effectiveness as are facts and problem solving. Managers also should remember that some people perform better in one type of role; some are inclined toward social concerns and others toward task concerns. A well-balanced team will do best over the long term because it will be personally satisfying for team members and permit the accomplishment of team tasks.

**dual role**
A role in which the individual both contributes to the team's task and supports members' emotional needs.

**nonparticipator role**
A role in which the individual contributes little to either the task or members' socioemotional needs.

Exhibit 21.4

**Team Member Roles**

| | Low ← Member Social Behavior → High |
|---|---|
| **High**<br><br>Member Task Behavior<br><br>**Low** | **Task Specialist Role**<br>Focuses on task accomplishment over human needs<br><br>Important role, but if adopted by everyone, team's social needs will not be met | **Dual Role**<br>Focuses on task and people<br><br>May be a team leader<br><br>Important role, but not essential if members adopt task specialist and socioemotional roles |
| | **Nonparticipator Role**<br>Contributes little to either task or people needs of team<br><br>Not an important role—if adopted by too many members, team will disband | **Socioemotional Role**<br>Focuses on people needs of team over task<br><br>Important role, but if adopted by everyone, team's tasks will not be accomplished |

# Team Processes

Now we turn our attention to internal team processes. Team processes pertain to those dynamics that change over time and can be influenced by team leaders. In this section, we will discuss the team processes of stages of development, cohesiveness, and norms. The fourth type of team process, conflict, will be covered in the next section.

## Stages of Team Development

After a team has been created, there are distinct stages through which it develops.[44] New teams are different from mature teams. Recall a time when you were a member of a new team, such as a fraternity or sorority pledge class, a committee, or a small team formed to do a class assignment. Over time the team changed. In the beginning, team members had to get to know one another, establish roles and norms, divide the labor, and clarify the team's task. In this way, each member became part of a smoothly operating team. The challenge for leaders is to understand the stages of team development and take action that will help the group improve its functioning.

Research findings suggest that team development is not random but evolves over definitive stages. One useful model for describing these stages is shown in Exhibit 21.5. Each stage confronts team leaders and members with unique problems and challenges.[45]

### Forming

**forming**
The stage of team development characterized by orientation and acquaintance.

The forming stage of development is a period of orientation and getting acquainted. Members break the ice and test one another for friendship possibilities and task orientation. Team members find which behaviors are acceptable to others. Uncertainty is high during this stage, and members usually accept whatever power or authority is offered by either formal or informal leaders. Members are dependent on the team until they find out what the ground rules are and what is expected of them. During this initial stage, members are concerned about such things as "What is expected of me?" "What is acceptable?" "Will I fit in?" During the forming stage, the team leader should provide time for members to get acquainted with one another and encourage them to engage in informal social discussions.

### Storming

**storming**
The stage of team development in which individual personalities and roles, and resulting conflicts, emerge.

During the storming stage, individual personalities emerge. People become more assertive in clarifying their roles and what is expected of them. This stage is marked by conflict and disagreement. People may disagree over their perceptions of the team's mission. Members may jockey for position, and coalitions or subgroups based on common interests may form. One subgroup may disagree with another over the total team's goals or how to achieve them. Unless teams can successfully move beyond this stage, they may get bogged down and never achieve high performance. During the storming stage, the team leader should encourage participation by each team member. Members should propose ideas, disagree with one another, and work through the uncertainties and conflicting perceptions about team tasks and goals.

### Norming

**norming**
The stage of team development in which conflicts developed during the storming stage are resolved and team harmony and unity emerge.

During the norming stage, conflict is resolved, and team harmony and unity emerge. Consensus develops on who has the power, who are the leaders, and members' roles. Members come to accept and understand one another. Differences are resolved, and members develop a sense of team cohesion. This stage typically is of short duration. During the norming stage, the team leader should emphasize unity within the team and help clarify team norms and values.

Exhibit 21.5

## Five Stages of Team Development

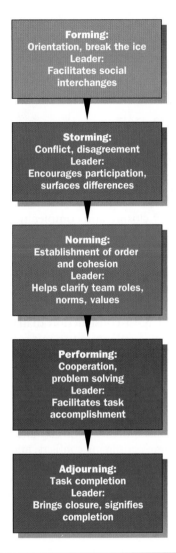

**Forming:**
Orientation, break the ice
Leader:
Facilitates social
interchanges

**Storming:**
Conflict, disagreement
Leader:
Encourages participation,
surfaces differences

**Norming:**
Establishment of order
and cohesion
Leader:
Helps clarify team roles,
norms, values

**Performing:**
Cooperation,
problem solving
Leader:
Facilitates task
accomplishment

**Adjourning:**
Task completion
Leader:
Brings closure, signifies
completion

## Performing

During the performing stage, the major emphasis is on problem solving and accomplishing the assigned task. Members are committed to the team's mission. They are coordinated with one another and handle disagreements in a mature way. They confront and resolve problems in the interest of task accomplishment. They interact frequently and direct their discussions and influence toward achieving team goals. During this stage, the leader should concentrate on managing high task performance. Both socioemotional and task specialists should contribute.

**performing**
The stage of team development in which members focus on problem solving and accomplishing the team's assigned task.

## Adjourning

The adjourning stage occurs in committees and teams that have a limited task to perform and are disbanded afterward. During this stage, the emphasis is on wrapping up and gearing down. Task performance is no longer a top priority. Members may feel heightened emotionality, strong cohesiveness, and depression or even regret over the team's disbandment. They may feel happy about mission accomplishment and sad about the loss of friendship and associations. At this point, the leader may

**adjourning**
The stage of team development in which members prepare for the team's disbandment.

## CONCEPT CONNECTION

*To accomplish their goals—whether in the business world or on the basketball court—teams have to successfully advance to the **performing stage of team development**. The WNBA's Phoenix Mercury teammates shown here blend their talents and energies so effortlessly that they play the game not like separate people but like a coordinated piece of a whole. Phoenix recently began using psychological testing as part of the appraisal of new coaches and potential draft picks. Managers think testing gives them another tool for building a high-performance team. As part-owner Anne Mariucci puts it, "If a person isn't dotting the I's and crossing the T's, we know why, and we can surround that person with people who complement that . . . . "*

wish to signify the team's disbanding with a ritual or ceremony, perhaps giving out plaques and awards to signify closure and completeness.

The five stages of team development typically occur in sequence. In teams that are under time pressure or that will exist for only a short period of time, the stages may occur quite rapidly. The stages may also be accelerated for virtual teams. For example, bringing people together for a couple of days of team building can help virtual teams move rapidly through the forming and storming stages. McDevitt Street Bovis, one of the country's largest construction management firms, uses an understanding of the stages of team development to put teams on a solid foundation.

**MCDEVITT STREET BOVIS**
**http://www.bovis.com**

The team-building process at McDevitt Street Bovis is designed to take teams to the performing stage as quickly as possible by giving everyone an opportunity to get to know one another; explore the ground rules; and clarify roles, responsibilities, and expectations. The company credits this process for quickly and effectively unifying teams, circumventing damaging and time-consuming conflicts, and preventing lawsuits related to major construction projects.

Rather than the typical construction project characterized by conflicts, frantic scheduling, and poor communications, Bovis wants its collection of contractors, designers, suppliers, and other partners to function like a true team—putting the success of the project ahead of their own individual interests. The team is first divided into separate groups that may have competing objectives—such as the clients in one group, suppliers in another, engineers and architects in a third, and so forth—and asked to come up with a list of their goals for the project. Although interests sometimes vary widely in purely accounting terms, there are almost always common themes. By talking about conflicting goals and interests, as well as what all the groups share, facilitators help the team gradually come together around a common purpose and begin to develop shared values that will guide the project. After jointly writing a mission statement for the team, each party says what it expects from the others, so that roles and responsibilities can be clarified. The intensive team-building session helps take members quickly through the forming and storming stages of development. "We prevent conflicts from happening," says facilitator Monica Bennett. Leaders at McDevitt Street Bovis believe building better teams builds better buildings.[46]

## Team Cohesiveness

**team cohesiveness**
The extent to which team members are attracted to the team and motivated to remain in it.

Another important aspect of the team process is cohesiveness. Team cohesiveness is defined as the extent to which members are attracted to the team and motivated to remain in it.[47] Members of highly cohesive teams are committed to team activities, attend meetings, and are happy when the team succeeds. Members of less cohesive teams are less concerned about the team's welfare. High cohesiveness is normally considered an attractive feature of teams.

## Determinants of Team Cohesiveness

Characteristics of team structure and context influence cohesiveness. First is *team interaction*. The greater the contact among team members and the more time spent together, the more cohesive the team. Through frequent interactions, members get to know one another and become more devoted to the team.[48] Second is the concept of *shared goals*. If team members agree on goals, they will be more cohesive. Agreeing on purpose and direction binds the team together. Third is *personal attraction to the team*, meaning that members have similar attitudes and values and enjoy being together.

*Go to the experiential exercise on page 795 that pertains to evaluating team cohesiveness.*

*Take A Moment*

Two factors in the team's context also influence group cohesiveness. The first is the presence of competition. When a team is in moderate competition with other teams, its cohesiveness increases as it strives to win. Finally, team success and the favorable evaluation of the team by outsiders add to cohesiveness. When a team succeeds in its task and others in the organization recognize the success, members feel good, and their commitment to the team will be high.

## Consequences of Team Cohesiveness

The outcome of team cohesiveness can fall into two categories—morale and productivity. As a general rule, morale is higher in cohesive teams because of increased communication among members, a friendly team climate, maintenance of membership because of commitment to the team, loyalty, and member participation in team decisions and activities. High cohesiveness has almost uniformly good effects on the satisfaction and morale of team members.[49]

With respect to team performance, research findings are mixed, but cohesiveness may have several effects.[50] First, in a cohesive team, members' productivity tends to be more uniform. Productivity differences among members are small because the team exerts pressure toward conformity. Noncohesive teams do not have this control over member behavior and therefore tend to have wider variation in member productivity.

With respect to the productivity of the team as a whole, research findings suggest that cohesive teams have the potential to be productive, but the degree of productivity depends on the relationship between management and the working team. Thus, team cohesiveness does not necessarily lead to higher team productivity. One study surveyed more than 200 work teams and correlated job performance with their cohesiveness.[51] Highly cohesive teams were more productive when team members felt management support and less productive when they sensed management hostility and negativism. Management hostility led to team norms and goals of low performance, and the highly cohesive teams performed poorly, in accordance with their norms and goals.

The relationship between performance outcomes and cohesiveness is illustrated in Exhibit 21.6. The highest productivity occurs when the team is cohesive and also has a high performance norm, which is a result of its positive relationship with management. Moderate productivity occurs when cohesiveness is low, because team members are less committed to performance norms. The lowest productivity occurs when cohesiveness is high and the team's performance norm is low. Thus, cohesive teams are able to attain their goals and enforce their norms, which can lead to either very high or very low productivity.

A good example of team cohesiveness combined with high performance norms occurred at the Ralston Foods plant in Sparks, Nevada.

# Exhibit 21.6

### Relationship among Team Cohesiveness, Performance Norms, and Productivity

| | | |
|---|---|---|
| **Moderate Productivity**<br>Weak norms in alignment with organization goals | | **High Productivity**<br>Strong norms in alignment with organization goals |
| **Low/Moderate Productivity**<br>Weak norms in opposition to organization goals | | **Low Productivity**<br>Strong norms in opposition to organization goals |

Team Performance Norms (High / Low)

Team Cohesiveness (Low / High)

RALSTON FOODS,
SPARKS, NEVADA
http://www.
ralstonfoods.com

When the Ralston Foods, Sparks, Nevada plant was being retrofitted from an operation that produced pet foods to one producing cereals, plant manager Daniel Kibbe wanted to also transform it into a team-based organization.

After gaining the support of divisional and top executives, Kibbe's first task was to put together the right management team. He put in place a small group of leaders who believed in and supported the idea of participative management. Next, before the plant ever made a pound of cereal, it spent millions of dollars training people how to work in teams and make the kinds of decisions once made by managers. Managers also received training that helped them create an environment of empowerment, trust, and credibility.

The plant's 150 or so workers were divided into six operating work groups, which were, in turn, divided into small teams of around 10 people. Managers wanted to keep teams small so people could get to know one another, develop bonds of trust and commitment, and manage themselves more easily. Some teams function entirely without designated leaders and handle all issues and problems that arise in their areas, including hiring and firing, scheduling, budgeting, quality, and disciplinary problems. Other teams have leaders assigned by management. Yet, in all cases, the teams function quite independently and have developed strong bonds that motivate them to perform well for the sake of the team. The teams that have progressed to total self-direction actually outperform teams with assigned leaders.[52]

At Ralston Foods, a combination of team cohesiveness and management support that created high performance norms from the beginning has led to record-breaking production output levels and generated significant cost savings.

## Team Norms

team norm
A standard of conduct that is shared by team members and guides their behavior.

A team norm is a standard of conduct that is shared by team members and guides their behavior.[53] Norms are informal. They are not written down, as are rules and procedures. Norms are valuable because they define boundaries of acceptable behavior. They make life easier for team members by providing a frame of reference for what is right and wrong. Norms identify key values, clarify role expectations, and facilitate team survival. For example, union members may develop a norm of not cooperating with management because they do not trust management's motives. In this way, norms protect the group and express key values.

Norms begin to develop in the first interactions among members of a new team.[54] Thus, it is important for leaders, especially those of virtual teams, to try to shape early interactions that will lead to norms that help the team succeed. Norms that apply to both day-to-day behavior and employee output and performance gradually evolve, letting members know what is acceptable and directing their actions toward acceptable performance. Four common ways in which norms develop for controlling and directing behavior are illustrated in Exhibit 21.7.[55]

Exhibit 21.7

**Four Ways Team Norms Develop**

## Critical Events

Often, *critical events* in a team's history establish an important precedent. One example occurred when an employee at a forest products plant was seriously injured while standing too close to a machine being operated by a teammate. This led to a norm that team members regularly monitor one another to make sure all safety rules are observed. Any critical event can lead to the creation of a norm.

## Primacy

*Primacy* means that the first behaviors that occur in a team often set a precedent for later team expectations. For example, at one company a team leader began his first meeting by raising an issue and then "leading" team members until he got the solution he wanted. The pattern became ingrained so quickly into an unproductive team norm that team members dubbed meetings the "Guess What I Think" game.[56]

## Carryover Behaviors

*Carryover behaviors* bring norms into the team from outside. One current example is the strong norm against smoking in many management teams. Some team members sneak around, gargling with mouthwash, and fear expulsion because the team culture believes everyone should kick the habit. Carryover behavior also influences small teams of college students assigned by instructors to do class work. Norms brought into the team from outside suggest that students should participate equally and help members get a reasonable grade.

## Explicit Statements

With *explicit statements*, leaders or team members can initiate norms by articulating them to the team. Explicit statements symbolize what counts and thus have considerable impact. Making explicit statements can be a highly effective way for leaders to influence or change team norms. At Warner Brother Television, Greg Berlanti, who is the head writer and "show runner" for the WB Network's popular *Everwood*, makes clear to his team of writers that they should "leave on a successful note."

Berlanti believes people are more creative when they're feeling upbeat, so whenever the team has been struggling and reaches a breakthrough, he ends the meeting so they can pick up at a high point the next day. Although the writers' rooms can get pretty nerve-wracking with deadlines approaching, Berlanti's explicit statements about starting from a positive place establish norms of taking needed breaks and down time.[57]

# Managing Team Conflict

The final characteristic of team process is conflict. Of all the skills required for effective team management, none is more important than handling the conflicts that inevitably arise among members. Whenever people work together in teams, some conflict is inevitable. Conflict can arise among members within a team or between one team and another. Conflict refers to antagonistic interaction in which one party attempts to block the intentions or goals of another.[58] Competition, which is rivalry among individuals or teams, can have a healthy impact because it energizes people toward higher performance.[59]

**conflict**
Antagonistic interaction in which one party attempts to thwart the intentions or goals of another.

## Balancing Conflict and Cooperation

Some conflict can actually be beneficial to teams.[60] A healthy level of conflict helps to prevent groupthink, in which people are so committed to a cohesive team that they are reluctant to express contrary opinions. Author and scholar Jerry Harvey tells a story of how members of his extended family in Texas decided to drive 40 miles to Abilene on a hot day when the car's air conditioning didn't work. Everyone was miserable. Later, each person admitted they hadn't wanted to go but went along to please the others. Harvey used the term *Abilene Paradox* to describe this tendency to go along with others for the sake of avoiding conflict.[61] Similarly, when people in work teams go along simply for the sake of harmony, problems typically result. Thus, a degree of conflict leads to better decision making because multiple viewpoints are expressed. Among top management teams, for example, low levels of conflict have been found to be associated with poor decision making.[62]

**groupthink**
The tendency for people to be so committed to a cohesive team that they are reluctant to express contrary opinions.

However, conflict that is too strong, that is focused on personal rather than work issues, or that is not managed appropriately can be damaging to the team's morale and productivity. Too much conflict can be destructive, tear relationships apart, and interfere with the healthy exchange of ideas and information.[63] Team leaders have to find the right balance between conflict and cooperation, as illustrated in Exhibit 21.8. Too little conflict can decrease team performance because the team doesn't benefit from a mix of opinions and ideas—even disagreements—that might lead to better solutions or prevent the team from making mistakes. At the other end of the spectrum, too much conflict outweighs the team's cooperative efforts and leads to a decrease in employee satisfaction and commitment, hurting team performance. A moderate amount of conflict that is managed appropriately typically results in the highest levels of team performance.

*Take A Moment*    *Go to the ethical dilemma on page 796 that pertains to team cohesiveness and conflict.*

## Causes of Conflict

Several factors can cause people to engage in conflict:[64]

Exhibit 21.8

## Balancing Conflict and Cooperation

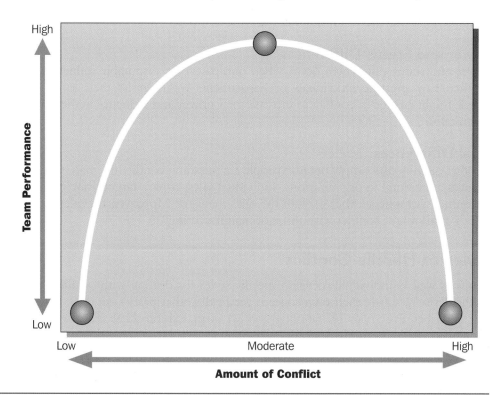

## Scarce Resources

Resources include money, information, and supplies. Whenever individuals or teams must compete for scarce or declining resources, conflict is almost inevitable. The introduction of fast-cycle teams, as described earlier, for example, frequently leads to conflict because it creates a new competition for resources.[65] Some projects may be delayed because managers reallocate resources to fast-cycle projects, leading to conflicts.

## Jurisdictional Ambiguities

Conflicts also emerge when job boundaries and responsibilities are unclear. When task responsibilities are well defined and predictable, people know where they stand. When they are unclear, people may disagree about who has responsibility for specific tasks or who has a claim on resources. Virtual teams are particularly susceptible to this area of conflict because the lack of regular interaction and on-site monitoring sometimes leads to uncertainty and disagreement regarding areas of task responsibility.

## Communication Breakdown

The potential for communication breakdown is also greater with virtual teams and global teams, but faulty communication can occur in any team. Poor communication results in misperceptions and misunderstandings of other people and teams. In some cases, information is intentionally withheld, which can jeopardize trust among teams and lead to long-lasting conflict.

## Personality Clashes

A personality clash occurs when people simply do not get along or do not see eye-to-eye on any issue. Personality clashes are caused by basic differences in personality, values, and attitudes. In one study, personality conflicts were the number-one reported cause preventing front-line management teams from working together effectively.[66] Some personality differences can be overcome. However, severe personality clashes are difficult to resolve. Often, it is a good idea to simply separate the parties so that they need not interact with one another.

### Power and Status Differences

Power and status differences occur when one party has disputable influence over another. Low-prestige individuals or departments might resist their low status. People might engage in conflict to increase their power and influence in the team or organization.

### Goal Differences

Conflict often occurs simply because people are pursuing conflicting goals. Goal differences are natural in organizations. Individual salespeople's targets may put them in conflict with one another or with the sales manager. Moreover, the sales department's goals might conflict with those of manufacturing.

## Styles to Handle Conflict

Teams as well as individuals develop specific styles for dealing with conflict, based on the desire to satisfy their own concern versus the other party's concern. A model that describes five styles of handling conflict is in Exhibit 21.9. The two major dimensions are the extent to which an individual is assertive versus cooperative in his or her approach to conflict.

Effective team members vary their style of handling conflict to fit a specific situation. Each of these five styles is appropriate in certain cases.[67]

1.  The *competing style* reflects assertiveness to get one's own way, and should be used when quick, decisive action is vital on important issues or unpopular actions, such as during emergencies or urgent cost cutting.
2.  The *avoiding style* reflects neither assertiveness nor cooperativeness. It is appropriate when an issue is trivial, when there is no chance of winning, when a delay to gather more information is needed, or when a disruption would be very costly.
3.  The *compromising style* reflects a moderate amount of both assertiveness and cooperativeness. It is appropriate when the goals on both sides are equally important, when opponents have equal power and both sides want to split the difference, or when people need to arrive at temporary or expedient solutions under time pressure.
4.  The *accommodating style* reflects a high degree of cooperativeness, which works best when people realize that they are wrong, when an issue is more important to others than to oneself, when building social credits for use in later discussions, and when maintaining harmony is especially important.
5.  The *collaborating style* reflects both a high degree of assertiveness and cooperativeness. The collaborating style enables both parties to win, although it may require substantial bargaining and negotiation. The collaborating style is important when both sets of concerns are too important to be compromised, when insights from different people need to be merged into an overall solution, and when the commitment of both sides is needed for a consensus.

The various styles of handling conflict are especially effective when an individual disagrees with others. But what does a manager or team leader do when a conflict erupts among others within a team or among teams for which the manager is

Exhibit 21.9

## A Model of Styles to Handle Conflict

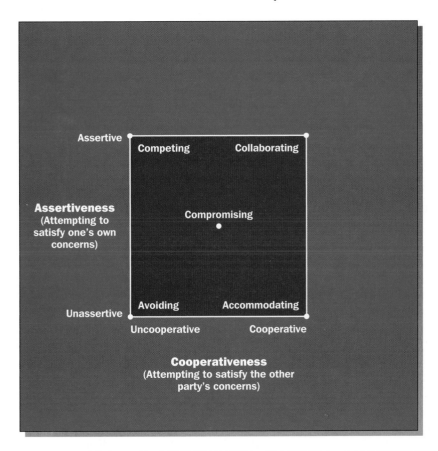

**SOURCE:** Adapted from Kenneth Thomas, "Conflict and Conflict Management," in *Handbook of Industrial and Organizational Behavior*, ed. M. D. Dunnette (New York: John Wiley, 1976), 900.

responsible? Research suggests that several techniques can be used as strategies for resolving conflicts among people or departments. These techniques might also be used when conflict is formalized, such as between a union and management.

### Superordinate Goals

The larger objective that cannot be attained by a single party is identified as a superordinate goal.[68] This is similar to the concept of vision. A powerful vision of where the organization wants to be in the future often compels people to overcome conflicts and cooperate for the greater good. Similarly, a superordinate goal requires the cooperation of conflicting team members for achievement. People must pull together. To the extent that employees can be focused on team or organization goals, the conflict will decrease because they see the big picture and realize they must work together to achieve it.

**superordinate goal**
A goal that cannot be reached by a single party.

### Bargaining/Negotiation

Bargaining and negotiation mean that the parties engage one another in an attempt to systematically reach a solution. They attempt logical problem solving to identify and correct the conflict. This approach works well if the individuals can set aside personal animosities and deal with the conflict in a businesslike way. Books, software, newsletters, and training seminars on negotiating have proliferated in recent years. Most emphasize that the key to effectiveness is to see negotiation not as a zero-sum game but as a process for reaching a creative solution that benefits everyone.[69]

**mediation**

The process of using a third party to settle a dispute.

## Mediation

Using a third party to settle a dispute involves mediation. A mediator could be a supervisor, higher-level manager, or someone from the human resource department. The mediator can discuss the conflict with each party and work toward a solution. If a solution satisfactory to both sides cannot be reached, the parties might be willing to turn the conflict over to the mediator and abide by his or her solution.

## Facilitating Communication

Managers can facilitate communication to ensure that conflicting parties hold accurate perceptions. Providing opportunities for the disputants to get together and exchange information reduces conflict. As they learn more about one another, suspicions diminish and improved teamwork becomes possible.

Four guidelines can help managers facilitate communication and keep teams focused on substantive issues rather than interpersonal conflicts.[70]

- *Focus on facts.* Keep team discussions focused on issues, not personalities. Working with more data and information rather than less can keep team members focused on facts and prevent meetings from degenerating into pointless debates over opinions. At Star Electronics, the top management team meets daily, weekly, and monthly to examine a wide variety of specific operating measures. Looking at the details helps team members debate critical issues and avoid useless arguments.
- *Develop multiple alternatives.* Teams that deliberately develop many alternatives, sometimes considering four or five options at once, have a lower incidence of interpersonal conflict. Having a multitude of options to consider concentrates team members' energy on solving problems. In addition, the process of generating multiple choices is fun and creative, which sets a positive tone for the meeting and reduces the chance for conflict.
- *Maintain a balance of power.* Managers and team leaders should accept the team's decision as fair, even if they do not agree with it. Fairness requires a balance of power within the team.
- *Never force a consensus.* There will naturally be conflict over some issues, which managers find a way to resolve without forcing a consensus. When there are persistent differences of opinion, the team leader sometimes has to make a decision guided by input from other team members. At Andromeda Processing, the CEO insisted on consensus from his top management team, causing a debate to rage on for months. Conflict and frustration mounted to the point where some top managers left the company. The group achieved consensus only at the price of losing several key managers.

# Benefits and Costs of Teams

In deciding whether to use teams to perform specific tasks, managers must consider both benefits and costs. Teams may have a positive impact on both the output productivity and satisfaction of members. On the other hand, teams may also create a situation in which motivation and performance actually decline.

## Potential Benefits of Teams

Teams come closest to achieving their full potential when they enhance individual productivity through increased member effort, members' personal satisfaction, integration of diverse abilities and skills, and increased organizational flexibility.

## Level of Effort

Employee teams often unleash enormous energy and creativity from workers who like the idea of using their brains as well as their bodies to accomplish an important goal. Teams are an important part of the move to the learning organization and more horizontal forms of organizing, as described in Chapters 2 and 10. To facilitate learning and problem solving, managers are breaking down barriers, empowering workers, and encouraging employees to use their minds and creativity. Research has found that working in a team often increases an individual's motivation and performance. Social facilitation refers to the tendency for the presence of others to enhance one's motivation and performance. Simply being in the presence of other people has an energizing effect.[71]

**social facilitation**
The tendency for the presence of others to influence an individual's motivation and performance.

## Satisfaction of Members

As described in Chapter 19, employees have needs for belongingness and affiliation. Working in teams can help meet these needs. Participative teams reduce boredom and often increase employees' feeling of dignity and self-worth because the whole person is employed. At Radius, a Boston restaurant, for example, two-person kitchen teams have full responsibility for their part of a meal, which gives them a greater sense of accomplishment and importance.[72] People who have a satisfying team environment cope better with stress, enjoy their jobs, and have a higher level of organizational commitment.

## Expanded Job Knowledge and Skills

The third major benefit of using teams is the empowerment of employees to bring greater knowledge and ability to the task. For one thing, multiskilled employees learn all of the jobs that the team performs. Teams gain the intellectual resources of several members who can suggest shortcuts and offer alternative points of view for team decisions. Teams at Radius work for six weeks at one station and then rotate to another. This makes the work experience fun, exciting, and educational, as well as enables employees to learn a broad range of skills.

## Organizational Responsiveness

Employee teams enhance flexibility because workers can be reorganized and employees reassigned as needed. People work closely together, learn a variety of skills, and can exchange jobs as needed to accomplish the team's task. In addition, teams can break down traditional organizational boundaries so that people collaborate across functional and hierarchical lines, which enables the organization to rapidly respond to changing customer needs.

© MICHAEL HART

*Cooper Industries' Bussmann division has first-hand knowledge of the **benefits of teams**. Angelina Bernardi, Steve Goble, Ed Haworth, and Lynne Sanick worked on Bussmann's first experimental team to develop the new line of Optima overcurrent protection modules, which combine a fuse and fuseholder in a single, easy-to-use power protection system. The team introduced the line in 10 months compared to the average 24-month cycle time. The enhanced flexibility and rapid response to customer needs led Bussmann to create Rapid Development Teams for each of its major market segments. The teams consistently cut new-product development time in half.*

# Potential Costs of Teams

Managers must also assess certain costs or liabilities associated with teamwork. When teams do not work very well, the major reasons usually are power realignment, free riding, coordination costs, or system revisions.

## Power Realignment

When companies form front-line employees into teams, the major losers are low- and middle-level managers. These managers are sometimes reluctant to give up power. Indeed, when teams are successful, fewer supervisors are needed. This is especially true for self-directed teams, because workers take over supervisory responsibility. The adjustment is difficult for managers who fear the loss of status or even their jobs and who have to learn new, people-oriented and team leadership skills to survive.[73]

## Free Riding

The term free rider refers to a team member who attains benefits from team membership but does not do a proportionate share of the work.[74] Free riding sometimes is called *social loafing*, because members do not exert equal effort. One study of global virtual teams found a greater propensity among members for shirking their duties or giving less than their full effort.[75] Also, in large teams, some people are likely to work less. For example, research found that the pull exerted on a rope was greater by individuals working alone than by individuals in a group. Similarly, people who were asked to clap and make noise made more noise on a per person basis when working alone or in small groups than they did in a large group.[76] The problem of free riding has been experienced by people who have participated in student project groups. Some students put more effort into the group project than others do but often it seems that no members work as hard for the group as they do for their individual grades.

## Coordination Costs

The time and energy required to coordinate the activities of a group to enable it to perform its task are called coordination costs. Groups must spend time getting ready to do work and lose productive time in deciding who is to do what and when.[77] Once again, student project groups illustrate coordination costs. Members must meet after class just to decide when they can meet to perform the task. Schedules must be checked, telephone calls made, and meeting times arranged in order to get down to business. Hours may be devoted to the administration and coordination of the group. Students often feel they could do the same project by themselves in less time. Teams typically have frequent meetings throughout a project, so leaders have to know how to keep meetings focused and productive. This chapter's Shoptalk box offers some tips for running a great meeting.

## Revising Systems

Implementing teams also requires changes in other parts of the organization. In particular, performance appraisal and reward systems have to be carefully revised to reflect the new team approach; otherwise, teamwork will fail. Managers should be aware that a shift to teams requires that time and resources be invested to develop new systems that support and reinforce collaboration, sharing of information, and empowerment rather than pitting team members against one another.

## Manager's Solution

Several important concepts about teams were described in this chapter. Organizations use teams both to achieve coordination as part of the formal structure and to encourage employee involvement. Formal teams include vertical teams along the chain of command and horizontal teams such as cross-functional teams and committees. Special-purpose teams are used for special, large-scale, creative projects. Employee involvement via teams is designed to bring lower-level employees into decision processes to improve quality, efficiency, and job satisfaction. Companies typically start with problem-solving teams, which may evolve into self-directed teams that take on responsibility for management activities. New approaches to teamwork include virtual teams and global teams. These teams may include contingent workers, customers, suppliers, and other outsiders. Although team members sometimes meet face to face, they use advanced information and telecommunications technology to accomplish much of their work.

Most teams go through systematic stages of development: forming, storming, norming, performing, and adjourning. Team characteristics that can influence organizational effectiveness are size, diversity, cohesiveness, norms, and members' roles. All teams experience some conflict because of scarce resources, ambiguous

## Turbulent Times

# manager's Shoptalk

## How to Run a Great Meeting

Many managers think meetings are a waste of time. Busy executives may spend up to 70 percent of their time in meetings where participants doodle, drink coffee, tap away on their laptops, and think about what they could be doing back in their offices.

However, effective meetings help people process important information and solve problems. Good meetings don't just happen; they are designed through careful thought and planning. The success of a meeting depends on what is done in advance of, during, and after it.

### Prepare in Advance

Advance preparation is the single most important tool for running an efficient, productive meeting. Advance preparation should include the following:

- *Define the purpose.* The leader should be very explicit in setting goals and communicating them clearly and meaningfully. If a meeting isn't essential, don't have it.
- *Prepare an agenda.* The agenda is a simple list of the topics to be discussed. It is important because it lets people know what to expect and keeps the meeting on track.
- *Issue invitations selectively.* If the group gets too big, the meeting will not be productive. However, be sure every department with a stake in the topic is represented.
- *Set a time limit.* The ending time for the meeting should be announced in advance, and the agenda should require things to move along at a reasonable pace.

### During the Meeting

If the leader is prepared in advance, the meeting will go smoothly. Moreover, certain techniques will bring out the best in people and make the meeting even more productive:

- *Start on time.* Although this sounds obvious, many meetings get started 10 or 15 minutes late. Starting on time has symbolic value,

because it tells people that the topic is important and that the leader values their time.
- *Outlaw cell phones and laptops.* Having the flow of discussion interrupted by the ringing of a cell phone can throw the meeting completely off-track. Unless they will be used for the purposes of the meetings, laptops should not be allowed.
- *State the purpose and review the agenda.* The leader should start the meeting by stating the explicit purpose and clarifying what should be accomplished by the time the meeting is over.
- *Encourage participation.* Good meetings contain lots of discussion. If the leader merely wants to present one-way information to members, he or she should send a memo. A few subtle techniques go a long way toward increasing participation:
  - *Draw out the silent.* This means saying, "Bob, what do you think of Nancy's idea?"
  - *Control the talkative.* Some people overdo it and dominate the discussion. The chairperson's job is to redirect the discussion toward other people. One organization has a rule called NOSTUESO (No one speaks twice until everyone speaks once).
  - *Encourage the clash of ideas.* A good meeting is not a series of dialogues but a crosscurrent of discussion and debate. The leader listens, guides, mediates, stimulates, and summarizes this discussion.
- *Stick to the purpose.* Encouraging a free flow of ideas does not mean allowing participants to sidetrack the meeting into discussions of issues not on the agenda. This can waste valuable time and prevent the group from reaching its goals.

### After the Meeting

The actions following the meeting are designed to summarize and implement agreed-upon points.

- *End with a call to action.* The last item of the meeting's agenda is to summarize the main points and make sure everyone understands his or her assignments.

# manager's Shoptalk

## Turbulent Times

- *Follow up*. Send minutes of the meeting to all participants. Use this memorandum also to summarize the key accomplishments of the meeting and suggest schedules for agreed-upon activities.

SOURCES: Based on Jeff Siegel, "Mending Your Meetings," *Southwest Airlines Spirit* (March 2004), 46-49; Edward Michaels, "Business Meetings," *Small Business Reports* (February 1989), 82-88; Daniel Stoffman, "Waking Up to Great Meetings," *Canadian Business* (November 1986), 75-79; Antoney Jay, "How to Run a Meeting," *Harvard Business Review* (March-April 1976), 120-134; Jana Kemp, "Avoiding Agenda Overstack," *Corporate University Review* (May-June 1997), 42-43; and Jeffrey L. Seglin, "We've Got to Start Meeting Like This," *CIO* (March 1, 2001), 168-170.

responsibilities, communication breakdown, personality clashes, power and status differences, and goal conflicts. Some conflict is beneficial, but too much can hurt the team and the organization. Techniques for managing and resolving conflicts include superordinate goals, bargaining, mediation, and communication. Techniques for facilitating team communication to minimize conflict are to focus on facts, develop multiple alternatives, maintain a balance of power, and never force a consensus. Advantages of using teams include increased motivation, diverse knowledge and skills, satisfaction of team members, and organizational responsiveness. Potential costs of using teams are power realignment, free riding, coordination costs, and the need to revise systems.

Returning to the opening example of Rowe Furniture, Charlene Pedrolie believed teamwork could be the answer for helping Rowe meet the challenges of a fast-paced, competitive environment. She eliminated most supervisory positions, cross-trained employees to perform the different tasks required to build a piece of furniture, and then asked front-line workers to form horizontal clusters, or cells, to design the new production system. Each group selected its own members from the various functional areas, then created the processes, schedules, and routines for a particular product line. The assembly line was a thing of the past. Five hundred workers who had been accustomed to standing in one place and having the furniture come to them were suddenly working in teams, wandering from one partially assembled piece to another, performing a variety of tasks. Every team had instant access to up-to-date information about order flows, output, productivity, and quality. The sense of personal control and responsibility eventually led to a dramatic change in workers, who began holding impromptu meetings to discuss problems, check each other's progress, or talk about new ideas and better ways of doing things. Productivity and quality shot through the roof. Before long, the factory was delivering custom-made pieces within a month. Only a few months later, that lead time had decreased to a mere 10 days.[78]

# Discussion Questions

1. Volvo went to self-directed teams to assemble cars because of the need to attract and keep workers in Sweden, where pay raises are not a motivator (high taxes) and many other jobs are available. Is this a good reason for using a team approach? Discuss.

2. During your own work experience, have you been part of a formal vertical team? A task force? A committee? An employee involvement team? How did your work experience differ in each type of team?

3. What are the five stages of team development? What happens during each stage?

4. How would you explain the emergence of problem-solving and self-directed teams in companies throughout North America? Do you think implementation of the team concept is difficult in these companies? Discuss.

5. Assume that you are part of a student project team and one member is not doing his or her share. Which conflict resolution strategy would you use? Why?

6. Do you think a moderate level of conflict might be healthy for an organization? Discuss.

7. When you are a member of a team, do you adopt a task specialist or socioemotional role? Which role is more important for a team's effectiveness? Discuss.

8. What is the relationship between team cohesiveness and team performance?

9. Describe the advantages and disadvantages of teams. In what situations might the disadvantages outweigh the advantages?

10. What is a team norm? What norms have developed in teams to which you have belonged?

11. One company had 40 percent of its workers and 20 percent of its managers resign during the first year after reorganizing into teams. What might account for this dramatic turnover? How might managers ensure a smooth transition to teams?

# Management in Practice: Experiential Exercise

## Is Your Group a Cohesive Team?

Think about a student group with which you have worked. Answer the questions below as they pertain to the functioning of that group.

Disagree Strongly                    Agree Strongly

1    2    3    4    5

1. Group meetings were held regularly and everyone attended.  1  2  3  4  5

2. We talked about and shared the same goals for group work and grade.  1  2  3  4  5

3. We spent most of our meeting time talking business, but discussions were open-ended and active.  1  2  3  4  5

4. We talked through any conflicts and disagreements until they were resolved.
   1  2  3  4  5

5. Group members listened carefully to one another.
   1  2  3  4  5

6. We really trusted each other, speaking personally about what we really felt.  1  2  3  4  5

7. Leadership roles were rotated and shared, with people taking initiative at appropriate times for the good of the group.  1  2  3  4  5

8. Each member found a way to contribute to the final work product.  1  2  3  4  5

9. I was really satisfied being a member of the group.  1  2  3  4  5

10. We freely gave each other credit for jobs well done.  1  2  3  4  5

11. Group members gave and received feedback to help the group do even better.
    1  2  3  4  5

12. We held each other accountable; each member was accountable to the group.
    1  2  3  4  5

13. Group members really liked and respected each other.  1  2  3  4  5

**Total Score** _____

The questions here are about team cohesion. If you scored 52 or greater, your group experienced authentic teamwork. Congratulations. If you scored between 39 and 51, there was a positive group identity that might have been developed even further. If you scored between 26 and 38, group identity was weak and probably not very satisfying. If you scored below 26, it was hardly a group at all, resembling a loose collection of individuals.

Remember, teamwork doesn't happen by itself. Individuals like you have to understand what a team is and then work to make it happen. What can you do to make a student group more like a team? Do you have the courage to take the initiative?

# Management in Practice: Ethical Dilemma

## Consumer Safety or Team Commitment?

Nancy was part of a pharmaceutical team developing a product called loperamide, a liquid treatment for diarrhea for people unable to take solid medicine, namely infants, children, and the elderly. Loperamide contained 44 times the amount of saccharin allowed by the FDA in a 12-ounce soft drink, but there were no regulations governing saccharin content in medication.

Nancy was the only medical member of the seven-person project team. The team made a unanimous decision to reduce the saccharin content before marketing loperamide, so the team initiated a three-month effort for reformulation. In the meantime, management was pressuring the team to allow human testing with the original formula until the new formula became available. After a heated team debate, all the team members except Nancy voted to begin testing with the current formula.

Nancy believed it was unethical to test on old people and children a drug she considered potentially dangerous. As the only medical member of the team, she had to sign the forms allowing testing. She refused and was told that unless she signed, she would be removed from the project, demoted, and seen as a poor team player, nonpromotable, lacking in judgment, and unable to work with marketing people. Nancy was aware that no proof existed that high saccharin would be directly harmful to potential users of loperamide.

## What Do You Do?

1. Refuse to sign. As a medical doctor, Nancy must stand up for what she believes is right.
2. Resign. There is no reason to stay in this company and be punished for ethically correct behavior. Testing the drug will become someone else's responsibility.
3. Sign the form. The judgment of other team members cannot be all wrong. The loperamide testing is not illegal and will move ahead anyway, so it would preserve team unity and company effectiveness to sign.

Source: Based on Tom L. Beauchamp, *Ethical Theory and Business*, 2d ed. (Englewood Cliffs, N.J.: Prentice-Hall, 1983).

# Surf the Net

1. **Self-Directed Work Teams.** Use your search engine to find a site such as *http://www.teamtechnology.co.uk/tt/h-articl/tb_basic.htm* that will provide information on the team-building process. Another good site can be found at *http://ianrpubs.unl.edu/misc/cc352.htm*, where you can click on categories such as team effectiveness and focused teams. Select three ideas that you could apply to improve the performance of a team that you are currently a member of—an employee group, an athletic team, a campus or community organization, etc. Report to your class the ideas you implemented and what impact they had on your team's performance.

2. **Team Meetings.** The communication process used frequently in the team environment is group meetings. Productive meetings don't just automatically happen. One Web site loaded with excellent ideas and links to information about improving the meeting process can be found at

*http://www.effectivemeetings.com/teams/teamwork/bens.asp*. Find information on issues such as: (a) preparation, (b) technology, and (c) productivity.

3. **Team Performance.** Something very evident among athletic teams is the importance of keeping the team members motivated to achieve their goal of winning the game. Assume the role of "chief motivator" for a work team and design a one-page flyer to be given to each team member in which you include the best advice you can find for enhancing team performance. A good starting point for finding information for your flyer is *http://www.brightquotes.com* (select the heading of "Teamwork"). You can copy and paste those items from this site or other sites into your word processing program to create your flyer.

# Case for Critical Analysis

## Acme Minerals Extraction Company

Several years ago, Acme Minerals Extraction Company introduced teams in an effort to solve morale and productivity problems at its Wichita plant. Acme used highly sophisticated technology, employing geologists, geophysicists, and engineers on what was referred to as the "brains" side of the business, as well as skilled and semi-skilled labor on the "brawn" side to run the company's underground extracting operations. The two sides regularly clashed, and when some engineers locked several operations workers out of the office in 100-degree heat, the local press had a field day. Suzanne Howard was hired to develop a program that would improve productivity and morale at the Wichita plant, with the idea that it would then be implemented at other Acme sites.

Howard had a stroke of luck in the form of Donald Peterson, a long-time Acme employee who was highly respected at the Wichita plant and was looking for one final, challenging project before he retired. Peterson had served in just about every possible line

and staff position at Acme over his 39-year career, and he understood the problems workers faced on both the "brains" and the "brawn" sides of the business. Howard was pleased when Peterson agreed to serve as leader for the Wichita pilot project. There were three functional groups at the Wichita plant: operations, made up primarily of hourly workers who operated and maintained the extracting equipment; the "below ground" group, consisting of engineers, geologists, and geophysicists who determined where and how to drill; and the "above ground" group of engineers in charge of cursory refinement and transportation of the minerals. Howard and Peterson decided the first step was to get these different groups talking to one another and sharing ideas. They instituted a monthly "problem chat," an optional meeting to which all employees were invited to discuss unresolved problems. At the first meeting, Howard and Peterson were the only two people who showed up. However, people gradually began to attend the meetings, and after about six months they had become lively problem-solving discussions that led to many improvements.

Next, Howard and Peterson introduced teams to "select a problem and implement a tailored solution," or SPITS. These were ad hoc groups made up of members from each of the three functional areas. They were formed to work on a specific problem identified in a chat meeting and were disbanded when the problem was solved. SPITS were given the authority to address problems without seeking management approval. There were some rocky moments, as engineers resented working with operations personnel and vice versa. However, over time, and with the strong leadership of Peterson, the groups began to come together and focus on the issues rather than spending most of their time arguing. Eventually, workers in Wichita were organized into permanent cross-functional teams that were empowered to make their own decisions and elect their own leaders. After a year and a half, things were really humming. The different groups weren't just working together; they had also started socializing together. At one of the problem chats, an operations worker jokingly suggested that the brains and the brawn should duke it out once a week to get rid of the tensions so they could focus all their energy on the job to be done. Several others joined in the joking, and eventually, the group decided to square off in a weekly softball game. Peterson had T-shirts printed up that said BRAINS AND BRAWN. The softball games were well attended, and both sides usually ended up having a few beers together at a local bar afterward. Productivity and morale soared at the Wichita plant, and costs continued to decline.

Top executives believed the lessons learned at Wichita should make implementing the program at other sites less costly and time-consuming. However, when Howard and her team attempted to implement the program at the Lubbock plant, things didn't go well. They felt under immense pressure from top management to get the team-based productivity project running smoothly at Lubbock. Because people weren't showing up for the problem chat meetings, attendance was made mandatory. However, the meetings still produced few valuable ideas or suggestions. Although a few of the SPITS teams solved important problems, none of them showed the kind of commitment and enthusiasm Howard had seen in Wichita. In addition, the Lubbock workers refused to participate in the softball games and other team-building exercises that Howard's team developed for them. Howard finally convinced some workers to join in the softball games by bribing them with free food and beer. "If I just had a Donald Peterson in Lubbock, things would go a lot more smoothly," Howard thought. "These workers don't trust us the way workers in Wichita trusted him." It seemed that no matter how hard Howard and her team tried to make the project work in Lubbock, morale continued to decline and conflicts between the different groups of workers actually seemed to increase.

## Questions

1. What types of teams described in the chapter are represented in this case?
2. Why do you think the team project succeeded at Wichita but isn't working in Lubbock?
3. What advice would you give Suzanne Howard and her team for improving the employee involvement climate at the Lubbock plant?

Source: Based on Michael C. Beers, "The Strategy That Wouldn't Travel," *Harvard Business Review*, November–December 1996, 18–31.

# Endnotes

1. Thomas Petzinger, Jr., *The New Pioneers: The Men and Women Who Are Transforming the Workplace and Marketplace* (New York: Simon & Schuster, 1999), 27–32.
2. "Team Goal-Setting," *Small Business Report* (January 1988), 76–77; Frank V. Cespedes, Stephen X. Dole, and Robert J. Freedman, "Teamwork for Today's Selling," *Harvard Business Review* (March–April 1989), 44–55; Victoria J. Marsick, Ernie Turner, and Lars Cederholm, "International Managers as Team Leaders," *Management Review* (March 1989), 46–49;

and Terry Adler, Janice A. Black, and John P. Loveland, "Complex Systems: Boundary-Spanning Training Techniques," *Journal of European Industrial Training* 27, no. 2–4 (2002), 111+.
3. J. D. Osburn, L. Moran, E. Musselwhite, and J. H. Zenger, *Self-Directed Work Teams: The New American Challenge* (Homewood, IL: Business One Irwin, 1990).
4. Linda I. Glassop, "The Organizational Benefits of Teams," *Human Relations* 55, no. 2 (2002), 225–249.
5. Carl E. Larson and Frank M. J. LaFasto, *TeamWork* (Newbury Park, Calif.: Sage, 1989).

6. "'Golden Hour' Crucial Time for Surgeons on Front Line," *Associated Press* report in *Johnson City Press* (April 1, 2003), 9.

7. Eric Sundstrom, Kenneth P. DeMeuse, and David Futrell, "Work Teams," *American Psychologist* 45 (February 1990), 120–133.

8. Deborah L. Gladstein, "Groups in Context: A Model of Task Group Effectiveness," *Administrative Science Quarterly* 29 (1984), 499–517.

9. Dora C. Lau and J. Keith Murnighan, "Demographic Diversity and Faultlines: The Compositional Dynamics of Organizational Groups," *Academy of Management Review* 23, no. 2 (1998), 325–340.

10. Thomas Owens, "Business Teams," *Small Business Report* (January 1989), 50–58.

11. "Participation Teams," *Small Business Report* (September 1987), 38–41.

12. Susanne G. Scott and Walter O. Einstein, "Strategic Performance Appraisal in Team-Based Organizations: One Size Does Not Fit All," *Academy of Management Executive* 15, no. 2 (2001), 107–116.

13. Larson and LaFasto, *TeamWork*.

14. V. K. Narayanan, Frank L. Douglas, Brock Guernsey, and John Charnes, "How Top Management Steers Fast Cycle Teams to Success," *Strategy & Leadership* 30, no. 3 (2002), 19–27.

15. James H. Shonk, *Team-Based Organizations* (Homewood, Ill.: Business One Irwin, 1992); and John Hoerr, "The Payoff from Teamwork," *BusinessWeek* (July 10, 1989), 56–62.

16. Gregory L. Miles, "Suddenly, USX Is Playing Mr. Nice Guy," *BusinessWeek* (June 26, 1989), 151–152.

17. Jeanne M. Wilson, Jill George, and Richard S. Wellings, with William C. Byham, *Leadership Trapeze: Strategies for Leadership in Team-Based Organizations* (San Francisco: Jossey-Bass, 1994).

18. Ruth Wageman, "Critical Success Factors for Creating Superb Self-Managing Teams," *Organizational Dynamics* (Summer 1997), 49–61.

19. Thomas Owens, "The Self-Managing Work Team," *Small Business Report* (February 1991), 53–65.

20. Bradley L. Kirkman and Benson Rosen, "Powering Up Teams," Organizational Dynamics (Winter 2000), 48–66.

21. Vanessa Urch Druskat and Jane V. Wheeler, "Managing from the Boundary: The Effective Leadership of Self-Managing Work Teams," *Academy of Management Journal* 46, no. 4 (2003), 435–457.

22. Donald Vredenburgh and Irene Yunxia He, "Leadership Lessons From a Conductorless Orchestra," *Business Horizons* (September–October 2003), 19–24.

23. Curtis Sittenfeld, "Powered by the People," *Fast Company* (July/August 1999), 178–189.

24. The discussion of virtual teams is based on Wayne F. Cascio and Stan Shurygailo, "E-Leadership and Virtual Teams," *Organizational Dynamics* 31, no. 4 (2002), 362–376; Anthony M. Townsend, Samuel M. DeMarie, and Anthony R. Hendrickson, "Virtual Teams: Technology and the Workplace of the Future," *Academy of Management Executive* 12, no. 3 (August 1998), 17–29; and Deborah L. Duarte and Nancy Tennant Snyder, *Mastering Virtual Teams* (San Francisco: Jossey-Bass, 1999).

25. Jessica Lipnack and Jeffrey Stamps, "Virtual Teams: The New Way to Work," *Strategy & Leadership* (January/February 1999), 14–19.

26. Based on Bradley L. Kirkman, Benson Rosen, Cristina B. Gibson, Paul E. Tesluk, and Simon O. McPherson, "Five Challenges to Virtual Team Success: Lessons From Sabre, Inc.," *Academy of Management Executive* 16, no. 3 (2002): 67–79; Wayne F. Cascio and Stan Shurygailo, "E-Leadership and Virtual Teams," *Organizational Dynamics* 31, no. 4 (2002): 362–376; Ilze Zigurs, "Leadership in Virtual Teams: Oxymoron or Opportunity?" *Organizational Dynamics* 31, no. 4 (2002): 339–351; and Manju K. Ahuja and John E. Galvin, "Socialization in Virtual Groups," unpublished manuscript.

27. Kirkman et al., "Five Challenges to Virtual Team Success."

28. Terri L. Griffith and Margaret A. Neale, "Information Processing in Traditional, Hybrid, and Virtual Teams: From Nascent Knowledge to Transactive Memory," *Research in Organizational Behavior* 23 (2001), 379–421.

29. Vijay Govindarajan and Anil K. Gupta, "Building an Effective Global Business Team," *MIT Sloan Management Review* 42, no. 4 (Summer 2001), 63–71.

30. Charlene Marmer Solomon, "Building Teams Across Borders," *Global Workforce* (November 1998), 12–17.

31. Jane Pickard, "Control Freaks Need Not Apply," *People Management* (February 5, 1998), 49.

32. Cristina B. Gibson, Mary E. Zellmer-Bruhn, and Donald P. Schwab, "Team Effectiveness in Multinational Organizations: Evaluation Across Contexts," *Group and Organizational Management* 28, no. 4 (December 2003): 444–474.

33. Sylvia Odenwald, "Global Work Teams," *Training and Development* (February 1996), 54–57; and Debby Young, "Team Heat," *CIO*, Section 1 (September 1, 1998), 43–51.

34. Reported in "Vive La Difference," box in Julie Connelly, "All Together Now," *Gallup Management Journal* (Spring 2002), 13–18.

35. Ray Oglethorpe in Regina Fazio Maruca, ed., "What Makes Teams Work" (Unit of One column), *Fast Company* (November 2000), 109–140.

36. For research findings on group size, see M. E. Shaw, *Group Dynamics*, 3d ed. (New York: McGraw-Hill, 1981); and G. Manners, "Another Look at Group Size, Group Problem-Solving and Member Consensus," *Academy of Management Journal* 18 (1975), 715–724.

37. Warren E. Watson, Kamalesh Kumar, and Larry K. Michaelsen, "Cultural Diversity's Impact on Interaction Process and Performance: Comparing Homogeneous and Diverse Task Groups," *Academy of Management Journal* 36 (1993), 590–602; Gail Robinson and Kathleen Dechant, "Building a Business Case for Diversity," *Academy of Management Executive* 11, no. 3 (1997), 21–31; and David A. Thomas and Robin J. Ely, "Making Differences Matter: A New Paradigm for Managing Diversity," *Harvard Business Review* (September–October 1996), 79–90.

38. J. Stuart Bunderson and Kathleen M. Sutcliffe, "Comparing Alternative Conceptualizations of Functional Diversity in Management Teams: Process and Performance Effects," *Academy of Management Journal* 45, no. 5 (2002): 875–893; and Marc Orlitzky and John D. Benjamin, "The Effects of Sex Composition on Small Group Performance in a Business School Case Competition," *Academy of Management Learning and Education* 2, no. 2 (2003): 128–138.

39. Watson et al. "Cultural Diversity's Impact on Interaction Process and Performance."

40. George Prince, "Recognizing Genuine Teamwork," *Supervisory Management* (April 1989), 25–36; K. D. Benne and P. Sheats, "Functional Roles of Group Members," *Journal of Social Issues* 4 (1948), 41–49; and R. F. Bales, *SYMLOG* Case Study Kit (New York: Free Press, 1980).

41. Robert A. Baron, *Behavior in Organizations*, 2d ed. (Boston: Allyn & Bacon, 1986).

42. Ibid.

43. Avan R. Jassawalla and Hemant C. Sashittal, "Strategies of Effective New Product Team Leaders," *California Management Review* 42, no. 2 (Winter 2000), 34–51.

44. Kenneth G. Koehler, "Effective Team Management," *Small Business Report* (July 19, 1989), 14–16; and Connie J. G. Gersick, "Time and Transition in Work Teams: Toward a New Model of Group Development," *Academy of Management Journal* 31 (1988), 9–41.

45. Bruce W. Tuckman and Mary Ann C. Jensen, "Stages of Small-Group Development Revisited," *Group and Organizational Studies* 2 (1977), 419–427; and Bruce W. Tuckman, "Developmental Sequences in Small Groups," *Psychological Bulletin* 63 (1965), 384–399. See also Linda N. Jewell and H. Joseph Reitz, *Group Effectiveness in Organizations* (Glenview, Ill.: Scott, Foresman, 1981).

46. Thomas Petzinger Jr., "Bovis Team Helps Builders Construct a Solid Foundation," (The Front Lines column), *The Wall Street Journal* (March 21, 1997), B1.

47. Shaw, *Group Dynamics*.

48. Daniel C. Feldman and Hugh J. Arnold, *Managing Individual and Group Behavior in Organizations* (New York: McGraw-Hill, 1983).

49. Dorwin Cartwright and Alvin Zander, *Group Dynamics: Research and Theory*, 3d ed. (New York: Harper & Row, 1968); and Elliot Aronson, *The Social Animal* (San Francisco: W. H. Freeman, 1976).

50. Peter E. Mudrack, "Group Cohesiveness and Productivity: A Closer Look," *Human Relations* 42 (1989), 771–785. Also see Miriam Erez and Anit Somech, "Is Group Productivity Loss the Rule or the Exception? Effects of Culture and Group-Based Motivation," *Academy of Management Journal* 39, no. 6 (1996), 1513–1537.

51. Stanley E. Seashore, *Group Cohesiveness in the Industrial Work Group* (Ann Arbor, Mich.: Institute for Social Research, 1954).

52. Daniel R. Kibbe and Jill Casner-Lotto, "Ralston Foods: From Greenfield to Maturity in a Team-Based Plant," *Journal of Organizational Excellence* (Summer 2002): 57–67.

53. J. Richard Hackman, "Group Influences on Individuals," in *Handbook of Industrial and Organizational Psychology*, ed. M. Dunnette (Chicago: Rand McNally, 1976).

54. Kenneth Bettenhausen and J. Keith Murnighan, "The Emergence of Norms in Competitive Decision-Making Groups," *Administrative Science Quarterly* 30 (1985), 350–372.

55. The following discussion is based on Daniel C. Feldman, "The Development and Enforcement of Group Norms," *Academy of Management Review* 9 (1984), 47–53.

56. Wilson, et al., *Leadership Trapeze*, 12.

57. Emily Nelson, "TV Guide: Think You've Got a Tricky Staff? Try Herding Writers," *The Wall Street Journal* (May 16, 2003), A1.

58. Stephen P. Robbins, *Managing Organizational Conflict: A Nontraditional Approach* (Englewood Cliffs, N.J.: Prentice-Hall, 1974).

59. Daniel Robey, Dana L. Farrow, and Charles R. Franz, "Group Process and Conflict in System Development," *Management Science* 35 (1989), 1172–1191.

60. Dean Tjosvold, Chun Hui, Daniel Z. Ding, and Junchen Hu, "Conflict Values and Team Relationships: Conflict's Contribution to Team Effectiveness and Citizenship in China," *Journal of Organizational Behavior* 24 (2003): 69–88; C. De Dreu and E. Van de Vliert, *Using Conflict in Organizations* (Beverly Hills, CA: Sage, 1997); and Kathleen M. Eisenhardt, Jean L.

Kahwajy, and L. J. Bourgeois III, "Conflict and Strategic Choice: How Top Management Teams Disagree," *California Management Review* 39, no. 2 (Winter 1997): 42–62.

61. Jerry B. Harvey, "The Abilene Paradox: The Management of Agreement," *Organizational Dynamics* (Summer 1988): 17–43.

62. Eisenhardt et al., "Conflict and Strategic Choice."

63. Koehler, "Effective Team Management"; and Dean Tjosvold, "Making Conflict Productive," *Personnel Administrator* 29 (June 1984), 121.

64. This discussion is based in part on Richard L. Daft, *Organization Theory and Design* (St. Paul, Minn.: West, 1992), Chapter 13; and Paul M. Terry, "Conflict Management," *The Journal of Leadership Studies* 3, no. 2 (1996), 3–21.

65. Narayanan et al. "How Top Management Steers Fast Cycle Teams to Success."

66. Clinton O. Longenecker and Mitchell Neubert, "Barriers and Gateways to Management Cooperation and Teamwork," *Business Horizons* (September–October 2000), 37–44.

67. This discussion is based on K. W. Thomas, "Towards Multidimensional Values in Teaching: The Example of Conflict Behaviors," *Academy of Management Review* 2 (1977), 487.

68. Robbins, *Managing Organizational Conflict*.

69. Rob Walker, "Take It Or Leave It: The Only Guide to Negotiating You Will Ever Need," *Inc.*, (August 2003), 75–82.

70. Based on Kathleen M. Eisenhardt, Jean L. Kahwajy, and L. J. Bourgeois III, "How Management Teams Can Have a Good Fight," *Harvard Business Review* (July–August 1997), 77–85.

71. R. B. Zajonc, "Social Facilitation," *Science* 149 (1965), 269–274; and Erez and Somech, "Is Group Productivity Loss the Rule or the Exception?"

72. Gina Imperato, "Their Specialty? Teamwork," *Fast Company* (January–February 2000), 54–56.

73. Aaron Bernstein, "Detroit vs. the UAW: At Odds over Teamwork," *BusinessWeek* (August 24, 1987), 54–55.

74. Robert Albanese and David D. Van Fleet, "Rational Behavior in Groups: The Free-Riding Tendency," *Academy of Management Review* 10 (1985), 244–255.

75. Debra L. Shapiro, Stacie A. Furst, Gretchen M. Spreitzer, and Mary Ann Von Glinow, "Transnational Teams in the Electronic Age: Are Team Identity and High Performance at Risk?" *Journal of Organizational Behavior* 23 (2002): 455–467.

76. Baron, *Behavior in Organizations*.

77. Harvey J. Brightman, *Group Problem Solving: An Improved Managerial Approach* (Atlanta: Georgia State University, 1988).

78. Petzinger, *The New Pioneers*, 27–32.

# Video Case

## Chapter 17: CVS Stands for Consumer Value Store

When the first CVS store opened in Lowell, Massachusetts, in 1963, customers knew it as the Consumer Value Store. But as the store itself caught on with consumers, so did the abbreviation CVS. Today, CVS—which has acquired other stores such as Peoples Drug, Revco D.S., and Arbor Drugs—employs more than 80,000 workers nationwide, including 12,000 pharmacists in 4,200 stores. In addition, when CVS acquired Soma.com of Seattle, Washington, it became the first company in the nation to launch an Internet pharmacy site. One way that the company has managed to grow and continue to offer value to its customers is through a heavy emphasis on continuous learning throughout the organization.

Training is paramount at CVS. The company offers an Emerging Leaders Program several times a year for managerial candidates; but perhaps more importantly, CVS considers every employee to have the potential to grow. Thus, employees at every level are offered opportunities to learn the skills they will need for their next job at CVS. With formal training programs, mentoring, and other methods of learning, CVS employees have a greater chance of achieving person-job fit as they move up in the company than they might have if they were simply promoted without preparation and support.

The Emerging Leaders Program is offered to about 90 district manager candidates and 10 regional manager candidates at each session. According to CVS spokesperson Seth B. Kamen, candidates ideally enter the program about a year and a half before they are ready for a promotion. Participants gather at the company's Store Support Center for a two-day kickoff session; then they return to the field to complete 23 training activities. Participants receive regular feedback from their managers and communicate regularly with peers for continual learning. Throughout the program, participants gain experience in planning and organizing, customer service, interviewing and selection, loss prevention, laptop computer skills, pharmacy regulations, merchandising, and more. During the first year of the program, 21 out of 27 participants actually achieved their desired promotions. Response to the new program has been positive. "By working with the Emerging Leader Program, I have learned new insights on my own job," says one participant. "The exposure I have to my regional manager has been great to help me understand expectations," reports another.

Kamen believes that the value of the program goes beyond the boundaries of its initial intention. Leader-led training blended with actual job experience—the field activities—create a stronger result than might be achieved with one or the other alone. He observes that the program has influenced other programs and practices at CVS. "We developed a new process and tools for field managers to use to conduct store visits that are tied directly to the capability model we present through the program," he explains. And "when new projects, critical assignments, focus groups, and so forth come up, participants in the Emerging Leaders Program are among the first people the organization considers."

CVS also uses THINQ Training Server, a learning management system, to help manage its training efforts. The system has helped CVS employees adapt to standardized training that is designed not only to help them advance but also to increase the consistency of customer service and improve their overall knowledge of the pharmacy industry and the company. With the help of the system, CVS employees have a pass rate of 97 percent on a national pharmacy exam, which exceeds the national average of 81 percent.

CVS's commitment to learning extends throughout the company, at every level. Employees appreciate the opportunities available to them and work hard to perform their best. This is how loyalty is built: when learning never stops. One Emerging Leaders graduate sums it up this way: "CVS is very interested in my success!"

### Questions

1. In what ways do you think the Emerging Leaders Program helps achieve good person-job fit at CVS?
2. How might CVS's training programs help develop positive work-related attitudes among employees?
3. How does the model of the learning process in Exhibit 17.10 apply to the Emerging Leaders Program?

Sources: Company Web site, *http://www.cvs.com*, accessed March 18, 2002; Don Steinberg, "The Smart Business 50," *Tech Update, ZDNet, http://techupdate. zdnet.com*, accessed March 18, 2002; "Case Study: CVS/pharmacy," *Thinq, http://learning.thinq.com*, accessed March 18, 2002.

# Video Case

Chapter 18: Donna Fernandes: She's the Leader of the Pack

Donna Fernandes isn't your average MBA. Her expertise lies in the behavior of slugs—real ones, not the human kind. She also holds a Doctor of Sciences degree from Princeton, she's worked at the Franklin Park Zoo in Boston, led wildlife tours through Kenya and Tanzania, hosted her own educational television show, and now she's the director of the Buffalo Zoo in upstate New York, where her clients include elephants, gorillas, hyenas, polar bears, and more.

When Fernandes arrived at the 23-acre zoo a couple of years ago, it was a mess. "Most of what I found about the current state of the zoo was negative," she recalls. The 125-year-old park, the third-oldest zoo in the country, was in a terrible state of disrepair and was in danger of losing its accreditation. The management and board of directors were considering moving the zoo from its home in the Delaware Park area of Buffalo and relocating it to an industrial neighborhood along the Buffalo River. But the community rallied against the move, and it was postponed. Still, something had to be done to bring the zoo back to life. Fernandes quickly found that her base of support as a leader would come from the community and from volunteers and workers at the zoo. "As soon as I walked through the gates of the zoo, I just felt at home," she says. "The people were really friendly. . . . It seemed like people all wanted to improve the zoo. The amount of grass roots support for this zoo is phenomenal."

Fernandes used her position power to put forth a vision for improvement, but she quickly developed personal power as well. People liked her and respected her from the outset. She immediately outlined plans to bring the zoo back up to the standards of the American Zoo and Aquarium Association, which were backed by a pledge of $350,000 from Governor George Pataki. More funding was needed, so the board undertook a massive fundraising effort. Fernandes noted that as the zoo was upgraded she would place more emphasis on children and education through programs at the zoo. "I will also focus on trying to increase family visitors by making exhibits the right height for children in strollers and people in wheelchairs." In addition, she planned to create more natural settings for the animals, with an emphasis on wildlife habitats rather than cages. "These are issues to which I am very sensitive," she explained.

With strong support for Fernandes's vision, plans to relocate the zoo were abandoned, though she was careful to say that she understood the reasons why the board had considered it. Today, visitors enjoy the giraffe feeding station, guided tours, and especially the WILD place, where curious—and brave—participants can wash an elephant or even watch one paint. (Daryl Hoffman, the elephant keeper and head of the animal training committee at the zoo, has instituted a program called Art Gone Wild, in which the zoo sells "artwork" created by elephants, primates, and big cats.) The zoo's outreach program includes the Zoomobile and Distance Learning, both of which take the zoo's mission outside the grounds to people who might not be able to visit the zoo in person.

Fernandes's democratic leadership style encourages input from staff, groundskeepers, volunteers, the community, and the board of directors. She likes people to stop by her office to give her feedback, suggestions, and even complaints. But this open atmosphere didn't exist before Fernandes arrived, so she had to cultivate it. The change began almost by accident. In the days following the events of the September 11, 2001, attacks on the Pentagon and the World Trade Center, everyone around the zoo was shaken. So on a whim, Fernandes decided to bring her new puppy into the office to cheer up herself and others. Pretty soon people were stopping by to see the puppy and have a chat. Before long, Fernandes was receiving valuable feedback from people who would never have otherwise felt comfortable providing it—and a whole new line of communication had opened up between Fernandes and her staff. The puppy, who is rapidly growing, now makes regular appearances at the office, and Fernandes lets everyone know that she likes her employees to visit whenever they want.

Fernandes is happy with her work and seems comfortable in her leadership role. Of the 186 accredited zoos in the country, only 20 have female directors; so she is aware of her mentoring role as well. "I believe this is probably the most important thing I will ever do, being in this position in a community at a juncture where they want to rebuild their zoo," she says. "When I interviewed for this job, I did a presentation to the board on my vision for the zoo. I told them it would take 10 to 25 years of a shared dream, rather

# Chapter 18: Donna Fernandes: She's the Leader of the Pack (continued)

than just my vision, to restore the Buffalo Zoo to its greatness." Fernandes truly believes that her zoo will enjoy a second golden age—within limits. "I won't promise the world in rebuilding this zoo, but if I promise a continent, you'll get a continent." Which is plenty of ground for everyone.

**Questions**

1. In what ways do you believe Fernandes exhibits both expert power and referent power?

2. Using Exhibit 18.2 in the chapter, create a profile of Fernandes's personal characteristics.

3. Would you characterize Fernandes's leadership style as appropriate for building a learning organization? Why or why not?

Sources: Buffalo Zoo Web site, *http://www.buffalozoo.org*, accessed March 20, 2002; Christina Abt, "Donna Fernandes, Director, Buffalo Zoological Society," *Eve Magazine*; "Governor Pataki Announces $350,000 for Buffalo Zoo," May 22, 2001, *http://www.state.ny.us*.

# Video Case — Chapter 19: Motivation Is a Wild Experience at the Buffalo Zoo

At the Buffalo Zoo in upstate New York, you can buy a painting by an elephant, primate, or big cat. You can visit the giraffe feeding station, bathe an elephant, take a starlight safari, tour the conservation station, and take in the vanishing animals exhibit. You'll find renovated buildings, naturalized habitats, clean grounds. You'll be one of 340,000 people annually to enjoy the zoo. Much of this is the work of zoo director Donna Fernandes, her staff, volunteers, and the community of Buffalo. How she got everyone to transform the run-down, sparsely visited zoo in the space of just a few years is a story of motivation.

Fernandes herself is a motivated leader who believes in empowering everyone—inside and outside the organization—to turn the Buffalo Zoo into the very best it can be. She believes that her plans are "a shared dream, rather than just my vision, to restore the Buffalo Zoo to its greatness." When Fernandes first arrived at the zoo, employees were unenthusiastic about their jobs. A senior manager had adopted an autocratic leadership style that had reduced morale. Employees were often reprimanded and threatened with suspension for minor infractions of strict rules. Many felt that they were not given the freedom and respect to do their jobs as well-educated, specialized experts in the care of animals. Communication was lacking, information and ideas were not shared, and the zoo had begun to languish.

Fernandes has a doctorate from Princeton in animal behavior; she's worked at several large zoos; she is interested in education; she can communicate with and relate to her staff, who know and care so much about animals. She also has a business degree, so she can understand the thinking and decisions of the zoo's board of directors. And when she arrived, she knew she had to motivate both staff and board members in order to save the zoo, which was in danger of losing its accreditation with the American Zoo and Aquarium Association. One of her first actions as president and CEO of the zoo was to dismiss the senior manager and abolish the rigid policies that actually interfered with workers' freedom to get their jobs done. "Things happen. Your car breaks down, your kid is sick, it's no big deal," she explains. "It's not like we have a real problem with [attendance] anyway." By removing rules that prevented people from caring for a sick child or accompanying a parent to the doctor's office, Fernandes showed employees that she respected them as individuals who were trying to balance their family lives with their jobs.

Fernandes believed that there was too little communication and knowledge sharing among the departments at the zoo. Under the old management, employees actually hoarded information because they were afraid they would not receive any recognition for their work. So Fernandes established weekly staff

# Chapter 19: Motivation Is a Wild Experience at the Buffalo Zoo (continued)

meetings with vets, animal keepers, and trainers from all parts of the zoo. Here people share ideas and knowledge, take part in training, and openly share concerns with management. Fernandes also includes staff demonstrations in the meetings to give employees an opportunity to showcase new projects and developments in their areas of expertise. Fernandes observes that these demonstrations not only give recognition for a job well done but also allow the valuable sharing of information. Fernandes expands her motivating leadership to the board of directors and the community at large, who have been engaged in fundraising to renovate the zoo. The board of directors, once considered a stagnant bunch, is now one of the most sought-after groups for community involvement in upstate New York.

These days, the atmosphere at the Buffalo Zoo is much more upbeat. Employees are happier in their jobs, they feel free to offer ideas, and they have the authority to make decisions in their jobs. They also enjoy communication with the Top Dog herself. After September 11, 2001, Fernandes began bringing her new puppy to the office just to make herself—and everyone else—feel better. It didn't take long for people to stop in, pet the puppy, and chat with Fernandes about whatever was going on around the zoo. Fernandes finds these puppy visits as valuable as the staff meetings. It's not surprising that she talks with people as easily as she talks with her animals.

## Questions

1. What types of intrinsic rewards are workers now receiving from their jobs at the Buffalo Zoo?
2. In what ways might the human resource department at the Buffalo Zoo use job design to increase motivation among zoo workers?
3. How important is empowerment to motivation at the Buffalo Zoo?

Sources: Buffalo Zoo Web site, *http://www.buffalozoo.org*, accessed March 20, 2002; Christina Abt, "Donna Fernandes, Director, Buffalo Zoological Society," *Eve Magazine*; "Governor Pataki Announces $350,000 for Buffalo Zoo," May 22, 2001, *http://www.state.ny.us*.

# Video Case

Perhaps the most important part of a manager's job is communication. Bob van den Oord, assistant general manager at Boston's luxury Le Meridien hotel, would agree. Most of his job involves communicating—with department heads, staff, guests, suppliers, the general manager, and senior managers of the hotel chain based in London. That's why he spends so much time developing both the formal and informal channels of communication at the hotel. "There are a number of things we've done to improve communication at Le Meridien," van den Oord notes. One of the most important parts of his day takes place between 9:30 and 9:45, during which he and his managers hold an operational meeting to discuss the day's events, timeline, and staffing requirements. "It's quite casual," says van den Oord. "Everyone has a cup of coffee and talks." In those fifteen minutes, a great deal of communication is accomplished because managers have learned how to present their messages clearly, listen, and help each other come to a resolution when necessary.

Daily operational meetings aren't the only communication channels at Le Meridien. Van den Oord also holds weekly departmental meetings, such as the food and beverage meeting, in which managers may discuss their schedule of events, supply needs, or paperwork for group dinners; interdepartmental meetings; and yearly staff meetings during which all employees in attendance have an opportunity to ask questions and learn about the hotel's future plans and to review results for the year. Van den Oord calls this annual gathering a team-building opportunity as well. Other channels include the daily briefing sheet—literally a sheet of paper—that staff members can pick up near the hotel lobby to learn about the day's VIP visitors or groups, special events, restaurant promotions, and the like. Also, all managers have access to e-mail on the hotel's intranet.

Clearly, Bob van den Oord prefers the channel richness of face-to-face communication. Although he concedes that e-mail is convenient—and necessary—he is quick to point out that it is not a substitute for personal interaction. If there is a conflict, he wants it resolved either by phone or in person so that both parties have the opportunity to listen and understand each other's words and gestures. Instead of relying on

e-mail, van den Oord prefers what he calls "management by walk about," or simply walking through the hotel's different departments to see how things are going. "It gives the staff a chance to talk to me," he explains. "They like it. They like to see that the manager is not just sitting in his office. . . . All the one-on-one, constant feedback is important." During his daily walks through the hotel, van den Oord can easily pick up the news that is traveling through the grapevine.

Michiel Lugt, the hotel's room service and stewarding manager, wholeheartedly agrees. "E-mail facilitates the communication process, but it's not the solver of all problems," he says. Lugt notes that it's very easy for someone who sends an e-mail to assume that the recipient actually received and understood the message—and will act on it if necessary—when in fact the person might not have received or understood the message, or might have underestimated its importance. Lugt echoes van den Oord's concern with communication throughout the hotel. "We have so many departments, and they all need to perform. If one department doesn't communicate, everyone struggles." For instance, if the person taking dinner reservations oversells the restaurant so that people must wait for tables or the kitchen is not prepared with the right amount of food, all departments suffer. "Communication is key in our industry," Lugt concludes.

Van den Oord and Lugt understand well that part of their job as communicators is to influence their employees—to motivate them to perform at the highest level. One of the ways they do this is by setting an example of their own commitment and performance. "You need to be present," notes Lugt. "You are leading by example." Lugt is quick to help out wherever he is needed, whether it's filling in a service gap by serving morning coffee to guests at the restaurant or taking meal orders. By doing so, he communicates to his staff that they are all part of a team running the hotel together.

Van den Oord views good communication as part of good business. Good communication contributes to a happy staff, he believes. "A happy staff equals happy guests," he notes with a smile. "And happy guests help us meet our business objectives."

## Chapter 20: Communication Is Paramount at Le Meridien (continued)

**Questions**

1. How important is nonverbal communication to a hotel manager such as Bob van den Oord or Michiel Lugt?
2. Why is feedback an important part of Bob van den Oord's daily process of management by walk about?
3. In the video, assistant general manager Bob van den Oord has to work with another manager to clear up a misunderstanding about the staff's vacation schedule. Put yourself in Bob's shoes and write a brief outline of how you would communicate with the manager to solve the problem. Hint: You might want to refer to the Manager's Shoptalk box, "How to Be a Master Communicator," for ideas.

Source: Company Web site, *http://www.lemeridien-hotels.com*, accessed January 4, 2002.

# Video Case

## Chapter 21: Cannondale: Teams Perform in the Race for the Perfect Bicycle

High-performance bicycles are finely tuned machines that are tailored to their riders for peak performance. The search for the perfect bicycle is a never-ending race that pits a material's strength against its weight. Cannondale Corporation, based in Bethel, Connecticut, constantly runs that race and wins—through dedicated teamwork.

The company has come a long way from its beginnings in 1971 in a loft above a pickle factory. From the company's early efforts in manufacturing bicycle trailers and cycling apparel, it expanded to high-performance bicycle design and production in the 1980s. And it hasn't looked back since. The company became renowned early on for its innovative introduction of aluminum bicycle frames, combining strength, flexibility, and light weight. Competitors then constructed their frames of much heavier steel. Today, Cannondale is the leading manufacturer of aluminum bicycles, selling more than 80 models in 60-plus countries worldwide. And with the turn of the 21st century, the company ventured into the design and manufacture of motocross motorcycles and all-terrain vehicles. As Cannondale's Web site proudly proclaims, its "passion is to be the best cycling and off-road motorsports company in the world." Cycling experts would agree it is well on its way.

Maintaining its position in the competitive cycling market isn't easy. Cannondale must continually create new designs that boost performance. To do so, it relies on the best of art and science—the creativity of teams of engineers and experienced production craftsmen combined with the speed and precision of computer technology. The company forms special-purpose teams to create its designs. Design engineers for the teams are selected based on their particular areas of expertise—some are materials experts, others skilled at drawing, and still others experienced at proofing the designs to ensure that all the pieces fit so that they can be built. Cannondale also encourages engineers to volunteer for projects based on their interest in the particular product being considered. For example, a carbon fiber materials specialist may get involved in a project to contribute to the design because he or she wants to help or has a unique idea. The goal of these design teams is to work creatively to solve a particular design problem and produce innovative products. Usually two to four engineers team up for a design.

The design engineers also rely on technology to execute their ideas. Engineers draw their designs on a computer-aided design (CAD) system called Pro/Engineer and can generate a plastic prototype to check the overall design concept. From there, the engineers transmit their designs electronically to the production teams based in two company-owned factories in Bedford, Pennsylvania. John Horn, research

# Chapter 21: Cannondale: Teams Perform in the Race for the Perfect Bicycle (continued)

and development project manager at Cannondale says, "The design and production teams are separated by roughly 400 miles, but the communication is instantaneous." Production teams can generate a single prototype bicycle using the CAD system and actual materials to test its performance—strength, durability, flexibility, and dimensions. Frames are at the heart of Cannondale bicycles, and they undergo 12 to 15 different tests before a design is approved for production.

With all of its high-tech capabilities, Cannondale doesn't ignore the human touch in its manufacturing process. The company relies on skilled craftspeople to weld, sand, paint, and finish its bikes. "Aluminum is not an easy material to weld," says Horn. "It's more difficult than steel." So the company hires, trains, and certifies its welders to perform at their peak. The welders' jobs are coveted at the company—they carry prestige and high pay. After the welds are completed, the weld joints are sanded smooth—a mark of quality that Cannondale bikes carry over their competition. Then frames are machined to finish edges and prepare them for additional parts such as cranks and wheels. After that, the bikes are hand painted, matte or gloss finish is applied, and decals are added to customer specifications or sales demand.

Cannondale believes in the quality of human workmanship and relies on assembly line work teams, instead of robotic lines stamping out 10,000 copies at a time. Individual attention to each bicycle allows the company to monitor sales and be extremely flexible to meet customer demands—for a particular model, in a particular size, and in a particular color and finish. Such attention to detail creates pride in Cannondale's work teams—from design through production—and satisfies customers. As the company's Web site states, "We concentrate on detail, because the last 5 percent is often the difference between success and failure." Cannondale is proving that one bike and one rider at a time.

## Questions

1. Cannondale uses special-purpose teams to design and produce its bicycles. What are some benefits to that approach?
2. What could be some drawbacks to Cannondale's team approach?
3. How does Cannondale make use of virtual teamwork to produce its products?

Sources: Interview with John Horn, research and development product manager at Cannondale Corporation, April 9, 2002; Cannondale Web site, *http://www.cannondale.com,* accessed March 22, 2002.

# Part 6: Ford Enters a New Era of Leadership

# ..Continuing Case

Leaders come in all shapes and sizes. They come from different countries and cultures. They exhibit different personality traits. They practice different leadership styles. They may be team players or loners. They may have legitimate power, like Jac Nasser and Bill Ford. They may practice coercive power, as Nasser did with his controversial performance appraisal system. They often have personal power, as demonstrated by Bill Ford in his commitment to good relationships with union workers. They may possess different visions for the same company, but they all want to motivate their managers and employees toward that vision. And, they look for ways to communicate their goals.

Jac Nasser's entire tenure as CEO of Ford Motor Company was driven by his goal for the company to become "the world's leading consumer company for automotive services and products." He began by slashing costs and reducing payrolls, earning the nickname "Jac the Knife." Then he diversified Ford's business activities around the world, to the dismay of critics who believed he was carrying the company too far afield from its core business of building and selling cars and trucks. He professed to be a believer in teams and open communication, stating in one interview, "You let your teams have room to work and give them air cover. I'm not a believer in telling people [exactly] what to do. If you start giving people a cookbook, you start to get very narrow solutions." Despite cutting a number of jobs, Nasser claimed to be looking for the best people within the company, seeking to motivate them and move them up. "We are spending more time and effort developing leaders from inside the company," he said. "We're trying to strengthen the team. Like any sports team, if you stop recruiting, over time, you'd lose your competitiveness. If you look at the team we've got today, there's a tremendous mix of different backgrounds, even among the people who came up through Ford Motor Co." But Nasser also had a reputation for being an intimidating leader who kept tight controls on his managers—he had 16 senior managers reporting directly to him instead of creating a team of top executives with the authority to make decisions.

Bill Ford is a completely different type of leader, one who actually sees himself on par with the rank-and-file workers instead of heir to a family dynasty. His personal power is partly expert—he not only grew up in the business (as did Nasser) but prepared to take over the chairmanship by heading up the company's finance committee—and partly referent. People at all levels of the organization genuinely like him. "You can't get mad at Bill Ford," says Lincoln-Mercury dealer Martin J. McInerney. "He's just too nice a guy." He truly believes that Ford Motor Co. can—and should—have a positive relationship with all its workers and associated unions, and he is passionate about the environment. He sees no reason why the company cannot set an example as an environmentally friendly auto manufacturer. "I've staked much of my personal reputation on the environment," he says. "Sometimes I wake up wondering whether I'm taking the company on a diversionary course that won't pay off . . . but on other nights I wake up thinking we're not doing enough." Since taking over as CEO, Ford has redrawn the lines of communication within the company, establishing an executive team that he believes will work well together. "I expect the three of us [Ford, Nick Scheele, and Carl Reichardt] will have an easygoing relationship," predicts Ford.

Ford tried to share the leadership role when he took over the chairmanship position while Jac Nasser was still CEO. The company's board of directors urged the two men to hammer out an arrangement to share power to benefit the company. "You guys need each other," the directors said to each man in separate meetings. So the two tried to establish their roles. "We wanted to ensure that there was clear accountability and clarity with the roles so that we didn't confuse the organization," said Nasser at the time. The result was an arrangement that continued Nasser's primary responsibility for running the company's day-to-day operations and tied Ford more closely to management, but it lasted for only a few short months.

By November 2001, Nasser was out. Some reports say he resigned; others say he was fired. Chances are, both are true. Although Bill Ford certainly had a hand in Nasser's departure, he also takes responsibility for waiting perhaps too long to replace Nasser as the company was stumbling. "I'll always accept my share of the blame," he concedes. Although skeptics are waiting to see whether Bill Ford is tough enough to be the transformational leader that they believe the company now needs, he does have a vision for the company's role not only as a high-quality auto manufacturer but also as an agent of change. "I'm in this for my children and my grandchildren," he explains. "I want them to inherit a legacy they're proud of. I don't want anybody, whether it's my grandchildren or any of our employees' grandchildren, to have to apologize for working for Ford Motor Co. In fact, I want the opposite. I want them to look and say, 'What a difference we made!'"

## Questions

1. Using Exhibit 18.2 in Chapter 18, make a chart showing what you believe are the personal characteristics of leaders that Bill Ford and Jac Nasser possess.
2. Do you think Bill Ford and Jac Nasser are effective communicators? Explain your answer for each.
3. In what ways might Bill Ford use problem-solving teams to benefit his organization? Give one example describing a problem-solving team that might be effective at Ford Motor Co.

Sources: Alex Taylor, "Car Jacqued!" *Fortune* (November 26, 2001), *http://www.fortune.com*; David Booth, "FoMoCo on Firmer Ground with Family Back at Helm," *Financial Times* (November 16, 2001), *http://globalarchive.ft.com*; "Bill Ford Takes the Wheel," *BusinessWeek Online* (November 1, 2001), *http://www.businessweek.com*; Doron Levin, "Bill Ford Jr. Got His Wish, and Has Much to Prove," *Bloomberg.com* (October 31, 2001), *http://quote.bloomberg.com*; "Getting Ford Round the Corner," *Financial Times* (July 30, 2001), *http://news.ft.com*; Mary Connelly, "Where Jacques Nasser Went Wrong," *Automotive News* (October 15, 2001), *http://www.autonews.com*; Jeffrey E. Garten, "The Mind of the C.E.O.," *BusinessWeek Online* (February 5, 2001), *http://www.businessweek.com*; Keith H. Hammonds, "Grassroots Leadership—Ford Motor Company," *Fast Company* (April 2000), *http://www.fastcompany.com*; Alex Taylor, "The Fight at Ford," *Fortune* (April 3, 2000), *http://www.fortune.com*; Betsy Morris, "Idealist on Board," *Fortune* (April 3, 2000), *http://www.fortune.com*.

Glossary

**360-degree feedback** A process that uses multiple raters, including self-rating, to appraise employee performance and guide development.

## A

**accountability** The fact that the people with authority and responsibility are subject to reporting and justifying task outcomes to those above them in the chain of command.

**achievement culture** A results-oriented culture that values competitiveness, personal initiative, and achievement.

**activity ratio** A financial ratio that measures the organization's internal performance with respect to key activities defined by management.

**adaptability culture** A culture characterized by values that support the company's ability to interpret and translate signals from the environment into new behavior responses.

**adjourning** The stage of team development in which members prepare for the team's disbandment.

**administrative model** A decision-making model that describes how managers actually make decisions in situations characterized by nonprogrammed decisions, uncertainty, and ambiguity.

**administrative principles** A subfield of the classical management perspective that focuses on the total organization rather than the individual worker, delineating the management functions of planning, organizing, commanding, coordinating, and controlling.

**affirmative action** A policy requiring employers to take positive steps to guarantee equal employment opportunities for people within protected groups; government mandated programs that focus on providing opportunities to women and members of minority groups who have previously experienced discrimination.

**ambiguity** A condition in which the goal to be achieved or the problem to be solved is unclear, alternatives are difficult to define, and information about outcomes is unavailable.

**Angel financing** Financing provided by a wealthy individual who believes in the idea for a start-up and provides personal funds and advice to help the business get started.

**application form** A device for collecting information about an applicant's education, previous job experience, and other background characteristics.

**assessment center** A technique for selecting individuals with high managerial potential based on their performance on a series of simulated managerial tasks.

**attitude** A cognitive and affective evaluation that predisposes a person to act in a certain way.

**attributions** Judgments about what causes a person's behavior—either characteristics of the person or of the situation.

**authoritarianism** The belief that power and status differences should exist within the organization.

**authority** The formal and legitimate right of a manager to make decisions, issue orders, and allocate resources to achieve organizationally desired outcomes.

## B

**balance sheet** A financial statement that shows the firm's financial position with respect to assets and liabilities at a specific point in time.

**balanced scorecard** A comprehensive management control system that balances traditional financial measures with measures of customer service, internal business processes, and the organization's capacity for learning and growth.

**B2B marketplace** An electronic marketplace set up by an intermediary where buyers and sellers meet.

**BCG matrix** A concept developed by the Boston Consulting Group that evaluates SBUs with respect to the dimensions of business growth rate and market share.

**behavior modification** The set of techniques by which reinforcement theory is used to modify human behavior.

**behavioral sciences approach** A subfield of the humanistic management perspective that applies social science in an organizational context, drawing from economics, psychology, sociology, and other disciplines.

**behaviorally anchored rating scale (BARS)** A rating technique that relates an employee's performance to specific job-related incidents.

**benchmarking** The continuous process of measuring products, services, and practices against major competitors or industry leaders.

**biculturalism** The sociocultural skills and attitudes used by racial minorities to move back and forth between the dominant culture and their own ethnic or racial culture.

**Big Five personality factors** Dimensions that describe an individual's extroversion, agreeableness, conscientiousness, emotional stability, and openness to experience.

**blog** Web log that allows individuals to post opinions and ideas.

**bottom-up budgeting** A budgeting process in which lower-level managers budget their departments' resource needs and pass them up to top management for approval.

**boundary-spanning roles** Roles assumed by people and/or departments that link and coordinate the organization with key elements in the external environment.

**bounded rationality** The concept that people have the time and cognitive ability to process only a limited amount of information on which to base decisions.

**brainstorming** A technique that uses a face-to-face group to spontaneously suggest a broad range of alternatives for decision making.

**bureaucratic control** The use of rules, policies, hierarchy of authority, reward systems, and other formal devices to influence employee behavior and assess performance.

**bureaucratic organizations** A subfield of the classical management perspective that emphasizes management on an impersonal, rational basis through such elements as clearly defined authority and responsibility, formal recordkeeping, and separation of management and ownership.

**business incubator** An innovation that provides shared office space, management support services, and management advice to entrepreneurs.

**business intelligence** The high-tech analysis of data from multiple sources to identify patterns and relationships that might be significant.

**business-level strategy** The level of strategy concerned with the question "How do we compete?" Pertains to each business unit or product line within the organization.

**business plan** A document specifying the business details prepared by an entrepreneur prior to opening a new business.

## C

**CAD** A production technology in which computers perform new-product design.

**CAM** A production technology in which computers help guide and control the manufacturing system.

**capacity planning** The determination and adjustment of the organization's ability to produce products and services to match customer demand.

**capital budget** A budget that plans and reports investments in major assets to be depreciated over several years.

**cash budget** A budget that estimates and reports cash flows on a daily or weekly basis to ensure that the company has sufficient cash to meet its obligations.

**cellular layout** A facilities layout in which machines dedicated to sequences of production are grouped into cells in accordance with group-technology principles.

**central planning department** A group of planning specialists who develop plans for the organization as a whole and its major divisions and departments and typically report to the president or CEO.

**centralization** The location of decision authority near top organizational levels.

**centralized network** A team communication structure in which team members communicate through a single individual to solve problems or make decisions.

**ceremony** A planned activity that makes up a special event and is conducted for the benefit of an audience.

**certainty** The situation in which all the information the decision maker needs is fully available.

**chain of command** An unbroken line of authority that links all individuals in the organization and specifies who reports to whom.

**change agent** An OD specialist who contracts with an organization to facilitate change.

**changing** An intervention stage of organizational development in which individuals experiment with new workplace behavior.

**channel** The carrier of a communication.

**channel richness** The amount of information that can be transmitted during a communication episode.

**charismatic leader** A leader who has the ability to motivate subordinates to transcend their expected performance.

**chief ethics officer** A company executive who oversees ethics and legal compliance.

**classical model** A decision-making model based on the assumption that managers should make logical decisions that will be in the organization's best economic interests.

**classical perspective** A management perspective that emerged during the nineteenth and early twentieth centuries that emphasized a rational, scientific approach to the study of management and sought to make organizations efficient operating machines.

**closed system** A system that does not interact with the external environment.

**coalition** An informal alliance among managers who support a specific goal.

**code of ethics** A formal statement of the organization's values regarding ethics and social issues.

**coercive power** Power that stems from the authority to punish or recommend punishment.

**cognitive dissonance** A condition in which two attitudes or a behavior and an attitude conflict.

**committee** A long-lasting, sometimes permanent team in the organization structure created to deal with tasks that recur regularly.

**communication** The process by which information is exchanged and understood by two or more people, usually with the intent to motivate or influence behavior.

**communication apprehension** An individual's level of fear or anxiety associated with interpersonal communications.

**compensation** Monetary payments (wages, salaries) and nonmonetary goods/commodities (benefits, vacations) used to reward employees.

**compensatory justice** The concept that individuals should be compensated for the cost of their injuries by the party responsible and also that individuals should not be held responsible for matters over which they have no control.

**competitive advantage** What sets the organization apart from others and provides it with a distinctive edge in the marketplace.

**competitors** Other organizations in the same industry or type of business that provide goods or services to the same set of customers.

**conceptual skill** The cognitive ability to see the organization as a whole and the relationship among its parts.

**concurrent control** Control that consists of monitoring ongoing activities to ensure their consistency with standards.

**conflict** Antagonistic interaction in which one party attempts to thwart the intentions or goals of another.

**consideration** A type of leader behavior that describes the extent to which a leader is sensitive to subordinates, respects their ideas and feelings, and establishes mutual trust.

**consistency culture** A culture that values and rewards a methodical, rational, orderly way of doing things.

**content theories** A group of theories that emphasize the needs that motivate people.

**contingency approach** A model of leadership that describes the relationship between leadership styles and specific organizational situations.

**contingency plans** Plans that define company responses to specific situations, such as emergencies, setbacks, or unexpected conditions.

**contingency view** An extension of the humanistic perspective in which the successful resolution of organizational problems is thought to depend on managers' identification of key variables in the situation at hand.

**contingent workers** People who work for an organization, but not on a permanent or full-time basis, including temporary placements, contracted professionals, or leased employees.

**continuous improvement** The implementation of a large number of small, incremental improvements in all areas of the organization on an ongoing basis.

**continuous process production** A type of technology involving mechanization of the entire workflow and nonstop production.

**continuous reinforcement schedule** A schedule in which every occurrence of the desired behavior is reinforced.

**controlling** The management function concerned with monitoring employees' activities, keeping the organization on track toward its goals, and making corrections as needed.

**coordination** The quality of collaboration across departments.

**coordination costs** The time and energy needed to coordinate the activities of a team to enable it to perform its task.

**core competence** A business activity that an organization does particularly well in comparison to competitors.

**corporate governance** The system of governing an organization so the interests of corporate owners are protected.

**corporate-level strategy** The level of strategy concerned with the question "What business are we in?" Pertains to the organization as a whole and the combination of business units and product lines that make it up.

**corporate university** An in-house training and education facility that offers broad-based learning opportunities for employees.

**corporation** An artificial entity created by the state and existing apart from its owners.

**cost leadership** A type of competitive strategy in which the organization aggressively seeks efficient facilities, cuts costs, and employs tight cost controls to be more efficient than competitors.

**countertrade** The barter of products for other products rather than their sale for currency.

**courage** The ability to step forward through fear and act on one's values and conscience.

**creativity** The generation of novel ideas that may meet perceived needs or offer opportunities for the organization.

**cross-functional team** A group of employees from various functional departments that meet as a team to resolve mutual problems.

**cultural leader** A manager who uses signals and symbols to influence corporate culture.

**culture** The set of key values, beliefs, understandings, and norms that members of a society or an organization share.

**culture shock** Feelings of confusion, disorientation, and anxiety that result from being immersed in a foreign culture.

**culture/people change** A change in employees' values, norms, attitudes, beliefs, and behavior.

**customer relationship management (CRM) systems** Systems that help companies track customers' interaction with the firm and allow employees to call up information on past transactions.

**customers** People and organizations in the environment who acquire goods or services from the organization.

**cycle time** The steps taken to complete a company process.

## D

**data** Raw, unsummarized, and unanalyzed facts and figures.

**data warehousing** The use of a huge database that combines all of a company's data and allows users to access the data directly, create reports, and obtain answers to what-if questions.

**debt financing** Borrowing money that has to be repaid at a later date in order to start a business.

**decentralization** The location of decision authority near lower organizational levels.

**decentralized control** The use of organization culture, group norms, and a focus on goals, rather than rules and procedures, to foster compliance with organizational goals.

**decentralized network** A team communication structure in which team members freely communicate with one another and arrive at decisions together.

**decentralized planning** Managers working with planning experts to develop their own goals and plans.

**decision** A choice made from available alternatives.

**decision making** The process of identifying problems and opportunities and then resolving them.

**decision styles** Differences among people with respect to how they perceive problems and make decisions.

**decision support system (DSS)** An interactive, computer-based system that uses decision models and specialized databases to support organization decision makers.

**decode** To translate the symbols used in a message for the purpose of interpreting its meaning.

**delegation** The process managers use to transfer authority and responsibility to positions below them in the hierarchy.

**departmentalization** The basis on which individuals are grouped into departments and departments into total organizations.

**dependent demand inventory** Inventory in which item demand is related to the demand for other inventory items.

**descriptive** An approach that describes how managers actually make decisions rather than how they should.

**devil's advocate** A decision-making technique in which an individual is assigned the role of challenging the assumptions and assertions made by the group to prevent premature consensus.

**diagnosis** The step in the decision-making process in which managers analyze underlying causal factors associated with the decision situation.

**dialogue** A group communication process aimed at creating a culture based on collaboration, fluidity, trust, and commitment to shared goals.

**differentiation** A type of competitive strategy with which the organization seeks to distinguish its products or services from that of competitors.

**digital technology** Technology characterized by use of the Internet and other digital processes to conduct or support business operations.

**direct investing** An entry strategy in which the organization is involved in managing its production facilities in a foreign country.

**discretionary responsibility** Organizational responsibility that is voluntary and guided by the organization's desire to make social contributions not mandated by economics, law, or ethics.

**discrimination** The hiring or promoting of applicants based on criteria that are not job relevant.

**distribution** Moving finished products to customers; also called order fulfillment.

**distributive justice** The concept that different treatment of people should not be based on arbitrary characteristics. In the case of substantive differences, people should be treated differently in proportion to the differences among them.

**diversity awareness training** Special training designed to make people aware of their own prejudices and stereotypes.

**divisional structure** An organization structure in which departments are grouped based on similar organizational outputs.

**downsizing** Intentional, planned reduction in the size of a company's workforce.

**downward communication** Messages sent from top management down to subordinates.

**dual role** A role in which the individual both contributes to the team's task and supports members' emotional needs.

## E

**e-business** Work an organization does by using electronic linkages; any business that takes place by digital processes over a computer network rather than in a physical space.

**e-commerce** Business exchanges or transactions that occur electronically.

**E→P expectancy** Expectancy that putting effort into a given task will lead to high performance.

**economic dimension** The dimension of the general environment representing the overall economic health of the country or region in which the organization operates.

**economic forces** Forces that affect the availability, production, and distribution of a society's resources among competing users.

**economic order quantity (EOQ)** An inventory management technique designed to minimize the total of ordering and holding costs for inventory items.

**economic value-added (EVA) system** A control system that measures performance in terms of after-tax profits minus the cost of capital invested in tangible assets.

**effectiveness** The degree to which the organization achieves a stated goal.

**efficiency** The use of minimal resources—raw materials, money, and people—to produce a desired volume of output.

**electronic brainstorming** Bringing people together in an interactive group over a computer network to suggest alternatives, sometimes called *brainwriting*.

**electronic data interchange (EDI)** A network that links the computer systems of buyers and sellers to allow the transmission of structured data primarily for ordering, distribution, and payables and receivables.

**employee network groups** Groups based on social identity, such as gender or race, and organized by employees to focus on concerns of employees from that group.

**employment test** A written or computer-based test designed to measure a particular attribute such as intelligence or aptitude.

**empowerment** The delegation of power and authority to subordinates.

**encode** To select symbols with which to compose a message.

**enterprise resource planning (ERP)** Systems that unite a company's major business functions—order processing, product design, purchasing, inventory, and so on; a networked information system that collects, processes, and provides information about an organization's entire enterprise, from identification of customer needs and receipt of orders to distribution of products and receipt of payments.

**entrepreneur** Someone who recognizes a viable idea for a business product or service and carries it out.

**entrepreneurship** The process of initiating a business venture, organizing the necessary resources, and assuming the associated risks and rewards.

**entropy** The tendency for a system to run down and die.

**equity** A situation that exists when the ratio of one person's outcomes to inputs equals that of another's.

**equity financing** Financing that consists of funds that are invested in exchange for ownership in the company.

**equity theory** A process theory that focuses on individuals' perceptions of how fairly they are treated relative to others.

**ERG theory** A modification of the needs hierarchy theory that proposes three categories of needs: existence, relatedness, and growth.

**escalating commitment** Continuing to invest time and resources in a failing decision.

**ethical dilemma** A situation that arises when all alternative choices or behaviors have been deemed undesirable because of potentially negative ethical consequence, making it difficult to distinguish right from wrong.

**ethics** The code of moral principles and values that govern the behaviors of a person or group with respect to what is right or wrong.

**ethics committee** A group of executives assigned to oversee the organization's ethics by ruling on questionable issues and disciplining violators.

**ethics training** Training programs to help employees deal with ethical questions and values.

**ethnocentrism** A cultural attitude marked by the tendency to regard one's own culture as superior to others; the belief that one's own group or subculture is inherently superior to other groups or cultures.

**ethnorelativism** The belief that groups and subcultures are inherently equal.

**euro** A single European currency that replaced the currencies of 12 European nations.

**event-driven planning** Evolutionary planning that responds to the current reality of what the environment and the marketplace demand.

**executive information system (EIS)** A management information system designed to facilitate strategic decision making at the highest levels of management by providing executives with easy access to timely and relevant information.

**exit interview** An interview conducted with departing employees to determine the reasons for their termination.

**expatriates** Employees who live and work in a country other than their own.

**expectancy theory** A process theory that proposes that motivation depends on individuals' expectations about their ability to perform tasks and receive desired rewards.

**expense budget** A budget that outlines the anticipated and actual expenses for each responsibility center.

**expert power** Power that stems from special knowledge of or skill in the tasks performed by subordinates.

**exporting** An entry strategy in which the organization maintains its production facilities within its home country and transfers its products for sale in foreign countries.

**external locus of control** The belief by individuals that their future is not within their control but, rather, is influenced by external forces.

**extranet** An external communications system that uses the internet and is shared by two or more organizations.

**extrinsic reward** A reward given by another person.

## F

**fast-cycle team** A multifunctional team that is provided with high levels of resources and empowerment to accomplish an accelerated product development project.

**feedback** A response by the receiver to the sender's communication; using communication and evaluation to help the organization learn and improve.

**feedforward control** Control that focuses on human, material, and financial resources flowing into the organization; also called *preliminary* or *preventive control*.

**femininity** A cultural preference for relationships, cooperation, group decision making, and quality of life.

**finished-goods inventory** Inventory consisting of items that have passed through the complete production process but have yet to be sold.

**first-line manager** A manager who is at the first or second management level and is directly responsible for the production of goods and services.

**fixed-position layout** A facilities layout in which the product remains in one location and the required tasks and equipment are brought to it.

**flat structure** A management structure characterized by an overall broad span of control and relatively few hierarchical levels.

**flexible manufacturing system** A small- or medium-sized automated production line that can be adapted to produce more than one product line.

**focus** A type of competitive strategy that emphasizes concentration on a specific regional market or buyer group.

**force field analysis** The process of determining which forces drive and which resist a proposed change.

**formal communication channel** A communication channel that flows within the chain of command or task responsibility defined by the organization.

**formal team** A team created by the organization as part of the formal organization structure.

**forming** The stage of team development characterized by orientation and acquaintance.

**franchising** A form of licensing in which an organization provides its foreign franchisees with a complete assortment of materials and services; an arrangement by which the owner of a product or service allows others to purchase the right to distribute the product or service with help from the owner.

**free rider** A person who benefits from team membership but does not make a proportionate contribution to the team's work.

**frustration-regression principle** The idea that failure to meet a high-order need may cause a regression to an already satisfied lower-order need.

**functional-level strategy** The level of strategy concerned with the question "How do we support the business-level strategy?" Pertains to all of the organization's major departments.

**functional manager** A manager who is responsible for a department that performs a single functional task and has employees with similar training and skills.

**functional structure** The grouping of positions into departments based on similar skills, expertise, and resource use.

**fundamental attribution error** The tendency to underestimate the influence of external factors on another's behavior and to overestimate the influence on internal factors.

## G

**general environment** The layer of the external environment that affects the organization indirectly.

**general manager** A manager who is responsible for several departments that perform different functions.

**glass ceiling** Invisible barrier that separates women and minorities from top management positions.

**global outsourcing** Engaging in the international division of labor so as to obtain the cheapest sources of labor and supplies regardless of country; also called *global sourcing*.

**global team** A work team made up of members of different nationalities whose activities span multiple countries; may operate as a virtual team or meet face to face.

**globalization** The standardization of product design and advertising strategies throughout the world.

**goal** A desired future state that the organization attempts to realize.

**goal-setting theory** A motivation theory in which specific challenging goals increase motivation and performance when the goals are accepted by subordinates and these subordinates receive feedback to indicate their progress toward goal achievement.

**grand strategy** The general plan of major action by which an organization intends to achieve its long-term goals.

**grapevine** An informal, person-to-person communication network of employees that is not officially sanctioned by the organization.

**greenfield venture** The most risky type of direct investment, whereby a company builds a subsidiary from scratch in a foreign country.

**groupthink** The tendency for people to be so committed to a cohesive team that they are reluctant to express contrary opinions.

**groupware** Software that works on a computer network or the Internet to facilitate information sharing, collaborative work, and group decision making.

## H

**halo effect** An overall impression of a person or situation based on one characteristic, either favorable or unfavorable; a type of rating error that occurs when an employee receives the same rating on all dimensions regardless of his or her performance on individual ones.

**Hawthorne studies** A series of experiments on worker productivity begun in 1924 at the Hawthorne plant of Western Electric Company in Illinois; attributed employees' increased output to managers' better treatment of them during the study.

**hero** A figure who exemplifies the deeds, character, and attributes of a strong corporate culture.

**hierarchy of needs theory** A content theory that proposes that people are motivated by five categories of needs—physiological, safety, belongingness, esteem, and self-actualization—that exist in a hierarchical order.

**high-context culture** A culture in which communication is used to enhance personal relationships.

**horizontal communication** The lateral or diagonal exchange of messages among peers or coworkers.

**horizontal linkage model** An approach to product change that emphasizes shared development of innovations among several departments.

**horizontal team** A formal team composed of employees from about the same hierarchical level but from different areas of expertise.

**human capital** The economic value of the knowledge, experience, skills, and capabilities of employees.

**human relations movement** A movement in management thinking and practice that emphasizes satisfaction of employees' basic needs as the key to increased worker productivity.

**human resource information system** An integrated computer system designed to provide data and information used in HR planning and decision making.

**human resource management (HRM)** Activities undertaken to attract, develop, and maintain an effective workforce within an organization.

**human resource planning** The forecasting of human resource needs and the projected matching of individuals with expected job vacancies.

**human resources perspective** A management perspective that suggests jobs should be designed to meet higher-level needs by allowing workers to use their full potential.

**human skill** The ability to work with and through other people and to work effectively as a group member.

**humanistic perspective** A management perspective that emerged around the late nineteenth century that emphasized understanding human behavior, needs, and attitudes in the marketplace.

**humility** Being unpretentious and modest rather than arrogant and prideful.

**hygiene factors** Factors that involve the presence or absence of job dissatisfiers, including working conditions, pay, company policies, and interpersonal relationships.

## I

**idea champion** A person who sees the need for and champions productive change within the organization.

**idea incubator** An in-house program that provides a safe harbor where ideas from employees throughout the organization can be developed without interference from company bureaucracy or politics.

**implementation** The step in the decision-making process that involves using managerial, administrative, and persuasive abilities to translate the chosen alternative into action.

**income statement** A financial statement that summarizes the firm's financial performance for a given time interval; sometimes called a profit-and-loss statement.

**individualism approach** The ethical concept that acts are moral when they promote the individual's best long-term interests, which ultimately leads to the greater good.

**influence** The effect a person's actions have on the attitudes, values, beliefs, or behavior of others.

**information** Data that have been converted into a meaningful and useful context for the receiver.

**information reporting system** A system that organizes information in the form of prespecified reports that managers use in day-to-day decision making.

**information technology** The hardware, software, telecommunications, database management, and other technologies used to store, process, and distribute information.

**infrastructure** A country's physical facilities that support economic activities.

**initiating structure** A type of leader behavior that describes the extent to which the leader is task oriented and directs subordinates' work activities toward goal attainment.

**instant messaging** Electronic communication that allows users to see who is connected to a network and share information instantly.

**interactive leadership** A leadership style characterized by values such as inclusion, collaboration, relationship building, and caring.

**internal environment** The environment that includes the elements within the organization's boundaries.

**internal locus of control** The belief by individuals that their future is within their control and that external forces will have little influence.

**international dimension** Portion of the external environment that represents events originating in foreign countries as well as opportunities for U.S. companies in other countries.

**international human resource management (IHRM)** A subfield of human resource management that addresses the complexity that results from recruiting, selecting, developing, and maintaining a diverse workforce on a global scale.

**international management** The management of business operations conducted in more than one country.

**Internet** A global collection of computer networks linked together for the exchange of data and information.

**intrinsic reward** The satisfaction received in the process of performing an action.

**intuition** The immediate comprehension of a decision situation based on past experience but without conscious thought.

**inventory** The goods that the organization keeps on hand for use in the production process up to the point of selling the final products to customers.

**involvement culture** A culture that places high value on meeting the needs of employees and values cooperation and equality.

**ISO 9000** A set of international standards for quality management, setting uniform guidelines for processes to ensure that products conform to customer requirements.

## J

**job analysis** The systematic process of gathering and interpreting information about the essential duties, tasks, and responsibilities of a job.

**job characteristics model** A model of job design that comprises core job dimensions, critical psychological states, and employee growth-need strength.

**job description** A concise summary of the specific tasks and responsibilities of a particular job.

**job design** The application of motivational theories to the structure of work for improving productivity and satisfaction.

**job enlargement** A job design that combines a series of tasks into one new, broader job to give employees variety and challenge.

**job enrichment** A job design that incorporates achievement, recognition, and other high-level motivators into the work.

**job evaluation** The process of determining the value of jobs within an organization through an examination of job content.

**job rotation** A job design that systematically moves employees from one job to another to provide them with variety and stimulation.

**job satisfaction** A positive attitude toward one's job.

**job simplification** A job design whose purpose is to improve task efficiency by reducing the number of tasks a single person must do.

**job specification** An outline of the knowledge, skills, education, and physical abilities needed to adequately perform a job.

**joint venture** A strategic alliance or program by two or more organizations; a variation of direct investment in which an organization shares costs and risks with another firm to build a manufacturing facility, develop new products, or set up a sales and distribution network.

**justice approach** The ethical concept that moral decisions must be based on standards of equity, fairness, and impartiality.

**just-in-time (JIT) inventory system** An inventory control system that schedules materials to arrive precisely when they are needed on a production line.

### K

**knowledge management** The efforts to systematically find, organize, and make available a company's intellectual capital and to foster a culture of continuous learning and knowledge sharing; the process of systematically gathering knowledge, making it widely available throughout the organization, and fostering a culture of learning.

**knowledge management portal** A single point of access for employees to multiple sources of information that provides personalized access on the corporate intranet.

### L

**labor market** The people available for hire by the organization.

**large-group intervention** An approach that brings together participants from all parts of the organization (and may include key outside stakeholders as well) to discuss problems or opportunities and plan for major change.

**law of effect** The assumption that positively reinforced behavior tends to be repeated and unreinforced or negatively reinforced behavior tends to be inhibited.

**leadership** The ability to influence people toward the attainment of organizational goals.

**leadership grid** A two-dimensional leadership theory that measures a leader's concern for people and concern for production.

**leading** The management function that involves the use of influence to motivate employees to achieve the organization's goals.

**lean manufacturing** Manufacturing process using highly trained employees at every stage of the production process to cut waste and improve quality.

**learning** A change in behavior or performance as the result of experience.

**learning organization** An organization in which everyone is engaged in identifying and solving problems, enabling the organization to continuously experiment, improve, and increase its capability.

**legal-political dimension** The dimension of the general environment that includes federal, state, and local government regulations and political activities designed to influence company behavior.

**legitimate power** Power that stems from a formal management position in an organization and the authority granted to it.

**licensing** An entry strategy in which an organization in one country makes certain resources available to companies in another in order to participate in the production and sale of its products abroad.

**line authority** A form of authority in which individuals in management positions have the formal power to direct and control immediate subordinates.

**liquidity ratio** A financial ratio that indicates the organization's ability to meet its current debt obligations.

**listening** The skill of receiving messages to accurately grasp facts and feelings to interpret the genuine meaning.

**locus of control** The tendency to place the primary responsibility for one's success or failure either within oneself (internally) or on outside forces (externally).

**logistics** The activities required to physically move materials into the company's operations facility and to move finished products to customers.

**long-term orientation** A greater concern for the future and high value on thrift and perseverance.

**low-context culture** A culture in which communication is used to exchange facts and information.

**LPC scale** A questionnaire designed to measure relationship-oriented versus task-oriented leadership style according to the leader's choice of adjectives for describing the "least preferred coworker."

### M

**Machiavellianism** The tendency to direct much of one's behavior toward the acquisition of power and the manipulation of others for personal gain.

**management** The attainment of organizational goals in an effective and efficient manner through planning, organizing, leading, and controlling organizational resources.

**management by objectives** A method of management whereby managers and employees define goals for every department, project, and person and use them to monitor subsequent performance.

**management by wandering around (MBWA)** A communication technique in which managers interact directly with workers to exchange information.

**management information system (MIS)** A computer-based system that provides information and support for effective managerial decision making

**management science perspective** A management perspective that emerged after World War II and applied mathematics, statistics, and other quantitative techniques to managerial problems.

**manufacturing organization** An organization that produces physical goods.

**market entry strategy** An organizational strategy for entering a foreign market.

**masculinity** A cultural preference for achievement, heroism, assertiveness, work centrality, and material success.

**mass production** A type of technology characterized by the production of a large volume of products with the same specifications.

**matching model** An employee selection approach in which the organization and the applicant attempt to match each other's needs, interests, and values.

**material requirements planning (MRP)** A dependent demand inventory planning and control system that schedules the precise amount of all materials required to support the production of desired end products.

**matrix approach** An organization structure that utilizes functional and divisional chains of command simultaneously in the same part of the organization.

**matrix boss** A product or functional boss, responsible for one side of the matrix.

**mentor** A higher-ranking, senior organizational member who is committed to providing upward mobility and support to a protégé's professional career.

**merger** The combination of two or more organizations into one.

**message** The tangible formulation of an idea to be sent to a receiver.

**middle manager** A manager who works at the middle levels of the organization and is responsible for major departments.

**mission** The organization's reason for existence.

**mission statement** A broadly stated definition of the organization's basic business scope and operations that distinguishes it from similar types of organizations.

**modular approach** The process by which a manufacturing company uses outside suppliers to provide the large components of the product, which are then assembled into a final product by a few workers.

**monoculture** A culture that accepts only one way of doing things and one set of values and beliefs.

**moral leadership** Distinguishing right from wrong and choosing to do right in the practice of leadership.

**moral-rights approach** The ethical concept that moral decisions are those that best maintain the rights of those people affected by them.

**most favored nation** A term describing a GATT clause that calls for member countries to grant other member countries the most favorable treatment they accord any country concerning imports and exports.

**motivation** The arousal, direction, and persistence of behavior.

**motivators** Factors that influence job satisfaction based on fulfillment of high-level needs such as achievement, recognition, responsibility, and opportunity for growth.

**multicultural teams** Teams made up of members from diverse national, social, ethnic, and cultural backgrounds.

**multidomestic strategy** The modification of product design and advertising strategies to suit the specific needs of individual countries.

**multinational corporation (MNC)** An organization that receives more than 25 percent of its total sales revenues from operations outside the parent company's home country; also called global corporation or transnational corporation.

**Myers-Biggs Type Indicator (MBTI)** Personality test that measures a person's preference for introversion vs. extroversion, sensation vs. intuition, thinking vs. feeling, and judging vs. perceiving.

### N

**need to achieve** A human quality linked to entrepreneurship in which people are motivated to excel and pick situations in which success is likely.

**neutralizer** A situational variable that counteracts a leadership style and prevents the leader from displaying certain behaviors.

**new-venture fund** A fund providing resources from which individuals and groups can draw to develop new ideas, products, or businesses.

**new-venture team** A unit separate from the mainstream of the organization that is responsible for developing and initiating innovations.

**nonparticipator role** A role in which the individual contributes little to either the task or members' socioemotional needs.

**nonprogrammed decision** A decision made in response to a situation that is unique, is poorly defined and largely unstructured, and has important consequences for the organization.

**nonverbal communication** A communication transmitted through actions and behaviors rather than through words.

**norm** A standard of conduct that is shared by team members and guides their behavior.

**normative** An approach that defines how a decision maker should make decisions and provides guidelines for reaching an ideal outcome for the organization.

**norming** The stage of team development in which conflicts developed during the storming stage are resolved and team harmony and unity emerge.

### O

**office automation systems** Systems that combine modern hardware and software to handle the tasks of publishing and distributing information.

**on-the-job training (OJT)** A type of training in which an experienced employee "adopts" a new employee to teach him or her how to perform job duties.

**open-book management** Sharing financial information and results with all employees in the organization.

**open communication** Sharing all types of information throughout the company, across functional and hierarchical levels.

**open innovation** Extending the search for and commercialization of new ideas beyond the boundaries of the organization.

**open system** A system that interacts with the external environment.

**operational goals** Specific, measurable results expected from departments, work groups, and individuals within the organization.

**operational plans** Plans developed at the organization's lower levels that specify action steps toward achieving operational goals and that support tactical planning activities.

**operations information system** A computer-based information system that supports a company's day-to-day operations.

**operations management** The field of management that focuses on the physical production of goods or services and uses specialized techniques for solving manufacturing problems.

**operations strategy** The recognition of the importance of operations to the firm's success and the involvement of operations managers in the organization's strategic planning.

**opportunity** A situation in which managers see potential organizational accomplishments that exceed current goals.

**organization** A social entity that is goal directed and deliberately structured.

**organization chart** The visual representation of an organization's structure.

**organization structure** The framework in which the organization defines how tasks are divided, resources are deployed, and departments are coordinated.

**organizational behavior** An interdisciplinary field dedicated to the study of how individuals and groups tend to act in organizations.

**organizational change** The adoption of a new idea or behavior by an organization.

**organizational citizenship** Work behavior that goes beyond job requirements and contributes as needed to the organization's success.

**organizational commitment** Loyalty to and heavy involvement in one's organization.

**organizational control** The systematic process through which managers regulate organizational activities to make them consistent with expectations established in plans, targets, and standards of performance.

**organizational development (OD)** The application of behavioral science techniques to improve an organization's health and effectiveness through its ability to cope with environmental changes, improve internal relationships, and increase learning and problem-solving capabilities.

**organizational environment** All elements existing outside the organization's boundaries that have the potential to affect the organization.

**organizing** The management function concerned with assigning tasks, grouping tasks into departments, and allocating resources to departments; the deployment of organizational resources to achieve strategic goals.

### P

**P→O expectancy** Expectancy that successful performance of a task will lead to the desired outcome.

**partial productivity** The ratio of total outputs to the inputs from a single major input category.

**partial reinforcement schedule** A schedule in which only some occurrences of the desired behavior are reinforced.

**partnership** An unincorporated business owned by two or more people.

**path-goal theory** A contingency approach to leadership specifying that the leader's responsibility is to increase subordinates' motivation by clarifying the behaviors necessary for task accomplishment and rewards.

**pay-for-performance** Incentive pay that ties at least part of compensation to employee effort and performance.

**peer-to-peer (P2P) file sharing** File sharing that allows PCs to communicate directly with one another over the Internet, bypassing central databases, servers, control points, and Web pages.

**perception** The cognitive process people use to make sense out of the environment, by selecting, organizing, and interpreting information.

**perceptual defense** The tendency of perceivers to protect themselves by disregarding ideas, objects, or people that are threatening to them.

**perceptual distortions** Errors in perceptual judgment that arise from inaccuracies in any part of the perceptual process.

**perceptual selectivity** The process by which individuals screen and select the various stimuli that vie for their attention.

**performance** The organization's ability to attain its goals by using resources in an efficient and effective manner.

**performance appraisal** The process of observing and evaluating an employee's performance, recording the assessment, and providing feedback to the employee.

**performance gap** A disparity between existing and desired performance levels.

**performing** The stage of team development in which members focus on problem solving and accomplishing the team's assigned task.

**permanent teams** A group of participants from several functions who are permanently assigned to solve ongoing problems of common interest.

**person-job fit** The extent to which a person's ability and personality match the requirements of a job.

**personal communication channels** Communication channels that exist outside the formally authorized channels and do not adhere to the organization's hierarchy of authority.

**personality** The set of characteristics that underlie a relatively stable pattern of behavior in response to ideas, objects, or people in the environment.

**personal networking** The acquisition and cultivation of personal relationships that cross departmental, hierarchical, and even organizational boundaries.

**plan** A blueprint specifying the resource allocations, schedules, and other actions necessary for attaining goals.

**planning** The management function concerned with defining goals for future organizational performance and deciding on the tasks and resource use needed to attain them; the act of determining the organization's goals and the means for achieving them.

**planning task force** A group of managers and employees who develop a strategic plan.

**pluralism** An environment in which the organization accommodates several subcultures, including employees who would otherwise feel isolated and ignored.

**point-counterpoint** A decision-making technique in which people are assigned to express competing points of view.

**political forces** The influence of political and legal institutions on people and organizations.

**political instability** Events such as riots, revolutions, or government upheavals that affect the operations of an international company.

**political risk** A company's risk of loss of assets, earning power, or managerial control due to politically based events or actions by host governments.

**portfolio strategy** The organization's mix of SBUs and product lines that fit together in such a way as to provide the corporation with synergy and competitive advantage.

**power** The potential ability to influence others' behavior.

**power distance** The degree to which people accept inequality in power among institutions, organizations, and people.

**pressure group** An interest group that works within the legal-political framework to influence companies to behave in socially responsible ways.

**problem** A situation in which organizational accomplishments have failed to meet established goals.

**problem-solving team** Typically 5 to 12 hourly employees from the same department who meet to discuss ways of improving quality, efficiency, and the work environment.

**procedural justice** The concept that rules should be clearly stated and consistently and impartially enforced.

**process** An organized group of related tasks and activities that work together to transform inputs into outputs and create value.

**process control system** A computer system that monitors and controls ongoing physical processes, such as temperature or pressure changes.

**process layout** A facilities layout in which machines that perform the same function are grouped together in one location.

**process theories** A group of theories that explain how employees select behaviors with which to meet their needs and determine whether their choices were successful.

**procurement** Purchasing supplies, services, and raw materials for use in the production process.

**product change** A change in the organization's product or service output.

**product layout** A facilities layout in which machines and tasks are arranged according to the sequence of steps in the production of a single product.

**product life-cycle management** Manufacturing software that manages a product from creation through development, manufacturing, testing, and even maintenance in the field.

**productivity** The organization's output of products and services divided by its inputs.

**profitability ratio** A financial ratio that describes the firm's profits (for example, sales or total assets).

**programmed decision** A decision made in response to a situation that has occurred often enough to enable decision rules to be developed and applied in the future.

**project manager** A manager responsible for a temporary work project that involves the participation of other people from various functions and levels of the organization; a person responsible for coordinating the activities of several departments on a full-time basis for the completion of a specific project.

**projection** The tendency to see one's own personal traits in other people.

## Q

**quality circle (QC)** A group of 6 to 12 volunteer employees who meet regularly to discuss and solve problems affecting the quality of their work.

## R

**raw materials inventory** Inventory consisting of the basic inputs to the organization's production process.

**realistic job preview (RJP)** A recruiting approach that gives applicants all pertinent and realistic information about the job and the organization.

**recruiting** The activities or practices that define the desired characteristics of applicants for specific jobs.

**reengineering** The radical redesign of business processes to achieve dramatic improvements in cost, quality, service, and speed; bringing together all elements of a single business process to eliminate waste and delays.

**referent power** Power that results from characteristics that command subordinates' identification with, respect and admiration for, and desire to emulate the leader.

**refreezing** The reinforcement stage of organizational development in which individuals acquire a desired new skill or attitude and are rewarded for it by the organization.

**reinforcement** Anything that causes a given behavior to be repeated or inhibited.

**reinforcement theory** A motivation theory based on the relationship between a given behavior and its consequences.

**reorder point (ROP)** The most economical level at which an inventory item should be reordered.

**responsibility** The duty to perform the task or activity an employee has been assigned.

**responsibility center** An organizational unit under the supervision of a single individual who is responsible for its activity.

**revenue budget** A budget that identifies the forecasted and actual revenues of the organization.

**reward power** Power that results from the authority to bestow rewards on other people.

**risk** A situation in which a decision has clear-cut goals, and good information is available, but the future outcomes associated with each alternative are subject to chance.

**risk propensity** The willingness to undertake risk with the opportunity of gaining an increased payoff.

**role** A set of expectations for one's behavior.

**role ambiguity** Uncertainty about what behaviors are expected of a person in a particular role.

**role conflict** Incompatible demands of different roles.

### S

**satisficing** To choose the first solution alternative that satisfies minimal decision criteria, regardless of whether better solutions are presumed to exist.

**scenario building** Looking at trends and discontinuities and imagining possible alternative futures to build a framework within which unexpected future events can be managed.

**schedule of reinforcement** The frequency with which and intervals over which reinforcement occurs.

**scientific management** A subfield of the classical management perspective that emphasized scientifically determined changes in management practices as the solution to improving labor productivity.

**search** The process of learning about current developments inside or outside the organization that can be used to meet a perceived need for change.

**selection** The process of determining the skills, abilities, and other attributes a person needs to perform a particular job.

**self-directed team** A team consisting of 5 to 20 multiskilled workers who rotate jobs to produce an entire product or service, often supervised by an elected member.

**self-serving bias** The tendency to overestimate the contribution of internal factors to one's successes and the contribution of external factors to one's failures.

**semantics** The meaning of words and the way they are used.

**servant leader** A leader who works to fulfill subordinates' needs and goals as well as to achieve the organization's larger mission.

**service organization** An organization that produces nonphysical outputs that require customer involvement and cannot be stored in inventory.

**service technology** Technology characterized by intangible outputs and direct contact between employees and customers.

**short-term orientation** A concern with the past and present and a high value on meeting social obligations.

**single-use plans** Plans that are developed to achieve a set of goals that are unlikely to be repeated in the future.

**situation analysis** Analysis of the strengths, weaknesses, opportunities, and threats (SWOT) that affect organizational performance.

**situational theory** A contingency approach to leadership that links the leader's behavioral style with the task readiness of subordinates.

**Six Sigma** A quality control approach that emphasizes a relentless pursuit of higher quality and lower costs.

**skunkworks** A separate small, informal, highly autonomous, and often secretive group that focuses on breakthrough ideas for the business.

**slogan** A phrase or sentence that succinctly expresses a key corporate value.

**small-batch production** A type of technology that involves the production of goods in batches of one or a few products designed to customer specification.

**social entrepreneurs** Entrepreneurial leaders who are committed to both good business and changing the world for the better.

**social facilitation** The tendency for the presence of others to influence an individual's motivation and performance.

**social forces** The aspects of a culture that guide and influence relationships among people—their values, needs, and standards of behavior.

**social responsibility** The obligation of organization management to make decisions and take actions that will enhance the welfare and interests of society as well as the organization.

**sociocultural dimension** The dimension of the general environment representing the demographic characteristics, norms, customs, and values of the population within which the organization operates.

**socioemotional role** A role in which the individual provides support for team members' emotional needs and social unity.

**sole proprietorship** An unincorporated business owned by an individual for profit.

**span of management** The number of employees reporting to a supervisor; also called *span of control*.

**special-purpose team** A team created outside the formal organization to undertake a project of special importance or creativity.

**staff authority** A form of authority granted to staff specialists in their areas of expertise.

**stakeholder** Any group within or outside the organization that has a stake in the organization's performance.

**standing plans** Ongoing plans that are used to provide guidance for tasks performed repeatedly within the organization.

**stereotyping** Placing an employee into a class category based on one or a few traits or characteristics; the tendency to assign an individual to a group or broad category and then attribute generalizations about the group to the individual.

**storming** The stage of team development in which individual personalities and roles, and resulting conflicts, emerge.

**story** A narrative based on true events that is repeated frequently and shared among organizational employees.

**strategic business unit (SBU)** A division of the organization that has a unique business mission, product line, competitors, and markets relative to other SBUs in the same corporation.

**strategic conversation** Dialogue across boundaries and hierarchical levels about the team or organization's vision, critical strategic themes, and the values that help achieve important goals.

**strategic goals** Broad statements of where the organization wants to be in the future; pertain to the organization as a whole rather than to specific divisions or departments.

**strategic management** The set of decisions and actions used to formulate and implement strategies that will provide a competitively superior fit between the organization and its environment so as to achieve organizational goals.

**strategic plans** The action steps by which an organization intends to attain its strategic goals.

**strategy** The plan of action that prescribes resource allocation and other activities for dealing with the environment, achieving a competitive advantage, and attaining organizational goals.

**strategy formulation** The stage of strategic management that involves the planning and decision making that lead to the establishment of the organization's goals and of a specific strategic plan.

**strategy implementation** The stage of strategic management that involves the use of managerial and organizational tools to direct resources toward achieving strategic outcomes.

**stress** A physiological and emotional response to stimuli that place physical or psychological demands on an individual.

**structural changes** Any change in the way in which the organization is designed and managed.

**substitute** A situational variable that makes a leadership style redundant or unnecessary.

**subsystems** Parts of a system that depend on one another for their functioning.

**superordinate goal** A goal that cannot be reached by a single party.

**suppliers** People and organizations who provide the raw materials the organization uses to produce its output.

**supply chain management** Managing the sequence of suppliers and purchasers, covering all stages of processing from obtaining raw materials to distributing finished goods to final customers.

**survey feedback** A type of OD intervention in which questionnaires on organizational climate and other factors are distributed among employees and the results reported back to them by a change agent.

**sustainability** Economic development that meets the needs of the current population while preserving the environment for the needs of future generations.

**symbol** An object, act, or event that conveys meaning to others.

**synergy** The condition that exists when the organization's parts interact to produce a joint effect that is greater than the sum of the parts acting alone; the concept that the whole is greater than the sum of its parts.

**system** A set of interrelated parts that function as a whole to achieve a common purpose.

**systems theory** An extension of the humanistic perspective that describes organizations as open systems that are characterized by entropy, synergy, and subsystem interdependence.

## T

**tactical goals** Goals that define the outcomes that major divisions and departments must achieve in order for the organization to reach its overall goals.

**tactical plans** Plans designed to help execute major strategic plans and to accomplish a specific part of the company's strategy.

**tall structure** A management structure characterized by an overall narrow span of management and a relatively large number of hierarchical levels.

**task environment** The layer of the external environment that directly influences the organization's operations and performance.

**task force** A temporary team or committee formed to solve a specific short-term problem involving several departments.

**task specialist role** A role in which the individual devotes personal time and energy to helping the team accomplish its task.

**team** A group of participants from several departments who meet regularly to solve ongoing problems of common interest; a unit of two or more people who interact and coordinate their work to accomplish a specific goal.

**team-based structure** Structure in which the entire organization is made up of teams that coordinate their work and work directly with customers to accomplish the organization's goals.

**team building** A type of OD intervention that enhances the cohesiveness of departments by helping members learn to function as a team.

**team cohesiveness** The extent to which team members are attracted to the team and motivated to remain in it.

**team norm** A standard of conduct that is shared by team members and guides their behavior.

**technical complexity** The degree to which complex machinery is involved in the production process to the exclusion of people.

**technical core** The heart of the organization's production of its product or service.

**technical skill** The understanding of and proficiency in the performance of specific tasks.

**technological dimension** The dimension of the general environment that includes scientific and technological advancements in the industry and society at large.

**technology change** A change that pertains to the organization's production process.

**telecommuting** Using computers and telecommunications equipment to perform work from home or another remote location.

**tolerance for ambiguity** The psychological characteristic that allows a person to be untroubled by disorder and uncertainty.

**top-down budgeting** A budgeting process in which middle- and lower-level managers set departmental budget targets in accordance with overall company revenues and expenditures specified by top management.

**top leader** The overseer of both the product and the functional chains of command, responsible for the entire matrix.

**top manager** A manager who is at the top of the organizational hierarchy and is responsible for the entire organization.

**total factor productivity** The ratio of total outputs to the inputs from labor, capital, materials, and energy.

**total quality management (TQM)** A concept that focuses on managing the total organization to deliver quality to customers. Four significant elements of TQM are employee involvement, focus on the customer, benchmarking, and continuous improvement. An organizationwide commitment to infusing quality into every activity through continuous improvement.

**traits** Distinguishing personal characteristics, such as intelligence, values, and appearance.

**transactional leader** A leader who clarifies subordinates' role and task requirements, initiates structure, provides rewards, and displays consideration for subordinates.

**transaction processing system** A type of operations information system that records and processes data resulting from routine business transactions such as sales, purchases, and payroll.

**transformational leader** A leader distinguished by a special ability to bring about innovation and change.

**transnational strategy** A strategy that combines global coordination to attain efficiency with flexibility to meet specific needs in various countries.

**two-boss employee** Employees who report to two supervisors simultaneously.

**type A behavior** Behavior pattern characterized by extreme competitiveness, impatience, aggressiveness, and devotion to work.

**type B behavior** Behavior pattern that lacks Type A characteristics and includes a more balanced, relaxed lifestyle.

## U

**uncertainty** The situation that occurs when managers know which goals they wish to achieve, but information about alternatives and future events is incomplete.

**unfreezing** A stage of organization development in which participants are made aware of problems in order to increase their willingness to change their behavior.

**upward communication** Messages transmitted from the lower to the higher level in the organization's hierarchy.

**utilitarian approach** The ethical concept that moral behaviors produce the greatest good for the greatest number.

## V

**valence** The value or attraction an individual has for an outcome.

**validity** The relationship between an applicant's score on a selection device and his or her future job performance.

**venture capital firm** A group of companies or individuals that invests money in new or expanding businesses for ownership and potential profits.

**vertical team** A formal team composed of a manager and his or her subordinates in the organization's formal chain of command.

**virtual network structure** An organization structure that disaggregates major functions to separate companies that are brokered by a small headquarters organization.

**virtual team** A team made up of members who are geographically or organizationally dispersed, rarely meet face to face, and do their work using advanced information technologies.

**vision** An attractive, ideal future that is credible yet not readily attainable.

**Vroom-Jago model** A model designed to help managers gauge the amount of subordinate participation in decision making.

## W

**wage and salary surveys** Surveys that show what other organizations pay incumbents in jobs that match a sample of "key" jobs selected by the organization.

**whistle-blowing** The disclosure by an employee of illegal, immoral, or illegitimate practices by the organization.

**wholly owned foreign affiliate** A foreign subsidiary over which an organization has complete control.

**workforce diversity** Hiring people with different human qualities or who belong to various cultural groups.

**work-in-process inventory** Inventory composed of the materials that still are moving through the stages of the production process.

**work redesign** The altering of jobs to increase both the quality of employees' work experience and their productivity.

**work specialization** The degree to which organizational tasks are subdivided into individual jobs; also called division of labor.

**World Wide Web (WWW)** A collection of central servers for accessing information on the Internet.

# Indexes

Name Index
Company Index
Subject Index

# Name Index

# Company Index

# Subject Index